THE BEST OF

LONDON

Seventh Edition

Editor-in-Chief
André Gayot

Editor
Mary Anne Evans

Managing Editor
Mary Lu Abbott

Contributing Editors
Hugo Arnold, Matthew Barker, Jane Berkeley, Andrew Campbell,
Louis Charles, Guy Dimond, George Dorgan, Robin Dutt, David Evans,
Sylvie Greil, Carole Hirschhorn, Ossi Laurila Sandrae Lawrence,
Susan Low, Lisa Messinger, Michael North, Sudi Pigott, Christi Solomon,
Caroline Stacey, Emile Toyag, Ian Wisniewski, David Wolfe

Coordination
Sophie Gayot

Publisher
Alain Gayot

● www.gayot.com ●

GAULT·MILLAU

Los Angeles ■ New York ■ San Francisco
London ■ Munich ■ Paris ■ Vienna

GAYOT

GAULT·MILLAU

The Best of Beverly Hills
The Best of Chicago
The Best of Florida
The Best of France
The Best of Germany
The Best of Hawaii
The Best of Hong Kong
The Best of Italy
The Best of Las Vegas
The Best of London
The Best of Los Angeles

The Best of New England
The Best of New Orleans
The Best of New York
The Best of Paris
Paris, Ile-de-France & The Loire Valley
Paris & Provence
The Best of San Francisco
The Best of Thailand
The Best of Toronto
The Best of Washington, D.C.
The Best Wineries of North America

Los Angeles Restaurants
New York City Restaurants
San Francisco Restaurants

Tastes Newsletter, The Food Paper
www.gayot.com

Published by GaultMillau, Inc.
5900 Wilshire Blvd.
Los Angeles, CA 90036

Please address all comments regarding
THE BEST OF LONDON to:
GaultMillau, Inc.
P.O. Box 361144
Los Angeles, CA 90036
E-mail: gayots@aol.com

Operations: Harriet Callier
Production: Susan Cranston
Page Layout & Design: Mad Macs Communications
Cover Photo: ©2000 Mike McQueen/Stone

ISSN 1520-3514
ISBN 1-881066-58-4
Printed in the United States of America

CONTENTS

INTRODUCTION   5

MAPS   7

An overview of London's **Underground** system and **landmarks** of the city.

RESTAURANTS   11

Candid, penetrating, witty reviews of the top, the new—and the newly discovered—restaurants in London. Listed by area. Includes our famous **Toque Tally**.

QUICK BITES   103

Where to get a square meal for a square deal—**ethnic restaurants, cafés, pub-grub**, and the best **in-store eateries** for your shopping breaks. Plus where to take **tea** the English way.

HOTELS   151

A guide to London's hotels—for every taste and pocketbook. Includes our **Key** ratings.

NIGHTLIFE   203

For after dark: The best **pubs, wine bars, casual & sophisticated bars.** Plus **comedy & music clubs.**

Shopping 225

From **antiques** to **high-tech furniture**—from **Savile Row tailors** to trendy boutiques—we'll direct you to where to shop for the best.

Arts & Leisure 351

The best **art galleries** and **museums**, plus **sightseeing** from the **Tower of London** to the **Changing of the Guard**. Where to indulge in your favorite **sports & hobbies**, and enjoy **concerts & theatre**. In search of the unusual? You'll find it right here.

Out of London 413

All you need to spend a day or so outside London in England's sylvan countryside: **Bath, Oxford, Windsor & York.**

Basics 429

Everything you need to know about getting around London.

Menu Savvy 441

Glossaries of international cuisine terms.

Index 448

BRIDGES OVER THE CENTURIES

It's a new millennium and a new excitement has hit London. Not since the 18th century has there been such an outpouring of creativity in all fields in Britain's great capital city. It shows in the buzz of London's cultural life, in the rejuvenation of many splendid old buildings and institutions and the creation of new venues. It also shows in the new hotels that are being opened all over town from Docklands to Notting Hill, in newly discovered and reinvented areas like Clerkenwell and Smithfield; it shows even more in the wealth of culinary experiences on offer in every part of the capital. The capital hums with a cosmopolitan verve as the nations of the world come to see what is happening here.

For decades London has turned its back on the river which brought such wealth to the city. Today, Londoners are rediscovering this jewel in the crown. The biggest expansion ever of the great museums and galleries, is underway, largely funded by the national lottery. With the refurbishment of Somerset House, the creation of Shakespeare's Globe and the opening of the new Tate Modern on Bankside, these elements have magnificently come together. Bankside power station, designed in 1947 but completed only in 1963 houses one of the most important new international modern art galleries in the world, a fact recognised by private collectors who are sending works on permanent loan to the new gallery. Somerset House now hosts the Gilbert Collection, acknowledged as one of the best private collections of decorative arts in existence and given to the nation by Sir Arthur Gilbert in 1999. A permanent exhibition from the Hermitage in Russia opens in the second refurbished riverside wing of Somerset House.

Three new footbridges help the flow between the opposite banks. The first to open (and the first new Thames crossing in central London since Tower Bridge opened in 1894), is a new footbridge running from St. Paul's to Tate Modern. Spanning the river a little upstream and running beside Hungerford Bridge are two new footbridges, linking London's great South Bank cultural centre to the area around Charing Cross.

Other great institutions are celebrating new plans and projects. The National Maritime Museum has added eleven new galleries under a vast glass atrium roof; the British Museum's Great Court, under a roof which is the biggest glass span in Europe, opens at the end of 2000; the National Portrait Gallery has 50 percent more exhibition space and a great new restaurant; Dulwich Picture Gallery reopens after a major renovation; the new Wellcome Wing at the Science Museum is on track to become the world's leading centre for the presentation of contemporary science and technology; a new gallery is dedicated to the Holocaust at the Imperial War Museum, and the Wallace Collection is being refurbished. These are the big names; you'll also see innovative new developments in the smaller museums and galleries all publicly funded. The juxtaposition of old and new sums up London's attraction to many visitors who come to look at the past in the form of London's venerable buildings, streets and institutions, while marveling at how the new is made to fit seamlessly into this history.

Private projects are equally as exciting and cover all aspects of life, so the visitor is spoilt for choice whatever he or she is looking for. Your hotel room can be the most luxurious in the world, or the chicest, or the cosiest, depending on your taste and pocket. Should you want to savour London life more closely, rent an apartment, or stay with a family on a "bed and breakfast" basis. For the inveterate shopper, the big designer names continue to recognise the importance of London in the world scheme and continue to open the smartest shops in and around Bond and Sloane Streets; while smaller up-and-coming young designers choose chic enclaves like Notting Hill Gate, or the booming area called 'Belgravia Village'. An evening's entertainment can span a wide spectrum. London's theatres continue to offer some of the best experiences in the world, from big-time musicals to new productions from the vibrant fringe, where you may well see some of the big American stars eager to tread the boards. All the big orchestras and all the great musicians visit London during the year, confirming the city as a world musical centre. And the restaurants continue to astonish with their excellence and their diversity.

It is this diversity and choice that sets London among the most appealing cities of the world. By the same token, it makes the production of a guide such an exciting and challenging task. In *The Best of London* we present London in all its various and intriguing forms, covering every aspect, large and small, major and minor, world famous or known only to the insider. So whether you are a first-time visitor or returning for the umpteenth time, you'll always discover something new.

Welcome to London!

Andre Jot

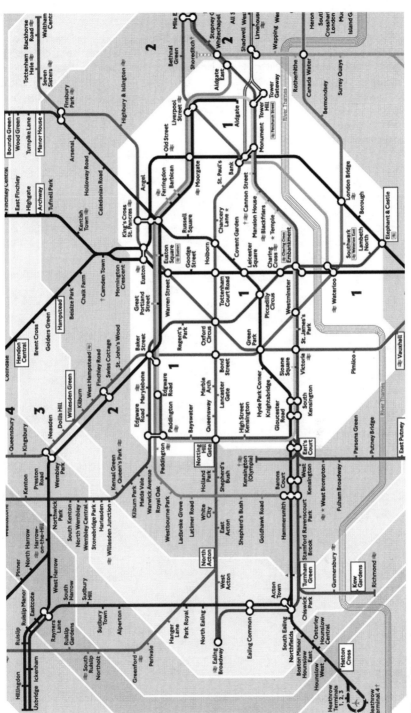

© London Transport

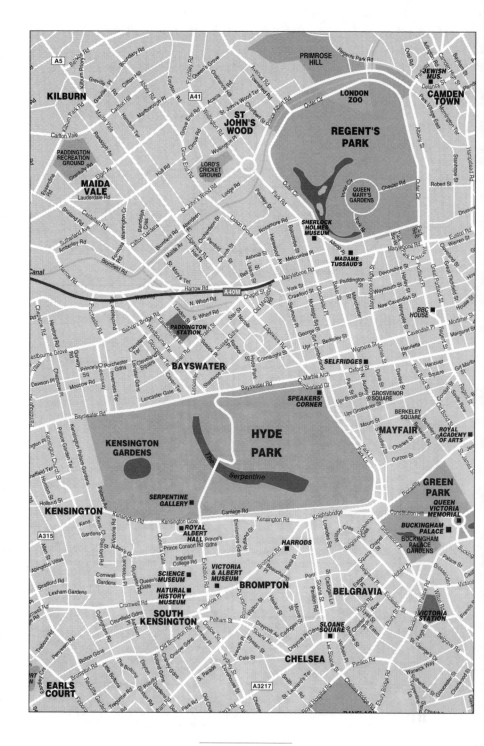

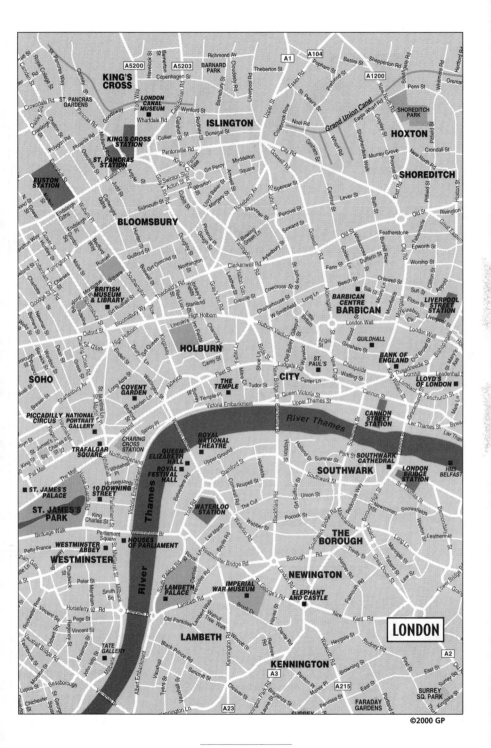

LONDON

©2000 GP

THE BEST OF
LONDON

We thank you for your interest in Gayot guides, and we welcome your remarks and recommendations about restaurants, hotels, nightlife, shops, services, etc. Please direct your questions or comments to:

GaultMillau, Inc.
P.O. Box 361144
Los Angeles, CA 90036
E-mail: gayots@aol.com

RESTAURANTS

CONTENTS

INTRODUCTION 12
RESTAURANT SAVVY 13
ABOUT THE REVIEWS 13
TOQUE TALLY 15
RESTAURANTS BY CUISINE 17
RESTAURANTS
   BY NOTABLE FEATURES 19
RESTAURANTS
   BARNES 22
   BATTERSEA 22
   BAYSWATER 23
   BELGRAVIA 24
   BERMONDSEY 26
   BLOOMSBURY 27
   CHALK FARM 27
   CHELSEA 27
   CHINATOWN 31
   CHISWICK 33
   THE CITY 34
   CLERKENWELL 38
   COVENT GARDEN 40
   DULWICH 45
   EALING 46
   FULHAM 46
   GOLDERS GREEN 48
   HAMMERSMITH 48
   HAMPSTEAD 48
   HIGHGATE 49
   HOLLAND PARK 50
   ISLINGTON 50

KENNINGTON 51
KENSINGTON 52
KEW 55
KNIGHTSBRIDGE 55
LONDON BRIDGE 59
MARBLE ARCH 59
MARYLEBONE 60
MAYFAIR 62
NOTTING HILL GATE 72
PICCADILLY CIRCUS/REGENT ST .74
PIMLICO 78
PRIMROSE HILL 78
PUTNEY 79
RICHMOND 79
ST. JAMES'S 80
ST. JOHN'S WOOD 84
SHEPHERD'S BUSH 85
SHOREDITCH 85
SOHO .86
SOUTH BANK 91
SOUTH KENSINGTON 92
SOUTH NORWOOD 95
STRAND 95
TOTTENHAM COURT ROAD . .96
TOWER BRIDGE 98
VICTORIA 99
WANDSWORTH 100
WILLESDEN 100
WIMBLEDON 101

INTRODUCTION

GASTRONOMY FOR THE PUNTER

The new millennium has already produced some major changes on the London restaurant scene, with interesting side effects. First of all, two of London's best chefs have voluntarily withdrawn from the top league. Marco Pierre White has hung up his toques at The Oak Room to become a full-time restaurateur developing new restaurants and overseeing their menus rather than cooking, and Nico Ladenis has simplified the menu at his restaurant on Park Lane, and renamed it Chez Nico. While two do not a trend make, it is indicative of a general move among many restaurants to stop aiming for the heights and to become more accessible to the ordinary punter. So where does one go for the very best? While there are still some individuals up there, namely Pierre Koffmann at La Tante Claire, Philip Howard at The Square, Gordon Ramsay, Michel Roux at Le Gavroche in London, and outside London the superlative Raymond Blanc at Le Manoir aux Quat'Saisons near Oxford, and the older Michel Roux at The Waterside Inn at Bray, it is to hotel restaurants like The Connaught that you must look for more formal dining where luxury ingredients and classic methods of cooking still hold sway. In the meantime, competition among other big restaurants is hotting up. While Sir Terence Conran continues to produce the kind of big, sophisticated, brasserie-style eating that has become so much a part of the London restaurant scene, others like Oliver Peyton have taken the plunge with his Isola in Knightsbridge and the recenetly opened Admiral in Somerset House. All this is good news for the punter.

There's more good news also in the form of young chefs coming up fast through the ranks. Many are continuing the trend of opening gastro-pubs, former pubs which have been given a makeover, often fairly simple, and re-opened as places where food is of paramount importance. And the individual continues to fly the flag of independence, often against stiff competition from big breweries and other large voracious companies whose search for prime sites and big bucks buying power can put huge pressure on these small establishments. And as ever, London's ethnic eating scene is buoyant, with Chinatown as lively an area as ever, and London's Thai and Indian restaurants providing some wonderful food. What is in fashion in the culinary stakes? Fusion continues to both fuse and confuse people with places like the Sugar Club leading the right way, and Nobu offering a unique experience. Spanish and North African cooking have certainly made people sit up and take notice and look set to become a permanent feature. And contemporary Italian, a modern, lighter version of classic Italian cuisine, has also become a major force. On the down side, the search for good staff is as cutthroat as ever, especially at front-of-house. And some bad habits like turning tables every two hours to maximise profits is still practised. Combined with the slow but steady rise in prices this year, in both fixed price menus and à la carte, this is to be deplored. All of the above comes from a booming city where the upside greatly outshines any disadvantages. London continues to be a restaurant city *par excellence* that surprises with its vitality and astonishes with its expansion. It's a great place to eat out, offering a diversity difficult to find in any other city in the world.

We wish you Bon Appétit!

RESTAURANT SAVVY

You will have to **book the top restaurants** in advance, and some might require a few weeks' notice. Be prepared to give your telephone number and expect the restaurant to re-confirm the booking. There have been so many cases of no-shows in the past that restaurants have found themselves with empty tables on busy nights that they can ill afford.

Dress is fairly casual, though at the better restaurants women may feel out of place in pantsuits. Men also, might prefer to wear a jacket and tie. Although there is seldom any formal dress code, many people these days dress up for an evening out, so you may feel out of place if too casually dressed.

At any of the top restaurants, it is always a good idea to **ask the head waiter for suggestions**. Remember, too, that the **wine waiter** is there to offer expert advice, so never be afraid to ask.

Lunch is generally served from 12.30pm to around 2.30pm; **dinner** usually from 7pm onwards. However, many restaurants now offer pre- or post-theatre menus. These can be very good value. Another established practice (though centuries-old in Chinese restaurants) is the prix-fixe menu, which can offer good value and often the best efforts of the chef.

Some restaurants add a **service charge** (this should be printed on the menu); others will leave the service charge up to you. Fifteen percent has become the norm. But always double check your bill as cases are recorded of the practice of adding on the service charge but leaving the final total free in the hopes that the unsuspecting customer will add yet more to what should be a final total.

In today's rapidly changing world, **chefs change** too, which means a restaurant might not be as described in this book. Chef-owned restaurants are generally more stable, though they can also change. If you experience any of this, please don't hold us responsible.

ABOUT THE REVIEWS

USING OUR RATING SYSTEM

Our rating system works as follows: restaurants are ranked in the same manner that French students are graded, on a scale of one to twenty.

THE RANKINGS REFLECT ONLY OUR OPINION OF THE FOOD. THE DECOR, SERVICE, AMBIENCE AND WINE LIST ARE COMMENTED UPON WITHIN EACH REVIEW.

Sample Review

The following key explains the information provided in our reviews.

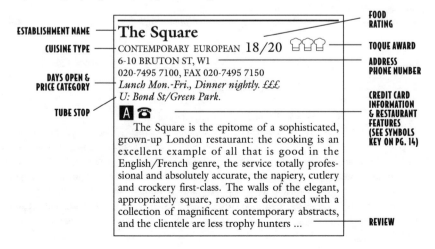

FOOD RATING

ESTABLISHMENT NAME — **The Square**

CUISINE TYPE — CONTEMPORARY EUROPEAN 18/20 — TOQUE AWARD

6-10 BRUTON ST, W1 — ADDRESS PHONE NUMBER

DAYS OPEN & PRICE CATEGORY — 020-7495 7100, FAX 020-7495 7150
Lunch Mon.-Fri., Dinner nightly. £££
U: Bond St/Green Park.

TUBE STOP — CREDIT CARD INFORMATION & RESTAURANT FEATURES (SEE SYMBOLS KEY ON PG. 14)

The Square is the epitome of a sophisticated, grown-up London restaurant: the cooking is an excellent example of all that is good in the English/French genre, the service totally professional and absolutely accurate, the napiery, cutlery and crockery first-class. The walls of the elegant, appropriately square, room are decorated with a collection of magnificent contemporary abstracts, and the clientele are less trophy hunters ... — REVIEW

Restaurants that are ranked 13/20 and above are distinguished with toques (chef's hats) according to the table below:

Exceptional *(4 Toques)*

(ratings of 19/20)

Excellent *(3 Toques)*

(ratings of 17/20 and 18/20)

Very good *(2 Toques)*

(ratings of 15/20 and 16/20)

Good *(1 Toque)*

(ratings of 13/20 and 14/20)

Keep in mind that we are comparing London's restaurants to the very best in the world. Also, these ranks are relative. A 13/20 (one toque) may not be a superlative ranking for a highly reputed (and very expensive) restaurant, but it is quite complimentary for a small place without much culinary pretension. We know that diners often choose a restaurant for reasons other than the quality of the food because of its location, type of cuisine or just because it's a fun place to spend an evening.

OUR PRICING SYSTEM

Prices for a three-course meal for one with coffee and service, but no beverages:

£—under £25	£££—£35-£50
££—£25-£35	££££—over £50

SYMBOLS

All credit cards taken . . . . **A**

Visa . . . . **VISA**

MasterCard . . . . **MasterCard**

American Express . . . .

Diners Club . . . .

Reservations suggested . . . . ☎

Valet parking . . . . 🚗

Ties suggested . . . .

Romantic setting . . . .

View . . . . 📷

Outdoor dining . . . .

🎩 THE TOQUE, CIRCA 1700 🎩

Have you ever wondered about the origin of that towering, billowy (and slightly ridiculous) white hat worn by chefs all over the world? Chefs have played an important role in society since the fifth century B.C., but the hats didn't begin to appear in kitchens until around the eighteenth century A.D. The toque is said to be of Greek origin; many famous Greek cooks, to escape persecution, sought refuge in monasteries and continued to practice their art. The chefs donned the tall hats traditionally worn by Orthodox priests, but to distinguish themselves from their fellows, they wore white hats instead of black. The custom eventually was adopted by chefs from Paris to Peking.

TOP RESTAURANTS: FOOD RATING
TOQUE TALLY

19/20 ♟♟♟♟

La Tante Claire *(Knightsbridge)*
Le Manoir aux Quat'Saisons (*Great Milton*, see *Oxford*)

18/20 ♟♟♟

Chez Nico *(Mayfair)*
Gordon Ramsay *(Chelsea)*
The Square *(Mayfair)*
Waterside Inn (*Bray-on-Thames*,
see *Windsor*)

17/20 ♟♟♟

Fat Duck (*Bray-on-Thames*, see *Windsor*)
Le Gavroche *(Mayfair)*
Lettonie *(Bath)*
Nobu *(Mayfair)*
The Oak Room *(Piccadilly Circus/ Regent Street)*
Tatsuso *(The City)*

16/20 ♟♟

Aubergine *(Chelsea)*
The Capital *(Knightsbridge)*
Chez Bruce *(Wandsworth)*
City Rhodes *(The City)*
Club Gascon *(The City)*
The Connaught Grill Room
& Restaurant *(Mayfair)*
Gaudi *(Clerkenwell)*
The Glasshouse (*Kew*)
Orrery *(Marylebone)*
Pétrus *(St. James's)*
Restaurant One-O-One *(Knightsbridge)*
Richard Corrigan at Lindsay House *(Soho)*
Roussillon *(Belgravia)*
Sabras *(Willesden)*
Sarkhel's *(Wimbledon)*
Stefano Cavallini at The Halkin *(Belgravia)*

15/20 ♟♟

Café Japan *(Golders Green)*
Cambio de Tercio *(South Kensington)*
Clarke's *(Kensington)*
Foliage *(Knightsbridge)*
Isola *(Knightsbridge)*
Mantanah *(South Norwood)*
Matsuri *(St. James's)*
Mirabelle *(Mayfair)*
Moro *(Clerkenwell)*
New End *(Hampstead)*
1 Lombard Street *(The City)*
Pied-à-Terre *(Tottenham Court Road)*
The River Café *(Hammersmith)*
Tatsuso Teppan Room *(The City)*
Vong *(Knightsbridge)*
Windows *(Mayfair)*
Zen Chelsea *(Chelsea)*

14/20 ♟

Alastair Little Lancaster Gate
(Notting Hill Gate)
Al Hamra *(Mayfair)*
Amandier *(Bayswater)*
Aroma *(Chinatown)*
Assaggi at The Chepstow *(Notting Hill Gate)*
Axis *(Covent Garden)*
Bali Sugar *(Notting Hill Gate)*
Bank *(Covent Garden)*
Base *(Hampstead)*
Bath Priory *(Bath)*

The Belvedere *(Kensiugton)*
Bibendum *(South Kensington)*
Boisdale *(Victoria)*
Chinon *(Shepherd's Bush)*
Chutney Mary *(Fulham)*
Claridge's *(Mayfair)*
Coast *(Mayfair)*
1837 *(Mayfair)*
The English Garden *(Chelsea)*
The Feathers Hotel (*Woodstock*, see Oxford)
The Fifth Floor *(Knightsbridge)*
Floriana *(Knightsbridge)*
French House Dining Room *(Soho)*

Fung Shing *(Chinatown)*
Hilaire *(South Kensington)*
The House *(Chelsea)*
The Ivy *(Covent Garden)*
J Sheekey *(Covent Garden)*
Kensington Place *(Kensington)*
Kiku *(Mayfair)*
Le Caprice *(St. James's)*
L'Escargot *(Soho)*
L'Oranger *(St. James's)*
Le Pont de la Tour *(Tower Bridge)*
Ma Goa *(Richmond)*
Mandarin Kitchen *(Bayswater)*
Ming *(Chinatown)*
Mr Kong *(Chinatown)*
Noble Rot *(Mayfair)*
Novelli Restaurant *(Clerkenwell)*
Odette's *(Primrose Hill)*
Olive Tree *(Bath)*
Osteria Isola *(Knightsbridge)*
Ozer *(Piccadilly Circus/Regent Street)*
Parade *(Ealing)*
Poons & Co *(Chinatown)*
Prism *(The City)*
Putney Bridge *(Putney)*
Quo Vadis *(Soho)*
Ransome's Dock *(Battersea)*
The Real Greek *(Shoreditch)*
Redmond's *(Richmond)*
Rhodes in the Square *(Pimlico)*
The Ritz Restaurant *(St. James's)*
Saga *(Mayfair)*
Saint M *(Covent Garden)*
St. John *(Clerkenwell)*
Sartoria *(Piccadilly Circus/Regent Street)*
Sonny's *(Barnes)*
Stephen Bull *(Marylebone)*
Stepping Stone *(Battersea)*
Sugar Club *(Soho)*
Suntory *(St. James's)*
Tentazioni *(Tower Bridge)*
The Tenth *(Kensington)*
Turner's *(South Kensington)*
Twentyfour *(The City)*
The Vineyards at Stockcross
   Restaurant (*Near Newbury*, see *Bath)*
Zafferano *(Belgravia)*
Zaika *(Fulham)*
Zen Garden *(Mayfair)*

13/20 ♗

Alastair Little *(Soho)*
Al Duca *(St. James's)*
Al San Vincenzo *(Marble Arch)*
Aurora *(The City)*
Avenue *(St. James's)*
Belair House *(Dulwich)*
The Birdcage *(Tottenham Court Road)*
Bluebird Restaurant *(Chelsea)*

Blue Print Café *(Tower Bridge)*
The Brackenbury *(Shepherd's Bush)*
Busabong Tree *(Chelsea)*
Café du Jardin *(Covent Garden)*
Café Spice Namaste *(The City)*
Cassia Oriental *(Mayfair)*
Chez Max *(Fulham)*
Chez Moi *(Holland Park)*
Cibo *(Kensington)*
Circus *(Soho)*
County Hall Restaurant *(South Bank)*
The Crescent *(Marble Arch)*
Criterion Marco Pierre
   White *(Piccadilly Circus/Regent Street)*
Delfina Studio Café *(Bermondsey)*
Granita *(Islington)*
Grano *(Chiswick)*
The Greenhouse *(Mayfair)*
Gresslin's *(Hampstead)*
The Grill Room *(Mayfair)*
Ibla *(Marylebone)*
Idaho *(Highgate)*
Indigo *(Covent Garden)*
Itsu *(South Kensington)*
Kaspia *(Mayfair)*
Langan's Brasserie *(Mayfair)*
Le Colombier *(Chelsea)*
Le Petit Blanc *(Oxford)*
Le Soufflé *(Mayfair)*
Lola's *(Islington)*
Matsuri Teppan Room *(St. James's)*
Mela *(Covent Garden)*
Melton's *(York)*
Middlethorpe Hall *(York)*
The Moody Goose *(Bath)*
New Diamond *(Chinatown)*
The Oriental *(Mayfair)*
Orso *(Covent Garden)*
Oxo Tower Restaurant Bar
   & Brasserie *(South Bank)*
Pacific Oriental *(The City)*
Pharmacy *(Notting Hill Gate)*
Phoenicia *(Kensington)*
Quadrato *(The City)*
Quality Chop House *(Clerkenwell)*
Quilon *(Victoria)*
Rasa Samudra *(Tottenham Court Road)*
Rasa W1 *(Mayfair)*
Red Fort *(Soho)*
The Red Room *(Piccadilly Circus/
   Regent Street)*
The Rib Room & Oyster Bar *(Belgravia)*
Riva *(Barnes)*
The River Room *(Strand)*
Rules *(Covent Garden)*
The Stafford *(St. James's)*
Tajine *(Marylebone)*
Tamarind *(Mayfair)*
Terrace *(Kensington)*
Wiltons *(St. James's)*
Zen Central *(Mayfair)*

RESTAURANTS BY CUISINE

There are so many cross-overs in modern cooking that it is difficult to pinpoint the inspiration behind many restaurants. However we have taken the predominant tastes to classify restaurants by their cuisine.

AMERICAN
Christopher's American Grill *(Covent Garden)*
Idaho *(Highgate)*
Joe Allen *(Covent Garden)*

BELGIAN
Belgo Noord *(Chalk Farm)*

BRITISH
French House Dining Room *(Soho)*
Green's Restaurant & Oyster Bar *(St. James's)*
The Grill Room *(Mayfair)*
The Rib Room & Oyster Bar *(Belgravia)*
Rules *(Covent Garden)*
Simpson's-In-the-Strand
  Grand Divan *(Strand)*
Wiltons *(St. James's)*

CALIFORNIA/MODERN BRITISH
Clarke's *(Kensington)*

CHINESE
Aroma *(Chinatown)*
Cassia Oriental *(Mayfair)*
Fung Shing *(Chinatown)*
London Jade Garden *(Chinatown)*
Mandarin Kitchen *(Bayswater)*
Ming *(Chinatown)*
Mr Kong *(Chinatown)*
New Diamond *(Chinatown)*
The Oriental *(Mayfair)*
Poons in the City *(The City)*
Poons & Co *(Chinatown)*
Zen Central *(Mayfair)*
Zen Chelsea *(Chelsea)*

CONTEMPORARY EUROPEAN
Alastair Little Lancaster
  Road *(Notting Hill Gate)*
Aurora *(The City)*
Base *(Hampstead)*
Bath Priory *(Bath)*
Belair House *(Dulwich)*
The Belvedere *(Kensington)*
The Brackenbury *(Shepherd's Bush)*
Café du Jardin *(Covent Garden)*
The Crescent *(Marble Arch)*
Euphorium *(Islington)*
The Feathers Hotel *(Oxford)*
The Fifth Floor *(Knightsbridge)*
Foliage *(Knightsbridge)*

The Glasshouse *(Kew)*
Granita *(Islington)*
The Greenhouse *(Mayfair)*
Indigo *(Covent Garden)*
Langan's Brasserie *(Mayfair)*
Lemon Tree *(Oxford)*
Lola's *(Islington)*
Melton's *(York)*
New End *(Hampstead)*
Noble Rot *(Mayfair)*
192 *(Notting Hill Gate)*
1 Lombard Street *(The City)*
Oxo Tower Restaurant Bar
  & Brasserie *(South Bank)*
Pharmacy *(Notting Hill Gate)*
Prism *(The City)*
Putney Bridge *(Putney)*
Quaglino's *(St. James's)*
Redmond's *(Richmond)*
Soho Soho *(Soho)*
The Square *(Mayfair)*
Station Grill *(Kennington)*
The Vineyard at Stockcross Restaurant *(Bath)*

DANISH
Lundum's *(South Kensington)*

FRENCH
Amandier *(Bayswater)*
Aubergine *(Chelsea)*
Bibendum *(South Kensington)*
Brasserie St. Quentin *(Knightsbridge)*
Browns *(Bath)*
The Capital *(Knightsbridge)*
Chez Bruce *(Wandsworth)*
Chez Max *(Fulham)*
Chez Moi *(Holland Park)*
Chez Nico *(Mayfair)*
Chinon *(Shepherd's Bush)*
Club Gascon *(The City)*
Criterion Marco Pierre
  White *(Piccadilly Circus/Regent Street)*
1837 *(Mayfair)*
Fat Duck *(Bray-on-Thames, see Windsor)*
La Tante Claire *(Knightsbridge)*
Le Colombier *(Chelsea)*
Le Coq d'Argent *(The City)*
L'Escargot *(Soho)*
Le Gavroche *(Mayfair)*
Lettonie *(Bath)*
Le Manoir aux
  Quat'Saisons *(Great Milton, see Oxford)*
L'Odéon *(Piccadilly Circus/Regent Street)*
L'Oranger *(St. James's)*
Le Palais du Jardin *(Covent Garden)*
Le Petit Blanc *(Oxford)*
Le Pont de la Tour *(Tower Bridge)*
Le Soufflé *(Mayfair)*
The Oak Room *(Piccadilly Circus/Regent Street)*

Pétrus *(St. James's)*
Pied-à-Terre *(Tottenham Court Road)*
Mirabelle *(Mayfair)*
Mon Plaisir *(Covent Garden)*
Novelli Restaurant *(Clerkenwell)*
No. 5 Bistro *(Bath)*
Orrery *(Marylebone)*
The River Room *(Strand)*
Roussillon *(Belgravia)*
Saint M *(Covent Garden)*
Turner's *(South Kensington)*
Waterside Inn *(Bray-on-Thames,* see *Windsor)*
Windows *(Mayfair)*

FRENCH/BRITISH
Claridge's *(Mayfair)*
Clos du Roy *(Bath)*
The Connaught Grill Room
 & Restaurant *(Mayfair)*
The Ritz Restaurant *(St. James's)*

FRENCH/THAI
The Birdcage *(Tottenham Court Road)*
Vong *(Knightsbridge)*

GREEK
The Real Greek *(Shoreditch)*

INDIAN
Bombay Brasserie *(South Kensington)*
Café Spice Namaste *(The City)*
Chor Bizarre *(Mayfair)*
Chutney Mary *(Fulham)*
La Porte des Indes *(Marble Arch)*
Ma Goa *(Richmond)*
Mela *(Covent Garden)*
Old Delhi *(Bayswater)*
Quilon *(Victoria)*
Rasa W1 *(Mayfair)*
Rasa Samudra *(Tottenham Court Road)*
Red Fort *(Soho)*
Sabras *(Willesden)*
Sarkhel's *(Wimbledon)*
Star of India *(South Kensington)*
Tamarind *(Mayfair)*
Vama *(Chelsea)*
Veeraswamy *(Piccadilly Circus/Regent Street)*
Zaika *(Fulham)*
Zen Garden *(Mayfair)*

INTERNATIONAL
Atlantic Bar & Grill *(Piccadilly Circus/ Regent Street)*
Asia de Cuba *(Covent Garden)*
Avenue *(St. James's)*
Bali Sugar *(Notting Hill Gate)*
Browns *(Oxford)*
Che *(St. James's)*
Coast *(Mayfair)*
First Floor *(Notting Hill Gate)*
Gresslin's *(Hampstead)*
Odette's *(Primrose Hill)*

Pomegranates *(Pimlico)*
Searcy's at the Barbican *(The City)*
Spoon+ at Sanderson *(Tottenham Court Road)*
The Tenth *(Kensington)*
Titanic *(Piccadilly Circus/Regent Street)*

ITALIAN
Al Duca *(St. James's)*
Al San Vincenzo *(Marble Arch)*
Assaggi at The Chepstow *(Notting Hill Gate)*
Bertorelli's Café Italian *(Tottenham Court Road)*
Cibo *(Kensington)*
Daphne's *(South Kensington)*
Del Buongustaio *(Putney)*
Floriana *(Knightsbridge)*
Grano *(Chiswick)*
Great Eastern Dining Room *(Shoreditch)*
Ibla *(Marylebone)*
Il Forno *(Soho)*
Isola *(Knightsbridge)*
Olivo *(Belgravia)*
Orso *(Covent Garden)*
Osteria Antica Bologna *(Battersea)*
Osteria Isola *(Knightsbridge)*
Quadrato *(The City)*
Riso *(Chiswick)*
Riva *(Barnes)*
The River Café *(Hammersmith)*
Sartoria *(Piccadilly Circus/Regent Street)*
Stefano Cavallini at The Halkin *(Belgravia)*
Teca *(Mayfair)*
Tentazioni *(Tower Bridge)*
Vasco & Piero's Pavilion *(Soho)*
Zafferano *(Belgravia)*

JAPANESE
Café Japan *(Golders Green)*
Itsu *(South Kensington)*
Kashinoki *(St. John's Wood)*
Kiku *(Mayfair)*
Miyama *(Mayfair)*
Suntory *(St. James's)*
Tatsuso Teppan Room *(The City)*

JAPANESE/SUSHI
Matsuri *(St. James's)*
Saga *(Mayfair)*
Tatsuso *(The City)*

JAPANESE/INTERNATIONAL
Nobu *(Mayfair)*

LEBANESE
Al Hamra *(Mayfair)*
Al-Shami *(Oxford)*
Phoenicia *(Kensington)*

MODERN BRITISH
Alastair Little *(Soho)*
Alfred *(Bloomsbury)*

Axis *(Covent Garden)*
Bank *(Covent Garden)*
Beak Street *(Soho)*
Bibendum Oyster Bar *(South Kensington)*
Bluebird Restaurant *(Chelsea)*
Blue Print Café *(Tower Bridge)*
Butlers Wharf Chop House *(Tower Bridge)*
Le Caprice *(St. James's)*
Cherwell Boathouse *(Oxford)*
Circus *(Soho)*
City Rhodes *(The City)*
Clarke's *(Kensington)*
County Hall Restaurant *(South Bank)*
Delfina Studio Café *(Bermondsey)*
The English Garden *(Chelsea)*
Gordon Ramsay *(Chelsea)*
Hilaire *(South Kensington)*
The House *(Chelsea)*
The Ivy *(Covent Garden)*
Kensington Place *(Kensington)*
Launceston Place *(Kensington)*
Le Caprice *(St. James's)*
Mezzo *(Soho)*
Middlethorpe Hall *(York)*
The Moody Goose *(Bath)*
Nicole's *(Mayfair)*
Olive Tree *(Bath)*
Parade *(Ealing)*
Quality Chop House *(Clerkenwell)*
Quo Vadis *(Soho)*
Ransome's Dock *(Battersea)*
The Red Room *(Piccadilly Circus/
    Regent Street)*
Rhodes in the Square *(Pimlico)*
The Room at The Halcyon *(Holland Park)*
St. John *(Clerkenwell)*
Sonny's *(Barnes)*
The Stafford *(St. James's)*
Stephen Bull *(Marylebone)*
Stephen Bull Smithfield *(Clerkenwell)*
Stepping Stone *(Battersea)*
Terrace *(Kensington)*
Twentyfour *(The City)*
Villandry *(Marylebone)*
The White House *(Oxford)*
Woods *(Bath)*

MODERN BRITISH/IRISH
Richard Corrigan at Lindsay House *(Soho)*

NORTH AFRICAN
Momo *(Piccadilly Circus/Regent Street)*
Tajine *(Marylebone)*

PACIFIC RIM
Pacific Oriental *(The City)*
Sugar Club *(Soho)*

PAKISTANI
Salloos *(Belgravia)*

RUSSIAN
Firebird *(Mayfair)*
Kaspia *(Mayfair)*
Soviet Canteen *(Chelsea)*

SCOTTISH
Boisdale *(Victoria)*

SPANISH
Cambio de Tercio *(South Kensington)*
Gaudi *(Clerkenwell)*
Lomo *(Chelsea)*

SPANISH/NORTH AFRICAN
Moro *(Clerkenwell)*

THAI
Busabong Tree *(Chelsea)*
Blue Elephant *(Fulham)*
Mantanah *(South Norwood)*
Thai Pavilion *(Soho)*

TURKISH
Ozer *(Piccadilly Circus/Regent Street)*

RESTAURANTS BY NOTABLE FEATURES

SEAFOOD
Restaurants serving fish exclusively or with a
major bias, as in many Japanese restaurants.
Bank *(Covent Garden)*
Bibendum Oyster Bar *(South Kensington)*
fish! *(London Bridge)*
J. Sheekey *(Covent Garden)*
Livebait *(Covent Garden)*
Rasa Samadra *(Tottenham Court Road)*
Restaurant One-O-One *(Knightsbridge)*
Rib Room & Oyster Bar *(Knightsbridge)*

VEGETARIAN
Most restaurants have one or two dishes for
appetisers and main courses. We have listed
here only restaurants serving a substantial
number of vegetarian dishes or with a separate
vegetarian menu. Most Indian and Chinese
restaurants also carry vegetarian menus.
Al Hamra *(Mayfair)*
Amandier *(Bayswater)*
Beak Street *(Soho)*
The Blue Elephant *(Fulham)*
Bombay Brasserie *(South Kensington)*
Ma Goa *(Richmond)*
Rasa W1 *(Mayfair)*

Rasa Samadra (*Tottenham Court Road*)
Roussillon (*Belgravia*)
Sabras (*Willesden*)
Star of India (*South Kensington*)

LATE NIGHT
Most restaurants, with the exception of those
in the City, now have last orders at 11pm.
Listed here are restaurants with last orders at
11.30pm or later, though double-check. If it's
a quiet night, the restaurant may close earlier
than its stated time.
Alfred (*Bloomsbury*)
Al Hamra (*Mayfair*)
Aroma (*Chinatown*)
Asia de Cuba (*Covent Garden*)
Atlantic Bar & Grill (*Piccadilly Circus/
    Regent Street*)
The Avenue (*St. James's*)
Axis (*Covent Garden*)
Bank (*Covent Garden*)
Belgo Noord (*Chalk Farm*)
Bibendum (*South Kensington*)
Blue Elephant (*Fulham*)
Bombay Brasserie (*South Kensington*)
Café du Jardin (*Covent Garden*)
Cambio de Tercio (*South Kensington*)
Chor Bizarre (*Mayfair*)
Christopher's American Grill (*Covent Garden*)
Chutney Mary (*Fulham*)
Circus (*Soho*)
Coast (*Mayfair*)
Criterion Marco Pierre
    White (*Piccadilly Circus/Regent Street*)
Daphne's (*South Kensington*)
The Fifth Floor (*Knightsbridge*)
Fung Shing (*Chinatown*)
The Ivy (*Covent Garden*)
Joe Allen (*Covent Garden*)
J Sheekey (*Covent Garden*)
Kensington Place (*Kensington*)
La Porte des Indes (*Marble Arch*)
Langan's Brasserie (*Mayfair*)
Launceston Place (*Kensington*)
Le Caprice (*St. James's*)
Le Palais du Jardin (*Covent Garden*)
Le Pont de la Tour (*Tower Bridge*)
L'Escargot (*Soho*)
Livebait (*Covent Garden*)
Lomo (*Chelsea*)
London Jade Garden (*Chinatown*)
Mandarin Kitchen (*Bayswater*)
Mezzo (*Soho*)
Mirabelle (*Mayfair*)
Mr Kong (*Chinatown*)
New Diamond (*Chinatown*)
192 (*Notting Hill Gate*)
Orso (*Covent Garden*)

Osteria Isola (*Knightsbridge*)
Oxo Tower (*South Bank*)
Phoenicia (*Kensington*)
Poons & Co (*Chinatown*)
Quaglino's (*St. James's*)
Quality Chop House (*Clerkenwell*)
Quo Vadis (*Soho*)
Rules (*Covent Garden*)
Saint M (*Covent Garden*)
Soho Soho (*Soho*)
Star of India (*South Kensington*)
Tamarind (*Mayfair*)
Tentazioni (*Tower Bridge*)
Titanic (*Piccadilly Circus/Regent Street*)
Vama (*Chelsea*)
Veeraswamy (*Piccadilly Circus/Regent Street*)
Vong (*Knightsbridge*)
Windows (*Mayfair*)
Zen Central (*Mayfair*)
Zen Chelsea (*Chelsea*)
Zen Garden (*Mayfair*)

OPEN ON A SUNDAY
(L) means lunch only, (D) means dinner only.
Al Hamra (*Mayfair*)
Aroma (*Chinatown*)
Asia de Cuba (D) (*Covent Garden*)
Assaggi at The Chepstow (D) (*Notting
    Hill Gate*)
    Atlantic Bar & Grill (D) (*Piccadilly
    Circus/Regent Street*)
Aurora (L) (*The City*)
Avenue (*St. James's*)
Bali Sugar (*Notting Hill Gate*)
Bank (*Covent Garden*)
Base (*Hampstead*)
Belair House (*Dulwich*)
Belgo Noord (*Chalk Farm*)
Bibendum (*South Kensington*)
Bibendum Oyster Bar (*South Kensington*)
The Birdcage (*Tottenham Court Road*)
Bluebird (*Chelsea*)
Blue Elephant (*Fulham*)
Blue Print Café (L) (*Tower Bridge*)
Bombay Brasserie (*South Kensington*)
The Brackenbury (L) (*Shepherd's Bush*)
Brasserie St. Quentin (*Knightsbridge*)
Busabong Tree (L) (*Chelsea*)
Butlers Wharf Chop House (L) (*Tower
    Bridge*)
Café Spice Namaste (*Battersea*)
Café du Jardin (*Covent Garden*)
Café Japan (*Golders Green*)
Cambio de Tercio (*Knightsbridge*)
The Canteen (L) (*Chelsea*)
The Capital (*Knightsbridge*)
Che (D) (*St. James's*)
Chez Bruce (L) (*Wandsworth*)

Claridge's *(Mayfair)*
Chor Bizarre *(Mayfair)*
Christopher's American Grill (L) *(Covent Garden)*
Chutney Mary *(Fulham)*
Cibo (L) *(Kensington)*
Circus *(Soho)*
Claridge's *(Mayfair)*
Coast (L) *(Mayfair)*
The Connaught Grill Room & Restaurant *(Mayfair)*
County Hall Restaurant *(South Bank)*
The Crescent (D) *(Marble Arch)*
Criterion Marco Pierre White (D) *(Piccadilly Circus/Regent Street)*
Daphne's *(South Kensington)*
Del Buongustaio *(Putney)*
Euphorium (L) *(Islington)*
The Fifth Floor (L) *(Knightsbridge)*
First Floor *(Notting Hill Gate)*
Floriana *(Knightsbridge)*
Fung Shing *(Chinatown)*
The Glasshouse (L) *(Kew)*
Granita *(Islington)*
Grano (L) *(Chiswick)*
The Greenhouse *(Mayfair)*
Green's Restaurant & Oyster Bar *(St. James's)*
Gresslin's (L) *(Hampstead)*
The Grill Room *(Mayfair)*
Idaho (L) *(Highgate)*
Indigo *(Covent Garden)*
Isola *(Knightsbridge)*
Itsu *(South Kensington)*
The Ivy *(Covent Garden)*
J Sheekey *(Covent Garden)*
Joe Allen *(Covent Garden)*
Kashinoki *(St. John's Wood)*
Kensington Place *(Kensington)*
Launceston Place (L) *(Kensington)*
La Porte des Indes (L) *(Marble Arch)*
Le Caprice *(St. James's)*
Le Colombier *(Chelsea)*
Le Coq d'Argent (L) *(The City)*
Le Palais du jardin *(Covent Garden)*
Le Pont de la Tour (D) *(Tower Bridge)*
Le Soufflé (L) *(Mayfair)*
Lola's *(Islington)*
Lomo *(Chelsea)*
London Jade Garden *(Chinatown)*
Lundum's *(South Kensington)*
Mandarin Kitchen *(Bayswater)*
Mantanah (D) *(South Norwood)*
Ma Goa *(Richmond)*
Mezzo *(Soho)*
Mirabelle *(Mayfair)*
Momo *(Piccadilly Circus/Regent Street)*
Mr Kong *(Chinatown)*
Miyama (D) *(Mayfair)*
New Diamond *(Chinatown)*

New End *(Hampstead)*
Nobu (D) *(Mayfair)*
Old Delhi *(Bayswater)*
Olivo (D) *(Belgravia)*
Orrery *(Marylebone)*
192 *(Notting Hill Gate)*
Orso *(Covent Garden)*
Osteria Antica Bologna *(Battersea)*
Osteria Isola *(Knightsbridge)*
Oxo Tower Restaurant Bar & Brasserie *(South Bank)*
Pharmacy *(Notting Hill Gate)*
Phoenicia *(Kensington)*
Poons & Co *(Chinatown)*
Putney Bridge *(Putney)*
Quaglino's *(St. James's)*
Quadrato *(The City)*
Quality Chop House *(Clerkenwell)*
Quo Vadis *(Soho)*
Ransome's Dock (L) *(Battersea)*
Rasa (D) *(Mayfair)*
Red Fort *(Soho)*
Redmond's (L) *(Putney)*
Restaurant One-O-One *(Knightsbridge)*
Rib Room & Oyster Bar
Riso *(Chiswick)*
The Ritz Restaurant *(St. James's)*
Riva *(Barnes)*
River Café (L) *(Hammersmith)*
The River Restaurant *(Strand)*
Rules *(Covent Garden)*
Sabras (D) *(Willesden)*
Saint M (D) *(Covent Garden)*
Sartoria *(Piccadilly Circus/Regent Street)*
Searcy's at the Barbican *(City)*
Simpson's-in-the-Strand Grand Divan *(Strand)*
Soho Soho *(Rôtisserie only) (Soho)*
Sonny's (L) *(Barnes)*
The Square (D) *(Mayfair)*
The Stafford (D) *(St. James's)*
Star of India *(South Kensington)*
Station Grill (L) *(Kennington)*
Stefano Cavallini at The Halkin (D) *(Belgravia)*
The Stepping Stone (L) *(Battersea)*
Sugar Club *(Soho)*
Tamarind *(Mayfair)*
The Terrace (L) *(Kensington)*
Thai Pavilion *(Soho)*
Vama *(Chelsea)*
Veeraswamy *(Piccadilly Circus/Regent Street)*
Villandry (L) *(Marylebone)*
Vong *(Knightsbridge)*
Wiltons *(St. James's)*
Windows (L) *(Mayfair)*
Zen Central *(Mayfair)*
Zen Chelsea *(Chelsea)*
Zen Garden *(Mayfair)*

BARNES

Riva

ITALIAN   13/20   ♟
169 CHURCH RD, SW13, 020-8748 0434
Lunch Sun.-Fri., Dinner nightly. ££
Rail: Barnes.

🅰 ☎ ⬙

The unshowy exterior belies the extremely serious intent of Andreas Riva's North Italian gastronomic haven which attracts celeb locals in discreet droves. The mixed fish antipasta is brilliant, especially the salt cod cakes, as is beef carpaccio and particularly fine pasta dishes prepared by the Cipriani-trained chef such as spaghetti with bottarga, mussels and clams. Calf's liver of superlative tenderness comes with a punchy garlic polenta, whilst more adventurous mains include sturgeon fillets with black truffle and juniper. Alongside excellent Italian standards of pannacotta and tiramisù, delicately fragrant sweet milk gnocchi stands out among desserts. The austere narrow room decorated with architectural prints can seem intimidating, especially as service favours the many regulars. The all-Italian wine list includes plenty of stickies and grappa.

Sonny's

MODERN BRITISH   14/20   ♟
94 CHURCH RD, SW13
020-8748 0393, FAX 020-8748 2698
Restaurant: Lunch daily, Dinner Mon.-Sat.
Café: daily 10.30am-4pm. ££
Rail: Barnes Bridge.

🅰 ☎

Fashionable and contemporary without being showy, the owners of Sonny's have a canny knack of providing what is vastly appealing to local gliteratti and neighbourhood diners across the generations. Its recent refit only adds to its charms: some serious modern art, comfortable Swedish blue banquettes, flattering lighting and a stunning modern fireplace plus admirably attentive, yet laidback waiting staff. Chef Lee Diggins' modish menu evolves daily with plenty to tempt. An autumnal meal offered sublime chanterelle risotto with melt-in-the-mouth tender breast of wood pigeon to start, and red mullet arrestingly served with a pumpkin seed and lemon grass broth. A perfect chargrilled chunk of halibut came robustly accompanied by an original tomato and mussel cassoulet, whilst breast of pheasant was simply served with a tasty game sausage and chestnut purée. Delectably light, warm, bitter chocolate cake was pronounced as moreish, as was the more seasonal quince bakewell tart with quince ice cream. A savvy wine list has plenty of interest at fair prices. Set 2-course lunch £12, 3 courses £15, 3-course Sun. lunch £18.50.

BATTERSEA

Osteria Antica Bologna

ITALIAN   12/20
23 NORTHCOTE RD, SW11
TEL/FAX: 020-7978 4771
Lunch & Dinner daily. £
Rail: Clapham Junction.

💳 💳 📷 ☎ ⬙

A likeable and distinctive, somewhat scruffy rustic Italian trattoria where chef/proprietor Aurelio Spagnuolo serves up some inventive dishes. Start with an assagi of starters including stuffed artichoke with honey, nut and coriander sauce, and Napoli sausage with warm lentils and fennel. Ancient Roman recipes are a speciality which leads to some interesting sweet and savoury combinations. Kid stew with almond sauce is a signature dish. Rabbit with rosemary, pancetta, pepper, cloves and cinnnamon exemplifies the imaginative yet robust approach. Stuffed dates with 'Roman custard' outshone a sloppy tiramisù for dessert. Interesting and inexpensive all-Italian wine list. Tables are rather crammed together, decibels are loud and service can be chaotic when the place is heaving. Set 2-course lunch Mon.-Sat. £8.50.

Ransome's Dock

MODERN BRITISH   14/20   ♟
35-37 PARKGATE RD, SW11
020-7223 1611, FAX 020-7924 2614
Restaurant: Lunch Mon.-Fri., Sat. 11am-midnight, Sun. 11.30am-3.30pm.
Bar: Mon.-Sat. 11am-11pm, Sun. noon-3.30pm. ££
U: None nearby.

🅰 ☎ ⬙

Chef-patron Martin Lam calls himself an artisan, not an artist. But many of his trade (some describing themselves as artists) pay him the ultimate tribute by regularly eating here. The dock outside the restaurant can be oddly attractive especially for summer lunch, while vibrant blue walls with intriguing pictures contribute to a lively but not brash ambience. Service is relaxed and friendly. The menu has just enough excursions to foreign parts to justify the description Modern British, but on one summer day only a Mexican chilli went further than the Mediterranean—in piquillo butter with grilled chicken. The two-course set lunch, great value at £12.50 with three choices in each course, might include avocado and mango salad, navarin of lamb with couscous, braised chicory with Serrano ham and the listed British Heritage dish, cod and chips with tartare sauce. Totally home-grown in the à la carte are Norfolk smoked eel, Morecambe Bay potted shrimps, Trelough duck and Guernsey veal, while exotic Dutch calf's liver is domesticated by Cumbrian smoked bacon, bubble and squeak and shallot sauce. The modestly priced wines are skillfully chosen and include a wide range by the glass. Unfashionable but recommended with this food are the Lustau Almacenista sherries. Set 2-course lunch Mon.-Fri. £12.50.

Stepping Stone

MODERN BRITISH   14/20
123 QUEENSTOWN RD, SW8
020-7622 0555, FAX 020-7622 4230
Lunch Sun.-Fri., Dinner Mon.-Sat. ££
U: None nearby.

Battersea is not usually associated with style or gastronomy, although this particular stretch of Queenstown Road has always had a sterling culinary provenance, accommodating superchefs Nico Ladenis and Christian Delteuil during the 1980s. While the Stepping Stone is not pitched at that level, it is a prime example of a superior neighbourhood restaurant. Having cornered the local market, which means upmarket 30-somethings who also bring in their parents and friends, the sociodemographics are as much SW3 as SW8. Décor is minimal in design though maximum in delivery. A simple formula combines stretches of white with blocks of vivid colour, creating effective contrasts, and a fresh, contemporary setting that showcases the diner rather than the designer. A recent extension has also created a separate bar area, so apéritifs can be taken at the counter rather than at the table. Staff are professionally friendly, and speak knowledgeably about dishes, which is important as the menu's purely factual nature

belies the creativity of presentation and skillful integration of flavours: warm salad of chorizo, morcilla black pudding and poached egg; roast duck breast, braised red cabbage, fondant potato, and rhubarb crumble tart, thick custard deliver far more on the palate. Moreover, a great value 2-course set lunch is £12.50, with plenty of wines by the glass at £3.75 including new world stars. Set 2-course lunch £12.50; set 3-course Sun. lunch £16.50.

BAYSWATER

Amandier

FRENCH   14/20
26 SUSSEX PL, W2
020-7262 6073, FAX 723 8395
Lunch Mon.-Fri., Dinner Mon.-Sat. ££
U: Lancaster Gate.

Daniel Gobet's new venture is in a smarter part of town than his previous restaurant La Ciboulette—a basement in the King's Road, and his already fastidious cooking has also gone up a notch. The pale cream and green ground-floor dining room is a restful space; staff are charmingly French and knowledgeable. Of seven starters offered, a delicate ravioli of goats cheese with tender baby leeks and garlic butter sauce had an apt edge to the dish was masterly; the pâté of quail and wild mushrooms packed more of a punch, and a Tatin of shallots over crumbling pastry laid on a balsamic vinegar-drizzled plate was meltingly sweet. The six main courses, with meat and fish given equal billing, offer just as much in the way of both variety and expertise. A tender baked guinea fowl breast was accompanied by Savoy cabbage wrapped in light pastry and baked in the oven and a piquant mushroom sauce; pan-fried sea bass came with soufflèed aubergine caviar and was given an Oriental twist with ginger and soya oil. Desserts are more classically inclined—as in passion fruit crème brûlée, but equally well executed. To really see Monsieur Gobet's talents to the full, go for the 4-course Menu Découverte at £37. For a lighter lunch, there's an excellent 2-course menu at £15.50 and three courses at £18.50, which judging from our last visit, is delighting the local regulars. Bistro Daniel in the basement offers simpler fare (see Quick Bites). Set 2-course lunch £15.50, 3 courses £18.50; 2-course menu £25.50, 3 courses £29.50; Menu Découverte £37.

Mandarin Kitchen

CHINESE   14/20

14-16 QUEENSWAY, W2
020-7727 9012, FAX 020-7727 9468
Open daily noon-11.30pm. ££
U: Queensway.

A few minutes' walk from Kensington Gardens, in London's most ethnically mixed thoroughfare, is this Chinatown-style restaurant. It is always packed, and even a reservation does not guarantee a table within twenty minutes of the specified time. Staff, dressed in silver-grey, are fast, generally efficient, and sometimes friendly. Tables in the front are more desirable than those in the cavern at the rear. But what matters is the food, which is usually excellent. Although fifty meat, chicken and duck dishes are offered too, seafood is the meat of the menu. Lobsters prepared in six ways, although wild and Scottish, will sing, but won't play bagpipes. Crabs, from the south or south west coast may be baked, but the wonderful signature dish—pot of crab with bean noodles and dry shrimps in chilli sauce—requires fingers as well as spoon and chopsticks as eating implements. Scallops, mussels and squid appear too, along with abalone, Alaskan king clam or geoduck, and occasionally razor-shells and other rarities. The menu lists as fish normally served: sea bass, Dover sole, live eels, live carp, monkfish, pomfret and yellow croakers. Set dinners are unexciting, so are desserts. House wines are acceptable. Set meals £10.90-£30.

Old Delhi

INDIAN   11/20

48 KENDAL ST, W2, 020-7723 3335
Lunch & Dinner daily. ££
U: Marble Arch.

The Iranian owner and his Iranian chef proudly present a menu evenly divided between Indian and Persian cuisines. Indian dishes are well executed, if conventional, and flair and national pride are more evident in Persian specialities. Lamb or chicken kebabs are accompanied by fine saffron rice, while many other Persian dishes, however romantically named, are basically, stews—which is high praise. Gorgeous gormeh (which may be a version of 'gourmet') sabsi (vegetables) is actually lamb cooked with a gardenful of green herbs, while fesenjune is duck, roasted, then sliced and finished in a walnut and pomegranate sauce. Crisp pomegranate seeds sparkle brilliantly and pinkly as a garnish on several dishes. Vegetable-based Persian starters include tasty variations of the ubiquitous Middle Eastern aubergine paste, including one with egg and garlic. The restaurant is sumptuously furnished in Middle Eastern style, and service is as suave and skilled as it should be when the ambitious wine list extends to top clarets at well over £1,000. However, very good house wines are £11.50. An extra touch of luxury is live music on Wednesday and Friday evenings.

BELGRAVIA

Olivo

ITALIAN   12/20

21 ECCLESTON ST, SW1, 020-7730 2505
Lunch Mon.-Fri., Dinner nightly. ££
U: Sloane Sq/Victoria.

This Sardinian 'local' on the smart Chelsea borders offers a decent Italian meal in decidedly jolly surroundings: colours are yellows and blues, service is brisk. The menu, which is standard rather than innovative, starts with salads and pastas, beef or tuna carpaccio and marinated chargrilled Mediterranean vegetables, smokey and appealing. Chargrilling continues as the main method of cooking, as in fish (tuna or swordfish), and meat (marinated lamb with rosemary, pork fillet), but the Sardinian spaghetti alla bottarga (dried red mullet roe grated over a bowl of spaghetti) makes a welcome alternative. Sardinia appears again in the desserts in the form of sebada, deep-fried pastry filled with cheese and drizzled with honey. If you prefer, there are dishes like pannacotta and fruit tarts. Cheeses are Italian, so is the wine list. Olivo has a great buzz and sparkle, and makes a good informal night out. Set 2-course lunch £15, 3 courses £17.

The Rib Room & Oyster Bar

TRADITIONAL BRITISH   13/20

HYATT CARLTON TOWER, 162 SLOANE ST, SW1
020-7858 7053, FAX 020-7235 9129
Lunch & Dinner daily. £££
U: Knightsbridge.

A ☎

The Rib Room is one of those places that seem to have been around since the beginning of time, so it caused quite a frisson among its well-heeled regulars when it closed for refurbishment. And a collective sigh of relief went up when it re-opened, refurbished certainly (the old décor was creaking a bit), and with a spanking new oyster bar at one end and a club-like bar at the other, but still both comfortable and traditional. The menu now offers more fish—dozens of fat, succulent oysters coming with different sauces in varying degrees of sharpness (try the guacamole with jalapeño peppers), and grilled or roasted seafood as in turbot with olive relish, or whole sea bass with lemon, herbs and garlic at £42 for two. But despite all this, and the veal chops, Aylesbury ducks et al, this is the place for beef, which appears triumphantly cooked on the bone. So all is well with the world. And the beef is superb. It's from the Duke of Buccleuch and Queensbury's estates in Scotland, so it has the right pedigree, and is cooked perfectly. Go for the Yorkshire pudding and baked potato (but go carefully on the searingly hot horseradish sauce), and you'll understand why the British are proud to be les rosbifs. If you have room, try the oven-baked Bramley apple with Calvados and vanilla sabayon.

Roussillon

FRENCH   16/20

16 ST. BARNABAS ST, SW1, 020-7730 5550
Lunch Mon.-Fri., Dinner Mon.-Sat. £££
U: Sloane Sq.

A ☎

Definitely a destination restaurant, partly because there is no other reason to go down this elegant, residential street, Roussillon has already fulfilled its destiny—elevating vegetarian dishes to gourmet status. But coming to veg out only accounts for part of the restaurant's appeal, as rustic chic dishes make just as much of fish and meat, accompanied by impeccable matching accessories: sautéed foie gras; persimmon chutney and black radish,

warm brioches; simmered sea-bream, fricassée of Jerusalem artichokes and Swiss chard, herb aromatic sauce; spicy soufflé of organic duck egg, gingerbread fingers and maple infusion. Service is unmistakeably French, meaning prompt and self-assured (they know exactly how and when to pitch it.) The décor is similarly nationalistic, utilising that winning combination: a little bit of Provence, a hint of château, a touch of Paris, with a palete of autumnal browns and tans, a stretch of hessian here and there, and some botanical prints. The result is not surprising in any way, but that's a compliment. It immediately feels familiar, without being predictable—a combination that suits the discerning regulars, who are coiffed and buffed rather than suited and booted. Set 2-course lunch £13.50, 3 courses £16; set 2-course dinner £25, 3 courses £28.50, vegetarian £26.50, 6 courses £38.

Salloos

PAKISTANI   12/20

62-64 KINNERTON ST, SW1, 020-7235 4444
Lunch & Dinner Mon.-Sat. ££
U: Hyde Park Corner/Knightsbridge.

A ☎

Little ever changes in this first-floor mews room near the Berkeley Hotel and even if the long promised redecoration comes in 2000, it will hardly be noticeable. London's first luxury 'Indian' restaurant is in fact authentically Pakistani, so the menu's emphasis is on meat and the 'Vegetables etc.' section looks like an afterthought. Fine tandoori dishes take time to arrive as they are cooked to order and are best as a separate course, with curries or other Salloos's specialities to follow. Most are familiar, but not chicken in cheese, a sort of chicken and cheese soufflé. Stranger still is haleem akbari, 'Salloos's unique speciality from the days of the Moghul emperors'. Shredded lamb is cooked in whole wheat germ, lentils and spices; the resulting porridge-like texture is curious. The claim that no two dishes are identically spiced is born out by distinct tastes in masalas of gurda (lamb's kidneys), and jhingha (prawns). Despite disapproving Brussels officialdom, warm carrot halwa is garnished with silver leaf to please both eye and palate. The exalted prices of rather conventional wines are not always reflected in their service, which remains the least gracious aspect of an otherwise excellent restaurant. Set 3-course lunch £16.

Stefano Cavallini at The Halkin

ITALIAN   16/20   ♟♟

THE HALKIN, 5-6 HALKIN ST, SW1
020-7333 1234/1000, FAX 020-7333 1100
Lunch Mon.-Fri., Dinner nightly. £££
U: Hyde Park Corner.

A ☎

In this age of TV, celebrity and super-chefs, it's refreshing to find a top-flight chef who keeps doing exactly what he does best. The cuisine is Italian, not of the trattoria-style, tomato sauce-with-everything sort, but of the uncompromisingly Italian sort and, as such, it's some of the best in London. Proper Italian ingredients, such as mostarda (a fruit and mustard preserve) and bottarga (grated grey mullet roe) are menu staples. Pasta dishes (such as chocolate pasta with pigeon and potato sauce) are wonderful, the own-made pasta feather light. But it is perhaps the quality of the sauces that goes furthest in proving Cavallini's prowess as an outstanding chef. The red wine sauce with the fillet of beef in a salt crust was beautifully reduced to the point of perfect unctuousness, without being cloying. The dining room at The Halkin is at the comfortable end of the minimalist spectrum and designer-clad service is of a very high standard. Such precision comes at a price (about £100-plus for two), but the food is memorable. Set 3-course lunch £23; set 5-course dinner £55.

Zafferano

ITALIAN   14/20   ♟

15 LOWNDES ST, SW1
020-7235 5800, FAX 020-7235 1971
Lunch & Dinner Mon.-Sat. £££
U: Knightsbridge.

Being in such a smart neighbourhood makes this essentially local restaurant all the more surprising. Prices remain reasonable, particularly at lunchtime, while the food is sensational, easily making Zafferano one of the top five Italian restaurants in the capital. Two interconnecting rooms with their tiled floors are business-like and watched over by calm and enthusiastic staff, much as they would be in Italy. If the menu sounds pedestrian, prepare to be surprised, effort here goes into first-rate ingredients and minimal, carefully judged exe-

cution. Georgio Locatelli scans all of Italy, and some of France, in search of inspiration, picking and choosing with care as he goes. Wind-dried tuna, the sea salty tang cut perfectly by fine beans and tomato-enriched olive oil, was so simple, yet utterly balanced. Pasta is one of Locatelli's strong points, ravioli stuffed with osso buco perhaps, or stuffed with wild herbs and served with a sage butter. You are unlikely to find a better risotto in London, whether it is saffron or summer truffle. Fish is treated simply and with respect, sea bass with fennel and olive oil perhaps, while meat, loin of pork maybe, will be given the same treatment. Lest you fear a boring hunk of meat, however, steal yourself for something moist, succulent, well-rounded and full of flavour; much is in the cooking but even more in the sourcing and this was first rate. Desserts bow to modernity: tiramisù is present, but so too are excellent tarts and ices. The all-Italian wine list requires knowledge to reveal the gems, but there is help at hand should you need it. Set 2-course lunch £18.50, 3 courses £21.50; set 2-course dinner £29.50, 3 courses £35.50, 4 courses £39.50.

BERMONDSEY

Delfina Studio Café

MODERN BRITISH   13/20   ♟

50 BERMONDSEY ST, SE1, 020-7357 0244
Lunch Mon.-Fri. ££
U: London Bridge.

A ☎

The space is vast, with its pale wooden floor and acres of white walls displaying modern art. The coffee bar on the right as you enter suggests an informal café but the kitchen at the back delivers serious lunches (closed in the evening) to the various tables scattered about. Flavours are robust and delivered with style and panache, a roasted tomato soup with Indian-style spicing, or home-cured beef with celeriac rémoulade for example, the latter adding punch and richness. Main courses might be chicken, well roasted, and served with a winter bean stew and wilting salad leaves, or monkfish with chilli, chickpeas and chorizo. Flavourings from the Levant play their part, but overall Maria Elia treads an independent route with tremendous verve and usually success. Desserts are less inspiring, but no less well-executed than you might expect: quince and amaretto tart for example, or an old-fashioned chocolate and walnut roulade. The wine list canters about the world and is reasonably priced; service is relaxed, willing and efficient.

BLOOMSBURY

Alfred

MODERN BRITISH   11/20
245 SHAFTESBURY AVE, WC2
020-7240 2566, FAX 020-7497 0672
Lunch Mon.-Fri., Dinner Mon.-Sat. £
U: Tottenham Court Rd.

🅰 ☎ 🍴

No-holds barred, unfussy British cooking is what you can expect from Alfred. The room looks more like a caff than a proper restaurant with formica- and marble-topped tables, but there's nothing greasy spoon-like about the cooking. The menu looks you in the eye and talks straight. Start with leek and potato soup, potted duck with roast pickles and chutney or even haggis and neeps. Follow with braised duck leg served with champ and spinach, and candied orange of Welsh lamb shank with garlic mash and tomato and olive sauce. There's no nonsense in the puddings either—Trinity College burnt cream (bah humbug to the foreigners who call it crème brûlée), hot apple pie or gingerbread and custard. The wine list has plenty of medium-priced, interesting wines, and there's also a list of real ales. As is the way with English food, it's hearty fare. You're pretty well guaranteed not to need to eat for a day if you manage all three courses. Set lunch £10; set 2-course dinner £13.90, 3 courses £17.

CHALK FARM

Belgo Noord

BELGIAN   11/20
72 CHALK FARM RD, NW1
020-7267 0718, FAX 020-7267 7508
Lunch & Dinner daily. £
U: Chalk Farm.

🅰 ☎

The original Belgo still keeps our vote as the best of the group, though Covent Garden comes a very close second. A concrete entrance leads you into a Dante-esque space— you see the heaving, fiery kitchens from above before descending into a cavernous room where names and expressions are massively carved into the concrete. Mussels, beer and chips is the raison d'être for the Belgo group and mighty satisfying too, are these steaming bowls of moules prepared in different ways— Provençale, classic, with mustard, served in platters or pots and all coming with frites and mayonnaise. But the menu doesn't stop here: there are salads, grills and specials like game in season, perhaps partridge braised in an Abbey beer with Ardennes ham, Savoy cabbage and filling parsley mash. Beer fans swear by its list—some hundred Belgian beers, followed by schnapps served in small glasses and held aloft in wooden carriers by hard-working staff. There's a great £5 lunchtime deal, plus set meals at Belgo branches running from £13.95 (Belgo Zuid) to £15.95 (Belgo Noord). Also in **Covent Garden** at Belgo Centraal, 50 Earlham St, WC2, 020-7813 2233; **Notting Hill Gate** at Belgo Zuid, 124 Ladbroke Grove, W10, 020-8982 8400. Bierodrome is in **Clapham** at 44-48 Clapham High St, SW4, 020-7720 1118; **Islington** at 173-174 Upper High St, N1, 020-7226 5835 (see *Bars*).

CHELSEA

Aubergine

FRENCH   16/20   👨‍🍳👨‍🍳
11 PARK WALK, SW10
020-7352 3449, FAX 020-7351 1770
Lunch Mon.-Fri., Dinner Mon.-Sat. £££.
U: Sloane Sq.

🅰 ☎ 🍴

Post-Gordon Ramsey, this impeccable Chelsea address seems to have lost none of its allure and is almost as hard to book as ever. Chef William Drabble cooks haute modern French cuisine to exacting standards with considerable flair and artistry, producing some dishes close to perfection. Boudin of pigeon with foie gras, morels and truffle jus is a fabulous assault on the tastebuds and looks stunning—arranged petal-like on the plate. Seared scallops with pea purée is an exquisitely delicate balance of sweetness and earthiness. Only roasted cod with braised lettuce and morels was less thrilling. Mallard with foie gras and caramelised turnip had superb flavour. A dessert of caramelised pineapple millefeuille with coconut ice cream tasted a trifle over sweet, a fig compote was infinitely more successful. The room seems rather dated with apricot rag-rolled walls, and the lack of view or daylight may disappoint at lunch, though the set menu offers a great deal. For the total gastronomic experience, an awesome six-course truffle menu is offered in season. The wine list is weighted towards serious spending on French vintages. Service is immensely knowledgeable and thoughtful. Set 2-course lunch £16, 3 courses £19.50; set 3-course dinner £45; Menu Dégustation £59.50.

Bluebird Restaurant

MODERN BRITISH   13/20   ♔
350 KING'S RD, SW3
020-7559 1000, FAX 020-7559 1111
Lunch & Dinner daily. £££
U: Sloane Sq.

🅰 ☎

Only Conran could make eating in a former classic 1930s garage glamorous. The dazzlingly airy Bluebird with its steel girder roof, fluttering blue banners, extraordinary light, and trademark crustacea altar invariably has a good buzz. Andrew Sargent is now well into his stride in the kitchen and his deceptively simple approach with far less emphasis on fusion for fusion's sake is definitely a marked improvement, as are the hugely generous portions. The lightest of vine-wrapped sheep ricotta served with grilled peppers and Poilane toast made for a stylish starter. Equally satisfying was a creamy Jerusalem artichoke soup judiciously flavoured with cèpes. Preserved lemon gave a good piquancy to sea bass en papillote, whilst wood-roasted salmon with red onion and coriander made for a more raunchy dish. The wood-roasted vegetable side order is a delicious must. Only a bland pavlova—not gooey enough in the centre—disappointed; far better was an abundant platter of exotic fruit with a nicely citrus lemon parfait. The wine list is sassy, cosmopolitan and with a decent range by the glass. Service is informal, efficient yet rather impersonal. Good for family Sunday brunches. Set 2-course lunch Mon.-Fri. £12.75, 3 courses £15.75, set 3-course Sun. lunch £17.50; children's meals £4.50, £5; set 2-course dinner (6pm-7pm) £12.75, 3 courses £15.75.

Busabong Tree

THAI   13/20   ♔
112 CHEYNE WALK, SW10
020-7352 7534, FAX 020-7352 6661
Lunch daily, Dinner Mon.-Sat. £
U: None nearby.

🅰 ☎ ⛾

Feng Shui buffs point to Busabong Tree as an example of their art—or science. A practitioner supervised the recent makeover involving a colour change from blue to pale daffodil, set off by colourful fabrics and artefacts. The more serene ambience may well be the result of rearranging the tables, but the flowery courtyard, always delightful in summer, is unchanged, as is the charming service led by owner Mini. Starters more interesting than the usual versions are satay beef, chicken or prawns with a creamy garlic sauce, plus the usual peanut sauce, toast and cucumber; and chicken wings stuffed with crab meat, chopped chicken, coriander roots and glass noodles. Black tiger prawns grilled on sticks, jacketed prawns, and fish cakes are simpler options. The Moral Maze of 'Chef's specials' includes scallops with mange-touts in coconut sauce with red curry and holy basil; devil monkfish in green curry sauce; and 'passion killer' stir-fried king prawns in fish sauce with garlic, coriander and black pepper. There are about twenty vegetarian dishes. Many of the forty well-chosen wines are well suited to the food. Set lunch £9.95; set 3-course dinner £22.25 & £27.

The English Garden

MODERN BRITISH   14/20   ♔
10 LINCOLN ST, SW3
020-7584 7272, FAX 020-7584 1961
Lunch & Dinner Mon.-Sat. ££
U: Sloane Sq.

🅰 ☎

Culinary proof that the best in life often comes in small packages and a welcome antidote to the 90s big-is-better brasserie. The petite English Garden has been drastically repackaged—the chintz and fussy cooking has been replaced by a svelte contemporary scheme of taupe and suede with a pleasing glazed conservatory roof at the rear and excellent modern Irish cuisine by Malcolm Starmer, formerly long-standing sous-chef to Richard Corrigan. Delectable terrine of game birds with foie gras and fig fondant, and a striking combination of goat cheese ricotta, black pig ham and sherry dressing were first-rate starters. A pretty 'tasting' assembly of shoulder and belly of pork with crubeens (pig's trotter), black pudding and sauerkraut had plenty of flavourful impact without being too full-on, whilst Beaufort cheese was an inspired pungent addition to baked cod with ventreche. Perfect gooey-centred chocolate fondant with retro caramelised oranges and notable cheeses from a separate cheese menu, plus a well-thought out wine list and assured service, completed a most promising meal. Set 3-course lunch including half bottle of wine £19.50.

Gordon Ramsay

MODERN BRITISH   18/20   ♟♟♟
68 ROYAL HOSPITAL RD, SW3
020-7352 4441, FAX 020-7352 3334
Lunch & Dinner Mon.-Fri. ££££
U: Sloane Sq.

🅰 ☎ ❢

The entrance to what was La Tante Claire is as before, down a long corridor off the street and into a small drinks area. The colour scheme, however, has been reworked and as with the square room, everything is brighter and sharper, glass playing a predominant role—mirrored, sculpted and frosted. The food is decidedly French in style, but with contemporary twists and turns, as in lemon grass appearing in a shellfish bisque accompanying crab ravioli. The kitchen certainly works and effort from various quarters will appear on each plate: a starter of raw scallop, diced and fashioned into towers with caviar, cucumber and basil consommé to set it off for example, or a more traditional, but nonetheless excellent, terrine of foie gras. Amuses have transferred from his former restaurant, Aubergine, as in cappuccino of haricots blancs, with success. Main courses vary from the robust: braised shin of beef with pomme purée, that latter as rich as rich can be, to more elegant but still sturdy turbot poached in red wine, the wine appearing as a rich (again) reduction on the plate. Other main courses might be pigeon, served with a choux farcis, or sea bass, the skin roasted to a crisp and served with langoustine. Desserts come with a flourish, vanilla crème brûlée with jus Granny Smith, pistachio soufflé or a terrine of citrus fruits with accompanying sorbets for example. Service is impeccable, the wine list largely French and although hardly a bargain, there is a some-

thing-for-everyone approach. Set 3-course lunch £28; set 3-course dinner £55, 7 courses £70.

The House

MODERN BRITISH   14/20   ♟
3 MILNER ST, SW3
020-7584 3002, FAX 020-7581 2848
Lunch Mon.-Fri., Dinner Mon.-Sat. £
U: Sloane Sq.

🅰 ☎

Formerly The English House, the menu is more English than ever now it's part of the restaurant group owned by Richard Corrigan (of Lindsay House fame, see below). Chef/patron Graham Garrett works in a style similar to Corrigan's, which might just as well be called *rus in urbe*, bringing as it does a bit of the country into city cooking. The décor, however, has not changed, so there are still flower-patterned, fabric-covered walls and all that goes with it, which either grows on you or irritates you; this may evolve or it may not change at all. Either way, the cooking is just where it should be—gutsy, flavourful food informed by a refined sensibility. Don't you just love a paradox. The menu changes frequently but recent hits included goose rillettes with tomato and onion chutney; cold poached skate, potato, parsley and caper salad. Mains run to roast rump of lamb and balsamic roasted red onions; and a real winner in ballotine of pheasant, confit of belly pork with fondant potato (is Alain Ducasse reading this?) and black pudding-stuffed apple. Good cheeses, worthwhile desserts, well-chosen wines and service organised by Dieter Jurgensen cannot be faulted. Set 3-course lunch £14.50; 3-course dinner £21.

Le Colombier

FRENCH   13/20   ♟
145 DOVEHOUSE ST, SW3
020-7351 1155, FAX 020-7351 0055
Lunch & Dinner daily. ££
U: Sloane Sq/South Kensington.

🅰 ☎ 🍷

A new Gallic classic. Didier Garnier, former manager of Brasserie St. Quentin has created a worthy successor which feels more contemporary—an airy blue-and-white dining room reincarnation of a run-down pub—whilst remaining true to quality ingredients simply prepared. Starters include an authentic, garlicky fish soup and snails in puff pastry. Dishes like sea bass baked with thyme, and monkfish with red wine sauce and bacon exemplify the maxim that fish at its finest needs little elaboration. The set lunch is a steal. The terrace with smart stripy awning is a real draw in the summer. Set 2-course lunch, 6.30pm-7.30pm £13.

Lomo

SPANISH   11/20
222 FULHAM RD, SW10, 020-7349 8848
Mon.-Sat. noon-midnight, Sun. 10am-11pm. £
U: Fulham Broadway.

Swinging Chelsea says salud to jumping Madrid or bounding Barcelona in this super tapas bar. Lively young(ish) people crowd into a room accommodating only 48 on bright orange-backed steel chairs at tables and pillars. Super tapas are raciones, twice the size of ordinary tapas and some involving several ingredients. Cantabrian anchovies come with toast and shallots; lomo embuchado is smoked pork loin with goat cheese, roast peppers and tapenade wrapped in soca, a thin rolled pancake. Olives and fresh capers come with bread, and there are some more substantial dishes such as sizzling chicken with parsley and garlic, or fillet steak hogazas (sandwiches) with rocket and manchego cheese. The £5 lunch menu offers any three from six items which might be grilled mackerel, Serrano ham, escalivada (marinated roasted vegetables), green salad, and patatas bravas or allioli. Breakfast delicacies include the expected churros, and scrambled egg with unexpected real caviar from Spain. Interesting wines, mostly under £17, are mostly Spanish, and the true Andalusian taste can be indulged with fino sherry or Manzanilla from chilled half-bottles. Service is friendly but not exaggeratedly Spanish so orders arrive well before mañana.

Soviet Canteen

RUSSIAN   12/20
430 KING'S RD, SW10, 020-7795 1556
Dinner Mon.-Sat. Lunch by special booking. £
U: Sloane Sq.

Here we have an engagingly eccentric Russian basement down in World's End that takes its interior design cue from early 1970s Muscovite milk bar chic, complete with garish

soft furnishings and metal-top table functionalism, pop prints of Lenin and a chandelier made up of re-cycled kitchen utensils. It's comfortable enough though, and thankfully there's enough content behind the style. Chef Mike Scutar's cooking is both revelation and revolution: a decadent helping of zakuski (smoked salmon and chive cream, quail eggs and Oscietra caviar with smoked sturgeon, served with a shot of vodka, natch); Georgian roast wild pigeon and, but of course comrade, beef stroganoff ('served with chipski'). Wash it all down with a Molotov cocktail or a Siberian sling. Set-course dinner 6.30pm-8pm £12.50, 3 courses £15.50, both include a glass of house wine.

Vama

INDIAN   12/20
438 KING'S RD, SW10
020-7351 4118, FAX 020-7565 8501
Lunch & Dinner daily. ££
U: Sloane Sq.

Vama may look like an Italian restaurant with its Tuscan hues, flagstone floor and French windows opening onto the busy King's Road, but the menu is Indian. The dishes are unusually well-prepared and a good range of Indian cooking styles is showcased. The meat cookery from the north-west of the sub-continent is particularly reliable: try the baby lamb marinated in ginger and coriander (adraki gosht, £9.95), perhaps with one of the breads (such as the curiously elastic roomali roti, £2.50). Vegetarians needn't feel left out, as vegetarian dishes are given equal prominence, and are refreshingly interesting: marrow is cooked with cumin and tomatoes (£6.50 as a main course). Service is attentive, and managed by an engaging Indian woman who is happy to explain the dishes. Set lunch £6.95, £9.95.

Zen Chelsea

CHINESE   15/20
CHELSEA CLOISTERS, SLOANE AVE, SW3
020-7589 1781
Lunch & Dinner daily. ££
U: South Kensington.

New management has transformed the Zen group's revered, but tired, ancestral home into a thrusting new generation, deluxe restaurant in 90s Hong Kong style. The warmer, lighter décor is welcome and welcoming, as are smiling, efficient staff. The whole menu asks to be quoted which would fill too many of our pages. The main list includes such delicacies as supreme shark's fins in imperial sauce, whole suckling pig and various fresh fish and lobsters prepared nine ways. Fifty more 'chef's recommendations' include remarkable soups ranging from double-boiled quails, snow fungi and almond at £16 for four people, to braised superior mixed dried seafood hot pot at £198 for twelve. With so many temptations, it is wise to let manager Philip Chan choose, saying at the outset what you expect to spend. At lunch the selection is equally wide, but dim sum from £2.20 make it easier on the pocket; the lunch special noodle menu offers one-dish meals from £6, and there are even afternoon tea (2.30pm-5pm) menus for dim sum and soup noodle combinations from £6.80. On weekends there are extra dim sum treats and snacks such as stewed pork skin with fish ball and turnip. Set menus from £8.80.

CHINATOWN

Aroma
CHINESE　　　14/20

118 SHAFTESBURY AVE, W1
020-7437 0370, FAX 020-7437 0377
Open Mon.-Sat. noon-midnight, Sun. noon-10.30pm. £
U: Leicester Sq.

In many ways one is overburdened with choice of Chinese restaurants around Gerrard Street, but the quality of these establishments is variable, and price is not necessarily an indication. The original Aroma Restaurant is one of the better restaurants on Gerrard Street but the younger branch around the corner in Shaftesbury Avenue is rather the better of the two. The normal collection of set menus is available, but as ever they offer good value but hold little interest. Go deeper into the menu and you'll find proper preparation and careful cooking. All the usual suspects are there: baked lobster with ginger and spring onion, platters of starters, crispy beef in garlic sauce, but there's also an astonishing range of dishes not usually offered to the general public. Here they are prepared to make you a real shark's fin soup, pig crackling with turnips and chives or baked quails with spicy salt and pepper.

Service is professional and friendly, something almost unknown in Chinatown, and the restaurant is clean, comfortable and reasonably elegant, which is equally unusual. Set meals £13.50-£22.

Fung Shing
CHINESE　　　14/20

15 LISLE ST, WC2
020-7437 1539, FAX 020-7734 0284
Open noon-11.30pm. £
U: Leicester Sq.

This long top-rated Chinatown kitchen now has a worthy successor to the late lamented Chef Wu. Mr. Chung was chef-patron of the Mayflower in Shaftesbury Avenue when it was an informal dining club for London's top European chefs. His style here could set a trend for 'cuisine haute paysanne'. For although the menu offers luxuries such as lobster and fresh abalone, its most striking successes are powerfully flavoured home-style dishes. Vegetables include spicy aubergine with minced meat in a clay pot, and water spinach (ung choy) with balachan (dried shrimp) sauce. Fish lovers are not neglected in the special à la carte menu, offering razor clams with garlic sauce, stewed stick bean curd with turbot, and chilli spicy fish which might be a whole, filleted, fried sea bass in a chilli-hot, not over-sweet, variation on a sweet/sour sauce. Carnivores find that ostrich with ginger and spring onion demonstrates the big bird's resemblance to beef fillet in tenderness and flavour. The £30 set meal, while not too challenging for delicate western palates, includes 'special cold combo', lobster with noodles, and shark's fin with crab meat soup. Despite the pressures of an ever busy restaurant, service is generally cheerful and skilled, and the pleasant décor is well maintained. In a decent wine list, Guigal's Côtes du Rhône perfectly complements robust Cantonese dishes. Set 2-course lunch £16; set dinners £16-£50.

London Jade Garden
CHINESE　　　12/20

15 WARDOUR ST, W1, 020-7437 5065
Open Mon.-Fri. noon-11.30pm, Sat. noon-11.45pm, Sun. 11am-10.15pm. £
U: Leicester Sq.

Confusion does not only mean disorientated Oriental dishes. Here it starts with the restaurant's name; they call themselves London Jade Garden or simply Jade Garden. It extends to the service—sometimes gracious and helpful, sometimes surly and baffled by occidental mysteries, such as the English language. Dishes arrive with startling speed or after long delays and it is not always apparent that what does arrive is what was ordered—enigmatic morsels are perhaps intended for other tables. In theory the staff can't be blamed because dim sum are ordered by the customer ticking choices on a paper menu which lists them only in Chinese, although helpfully they are numbered too. Arrive early for lunch to get a balcony table overlooking the hubbub below. Steamed dim sum include a full range of buns and dumplings, spareribs in various sauces, and noodle rolls. The many and varied fried ones oddly include some grilled items. Congee, rice porridge with various garnishes, is a speciality which makes a good snack, on its own or accompanied by a few dim sum. In the evening, the long conventional à la carte is generally acceptable, and to drink there are very fine special teas. Set menus for minimum of 2 people £11-£25.

Ming

CHINESE   14/20   ♟

35-36 GREEK ST, W1, 020-7734 2721
Lunch & Dinner Mon.-Sat. ££
U: Leicester Sq.

A ☎

This delightful, small Chinese restaurant has consistently served good food for many years. Its owner, Christine Yau, has also worked tirelessly to build up a loyal following by offering advice to customers who might feel daunted by the menu. In addition, the service is charming and the stunning décor, with its sea green coloured walls, makes it the smartest Chinese restaurant in Chinatown; although it seems to appeal more to Westerners than the local Chinese community. The cooking, however, is thoroughly authentic and specialises in dishes from the Northern provinces, although other regional dishes appear on the menu. Favourites include double-braised pork; empress beef and prawn cakes; lobster with spiced salt (there are six lobster dishes on offer) and duck breast sliced with orange and spices. Added to this is the pleasure of tasting the other homemade additions like pickles and dumplings. There are four set menus and a lengthy à la carte, and there is a good wine list to juggle with your food. Set menus £15-£35.

Mr Kong

CHINESE   14/20   ♟

21 LISLE ST, WC2
020-7437 7341, FAX 020-7437 7923
Open daily noon-3am. £
U: Leicester Sq.

A ☎

Mr. Kong's strong points are neither décor nor ambience although both exceed local norms. Nor, although they may be above average, should one order set dinners with crispy aromatic duck and sweet and sour pork. Consider instead 'chef's special' and 'To-Day Chef's Special' menus, or ask the manager for suggestions. They might be deep-fried crispy aubergine with yam paste, miraculously transmuting two bland ingredients into a richly flavoured dish, which, by the way, comes with a not too sweet sweet-sour sauce, or steamed stuffed prawns with prawn paste in garlicky sauce. If you are fortunate, you might find something as wonderful as our braised eels with Chinese cucumber and roasted pork in hot-pot, the white Chinese cucumber soft yet crisp, the eel thick and succulent. It's not always on the menu so ask for ung choy (water spinach) with garlic, chilli and shrimp paste. The range of seafood is wide and the adventurous will find surf clam, razor clam and top shell. For the less adventurous (or foolhardy), there are such delicacies as sautéed chicken with fresh mango and asparagus. And for the incorrigibly audacious there is fried cuttlefish cake with angled loofah and black fungus. Set menus for minimum of two people £9.30 to £22 (minimum four people).

New Diamond

CHINESE   13/20   ♟

23 LISLE ST, WC2, 020-7437 2517
Open daily noon-3am. £
U: Leicester Sq.

A ☎

Those who wish to know what TV and celebrity chefs actually eat should dine late (it's open until about 3am), for the chance to watch them enjoying gutsy peasant cooking very different from their own here at the New Diamond. It is Cantonese with hardly any westernisation except in the dull set menus. Soups as familiar as wonton, or unusual as diced winter melon with mixed meat are more interesting than 'hors d'œuvres', although the latter includes rarely seen geoduck clam with jellyfish. At least some dishes once only in the written 'Chinese menu' now appear on the printed list. Hot pots include much acclaimed stewed duck with yam, and for the really brave, stewed fish head with bean curd. Diced chicken in hot sauce lives up to its name, with water chestnuts providing a happy contrast of textures. Untypical for Chinatown, the black-and-white décor is well maintained, and the service is even more unusual in being positively friendly—one waiter was so friendly to the female customers that he might have previously worked in an Italian restaurant. Set menus for minimum of two people £10 to £16.

Poons & Co

CHINESE   14/20   ♟
27 LISLE ST WC2, 0171 437 4549
Open daily noon-11.30pm. £
U: Leciester Sq/Piccadilly Circus.

The promotion of 'little Poons' from our Quick Bite section does not mean that it has become more luxurious or more expensive. It remains a simple eating house, its four tiny rooms, plainly furnished and decorated serving excellent food. It also remains remarkable value for a quick lunch or dinner. Poons' wind-dried duck, Chinese sausages and bacon were brought to London in the restaurant's early days and are still among the city's best. Another innovation was 'original hot-pots' with chicken and Chinese mushrooms, minced beef and egg, or sparerib in black bean sauce which arrive at table in a steel pot. One on its own makes a meal for two, perhaps with soup on the side. Stick to authentic Cantonese dishes and eschew crispy duck or the starters so common elsewhere. Single dish meals include a wide variety of noodles, in soup, or braised and plates of rice with meat or fish. Don't expect lobsters but enjoy crab with spring onion and ginger or with chilli and black bean sauce. Set menus are not bad but don't include hot-pots, wind-dried foods or other specialities. Service is friendly and helpful. Set menus £7.50-£16.

CHISWICK

Grano

ITALIAN   13/20   ♟
162 THAMES RD, W4, 020-8995 0120
Lunch Sun., Tues.-Fri., Dinner Mon.-Sat. ££
U: Gunnersbury.

A room without a view despite its riverside location may disappoint, yet the well-thought out, robust regional Italian food makes amends. Alessio Brusadin's homemade pasta is outstanding: especially guinea fowl ravioli with a divine, creamy, truffle oil-infused potato purée. Gutsy mains include rabbit with black olive and thyme, and seared tuna with a serious balsamic jus. Desserts such as Marsala mousse with chocolate meringue maintain the good sense of balance and Italian authenticity. The entirely Italian wine list has some prestigious bottles worth investing in. The bare brick and wooded floorboard interior made more formal with crisp linen and astute, welcoming staff, ensures attention does not wander too far from the intelligent and diligent cooking. Set 2-course lunch £15, 3 courses £19; set 2-course dinner £19, 3 courses £24.

Riso

ITALIAN   12/20
76 SOUTH PARADE, W4, 020-8742 2121
Lunch Sat.-Sun., Dinner Tues.-Sun. £
U: Turnham Green.

Despite its unprepossessing site, this promising, new, informal neighbourhood restaurant offers simple, modern Italian food charmingly served at hard-to-quibble prices. Starters are little more than well-shopped assemblies: anchovies with grilled courgettes, decent grilled vegetables. Homemade pasta is where the kitchen really excels: delicate pumpkin ravioli served simply with butter and sage was outstanding. Skate with balsamic vinegar and faultless, ultra-smooth mash was confidently cooked too. Desserts falter: cloying white chocolate pudding with orange sauce, and insipid poached pear unsubtly lashed with amaretto. Good simple Italian wine list. Set 2-course menu £15, 3 courses £19.

THE CITY

Aurora

CONTEMPORARY EUROPEAN   **13/20**   ♕
GREAT EASTERN HOTEL, LIVERPOOL ST, EC2
020-7618 7000, FAX 020-7618 7001
*Breakfast Mon.-Fri., Lunch Sun.-Fri., Dinner
Mon.-Sat. £££*
U: Liverpool St.

A ☎

Yet again, Sir Terence Conran displays his canny knack for rescuing forgotten splendid buildings which have fallen on hard times. The restoration of The Great Eastern Hotel's flagship dining room is no exception. It is a grandiose, pillared room of dramatic proportions with painted murals and an attention-grabbing, stained glass cupola which is seductively back-lit at night. This is a sophisticated haute cuisine operation with impeccably drilled staff, so expectations are sky-high. The menu reads superbly. Pity then that tian of crab comes with tired, over-fried soft-shell crab, and the appealing-sounding, chilled lemon grass velouté is too heavily spiked with ginger. Cappuccino of morels lacked intensity as well as the anticipated froth, but was partnered with heavenly roast scallops and braised leeks. Exquisitely tender French pigeon is served with a masterful endive tarte Tatin and what looks like a Scotch egg filled with foie gras and a rich Madeira jus. Veal sweetbreads caramelised in aged Xeres vinegar sauce were disappointingly fatty but accompanied by superb braised salsify. The cheese trolly is truly exceptional with a stunning selection of cheeses in superb condition. Puddings excel too: both definitive tarte Tatin with cinnamon ice cream and a more fanciful glass plate of delectable chocolate desserts. Serious consideration has been given to a weighty wine list. Aurora should mature into a premier gastro-destination.

Café Spice Namaste

INDIAN   **13/20**   ♕
16 PRESCOT ST, E1
020-7488 9242, FAX 020-7488 9339
Lunch & Dinner Mon.-Fri. £
U: Tower Hill.

A ☎

A riot of vivid south Indian colours throughout the restaurant does not imply a boring sameness, for the vivid purples and reds of fabrics in the front area contrast with softer orange and green in the back room. The menu is equally diverse, both in ingredients and in their preparation. Weekly specials might include milkfish, Swedish elk or, as on our last visit, swordfish, beautifully marinated before roasting in the tandoor. In the main menu, sea bass, monkfish, scallops, tuna and wild Scotch salmon jostle with conventional meats as well as venison, Barbary duck, and wild boar in the form of sausages. Dishes of widely varied origin represent north India, Gwalior, the Punjab, south India, even Thailand and China. But the emphasis is on Goa and, of course, on the cuisine of chef-patron Cyrus Todiwala's own Bombay Parsee community. The most refreshingly sour lassi, the crispest popadoms, the most piquant pickles are additional pleasures. Vegetables include challengingly hot channa chutt putti—a street speciality of Dhaka, Bangladesh, based on succulent chickpeas sauced and garnished with chilli, yoghurt, shallots, tamarind and crushed poories. The wine list expertly guides diners towards what best complements the cuisine.

Also in **Battersea** at 247 Lavender Hill, SW11, 020-7738 1717.

City Rhodes

MODERN BRITISH   **16/20**   ♕♕
1 NEW ST SQ, EC4, 020-7583 1313
Lunch & Dinner Mon.-Fri. £££
U: Chancery Lane.

A ☎

It's all credit to the spiky one—despite yet more TV & getting the Rhodes & Co brasserie concept on the road, his flagship enterprise remains stellar with sublime, sophisticated British cuisine given a modern spin, and well-informed, exemplary staff who seem more than content to work for our Gary in absentia. Twice-baked truffle soufflé lifted a creamy celeriac soup into the realm of something thrilling. Both delicately flavoured poached loin of lamb with foie gras and shallot Tatin, and a delectably tender partridge on foie gras toast (no stinting on luxury ingredients here) were perfectly executed with no unnecessary adornments. Puddings are extremely fine: dark chocolate soufflé and warm lemon pudding with raspberries provoked raptures. A carefully constructed wine list and a considerate sommelier add to the pleasures. Only the rather soulless modern décor of the obscurely located first-floor dining room, which already seems dated, disappoints—especially for lingering evening visits. More a venue for larger groups and lunchtime meets.

Club Gascon

FRENCH   **16/20**
57 WEST SMITHFIELD, EC1
020-7253 5853, FAX 020-7796 0601
Lunch Mon.-Fri., Dinner Mon.-Sat. ££
U: Barbican/Farringdon.

Since it opened in 1998, this has been garlanded with awards. And for originality, and some outstanding dishes, rightly so. It's a joy to find somewhere devoted to the rich, earthy regional delicacies for which Gascony is famous. The menu is not structured conventionally. Dishes are scaled down to allow sampling of around four or five savouries and even (though unlikely) two desserts. No one should miss out on the glorious griddled foie gras with grapes and onion marmalade, or smoked eel with horseradish cream. Chips cooked in duck fat can be outrageously good. Or not, we've had the odd dish that misses the target. And some dishes such as cassoulet are odd in miniature; there's a risk a meal doesn't get into its stride. But it's a risk worth taking for remarkable high spots. Another attraction is the delightful setting just off Smithfield meat market (somehow appropriate). With marble walls, a silver ceiling and simple furnishings, it's a beguiling place. From the moment you try to book (do so well in advance), service can be patchy. Wines are mostly resolutely regional and often unusually powerful reds. Set 5-course meal £30, with 5 glasses of wine £50.

Le Coq d'Argent

FRENCH   **12/20**
NO.1 POULTRY, EC2
020-7395 5000, FAX 020-7359 5050
Breakfast Mon.-Fri., Lunch Sun.-Fri., Dinner Mon.-Sat. £££
U: Bank.

Conran's City restaurant roosts at the top of No.1 Poultry, James Stirling's pink stone bulwark opposite the Bank of England. Whisked up in a glass lift onto an outdoor roof terrace, you reach a stunning summer eyrie for al fresco dining. The wood-panelled restaurant with tables laid with heavy silver (and characteristic of Conran, conspicuous ashtrays), is aimed at high rollers, not all of them male, but all comfortable in surroundings that suggest that money and masculinity go handsomely together. The menu is correspondingly traditional: dressed crab, coq au vin, entrecôte au poivre, and simple: caviars, oysters and lobster mayonnaise. It doesn't set out to be exciting, but it would be commendable if the kitchen could give it more gravitas. As it is, the cooking has less lustre than the cutlery. And the prices for food that has a little of the production line lack of character are high. An oxtail soup was a broth with bits of vegetable bobbing about, and, inexplicably, what seemed to be a chicken bone. Lobster mayonnaise and steak béarnaise were acceptable but unexceptional. The fine selection of French cheeses is a good alternative to unchallenging desserts. Staff, in a hierarchy of uniforms from white tunics to hotel personnel jacket and tie, are plentiful and well-drilled. Set 2-course Sun. lunch £17.50, 3 courses £20.

I Lombard Street

CONTEMPORARY EUROPEAN   **15/20**
1 LOMBARD ST, EC3
020-7929 6611, FAX 020-7929 6622
Lunch & Dinner Mon.-Fri. £££
U: Bank.

Deep in banking territory, just near the Bank of England and Mansion House and opposite Conran's Le Coq d'Argent (see above), this is one of the many serious restaurants opening in an area of London which hitherto has offered very little by way of gastronomic seriousness. It's pitched itself just right: at the front, there's a large, impressive (this was a former bank, too) noisy brasserie where young traders come to down the bubbly and eat off a menu of robust dishes. Starters like salmon carpaccio with an Oriental salad and Thai vinaigrette, fish soup, and caviar, and main dishes which take in grilled lobster, a flavourful, rich coq au vin or blackened wood pigeon with roasted root vegetables are served at tables grouped around the large central bar. The menu is large, but the cooking is good. At the back, there's a smaller, more expensive and serious restaurant where heavier deals can be done in relative privacy. The menu here offers more complex cooking, as in seared foie gras with celeriac rémoulade and a pungent truffle vinaigrette; sauté of scallops with ginger and lime beurre blanc and Oriental cannelloni or tender roast rack of lamb with truffled potatoes. Chef Herbert Berger has found his niche here; long may he continue. Brasserie: 2-course dinner £18, 3 courses £18.50. Restaurant: 2-course lunch £32, 3 courses £38.

Pacific Oriental

PACIFIC RIM   **13/20**   🍷
1 BISHOPSGATE, EC2, 020-7621 9988
Lunch & Dinner Mon.-Fri. ££
U: Liverpool St.

A ☎

Lively but civilised, this prime City location has its own micro-brewery in the ground floor bar, which does some snacks and light dishes, but the main dining room is on the first-floor balcony. This is an urbanely masculine dining space—comfortable, poised, well-appointed. Service is unfailingly helpful, informed and correctly polite. The bits of the Pacific the menu draws most heavily on are Japan, China, Indonesia, Thailand and Mexico. So for starters expect to find the likes of lobster and mango sushi; Peking duck spring rolls with hoisin sauce; or quesadilla with salmon, Monterey Jack cheese and sambal. Main courses carry on the theme with dishes like five-spiced rib-eye steak with garlic mash; Chinese spiced lamb rump, grilled pumpkin, shiitakes and anise jus, and Caesar salad with smoked chicken and chilli aioli. Chef Darren Wightman's cooking is accomplished, but with a frequently changing menu it is inevitable that there are some misses along with the hits. Set 2-course menu £23, 3 courses £27.

Poons in the City

CHINESE   **12/20**
2 MINSTER PAVEMENT, MINSTER COURT
MINCING LANE, EC3
020-7626 0126, FAX 020-7626 0526
Open Mon.-Fri. 11.30am-10.30pm. Restaurant ££, Café £
U: Monument.

A ☎ 🍴

Despite its location in the lower mall of a glass and steel office building with sculpted horses rearing outside, this restaurant's seriousness, even solidity, is more reminiscent of the nineteenth than the twenty-first century. The décor is Chinese without dragons; seats at the large tables are wide and comfortable. The cooking too is soundly based. The shortish menu offers many standard items, even if their names suggest something more recherché.

Kow lo yuk for example translates as sweet and sour pork, while see chew beef is in black bean sauce with red and green peppers—and is pleasingly tender. Specialities include lap yuk soom—finely chopped vegetables with wind-dried meat eaten wrapped in a lettuce leaf. Another intriguing 'Bill Poon Special' is Cantonese beef hotpot—braised brisket in a sauce involving yellow beans, fermented red beans and a Chinese liqueur. His mastery of subtle culinary technique shows in spicy garlic prawns, stir-fried with garlic chilli and Chinese wine after being deep-fried—and they stay crisp. Interesting vegetarian specials include honeycomb roundels of starch-free wheat flour dough variously cooked. Partly outside, but under the glass atrium, is a (comparatively) fast food snack bar. Restaurant: Set menus for minimum of two people £22.50, £26.50, £30.80.

Prism

CONTEMPORARY EUROPEAN   **14/20**   🍷
147 LEADENHALL ST, EC3, 020-7256 3888
Lunch & Dinner Mon.-Fri. £££
U: Bank/Monument.

A ☎ 🍴

Harvey Nichols (see Oxo Tower above), is responsible for the conversion of the former Bank of New York into this magnificent, white-pillared dining room which dwarfs the red leather Mies van der Rohe chairs around well-spaced tables—a luxury in the City where space is at a premium. Inevitably, given the imposing building, and the fact that it's a long way from the mother ship, it's a little lacking in soul. The cooking has more than might be expected, though. It doesn't play safe for a conservative clientele, but brings some delicacy and individuality to down-to-earthy ingredients, resulting in clear, bold, unusual flavours in relatively hearty portions. Witness the lightly battered Whitby cod on a vivid pat of delicately mushed peas—even though it's called tempura of cod with pea purée. Another striking starter was a paella-meets-risotto plate of Arborio rice with chorizo and juicy prawns. Calf's liver with soft polenta and grilled pancetta made a classy, comforting trio of textures and tastes. Fish soup is a classic version; skate with capers and brown butter is another unmessed-with dish. Desserts are as various as apple strudel, rum baba or a more wayward plate of citrus fruits around mango and chilli sorbet. Service is enthusiastic and well informed.

Quadrato

ITALIAN   **13/20**

FOUR SEASONS CANARY WHARF
46 WESTFERRY CIRCUS, E14
020-7510 1857, FAX 020-7510 1998
Lunch & Dinner daily. ££
U: Canary Wharf.

A ☎

You'll find agreeably authentic Northern Italian cuisine at this enjoyably swanky hotel dining room overlooking the second coming of Canary Wharf. Chef Marco Bax learnt his trade at the Four Seasons Milan and oversees a confident menu with specialities including garganelli with braised endive, spinach and chicken fillets, and a roasted rack of lamb with caramelised shallots and figs. Elsewhere squid ink taglionini with pesto, warm ricotta and winter truffle salad, and a splendid veal Milanese (it would need to be of course) show plenty of verve. There's a good selection of vegetarian options, too. You can watch Signor Bax through a glass panel to the front of the kitchen, a neat counterpoint to the low-lit interior, all hues of black currant and brown set off with a cube motif. Italian wines to the fore and front-of-house have an efficient charm. Set 2-course lunch £18, 3 courses £22; set 2-course dinner £24, 3 courses £28.

Searcy's at the Barbican

INTERNATIONAL   **11/20**

BARBICAN CENTRE, LEVEL 2, SILK ST, EC2
020-7588 3008, FAX 020-7382 7247
Lunch Sun.-Fri., Dinner nightly (to 7pm Sun). ££
U: Barbican.

A ☎

Searcy's has put a considerable amount of effort into making this restaurant work. One of the problems it has had to overcome has been how to keep its diverse clientele, city types on the one hand, patrons of the Barbican on the other, all happy. In this it has largely succeeded through the excellent cooking designed to appeal to everyone. Former chef Richard Corrigan has left his trademark— modern British with a hint of Irish—on the menu, in dishes like braised collar of bacon, Savoy cabbage with cream and grain mustard sauce. But there is also more than a nod in the direction of Italy, with various risottos and a paupiette of veal with mozzarella and sage, roasted peppers and a red onion jus on offer too. The short à la carte, five starters and main courses, is supplemented by a daily menu at £18.50 and £21.50. The service is efficient and respectful; the wine list is adequate. But Searcy's—who are expanding all around town at the moment—must pay attention to this operation if they want to keep it working properly. Set lunch & dinner menus 2 courses £18.50, 3 courses £21.50.

Tatsuso

JAPANESE   **17/20**

32 BROADGATE CIRCLE, EC2
020-7638 5863, FAX 020-7638 5864
Lunch & Dinner Mon.-Fri. £££
U: Liverpool St.

A ☎

This traditionally elegant Japanese establishment offers a wealth of set menus which makes it easy to order, although in normal Japanese style most items are described only by how they are cooked. The Fuji menu (£58) features toban yaki—sliced beef cooked at the table in a neat miniature casserole; it is preceded by appetisers: clear soup, sashimi, tempura, and Japanese salad. More modest sukiyaki, shabu-shabu or sashimi menus offer those centrepieces with four courses beforehand. The long à la carte starts with small seasonal dishes which many consider the superstars of Japanese gastronomy. There is simple perfection in ohitashi, seasonal vegetables, usually spinach or watercress, with shaved bonito in a soy and mirin sauce. If you prefer to hoe a different row, try salmon roe with grated mooli; crabmeat and its own roe; or marinated herring roe. Sashimi is all it should be and egg shell crisp tempura may include a sprig of ultra-fine pasta. A rare speciality is chopped fish, prawn and eel rolled in noodle paste coloured and flavoured with green tea. Don't overlook sunamono, lightly vinegared relishes with seaweed and a choice of scallop, squid, mackerel or jelly fish. The teppan room on the upper floor features the finest meat and seafood prepared by specialists in cooking, not in knife-juggling. Kashinoki (see above) and Hiroko in Kensington are now owned by Tatsuso. Lunch menus £37-£80, dinners £42 to £80; Teppan lunch menus £28 to £80, dinners £43 to £80.

Tatsuso Teppan Room

JAPANESE   15/20

32 BROADGATE CIRCLE, EC2, 020-7638 5863
Lunch & Dinner Mon.-Fri. £££
U: Liverpool St.
   For set menus *see above.*

Twentyfour

MODERN BRITISH   14/20

LEVEL 24, TOWER 42, OLD BROAD ST., EC2
020-7877 2424, FAX 020-7877 7788
Lunch & Dinner Mon.-Fri. ££
U: Bank.

The Roux Brothers are literally reaching for the sky at this 24th-floor restaurant with aspirations to match. These are fairly convincingly achieved. Of course, the panoramic view across the City, taking in St. Paul's and Tower Bridge, helps immensely in creating drama. Quite correctly, the interior design does not try to compete against this but makes a virtue of good materials, clean lines and interesting curves, keeping chairs and tabletop items below sight lines in both the spacious bar and dining room. Service is professional, correctly unobtrusive and staff are well-informed and enthusiastic about the menu. This is kept sensibly short with seven starters and eight mains, supplemented by two or three daily specials at each course. Good cooking is what one would expect from a stablemate of Le Gavroche and the Waterside Inn—confident and well chosen with good contrapuntal harmony between ingredients. Some are classics like starters of seared scallops, wonderfully caramelised on the surface, with a fettucini of vegetables and lobster butter sauce. Others are interesting variations, like the starter of boudin of foie gras and green peppercorns served with a salad of French beans and sherry vinaigrette. And some dishes are altogether surprising, like the saffron steamed halibut with a ragoût of mussels, clams and trompettes de la mort, the whole assembly working wonderfully together. Desserts, such as molten chocolate cake, do not let the side down. Wines are very well chosen and staff are also knowledgeable in this area. Set 3-course lunch £26.50.

CLERKENWELL

Gaudi

SPANISH   16/20

63 CLERKENWELL RD, EC1
020-7608 3220, FAX 020-7250 1057
Lunch & Dinner Mon.-Fri. ££
U: Farringdon.

The décor may not suit all tastes and particularly in daylight might seem excessively gaudy, but the amiable service conquers all reservations. And even if the service were by snarling serfs in a broken-down shed, all could be forgiven for the excellence of the cooking. Amuse-gueules which really amuse are tiny brochettes of chive-sprinkled melon and ham, then chorizo in filo pastry which give a whole new meaning to 'sausage roll'. Chef Nacho Martinez' skill in execution equals his flair and imagination in such dishes as duck foie gras in escabèche with warm vegetable salad, or Castilian garlic soup with poached quail eggs, Serrano ham and cheese croûton. Similarly unlikely combinations succeed in sea bream baked in salt on red cabbage with aioli, pine nuts and sultanas, or herbed loin of wild boar garnished with wild mushrooms and small glazed white scallions filled with aubergine paste. That these garnishes are neither so meagre as to make you feel cheated, nor large enough to outstay their welcome, confirms his sound judgement. Equally tempting desserts include the penultimate gastronomic hedonism in the warm walnut sauce accompanying deep-fried cream, but the ultimate is the Pedro Ximenez ice cream with turron soufflé. The Spanish wine list shows a sharp eye for quality from house wines at £11.50 to rare old reservas extending to Vega Sicilia 1981 at £225.00. Set 2-course lunch £10.

Moro

SPANISH/NORTH AFRICAN 15/20

34-36 EXMOUTH MARKET, EC1
020-7833 8336, FAX 020-7833 9338
Lunch & Dinner Mon.-Fri. ££
U: Farringdon.

This coming together of Spanish and north African food gastronomically echoes Cordoba's cathedral built inside a great mosque. Tapas at the bar, perhaps with a glass of superb sherry, or at table while choosing from the short, stimulating menu, are pure Spanish, with tortilla and morcilla adding new lustre to 'omelette' and 'black pudding' respectively. Moorish influence shows in fruits and spices in such dishes as boquerones with roast squash and braised chicory, or deep-fried potato cakes with ground lamb and cinnamon. Partridge with pancetta and chestnuts was stuffed with a sprig of thyme and roasted on a vine leaf in the wood-fired oven, with some of the chestnuts transmuted into a glorious sauce. Another favoured cooking method is charcoal grilling as in tender lamb with spiced chickpeas in a subtle tomato dressing. From the tempting desserts list we chose chocolate and apricot tart. The two ingredients melded into the sort of new flavour one hopes to find once in a decade, and made up for eschewing rosewater and cardamom ice cream, or yoghurt cake with pistachios and pomegranates. Mainly Spanish wines include a modestly priced but excellent red, Almansa Reserva 1993. Service is courteous, efficient, but above all, knowledgeable. Of the décor one can say little other than that its harsh minimalism is favoured, or perhaps ignored, by all those who wisely make this one of London's busiest restaurants.

Novelli Restaurant

FRENCH   14/20   🍴
31 CLERKENWELL GREEN, EC1
020-7251 6606, FAX 020-7490 1083
Lunch Mon.-Fri., Dinner Mon.-Sat. ££
U: Farringdon.

🅰 ☎ 🍴

Jean-Christophe Novelli is behind the stove and actually cooking in his restaurant. He's back from his wanderings around the world, and we are assured that he intends to stay there. This is very good news for diners in the Clerkenwell area. Jean-Christophe is not only the Adonis of the restaurant world, he's also a very good cook, and his restaurant has rather suffered in his absence. His cooking seems to have grown up in his travels. There are less silly pretentions, less confusion on the plate and less of the ubiquitous truffle oil than there has been previously. Instead, he is using good ingredients and letting them speak for themselves, with one or two flights of fancy which seem to hang together better than they did of late. Ham hock is served with a marinated leek and a gribiche sauce; a haricot blanc velouté is garnished with grilled scallops; turbot is poached in anise-flavoured broth and served with hollandaise. Customers are looking happy and well fed.

Quality Chop House

MODERN BRITISH   13/20   🍴
92-94 FARRINGDON RD, EC1
020-7837 5093, FAX 020-7833 8748
Lunch Sun.-Fri., Dinner nightly. £
U: Farringdon.

A decade after the Victorian 'working class caterer' (with hard bench seating and anaglypta walls and even ketchup bottles faithfully in place) was taken over by ex-Le Caprice chef Charles Fontaine, it has expanded into a faithfully replicated room next door calling itself the Quality Fish House but sharing the same menu, also extended to take in far more seafood. Joining the Caesar salad, bang bang chicken, corned beef hash with fried egg and lamb chops which mark this out as a posh caff where champagne or ale are equally at home, the seafood also runs the gamut from trad, gor-blimey fare like jellied eels, through potted shrimps and crab salad to upper-class beluga caviar with blinis. Somewhere in the middle, a cannonball-sized salmon fishcake is subtly spiced with mace, and graced by a refined sorrel sauce. Braised plaice surrounded by lightly cooked tomatoes, black olives and shredded basil is fresh and direct; all good stuff, typical of a place that cuts across class divisions and suits all sorts. The chips are heavenly. A wonderful light chocolate and espresso sponge in a lake of dark chocolate sauce gave grown-up meaning to a retro pudding.

St. John

MODERN BRITISH   14/20   🍴
26 ST. JOHN ST, EC1
020-7251 0848, FAX 020-7251 4090
Lunch Mon.-Fri., Dinner Mon.-Sat. ££
U: Farringdon.

🅰 ☎

The belief that no-one eats better than farmers is confirmed by the repertoire of this bare, white, classy canteen, with its pleasant relaxed service which is far from rustic. St. John may have strayed to the Mediterranean but his menu is British with only odd excursions to a neighbour for leg of kid with fennel, or aioli with deep-fried ling. Among salad starters are pigeon and sweet cicely, and the inspired combination of cucumber, samphire and pickled walnut. Fish lovers wallow among whelks or whole crab mayonnaise to start, and main dishes of roast turbot and garlic, and skate with broad beans and bacon. The variety meats (the American term is perhaps more accurate than the English 'offal') might include, even in mid-summer, duck livers or lambs' sweetbreads with peas and mint, and as a starter the signature dish of roast bone marrow. Vegetables are less caringly prepared. In desserts simplicity rules, as in hazelnut terrine and roast peaches, or other luxuries of the simple life such as a bowl of cherries, vanilla cream and strawberries, or treacle tart and Jersey cream, nearly as mother used to make it. There are many decent wines by the glass in a shortish list.

Stephen Bull Smithfield

MODERN BRITISH   12/20
71 ST. JOHN ST, EC1
020-7490 1750, FAX 020-7490 3128
Lunch Mon.-Fri., Dinner Mon.-Sat. ££
U: Barbican/Farringdon.

A **☎**

In this lively, modern place with its brightly coloured, three-dimensional art works, the Stephen Bull magic touch produces food which he calls 'grown-up'; we say it displays the finesse expected of a serious restaurant. The short menu is eclectic, not eccentric, with several dishes offered as either starters or main courses. Mediterranean contributions include lamb kofte with couscous and citrus labne, panzanella—Italian bread salad, pea and mint risotto, and the signature 'delicacies from Spain'. Eastern influence shows in caramelised pork belly with coconut and soba noodle laksa, while more difficult to pin down exotica are smoked eel with apple and celeriac; polenta-crusted skate with red onion and tomato galette; and subtly flavoured Szechuan-cured salmon with sweet mustard dressing. Guaranteed to offend both Cumbrians and Toulousians—until they taste it—is confit of duck with Cumberland cassoulet and poached leeks. The light cooking makes it easy to be tempted by such desserts as caramelised apples with Calvados cream palmier, or raspberry and white chocolate cheesecake; for more delicate appetites, homemade ice creams and sorbets are strongly recommended. Wines are always a feature of Mr. Bull's restaurants. The English dessert wine, Thorncroft Noble Harvest 1994, is here for its quality, not for xenophobia. And there's friendly well-trained service.

COVENT GARDEN

Asia de Cuba

INTERNATIONAL   12/20
ST. MARTINS LANE
45 ST. MARTIN'S LANE, WC2, 020-7300 5588
Lunch Mon.-Fri., Dinner nightly. £££
U: Leicester Sq.

A **☎**

Even the most jaded and seasoned London diner should expect all preconceptions to be swept aside by this Philippe Starck-inspired crazily eclectic homage to Cuba. Think of it as a fun, wacky experience (and never mind the authenticity), to approach it with the right frame of mind. The décor mixes high camp with stark modernism to curiously good effect: bare light bulbs hang over extra wide tables designed to promote the sharing ethic; pillars are decorated with Cuban photographic images, vintage books and radios; staff are dressed to party and the voltage is high. The menu defies categorisation, though reflects the fact that Cuban cuisine is heavily influenced by Chinese ingredients. An unlikely salad mixing banana and cashew nuts had a mushy consistency but delicious, tiny, crispy calamari. The Tex-Mex presentation of spiced duck was rather naff but mitigated by a likeable sweet piquant sauce. A main of tuna was disappointingly tough and tasteless, but Thai-inclined beef stood out. A side order of plantain and avocado is a must. Exceptional desserts are the high point, especially a chilli-spiked pannacotta with wild berry compote. Service is pretentiously over-mannered and inclined to irritate.

Axis

INTERNATIONAL   14/20   ♟
ONE ALDWYCH, 1 ALDWYCH, WC2
020-7300 0300, FAX 020-7300 0301
Lunch Mon.-Fri., Dinner Mon.-Sat. £££
U: Covent Garden/Temple (closed Sun.)

A **☎**

Axis is the drop-dead glamorous, stand-alone restaurant of one of London's most feted modern luxury hotels. Beyond the grand entrance, stairs descend past a bar with a leather floor to an ultra-slick, chic dining room where one encounters a huge Vorticist-style mural of Manhattan and gorgeous leather seating at beautiful contemporary table settings. Mark Gregory's cooking is going from strength to strength. A delicate, beautifully presented starter of poached haddock and cheese soufflé tart was hugely successful, as was an unusual double-cooked potato terrine generously studded with black truffle and served on a subtle red onion compote. Mains move from the witty takes on modern British food: grilled chicken breast with a toothsome green bean, rosemary and lemon risotto to encompass more rarified Eastern flavours in excellent Japanese grilled Saikyo cod with udon noodles, ginger shoot, pumpkin and dashi. Puddings are memorable: his signature 1880s' trifle and an exquisite elderflower jelly with champagne sorbet. Service is charming and well-informed. The wine list includes some stunning fine wines, available in very limited quantities. Set lunch and pre-theatre 6pm-7.15pm £15.75 2 courses, 3 courses £19.75.

Bank

MODERN BRITISH   14/20   ♔
1 KINGSWAY, WC2
020-7234 3344, FAX 020-7234 3343
Breakfast Mon.-Fri., Lunch & Dinner daily. ££
U: Covent Garden/Holborn.

🅰 ☎

It could be Conran, but isn't. Underneath a dramatic if unsettling ceiling made of dangling shards of glass, Bank is a bold, bright vision of large-scale dining with, visible behind a wall of glass, a kitchen that meets consistently high standards. The single page carte covers all European-with-dashes-of-the-East bases; sections devoted to caviar, crustacea and fish give away the fact that the owners of what is fast becoming a major player on the restaurant scene (fish! see *London Bridge* is also owned by the group as is the newly opened Zander in the Crowne Plaza St. James Hotel, and another Bank opens in Birminghan in 2000), are also fish wholesalers. Chicken and shrimp nam rolls with chilli sauce, or honey and soy quail, frisée and bacon salad for starters; glazed belly of pork with Chinese cabbage, or braised beef with parsnip purée as meaty mains are unlikely to disappoint. But it's the fish which you can really be sure has been expertly chosen and cooked. Seared mullet with wok-fried greens and tamarind dressing might be one example. Fish and chips with mushy peas is irreproachable—as it should be for £16.95. Swift service is geared to business lunching (where Bank also scores is its location, poised between the West End and the City and it's even open for breakfast and weekend brunches), and the din-

ing room can be noisy. Set lunch Mon.-Fri. & dinner before 7pm 2 courses £13.90, 3 courses £17.50.

Café du Jardin

CONTEMPORARY EUROPEAN   13/20   ♔
28 WELLINGTON ST, WC2
020-7836 8769, FAX 020-7836 4123
Lunch & Dinner daily. £
U: Covent Garden.

🅰 ☎ ♟

This buzzing, noisy brasserie appeals to a wider audience than young Covent Gardeners. The additional attraction is real food, generally good enough to please more mature customers. In an international menu, typical starters in the European tradition include smoked salmon and scrambled eggs on potato and horseradish blini with chive oil; smoked goose breast with sweet potato and roasted pumpkin seed salad. Vegetarians enjoy wild mushrooms and soft poached egg on toasted brioche, or grilled winter root vegetables with candied walnuts and parsnip chips. A few of the fifteen omnivorean main dishes demonstrate the chef's command of Oriental exoticism: as in double-baked shank of lamb brushed with red Thai curry spices, with bok choy and soy jus. Sautéed veal escalopes with rosemary-scented polenta and Puy lentil sauce, or rare grilled tuna with garlic, are unsurprising but good, while calf's liver is enlivened by pink turnip pickle; and thyme- and honey-glazed confit of duck leg meets bubble and squeak with a red wine jus, perhaps for the first time. Set menus offer exceptional value outside the busy dinner period. The long, eclectic wine list offers many treats under £20. Set lunch & pre- and post- theatre menus 2 courses £9.95, 3 courses £13.50.

Christopher's American Grill

AMERICAN   12/20
18 WELLINGTON ST, WC2
020-7240 4222, FAX 020-7836 3506
Lunch Mon.-Fri., Dinner Mon.-Sat., Brunch Sat.-Sun. noon-3pm. ££
U: Covent Garden.

🅰 ☎

This majestic restaurant in Covent Garden overlooking Waterloo Bridge and the Thames has been a remarkable success, opening as it did in the height of the last recession. This has as much to do with the aristocratic and politiocratic connections of its proprietor, the Hon. Christopher Gilmour, as the style of restaurant which, when it opened, was the only decent, expense account-driven restaurant on this side of Covent Garden, and almost the only dining oasis from Covent Garden to the City. It found a horde of hungry mouths to feed with its East Coast offerings of top quality beef and lobster. Possibly due to the amount of new competition in the area, Christopher's has been through a major refurbishment—the spacious, comfortable downstairs bar has been turned into extra restaurant space and the bar is now a cramped, dark corner in the basement. And though the original chef Adrian Searing is still in residence, the quality of the cooking and the inspiration seem to have slipped. Lobster is absolutely—though seemingly impossibly—flavourless, and the Caesar salad insipid. Every restaurant has its ups and downs. We look forward to the time when Christopher's American Grill comes up to scratch again. Pre-theatre dinner to 7pm 2 courses £14.50, 3 courses £17.50.

Indigo

CONTEMPORARY EUROPEAN 13/20
ONE ALDWYCH, 1 ALDWYCH, WC2
020-7300 0400
Breakfast, Lunch & Dinner daily. ££
U: *Covent Garden.*

The stylish second in-house restaurant on the mezzanine of the breathtaking lobby of hugely fashionable One Aldwych with its oversized sculptures, stunning flower arrangements and arched windows. Food is designed to safely appeal to a cosmopolitan palate and so takes few risks with well-prepared comfort dishes with a twist. Risottos such as shallot and thyme are cooked to perfection. Good starter tarts include a leek and truffle, and goat cheese and sweet pepper variant. Several dishes such as a main dish of pan-fried sea bream with parsnip purée and mixed pepper vinaigrette, and farfalle with cherry tomatoes and basil are annotated on the menu as specifically light and healthy for sophisticated, health-conscious diners. Nevertheless, the best puddings are extremely indulgent: crunchy chocolate tart innovatively partnered with fresh honeycomb, and a smartly executed tart Tatin with vanilla and Calvados sauce. Great wines and superb, suave service. Set lunch and pre-theatre to 7pm 2 courses £15.50, 3 courses £19.50.

The Ivy

MODERN BRITISH 14/20
1 WEST ST, WC2
020-7836 4751, FAX 020-7240 9333
Lunch & Dinner daily. ££
U: *Leicester Sq.*

Notoriously difficult to get into, but once there you are cosseted and pampered with sheer professionalism—this is one of the best-run dining rooms in London and the kitchen is more than a match. Book ahead, months ahead, go for brunch at the weekend (amazing value), or opt for a table in the bar area and be prepared to tuck your legs in. Oak paneling abounds and with the stained glass windows, the outside world seems miles away. If you feel you know the other diners don't be too surprised, this is one place celebrities really do feel at home and there tends to be a lot of them. The menu follows a bistro formula with recognisably classic dishes like potted shrimps, risotto Nero and eggs Benedict sitting comfortably alongside more modern interpretations like chargrilled tuna with a pile of exquisite Mediterranean vegetables; pork with a sharp and creamy lemon polenta or an Eastern spiced sea bass with fragrant rice and soy. Desserts, too, tread a successful path between nursery favourites—bakewell tart, spotted dick or bread and butter pudding—and more modern items like an elder flower jelly with summer fruits. Cost varies wildly: you can, with careful selection, eat for very little, or you can spend serious sums. The wine list is cautious and comforting. Set weekend 3-course lunch £15.50.

J. Sheekey

FISH & SEAFOOD 14/20
28-32 ST. MARTIN'S CT, WC2
020-7240 2565, FAX 020-7240 8114
Lunch & Dinner daily. ££
U: *Leicester Sq.*

A long-established fish restaurant in theatreland has been gloriously revived by the owners of The Ivy and Le Caprice to give the row of interconnecting rooms a timeless lustre. Lunch is less frantic than dinner when, from the moment the doorman lets you in, you're swept into a theatrical hubbub. Service is almost uncannily swift which contributes to the mood of buoyancy. Cooking maintains the momentum that makes dining here uplifting. Perfect fritto misto with mayonnaise; succulent and massive skate, and 'Sheekey's' fish pie, which wasn't hugely better than anybody else's (though reasonably priced at £9.50), were matched by far from ordinary vegetables. Why don't more restaurants take the trouble to make a tomato salad so much more interesting by combining beef, plum, green, yellow and cherry varieties with an aromatic basil dressing? This, and green beans, were boldly but not excessively salted. Of a trad selection of puddings: treacle tart and jam roly poly are typical—a blackcurrant tart was more of a mousse and very pretty. The cover charge is anachronistic. Not just the history but everything about Sheekey's is so polished it generates a satisfied glow. Set Sat.-Sun. lunch 2-course £9.50, 3 courses £13.50.

Joe Allen

AMERICAN   11/20
13 EXETER ST, WC2, 020-7836 0651
Lunch & Dinner daily. £
U: Covent Garden.

This old-stager in Covent Garden just goes on doing what it does very well. Difficult to find via a rather dingy door in a Covent Garden back street, you descend into a heaving mass of people, reveling in the brick-walled, rabbit warren space with its wooden tables and chairs, photographs of thespians on the walls and a pianist in the evenings. Real live thespians—both established and budding—make up quite a lot of the clientele who tuck into standards like pecan-crusted goat cheese with sweet chilli jelly, Caesar salads, eggs Benedict, crispy duck confit with sautéed bok choy and mango sauce, grilled lamb cutlets with basil mashed potatoes, broccoli and mint vinaigrette. Nothing surprises, but nothing disappoints. Joe Allen remains fun. Set weekday lunch & pre-theatre 2 courses £12, 3 courses £14; set weekend lunch 2 courses £14.50, 3 courses £16.50.

Please excuse us...(and the chefs). Menus are subject to the winds of change, so the dishes we've described may no longer be available when you visit.

Le Palais du Jardin

FRENCH   12/20
136 LONG ACRE, WC2
020-7379 5353, FAX 020-7379 1846
Lunch & Dinner daily. ££
U: Covent Garden.

This precursor of Covent Garden gastro-palaces once provided much innocent amusement in its bi-lingual menu. Now the futility of trying to be French and English simultaneously is confirmed only by the translation of purée de légumes as bubble and squeak. Happily it proved to be an authentic version of that English classic. This 'modern mid-Channel brasserie food' does credit to its mixed parentage. Seafood platters with lobster, crab, a variety of prawns, and much more, still surprise by their outstanding value. Other choices range from standard starters such as tomato and goat cheese tart, or carpaccio of beef with a truffled vinaigrette, to prawn guacamole with a mango and mint dressing. Main dishes include notable steaks; more ambitious notions range from lamb sautéed with button onions and mushrooms in mustard sauce; seared cod on courgette ribbons and cherry tomatoes with tapenade, and five ways of cooking lobsters. Service is generally as bright and cheerful as the buzzing crowd of all ages who fill the 350 seats—with more in the café at the front. The back of the balcony is marginally quieter than downstairs and tables at the rail enjoy an entertaining overview of those below.

Livebait

SEAFOOD   12/20
21 WELLINGTON ST, WC2
020-7836 7161, FAX 020-7836 7141
Lunch & Dinner Mon.-Sat. ££
U: Covent Garden.

Livebait was the first to blow a huge hole in the theory that fish restaurants had to be either a) redolent with the fug of old chip fat, or b) stuck in a 1970s time warp. Although there have been a lot of changes since the original Livebait opened in Waterloo's The Cut— being bought by Groupe Chez Gérard, for one, and the departure of talented, idiosyncratic chef Theodore Kyriakou to the Real Greek (see above), for another—it remains London's most adventurous fish restaurant, despite growing competition. Although main courses seem to have lost the tendency to use the unusual ingredients and spicing that was Kyriakou's trademark, dishes are nonetheless inventive. Pan-roast sea bass fillet with steamed cavalo nero, gravlax and dill beurre blanc (£16.10), and chargrilled swordfish loin with colcannon mash and red onion marmalade (£15.85), use flappingly fresh fish as their basis and provide plenty of interest. Simpler crustacea such as oysters, cockles, whelks, winkles, crabs, crevettes are served simply, either on their own or with mayonnaise. The green-and-white tiled walls and simple seating are suitably cheerful and casual, while professional service generally keeps up with the quick pace. Groupe Chez Gérard has big plans to expand this winning formula in 2000 and 2001. Set lunch, pre- and post-theatre menu £15.50.

Also at **Waterloo** at 43 The Cut, SE1, 020-7928 7211; **Notting Hill Gate** at 175 Westbourne Grove, W11, 020-7727 4321.

Mela

INDIAN   13/20   🍴

152-156 SHAFTESBURY AVE, WC2, 020-7836 8635
Lunch & Dinner daily. £
U: Leicester Sq.

The Hindi word Mela means 'funfair' and it befits a restaurant so colourful in its décor. Charming staff please an assorted clientele ranging from pre- and post-theatregoers, young and old, to celebrating Indian families. From the glass-fronted kitchen by the entrance comes reasonably priced country-style cuisine, and its liveliness and fine flavours will appeal especially to those who find much Indian food too heavy or too highly spiced. In a shortish menu most main dishes are from the tandoor, or the tawa grill; only five 'curries' are listed—including a version of chicken tikka masala. Not to be missed is the tandoori boned chicken leg marinated in beetroot juice to give the sensuously tender meat a rich colour. Finish the meal with rasmalai, light cheese dumplings in reduced milk, or the original and delicious tandoori fruit kebab. Set 3-course dinner £15.

Mon Plaisir

FRENCH   12/20
21 MONMOUTH ST, WC2
020-7836 7243, FAX 020-7240 4774
Lunch Mon.-Fri., Dinner Mon.-Sat. ££
U: Covent Garden/Tottenham Court Rd.

Mon Plaisir briefly closed after a fire, then re-opened looking much the same as before, following the old adage, if it works, why fix it? So this charming, quintessential, busy French bistro in Covent Garden keeps on with its splendid and traditional snails in garlic, coquilles St. Jacques meunière, coq au vin, and tarte maison du jour. But owner Alain Lhermitte doesn't rest on his laurels and has introduced dishes like red mullet escabèche with a mesclun salad, tapenade and crostini; braised brill with baby squid, oyster and chervil sauce, and roast duck breast in Szechuan pepper, beetroot and onion marmalade, parsnip purée and Armagnac jus. Such forays beyond the traditional work well with the more adventurous. It all takes place in a series of small rooms, still decorated with banquette seating and wooden floors, old posters on the walls and Piaf on the gramophone (Mon Plaisir brings out that kind of old-fashioned touch). Long may it last. Set 3-course lunch £14.95, pre-theatre 6pm-7.15pm 2 courses £11.95, 3 courses £14.95.

Orso

ITALIAN   13/20   🍴
27 WELLINGTON ST, WC2
020-7240 5269, FAX 020-7497 2148
Open daily noon-midnight. ££
U: Covent Garden.

Orso is set in a basement in the heart of theatreland. Richard Polo, who owns the restaurant, and the team who run it, have understood the point that many people would rather return again and again to an establishment which offers no great changes, than experiment with new ones. Orso always looks pristine, it is well run, exudes an air of confidence, and with its tiled floor and vibrantly coloured, chipped crockery, evokes all the warmth of a superior Mediterranean trattoria. It continues to be frequented by a theatrical crowd, both audiences and actors, and over the years has extended its hours from lunch all the way through to after midnight for post-theatre diners. The menu is divided into appetizers, pizzas, first courses and entrées. Although there is nothing particularly clever about the cooking, it is devised and executed with considerable knowledge and care. The pizzas, suited to the idea of all-day eating, are excellent and varied: here are pizzas with rock shrimps, hot pepper, parsley, arugula and tomato and goat cheese, roasted garlic, oregano and tomato. The menu is written daily but only a few of the dishes actually change. The wine list, save the champagnes, is entirely Italian. Set Sat.-Sun. lunch (noon-5pm) 2 courses £15, 3 courses £17; pre-theatre menus (5pm-7pm) 2 courses £14.50, 3 courses £16.50.

Rules

TRADITIONAL BRITISH   13/20

35 MAIDEN LANE, WC2, 020-7836 5314
Open daily noon-11.30pm.
U: Covent Garden.

Rules is an odd place, a restaurant that opened its doors over 200 years ago, and which has seen the great and the good, the famous and infamous and latterly, tourists in droves pass through its doors. It has a décor that shouts 'history' in a stained-glass, wood-paneled, walls-hung-with-cartoons way, and you just know that Charles Dickens ate here. Some years ago it was really creaking, then the old dear was bought by one John Mayhew who, usefully, owns an estate from which much of the exemplary game comes from. He, most perspicaciously, employed David Chambers who was at the Hilton on Park Lane and the place has recovered superbly. The game here really is good, so go for whatever is in season—ptarmigan, wild duck, pheasant, teal, all served with trad British accompaniments like proper game chips, quince marmalade and well-cooked root vegetables. British savouries are here in force, or go for tried and tested puddings like crumbles and fruit pies. The wine list is good, the service amazingly friendly.

> **Ratings** are based solely on the restaurant's cuisine. We do not take into account the atmosphere, décor or service; these are commented on in the review.

Saint M

FRENCH   14/20

45 ST. MARTIN'S LANE, WC2, 020-7300 5544
Lunch Mon.-Fri., Dinner nightly. ££
U: Leicester Sq.

Saint M is the second, slightly less expensive (if you go à la carte), and hugely less pretentious restaurant of that achingly fashionable hotel of Ian Schrager's, St. Martins Lane. Presumably Philippe Starck had his hands nailed down when designing this room—it's relatively conservative compared to the rest of the hotel. A huge central bar takes pride of place, with the tables partitioned off on four sides by wooden dividers with seating. Mirrors run above the tables down one wall, it's open to an outdoor terrace down another. The staff is young, friendly and efficient; the customers are—at least at lunch—a good cross-section of London diners, so you *can* dress how you want. And the food? The food is very good. A game terrine with Madeira jelly came with Poîlane bread and was flavourful and gutsy, while a risotto of sea scallops with hollandaise sauce topped with crisp-fried Parmesan was suitably nutty. Mains continue the good work, as in simply grilled veal chop with tomato chutney and mushrooms that were wild and woody. Tuna came crusted in fennel and cumin with watercress risotto and a spiced fish-based cream sauce. Desserts revert to the traditional—sticky toffee pudding with butterscotch sauce and vanilla ice cream, treacle tart with clotted cream. Set lunch & pre-theatre dinner (5.30pm-7pm) 2 courses £14.95, 3 courses £17.95.

DULWICH

Belair House

CONTEMPORARY EUROPEAN   13/20

GALLERY RD, SE21
020-8299 9788, FAX 020-8299 6793
Lunch & Dinner daily. £££
Rail: Dulwich West.

One of the most beautifully situated dining rooms in London overlooking rolling parkland, this fine Georgian-listed building has been tastefully restored by actor Gary Cady (the rather lurid colours are apparently authentic to the period), to offer civilised fine dining without the rigours of negotiating West End parking. Cooking courtesy of Colin Barnett eschews the modish for modish sake but remains interesting and sometimes challenging. Good starters include cured duck breast with mustard pears. Mains veer from the complex: vanilla marinated lobster, mango and tomato tian with herb salad to more straight-forward variations on the Sunday roast theme. Puddings are adventurous and homemade ices particularly notable. Staff are attentive and encourage diners to linger and feast on the vista. The outside terrace is wonderful when the weather is clement. Set 2-course lunch £14.50, 3 courses £17.50; set 3-course dinner Mon.-Thurs. & Sun. £24.95.

EALING

Parade

MODERN BRITISH   14/20
18-19 THE MALL, EALING W5
020-8810 0202, FAX 020-8810 0303
Restaurant: Lunch & Dinner daily. Bar/Café: daily noon-4pm, 6.30pm-10pm. £
U: Ealing Broadway.

Despite the modest neighbourhood address among a row of undistinguished shops, the uncompromisingly contemporary frontage prepares diners for an extraordinary meal. Rob Jones has spent formative time at The Square and it shows: this is superbly accomplished cooking that holds its own with the major West End players. He has a rare knack for combining flavours that really resonate, whether rich and gutsy like a starter of ox tongue with chorizo and cannellini beans with a sweet, sticky bite, or exquisitely delicate, as in fennel- and tarragon-infused ragoût of oysters, mussels and salmon. Mains are handled with considerable dexterity too. Rabbit stuffed with surprisingly light black pudding was marred only by a somewhat salty Savoy cabbage, bacon and cannellini beans accompaniment. Sublimely tender haunch of venison partnered a light creamy celeriac purée with candied chunks of celeriac to give further definition to a stunning dish. White chocolate mousse was supremely refined and looked a picture with barely poached rhubarb whose flavour was accentuated by shards of candied orange peel. Inspiring wine list, extremely good, affable front-of-house and ultra-stylish

interior enlivened with excellent modern art forge the link with the big sibling, Sonny's (see *Barnes*). Set 2-course lunch £12, 3 courses £15; set 2-course dinner £18.50.

FULHAM

Blue Elephant

THAI   12/20
4-6 FULHAM BROADWAY, SW6
020-7385 6595, FAX 020-7386 7665
Lunch Sun.-Fri., Dinner nightly. £££
U: Fulham Broadway.

The sideways expansion of this already vast place has been promised for longer than the pregnancy of any colour elephant but might be complete when this guide appears. It will certainly not diminish the spectacle of the jungle complete with pools, and burgeoning Thai blooms as colourful as the charming waitresses' national dress. The presentation of dishes is often dazzling, with carved fruits and vegetables, and yet more flowers, on attractive tableware. All this makes the restaurant an entertainment in itself. The cooking, if not totally reliable, usually produces the goods in the form of Thai favourites, starting with crisp and spicy prawn crackers, followed by such starters as satay, fish cake, spring rolls and dim sum. More exotic are the menu's 'suggestions' of banana flower, prawn and coconut salad, Chinese-style soup with minced pork and beancurd, and lobster steamed with garlic, ginger and perfumed mushroom. Elephant symbols for hotness gambol across the menu, but as the food is designed for westerners, you might need extra chillies to balance the sweetness of the sauces. Set menus are amazingly lavish in the number of dishes: Royal Thai, or vegetarian Royal Siam Promenade banquets from £29; Kingdom of Siam banquet at £45; Sun. brunch buffet adult £16.75, child £6.26-£8.25; set banquets £29, £34, £45.

Chez Max

FRENCH   13/20
168 IFIELD RD, SW10
020-7835 0874, FAX 020-8244 0620
Lunch Tues.-Fri., Dinner Tues.-Sat. ££
U: Earls Court.

Tucked away in Ifield Road, Chez Max has

been ploughing a rather successful French hoe for years. It's in a cramped basement, reminiscent of 60s student days with its small wooden tables and chairs, and menus and wine lists on the walls. Owner Graham Thomson likes to explain the dishes in detail, so take your time and enjoy the home-baked olive oil bread, olives and good French (Charentais) butter while listening. This is classic French cooking, a tad old-fashioned perhaps, but done very well. A starter of risotto of wild mushrooms comes with a spicy roquette salad and shaved Parmesan; a foie gras and gibier terrine is suffused with truffles; duck is partnered by a boudin noir with a cèpe sauce. Desserts are rich and fulfilling, and the apple and Calvados crème brûlée a real killer. The wine list is predominantly French. Prices are quite high, so it's a place for a lengthy evening meal, perhaps recalling past French meals in Paris, or to judge from the well-heeled clientele, in that wonderful little restaurant somewhere in the Dordogne. Set meals 2 courses £23.50, 3 courses £27.50.

Chutney Mary
INDIAN   14/20   🍷
535 KING'S RD, SW10
020-7351 3113, FAX 020-7351 7694
Lunch & Dinner daily. ££
U: None nearby.

🅰 ☎ 🔧

The replacement of the ground floor bar by a private party room signals change here. The conservatory uses more vivid fabrics on the comfortable banquettes. More important is the arrival of friendly, skilled waiting staff, but happily unchanged is the welcome of owner Namita Punjabi, and manager Eddie Khoo's attention to detail. His grasp of the menu makes his advice indispensable to customers interested in wine even half as much as he is. The list is set out to help choose styles to match the food, and includes exciting discoveries. Changes in the kitchen staff have also brought improvement. The traditional cuisine makes one concession to modernity by including rice, basmati, pulao or lemon with most dishes. Regional specialities reflect regions featured in the occasional festivals. From Hyderabad came dum ka murgh, chicken baked in yoghurt, poppy seeds, green chillies and caramelised onion—as satisfyingly rich as it sounds. Note also tasty tandoori seekh kebabs, Malabar calamari, and Kerala chicken curry with coconut milk, red chillies and sub-

tly under-emphasized cinnamon. Notable vegetables include stuffed baby aubergines, and Chettinad crisp-fried okra and banana. Recalling the departed 'Anglo-Indian' style is Hill Station bread and butter pudding, but fruity not too sweet, homemade mango Martini kulfi garnished with pomegranate seeds is lighter. Lunch Mon.-Sat. set 2 courses £12.50, 3 courses £14.50; Sun. 3-course brunch £15.

Zaika
INDIAN   14/20   🍷
257-259 FULHAM RD, SW3
020-7351 7823, FAX 020-7376 4971
Lunch Mon.-Fri., Dinner Mon.-Sat. ££
U: South Kensington.

🅰 ☎

Vineet Bhatia, once star chef at the Star of India (see *South Kensington*), opened Zaika with a blast of hype hard to justify—but on the whole it does so. The décor is cool with elegantly displayed artefacts and fine pastel-coloured fabrics softening modern austerity. White cloths, large napkins, and tableware look well, but tables are small for main dishes in pots for sharing. Service is sophisticated, its expertise extending to proper handling of wines from the short, intelligent list. In the sensibly short menu the acclaimed speciality is tandoori home-smoked salmon with mustard and dill: the skin is satisfyingly crisp, the flesh just hints at rareness. Notable, too, is lamb biryani cooked in a pot sealed with crisp, perfectly browned pastry. But duck breast in peppery tomato sauce proves yet again that in all Asia only the Chinese can make a delicacy of duck. Excellent vegetables include a south Indian stir-fry more exciting than it sounds, while dal tadka, a yellow lentil and turmeric stew with garlic and cumin seed is even more exciting. Outstanding details include mango chutney with roasted onion seeds, and pudina paratha, bread delicately flavoured with mint. Coffee is the real thing. The set jugalbandi menu for at least two is £20 or £28 with wine. Set dinner £30.

GOLDERS GREEN

Café Japan

JAPANESE   15/20   🍴🍴
626 FINCHLEY RD, NW11, 020-8455 6854
Lunch Wed.-Sun., Dinner nightly. £
U: Golders Green.

VISA **MasterCard** ☎

The décor is basic, and cleaner than suggested by the drooping damp-stained canvas ceiling, unchanged for years. Japanese pop music is rather noisy, while Japanese waitresses are friendly and efficient with few language problems. Sit at the sushi and yakitori bar or at plain wooden tables for outstanding Japanese food. The style is neither haute cuisine, nor rough and ready, still less fast food. It is comparable with the best old-style French bistros with reasonable prices for generous portions. There is much of the standard Japanese repertoire—sashimi, sushi, yakitori, tempura, and 'robatayaki grills'; sukiyaki and shabu-shabu, too, but the tables are too small to make that a comfortable notion. Weekly specials might include fried horse mackerel marinated in sauce, or fried plaice with ponzu sauce, its bones crisp enough to crunch. Among varied yakitori skewers are pork with aromatic shiso leaves, and succulent marinated tuna. The sushi menu displays the one hint of westernisation—sushi rolls with mayonnaise—although they would not be out of place in modern Tokyo. The clientele of mixed ages and origins is mainly local—but local here means all London, for many consider this food justifies a long journey. Set dinner £18.50, £19.50.

HAMMERSMITH

The River Café

ITALIAN   15/20   🍴🍴
THAMES WHARF STUDIOS, RAINVILLE RD, W6
020-7381 8824, FAX 020-7381 6217
Lunch daily, Dinner Mon.-Sat. ££££
U: Hammersmith.

A ☎ 📷

The view of the river is, sadly, only to be had by strolling in the grounds outside this functional building down a warren of side streets in Hammersmith. Once through the doors however, your senses easily succumb to the charms of the room. A huge stainless steel bar runs down the back wall, plates of roasted and grilled vegetables seemingly scattered nonchalantly at one end near the wood-fired oven. Opposite, glass doors look out over the garden so while you may not actually be outside, you feel as if you are. Sourcing is everything with chefs and co-owners Ruth Rogers and Rose Gray, much of what is cooked coming straight from Italy, where, even there, their reputation goes before them. Mozzarella is full-flavoured, rich and delicate, tomatoes shriek of sunshine, even the olive oil packs a fair punch. Ingredients lead in the likes of bruschetta topped with a purée of fresh broad beans and mint, or Cornish crab rich in tarragon. Risottos are flawless, pasta as good as the best in Italy, whether it is with a sardine sauce, or doused in shavings of white truffle. Main courses swing from the robustness of bollito misto, as rich and earthy as can be, to the more delicate, but still gutsy, roasted sea bass with gremolata and roasted vegetables. Desserts range from poached fruit, to tarts, to a chocolate Nemesis that one inspector referred to as faultless. Service comes with attitude and style, give as good as you get. The all-Italian wine list couples the familiar with the less so. Used wisely, it offers seriously good drinking.

HAMPSTEAD

Base

CONTEMPORARY EUROPEAN   14/20   🍴
71 HAMPSTEAD HIGH ST, NW3
020-7431 2224, FAX 020-7433 1262
Lunch & Dinner daily. ££
U: Hampstead.

A 🚇

Hampstead is still something of a culinary backwater, so it's a welcome sign to see Pierre Khodja setting up here in this affluent part of London, along with other young and exciting chefs (see below). Base is a pretty, sand- and ochre-coloured dining room, with a pale wooden floor, crisp linen and some very good modern art on the walls that complements the natural feel of the room. Khodja has cooked with Bruno Loubet, and like that chef, his basis is classical French. So goat cheese crotin comes on grilled vegetables and rocket salad, and meltingly tender roast salmon seared crisp on the outside, is accompanied by lobster mash, lime and tarragon jus. But North Africa also has its place and this first-generation French-Algerian chef makes subtle use of spices like cardamom, cinnamon and ginger. Pan-fried prawns come on aubergine and tabouleh, with haloumi cheese adding a delicious sharpness; best end of lamb comes with a saffron mash, spiced roast fennel and cinnamon jus. Desserts, too, get the same treatment, as in poached pear with fig or cinnamon ice cream. During the day, the café next door offers take-away and the café menu is served in the main restaurant. But it's in the evening when the place comes into its own.

Gresslin's

INTERNATIONAL **13/20**
13 HEATH ST, NW3
020-7794 8386, FAX 020-7433 3282
Lunch Tues.-Sun., Dinner Mon.-Sat. ££
U: Hampstead.

The first of the serious chefs to set up shop in Hampstead, Michael Gresslin continues to offer an adventurous menu that surfs the world for inspiration. Try sautéed lambs kidney with couscous and teriyaki sauce, or spicy tiger prawns with Oriental noodle salad as starters, and seared tuna with rice vermicelli 'Chow Mein' and crispy seaweed, or a more European pan-fried lemon marinated chicken breast with Puy lentils and sweet potato as a main dish. These bold combinations work well in the main while still allowing the principal ingredient to shine through, though there is the occasional collision, as in a roast cod dish with curly kale, carrot bubble and squeak and a sweet pea guacamole and tomato salsa. It's all delivered in a bright, narrow restaurant with service that is generally very good. The wine list is small but apt for the food, matching the often strong flavours. Wines are generally well priced, with a 'connoisseurs' choice list of some fine wines. Set lunch Tues.-Sat. 2 courses £8.95, 3 courses £11.95; set lunch Sun. 2 courses £14.95, 3 courses £17.95; set dinner Mon.-Thurs. 2 courses £14.95, 3 courses £17.95.

New End

CONTEMPORARY EUROPEAN **15/20**
102 HEATH ST, NW3, 020-7431 4423
Lunch Wed.-Sun., Dinner Tues.-Sun. ££
U: Hampstead

New End is the third in the triumvirate of serious Hampstead restaurants and if critical mass has any value, then finally this wealthy area is prepared to accept and encourage serious dining, something which strangely it has heretofore not done. A slew of admiring reviews within the second week of its opening made bookings red hot, but sensibly the restaurant stuck to its policy of not turning tables. The restaurant itself is pretty, light and airy with a high ceiling and a glass frontage, just the kind of casual décor that will not frighten Hampstead folk. But the point here, of course, is the cooking, which is extremely accomplished. The menu looks like a real foodie's paradise—with dishes like braised pig's cheek with garlic and parsley mash, and roast fillets of John Dory with crisp Serrano ham, red wine jus. Such seemingly uncompromising dishes turn out to be sublime examples of how good this chef is. We began with a little amuse-bouche of light beetroot soup with aged vinegar. The goat cheese soufflé (from the four-choice vegetarian menu), was beautifully crisp on the outside with the cheese inside correctly firm; while a foie gras and pigeon terrine with toasted brioche would have passed muster in the most expensive West End restaurant. Roast loin of lamb came perfectly pink, with a 'turnip' confit, in fact, a julienne of turnip. John Dory came with langoustine on spinach and with salsify. Desserts were as masterly, a bitter chocolate fondant with white chocolate ice cream, the richness cut by a passion fruit sauce, and a poached rhubarb, ginger and lemon grass pannacotta. The wine list is currently small, but being updated and expanded, but the mark ups are very reasonable. Set 2-course lunch £12.50, 3 courses £15, set 3-course dinner £35.

HIGHGATE

Idaho

AMERICAN SOUTH WEST **13/20**
13 NORTH HILL, N6
020-8341 6633, FAX 020-8341 5533
Lunch & Dinner daily. ££
U: Highgate.

Here you have wildly inventive south-west American cuisine in deepest Highgate in a refurbished pub with wonderful wooden beams and dramatic lighting and a definitely hip, laidback feel. The restaurant is somewhat pretentiously divided into distinct areas: water (formal dinner only), forest (private dining room), great outdoors (tree-lined terrace), and earth (brasserie). But food is expertly prepared from the most delicious all-day breakfast with black beans and ranchero sauce, to more exotic fare like swordfish ceviche with plantain crisps; grilled mahi mahi; yucutan pepper stew; mesquite-grilled green onions, tamarind-grilled chicken with wild rice salad. Adventurous puddings taste as exotic as they sound—like coconut tamale with pineapple-aniseed salsa and toasted coconut. Excellent cocktails and a well put-together wine list divided into light, medium and full is matched by charming, high-fashion service. It's very popular with well-heeled families at weekends.

HOLLAND PARK

Chez Moi

FRENCH **13/20**

1 ADDISON AVE, W11
020-7603 8267, FAX 020-7603 3898
Lunch Mon.-Fri., Dinner Mon.-Sat. ££
U: Holland Park.

The theatrical backdrop of this thirty-year old institution—all blood-red walls, gold mirrors and faux tiger skin banquettes—forewarns of expectations, but there's substance behind the style. Our starter of 'oursins'—deep-fried scallops, scampi and prawn sculpted with angel-hair pasta and a side dash of mustard di frutta was heavenly, so too was the sea bass Oriental with chilli and ginger and bok choy braised in oyster sauce. Classic dishes such as shin of pork with poached vegetables, or Dutch veal kidneys in Dijon mustard sauce, balance modern forays. Puddings are pretty concoctions. The wine list draws on noble French vineyards, some at a price, but the New World house at £10 doesn't disappoint. The set three-course lunch, always with a fish course, is superb value, and service is attractive. Set 3-course lunch £15.

The Room at The Halcyon

MODERN BRITISH **12/20**

THE HALCYON, 129 HOLLAND PARK AVE, W11
020-7221 5411, FAX 020-7229 8516
Lunch Mon.-Fri., Dinner Mon.-Sat. ££
U: Holland Park.

The Halcyon is a discreet townhouse hotel in one of London's smartest addresses—

Holland Park. The downstairs restaurant, somewhat unimaginatively called The Room at The Halcyon, is a large, airy room with a stone-paved floor and a small terrace at the back. It's been through some changes recently with the arrival of young Toby Hill, formerly at Gordleton Mill in Lymington, Hampshire, then at Gordon Ramsay. Fish is now a clear favourite: a list of seven starters included a startlingly good red mullet and saffron soup with croûtons and rouille, and ravioli of lobster and langoustine with a shellfish vinaigrette (with a £5 supplement). From the main courses of four fish and three meat dishes, a sauté of John Dory was perfectly timed, coming with crispy bacon, braised lettuce and a chicken and foie gras velouté; while the caramelised breast of duck comes with baby vegetables and Chinese five-spice sauce, reinforcing the light spicy marinade of the duck. Hill has made a name for his desserts, but these are overcomplicated in presentation and incorporate too many tastes, with spun sugar spinning everywhere in his pistachio parfait with caramelised fruit and rum syrup. Hill has also transformed the bar menu which now incorporates dishes like tempura of vegetables and king prawns with soya sauce along with the old favourites of battered cod with chips with a pea and truffle purée. Set 2-course lunch £18, 3 courses £23; set 2-course dinner £35, 3 courses £43; Bar menu 3 courses £17.50.

ISLINGTON

Euphorium

CONTEMPORARY EUROPEAN **12/20**

203 UPPER ST, N1
020-7704 6909, FAX 020-7704 6089
Lunch daily, Dinner Mon.-Sat. ££
U: Angel.

The daytime bakery and café attract the queue at this multi-purpose Islington mini food emporium. And the breads and pastries, savoury and sweet, are even more appetising than the dinners served in the restaurant at the back, with a wall of glass looking out onto a floodlit courtyard. In the evening you pass through a smoky bar to reach the minimal but not austere dining room patronised by a fashionable but not relentlessly youthful clientele. The menu is equally modern and unadorned. Big prawns and tomato chilli jam, 'mixed grill with offally bits and poached egg', show an unpompous approach to ingredients. Many-flavoured breads from the in-house bakery make a promising start, but the cooking can be a little too relaxed; greater precision would have improved lamb sweetbreads, spinach and poached egg which suffered from overcooking and watery juices. Dishes such as roast cod, herb crust and ratatouille, or leg of lamb with garlic mash usually strike the right notes—but not always without wobbles. The limited selection of puddings can be disappointing. An apple crumble was fine but with no distinguishing features. Prices compare with the cream of Islington restaurants but execution doesn't always follow.

Granita

MODERN EUROPEAN   13/20   ♟

127 UPPER ST, N1
020-7226 3222, FAX 020-7226 4833
Lunch Wed.-Sun., Dinner Tues.-Sun. £
U: Angel.

Behind the stern, sandcast and glass exterior is a consistently bright star in Islington, where any reservations about the austerity of the long, unadorned room are dispelled by the zesty cooking. There are no pictures, no tablecloths, no carpet, but the attention simply to what tastes right is immediately and pleasingly evident from the mixed bread and tub of French country butter that arrives at each table. What follows is characterised by the clarity with which ingredients are assembled. Mojama (wind-dried tuna), Garroxta (goat cheese) and sambusak (crisp, cheesy pastries) show it's still in the vanguard. The emphasis is mainly on the Mediterranean but with some of the flavours of the Middle East getting the pared-down Granita treatment. Take grilled aubergine, mint, chilli, yoghurt and flat bread, as an example. The salady tendency is illustrated by baby artichokes, parsley, basil, white wine and toast. Meat and fish are often chargrilled, as in chump of lamb with chickpeas, courgettes and rocket, or chicken with lentils, porcini, red wine broth. Female staff in androgynous uniforms are friendly, informed and contribute to relaxing and rewarding eating. The wine list is focussed, with an equal emphasis on the old and new worlds. Set lunch Wed.-Sat. 2 courses £11.95, 3 courses £13.95; set lunch Sun. 2 courses £12.50, 3 courses £14.50.

Lola's

CONTEMPORARY EUROPEAN   13/20   ♟
THE MALL BUILDING, 359 UPPER ST, N1
020-7359 1932, FAX 020-7359 2209
Lunch & Dinner daily. ££
U: Angel.

Above an antiques arcade in a former Victorian tramshed, this airy, skylit restaurant generates an old-fashioned sense of occasion with a jazzy pianist and professional, fairly formal service overseen by the well-dressed women proprietors. Just as unpretentious and refusing to dumb down is the constantly changing menu—an intelligent reading of contemporary tastes for the Mediterranean stretching into the Middle East. Look out for the Middle Eastern flat bread which often accompanies a starter, while a main course from the same region might be lamb steak with hummus, harissa and couscous tabouleh. Other, European dishes—often assemblies of fine ingredients, don't strive for effect, but simply present well-considered combinations. Warm salad of duck, figs and pancetta; and grey mullet, roast cherry tomatoes, broccoli and anchovy dressing, are examples. Sometimes flavours pull their punches, but there's never anything to jar. And desserts such as blackcurrant fool or summer fruit pavlova are invariably winning. Alternatives such as British cheeses or vin santo and Cantuccini illustrate how sourcing and serving the best produce is valued as much as complicated cooking. Set lunch Mon.-Fri. 2 courses £10.

KENNINGTON

Station Grill

CONTEMPORARY EUROPEAN   12/20
2 BRAGANZA ST, SE17, 020-7735 4769
Lunch Sun., Dinner nightly. £
U: Kennington.

This is a thoroughly traditional, long-established restaurant du quartier—in its location (just by Kennington underground), welcoming family ambience, and modest prices. But its appearance has recently been transformed. Behind the painted glass façade are cream walls with deep aubergine fabric-covered panels, and white-clothed tables seating forty in three linked spaces. Tables bear fresh flowers, white china and good glasses lit by tiny silver-shaded candles. The equally new menu changes monthly. 'Modern European' in style, it is elegantly executed, with well-balanced main ingredients, sauces and vegetables. Poached quail eggs came with chicken liver so meltingly tender it could have been called 'chicken foie gras', with its port, orange and ginger sauce. Braised beef in Guinness with a mustard seed dumpling, new potatoes and root vegetables was as successful as more exotic steamed squid filled with chorizo, smoked pork and braised canellini beans. Desserts such as warm chocolate fondue filled with raspberries may be over-rich for some, but homemade ice creams and sorbets are notable. The wine list is uninformative about shippers but Alsace Riesling at £12.50 turned out to be a beauty from Kuentz-Bas. Set 2-course dinner £14.95, 3 courses £19.95.

KENSINGTON

The Belvedere

CONTEMPORARY EUROPEAN 14/20 ♟
ABBOTSBURY RD, W8, 020-7602 1238
Lunch & Dinner daily. £££
U: High St Kensington.

A

The Belvedere has long been one of those restaurants that was almost successful. Certainly its location is perfect—in leafy Holland Park away from the roar of London traffic and in summer within earshot of the nearby open-air opera festival. What it clearly needed was a name or two, and now it has them. The Belvedere is owned by restaurateur Jimmy le Houd, whose other ventures—co-owned with chef-turned-restaurateur Marco Pierre White—include L'Escargot (see *Soho*), Quo Vadis (see *Soho*), and Mirabelle (see *Mayfair*), and the chef, Jeremy Hollingsworth, is ex-Quo Vadis and The Oak Room. The restaurant has been refurbished and now sports a wood-floored ground-level alcove bar and a dining room on two levels with a roof terrace off the second floor. The impression is one of sophisticated intimacy, though even after a few months some of the glitz has worn off the refurbishment. If the menu seems familiar, then think of the other Marco Pierre White-related restaurants and you've got it. So expect impeccable dishes like terrine of foie gras with green peppercorns, gelée of

Sauternes with toasted Poilâne brioche, and ceviche of sea scallops with chives, ginger and fresh coriander for starters; sea bass with aubergine caviar, and a sauce vierge with fresh basil, and honey roast duck with Thai spices, caramelised endives, and a Thai sauce for main dishes. Desserts also hoe a familiar row, with a splendid caramelised apple tart with vanilla ice cream and caramel sauce and that now famous and excellent and ubiquitous lemon tart. Standards are as high as you would expect; these are good menus well-cooked by well-trained chefs, and the consistency among these restaurants is to be applauded. The wine list is even-handed in its offerings and fair in its pricing, and the service is charming. Set lunch S. £14.95.

Cibo

ITALIAN 13/20 ♟
3 RUSSELL GDNS, W14
020-7371 6271, FAX 020-7602 1371
Lunch Sun.-Fri., Dinner Mon.-Sat. ££
U: Kensington (Olympia).

A ☎ ⬤

Cibo opened some ten years ago in the vanguard of decent Italian cuisine. Critics raved (rightly so), film stars and fashionistas flocked, and you couldn't get a table. Competition has thinned the buzz (no bad thing), but the cooking remains resolutely good. Servings—on brightly coloured Mediterranean china—are vast. We kicked off with snappily fresh crab and rocket salad, and seductively sautéed wild mushrooms, potatoes and Asiago cheese. Seafood is a strong bias here: the next table was enraptured with their grilled swordfish with roast baby tomatoes and capers, and spaghetti al'Arogosta (spaghetti with lobster in its own sauce). We chose a marvelously gamey and lip-smacking Piedmontese partridge and pheasant stew, accompanied by a decent I Sistri Chardonnay. The closing zabaglione alla frutta revealed toothsome layers of rich and light. It is a pretty, creamy coloured restaurant where eccentric art adorns the walls. Service is sweet and obliging. Cibo is definitely value for money. Put it firmly on your list. Set lunch Mon.-Fri. 2 courses £12.50; set lunch Sun. 2 courses £17.95, 3 courses £21.95.

Clarke's

CALIFORNIA/MODERN BRITISH 15/20 🍴🍴
124 KENSINGTON CHURCH ST, W8
020-7221 9225, FAX 020-7229 4564
*Summer: Lunch & Dinner Mon.-Sat.; Winter:
Lunch & Dinner Mon.-Fri. £££*
U: Notting Hill Gate.

[VISA] [MasterCard] [💳] [☎]

There is a direct simplicity in the décor, both up and downstairs: pale walls, fresh flowers and lots of white linen which is mirrored in the food. Upstairs is somewhat quieter while the basement nestles up to the kitchen, although the largely female team is one of the quietest in town. Ingredients lead the way, with an elegant simplicity in the cooking which belies the technique and attention required. There is a short carte at lunchtime; in the evening a no-choice four-course format which has its detractors, but has been successful for a decade and a half now. First courses might be a beetroot and vine tomato soup of such intensity and lightness as to astonish. While smoked eel, gently warmed and served with a salad of intense leaves and fruity olive crostini, was simply stunning. So, too, was a tart of girolles, the mushrooms leading the way. Main courses favour the chargrill, lamb for example served with a summer salad of beans and spinach was a delight, while scallops were rendered crispy yet succulent. If Chez Panisse in California springs to mind it will be no surprise to find that Sally Clarke worked there for a time. Cheese will follow in the evening, usually English or Irish and in impeccable condition. For dessert, elegantly poached pears, a sensational tart perhaps, or something as old-fashioned as trifle, here rendered elegant and light. The wine list majors on California, following up quickly with France and Italy, all impeccably chosen. Service is cool and slick. Set 4-course dinner £44.

Kensington Place

MODERN BRITISH 14/20 🍴
201-209 KENSINGTON CHURCH ST, W8
020-7727 3184, FAX 020-7229 2025
Lunch & Dinner daily. ££
U: Notting Hill Gate.

[VISA] [MasterCard] [💳] [☎]

The room is vast, with a wall of glass facing onto the street and a large mural dominating one wall. The noise level comes in for criticism and there is no doubting that this is not a room for a cosy chat, but that apart, it buzzes with atmosphere; service is on the ball if a little impersonal, and the food is consistently good. The bulk of it is typed up, with a dish or two handwritten on to the end depending on what chef Rowley Leigh has been offered from suppliers. Seasons are the driving force, with ingredients gently or robustly accompanied depending on requirements. Scallops for example, get a delightful pea purée and mint vinaigrette in summer, foie gras comes with a sweet corn pancake in the autumn. Classics get a showing, omelette fines herbs for example, or a braised haunch of hare, while sea bass is accompanied by meltingly soft Swiss chard, guinea fowl by a tagine of vegetables powerfully infused with saffron. Desserts can be unusual—grilled pineapple with a chilli syrup, or traditional—bread and butter pudding or pannacotta, although the pudding is made with panettone, and the pannacotta with coffee and mascarpone. The wine list is in the something-for-everybody mode, with prices to match. Set 3-course lunch Sun.-Fri. £14.50.

Launceston Place

MODERN BRITISH 12/20
1A LAUNCESTON PL, W8
020-7937 6912, FAX 020-7938 2412
Lunch Sun.-Fri., Dinner Mon.-Sat. ££
U: High St Kensington.

[VISA] [MasterCard] [💳] [☎] [🏃]

This corner site in leafy Kensington is in direct contrast to its more feisty sister Kensington Place (see above), preferring to quietly sell itself under cover of muted shades and pastels. The space is intimate, yet large—a series of interconnecting rooms giving a quaintly personal touch to the otherwise efficient and professional service. The food encompasses both classic and modern British with equal aplomb, serving up various roasts on Sundays alongside dishes like sweetbreads with salsa verde. Somewhere to take your mother or your girlfriend—both would be impressed. The cooking is assured and confident rather than ground-breaking. Dishes like peppers Piedmontese, twice-baked cheese soufflé, and a roasted pepper and mozzarella terrine with rocket salad might start a meal. Main courses swing between seared scallops with red peppers, sea bass with gremolata and a 'sort of bean stew', and more daring items involving Eastern spicing—sweet and sour duck, and north African flavourings—lamb with a fruit-laden couscous. Desserts are simple, well executed and refreshing: an almond tart, poached peaches, zabaglione. The wine list hops and skips with assured confidence offering good value for all budgets. Set lunch Mon.-Fri. and before 8pm 2 courses £14.50, 3 courses £18.50.

Phoenicia

LEBANESE   **13/20**
11-13 ABINGDON RD, W8
020-7937 0120, FAX 020-7937 7668
Open daily noon-midnight. £
U: High St Kensington.

This sector of Kensington has long drawn locals and others from further afield to its family-owned and managed restaurants. In this one, the Middle Eastern décor with comfortable tub chairs at well-spaced tables offers a warm ambience and friendly service and guidance through the menu for those new to the cuisine. The reasonably priced menu includes main course kebabs and other grills and some delectable stews. But many diners prefer to stay in the wonderful world of meze, cold and hot. Aubergines are a highlight. They appear

---

Dining & Dancing

Tripping the light fantastic in London's restaurants has always been popular. The best evenings are, naturally, at the end of the week and some restaurants restrict their dinner dances to those times. Telephone for information and for booking.

Claridge's, Brook St, W1, 020-7629 8860

The Conservatory, The Lanesborough, Lanesborough Pl, SW1, 020-7259 5599

London Showboat, Westminster Pier, SW1, 020-7237 5134

Le Soufflé, Inter-Continental Hotel, Hyde Park Corner, W1, 020-7409 3131

The River Room, The Savoy, Strand, WC2, 020-7836 4343

The Tenth, Royal Garden Hotel, 2-24 Kensington High St, W8, 020-7937 8000

Windows, London Hilton on Park Lane, W1, 020-7493 8000

---

as mutabal paste, also as monk's aubergine, or cracked or pickled. Beans and other vegetables come in tasty oil and citrus dressings. Tajin, an unusual dish, seemingly unconnected with Moroccan tajine, is a sesame paste with onions, embedding fish. Another delicacy is rkakat—the cheese- and vegetable-filled 'spring roll' which crackles as much in the eating as in the saying. Meat and offal includes superb kafta nayeh—lamb tartare; also sausages and beautifully dressed liver, kidneys, sweetbreads and chicken wings. Hidden in the menu as 'homemade sweets' is osmaliye, a glorious Lebanese twist to cheesecake, flavoured with chopped nuts and sauced with aromatic rose syrup. Drink raki, Lebanese wine, Arabic coffee. Buffet lunch Mon.-Sat. £10.95, Sun./Bank Hol. £16.80; set meals £25.49-£30.95.

Terrace

MODERN BRITISH   **13/20**
33C HOLLAND ST, W8
020-7937 3224, FAX 020-7937 3323
Lunch daily, Dinner Mon.-Sat. ££
U: High St. Kensington.

Those who prefer a privately owned, small restaurant to a branch of a mega-gastropolis will find their prejudice reinforced here. Design is simple but not austere, and, with only about twenty seats (and about the same on the terrace in summer), booking is essential. Service is charming. The menu offers about six choices in each course, described in plain English, with daily specials added verbally. Ingredients, too, are mainly indigenous and presentation is elegant and unfussy. Starters might include Jerusalem artichoke soup with chives and truffle oil; natural smoked haddock kedgeree; and game terrine with quince jelly. Typical main dishes are braised lamb shank with white beans, tomatoes and a rosemary jus; roasted skate wing with curly kale and caper butter; and a vegetarian wild mushroom risotto with Parmesan and white truffle oil. 'Puddings'—that's what the menu calls them—include apple compote with Calvados sorbet, steamed sticky toffee pudding with ginger ice cream and fudge sauce and always a plate of British cheese. Eighty well-chosen wines include half a dozen by the glass, and the policy is to add a maximum of £15 to the cost. Set lunch menus offer small choice but great value. Set weekday 2-course lunch

£12.50, 3 courses £14.50, Sat. lunch £16.50, Sun. lunch £19.50.

The Tenth

INTERNATIONAL **14/20**
ROYAL GARDEN HOTEL
2-24 KENSINGTON HIGH ST, W8, 020-7937 8000
Lunch Mon.-Fri., Dinner Mon.-Sat.
U: High St Kensington.

A

On the tenth floor of the Royal Garden Hotel, the views over Kensington Gardens are stunning, so ask for a window table. There is a bar at one end with comfortable chairs, while the restaurant occupies a two-tiered space, which comes into its own on Saturdays when the John Wilson band play (full band on the last Saturday of the month; smaller group every other Saturday). The space needs people to fill it, otherwise its hotel décor style can be gloomy. The same cannot be said for the cooking, which is done well with exuberant flourishes. Expect starters like wild mushroom boudin with a fricassée of butter beans and truffle, or tiger prawns sautéed with a coconut and galangal broth; main courses such as the now-fashionable herbed baked cod, which comes here with a sufficiently tart gravad lax sauce, or confit of duck with oriental flavours as in ginger and coriander and braised bok choy. Desserts might include passion fruit cream with orange sable, or chocolate pudding with a masterly marbled chocolate ice cream. Service is excellent, friendly and professional; the wine list covers the world. Set 2-course lunch £12.50, 3 courses £17.75; set 3-course dinner £34.

KEW

The Glasshouse

CONTEMPORARY EUROPEAN **16/20**
14 STATION PARADE, KEW, SURREY
020-8940 6777
Lunch daily, Dinner Mon.-Sat. ££
U: Kew Gardens.

The Glasshouse, which opened to rapturous applause in 1999, has proved to be an outstanding establishment, one about which everyone seems to agree. It remains a really top restaurant, serving assured and interesting food, with exemplary service, at reasonable prices. The lunch table d'hôte menu, offering a choice of six starters and main courses is £19.50, while the more elaborate and slightly more extensive menu is still excellent value at £25. The plainly worded menus of chef Bruce Poole (see *Chez Bruce*, above), list temptingly contemporary dishes such as pumpkin and Parmesan risotto but the predominant influence is French. Warm salad of wood pigeon with deep-fried truffled egg, whole lemon sole à la grenobloise, pot roast pheasant with leek, cèpe and potato gratin, and comforting dishes such as duck confit with parsnip purée and pommes sarlardaise, and slow roast pork belly with choucroute, Toulouse sausages and salsa verde. The duck confit is simply delicious, succulent and full of flavour, and the presentation is confident and assured. The wine list is extensive and well chosen, with many wines to be ordered by the glass, including five dessert wines. The Glasshouse (only one side is actually glass) is in the village across from the green and seats 65. Set 1-course lunch £15, 2 courses £17.50, 3 courses £19.50; set 3-course Sun. lunch £21.50; set 3-course dinner £25.

KNIGHTSBRIDGE

Brasserie St. Quentin

FRENCH **11/20**
243 BROMPTON RD, SW3
020-7589 8005, FAX 020-7584 6064
Lunch & Dinner daily. ££
U: South Kensington.

Brasserie St. Quentin continues its French way, unperturbed by modern fashion, still serving a traditional menu which goes down well with the establishment clients it continues to attract. The setting is pretty, with mirrors and chandeliers, plenty of wood, and red and gilts colours. Tables are too close together for comfort, but the place fairly bustles along. Cooking is standard, with some dishes succeeding well enough like duck liver terrine with Sauternes jelly and toasted brioche, pan-fried salmon with sorrel sauce, and a very good grilled calf's liver with mustard mash and Bourguignone sauce. But such cooking should pass muster, the Brasserie has been here for a long time and despite changes of ownership (it's now Groupe Chez Gérard), the formula remains the same. Set lunch & pre-theatre dinner 2 courses £11.50.

The Capital

FRENCH   16/20   ♨♨
THE CAPITAL, 22-24 BASIL ST, SW3
020-7589 5171, FAX 020-7225 0011
Lunch & Dinner daily. ££££
U: Knightsbridge.

Right in the heart of Knightsbridge is this family-run hotel that has oodles of style and the kind of service most hotels are left dreaming about. Guests come time and again, both to stay, and to eat in the small, intimate dining room, where a neutral beige décor showcases wooden sculptures and mirrors. The Capital has gained hugely from the arrival of Eric Chavot, a chef who deserves our attention. Settling happily into The Capital, he seems to be reaching a new maturity in his warm, gutsy style, reminiscent of his native France, yet rendered with a light hand. We liked dishes such as the pan-fried salmon with choucroute and horseradish, and his daube of beef, black as squid ink, melting and succulent, yet the accompanying root vegetables were simply steamed and allowed to act as the perfect counterpoint. Other main courses might be roast pigeon with lentils and braised cabbage; turbot, on the bone, with artichokes and jus; or gigot of rabbit with a tomato and black olive farce. Starters may be more delicate in presentation, but are equally robust in delivering flavours: pan-fried foie gras with girolles, haricots blancs and jus; warm smoked haddock and potato salad with caviar and quail eggs, or roast scallops with chives, ginger and onion. Desserts are delivered with panache: walnut biscuit, chicory mousse and Hoegaarden sorbet; dark chocolate vacherin with fresh peppermint; or spiced apple millefeuille with cranberries. Service charms and delivers; the wine list is superb and not unfairly priced. Set 3-course lunch £24.50; set 5-course dinner £60.

Foliage

CONTEMPORARY EUROPEAN 15/20   ♨♨
MANDARIN ORIENTAL HYDE PARK
66 KNIGHTSBRIDGE, SW1, 020-7235 2000
Lunch Mon.-Fri., Dinner Mon.-Sat. ££££
U: Knightsbridge.

Foliage is everything a hotel dining room should be. Its design is contemporary without being startlingly modern, starting with the entrance which takes you past two glassed-in

rooms holding over 5,000 bottles into a split-level room with views onto Hyde Park. Lighting is gentle; fabrics are luxurious; tables are well-spaced, and the noise level agreeably low. Service is very good, the young staff eager to please, which makes up for any occasional lapse. The wine list is suitably serious, the emphasis on France with more than a passing nod to the New World and priced to suit most pockets. Chef David Nicholls had already made quite a reputation for himself by the time the hotel closed for refurbishment late 1999; now he more than justifies the significant outlay the Mandarin Oriental group has made. His cooking, always ambitious, has gone up a notch, though his dishes may sometimes go a taste too far. Roast scallops came with a delicate turnip purée, finely chopped and creamed parsley, and steamed cèpes and snails, the whole working perfectly in textures, looks and taste; millefeuille of crisp artichokes were layered with asparagus and truffles and a game dressing. In the main dishes, a beautifully cooked spiced loin of venison came on a bed of shredded, crushed sweet peppers, and with pancetta, crisp bone marrow fondants and roast endive. Quite delicious, but too many tastes were involved here, and the roast endive, presumably intended to give a slightly bitter counterpoint of taste, failed to hold its own. More successful was a pan-fried sea bass with lobster tortellini, braised celery hearts and a gently savoury and sweet raisin and caper vinaigrette. Baked apple and Calvados soufflé accompanied by a pain d'épices ice cream was masterful, cooked to perfection; glazed organic lemon tart came with a lemon soufflé and a lemon sorbet—perfect accompaniments. The presentation is superb—colourful and beautifully arranged. Any small glitches will soon be ironed out, giving Foliage a top placing among London's restaurants. Set 2-course lunch £9.95, 3 courses £23.50; coffee and petits fours £2.50.

The Fifth Floor

CONTEMPORARY EUROPEAN 14/20   ♨
HARVEY NICHOLS, KNIGHTSBRIDGE, SW1
020-7235 5250, FAX 020-7823 2207
Lunch daily, Dinner Mon.-Sat. ££
U: Knightsbridge.

An upper floor devoted entirely to eating and drinking (a wine shop, bar and café and this restaurant glassed-off from the smart food market) has earned Harvey Nichols as much of a reputation as have the other floors of fashion. The restaurant has more substance than might be expected of somewhere that feeds the AbFab brigade. In veteran restaurant designer Julyan Wickham's colourful, postmodern room, the food keeps pace with informed tastes without slavishly following fashion. Henry Harris produces a menu inspired by ingredients more than fads. Spain seems to be exerting a pull currently, with nutty, piquant Romesco sauce on chargrilled baby leeks and goat cheese, and Iberian acorn-fed black pig ham. Other starters such as smoked eel and salmon roe with potato pancake, crème fraîche and chives, or the richness of pan-fried foie gras sharply partnered with a bitter orange sauce bigarade are generous, powerfully flavoured and pleasurable. The enjoyable, confident style follows through into mains: Dover sole with brown butter, winkles and cucumber; grilled veal chop with Roquefort butter. The geographic and price range of the wine list reflects the buying clout of the shop on the same floor. Set 3-course lunch £23.50.

Floriana

ITALIAN   14/20   🍽

15 BEAUCHAMP PL, SW3
020-7838 1500, FAX 020-7584 1464
Lunch Tues.-Sat., Dinner nightly. £££
U: Knightsbridge.

🅰 📞 📷

An exciting new contender for best modern Italian cuisine in the capital. Chef Fabio Trabocchi is creating waves with sensational cooking in a beautiful contemporary taupe and chocolate dining room by designer Emily Todhunter with particularly glittering lighting, luxurious seating and some gorgeous art. Exquisitely understated semi-transparent crab ravioli is served with barely poached slivers of egg and langoustine; salad of spring vegetables is served with the lightest cucumber sorbet. Wild sea bass is perfumed with shavings of white truffle and daringly partnered with a red wine and herb jus, whilst lamb fillet is presented in a cèpe consommé flavoured with thyme, albeit slightly too peppery. Desserts are equally well conceived, particularly fruit brochette with lavender sorbet. Service is smooth, suave and professional. Wines, mainly Italian and French classics, like the menu are priced to suit those who are not cost-conscious. An extremely elegant address where attention to detail really matters and the clientele dress to

impress. Set 1-course lunch £10, 2 courses £15, 3 courses £19.50; Grand menu £55.

La Tante Claire

FRENCH   19/20   🍽🍽🍽

THE BERKELEY, WILTON PLACE, SW1
020-823 2003, FAX 020-7823 2001
Lunch Mon.-Fri., Dinner Mon.-Sat. ££££
U: Hyde Park Corner.

🅰 📞

The agonizing question for admirers of Pierre Koffmann and his intimate restaurant in Chelsea was: How would this scrupulous artisan manage in a grand institution? After all those years of craftsmanship, Pierre has abandonned the scarce tables of his old Tante Claire for the grandiose setting of the Berkeley Hotel, but not his passion for goldsmith-like work. On a sumptuous pale green, blue, mauve, silky stage, Koffmann thrives—discreet, assiduous as ever and looking even younger. A visible but restrained enthusiasm brightens new young staff, already au fait with service in the grand style, devoted to following a master who seeks perfection. They bring you fifteen different petits pains and six varieties of large ones. Difficult to resist sampling the tomato, the olive, the nut-flavored ones, the fougasse, and other bakery delights like Kamat bread made with a rare Egyptian flour. Resisting all the current gastronomy fads—the fusions and the confusions—Koffmann remains as French as it gets. Grey truffles from Burgundy on a thin slice of bread gently enhances one of the best foie gras we have ever eaten. On the menu his dishes sound simple: filet of turbot with shallots and coriander; sea bass braised in red wine and fricassée of cèpes; supreme of Challand duck confit. But what finesse is based on such well chosen, assembled and cooked raw ingredients. This is great art emerging from behind a curtain of simplicity. With equal pleasure we savoured the signature dishes so often copied by others: stuffed pig's trotter, or the scallops in squid ink that fill your palate so memorably. Dishes and tastes such as the light bitter chocolate in red wine sauce accompanying venison will last forever, for they are a fixed feature in gastronomy's inventory. It's impossible to refuse when thirty varieties of odoriferous cheeses are brought to the table. The only good reason would be to save space for the sweet of three chocolates or the wonderful dacquoise au café with caramel. Needless to say, the wine list is overwhelming with its naturally expensive treasures, but some good deals can be found among the regional wines. Prices are stiff, but the lunch menu is a steal. Set 3-course lunch £28.

Isola

ITALIAN   15/20   ♟♟

145 KNIGHTSBRIDGE, SW1
020-7838 1044, FAX 020-7838 1099
Lunch & Dinner daily £££
U: Knightsbridge.

A ☎

Ubiquitous restaurateur Oliver Peyton has joined forces with leading French chef Bruno Loubet to create this vast, plate-glassed Italian restaurant which manages to twin aching fashionability with 'serious cuisine'. The chef's Gallic antecedents have been deftly transposed; the six-course £50 'gustatzione' which included a ceviche of sea bass, zuppe, filetti di triglia on a bed of julienne, squab pigeon with gnocchi and pescespeda, revealed one strand after another of delicacy and depth with flavour harmoniously chasing flavour. Our arrostto d'agnello al Romano—sweet and tender cuts of lamb, glowingly pink—were masterly, and the torta di mela cotogna (upside-down caramelised quince tart with verbena ice cream) ended the meal on an ambrosial high note. The all-Italian wine list is far-ranging and regionally impressive, particularly to be appreciated are the seventy selections offered by the glass. Diners take pleasure in a room strikingly designed with sophisticated retro-sixties idiom. Waiters glide around it solicitously. You leave with a sense of having been somewhere 'hot' and, if you go the whole hog, a lighter wallet—but why not? Set 3-course lunch £25, gourmet 6-course dinner £50.

Osteria Isola

ITALIAN   14/20   ♟

145 KNIGHTSBRIDGE, SW1, 020-7838 1055
Open daily noon-midnight ££
U: Knightsbridge.

A ☎

The lower half of the long-awaited (two-and-a-half years and £4 million in the making) Knightsbridge showcase for Italian food has less elevated aspirations than upstairs Isola, though prices are still high. Osteria is a state-of-the-art diner with the kitchen visible at the back. Yet tables and booth-backed seats are cleverly arranged at different levels and angles

so that you feel shielded from neighbours (Conran, are you reading this?) Under the direction of gifted Frenchman Bruno Loubet, Italian country dishes, loosely arranged into courses, have a smooth assurance. No expense has been spared sourcing ingredients, and from the olive oil with homemade grissini and breads to the cheeses, they are impeccable. This is evident in glorious ravioli stuffed with beetroot, sage and horseradish, and mouth-watering secondi such as steamed clams, mussels and cockles with vermouth, chilli and garlic; slow-roast lamb with anchovies and olives Roman-style, or Livornese fish stew for around £15. The all-Italian wine list is mind-boggling. It could be more helpfully arranged, but groups of taster glasses are a marvelous introduction to what's available. Fun, informal Italian dining, but deeply serious about the country's food and wines.

Restaurant One-O-One

SEAFOOD   16/20   ♟♟

SHERATON PARK TOWER, WILLIAM ST, SW1
020-7290 7101, FAX 020-7235 6196
Lunch & Dinner daily. £££
U: Knightsbridge.

A ☎

Few chefs profess their passion for poisson as persuasively as Breton Pascal Proyart whose menu is entitled 'cuisine de mer' and who cooks ambitious piscean dishes using abundant luxury ingredients with considerable aplomb. A daring combination of perfect carpaccio of tuna with pan-fried foie gras with a balsamic and hazelnut dressing was truly stunning, whilst smoked foie gras accompanied a luscious dish of scallops glazed with a light truffle sauce. Sea bass of superlative quality features prominently: roast with its skin on with truffle herb mash, brussels sprout chiffonade and girolle jus a ridiculously fancy-sounding dish which worked a treat, while two can share a whole sea bass in a sea-salt crust with olive oil and flat parsley. Steamed Dover sole of sublime delicacy with Oscietra caviar and shallot cream emulsion was artfully presented to look as decadent as it tasted. Desserts are stellar too, especially a marvelously light pear chocolate millefeuille with coffee and praline cream. Pity only that the oceanic redesign of the dining room is rather harshly lit and lacks warmth. Service is perfectly groomed if over-solicitous. The wine list is conservative with little to excite outside Burgundy. Proyart surely deserves real acclaim for such haute piscean cuisine. Set 2-course lunch £21, 3 courses £25; set 4-course dinner £42, 5 courses £55.

Vong

FRENCH/THAI **15/20**

THE BERKELEY, KNIGHTSBRIDGE, SW1
020-7235 1010, FAX 020-7235 1011
Lunch & Dinner daily. £££
U: Knightsbridge.

So goes the life: The London outpost of New York-based Jean-Georges Vongerichten's enterprise may seem to some a tad less startling a resident of the Berkeley Hotel as it did when it opened. Once in the vanguard of fusion, it's still a shining exponent of that style of cooking. Here French finesse applied to Asian ingredients often produces dishes that seem as if they were meant to be, and the repertoire is well honed. Crisp crab spring rolls stand out among starters; scallops with pickled cauliflower and caper and raisin sauce was less appealing. Main courses such as cod with curried artichokes, rabbit curry, and sweetbreads threaded on a liquorice stick, are protein-rich and rewarding, although the spicing is pallid compared with true Thai cooking. The international customers' jewellery and the richly coloured fabrics give a warm glow to the cool stone from which the imposing room, and even the tables, are fashioned. East and West fuse most deliciously in desserts like the warm Valrhona chocolate cake, melting in the middle, baked on the outside, with coconut ice cream. Staff in gorgeous waistcoats are very obliging, the atmosphere one of smart informality. Set lunch £15-£19.50; set 3-course dinner 6pm-7pm £17.50, set dinner £45.

LONDON BRIDGE

fish!

SEAFOOD **12/20**

CATHEDRAL ST, SE1, 020-7836 3236
Lunch & Dinner Mon.-Sat. £
U: London Bridge.

As steakhouses used to in the past, fish! takes a straightforward approach to serving its chosen protein. The menu which doubles as a disposable place mat is little more than a tick-list on one side and policy statement on the other. Fish! is part of a group that includes Bank restaurant, and fish supplier, Cutty. It supports sustainable and responsible fishing practices, and prices for what is essentially a contemporary fish and chip operation reflect the care taken with sourcing. With Southwark Cathedral on one side and Borough fruit and veg market on the other, the surroundings are atmospheric and the interior of the Victorian glasshouse that of a metallic modern diner. Starters include an excellent fish soup with croûtons and rouille, devilled whitebait, both crunchy and fleshy, prawn cocktail and potted shrimps all of the highest calibre. Then a choice of a score of fish, ticked where available, is offered steamed or grilled with a choice of salsa, hollandaise, herb butter, olive oil dressing or red wine gravy. It's not ambitious cooking, but it's nevertheless spot on. There are also fishcakes and fish pie. Chips are the tops. Nursery puddings, such as sponge and custard, are also the best of their type. Frill-free and fun, it's a big hit with City types slipping south of the river for a fish supper, and at weekends caters admirably for families

MARBLE ARCH

Al San Vincenzo

ITALIAN **13/20**

30 CONNAUGHT ST, W2, 020-7262 9623
Lunch Mon.-Fri., Dinner Mon.-Sat. ££
U: Marble Arch.

This is a somewhat surprising 'local' to find in such a well-heeled area, but it's clearly a great favourite with its regulars. It's small, only seating around 24, with pale walls covered in black and white photographs run by husband-and-wife team Vincenzo (who does the cooking) and Elain (who looks after front of house) Borgonzolo. The regularly changing menu offers simple, rustic Italian cooking, but of a standard which is a delight. Expect perhaps pan-fried prawns with a variety of sides like chilli and pepper, a pasta dish which might be penne with pork ragoût, and a robust stuffed pig's trotter with lentils. In a city where modern Italian cooking is capturing the imagination and the headlines, it's good to find such a family-run, straightforward Italian restaurant doing so well. There's a short Italian wine list, reasonably priced. Set lunch & dinner 2 courses £25, 3 courses £31.

The Crescent

CONTEMPORARY EUROPEAN 13/20 ♟
THE MONTCALML, GREAT CUMBERLAND PL, W1
020-7402 4288, FAX 020-7724 9180
Lunch Mon.-Fri., Dinner nightly. ££
U: Marble Arch.

A ☎

A calm and elegant hotel dining room in search of a chef who'll stay the course after frequent changes in the kitchen. Chef Steve Whitney (ex Mosimann's and The Savoy) is the latest, and judging by the number of diners, is creating a name for himself for accomplished complex dishes with plenty of visual excitement. But not every dish fires on all cylinders: creamed soup of oysters, leeks and champagne sabayon had a heavenly velvet texture with the surprise of shredded leeks, but a rather tasteless seared blue fin tuna was only mitigated by an unusual bok choy and bean salad. Slightly overcooked red mullet fillets undermined a delicious combination of tomato, basil and flaked crab meat in a promising main, whereas a rather mushy tomato and herb risotto didn't enhance crisp-fried sea bass. Desserts are impressively decorative—chocolate teardrop with citrus fruit salad and rhubarb sorbet required a sweet tooth whilst simpler sorbets such as orange and black currant are a treat. The extensive wine list is well researched. Courteous staff, well-spaced tables, a sophisticated, neutral revamp of the room plus an extremely good lunch deal including wine make for a very appealing restaurant, which after a little tuning is on its way to becoming a gastro destination. Set 3-course lunch & 2-course dinner £20, 3 courses £25.

La Porte des Indes

INDIAN 12/20
32 BRYANSTON ST, W1
020-7224 0055, FAX 020-7224 1144
Lunch Sun.-Fri., Dinner nightly. ££
U: Marble Arch

A ☎ 🏃

The staircase down to the lower level is imposing enough to be descended on an elephant, which would be appropriate for this is the one Indian restaurant of the Thai Blue Elephant international chain. The cooking rarely ascends to the height of the marble waterfall which is just one of the features of this maharaja's palace (which is no place for

nouveaux pauvres), but it can be pretty good. It shows best during the festivals which are regularly held, a recent one being a four weddings feast offering nuptial banquets from four major regions. Magret de canard pulivaar, calamars à la façon de Mahé and a vegetarian main dish of rougail d'aubergine with chilli, ginger and fresh lime, show the Gallic influence on the cuisine of the former French colony of Pondicherry. From the menu's 'voyage of discovery round India' come Hyderabadi biryani, Goanese pork vindaloo and from the country's most western outpost, chicken tikka masala. The long, if expensive, wine list would not discredit a French restaurant, except for the inclusion of 'Chablis', an Indian white wine as authentic as might be a French chef's attempt at a 'curreil de l'Inde'. Set weekday buffet lunch £16.50, weekend £17.50; set dinner £30-£40.

MARYLEBONE

Ibla

ITALIAN 13/20 ♟
89 MARYLEBONE HIGH ST, W1
020-7224 3799, FAX 020-7486 1370
Lunch & Dinner Mon.-Sat. ££
U: Baker St.

A MasterCard ☎

Choose from a radiant green in the front room, or the more library red in the rear—each have their followers but both have a warm intimacy which is a welcome relief given the plethora of so many large, impersonal restaurants. Tables are elegantly laid with best white linen, a perfect stage for cooking which draws its inspiration from the Italian home, but executes it with wit and style. A first course might be egg-rich pasta tossed with crab and chilli, the whole perfectly balanced. Main courses might be stuffed squid, sweet and sticky, served with mussels and an elegant tomato broth. Other main courses might be duck served with an inky black sauce spiked with citrus fruits, or red mullet served with a light and fresh caper sauce and wilted spinach. Desserts are more French in style, a delicious pear tart with mascarpone, or a lime mousse, delicate but intense. The almost all-Italian wine list climbs steeply, but is unusual and different and worth exploring with the extremely helpful sommelier. Service overall is charming, willing and efficient. Set 2-course lunch £15, 3 courses £18; set 2-course dinner £23, 3 courses £27.

Orrery

FRENCH 16/20 ♟♟

55 MARYLEBONE HIGH ST, W1,
020-7616-8000, FAX 020-7616-8080
Lunch & Dinner daily. ££££
U: Baker St/Regent's Park.

A **☎**

This is arguably Sir Terence Conran's best restaurant, and it's also his least well-known—which is great news, because it means you get a top-class restaurant experience without any difficulty in booking, and without having to leave your table after two hours. The whole operation is flawlessly professional, from charming staff to faultless food. The large first-floor dining room lies above the Conran Shop, and during the summer there's some outdoor seating on a hemmed-in roof terrace. Chef Chris Galvin prepares his ambitious and hautey menu with an assured touch, be it a starter of saddle of rabbit with black pudding, cèpes and parsley dressing (£9.50), or a main course of red mullet, herb risotto and wood-roasted pepper oil (£19.50). The high prices extend to the desserts, which cost between £7 and £8.50, but at least there's a set lunch at £23.50 for three courses, a Sunday set dinner for £28.50, and a bar menu served in the small and cosy bar. The wine list has many excellent bottles, but few cost under £20. Set 3-course lunch £23.50, Sun. 3-course dinner inc. glass of Champagne £28.50; 5-course Menu Gourmand dinner £45, or £75 with wine at each course.

Stephen Bull

MODERN BRITISH 14/20 ♟

5-7 BLANDFORD ST, W1
020-7486 9696, FAX 020-7224 0324
Lunch Mon.-Fri., Dinner Mon.-Sat. ££
U: Baker St.

'Grown up restaurants' is how Mr. Bull thinks of his establishments. That does not suggest that the younger generation is excluded; happy families dining here include young children who are as well looked after as the more typical mature clientele. Mr. Bull's 'grown up' means an ever-changing, short, three-course set price menu of serious western European dishes. It is far from 'fast food', so patience is called for, but Roger Gorman's accurate cooking produces strong but not overpowering flavours which make any wait

well worthwhile. Starters might include twice-baked goat cheese soufflé with parsley, coriander and olive salad, or seared scallops, creamed endive and wilted roquette. Equally successful main dishes were fried calf's liver and kidney, mustard sauce and creamed potatoes, and guinea fowl with roast shallots and apples. In the desserts the choice is wider and of a quality, and quantity, to satisfy the child in every man or woman. Steamed ginger pudding is made with the traditional suet, while warm baked pumpkin cheesecake proves that two usually bland ingredients can be combined in a remarkably full-flavoured partnership. The wide-ranging, carefully selected wine list is divided by style, not geography, and prices are reasonable. Set 2-course lunch £22, 3 courses £26; set 3-course dinner £27.50.

Tajine

NORTH AFRICAN 13/20 ♟

7A DORSET ST, W1, 010-7935 1545
Lunch Mon.-Fri., Dinner Mon.-Sat. ££
U: Baker St.

In this charming Moroccan restaurant, owner Mehdi Barradi looks after front-of-house while his Turkish fiancé, Gonal Ozturk, cooks. The warmth of welcome and ambience is reflected in the décor of terracotta walls with mirrors, prints and travel posters. Ms. Ozturk's success in the kitchen allows her to offer a wider than usual range of classic dishes. Starters include lentil salad, aubergine zaalouk, and carnivorean temptations such as fried kidneys in mustard sauce, or liver with fresh herbs. But b'stilla is irresistible with a choice of chicken, pigeon or seafood. Among couscous variations are chicken and vegetable, chicken Kedra with onions, raisins and chickpeas, and lamb, merguez or mixed. Tajine lovers—and aren't we all?—choose from ten, including lamb with caramelised pear, or with caramelised prunes and almonds; while chicken comes with carrots, green olives and preserved lemon, or with ginger, parsley, courgette, and garlicked red pepper. Portions are large, so desserts, other than Moroccan pastries, may be out of the question. Then there is the difficult choice between Turkish coffee, or mint tea traditionally poured from a height into gilded tumblers. The short interesting wine list includes full-bodied rosés and reds from Morocco and many other countries. Set 2-course lunch £7.50.

Villandry

MODERN BRITISH   12/20
170 GT. PORTLAND ST, W1
020-7631 3131, FAX 020-7631 3030
Lunch daily, Dinner Mon.-Sat. ££
U: Oxford Circus.

The all-white room is spacious and airy, particularly so if you arrive through the shop, decked out as it is in all manner of vegetables, cheeses, and tinned, jarred and beautifully packaged items. In Paris many of these are run of the mill, yet in London they seem to instill cries of pleasure and pain at the quality and price in equal measure. The restaurant maintains the concentration on ingredients: tuna and couscous, belly of pork and root vegetables—no fancy footwork here, simply accurate and well-judged execution. The menu allows for lighter eating, in perhaps a salad to start followed by a savoury tart of mushrooms or broccoli, while those with larger appetites are also catered for: an earthy pumpkin soup, or wilted fennel salad with pecorino in winter perhaps, followed by grilled sea bass and leeks with salsa verde, or roast rabbit with caramelised shallots and roasted roots. Desserts tend towards the very simple: tart Tatin, chocolate mousse or ricotta cheesecake, while the wine list too, gains strength from its simplicity. Service is enthusiastic, if a little slow. Pre-theatre 6pm-7pm 2-course dinner £12.50, 3 courses £15.50.

MAYFAIR

Al Hamra

LEBANESE   14/20
31-33 SHEPHERD MARKET, W1
020-7493 1954, FAX 020-7493 1044
Lunch & Dinner daily. ££
U: Green Park.

This long-established front runner among London's Lebanese restaurants is located in mid-Mayfair and priced appropriately. Service tends to the stiff and formal, but recorded cabaret music and the buzz of conversation is always lively. We can only speculate on why Lebanese restaurants differ from the rest in that the more luxurious they are the more the tables are crammed into a minimal space. Here you may find only a narrow flower trough separating you from your neighbours, sometimes not even that. There are few surprises on the menu with its long list of meze which includes a wide range of vegetables: leeks, aubergine, and beans—both French and broad—come cold with olive oil dressings. Hot meze include most of the same ingredients as well as stuffed pastries and 'pizzas'. Meat eaters relish raw lamb, and its liver and tongue in salads, and hot offal includes variously prepared sweetbreads, liver, kidney, and sausages. Main dishes are the usual chicken and lamb kebabs, with vegetable garnishes. Lebanese pastries are not listed but always available and not to be missed. There are some classy, if expensive wines, also some Lebanese, and for apéritifs a choice of several sorts of arak. Set lunch & dinner £20.

Cassia Oriental

CHINESE   13/20
12 BERKELEY SQ, W1, 020-7629 8886
Lunch & Dinner daily. ££
U: Green Park.

Surprises abound in this luxurious yet modestly priced first-floor restaurant and bar in Berkeley Square although sadly there is no view of that fabled aviary where the nightingales sang. The cool modern décor cleverly combines wooden panelling with pale beige and silver-gray colours, and a deep carpet makes this modern place quieter than most. Service is charming in the best Asian tradition, and both tableware and elegant presentation please the eye. The set-price menu includes delicacies from China, Japan, Vietnam and Thailand among its fourteen starters and fourteen main dishes. But despite its sophisticated westernisation, you shouldn't choose a western-style course meal. Main dishes are substantial, so as in other Chinese restaurants they should be shared, preferably by at least four people—although fewer can eat well especially from the shorter lunch menu. A skilfully selected list encourages the enjoyment of wine. Set 2-course lunch £10; set 2-course dinner £15, 3 courses £19, 4 courses £23.

Chez Nico

FRENCH   18/20   🍳🍳🍳
LE MERIDIEN GROSVENOR HOUSE
90 PARK LANE, W1
020-7409 1290, FAX 020-7355 4877
Lunch Mon.-Fri., Dinner Mon.-Sat. ££££
U: Hyde Park Corner.

🅰 ☎ 🍴

The intention of Nico Ladenis in his newly 'down to earth' restaurant is to put the 'g' back in 'gastronomy'. Service by informally uniformed staff, is attentive as ever, but more relaxed. The slightly longer menu is à la carte at lunch so guests can choose two or three courses, or even a single dish; at dinner the same list becomes table d'hôte at £48 for three courses. The food is lighter, but happily unchanged in that fine cooking takes precedence over luxurious ingredients, although foie gras, caviar and truffles still have their place, as does Balik smoked salmon, arguably a touch bland for some London tastes. In the elegantly balanced seven-course gastronomic menu, (£62), standards are set by risotto perfumed by minute specks of black truffle. Other highlights include grilled scallops, and langoustine tortellini, their cream sauces satisfying both traditionalists and those seeking twenty-first century lightness. Seared sea bass with fennel in basil oil was one example of great provençale cuisine; another was herb-crusted slices of lamb saddle, topped by a fan of crisp potato, on a base of tomato, courgettes and aubergine. In the mini-assiette of four desserts some flavours seemed too delicate for forgivably tiring palates. Maestro Ladenis' **other ventures** now include Incognito, 177 Shoftesbury Ave., WC2, 020-7836 8866, and others, opening as we go to press. Set 3-course dinner £48, 7 courses £62.

Chor Bizarre

INDIAN   12/20
16 ALBEMARLE ST, W1
020-7629 9802, FAX 020-7493 7756
Lunch & Dinner daily. ££
U: Green Park.

🅰 ☎

The instant appeal here is the eccentric décor which fulfils the promise of the name, a pun on chor bazaar, the thieves' market of Delhi and other Indian townships. A multitude of wondrous 'antiquities', ancient and modern, include tables of wrought iron, or perforated stone panelling, even one made from a four-poster bed; seats may be ivory armed or silvered thrones. All are for sale. Service is friendly, if Nelsonian in its reactions to diners seeking attention. The long menu is divided into sections, some as familiar as tandooris, others less familiar such as tak-a-tak dishes. The simplest way to explore it is to order one of the non-vegetarian thali set meals, or the vegetarian version on a silver thali, offered under the sexist name 'Maharani'; it is described as 'dainty' and includes okra, wild mushrooms, spinach, lotus roots, lentils and a saffron pulao. Excellent ingredients are cooked with more care than flair, and flavours sing less clearly than the film music which plays all the time. The wines, chosen by wine writer Charles Metcalfe are interesting as are his dish-by-dish recommendations, although some would find the bias towards white wines controversial. Set lunch £24; set pre-theatre 2-course dinner £24 inc. cab to a West End theatre.

Claridge's

FRENCH/BRITISH   14/20   🍳
CLARIDGE'S, BROOK ST, W1
020-7629 8860, FAX 020-7499 2210
Lunch & Dinner daily. ££££
U: Bond St.

🅰 ☎ 🍴

This elegant Art Deco gilded dining room is aristocratic, formal yet surprisingly innovative in its culinary approach, thanks to chef John Williams, as classic dishes are given enough twist to satisfy the more free-thinking captains of industry and dowagers. Synchronised domes are de rigeur, but underneath lurk some superb creations: a classy trio of foie gras with the lightest elderflower sauce and aromatic spiced bread; superlative flavoured truffled lobster with polenta, rocket salad and walnut dressing. Mains of Barbary duck with braised Savoy cabbage and green pepper sauce, or guinea fowl given the confit treatment with girolles in a truffle bouillon exemplify the menu moving with the times yet retaining that luxurious pampering edge. Desserts are brought round on a chariot and grazing on several puds is encouraged: caramelised apple millefeuille is stylishly partnered with star anise ice cream. Wines are grand and service suitably gracious without too much hauteur. A memorable, utterly British experience. Set lunch £29.50; set dinner £39.

Coast

INTERNATIONAL   14/20   🍽
26B ALBEMARLE ST, W1
020-7495 5999, FAX 020-7495 2999
Lunch daily, Dinner Mon.-Sat. £££
U: Green Park.

🅰 ☎

It will come as no surprise that this was once a car showroom, yet the design takes it light years away from paintwork and chrome bumpers. The plate-glass window stretches the entire width of the restaurant, with 'coast' engraved across it in a specially designed typeface. If you are a group you may be ushered into one of the fairground-like booths, teacup shaped for comfort and privacy, or one of the specially commissioned open tables that rise, pod-like, from the parquet floor. Once past the door staff—long on attitude and short on charm—the mood is decidedly hip and trendy, with noise echoing around the room to good, if sometimes loud, effect. Stephen Terry is back in the kitchen once more and serving up eclectic, sometimes wacky, combinations to a well-heeled set of bright and fashionable young things. He has mellowed somewhat though, with starters like ravioli of salmon and crab in lemon grass and ginger bouillon; a salad of ironbark pumpkin, crispy artichokes and Parmesan; and smoked eel, with caramelised pineapple, pancetta and red wine sauce. The twists on dishes remain in main courses, as in Welsh black beef, foie gras, chips and a fried quail's egg; or lamb, again Welsh, with tapenade, courgette fries and tomato. Desserts tend to be classical—tarts and ices. The wine list is a delight, a reflection of owner Oliver Peyton's passion.

The Connaught Grill Room & Restaurant

BRITISH/FRENCH   16/20   🍽🍽
THE CONNAUGHT, CARLOS PL, W1
020-7499 7070, FAX 020-7495 3262
Restaurant: Lunch & Dinner daily; Grill:
Lunch Sun.-Fri., Dinner nightly. ££££
U: Bond St.

🅰 ☎

While the rest of London is busy simplifying its menus and generally dumbing down on prices and complexity, the Connaught continues its magisterial path, offering the very best in a style of classic cooking which has changed little in the now 25 years that the splendid Michel Bourdin, Maître Cuisinier de France, has been chef here. The rooms, too, offer a formal dining experience increasingly difficult to find. In the Restaurant, the polished wood paneling gleams; the silver trolleys roll; the service is stately. The smaller Grill is intimate in the way that a dining room in a stately home is intimate: rather grand with all pretty pastel shades, luxurious curtains and well-spaced, beautifully laid tables. The menu is the same in both restaurants, an object lesson in grand dining on an Edwardian scale. The list is long, with the emphasis on the very best ingredients (Bourdin's devotion to truffles is legendary; this is the place to go during the truffle season for top menus which given the price of the noble fungus, are top value). Starters like asparagus, kipper pâté, smoked Scotch salmon compete with the grander pâté de turbot froid au homard, sauce pudeur, and consommé Prince of Wales. Les Poissons include sole jubilee, turbot done various ways, and Scottish lobster done 'My Way'. La chasse includes roast grouse 'Old England', and quite the best wild duck we have ever tasted. Les Entrées range from the regular luncheon dishes in the chariot (roast Kentish lamb on a Thursday, Irish stew and braised loin of pork with apples and prunes on a Tuesday, always), to Kent lamb 'Forestière', even mixed grill. And of course there are those traditional British savouries like deviled sardines, Scotch woodcock, mushrooms on toast. For dessert? It must be a bread and butter pudding, or sorbets or mousses if you insist. The wine list is, as you would expect, splendid, with splendid prices to match, heavy on France but with more than a nod to the New World. There are those who would disparage The Connaught, but this is a place which demonstrates what classic French and British cooking should be like, and provides a yardstick in an increasingly un-selfconfident world. Long may it continue in the same vein. Set 3-course lunch £27.50; 3-course dinner £58.

1837

FRENCH   14/20   🍽
BROWN'S HOTEL, 33 ALBEMARLE ST, W1
020-7408 1837, FAX 020-7493 9381
Lunch Mon.-Fri., Dinner Mon.-Sat. ££££
U: Green Park.

🅰 ☎

Step from busy Dover Street into Brown's and the hustle and bustle of London disappears. This is more country than town, with wood paneling throughout and soft, patterned carpets. 1837 is a large room and staff pad about with surprising speed and deftness. Service is impeccable: attentive and professional. Chef Andrew Turner arrived at the end of 1999 from The Berkeley along with a sizable part of his brigade, changed the menu structure and content and almost instantly created a buzz. Getting a table on a Thursday was surprisingly difficult. Watercress soup, with upfront intensity, comforting and served in a teacup, not the more usual intensely trufflised espresso cup, kicked things off well. A salad of lobster with minted scallions, tamarind and mesclun leaves was suitably sweet and sour, packing punch and elegance in equal proportion. Other choices might have been roast foie gras with mango-crushed potatoes and truffled champagne vinaigrette, or tuna classic fish soup with paprika straws. Fillet of black Angus beef, salsify, wild mushrooms and a sweet meat glaze was hearty without being heavy. Other choices might have been saddle of rabbit, potato purée, spinach and baby onions, or herb-coated John Dory with artichokes, spinach and an olive and tomato sauce. Cheese is one of the better boards in London, while desserts might be straight tart Tatin, or chocolate indulgence with chilled apricot cream, the latter suitably wicked. The wine list is one of the best in London with sommelier John Gilchrist knowledgeable, astute and stylish. Let him match each course, you will be amazed. 7-course lunch & dinner Menu Dégustation £55. 'Grazing' menus with small portioned dishes from the carte: 7 courses £34, 8 courses £39, 9 courses £45.

Firebird

RUSSIAN   12/20
23 CONDUIT ST, W1
020-7493 7000, FAX 020-7493 7088
Lunch Mon.-Fri., Dinner Mon.-Sat. £££
U: Oxford Circus.

A ☎

It's rare to find a restaurant boasting a new cuisine concept, but pre-revolutionary Russian is a retro style new to the capital. Harking back to a time when the best Russian households employed French chefs, Firebird, which already has a successful sister establishment in New York, briefed French chef Alain Allard, formerly at L'Oranger, to immerse himself in Russian cuisine and evolve a lighter, more sophisticated modern French approach. Don't

come expecting authenticity. Do expect opulence and mostly highly accomplished cooking. A decadent dish of exceptionally plump lightly poached oysters with caviar and wilted lettuce was a total delight. Zakuski, supposedly Russian mezedes, were more variable: excellent herring in sour cream and fresh blini, but mediocre baked mushrooms and aubergine caviar. Uzbeck squab breast was delectably tender and well partnered with celeriac blini, chanterelles and spinach. Roast venison with beetroot, pumpkin, sweet and sour berries however was lacklustre with meat of indiscriminate taste. Stunning caramelised walnut ice cream lifted a drab 'Bolshoi' chocolate cake, whilst orange and mandarin paska was rather too mousse-like and lacked bite. The townhouse is luxuriously (over) decorated with handblocked wallpaper, original Fabergé eggs and photographs. Service by formally dressed staff is knowledgeable and courteous, if a little nervously over-eager. Unsurprisingly there is a fine selection of vodka, including a delectable honey vodka. Set 2-course lunch £15, 3 courses £18.95.

The Greenhouse

CONTEMPORARY EUROPEAN 13/20 ☺
27A HAYS MEWS, W1
020-7499 3331, FAX 020-7499 5368
Lunch Sun.-Fri., Dinner nightly. £££
U: Green Park.

A ☎

Housed as it is on the ground floor of a very ugly block of flats, the Greenhouse is a surprisingly attractive looking restaurant, all plants and painted trelliswork, but the décor is not the reason to visit. If you want to know what British cooking is about, this is a good place to start. It was here that Gary Rhodes first grabbed the headlines for real British cooking. Paul Merrett has now taken over the reins as chef, and though he intends to make his own impression, he'll keep the flag flying. He's a young man of considerable talent and when he cooks well it's very good. The Greenhouse looks as though it will suit him well. You'll find classics like smoked haddock fish cakes enhanced by the addition of a mussel butter broth; pot-roasted guinea fowl with cornbread and chestnut stuffing, served on a bed of cabbage and bacon, and baked rice pudding with apple mash and butterscotch sauce. Occasionally the kitchen has its aberrations, but that's only to be expected in young talented cooks who experiment. Set 2-course lunch

£19.50, 3 courses £22.50; set Sun. 3-course lunch £19.50.

The Grill Room

BRITISH   13/20   ♟
THE DORCHESTER, 54 PARK LANE, W1
020-7629 8888, FAX 020-7317 6464
Lunch & Dinner daily. £££
U: Hyde Park Corner.

A ☎ ❙

Even institutions seemingly as impervious to change as the palatial Spanish-styled Dorchester Grill Room do evolve. Henry Brosi is only the seventh chef to inherit the mantle of Executive Chef in the seventy years of the hotel's existence. Although classics such as the lobster soup and unimpeachable roast Angus beef and Yorkshire pudding from the silver galleon remain, Brosi is already making his presence felt with some lighter modern British dishes on the daily menu which are immaculately executed and stylishly presented. The Stilton bread carved to order remains impressive on the bread trolley. A starter salad of duck with sweet onion marmalade prettified with red pepper was delicate with a likeable hint of earthiness. Impeccable grilled scallops, langoustine and halibut came with eye-catching, stripy beetroot-filled ravioli though a disappointing, over-peppered ratatouille-like timbale with somewhat bitter, undercooked aubergine. A fabulous apple tart scattered with pistachios adorned with unseasonally exotic fruits and extraordinary chocolate doves was sensational. Service is unpompous and enthusiastic yet efficient to the point of invisibility. The wine list is magnificent, though mostly stratospherically priced. Set 3-course lunch £19.50; set 3-course dinner £29.50.

Kaspia

RUSSIAN   13/20   ♟
18/18A BRUTON PL, W1, 020-7493 2612
Lunch & Dinner Mon.-Sat. £££
U: Green Park/Bond St.

A ☎

A fresh lick of paint has lightened the tone of this clubby Mayfair institution tucked away around the corner from Berkeley Square and famed for its splendid caviar list and old school charm. If that all sounds a mite intimidating, fear not: everyone gets treated royally (the ladies-who-lunch have cottoned on to its handy proximity to the delights of nearby Bond Street), and there's a placid purr of contented chat about the place. Beluga, Oscietra, Sevrugra, pressed and salmon caviar are all available, served with a variety of accompaniments (can't go wrong with blinis or toast of course). Chef Anabelle Job has plenty of other tricks up her sleeve: pasta roulade filled with wild mushrooms, spinach and sage butter; fresh foie gras and salmon fishcakes with lobster sauce. There are 40 different vodkas to tuck into as well, which can't be bad. Set menus £36, £72 and £128.

Kiku

JAPANESE   14/20   ♟
17 HALF MOON ST, W1, 020-7499 4208
Lunch & Dinner Mon.-Sat. £££
U: Green Park.

A ☎

Japanese minimalism is hundreds of years older than its western counterpart—which may be why it more easily creates a warm ambience. This large rectangular room has slate flooring, black wooden tables and neutral coloured seats, but one wall is covered with light paneling, and plants on the window sills add colour. It is noisy, but the sushi bar is a cosy refuge. It offers classical cuisine with superb sushi including such rarities as scallop and flying fish roe; subtly flavoured maki roll of pickled plum and shiso leaf and succulent hamachi, yellowfish, worth its high price. Set dinner menus from £34.50 traditionally list only the way dishes are cooked not their ingredients. At lunchtime menus are from £10 and makonouchi bento boxes from £20. The à la carte is long and a few seasonal dishes written in Japanese are willingly translated. Note aji tataki, a sort of sashimi of horse mackerel chopped with onion, ginger and herbs. As well as the standards, less usual delicacies include dengaku konnyaku, devil's tongue plant with miso paste, and under 'casseroles' a superb nimono of poached mooli and chicken. The deep flavoured house saké is excellent and there are about 30 sensibly priced wines. Set lunch menus from £10, bento boxes from £20; set dinner from £34.50.

For a complete guide to our **restaurant ranking system,** see *'About the Reviews'* in the introduction to the Restaurants chapter.

Langan's Brasserie

MODERN EUROPEAN   13/20   🍺
STRATTON ST, W1
020-7491 8822, FAX 020-7493 8309
Lunch Mon.-Fri., Dinner Mon.-Sat. ££
U: Green Park.

Ⓐ ☎

Twenty-five years after it opened, this large, glamorous brasserie—one of London's first—still casts a spell despite cynical claims that the cooking has lost its magic and the crowd is less 'movers 'n' shakers' and more 'bridge 'n' tunnel'. Nonsense. The Anglo-French fare may not be haute cuisine, but it offers a pleasing exactitude: a beautifully judged soufflé aux épinards with plentiful sauce anchoise to start, then delicious pan-fried monkfish with bacon and leeks (both meaty and briny) and roast duck with onion stuffing (crispy skin enclosing succulent flesh). Desserts—'nursery food', such as treacle tart and spotted dick with crème anglaise were greedily gobbled up. The wine list delivers a good balance of French, European and New World; our nicely perfumed Gewürtztraminer '98 Leon Beyer didn't disappoint. Service has a professional bustle. The downstairs room—walls strewn with notable pictures—has a distinctive buzz, even exuberance. The upstairs room has sedate charms, including tender English roast lamb from the trolley.

Le Gavroche

FRENCH   17/20   🍺🍺🍺
43 UPPER BROOK ST, W1
020-7408 0881, FAX 020-7491 4387
Lunch & Dinner Mon.-Fri. ££££
U: Bond St.

Ⓐ ☎ 🍷

Le Gavroche is a real London institution. It first opened on a previous site in the 60s and has been preparing haute cuisine for a discerning, well-heeled clientele ever since. With Albert Roux at the helm is was the spawning ground of generations of chefs around Britain. Albert retired from the kitchen some years ago, and his son Michel now wears the toque. Through the five years of changeover period, Le Gavroche had its less than perfect days—unbalanced menus, over-rich sauces. Like an old galleon, it took a long time to change its direction, but now Michel has put his own mark on the place, and the ship is in full sail again. He still offers fantastically good luxury ingredients—foie gras, turbot etc. But arguably his best dishes are his most humble—a perfect navarin of lamb, or his version of the restaurant classic, caneton Gavroche, which delivers duck poached in duck broth. Service, still led by Silvano Giraldin is superb, and Thierry, the sommelier, is one of the only men of his profession who puts his customers at ease. Dinner is a grand affair, but lunch is a steal. Set 3-course lunch £38.50.

Le Soufflé

FRENCH   13/20   🍺
INTER-CONTINENTAL HOTEL, 1 HAMILTON PL
HYDE PARK CORNER, W1
020-7409 3131, FAX 020-7409 7460
Lunch Sun.-Fri., Dinner Tues.-Sat. ££££
U: Hyde Park Corner.

Ⓐ ☎

There's definitely life beyond the soufflé at Peter Kromberg's severely dated sage, beige and defiantly 80s hotel dining room. That's not to say the soufflés should necessarily be eschewed, though a starter of cèpe and tarragon soufflé with a gratin of goat cheese did not live up to the fluffy perfection anticipated. It's the organic menu which may put this destination back on the gastro-map. Not only is every detail organic: including the bread, rolls, wine, coffee and chocolate, but the dishes are confidently cooked using excellent, flavoursome ingredients. Smoky brochette of scallops on roasted aubergine with a fragrant tomato fondue, and roasted sea bass with shiitake mushrooms and a Savoy cabbage emulsion were supremely confident dishes. A sweet soufflé of red berries was simply stunning. The wine list is classic with little of excitement in the lower echelons. Service is old-fashioned and cossetting though did seem a little overbearing.

Mirabelle

FRENCH   15/20   🍺🍺
56 CURZON ST, W1
020-7499 4636, FAX 020-7499 5449
Lunch & Dinner daily. ££
U: Green Park.

Ⓐ ☎ 🍽

A rarified operation with more than a touch of Marco Pierre White's culinary brilliance. This is haute cuisine stunningly presented in superlative Art Deco surroundings, restoring this distinguished society venue to central stage. An elegant bar gives way to one of the most beautiful dining rooms in London with trompe l'œil paintings, tasselled lights, opulent flower arrangements and no inferior tables, which together with scrupulously attentive service makes for extremely pleasurable special occasion dining. The menu offers expertly refined classics, stunningly presented. Starters showcase peerless rich, buttery omelette 'Arnold Bennett' with flaky haddock, or sensationally smooth foie gras terrine with gelée de Sauternes and brioche. Mains include a delicate sea bream with citrus fruits, olive oil, coriander, melt-in-the-mouth liver and bacon with definitive mash, and a divine eponymous pork dish with mirabelles and apple sauce. Desserts are equally memorable, especially a delightful hot caramel soufflé, and top-ranking lemon tart. The set lunch is presently an absolute steal. At dinner the temptation of some stratospheric bottles from an extraordinary list can make for an extravagant evening. Set 2-course lunch £14.95, 3 courses £17.95.

Miyama

JAPANESE   12/20
38 CLARGES ST, W1
020-7499 2443, FAX 020-7493 1573
Lunch Mon.-Fri., Dinner nigthly. ££
U: Green Park.

🅰 ☎

In interior decor, as elsewhere, forerunners are destined to be overtaken. Miyama's smart white décor with Italian tri-dimensional pictures on the walls is now more restful than piquant. Elegant Japanese tableware here extends to individual saké cups chosen by the customer from a tray proffered by a waitress in national costume. The menu is conservative with set courses incorporating classic sashimi, sushi, tempura, teriyaki and sukiyaki (or shabu-shabu, the more health-conscious, poached version), at £38 to £42. Those who enjoy teppan dishes, griddled on a steel sheet, can enjoy them either at the single teppan downstairs, or have them brought to table in the main restaurant. 'Unusual but healthy minded' offerings in the 'one more step forward' menu include sea bass or salmon cooked in foil with asparagus and oyster mushrooms and kaisen salad of luxurious shellfish with a vinaigrette dressing instead of the slightly sweetened vinegar of traditional sunamono, although that is available too. Yakitori, a skewer of chicken grilled with onion, takes up to 15 minutes to prepare says the menu, and jus-

tifies the wait. To occupy the time, try some of the many intriguing small dishes, some alas, listed only on a short supplementary Japanese language menu. Set lunch from £12; set dinner from £34.

Nicole's

MODERN BRITISH   12/20
158 NEW BOND ST, W1
020-7499 8408, FAX 020-7409 0381
Lunch & Dinner Mon.-Fri. ££
U: Green Park.

🅰 ☎

Nicole Farhi's eponymous restaurant is located in the basement of her flagship Bond Street clothing store. The best time to come is lunchtime, when the smart ladies-who-lunch crowd descend the stairs to sample the delicious modern British-meets-Mediterranean cooking. Roasted vegetables vie with an interesting selection of salads, including fennel and feta; even the simple green salads are excellent. The menu, though mainly light in conception, also includes heartier items such as calf's liver and mashed potato. One of the most popular dishes remains the cornmeal pancakes with smoked salmon and crème fraîche. The desserts are tempting, in particular a meltingly sweet and delicious apple and blackberry crumble served with cream. But like the clothes and home accessories upstairs, nothing on the menu is cheap.

Noble Rot

CONTEMPORARY EUROPEAN 14/20   🍷
3-5 MILL ST, W1
020-7629 8877, FAX 020-7629 8878
Lunch Mon.-Fri., Dinner Mon.-Sat.
U: Bond St.

🅰 ☎

This, the second of Soren Jessen's restaurants (see 1 Lombard Street in *The City* for the first), is in a back street in Mayfair on a site which has not been blessed for restaurateurs. Happily, with the arrival of Noble Rot and chef Matthew Owsley-Brown (who's worked with Anton Mosimann, Rick Stein and Henry Harris at the Fifth Floor, see *Knightsbridge*), this is set to change. Once past the unprepossessing, bare entrance and the staircase down to the private-members club, you emerge into a long narrow room which curves into a smaller dining area, has windows down one side, crisp linen (which stretches to the trendy chair covers), and a stone floor. It's sophisticated without being overwhelming, which could also describe the cooking. A starter of terrine of foie gras, artichoke and green peppercorn comes with a quite delicious, rich noble rot jelly; pot roast quail with red cabbage, raisins and pine nuts with a sherry vinegar was suitably gutsy. Mains present a difficult choice: here is a menu offering relatively straightforward dishes, all of which sound appealing and are knock-outs when they appear. Try confit of duck with braised red cabbage and Spätzle (on the set lunch menu); perfectly rendered pan-fried scallops with creamed macaroni in a basil infusion, or tender breast of pheasant with a light truffle mash, caramelised chestnuts and rich game gravy. Save room for desserts, perhaps a chocolate marquise with chocolate sorbet and pistachio sauce, or a refreshing, tart orange soufflé glacé with rhubarb compote and orange sauce. Not only are these desserts extremely good, they also give an excuse for venturing into the sweet wine list which offers 26 by the glass, ranging from £4.50 to £33, and 29 by the bottle, from £12.50 to Château d'Yquem, 1986 at £385 (not available by the glass). The main wine list is good, service is delightful. Set 2-course lunch £15, 3 courses £20.

Nobu

JAPANESE/INTERNATIONAL 17/20 ⵖⵖⵖ
METROPOLITAN HOTEL, 19 OLD PARK LANE, W1
020-7447 4747, FAX 020-7447 4749
Lunch Mon.-Fri., Dinner nightly. £££
U: Hyde Park Corner.

🅰 📷 📷

The cooking at this restaurant is the big attraction—it's certainly not the bland hotel interior which resembles a business hotel in Kuwait, or the overly gushing service which seems just at little too Hollywood (and yes, a scene from Notting Hill was filmed here). Chef Mark Edwards follows a formula created by his globe-trotting Japanese American head chef Nobuyuki Matsuhisa ('Nobu'), and boy, Edwards does it well. Signature dishes include the black cod with miso; the 'new-style' sashimi, which—atypically—incorporates garnishes, dressings and marinades; and uniquely Nobu fusion dishes such as 'Anti-Cucho Peruvian Style Spicy Chicken Skewer', anit-cucho being the Peruvian equivalent of yakitori—marinated meat grilled on a stick. It's best, though to order the chef's choice (omakase, £60) which gives you a tour of the extraordinary Nobu

repertoire. Even if you know Japanese food, you'll never have had dishes like this before—except, perhaps, at one of the growing number of Nobu branches around the world. Set lunch £40; set dinner £60; set sushi lunch box £25.

The Oriental

CHINESE 13/20 ⵖ
THE DORCHESTER, 55 PARK LANE, W1
020-7629 8888
Lunch Mon.-Fri., Dinner Mon.-Sat. £££
U: Hyde Park Corner.

🅰 📷

The Oriental is a grand hotel restaurant with no expense spared to make it the finest Chinese dining room in London. The spacious restaurant has several dining areas, including private rooms beautifully decorated with chinoiserie. Service tends towards formal, with no detail overlooked. The dishes, in contrast, are surprisingly tame if you're used to ferreting around in the entrails and 'texture foods' that you will find in Chinatown restaurants around the world; the shock factor has been eradicated from this menu. Instead you get MSG-free dishes which are impeccably prepared and presented, such as a starter of boiled prawn and chicken dumplings with ginger and spring onion sauce (£9.50) or main courses such as sautéed lobster with asparagus and black pepper (a sobering £38 for the whole lobster). The dim sum set lunch seems a bargain in comparison, at only £25 per head. Delightful maybe, but a bowdlerised version of Chinese food. Set dim sum lunch £25; set meals £47-£90.

Rasa W1

INDIAN VEGETARIAN 13/20 ⵖ
6 DERING ST, W1, 020-7629 1346
Lunch Mon.-Sat., Dinner nightly. £
U: Bond St.

🅰 📷

This is the West End branch of chef/owner Das Sreedharan's original, less accessible Stoke Newington Rasa, so the décor is a bit more upmarket, done in Indian temple style with lots of gods and godesses adorning the walls and staircase. And then there's the trademark shocking pink. Looking in the window at the packed tables, you'd never believe this is a non-smoking, vegetarian restaurant—the sock-and-sandal brigade are scarcely in evidence—

with the clientele drawn from the film and music biz centre in nearby Soho. Das has published a well-received cookbook of his Keralan recipes and his chefs all get sent to his mom in Kerala for their final training, so the cooking makes even die-hard carnivores forget there is no meat on offer. Blissful flavours accompany some of the most unlikely sounding curries, like the spinach and beetroot thoran and the garlic curry. And don't miss the crunchy poppadom-alternatives accompanied by their own pickles and chutneys. The selection of wines lives up to the menu. Set lunch & dinner £22.50.

Saga

JAPANESE/SUSHI **14/20**

43 SOUTH MOLTON ST, W1
020-7408 2236, FAX 020-7629 7507
Lunch & Dinner Mon.-Sat. ££
U: Bond St.

A ☎

One of London's oldest Japanese restaurants has been reborn under new owners, manager Mr. Leroy and chef Mr. Funakoshi. Off-white walls and brown woodwork preserve the ambience of a rustic inn but it is now brighter with larger tables and fewer partitions. Private rooms, not tatami, seat five to twelve at tables with comfortable chairs instead of backrests. There are set dinners from £26 to £42 and lunches from £8.50 to £25. In the long à la carte, side dishes and starters are rather confusingly listed under various headings. The frequently changed 'recommendations' might include marinated herring in rice vinegar, oil and seaweed, its flavour resembling mildly salted Scandinavian herring; or full-flavoured, grilled fillet of beef with miso paste, garnished with marinated onion and carrot. But finesse is the keynote of Funakoshi's kitchen, as seen in the wappa dishes (seasoned rice with various toppings steamed and served in cedar bowls), or in ultra-delicate chawan mushi, savoury custard. An unusual soup is asari jiru (soya with clams). The long menu of the ground-floor sushi bar is also available downstairs. Abalone, boiled and marinated, is one of the specialities. Drink a special saké, perhaps the superlative warm 'very clear' Masumi with its exquisite flowery-fruity aroma and matching flavour. Set lunch from £8.50; set dinner from £26.

The Square

CONTEMPORARY EUROPEAN **18/20**
6-10 BRUTON ST, W1
020-7495 7100, FAX 020-7495 7150
Lunch Mon.-Fri., Dinner nightly. £££
U: Bond St/Green Park.

A ☎

The Square is the epitome of a sophisticated, grown-up London restaurant: the cooking is an excellent example of all that is good in the English/French genre, the service totally professional and absolutely accurate, the napiery, cutlery and crockery first-class. The walls of the elegant, appropriately square, room are decorated with a collection of magnificent contemporary abstracts, and the clientele are less trophy hunters (The Square has a number of accolades and awards to its name), than a well-heeled, well-dressed businessy crowd. It seems pernickety to make criticism of such an elegant and professional establishment, and in fact there's absolutely nothing to complain about. As you would expect, there are plenty of luxury ingredients like foie gras and caviar—mash potatoes will probably come garnished with a slice of truffle, pasta served with scallops and langoustine—it's just that its smooth professionalism means that though a meal at The Square will give you everything to write home about, that 'Wow' rush of excitement that you might hope for can be missing, especially given the top-dollar prices. Happily, The Square is open on weekends, when the business crowd melts away and a jollier clientele takes over, giving the restaurant a lighter, buzzier atmosphere. If you have to visit without benefit of your expense account, this is the time to go. Set 2-course lunch £20, 3 courses £25; set 3-course dinner £45.

Tamarind

INDIAN **13/20**

20 QUEEN ST, W1
020-7629 3561, FAX 020-7499 5034
Lunch Sun.-Fri., Dinner nightly. £££
U: Green Park.

A ☎

This sophisticated restaurant has a flair suited to its Mayfair location. Tables are large and well-spaced; seating is comfortable, and elegant tableware includes fine copper showplates. The main decorative colours are the silks in the display windows. Service is smooth. Cooking is classical Indian without resort to disorientated 'fusion'. Everything comes on, or in, its own dish or bowl, and you choose the rice, or bread. The spicing is subtle and even dishes marked in the menu with a flame symbol are not too hot, although an enticing chilli bite may lurk under the clear flavours of main ingredients, polished by spices and herbs. Vegetarians have ample choice, perhaps starting with hara kebab—crisp cakes of chickpeas, lentils, spinach and potatoes. A tandoori sheekh kebab gilafi clearly demonstrates the sureness of the spicing. Fish plays a comparatively minor role, but fresh tasting jingha Khyber prawns come in a ginger, yoghurt, sunflower and sesame seed sauce, which does not overwhelm them. Rogan josh, the classic rich lamb curry, is happily complemented by plain rice, or bread, especially roomali roti—thin as a chappati and with the lightness of naan. Wines are mainly French with decent house wines from £14.50. Set 2-course lunch £10, 3 courses £14.95; set 3-course pre-theatre dinner (6pm-7pm) £22.50; set 3-course dinners £28.50, £34.50, £40.

Teca

ITALIAN   12/20
54 BROOKS MEWS, W1
020-7495 4774, FAX 020-7491 3545
Restaurant: Lunch & Dinner Mon.-Sat.; Bar:
Mon.-Sat. noon-midnight. £££
U: Bond St.

Tucked in a mews at the back of Bond Street, this bright, airy corner site could do with a better view than the row of motorbikes parked outside. The room, however, is comfortable, minimal and tastefully done out in bright colours and pale wood with a vast expanse of large windows allowing plenty of daylight in. The menu is refreshingly short, playing three or four risotto and pasta melodies, and splitting main courses equally into fish and meat. Extras are announced as menus are handed out, and at our dinner, included a deliciously rich dish of pasta dressed with skate and capers. The skate also turns up in ravioli, with artichoke, the pasta dressed in a sea-fresh butter sauce. Other starters might be salmon with spring onion and wilted lettuce or a salad of grilled summer vegetables. Mains might be a saddle of rabbit wrapped in Parma ham and roasted to a moist, delicate finish or sea bass, roasted so the skin was cracklingly crispy and served with a chickpea purée of real mealiness. Desserts play in a

successful duet mode: chocolate mousse with cherry compote, chocolate-stuffed dates with mint sauce. The wine list is impeccable and all-Italian, the white coming direct from the glass-fronted teca, or cave at the back of the room, which also stocks a first-rate supply of cigars. Service is charming and efficient. Set 2-course lunch £16, 3 courses £19; set 2-course dinner £19, 3 courses £23.50.

Windows

FRENCH   15/20
LONDON HILTON ON PARK LANE
22 PARK LANE, W1
020-7208 4021, FAX 020-7208 4142
Lunch Sun-Fri., Dinner Mon.-Sat. £££
U: Hyde Park Corner.

Year after year, Windows, perched atop the recently refurbished London Hilton, confirms its status as one of the restaurants in town to value. An evening there is a complete experience. Behind the huge windows, indeed a whole glass wall, London displays her gems, especially at night. What an entrancing cocktail for the senses with all those shimmering lights showcasing the jewels of Buckingham Palace against the dark shade of Green and Hyde Parks. Angelo, surely the most charming maître d' in town, and his well-disciplined young team know how to retain the seductive magic in this elegant room. Trust him to guide you expertly through the many choices offered by Jacques Rolancy. Jacques won the much envied title of Meilleur Ouvrier de France, and he only gets better as time goes on. Watching him for several years now, we've seen him reach a new level of serenity and confidence as a master of his art. His craftsmanship shows from the start in a dish of pan-fried langoustines, cooked to the right degree of firmness and delightfully complemented by herbs, while scallops melt in the mouth. In the appealing Menu Dégustation, the venison and foie gras marbled with wild mushroom salad and accompanied by a beetroot vinaigrette is a delicacy to remember. For the calorie-conscious, he has a few options, like pan-fried fillet of brill with a salad of confit of fennel, and a sauce flavoured with Jerusalem artichokes—a dish which offers flavour and rejects the sin. Because it is so lightly roasted, a wild duck in lavender sauce with salsify, artichokes and Paris mushrooms leaves you feeling only partially guilty. To make the evening perfect, you find—at a price—a marvel of a wine list, but a few reasonable choices are also available. Set 5-course dinner £44.

Zen Central

CHINESE   13/20

20 QUEEN ST, W1
020-7629 8089/8103, FAX 020-7493 6181
Lunch & Dinner daily. £££
U: Green Park.

When this restaurant opened in the 1980s the décor was ahead of its time with black furniture, and lots of glass and steel, while along one wall was a long waterfall, now long dried up. Currently opinions are divided, but those who feel that it is time for change will welcome the refurbishment promised for 2000. Unlikely to change is the well-executed, modern, deluxe Hong Kong cooking style. That calls for such delicacies as supreme shark's fin; whole abalone; whole suckling pig; lobster in three conventional styles or, less conventionally, with South Sea curry sauce. Other postmodern twists appear in duck fillets with orange Cointreau sauce; prawn fillets in red curry sauce, and crisp seaweed with pine kernels. On the other hand the menu now offers some more basic, homely dishes, particularly various clay hot-pots such as braised mixed seafood; crab meat and rice vermicelli, and chicken fillets with shallots and spring onions. Vegetables are carefully prepared, especially the zingy spinach sautéed with chilli and preserved beancurd sauce. Among conventional desserts, the ginger sorbet shines out. The sumptuous wine list ascends the heights of French classics but house wines, also French, are fairly priced at £16. Set 2-course lunch £15, 3 courses £30; set dinner £25-£38.

Zen Garden

CHINESE   14/20

15 BERKELEY ST, W1, 020-7493 1381
Lunch & Dinner daily. £££
U: Green Park.

Here is Hong Kong luxury in London. Impressive kitsch, deluxe décor in the windowless room includes fine Chinese fabrics and porcelain. Suave skillful service is surprisingly sympathetic. The long menu offers classics of Chinese haute cuisine including whole suckling pig, birds' nest soup with coconut or almond flavours, and superior tiger shark's fin in crown style with two kinds of gravy—at £130 for two. Lobster, sea bass, turbot and Dover sole variously prepared are charged by the pound—or possibly the kilo nowadays. There are a few 'modern eclectic' dishes such as nori scrolls Japanese seaweed rolls, and coffee spareribs. Set menus from £29.50 to £138 per person suggest unlimited luxury, but Chinese earthiness can be found too, in mixed vegetable and roasted duck in a clay pot, and perhaps in 'flaming drunk pork'. Less expensive are lunchtime dim sum, ordered by ticking choices on a paper menu. Among mainly familiar items, the unpromisingly named pan-fried Chinese turnip cake is enjoyed by almost everybody; 'mixed cannelloni' are what Chinatown calls cheung fan noodle rolls. A wide range of carefully prepared vegetables pleases vegetarians. Set lunch £15.50, set dim sum £13.50; set dinner from £29.50.

NOTTING HILL GATE

Alastair Little Lancaster Gate

CONTEMPORARY EUROPEAN   14/20

136A LANCASTER RD, W11, 020-7243 2220
Lunch & Dinner Mon.-Sat. ££
U: Ladbroke Grove.

Modern British- and Italian-influenced food is something that Alastair Little has championed for the last dozen years and in this, his second eponymous restaurant, you can get a feel for what all the fuss is about. The menu, which changes with every service and is therefore genuinely market—and weather-led, is full of enticing dishes—artichoke soup, seafood bourride, pappardelle al salmis, pecorino and pear salad. Alastair's food is so much imitated that a menu like this may not seem unusual in modern-day London, but more thought tends to go into its preparation here on a daily basis. Occasionally you'll be served a clanger of a dish, but more usually it's very good. The downside is the staff with a laissez-faire Notting Hill attitude and the room—plain and bare with white walls and plate-glass frontage, which is fine when the restaurant is busy, but rather dull when there are only a few customers. Set 2-course dinner £23.50, 3 courses £27.50.

Assaggi at The Chepstow

ITALIAN 14/20

39 CHEPSTOW PLACE, W2, 020-7792 5501
Lunch & Dinner Mon.-Sat. £££
U: Notting Hill Gate.

The room, above a pub, has an elegant simplicity about it, the floor-to-ceiling windows looking out over a leafy Notting Hill residential street. Bare floorboards combine with walls adorned with square canvases of strong colours to give a slightly surreal feel. The food however, is anything but surreal—more honest, homely and robust. Ingredients are first rate, the prosciutto thin as lace and unadorned, to be enjoyed with excellent bread. Pasta is noteworthy, perhaps wrapped, Swiss-roll style, around cheese and vegetables or dressed simply with mushrooms or maybe bottaga (dried tuna or grey mullet roe). Main courses might be a veal chop, simply grilled and served with sage and butter, or red mullet, perfectly timed, with some wilted leaves and olive oil. Desserts are straightforward, and none the worse for that: ice cream, a tart and maybe some pannacotta. The wine list's loyalty is to Italy, with good and unusual effect. Service is charming, yet matter of fact.

Bali Sugar

INTERNATIONAL 14/20

33A ALL SAINTS RD, W11
020-7221 4477, FAX 020-7221 9995
Lunch & Dinner daily. ££
U: Westbourne Park.

The original Sugar Club is firmly established in Soho (see above), while its successor here, Bali Sugar, continues to feed the boho trendies of Notting Hill Gate in a sparse setting, with stripped floorboards and plain yellow walls. The honours come from Claudio Aprile who succeeded Peter Gordon. Other restaurants in London offer 'fusion' cooking with greater or lesser success; here you get the real thing. A starter of pan-fried quail with crispy noodles and green mango salad that sounds uncomplicated works as well at producing an outstanding combination of flavours as the warm mushroom nori roll with jicama salad and yuzu. Don't be afraid to ask the laid-back and friendly staff what the ingredients are (jicama is a tuber known as yam bean from southeast Asia and makes a particularly good

salad with its crisp, starchy flesh; yuzu is a Japanese citrus fruit). For mains a seared sea bass came with smoked trout mash, baked lemon dressing and a hot pepper tapenade; duck breast marinated in soy and ginger was perfectly matched with Chinese broccoli and a rich star anise-plum sauce. For desserts, try fruit poached in ginger. Flavours and combinations work powerfully together and many other chefs could learn some good lessons here in what is possible. The wine list is similarly wide ranging.

First Floor

INTERNATIONAL 12/20

186 PORTOBELLO RD, W11
020-7243 0072, FAX 020-7221 9440
Lunch & Dinner daily. ££
U: Notting Hill Gate.

This Notting Hill stalwart was here at the beginning, serving up Pacific Rim fusion fancies to a new breed of trend-setting pioneers when they began heading west at the start of the 1990s. Now that the funky gentrification of Portobello Road is almost complete (give or take the occasional kebab shop and dodgy pub), time has started to catch up and there's plenty of hot competition in the area. A new menu takes a meatier approach, with dishes such as pecan-crusted lamb rump, oven-roasted monkfish with celeriac mash and smoked salmon. Duck is a regular feature, too. The décor is very W11, all wrought-iron, treated wood and candles.

192

CONTEMPORARY EUROPEAN 12/20

192 KENSINGTON PARK RD, W11
020-7229 0482, FAX 020-7229 3300
Lunch & Dinner daily. ££
U: Notting Hill Gate.

Past the long bar with its embedded fibre optics playing light games, the restaurant opens out as a series of rooms, two at street level and the rather inferior one downstairs. Lots of glass means that even on sunny days the room is bright and airy, with large flower arrangements and a rather clever design which is both modern and classic. 192 is frequented by locals who treat it rather as their own club, into which you are welcomed on arrival with charm and efficiency. The menu changes twice a day and caters both for those in search of a three-course meal, and those who may only want one dish. Salads are popular, and usually come in a number of forms, seasonal as well as the likes of Caesar or Niçoise. Other starters might be a terrine, seared scallops or steamed mussels, either finished with a classic cream and wine sauce, or with something more Oriental. Main courses include lamb shanks with couscous, steak with béarnaise and spinach or roast sea bass with beurre blanc and celeriac purée. Desserts wander from classic English, as in bread and butter pudding or steamed ginger sponge, to more classic tarts, ices and sorbets. The wine list is extensive, with much to offer from around the world at reasonable prices and with a good collection by the glass. Set 2-course Mon.-Fri. lunch £11.50, Sun. lunch £12.50.

Pharmacy

CONTEMPORARY EUROPEAN 13/20
150 NOTTING HILL GATE, W11, 020-7221 2442
Lunch & Dinner daily. £££
U: Notting Hill Gate.

A ☎

This is the restaurant that Damien Hirst designed to look like a chemist's, so much so that the Royal Pharmaceutical Society tried to make it change its name. The downstairs bar is indeed as sterile as any medicine dispensary, with barstools resembling gigantic round white aspirins and slim glass cabinets on the walls piled high with packets of pills and plasters and boxes of balms and bandages. The food, however, is thrather cosier: baked beans on toast with bacon and Welsh rarebit is typical. Upstairs, via a concreted fire escape, is the restaurant which is plusher and more luxurious than one might expect. Here you'll come face to face with Damien Hirst's famous DNA mobile and attractive butterfly paintings on the walls. The menu is ambitious, and most dishes succeed, as in an unctuously rich beef stew, a fish carpaccio with nobu dressing, and roast lobster en cocotte. You'll be surrounded by fashion victims and a few famous names. Set 2-course lunch £15.50, 3 courses £17.50

Please excuse us...(and the chefs).
Menus are subject to the winds of change, so the dishes we've described may no longer be available when you visit.

PICCADILLY CIRCUS/REGENT STREET

Atlantic Bar & Grill

INTERNATIONAL 12/20
20 GLASSHOUSE ST, W1, 020-7734 4888
Lunch Mon.-Fri., Dinner nightly. ££
U: Piccadilly Circus.

A ☎

When Atlantic Bar and Grill first opened, London's fashionable crowd flocked through its doors. There was a bouncer only allowing the best-dressed, most beautiful people in. It was, in short, the sine qua non of the London restaurant scene. The fact that it is still open, still doing good business and still considered a desirable place to drink or dine in is testament to its (then) youthful proprietor Oliver Peyton. Most people visit Altantic for the bar, where you will see pretty teenage girls flirting with famous footballers, but the restaurant itself should not be forgotten. The cooking has been simplified since the early days, leaving the menu with a classic bias, but with plenty of buzzwords. Try salmon tuna and crabcake with honey-roast tomatoes and langoustine sauce or confit of Gressingham duck with Suffolk Blackshin rasher. Décor is 20s liner style (hence the name), and it's not to be confused with its arch emeny, the Titanic, which is to be found upstairs. Set 3-course lunch £14.50.

Criterion
Marco Pierre White

FRENCH 13/20
PICCADILLY CIRCUS, W1
020-7930 0488, FAX 020-7930 8380
Lunch Mon.-Sat., Dinner nightly. ££
U: Piccadilly Circus.

A ☎

This restaurant is perhaps the most attractive in London—high ceilings and Byzantine-looking gold mosaics have been a feature here for many years, and, through a sympathetic interior design, have been enhanced rather than exploited by the present incumbents. The place is immediately soothing. Marco Pierre White's restaurant group expertly runs both the kitchen and front of house. Perhaps because it is still referred to as a brasserie, the MPW group has deliberately kept the prices to an affordable level, and the cuisine is classic Anglo-French. Though Marco Pierre White has his finger in many restaurant pies, both good and bad, this is the most accessible of the former breed. There's always something on the menu that'll tickle the taste buds, and you'll generally find an unusual dish or two. There's a well-priced set menu at lunch and, if you're careful with the extravagant wine list, you'll come out with a genuine bargain. The only real complaint is of snooty reception staff and of waiters who work too hard at up-selling. Set 2-course lunch & Mon.-Sat. to 6.30pm £14.95, 3 courses £17.95.

Momo

NORTH AFRICAN   12/20
25 HEDDON ST, W1
020-7434 4040, FAX 020-7287 0404
Lunch & Dinner daily. ££
U: Piccadilly Circus.

A ☎

There are other places to eat couscous as good as you'll get here—and much more reasonably priced. But nowhere else in London captures as convincingly as Momo the heady, mesmerising allure of North Africa and takes Maghreb cooking to such lengths. The music sets the tone, the restaurant looks the part—not themed, but as if it has been airlifted from Marrakesh—with low seats and banquettes that are a challenge for the longer-legged. A new chef seems to have introduced more ambition to the menu which, though redolent with the expected flavours of cinnamon, figs, almonds, chickpeas and dried fruits, displays some original, if inauthentic, ideas. Examples might be deep-fried labna (ewe's milk cheese) with a coating of spices and seeds on a bed of rocket, beetroot and sultanas, or sea bream with curried French toast, shallots and fennel salad. The classic couscous Momo, the fluffy grains served separately, with a plate of tender lamb, merguez sausage and brochette, and another bowl of broth to lubricate, is the business (as it should be for £15). Diverse tagines, such as duck with quince and apple, are piping hot when the funnelled lid of the clay pot is removed revealing a melting medley of meat and sweetly spiced juices. The clientele is painfully fashionable, and telephone booking can take perseverence. Set 2-course lunch £12.50, 3 courses £18.

The Oak Room

FRENCH   17/20 ♟♟♟
LE MERIDIEN, 21 PICCADILLY, W1
020-7437 0202, FAX 020-7437 3574
Lunch Mon.-Fri., Dinner Mon.-Sat. ££££
U: Piccadilly Circus.

A ☎ ▮

Marco Pierre White has hung up his toque to become a full-time restaurateur and left the Oak Room to the charge of his former head chef, Robert Reid, who was without doubt already in charge on the occasions when the master was absent, setting up the Mirabelle, Titanic, and more. So it had to be bad luck that on the night we went, the cooking was not as consistently polished as on previous occasions, for Robert Reid is a very accomplished and experienced chef. The menu has changed little, and all those familiar dishes still appear, as they do in various of his other places—like terrine of foie gras with Sauternes gelée. But back to the Oak Room, a splendid if slightly overpowering restaurant with its high ceiling, Edwardian grandeur, lime-oaked wood panels and huge glass chandeliers, now somewhat relieved by oil paintings chosen by Marco Pierre White. The maître d' is superb, a charming Frenchman whose concerned but not too serious approach lightens what might otherwise seem an oppressive temple of gastronomy. A 'soup' of shellfish as an amuse-gueule with diced vegetables was a little too buttery and rich. The millefeuille of crab and tomato, however, was a real treat, creamy without being cloying, but the terrine of leeks came with large chunks of truffle on top, which did nothing for what was otherwise a remarkable terrine. Lobster was served with a garlic-heavy sauce, although the lobster was perfectly cooked, even if the sauce was biting. However, fillet of lamb was not so well done. A dessert of caramelised pineapple with vanilla and spice is another well-known Oak Room favourite, but was overdone. Perhaps stick to the lemon tart classic. The cheese board is good and offers a wide range. The wine list is impressive, as you would expect, and also astronomical in price. A meal here is an expensive occasion, and at these prices, the cooking should be thoroughly consistent. Set 3-course lunch £30; set dinners £55, £80, £90.

L'Odéon

FRENCH   12/20
65 REGENT ST, W1, 020-7287 1400
Lunch & Dinner Mon.-Sat. £££
U: Piccadilly Circus

A **☎**

This large, bustling restaurant looking out over Regent Street is cleverly laid out—the long room with windows running down the whole of the front is divided by screens so you don't feel lost. And for such a space, the noise level is refreshingly muted. The menu is a mix of styles, French-based with modish ingredients, perhaps a gazpacho with dressed crab, or grilled vegetable terrine with a tomato salsa to start, followed by confit of salmon with warm potato salad and aïoli, or pork knuckle with nutty Puy lentils and beetroot marmalade to follow. With vegetables as extras, prices can mount, which makes the set menus good value for the type of competent cooking that prevails here. The wine list can also mount sharply, but the service is good and the whole package delivers an elegant experience that keeps the sophisticated regulars coming back for more. Set 2-course lunch & dinner £15.50, 3 courses £19.50

Ozer

MODERN TURKISH   14/20   ♟
5 LANGHAM PL, W1, 020-7323 0505
Lunch Mon.-Fri., Dinner Mon.-Sat. £££
U: Oxford Circus.

A **☎**

Modern Ottaman sounds ingenuous. The strategy being to bring a Vong-style fusion of Turkish and French cuisine to Marylebone, and, if this sounds a touch contrived, be on guard. Certainly the initial impact is stunning. Entry is through bronze grills and a studded heavy timber door, and the walls decorated in ruby-polished plaster curve sensuously past a haremesque bar of louche, yet uncomfortable, pouffes to a well-spaced limestone dining area with unusual copper tube and glass lantern lighting, said to be inspired by something similiar in Istanbul's Blue Mosque. The French chef, Jerome Tauvron, has impeccable acclaimed credentials. First impressions are good. Chilli-flavoured oil plus well-spiced hummus in which to dip onion, walnut and raisin bread is proffered. The menu, which promises a more exciting taste sensation than it mostly delivers and is dwarfed by the sump-

tuous setting and outlandish prices for basically simple fare, is very compact and practically limited to fish, lamb and vegetables. Coriander langoustine with pomegranate looked a treat, but would've been tastier without the tempura batter which wasn't mentioned on the menu. Vegetables with delectable smoky aubergine were sensational. A meagre main of grilled red mullet fillets was competently cooked but came with a suspiciously similar aubergine accompaniment. Brill with saffron potatoes was frankly insipid and uninspired. Lamb enticingly partnered with spiced bread and lentils looked to be a better choice. A dessert of distinctly un-Turkish pain perdu with pepper ice cream was unmistakenly delicious. The decent wine list even offers one Turkish choice. Service is irritatingly oversolicitious and possibly aware of the present victory of style over content. Set 2-course lunch £14.95, 3 courses £17.95.

The Red Room

MODERN BRITISH   13/20   ♟
WATERSTONE'S, LOWER GROUND FLOOR
203-206 PICCADILLY, W1
020-7851 2464, FAX 020-7851 2469
Lunch Mon.-Fri., Dinner Mon.-Sat., Brunch Sat.-Sun. ££
U: Piccadilly Circus.

A **☎**

A serious restaurant in a book shop may sound rather bizarre, but Waterstone's new flagship bookstore on Piccadilly rather warrants it, spread as it is over the whole of what used to be the rather grand clothes shop, Simpson's. There are various refreshment spots throughout the building where you can feed the stomach as well as the brain cells but arguably the Red Room is the only one worth making an effort to visit. It's a proper restaurant with white-linen tablecloths and napkins and a predictably red colour scheme, where a civilised bookish clientele congregate to eat hearty, mostly British cooking—smoked salmon with soda bread, pan-fried veal liver with roast root vegetables. Bad accoustics allow you to hear other diner's conversations, and they to hear yours, so talk about something innocuous or just enjoy reading your recent purchases. Set lunch & dinner 2 courses £15.50, 3 courses £18.50.

Sartoria

ITALIAN   14/20   ⌐

20 SAVILE ROW, W1
020-7534 7000, FAX 020-7534 7070
Lunch & Dinner daily. ££££
U: Piccadilly Circus.

A ☎

The room is elegant and long, a row of windows running down all of one side. Tables are well-spaced, chairs comfortable, glassware and cutlery of the right order. The mood and atmosphere is decidedly luxurious, playing somewhat overtly on the name, to the point where your bill arrives on a pincushion. Theme aside however, the largely Italian menu manages to please, with dishes like antipasti, risotto and pasta kicking things off. Crab comes infused with lemon and herbs, veal sweetbreads and artichokes wrapped in a light, crispy batter, and artichokes with boiled lemon and almonds. If the latter sounds intriguing, it is, as it is delicious and straight from the River Café, where chef Darren Simpson trained. The influence is marked and continues in main courses like roast pork with a salsa of chopped, roasted red peppers and tomatoes, or osso buco as classic and straightforward as it should be. Desserts swing from austere but delicious tarts to full-blown rich chocolate Nemesis. The wine list sports super Tuscans by the bucketful and will relieve you of your money in the same receptacle if you are not careful. Service is efficient if a little austere. Set 2-course lunch £15.

Titanic

INTERNATIONAL   12/20

8 BREWER ST, W1, 020-7437 1912
Dinner Mon.-Sat. ££
U: Piccadilly Circus.

A ☎

The Titanic opened to such celebrity fanfare, and such emphasis was given to its fabulous bar, that the cooking was inevitably accorded third-class passenger status in spite of being captained by the great Marco Pierre White. But many have reported back that the cooking is consistently very good, and indeed it is. The menu reads like a collation of the most popular items from the top-twenty London restaurants from the last three decades. It offers fourteen starters, fifteen main courses dishes that encompass a vast array of styles and cuisines, including Spanish, French, and

Moroccan, whilst the last words of the captain of the Titanic are ironically quoted at the bottom of the menu: 'Be British'. There is obvious glee at the inclusion of updated versions of prawn cocktail, macaroni and cheese and Black Forest gâteau. Marco Pierre White's joke even extends to the infamous burger, with a steak haché à la McDonalds—and it's about as good as a burger gets. The bar, which dominates the room, is hugely popular in the evenings, so beware. The wine list is extensive, reasonably priced and well-chosen.

Veeraswamy

INDIAN   12/20

VICTORY HOUSE, 101 REGENT ST, W1
020-7734 1401
Lunch & Dinner daily. ££
U: Piccadilly Circus.

A ☎

The vivid contemporary transformation of London's oldest Indian restaurant has been an unqualified success, injecting new life into this prime Regent Street location. The interior dazzles with jewel-like colours, gorgeous fabrics and covetable decorative artifacts and sets off the inventively spiced, regional Indian food admirably presented in modern style. Among starters, delicately flavoured stir-fried oysters with sweet kerala spices and pani puri with a sympathetic tamarind scent show no corners have been cut in preparation. A sophisticated dish of Hyderabad lamb curry with caramelised onions and plums is sensational, and Malabar prawn curry with mango and tumeric is also full of subtle appeal. Caramelised carrot tart is an excellent new take on the Tatin concept; otherwise go for refreshing sorbets and ices. An extremely well-researched wine list finely complements the complexity of flavours on the menu. Service is slick, stylish and multicultural. Set lunch Mon.-Sat. 2 courses £11, 3 courses £14, Sun. 3-course lunch £13.95.

PIMLICO

Pomegranates

INTERNATIONAL   **12/20**
94 GROSVENOR RD, SW1, 020-7828 6560
Lunch Mon.-Fri., Dinner Mon.-Sat. ££
U: Pimlico.

A ☎

For a sneak preview of Parliamentary scandals of 2010, look around you at Pomegranates, in the basement below Dolphin Square, but don't expect startling disclosures from host Patrick Gwynn-Jones who is as discreet as he is buoyant. But he willingly discourses about his food and wines and is rightly proud of the restaurant, most of its staff, its style and almost every dish that has stood the test of time. The origins of those dishes include Spain, Mauritius, Sweden, Denmark, Southeast Asia, Turkey, Sudan and—oh, yes, France and England—and that's only in the starters. Add crispy breast of lamb from China, curried goat with plantain from the West Indies, Welsh salt duck, and, from Scotland, a carnivorean rampage of Aberdeen beef, including three versions of steak tartare. The à la carte menu makes it possible to enjoy a starter followed by fish for £21.50; meat will make it £2-£3 more, very reasonable for such a comfortable sophisticated place. These prices include crudités with aioli, bread, and all vegetables. Three British cheeses are listed together with treacle tart, homemade honey and Cognac ice cream, and the 'bottomless' coffeepot with chocolates. Set 2-course lunch & dinner £11.95, 3 courses £14.95.

Rhodes in the Square

MODERN BRITISH   **14/20**   ♕
DOLPHIN SQUARE, CHICHESTER ST., SW1
020-7798 6767, FAX 020-7798 5685
Lunch Tues.-Fri., Dinner Tues.-Sat. £££
U: Pimlico.

A ☎

Modern British Gary Rhodes-style goes Art Deco at this discreet restaurant within a smart Pimlico apartment complex. It has well-spaced tables and is much frequented by MPs. The sleek navy, chrome and mirrored décor and windowless interior makes one feel aboard an ocean liner, as does the cossetting, well-informed, if sometimes gauche (forget the Gary Rhodes mannerisms please), service. Meticulously executed signature dishes include

a hugely flavoursome faggot of spiced pigeon and stunning lobster thermidor omelette to start. Good fish choices include herb-crusted cod with velvet mash, whilst calf's liver comes with an impactful blue cheese and bacon gnocchi. Puddings are exemplary: chocolate brioche with banoffi ice cream and the jaffa cake ensemble are memorable; the British cheese selection is good. An appealing wine list includes an adventurous choice by the glass. Set lunch Mon.-Fri. 2 courses £16.50, 3 courses £19.50; set 3-course Sun. lunch £19.50; set 3-course dinner £28.50.

PRIMROSE HILL

Odette's

INTERNATIONAL   **14/20**   ♕
130 REGENT'S PARK RD, NW1
020-7586 5486, FAX 020-7586 2575
Lunch Mon-Fri, Dinner Mon.-Sat. ££
U: Chalk Farm.

A ☎ 📺 🏃

Londoners who believe the far north begins at Regent's Park are pleasantly surprised by this bastion of civilisation just beyond that frontier. Odette's satisfies all criteria. Ambience and décor are soothing even with enough mirrors for a (minor) hall of Versailles; and service is suave, discreet and efficient. The unpretentious menu succinctly describes dishes in English. Where it strays into a foreign tongue as in potatoes 'Pont-Neuf', it adds 'fried in duck fat'. Four vegetarian options among a dozen starters include varying soup, and a main dish of gnocchi, black trumpet mushrooms, girolles and Cabernet Sauvignon dressing might divert even committed carnivores. Or they could choose a first course of warm rabbit salad with pancetta, kidney and liver; crab, salmon and chive sushi with tuna sashimi, or risotto of roasted pumpkin, langoustine and scallops. Main dishes are as simply classic as fillet of halibut, grilled, with stir-fried greens; or roasted free-range chicken, Puy lentils and Savoy cabbage on a potato galette; or more exotic as in Gressingham duck with caramelised endive, Szechuan pepper and fondant potatoes. Desserts are equally impressive; and a long, clearly arranged, well-chosen wine list incorporates a wide range by the glass for butterfly-drinkers. Set 3-course lunch Mon.-Fri. £10.

PUTNEY

Del Buongustaio

ITALIAN   12/20
283 PUTNEY BRIDGE RD, SW15, 020-8780 9361
Lunch Sun-Fri, Dinner nightly. ££
U: Putney Bridge.

A satisfying local osteria, Del Buongustaio meanders throughout Italy for its inspiration, with some of the dishes genuinely researched from the Renaissance. The cooking is good, with interesting pastas appearing, such as sheets enclosing a light, creamy spinach, rocket and cheese mixture served with a tomato and basil sauce. Main courses run the gamut from lamb to veal, sea bass to calf's liver cooked clasically with butter, sage and Marsala. Desserts might include a pannacotta with pine nuts and red berries, and ice creams which accompany treats like chocolate torte are equally satisfying. Eleven dessert wines by the glass exemplify the careful and authentic approach of the restaurant. And it all appears in a pleasant, light dining room where the staff is anxious to please. Set 2-course lunch £9.75; set 3-course dinner £12.75, 5 courses £26.95.

Putney Bridge

CONTEMPORARY EUROPEAN 14/20
EMBANKMENT, SW15
020-8780 1811, FAX 020-8780 1211
Lunch Tues.-Sun., Dinner Tues.-Sat. £££
U: Putney Bridge.

Location counts for a lot with restaurants, and they don't come any more 'riverside' than this: the award-winning modernist architecture of Putney Bridge looks out over the Thames and the solid span of its namesake. The spacious ground floor is agreeably smart, with doormen, coat-takers, a decent cocktail list and terrace seating in the summer; while the first floor has the best views and a French restaurant. Anthony Demetre's dishes are in the contemporary European mould, but often use hautey flourishes and luxury ingredients: for example, fillet of zander is served with young vegetables, but the sauce is infused with juniper berries. Starters might include duck confit and foie gras with a creamed walnut dressing; while puddings might include a quince tarte with lemon-thyme ice cream. Set 3-course lunch £19.50; set 3-course a la carte dinner £35, 5-course Menu Gourmande £50.

RICHMOND

Ma Goa

INDIAN   14/20
244 UPPER RICHMOND RD, SW15
020-8780 1767, FAX 020-8246 6878
Lunch & Dinner Tues.-Sun. £
U: East Putney.

'Nothing beats mother's cooking'—proved again in this family restaurant where Dee Kapur shares the kitchen with his parents, while also looking after front-of-house with his wife Ela. In two simple, pleasant rooms with sepia photographs on the walls, they offer flavours and textures to tease and tempt the palate. This captivating diversity comes in a menu which is virtually pure Goanese. Starters include sorpotel—pork, lamb's liver and kidney in a minimal sauce; and stuffed papard—lentil flour parcels filled with herby-spicy potatoes. Ma's fish caldin amazingly makes swordfish a gastronomic delight, and the Portuguese heritage appears in vindaloo, subtly combining the taste of pork with palm vinegar, red chilli garlic and roasted spices. The short menu is supplemented by a main dish, vegetable and dessert of the day, and at our last visit these 'blackboard specials' were the high points of a memorable meal. The vegetable was spinach and potato, transmuted from 'sag aloo' by the addition of fenugreek. Equally notable was mango rice pudding transcending hope and expectation of those three words, singly or together. The short wine list is cleverly chosen and indigenous drinks include feni liqueur based on cashews. Set 2-course dinner Mon.-Thurs. 7-8pm £8.95.

Redmond's

CONTEMPORARY EUROPEAN 14/20
170 UPPER RICHMOND RD WEST, SW14
020-8878 1922, FAX 020-8878 1133
Lunch Mon.-Fri. & Sun., Dinner Mon.-Sat. ££

An exemplary neighbourhood restaurant whose eclectic, contemporary style is more than a match for many fashionable West End openings. Chef proprietor Redmond Haywood is justly renowned for his fish soup brimming with vibrantly fresh fish and crustaceans with just the right hint of lemon grass and Thai spicing. Roast pigeon with foie gras, balsamic and butternut squash is flavoursome, as is a well-conceived lighter dish of chicken breast with parsley oil and olive oil mash. The small kitchen and tiny staff overseen by Pippa Heywood can lead to longish waits between courses on busy nights, but an extremely well-researched wine list makes amends for most hiccups in service. Outstanding puddings include exemplary tarte Tatin. The cheery blue and yellow décor is enhanced with a changing gallery of often excellent paintings for sale. Set 2-course lunch £16.50, 3 courses £21; set 2-course dinner £22, 3 courses £26.50.

ST. JAMES'S

Al Duca

ITALIAN   13/20

4/5 DUKE OF YORK ST, SW1
020-7839 3090, FAX 020-7839 4050
Lunch & Dinner Mon.-Sat.
U: Green Park.

The changeover from the antediluvian Colombina restaurant to the smart, affordable and authentically contemporary Al Duca in St. James's sums up everything that is good in London. Al Duca is the brainchild of Claudio Pulze, who was instrumental in setting up Zafferano with Giorgio Locatelli (see *Belgravia*), Spiga and La Spighetta (see *Quick Bites*). He is one of those knowledgeable restaurateurs who has brought a style of Italian cooking to London that his native country-men recognise and applaud as the real thing. Al Duca's décor is relatively plain—a smallish room decorated with mirrors, filled wine racks on the walls, pale wood and pink floor tiles. The cooking and presentation are also relative-ly plain—in the very best sense of the word. Here, sensation and ostentation has been rejected in favour of well-sourced ingredients and impeccable cooking. And with the four-course menus so attractively priced, you can do the meal properly Italian-style. Start with a simple but excellent salad, perhaps bresaolo with rocket and goat cheese, then move on to a pasta, such as a perfectly proportioned penne with veal ragoût and wild mushrooms. For mains, a duck leg confit came with perfectly cooked, al dente lentils and attractive mixed leaves; chargrilled pork medallions were of the right smokiness and came with a piquant rata-touille. A sharp lemon tart was accompanied by fresh raspberries. The wine list is short and

to the point, completely Italian, and, like the rest of the meal, both affordable and carefully chosen. In a city where prices are creeping up, Al Duca is a very welcome newcomer. Set 2-course lunch £14.50, 3 courses £17.50, 4 courses £20; set 2-course dinner £16, 3 cours-es £19, 4 courses £22.

Avenue

INTERNATIONAL   13/20

7-9 ST. JAMES'S ST, SW1
020-7321 2111, FAX 020-7321 2500
Lunch & Dinner daily. £££
U: Green Park.

The room is vast and white, a bank of large screens showing hip television clips adorns one wall as you enter, the bar stretching down towards the back of the room on the other. Were it not for the skylight running down one side, the room might be oppressive, but its starkness lends an airy, summery feel. Suits dominate, but the mood is relaxed and infor-mal, the service efficient and polite. Menu descriptions are sparse; the style concentrates on light Mediterranean-inspired ingredients for its general direction. A pasta or risotto to start perhaps, or an excellent Gorgonzola tart, meltingly smooth with good crunchy pastry. Main courses lean more toward the cooking of France with a twist on the English nursery theme thrown in: coq au vin perhaps, or a daube of beef alongside the best fishcakes served with delicious buttered vegetables. Additional fish gets simple treatment, seared and served with a salsa in the case of tuna, or roasted in the case of sea bass. Desserts lend a classical note: well-made tarts, good ice creams and excellent crème brûlée. The wine list casts a wide net, although anyone open to tempta-tion should beware, it is easy to trade up. Set 2-course Mon.-Sat. lunch £17.50, 3 courses £19.50; set dinner 5.45pm-7.30pm & 10.15pm-closing 2 courses £14.50, 3 courses £16.50.

Che

INTERNATIONAL   12/20

23 ST. JAMES'S ST, SW1, 020-7747 9380
Lunch Mon.-Fri., Dinner nightly, Brunch Sat. ££
U: Green Park.

Natty restaurant, bar and cigar room housed in the old Economist building, a suitably groovy example of listed 1960s architecture on the fringes of St. James's. The large, buzzing, bountifully stocked cocktail bar is your first port of call, staffed by a squad of enthusiastic mixologists that oversees a long list of intoxicating diversions. The restaurant, at the top of a set of original escalators, keeps up the good work, with impressive views and service brimming with affable efficiency. New chef Julian Marshall inherited a 'greatest hits' menu and has yet to make any major changes. So expect plenty of diligently prepared bloke-ish comfort food at one end (Thai green chicken curry, fish and chips) and game specials at the other (foie gras, duck). Back down the escalator, the comfy environs of the cigar divan have a pleasingly informal air, but still allow for some serious stogie smoking.

Green's Restaurant & Oyster Bar

BRITISH   12/20
36 DUKE ST, SW1
020-7930 4566, FAX 020-7930 2958
Lunch & Dinner daily. ££
U: Green Park/Piccadilly Circus.

Green's is one of those restaurants that tend to get overlooked when it comes to dishing out accolades, which is a shame as it produces very good, straightforward British cooking. This is the place for classic crab bisque with garlic croûtons, smoked Scottish salmon with soda bread, even a retro prawn cocktail. For mains, go for good old bangers and mash with bacon and onion gravy; top Scottish sirloin steak; a delectable sea trout with creamed leeks and truffle oil; plain grilled Dover sole or fillet of John Dory with a tangy mint and cider sauce. Seasonal game dishes are always worth ordering. With a nod to modernity, the roast breast of duck comes with sesame bok choy and spiced cranberry sauce, but it's just a nod. Puddings are puddings, with treacle tart and custard coming out tops. This is a restaurant for the establishment with attentive service in a suitably club-like setting—all paneling, prints on the walls, and seating in booths. But despite this and its location in St. James's, it is neither snooty nor off-putting, but welcomes all comers with equal grace. Owner Simon Parker Bowles is a former wine merchant; the wine list is solid and well notated.

Le Caprice

MODERN BRITISH   14/20
ARLINGTON HOUSE, ARLINGTON ST, SW1
020-7629 2239, FAX 020-7493 9040
Lunch & Dinner daily. ££
U: Green Park/Piccadilly Circus.

Seemingly unaffected by the capriciousness of food fashion, Le Caprice remains confidently consistent in offering supreme service even to those of us who are not celebrities, as well as dishing up expertly executed Modern British dishes. The constant welcoming presence of owners Corbin & King (despite the sell-out to the Belgo Group), adds warmth to what is now a fairly dated monochrome room beneath an office block with tinted windows and enlivened with framed celeb photos. The vicarious glamour of eating among the film and theatre A-list definitely adds to the culinary experience. Benchmark dishes such as tomato and basil galette, first-rate salmon fish-cakes with sorrel sauce and signature Scandinavian iced berries with white chocolate sauce remain for dessert flawless. Simple risottos are always impeccably prepared. Glitches can occur: a lacklustre crispy duck salad; slightly tough roast hake with punch clams and chorizo. Sunday brunch, with faultless kedgeree and eggs Benedict plus pitchers of Bloody Mary, is recommended. The sophisticated wine list is not priced too greedily. Famous names can secure a last-minute table, whilst mere mortals need to book well in advance.

L'Oranger

FRENCH   14/20
5 ST. JAMES'S ST, SW1
020-7839 3774, FAX 020-7839 4330
Lunch Mon.-Fri., Dinner Mon.-Sat. ££
U: Green Park/Piccadilly Circus.

Addresses don't come much more British establishment than this, so it's refreshing to find an unequivocally Provençal French restaurant among the wine merchants and hatters. Kamel Benemar now heads the kitchen, utilising Provençal ingredients to exciting, though not slavishly fashionable, effect. Presentation, with a tendency to towers, impresses on arrival, though a liking for chopping ingredients into tiny pieces reduces the intensity of some dishes. An inventive first course of salted cod and potato tartelette with shallots and tomato was faultless, though a foie gras and duck terrine was somewhat flabby. Perfectly cooked brill cleverly coated with crispy potato slices was let down by a timid Perigord sauce, and John Dory with crushed potato and tomato also lacked bite. Desserts shine, especially an outstanding pear and quince tart with cinnamon ice cream. Exceptionally accomplished and plentiful petits fours end a meal on a high and exemplify Kamel's classical training. Courteous service is multi layered, formal and French. The wine list is thoughtfully chosen with some unusual Rhône and Burgundy options. The room exudes luxury, but despite the pleasing atrium roof, the mix of wood-panelling, brass rails, mirrors and Toulouse-Lautrec prints is a disappointingly staid backdrop to such accomplished cuisine. Set 2-course lunch £20, 3 courses £24.50; set 3-course dinner £37.

Matsuri

JAPANESE/SUSHI BAR	15/20	🍴🍴
TEPPAN ROOM	13/20	🍴

15 BURY ST, SW1
020-7839 1101, FAX 020-7930 7010
Lunch & Dinner Mon.-Sat. ££
U: Green Park.

A ☎

An example of the Japanese genius for absorbing new into old appears in Matsuri's elegant, traditional, intimate sushi bar. Behind its counter, a microwave oven (used only for eel) signifies the readiness of its contents by displaying the message 'enjoy your meal'. And you will, if you choose from chef Hashiba's sparkling array of fresh fish, shellfish and crustaceans for sashimi or sushi. Intriguing appetisers include edamame—salted green soya beans, and, when available, warm, marinated turbot fins in a light broth—infinitely more delicious than they sound. The main area of the colourfully decorated restaurant is a large teppan room and you can mix and match by choosing grill in the sushi bar, or sushi in the teppan room. Standards, and prices, are high, but lunchtime menus start at £10 with 'okonomi-pizza Hiroshima-style' snacks from £6.50. The wine list has some well-known names, most highly priced, but useful New World bottles are mainly under £20. Better still is fine saké, drunk well-chilled. In subtlety and variety, it compares with single malt whisky. A dozen are listed by the glass from

£5.25 to £14.50 for a superb Kubota—pale, light and clean tasting, with a delicate grainy undertaste. Set menus £20-£55.

Pétrus

FRENCH	16/20	🍴🍴

33 ST. JAMES'S ST, SW1, 020-7930 4272
Lunch Mon.-Fri., Dinner Mon.-Sat. £££
U: Green Park/Piccadilly Circus

A ☎ ▮

Pétrus, as its name suggests, sets out to be a serious French restaurant. How serious is evident when you look at the wine list: the '47 Pétrus is £12,300. The surroundings, too, announce an expensive establishment: well-spaced tables, huge 'Old Master' oils on the walls, top napiery, cutlery and glassware, enough staff to run a restaurant twice the size and well-heeled customers. On to the menu where dishes offer plenty of luxury ingredients: eight starters included a stunning but simple carpaccio of tuna and swordfish, lemon oil vinaigrette and white radish salad; and a more complex pan-fried red mullet with peas à la crème and lentil velouté. Of the four main fish dishes, roasted sea bass with oysters, braised lettuce and a velouté of chervil with oyster sauce was flavourful; of the four main meat dishes, the cannon of lamb with baby onions, fried aubergines and black olives and basil jus evoked the best Provençal tastes. Desserts, which are rich, included a not wholly successful mix of tastes in a pistachio parfait with chocolate tuile and banana ice cream, and a truly wonderful caramel and praline mousse layered with chocolate thins with a caramel sauce. The chef, Marcus Wareing, was previously down the road at L'Oranger, and is financially backed here by Gordon Ramsay (see *Chelsea*). With such ingredients and polished cooking, the prices are still a very good value (though dinner is up from £28 last year). Service is oversolicitous, even though you often wait too long for your main course. The Pétrus on the wine list starts at £370 and goes sky-high, but you can enjoy non Pomerol wines at fair prices. It seems churlish to quibble at such an establishment, but Marcus Wareing is a better chef than shows currently at Pétrus. Perhaps he should spread his wings a little, become less impeccably French and more adventurous. Set 3-course lunch £22; set 3-course dinner £35, 6-course tasting menu £45.

Quaglino's

CONTEMPORARY EUROPEAN   11/20
16 BURY ST, SW1
020-7930 6767, FAX 020-7836 2866
Lunch & Dinner daily. £££
U: Green Park/Piccadilly Circus.

A ☎

Vast, buzzing and full of life, Quags has its detractors but it is hard not to be impressed both by its sheer scale and style. From street level you descend, first to a bar area where you can snack and sip and then, via a broad, sweeping, central stairway to the dining room proper. Dress to impress, everyone else does, and expect to be clocked as you descend. That this is a basement will surprise, the room is bright and airy and somehow seemingly infused with sunshine, the enormous central skylight bathing diners in its glow. Much is right, from the marble floor to the leather banquettes and the bevy of attendants who will descend on you once you are seated. The menu comes as an extended card and runs the whole gamut from seafood, magnificently displayed at the back of the room, through trusty bistro dishes to more haute cuisine. Calf's liver and bacon rubs shoulders with squid and hummus. If you opt for seafood, tread warily, the cost can shoot up. On the other hand, you may be happy with Caesar salad, or scallops served with an onion cream sauce. Main courses might be humble fish and chips, peppered rib of beef, or more elaborate items like chicken and snail Bourguignon or duck confit with baked chicory and apple. Desserts follow the classic mode, tarts and ice creams along with a few more English puddings, in keeping with the St. James's setting perhaps. Wines are international, climbing steeply and quickly. Set lunch & dinner (daily 5.30pm-6.30pm, or Mon.-Thurs. all evening) 2-course £12.50, 3 courses £15

The Ritz Restaurant

BRITISH/FRENCH   14/20   ♟
THE RITZ, PICCADILLY, W1
020-7493 8181, FAX 020-7493 2687
Lunch & Dinner daily. ££££
U: Green Park/Piccadilly Circus.

A ☎ **ⵏ** 🍷

The Ritz is unquestionably one of the most beautiful dining rooms in London. It's grand stately home style, awash with pinks and golds, sporting a magnificent trompe l'œil painted ceiling and floor-to-ceiling windows looking out onto the terrace where you can eat in the summer. Service is pretty stately, too, with waiters gliding around to cater to your every wish. Chef Giles Thompson has been faced with that classic hotel dining conundrum: how to keep the regulars happy while enticing a new, more adventurous clientele. Happily, he has achieved this balancing act remarkably well. While the à la carte menu emphasises classic starters: seared scallops with spiced leaves; Scottish smoked salmon; caviar and lobster bisque, the set menu offers a more cosmopolitan choice: bresaola with potato and watercress salad and wild rocket pesto; mousseline of smoked salmon with celeriac-wafers and citrus cream. Main courses include dishes like pot-roasted monkfish with red wine and pancetta and supreme of pheasant with braised red cabbage and Normandy apples and Calvados. And then there are the daily specialities from the trolley to hoe the British path: saddle of lamb en croûte; beef Wellington; and braised gammon. Desserts have mixed parentage: such as rhubarb compote comes with strawberries poached in green peppercorns and pistachio tuile. Why not just go the whole Edwardian hog with crêpes Suzette prepared at your table—one of the very few places in London still serving this old-fashioned masterpiece. The wine list is long and expensive, as is the whole experience, but it is quite an experience. Set 3-course lunch £35; set 3-course dinner £43, 4 courses £51 (Mon.-Thurs., Sun.), 5 courses £55 (Fri., Sat.).

The Stafford

MODERN BRITISH   13/20   ♟
THE STAFFORD, ST. JAMES'S PLACE, SW1
020-7493 0111, FAX 020-7493 7121
Lunch Sun.-Fri., Dinner nightly. ££
U: Green Park/Piccadilly Circus.

A ☎ **ⵏ**

The Stafford Hotel's location (tucked off St. James's), and the presence of its ebullient general manager, Terry Holmes, have ensured its ongoing success. It's a gem of a hotel, with a rather formal, pretty restaurant and the very good American Bar. Chris Oakes in the kitchen continues to cook with verve, producing a menu that is basically traditional, albeit occasionally enlivened by the odd nod to today's preoccupation with spicier tastes. Expect starters like duck liver, wild mushroom and garlic terrine with a tomato 'jam', and sautéed tiger prawns on mixed leaves with a dribble of chilli dressing. Mains continue the same path, perhaps a classic roast rump of lamb with Provençal vegetables or a fillet of brill on lightly crushed potatoes and flavoured with prawns, capers and a zingy cherry tomato salsa. Puddings stick to the British mode, as in a chocolate bread and butter version which comes richly surrounded by chocolate and vanilla sauce and topped with an orange sorbet. The experience is extremely satisfying. Set 2-course lunch £23.50, 3 courses £27; set 2-course dinner £27, 3 courses £32.50.

Suntory

JAPANESE   14/20   🍴
72-73 ST. JAMES'S ST, SW1
020-7409 0201, FAX 020-7499 0208
Lunch & Dinner daily. £££
U: Green Park/Piccadilly Circus.

🅰 ☎

A full-scale refurbishment is promised for 2000, but already the bar and the classic restaurant have been made brighter by opening up the windows previously obscured by wooden panels. Service, too, has improved, displaying more skill and attentiveness, while remaining friendly and helpful. The food is reliable as ever and often inspired. Some recent experiences are as enjoyable as they are unusual. Roasted gingko nuts—a delightful nibble with a pre-dinner sake—look like tiny gull's eggs, with white shells half broken away, and a soft 'nut' with a subtle flavour and texture. The seasonal menu might offer persimmon and smoked salmon where small cubes of the under-ripe fruit with dice of the mild fish are lightly dressed with white sesame sauce in a pleasing 'fusion' dish. Braised mooli is an inadequate name for a glorious nimono, a broth which also included fishcake, prawn and kabocha pumpkin. Boiled marinated abalone comes in its gleaming shell; and grilled lobster is precisely cooked. All the standards—sushi, sashimi, tempura, sukiyaki, shabu-shabu—are offered à la carte and in set menus from £53. Best value is at lunchtime with single dish meals from £11.50 for chicken teriyaki on rice with salad, miso soup and pickles. Set lunches from £11.50 ; set dinners from £54.

Wiltons

TRADITIONAL BRITISH   13/20   🍴
55 JERMYN ST, W1
020-7629 9955, FAX 020-7495 6233
Lunch & Dinner Sun.-Fri. £££
U: Green Park.

🅰 ☎ 🍴

'Tradition' is the tradition at Wiltons, and as far as the décor and above all the clientele are concerned, it is stoutly maintained. Diners in discreet alcoves look as if they have been governing great companies—or great societies—for decades. The ferocious discipline which the waitresses used to impose is now more relaxed. Although a few ingredients and combinations, such as superb green-olive ciabatta bread, or chargrilled tuna with tomato, red onion and coriander salad are of the late twentieth century, most of the fish and game menus, would not have seemed out of place hundred years ago. But some departures from the classical may surprise the older generation. Superb Colchester oysters are served on the half shell, but drained, so they are without the 'liquor' relished by oyster-lovers. Equally heretical, they sprinkle bread crumbs on the bread sauce rather than beside it. This was with grouse ordered medium-rare, but unskillfully cooked so it was dry under the skin, but blue in its depths. In one aspect, Wiltons remains ahead of the pack: uniquely English savouries never disappeared from its menu. Among them are anchovies on toast, Welsh rarebit and angels on horseback. Wines remain largely French and emphasise the classic, and expensive, Burgundy and Bordeaux regions. Set Sun. 3-course lunch £19.75.

ST. JOHN'S WOOD

Kashinoki

JAPANESE   12/20
JURY'S INTERNATIONAL REGENT PARK HOTEL
18 LODGE RD, NW8 020-7722 7722
Lunch & Dinner Tues.-Sun. ££
U: St. John's Wood.

🅰 ☎

Surprisingly, this restaurant in a large hotel seats only 40 plus five at the sushi bar. Mirrored alcoves and colourful pictures contribute to a vivid ambience, less austere than most classic Japanese places. The quite short à la carte offers a choice of standard dishes, with less common delicacies in the chef's specials. Recommended are edamame—boiled green soybeans; saba shioyaki—grilled mackerel with salt and hirame engawa tatsutaage—a masterpiece composed of deep-fried marinated turbot fins. But tsukimi tororo—grated yam with raw egg is perhaps best left to those who share a yen for viscous textures. Unusual in offering just one set menu at £32, but more unusual still, it offers a choice of sashimi or yakitori—grilled chicken as one of four courses preceding the main dishes—no less than seven options, which include sushi, steak, beef teriyaki and grilled lemon sole with mushroom and onion. Devotees of fine saké, always drunk chilled, will be refreshed by finding it here at the same price as the ordinary, warmed version. This restaurant, like Hiroko in the Kensington Hilton, is owned by Tatsuso (see above). Set 2-course lunch & dinner from £18, 3 courses £32.

SHEPHERD'S BUSH

The Brackenbury

CONTEMPORARY EUROPEAN 13/20   ♟
129-131 BRACKENBURY RD, W6
020-8748 0107, FAX 020-8741 0905
Lunch Sun.-Fri., Dinner Mon.-Sat. £
U: Goldhawk Rd.

🅰 ☎ 🖃

This is a perfect example of the kind of restaurant every neighbourhood should have, one that offers unpretentious, well-cooked meals at reasonable prices. Consisting of two small shops knocked into one, the restaurant front opens right up in the summer for al fresco dining beneath a shady dark green canopy at the corner of a quiet residential street in fashionable 'Brackenbury village'. The interior is simply and informally decorated with plain wooden floors, small but ample chairs and wooden tables. The atmosphere is usually humming since it is popular with locals; book at least a week ahead. The menu is a mix of Modern British with European influences; it changes daily but dishes are consistently good and flavoursome, such as pan-fried sweetbreads with artichoke purée and truffle oil, grilled radicchio and Gorgonzola risotto. Puddings include pannacotta, crème brûlée and a decent version of bread-and-butter. There's an excellent value set menu. The wine list is well-judged and modest mark-ups ensure

reasonable prices. Service is pleasantly casual. Set 2-course lunch £10.50, 3 courses £12.50.

Chinon

FRENCH   14/20   ♟
23 RICHMOND WAY, W14
020-7602 5968, FAX 020-7602 4082
Dinner Mon.-Sat. ££
U: Shepherd's Bush.

Chinon, located in a residential backwater, continues to quietly delight, enjoyed by locals and those in the know. The chef/owner and his manager wife are French-trained and clearly dedicated. Let's start with a typical three-course £16 set menu where price doesn't ever seem to cheat on quality or quantity. Superb homemade breads and then rillettes of goose with capers and walnuts, followed by tangy fried squid with pesto and mash, and lastly a toothsome vanilla bavarois. Presentation is well thought-out and each flavour impacts. Cooking also nods to modish tastes: rack of lamb with couscous, harissa and black olives; sea bass with sweet soy, bok choy and lemon chutney. Wines—half French, half New World—are thoughtfully selected and presented. Service can be a tad opinionated, but it's well-meaning. The décor has a pleasantly French provincial feel. Take a table upstairs by the large window overlooking a leafy courtyard or sit out there in summer. Here is a restaurant de quartier that's worth seeking out.

SHOREDITCH

Great Eastern Dining Room

ITALIAN   12/20
54-56 GT EASTERN ST, EC2
020-7613 4545, FAX 020-7613 4137
Open Mon.-Fri. noon-midnight, Sat. 6.30pm-midnight. £
U: Old St.

🅰 ☎

Studiedly brown, dimly lit, acoustically challenging, the Great Eastern Dining Room is aggressively fashionable in its chocolate leather, 70s-Sputnik chandelier and dark-wood cladding. Through a spacious and smoky bar, the restaurant becomes packed thanks to its cutting-edge Shoreditch location and prices that are extremely keen for food that gives a general impression of being Italian, albeit arguably via Australia. They're not skimping on ingredients: to serve tuna carpaccio with pomegranate and lime dressing for £6, and sea bass for £10 is admirable. But at these prices allowances have to be made and the execution isn't always what it should be. Seasoning seemed hit and miss—some dishes were sweet, some too salty; the sea bass on top of sweet potato, with a dollop of almond and rocket pesto on top was both and a peal shame. Butternut and ricotta lasagne was a tad stodgy, and some examples, like the side order of broccoli with mozzarella and pine nuts, and halibut with braised leek, lemon and sage butter, overdo the oil. But luck and careful ordering can result in excellent red pepper stuffed with tomato, goat cheese and anchovies. And who can complain about nicely grilled calf's liver with creamy polenta and crisp-fried sage leaves for £8.50? A laudable and not unsuccessful attempt to bring modish food within more diner's price ranges.

The Real Greek

GREEK   14/20   ♟
15 HOXTON MARKET, N1, 020-7739 8212
Lunch Mon.-Fri., Dinner Mon.-Sat. £

Good Greek food in London was regarded as an oxymoron before The Real Greek arrived in newly groovy and fashionable Hoxton, just north of the City. Theodore Kyriakou, the chef/proprietor, is not new on the restaurant scene. It is he who brought us Livebait, the restaurant that introduced new and interesting ways of preparing fish (see above). His move from there to The Real Greek was bound to produce great excitement. Expect no thrills and frills from the décor of the restaurant—its plain, simple, inexpensive interior allows for less effort in the upkeep and keeps the emphasis on the food, which is terrific. Mezze are divided up into well-matched plates of three or four dishes, perfect to share. If you prefer to keep your food to yourself, try one of their individual starters—wild boar sausages with prunes and apricots or octopus stifado. Main courses are top class—fish soup with fish terrine, roast loin of pork with honeyed quince—not a moussaka in sight! Only a Greek oenophile would know his way around the wine list, but the staff is very helpful. Set 2-course lunch £10.

SOHO

Alastair Little

MODERN BRITISH   13/20   ♟
49 FRITH ST, W1
020-7734 5183, FAX 020-7792 4504
Lunch Mon.-Fri., Dinner Mon.-Sat. £££
U: Tottenham Court Rd.

The room is intimate, but not overly cosy, the pale walls now adorned with paintings where before they were plain. The food is deceptively simple, reading like so many other restaurants, but there is a rigour, both in the design and execution of the menu which you cannot fail to miss when you eat. Allegiance is firmly to Italy, but the Far East also gets a nod. Flavours are strong and robust, as are textures, but there is always balance. A pizzetta bianca, perhaps with mozzarella, rocket and tomatoes, is thin-based, the topping getting star billing; a robustly flavoured chickpea soup was silky smooth; grilled mackerel, Japanese style, came with just the right amount of soy to cut the richness. Main courses continue the theme: sea bass with spicy tomato sauce; calf's liver with a potato cake and caramelised shallots. Desserts might be tiramisù, crème caramel with blood orange salad or a deliciously nutty apple and amaretti tart with crème fraîche. The global wine list climbs above £20 quickly. Service has attitude, not always of the right kind. Set 3-course lunch £25; set 3-course dinner £33.

Beak Street

MODERN BRITISH   12/20
41 BEAK ST, W1
020-7287 2057, FAX 020-7287 1767
Lunch Mon.-Fri., Dinner Mon.-Sat. ££
U: Oxford Circus.

Beak Street is the new name of the former Leith's Soho, reflecting a change of ownership (now Nick Tarayan and the Kemps of the estimable Firmdale Hotels group). Leith's Soho quickly became a popular institution; perhaps Beak Street will return to its exciting beginnings, rather than remain resting on its less-than-good value laurels, as it so far has done. Certainly their heart is in the right place: a note at the top of the menu encourages customers to ask for something 'really simple', if that's what is wanted, and they will do their best to produce it. Otherwise, choose from a starter of perhaps a light velouté of cèpes with a soft poached egg or their ever popular and excellent retro prawn cocktail. Mains include modish dishes like guinea fowl with sweetcorn and Parma ham and creamed cabbage, and braised pork belly with spiced, crab beignet and bok choy. Vegetarians swear by the cooking. The wine list is good; many are offered by the glass; service is helpful. Set 2-course lunch & 6pm-7pm £17.50, 3 courses £19.50.

Circus

MODERN BRITISH   13/20   ♟
1 UPPER JAMES ST, W1
020-7534 4000, FAX 020-7534 4010
Lunch Mon.-Fri., Dinner Mon.-Sat. ££
U: Piccadilly Circus.

A **☎**

A baby brother to the Avenue (see *St. James's*), which shares the same sense of minimalism. Here brown gets a viewing in the shape of beige chairs, but the overall colour scheme remains resolutely white. Service can be intimidating, in part to protect the members-only bar downstairs, but once seated in the dining room, all of this slides comfortably away. The menu treads a predictable modish path, but there are interesting twists, first-rate ingredients and a restraint which is refreshing. Starters might be good onion soup, even better ravioli stuffed with crab and served with roasted artichokes—never mind authenticity—this was delicious, as was a good duck terrine. Attention to detail marks the cooking and this continues into the main courses, as in crisply roasted cod on a salad of various beans, a good chicken breast served with seasonal morels. Some desserts are given modern twists—a poached pear, the liquor including Asian spicing, the accompanying ice cream decidedly Thai in character, while others follow a more traditional path: chocolate torte with berries, for example. Service is attentive, if at times a little clumsy. The wine list shows serious intent. Set 2-course lunch £10.50, 3 courses £12.50; set à la carte 2-course lunch & dinner £17.50, 3 courses £19.50.

> **Ratings** are based solely on the restaurant's cuisine. We do not take into account the atmosphere, décor or service; these are commented on in the review.

French House Dining Room

BRITISH   14/20   ♟
49 DEAN ST, W1
020-7437 2477, FAX 020-7287 9109
Lunch & Dinner Mon.-Sat. £
U: Leicester Sq.

A **☎**

Now a stalwart of Soho, this restaurant above an eccentric pub (with which it shares lavatories down some rickety stairs, so beware) appears to have been here long before the current generation of bohos were born but, in fact, dates back less than a decade. The small, bareboards upstairs room with tortoiseshell laquered walls is intimate, with an almost conspiratorial atmosphere generated by the kind of customer who doesn't belong in the brash new world of media West End. If the surroundings are a little louche, the cooking is quite the opposite. It's British and resolutely seasonal, but not an exercise in heritage. The menu is uncompromisingly direct: grilled squid and aioli; grilled lamb and chickpea, potato, artichoke and olives. Each will be cooked simply and honestly, but nevertheless skillfully, producing generously proportioned, full-flavoured dishes. Expect something like chocolate pot or prune and Armagnac ice cream for desserts. Wines are a good, sturdy selection from France. Prices, too, especially for Soho, are another example of the French House's disarming integrity: they're lower than they need be.

Il Forno

ITALIAN   12/20
63-64 FRITH ST, W1
020-7734 4545, FAX 020-7387 8624
Lunch Mon.-Fri., Dinner nightly. £
U: Tottenham Court Rd.

A **☎**

In its new guise, this restaurant appears to have overcome the problems of this difficult site, just too far north of the main part of Frith Street to attract much passing trade. Although the previous incarnation, the excellent Frith Street, sadly lasted only a short time, now owner Claudio Pulze and chef Marco Stucchi from Al Duca, another Pulze restaurant, have produced what seems to be a winning formula—affordable, good contemporary Italian cooking in a relaxed setting. A starter of organic polenta with four cheeses was rich without being overwhelming; beautifully roasted firm cod came on white beans with spring onions to give it an edge, mackerel char-grilled (a favoured cooking method), came on rocket and tomato and was refreshing and oil-free. Prices and dishes are designed to attract those after a casual lunch, as in plenty of pasta choices and a newly built pizza oven producing excellent, thin-based pizzas, perhaps with tomato, bresaola, rocket and goat cheese (£7), or with garlic smoked swordfish and mixed leaves (£7.50), as well as more serious evening diners. Desserts at £3.50 are superb: try the lemon tart with its thin meringue topping and fresh raspberries, splendidly alcoholic tiramisù in a cup, or a rich chocolate and almond cake with vanilla ice cream. Presentation is not sacrificed for economy, and the service is delightful.

L'Escargot

FRENCH   14/20

48 GREEK ST, W1
020-7432 2679, FAX 020-7437 0790
Lunch Mon.-Fri., Dinner Mon.-Sat. ££
U: Leicester Sq.

L'Escargot has been feeding Soho for generations—it was fashionable as long ago as the twenties. During the intervening years it has been through several different owners and several good and bad patches. At the moment the patch is good. The premises as ever is divided into two, with a large bustling restaurant on the ground floor and a small, grand restaurant upstairs. Both have recently been refurbished and it pays to take some time to look around—the collection of works by David Hockney, Chagall and Matisse which adorns the downstairs restaurant is astonishing; the restaurant upstairs is referred to as the Picasso Room, and you only have to look at the dress plates to understand why. Andrew Thompson is the chef and he's lightened the cooking to make it more palatable to trendy Soho tastes—sweet sticky sauces are replaced with simple jus, there's lots of fish, and always interesting vegetarian options. In keeping with the premises, the menu is French-based, offering anything from sauté of foie gras with sweet corn madelaines, or roast fillet of sea bass with velouté of crab and oyster beignet and choucroute paysanne on the ground floor. The Picasso menu is slightly grander—expect dishes like assiette of lamb or skate and new potato terrine with lime and caper vinaigrette.

Ground Floor: Set 2-course lunch & 6pm-7.30pm £14.95, 3 courses £17.95. Picasso Room: Set 2-course lunch £29.50.

Mezzo

MODERN BRITISH   12/20

100 WARDOUR ST, W1
020-7314 4000, FAX 020-7314 4040
Lunch & Dinner daily. £££
U: Piccadilly Circus.

Mezzo, the downstairs restaurant, is big, brash, stylish, a typical Conran venture—but here without the master's touch in the kitchen that lifts Le Pont de la Tour, Orrery and Bluebird into another sphere (for all see index). It's not bad; it's just not that good. Other gripes include very loud live music at certain times for which you pay a cover charge whether you like it or not, and cloakroom attendants who attempt to spray you with perfume and charge you a £1. All of which is fine if you're in a group having a good time, but this is not the place for intimate or fine dining. Starters range from a decent chicory, walnut, Roquefort and orange salad, to £12 for a foie gras terrine, with a Sauternes and Bramley jelly. (Forget the caviar menu, that's out of most diner's price league). Mains go from £11.25 for pappardelle with mushrooms, pesto and Parmesan to a plateau de fruits de mer (which is magnificent) for two at £29.50 per person. In between, main dishes take in all the usual modish favourites like braised rabbit leg with cumin-spiced aubergine; swordfish, sea scallops and more. Vegetables are charged on top of this. The best bets are the simplest: salads, the fruits de mer, grills. The upstairs Mezzonine continues to tour the East with a long menu, offering something for everyone. Mezzo: Set lunches and pre-theatre 6pm-7.15pm, 2 courses £12.50, 3 courses £15.50.

Richard Corrigan at Lindsay House

MODERN BRITISH/IRISH   16/20

21 ROMILLY ST, W1
020-7439 0450, FAX 020-7437 7349
Lunch Mon.-Fri., Dinner Mon.-Sat. £££
U: Leicester Sq.

A cult figure among hard-core foodies, Richard Corrigan is an original. The Lindsay

House is unlike any other restaurant: an antidote to big, brash eateries with unknown chefs. You ring a bell to enter the eighteenth-century Soho townhouse with bare floorboards, original fireplaces and a plain, cream-coloured elegance. Corrigan's rural Irish upbringing informs his cooking, and there can be few places this side of the Irish Sea to eat crubeens, a sausage made from pig's trotter, especially not served with suckling pig, black pudding and choucroute. Each component is as tidy as a petit four, a meaty story in itself. He may pair seafood and meat as in red snapper with merguez sausage, and though a few of his dishes err on the wild side, the best are simply outstanding—Corrigan works his earthy ingredients into feats of depth and complexity. His risotto of veal kidney and girolles is an archetypical success. He's also an experienced hand with game and pasta—and the two combined, as in glorious teal ravioli with game consommé. Desserts respect the seasons, too, and suggest he does not have a particularly sweet tooth. The chocolate fondant is peerless; chocolate sorbet accompanies caramelised pumpkin for a robust ending to what should be a magnificent meal. The intimate and appreciative, but not reverential, atmosphere is encouraged by delightful and unaffected service. The list of wines is long, inspiringly grouped and lovingly annotated—a joy, like so much of the food. Set 3-course dinner £42.

Quo Vadis

MODERN BRITISH   14/20   ♕
26-29 DEAN ST, W1
020-7437 9585, FAX 020-7439 1933
Lunch Sun.-Fri., Dinner daily. £££
U: Leicester Sq.

🅰 ☎

Quo Vadis is one of those legendary restaurants in London that have recently been restored to their former glory. There are a few disappointing aspects to the latest makeover, however, including some gimmicky art on the walls, courtesy of Marco Pierre White, and the

first floor bar which has become isolated as a members-only club. The transition over the past three years, since Marco Pierre White took over the restaurant, has not been smooth, but the restaurant seems now to be back on top form, not surprising since the chef is Spencer Patrick and the manager is Fernando Peire. The menu is divided into soups and salads, hors d'œuvres, egg, pasta and risotto, fish and seafood and roast and grills. The cooking is superb, as in dishes such as the escalope of veal saltimbocca with fresh noodles and roasting juices where the meat is perfectly cooked and the cohesiveness of the ensemble is a joy. One cannot help thinking that a braver attempt to edit the menu would benefit the kitchen and the restaurant. The menu currently lists sashimi of salmon with chives and ginger next to a terrine of foie gras; spaghettini alle vongole next to omelette Arnold Bennett. But the cooking is superb. The wine list is well chosen and a delight. Set 2-course lunch, pre-theatre £14.50, 3 courses £17.

Red Fort

INDIAN   13/20   ♕
77 DEAN ST, W1, 020-7437 2115
Lunch & Dinner daily. ££
U: Leicester Sq.

🅰 ☎

This was one of the first upmarket Indian eateries and while the décor is getting a bit tired (although moves are afoot to address this), the kitchen has been given a new lease on life with the arrival of two of the Quereshi clan-chefs. They are part of a 200-year old family tradition of cooking for the Nawabs of Avadh, with recipes handed down from father to son and are famous for their dum pukht dishes and their way with kebabs. So start with galauti kebab, lamb tenderised with raw papaya and flavoured with rose petal and kewra essence; or murgh-e-seekhpa, minced chicken flavoured with cardamom and stuffed with cream cheese, mint and coriander. The one dish not to miss is the biryani—rice, lamb and spices cooked in a sealed pot—a dish which their family can fairly claim to have invented. Also try the murgh dum handi, chicken cooked in a sealed pot with cardamom, coriander, chillies and saffron; and the murgh bemissal, which means 'incomparable'; and, as no Indian meal is complete without dal (lentils), try the dal dum pukht Quereshi, also cooked in a sealed pot with yoghurt and roasted garlic. Set menus £25, £35.

Soho Soho

CONTEMPORARY EUROPEAN   12/20
11-13 FRITH ST, W1
020-7494 3491, FAX 020-7251 3091
Restaurant: Lunch Mon.-Fri., Dinner Mon.-Sat. Rôtisserie: Lunch & Dinner daily. ££
U: Leicester Sq.

A ☎

The bustling ground-floor rôtisserie is where a mainly young crowd enjoy spit-roast chicken or suckling pig plus brasserie staples—omelettes, moules marinières, onglet or entrecôte béarnaise. Fish include tuna, mullet, salmon and gâteau d'églefin fume—better known as the English brasserie favourite, smoked haddock fishcake. Upstairs, which is a little less noisy, appeals to a varied clientele who appreciate serious cooking and attention to detail. Note, for example, how the deep colours of the show-plates match the seating, while elegant tableware typifies this restaurant's style. Service is professional but relaxed and the kitchen takes time to prepare and present real food. The French menu is (usually) accurately translated into English, and most dishes have an unexpected extra—for example in the smooth, pink pâté of its liver with salad of marinated pigeon breast, or batons of courgette, potato and carrot with rabbit leg stuffed with buttered leeks and bacon. Adventurous desserts are skillfully executed, and a sensibly small board offers cheese in good condition. The wine list is entirely Mediterranean and includes a few surprises such as a really mature red from, of all places, the Costa Brava. Set 2-course dinner 5.30pm-7.30pm & 10.15pm-11.30pm £12.50, 3 courses £15.50.

Sugar Club

PACIFIC RIM   14/20   ♟
21 WARWICK ST, W1
020-7437 7776, FAX 020-7437 7778
Lunch & Dinner daily. ££
U: Piccadilly Circus.

A ☎

Sugar Club has taken to its new home in Soho like a fish to water—though such mundane juxtapositions as fish and water are rare at this fashionable restaurant. Sugar Club and its well-travelled, Kiwi-born chef Peter Gordon went some way to bringing Pacific Rim 'fusion food' to London. Signature dishes such as the starter of grilled scallops with sweet chilli sauce and crème fraîche seem tame compared to a globe-trotting dish of roast corn-fed chicken breast on braised Swiss chard and cassava chips with smoked paprika and feta pesto as a main dish. Although the dishes sound like the culinary equivalent of Esperanto, the flavours are so well judged that the dishes appear as a blend of complementary contrasts, rather than a series of weird ingredients chucked together by chance. Simple pale walls and plain floor boards allow you to concentrate on what's on the plate, though, when busy, this place can be noisy. Service is largely Antipodean and staff usually copes well, even during crowded lunchtimes. The wine list is well-chosen and turns up a couple of one-of-a-kind New Zealand wines you're unlikely to find elsewhere in the UK.

Thai Pavilion

THAI   11/20
42 RUPERT ST, W1, 020-7287 6333
Lunch & Dinner daily. £
U: Leicester Sq.

A ☎

The basement room is decorated in restrained Thai style with a seashell fountain and colourful prints, while the first floor feels more tropical with bamboo furniture. On the second floor in a traditional khantok room, you recline on the floor with back supports. Thai orchids glow everywhere. Gracious service is a feature of the calm ambience, very different from nearby Chinatown. The menu explains exotic Thai flavourings, and how to order a balanced meal from a long list in which main course curries, grills and stir-fried dishes produce the most excitement. Many offer a choice of ingredients; a classic green curry, for example, might contain chicken, duck, beef, fish, prawns or vegetables. Most are mild, but they will happily add chillies to the desired degree. 'Chef's recommendations' include famous Thai salads, som tum with papaya, and laarb, again with a choice of ingredients; and special soups such as chicken broth with banana blossoms. There is a long special vegetarian menu too. The 80-strong wine list deserves exploration, for crisp whites from the Loire, fruitier whites from Alsace and powerfully flavoured reds from anywhere that go better with Thai curries than many would ever believe. Set meals from £10.95 to £26.

Vasco & Piero's Pavilion

ITALIAN   12/20
15 POLAND ST, W1, 020-7437 8774
Lunch Mon.-Fri., Dinner Mon.-Sat. ££
U: Oxford Circus/Tottenham Court Rd.

A ☎

While the rest of the city revels in having 'discovered' Italian cooking, this establishment, with its quietly modern interior, continues to turn out the same family-style food it has done for the last twenty years. While not exactly cutting-edge, it has a lead over many others, with excellent freshly prepared pastas, as well as more elaborate dishes. Start with a sweet and sour Sicilian salad of cauliflower heady with saffron, or a duck salad replete with mostarda di Cremona, or simple carpaccio, delicately flavoured and accompanied by peppery rocket and tingling Parmesan shavings. Roast monkfish with sautéed potatoes and spaghetti strands of courgettes might follow, or perfectly prepared calf's liver with beautifully crisped large sage leaves. Desserts are of the semi-freddo and crema Cataluna variety. The wine list is all Italian, does desserts a service and rewards the adventurous. Service is old-style Italian—warm, friendly and helpful—and you are encouraged, for a moment, to become part of the family. Set 2-course dinner £16.50, 3 courses £19.50.

SOUTH BANK

County Hall Restaurant

MODERN BRITISH   13/20   🍳
LONDON MARRIOTT COUNTY HALL
QUEENS WALK, SE1
020-7902 8000, FAX 020-7928 5300
Breakfast, Lunch & Dinner daily. ££
U: Waterloo.

A ☎ 📷

This restaurant, annexed to the London Marriot Hotel, although not owned by it, is surprisingly good but sadly seems to be neglected by many Londoners who don't even know it exists. Rather, it is patronised by the hotel's guests and employees of the many local businesses and corporations who enjoy spectacular views of the Thames, Houses of Parliament, and now the new London Eye from the comfort of the beautiful bar and dining room. The principally Modern British slant of the restaurant's menu focuses on sea-

sonal ingredients, and the chef, David Ali, clearly enjoys cooking seafood. Other excellent dishes include ballotine of foie gras with Sauternes jelly and toasted brioche; fillet of seabream with crushed new potatoes and sauce verge; ribeye of beef, artichoke barigoule and Cabernet Sauvignon jus and white chocolate crème brûlée with pineapple. The bar features a large selection of oysters. Set 3-course lunch £19.50; pre-theatre 2 courses £16.50, 3 courses £21.50.

Oxo Tower Restaurant Bar & Brasserie

CONTEMPORARY EUROPEAN   13/20   🍳
OXO TOWER WHARF, BARGEHOUSE ST, SE1
020-7803 3888, FAX 0171 803 3838
Restaurant: Lunch & Dinner daily. Brasserie Mon.-Sat. 11am-11.30pm, Sun. 11am-10.30pm. £££
U: Waterloo.

A ☎ 📷 🍷

Who said south London wasn't fashionable? Okay, so it's only just south of the Thames—on the riverbank, in fact—which affords some of the most wonderful, sweeping river views in the capital. Located a stone's throw from the massive IPC publishing house, the Oxo Tower is a favourite with journos and other media types. As part of the burgeoning Harvey Nichols Restaurants Ltd. (which also launched Prism in 1999 (see *The City*), Oxo Tower fits right in: it's big, it's incredibly design-conscious and it's firmly aimed at moneyed, expense-account dining. Take the speedy lift all the way up to the top floor and you can choose between the airy, light-filled bar, the buzzing brasserie (tables out on the balcony with stunning river views during summer months), or the more haute cuisine-ish restaurant. There have been reports of sniffy service, but on our visit, service was exemplary, though staff was kept very busy. Starters such as sauté of lambs' sweetbreads, chorizo, potato, sherry, parsley and garlic, or mains of open ravioli of pan-fried monkfish with mussels, prawns and leeks in a cider velouté are well-executed and, as you'd expect, beautifully presented, though rarely as memorable as that stunning view. Restaurant set 3-course lunch £27.50.

SOUTH KENSINGTON

Bibendum

FRENCH   14/20   ♔
MICHELIN HOUSE, 81 FULHAM RD, SW3
020-7581 5817, FAX 020-7823 7925
Lunch & Dinner daily. £££
U: South Kensington.

A ☎

Named after the jauntily obese Michelin man himself, and sitting atop the original Michelin building, this is now a temple to life as Sir Terence Conran would have us live it (there's an oyster bar in the downstairs foyer, a florist out front and the Conran shop next door). The light, airy dining room, offset by stained glass windows featuring etchings of Gallic street plans, remains one of London's most enjoyable, although service can sometimes be a touch iffy. No such problems with the menu, which combines classic French with mod Med touches. Grilled Bresse pigeon with shallots, thyme and balsamico is as good as it sounds; ditto fillet of sea bass with oysters and Champagne sauce. Matthew Juke's adventurous wine list is one of the capital's finest. A more affordable and casual late-night supper menu of one or two courses is available from 9.30pm. Set 2-course lunch £23, 3 courses £27.50.

Bibendum Oyster Bar

MODERN BRITISH   12/20
MICHELIN HOUSE, 81 FULHAM RD, SW3
020-7823 7925
Lunch & Dinner daily. ££
U: South Kensington.

A 🍴

This is the best place for eating all manner of shellfish, especially oysters in Chelsea. The premises, formerly the London headquarters of the Michelin tyre people, may seem a little cold and echoey as you arrive, not surprising given that marble tables and wicker chairs are the only adornment of the old shop floor. But there's always a buzzy atmosphere, and if you're lucky you may be able to get a seat inside the bar itself, a little room on the left. Though there are a couple of meat dishes on the menu, but to ignore the shellfish would make a visit here a pointless exercise. Crab is served whole for those who enjoy the challenge, or dressed for the Gucci-clad customers. Oysters come in several different vari-

eties. The plateau of fruits de mer is a real treat. The only surprise is that there is generally no hot seafood on the menu. The wine list is appropriately white heavy and the service is professional. Bibendum Oyster Bar is a great fuelling point for shopping.

Bombay Brasserie

INDIAN   11/20
COURTFIELD CLOSE, COURTFIELD RD, SW7
020-7370 4040, FAX 020-7835 1669
Lunch & Dinner daily. ££
U: Gloucester Rd.

 🏃

This long-standing South Ken Indian, once quite the trailblazer, is guilty of late of a spot of laurel-resting. However, a recent(ish) refurbishment and the arrival of new faces in the kitchen should herald the start of a new period of innovation. The Brasserie has always prided itself on playing host to a myriad of flavours from all points on the Indian subcontinent, introducing the capital to the wonders of Goan cuisine a good few years before it enjoyed such fashionable status. The lighter side of things certainly tends to work the best: dishes to look out for include Goan fish curry, mulligatawny (lentil) soup, and crab malabari with coconut and assorted spices. Dining in the grand colonial surrounds of the conservatory can still be quite an experience, despite the occasional grumpy waiter. Reliable seems to be the word here—a shame given the impressive décor and illustrious past. Set buffet lunch and dinner £15.95.

Cambio de Tercio

SPANISH   15/20   ♔♔
163 OLD BROMPTON RD, SW5
020-7244 8970, FAX 020-7373 8817
Lunch & Dinner daily. ££
U: Knightsbridge.

For food that respects its fundamental style but does not eschew novelty, look to the frontiers of the old world. In this Iberian outpost the perfect tapa with apéritifs is arguably the world's finest ham, accredited 'JJJJJ' Jabugo, from black leg pigs fed on acorns all their adult life. Follow with starters as traditional as Galician octopus and potato dressed with paprika and olive oil, or eggs scrambled with Burgos black pudding; or as modern as large ravioli filled with a liquid spring onion mousse with pig's trotter terrine. Main dishes include quail cooked in red wine with a voluptuous risotto of Mahon cheese and bone marrow, and the 'signature' suckling pig Segoviana. Fish lovers can choose monkfish with spinach and almonds, sea bass with fennel, asparagus and mojama—air-dried tuna. Delectable desserts include convent-style egg puddings, and citrus infusion, unsweetened grapefruit soup with lemon sorbet. Vegetarians have limited choices and will not appreciate the décor based on the colours and artefacts of the bullring. Courteous Spanish service and the all-Spanish wine list are other attractions. As well as highly priced modern classics, there are such gems as white Rueda de Borros at £12.90 and a fine Ribeiro de Douro Callejo 1996 at £15.50.

Daphne's

ITALIAN   11/20
112 DRAYCOTT AVE, SW3
020-7589 4257, FAX 020-7581 2232
Lunch & Dinner daily. ££
U: South Kensington.

No longer quite the 'happening' restaurant it was when owned by Mogens Tholstrup, Daphne's still retains a fairly sassy profile. It continues to be favoured by the ladies-who-lunch crowd, evident from the preponderance of bottles of mineral water on the tables; while in the evenings one can still spot the odd honcho or film star. Divided into two rooms, the back one is a pleasant, leafy conservatory with brick walls, tiled floors and warm, muted colours—welcoming even in winter, when the fire is lit. The waiters and meeters and greeters are all good looking, smartly attired but, at times, a little off-hand. The menu is divided into pastas and risottos, grills and roasts. Fish is particularly popular and dishes include sea bass with fennel and chargrilled swordfish with lemon and olive oil. The best dishes are those in which ingredients have been prepared simply and straighforwardly using good Italian produce. The wine list includes French and New World wine, though it is predominantly Italian.

Hilaire

MODERN BRITISH   14/20
68 OLD BROMPTON RD, SW7
020-7584 8993, FAX 020-7581 2949
Lunch Mon.-Fri., Dinner Mon.-Sat. ££
U: South Kensington.

In this civilised restaurant the ground floor is usually bustling, so those seeking quiet and discretion might prefer the basement and particularly the cosy alcoves. Susan Webb is the welcoming hostess, while spouse chef/patron Bryan rarely ventures from the kitchen. Modern British may be his style, but classic virtues, and classic dishes are not forgotten. Mousseline of pike with lobster sauce recalls quenelles de brochet, but comes as a slice on a bed of chopped lobster, not in moulded spoonfuls. It seems, and is, very luxurious but there are no supplements in the set price of £37.50 for three courses with variations for lighter appetites. Exotic ingredients are used discreetly in the chilli oil accompanying fillets of mullet with aubergine, or elegantly balanced sweet, sharp and hot Thai dip with crisp goujons of plaice. A tender roast partridge came with bread sauce, game chips and green grapes in the well-bred gravy. There was cabbage, too, and only unreconstructed traditionalists could regret the absence of the liver croûton. Other classics are turbot with shrimps and watercress sauce, fillet steak au poivre and saddle of venison. Equal skill and delicacy show in tempting desserts, and spectacularly so in the grapefruit and Campari sorbet. The wine list is well balanced between the classics and New World with a wide choice by the glass. Set 2-course lunch £18.50; set 2-course dinner 6.30pm-7.30pm & 10pm-11.15pm £18.50, 3 courses £33.

Itsu

JAPANESE   13/20
118 DRAYCOTT AVE, SW3
020-7584 5522, FAX 020-7581 8716
Lunch & Dinner daily. ££
U: South Kensington

No bookings.
This bright corner site is the ultimate in casual dining; eat, anytime of the day, as much or as little as you like with each dish priced from £2.50 to £3.50 depending on ingredi-

ents. The room is bright white with stainless steel providing the relief. While gazing out on this exclusive part of Kensington as passersby peer at you through the large plate-glass windows, you sit at a conveyor belt as staff busy themselves in front of you. It's public display of excess or frugality, depending on your approach. The loose theme is Japanese with attitude, resulting in dishes like salmon sashimi, eel roll and seared tuna with mustard and tuna, but also spinach given an Eastern treatment of soy and sesame, avocado partnered with fish eggs and marinated beetroot. Chef Clive Fretwell (from Le Manoir aux Quat'Saisons; see *Oxford*), rightly concentrates on first-rate ingredients and does as little as possible to them while still managing to transform the individual flavours into a whole. Dessert seems somewhat unnecessary, but mini versions of custards and puddings provide the sweet finale should you want one. The wine list is cursory; service non-existent given you help yourself.

Lundum's

DANISH   11/20

119 OLD BROMPTON RD, SW7
020-7373 7774, FAX 020-7373 4472
Lunch & Dinner daily. ££
U: South Kensington.

Londoners have slowly come around to the idea of this Kensington Danish. A family-run establishment with a refined, dare one say old-fashioned, interior and almost eccentric genteel charm (Gerry & the Pacemaker's Greatest Hits soothingly serenading diners during one visit). Anyone believing Scandinavian cuisine begins and ends with meatballs and herrings will be surprised by the variety of what's offered here. And the menu selection has gained in confidence considerably since the restaurant's opening a couple of years ago: roast fillet of lamb; beef stroganoff; warm liver pâté with mushrooms and crispy bacon and a celebrated selection of fresh salmon. If it's on the list, be sure to try the duck (Spraengt And)—cured for 52 hours (no more, no less) and served in a honey sauce. Set 3-course lunch £15.50; set 2-course dinner £21.50; Sun. buffet brunch £14.50.

Star of India

INDIAN   12/20

154 OLD BROMPTON RD, SW5
020-7373 2901, FAX 020-7373 5664
Lunch & Dinner daily. ££
U: Gloucester Rd.

More than the proverbial 'location, location, location' makes a successful restaurant. 'Personality, personality, personality' is needed, too, and it is found here in abundance. It starts with the décor, a sort of kitsch Italianate trompe l'œil and continues with co-owner (the flamboyant Reza Mahammad), who often appears in one guise or another to welcome and entertain guests. The cooking under the new chef shows a style of its own with a happy lightness of touch so that even after a substantial meal—and portions are generous—one leaves light of heart and stomach. Some of the cuisine is still a touch tentative like samosas filled with a mixture of three cheeses (is three always better than one?), but like other dishes it is much enhanced by a subtle chutney, in this case, spiced tomato and chive. While understated flavours reflect local preferences, Indian traditions are maintained in enticing vegetables such as crunchy cubes of okra in yoghurt, and okra again, fried with shreds of red onion. Delicate and well-balanced lamb biryani comes in a pastry sealed pot, and there is a wide choice of breads. Among hearty reds, the Australian Shiraz is ideal for Indian food.

Turner's

FRENCH   14/20

87-89 WALTON ST, SW3
020-7584 6711, FAX 020-7584 4441
Lunch & Dinner Mon.-Sat. £££
U: South Kensington.

Located at the Brompton Cross end of Walton Street, the room manages to be both formal and intimate, done in pale yellow and blue with subdued cloth covering the seats and comfortable banquettes. While many restaurants seem satisfied to compose dishes on the plate, Brian Turner's pedigree of hotel and fine dining shows through in well-worked and complex dishes—an intense foie gras terrine, for example, alongside a crab salad infused with herbs and possibly spices. Meat is a strong point, particularly offal, but not to the detriment of fish, which might be perfectly cooked turbot in an accurately reduced sauce, or monkish, roasted and served with garlic and a medley of perfectly turned root vegetables. Meat, however, remains a passion, whether it is pink and juicy veal kidneys or a rack of lamb with haricots. Desserts show serious pastry work, as in almond tart—nutty and crunchy— while anyone undecided might opt for the selection, which is a worthwhile tour. Wines reward expenditure, with France getting particularly good coverage. Set 3-course lunch £17.50; 3-course dinner £29.50.

SOUTH NORWOOD

Mantanah

THAI   **15/20**

2 ORTON BUILDING, PORTLAND RD, SE25
020-8771 1148
Dinner Tues.-Sun. £
R: Norwood Junction.

'Worth a special journey' traditionally defines an outstanding restaurant. Mantanah is outside central London but those determined enough to find it are rewarded by some of London's finest Thai cooking. It is a family business where Tym Yeoh cooks and husband Tony leads service in the simple, but pleasantly furnished room, seating just 24. The menu is infinitely varied. Don't miss soup, a major feature of Thai meals soup properly served as a side dish with the main course. Tom yum is hot and sour, highly aromatic, with chicken, beef or prawns. Something to dive for is the mixed seafood tom yum which comes in a steamboat. Curries are generally milder than soups but made hotter to order; choose from green, red, 'jungle' or regional specialities. Other treasures include aptly named 'yum yum', chilli hot salads and varied stir-fries and grills; these are not usually dry, for they too are spicily sauced. The national 'signature dish' is Pad Thai, fried rice noodles with prawns, egg, beanshoots and ground peanuts. Brown or sticky rice also makes a superb background for the subtle spicing of the curries. Vegetarians can choose from a special menu listing 30 options.

STRAND

The River Room

FRENCH   **13/20**

THE SAVOY, STRAND, WC2, 020-7836 4343
Lunch & Dinner daily. ££££
U: Covent Garden/Embankment.

The River Room is indelibly old-fashioned yet with the timeless charm of an elegant ocean liner which glides on safe in the knowledge that age does not wither the frisson of excitement of dining in such splendidly grand surroundings with utterly impeccable, pleasingly unobsequious service. The menu is not high-definition fashion, but interestingly eclectic with nods to maître chef Anton Edelmann's Germanic heritage as well as the necessary luxury ingredients. Domes are still lifted in unison to reveal successful starters such as admirably refined scallop ravioli topped with roasted scallop on a frothy saffron broth, and a macho, richly defined dish of kidneys and sweetbreads with cockcomb and deconstructed vol-au-vent. Roast suckling pig with bread dumplings was wonderfully savoury with particularly good parsnip and swede purée accompaniments. A vegetarian casserole, including brussels sprouts, broad beans, carrots and baby turnips, came with a delectable truffle cream adorned with generous slivers of Périgord black diamond. Only desserts from the trolley were disappointingly mediocre—both apple strudel and almond and pear tart belonged to a second-rate pâtissier. There is a reasonable choice of wines by the glass and a plump wine list not wholly dedicated to French classics with a respectable number of contemporary producers from further afield. Book well ahead for a privileged view of the Thames and the Millennium wheel. Set lunch £29.50; set dinner Mon.-Thurs. £39.50, Fri.-Sat. £44.50

> **Ratings** are based solely on the restaurant's cuisine. We do not take into account the atmosphere, décor or service; these are commented on in the review.

Simpson's-In-The-Strand Grand Divan

TRADITIONAL BRITISH   **12/20**
100 STRAND, WC2
020-7836 9112, FAX 020-7836 1381
Breakfast Mon.-Fri. 7am-11am, Lunch &
Dinner daily. ££
U: Covent Garden/Embankment.

A ☎

At an age exceeding 150 years, Simpson's Grand Divan could be excused for moving slowly. But it doesn't. As soon as beef on the bone was liberated, the famous silver trolleys (not to be confused with Zimmer frames) were loaded with whole ribs of Aberdeen Angus beef. Ancient curmudgeons might complain that it is not invariably cut as razor thin as it used to be, and may, or may not, regret that cabbage is now an optional vegetable, not a compulsory penance. Other roasts offered à la carte or as daily specials include lamb, suckling pig, duck, capon and game in season, while Thursday's special is boiled salted silverside, brisket and tongue with dumplings and stuffed cabbage—possibly a distant English relative of Italian bollito misto. Starters such as oysters, smoked salmon or excellent cream of lobster soup also fly the national flag. More traditional still are savouries and puddings such as treacle tart with custard or plum crumble tart with clotted cream. All this in a room which recalls the splendours of a gentleman's club, with discreet alcoves for politicians and captains of industry and long tables in the centre for the hordes of tourists. Wines are mainly classical French, well suited to the cooking. Set 2-course lunch and to 7pm £14.50, 3 courses £17.75.

TOTTENHAM COURT ROAD

Bertorelli's Café Italian

ITALIAN   **11/20**
19 CHARLOTTE ST, W1
020-7636 4174, FAX 020-7467 8902
Lunch Mon.-Fri., Dinner Mon.-Sat. ££
U: Goodge St.

A ☎

Arranged around the stairwell, all the first floor restaurant is visible, although some areas are psychologically separated by glass partitions. More solid walls are painted a warm terra cotta. The clientele represents all ages and assorted occupations. Service is oddly confused. While generally amiable, it may be as stretched as the intervals between courses. The cooking is also variable with first-class starters such as the freshest flavoured minestrone or a warm salad harmonising squid, chorizo, chickpeas, baby red chard, black olive and onion salsa. Pastas, too, are excellent, although precisely cooked rigatoni, chicken livers, roast red onions, tomatoes and chilli cheese lacked the last mentioned. Such omissions are not uncommon in menus which list every ingredient in each dish. Main dishes are clumsy, trying to cover lack of cooking skills with extraordinarily large portions. We conclude that the busy downstairs café might be the most successful part of the operation. Here the menu includes the same antipasti and pasta as upstairs, together with pizzas ranging from the classic Margherita or Mediterranean, to smoked salmon or smoked chicken variations. The Italian wines are carefully chosen mostly at under £20, with light house wines from Verona at £9.95.

Also at 44a Floral St, Covent Garden at Tower Bridge, WC2, 020-7836 3969.

The Birdcage

FRENCH/THAI   **13/20**   ♟
110 WHITFIELD ST, W1
020-7323 9655, FAX 020-7323 9616
Lunch Mon.-Fri., Dinner Mon.-Sat. ££
U: Goodge St.

A ☎ 🏃

Unexpected Bohemian exoticia in the heart of Fitzrovia, Michael von Hruska's theatrically decorated jewel of a restaurant filled with global artefacts serves idiosyncratic fusion cuisine with a strong SouthEast Asian slant reflecting his previous position at I-Thai at The Hempel. Dishes are opulently described and presented, but tastes don't necessarily match up to the almost illegible purple prose of the menu. The inventive bread basket is extraordinairly good. Successful dishes include a tom yam soup, Thai-spiced coconut chicken with couscous and cinnamon lamb with cèpes, but the truly adventurous can try myrtle shark risotto with cumin marscapone. Delicious, visually mesmerising ice concoctions for dessert. The origami-style wine list is presented in a gilded birdcage. Service can be unpredictable—even downright eccentric. Set 2-

course lunch £19.75, 3 courses £26.50; set 2-course dinner £28, 3 courses £36.50.

Pied-à-Terre

FRENCH   15/20   🍴🍴
34 CHARLOTTE ST, W1
020-7636 1178, FAX 020-7916 1171
Lunch Mon.-Fri., Dinner Mon.-Sat. £££
U: Goodge St.

🅰 ☎

The abrupt departure of Tom Aikens from Pied-a-Terre was a shock to one and all. But his sous chef, Shane Osborn, has taken over the reins with remarkable aplomb. Although it is still early, and the menu remains almost identical, there seems to be a definite lightening of the more complex manoeuvres of his predecessor. At a recent lunch, a boudin of guinea fowl with a nicely crunchy green bean and asparagus salad and foie gras roulade was masterly, showing that the new hand can use luxury ingredients with as much assurance as before, while a roasted scallops with onion purée, shallot emulsion and caramelised baby onions (from the more expensive 2-course £39.50 menu) was meltingly sweet. Sole fillets came lightly poached in a Champagne velouté with asparagus, oysters and caviar—a £7 supplement to the £9.50 menu, but well worth the extra. Roasted pork fillet with stuffed trotter and braised pork belly with celeriac purée was suitably rich. The restaurant is pleasant—a long, light room. The wine list is good and suggestions from the sommelier are invariably apt without pushing you into spending more than you might like; service is remarkably fresh and young for such a serious place. Set 2-course lunch £19.50; set 3-course dinner £39.50.

Spoon+ at Sanderson

INTERNATIONAL   11/20
SANDERSON, 50 BERNERS ST, W1, 020-7300 1444
Breakfast, Lunch & Dinner daily 7am-11.30pm. ££££
U: Oxford Circus/Tottenham Court Rd.

🅰 ☎

Every year there is always at least one new restaurant that is hyped way beyond its ability to satisfy expectations, with an elitism that makes it intensely fashionable—and Spoon+ at Sanderson is the current emperor's new clothes. It's not a bad restaurant, but it is fantastically overpriced (cappuccino costs £4.50—plus 15 percent service), and it's far too flawed to justify the hugely inflated costs. The French staff may have model good looks, but they're also blasé and service is painfully slow. The Starck-designed dining room and Long Bar are pretty enough, but the cooking just doesn't live up to the promise. Head chef Alain Ducasse's menu at Spoon+ unfortunately isn't the stuff that's won him great critical acclaim back home in France. This Spoon+ menu resembles his Paris bistro Spoon Food & Wine in that it's a mix-and-match mongrel of global dishes, sometimes put together for shock or novelty value. For example, you can mix iceberg lettuce with pickled eggplant and sautéed beef—but why would you want to? Stick to the more classically inspired French dishes (which are well-rendered, such as the frogs' leg soup), and to the desserts (which are excellent, such as the cheesecake or the 'chocolate pizza'). Like the dishes, the wine list is very expensive, largely because of hefty mark-ups.

Rasa Samudra

INDIAN/SEAFOOD/VEGETARIAN 13/20   🍴
5 CHARLOTTE ST, W1, 020 7637 0222
Lunch & Dinner Mon.-Sat.
U: Tottenham Court Rd.

[VISA] [MasterCard] 🔶 ☎

This is a real first which reflects the growing diversity and authenticity of London's Indian food offerings, and the Capital's diners-out have reacted with enthusiasm. Now that it's open it seems such an obviously winning idea to highlight Indian seafood, or, more correctly, Keralan seafood as this is one of Das Sreedharan's trio of restaurants. Although Charlotte Street is full of restaurants, this stands out in more ways than one. Starting from the shocking pink exterior (a group trademark colour), to the dominating cool sea blues and greens downstairs in several small rooms, to the dramatic reappearance of hot pink upstairs, this restaurant provides living colour for the palate as well. Everything that swims or scuttles across the sea is offered here—Samudra means sea in Tamil. So you can start with the Keralan bouillabaisse called rasam—a medley of prawn, crab, mussel and squid swimming in sour rice water and move on to lemon sole with tamarind, pomfret with Indian shallots, crab in coconut milk or whole lobster with lemon rice and beetroot curry. Service is charming and wines are well-selected. Set meals: vegetarian £22.50, seafood £30.

TOWER BRIDGE

Blue Print Café

MODERN BRITISH   13/20   ♟

DESIGN MUSEUM, BUTLERS WHARF, SE1
020-7378 7031, FAX 020-7357 8810
Lunch daily, Dinner Mon.-Sat. ££
U: Tower Hill.

🅰 ☎ 📷

The view of the river is stunning, provided
you are sitting on the now glassed-in balcony
or very near it; otherwise this low-ceilinged
room can be a little claustrophobic. At night,
Tower Bridge is visible, floodlit in all its glory.
The menu follows a Cal-Ital theme, with
much use made of the chargrill and attention
to detail, particularly in the sourcing of ingredients. An early summer starter might include
a good selection of leaves along with broad
beans; risottos and pastas are good, squid ink
in the former of just the right intensity. Main
courses have included a perfectly cooked rump
of beef; cod dressed with mussels and served
with aioli, and a generous hunk of turbot
accompanied by an aniseed-enriched fennel
purée. Desserts tend toward the traditional:
gooseberry, lemon or almond tart, ice creams
and something chocolatey, truffle cake perhaps, delicate and rich, or petit pot au chocolate, gloriously intense. Service can be clumsy
and inattentive; the wine list is to the point,
but holds no surprises.

Butlers Wharf Chop House

MODERN BRITISH   12/20

BUTLERS WHARF BUILDING, 36E SHAD THAMES, SE1
020-7403 3403, FAX 020-7403 3414
Lunch Sun.-Fri., Dinner Mon.-Sat. £££
U: Tower Hill.

🅰 ☎ 📷

Of all the Conran restaurants along this
stretch of the river, the Chop House is the
most informal, with plain wooden tables giving it a relaxed air. The theme is solidly
British, with all the best this island has to offer
given due care and consideration. The view of
Tower Bridge is as splendid as the next door
Le Pont de la Tour, yet here you can snack at
the bar, have a substantial but quick one-
course meal, or go the whole hog, so to speak,
and spend hours over several courses.
Ingredients tend to speak for themselves:
smoked salmon, oysters, carrot soup or maybe

chicken livers on toast at lunch while in the
evening the chicken livers are fashioned into a
terrine and a salad might join the list. Mains
run from the likes of sausage and mash with
onion gravy; lamb chops with watercress and
chips, or straight roast beef, with lashings of
gravy and Yorkshire puddings. Spit roasts are
popular, and grills come in various shapes and
sizes. Roast monkfish comes with fennel and
leeks, while lobster is simply grilled and served
with garlic butter. Desserts maintain the
British theme: burnt cream, bread-and-butter
pudding. The wine list has a rather British
tone to it, in keeping with the theme, claret
being particularly emphasised. Service is slick
and professional. Set 2-course lunch £19.75, 3
courses £21.75.

Le Pont de la Tour

FRENCH   14/20   ♟

36D SHAD THAMES, BUTLERS WHARF, SE1
020-7403 8403, FAX 0171-403 0267
Lunch Sun.-Fri., Dinner daily. ££££
U: Tower Hill.

🅰 ☎ 📷

There is an element of style and sophistication as you glide through the bar (above average snack menu) and into this elegant dining
room with windows looking out on to the
Thames and floodlit Tower Bridge, for the
lucky few. The theme is Anglo-French, with
the best from both sides of the Channel championed. Dover sole, simply grilled; beef with
béarnaise; or rump of lamb with haricot beans.
Inspiration creeps in from further afield in
dishes like ravioli with pumpkin and ricotta,
but on the whole the tried and tested are
served up adequately well. Desserts follow the
crème brûlée route with success. Criticism is
raised at the extra charge for vegetables which
can add to the already steep prices, although
excellent value is to be had outside prime-time
on the prix fixe menu. Tables are rather too
tightly packed for some and service is brisk to
the point of indifference. The same cannot be
said for the sommeliers, whose knowledge and
enthusiasm can be infectious. Choose carefully, either from the full or abridged wine list.
Set 3-course lunch Mon.-Fri. £28.50; set 3-
course dinner 6pm-6.45pm & 10.30pm-
11.30pm £19.50.

Tentazioni

ITALIAN   14/20

MILL ST, LLOYD'S WHARF, SE1
020-7237 1100
Lunch Tues.-Fri., Dinner Mon.-Sat. ££
U: Tower Hill.

True to the restaurant's name, temptations here start with bread and olive oil and continue to post-prandial grappa or the delicately pear-flavoured distillato. The classic Italian discipline of using seasonal ingredients is strictly observed, both in the five-course Menu Degustazione (£35) and in the à la carte with six choices in each course. Autumnal favourites include crema di ceci (cream of tender whole chickpeas and crab-stuffed tortelli); red mullet with artichokes alla Romana and crisp herb-flavoured polenta; and saddle of rabbit stuffed with sun-dried tomatoes and aubergine on spinach with roast potatoes. Among desserts was pannacotta with grappa and fruits of the forest; and a peak of Italian gastronomy for many of its devotees, cheese with fruit—more precisely Parmesan with pears and walnuts. The lunch menu at £15 for two courses, £19 for three, is a simplified version of dinner. Service is the optimal Italian, friendly and enthusiastic yet sophisticated. The restaurant has been redecorated in restful stone colours. In the all-Italian list, good house wines are £12.50 and there are nine by the glass, as well as, yes, very tempting dessert wines. Set 2-course lunch £15, 3 courses £19; set 5-course dinner £35.

VICTORIA

Boisdale

SCOTTISH   14/20

15 ECCLESTON ST, SW1, 020-7730 6922
FAX 020-7730 0548
Lunch Mon.-Fri., Dinner Mon.-Sat. £££
U: Victoria.

The menu proudly claims beef, lamb, game, salmon and shellfish sourced direct from Scotland, and also notes that 'we have no microwave'. Instead they make macrowaves with mostly traditional dishes, although foie gras, or avocado, goat cheese and pancetta salad acknowledge the wider world. Haggis which deserves its acclaim by Burns as 'great chieftain o' the puddin' race', stars in a two-course £12.90 menu, with a vegetable soup and a noggin of whisky for £1. A note encourages switching between the carte and the £16.90 two-course menu, perhaps including smoked venison salad, or Orkney salmon gravad lax, and homely main dishes from homemade sausages, fishcakes with spinach, crème fraîche and chives, to sirloin steak béarnaise. A la carte offerings include potted lobster, grilled scallops with fennel and mussels, and oysters, which oddly are Irish. Daily specials include game, fish or offal. Haggis reappears as a savoury, while raspberry cranachan with 16-year-old malt whisky is a tempting dessert. The long, many splendoured wine list is supplemented by hundreds of malt whiskies, cocktails and cigars, a major feature in the Macdonald bar. The main feature of the décor, which is not obtrusively Scottish, is the collection of paintings and prints covering every subject and period. Set meals £12.90, £17.45.

Quilon

INDIAN   13/20

CROWNE PLAZA ST. JAMES'S
41 BUCKINGHAM GATE, SW1, 020-7821 1899
Lunch Mon.-Fri., Dinner Mon.-Sat. ££
U: Victoria

It's rare for waiters to steer diners off certain dishes as we experienced at Quilon, owned by Taj International Hotels and masterminded by Bombay Brasserie's Adi Modi, so such lukewarm endorsement among staff is surprising. The culinary theme is the coastal cooking of southern India with Chef Aylur V. Sriram formerly of The Taj Hotel in Bangalore. The menu scores on unusual sophisticated extras: raita-like okra with yoghurt and cumin; rasam (a spicy tamarind-sour broth served mid-course) and outstanding appams (lacey rice flour pancakes), but elsewhere execution is hit and miss. Among starters, Malabar potato roast had an appearance distressingly similiar to chicken nuggets and tasted as bland, though lime-marinated partridge stood up well to an intricate roast Marsala. Aleppy fish curry with coconut, chilli and raw mango gravy had an unpleasant sourness; chargrilled trout with fenugreek, lime, chilli and tumeric had more finesse, but a crispier skin better impregnated with spices would transform the dish. Good desserts include bibinca (a nutmeg-infused layered pancake dish). The saffron and blue colour scheme, evocative of the subcontinent, gives the dining space a contemporary edge; and restrained prices on wines well matched to the spiced menu suggest Quilon is here to stay. Set 2-course lunch £12.50, 3 courses £15.95.

For a complete guide to our **restaurant ranking system,** see "About the Reviews" in the introduction to the Restaurants chapter.

WANDSWORTH

Chez Bruce

FRENCH   16/20   🍴🍴
2 BELLEVUE RD, SW17, 020-8672 0114
FAX 020-8767 6648
Lunch daily, Dinner Mon.-Sat. ££
Rail: Wandsworth Common.

[A] [MasterCard] [Diners Club International] ☎

This room on the edge of Wandsworth Common is both warm and intimate—a shame, really, it doesn't have more of a view. Closely packed tables sit under a vaulted ceiling, the fixed-price menu ensuring a packed house most of the time. Service is relaxed and efficient, a perfect backdrop to serious, French-inspired cooking which is long on robust flavours, short on hype, and delivers with a punch. An assiette of charcuterie for example, came laden with homemade pâté and partfaits, chutneys and pickles, making the odd slice of bought-in salami of the highest quality in perfect company. A well-balanced terrine of smoked and cured fish comes with a perfectly balanced relish of beetroot and horseradish, while fried sardines come crisp as anything with a piquant caper mayonnaise. Main courses might be rump of lamb with couscous, merguez and hummus; or with a potato galette sarladaise. Fish is also deftly handled, a prime chunk of thick cod with olive oil-infused mashed potato, or halibut with herb-infused noodles. The cheese board is

notably stunning, while deserts are impressive: ice cream slowly dissolving over a chocolate pudding, or a light and delicately balanced clafoutis of plum, along with stalwarts like crème brûlée or tart Tatin all well up to the mark. The wine list is a model of restraint and excess, the buyer deciding on the field of activity, but whichever end of the scale you wish to play, there is a tightly focused something-for-everyone approach. Set 3-course lunch Mon.-Sat. £21.50, Sun. £23.50; set 3-course dinner £27.50.

WILLESDEN

Sabras

INDIAN/VEGETARIAN   16/20   🍴🍴
263 WILLESDEN HIGH RD, NW10, 020-8459 0340
Dinner Tues.-Sun. £
U: Dollis Hill.

[A] ☎

Sabras remains a simple spot, but now looks neater with its framed pictures and newspaper cuttings on plain white walls. Tables have black tops; chairs are more comfortable. But Mrs Desai's cooking is unchanged, or marginally better than before. The menu no longer lists dishes varying according to the day of the week, and because only main vegetable, cheese and lentil 'curries' are prepared in advance, time must be allowed for other dishes to arrive at table. They include Mumbai (formerly Bombay) beach snacks—kachori, a crushed pea 'rissole'; patra (yam leaves rolled, steamed and sliced before frying), and crackling crisp onion bhajiyas. Bel poori and sev-poori puffs explode on the tongue while spectacular dosas—south Indian pancakes, plain or variously stuffed, appeal equally to eyes and palate. Main dishes offer a wide range of ingredients and textures; all are packed with spicy flavours, but few are chilli-hot. Kasmiri pulau rice is another visual delight with its pink pomegranate pearl garnish. Finish with kulfi ice cream or shrikhand, (sweet yoghurt with saffron, cardomom, and pistachios); or a sweet stuffed baked chapati. There are Indian beers and a short wine list, while subtly spiced and salted lassi is exceptionally well made. Set dinner £6.50-£15.50.

Sarkhel's

INDIAN　　　　16/20　

199 REPLINGHAM RD, SOUTHFIELDS, SW18
020-8870 1483
Lunch Sun., Dinner Tues.-Sun. £
U: Southfields.

For lovers of real Indian food, it is definitely worth a special trek to Southfields, near Wimbledon, because the eponymous chef/owner, Udit Sarkhel, is arguably the finest traditional Indian chef in the UK, trained by the Taj Group across India. The restaurant won the Carlton (television) award for Best Indian restaurant in 1999 and has received widespread critical and popular acclaim, so book in advance. It has just gone through an expansion—Udit and his wife, Veronica (who runs the front of house), got tired to turning away up to 200 customers a night—so the restaurant is comfortably smart. And what delights await you. You might start with king prawns peri peri, flash-fried with onion, chilli, tomato and just enough richly spiced peri peri sauce to make the tastebuds tingle. Or go for the soft shell crabs, crisply fried in gram-flour batter to contrast with the succulent crabmeat underneath. Alternatively, ask if there are any cold pickled lamb chops—a frequent off-menu special that regulars always request. Moving along, do try the dum ka biryani, properly cooked in a sealed pot—moist, subtly perfumed and utterly lip-smacking. Just like the lamb chops, the lamb shank is another off-menu winner, cooked slowly with Ayurvedic spices in a gravy enriched by marrow. The runaway favourite veg dish is the palak pakodi curry, spinach fritters floating in turmeric and curry leaf-scented yoghurt gravy. Service is warm and friendly, wines have been given serious consideration.

GAYOT

on the *Internet*

Visit Gayot online at www.gayot.com for the latest travel, food and wine news, including information on hotels, worldwide events for gourmets and wine tasting notes. In cooperation with AOL's Digital City, Gayot also presents the latest dining reviews and restaurant news in more than 60 U.S. cities.

We welcome your questions and comments at our e-mail address:

gayots@aol.com

   AOL Keyword: GAYOT

QUICK BITES

CONTENTS

CAFÉS & ETHNIC RESTAURANTS .104
    ARCHWAY 104
    BANKSIDE 104
    BATTERSEA 104
    BAYSWATER 105
    BETHNAL GREEN 106
    BLOOMSBURY 106
    CAMDEN TOWN 107
    CHALK FARM 109
    CHELSEA 110
    CHINATOWN 111
    CHISWICK 112
    THE CITY 112
    CLAPHAM 114
    CLERKENWELL 114
    COVENT GARDEN 115
    DOCKLANDS 118
    EUSTON 119
    FINCHLEY 119
    FULHAM 119
    HACKNEY 120
    HAMPSTEAD 121
    ISLINGTON 121
    KENSAL GREEN 123
    KENSINGTON 123
    KILBURN 124
    KNIGHTSBRIDGE 124

    MAIDA VALE 125
    MARYLEBONE 126
    MAYFAIR 128
    NOTTING HILL GATE 129
    OXFORD CIRCUS 132
    PARSON'S GREEN 132
    PICCADILLY CIRCUS 132
    PRIMROSE HILL 134
    ST. JOHN'S WOOD 136
    SHEPHERD'S BUSH 137
    SHOREDITCH 138
    SOHO 138
    SOUTHALL 142
    SOUTH BANK 142
    SOUTH KENSINGTON 142
    STOKE NEWINGTON 143
    TOOTING 143
    TOTTENHAM COURT ROAD . .143
    TRAFALGAR SQUARE 144
    VAUXHALL 144
    VICTORIA 144
    WANDSWORTH 145
    WESTMINSTER 145
    WIMBLEDON 146
IN-STORE RESTAURANTS 146
TEA TIME 147

Spots where you can grab a bite and a drink at reasonable prices. Categorized by geographic area.

CAFÉS & ETHNIC RESTAURANTS

ARCHWAY

Paris-London Café

FRENCH
5 JUNCTION RD, N19, 020-7561 0330
Open Mon.-Sat. 9am-11pm, Sun. 9am-10.30pm.
U: Archway.

The restaurant may have moved to larger premises next door and added a huge mural on one wall of a typical Parisian scene, but the Gallic atmosphere and food remain pretty much the same. It's a cheerful place, much loved by regulars who still comprise medical staff from the nearby Whittington Hospital and Highgate residents on a cheap night out, all enjoying the very French bistro fare, which presumably reminds them of French holidays. Here you'll find all the frogs' legs, well garlicked snails and monkfish with green peppercorn sauce you could ever want. Don't expect top cooking; do expect friendly service and a respite from the surrounding fast food shops. A 3-course set meal is £9.95, or indulge in 5 courses for £17.95.

St. Johns

PUB/INTERNATIONAL
91 JUNCTION RD, N19, 020-7272 1587
Open Mon.-Sat. 11am-11pm, Sun. noon-10.30pm.
U: Archway.

Shock horror! A gastro-pub near Archway. But wait, this might once have been a pretty dire area for restaurants, but it's steadily, if a little slowly, going upmarket (helped by projects like the private housing created in the former church nearby). But even without the local gentrification, St. Johns would succeed, as it combines serious food with a friendly, local pub atmosphere. On our Sunday visit, at one end a grandfather was playing chess with his grandson while waiting for their traditional roast with Yorkshire pudding and all the trim-

mings (£10). On the other side, a media type was writing a script and diving into his seafood risotto with tomatoes, chillies and garlic (£9). The most expensive item on the chalkboard menu was pan-fried John Dory with mash, spinach, clam, leek and parsley sauce for £14. The menu covers all cuisines with equal gusto.

BANKSIDE

Cantina Vinopolis

MODERN EUROPEAN
1 BANK END, SE1
020-7940 8333, FAX 020-7940 8302
Lunch daily, Dinner Mon.-Sat.
U: London Bridge/Blackfriars/Mansion House.

Cantina Vinopolis is the cavernous-ceilinged restaurant attached to Vinopolis, the vinously themed attraction the appeal of which is dubious enough to make the Dome look like a crowd-pleaser. It occupies part of the brick-lined vaults, behind a small wine bar, and the wine list is as great an attraction as the food. All 200-plus odd bins are available by the glass, and they're generally accessibly priced. It has more breadth than depth. The emphasis is on modern production and, among more unusual choices, there are a number of Greek wines. Food is robust and Mediterranean: warm salad of chorizo, new potatoes and haricot beans; tomato risotto fritters with rocket and Parmesan; roast cod with courgette, onion and pepper ragoût. Provides scope for unpretentious food- and wine- matching at around £20 per person.

BATTERSEA

Beyoglu

TURKISH
50 BATTERSEA PARK RD, SW11, 020-7627 2052
Dinner nightly.
Rail: Battersea Park.

This friendly local goes from strength to strength, much to the delight of Battersea residents. The interior is bright with plenty of that pretty shade of blue that reminds you of the Mediterranean. The menu is predictable, but the sourcing and execution of such staples as taramasalata, combination platter of karisik izgara and kebabs lift this restaurant above the norm. Grilled meats are tender and cooked well; salads served with them are delightfully fresh. The meze is always a good bet. The set dinner for a minimum of two at £10.50 per person is good value.

Duke of Cambridge

PUB/MODERN BRITISH
228 BATTERSEA BRIDGE RD, SW11
020-7223 5662
Pub: Mon.-Sat. 11am-11pm, Sun. noon-10.30pm. Lunch & Dinner daily.
Rail: Clapham Junction.

Here is a prize-winning, spacious gastro-pub with a comfortable country feel offering large sofas to lounge in alongside the obligatory stripped floors and antiquarian objets. Delicate chilled melon and mint soup, chargrilled swordsteak, rump of lamb with polenta, spinach and olives and superlative walnut tart are dishes to expect. Handy for post-Battersea Park dining.

Masons Arms

PUB/INTERNATIONAL
169 BATTERSEA PARK RD, SW8, 020-7622 2007
Lunch & Dinner daily.
Rail: Battersea Park.

A happy-go-lucky-local that follows the usual gastro-pub template (all that wood, dubious artwork and trendy young clientele), but with a nicely balanced menu that goes way beyond the usual bangers 'n' mash fare. Unfortunately, this comes at a price, which is undoubtedly high for this kind of establishment. Still, when the quality of cooking is as good as it is here (homemade ravioli filled with ricotta and butternut squash; chargrilled lamb and thyme burgers), you can't complain too much.

BAYSWATER

Bistro Daniel

FRENCH
26 SUSSEX PL, W2
020-7262 6073, FAX 020-7723 8395
Lunch Mon.-Fri., Dinner Mon.-Sat.
U: Lancaster Gate.

This small basement bistro-style restaurant under its big sister Amandier (see Restaurants)

offers good French cooking at a reasonable price. The menu is long, but simple starters like assiette of French charcuterie (£6.50) and crab-fish soup (£5.30) are well-sourced and prepared. Main dishes run from braised knuckle of lamb with confits, garlic and thyme jus (£8.50), to pan-fried lemon sole simply meuniere and garnished with capers and lemon (£11.50). The 2-course lunch menu is a steal at £9.95 (3 courses £12.95). The room is a little gloomy, but tries hard with bright furnishings; the staff's welcome is truly genuine.

The Café at Phillips

CAFÉ
PHILLIPS BAYSWATER, 10 SALEM RD, W2
020-7229 9090
Open Mon.-Sat. 9am-4.30pm, Sun. 11am-4.30pm.
U: Bayswater.

Their avowed aim is to 'demystify the auction business', and the refurbishment of Phillips' second London saleroom does a good job. Part of the demystifying process is to include a coffee bar that serves lunch in the gift shop where you can take a cappuccino as a break from the heady (and often nerve wracking), business of bidding. You're not that removed, there's a glass wall between you and the adjoining sale room. Lot numbers are relayed over the PA so you don't miss the action while snacking on sandwiches and salads.

Maison Bouquillon

CAFÉ
41 MOSCOW RD, W2, 020-7727 4897
Open Mon.-Sat. 8am-8.30pm, Sun.8am-7.30pm.
U: Bayswater.
No cards. No bookings.
Small, friendly patisserie with a Middle European clientele and feel due to its proximity to the Russian Orthodox church, which was built for the large Russian population that once lived here and gave its name to the area. Now it's completely cosmopolitan, and, for its superlative cakes and pastries worth that extra walk if you're in or around Queensway. The small room, free provided newspapers and café-style tables and chairs make it a welcoming place.

BETHNAL GREEN

S & R Kelly

BRITISH/PIE & MASH
284 BETHNAL GREEN RD, E2, 020-7739 8676
Open Mon.-Thurs. 10am-2.30pm, Fri. 10am-6.30pm, Sat. 10am-4pm.
No underground nearby.
No cards. No bookings.

A traditional piece of the old East End survives at S & R Kelly, where the pie and mash or eels and mash show you what this particularly British dish and longtime staple of working-class life is like. Go on, try the eels. For other such establishments, try G Kelly, 414 Bethnal Green Rd, E2, 020-7739 3606, and G Kelly, 526 Roman Rd, E3, 020-8980 3165, both in the traditional East End of London. They all also do takeaway in case you want to sample this delicacy in the privacy of your own room.

BLOOMSBURY

Coffee Gallery

CAFÉ
23 MUSEUM ST, WC1, 020-7436 0455
Open Mon.-Fri. 8am-5.30pm, Sat. 10am-5.30pm, Sun. noon-5.30pm.
U: Tottenham Court Rd.

Excellent, small, family-managed café serves locals and visitors alike. Standouts: baking from Clarke's; fantastic coffee; freshly made, good salads; imaginative sandwiches, pastas and soups like butternut squash, or potato, celery, borlotti beans and broccoli. Changing artwork on the walls (all for sale) makes for a bright jolly décor. This is certainly the best café in the area around the British Museum, which is full of small cafés. The owners also run the Table Café at the two Habitat shops, and the small café at the Courtauld, but for us this is their best venue.

Townhouse Brasserie

INTERNATIONAL
24 COPTIC ST, WC1
020-7636 2731, FAX 020-7580 1028
Open Mon.-Fri. noon-11.30pm, Sat. 3pm-11.30pm, Sun. noon-8pm.
U: Tottenham Court Rd.

A long thin room widening out at both ends makes for a slightly uncomfortable space, but the décor is pretty—light wood and colourful prints. The cooking is crackingly good at this small, family-run restaurant just off New Oxford Street. It's an excellent lunchtime spot for British Museum visitors and a good dinner venue for anyone staying in the area. The menu travels around the world. There are starters like potted duck with nutmeg and rosemary served with crusty country bread and simple crostini with fresh tomatoes, basil and olive oil. The kitchen staff's way with fish is distinguished such as a baked sea bream with a warm ginger, basil and tomato salsa. There is a 'casse-croûte', or light meal menu, allowing for excellent midday snacking on such choices as chargrilled duck breasts on Chinese-style vegetables at £6.95. Prices overall are very good indeed for this high level of cooking—the brasserie is well worth seeking out.

Wagamama

JAPANESE
4 STREATHAM ST, WC1
020-7323 9223, WWW.WAGAMAMA.COM
Open Mon.-Sat. noon-11pm, Sun. 12.30pm-10.30pm.
U: Tottenham Court Rd.

The original that started the fashion for cheap and cheerful, but stylish Japanese noodle bars packs in businessmen, people up from the country, visitors and students. Guests sit at long wooden benches and tables while the servers with mini computers take orders. Portions are generous, and tastes cater to the adventurous. The teppan-fried yaki soba is the best; freshly 'squeezed-to-order' juices are great. This, the original Wagamama, is a great fuelling stop for the British Museum, while the others are good for shopping forays, and prices are reasonable. It's all very reasonable (dishes around £5-£8) and great fun.

Also in **Soho** at 10A Lexington St, W1, 020-7292 0990; the **West End** at 101a

Wigmore St, 020-7409 0111; **Camden Town** at 11 Jamestown Rd, NW1, 020-7428 0800; **Kensington** at 24-30 Kensington High St, W8, 020-376 1717.

CAMDEN TOWN

Andy's Taverna

GREEK CYPRIOT
81-81A BAYHAM ST, NW1, 020-7485 9718
Lunch Mon.-Fri., Dinner Mon.-Sat.
U: Camden Town/Mornington Crescent.

Along with Daphne and Nontas, this is a long established Greek restaurant in this heavily Greek Cypriot area, Andy's has quietly expanded over the years. The loyal clientele come for well-cooked classics—light, creamy tarama, zingy tzatziki, kebabs, which retain their flavour and texture and wonderful sticky desserts which threaten to pull out your fillings. Andy's has the added advantage of a delightful back yard. Prices, as in all the Camden Town Greek restaurants, are good value, with a £6.50 3-course lunch and set 3-course dinner at £9.95.

Asakusa

JAPANESE
266 EVERSHOLT ST, NW1, 020-7388 8533
Dinner Mon.-Sat.
U: Mornington Crescent/Camden Town.

Amazingly low prices (set dinners from £5.20), excellent food, sociable customers, and mama-san's warm welcome. What more can you ask of an authentic Japanese restaurant? Décor? It's best forgotten; but, if you can't read the seasonal items on the wall posters, you can enjoy the calligraphy. Sushi from a tiny bar is good, but lacks the inspiration of other dishes. As well as familiar dishes, you might find tender cuttlefish tempura; kazunoko (diced herring roe in savoury broth); duck with satoimo (taro with ginger in a concentrated sauce); sunamono (the Japanese equivalent of a ceviche) of 'sardines' small as whitebait.

Camden Brasserie

FRENCH
216 CAMDEN HIGH ST, NW1, 020-7482 2114
Lunch & Dinner daily.
U: Camden Town.

A model in how a successful, local restaurant should be run, the Camden Brasserie continues to keep its clientele very happy indeed. The restaurant is a long room, with prized tables in the window (though the local Camden life outside can be a touch on the rough side), an open fireplace and open grill. The décor fits the concept perfectly—white-plastered walls featuring photographs, wood floor, wood tables and chairs and exposed brick walls. Food is satisfying, still best from the flaming grill with dishes like spicy Italian sausages with potato mash and onion marmalade or superb beef with béarnaise sauce. Frites are excellent, but are now counted as a separate item. Also good are seared tuna tataki with salad and Scottish salmon with sorrel sauce. Good, short wine list and friendly service—the owners are still here all the time.

Café Delancey

FRENCH
3 DELANCEY ST, NW1, 020-7387 1985
Open Mon.-Sat. 9am-11.30pm, Sun. 9am-10pm.
U: Camden Town/Mornington Crescent.

Slightly off Camden Town High Street, Café Delancey caters as much for regulars who know its location as for visitors who find it by chance. Consequently, it has a local feel that fits in well with its successful French brasserie theme—wood floors, wood chairs and blackboards proclaiming specials. The menu changes weekly and does not contain GM ingredients. There is a delicious warm seafood salad with truffle oil, baby spinach and mixed herbs garnished with crab, mussels and langoustine; and La Salade Delancey, a warm pasta salad with roasted peppers, fresh herbs, Parmesan, olives, capers and tomatoes. There's plenty to satisfy traditional meat-eaters too, like entrecôte au poivre vert. Coffee and pastries are good, too.

The Crown & Goose

PUB/MODERN BRITISH
100 ARLINGTON RD, NW1, 020-7485 2342
Lunch & Dinner daily.
No cards.

Slightly rough-and-ready with its retro, but not chic, décor, the Crown and Goose suits an area to which the young flock in the evenings. Friendly staff work hard and cheerfully, serving generous portions of mix-and-match cuisine like salmon, dill and potato cakes in a sharp watercress sauce; pasta; and vegetarian options. Daily specials supplement the short main menu and are more elaborate like chicken supreme in coriander sauce, or the Sunday roast. Bar snacks include ciabatta roll with either mozzarella with fried onions or chicken with Dijon mustard. The music gets loud in the evenings. Not a place for the retiring.

Daphne

GREEK CYPRIOT
83 BAYHAM ST, NW1, 020-7267 7322
Lunch & Dinner Mon.-Sat.
U: Camden Town/Mornington Crescent.

There's pretty décor, which avoids the usual garishly coloured pictures and bottles around the place. The roof terrace for outdoor dining, ensures that a large regular clientele keeps coming back for more of the freshly prepared and carefully cooked Greek classics. From tarama to kebabs to dishes like chargrilled sword fish. The dishes are distinguished. The charcoal grills are always good. Specials are written on the menu board. Friendly service and a great value 2-course lunch at £5.75, plus meat meze selection at £10.75 and fish selection at £15.50.

Mango Room

CARIBBEAN
10 KENTISH TOWN RD, NW1, 020-7428 5065
Lunch Tues.-Sun., Dinner nightly.
U: Camden Town.

Located in trendy Camden, the Mango Room is a relaxed and welcoming restaurant with brick walls hung with paintings. It has been serving traditional and modern Caribbean cooking to a varied clientele for a couple of years. The secret of the restaurant's success is attitude—it has figured out what it wants to be and does it well. The menu offers familiar Caribbean dishes like jerk chicken (£8) and spicy curry coat with hot pepper, scallions, garlic and pimento (£7.80). There are exciting dishes for vegetarians like baked baby squash with courgettes, plantain, red beans, spring onions, cashew nuts and rice (£8.50). Fish lovers can entertain themselves with Creole snapper with mango and green pepper sauce (£8.50), grilled barracuda with coconut sauce (£8.50) or yellow fin tuna steak (£10.50). The Mango Room is not cheap, but it serves food in an atmosphere that brings a warm smile to your face.

Marine Ices

ITALIAN/ICE CREAM PARLOUR
8 HAVERSTOCK HILL, NW3, 020-7482 9000
Open Mon.-Sat. 10.30am-11pm, Sun. 11am-10pm.
U: Chalk Farm.

One of north London's favourite institutions, Marine Ices was producing the best Italian ice cream in London way before that delicious food became so sexy. There are lots of varieties, including cassata, bombes and sundaes as well as single scoops. They do serve solid Italian fare, but it's the ice cream that is famous. You can also stand at the window and get ice creams to take away, particularly popular on warm weekends when the nearby Camden Lock shopping area gets a bit too crowded.

Sauce Bar Organic Diner

BRASSERIE
214 CAMDEN HIGH ST, NW1, 020-7482 0777
Open Mon.-Sat. noon-11pm, Sun. noon-4pm.
U: Camden Town/Mornington Crescent.

In the fight for purity, it's sometimes overlooked that organic food includes meat and, therefore, is not just for vegetarians. From the same owners as the excellent Camden Brasserie upstairs (see above), Sauce features dishes like saffron lamb with peppers and onions over polenta (£10.95), rib-eye steak with braised shallots (£11.50) and farm pork sausages (£8.95). The vegetarian selections include sesame-glazed tofu with stir-fried vegetables and brown rice (£8.50), burger with lentils, nuts and seeds (£6.50) and salads with a topping of your choice. The children have their own menu and the restaurant even stocks Baby Organics brand baby food. The drink list includes organic wines, beers and freshly squeezed fruit and vegetable juices. If you don't want to go wholly healthy there are nonorganic cocktails.

Yima

MOROCCAN
95 PARKWAY, LONDON, NW1, 020-7267 1097
Open Mon.-Sat. 11am-9.30pm.
U: Camden Town.
No cards. No bookings.

This family-run Moroccan tearoom has a pleasantly coloured cosy downstairs lounge with comfortable cushions to recall warm Moroccan hospitality. The small upstairs room looks more like an average sandwich shop, except for the red fez lampshades and food counter offering North African delicacies. All the classic Moroccan dishes are available on the short, but varied menu: spicy harira soup (£2.95), Zaalouk salad with aubergines (£2.80), b'stilla (chicken baked in almonds and cinnamon pie, £6.90), tagine either with lamb or chicken (£6.50) or vegetables (£5.50). A good dessert is seffae (sweet couscous with cinnamon and nuts). All this should be washed down with a pot of strong, refreshing mint tea. Yima serves a special vegetarian lunch for £5 and has takeaway.

CHALK FARM

Thanh Binh

VIETNAMESE
14 CHALK FARM RD, NW1 020-7267 9820
Lunch & Dinner Tues.-Sat., Sun. noon-10pm.
U: Chalk Farm.

Not withstanding their famous pigs, the Vietnamese are as much beef-eaters as the British, although the favoured Sunday dinner is soup not roast. Here pho bo is all it should be. The large bowl of al dente rice noodles in soup comes with sliced beef, beanshoots, coriander and mint. The beef is sliced thick enough to stay tender and tasty when immersed in the soup. Other dishes are variations of Chinese favourites: spring rolls, king prawn cakes, bean curd and much else. This pleasant owner-run ethnic-eating house is ideally located for shoppers at Camden Lock across the road.

Eating in Museums & Galleries

There are some pretty good restaurants and cafes now attached to London's museums and galleries. Here is the pick of the bunch:

Museum of Garden History, housed in the old church of St. Mary-at-Lambeth, Lambeth Palace Rd, SE1, 020-7261 1891, has a small café serving snacks. It's very attractive in summer when you can take your tea and cakes outside to the tiny churchyard with its 17th century herb garden.

The Sainsbury Wing Brasserie at the *National Gallery*, Trafalgar Sq, WC2, 020-7839 3321, looks out onto the Square.

The *National Portrait Gallery*, St. Martin's Pl, WC2, 020-7306 0055, now has a serious place, **The Portrait Restaurant & Bar**, with top catering from Searcy's who are expanding all over the place at the moment, and stunning views of Nelson and across Whitehall to the river.

At the **Royal Academy of Arts**, Burlington House, Piccadilly, W1, 020-7287 0752, the restaurant is usually full of ladies up from the country, 'doing' the latest exhibition. It can get very crowded, but it's a relaxed place and the food is good.

Shakespeare's Globe, Bankside, SE1, 020-7902 1500 offers a restaurant and separate café overlooking the Thames.

Somerset House has **The Admiralty**, a new restaurant from Oliver Peyton, plus cafés overlooking the Thames.

The restaurant at **Tate Britain**, Millbank, SW1, 020-7887 8877 goes in and out of favour and fashion. Whatever the state of the kitchen, it's a wonderful room with Rex Whistler's famous mural on one wall and a wine list which is well worth perusing.

Tate Modern, Bankside, SE1, 020-7887 8000, has three cafés, including one overlooking the river.

The Victoria & Albert Museum, Cromwell Rd, SW7, 020-7938 8500 has a well run restaurant.

CHELSEA

Admiral Codrington

PUB/MODERN EUROPEAN
17 MOSSOP ST, SW3, 020-7581 0005
Lunch & Dinner daily
U: South Kensington.

The Admiral Codrington has had a dramatic makeover and is now barely recognisable as the former, famously 'Hooray Henry' hangout of old. The circular bar has been stripped of its overhanging glass shelf and dividing partitions making it an island in an open space. This is now a modern gastro-pub-style bar with a smart restaurant in the rear designed by interior decorator Nina Campbell, who has bordered it with a row of banquettes and topped it with a retractable glass roof. The food is minimal and Modern British, though the sausages are Toulouse.

Big Easy

AMERICAN
332-334 KING'S RD, SW3, 020-7352 4071
Open Mon.-Sat. noon-11.30pm, Sun. noon-10.30pm.
U: Sloane Sq.

If it's themed restaurants you're after, go for the Big Easy. Subtle it ain't, but fun it is, with wooden décor (everywhere), kitsch on the walls in the form of notices and U.S. license plates, big portions and a great welcome. Chargrilling figures heavily; seafood comes in all forms; there are a wide range of sauces and dips. Their famous snow crab claws come with a mustard-honey dip (£11.95). Main dishes range from burgers with all the trimmings (£4.95-£6.95), to seafood baskets and surf-and-turf variations (£8-£13). The set lunch at two courses for £4.95 (Monday-Friday noon to 5pm) is great value.

Bluebird Café

CAFÉ
350 KING'S RD, SW3, 020-7559 1000
Open Mon.-Sat. 8am-11pm, Sun. noon-6pm.
U: Sloane Sq.

The café is in on side of the fabulous Conran development of the old Bluebird Garage in the King's Road and spills its seats onto the forecourt in sunny weather. The old pumps have been replaced by a long and abundant fruit and vegetable display with flaming torches at either end to counter the village market look. The café serves a wide range of light snacks and meals, plus very good coffee, all very modish and all highly suitable for the Chelsea designer families who have adopted the place as their own. Expect to want for tables in the summer.

Builder's Arms

PUB/MODERN EUROPEAN
13 BRITTEN ST, SW3
020-7349 9040, FAX 020-7351 3181
Open daily Lunch & Dinner.
U: Sloane Sq/South Kensington.

Taken over by the group that also runs the Queens in Primrose Hill and the Duke of Cambridge in Battersea (see above), the Builder's Arms has been subjected to the same gentrification process and is now a full member of the gastro-pub scene. Pleasant interior, with sisal on the floor, wooden chairs plus some upholstered in coloured dogtooth material and books on the drawing room-style shelves put the diner in a relaxed mood. Cooking is good Modern British with dishes like duck carpaccio with chilli couscous and plum sauce (£6.95 as starter, £8.95 as a main), pork sausages and mash and shallot gravy and entrecôte steak. Great wine list, the right kind of beers and pleasant staff.

Chelsea Ram

PUB/INTERNATIONAL
32 BURNABY ST, SW10, 020-7351 4008
Lunch & Dinner daily.
U: None nearby.

Invariably packed with Chelsea locals (booking is essential at weekends), this glorified gastro-pub has de rigeur stripped floorboards and dusty antiquarian books. The cheery Antipodian staff happily serve unpretentious Modern British dishes: confit of salmon with bacon and thyme potatoes; good pasta; roasts and brunch-style dishes everyday; plus first-rate puds like chocolate and hazelnut terrine with sour cream. Wines by the glass and decent beers, too.

The Garden Restaurant
General Trading Company

CAFÉ

144 SLOANE ST, SW1, 020-7730 2001
*Open Mon.-Tues. & Thurs.-Fri. 9.30am-6pm,
Wed. 9.30am-7pm, Sat. 9.30am-5pm.
U: Sloane Sq.*

Packed with Chelsea Sloane Rangers, discussing, it seems, either their wedding plans or their divorce settlements, the Garden Restaurant fits seamlessly into the GTC/Chelsea scene. The food is good, with hot dishes served at lunchtime, plus excellent salads, and outstanding cakes and coffee at other times of the day. There's a garden in the back, which is wonderful on a warm summer's day; inside it tends to get very crowded.

La Delizia

ITALIAN PIZZERIA

FARMERS MARKET, SYDNEY ST, SW3
020-7351 6701
*Open Mon.-Sat. 12.30pm-11.30pm.
U: Sloane Sq.*

This is a smart, glass-fronted, marble-tabled pizzeria handy for the King's Road. There are more than adequate pizzas with good salami and roasted vegetable toppings and well-prepared baked pasta dishes. Longish waits and distracted staff can sour the experience. Salads and puddings of the ice cream variety are mediocre.

Tiger Lil's

ASIAN

500 KING'S RD, SW10
020-7376 5003; WWW.TIGERLILS.COM.
*Open Mon.-Fri. Dinner, Sat.-Sun. noon-
midnight.
U: Sloane Sq.*

You can't miss the flaming woks as you go past any of the branches of Tiger Lil's; they flare up dramatically every few minutes. This is one of the decent semi self-service places in London; you help yourself from a large selection of meat, fish and vegetables, then get it cooked with flavours like garlic and chilli. It can taste metallic; but it's fun so no one seems to mind, and multiple returns to the counter

can be good value at £11.50 per person and £5.50 for children. Drinks come via servers. It's a good place for families.

Also in **Clapham** at 16a Clapham Common South Side, SW4, 020-7720 5433; in **Islington** at 270 Upper St, N1, 020-7226 1118.

CHINATOWN

London Hong Kong

CHINESE

6-7 LISLE ST, WC2
020-7287 0352, FAX 020-7287 9028
*Open daily noon-11.30pm, dim sum daily noon-
5pm.
U: Leicester Sq.*

This bright place offers something rare in the area—charming service. Good efforts, sometimes successful, are made to translate the Chinese special dim menu. That may include sumai with three seasonal garnishes such as New Year black moss, black mushroom and dried oyster or steamed pork balls with pork tongue. Standard dim sum such as noodle rolls, turnip paste and harkau—(prawn dumplings) are at least acceptable, which suggests they are homemade and not brought in. The best drink with these modestly priced snacks is soft full-bodied po-li tea.

Tokyo Diner

JAPANESE

2 NEWPORT PL, WC, 020-7287 8777
*Open daily noon-midnight.
U: Leicester Sq.*

No bookings.

London's first cheap Japanese is still one of the best and cheapest. Donburi dishes on rice are from £3.90 (that is for Japanese omelette) and miso soup and fruit are included until 5.30pm. Bento lunch boxes start at £9.90. Tips are not accepted. At such prices something has to give, and, dear reader, it may be you—if you are long or large—for tables and chairs are minuscule. But they fit the authentic décor and layout of this warren of tiny rooms on a Soho corner.

> The **prices** in this guide
> reflect what establishments were
> charging at press time.

CHISWICK

The Chiswick

PUB/MODERN BRITISH
131 CHISWICK HIGH RD, W4, 020-8994 6887
Lunch Sun.-Fri., Dinner Mon.-Sat.

It helps to like lilac at this minimalist Modern British eatery with few decorative frills, hard acoustics and uncomfortably small tables. Kate and Adam Robinson (of Brackenbury success), have taken over the excellent no-fuss food (impressively, the menu changes twice daily), so the unforgiving décor doesn't grate. Starters often include brilliant charcuterie/terrines with homemade chutney followed by robust, fresh-flavoured roasted halibut with red wine sauce or calves liver and melted onions. Good cheeses, and trad puds with delicious ice creams finish the meal. The 'one-hour lunch menu' (also 7pm-8pm) is excellent value at two courses for £9.50 and three for £12.95. Service is keen yet informal and there are plenty of modestly priced wines.

Springbok Café

SOUTH AFRICAN
42 DEVONSHIRE RD, W4, 020-8742 3149
Dinner Mon.-Sat.
U: Turnham Green.

How could any food lover resist the chance to try zebra carpaccio? There is always a good assortment of exotic game. A recent menu included springbok loin fillet wrapped in guinea fowl served on a pumpkin and sage risotto and chargrilled warthog with dandelion leaves, Cape apricot chutney and roast red onion. There is a whole range of exotic vegetables. A three-course meal for two is around £35. Good South African wines, friendly and relaxed ambience.

THE CITY

Arkansas Café

AMERICAN
UNIT 12, OLD SPITALFIELDS MARKET, E1
020-7377 6999
Lunch Sun.-Fri.
U: Liverpool St.

Pretty basic décor, but the canvas chairs and plastic plates should not put you off, for this is one of the best places in London for barbecued meat. Bubba Helberg and his wife have been pleasing City traders, establishment figures and grateful North American visitors for years with steaks that Bubba chooses for texture and taste from nearby Smithfield Market. American and Irish beef come mainly in juicy, tender rib-eye steaks (around £12); also making spectacular appearances are lamb, excellent sausages and chicken sandwiches. Wonderful homemade sauce accompanies it all. Short wine list, long beer list and hefty U.S. puddings (£2). Sit inside or move outside and watch the hubbub of the market.

Bengal Trader

INDIAN
1 PARLIAMENT COURT, 44 ARTILLERY LANE, E1
020-7375 0072; WWW.BENGALRESTAURANTS.CO.UK
Lunch & Dinner Mon.-Fri.
U: Liverpool St.

A good alternative to Brick Lane and conveniently closer to Liverpool Street, this restaurant is bright and breezy and the upstairs neon-lit bar is a good place for quick Indian snacks like tikkas and Indian street foods. The dining room suffers slightly from downstairsitis, but is bright and the walls are hung with interesting modern Bengali art. Try the Bangladeshi specialties like arakan gosht (lamb with small hot chillies and shatkora, which are wild Bengali lemons. Good Goan crab curry. Surprisingly good wine list.

Moshi Moshi Sushi

JAPANESE/SUSHI BAR
UNIT 24, LIVERPOOL ST STATION, EC2
020-7247 3227
Open Mon.-Fri. 11am-9pm.
U: Liverpool St.

This was the first of London's many kaiten bars with prices denoted by the colours of dishes picked off the conveyor belt. It remains among the best and least expensive, while its location overlooking the rail tracks is an added attraction. At tables away from the counter you can enjoy set 'geta' meals. The geta is a board, fancifully likened to a wooden slipper. On it you may have various combinations of sashimi, hand-rolled sushi or nigiri and vegetarian selections, too. Tea is free, but there is a

50p cover charge, presumably for lubricating the conveyor belt.

Also in **Docklands** at Level 2, Cabot Place East, Canary Wharf, E14, 020-7512 9911; in **The City** at 7-8 Limeburner Lane, EC4, 020-7248 1808.

New Tayyab

PAKISTANI
83 FIELDGATE ST, E1, 020-7247 9543
Dinner nightly 5pm-midnight.
U: Whitechapel.
No cards.

The 'Old' Tayyab, almost next door and open for lunch, is as basic an eating house as any in London. New Tayyab, a little less basic, serves dinner while Tayyab's itself is the pastry shop in between. New Tayyab offers remarkably economically priced Pakistani punjabi chicken, mutton or fish as kebabs or from the tandoor. The many curries are called karahis here, which is also the name of the metal pots in which they arrive. There are daily specials and intriguing vegetarian curries: for a new taste, try lentils with bitter melon. Prices are reasonable—around £20 for two. It's closed for the month of Ramadan. No alcohol is served, but you can bring your own. Otherwise drink salted, sweet or fruit lassi.

The Place Below

VEGETARIAN
ST. MARY-LE-BOW CHURCH, EC2, 020-7329 0789
Open Mon.-Fri. 7.30am-2.30pm.
U: Bank/St. Paul's.

Tucked below St. Mary-le-Bow Church is this delightful unlicensed (for liquor) and very smart vegetarian and vegan café. It serves generous portions of imaginative food with Mediterranean and Asian spicing to City traders who presumably appreciate a healthy side to their otherwise unhealthily hectic existences. There is both take-away and eat in; plus unlimited tea and coffee for £1. This is a popular place, so avoid the main lunchtime hours.

> The **prices** in this guide reflect what establishments were charging at press time.

Saigon Times

VIETNAMESE
20-22 LEADENHALL MARKET, EC3
020-7621 0022, FAX 020-7623 0028
Breakfast, Lunch & Dinner Mon.-Fri.
U: Bank/Monument.
No cards.

The Saigon Times occupies ground floor and basement premises right in the middle of Leadenhall Market (a wonderful Victorian edifice). The restaurant is owned by the company that also owns the classic French Luc's Restaurant on the first floor and a French influence is evident on this menu, too, notably a French section which includes grilled lamb chop with chickpea purée and supreme of chicken. The basement restaurant gets crowded at lunchtimes, but seldom in the evenings, although this is gradually changing as The City generally, and this area in particular, is also being transformed.

Tao

CHINESE
11 BOW LANE, EC4
020-7248 5833, FAX 020-7329 1446
Lunch & Dinner Mon.-Fri. Bar: Mon-Fri.
11.45am-11pm.
U: Mansion House/Bank/St. Paul's.

Chic and cheerful City Chinese with an Italian front-of-house and management. Confused? How about the décor, which is the last word in black-and-white Japanese minimalism, or the chef Bruce Warwick, who's English. The menu echoes the multinational mix: potted king prawns with fennel and vanilla; crackling pork with bok choy and apple crisps. The ground floor bar buzzes nicely come evening time. There's a set menu at lunch from £18.50; bar platters are from £6.50.

Terminus

BRASSERIE
GREAT EASTERN HOTEL, LIVERPOOL ST, EC2
020-7618 7400, FAX 020-7618 7401
Open daily 6.30am-midnight.
U: Liverpool St.

A

The casual restaurant in the newly refurbished Great Eastern Hotel, Terminus brings more Conran style to the city. The restaurant runs along the façade of the hotel with a black granite bar running the length of the room at the back. You can sit in the window seats watching the City go by from 6.30am when the traders start with continental breakfasts. The pace quickens at lunch where a simple menu offers a universal appeal. Main dishes of Thai seafood green curry with steamed rice for those dealing with Asia at £11.50; roast belly pork and roast root vegetables with pomme purée for a closer-to-home feel at £13.50. One of the few places staying open until midnight, it's invariably packed.

CLAPHAM

Eco Pizzeria

ITALIAN
162 CLAPHAM HIGH ST, SW4, 020-7978 1108
Lunch & Dinner daily.
U: Clapham Common.

A ☎

Eco was one of the first fashionable restaurants in Clapham, an area which has since sprouted several hip eateries catering for young professionals moving to the area. The pizzas are undeniably good, but be warned that dining here isn't a relaxing experience—the noise levels can be very high (not helped by loud dance music) and turnover is swift (staff seem to want you in and out fast). Make sure you book—and be prepared to wait for a table even if you do.

Gastro

FRENCH
67 VENN ST, SW4, 020-7627 0222
Open daily 8am-midnight.
U: Clapham Common.
No cards. No bookings.

For a local French neighbourhood restaurant in London, you can't do much better than Gastro. The no-booking policy means that it's advantageous to arrive early. If you're a party of four, you are allowed to sit at the front, opposite the bar, but any other number is likely to be sat in the back around the communal table. If the restaurant is busy, you may be relegated to an ugly corridor. The food is unreconstructed French—moules, poulet au cidre, fromages and good pâtisserie. You might be unlucky, but, generally, the food lives up to the place, remarkable given the size of the open-plan kitchen.

The Sequel

PUB/PACIFIC RIM
VENN ST, SW4, 020-7622 4222
Dinner nightly, Brunch Sat.-Sun.
U: Clapham Common.

A

This newcomer has upped the stakes in otherwise cosy Clapham. It's right next to the Clapham Picture House cinema and consequently attracts the same young, trendy clientele. The interior is expensively designed with suede seats, steel fittings and a large TV screen silently playing films. The menu is Global-Gone-Mad: Peruvian sauces are mixed with Thai curries and European fish. This could all end in tears, but the unusual dishes usually work well. Prices are fair, and service is generally good too. Worth a look, as long as it's not too busy—which may be often.

CLERKENWELL

Al's Café & Bar

CAFÉ
11-13 EXMOUTH MARKET, EC1, 020-7837 4821
Open Mon.-Tues. 8am-midnight, Wed.-Fri. 8am-2am, Sat. 10am-2am, Sun. 10am-11pm.
U: Angel.

Al's manages to look like a cross between a trendy, though somewhat rough and ready, U.S. bar in Greenwich village and a worker's café, albeit a superior one. It serves a pretty wide menu, too, from English breakfasts to Mexican tortillas. A happy blend of good beers on draught and cups of tea sum up the place, which caters to just about everybody. It's a useful pit stop after an evening of culture at nearby Sadler's Wells.

Clark & Sons

PIE & MASH
46 EXMOUTH MARKET, EC1, 020-7837 1974
Open Mon.-Thurs. 10.30am-4pm, Fri. 10.30am-5.30pm, Sat. 10.30am-5pm.
U: Farringdon.
No cards. No bookings.

The area might be up-and-coming, but Clark's recalls the old days of Farringdon, when the market prospered and this was a distinctly working-class kind of place. With all the newer restaurants opening to feed the trendies, Clark's remains an old-fashioned spot, serving crisp-pastried meat pies and mash, and, for those newcomers who wish to be genuinely adventurous, eels and mash.

Bleeding Heart

MODERN EUROPEAN
BLEEDING HEART YARD, OFF GREVILL ST, EC1
020-7242 8238, FAX 020-7831 1402
Lunch & Dinner Mon.-Fri.
U: Chancery Lane/Farringdon.

City suits dominate this series of interconnecting basement rooms (there is a bistro on the first floor) where wooden floors, brick walls and linen tablecloths lend a curiously timeless air. The excellent and reasonably priced wine list, much of it decanted, may be the starting point, but is closely followed by a solid menu that feature lots of fish and meat. Starters might be a salad with lardons, smoked salmon or scallops; while main courses range from fishcakes to rump of lamb. Cheese is worth saving space for, as much for itself as an opportunity to plunder the wine list once again. Service is curt, yet efficient. Prices are around £4.50 for starters, £8 up for mains.

Eagle

PUB/MEDITERRANEAN
159 FARRINGDON RD, EC1, 020-7837 1353
Bar: Mon.-Sat. noon-11pm. Lunch daily,
Dinner Mon.-Sat.
U: Farringdon.

No cards.

Often cited as London's first true 'gastropub', the Eagle still manages to get the balance right between a place to drink and a place to eat. The Iberian-influenced dishes are wholesome and good. The beers include real ales and summery white beer. The Eagle is absurdly busy and you're well advised to get their early if you want a seat. In the last year, the service has also deteriorated markedly and complaints about rudeness are common. Still, it is worth it to see the role model that launched a hundred chalkboard-menu gastropubs. Starters are around £4-£5, main dishes hover around £8.

Medina's

ITALIAN
10 CLERKENWELL GREEN, EC1, 020-7490 4041
Lunch & Dinner Mon.-Sat.
U: Farringdon.

This large, attractive restaurant on Clerkenwell Green opened just as the area got into its stride as one of the hippest places in London, a dubious award since the trendiness has moved eastwards and into Hoxton and Shoreditch. But Medina's has gone on serving good, traditional pizzas at reasonable prices (around £6), satisfying the local business community as well as clubbers and ravers from the nearby warehouse buildings.

Tinseltown

AMERICAN
44-46 ST. JOHN ST, EC1, 020-7689 2424
Open 24 hours daily.
U: Farringdon.

A basement diner, sign posted from the main road, offers all-night noshing in an area where the clubbers gather in force. It's licensed for liquor until midnight; otherwise, stay on for coffee, milkshakes, burgers and pastas.

COVENT GARDEN

Browns Restaurant & Bar

BRASSERIE
82-84 ST. MARTIN'S LANE, WC2, 020-7497 5050
Open Mon.-Thurs. noon-midnight,
Fri.-Sat. noon-12.30am, Sun. noon-11pm.
U: Leicester Sq.

Browns may not be individually owned any more, but the brand remains much the same. After all, if it works, why change it? Success partly comes from the different venues—each of the Browns are converted from unusual purpose-built buildings. The one on Maddox Street was a tailor's; this one was an old courthouse. Cream-coloured walls, wooden chairs and marble-topped tables help the atmosphere and much greenery in the form of huge plants, as does the friendly and professional service. The food is pretty good and the choice wide in standard brasserie style (traditional fish

Juice, The Latest Thing

Have the Brits gotten healthier, or is this just a marketing triumph? Whatever the reason, get refreshed in London at any of the excellent juice bars that are springing up. And the good news is that most of them open early—around 8am.

Creative Juice Bar at Waterstone's, 2nd Floor, 203-206 Piccadilly, W1, 020-7851 2447. On the same floor as the children's book department, you get a good selection of juices and smoothies as well as teas, coffees and pastries. And it's open to 11pm. **Crussh** in The City at 48 Cornhill, EC3, 020-7626 2175, and in Mayfair at Curzon St, W1, offers all the usual suspects, plus their popular Lovejuice, made out of strawberries, bananas, peaches and orange juice. **Farmacia** at 169 Drury Lane, WC2, 020-7831 0830, and **Farmacia II** at 42 Short's Gardens, WC2, 020-7836 3179, may be best known for their general nutritional and beauty items (see *Shopping*), but it also delivers great juices, including the Power Boost which has fruit and carrot as well as ginseng, schisandra and damiana. Check them out on www.farmacia.co.uk.

Fluid at 206 Fulham Rd, SW10, 020-7352 4372, and in Notting Hill at 13 Elgin Crescent, W11, 020-7229 4871, has some pretty ace combinations which you can also take away by the litre. **Juicemoose** at 4 Upper James St, W1, 020-7734 9773, 13 Coopers Row, EC3, 020-7488 9008, and in Holmes Place Health Club at The Plaza Centre, 120 Oxford St, W1, 020-7637 8028, aims to cure your ailments or feed your hypochondria. There are juices for colds and flus, for detoxifying as well as milk shakes for the already healthy. And finally, **Squeeze** at 27 Kensington High St, W8, 020-7376 9786, delivers the usual squeezed goods as well as frozen yoghurts and snacks like sandwiches and soups, many of them organic.

soup, moules marinières, pastas, salads, venison steak); and children get a great deal.

Also in **Mayfair** at 47 Maddox St, W1, 020-7491 4565; **Chelsea** at 114 Draycott Ave, SW3, 020-7584 5359; **Barnes** at 201 Castelnau, SW13, 020-8748 4486.

Café des Amis du Vin

FRENCH BRASSERIE
11-14 HANOVER PL, WC2
020-7379 3444, FAX 020-7379 9124
Open Mon.-Sat. 11.30am-11.30pm.
U: Covent Garden.

Although one of the oldest wine bars in London has recently had a makeover to bring it kicking and screaming into the twenty-first century, it will take a while to recreate the patina of nicotine stains that have adorned it for twenty years. On the ground floor, is a so-so restaurant with an ambitious menu, popular with Covent Garden businessmen and tourists. Downstairs, you'll find the fun, unpretentious wine bar patronised by much of the chorus and orchestra from the neighbouring Opera House. Have a glass of wine, one of their weekly specials and a helping of really good cheese. If you can, sit at the bar—the tables, stools and banquettes are miserably uncomfortable.

Chez Gérard at the Opera Terrace

FRENCH
FIRST FLOOR, OPERA TERRACE
CENTRAL MARKET, WC2
020-7379 0666, FAX 020-7497 9060
Lunch & Dinner daily.
U: Covent Garden.

Steak and frites and Chez Gérard have become inseparable, and, why not, they are both very good. Steaks come in a whole range of cuts and prices and are cooked just as you want them. Frites are thin and tasty. You can have other French dishes—lamb brochettes, fish soup, and so on, but steak frites is the raison d'être of the chain. All the restaurants in the group are well designed, but the Covent Garden branch wins with its long bar—inevitably heaving in the evenings—and its superb outdoor terrace looking out at the new Royal Opera House. There's a good value lunch and pre-theatre menu at £12.95 and a 3-course dinner menu at £15.95.

Also in **Mayfair** at 31 Dover St, W1, 020-7499 8171; **The City** at 119 Chancery Ln, WC2, 020-7405 0290; **The City** at 64 Bishopsgate, EC2, 020-7588 1200; **The City** at 14 Trinity Sq, EC3, 020-7480 5500; **Fitzrovia** at 8 Charlotte St, WC1, 020-7636 4975; **Clerkenwell** at 84 Roseberry Ave, EC1, 020-7833 1515; **Knightsbridge** at 3 Yeomans Row, SW3, 020-7581 8377; **Waterloo** at The White House, Belvedere Rd, SE1, 020-72902 8470.

Corney & Barrow

WINE BAR
116 ST. MARTIN'S LANE, WC2, 020-7655 9800
Open Mon.-Sat. 11am-11.15pm, Sun. noon-4pm.
U: Leicester Sq.

A

Corney & Barrow is a long-established wine merchant with a string of modern, stylish bars in the City. Its West End flagship opposite the English National Opera replaces the candles, dark wood panelling and cobwebs usually associated with wine bars with cool stone, leather and teak. There's much hustle and bustle on the ground floor—as people rendezvous after work and reassemble after the shows—and not enough places to sit. Mid-evening it's easier to study at leisure the marvellous list of 60 wines, 35 of which are sold by the glass. They are also helpfully grouped by grape variety and feature jaunty tasting notes. Downstairs is a clubby Champagne bar, while upstairs (and often unnoticed by the crowd below) an informal restaurant serves robust and flavoursome European food at reasonable prices—making it worth seeking out for a West-End meal without the usual outlay. A menu that changes monthly matches wines to four courses for £47, although the setting is not as plush as you'd expect for a wine-led dinner.
Branches throughout London.

Telephone numbers in England have eleven digits, beginning with a zero. The initial zero must be omitted if you are calling England from abroad. Within the country, dial the entire eleven digits.

Food for Thought

VEGETARIAN
31 NEAL ST, WC2, 020-7836 0239
Breakfast, Lunch & Dinner Mon-Sat.
Lunch Sun.
U: Covent Garden.

No cards.

Queues spilling out onto the pavement confirm this tiny vegetarian basement restaurant's continuing popularity. Great salads here at around £2.50, or go for a hot dish like lentil and vegetable bake. There's an equally crowded take-away bar upstairs.

Monmouth Coffee House

CAFÉ
27 MONMOUTH ST, WC2, 020-7836 5272
Open Mon.-Sat. 9am-6pm
U: Covent Garden/Tottenham Court Rd.

Monmouth is a simple old coffeehouse selling great and varied coffees in the front, and with tables for tasting in the back. All accompanied by excellent baking—croissants, pain au chocolat, etc., making this a good, casual meeting place.

Neal's Yard Bakery & Tearoom

CAFÉ
6 NEAL'S YARD, WC2, 020-7836 5199
Open Mon.-Sat 9.30am-4.30pm.
U: Covent Garden.

No cards.

Delicious salads, great breads baked on the premises and good soups make this small converted warehouse a treat in Neal's Yard. The area has become something of a food oasis with its many small cafés spilling out into the yard at all times of the year.

The Poetry Café

CAFÉ
22 BETTERTON ST, WC2, 020-7420 9888
WWW.POETRYSOC.COM
E-MAIL: EPOETRYSOC@DIAL.PIPEX.COM.
Open Mon.-Fri. 11am-11pm, Sat. 6.30pm-11pm.
U: Covent Garden.
No cards.

A delightful small café on the ground floor with wooden floors, large tables and chairs and black- and-white photographs of—yes, poets—on the walls. Salads, quiches and snacks like anchovy toasts (£3-£5). All that and the good puds makes this a good, peaceful stop. Events take place downstairs and you might find yourself reading your own works.

Prospect Grill

AMERICAN
4-6 GARRICK ST, WC2, 020-7379 0412
Lunch & Dinner Mon.-Fri., Sat. 11.45am-midnight
U: Covent Garden.

The outlook for this newcomer ought to be rosy. It has an assurance and simplicity that may not make it especially newsworthy, but do make it a slightly sombre, reliable and rewarding place to eat for a reasonable price. From a New York-like menu free of fashionable excesses, well-sourced ingredients get on with the job. Choose potted shrimps; rosemary and lemon free-range chicken with gratin dauphinoise and chocolate brownie with vanilla ice cream with fudge sauce for simple satisfaction. And put money on the burger being a contender for the title of best in the capital. The wine list is short and neat. Prospect Grill is a place that gets things right. This timeless, East Coast look, with individual table lamps, adds to its appeal as a rendezvous. (£20-£25 a head.)

Punjab

INDIAN
80-82 NEAL ST, WC2, 020-7836 9787
Lunch & Dinner daily.
U: Tottenham Court Rd.

The benevolent Mr. Maan presides over this delightful Indian restaurant at the north end of Covent Garden, established here since 1951. Forget the hot colours and jazzy décors of many of London's newer Indian places, Punjab remains a delightful old-fashioned outpost with its dark colours, fretwork wooden partitions and old photographs on the walls. Among the first to bring tandoori cooking to Britain, they still produce excellent marinated and tandoor meats and fish. But they've also introduced delightful specials: one of their great dishes is meat flavoured with pomegranate, and dishes that are pickled in special Punjabi spices, then cooked—as in acharri

gosht (pickled lamb) and acharri murgha (pickled chicken). But be warned—these dishes are not always available. All the cooking is carefully spiced, so individual flavours come through. This is a restaurant to put on your must-go list.

Sofra

TURKISH
36 TAVISTOCK ST, WC2, 020-7240 3773
Open daily noon-11.45pm.
U: Covent Garden.

A

Huseyin Ozer, founder of the Sofra chain, and the recently opened Ozer (see Restaurants), is a busy man, but he's often to be found here, in this two-storey, light and airy restaurant. The cooking, concentrating on classic Middle Eastern tastes, is generally good, though can sometimes disappoint. Best bets are the meze at £8.45 (called the 'Healthy Lunch'), which gives you the usual array of small dishes filling the table: humus and taramasalata, kisir, imam bayildi, tabouleh and a whole lot more. There is even a surprising Turkish wine list. Service can be chaotic, but the bottom line is that this friendly place is a godsend in Covent Garden.

Also in **Mayfair** at 18 Shepherd St, W1, 020-7495 3320; near **Oxford Street** at 1 St. Christopher's Pl, W1, 020-7224 4080; plus **Sofra Bistro**, 18 Shepherd Market, W1, 020-7493 5940.

DOCKLANDS

Yellow River Café

CHINESE
NORTH COLONNADE, 10 CABOT SQ
CANARY WHARF, E14
020-7715 9515, FAX 020-7715 9528
Open Mon.-Fri.: Bar noon-11pm, Café & Restaurant noon-9.30pm; Sat. Bar & Café noon-8pm.
DLR: Canary Wharf.

With a menu overseen by famed chef Ken Hom, this is—surprisingly—more Chinese than Malaysian or Singaporean. But that's a quibble. This is a well-thought and handsome operation. Entrance and bar/brasserie downstairs is bright (yellow and red, broken by neutral wood). The upstairs restaurant is in soothing neutrals with curtained alcoves for private parties. For starters, try Hong Kong salt-and-pepper prawns, steamed scallops with black bean sauce and double-boiled shark's fin soup. As an intermezzo, try spring onion and ginger lobster with noodles, Peking duck or tender abalone with Chinese mushrooms and broccoli. Sea bass is steamed with ginger, spring onion, soy and Chinese wine. Good wine list and service. A 3-course meal in the restaurant is around £25 per person; in the bar, around £15 per person.

Also in **Twickenham** at 33-35 London Rd, 020-8891 3611; in **Chiswick** at 12 Chiswick High Rd, 4, 020-8987 9791.

EUSTON

Diwana Bhel Poori House

INDIAN VEGETARIAN
121 DRUMMOND ST, NW1, 020-7387 5556
Open daily noon-11.30pm.
U: Euston.

This pioneer of Drummond Street's bhel poori houses has maintained its high standards over decades. South Indian vegetarian snacks such as bhel poori (puffed rice and crackers with various toppings and flavourings), dosais (sculpted pancakes usually filled with spicy potato mash) and vegetable curries seldom cost more than around £10 per head. The interior is basic, café-style and stuck in the varnished pine era, but this doesn't detract from the cheer engendered by low prices and good food. It's BYO alcohol.

Great Nepalese

INDIAN
48 EVERSHOLT ST, NW1, 020-7388 6737
Lunch & Dinner daily.
U: Euston.

Great in character, but no megagastrodome, this friendly restaurant seats about 50. It is a family business, owned and hosted by Gopal P Manandhar and his sons. Like the décor, which emphasises the Gurkha connection, and the chef, they are Nepalese, so although conventional curry-house dishes are offered, discriminating regulars choose that country's cuisine. Kalezo ra chyau is thinly sliced chicken liver with mushroom and onions; its subtle spicing is a reminder that Nepal borders both China and India. Other starters include

mamocha, Nepalese ravioli and black lentil pancakes. Dumba (mutton curry) is the signature main dish; and there are a dozen vegetarian options. Tandooris are enhanced by sensational mint chutney.

FINCHLEY

Two Brothers Fish Restaurant

BRITISH
297-303 REGENT'S PARK RD, N3, 020-8346 0469
Lunch & Dinner Tues.-Sat.
U: Finchley Central.

One brother is away for two years sailing round the world, presumably looking for new fish to fry. Meanwhile, this simple, spacious English eating-house offers incomparable fresh fish, fried in batter or matzo meal or grilled. Crisp, hand-cut chips, homemade tartare sauce and the best tomato ketchup are additional pleasures. Fish range from fishcakes via cod and skate, to Dover sole, while starters include English fish soup, moules marinières, or dressed crab. Monkfish or grilled sardines might be among the daily specials. Wines include crisp white and dry, fruity pink from the brothers' own Côtes-de-Duras property. You may have to wait for a table, but it's worth it.

FULHAM

The Atlas

PUB/MEDITERRANEAN
16 SEAGRAVE RD, SW6, 020-7385 9129
Lunch & Dinner daily.
U: West Brompton.

Run by a team who first met at the groundbreaking The Eagle in Farringdon, The Atlas is the quintessential London gastro-pub. Located in a rather far-flung spot on the edge of Fulham, it retains its pub ambience, but serves some of the best pub grub in the capital. The cooking reflects Mediterranean-Moorish-Iberian influences. Spicing is good and ingredients (as in pot-roasted partridge with tomato, pomegranates and parsley, £8.50) go well beyond the traditional pub menu. The beers are good, wine lovers are particularly well-catered for with the excellent wine list and prices are reasonable. A rarity.

Nayab

INDIAN
309 NEW KING'S RD, SW6, 020-7731 6993
Lunch & Dinner daily.
U: Parsons Green.

Vivid Indian colours and a warm welcome add to the pleasures of this excellent curry restaurant. Successful specialties include crisp baingan pakoras, aubergine roundels stuffed with cheese and herbs at £3.50; lamb kallia, a thickish, mild, tender lamb curry; and regional dishes from Mangalore, Hyderabad and Delhi. Tandooris include cheese, scallops, and monkfish. Those who love the 'old curry house favourites' are asked to choose any one of a dozen varieties—such as vindaloo, bhuna, dhansak, Madras—to be applied to chicken, lamb, prawns, monkfish and scallops. Main dishes run from £5.95 to £9.95. Finish with homemade creamy mango kulfi prepared by a local Pakistani housewife. Wines are well chosen to match the food.

Vingt-Quatre

INTERNATIONAL
325 FULHAM RD, SW10, 020-7376 7224
Open daily 24 hours.
U: South Kensington, then bus: No 14, or N14.

Owned by Longshot Ltd (which also owns the Admiral Codrington, see above), a company founded by Joel Cadbury, Vingt-Quatre has become quite the place for the Sloane Rangers who haunt the area. The décor is a pretty bizarre mix—providing no help at all to those attempting to clear up a hangover with the all-day breakfast (£7.75), which includes fried bread that great toxin sponge. Fishcakes, steak and fries, vegetarian salad and a drinks list which includes the infamous Mars Bar Vodka Shot complete the picture.

HACKNEY

F Cooke

BRITISH
9 BROADWAY MARKET, E8, 020-7254 6458
Open Mon.-Thurs. 10am-7pm, Sat. 10.30am-8pm.
Rail: Cambridge Heath.
No cards. No bookings.
If it's a genuine slice of London's culinary tradition you're after, this is the place to go.

The décor is authentic—green-and-white tiles, marble-topped tables and benches, but luckily the food is old-fashioned enough to keep the relentlessly increasing trendy crowd at bay. Try eels with mash for authenticity, or stick to the excellent pies which at around £2 with mash, are some of London's great bargains.

> **Telephone numbers** in England have eleven digits, beginning with a zero. The initial zero must be omitted if you are calling England from abroad. Within the country, dial the entire eleven digits.

Faulkener's

FISH & CHIPS
424 KINGSLAND RD, E8, 020-7254 6152
Lunch & Dinner Mon.-Fri., Sat. 11.30am-10pm, Sun. noon-9pm.
Rail: Dalston Kingsland.
No cards. No bookings.

All the trappings of a genuine local restaurant are here. It's a proper locale, quite smart in fact, with old photos, a tiled floor, a takeaway and a list of fish from reliable cod, to haddock, to Dover sole bought fresh from Billingsgate market. Started by Mr. Faulkener after he sold the Seashell in Lisson Grove (see below), Faulkner's does a good job of providing for both its neighbours and for those coming from the East End and lively Ridley Road Market (about ten minutes' walk away).

Shanghai

CHINESE
41 KINGSLAND HIGH ST, E8, 020-7254 2878
Lunch & Dinner daily.
Rail: Dalston Kingsland.

In the front room, once a typical old London eel and pie shop, choose from over a hundred, mostly conventional dishes at prices low even for this area. The lunch buffet is £4.90 Monday-Friday; £5.90 weekends. In the more spacious back room, enjoy a serious meal with cooking far surpassing our Quick Bite norm. A few Shanghai dishes are listed and aficionados of the style should request them prepared in their full pungency, rather

Cafés & Ethnic Restaurants - **Quick Bites**

than 'inoffensively for Westerners'. The highlight of our £15 per head feast was tai chi crab—the shell filled with the meat and scarlet coral, steamed with garlic and Chinese wine; the legs and claws deep-fried with salt and pepper giving an intriguingly smoky flavour.

HAMPSTEAD

Babe Ruth's

INTERNATIONAL
02 COMPLEX, FINCHLEY RD, NW3
020-7433 3388, FAX 020-7433 3432
Open Mon.-Sat. noon-11pm, Sun. noon-10.30pm.
U: Finchley Road.

Huge TV screens showing just about every sport, memorabilia of sporting greats and a bar and game table area make for a jolly atmosphere, particularly good for families with restless children. The menu is broad, from blackened swordfish to Philadelphia steak sandwich, jambalaya and chicken quesadillas, with plenty of Asian stir-frying and spices in evidence. This mix-and-match approach, probably not pleasing the purists, seems to go down well with the locals. Cocktails are great. The view from the curved floor-to-ceiling glass window offers continuous entertainment.

Also in **Wapping** at 172-176 The Highway, E1, 020-7481 8181.

Giraffe

BRASSERIE
46 ROSSLYN HILL, NW3, 020-7435 0343
Lunch & Dinner daily.
U: Hampstead.

Hampstead seems to be an area cursed with mediocre cafés, but Giraffe is an agreeable deviation from the norm. The brightly lit interior has chirpy staff who play world music CDs and serve global, vegetarian-oriented dishes at fair prices. You can just drop in for a fruit juice or coffee or have a full meal with wine. Prices are low, too, which is probably why Giraffe doesn't attract the conspicuously gilded youth that crowd every other café on Rosslyn Hill. The branch near Marylebone High Street follows the same formula, as does the new one in Islington.

Also in **Marylebone** at 6-8 Blandford St, W1, 020-7935 2833; **Islington** at 29/31 Essex Rd, N1, 020-7359 5999.

Halepi

GREEK
48-50 BELSIZE LN, NW3, 020-7431 5855
Lunch Wed.-Sat., Dinner Mon.-Sat.,
Sun. noon-11pm.
U: Belsize Park.

There are only a few good Greek restaurants in London, which makes Halepi even more of a find. It's in a quiet, residential part of north London, and has an interior that's stripped bare of Hellenic kitsch, allowing you to concentrate on the first-rate ingredients, simply but well-prepared. The classic dishes (taramasalata, Greek salad, spanakopitta) are fine examples, but go for the less obvious choices if you want a surprise. Maybe the broad beans cooked with onions and (inevitably) olive oil (goutsia, £2.75) or market-fresh fish are also good choices.

Also in **Bayswater** at 18 Leinster Terrace, W2, 020-7723 4097.

Louis Pâtisserie

CAFÉ
32 HEATH ST, NW3, 020-7435 9908
Open daily 9am-6pm.
U: Hampstead.
No cards.

Louis is a small tearoom at the back of the eponymous cake shop where you seem to be in Hampstead circa 1960. Small tables close together, leather seating along the walls and a waitress who brings you a tray of those great cakes in the window. Long may it last—while the rest of London changes to all those large, minimalist, designed places, Louis remains exactly the same.

ISLINGTON

Centuria

GASTRO PUB/MODERN EUROPEAN
100 ST. PAUL'S RD, N1, 020-7704 2345
Lunch Mon.-Fri., Sat. 12.30pm-11pm,
Sun. 12.30pm-10.30pm.
U: Highbury & Islington

This extremely popular dining room behind a modern pub that's all bold art and bare

121

boards is well placed to attract customers from Islington, Highbury and Stoke Newington. Not as cosy as some gastro-pubs, chefs in full view in the behind-the-counter kitchen rustle up a muscular Italian-inspired repertoire accompanied by pyrotechnic displays. After bread and olive oil, portions are enormous, and a rather free hand with the cream—in a sauce for pumpkin ravioli with sage, for example—make for a satisfying and filling full meal for around £20. Seared tuna, chicken or squid are also menu staples.

Duke of Cambridge

PUB/MODERN EUROPEAN
30 ST. PETER'S ST, N1, 020-7359 3066
Lunch & Dinner Mon.-Sat.
U: Angel.

'London's first organic pub' is the boast of this handsome Victorian conversion in Islington. Yep, that even includes the additive-free beers, such as Eco Warrior (£3) and Freedom lager (£2.70). There's a daily-changing blackboard menu from which you can order solid fare such as vegetable soup (cheekily priced up to £5) or main courses such as risottos and stews (under £10). You can even buy organic cigarettes (presumably so you can give yourself organic lung cancer). Prices here are on the high side overall, but the Islington locals don't seem to mind.

Japanese Canteen

JAPANESE
394 ST. JOHN ST, EC1, 020-7833 3222
Lunch & Dinner Mon.-Sat.
U: Angel

A minimalist fueling station offering simple refectory-style dining from a menu that covers all bases of fast Japanese, albeit somewhat Anglicised, food. There's not much finesse, and you'll find better sushi elsewhere, but the lunchtime donburi dishes in a box are great value at £3.95. Bento boxes—a tray with a main course of, say, tempura, chicken teriyaki or tuna steak, plus rice, seaweed salad and fruit with a little bowl of miso soup—offer a well-balanced, healthy and filling meal for £7.95. Service does not have the grace usually associated with Japanese restaurants.

Also in **Clerkenwell** at 19 Exmouth Market, EC1, 020-7833 3521; **Marylebone**

at 5 Thayer Street, W1, 020-7487 5505; **Notting Hill Gate** at 305 Portobello Road, W10, 020-8968 9988.

Pasha

TURKISH
301 UPPER ST, N1, 020-7226 1454
Lunch & Dinner Mon.-Fri., Sat.-Sun. noon-midnight.
U: Angel.

Though there are other more authentic Turkish restaurants nearby, this one is wildly popular with the more price-conscious denizens of Islington. As is typical of the region, the food is generously served and priced, which belie the smartness of the restaurant. Set menus are at £9.95 and a feast at £15.95; starters from the à la carte around £3-£4, mains £8-£10. We can vouch for the juicy tenderness of the incik (slow-cooked lamb on the bone with potatoes and rosemary-flavoured juices), and this and other main courses—of which, this being trendy Islington, there are several vegetarian choices—are very reasonably priced.

Upper Street Fish Shop

BRITISH
324 UPPER ST, N1, 020-7359 1401
Lunch Tues.-Sat., Dinner Mon.-Fri.
U: Angel.
No cards.

The quintessential British fish and chips restaurant, albeit with an Islington twist—how many other chip shops do people bring their own bottles of Champagne to? Like all the best seafood cookery, dishes are kept simple, though portions are unfeasibly large. The haddock and chips (£8.50) is large enough to worry Captain Ahab, so you probably will be hard-pressed to make it as far as the calorific puds such as treacle tart and custard (£3). If you fancy something a bit more—well, fancy—the lemon sole stuffed with scallops and crabmeat in cheese sauce (£9) is a winner. There's also a takeout counter.

White Onion

FRENCH
297 UPPER ST, N1
020-7359 3533, FAX 020-7359 3533
Lunch Sat.-Sun., Dinner nightly.
U: Angel

While its elder sister the Red Pepper in Maida Vale concentrates on pizza and pasta, the White Onion is somewhat upscale market in its approach. Crisp linen underscores the theme for largely Mediterranean dishes like guinea fowl with pancetta, grilled vegetables and salsa or steamed brill with a somewhat old-fashioned cream and wine sauce. Cooking is generally good, dishes delivering as promised. Service is efficient to the point of being intrusive. There's a Saturday set 2-course lunch at £12.50 and 3 courses £14.50, and on Sunday main meals are 2 courses for £15, 3 courses for £19.50.

KENSAL GREEN

William IV

PUB/INTERNATIONAL
786 HARROW RD, NW10, 020-8969 5944
Lunch & Dinner daily.
U: Kensal Green.

This rough and ready converted 1930s pub in increasingly trendy Kensel Rise has a bright yellow and green dining area, battered leather chesterfields and small, heated back terrace serves high quality food in hearty portions. The norm: squid with noodles, bok choy and mango salsa and chargrilled sardines on focaccia with humus and olives. Scrumptious puds include chocolate parfait with rich chocolate ice cream. Staff can be irritatingly laid-back so this is not a place to eat in a hurry.

KENSINGTON

Alounak

IRANIAN
10 RUSSELL GARDENS, W14, 020-7603 1130
Open daily noon-midnight.
U: Olympia

Skewered meats are the sine qua non of Persian cuisine: here the diced marinated fillets and minced lamb are always meltingly tender and options such as barbecued swordfish with herbs are especially fresh. Scoop it all up with traditional steamed rice and just-made bread. The attractive brick dining room buzzes—often with Iranians—surely a sign of authenticity. Expect to pay about £30 for two, and, as it's unlicensed, bring your own wine.

The Orangery

CAFÉ
KENSINGTON PALACE, KENSINGTON GARDENS, W8
020-7376 0239
Open Oct-Easter: daily 10am-4pm; Easter-Sept: daily 10am-6pm.
U: High St Kensington.

This gracious eighteenth-century building, designed as a greenhouse by Sir John Vanbrugh, is a rather austere setting with its huge ceilings and large windows. Everybody is rather well-behaved, as a result, and it's a bit like going to tea with a respected aunt. Light lunch dishes such as sandwiches and salads are delicious, but the place really comes into its own at teatime when glorious cream cakes make an appearance.

Sticky Fingers

AMERICAN
1A PHILLIMORE GDNS, W8
020-7938 5338, FAX 020-7937 7238
Open Mon.-Sat. noon-11.30pm, Sun. noon-11pm.
U: High St Kensington.

Pretty standard U.S. fare from burgers to steaks. Standards of cooking are high here—juicy, well-cooked naked burgers; others sporting cheese, bacon and fried onions on top, plus great steaks and imaginative, fresh salads. Sticky Fingers remains one of the favourite spots of the masses and service is correspondingly indulgent to families.

We're always interested to hear about your discoveries and to receive your comments on ours. Please let us know what you liked or disliked; **e-mail us** at gay-ots@aol.com.

Yas

IRANIAN
7 HAMMERSMITH RD, W14, 020-7603 3980
Open daily noon-2am.
U: Olympia.

This pretty, prize-winning Iranian restaurant went off the boil a while back, but regained some of its old sparkle. Bread comes straight from the clay oven and garnished with pickles and crudités. We nibbled them with refreshing doogh, a yoghurt drink. Starters of kashk bademjan (grilled aubergines and whey) and bal e morgh (chargrilled chicken wings) played well and our khoresh e ghorme sabzi (stewed lamb with kidney beans) delivered flavourful, herby depths. Accompanying saffron rice was nicely delicate. It's conveniently situated opposite Olympia Exhibition Halls, the venue for many prestigious antiques and trade fairs. This is a place to value for a decent meal for two at £35 including house wine.

KILBURN

Organic Café

INTERNATIONAL
21-26 LONSDALE RD, NW6, 020-7372 1232
Open daily 9.30am-5pm & 7pm-11.30pm.
U: Queen's Park
No cards. ☎ ⍭

Down an unlikely mews in what once must have been stables or garaging lies this unlikely venue for a café. The style is very relaxed, with wooden tables and floor and whitewashed walls. In summer, the doors open out onto the cobbled street, giving it something of a New York feel. The breakfast/brunch lasts until late afternoon: BLT, eggs Florentine and various salads. At night, there are pasta main courses, steak and chips and various mainland European-inspired dishes. The wine list maintains the organic theme. Staff is friendly, if seemingly a little bemused by it all.

> Looking for an address?
> Refer to the index.

KNIGHTSBRIDGE

The Fifth Floor Café

BRASSERIE
HARVEY NICHOLS, KNIGHTSBRIDGE, SW1
020-7823 1839
Open Mon.-Sat. 10am-10.30pm, Sun. noon-6pm.
U: Knightsbridge.

🅰 ☎ ⍭

This little sister (though not so little) of the very grown up Fifth Floor Restaurant (see Restaurants), bustles and buzzes all day with a smart crowd. They happily lay aside their designer bags to eat either in the main room—or better still on a fine day (though they do, of course, have overhead heaters)—on the roof terrace. The à la carte menu offers smoked salmon, soups, and salads as starters and dishes like seared tuna with crispy noodles and bok choy with tangy cucumber and spring onion salad for mains. Prices seem steep for a café, but this is Harvey Nichols and it is very stylish: starters from £4.50 to £8, mains from £12 to £14 (with vegetables extra). Or take advantage of the set menus: 2 courses for £15.50, three for £18.50 (worth the extra £3 for the rum cheesecake).

Le Métro

MODERN BRITISH
L'HOTEL, 28 BASIL ST, SW3, 020-7591 1213
Open Mon.-Sat. 7.30am-10.30pm.
U: Knightsbridge.

🅰 ☎

This chic wine bar gets somewhat crowded with guests from L'Hôtel upstairs, and locals and tourists dropping in and can be very noisy. Le Métro has made its name on its considerable and excellent wine list, with some 50 wines by the glass. The food is sharp, too, starting with breakfast (continental with great pastries, or an English hearty fry-up for £6.50). Then, a lunch and dinner menu including seasonal soupe du marché (£4.95) and fish and chips (£7.50). A smaller snack menu around teatime offering savouries like smoked salmon bagels and desserts, which, if you're lucky, include a great sticky toffee pudding. Service, however, can be chaotic and the seating uncomfortable.

Pizza on the Park

PIZZERIA
11 KNIGHTSBRIDGE, SW1, 020-7235 5273
Open Mon.-Sat. 8.15am-midnight,
Sun. 9.15am-midnight.
U: Knightsbridge.

Pizza on the Park remains one of our favourites, for its location (looking out onto Knightsbridge from the front of the ground floor room) and for its continuing top jazz and cabaret acts, nightly in the basement music room. Pizzas are classic and decent, but it's really the ambience, the music and entertainment—nothing too startling or uncomfortable—that most people seem to enjoy the most.

MAIDA VALE

Ard Ri Dining Room

PUB/IRISH
O'CONNOR DON
88 MARYLEBONE LANE, W1, 020-7935 9311
Lunch & Dinner Mon.-Fri.
U: Bond St.

If you want a decent pint of Guinness, the O'Connor Don is the place for you. It's an Irish pub owned and run by a charming Irishman, rather than by a big corporation, and the quality of drink is clearly important to him. Hearty sandwiches, gammon and champ are served in the bar, but if you want something slightly more delicate head upstairs to the Ard Ri Dining Room where you'll find remarkably good Irish cooking—hot buttered oysters, roast monkfish, the inevitable Irish stew—and a decent wine list. In keeping with the rest of the place, the room looks a little eccentric and the service is haphazard but well meant.

Don Pepe

TAPAS BAR
99 FRAMPTON ST, NW8, 020-7262 3834
Lunch & Dinner Mon.-Sat.
U: Edgware Rd.

What is probably London's oldest Spanish restaurant and first tapas bar, has a warm feeling. Although the restaurant's cooking can be

variable, no one should miss the signature dish, Pepe's favourite lubina à la sal (whole sea bass baked in salt, carefully served and filleted). More consistent is the simple front bar, offering more than 40 tapas including steamed clams, kidneys cooked in sherry, octopus salad, fabada (a Spanish cassoulet), and serrano ham, not the classic, expensive black-foot, but nonetheless succulent. Drink sherry, Galician wine or Rioja—or, for over £100 a bottle, the great Araganza wines of Villafranca del Bierzo.

The Green Olive

ITALIAN
5 WARWICK PL, W9
020-7289 2469, FAX 020-7289 4178
Lunch Sat.-Sun., Dinner nightly.
U: Warwick Ave.

The Green Olive is a relaxed, informal, neighbourhood restaurant where pale walls, wood floors and neatly adorned tables set the scene for competent, well-executed cooking. Choose from the set menu, two, three or four courses in the evening (£20.50-£26); à la carte at lunch. Cod is simply roasted and served with sun-dried tomatoes and the jus from the fish; saffron risotto accompanies salmon; and pork loin is roasted to mouthwatering tenderness. Desserts play classic Italian; the ices being particularly good. Service is charming and willing.

The Red Pepper

ITALIAN
8 FORMOSA ST, W9
020-7266 2708, FAX 020-7289 4178
Lunch Sat.-Sun., Dinner nightly.
U: Warwick Ave.

Nestling on a quiet, shop-lined street in this Maida Vale backwater, the Red Pepper has carved a niche by making surprisingly good pizzas in its wood-fired oven downstairs (it was one of the first in London). Decoration is sparse, tables tightly packed in the ground floor room, but locals swear by it. Pizzas change constantly, or you can choose from equally varied pasta. For those in search of something more elaborate, there might be choices like grilled tuna with rocket, grilled peppers and black olives. The wine list is Italian; service somewhat abrupt.

The Vale

PUB/MODERN EUROPEAN
99 CHIPPENHAM RD, W9
020-7266 0990, FAX 020-7286 7224
Lunch Tues.-Fri., Brunch Sun., Dinner nightly.
U: Westbourne Park

A

As gentrification transforms the urban land-scape in its sweep towards Kilburn from ultra-trendy Notting Hill, new eateries are springing up like mushrooms after an autumn rain. Among them is The Vale, which opened in early 1999. The Vale conforms to the mould of late-nineties Modern European—pale wood with matte silver detail and lots of frosted glass, and a trendy basement bar. The menu changes daily, trawling Europe and beyond for culinary influences. The cooking tends to be satisfactory rather than exemplary, but the short wine list deserves praise for well-chosen selections (eleven available by the glass). Set menus are good value at £7.50 for a 2-course lunch, £10.50 for three courses, and a 3-course dinner at £13.50.

MARYLEBONE

Back to Basics

SEAFOOD
21A FOLEY ST, W1, 020-7436 2181
Lunch & Dinner Mon.-Fri.
U: Goodge St.

In an increasingly fashionable part of town that used to be at the heart of the rag trade, Back to Basics appears to have more than a usual natty and apt name. Basics is a small and invariably crowded, neighborhood restaurant, surprisingly close to anonymous Oxford Street. In food terms, Basics means fish, that great food which much of the great British public still ignores. Fish come from around the world, from good old British cod and plaice to mahi mahi, swordfish and other exotic varieties and the 'Catch of the Day' is written on the blackboard. Expect to pay from £10-£14 for flappingly fresh, well-cooked fish.

Golden Hind

SEAFOOD
73 MARYLEBONE LANE, W1, 020-7486 3644
Lunch Mon.-Fri., Dinner Mon.-Sat.
U: Bond St.

A ☎

This inestimable fish and chips shop was first opened by an Italian in 1914 and is now run by Greeks. Sadly after a fire a couple of years ago, they no longer use their glorious 50s fryers that make up one wall of the restaurant, preferring instead to do the cooking in the back room. But, arguably, their fish and chips are even better than they were and the cod is definitely the favourite. Don't expect any frills, just bring a healthy appetite—the portions are generous. It's unlicensed, but there are two good wine shops within 50 yards.

Mandalay

BURMESE
444 EDGWARE RD, W2, 020-7258 3696
Lunch & Dinner Mon.-Sat.
U: Edgware Rd.

A ☎

The road to this Mandalay for the Ally family was via Oslo, where theirs was the only Burmese restaurant. Now it is the only one in the UK, which is sad because the amiable Allys and their cooking keep their inexpensive but bright little restaurant extremely busy. (Dishes run £1.90 to £6.50.) The cuisine reflects the country's location between India, China and Thailand. So curries, salads, soups and stir-fries jostle in a menu which features bottle gourd, long beans and snow peas. Starters include samosas and spring rolls and the specialty fritters of calabash: shrimp and bean sprouts, chicken and vegetables and 'leafy green'. Balachaung (shrimp relish) adds zing to otherwise generally restrained spicing. Set lunches are remarkable value at one course for £3.50 and three for £5.90.

Purple Sage

ITALIAN
92 WIGMORE ST, W1
020-7486 1912; FAX 020-7486 1913
Lunch & Dinner Mon.-Sat.
U: Bond St.

This is a trendy, informal Italian restaurant in the quieter backwaters behind Oxford Street. Bread and olive oil greet you, as do irresistible scents from the wood-burning pizza oven. It's a shame they're not available at lunchtime when you'll pay more for some interesting antipasti such as broccoli croquettes or cabbage, spring onion, Parmesan and saffron timbale. The straightforward main courses like veal chop with rosemary sautéed potatoes and tomato salad with prices that nevertheless make a useful but not bargain rendezvous in the West End away from the crowds. Be warned, the high-ceilinged, brick-walled room itself is noisy.

RK Stanley's

BRITISH
6 LITTLE PORTLAND ST, W1, 020-7462 0099
Lunch & Dinner Mon.-Sat.
U: Oxford Circus.

Sausage and mash and other filling British nosh is served in this extraordinary diner close to Oxford Circus tube. The interior resembles a 1970s Soviet airport with its concrete walls

Soup of the Evening, and Morning, and Lunch. . .Beautiful Soup.

Another fashion hits London. The idea of places dedicated to soup is not new by any means, but the execution is. Now we have several soup chains starting up just as sandwich bars, coffee bars and juice bars have, offering bright décor and good food. Many offer tastings before you buy and serve coffee, tea, soft drinks and juices.

Soup, 37 Marylebone High St, W1, 020-7935 5008, the retail branch of the well-known New Covent Soup Company, offers those soups most of us have bought in the better supermarkets like carrot and coriander, wild mushroom and more. Also in Hammersmith at Food Court, King's Mall Shopping Centre, King St, W6, 020-8563 2588; Clerkenwell at 158 Clerkenwell Rd, 020-7278 6813; The City at 23 Fleet St, EC1, 020-7353 3711. www.coventgarden-soup.co.uk.

Soup Opera, 2 Hanover St, W1, 020-7629 0174, has soups in three sizes: 'Peckish' (12 ounces), 'Hungry' (16 ounces), and 'Ravenous' at (32 ounces). Never mind the cute language, here are vegetable delights like lentils and grilled artichoke, meat in the form of chicken pot-pie and Hungarian goulash, and seafood in the favourite Manhattan clam chowder. Ranging from £2.95 (corn chowder) to £9.55 (smoked haddock chowder); the price includes fruit and a choice of breads. Also in The City at 56-57 Cornhill, EC3, 020-7621 0065; Covent Garden at 17 Kingsway, WC2, 020-7379 1333; Docklands at Concourse level, Cabot Pl, Canary Wharf, E14, 020-7513 0880; King's Cross at Platform 8, King's Cross Railway Station, N1, 020-7713 1137. w w w . s o u p o p e r a . c o . u k . **Soup Works**, 9 D'Arblay St, W1, 0207439 7687, offers four sizes of soup, small to extra large, with free garnishes of crackers, croutons or sour cream, ranging from chilled gazpacho to bœuf bourgignon. Seasonally led, complimentary fruit and good range of breads. Also in Covent Garden at 29 Monmouth St, WC2, 020-7240 7687, near Tottenham Court Rd at 56 Goodge St, W1, 020-7637 7367, www.soupworks.co.uk.

Soupdouper, Victoria Station, SW1, 020-7828 7473. Operating only at Railway stations, these fast food outlets offer good changing soups, like carrot and coriander, and Moroccan lamb, plus organic soups. The breads are good. Also in Euston at Euston Station, NW1, 020-7383 3715; Marylebone at Baker St Station, NW1, 020-7486 8446 and Marylebone Station, Harwood Ave, NW1, 020-7723 1511; Victoria at Victoria Station, SW1, 020-7828 7473.

and wipe-clean vinyl seats, but it's intentional tongue-in-cheek post-modernism. As for food, these are top bangers: bratwurst is served with choucroute, champ mash and even some caramelised pears (£7.95). If sausages fail to excite, try seafood and take a diversion to meatloaf and scallops. Desserts are old-school and boring. There are some excellent artisan bottled beers to go with the hearty food. Service is enthusiastic and young. The wine list is adequate.

La Spighetta

ITALIAN
43 BLANDFORD ST, W1, 020-7486 7340
Open daily Lunch & Dinner.
U: Baker St.

This unlikely basement off Marylebone High Street is surprisingly spacious with exposed brickwork and minimal decoration giving it something of a Tuscan feel. Pizzas are the items to order, with unusual toppings like beet root, seafood and, on one occasion, palm hearts. Pasta, too, is excellent. There are old stalwarts like calf's liver, here rendered perfectly pink and juicy with a lightly dressed rocket salad; and cod, perfectly roasted in the wood-fired oven and served with unusually spiced lentils. The mostly Italian wine list is short and to the point.

Union Café

MODERN EUROPEAN
96 MARYLEBONE LANE, W1, 020-7486 4860
Lunch & Dinner Mon.-Sat.
U: Bond St.

Since a change of ownership, Union Café has lost a little of the lustre that emanated from the open kitchen. Good value and lively food, professional service and, particularly, the incredibly low mark-ups on well-chosen wines like the house wine at £6.50 creates a happy hubbub. The cooking is mostly Mediterranean with a dash of Asia. Although unlikely to stop anyone in his tracks, it completes an attractive package very well. Typical: chargrilled calamari salad, or chargrilled baby artichokes and leeks with rocket and Parmesan; crab cakes with mango and spring onion; or duck confit.

MAYFAIR

Condotti

ITALIAN
4 MILL ST, W1, 020-7499 1308
Open Mon.-Sat. 11.30am-midnight.
U: Bond St.

A

This is one of the three London restaurants of the founder of the Pizza Express chain, Kettners and Pizza on the Park, Peter Boizot. A surprisingly spacious spot, Condotti has two floors with good art on the walls and an open kitchen. Being Mayfair, it's pretty posh. The pizzas are reminiscent of the old Pizza Express days—beautifully cooked with the best ingredients. Definitely one to seek out if you're shopping nearby.

Coffee Mania

Perhaps it was inevitable that coffee should become so wildly popular in London and Britain for a slightly older generation who spent their teens slurping frothy coffee in dubious coffee bars, but it seems to have caught the younger generation by surprise. Huge American chains have dominated, but there are a few smaller places well worth checking out.

Caffè Nero, 39 Floral St, WC2, 020-7379 0855, keeps the clubbers happy in the small hours, serving good coffee, snacks—pizza slices are popular—and cakes. Also at 28-29 Southampton St, WC2, 020-7240 3433, and many other branches.

Canadian Muffin Company, 9 Brewer St, W1, 020-7287 3555, is a cheerful chain with some great pastries and snacks. Also in Covent Garden at 5 King St, WC2, 020-7379 1525; Fulham at 353 Fulham Rd, SW10, 020-7351 0015; Islington at 13 Islington High St, N1, 020-7833 5004; The City at 19 Rotterdam Drive, E14, 020-7538 1667.

Leith's at Dartmouth House

INTERNATIONAL
ENGLISH SPEAKING UNION, 37 CHARLES ST, W1
020-7493 3328
Lunch Mon.-Fri.
U: Green Park.

This is a somewhat surprising, but delightful, venture—a public restaurant in the headquarters of the English Speaking Union. The Revelstoke Room is a cross between a hotel drawing room and a club. Portraits hang on the deep-red walls, chairs upholstered in red, carpet muffles the noise and the linen is finely starched. You get a very good lunch indeed (though note that this is not under the same ownership as Leith's Soho, (see below), and Leith's in Kensington, see Restaurants). Two courses at £14 or three at £17 bring mod dishes like roasted red pepper soup with pesto or fresh, seasonal salads as starters. For mains, there are chargrilled meats accompanied by the likes of pancetta and rosemary risotto and fish. For a savoury finish, there are puddings of the satisfying-but-not-too-heavy variety, homemade ice creams with biscuits or an imaginative brie with gooseberry compote. There's the added advantage in summer of a beautiful, outdoor courtyard.

Sotheby's Café

MODERN EUROPEAN
34-35 NEW BOND ST, W1, 020-293 5000
Open Mon.-Fri. 9.30am-5pm, Sun. noon-4pm.
U: Bond St.

Seek out this small café in the venerable auction house, for it's a real find. Sitting in the small room, hung with mirrors and black-and-white Cecil Beaton photographs, you can watch the comings and goings of buyers and sellers. The café does everything well, there's excellent fresh brioches and croissants for breakfast with good, strong coffee (perhaps to steady the nerves of those about to part with the odd million?). The lunches feature the famous lobster club sandwich still having pride of place among a Modern British selection of dishes. Teatime, which at £4.95, £9.50 and £14.95 (with Champagne to celebrate that buy?) is one of the best deals in town. It has an exceptional wine list, which given the fact that wine expert Serena Sutcliffe, MW, is the

resident Sotheby's wine expert, should not come as a surprise.

NOTTING HILL GATE

Books for Cooks

CAFÉ
4 BLENHEIM CRESCENT, W11, 020-7221 1992
Café: Lunch Mon.-Sat. Bookshop: Mon.-Sat. 9.30am-6pm.
U: Ladbroke Grove.

It's surprising no one else does this, creating a tiny café in a bookshop which only stocks food and wine books. Given its phenomenal success, even more surprising that the idea hasn't been copied. The 3-course £10 meal is produced from the recipe books stocked in the shop, so the variety is huge. It's cooked by a changing rota of chefs, who always manage to produce great results, ranging from a soup, through three simple lunch dishes, to a choice of two or three desserts. It's a mecca for every self-respecting foodie and the knowledgeable staff is always happy to discuss and advise on dishes (and, of course, sell you the book which inspired your meal).

Café Med

MEDITERRANEAN
184A KENSINGTON PARK RD, W11, 020-7221 1150
Open Mon.-Sat. 10am-11.30pm, Sun. noon-10.30pm.
U: Ladbroke Grove/Notting Hill Gate.

The somewhat idiosyncratic décor suits the trendies of Notting Hill. But it's not only those of Notting Hill worthy of the trend; a whole clutch of Café Meds has subsequently sprung. While the atmosphere might be original, the culinary inspiration comes originally from the Camden Brasserie (see above). Vaguely Mediterranean dishes using goat cheese, rocket and other such ingredients in the starters are followed by good chargrilled meat and fish, which come with a huge wooden bowl of french fries, pastas and salads. There are pavement tables at this branch; St. John's Wood has a delightful spacious terrace; Chiswick has a garden; at Battersea, children eat free during Saturday lunch. All in all, the Café Meds do a very good job.

Also in **Chelsea** at 2 Hollywood Rd, SW10, 020-7823 3355; **Clerkenwell** at 370

St, John St, EC1, 020-7278 1199;
Hammersmith at 320 Goldhawk Rd, W6,
020-8741 1994; **St. John's Wood** at 21
Loudon Rd, NW8, 020-7625 1222; **Soho** at
22-25 Dean St, W1, 020-7287 9007;
Wandsworth at 2 Northside, Wandsworth
Common, SW18, 020-7228 0914.

Calzone

ITALIAN
2A KENSINGTON PARK RD, W11, 020-7243 2003
*Open Mon.-Sat. noon-midnight, Sun noon-
10pm.*
U: Notting Hill Gate.

Good pizza and pasta from this small, reliable chain. Try the calzone (a pizza folded in
half, toppings inside) or just go for the classics
on an open base. Calzone is a useful pit stop
for hungry families since children are very welcome.

Also in **Fulham** at 335 Fulham Rd, SW10,
020-7352 9797; **Hampstead** at 66 Heath St,
NW3, 020-7794 6775; **Islington** at 35 Upper
St, N1, 020-7704 0111.

Costas Fish Restaurant

GREEK/FISH & CHIPS
18 HILLGATE ST, W8, 020-7727 4310
Lunch & Dinner Tues.-Sat.
U: Notting Hill Gate.

No cards. ☎

Join the queues at the takeaway, or indulge
yourself in the back room of this chippie,
which has changed little since its early days.
Go for the freshest of British fishes—sole, haddock and cod, served with unbelievably good
chips. But there's a difference here, the Greek
influence comes in calamares and Retsina,
though it's debatable whether Greek wine
really goes with chips and vinegar.

The Cow Dining Room

PUB/MODERN BRITISH
89 WESTBOURNE PARK RD, W2, 020-7221 0021
Lunch Sun., Dinner nightly.
U: Westbourne Park.

Very Notting Hill here, with its crowded bar
and small first-floor dining room with modern
art prints. The kitchen has recently been taken
over by Juliet Peston, who comes with great
credentials (Alastair Little in Soho and Lola's

in Islington) and who is raising the stakes in
gastro-pub food. A daily changing menu takes
in various influences as in lamb tagine with
couscous, roast fillet of beef served with excellent chips and chargrilled chicken with similarly chargrilled Mediterranean vegetables. The
venture belongs to Tom Conran (Sir Terence's
son) who moves between the pub and his
excellent deli nearby (see Food in Shopping).
There are plans to open at lunchtime during
the week, so check first.

De Baere

CAFÉ
101 NOTTING HILL GATE, W11, 020-7792 8080
*Open Mon.-Sat. 8.30am-6.30pm, Sun. 9am-
1pm.*
U: Notting Hill Gate.

A

Belgian chocolate makers really do know
their stuff, and nowhere more so than at the
various De Baere's dotted around the richer
parts of town. Their bitter chocolate mousse is
to-die-for, but all their pastries are fantastic,
too. There's a pastry shopping section, and a
delightful tearoom where they serve all day
from continental breakfasts to scrumptious
teas.

Also in **Knightsbridge** at 5-6 William St,
SW1, 020-7235 4040; in **South Kensington**
at 24 Bute St, SW7, 020-7591 0606; **Mayfair**
at 3 Shepherd St, W1, 020-7408 1991.

Geales

BRITISH/FISH & CHIPS
2 FARMER ST, W8, 020-7727 7528
Lunch daily, Dinner Mon.-Sat.
U: Notting Hill Gate.

This old timer has been sold, but retains its
former feel even though it has been refurbished. Food is more ambitious than you
might first expect, with excellent fish soup
with garlicked rouille and croutons and oak
smoked Scottish salmon. The basis remains
good fish and chips, using cod, haddock,
plaice, skate and more, fried or grilled, with
mushy peas and great chips. Desserts run from
sticky toffee pudding with toffee sauce (a real
killer!), to sunken chocolate cake—which does
the same to you. Good wine list including
Champagne, Pouilly Fumé, Beaujolais, 'Jolly
Good Claret' from Laytons and more.

Lisboa Pâtisserie

CAFÉ
57 GOLBORNE RD, W10, 0181-968 5242
Open daily 8am-8pm.
U: Ladbroke Grove.

No cards

A real institution, Lisboa is still the place in
Notting Hill to go on a sunny day. Savouries
are freshly made so you need to get there
early. Prices are very reasonable and it's fun.

The Market Thai

THAI
1ST FLOOR, 240 PORTOBELLO RD, W11
020-7460 8320
Lunch & Dinner Mon.-Fri. & Sun., Sat. noon-
10.30pm.
U: Westbourne Park/Ladbroke Grove.

Above the permanently hip Market Bar at
the heart of Notting Hill, The Market Thai
has found a successful formula. The restaurant
shares its rather Gothic interior style with the
main bar downstairs, and there is no extra
Thai paraphernalia to underline the menu.
Sturdy tables and dark wooden objects decorate the room. Our three main courses: Pad
Thai (prawns and fried noodles with bean
curd, ground peanuts and bean sprouts), vegetarian Kaeng Kiew (green curry cooked with
coconut milk, herbs and Thai aubergines) and
Kai Ma Muang (stir-fried chicken with cashew
nuts, fried chilli and spring onion) were good.
The prices are generally customer-friendly,
with starters from £3.50, soups from £3.25
and main courses from £4.25. The set menu
(£13.95), for a minimum of two, includes a
starter, soup and a main course with one side
dish. A selection of starters for two is £9. The
Market one-plate express menu is available
noon-3pm (6pm on Sat). It has selected dishes
from the main menu for about £5.

Prince Bonaparte

PUB/MODERN EUROPEAN
80 CHEPSTOW RD, W2, 020-7229 5912
Lunch Sat.-Sun., Dinner nightly.
U: Notting Hill Gate.

This is one of many gastro-pubs in Notting
Hill Gate, which is packed in the evenings and
on weekends. The décor is a formulaic re-

incarnation of many a Victorian pub, and will
be instantly familiar to people who like such
establishments. Its owners, Bass, have kept on
the services of Beth Coventry, who oversees
the kitchen to ensure that the high quality of
the food is maintained. Indeed, it is far better
than many similar pubs. The daily menu is
hand-written on the blackboard and includes
many robust dishes: a daily soup, salads and
pastas, such as spinach salad with shaved
Parmesan and pancetta, and penne with roasted aubergine and pesto.

Rôtisserie Jules

FRENCH
133A NOTTING HILL GATE, W11, 020-7221 3331
Open daily noon-11.30pm.
U: Notting Hill Gate.

Open kitchens may not be the keys to success, but they come into play at all three
restaurants in this highly successful little chain.
Flame-grilled chicken is the raison d'être here,
at remarkably reasonable prices: from £4.95
for a quarter of a chicken, and £5.75 for a
half. Gratin dauphinoise is a treat with the
bird; otherwise, try the good frites. There's
more here, too, in the form of Caesar salad,
lamb or duck, plus desserts like chocolate
mousse and Ben & Jerry's delicious ice
creams. They also do take-away which keeps
the places even busier.

Also in **Chelsea** at 338 King's Rd, SW3,
020-7351 0041; **South Kensington** at 6-8
Bute St, SW7, 020-7584 0600.

The Westbourne

PUB/INTERNATIONAL
101 WESTBOURNE PARK VILLAS, W2
020-7221 1332
Lunch Tues.-Sun., Dinner nigthly.
U: Royal Oak/Westbourne Park.

Very hip and happening here, so don't venture in unless you're looking the part in
designer gear, or feeling mighty confident.
The Mediterranean food is confident and satisfies the Notting Hillbillies who eat happily on
well-sourced ingredients simply cooked.

OXFORD CIRCUS

Carluccio's Caffè

CAFÉ
8 MARKET PL, W1, 020-7636 2228,
FAX 020-7636 9650
Open Mon.-Sat. 8am-11pm, Sun. 11am-10pm.
U: Oxford Circus.

This newcomer promises much and delivers it all. The inspiration of Priscilla Carluccio, it's modeled directly on the Italian café/deli/restaurant concept and is brilliantly done. It's et in Market Place, just north of Oxford Street, an area rapidly becoming full of trendy restaurants (it's rather coyly called 'Oxford Market'). There are chairs and tables outside, a small shop in the immediate entrance, then a long stainless-steel bar down one side of the café and tables and chairs opposite. It buzzes and hums with customers all day, while the deli side, not surprisingly given the Carluccios' expertise, is booming (see Food in Shopping). Food is freshly prepared and runs from mushroom soup or hearty pasta and bean soup from Sardinia (£3.50) to lasagnes, salads, antipasti and cheeses. Reckon to spend anything from £2 for coffee to around £14 for 3 courses. Soon after they opened, they extended their hours to cope with the success. Fortunately, they plan to roll out more of these cafés in the near future.

PARSON'S GREEN

The White Horse

PUB/MODERN EUROPEAN
1-3 PARSON'S GREEN, SW6, 020 7736 2115
Lunch & Dinner daily.
U: Parson's Green.

Known affectionately to regulars as The Sloaney Pony, this classically perfect pub has always concentrated on food more than most other pubs. It's also built up an outstanding list of beers (over 60 unusual and worthwhile bottled varieties), as well as an impressive wine list with over 20 wines by the glass. After a recent renovation, the pub is looking even better and there is a dedicated non-smoking restaurant in the former coach house, as well as a sparkling new kitchen. Owner Mark Dorber has rightly reasoned that good wines

and beers show off well with good food, so expect fine charcuterie, cheeses, smoked salmon with rosti potatoes, roast rump of lamb with artichoke and aubergine couscous and hake with chorizo.

PICCADILLY CIRCUS

Café Flo

FRENCH
11-12 HAYMARKET, SW1, 020-7976 1313
Open Mon.-Sat. 10am-11.30pm, Sun. 10am-11pm.
U: Piccadilly Circus.

Whether for a well-made cappuccino or a full meal—soupe de poissons, Toulouse sausages with pommes purée and fried onions rings and crème brûlée or île flottante—Café Flo does the job deftly. In between, the poulet foccacia (chicken, lots of crispy bacon, well-seasoned guacamole and perky salad leaves on notably good, fresh, herby focaccia bread for £6.75) is typical of the value and freshness offered. Not as child-friendly as it could be, but with its bold Matisse prints and, in this branch, its palm trees and silver bar bedecked by large vases of flowers, Flo is le mot juste for lunch or anytime.

Also in **Chelsea** at 89 Sloane Ave, SW3, 020-7225 1048; **The City** at 40 Ludgate Hill, EC4, 020-7329 3900; **Covent Garden** at 51 St. Martin's Lane, WC2, 020-7836 8289; **Fulham** at 676 Fulham Rd, SW6, 020-7371 9673; **Hampstead** at 205 Haverstock Hill, NW3, 020-7435 6744; **Islington** at 334 Upper St, N1, 020-7226 7916; **Kensington** at 127 Kensington Church St, W8, 020-7727 8142; **Marylebone** at 13 Thayer St, W1, 020-7935 5023; **Soho** at 103 Wardour St, W1, 020-7734 0581; **South Kensington** at 23-25 Gloucester Rd, SW7, 020-8225 1048.

China House

CHINESE
GROUND FLOOR, 160 PICCADILLY, W1
020-7499 6996, FAX 020-7499 7779
WWW.CHINAHOUSE.CO.UK
Open Mon.-Sat. noon-midnight, Sun. noon-11.30pm.

Housed in the magnificent domed former banking hall of Barclays Bank, China House incorporates an upstairs restaurant, a retail outlet and a casual ground floor bar and café. It serves what it calls modern Chinese 'express food' with Western influences, which translates into a menu ranging from squid with mustard sauce to dumplings in chilli soy, all at £3. Main dishes at £6.50 might be a seafood bowl of prawns, crab, squid, and vegetables with Szechuan cabbage or roast duck with vegetables and shallot crisps, served with wet or dry noodles or rice. Children, thankfully, have smaller ('panda') portions at £4.50. More Western and child-friendly influences come in the £3.50 desserts—ice creams, frozen yoghurts, chocolates and fruit. But don't treat this as just a café, there's a minimum charge of £6.50 per person.

Fountain Restaurant

INTERNATIONAL
FORTNUM & MASON, 181 PICCADILLY, W1
020-7973 4140
Open Mon.-Sat. 9am-6pm.
U: Piccadilly Circus.

The Fountain Restaurant has changed from serving a menu which had everything on it (and was more like a book), to one which offers a little bit of everything. It's surprising that salads don't figure more strongly here, given the ladies-who-lunch clientele. It's on the expensive side (Cumberland sausage and mash, red onion marmalade and gravy for £8.75), but portions are generous and this is Fortnum's, after all. It's also good for breakfast and teas—and the old-fashioned décor, with its walls painted with neo-colonial scenes and its predominately pastel colour—scheme suits the genteel serving of plates of pastries and cups of Darjeeling. Oh joy, it also serves great, old-fashioned sundaes like the maple dipper and the Piccadilly poppet. Fortnum's also has an excellent Salmon and Champagne Bar, the Patio Restaurant and the St. James's Restaurant.

Hard Rock Café

AMERICAN
50 OLD PARK LANE, W1
020-7629 0382, FAX 020-7629 8702
Open Mon.-Thurs. & Sun. 11.30am-12.30am,
Fri.-Sat. 11.30am-1am.
U: Hyde Park Corner.

What can we say about one of the most famous brand names in the world? Only that

after 28 years, this remains one of London's best burger joints (but try to eat upstairs, downstairs can be dire, noisy and hot) with its legendary queues, memorabilia on the walls and famous burgers. They do other things, too, like excellent steaks. This is one of those places everyone goes to once in their life, but it has its fair share of regulars, too.

Jus Café

CAFÉ
30-32 FOUBERT'S PL, W1
020-8870 7346 (CENTRAL OFFICE NUMBER)
Open Mon.-Sat. 7am-6pm.

Arguably, the most appetising of the growing number of juice bars. This had as its con-

Smashing Sandwiches

London's sandwich bar scene is booming as locals go for the exotic fillings and fresh breads that the new breed offer.

A rare one-off of a high standard is **Eyre Bros**, 34/42 Charlotte Rd, EC2, 020-7739 5345, where David Eyre, originally from The Eagle (see Tkabove/below), has found a good audience for his excellent sandwiches, casseroles and soups to take away. Of the chains, we recommend the following.

EAT, 16a Soho Sq, W1, 020-7287 7702, won the British Sandwich Association's UK Sandwich Bar of the Year Award in 1998 and 1999. That's serious in the world of sandwiches. The minimalist, high-tech, high-fashion interior raises your expectations, which are more than usually satisfied with their range of international flavours. Or go for light offerings, like Thai chicken peanut noodles in the summer, or watercress, herb and potato soup in the winter. Puddings please like ginger lemon cheesecake; juices are freshly squeezed. Branches throughout London.

Always reliable are the **Prêt-à-Manger** outlets, offering freshly made sandwiches, sushi, a limited range of salads, puds, juices and good coffee. Branches throughout London.

sultant, Philip Howard, chef of The Square (see Restaurants), and it means that the food is more interesting than the juices, refreshing as they are. His influence is evident in a delicious lamb, salsa verde and sun-dried tomato sandwich and a pannacotta that could grace a restaurant were it not in a plastic pot. These, plus salads—does anywhere else do Lyonnaise with ham hock and mustard?—and desserts like cherry and cranberry trifle or apricot fool are a significant advance on most lunchtime takeaways. Not immediately apparent is that there's plenty of seating at chunky arty-crafty chairs and tables in a room upstairs.

Also in **Covent Garden** at 13 New Row, WC2, 020-8870 7346.

Mô

CAFÉ
25 HEDDON ST, W1, 020-7734 3999
Open Mon.-Sat. 11am-11pm
U: Oxford Circus/Piccadilly Circus.

A

A quirky oasis, an offshoot of Momo next door, in a quiet backwater off Regent Street. Like a North African souk stall and tearoom, it doesn't just serve unusual food and drinks, everything in the room has a price. Before you leave with a rug or lampshade, try one of the delicious, exotic teas such as Egyptian arcadee, a ruby-red infusion of dried hibiscus flowers. Or genuine Moroccan mint tea made with the freshest, sweetest leaves. Snacks such as grilled peppers, cubes of lamb with apricots, pigeon with cinnamon and feta cheese with basil—as sandwich fillings or on a pottery meze plate— are also unusual and tempting. Mesmerising music helps time drift by. Not for those in a rush, but a delightful retreat, if too many others haven't got there first.

Planet Hollywood

AMERICAN
TROCADERO, 13 COVENTRY ST, W1
020-7287 1000, FAX 020-7734 0835
Open Mon.-Sat. noon-1am, Sun. noon-11.30pm.
U: Piccadilly Circus.

A

This is one of the best theme restaurants around, with great memorabilia around the place from favourite films and equally favourite stars, videos and cheerful staff. Planet Hollywood delivers a good range of classic American dishes. Expect salads, steaks, burgers, good fish, a great range of starters like potato skins and desserts like dark chocolate brownies or that to-die-for cheesecake. Portions are gargantuan; cocktails are impressive. All in all, despite recent financial earthquakes, this branch of Planet Hollywood seems pretty set to continue in the same vein.

Royal Academy Restaurant

BRITISH
ROYAL ACADEMY OF ARTS, BURLINGTON HOUSE, W1
020-7439 7438
Open daily 10am-5.30pm.
U: Green Park/Piccadilly Circus.

In a suitably solemn and impressive room, high-ceilinged and with murals painted by past members of the Royal Academy, the restaurant has a slightly school canteen feeling, which is a shame given its excellent food. Perhaps the retro feel comes from the clientele—all very middle England and tweed, twin-sets and sensible shoes up from the country. They tuck in with vigour to a daily changing homemade soup with crusty bread, light quiches and salads and hot dishes like casserole of chicken. The cakes are superb. The whole place rather genteel.

PRIMROSE HILL

The Black Truffle

MODERN EUROPEAN
40 CHALCOT RD, NW1
020-7483 0077, FAX 020-7483 0088
Lunch Sun.-Fri., Dinner nightly.
U: Chalk Farm

A 🍴

The Black Truffle opened in January. It is the latest in the Red Pepper, White Onion, Purple Sage and Green Olive group (see above). With four tables at entry level, the lower room has dark wood tables, stone floors and stainless-steel lights, all very modern for Primrose Hill which so far has steered clear of 'designed' restaurants. But the formula fits perfectly, just as it did originally in Maida Vale. North Italian cooking offers robust dishes like a starter of chargrilled cuttlefish in its black ink sauce, and to follow, roast saddle of lamb with polenta and trevisano. Strong flavors seem to suit the local residents, as do the prices—a 2-course lunch is £12.50, and dinners run from

£16.50, to £19.50 and £21.50. Tables outside in summer just clinch the deal.

The Engineer

PUB/MEDITERRANEAN
65 GLOUCESTER AVE, NW1, 020-7722 0950
Breakfast, Lunch & Dinner daily.
U: Chalk Farm.

A real favourite among the local inhabitants and well worth seeking out if you're enjoying the open-air expanse of nearby Primrose Hill with its fabulous views stretching over London. You can dine either in the bar, in the garden, an upstairs room or a small dining room, but you'll get the same accomplished cooking. Breakfast scores with the Engineer smoothie for the healthy, and the full breakfast for the hungry (and the healthy, it's all cor-

rectly organic). At other times, starters include excellent soups such as celeriac, leek and courgette served with homemade bread (£3.75) and ambitious salads (try mizuna, roast red pepper, red onion, pine nuts, mango and mint served with a chilli dressing at £5.50). Continue with mains such as spiced roast lamb with cous cous or duck confit with Puy lentils, pan-fried bok choy and a star anis jus (£11.95).

The Lansdowne

PUB/MEDITERRANEAN
90 GLOUCESTER AVE, NW1, 020-7483 0409
Lunch Tues.-Sun., Dinner nightly.
U: Chalk Farm.

This corner pub has enormous plain windows looking out over leafy Primrose Hill, the

---

Breakfast

Long gone are the days when if you wanted to eat well in London, you ate breakfast three times a day, but breakfast is still a meal to be treasured.

For a high-energy, quick, stand-up breakfast, try **The Cinnamon Bar** at One Aldwych, WC2, 020-7300 0800, belonging to, but not attached to, the highly fashionable *One Aldwych Hotel*. Standouts: light food, high-energy juices and shakes, good coffee and fresh macaroons in different flavours. For more serious fare, it has to be *Simpson's-in-the-Strand Grand Divan*, 100 Strand, WC2, 020-7836 9112 and their **Seven Deadly Sins Breakfast**, complete with newspapers. A little closer to the square mile, **Bank**, 1 Kingsway, WC2, 020-7379 9797, from 7am-11.30am, has become known for its power breakfasts. City working breakfasts don't come much smoother than at **Terminus**, *Great Eastern Hotel*, Liverpool St, EC2, 020-7618 7400, open from 6.30am and offering just about everything you can imagine. Or rub shoulders with Smithfield porters on one hand and movers and shakers from The City on the other at either **The Cock Tavern**, Poultry Market, Central Market, EC1, 020-7248 2918, serving breakfast from 6am to 10.30am, or **The Fox & Anchor**, 115 Charterhouse St, EC1, 020-7253

4838, from 7am. Also in this neck of the woods is **Saigon Times**, 20-22 Leadenhall Market, EC3, 020-7621 0022, which surprisingly serves French-influenced Vietnamese food during the day, but a hearty British breakfast earlier.

In the West End, make for **Carluccio's Caffè**, 8 Market Pl, W1, 0120-7636 2228, for some heart-stoppingly strong coffee and excellent pastries. And you can eat outside on a warm morning. If you get to the British Museum before it opens at 10am as many do, don't despair, just nip down Museum Street to the **Coffee Gallery**, 23 Museum St, WC1, 020-7436 0455. You can get Clarke's pastries (there's usually stiff competition for the brioches and plum danish), excellent coffee, newspapers to read and the chance to see the odd famous faces (it's surprising who lives around here). **Baker & Spice**, 46 Walton St, SW3, 020-7589 4734, attracts people by the busload to its door. Luckily, most of them are buying breads and pastries to take with them, but on a sunny day, the smell of baking will lure you to the few tables outside. And over in fashionable Brompton Cross, **The Brasserie**, 272 Brompton Rd, SW3, 020-7581 3089, caters to the locals and a trendy young crowd.

---

street thankfully mostly devoid of traffic. The mismatching chairs and tables are well-spaced; the menu chalked on a blackboard above the fireplace. Warm salads, soups and perhaps a tart to start, followed by sausages and mash, grilled fish with marinated vegetables and a pasta dish. Flavours are gutsy and robust, colours strong. Sunday means all three courses, the rest of the week you can pick and choose. Order and pay at the bar, but there are no tabs, which discourages further ordering, particularly when it is busy.

Lemonia

GREEK
89 REGENT'S PARK RD, NW1, 020-7586 7454
Lunch Sun.-Fri., Dinner Mon.-Sat.
U: Chalk Farm.

Still one of our favourites, this now 20-year old restaurant never fails to deliver the goods. First the décor welcomes, a large room with a greenery-filled conservatory area, and bench seating around the outside. More trailing plants cover walls and the floors are of warm red terra-cotta tiles. The food, too, is a cut above the usual taverna, with creamy taramasalata, nutty Greek salad, fresh, definitely unrubbery calamari. Kebabs are well cooked, and shieftalies a delight. If you're undecided, the meze is at £13.50 per person is a feast. With friendly service, this buzzing restaurant is a well-established delight and you must book at weekends and popular times.

Limani

GREEK
154 REGENT'S PARK RD, NW1, 020-7483 4492
Lunch Sat., Dinner Tues.-Sun.
U: Chalk Farm.

The grown-up relative of Lemani, this is a small, intimate restaurant with tables on the ground floor and up stairs on small landings. The menu is in the same classic tradition, though not quite up to the same level. Never mind; the standard kebabs are pretty good, and the moussaka is deliciously creamy. The meze at £11.75 per person is a good bet, as is the fish meze at £14.95 per person. The staff is as obliging as Lemonia's and, once when accompanied by a small restless boy, the owner entertained us for a good twenty minutes with various highly entertaining tricks.

Primrose Pâtisserie

CAFÉ
136 REGENT'S PARK RD, NW1, 020-7722 7848
Open daily 8.30am-9pm
U: Chalk Farm.

No cards. 🔔

With a back room looking like someone's private living room and a small front area where the large counter fights for space with a few tables, this local pâtisserie offers very good pastries. The lemon cake, cheesecake and more along with excellent coffee are to-die-for. Being Primrose Hill, it's a great place for people watching. Even the occasional blip in the good will of the staff doesn't spoil the place.

The Queens

MODERN EUROPEAN
49 REGENT'S PARK RD, NW1, 9020-7586 0408
Lunch & Dinner daily.
U: Chalk Farm.

This delightful pub looks over towards Primrose Hill and the upstairs restaurant has the advantage of a small terrace, which gives a satisfying glow of instant superiority to those lucky enough to find a seat. It's always been a Primrose Hill favourite, but its refurbishment a few years ago by the owners of the Duke of Cambridge in Battersea and the Builder's Arms in Chelsea has only added to its charms. Now the restaurant serves serious food including pastas, salads and good risottos as well as a daily special. Desserts are old-fashioned. The whole experience on a summer's day is a real treat.

ST. JOHN'S WOOD

Maison Blanc

CAFÉ
37 ST. JOHN'S WOOD HIGH ST, NW8
020-7586 1982
Open Mon.-Sat. 8.30am-6.30pm, Sun. 9am-6pm.
U: St. John's Wood.

More than just a pâtisserie, though many— with justification—come to Maison Blanc just for their rich, handmade French chocolate cakes, the café offers savoury treats in the form of light stuffed croissants and salads. At St. John's Wood, mums sit with prams and friends in the back; the glass counter in the front is always busy with passing customers choosing from the wide range of goodies.

Also in **Chelsea** at 11 Elystan St, SW3, 020-7584 6913; **Fulham** at 303 Fulham Rd, SW10, 020-7795 2663; **Hampstead** at 62 Hampstead High St, NW3, 020-7431 8338; **Holland Park** at 102 Holland Park Ave, W11, 020-7221 2494; **Richmond** at 27B The Quadrant, Richmond, Surrey, 020-8332 7041, Turnham Green at 26-28 Turnham Green Terrace, W4, 020-8995 7220.

The Salt House

PUB/MODERN EUROPEAN
63 ABBEY RD, NW8, 020-7328 6626
Lunch & Dinner daily.
U: St. John's Wood.

This well-scrubbed pub conversion (run by the people behind the noteworthy Chiswick), is a welcome newcomer to London's burgeoning clutch of good gastro-pubs. You could just come in for a drink at the bar, which serves ales and some decent wines, but it would be a shame to miss out on the food. The menu changes daily and includes simpler dishes (such as rib-eye steak with chips and horseradish, £25.50 for two) along with more ambitious fare that's cooked to standards as high as you'd find in many a Modern European restaurant—with prices to match.

Seashell

BRITISH/FISH & CHIPS
49-51 LISSON GROVE, NW1, 020-7723 8703
Open Sun.-Fri. Lunch; Sat. noon-10.30pm.
U: Marylebone.

A takeaway to one side and a large restaurant to the other, with wooden partitions and walls decorated with murals, this is a favourite with taxi drivers, locals and tourists. The standard of frying is high, with proper nut oil used as is respect for the crisp batter coating the fresh halibut, sole, plaice or whatever is recommended. Fat chips and those British mushy peas complete the picture. Good service and a friendly atmosphere make the Seashell one of London's tried-and-trusted favourites.

SHEPHERD'S BUSH

Adam's Café

NORTH AFRICAN
77 ASKEW RD, W12, 020-8743 0572
Open daily 7pm-11pm.
U: Shepherd's Bush.
No cards.

Abdel and Frances Boukraa run two catering operations. At lunchtime an English café, in the evening an authentic North African restaurant. It offers friendly service, unpretentious but pleasant décor, and ingenious menus, all including appetisers. Menu 'rapide' is £9.95 for a main course plus tea or coffee; 'gourmet' offers main course and starter for £12.95 while 'gastronomique' at £14.95, is three courses. You choose from an unpriced à la carte. The surprise is the consistently excellent cooking. Start perhaps with brik (egg-filled crisp pastry); ojjia (Tunisian ratatouille); or brioutte (pastry filled with seafood). Main courses are grilled brochettes, couscous and tagines. Desserts include lemon or almond tart and pastries. Drink Tunisian or Moroccan wine, Tunisian digestifs, mint tea with pine nuts or Arabic coffee.

Anglesea Arms

PUB/MODERN BRITISH
35 WINGATE RD, W6, 020-8749 1291
Lunch & Dinner daily.
U: Goldhawk Rd.

Unusual these days for the gastro-pub, the Anglesea Arms is still very much a pub, with a bar where locals sink pints of Courage beer and smoke Sweet Afton cigarettes. The point, however, is Dan Evans'cooking, which is inventive, inspired, thorough, well-researched and remarkably cheap—most starters are under £5; most main courses under £10. The warm salad of chorizo that comes with shavings of foie gras is the result of astute buying and clever use of ingredients. A main course of grilled sea bass might come with a fennel and black olive salad, rouille and rocket. Desserts might be a blood orange sorbet, in season, or poached fruits with flavoured creams. The wine list rewards the cautious as well as the adventurous.

Chez Marcelle

MIDDLE EASTERN
36 BLYTHE RD, W14, 020-7603 3241
Open daily noon-midnight.
U: Kensington (Olympia).

Marcelle has returned to her restaurant, which specialises in good homey Lebanese food. Not that homey Lebanese food seems very different from the offerings of other Lebanese restaurants, plain or luxurious. A few recherché specialties have gone from the menu, perhaps in response to lack of demand. Marcelle hopes to replace the hard wooden bench seating with real chairs but no other changes are planned. The quality of the meze and grills and their very low prices make it useful for visitors to Olympia seeking sustenance more exciting than that found in that nearby building.

Rôtisserie

FRENCH
134 UPPER ST, N1, 020-7226 0122
Lunch Wed.-Fri., Dinner Mon.-Tues.,
Sat. noon-11pm, Sun. noon-10pm.
U: Angel.

The Rôtisserie has become a great success within the niche market of spit-roast and grill cooking. Famous for its steaks (sirloin, T-Bone and fillet), the restaurant also serves chicken, duck, marinated lamb chops, tiger prawns and halibut steaks. Ingredients are sound, the method simple and the idea appealing. It may be a market many have entered and failed in, but this company seems to have gotten the formula absolutely right—and it has two more outlets with more to follow.

Also in **Shepherd's Bush** at 56 Uxbridge Rd, W12, Tel, 020-8743 3028; 316 Uxbridge Rd, Hatch End, **Middlesex**, 020-8421 2878.

Wilsons

SCOTTISH
236 BLYTHE RD, W14, 020-7603 7267
Lunch Mon.-Fri., Dinner Mon.-Sat.
U: Goldhawk Rd/Shepherd's Bush.

Robert Wilson's kilt announces his unique combination of restaurant de quartier and Scottish ethnicity, and the yellow and blue room incorporates restrained tartans and Scottish and Buddhist artefacts. There may be recorded music, but Wilson sometimes plays the liveliest of bagpipes. Specialties include salmon fishcakes with parsley sauce; and haggis with tatties, swede and a dram. Other successes range from simple pork and ham sausages with homemade piccalilli, to more elaborate marinated chargrilled chicken with curried cream and Cognac sauce. Steamed syrup pudding is like Scottish mothers once made, and a few well-chosen wines are backed up by selected single malt whiskies. Expect to pay around £35-£40 for a three-course meal for two.

SHOREDITCH

F Cooke

BRITISH
150 HOXTON ST, N1, 020-7729 7718
Open Mon.-Thurs. 10am-7pm, Fri.-Sat.
9.30am-8pm.
U: Old St.
No cards. No bookings.

Not as old as it looks, this pie and mash joint is housed in a formerk. But it doough job with the décor, and the tiles and wooden chairs hit the right note. Go for the great pies and mash, around £2, both vegetarian and meat, all coming with rich brown gravy. Wash it down with copious cups of tea.

SOHO

Andrew Edmunds

MODERN EUROPEAN
46 LEXINGTON ST, W1, 020-7437 5708
Lunch & Dinner daily.
U: Piccadilly Circus.

Upstairs is much better than down in this somewhat cramped Soho institution. Andrew Edmunds has the winning formula of a good, inexpensive wine list crammed with specials, a short handwritten bistro-style menu, paper tablecloths and napkins and a regular customer base. Be sure to book, even if it is only for an early evening drink. Starters might be Parma ham, mussels or an earthy salad, while main courses might be tuna and couscous, or rump of lamb with piquant and herb-infused stewed beans. Desserts are tarts and ices and there is a good cheese board. Service is efficient and mostly friendly.

Aurora

MEDITERRANEAN
49 LEXINGTON ST, W1, 020-7494 0514
Open Mon.-Sat. Lunch & Dinner, 10am-noon for coffee only.
U: Oxford Circus/Tottenham Court Rd.

This is a longtime small Soho restaurant, with a tiny walled garden, not to be confused with the large new establishment, which has appropriated its name on the other side of the City. This Aurora is more eighteenth than twenty-first century in décor and ambience, and it almost would be no great surprise to find Dr. Samuel Johnson in one of its battered leather chairs. The short menu is modern enough to offer 'coconut fusion broth' as well as Chinese and Mediterranean (especially North African) ideas. Service is pleasant, but not the fastest, despite the policy of two dinner sittings. It is still unlicensed with a nominal corkage charge.

Bar Italia

CAFÉ
22 FRITH ST, W1, 020-7437 4520
Open Mon.-Sat. 24 hours, Sun. 7am-3am.
U: Leicester Sq/Tottenham Court Rd.

No cards.

One of Soho's great institutions which will probably be there after every other style of restaurant/bar/café has been tried and long gone, Bar Italia attracts a motley crew of customers who come to gaze at the huge video screen (particularly lively if Italy is playing football) in the back room or to get an outside table. People-watching is one of the attractions, being seen here is another, a third is the excellent coffee and the fresh juices. Large toasted sandwiches keep the night owls and clubbers going.

busaba eathai

THAI
106-110 WARDOUR ST, W1, 020-7255 8686
Open daily noon-11pm.
U: Leicester Sq.

This is a hugely popular, holistic, non-cranky, non-smoking, trendy Thai eating house in the middle of Soho. Beautiful, large, square, wooden communal tables dominate the wood-panelled room. Service is very quick, efficient and friendly. There is only one course (with side dishes) offered and the 'you are what you eat' philosophy means there is a good choice for vegetarians. Since as many ingredients as possible are organic, there is an extensive list of good, fresh-pressed juices. There is a short but food-friendly wine and beer list. Food choices centre around curries, noodle dishes and stir-fry items, all quite distinctive and distinctly convincing—green chicken or vegetable curry, phad thai, roasted cod curry, Thai beef laksa, fish dumpling vermicelli, chicken butternut squash stir-fry. Sides range from green papaya salad, to morning glory stir-fry. to Thai calamari. One to remember.

Café Mezzo

CAFÉ
100 WARDOUR ST, W1, 020-7314 4000
Open Mon.-Sat. 9am-11pm, Sun. 10am-10pm.
U: Piccadilly Circus.

Part of the immensely successful Conran empire, and particularly the Mezzo restaurant next door, this small but oh-so-fashionable café serves great pastries and coffee as well as lunchtime dishes like noodles and soups. Read the newspapers and magazines, watch the news broadcasts on TV monitors and enjoy the Conran formula at a fraction of the price you would pay at a more haughty Conran establishment.

Cranks

VEGETARIAN
8 MARSHALL ST, W1, 020-7437 9431
Open Mon.-Fri. 9am-8pm, Sat. 9am-9pm, Sun. 10am-8pm.
U: Covent Garden.

This long-established vegetarian café chain has shed its lentils and sandals and now sports citric colours and bright lighting to suggest that food is up-to-the-minute. Crunchy and varied salads—and, goodness knows, a worthy selection of these are hard enough to find anywhere in London—are often preferable to hot dishes such as stir-fried noodles or homity pie, which can be stodgy and dull-tasting. Cakes and puddings are okay. Service isn't exactly slick—though what do you expect in a pioneering veggie business, even one which is trying to convince you that it has a contemporary commercial edge?

Also in **Covent Garden** at 17-19 Great Newport St, WC2, 020-7836 5226; **Docklands** at Unit RP, 380-385 Concourse Level, 15 Cabot Pl, Canary Wharf, E14, 020-7513 0678; **Marylebone** at 23 Barrett St, W1, 020-7495 1340; near **Tottenham Court Road** at 9-11 Tottenham St, W1, 020-7631 3912; plus Cranks Express in **Covent Garden** at 9 Adelaide St, WC2, 020-7836 0660.

Kettners

INTERNATIONAL
29 ROMILLY ST, W1
020-7734 6112, FAX 020-7434 1214
Open daily noon-midnight.
U: Leicester Sq/Tottenham Court Rd.

Belonging still to Peter Boizot, the original Pizza Express man, Kettners is in a definite time-warp but fits seamlessly into Soho's idiosyncratic scene. Pizzas are strong on the menu here (around £8-£9), but so are burgers and meat from the charcoal grill. It's quite an experience to dine in this Edwardian drawing room, and the décor inspires a bohemian feel that would not have been out of place in the 20s and 30s. Great piano playing in the evening, great drinks and great staff make this a must.

Kulu Kulu Sushi

SUSHI
76 BREWER ST, W1
020-7734 7316, FAX 020-7734 6507
Lunch & Dinner Mon.-Sat.
U: Piccadilly Circus.

Not East meeting West, but old Japan encountering modern in what some consider London's outstanding kaiten—conveyor belt sushi bar. The sushi is prepared behind the counter, or in the kitchen in the back and the visible human element means that even if it is not on the conveyor you can ask for something special. A comparative rarity that was on the kaiten on our last visit was aji or horse mackerel, chopped with onions and herbs. Excellent sushi includes tuna, squid, octopus as well as some snacks that are not sushi at all: salmon sashimi, rice balls, even the odd salad.

Dishes range around £1.20 to £3.

Maison Bertaux

CAFÉ
28 GREEK ST, W1, 020-7437 6007
Open Mon.-Sat. 8.30am-8.30pm, Sun. 9.30am-7.30pm
U: Leicester Sq/Tottenham Court Rd.
No cards.

Tradition runs rampant here, from all of the ornaments, to the mix of students and Soho residents as customers. Great savoury quiches and sweet pastries are washed down with plenty of café latte; the smoking room upstairs is popular. This is a genuine blast from the past.

Pâtisserie Valerie

CAFÉ
44 OLD COMPTON ST, W1, 020-7437 3466
Open Mon.-Fri. 8am-7pm, Sat. 9pm-7pm, Sun. 9.30am-6pm.
U: Leicester Sq.

Pâtisserie Valerie has held its position as one of London's top cafés, starting in Soho on Old Compton Street and fanning out from there to conquer different parts of town. But, this old-fashioned, wool-panelled room continues to be our favourite. It may be less sophisticated than the Old Brompton branch in Knightsbridge, but it fits perfectly. Expect simple salads and club sandwiches, around £4-£5, plus pastries that are some of the greatest chocolate fixes in town. Top coffee, also.

Also in **Knightsbridge** at 215 Old Brompton Rd, SW3, 020-7823 9971; **Marylebone** at 105 Marylebone High St, W1, 020-7935 6240; **Royal Institute of British Architects** (RIBA), 66 Portland Pl, W1, 020-7631 0467.

Pizza Express

ITALIAN
10 DEAN ST, W1, 020-7437 9595
WWW.PIZZAEXPRESS.CO.UK
Open daily 11.30am-midnight.
U: Leicester Sq.

A

The first of the Pizza Expresses to play live jazz, the formula has been copied throughout London with phenomenal success, but this remains one of the best. Good pizzas, vibrant atmosphere, some of the best jazz around.

Also at 30 Coptic St, WC1, 020-7636 3232, and branches throughout London.

Randall & Aubin
BRASSERIE
16 BREWER ST, W1, 020-7287 4447
Open Mon.-Sat. 11am-11pm, Sun. 4pm-10pm.
U: Piccadilly Circus.

A **No bookings.**

Perch on stools looking out the window onto busy Soho, or at one of the marble-topped tables further into the room. Rôtisseries deliver perfectly roasted chickens; you can choose from the enticing seafood display, or go for something less visible from the bistrostyle menu. The general style is informal—bare wood floors, loud music and a sense of buzz. Success is more likely with the simpler dishes, like smoked salmon, baguettes filled with salt beef, eggs Benedict. The wine list is short and to the point; service somewhat indifferent and remarkably slow given the size of the room.

Soho Spice
INDIAN
124-126 WARDOUR ST, W1
020-7434 0808, FAX 020-7434 0799
Open Mon.-Wed. 12.30pm-midnight; Thurs.-Sat. 12.30pm-3am, Sun. 12.30pm-10.30pm.
U: Tottenham Court Rd/Leicester Sq.

A

This Indian brasserie, perfectly suited to its location, is radically different from the old-fashioned curry houses with their dreary décor, mercifully subdued music, unmercifully grim service and a predictable menu. Here bright young customers and appropriately noisy music complement zingy colours in both décor and the uniforms of staff whose professionalism includes smiles served along with the food. A well as à la carte, the short menu offers starters and main course selections for two, and there's a set lunch at £7.50 and set dinner at £15. Curries and tandooris are Euro-friendly, mostly mildly spiced and main dishes come complete with rice, bread, lentils and vegetables.

Spiga
PIZZA
84-86 WARDOUR ST, W1, 020-7734 3444
Lunch & Dinner daily.
U: Leicester Sq.

Tan and beige throughout with much use of wood and the low ceilings contribute to a busy buzzy atmosphere. The prices help, too, and the structure of the menu which rightly guides you toward excellent and unusually thin pizzas. Gorgonzola is teamed with speck, suckling pig with rocket. Pasta comes in the usual guises, but is above average, and if you need something more substantial, try fish and meat done the Italian way. The wine list is short and concise and the service somewhat haphazard, but willing.

Yo! Sushi/Yo! Below
SUSHI
52 POLAND ST, W1, 020-7287 0443
Open daily noon-midnight.
U: Oxford Circus.

Teeming every night with trendy young things, the sushi seems to play second fiddle to the singing waiters, the drink-serving robot, television screens playing Japanese TV and the snaking conveyor belt which delivers colour/price coded plates of sushi right to your seat. The atmosphere is distinctly un-Zen and the sushi tends to be mediocre, yet this place still deserves its reputation as a favoured re-fuelling station for committed Soho-ites and funky urban tourists. Queues can be long, particularly on Friday and Saturday nights, but this place provides enough theatre to keep you entertained while you wait. The basement bar (Yo! Below) serves bento boxes as well as Japanese lager on tap.

Also in **Hampstead** at 02 Centre, 255 Finchley Rd, NW3, 020-7431 4499; **Knightsbridge** at Fifth Floor, Harvey Nichols, Brompton Rd, SW1, 020-7235 5000; **Oxford Street** in Selfridges, 400 Oxford St, W1, 020-7318 3885.

SOUTHALL

Brilliant

INDIAN
72-74 WESTERN RD, SOUTHALL, MIDDLESEX
020-8574 1928
Lunch Tues.-Fri., Dinner Tues.-Sun.
Rail: Southall.

Run by the Anand family, the name hearkens back to The Brilliant Hotel, which their grandfather owned in Nairobi. This is simple, gutsy home cooking that never fails to please. They're famous for their butter, jeera (cumin) and chilli chicken starters and do have some fried mogo (cassava chips) with one of them. The menu is fairly extensive, but do not worry about this because they know how to cook here. Try some tilapia fish when it's available, along with methi (fenugreek) chicken cooked bhuna style (well cooked and more dry than soupy). Breads like rotis, rice and dals are all very good.

SOUTH BANK

Globe Café

CAFÉ
SHAKESPEARE'S GLOBE, NEW GLOBE WALK
BANKSIDE, SE1, 020-7902 1576
Open daily 10am-5.30pm (plus pre-theatre suppers during the theatre season, May-Sept.).
U: London Bridge.

This is a delightful small café with windows on three sides looking out over the river. Good choice of dishes, from sandwiches to soup, and hot meals like breast of chicken with

---

Internet Cafés

Internet cafés might not be the most glamorous, but they're very useful. First to set up was **Cyberia Café**, 39 Whitfield St, W1, 020-7681 4200, cyberia@easynet.co.uk. Also seek out **Intercafé**, 25 Gt. Portland St, W1, 020-76310063, managers@inter-café.co.uk, and **Portobello Gold's** upstair's internet café, 95-97 Portobello Rd, W11, 020-7460 4918.

---

tomatoes, chickpeas and cumin. There's a more formal restaurant upstairs.

Gourmet Pizza

PIZZA
GABRIEL'S WHARF, 56 UPPER GROUND, SE1
020-7928 3188, FAX 020-7401 8583
Open Mon.-Sat. noon-11pm, Sun. noon-10.30pm.
U: Waterloo.

The idea of those exotic fillings on pizzas already seems rather passé—after all, who really wants to add tuna or Cajun chicken to a classic base? Well, quite a few people, judging from the queues at the door. It could also be the view that helps—looking out over the Thames at one of the best points, and the location—it's just by the Royal Festival Hall so is ideal for concert-goers.

Also in **Docklands** at 18-20 Mackenzie Walk, Canary Wharf, E14, 020-7345 9192; **Mayfair** at 7-9 Swallow St, W1, 020-7734 5182; **Merton** at Merton Abbey Mills, Watermill Way, SW19, 020-8545 0310.

SOUTH KENSINGTON

Daquise

POLISH
20 THURLOE ST, SW7, 020-7589 6117
Open Mon.-Fri. 11.30am-11pm, Sat.-Sun. 10am-11pm.
U: South Kensington.

Still here, still serving the same classic fare, still the same take-it-or-leave it service, still the same muddled décor—we love it. This is the place for those traditional Polish fillers, in great portions: rich soups, pancakes, marinated pork knuckle, Vienna schnitzel with—yes, of course— fried egg triumphantly on top. Don't miss it.

La Brasserie

FRENCH
272 BROMPTON RD, SW3, 020-7584 1668
Open Mon.-Sat. 8am-11.30pm, Sun. 9am-11.30pm.
U: South Kensington.

It's had a much-needed makeover, but the strong Parisian atmosphere remains. It's smart, full of chic people, and serves all the great traditional dishes. Try moules, monkfish, steak frites and carré d'agneau, all accompanied by good French wines, and revel in what is a small corner of France in what is London's most French quartier.

STOKE NEWINGTON

Istanbul Iskembecisi

TURKISH
9 STOKE NEWINGTON RD, N16, 020-7254 7291
Open daily noon-5am.
Rail: Dalston.

Less basic, but as authentic as any of the numerous nearby competitors, this eating house offers the warmest of welcomes until 5am every day. Its 'signature dish' (after which it is named) is a bland tripe soup magically transfigured by chilli, salt, pepper, vinegar and lemon juice seasonings. The wide choice of mezes includes delicious vegetarian items emphasising artichokes, lentils, beans, aubergine. Omnivores enjoy a variety of kebabs and grills, as well as 'traditional Turkish dishes'. These are mostly lamb with vegetables such as fried aubergine stuffed with tomatoes, peppers, onions and meat. Drink ayran, (sour milk with herbs), modestly priced Turkish wines, and of course Turkish coffee.

TOOTING

Kastoori

INDIAN VEGETARIAN
188 UPPER TOOTING RD, SW17, 020-8767 7027
Lunch Wed.-Sun, Dinner nightly.
U: Tooting Bec/Tooting Broadway.

This longtime favourite with the local Asian community has been discovered by others as well. Run by the Thanki family, from Kathia Wahd in Gujurat via East Africa, there are many interesting and satisfying dishes to try. These range from simple starters like mogo (fried cassava chips with tamarind sauce), to green banana curry with chillies, to kasodi (corn cooked in coconut milk with peanut sauce), to tomato curry. There are also wonderful breads and rice dishes. The service is very sweet and charming. A real gem.

TOTTENHAM COURT ROAD

Ikkyu

JAPANESE
67 TOTTENHAM COURT RD, W1, 020-7636 9280
Lunch & Dinner Mon.-Fri.
U: Tottenham Court Rd.

The ground floor looks authentically Japanese, the first floor rather less so, more giving the impression of Chinatown than anything from the land of the rising sun. Authentic this is not, but done competently and sometimes excellently. Sushi and sashimi are hardly stunning, but much better than in many other places charging higher prices. Steer clear of risky items like tempura, the batter rather greasy, but revel in subtly flavoured ramens which hit the spot, particularly for the prices charged which are around £2-£6. Set meals are £6-£9.50 at lunch, £10-£14 at dinner.

Noho

ORIENTAL
32 CHARLOTTE ST, W1, 020-7636 4445
Open Mon.-Sat. noon-11.30pm, Sun. noon-11pm.
U: Goodge St.

This stylishly decorated canteen in Fitzrovia's prime restaurant street serves pan-Asian dishes, mostly noodle-based. Some of these (Thai fishcakes, £4.50; seafood laksa £7.95) are flavourful, while others are little better than Chinese takeaway fare (beef ho fun, £6.25). Still, the place has a buzz to it, helped along by nattily dressed staff, pop muzak and a crowd of young media types who congregate here at lunchtime and seem to appreciate the vibrant atmosphere and reasonably low prices.

Passione

ITALIAN
10 CHARLOTTE ST, W1
020-7636 2833, FAX 020-7636 2889
Lunch Mon.-Fri., Dinner Mon.-Sat.
U: Goodge St.

Charlotte Street is lined on both sides of the road with restaurants. With a few exceptions, they are less than inspiring, and Passione is definitely one of the exceptions. The menu, based firmly in the Italian camp, is inexpensive and appealing, offering pappardelle with wild mushrooms, caponata, gnocchi with pumpkin and the like, from £6-£8. There are occasional glitches with service, but it's so charming one is prepared to forgive. It gets very busy at lunchtime, so it's wise to book.

TRAFALGAR SQUARE

Café in the Crypt

INTERNATIONAL
ST.-MARTIN-IN-THE-FIELDS, DUNCANNON ST, WC2
020-7839 4342
Open Mon.-Sat.10am-8pm, Sun. noon-8pm.
U: Charing Cross.
No cards.

The brick-vaulted setting is attractive and there's the added pleasure of the brass rubbing centre and a small shop. A long counter keeps the hot dishes hot, but not necessarily fresh. There are also sandwiches, pastries and soups. You can have a cup of tea or a full meal, and it's a good place for single people waiting for a concert or just passing the time of day.

ICA Café

BRASSERIE
THE MALL, SW1
020-7930 8619, FAX 020-7930 8754
Open Mon. noon-11pm, Tues.-Sat. noon-1am,
Sun. noon-10.30pm.
U: Charing Cross.

Pay your £1.50 day membership to this private arts club and enter a realm of creative barflies propping up the mezzonine bar and creative cooking from the subterranean kitchen. Chef Phillip Owens is accomplished at producing simple but first-rate Italian dishes, but he's also versatile enough to turn out better Thai food than most of London's Thai restaurants do. Service can be flaky and slow, but some would say that's all part of the art-house charm.

VAUXHALL

Hot stuff

INDIAN
19 WILCOX RD, SW8, 020-7720 1480
Open Mon.-Sat. noon-10pm.
U: Vauxhall.

This neighbourhood gem has found its way into several London guidebooks for very good reasons. The home-style Indian cooking is wonderful, there's a warm, friendly, family atmosphere and the prices are hard to beat. All of which makes it just the kind of restaurant reviewers delight in recommending. Run by Bele and Abdul Ghafoor, Indian by way of Kenya, with assistance from their son and daughter there are some dishes you must have. Jeera (cumin) chicken wings are zingingly aromatic and Bele's paratha (bread) stuffed with potato is properly crispy outside and moist inside. If you go Wednesday through Friday, order the East African fish curry. Many regulars leave the ordering to the owners and, therefore, never go wrong.

VICTORIA

Ebury Wine Bar
International

139 EBURY ST, SW1, 020-7730 5447
Lunch & Dinner Mon.-Sat.
U: Victoria.

A busy room decorated with trompe-l'oeil books has been the setting for some masterful cooking from chef Josh Hampton. Now he's moving on, and we have yet to see his replacement in full form. But expect good cooking along with an excellent wine list, with many interesting wines by the glass at this bustling, friendly, trendy local in Pimlico.'

We're always interested to hear about your discoveries and to receive your comments on ours. Please let us know what you liked or disliked; **e-mail us** at gay-ots@aol.com.

Ichi-Riki Sushi House

JAPANESE/SUSHI
7B STRUTTON GROUND, SW1, 020-7233 1701
Lunch & Dinner Mon.-Fri.
U: *Victoria.*
No cards.

A wide range of real handmade sushi is just part of the menu in this lively dive just off Victoria Street. They also offer sashimi, and interesting side-dishes-cum starters. Of these, takoyaki is a stunning treat for the eyes. A substantial 'snack' of wheat balls stuffed with octopus are served warm with a sauce and katsuo (bonito flakes). As the warmth reaches the katsuo, the flakes start to wave as if influenced by a gentle breeze. Sushi sets from £8 to £12 include miso soup, while set meals based on sashimi, salmon teriyaki or yakitori chicken are £8.50; homesick Japanese businessmen join locals for noodle soups.

Jenny Lo's Tea House

CHINESE
14 ECCLESTON ST, SW1
020-7259 0399, FAX 020-7823 6331
Lunch & Dinner Mon.-Sat.
U: *Victoria.*
No cards.

This buzzing noodle bar seats 28 at communal tables in a minimalist white room enlivened by areas of strong colours. If the planned expansion downstairs comes to pass, they will consider taking credit cards. The food is Chinese plus a few Vietnamese items. There are fresh egg noodles, rice noodles and flat ho fun noodles. Rice comes with pork and chestnuts, bean curd and mushrooms, chicken with pine nuts and much more. Side dishes—not starters, for they take longer to arrive than main dishes—include wonton soup, spareribs, grilled dumplings, and stir-fried vegetables. Drink house wine or interesting tea from a list of herbal, therapeutic or just Chinese choices.

Marmaris

TURKISH
45 WARWICK WAY, SW1, 020-7828 5940
Open Mon.-Sat. noon-midnight, Sun. 6pm-midnight.
U: *Victoria.*

Murmurs of appreciation rise from discreet corners of this pleasant, but low-lit café as customers enjoy the standard Turkish repertoire of meze and kebabs. Meze from £2.20 (or a set combination at £11.50) suits both carnivores and vegetarians. Yoghurt and fried or spring onions enliven many of them, including lambs' liver, meat balls, Turkish sausage, aubergine and artichoke and a notable yoghurt salad with flat parsley. Turkish beer and wines are unmemorable but acceptable at the price, and good Turkish coffee is accompanied by Turkish Delight.

WANDSWORTH

Brady's

BRITISH/FISH & CHIPS
513 OLD YORK RD, SW18, 020-8877 9599
Dinner Mon.-Sat.
Rail: Wandsworth Town.
No cards. No bookings.

Luke Brady, the original owner, is back at the helm, and he's back in form, serving superb fish and chips at bargain prices. Too posh to be a normal chipper, but not swanky enough for a smart night out, Brady's is pitched just right for Wandsworth locals who relish slabs of haddock or cod in light, crispy batter, served with crunchy fat chips in a cosy bistro setting. Other dishes are also good—try the side dish of mushy peas, the starters (from fishcakes to shellfish) and hearty British puds such as treacle tart.

WESTMINSTER

Politico's

CAFÉ
8 ARTILLERY ROW, SW1, 020-7828 0010
Open Mon.-Fri. 9am-6.30pm, Sat. 10am-6pm, Sun. 11am-5pm.
U: *St. James's Park/Victoria.*

Iain Dale used to be a political lobbyist, now while running the hugely popular Politico's he's also writing books. He got the idea from a shop in Washington D.C. and opened this one just before New Labour got in in 1997. Downstairs is a huge selection of political journals, books, post cards and gift items; upstairs take your coffee and cakes and watch the goings-on in the House of Commons on large-screen television. And keep your eyes open, you never know who you might meet, though on the whole it's a steady stream of civil servants from the nearby government offices.

WIMBLEDON

Saigon Thuy

VIETNAMESE
189 GARRATT LN, SW18, 020-8871 9464
Dinner nightly.
Rail: Earlsfield/Wandsworth Town.

This charming, bright little eating house sometimes erects an unusual language barrier by employing Chinese waiters unfamiliar with Vietnamese specialties. There are many among the 80 dishes listed, some admittedly hard to describe although the menu tries hard. Hand-rolled crystal spring rolls need 27 words, but only a minute or two to enjoy. Papaya salads and fishcakes are reminders that Thailand is one neighbour; stir-fries that China is another. Tough but tasty goat meat satay confirms that Vietnam is also a long way from Wandsworth, but the respectable short wine list recalls the French connection. The exotic and welcome final touch is tiny green bean cakes, which come with the bill.

IN-STORE RESTAURANTS

In-store restaurants vary from the casual to the ambitious, with some as serious destination restaurants in their own right. **Nicole's** at **Nicole Farhi**, 158 New Bond St, W1, 020-7287 8787, is such an example, as is the **Fifth Floor Restaurant** at **Harvey Nichols**, Knightsbridge, SW1, 020-7235 5250 (for both see *Restaurants*). Also up here competing for a slice of the action is the **Fifth Floor Café**, another excellent watering hole and pit stop (see *Knightsbridge* above). Downstairs at this cutting-edge store is **The Foundation**, an elegant bar/restaurant serving a modern

> **Telephone numbers** in England have eleven digits, beginning with a zero. The initial zero must be omitted if you are calling England from abroad. Within the country, dial the entire eleven digits.

menu. Smart ladies who shop still flock to **Jo's** at **Joseph**, 16 Sloane St, SW1, 020-7235 9869, or they might go to **Emporio Armani Express** at 191 Brompton Rd, SW3, 020-7823 8818, where the waiters are so smart it's hard to distinguish them from the punters. **The Fountain Restaurant** in **Fortnum & Mason**, 181 Piccadilly, W1, 020-7734 8040, is a useful address (see *Piccadilly* above). The **St. James Restaurant** on the fifth floor is old-fashioned and comforting and more formal, the sort of place where an elderly relative will feel perfectly at home, while the **Salmon & Champagne Bar** attracts businessmen in loud pinstripe suits, serious shoppers and media types. In Bond Street, sit at the counter at ultra-trendy **DKNY**, 24 Old Bond St, W1, 020-7499 8089, and snack. The opening of **Waterstone's** at 203-206 Piccadilly, W1, has helped in-store dining no end, with the main restaurant **The Red Room** (see *Restaurants*), a juice bar, the **News Café** on the lower ground floor for sandwiches, salads, croissants for breakfast and the like, and the Studio Lounge on the fifth floor, with excellent views, drinks and tapas-style food. For all **Waterstone's** venues, 020-7851 2466.

Down in Knightsbridge, one of the most elegant in-store diners is **Alberta's Café** at **Alberta Ferretti**, 205-206 Sloane St, SW1, 020-7838 9777. Expensive but tops. And **The Garden Restaurant** at the **General Trading Company**, 144 Sloane St, SW1, 020-7730 0411, has an excellent small garden for summer days.

In the department stores, **Premier** on the third floor of **Selfridges**, Oxford St, W1, 020-7318 3155, designed by Conran, operates as restaurant and bar. **Dickins & Jones**, 224 Regent St, W1, 020-7734 7070, now has a new **Albert Roux Café**, serving everything from scones with Albert Roux jam and clotted cream (£2.95), to great fresh salads and dishes like chicken tortillas. **Harrods**, being Harrods, has eighteen places to eat. Check them out, and the huge **Georgian Restaurant** (complete with Scottish piper each day at 1pm) at Knightsbridge, SW1, 020-7730 1234. The **Table Café at Habitat**, 196 Tottenham Court Rd, W1, 020-7631 3880, is good for vegetarians. **Liberty**, 210 Regent St, W1, 020-7734 1234, has a delightful small café on the second floor next to the book section. **Fenwick**, 63 New Bond St, W1, 020-7495 5402, has a **Joe's** restaurant among the designer frocks where ladies from the nearby Vogue offices toy with lettuce leaves.

TEA TIME

Tea remains so much the quintessentially English drink that one imagines it to have been around forever. But as the diarist Samuel Pepys wrote 300 years ago: 'I did send for a cup of tea (a China drink) of which I never had drunk before'. Tea as an occasion in itself has come right back into fashion. Many London hotels, and other places, too, serve an elegant afternoon tea which, to qualify, should include thinly cut sandwiches (going beyond cucumber for the fillings), a selection of pastries, scones with clotted cream and jam and, of course, a wide choice of teas.

Many are the tales about the evolution of afternoon tea. Was it really invented by the seventh Duchess of Bedford who, finding herself peckish between an early lunch and a late dinner, invited her friends around for tea with light refreshments? And was the sandwich really invented by the Earl of that name who was so engrossed in a game of chance that he refused to get up from the table, preferring instead to slap a piece of beef between two slices of bread? Does it matter? It all adds to the rich history of afternoon tea in British life.

Tea is both a practical treat—if you're going to the theatre, a substantial tea will keep you going until after the show—and a positive pleasure. As soon as you sit down in front of a teapot, life slows down. Bookings are sometimes not taken for tea, but try to book if possible. If you cannot, arrive early, since once settled in the clientele does like to stay put. London's top hotels all do an excellent tea; here we recommend a few favourites. Most of them also offer a Champagne Tea, which includes a glass of bubbly and often strawberries and cream.

Basil Street Hotel

BASIL ST, SW1, 020-7581 3311
Open daily 3.30pm-5.45pm.
U: Knightsbridge.

This delightfully old-fashioned hotel serves cream teas in the antique-filled lounge. A great place with a particularly female clientele, this is a small oasis in busy Knightsbridge. (£11 per person.)

Bramah Tea & Coffee Museum

1 MAGUIRE ST, SE1, 020-7378 0222
Open daily 10am-6pm
U: London Bridge/Tower Hill.

Although this is a museum, there is a small café where you get, quite simply, probably the best cuppa in town. No use of the dreaded tea bag here; Edward Bramah who used to be a tea-taster, abhors the modern invention and insists on the real thing. Once tasted, it's difficult not to share his views on loose-leaf tea as opposed to the bag

Brown's Hotel

30-34 ALBEMARLE ST, W1, 020-7493 7020
Open daily 3.30pm-5.45pm.
U: Green Park.

The Brown's Hotel is one of the best and our favourite place to have tea in an old-fashioned drawing room. There are old glass in the windows, chintz-covered sofas and chairs, an open fire and wood panelling and waiters glide around with pots of tea and trays of cakes. The large tea selection includes Browns Afternoon Blend. (£19.95 per person.)

Cannizaro House

WEST SIDE, WIMBLEDON COMMON, SW18
020-8879 1464
Open daily 3pm-5.30pm.
Rail: Wimbledon.

Built in the early eighteenth century, Cannizaro House was patronised by Victorian figures like Lord Tennyson, Oscar Wilde and Henry James. In winter, the full tea is taken in the restaurant (£13.50 per person); in good weather (Spring onwards), you can sit on the terrace looking out over gardens and parkland.

> The **prices** in this guide reflect what establishments were charging at press time.

The Capital

BASIL ST, SW3, 020-7589 5171
Open daily 3pm-5.30pm.
U: Knightsbridge.

A ☎

Great place after battling in nearby Harrods to relax over a pot of tea and all the trimmings. It's served in the sitting room, and in winter, there's a fire burning in the hallway. (£16.50 per person.)

Claridge's

BROOK ST, W1, 020-7629 8860
Open daily 3pm-5.30pm.
U: Bond St.

A ☎

Tea in The Reading Room really does take you back to the days of Mrs. Claridge (who looks sternly down on you from a portrait hanging on the wall). But tea here is all grace and comfort. ('Lady' Claridge's Tea, £22 at weekends and £19.50 during the week.)

College Farm

THE TEA HOUSE, 45 FITZALAN RD, N3
020-8349 0690
Sun. 2.30pm-5.30pm.
No U or BR nearby.
No cards.

College Farm, a small farm in the middle of urban north London, is an eccentric place to find a delightful old dairy. Built in 1864, it became a teahouse in 1925 and restored a few years ago by the energetic Su Russell. There are blue-and-white Minton tiles on the walls of this octagonal building with windows looking out onto the farm and the fields, solid chairs and tables covered with lace tablecloths, proper teapots and old-fashioned china. If you take a child, they provide a tray of toys for them to play with. Scones are homemade, fresh clotted cream comes with the proper hard crust, and servers refill your teapot as often as you like. On the first Sunday of the month the farm has an open day, so it can get pretty busy. (Around £6 per person.)

The Connaught

CARLOS PL, W1, 020-7499 7070
Open daily 3.30pm-5pm.
U: Bond St.

A ☎

You feel as if you're in someone's rather grand country mansion, taking tea in the lounge at this illustrious hotel, which is close enough to Bond Street to make it a good post-shopping pit stop. (£19.50 per person.)

The Conservatory

LANESBOROUGH HOTEL
1 LANESBOROUGH PL, SW1, 020-7259 5599
Open daily 3.30pm-6pm.
U: Hyde Park Corner.

A ☎

A truly superlative experience in this most gracious of hotels in the extravaganza of the Conservatory, quite the best setting for a tea which comes from the samovar. Good afternoon tea both set or à la carte, offers all the staples, plus a variety of teas which include seasonal specialty teas. So you can get the first flush of whatever is in season. (Lanesborough Tea £20.50.)

County Hall Restaurant

QUEENS WALK, SE1, 020-7902 8000
Open daily 3pm-6pm.
U: Waterloo.

A ☎

After a spin around on the splendid British Eye wheel, you can take tea here looking out over the river and at the aforementioned attraction. (£16 per person.)

The Dorchester

53 PARK LANE, W1, 020-7629 8888
Open daily 2pm-6.30pm.
U: Hyde Park Corner.

A ☎

Tea is served in the gilded Promenade, so it's a great place to people watch. There's also a pianist. (£19.50 per person.)

Fortnum & Mason

PICCADILLY, W1, 020-7734 8040
Open Mon.-Sat. 3pm-5.15pm.
U: Piccadilly Circus.

A ☎

Just the place to take your great aunt or grandmother to, the dignified fourth floor restaurant feels more like someone's private drawing room than a shop. It's peaceful as surprisingly few people make their way up to this excellent time-warp. Motherly waitresses help, and you can buy the teas in the downstairs food hall afterwards. Afternoon tea is

£16.50, Fortnum's High Tea (which includes Welsh rarebit and scrambling Highlander) is £18.50, Champagne Afternoon Tea is £21.50. A more casual alternative is the downstairs Fountain Restaurant where set tea is £13.95.

The Four Seasons Hotel

HAMILTON PL., PARK LANE, W1, 020-7499 0888
Open daily 3pm-6pm.
U: Hyde Park Corner.

A ☎

The Four Seasons has really gone to town with its teas, introducing four seasonal afternoon teas a year. Eric Deblonde and Sam Twining select the teas and a menu to match. Not only are the fillings appropriate, what goes into the bread and cakes changes, too. So Spring might bring spiced duck and kumquat sandwiches on orange-flavoured bread, summer grilled tuna and vegetables on basil bread and so on. It's all quite delicious. Throwing all caution to the wind, the Four Seasons also has scones with chestnuts and French pastries with lavender and honey mousse. Accompanying the teas throughout the year is a sorbet served in a chocolate mini teacup—delightful! (£22 per person.)

The Goring

17 BEESTON PL., GROSVENOR GDNS, SW1
020-7396 9000
Open daily 3.30pm-5pm.
U: Victoria.

A ☎

Little has changed at this delightful family-run hotel near Victoria, a haven for those up from the country for shopping and wanting to stretch the day out a little further, and a godsend for thirsty visitors who have just been round Buckingham Palace in the summer. Afternoon tea in the quiet drawing-room with its splendid ornate mantlepiece and its two fluffy sheep is a special treat. But tea is usually served in the new Terrace, overlooking the gardens at the back. The waiters give a very good impression of family butlers. All in all, tea here is a special pleasure. (£15 per person.)

The Landmark

222 MARYLEBONE RD, NW1, 020-7631 8000
Open daily 3pm-6pm.
U: Baker St/Marylebone.

A ☎

You're likely to get a crick in your neck in this magnificent setting. The Winter Garden

where you have tea is in the middle of the eight-storey, palm-bedecked Atrium. (Landmark tea £17.)

Library Bar

THE MONTCALM
GT. CUMBERLAND PL, W1, 020-7402 4288
Open daily 2.30pm-5.30pm.
U: Marble Arch.

A

The Montcalm Hotel is a delightful place for tea, just north of Oxford Street near Marble Arch and set in a gracious crescent. Taking tea in the comfortable library bar, sitting on large sofas, includes a posh sandwich 'collection' plus all the usual trimmings. (£16 per person.)

Original Maids of Honour

KEW RD, KEW, SURREY, 0181-940 2752
Open Mon. 9.30am-1pm, Tues.-Sat. 9.30am-5.30pm.
Rail: Kew Gardens.
No bookings.

Bow-fronted windows look out onto Kew Gardens opposite, the perfect place for thoroughly English tea and cakes after admiring all those exotic foreign blooms. With cottage-style furniture and blue-and-white china, you could be in the country. The place is relaxed and friendly, the selection of cakes (which you also can buy on your way out) wide and the service excellent. (Set tea £4.65.)

The Palm Court

THE LANGHAM HILTON
1 REGENT ST, PORTLAND PL, W1, 020-7636 1000
Open daily 3pm-6pm.
U: Oxford Circus.

A ☎

A pianist playing gently in the Palm Court sets the tone here. It's a good, rather stately spot with a tea which includes York ham on its sandwich menu and a variety of pastries. (£16 per person.)

Palm Court

LE MERIDIEN WALDORF, ALDWYCH, WC2
020-7836 2400
Open daily 3pm-5.30pm.
U: Covent Garden.

A ☎

If you're feeling old-fashioned, or are a good dancer, this is the place to come on a weekend, when the band strikes up and their famous tea dances begin. It takes place in the magnificent Palm Court, all high British Empire Edwardian style and gilded walls. During the week, tea is £18 per person; for the tea dance, you pay £25 per person, or with a glass of Champagne (obligatory we should imagine, with all that exercise), it's £28 per person.

The Ritz Palm Court

THE RITZ, PICCADILLY, W1, 020-7493 8181
Open daily 3.30pm-5.30pm.
U: Green Park.

A ☎ **�**

You may have to book weeks in advance—a sign of the overwhelming popularity of tea in the legendary Palm Court of the Ritz Hotel. The oval setting is beautiful, the gold and red chairs a little uncomfortable, but tea at the Ritz is something everyone should do once in a lifetime. Service is impeccable; the experience unforgettable. It's the most expensive tea in London, but there is all that gilding to take care of. (£27 per person.)

The Savoy

STRAND, WC2, 020-7836 4343
Open daily 3pm-5.30pm.
U: Embankment/Charing Cross.

A ☎ **♦**

The Savoy afternoon tea menu is pretty, and informative enough to take away—they must lose a lot of them. A picture on the front shows a terrace with various elderly gentlemen entertaining various much younger ladies and bottles of Champagne on the table. Rather surprisingly, what look like Chinese junks sail up and down the Thames. Inside there's a little piece about the Thames Foyer (where you take tea), full of wonderful nuggets about the Savoy Orpheans, and the famous who came here. The actual menu seems rather meek compared to the rest, but the tea when it comes, brought by stately waiters to your armchair or sofa, is delicious. A tinkling pianist whiles away the afternoon. (£19.50 per person.)

Looking for an address?
Refer to the index.

HOTELS

CONTENTS

INTRODUCTION. 152
OUR HOTEL RATING SYSTEM 152
RENTING AN APARTMENT. 153
BED & BREAKFAST 155
HOTEL SYMBOLS. 155
TOP OF THE LINE. 156
LUXURY 161
TOWNHOUSE HOTELS. 177
MODERATE 185
ECONOMY. 196
THE CHAINS. 200
AIRPORTS. 200

INTRODUCTION

London's hotel scene is expanding as never before, at both ends of the spectrum—luxury and economy. There's also been major buy-outs of some hotels and chains, which have resulted in higher standards across the board. 'Designer' hotels also have become a major factor in the market, with Ian Shrager opening in St. Martin's Lane and in Berners Street, and the continuing expansion of the smaller town house market. All in all, it makes for a most exciting mix of properties, suited to everyone from pop stars to princes.

All top hotels now have state-of-the-art equipment, particularly important for business travellers. Business centres are improving and many are open 24 hours a day. Health clubs have become de rigueur and new swimming pools are being built in many hotels. Even among the smaller hotels, standards are very high indeed, suited for the international traveller.

LONDON HOTEL PRICES

It should be kept in mind that while published rack rates at top hotels appear high, there are many bargains to be had for the intrepid traveller. Check advance purchase packages before departure, investigate corporate rates offered to many businesses or, for the bold, negotiate on the spot. Weekend packages, small group bookings and seasonal savings abound. Our editorial comment will tell you what we think of the hotels, and price does not necessarily mean the best in terms of accommodation, service or ambience. So choose carefully.

RESERVATION SERVICE

If you arrive without having booked a hotel, the **Tourist Information Centres** run by the London Tourist Board at **Heathrow Airport**, **Liverpool Street Station** and **Victoria Station** can book a room for you, though they do not cover every hotel. There is a credit card booking hotline run by the LTB open Mon.-Fri. 9.30am-5.30pm, 020-7932 2020, Fax 020-7932 2021. The *Evening Standard's This is London* (www.thisislondon.com) has an agreement with HotelWorld (www.hotelworld.com) for selecting and reserving London hotel accommodations online.

TOWNHOUSE HOTELS

The townhouse hotel phenomenon is unique to London, and has seen incredible growth in the last five years. Townhouse hotels are converted private houses in leafy residential areas—Chelsea, South Kensington, Knightsbridge and Notting Hill Gate—that have been joined together and decorated with quality antiques. The service is usually very personal and caring. What townhouse hotels lack in size (most have fewer than 20 rooms), they make up for with charm, style, a very warm welcome and a genuinely personal touch. Most recently, townhouse hotels have started to appear in central London areas like Mayfair.

OUR HOTEL RATING SYSTEM

To help you easily find the hotel that best matches your needs and budget, we have listed establishments in sections that reflect price, service and amenities: **Top of The Line**, **Luxury**, **Townhouse** (see explanation below), **Moderate** and **Economy**. We also have listed Chain Hotels and Airport Hotels at the end of the chapter.

Our ranking of the décor, service, food, amenities and ambience of each hotel is expressed in Keys, from one to five. The number of Keys accompanying each review indicates the hotel's ranking according to the following system:

♪ *Just the basics:* A clean room and private bath, and that's about it.

♪♪ *Comfortable:* Adequate rooms, pleasant service and some amenities.

♪♪♪ *Very comfortable:* Good rooms, amenities and service; you can't complain.

♪♪♪♪ *Everything you need and more:* Excellent rooms, superb amenities and service—with style.

♪♪♪♪♪ *As good as it gets;* pure luxury: Where to stay if money is no object and you demand perfection. Among the very best hotels in the world.

RENTING AN APARTMENT

You might also consider the option of renting an apartment, particularly if you are contemplating a longer stay and are quite happy to stock your own fridge and discover your neighbourhood restaurants. Living like a Londoner can be great fun. Renting a house or apartment in London is becoming an increasingly popular option; and greater demand has consequently produced a wider range and choice. The apartments recommended here are only a few of those available in London. For further advice, contact your local British Tourist Authority office.

The BTA publishes a booklet listing recommended apartments and apartment services. When you enquire about an apartment, try to get as much information as you can, as they vary enormously even within the same apartment block. The rates given here, except where indicated otherwise, are for weekly rentals and are only an indication of the price. There are many options and special breaks and prices vary according to time of year and availability.

Most apartments also offer daily rates and do not restrict you to a weekly stay. If you stay longer, rates often decrease. Of the companies listed first here, all of which deal with large numbers of apartments, we particularly recommend In the English Manner for its delightful townhouses as well as its first-class apartments. They also rent houses outside London.

APARTMENT RENTAL SERVICES

The Apartment Service
5-6 FRANCIS GROVE, WIMBLEDON, SW19 4DT
020-8944 1444, FAX 020-8944 6744
WWW.APARTMENTSERVICE.COM

Barclay International Group
150 E. 52ND ST, NEW YORK, NY 10022
212-832-3777, TOLL-FREE 800-845-6636
FAX 212-753 1130

Home from Home
22 GLOUCESTER RD, SW7
020-7584 8914, FAX 020-7823 8433
E-MAIL: HOMEFROMHOME@COMPUSERVE.COM
Studio 1-2 people from £395; 3-bedroom 1-6 people from £1,250.

Highly organised, friendly group originally started by a qualified barrister and offering very good short-term lets of privately owned homes in prime London sites.

In the English Manner
LANCYCH, BONCATH, PEMBROKESHIRE SA37 0LJ
0123-969 8444, FAX 01559 371 601
WWW.ENGLISH-MANOR.CO.UK
IN U.S.: 515 SOUTH FIGUEROA ST, SUITE 1000,
LOS ANGELES, CA 90071
213-629-1811, TOLL-FREE 800-422-0799
FAX 213-689-8784;
4092 NORTH IVY RD, NE, ATLANTA, GA 30342
404-231-5837, FAX 404-231-9610

Park Lane Apartments
119/121 PARK LANE, W1Y 3AE
WWW.PARKLANE.CO.UK
E-MAIL: PARKLANE@CPD.CO.UK
Weekly: high season £575-£4,100, low season £520-£2,450.

Apartments in Park Lane and also throughout Mayfair and the City. Many complimentary services offered.

Westminster Apartment Services
16 LEINSTER SQ, W2 4PR
020-7221 1400, FAX 020-7229 3917

Many apartments all around London at a variety of prices.

RECOMMENDED APARTMENTS

Please note that all prices are exclusive of VAT, at 17.5% unless otherwise stated. A reduced rate of VAT is payable after 28 days.

The Ascott Mayfair
49 HILL ST, W1X 7FQ
020-7499 6868, FAX 020-7499 0705
WWW.SCOTTS.COM.SG
E-MAIL: ASCOTTMF@SCOTTS.COM.SG
56 apts: nightly £184-£550, weekly £1,240-£3,700, monthly £5,050-£14,900.
U: Bond St.

Luxurious apartments with complimentary continental breakfast included, with a very high standard of both apartments and service, plus health club, business services, lounge and bar.

Aston's Apartments

31 ROSARY GDNS, SOUTH KENSINGTON, SW7 4NQ
020-7590 6000, FAX 020-7590 6060
WWW.ASTONS-APARTMENTS.COM
E-MAIL: SALES@ASTONS-APARTMENTS.COM
U.S. TOLL-FREE 1-800-525-2810
60 apts £60-£160.
U: Gloucester Rd.

These apartments are well placed and well run and recommended for budget accommodations in a good Kensington location.

Beaufort House

45 BEAUFORT GDNS, KNIGHTSBRIDGE, SW3 1PN
020-7584 2600, Fax 020-7584 6532
WWW.BEAUFORTHOUSE.CO.UK
E-MAIL: INFO@BEAUFORTHOUSE.CO.UK
22 apts: low season nightly, £180-£490, weekly £1,225-£3,395; high season nightly £200-£550, weekly £1,365-£3,815.
U: Knightsbridge/Sloane Sq.

In pretty Beaufort Gardens near Harrods, these well-decorated and well-equipped suites are in an elegant old building and include 24-hour concierge, daily maid service and electricity. Longer lets available.

Citadines Barbican

7-21 GOSWELL RD, EC1
020-7566 8000, FAX 020-7566 8130
E-MAIL: BARBICAN@CITADINES.COM
129 apts £89-£135. Weekly rates also available.
U: Barbican.

This apartment hotel is owned by the French group Orion.

Also at 94-99 High Holborn, WC1, 020-7395 8800, Fax 020-7395 8799; 18-21 Northumberland Ave., WC2, 020-7766 3700, Fax 020-7766 3766.

Draycott House

10 DRAYCOTT AVE, CHELSEA, SW3 3AA
020-7584 4659, FAX 020-7225 3694
WWW.DRAYCOTTHOUSE.CO.UK
E-MAIL: SALES@DRAYCOTTHOUSE.CO.UK
13 apts: nightly £172-£416, weekly £1,234-£2,648.
U: Sloane Sq/South Kensington.

Well located in Chelsea, there's a friendly welcome here. In a charming, old red-brick building, many have their own balconies. Very well decorated in English country style.

Durley House

115 SLOANE ST, CHELSEA, SW1X 9PJ
020-7235 5537, FAX 020-7259 6977
WWW.FIRMDALE.COM
E-MAIL: DURLEY@FIRMDALE.COM
U.S. TOLL-FREE 1-800-553-6674
11 apts £240-£435
U: Sloane Sq.

Owned by the excellent Firmdale group which also owns Dorset Square, the Pelham Hotel, the Covent Garden Hotel and the new Charlotte Street Hotel. All thoroughly recommended by us, these delightful, well-decorated suites in a fashionable area, are among our favourites. Decoration is English country-style at its best. More an all-suite hotel than apartments with the additional comforts.

Flemings Mayfair

10 HALF MOON ST, MAYFAIR, W1Y 7RA
020-7493 2088, FAX 020-7629 4063
WWW.FLEMINGS-MAYFAIR.CO.UK/FLEMINGS
E: MAIL: RESERVATIONS@FLEMINGS-MAYFAIR.CO.UK
U.S. TOLL-FREE 1-800-348-4685
10 apts £165-£255.
U: Green Park.

Part of Flemings Hotel, the apartments in this Mayfair townhouse have all the hotel's amenities and a separate entrance. Ideally located.

Fountains

1 LANCASTER TERRACE, HYDE PARK, W2 3PF
020-7706 7070, FAX 020-7706 7006
WWW.LIVING-ROOMS.CO.UK
E-MAIL: SALES@LIVING-ROOMS.CO.UK
17 apts £171-£450. Weekly rates available.
U: Lancaster Gate.

These individually decorated apartments, just north of Hyde Park, overlook the Italian Water Gardens in the park.

Grosvenor House

GROSVENOR HOUSE HOTEL, PARK LANE, W1A 3AA
0171-499 6363, FAX 0171-493 3342
WWW.GROSVENORHOUSE.CO.UK
46 apts nightly £290-£485.
U: Hyde Park Corner.

Part of the Grosvenor House Hotel, though with its own entrance, the apartments are well decorated and guests can use the hotel's facilities such as the first-rate health club and pool. Long lets also.

Hyde Park Residence

55 PARK LANE, W1Y 3DB
020-7409 9000, FAX 020-7493 4041
WWW.HPR.CO.UK
E-MAIL: LETTINGS@HPRAPTS.DEMON.CO.UK
120 apts weekly basis only £1,100-£65,000.
U: Hyde Park Corner.
  Superb accommodation on London's Park Lane with views over Hyde Park. Some apartments are on long-term lets. The building has all the facilities of a five-star hotel.

Nell Gwynn House

SLOANE AVE, SW3 3AX
0202-7584 8317, FAX 020-7823 7133
200 apts: weekly £320-£800. Minimum let 22 nights.
U: Sloane Sq/South Kensington.
  Apartments individually owned but centrally managed. In an impressive 1930s building and recently refurbished, this is a popular location in Chelsea with a health club and garage.

One Thirty

130 QUEENSGATE, SOUTH KENSINGTON, SW7 5LE
020-7581 2322, FAX 020-7823 8488
WWW.ONETHIRTY.CO.UK
E-MAIL: SALES@ONETHIRTY.CO.UK
54 apts: nightly £126.50-£267, weekly £841.50-£1775.50.
U: Gloucester Rd/South Kensington.
  In a refurbished Victorian building near the museums and Hyde Park, the apartments are well furnished and some have balconies.

23 Greengarden House

23 GREENGARDEN HOUSE
ST. CHRISTOPHER'S PL, W1M 5HD
020-7935 9191, FAX 020-7935 8858
WWW.GREENGARDENHOUSE.COM
E-MAIL: INFO@GREENGARDENHOUSE.COM
23 apts: nightly £165-£260, weekly £1,155-£1,820.
U: Bond St.
  In a delightful, secluded courtyard behind Oxford Street, some of the apartments are quite small, but well decorated and the management is delightfully helpful.

BED & BREAKFAST

  This is proving a popular and good way to stay in London, in private houses where you are given a warm welcome. Many of the hotels in the following Economy section fit into this category. Contact these companies for vetted accommodations:

At Home in London

70 BLACK LION LANE, W6 9BE
020-8748 1943, FAX 020-8748 2701
WWW.ATHOMEINLONDON.CO.UK
E-MAIL: ATHOMEINLONDON@COMPUSERVE.COM

Bulldog Club

14 DEWHURST RD, W14
020-7371 3202, FAX 020-7371 2015
WWW.BULLDOG.COM

Uptown Reservations

50 CHRISTCHURCH ST, SW3 4AR
020-7351 3445, FAX 020-7351 9383
WWW.UPTOWNRES.CO.UK

Wolsey Lodges Ltd.

9 MARKET PL, HADLEIGH, IPSWICH, SUFFOLK IP7 5DL
BROCHURE REQUESTS: 01473-827500, ADMINISTRATION: 01473-822058, FAX 01473 827444
WWW.WOLSEY-LODGES.CO.UK
E-MAIL: WOLSEY@WOLSEYLO.DEMON.CO.UK

HOTEL SYMBOLS

  Before the text of each review, you'll find the following symbols:

A	All credit cards taken
	Visa
	MasterCard
	American Express
	Diners Club
	Health club and/or spa
	Tennis
	Golf
	Horseback Riding
	Swimming pool
P	Parking
	In-room faxes
	Meeting rooms
	Business center
	Complimentary continental breakfast

TOP OF THE LINE

The Berkeley ♪♪♪♪

WILTON PL, SW1X 7RL
020-7235 6000, FAX 020-7235 4330
WWW.SAVOY-GROUP.CO.UK
E-MAIL: INFO@THE-BERKELEY.CO.UK
56 stes £450-£2,600, 112 rms S £280, D £305-£365 plus VAT. 11 non-smoking stes, 17 non-smoking rms. Air cond. 24-hr rm service. Limousine service.
U: Hyde Park Corner/Knightsbridge.

🅐 🏋 ⇌ P 🛏 ♺

Since it opened in 1972, The Berkeley has remained in the vanguard of London's top hotels. Built of sandstone, it has mellowed well and has a timeless elegance while its location can't be beaten, being a few seconds from Knightsbridge and Hyde Park. Discreet, refined and superbly refurbished, it welcomes its celebrity guests as if they are long-lost friends. The entrance hallway is small but stylish, more in keeping with a grand house than a hotel. The rooms themselves are well sized and impeccably furnished in a grand country-house manner. Two of the top conservatory suites have their own saunas. Service is second to none. In keeping with the capital's status as a top restaurant city, **Vong** remains one of London's most fashionable hot spots, with a stylish frontage onto Knightsbridge and an entirely separate entrance (see *Restaurants*). Since the refurbished main restaurant came under the direction of Pierre Koffmann of **La Tante Claire**, The Berkeley has had a real edge on all hotels (see *Restaurants*). The Berkeley Health Club is fully equipped with one of the true pleasures of London—a swimming pool with both a retractable roof for fine weather and great views over London.

Claridge's ♪♪♪♪

BROOK ST, W1A 2JQ
020-7629 8860, FAX 020-7499 2210
WWW.SAVOY-GROUP.CO.UK
E-MAIL: INFO@CLARIDGES.CO.UK
79 stes £475-£3,500, 118 rms S £290, D £345-£360 plus VAT. 17 non-smoking stes, 30 non-smoking rms. Air cond. 24-hr rm, maid and valet service.
U: Bond St.

🅐 🏋 🛏 ♺

From its creation in 1853, when William Claridge put together six houses to let suites

as private apartments, Claridge's has been welcoming heads of state, dignitaries and the illustrious from around the world. They come for the discreet welcome and because this grand and dignified hotel manages so successfully to convey the feel of a private club, even down to a blazing log fire in the lobby in the winter. A major refurbishment has transformed parts of the hotel, while still retaining the feeling of old-fashioned comfort and luxury. Two penthouse suites on the seventh floor, both with two bedrooms, two bathrooms and sitting-rooms with terrace, have been created—the Davies Penthouse complete with original fireplace and a barrel-vaulted ceiling and the Brook Penthouse sporting all the elegance of the Art Deco era. Service is all you would expect and includes full butler services; this is truly living in the grand manner. The Royal Suites remain as sumptuous as ever, one complete with the grand piano that belonged to Richard d'Oyly Carte, founder of the Savoy Hotel and the Opera Company. Designed as three, they can make one suite of 50 separate rooms. The facilities are bang up-to-date, though décor can be anything from Scottish baronial to pure 1920s chic. **Claridge's** restaurant, originally designed in 1925-26 by Basil Ionides to provide an ambience in keeping with the jazz age, offers some good cooking (see *Restaurants*). Services include hairdressers for men and women and a society florist.

The Connaught ♪♪♪♪

CARLOS PL, W1Y 6AL
020-7499 7070, FAX 020-7495 3262
WWW.SAVOY-GROUP.CO.UK
E-MAIL: INFO@THE-CONNAUGHT.CO.UK
24 stes £695-£1,600, 66 rms S £290-£300, D £370-£380 plus VAT. Non-smoking rms available. Air cond in most rms. 24-hr rm service. Bentley & Rolls Royce limousine service.
U: Bond St.

🅐 🏋 🛏 ♺

Probably the most quintessentially English of London's top hotels, The Connaught has always attracted guests for the sort of understatement the nation is famed for; a rarefied hushed elegance and feeling of absolute top comfort and quality British service. From the outside it doesn't even look very much like a London hotel, with its low height and red brick façade fitting perfectly with its Mayfair neighbours. The ratio of staff to guests is very high and it shows. It has never sought to be fashionable; instead it has the feel of a grand country-house transplanted to London. Marble fireplaces, oak panelling and wonderfully ornate ceilings in the public areas, which are furnished with antiques and paintings, add to the atmosphere. Bedrooms are luxurious and decorated in appropriate English chintzes; bathrooms are marble, with masses of toiletries. While tradition is very much to the fore, the needs of the twenty-first century are not forgotten with ISDN telephone lines and the opening of a health club. There are two restaurants presided over by top chef Michel Bourdin, now here for a glorious 25 years: **The Connaught Restaurant** (very formal) and **The Grill Room** (Georgian-style), both serving a mix of traditional English and French cuisine (see *Restaurants*).

The Dorchester *ffff*

54 PARK LANE, W1A 2HJ
020-7629 8888, FAX 020-7409 0114
WWW.DORCHESTERHOTEL.COM
53 stes £450-£1,925, 195 rms S £275-£295, D £305-£335 plus VAT. Non-smoking rms available. Air cond. 24-hr rm service. Limousine service.
U: Hyde Park Corner.

From the day it opened in 1931, the Dorchester was hailed as the most modern and luxurious hotel in London and the total refurbishment of the late eighties has ensured that it still is. Just peruse the guest list—Woody Allen, Cindy Crawford, Sigourney Weaver, Karl Lagerfeld, Cecil B. De Mille, to name but a few, and details of all guests are meticulously recorded for future stays. The Rolls Royces, Daimlers and stretch Mercedes parked outside announce a celebrity clientele who frequently want publicity along with tight security and attention. Along with heads of state and international industrialists, they come here for personal service (a ratio of almost 3 staff per bedroom) plus the latest technology. The rooms are now among the best in London, restored to the remarkable standards of the past that made the hotel so famous. Triple-glazed bedroom windows, many looking out over Hyde Park, shut out the noise of London. Bedrooms are large and furnished with antiques in grand English country-house style. Some rooms have four-poster beds, swathed in fabrics and silks that are echoed around the windows. Paintings adorn the walls while touches like hand-embroidered cushions

scattered around add to the home-away-from-home—or perhaps palace-to-palace—feel. All the bathrooms, boasting the deepest baths in London (Charlton Heston claims they are the only ones big enough for him to put his knees under water), are decorated in white Italian marble and many have windows giving natural light. The Oliver Messel Suite is delightful and was restored by some of the same craftsmen who had worked on it in 1953, when it opened as the first luxury suite in a British hotel. The roof garden suites, restored to their original patterns, are stunning. The Promenade, just off the entrance lobby, stretches before you, a sea of marble and opulence perfect for morning coffee, afternoon tea, cocktails and light snacks. The bar is great for cocktails and a menu of light Italian dishes and has live jazz in the evenings. **The Oriental Restaurant** offers expensive Chinese food in spectacular décor, and also has three private dining rooms. Modelled on an old Spanish Palace, **The Grill Room** serves traditional British food, (see *Restaurants*). Anyone who has overindulged can work out in the Dorchester Spa.

47 Park Street *ffff*

47 PARK ST, W1Y 4EB
020-7491 7282, FAX 020-7491 7281
E-MAIL: RESERVATIONS@47PARKSTREET.COM
52 stes £275-£600 plus VAT. Air cond. 24-hr rm service from Le Gavroche.
U: Bond St.

Now flagship of Sofitel Demeure Hotels, you could describe this as a restaurant with rooms, as **Le Gavroche**, in the capable hands of young Michel Roux (Albert Roux's son), is probably the better known of the two institutions, (see *Restaurants*). But what rooms you find in this prestigious Mayfair address, a member of Relais et Châteaux. Suites are individually designed and range from the chintzy to the clubby. Each comes with one or two bedrooms plus a sitting room complete with dining table and chairs and a fully equipped kitchen for entertaining, or for those on longer stays when even Le Gavroche's attractions might pall. Antiques, interesting fabrics and objets d'art decorate the rooms. The marble bathrooms are all luxury and feature masses of Molton Brown toiletries and wonderful fluffy bathrobes and towels. Technophiles are well catered for with three telephone lines in each suite, plus private DDI phone/modem line. It's not chance that over sixty percent of their customers represent repeat business and may well be influenced by the fact that hotel guests get preferential booking for the restaurant.

The Four Seasons Hotel ✔✔✔✔

HAMILTON PL, PARK LANE, W1A 1AZ
020-7499 0888, FAX 020-7493 6629
WWW.FOURSEASONS.COM
26 stes £440-£1,800, 194 rms S £270-£300, D £315-£325 plus VAT. 9 non-smoking stes, 82 non-smoking rms. 2 rms for disabled. Air cond. 24-hr rm service.
U: Hyde Park Corner.

🅐 ⏹ P 🍽 ⭕ 🖥

Built in 1970, the simple façade belies a luxurious interior; and this hotel is both grand and welcoming with good views over Hyde Park. Though owned by an international chain, there is no lack of individuality here. Off the impressive wood-panelled lobby, a lounge offers light meals and our favourite seasonally changing **Four Seasons Tea**, voted 'London's 1999 Top Tea Place of the Year' by The Tea Council (see *Quick Bites*). Apart from the Conservatory rooms, which are delightful, and the very well-equipped suites, large bedrooms are decorated with style, many in soft colours. The furnishings are pretty, the sofas comfortable and the beds are renowned. The hotel has an enviable reputation for professional service and first-rate housekeeping, with baby-listening and baby-sitting services on hand. Lanes restaurant makes striking use of stained glass, dark blue marbling, wood panelling and rich colours. There is a spectacular buffet with an intricate glass sculpture as a centrepiece. Chefs Eric Deblonde and Shaun Watling offer a mix of exciting modern dishes with international influences while not neglecting old British favourites. The Cocktail Bar has an extensive Malt Whisky menu and a resident pianist. The fitness club offers state-of-the-art equipment.

We're always interested to hear about your discoveries and to receive your comments on ours. Please let us know what you liked or disliked; **e-mail us** at gay-ots@aol.com.

The Four Seasons Hotel Canary Wharf ✔✔✔

46 WESTFERRY CIRCUS, E14 8RS
020-7510 1999, FAX 020-7510 1998
WWW.FOURSEASONS.COM
14 stes £450-£1400, 128 rms S £240-£290, D £260-£310 plus VAT. 3 non-smoking stes, 43 non-smoking rms. 7 rms for disabled. Air cond. 24-hour rm service Limousine service.
U: Canaray Wharf, DLR: Westferry.

🅐 ⏹ P 🍽 ⭕ 🖥

It's taken a while, but the Docklands redevelopment area has finally taken off and the opening of this, London's second Four Seasons Hotel, pretty well confirms it. In the heart of Canary Wharf, London's major new financial centre and just ten minutes from London City Airport, it's spanking new and feels more Los Angeles than London. Indeed the whole area seems like a totally separate city and only the incredible views of the City of London remind you where you are. Designed for a largely corporate clientele, it is quite stark (except for the rather dubious choice of purple carpeting in the public areas), but very functional. Rooms are large with pale wood flooring and simple American walnut furniture, but equipped with every imaginable bit of technology: big flat-screened televisions with Internet access, CD players, play stations, multiline telephones and safes designed to hold a laptop. Bathrooms have excellent lighting, separate shower units, good deep baths and Bulgari toiletries. The more expensive rooms all have superb river views, while the Presidential Suite is the last thing in luxury: a massive 2,930 square feet (728sq.m), it features three bedrooms, walk-in closet, separate powder room, big sitting area, full kitchen and dining room for eight. The restaurant, **Quadrato** is under the direction of Milanese chef Marco Bax and offers a Northern Italian menu; chefs work in an 'exhibition' kitchen in the centre of the restaurant (see *Restaurants*). A small bar area to the left of the entrance serves cocktails, light meals and afternoon tea and in summer there is an open terrace for alfresco eating. Key staff have come from other Four Seasons hotels around the world, so ensuring high standards of service. Guests have access to a state-of-the-art fitness centre within the hotel and use of the adjacent Canary Riverside Health Club.

The Halkin 𝒥𝒥𝒥𝒥

5 HALKIN ST, SW1X 7DJ
020-7333 1000, FAX 020-7333 1100
E-MAIL: RES@HALKIN.CO.UK
11 stes £415-£575, 30 rms S/D £265-£345 plus VAT. Air cond. 24-hr rm service.
U: Hyde Park Corner.

A ☎ ♻

One of the first 'designer' hotels now springing up all over London, The Halkin is still impressive and comes as something of a surprise. Tucked away in very British Belgravia, it is pure Italian, from the minimalist décor to the Giorgio Armani staff uniforms. From the moment you enter the granite, marble-floored lobbies with Italian-designed leather sofas and chairs, you realise that chintz and the English country-house look have been rejected here in favour of clean, lean and very sophisticated lines. Large bedrooms each have their own seating area and the general scheme is minimal with much wood on the walls and plenty of mirrors. Most of the splendid all-marble bathrooms have their own walk-in showers. Rooms boast all the latest techno-gadgetry, from hands-free telephones and remote control lighting to CD players and videos, plus featuring high security key systems. The restaurant, called **Stephano Cavallini at The Halkin**, reflects the esteem this young chef is held in, and focuses on modern Italian cuisine (see *Restaurants*). It's first-class, with a handsome adjoining private dining room for parties up to twenty. The small bar adjacent to the lobby is invariably full of designer-clad guests.

The Hempel 𝒥𝒥𝒥𝒥

HEMPEL SQ, LANCASTER GATE, W1
020-7298 9000, FAX 020-7402 4666
E-MAIL: THE-HEMPEL@EASYNET.CO.UK
12 stes from £390-£1,200, 35 rms S/D £235-£275. Air cond. 24-hr rm service. Garden.
U: Lancaster Gate.

A ☎ ♻

Unlike the opulent and almost decadent air of Blakes Hotel, also owned by society designer Anouska Hempel, here minimalism reigns with more than a nod towards the Orient. This is one of those places which you enter and say 'Wow'—that is after you've found the front door of this ultra-discreet, oh-so-talked about hotel. Just two minutes from Hyde Park, and stretched over five townhouses which run along an entire garden square, it's all lightness, whiteness and sophistication with Portland stone rather than marble and designed so the fireplaces appear to float in the walls. The rooms are equally sophisticated, some might even say spartan in their approach, though they incorporate a wealth of high-tech 'must haves'. All the facilities are here, plus I-Thai, serving Italian/South East Asian food. The Shadow Bar with its special cocktail selection attracts a sophisticated clientele. There is a fitness club to keep that figure. Directly opposite, a further townhouse, number 17, is used for fashion shows and shoots and opens onto a Zen garden where peace supposedly reigns. Certainly it's delightfully tucked away.

The Hyatt Carlton Tower 𝒥𝒥𝒥𝒥

CADOGAN PL, SW1X 9PY
020-7235 1234, FAX 020-7235 9129
WWW.LONDON-HYATT.COM
60 stes £380-£2,750, 160 rms £280-£305 plus VAT. 64 non-smoking rms. Air cond. 24-hr rm service.
U: Hyde Park Corner.

A 🍴 ≈ P ☎ ♻ 💻

Overlooking leafy Cadogan Square, this refurbished sixties hotel is a favourite with Asian and Arab heads of state, with one of the most expensive suites in London—the eighteenth-floor Presidential Suite which is spectacular by any standards. From the bullet-proofed glassed-in conservatory style drawing room/dining room you look down over Chelsea's green squares; elsewhere the suite is opulent with a four-poster bed, panic buttons, its own sauna and Jacuzzi with a television built into the wall, plus personal butler with his own pantry area. But you don't have to go quite so high for great views and good-sized rooms. Try room 426 on the fourth floor with its own balcony for breakfast and a delightful gold-starred entrance. On the ninth floor, the Peak Health Club offers state-of-the-art equipment, work-out classes and an attractive lounge area for light meals. The business centre is impressive. As for restaurants, Grissini as its name implies offers Italian food, and **The Rib Room& Oyster Bar** is tops for traditional British beef (see *Restaurants*). Afternoon tea and drinks accompanied by a harpist are fun in the pretty Chinoiserie Lounge off the lobby.

The Lanesborough ✓✓✓✓✓

HYDE PARK CORNER, SW1X 7TA
020-7259 5599, FAX 020-7259 5606
WWW.LANESBOROUGH.COM
E-MAIL: INFO@LANESBOROUGH.CO.UK
43 stes £510-£4,000, 52 rms S £245-£295, D £325-£430 plus VAT. 30 non-smoking rms. Air cond. 24-hr room and butler service. Limousine service.
U: Hyde Park Corner.

A ☨ ☎ ♿

Opened in 1991, The Lanesborough rapidly became the place for the likes of Madonna and Michael Jackson, noted for having all the latest high-tech gadgetry, cunningly concealed behind a sea of mahogany furnishings. Indeed, façade is everything here, for this luxury hotel was created inside the gutted shell of the former St. George's Hospital, a beautiful white classical building that dominates the western side of Hyde Park Corner. Marketed as a stately country home in the heart of central London, it's all large-scale antique furniture, acres of marble, yards of impressive fabric and wonderful, huge flower arrangements. It may feel like a stately home of the 1820s, but the comforts of the twenty-first century are evident. Rooms have triple-glazed windows and are beautifully furnished in the aforementioned mahogany. Its arrival policy is singular: guests are taken to the room and introduced to their own butler who will unpack, run baths and, most importantly, explain the up-to-minute equipment which can be confusing—all in a very traditional British manner. **The Conservatory** is in a lavish, over-the-top, mini-Brighton-pavilion style, with massive urns, fountains and trees, particularly right for late evening supper dances, where chef Paul Gayler cooks an international cuisine. The wood-panelled **Library Bar**, complete with bookshelves, is a real delight and buzzes for drinks and light meals (see Bars); tea is served in The Conservatory which is decorated in wonderful muted gold (see *Quick Bites*). Service throughout is faultless, from personalised stationery to complimentary pressing by a 24-hour butler service on arrival. The Royal Suite includes the use of a Bentley and your own 24-hour butler.

The Ritz ✓✓✓✓✓

PICCADILLY, W1V 9DG
020-7493 8181, FAX 020-7493 2687
WWW.THERITZHOTEL.CO.UK
E-MAIL: ENQUIRE@THERITZHOTEL.CO.UK
22 stes £450-£1,500, 109 rms S £285-£385 D £325-£385 plus VAT. 6 non-smoking stes, 14 non-smoking rms. Air cond in stes and executive rms. 24-hr rm service. Limousine service.
U: Green Park.

A ☎ ♿

Built in 1906 by César Ritz, and the first reinforced steel and concrete building in London, The Ritz looks onto Piccadilly and Green Park. Recent refurbishment has enabled it to live up to its name and fortunately it is now as glitzy and ritzy (though in the best possible taste) as anyone could want. It's relatively small, with a mere 131 rooms, each one individually decorated in pretty pastels and gold leaf, full of antique furniture and fireplaces, and with plush marble bathrooms. Behind the tradition however, the needs of the twenty-first century are well catered to with UK/US ISDN modem lines in each room and plugs that all are dual voltage. Suites for private dining are stunning; the Trafalgar Suite looks over Green Park. Afternoon tea in this glorious hotel is a British institution, taken in the opulent **Palm Court** (see *Quick Bites*). The Louis XIV restaurant, generally referred to simply as **The Ritz Restaurant** (see *Restaurants*) is probably the most beautiful dining room in London and in summer has a terrace overlooking a small, artificially created walled garden. The hotel also has a fitness centre for those who cannot do without a daily workout.

The Savoy ✓✓✓✓✓

STRAND, WC2R 0EU
020-7836 4343, FAX 020-7240 6040
WWW.SAVOY-GROUP.CO.UK
E-MAIL: INFO@THE-SAVOY.CO.UK
71 stes £425-£1,370, 106 rms S £270, D £325-£345 plus VAT. 35 non-smoking stes, 50 non-smoking rms. Air cond. 24-hr rm service.
U: Charing Cross/Temple (closed Sun).

A ☨ ≋ ☎ ♿

Few hotels in London can be as famous as The Savoy, and it is truly something of a legend. This grand lady continues to hog the limelight, particularly after her multimillion pound refurbishment which took the suites back to their former glorious furnishings and removed the clutter of the cathedral-like lobby and brought back the original carvings and shape. Close to both the City and the West End, and within easy walking distance of theatres and Covent Garden, its position facing the Thames and overlooking Embankment Gardens is spectacular. For this is a view that inspired French Impressionist Claude Monet into producing some 70 paintings of London's bridges on three separate occasions at three different seasons from 1899 to 1901. From the sought-after rooms 310-311, you can see eight bridges over the River Thames. Thames-side suites with their views over the river come with top service at the touch of a button from maid, waiter or valet; classic furnishings are set off by deep pink velvet curtains; extravagant bathrooms include the famous 10-inch showerheads, and the other usual luxurious touches. Since opening in 1889, with Escoffier as head chef, The Savoy has always been known for restaurants, a tradition carried on by chef Anton Edelmann. **The River Room** restaurant overlooking the Thames with dancing in the evening is formal and old-fashioned (see *Restaurants*). The wood-panelled Grill Room is good for pretheatre suppers and serious business lunches and offers an extensive wine list. **The American Bar** is a great meeting place and afternoon tea or drinks in the Thames Foyer provides a good place for people-watching (see *Bars*). A Champagne-and-seafood bar is perched above the entrance drive. The elegant Fitness Gallery has a swimming pool, massage room, gym and sauna, unisex hairdresser and beauty treatments.

LUXURY

The Athenaeum ♪♪♪♪
116 PICCADILLY, W1V 0BJ
020-7499 3464, FAX 020-7493 1860
WWW.ATHENAEUMHOTEL.COM
E-MAIL: INFO@ATHENAEUMHOTEL.COM
43 stes £300-£750, 113 rms S £215-£250, D £225-£295 plus VAT. 21 non-smoking stes, 50 non-smoking rms. Air cond. 24-hr rm service. Limousine service.
U: Hyde Park Corner.

🅰 🍴 ☎ ⟳
Understated elegance is the keynote of this very well-run privately owned hotel. The Athenaeum is situated on Piccadilly, just past Hyde Park Corner and overlooks the green swathes of Green Park. Rooms are beautifully lit, and manage to radiate a golden glow with warm fabrics and fine furniture. They also offer all the amenities like two telephone lines, VCRs, CD players and the novelty in bathrooms of heated mirrors that never steam up. The Windsor Lounge, good for morning coffee or afternoon tea, has also been redecorated, and the hotel's famous bar continues to stock 56 different malt whiskeys. Bullochs, named after the ebullient marketing director, Sally Bulloch, serves modern European cuisine in a pretty downstairs room. You're likely to spot the odd celeb here, as it's particularly popular with some of the top film and theatre stars. In addition, they offer self-contained serviced apartments behind the hotel which are very popular, again with stars who are staying in London for any length of time.

Blakes Hotel ♪♪♪♪
33 ROLAND GDNS, SW7 3PF
020-7370 6701, FAX 020-7373 0442
WWW.BLAKESHOTEL.COM
E-MAIL: BLAKES@EASYNET.CO.UK
9 stes £495-£750, 42 rms S £155, D £220-£310 plus VAT. Non-smoking rms on request. Air cond in large stes and doubles. 24-hr rm service.
U: Gloucester Rd/South Kensington.

🅰 ▦ (in suites)
Not for the faint-hearted and definitely for travel connoisseurs, this theatrical hotel in a series of late-Victorian townhouses was the first venture of Anouska Hempel, a.k.a. Lady Weinberg, the wife of Sir Mark Weinberg, a leading city financier. The dramatic results reflect her fashion and acting background. Blake's style is esoteric with strong themes running through each room's décor, from Biedermeier furniture to black Oriental lacquer. There are lots of swagged curtains, trompe l'œil wall treatments and marble in the bathrooms. Each bedroom is different, startling and idiosyncratic, some with painted floorboards, others with fantasy beds. Some might accuse Hempel of over-decoration, and fans of minimalism should definitely steer clear, but it's enormous fun and, not suprisingly, goes down big with the media who make up most of the guests and no doubt appreciate the in-room CD and video players. Downstairs, Blakes restaurant continues Hempel's keen interest in the Orient with Japanese 'Kyoto Country Breakfasts' and an

expensive, but beautifully executed, international menu attracting a glamorous clientele. The hotel has an affiliation with Holmes Place health club.

Brown's Hotel   ♪♪♪

33 ALBEMARLE ST, W1A 4SW
0207-7493 6020, FAX 020-7493 9381
WWW.BROWNSHOTEL.COM
E-MAIL: BROWNSHOTEL@UKBUSINESS.COM
9 stes £250-£715, 118 rms S £199-£260, D £199-£290 plus VAT. Air cond. 24-hr rm service.
U: Green Park.

A ☎ ⟲

An ideal base for anyone seeking an England of a bygone era, Brown's now belongs to the group that owns Raffles Hotel in Asia. Having undergone a quiet refurbishment without changing its character, it remains a delightful, old-fashioned hotel, all stained-glass windows and oak panelling. It was opened by a retired gentleman's valet and Queen Victoria was a frequent visitor here. Running between Albemarle and Dover Streets, it originally had two entrances. Bedrooms are now done to a good standard and are cosy rather than grand. The Victorian Suite, room 161, for instance, is predominantly blue with chintz furnishings; other executive rooms have small lobbies leading to bedrooms. Some have four-poster beds; all have antiques (some reproduction), and top bathrooms. The refurbishment, renaming and redirecting of the restaurant has been met with enthusiasm. **1837 Restaurant**, with its separate entrance, is very good, with a particularly striking wine list (see *Restaurants*). Best of all, the lounge is delightful for afternoon tea, with comfortable sofas, a fireplace and a palpable feeling of the elegance of a past age; in the winter, particularly, it feels like a time warp with ladies up from the country. The clubby St. George's Bar with a stained glass window depicting the English hero, is a popular meeting place.

The Cadogan   ♪♪♪

75 SLOANE ST, SW1X 9SG
020-7235 7141, FAX 020-7245 0994
WWW.CADOGAN.COM
E-MAIL: INFO@CADOGAN.COM
4 stes £250-£330, 61 rms S £140-£195, D £190-£225. 1 non-smoking ste, 15 non-smoking rms. 24-hr rm service. Air cond.
U: Sloane Sq.

A ☎ ⟲

On walking into The Cadogan you could easily be forgiven for expecting to bump into Oscar Wilde or Lily Langtry, for the Historic House Hotel group has taken enormous pains to restore it to its Edwardian splendour. These two notorious figures frequently entertained their friends here and indeed it was the site of Oscar Wilde's arrest. Historic House Hotels have country-house hotels in Llandudno, Aylesbury and York, and the Cadogan is used like a London pied-a-terre. It sits well on Sloane Street, with its red brick façade and stained-glass ground-floor windows—and its refurbishment has left the lady in good order. Halfway between the Sloane Square and Harvey Nichols/Harrods triangle and overlooking Cadogan Gardens, the large rooms have double-glazed windows and are traditionally furnished with antique furniture; the bathrooms are beautifully done in white marble and some of the studio rooms have separate bath and shower rooms. Rooms have fax and modem points and 'brightner' light switches. The Cadogan restaurant is very pretty with floral prints and wood trim, and serves Modern British food at respectable prices, while the Langtry Drawing Room makes a pleasant afternoon tea break from shopping. The hotel has recently been licensed to perform marriages and it's hard to think of a more romantic spot.

The Capital   ♪♪♪

28 BASIL ST, SW3 1AT
020-7589 5171, FAX 020-7225 0011
WWW.CAPITALHOTEL.CO.UK
8 stes £310-£350, 40 rms S £160-£180, D £205-£235 plus V.AT. Air cond. 24-hr rm service. Limousine service.
U: Knightsbridge.

A P ☎ ⟲

It would be very easy to walk past The Capital, despite its excellent location a few steps from Harrods, but once inside, first impressions set the tone—you're welcomed by the doorman into a pretty front hall where a fire burns in the hearth on cold days. This is a personally run hotel, and it shows; owners David and Margaret Levin leave nothing to chance and membership of the prestigious Relais et Châteaux group underlines this. At this small, intimate hotel, the individually designed bedrooms are delightful in a subtle, pretty English country-style; some of the rooms have a more masculine feel, with darker colours and sober oil paintings on the walls. Egyptian cotton bed linens, handmade mattresses, beautiful fabrics at the windows and on the beds, lavish marble bathrooms with power showers, luxury toiletries and robes are all in the package. **The Capital** restaurant has always had an excellent reputation and new chef Eric Chavot shows every sign of maintaining it (see *Restaurants*). Décor is by society stylist Nina Campbell and uses, to great effect, mirrors from Viscount Linley. The Levins, who also own L'Hôtel, **The Greenhouse** restaurant (see *Restaurants*) and **Le Métro** wine bar (see *Quick Bites*), are firm believers in the good, but elegant, life.

The Churchill Inter-Continental ✔✔✔✔

30 PORTMAN SQ, W1A 4ZX
020-7486 5800, FAX 020-7486 1255
WWW.INTERCONTI.COM
E-MAIL: CHURCHILL@INTERCONTI.COM
40 stes £480-£3,500, 399 rms S/D £300-£350 plus VAT. 122 non-smoking rms. Air cond. 24-hr rm service.
U: Marble Arch.

Ⓐ P 🏊 ✿ 🖥

This grand hotel overlooking Portman Square may look modern from the outside, but inside it adopts a very British approach, with the overall English country-house hotel look working well. It is an extremely comfortable hotel and justifiably popular with business visitors. Clementine's, appropriately named after Sir Winston Churchill's wife, is an elegant, rather formal dining room with warm wood panelling, contemporary British art and nattily striped chairs; the food is modern Mediterranean and on Sundays there is live music. The Club Inter-Continental on the eighth floor has its own check-in, concierge and lounge, complimentary continental breakfast and valet service. The Churchill Bar and Cigar Divan is a place you can sink into, with deep, club-like leather sofas, Churchill prints

and memorabilia and the air of an interesting private study, concentrating on cigars and Cognac, which again reflects the great man's tastes. The Terrace is a more relaxed restaurant, open all day for breakfast, light lunches and afternoon teas with piano entertainment. Like all Inter-Continental hotels, the guests share all the advantages the group offers to frequent international travellers.

The Conrad ✔✔✔✔

CHELSEA HARBOUR, SW10 0XG
020-7823 3000, FAX 020-7351 6525
WWW.HILTON.COM
E-MAIL: LONCH-GM@HILTON.COM
160 stes £180-£190 plus VAT. 50 non-smoking stes. Air cond. 24-hr rm service.
No underground nearby.

Ⓐ 🍴 ⚓ P 🏊 ✿

A great riverside location, overlooking Chelsea Harbour, this luxury all-suite hotel is away from the mainstream hotel areas, but with plentiful taxis and many other advantages, this is not really a detraction. The Conrad is a splendid white stone building and part of the riverside Chelsea Harbour complex. The hotel is very quiet, being in a mainly residential area, and it has a large restful entrance foyer. Of particular appeal is the excellent health club, which has gym, sauna, steam bath, massage and swimming pool. Suites are two-roomed and very spacious, and many have wonderful river/harbour views. The newly refurbished restaurant, overlooking the river, is renamed Aquasia and offers a modern fusion menu in marina-style décor with porthole water features, a decorative floating glass top bar counter and decking. It's great Sunday brunch continues to attract appreciative brunchers. Drake's Bar has a terrace and is good for light snacks.

Crowne Plaza St. James's ✔✔✔✔

41 BUCKINGHAM GATE, SW1E 6AF
020-7834 6655, FAX 020-7630 7587
WWW.CROWNEPLAZA.COM
E-MAIL: SALES@CPLONSJ.CO.UK
18 stes £330, 333 rms S £217, D £240-£330 inc VAT. 2 non-smoking floors. Air cond. 24-hr rm service. Limousine service.
U: Victoria.

Ⓐ 🍴 ✿

Recently taken over by the Crowne Plaza group, the former St. James Court hotel has undergone a complete renovation. It is well located in Victoria, close to Buckingham Palace and St. James's Park. An impressive open-air courtyard connects the hotel bedrooms with an apartment complex of 82 suites, which are ideal for longer stays. There's a splendid lobby with a turn-of-the-century feel to it. Good sized, well-appointed bedrooms have modern furniture, two-line telephones, modem points and well-equipped bathrooms. Many of the tennis stars stay here during Wimbledon fortnight, but there are always a fair number of celebrities to spot. There are three very different restaurants: the casual Café Méditerranée featuring Modern British cooking, Zander, sister to the highly fashionable restaurant in the courtyard, Bank, and **Quilon** with modern Indian cuisine (see *Restaurants*). The Olympian Health Club offers beauty treatments in addition to the usual gym, saunas and Jacuzzis.

Dukes

ST. JAMES'S PL, SW1A 1NY
020-7491 4840, FAX 020-7493 1264
WWW.DUKESHOTEL.COM
E-MAIL: DUKESHOTEL@CSERVE.COM
12 stes £280-£525, 77 rms S £190-£200, D £210-£525 plus VAT. Air cond. 24-hr rm service.
U: *Green Park.*

Tucked away in a private, very quiet, gas-lamped cul-de-sac but just off busy St. James's Street, this red-brick Edwardian building houses a hotel opened in 1908 and retaining an Old World, almost club-like feel. Most taxi drivers know it but others might have difficulty finding it without detailed directions. Since David Naylor-Leyland originally took over Dukes, there was a splendid refurbishment and a cut in the prices, all of which is good news. But tradition remains the key element here in St. James, the heart of 'Gentlemans' London', known for its centuries-old shops, tailors and gentlemen's clubs. Many rooms have four-poster beds; all are of different shapes and décors though they all boast good antiques, oil paintings and marble bathrooms. The Penthouse suite has the bonus of a private roof terrace, which is used for parties. There is a lobby sitting room with a fireplace, comfortable sofas and newspapers you can read with your morning coffee, afternoon tea or drinks. The restaurant caters only to residents. The small cocktail bar, headed by a barman who

reputedly makes the best martinis in the country, also offers the discerning an extensive range of vintage Cognacs.

The Goring

17 BEESTON PL, GROSVENOR GDNS, SW1W 0JW
020-7396 9000, FAX 020-7834 4393
WWW.GORINGHOTEL.CO.UK
E-MAIL: RECEPTION@GORING.CO.UK
7 stes £255-£290, 68 rms S £150-£172, D £185-£260 plus VAT. Some rms air cond. 24-hr rm service.
U: *Victoria.*

Three generations of Gorings have run this hotel since it opened in 1910 and all that experience really shows in the extremely high levels of personal service. Owner George Goring's claim that he has slept in every room and really understands the intricacies of hotel management sums up the delightful and careful approach this hotel epitomises. It's close to Victoria Station and Buckingham Palace, and yet tucked away on a quiet side street. Even the façade with its attractive plants looks inviting. Quality is the buzzword here. Public rooms are delightful—a welcoming entrance area with marble floors and chandeliers, a pretty lounge and The Garden Bar overlooking gardens and the more formal dining room serving good, traditional British meals. Bedrooms are good size, with reproduction and antique furniture, while bathrooms are luxurious and well equipped. Some rooms have private balconies overlooking the pretty gardens at the back of the hotel. This is a delightful hotel, old-fashioned in the sense of offering courteous service yet bang up to date in terms of facilities such as ISDN telephone lines.

Great Eastern Hotel

LIVERPOOL ST, EC2 7QN
020-7618 5000, FAX 020-7618 5001
WWW.GREATEASTERN.HOTEL.CO.UK
E-MAIL: SALES@GREAT-EASTERN-HOTEL.CO.UK
21 stes £365-£515, 246 rms S £195, D £225-£255 plus VAT. 71 non-smoking rms. Air cond. 24-hour rm service.
U: *Liverpool St.*

It could only have been a matter of time before the indefatigable Sir Terence Conran extended his Midas tentacles from restaurants to hotels; the Great Eastern is the result. The only hotel within the square mile of the City of London, and representing the golden era of railway hotels, (Grade II listed), it is a clever blend of old and new. Corridors and public areas have been renovated to enhance all the building's 'listed' features, while rooms have been done in a very contemporary style. Clever play has been made of the business nature of the City, in the use of suiting fabric on upholstery, a theme that has been continued with dark wood panelling, rich colour schemes and leather upholstery. The past is recalled in nice touches like antimacassars and leather writing pads, while clever storage conceals all the mod cons—ISDN lines, modem points, fax machines, DVD/CD players. Bathrooms are pure white, tiled with black-and-white floors and have Frette linen. As you would expect, there's no shortage of restaurants, four in fact; **Aurora** harks back to the days of the grand Victorian station dining room—though food is thoroughly modern, (see *Restaurants*) **Terminus** is typical of the more relaxed Conran style of brasserie (see *Quick Bites*). The Fishmarket and Miyabi speak for themselves. Proximity to the burgeoning arts centres of Hoxton and Shoreditch has provided the basis for an expanding art collection. Gym and treatment rooms are first-rate, and for the less energetic there are even in-room aromatherapy facilities.

The Halcyon ♪♪♪♪
81 HOLLAND PARK, W11 3RZ
020-7727 7288, FAX 020-7229 8516
WWW.HALCYON-HOTEL.CO.UK
E-MAIL: SALES@HALCYON-HOTEL.CO.UK
18 stes £240-£700, 25 rms S £150-200, D £225-£240 inc VAT. Air cond. 24-hr rm service.
U: Holland Park.

Located in leafy Holland Park, with its wide streets and air of quiet wealth, the Halcyon Hotel has been created from several grand former private residences. There is an impressive wrought-iron awning over the entrance and the whole building has a delicate pink-wash. A high proportion of returning guests appreciate it for the fact that it's reliably private, discreet and luxuriously appointed. All the well-proportioned rooms are furnished with good antiques and delightful fabrics; some rooms have dramatic designs; many boast four-poster beds; and all the marble bathrooms are well appointed. The entrance hallway welcomes with an open fireplace. **The Room at The**

Halcyon (see *Restaurants*), has a Mediterranean-style décor and has achieved considerable acclaim under chef Toby Hill. There's a charming walled outdoor terrace which is perfect for intimate alfresco meals in warmer months; the Vodka Bar at the restaurant entrance serves caviar, salmon and lighter meals. Frequently there's a singer to entertain on Sunday evenings. The Halcyon has a place in the country, Fawsley Hall in Northamptonshire.

Holiday Inn Mayfair ♪♪♪
3 BERKELEY ST, W1X 6NE
020-7493 8282, FAX 020-7629 2827
WWW.HOLIDAYINN.COM
E-MAIL: HIMAYFAIR@EASYNET.CO.UK
4 stes £350-£600, 186 rms S/D £180-£230 inc VAT. Non-smoking floor. Air cond.
U: Green Park.

Occupying a prime site in the heart of Mayfair, between Berkeley Square and Piccadilly, this is very much the flagship of London's Holiday Inns. It has undergone extensive refurbishment in recent years, and has all the necessities of modern life: Internet access, direct fax lines, in-house movies, etc. There is a small entrance foyer with comfortable chairs and sparkling chandeliers giving an air of relaxed elegance. The restaurant, Nightingales, offers an international menu. Bedrooms are well furnished, and superior rooms have spa baths and king-size beds. The standards of service are all you would expect from a worldwide chain in such a prime location.

The Howard Hotel ♪♪♪♪
TEMPLE PL, STRAND, WC2R 2PR
020-7836 3555, FAX 020-7300 0234
WWW.THEHOWARDLONDON.COM
E-MAIL: SALES@THEHOWARDLONDON.COM
21 stes £329-£695, 114 rms S/D £ 299 inc VAT. 46 non-smoking rms. Air cond. 24-hr rm service.
U: Temple (closed Sun.).

Overlooking the River Thames, where the City meets Westminster, The Howard has one of the lowest profiles of all London's grand hotels, with discretion and privacy the formula for its success among serious captains of industry. Slightly old-fashioned and well-located for business, theatres and the Eurostar Terminal at Waterloo, it is tranquil with sumptuous eighteenth-century décorative touches—friezes, ornate ceilings and marbled pillars. Rooms are well appointed with French marquetry furniture and marble bathrooms with robes and slippers provided. Most have good views of the Thames, and many have twin rather than double beds. Three telephone lines and modem points are standard, while suites come equipped with 'power' desks, complete with computer, scanner, printer, etc. The Quai d'Or restaurant and Temple Bar overlook a charming floral courtyard and the restaurant serves a classical French and English repertoire. It is formal and comfortable with a predominantly green and pink décor. To emphasise the international business appeal, traditional Japanese breakfasts are available.

Inter-Continental Hotel ✓✓✓✓

1 HAMILTON PL, W1V 0QY
020-7409 3131, FAX 020-7493 3476
WWW.INTERCONTI.COM
E-MAIL: LONDON@INTERCONTI.COM
43 stes £375-£3,000, 415 rms S/D £290-£335 plus VAT. 275 non-smoking rms. Air cond. 24-hr rm service.
U: Hyde Park Corner.

🅰 'Ψ' P 🏢 ♻ 🖳

A large, modern hotel, situated at the crossroads of Park Lane, Piccadilly and Hyde Park Corner, and the flagship Inter-Continental property in the UK. On entering, there is a grand, marbled lobby with a useful lounge just off it. Bedrooms, which are fair-sized, are comfortably, but not ostentatiously, decorated, with the top floor rooms having great views of London. All the expected amenities are here, including plentiful seating areas, and, of course, double-glazed windows. Luxury suites feature good-sized drawing rooms and have butler service, CD players, videos, etc. The penthouse, The Palace, has a large drawing room, master bedroom with marbled bathroom and private entrance with a lobby. Particularly favoured by business people, the purpose-built Video Conferencing Suite is ideal for top business meetings and the business centre boasts four private meeting rooms. **Le Soufflé** restaurant under Peter Kromberg is suitably formal and expensive (see *Restaurants*), and has live piano music in the evenings. More informal meals may be taken in the Coffee House or the Observatory Lounge. Guests are offered all the advantages of an international hotel group when staying at an Inter-Continental, such as the Six Continents Club, air mile programmes and more. The Club on the dedicated seventh floor has 46 bedrooms and suites, private registration, shower room facilities and lounge with separate meeting space.

The Landmark ✓✓✓✓

222 MARYLEBONE RD, NW1 6JQ
020-7631 8000, FAX 020-7631 8080
WWW.LANDMARK.CO.UK
E-MAIL: SALES@THELANDMARK.CO.UK
47 stes £360, 252 rms S/D £285-£305 plus VAT. 25 non-smoking stes, 147 non-smoking rms. Air cond. 24-hr rm service.
U: Marylebone.

🅰 'Ψ' ≈ P 🏢 ♻ 🖳

One of the great old railway hotels (next door to Marylebone Station), The Landmark was completely restored in 1993. The Grade II-listed building is pure Victorian Gothic on the outside, but the inside was completely redesigned to great effect. The eight-storey central atrium is its most stunning feature with a mezzanine gallery overlooking the **Winter Garden Lounge** (see *Bars*). Also here is the formal restaurant, serving good Modern British dishes. The rooms, in a beige neutral palette, are among the largest in London, and are exceptionally well equipped with excellent bathrooms, many with separate shower cubicles. Top suites include the sixth-floor Penthouse and the fifth-floor Presidential which even has a grand piano. More casual is The Cellars bar with all-day light meals. The fitness facility has a small pool, sauna, steam room, massage and gym.

The Langham Hilton ✓✓✓✓

1 REGENT ST, PORTLAND PL, W1N 4JA
020-7636 1000, FAX 020-7323 2340
WWW.HILTON.COM
E-MAIL: LANGHAM@HILTON.COM
22 stes £670-£1200, 429 rms £280-£365 plus VAT. 12 non-smoking stes, 267 non-smoking rms. 2 rms for disabled. Air cond. 24-hr rm service.
U: Oxford Circus.

🅰 'Ψ' ≈ 🏢 ♻

Originally opened in 1865 and the pinnacle of Victorian style, the Langham played a key role in London society of the time—Oscar Wilde, Toscanini and Mark Twain were once guests. To this day, it continues to draw an intriguing crowd of celebrities. Totally reconstructed after decades as the headquarters of the BBC, it is impressive, with marble floors and pillars in public areas, and a particularly grand entrance hall, a peach-toned décor and American red oak furniture and fittings in guest rooms. Executive rooms and suites include English breakfast and a complimentary bar. All rooms have Playstations and Internet access through the T.V. Memories restaurant offers a menu of British classics and international influences and is particularly good for breakfast. Tsar's, decorated in rich royal Russian greens and golds, is a dark, rather enigmatic bar; it serves 107 types of vodka, caviar and seafood and boasts one of the most comprehensive collections of Louis Roederer Champagne in the world. The Chukka Bar's polo scenes and equipment are suitably sporty, and it is packed in the early evening and popular for luncheon buffets. **The Palm Court** is open from 6am to 2am for light refreshments, drinks and afternoon tea (see *Quick Bites*). The new health club is spectacular with sauna, state-of-the-art gym, steam room, solarium, and all kinds of treatments. There's also a hair and beauty salon, shop and theatre desk.

Le Méridien ♩♩♩♩

21 PICCADILLY, W1V 0BH
020-7734 8000, FAX 020-7851 3008
WWW.FORTE-HOTELS.COM
E-MAIL: GENERALSALES@FORTE-HOTELS.COM
35 stes £450-£650, 231 rms S £265-£295, D £305-£355 plus VAT. 90 non-smoking rms. Air cond. 24-hr rm service.
U: *Piccadilly Circus.*

A 'Ⴘ' ≈ P 🏨 ⟳ 🖳

Le Méridien's Piccadilly Circus location is one of the best addresses in London and the hotel is one of the most centrally located. Bedrooms, awash in pastel pinks and turquoise, boast good reproduction furniture, and the chic bathrooms (some with Jacuzzi) are splendid. Latest high-tech additions include the introduction of Playstations. Delightful afternoon tea in the lounge features a harpist and 40 different blends of tea. The formal **Oak Room** restaurant under chef Robert Reid continues to aspire to the standards set by Marco Pierre White (see *Restaurants*). An opulent and grand room, with splendid carved wood panelling and

impeccable service, its walls are lined with delightful paintings and portraits. The summery fourth-floor terrace, with its glass conservatory ceiling, overlooks Piccadilly and has recently appointed Michel Rostang as consultant chef. On sunny days, you can eat outside, enjoying the breeze and the view. The Burlington Bar is cosy and suitably club-like. With a keen eye to what's happening on the other side of the Atlantic, Le Méridien has just opened a Cigar Club and to complete the picture, there is a stunning Champneys health facility in the basement with gym, pool, squash court, massage and beauty treatments.

Le Méridien Grosvenor House ♩♩♩♩

90 PARK LANE, W1A 3AA
020-7499 6363, FAX 020-7493 3341
WWW.GROSVENORHOUSE.CO.UK
E-MAIL: 114033.1626@COMPUSERVE.CO.UK
72 stes from £417, 450 rms S from £267, D from £287 plus VAT. 8 non-smoking stes, 72 non-smoking rms. Air cond. 24-hour rm service.
U: *Marble Arch.*

A 'Ⴘ' ≈ P 🏨 ⟳ 🖳

Recently made part of Le Méridien group, the Grosvenor House Hotel first opened in 1927, built on the site of the former home of the Earl of Grosvenor. Overlooking Hyde Park on one side and Mayfair on the other, its location really can't be beaten. Its enormous, grand ballroom—the Great Room with a capacity of 2,000—attracts major balls and events like the annual June international Grosvenor House Art and Antiques Fair. Its size makes it slightly impersonal, but bedrooms are functional and filled with five-star amenities, indeed it claims to have been the first hotel in the world to offer its guests high-speed Internet access. Most bathrooms are luxurious and very well-equipped. A hotel of this massive size has a constant refurbishment programme, so check that you've got an up-to-date room when you book. The ground floor entrance now has a cosy wood-panelled library and plenty of armchairs. **Chez Nico** under Nico Ladenis (see *Restaurants*) remains one of London's top restaurants, despite a simplification of the menu and lessening of prices, and La Terraza, set on raised floors overlooking Park Lane and Hyde Park, offers breakfast (including a comprehensive Japanese breakfast), lunch and dinner. Go to the Royal Club on the seventh floor for executive perks, including a private boardroom and express check-in. Best rooms are the Sovereign Suites, which include limousine service to and from the airport. The health club has a large pool, gym, sauna and massage. A separate entrance leads to 140 serviced apartments in addition to the hotel rooms.

Le Méridien Waldorf ♫♫♫

ALDWYCH, WC2B 4DD
020-7836 2400, FAX 020-7836 7244
E-MAIL: LMPICCRES@FORTE-HOTELS.COM
28 stes £350, 292 rms S £235, D £255 plus VAT.
Non-smoking rms. Air cond. 24-hr rm service.
U: Covent Garden/Holborn.

A 🍴 🏢 ⟳

Opened in 1908 by King Edward VII, Le Méridien Waldorf still maintains a faintly raffish air, mainly due to its over-the-top, but wonderful Edwardian style. In the heart of theatreland, close to Covent Garden and convenient for the City, it recalls a bygone age of grand hotels. A landmark (Grade II listed) building, its rooms echo the Edwardian theme throughout, but it is the public areas which shine, literally, with rich wood panelling and stained-glass windows. Bedrooms have their own entrance lobby and the new décor, traditionally inspired, reflects the hotel's opulent past, with draped curtains and chandeliers. Bathrooms have period-style washbasins. This is an entertaining hotel, reflected in their brochure which gives you fun facts that bring home the huge organisation of a hotel. So '500 scones are served and 1,250 cups of tea poured every weekend, 1,089 pillows are fluffed each day; 15 tons of mineral water are consumed during conferences each year', and so on. The **Palm Court** restaurant is elegant, and on Sundays still holds Tea Dances which go in and out of fashion; otherwise a less energetic afternoon tea is served daily (see *Quick Bites*). Spices restaurant has an international menu with quite a few fusion dishes as well as more traditional British and French favourites and is open for pre- post-theatre dining. Drink either in the oak-panelled Club Bar or the rather ordinary Footlights Bar which tries hard to be a typical English pub and is always full of broadcasters from the famous BBC World Service just opposite. As part of the ongoing refurbishment, a new health club will be on line by the end of the year.

London Hilton on Park Lane ♫♫♫

22 PARK LANE, W1A 2HH
020-7493 8000, FAX 020-7208 4142
WWW.HILTON.COM
E-MAIL: GM-PARK-LANE@HILTON.COM
53 stes £495-£3095, 393 rms S/D £315-£395
plus VAT. 24 non-smoking stes, 144 non-smoking rms. Air cond. 24-hr rm service.
U: Hyde Park Corner.

A 🍴 **P** ⟳ 🖥

This was London's first skyscraper hotel, and when it opened, created a great deal of outrage that guests would be able to see into the gardens of Buckingham Palace. Times have changed, but it still has arguably the best views in London. The combination of its splendid Park Lane location and talented management by Rudi Jägersbacher and his team, makes this large hotel work beautifully. A massive £35 million refurbishment has placed the London Hilton among London's best hotels, with state-of-the-art facilities including TV, Internet access, Playstations and modem links. Bedrooms are spacious and have traditional mahogany furniture and plush fabrics and furnishings, and the bathrooms are very good. Six floors of executive rooms have their own private check-in, a clubby lounge area for complimentary continental breakfast, tea and drinks as well as a business centre. The Hilton is known for its excellent service and top efficiency, hence its popularity and large number of returning clients. The 28th floor **Windows** restaurant has the best view in town—a panorama of Hyde Park, Buckingham Palace and the rooftops of Mayfair and beyond. In the inspired hands of French chef Jacques Rolancy, the restaurant has gained a top reputation to add to the stunning views (see *Restaurants*). There's a pleasant, welcoming brasserie on the ground floor; St. George's Bar is the place for sporting enthusiasts with its six-foot TV screen. **Trader Vic's** Polynesian décor and menu is adventurous, fun, unusual and good value (see *Bars*). The newly opened **Zeta Bar** is very stylish and offers 'healthy' cocktails, full of fruit juices and good spices, with lengthy descriptions to take the guilt out. Also very good bar snacks. All in all, this makes Zeta a very formidable rival to the Met bar next door which operates a members-only policy after 5pm (see *Bars*).

London Marriott ♪♪♪

GROSVENOR SQ, W1A 4AW
020-7493 1232, FAX 020-7491 3201
WWW.MARRIOTT.COM
17 stes £450, 221 rms S/D £245 plus VAT. 17
non-smoking stes, 152 non-smoking rms. Air
cond. 24-hr rm service.
U: Bond St.

Ⓐ 🤸 ☎ ⟳ 🖥

Right on the corner of impressive Grosvenor
Square and bustling Duke Street, and a stone's
throw from the American Embassy, the
London Marriott is a popular choice with
international travellers. There is always an air
of activity in the public areas where the sofas
are set in little alcoves and backed by large
mirrors. Bedrooms are spacious, with comfortable armchairs and good writing desks, though
bathrooms can be small. Executive rooms and
suites have their own lounge. The Diplomat
plays many dining roles, from offering an
informal breakfast and lunch to a comprehensive international dinner menu. The pretty
adjacent Regent Lounge and Regent Bar are
good for a sumptuous afternoon tea buffet,
drinks and light meals.

London Marriott
County Hall ♪♪♪♪

COUNTY HALL, SE1 7PB
020-7928 5200, FAX 020-7928 5300
WWW.MARRIOTT.COM/MARRIOTT/LONCH
5 stes £360-£380, 195 rms S /D £215-£265 plus
VAT. 147 non-smoking rms. Air cond.
24-hour rm service.
U: Waterloo.

Ⓐ 🤸 ≈ P ⟳

Created from the former home of the
Greater London Council, the London
Marriott County Hall occupies a plumb riverside location right opposite the Houses of
Parliament and adjacent to London's newest
attraction, the London Eye, a giant Ferris
wheel built to celebrate the millennium. The
entrance is on the south side of Westminster
Bridge and has to be the grandest of any hotel
in London, occupying the whole of the original County Hall courtyard. Much has been
made of its municipal history, with the Noes
Lobby and the Leaders Cocktail Bar with its
collection of historical memorabilia of the
building. Bedrooms are well furnished in traditional style and many have river views; all
have satellite TV, modem points and voice-

mail. **The County Hall Restaurant** has unin-
terrupted Thames views, an oyster bar and
Modern British cooking (see *Restaurants*).
Health nuts will lap up the wonderful facilities
in the 24-hour Health Club, which include
pool, fitness centre and The Spa health and
beauty centre.

Lowndes Hyatt ♪♪♪♪

LOWNDES ST, SW1X 9ES
020-7823 1234, FAX 020-7235 1154
WWW.LONDON.HYATT.COM
E-MAIL: LOWNDES@HYATTINTL.COM
5 stes £282-£438, 73 rms S £182-£228, D £182-
£238 plus VAT. 2 non-smoking floors. Air cond.
U: Hyde Park Corner/Knightsbridge.

Ⓐ 🤸 ≈ ☎ ⟳

Very un-Belgravia and definitely un-Hyatt,
this intimate, unstuffy, well-run and friendly
hotel feels more privately owned than international chain. Bedrooms are decorated in
attractive blues, greens and pinks with good
wood furniture and are surprisingly spacious.
All have two telephone lines and modem
points. Five suites offer more luxury and are
very well appointed. The restaurant at the
Lowndes is informal, with its own bar and an
international menu, and it has al fresco tables
behind tubs of flowers on the pavement outside in summer for people-watching.
Traditional afternoon tea can be taken in the
inviting wood-panelled lounge. You can also
charge at the restaurants of the neighbouring
giant, the Hyatt Carlton Tower, where guests
can take advantage of the health club and
pool. And just next door, the Halkin Arcade is
full of shops selling good art, antiques and
design.

Mandarin Oriental
Hyde Park ♪♪♪♪

66 KNIGHTSBRIDGE, SW1Y 7LA
020-7235 2000, FAX 020-7235 4552
WWW.MANDARIN-ORIENTAL.COM
E-MAIL: RESERVEMOLON@MOHG.COM
22 stes £475-£2,500, 200 rms S£295-£375, D
£325-£375 plus VAT. 4 non-smoking stes, 44
non-smoking rms. Air cond. 24-hr rm service.
U: Knightsbridge.

Ⓐ 🤸 ☎ ⟳ 🖥

Since the Mandarin Oriental group took
over the Hyde Park Hotel in 1997, they have
undertaken a series of major refurbishments,
which have brought it bang into the twenty-

first century. The building began as gentlemens' apartments in 1892 and became a hotel in 1908 and like all grand hotels, it had its fair share of visiting celebrities, including Rudolph Valentino, who brought the whole of Knightsbridge to a halt when he appeared on the balcony. Today's celebrities include the three world-famous tenors, Pavarotti, Domingo and Carreras, as well as film stars. One of the first tall buildings in London, this splendid red-brick structure faces Harvey Nichols department store and is very close to Sloane Street and Harrods. The bedrooms at the back of the hotel have a wonderful view over Hyde Park itself. Major works have brought brand-new bathrooms to most of the rooms, beautifully decorated with marble tiles in a gracious style but with up-to-the-minute fittings. Some of the suites are made even more delightful by having their own terraces. All rooms have the modern equipment expected of a top hotel. Refurbishment in the public rooms has produced **Foliage,** a beautiful dining room looking out onto Hyde Park with a more contemporary look which is now the main showcase for David Nicholl's splendid cooking (see *Restaurants*), and the very pretty Café on the Park, which serves very good and varied menus from 7am to 11.30pm. A panelled bar to the back is more masculine in décor and contains a humidor for cigar lovers.

Mayfair Inter-Continental 🎵🎵🎵

STRATTON ST, W1A 2AN
020-7629 7777, FAX 020-7629 1459
WWW.INTERCONTI.COM
E-MAIL: MAYFAIR@INTERCONTI.COM
52 stes £600-£3,000, 238 rms S £265-£305, D £295-£335 plus VAT. 1 non-smoking floor. Air cond. 24-hr rm service. Limousine service. U: Green Park.

🅰 🏋 ≈ 🏢 ♻ 💻

A great position, in the heart of Mayfair and near Piccadilly and Green Park, plus a professional and enthusiastic staff, add up to making this a very personal hotel. There's an impressive entrance hall and bedrooms are a decent size, many with seating areas, comfortably though not lavishly furnished, with very well-equipped bathrooms. Some of the suites like the Penthouse and the Monte Carlo have two bedrooms, a good lounge, dining area and private lift from the street as well as a small roof garden. Opus 70, under Michael Coaker,

serves an excellent contemporary menu with Modern British, American and Asian influences. Jazz lovers should make a point of coming for Sunday brunch when live music is played. The small, clubby Château Bar with signed photographs of celebrities reinforces the general impression of friendliness and sophistication. The Mayfair Café is more relaxed and informal and serves breakfast and lunch from a Mediterranean-influenced menu. A small health club boasts a gym, solarium and pool. Frequent travellers enjoy all the international Inter-Continental group's facilities.

Metropolitan 🎵🎵🎵

19 OLD PARK LANE, W1Y 4LB
020-7447 1000, FAX 020-7447 1100
WWW.METROPOLITAN.CO.UK
E-MAIL: SALES@METROPOLITAN.CO.UK
19 stes £340-£1,750, 155 rms S £245-£255, D £280-£290 plus VAT. 39 non-smoking rms. 24-hr rm service. U: Hyde Park Corner.

🅰 🏋 ☎ ♻

Since being transformed by top interior designer Keith Hobbs, the Metropolitan (formerly The Londonderry) has become one of the hottest hotels in London. Hobbs has managed to create a contemporary masterpiece epitomising simple chic. From the moment you enter the lobby, with its startling space and beautifully arranged pots on the walls, you know that this is aimed at—and is very successful with—a particular clientele. Rooms are well decorated, comfortable and refreshing with their plain light wood fittings; bathrooms are all you would expect. Corner rooms have wonderful views over Hyde Park and Park Lane. Its informal, modern European style appeals to the international set from the advertising, entertainment and fashion worlds who want a London sanctuary which is a complete contrast to standard hotels. **Nobu** is still one of London's top, fashionable restaurants, owned by Nobuyuki Matsuhisa and Robert DeNiro, and offers stunning Japanese food (see *Restaurants*). Be warned: the **Met Bar** operates a discreet, informal membership policy after 5.30pm (see *Bars*).

Millennium Britannia

GROSVENOR SQ, W1A 3AN
020-7629 9400, FAX 020-7629 7736
WWW.BRITANNIAHOTEL.COM
E-MAIL: BRITTANNIARES@MILL-COP.COM
11 stes £500, 330 rms S £170, D £225-£245 plus VAT. Air cond. 24-hr rm service.
U: Bond St.

Now part of the Singapore Millennium group, this hotel has always been popular with local embassies and consulates, owing to its splendid location in the centre of Mayfair, overlooking beautiful Grosvenor Square. The main entrance is in Adam's Row, behind the square and you step down into a vast well of a main foyer which would benefit from a bit of refurbishment. Superior double rooms are spacious and well-equipped, many with separate seating areas and very good large bathrooms. Furnishings are in an antique style and luxurious. The Adams restaurant serves Modern British cuisine; the café has a respectable Anglo-American hot and cold buffet; and the excellent Shogun Japanese restaurant has a good sushi bar. There is also a pub called the Waterloo Dispatch, named after the announcement of victory at Waterloo on the site; the traditional piano bar is for drinks only and there is a cocktail lounge. You can shop in the Georgian shopping arcade at the florist, confectioner and men's wear shop. Front-of-house staff members are friendly and helpful.

The **prices** in this guide reflect what establishments were charging at press time.

The Millennium Knightsbridge

17-25 SLOANE ST, SW1X 9NU
020-7235 4377, FAX 020-7235 3705
WWW.MILL-COP.COM
E-MAIL: RESERVATIONS.CHELSEA@MILL-COP.COM
5 stes £550, 217 rms S £215, D £550 plus VAT. 84 non-smoking rms. Air cond. 24-hr rm service.
U: Knightsbridge.

From its location, bang in the middle of all the top Knightsbridge designer boutiques, the modern Millennium Chelsea is glossy enough to keep up with the neighbours. Bedrooms are rather small, but they have been refurbished to a high, modern standard and have smart marble bathrooms. An attractive central atrium has an impressive stairway up to the mezzanine level where you find a cocktail bar and The Chelsea restaurant. An informal brasserie style rules here at lunch which is excellent for Knightsbridge shoppers; there's a more formal air at dinner for the Provençal and Italian mixture of cooking. The Pavilion Lounge proves popular for afternoon tea, breakfast and snack lunches.

The Montcalm

GT. CUMBERLAND PL, W1A 2LF
020-7402 4288, FAX 020-7402 7977
WWW.MONTCALM.CO.UK
E-MAIL: SALES@MONTCALM.CO.UK
12 stes £295-£600, 108 rms S £220, D £240-£290 plus VAT. 74 non-smoking rms. 1 low-allergen rm. Air cond. 24-hr rm service.
U: Marble Arch.

Named after the eighteenth-century French general, the Marquis de Montcalm, this is something of a retreat, being just north of frenetic Marble Arch in a private Georgian crescent. Owned by the Japanese Nikko Hotels group, it is meticulously maintained and managed. A substantial refurbishment programme has brought the bedroom décor up to scratch and the duplex suites are comfortably spacious, if a bit tricky with narrow connecting spiral staircases. It also has one low-allergen room, where special materials have been used in the furnishings and the cleaning is meticulous. The light and airy conservatory-style **The Crescent** restaurant offers Contemporary European cuisine (and serves Japanese breakfasts to the high proportion of Japanese visitors (see *Restaurants*). The adjacent **Library Bar** is clubby and cosy with leather chairs, wood panelling, bookcases and a fireplace and proves a good place for afternoon tea (see *Quick Bites*). Service is pleasant and relaxed, though the first impression of the expansive marble lobby can be rather formal. This hotel is certainly a case of reality living up to the promotional material—it is one of London's best-kept secrets!

One Aldwych ♪♪♪♪

1 ALDWYCH, WC2B 4BZ
020-7300 1000, FAX 020-7300 1001
WWW.ONEADLWYCH.CO.UK
E-MAIL: RESERVATIONS@ONEALDWYCH.CO.UK
*12 stes £395-£795, 93 rms S £245-£300,
D £265-£320 plus VAT. 4 non-smoking stes, 36
non-smoking rms. Air-cond. 24-hr rm service.
U: Covent Garden.*

A ♥ ≈ ☎ ✿

One Aldwych was one of the first of
London's spectacular new luxury hotels. Its
location on the edge of Covent Garden, where
the West End meets the City, means that it has
equal appeal to the theatre-going tourist and
the high-powered business executive. The
Edwardian building was originally the home of
The Morning Post newspaper and was designed
by Mewès & Davis, the Anglo-French partnership responsible for the Ritz hotels in Paris,
London and Madrid. All the period details of
the exterior have been retained. The interior
design (by owner Gordon Campbell-Gray
with society interior designer Mary Fox-
Linton) offers something different—contemporary simplicity laced with classicism but
'without an inch of chintz in sight' where
'comfort and function are not sacrificed to
design'. The result is a luxury hotel that
reflects 'stealth wealth' rather than 'dripping
deluxe' with rich colours and plain fabrics.
There's a permanent collection of contemporary art and sculpture throughout the hotel
and in every bedroom. Flowers take centre
stage in public and guest rooms. Bathrooms
are state-of-the-art and even have mini-televi-
sions on stalks. The modern obsession with
fitness and health is met in the health club
(supervised by top London trainer Matt
Roberts), and pool; some suites feature private
gyms. Needless to say, every techno-gadget of
modern life is available—fax, modems, CD
players as standard and mobile phones on
request. This is an ultra-trendy hotel and
there's a private screening room downstairs,
which is becoming quite a status symbol
among London's newer hotels. The hotel has
three restaurants: **Axis** features modern
European cuisine and has become ultra-fashionable it own right, **Indigo** is great for
light lunches in an informal atmosphere and
the Cinnamon Bar for 'designer' sandwiches
and coffee (see *Restaurants* & *Quick Bites*).

The Park Lane Hotel ♪♪♪♪

PICCADILLY, W1Y 8EB
020-7499 6321, FAX 020-7499 1965
WWW.SHERATON.COM/PARKLANE
*39 stes £425, 266 rms S £275-£425, D £295-
£425 plus VAT. 70 non-smoking rms. Air cond.
24-hr rm service.
U: Green Park/Hyde Park Corner.*

A ♥ ☎ ✿

Opened in 1927 and now part of the
Sheraton group, this splendid Art Deco-influ-
enced hotel has provided the location for such
period pieces as Jeeves and Wooster, House of
Elliot and Brideshead Revisited. It has some
delightful suites like the Lord Peter Whimsey
Suite with a large bedroom, study that can be
turned into a second bedroom and limed-oak
drawing room with fireplace and balcony overlooking Green Park. All the bedrooms are
individually decorated and many of the large
marble-floored bathrooms have Jacuzzis. Most
of the deluxe rooms have separate showers and
many have double basins. All six Park Suites
look over Green Park. Its eponymous bar is
quite clubby, and the expansive, light 1920s
inspired Palm Court Lounge makes a good
meeting spot and is renowned for its afternoon teas. Citrus offers mediterranean dishes.
The Brasserie on the Park offers traditional
French dishes. There's a men's hair salon and
the Daniele Ryman shop sells aromatherapy
products, including anti-jet lag potions. The
splendid Art Deco ballroom can accommodate
up to 600 people for weddings, dinner dances
and antiques fairs.

Radisson Edwardian Mountbatten ♪♪♪♪

SEVEN DIALS, MONMOUTH ST, WC2H 9HD
020-7836 4300, FAX 020-7240 3540
WWW.RADISSON.COM
*7 stes £375, 120 rms S £175-£225, D £195-£290
plus VAT. 4 non-smoking stes, 60 non-smoking
rms. Air cond. 24-hr rm service.
U: Leicester Sq/Tottenham Court Rd.*

A ♥ ☎ ✿

The Earl Mountbatten of Burma provides
the theme for this Covent Garden spot owned
by the private group Radisson-Edwardian
hotels, and there are mementoes and tributes
to India throughout, creating an eclectic style.
Smallish rooms are well equipped with dark
wood furniture and all have marble bathrooms. Internet access is now available and

business-class rooms have well-equipped workstations. The country-house-style drawing room is good for afternoon tea and informal meetings. Ad Lib is informal and serves French cuisine plus good luncheon specials and pre- and post-theatre suppers; the Polo Bar is good for regular cocktails. There's also Centre Stage, an after-theatre supper club where you dine and listen to excellent cabaret from West End stars opens around 10pm and goes on until 1am.

The Radisson Hampshire ♪♪♪♪

31 LEICESTER SQUARE, WC2 7LH
020-7839 9399, FAX 020-7930 8122
WWW.RADISSON.COM
E-MAIL: RESHAMP@RADISSON.COM
22 stes £380, 102 rms S £290, D £320 plus VAT. 68 non-smoking rms. Air cond. 24-hr rm service.
U: Leicester Sq/Piccadilly Circus.

🅰 ᵞ 🕾 ⌂

Right in the heart of Leicester Square, this is a hotel that will have immediate appeal for cinema and theatregoers or anyone who thrives on being in the hub of a city. The whole area is a non-stop hive of activity with a 24-hour street personality and the Radisson-Edwardian-owned Hampshire is in the thick of it. Public rooms are quite intimate with an Oriental theme. Bedrooms are pleasant, in English country-house-style with pretty chintzes. Bathrooms are well-fitted out with Italian marble and mahogany. The new Celebrities restaurant serves Modern British food, while the small Drawing Room is good for afternoon tea and provides an invaluable central London meeting place. Suites are spacious, particularly the Penthouse on the seventh floor which is very popular with celebrities who adore its fabulous panoramic views.

> **Telephone numbers** in England have eleven digits, beginning with a zero. The initial zero must be omitted if you are calling England from abroad. Within the country, dial the entire eleven digits.

Radisson SAS Portman ♪♪♪♪

22 PORTMAN SQ, W1H 9FL
020-7208 6000, FAX 020-7208 6001
WWW.RADISSON.COM
E-MAIL: PORTMAN@LON2A.RDSAS.COM
8 stes £450-£650, 280 rms S/D £215-£250 plus VAT. 172 non-smoking rms. Air cond. 24-hr rm service.
U: Marble Arch.

🅰 ᵞ 🕾 ⌂ 🖵

Just behind Marble Arch and conveniently close to the Oxford Street shops, this hotel was completely refurbished and streamlined when taken over by Radisson SAS. You are assured of good-sized, standard bedrooms with a choice of Oriental, Scandinavian, British and Classic styles and a reasonable package of services and amenities, including an excellent security system and Internet access. The deluxe double bedrooms have sofa beds, which make this hotel a favourite with families. Some of the more expensive rooms include breakfast. There is also the novel innovation of the grab-and-run early morning breakfast of coffee and croissants in the lobby. The Portman Corner restaurant features a traditional English roast each day as well as a full à la carte menu, while afternoon tea is served beside an open fire in the lobby.

Royal Garden Hotel ♪♪♪♪

2-24 KENSINGTON HIGH ST, W8 4PT
020-7937 8000, FAX 020-7361 1991
WWW.ROYALGDN.CO.UK
E-MAIL: SALES@ROYALGDN.CO.UK
36 stes £335-£1,500, 400 rms S £210, D £260-£320 plus VAT. Air cond. 24-hr rm service.
U: High St Kensington.

🅰 ᵞ P ⌂ 🖵

Re-opened in April 1996, this hotel was transformed under the new ownership of the Singapore-based Goodwood Group. It is now a dramatic building, with some of the best views of London over Kensington Gardens, as well as down Kensington High Street. The marble lobby is impressive, with the raised Park Terrace restaurant to one end, and the bar and lounge area looking out onto the gardens. It has, of course, the latest state-of-the-art facilities in each room—in-house movies, two telephone lines, personally controlled air-conditioning and more. Rooms have good wood furniture and are furnished in a standard style, each one the same. One excellent feature is a sitting area by the huge windows, offering both good views and the feeling of being set apart from the main bedroom. Bathrooms are luxurious. **The Tenth** restaurant has created quite a stir under executive chef Steve Munkley (see *Restaurants*). The view is stunning, particularly at night when the lights of London shine. Every Saturday there is music, with the first Saturday of the month featuring the big band sounds of Manhattan from the John Wilson band, one of the best evening's entertainment on offer in a London hotel (see Bars). The health club is under the direction of top London trainer, Matt Roberts, and offers everything from eye zone treatment to reflexology.

Royal Horseguards Thistle ✔✔✔

2 WHITEHALL CT, SW1A 2EJ
020-7839 3400, FAX 020-7925 2263
WWW.THISTLEHOTELS.COM
E-MAIL: ROYALHORSEGUARDS.SALES@THISTLE.CO.UK
4 stes £475-£575, 276 rms S £217-£265, D £247-£295 inc VAT. 140 non-smoking rms. Air cond. 24-hr rm service.
U: Westminster.

🄰 🍽 ▣ ♻

Between Whitehall and the River Thames, this very grand Victorian Gothic building was once the home of the National Liberal Club and retains a club-like feel with its discreet entrance at the rear of the building. Thistle Hotels has an ongoing refurbishment programme and having updated all the bedrooms, has now opened a new bar and restaurant and six meeting rooms. All Rooms are of decent size and well-equipped with fax/modem points. Executive bedrooms are large and decorated with oak furniture and colourful chintz and have minibars, air conditioning and marble bathrooms; some have wonderful views. The Library Suite is, as it sounds, all leather, chenille and silk; the Egyptian Suite has a suitable black-and-gold colour scheme. Both have private cloakrooms and marble and ebony bathrooms. There's a pretty lounge with chandeliers and paintings, thoroughly in keeping with the general ambience of this pleasant hotel. The new restaurant, One Twenty One Two has a separate entrance and a modern, bright feel. The menu offers a European/ Asian mix as well as old British favourites. On summer afternoons, light meals are served in the Garden Terrace. Conference facilities for up to 250 people are available in sumptuous One Whitehall Place, which adjoins the hotel.

St. Martins Lane ✔✔✔

45 ST. MARTIN'S LANE, WC2N 4HX
020-7300 5500, FAX 020-7300 5515
WWW.HOTELBOOK.COM
204 stes & rms £300-£1,250, S £195-£215, D £280-£300. Non-smoking rms available. Air cond. 24-hour rm service.
U: Leicester Sq.

🄰 🍽 ▣ ▦ ♻ 🖵

Definitely the hippest new hotspot in town; if you're coming to London for the buzz, then this is the place to stay, though 'Cool Britannia' eat your heart out, it's owned by America hotel king Ian Schrager. Hats off, too, to designer Phillippe Starck, for transforming a soulless, sixties shell with such imagination. Having been greeted by a young, grey over coated doorman, you enter a vast, very twenty-first-century lobby, very modernist but with a surprise tribal art figure on your left—a theme which is echoed here and there in all the rooms. All the staff are young, enthusiastic and well-trained; many are American with other callings (arts, mostly) and, dare we say it, make a refreshing change from so many of London's hotel employees who barely seem to speak the language. Lifts have television screens on each side with fascinating pairs of eyes staring out at you or loftier cloud scenes. On arrival on a floor, the only hangover from the original building seems to be fairly uninteresting narrowish corridors, but when you enter your room, these are soon forgotten. All rooms have floor-to-ceiling windows and the higher you go the better it gets, with sixth-floor suites having stunning views— the top of Nelson's column, the London Eye, St. Martin's spire—and the effect of light is incredible. Though furniture is quite minimal (Perspex chairs), beds are sumptuous with great banks of pillows and the lighting can be changed at the flick of a switch from white to red to blue or green, depending on mood. Needless to say every high-tech amenity is on hand: state-of-the-art communications systems, Internet access etc. There are four restaurants/bars, **Saint M** and the **Asia de Cuba** which has rapidly become the place to see and be seen; the hotel has a high proportion of fashion/media guests and not surprisingly a few fashion victims (see *Restaurants*).

Sanderson ✓✓✓

50 BERNERS ST, W1P 4AD
020-7300 1400, FAX 020-73001401
E-MAIL: SANDERSON.IFUK@VIRGIN.NET.CO.UK
2 stes £495-2,500, 148 rms from £195-850

🅰 🍽 🛢 ↻ 🖥

Ian Schragers latest hip hotel in the former Sanderson building just off Oxford Street aims to create a lavish Urban Spa. Certainly, designed by Philippe Starck, it has some pretty extraordinary touches. Your first sight is of Salvador Dalí's red lips sofa which gives you an idea of the direction of the décor. There is much drapery in pale colours, large screen video monitors, and a mix of the old and the new as in 60s murals and mosaics with a giant Louis-XV armoire, and etched Venetian mirrors. The Courtyard Garden is a wonderful landscaped park open to the sky, surrounded by floor-to-ceiling glass walls and visible from anywhere in the lobby. Bedrooms follow the same fantastic inspiration, with silk curtains everywhere, electronically controlled, to separate the different spaces rather than walls. Furniture is also radically different: a silver-leafed nineteenth century sleigh bed, an egg-shaped stone as a footrest; its all designed to heighten your sense of theatricality. All the modern touches are here in-room, from DVD libraries to state-of-the-art telecommunications, portable computers, and mobile phones available on request. Dressing rooms/bathrooms are clear glass boxes with privacy areas behind mirrors, with a sink area designed like a boudoir; even the taps are designed by Starck as independent columns. **Spoon+** at Sanderson (see *Restaurants*), is inspired by Alain Ducasse's Spoon in Paris, and there are two bars: the Purple Bar which is a riot of purples, lavenders and violets, and the Long Bar serving tapas, oysters, sushi and Asian seafood, again under the control of Alain Ducasse. The Aqua Bathhouse spa is taken one step further from the original Aqua at Ian Schragers Delano. It's on two levels, and stresses spiritual as well as physical wellbeing. There's a 24-hour state-of-the-art gymnasium, steasium, steam rooms and a whole slew of top treatments from Eve Lom facials to Reiki. There are also production, wardrobe, makeup and casting rooms. This is a theatrical hotel which perfectly suits the media clientele.

Looking for an address?
Refer to the index.

Sheraton Belgravia ✓✓✓✓

20 CHESHAM PL, SW1X 8HQ
020-7235 6040, FAX 020-7259 6243
WWW.SHERATON.COM/BELGRAVIA
19 stes £375-£425, 70 rms S £275-£305, D £295-£325 plus VAT. 25 non-smoking rms. Air cond. 24-hr rm service.
U: Knightsbridge.

🅰 🍽 ≋ 🛢 ↻ 🖥

Surrounded by embassies in the heart of Belgravia, this is a relatively small hotel by Sheraton standards. There's distinctively personal service from the moment of check-in, when guests are seated at an antique leather desk in the lobby and served a glass of Champagne, so it's hard to imagine the hotel as part of the largest chain in the world. Service is slick and professional. There are several small public rooms, giving a charming impression of a private residence. Bedrooms are smallish but filled with amenities, even if it means the sofa is crammed into a corner. Chesham's restaurant is a pleasant surprise with an international cuisine, and again designed as a series of rooms, including a conservatory-style area. A friendly bar is an extension of the lobby with little nooks and crannies for private drinks or afternoon tea.

Sheraton Park Tower ✓✓✓✓

101 KNIGHTSBRIDGE, SW1X 7RN
020-7235 8050, FAX 020-7235 8231
WWW.STARWOOD.COM
47 stes £685-£1,505, 242 rms S £299-£399, D £319-£419 plus VAT. 50 non-smoking rms. Air cond. 24-hr rm service.
U: Knightsbridge.

🅰 🍽 ≋ 🛢 ↻ 🖥

Its position in the heart of Knightsbridge, within ambling distance of Harrods and Harvey Nichols and just by Hyde Park, plus Sheraton dependability, make this hotel a safe choice. Efficiency is the key here which makes the atmosphere rather functional, but hard to find fault with. Bedrooms and beds are large, security is good, and housekeeping impeccable. The executive-floor service with butlers is worth the extra cost and includes touches like valet unpacking, two-hour laundering and a special fast check-in service. All rooms have wonderful views from the circular tower, though the higher floors are obviously the best. **Restaurant One-O-One** has recently been refurbished and has a separate entrance on William Street, finally a suitably good setting for the excellent French—mainly fish—cooking of Pascal Proyart (see *Restaurants*). There are two comfortable bars, coffee shop, hair salon and gift shop.

The Stafford ♪♪♪♪

ST. JAMES'S PL, SW1A 1NJ
020-7493 0111, FAX 020-7493 7121
WWW.THESTAFFORD.CO.UK
E-MAIL: SALES@THESTAFFORD.CO.UK
14 stes £345-£700, 67 rms S £209, D £230-£295 plus VAT. Air cond in all rms.
24-hr rm service.
U: Green Park.

A 🕿 ⌗ ▯

The Stafford is another of those small London hotels which people discover and then keep to themselves. Despite this, it's been incredibly popular since World War II, when American and Canadian officers used it as a club. First rate service, led by Terry Holmes, one of London's most genial general managers and recent winner of the prestigious Hotel of the Year Award, is a key factor in the incredibly high number of returning guests. The Stafford is an elegant place, tucked away, like Duke's, behind St. James's. It's all very gracious, with individually furnished rooms in keeping with the traditional style of a refined country-house. Some rooms are in the Carriage House, built in the 1700s as stables for the aristocracy and looking out onto a small courtyard full of hanging baskets and tubs. The rooms—many beamed and oddly shaped—do make you feel in the country rather than in the heart of the capital. The Stafford also houses one of the largest wine cellars in London; if you get a chance, ask one of the staff to take you on a tour. **The Stafford** restaurant under Chris Oakes, is first-rate (see *Restaurants*). **The American Bar** is a convenient, convivial luncheon spot or pre-theatre rendezvous point (see *Bars*). Crammed with ties, caps and badges, its quirky décor goes down as a treat with guests.

Looking for an address?
Refer to the index.

Thistle Charing Cross ♪♪♪

THE STRAND, WC2N 5HX
020-7839 7282, FAX 020-7839 3933
WWW.THISTLE.CO.UK
E-MAIL: CHARING.X@THISTLE.CO.UK
238 rms S/D £210-£255 plus VAT. 140 non-smoking rms. Air cond. 24-hour rm service.
U: Charing Cross.

A 🕿 ⌗

A massive refurbishment by the Thistle group has brought this veteran station hotel bang into the twenty-first century. Its history, though, is fascinating: Jack the Ripper is rumoured to have been a guest and the original lift was one of the first 'rising rooms' in the country. Charing Cross is the official point from which all mileages are measured, so you can't get much more central, with Covent Garden and the theatre district right across the road and Trafalgar Square a couple of minutes in the other direction. The building is high Victorian, and key features such as the ornate ceiling in the Betjeman Room (available for private dining) have been beautifully restored. Many of the rooms on the upper floors have stunning views over the River Thames and even Strand-side rooms have interesting cityscape panoramas. There are two rooms specially equipped for disabled guests, and all rooms feature state-of-the-art techno-gadgetry that are high on security, with safes large enough for laptop computers and electronic deadlocks on the doors. The Strand bar is very popular with commuters and the Strand restaurant offers an international menu.

Thistle Tower Hotel ♪♪♪♪

ST. KATHARINE'S WAY, E1W 9LD
020-7481 2575, FAX 020-7481 3799
WWW.THISTLE.CO.UK
E-MAIL: TOWER.BUSINESSCENTRE@THISTLE.CO.UK
18 stes £188-£360, 802 rms S/D £84-£215 inc VAT. 7 non-smoking stes, 392 non-smoking rms. Air cond. 24-hr rm service.
U: Tower Hill.

A 🍴 P 🕿 ⌗

The Thistle Tower is a massive, modern tower block tucked between Tower Bridge and the colourful St. Katherine's Dock—which means there are spectacular views from both public and guest rooms. Besides separate check-in, City Club executive rooms (on the seventh and eighth floors) include superior, well thought-out amenities like ironing boards, irons, trouser presses and electronic safes, and luxurious bathrooms. The massive multilevel marble foyer is airily attractive. There are three restaurants: the Princes Room, named after the little princes murdered in the Tower of London, with an international menu, good views and weekend dining and dancing; The Carvery featuring traditional English roasts, and the Which Way West coffee shop/café serving a light menu throughout the day. The Thames Bar is a convivial place to enjoy that wonderful view. The location is handy for both the City and London's number-one tourist attraction, the Tower of London.

The Westbury

CONDUIT ST, W1A 4UH
020-7629 7755, FAX 020-7495 1163
WWW.WESTBURY-LONDON.CO.UK
E-MAIL: WESTBURYHOTEL@COMPUSERVE.COM
19 stes £245-£650, 225 rms S/D £175-£230 plus VAT. 9 non-smoking stes, 90 non-smoking rms. Air cond. 24-hr rm service.
U: Bond St.

When The Westbury opened in 1955, it was the first new hotel to be built in London for twenty years. It was named after the Long Island Polo Ground in New York and built by a keen polo player (Michael Phipps). Its enviable location—just steps from Bond Street and by the back door of Sotheby's—attracts a well-heeled clientele who love this particular Mayfair patch. Recently bought by Cola Holdings, it's now being rigorously scrutinised, and changes are in the offing. Bedrooms are elegant with dark-wood furniture and pretty floral touches, though sizes can vary from box-like to spacious. The restaurant is under the direction of chef Jonathan McCann who did part of his training with Alain Ducasse in Monaco. The Polo Lounge offers light meals all day and afternoon tea in front of an open fire and the Polo Bar serves drinks. Guests can use the nearby Metropolitan Club with its gym, sauna, aerobics classes and pool.

TOWNHOUSE HOTELS

The Beaufort

33 BEAUFORT GDNS, SW3 1PP
020-7584 5252, FAX 020-7589 2834
WWW.THEBEAUFORT.CO.UK
7 stes £295, 28 rms S £165, D £180-£260 plus VAT. Air cond. Modest rm service menu.
U: Knightsbridge.

From the outside, you would never guess that you were entering a hotel and, once inside, you are given your own front-door key and treated as a friend rather than a client. Located on a tree-lined residential square, and ideally situated just 100 yards away from Harrods and Knightsbridge, this privately owned hotel is unusually decorated with hundreds of original, English, twentieth-century floral water-colours. They set the tone for the individually designed rooms, with their mix of English country-house chintz and wood. Prices generously include sherry, chocolates, shortbread and Champagne, breakfast and drinks from the 24-hour bar, and membership at the local Nell Gwynn health club. Service is extremely friendly and helpful, and this charming hotel, which has won many international awards and accolades, offers a real home-away-from-home in central London. Guests booking suites are offered a complimentary one-way airport transfer.

Charlotte Street Hotel

15 CHARLOTTE ST, W1P 1HB
020-7806 2000, FAX 020-7806 2002
WWW.FIRMDALE.COM
E-MAIL: CHARLOTTE@FIRMDALE.COM
52 stes & rms. Air cond. 24-hour rm service. Limousine service.
U: Goodge St.

Just opened, this is the latest venture for Tim and Kit Kemp, who have an impressive track record with Dorset Square, The Pelham, Durley House and the Covent Garden Hotel. The new hotel has a brasserie, bar, gym and state-of-the art screening room—a sure-fire winner in this media-dominated part of London. Designer Kit Kemp has a distinctive style, but each new venture gives her scope for fresh ideas. The inspiration for wall coverings has come from the Bloomsbury Set and, as at the Covent Garden, she has made imaginative use of hand-embroidered fabrics; and there's lots of rich wood panelling. Rooms are extremely well equipped with all the latest technology and, as at their other hotels, this includes a cellular phone. Bathrooms are granite and mahogany with cast-iron tubs, separate showers, telephone and TV. Full business services are available and guests may work out in an up-to-the-minute gym.

The Cliveden Town House 🎜🎜🎜

26 CADOGAN GDNS, SW3 2RP
020-7730 6466, FAX 020-7730 0236
WWW.CLIVEDENTOWNHOUSE.CO.UK
E-MAIL: RESERVATIONS@CLIVEDENTOWNHOUSE.CO.UK
11 stes £295-£820, 24 rms S £130-£180, D £190-£235 plus VAT. 1 non-smoking ste, 6 non-smoking rms. 24-hr rm service. Air cond. U: Sloane Sq.

This handsome townhouse is in a quiet part of Cadogan Gardens, between Chelsea and Knightsbridge. Run by the owners of the top Cliveden hotel in Maidenhead, the former home of the Astors, their intention was to create a townhouse as an aristocratic family would have enjoyed all those years ago—and on all accounts they have succeeded. There's even a delightful old wooden board used for clocking in and out of the different rooms. The redecorated elegant interior is thoroughbred Edwardian with fine antique furniture, prints and oil paintings. It also has two public ground-floor rooms, a small library-type room at the front and a large, plush drawing room at the back overlooking gardens that is just right for afternoon tea. Bedrooms, named after actors such as Charles Laughton, vary in size (and some are quite small), have open fireplaces and are carefully decorated to remain in period; some overlook the quiet gardens. Bed linen is Sea Island cotton and the large beds are specially made to Cliveden's specification. They also offer decanters of vodka, whisky and gin and amenities such as VCRs, CD players and modem points. Concierge, limousine and nanny services are available twenty-four hours; and they can arrange to meet you at the airport. Though there's no restaurant, there are plenty of good ones within walking distance. The hotel has also taken over number 22 Cadogan Gardens, which has two meeting rooms and nine suites.

Covent Garden Hotel 🎜🎜🎜

10 MONMOUTH ST, WC2H 9 HB
020-7806 1000, FAX 020-7806 1100
WWW.FIRMDALE.COM
E-MAIL: COVENT@FIRMDALE.COM
3 stes £325-£595, 47 rms S £190, D £220-£280 plus VAT. Air-cond. 24-hr rm service. U: Covent Garden/Tottenham Court Rd.

Pioneer in an area not previously known for hotels, but where they now seem to be springing up every day, the Covent Garden Hotel remains a veritable jewel, and if you're feeling theatrical (or really are a thespian), it will fit you like a glove. This small hotel is one of the creations of Tim and Kit Kemp, who have cornered the market in small, individual townhouse hotels with character. A spacious entrance hall with a brasserie and bar leading off it takes you into the two-level reception area. Up a sweeping stone staircase (great for those dramatic entrances and exits), the drawing room with fireplace and adjacent library is the sort of place one dreams of owning. Bedrooms bear all the hallmarks of designer Kit Kemp's individual style. Handmade embroidered fabrics from China and India fill the rooms, all of which are large and have natural light. Bathrooms are in granite, not the ubiquitous marble. The Loft Suite (Number 303) has entrances on both the third and fourth floors. With its loft-style bedroom overlooking the drawing room, complete with fireplace, two bathrooms, dressing room and separate book-lined study, it is suitably dramatic. All rooms have CD players, VCRs, faxes, mobile phones and computer modem points. Brasserie Max has tripled its size and provides good light lunches in a long, pleasant room looking out onto the street. Due to its continuing popularity with the media crowd, a state-of-the-art screening room has been added and plans for six extra bedrooms and a gym are underway.

Dorset Square ♪♪♪

39/40 DORSET SQ, NW1 6QN
020-7723 7874, FAX 020-7724 3328
WWW.FIRMDALE.COM
E-MAIL: DORSET@FIRMDALE.COM
*1 ste £240, 37 rms S £98-£115, D £140-£240
plus VAT. Air cond in some rms.
24-hr rm service.
U: Marble Arch.*

Part of the rapidly expanding Firmdale Group set up by Tim and Kit Kemp and specialising in small townhouse hotels, Dorset Square is a prime example of the genre. A former pair of Regency residences, it is intimate and stylish and evokes a kind of quiet, country-house hotel mood with its pretty drawing rooms with cosy fireplaces. Lots of chintz, swagging, tapestry cushions piled on the beds, good antiques and bountiful floral touches. Private gardens—the original Lord's cricket ground—are accessible to guests, and are particularly pleasant for summertime drinks. The Potting Shed restaurant and bar offers modern international food in a pretty setting, decorated with gardening items you might find in a superior kind of...well...potting shed. Otherwise, try the 'Bedroom Picnic' in your own room, a pretty tray full of delights like continental meats, cheeses and fruits. As with all Firmdale hotels, cell phones are available in every room.

Egerton House ♪♪♪

EGERTON TERR, SW3 2BX
020-7589 2412, FAX 020-7584 6540
WWW.EGERTONHOUSEHOTEL.CO.UK
E-MAIL: BOOKINGS@EGERTONHOUSEHOTEL.CO.UK
*29 rms S £145, D £175-£225 plus VAT. Air
cond. 24-hr rm service.
U: Knightsbridge.*

The privately owned Egerton House opened in 1990 in the heart of Knightsbridge and is the true embodiment of the small luxury townhouse hotel. Spread over four floors, its rooms are of the English country-house-style; yet the hotel is at the same time unstuffy and intimate. There is no stinting on luxury, with most rooms overlooking private gardens and all with marble bathrooms. Sensible pricing is a major allure, particularly noting its proximity to Harrods, the Beauchamp Place designer shops and the South Kensington museums. An attractive drawing room and study is the ideal venue for afternoon tea or drinks. A dining room downstairs is available for meetings or private dinners for up to twenty and is used as a breakfast room.

The Fox Club

46 CLARGES ST, W1Y 7PJ
020-7495 3656, FAX 020-7495 3626
E-MAIL: FOXCLUB@CLUBHAUS.COM
*3 stes £228-£264, 6 rms S £144-£168, D £180-£228 plus VAT. Air cond.
U: Green Park.*

This elegant Georgian townhouse in the heart of Mayfair was once the home of Chales James Fox the eighteenth-century politician. It is, as its name suggests, a club, but temporary or overseas membership is available. Full membership is £360 per year and members get preferential room rates. Floors in the public areas are stripped pine with rugs scattered around. There is a long zinc-topped bar and this opens out into a comfortable lounge area—and to the side of this are tables where light meals may be taken. Rooms are tastefully and individually decorated in period style and some have open fireplaces and antique bedsteads; all have dual telephone lines, VCRs, safes and minibars. Staff is young, friendly and very helpful.

The Franklin ♪♪♪

28 EGERTON GDNS, SW3 2DB
020-7584 5533, FAX 020-7584 5449
WWW.THEFRANKLIN.CO.UK
E-MAIL: BOOKINGS@THEFRANKLIN.CO.UK
*6 stes £250-£295, 41 rms S £150, D £175-£230
plus VAT. Air cond. 24-hr rm service.
U: Knightsbridge.*

In the same ownership as Egerton House and Duke's, The Franklin overlooks a tranquil, leafy garden square, yet is only minutes from the shops of Knightsbridge. All rooms, which are of good size, have tasteful antique furnishings, original oil paintings, traditional fabrics and marble bathrooms; many also offer four-poster beds. Two telephone points and modems are standard. The drawing room has a small bar and opens directly onto the garden. Staff is extraordinarily friendly and professional. The dining room is also available for private lunch or dinner parties for up to 40 people.

The Gore ♪♪♪

189 QUEEN'S GATE, SW7 5EX
020-7584 6601, FAX 020-7589 8127
WWW.GOREHOTEL.CO.UK
E-MAIL: RESERVATIONS@GOREHOTEL.CO.UK
3 stes £255-£285, 50 rms S £115-£150, D £170-£275 plus VAT. Day-time rm service.
U: Gloucester Rd/South Kensington.

A ⟁

A hotel of great character, The Gore has really exploited its high Victorian Italianate buildings. The slightly more sophisticated big sister of Hazlitt's, it has retained its bohemian edge with an intelligent, interesting staff, quirky atmospheric décor—lived-in-look antiques, well-worn Oriental rugs, a fascinating collection of art—and an air of comfortable decadence. It's evident as soon as you walk into the long narrow hallway, its walls covered in prints, past the reception desk to the large, comfortable (residents-only) Green Room where sofas are drawn up beside the open fireplace. Club rooms have four-poster beds; the room to beg for is the Tudor Room, but the star struck can ask for the Venus Room, which has Judy Garland's bed. Bathrooms are wonderful and the Miss Ada room has a throne closet modelled on the one made for Queen Victoria by Thomas Crapper. In a wide avenue of lesser hotels and minor embassies, The Gore stands out on personality and its restaurants—Bistrot 190 for breakfast through dinner, and the fish- and seafood-dominated, restaurant Downstairs at 190.

Hazlitt's ♪♪♪

6 FRITH ST, SOHO SQ, W1V 5TZ
020-7434 1771, FAX 020-7439 1524
WWW.HAZLITTSHOTEL.CO.UK
E-MAIL: RESERVATIONS@HAZLITTSHOTEL.CO.UK
1 ste from £250, 22 rms S £130, D from £170 plus VAT.
U: Tottenham Court Rd.

A

A great spot for historians, wishing to conjure up ghosts of the past, Hazlitt's is best described as quirky. This Bohemian Soho haunt, was once owned by painter-turned-essayist William Hazlitt (born in 1778). All the rooms are named after eighteenth- and early nineteenth-century residents or visitors, so you might be Jonathan Swift, Sir Charles

Lamb or the Duke of Portland, as it were. There are creaky stairs, walls jammed with period pictures, antiques, mahogany, oak and pine everywhere and a general atmosphere of old-fashioned charm and character in this listed building. Rooms vary in size and standards with dark furnishings. Being in the middle of Soho, the clientele is mainly film and music celebrities, but of the low-key sort. Most request specific favourite rooms. They serve an excellent continental breakfast with noteworthy croissants and good coffee. The residents' sitting room is open for light refreshments but there is no liquor license. Nor is there a restaurant, although that would be superfluous—Hazlitt's is located in one of Soho's premier dining streets.

The Leonard ♪♪♪

15 SEYMOUR ST, W1H 5AA
020-7935 2010, FAX 020-7935 6700
WWW.THELEONARD.COM
E-MAIL: THE.LEONARD@DIAL.PIPEX.COM
20 stes £240-£500, 9 rms S £170, D £190 plus VAT. 3 non-smoking stes, 4 non-smoking rms.
24-hr rm service. Air cond.
U: Marble Arch.

A ☎

This small boutique hotel enjoys a great location, being just off Portman Square and north of Oxford Street. It has a delightful entrance, with a good-sized Café Bar to the left (excellent for dropping into if shopping in the area, or to meet someone for tea, a drink or a light lunch). The pretty drawing room comes complete with newspapers to read in front of the fire. Created from several townhouses, the whole place feels like a home-away-from-home. Individually decorated bedrooms and suites have excellent antiques and paintings, pretty chintzes, luxurious curtains and bedspreads. Marble bathrooms are good size and very well-appointed. Most impressive are the Grand Suites on the first floor. Number 14, for example, has a very large and comfortable main room, decorated in rich reds and with good antiques, and a large bedroom, luxuriously furnished and equipped with all the latest facilities.

L'Hôtel 𝄢𝄢

28 BASIL ST, SW3 1AS
020-7589 6286, FAX 020-7823 7826
WWW.CAPITALGRP.CO.UK
E-MAIL: LHOTEL@CAPITALGRP.CO.UK
1 ste £165, 11 rms S/D £145 plus VAT.
U: Knightsbridge.

A

Owned by David and Margaret Levin, who also own the more lavish Capital Hotel next door, L'Hôtel could almost be described as a very upmarket bed-and-breakfast. Just 100 metres from Harrods on a residential street, this charming hotel has a welcoming French pension ambience and the staff treat guests like members of an extended family. The rooms may seem small, but they are fully equipped and decorated in a rural French style, and some have open fireplaces. The bar and restaurant of The Capital are open to L'Hôtel's guests. The bustling **Le Métro** wine bar below carries a full menu, from croissants and coffee in the morning, to late-evening suppers (see *Quick Bites*).

London Outpost

69 CADOGAN GARDENS, SW3 2RB
020-7589 7333, FAX 020-7581 4958
WWW.CARNEGIEGROUP.CO.UK/LONDONOUTPOST
E-MAIL: LONDONOUTPOST@DIAL.PIPEX.COM
4 stes £250, 7 rms S £150, D £185-£220 plus VAT. Air cond. 24-hour rm service.
U: Sloane Sq.

A ⌘

The London Outpost of The Carnegie Club, owned by Peter de Savery, sets out to welcome you as if you were a house guest of Andrew Carnegie in the Edwardian era—and the overall feel is very much country-house-in-town rather than London hotel. In exclusive Cadogan Gardens, between Chelsea and Knightsbridge, there are just eleven rooms in a red bricked Edwardian townhouse. The entrance hall is painted in a warm, deep red with an interesting collection of eighteenth and nineteenth century prints on the walls. There is antique furniture throughout and some rooms have four-poster beds. In keeping with the Scottish connection (Skibo Castle in Scotland is a sister hotel and home of The Carnegie Club), many rooms have a tartan theme. There are drink trays in each room rather than minibars, and guests are offered Champagne and canapés in the elegant draw-ing room every evening. Breakfast and light meals are served in the pretty conservatory, and there is even a snooker room.

The Milestone 𝄢𝄢𝄢

1 KENSINGTON CT, W8 5DL
020-7917 1000, FAX 020-7917 1010
WWW.REDCARNATIONHOTELS.COM
E-MAIL: RESERVATIONS@MILESTONE.REDCARNA-TIONHOTELS.COM
12 stes £430-£800, 45 rms S £250-£290, D £305-£400 inc VAT. 4 non-smoking stes, 6 non-smoking rms. Air cond. 24-hr rm service. Limousine service.
U: High St Kensington.

A 🍴 ☎ ⌘

There's an attractive Victorian façade to this very grand late nineteenth-century former private residence, which has excellent views of Kensington Palace just opposite. It is also conveniently close to Knightsbridge's shops. Several of the stunning split-level suites and many of the rooms have king-size four-poster beds. All the rooms are spacious, individually decorated and graciously appointed with beautiful antique furniture. As a listed building, its restoration has been meticulously done according to English Heritage standards, which means original fireplaces, carved wood panelling, high ceilings and large ornate windows. Guests also enjoy very attentive, personal service from the staff. Chenestons restaurant takes its name from an early spelling of Kensington and has an eclectic modern European menu. Again, the décor is all Victorian country-house-style, with a Gothic feel to its plaster ceilings, a small private alcove off the main dining room and flickering candle-style lights. Start with an apéritif in the very comfortable drawing room, full of bookshelves and with a baronial-style fireplace, and you'll feel far removed from the bustle of Kensington just outside.

No 5 𝄢𝄢

5 MADDOX ST, W1R 9LE
020-7792 4070, FAX 020-7792 4003
E-MAIL: SALES@LIVING-ROOMS.CO.UK
12 stes: 1-bed £195-£275, 2-bed £345, 3-bed £495 plus VAT. 24-hour rm service. Air cond.
U: Oxford Circus.

A ☎

This small, all suite hotel is typical of a new breed of townhouse springing up all over

London: gone are the chintzes, dried flowers, etc. Instead, minimalism reigns, with the odd orchid being the only floral concession. Just off Regent Street, the entrance is a tiny door, so it comes as quite a surprise to find a much larger space within, and then an open glass-sided staircase before you really arrive. Stairs are a needed feature as there is no lift, but if you don't arrive with much more than a lap-top (we were told this is true of most of their guests), it shouldn't be too much of a prob-lem. Although there is 24-hour room service, all suites have a fully equipped kitchen com-plete with starter grocery pack. Guests tend to come from the worlds of fashion or music, but this would be a good choice for any business traveller, each suite having an pretty impressive workstation with fax and ISDN modem lines. Despite the general air of understatement, comfort is not neglected with fake sable throws on the beds, banks of pillows and open fires in the deluxe suites. They really do seem to have gotten it just right.

Number 41 ♪♪♪

41 BUCKINGHAM PALACE RD, SW1 0PS
020-7300 0041, FAX 020-7300 0141
WWW.SMALL-HOTEL.COM
4 stes £525-£615, 16 rms £325. 24-hour rm service.
U: Victoria.

A 🕿 💻 🛅

Opposite the Royal Mews of Buckingham Palace, Number 41 offers a totally inclusive luxury package. The flat rates include every item that's normally an extra: minibar drinks, snacks, telephone, fax and computer use and even selected meals and breakfasts; the Junior suites include round-trip airport transfers while the Executive suites offer full use of a chauffeur-driven Bentley. On arrival, you enter a mirrored reception area, before being whisked up to the executive lounge on the top floor. This mahogany-panelled room has an open fire, comfortable armchairs and sparkling chandeliers. After check-in, you are offered a snack while a butler does your unpacking. Bedrooms are elegantly furnished and have every conceivable comfort: open fireplaces, fax machines and printers, DVD players and US/UK modem lines. Bathrooms are suitably luxurious. There is a staff ratio of two-to-one; and while no formal restaurant, there is 24-hour room service and light meals are available in the lounge.

The Pelham ♪♪♪

15 CROMWELL PL, SW7 2LA
020-7589 8288, FAX 020-7584 8444
WWW.FIRMDALE.COM
E-MAIL: PELHAM@FIRMDALE.COM
3 stes £295-£595, 47 rms S £145, D £175-£235 plus VAT. Air cond. 24-hr rm service.
U: South Kensington.

A 🕿 ♻

Opened in 1989 by Kit and Tim Kemp, who have a keen design eye for the English coun-try-house-genre, the Pelham's tenth anniver-sary prompted the addition of thirteen new rooms in an adjacent building. Designer Kit Kemp has created a fresh new look for the extra rooms which mixes the modern (giraffe print chairs) with the more traditional (crewel-work, hand-embroidered fabrics). The overall effect of the main part of the hotel is cosy and stylish, from the profusion of flower arrange-ments (both fresh and creatively dried) and traditional floral prints, to fine original antiques and inviting four-poster beds, some of which come with matching teddy bears. Lots of ornaments like clocks, vases, pot pour-ri and objets d'art are fun, but may make some feel claustrophobic. Bathrooms are attractive and well-equipped, and concessions to the twenty-first century are gently concealed—minibars and TVs are hidden under chintz-covered tables. Each room is provided with a mobile phone. Kemps bar and restaurant, with a Mediterranean-style cuisine, is very pleasant and a good venue for a meal after visiting the nearby South Kensington museums.

The Portobello Hotel ♪♪♪

22 STANLEY GDNS, W11 2NG
020-7727 2777, FAX 020-7792 9641
12 stes £210-£280, 12 rms S £130, D £150-£160 inc VAT & CB. 6 rms air cond. 24-hr rm service.
U: Notting Hill Gate.

A 🛅

The Portobello may justly claim to be London's first townhouse hotel, having opened its doors more than 25 years ago. Made from two elegant, six-storey Victorian terraced houses in Kensington, its quirky eclecticism is a magnet for visiting rock and movie stars. Their smallest (cabin) rooms are very small (but inexpensive); other rooms have individual décors, some with delightful floor-to-ceiling windows, one with a Moroccan theme. Beds range from round to four-poster through half-tester and ship bunk. Four bedrooms have enormous Victorian bathing machines with intricate brass pipe work and glass screens. Two new suites have been created; the Colonial Suite, also known as Charlie's Room (it's dedicated to the Prince of Wales), is all British Raj, with Indian furniture, a ceiling fan, and empire bed; the Japanese Water Garden Suite features lots of jade, a Buddha and a cedar wood conservatory. One attic room with sloping ceilings boasts a mirror over the bed, which perhaps explains why the Portobello is often described as a sexy hotel. Not far from Portobello Market, it is also a short, pleasant walk to Kensington Gardens and Holland Park. Extra touches include goose-down duvets, 24-hour breakfasts and lavish room interiors. The informal restaurant/bar is open 24 hours. The owners also have the extremely popular Julie's restaurant and wine baron nearby Portland Road.

The Rookery

12 PETERS LANE, COWCROSS ST, EC1M 6DS
020-7336 0931, FAX 020-7336 0932
WWW.ROOKERY.CO.UK
E-MAIL: RESERVATIONS@ROOKERY.CO.UK
3 stes £250-£450, 30 rms S £160-£180, D £180-£195 plus VAT. 10 non-smoking rms.
24-hour rm service.
U: Farringdon.

The Rookery was the name given to this district in the eighteenth century; beyond the jurisdiction of the City of London, it became synonymous with thieves and lawlessness—this was Fagin's London. Today it's an area that's enjoying a great deal of rejuvenation with the redevelopment of Clerkenwell just to the north. Peter McKay and Douglas Blain, creators of Hazlitt's and The Gore, have taken a row of Georgian houses in a narrow lane and turned them into a little gem of a hotel; it's creaky and quaint and feels as if it's been there forever. There are open fires, flagstone floors and lots of wood panelling, and it's crammed with antiques (even the beds) and paintings. The star room has to be the Rook's Nest Suite; it's on two levels, has a 40-foot-ceiling and stunning views across the rooftops of the City of London; the bathroom is to die for, and has original Victorian fittings (as have all the rooms), but modern plumbing. Indeed, there's no shortage of twenty-first-century essentials like ISDN modem points, etc.,

though even the minibars and personal safes have been cunningly concealed in antique furniture. There is no restaurant, but this is an area with some particularly good ones within a couple of minutes' walk. Breakfasts are delicious with home-baked croissants and great coffee.

Sandringham Hotel

3 HOLFORD RD, NW3 1AD
020-7435 1569, FAX 020-7431 5932
E-MAIL: SANDRINGHAM.HOTEL@VIRGIN.NET
3 stes £150-£180, 17 rms S £75-£95, D £125-£140 inc breakfast & VAT. 24-hour rm service.
U: Hampstead.

Famous former Hampstead residents include John Keats and Sigmund Freud, indeed Hampstead is still regarded very much as the intellectuals quarter of London. It may seem a bit out of the way, but is actually easy to get to, including the fact that and the Sandringham is very close to Hampstead tube. Owners Jill and Michael von Grey took over this small hotel to offer a smart country-house-atmosphere. In a large red brick Victorian house, its public rooms overlook a garden. Bedrooms vary in style from pretty blues and florals to a more masculine décor with wood panelling. Many have views over the garden; many look out over the rest of London since Hampstead is at one of London's high points. Doubles have good size bathrooms. Breakfast is excellent, the welcome is friendly from this young couple and the location—if you want to be out of the city centre—is first-rate.

The Sloane Hotel

29 DRAYCOTT PL, SW3 2SH
020-7581 5757, FAX 020-7584 1348
WWW.PREMIERHOTELS.COM
E-MAIL: SLOANEHOTEL@BTINTERNET.COM
3 stes £225, 9 rms D £140-£225 plus VAT. Air cond. 24-hr rm service.
U: Sloane Sq.

Tucked away near the King's Road and Sloane Square, The Sloane Hotel is an absolute gem and the epitome of intimacy. The lavish décors are transportable too—in other words, you can buy most of the antiques from the bedrooms! The owners are inveterate collectors and decorate the hotel as if it were a private residence. The unusual interior design features vintage Vuitton cases, period military uniforms, beautiful carriage clocks, leopard-print fabrics, extravagant canopied beds, and antique lace. The mix of old and modern is ably executed with well-appointed bathrooms, and all suites are split-level with a separate sitting area. Service is charming and efficient. From the rooftop reception room and terrace (available for breakfast, light meals, afternoon tea or drinks), guests have mesmerising views of the Chelsea neighbourhood.

Sydney House Hotel ♪♪♪

9-11 SYDNEY ST, SW3 6PU
020-7376 7711, FAX 020-7376 4233
WWW.SYDNEYHOUSEHOTEL.COM
E-MAIL: SYDNEYHOUSEHOTEL@CSEE/LONDON.COM
23 rms S £150, D £180-£220 plus VAT. Air cond. 24-hr rm service.
U: South Kensington.

The brainchild of Swiss hotelier Jean-Luc Aeby, this whimsical townhouse hotel is situated at the Fulham Road end of Sydney Street and very close to Brompton Cross, with its trendy shops and restaurants. In a restored parade of mid-nineteenth-century townhouses, only a discreet brass plate and a couple of planters hint that it might be a hotel. Once inside, eclecticism reigns, as each room is individually designed with a different theme and has unusual details, rich colours and textures, creating a subdued modern mood. Noteworthy are the Chinese Leopard room with Biedermeier furniture, the Royale room with its gilded four-poster bed, the Penthouse with a large terrace, the Paris room with rich reds and toile de Jouy and the more traditional, pretty Wedgwood Blue room. Attentive service adds to the intimate atmosphere.

Ten Manchester Street ♪♪♪

10 MANCHESTER ST, W1M 5PG
020-7486 6669, FAX 020-7224 0348
WWW.10MANCHESTERSTREET.COM
E-MAIL: STAY@10MANCHESTERSTREET.FSNET.CO.UK
9 stes £195, 37 rms S/D £120-£150 inc VAT.
U: Bond St.

The newly opened Ten Manchester Street (under the same ownership as The Leonard), sets out to be a no-frills townhouse hotel—all the comforts in terms of décor, smart bathrooms, etc., but trimmed of expensive services like concierge, valet, room service—the result is very reasonable rates. A smart redbrick townhouse, dating from 1919, it's just around the corner from the fabulous Wallace Collection and within easy reach of the shops of Bond St., Oxford St. and Marylebone High St. Rooms are light and spacious and furnished in classical style; extras include minibars, stereos and satellite TV. Though the hotel has no restaurant, each room has a comprehensive dossier of restaurants, bars and night clubs, and helpful staff members available to make bookings. Continental breakfast is included and is served in the charming breakfast room downstairs.

22 Jermyn Street ♪♪♪

22 JERMYN ST, SW1Y 6HL
020-7734 2353, FAX 020-7734 0750
WWW.22JERMYN.COM
E-MAIL: TOGNA@22JERMYN.COM
13 stes £290-£325, 5 rms S/D £205 plus VAT. 24-hour rm service.
U: Green Park/Piccadilly Circus.

Winner of more accolades than most other hotels in London, this small clubby townhouse hotel continues to remain at the top of our list. Still very much like home as you wish it could be, 22 Jermyn Street is one of London's best private hotel secrets and you could quite easily pass it by, for discretion is the key here. No glittering signs, no uniformed valets, no shining Rolls Royces give you any clue as to what is inside. Owner Henry Togna has reshuffled this family property—located near Piccadilly Circus and in historic St. James's—into a hotel of charming suites and studios. Here you experience affordable elegance with antique furniture and granite bathrooms and gracious, but friendly, service. The rooms have every modern facility and reflect Togna's passion for technology, having CD Rom library, Internet access and even E-mail addresses for guests. The desks are the best equipped in town, with every conceivable staple, paper clip and notepad, as well as fresh flowers, monogrammed linen and a glass of Champagne on arrival. Furnishings are comfortable—country life-meets-sophisticated-central London but not over-chintzed. Everything is possible—from private fittings by nearby tailors, to unobtainable theatre tickets. Guests can use Champney's health club nearby for a nominal fee. Owner-managed, the staff could not be more friendly, professional and helpful and Togna's personal lists of shops and restaurants feature up-to-the-minute selections. A real gem.

Twenty Nevern Square ✔✔✔
20 NEVERN SQ, SW5
020-7565 9555, FAX 020-7565 9444
WWW.TWENTYNEVERNSQUARE.CO.UK
E-MAIL: HOTEL@TWENTYNEVERNSQUARE.CO.UK
1 ste £275, 20 rms S £130-£140, D £175-£195 plus VAT. 24-hour rm service.
U: Earls Court.

A

This smart new townhouse hotel, in a Victorian building, and overlooking the gardens of Nevern Square in Kensington, will appeal to anyone wanting to get away from the traditional tourist areas and get a true feel for London living, yet be within easy reach of the main tourist attractions. It is also just around the corner from the Earls Court Exhibition Centre. Bedrooms are individually designed and two of them have four-posters; attention to detail is good, with Egyptian cotton sheets, luxurious towelling bathrobes; even the toiletries are placed in little wooden chests. The Pasha suite features yards of gold silk fabrics and, if this isn't decadent enough, you can enjoy an alfresco breakfast on your own private roof terrace, overlooking the square. If you prefer to go deeper into the Orient, then try the Chinese room with Pagoda-style armoire and black silk bedspread dotted with red flowers. Café Twenty is an informal restaurant with a Mediterranean accent and has gained quite a strong local following.

MODERATE

Academy Town House ✔✔
17-21 GOWER ST, WC1E 6HG
020-7631 4115, FAX 020-7636 3442
WWW.ETONTOWNHOUSE.COM
E-MAIL: ACADEMY@AOL.COM
10 stes £185, 47 rms S/D £115-£185 plusVAT. Air cond. 24-hour rm service.
U: Euston Sq.

A ⟳

Well named, with its proximity to London University and the British Museum, its reason-

able rates make this hotel a firm favourite with many visitors. Originally three Georgian houses, it's an old-fashioned building, but brought bang-up-to-date. Service is efficient and friendly. Public rooms include the modern basement restaurant, The Alchemy, open for breakfast and lunch, plus a small patio garden for fine days and a cosy library. Bedrooms, which vary in size, are pretty with pastel shades and hung with good fabrics. Some beds are half-testers with fabrics draped from the wall to both sides of the bed. Bathrooms are en-suite except in a few singles, and are done in marble. Some are very small. If you want a quiet room, ask for a bedroom looking over the back. The owner has a good eye for paintings, which are hung everywhere. All in all, this is a very good place in an excellent location.

The Basil Street Hotel ✔✔✔
BASIL ST, SW3 1AH
020-7581 3311, FAX 020-7581 3693
WWW.ABSITE.COM/BASIL
E-MAIL: THEBASIL@AOL.COM
80 rms S from £125, D £185-£190 plus VAT. 24-hr rm service.
U: Knightsbridge.

A ⟳

Built in 1910, this privately owned, small hotel, has long been a favourite with ladies up from the country and indeed is home to the Parrot Club, a ladies-only club, a wonderful retreat for female guests and outsiders. Just yards from Harrods, and filled with antiques, rich carpets, tapestries and objets d'art, it has a very liveable feel. Compared to most Knightsbridge hotels, The Basil Street exudes an easy, comfortable and charming personality, rather than smart. Each room is a different size, shape, décor and mood, with lots of interesting nooks and crannies. The restaurant features a pianist in the evenings and also offers a light lunch menu. Traditional afternoon tea is served every day in the lounge and is very popular with Knightsbridge shoppers (see *Quick Bites*).

The **prices** in this guide reflect what establishments were charging at press time.

Berners Hotel

10 BERNERS ST, W1A 3BE
020-7666 2000, FAX 020-7666 2001
WWW.THEBERNERSHOTEL.CO.UK
E-MAIL: BERNERS@BERNERS.CO.UK
3 stes £300, 214 rms S £170, D £205-£250 inc VAT. 90 non-smoking rms. Air cond. 24-hr rm service.
U: Oxford Circus.

Being so close to Oxford Street, and midway between Oxford Circus and Tottenham Court Road, might suggest a hectic pace, but this hotel is an oasis of calm. Rooms are a jumble of sizes, but pleasantly decorated with a contemporary country-house theme, with double-glazed windows and bathrooms that have both showers and baths. The Club Floor has a private lounge where guests check-in and receive complimentary breakfast and a glass of Champagne and canapés every evening. A shower suite is available for guests arriving early in the morning, which is great for all those crack-of-dawn transatlantic flights. Particularly enjoyable is the Reflections restaurant, a stunning Edwardian dining room with high-carved ceilings and a traditional carvery, the original ballroom in the nineteenth-century private home of Joshua Berner. Afternoon tea in the lobby is a very civilised affair, being accompanied by a pianist. The Berners Bar is a good spot to unwind at the end of a hard day's sightseeing.

Blooms Hotel

7 MONTAGUE ST, WC1B 5BP
020-7323 1717, FAX 020-7636 6498
WWW.BLOOMSHOTEL.CO.UK
E-MAIL: RESERVATIONS@MONTAGUE.REDCARNATIONHOTELS.COM
27 rms S £130-£175, D £195-£205 inc breakfast & VAT. 24-hr rm service.
U: Holborn/Tottenham Court Rd.

An early eighteenth-century townhouse situated in Bloomsbury (London's literary corner) and very close to the British Museum and the theatre district, Blooms makes an excellent base for those visiting for business or pleasure. Smart planters line the entrance and this theme is continued inside with copious flower arrangements. There is a delightful walled garden overlooking the British Museum, where light meals can be taken. The lounge is well decorated in eighteenth-century style and there is an extensive library which guests are invited to use. There is no restaurant, though light snacks are available in the lounge, and guests can get preferential service at a number of nearby restaurants. A good selection of board games will keep adults and children amused on wet afternoons when even sightseeing seems too wearying. Bedrooms are well furnished and equipped with satellite TV, trouser presses and refreshment trays.

Cannizaro House

WEST SIDE, WIMBLEDON COMMON, SW19 4UF
020-8879 1464, FAX 020-8879 7338
WWW.THISTLE.CO.UK
E-MAIL: CANNIZARO.HOUSE@THISTLE.CO.UK
3 stes £328, 42 rms S/D £199-£288 inc VAT. 1 non-smoking ste, 21 non-smoking rms. 24-hr rm service.
No underground nearby.

Synonymous with tennis for most of the world, Wimbledon is better known to Londoners as a smart, upmarket neighbourhood and a wonderful location for this graceful Georgian mansion on the edge of Wimbledon Common surrounded by pretty Cannizaro Park. Cannizaro House is close to charming Wimbledon Village with its designer boutiques, trendy restaurants, tea shops and riding stables. Though slightly inaccessible to central London, the place is ideal for a retreat, small conference or pleasant experience of local 'village' life. Bedrooms display a tasteful mix of antique and reproduction furniture, but try to book in the original section of the building where the rooms are larger. The executive rooms boast four-poster beds. Public rooms resemble country-house drawing rooms with comfortable sofas, fireplaces and huge floral arrangements. The international menu in the **Georgian Dining Room** is strong on fish and game, and Sunday lunch followed by a stroll on the common is popular. Jacket and tie code is observed for gentlemen. Afternoon tea is a delight (see *Quick Bites*). Summertime evening concerts in the park, arranged by the local council, are a treat. Inevitably, the hotel is packed during Wimbledon tennis fortnight.

The Cavendish ♪♪♪

81 JERMYN ST, SW1Y 6 JF
020-7930 2111, FAX 020-7839 2125
WWW.LONDON-HOTELS.CO.UK
*16 stes from £259, 251 rms S from £175,
D from £205 plus VAT. 6 non-smoking stes, 89
non-smoking rms. Air cond. 24-hr rm service.
U: Green Park/Piccadilly Circus.*

The Cavendish has a great location, being on Jermyn Street, home to London's top shirtmakers and the heart of 'Gentleman's London'. The original Cavendish was where the redoubtable Rosa Lewis (the Duchess of Duke Street) reigned supreme and entertained royalty; the hotel is full of pictures and mementoes of the era and the lady. The current building is very sixties and the lobby is a bit of a testimony to this unfortunate period. Bedrooms, however, have been redecorated in a stylish manner with all modern facilities. En-suite bathrooms are marble floored and contain all the extras you'd expect. The top-floor suites have a wonderful view with sitting areas and spa baths. Leyton's brasserie serves light meals and sandwiches plus full meals from an international menu. Tea is served in the lounge from which window tables have a splendid view over Jermyn Street.

Chelsea Village Hotel ♪♪♪

STAMFORD BRIDGE, FULHAM RD, SW6 1HS
020-7565 1400, FAX 020-7565 1450
WWW.CHELSEAFC.CO.UK
E-MAIL: SALES@CHELSEAVILLAGE.CO.UK
*3 stes £195-£210, 288 rms S £140-£150, D
£160-£170. 144 non-smoking rms. Air cond.
24-hr rm service.
U: Fulham Broadway.*

Down towards Fulham Broadway and well known to football fans, the Chelsea Village Hotel has been developed by the Chelsea Football Club. It's a massive building, the centrepiece of the £100m redevelopment of the 12-acre Stamford Bridge site. Ken Bates, chairman of the club, reportedly wants to turn the area into the 'Covent Garden of Southwest London'. The hotel's entrance—all glass and steel—leads you into the lobby with restaurants off to different sides. Reception is upstairs. Bedrooms are fairly standard, though some are small; bathrooms are good. But prices are reasonable and, who knows, you might run into the odd international footballer. You'll certainly get close to them if you book into the massive main meeting and corporate hospitality suite which has an area for conferences and dining leading down to covered seating running the length of the pitch. Of the restaurants, Fishnets a moderately expensive seafood and crustacean restaurant with al fresco seating, is good; Arkles serves traditional Irish food; the King's Brasserie is the official hotel restaurant; The Shed Bar is casual, with banks of TV screens and leather chairs, good for watching sport of all kinds. Newly opened is a new building, The Court Hotel, adding another 131 rooms. Furnished to the same four-star standard as the Chelsea Village Hotel, it is equipped with the same facilities. The casual brasserie Le Bistro has a French emphasis.

The Chesterfield ♪♪♪

35 CHARLES ST, W1X 8LX
020-7491 2622, FAX 020-7491 4793
WWW.REDCARNATIONHOTELS.COM
E-MAIL: RESERVATIONS@CHESTERFIELD.REDCARNATIONHOTELS.COM
*13 stes £325-£475, 97 rms S £130-£195, D
£150-£205 plus VAT. 5 non-smoking stes, 31
non-smoking rms. Air cond. 24-hr rm service.
U: Green Park.*

The ongoing refurbishment of The Chesterfield is nearing completion and has brought this hotel up to the standards you would expect from such an excellent address. There's lots of wood panelling in the entrance hall and library (where afternoon tea is served) and the bar, too, has a very masculine clubby feel. The suites and about two-thirds of the rooms have found a new lease on life in classic townhouse style with new carpets, antique-look furniture and prints; it's worth requesting one of these. Little extras are good, with nightly turndown service, bathrobes, potpourri sachets and a fine range of toiletries. The Conservatory offers late breakfasts, light lunches or pre- and post-theatre suppers while there is also a more formal restaurant with dance floor and live music six nights a week. Staff are courteous and very helpful.

Clifton Ford Hotel ♪♪♪

47 WELBECK ST, W1M 8DN
020-7486 6600, FAX 020-7486 7492
WWW.DOYLE-HOTEL.IE
E-MAIL: MARK-BRAMLEY@JURYS.COM
4 penthouse stes £192-£270, 186 rms S £144-£180, D £160-£200 plus VAT. Air cond. 24-hr rm service.
U: Bond St.

A ᵞ ≈ **P** ⬡

On a relatively quiet street, just north of Oxford Street, this modern hotel is handy for shops and sightseeing. Bedrooms vary in size, but are comfortably outfitted with attractive, though modest, modern décor. The handful of suites, all on the seventh floor and with good views, are quite luxurious and highly recommended. The Howard De Walden restaurant is named after the former aristocrat who lived on the premises and serves a mixture of mainstream English and French dishes. It is informal and staff is very pleasant.

The Colonnade Town House ♪♪♪

2 WARRINGTON CRESCENT, W9 1ER
020-7286 1052, FAX 020-7286 1057
WWW.ETONHOUSE.COM
E-MAIL: RES.COLONNADE@ETONTOWNHOUSE.COM
6 stes £195, 37 rms S/D £110-£165 plus VAT. Non-smoking rms available. Air cond. 24-hour rm service.
U: Warwick Ave.

A 🛗

New sister to the Academy Hotel in Bloomsbury (see above), the Colonnade is regarded as the flagship for the Eton Town House group. Situated in the quiet residential area of Little Venice, yet within minutes of the Heathrow Express at Paddington, a mid-Victorian town house has been totally renovated to create this charming hotel. Antique furniture is dotted about the place and fabrics have been used to very good effect. Though the décor is traditional, the modern traveller is very well attended to with dual phones, modems, etc. Some of the rooms have private balconies, quite a rarity in London. There is a drawing room with open fire where afternoon tea and pre-dinner drinks are served before entering the restaurant in the conservatory.

The Cranley ♪♪

10-12 BINA GARDENS SW5 OLA
020-7373 0123, FAX 020-7373 9497
WWW.THECRANLEY.CO.UK
E-MAIL: THECRANLEY@WRITEME.COM
5 stes £185-£240, 37 rms S £130-£145, D £144-£160 inc VAT. Air-cond. All rooms inc kitch-enettes.
U: Gloucester Rd.

A

This smart townhouse in South Kensington has recently been very tastefully restored. Public areas have lots of antiques and modish arrangements of fresh and dried flowers. Rooms, each individual, have been decked out with antique furniture and oil paintings, as well as satellite television. Upgrading continues and rooms now have voice-mail and modem points; four-poster beds have been added to some rooms. For those not wanting to eat in the area's plethora of excellent restaurants, the Cranley also has cunningly concealed kitchenettes in every room with microwaves and refrigerators.

Cranley Gardens Hotel ♪♪

8 CRANLEY GARDENS, SW7 3DB
020-7373 3232, FAX 020-7373 7944
E-MAIL: CRANLEYGARDENS@AOL.COM
85 rms S £85, D £99-£109, inc breakfast & VAT. 24-hr rm service.
U: Gloucester Rd/South Kensington.

A ⬡

In South Kensington, handy for the museums and its short distance from Knightsbridge, this charming hotel represents very good value for the money. Originally four Georgian houses in residential Cranley Gardens, it has well-decorated bedrooms with built-in desks and TV with in-house movies. All rooms have en-suite facilities. The restaurant is pretty with swagged curtains and cane chairs, and there is a separate lounge area.

Cumberland Hotel ♪♪♪

MARBLE ARCH, W1A 4RF
020-7262 1234, FAX 020-7724 4621
WWW.CUMBERLAND.COM
3 stes £226, 886 rms S £165, D £196 inc VAT. 500 non-smoking rms. Some rms air cond. 24-hr rm service.
U: Marble Arch.

A ⬡

This is one of the largest hotels in the UK and, consequently, a long-time stalwart for package-tour operators; its central location (at the west end of Oxford Street just opposite Marble Arch, Speakers Corner and the wonderful expanse of Hyde Park) and the fact that it has very good housekeeping ensure its continued popularity. Recent renovation has greatly improved the Premier Club floors with the installation of air-conditioning; and 200 rooms are specifically designed for the business traveller. The Cumberland's lobby, all stainless steel and maroon carpets, can get hectic in the evening as business people arrive in droves to bed down after a hard day in the smoke, but the hotel is nevertheless a good bargain if you don't mind anonymous service. There's a mix of restaurants: Chinese (Sampans), British (Original Carvery) and an all-day coffee shop, plus four decent bars. No points for décor, in spite of the refurbishment. Rooms are functional and have interiors expected from this type of hotel, but with all the usual amenities of hair dryers, trouser presses, etc. The Premier Club rooms have well-lit working areas and access to the Premier Lounge with complimentary breakfast and all day snacks.

Durrants

GEORGE ST, W1H 6BJ
020-7935 8131, FAX 020-7487 3510
4 stes £260, 92 rms S £97.50, D £135-£175 inc VAT. Air cond in some rms. 24-hr rm service.
U: Baker St/Bond St.

A delightful family-owned hotel, situated north of Oxford Street, between Baker Street and Marylebone, and just off Manchester Square where you can browse through the fabulous Wallace Collection, Durrants is a refurbished series of Georgian townhouses giving the overall impression of a clubby, very English welcome. Some rooms are small but are well furnished in keeping with the style of the building. Staff is friendly and helpful, as you would expect at a hotel which has been in the same ownership for more than 70 years. Durrants restaurant is informal with a standard international menu selection. The George Bar is popular with residents.

Executive Hotel

57 PONT ST, SW1X 0BD
020-7581 2424, FAX 020-7589 9456
U: Knightsbridge.

At press time this hotel was undergoing total refurbishment but is due to reopen later in

2000. Bedrooms, and particularly bathrooms, needed updating. This is good news for the hotel because it is in an excellent location, a stone's throw from Harrods on elegant, turn-of-the-century Pont St. The entrance hall is very imposing with its original sweeping staircase, Wedgewood-style medallions and elaborately plastered ceiling.

Flemings Mayfair

HALF MOON ST, W1Y 7RA
020-7499 2964, FAX 020-7629 4063
E-MAIL: SALES@FLEMINGS-MAYFAIR.CO.UK
3 stes £255, 121 rms S £165, D from £195-£210 plus VAT. 30 non-smoking rms. Air cond. 24-hr rm service.
U: Green Park.

A super location in Mayfair and a snip of a price compared to its glossy Park Lane or Piccadilly neighbours, makes Flemings look like a pretty good bargain. It's a jumble of stairways and nooks and crannies, and some rooms can be a bit poky, but the next-door apartments offer good value-for-the money and have en-suite kitchens and dining areas. The basement-level restaurant has an inexpensive buffet lunch daily, plus there's a small bar and comfortable sitting room next to the lobby for afternoon tea and drinks.

The Forum

97 CROMWELL RD, SW7 4DN
020-7370 5757, FAX 020-7373 1448
WWW.INTERCONTI.COM
E-MAIL: FORUM.LONDON@INTERCONTI.COM
4 stes £280-£360, 906 rms S £150, D £170-£190 inc VAT. 176 non-smoking rms. Air cond. 24-hr rm service.
U: Gloucester Rd.

Despite being the biggest and tallest hotel in the country, The Forum somehow manages to maintain superb efficiency without being too impersonal. Perhaps it's due to its ownership by Inter-Continental Hotels. Bedrooms are functional and modestly equipped and are kept meticulously clean; bathrooms are good. The smart Tavern restaurant offers deli-style food, and the international Kensington Garden Café is open all day from buffet breakfast to dinner. The Tavern pub offers traditional pub fare and lively Sunday jazz brunches, while Oliver's Lounge next to the lobby does afternoon tea, drinks and snacks. About 10 percent of the clientele is Japanese, so there is a good range of specialist menus, including an extensive Japanese breakfast.

Gainsborough ♪♪

7-11 QUEENSBERRY PLACE SW7 2DL
020-7957 0000, FAX 020-7957 0001
WWW.EEH.CO.UK
E-MAIL: GAINSBOROUGH@EEH.CO.UK
4 stes £180-£210, 49 rms S £65, D £120-£145 plus VAT. Air cond in some rms.
U: South Kensington.

A

A great location in South Kensington, a couple of minutes from the Natural History, Science and Victoria and Albert museums, not to mention fashionable Brompton Cross and nearby Knightsbridge, this well-maintained hotel offers excellent value for the money. A deceptively large entrance lobby with lounge area has a welcoming clubby feel and cascades of plants enhance the whole of the reception floor. Reproductions of Gainsborough's paintings are scattered around and the standard of décor is very high, achieving a traditional English elegance. Dashing black and gold stripes adorn the breakfast room/bar where light meals are served all day. Bedrooms are individually decorated and bathrooms are particularly well-appointed with a wealth of marble and mahogany.

Gallery Hotel ♪♪

8-10 QUEENSBERRY PL, SW7 2EA
020-7915 0000, FAX 020-7915 4400
WWW.EEH.CO.UK; E-MAIL: GALLERY@EEH.CO.UK
2 stes £246-£293, 34 rms S £141, D £141-£170 inc breakfast & VAT. 24-hr rm service. Air cond most rms.
U: South Kensington.

A ☼ ▤

One of the best little bargains in town and sister to the Gainsborough (see above), this hotel offers the same good location and exceptional value for the money. There is a very welcoming mahogany-panelled lounge/bar area complete with chess set/table. As its name implies, there are art exhibitions in the 'Gallery Room'. All the public rooms have particularly attractive flower arrangements and the butlers and staff in general is exceptionally helpful. Bedrooms are very well furnished with

tasteful fabrics and, in the main, spacious (a rarity for smaller London hotels). One of the two suites even offers a roof terrace and whirlpool bath and both are air-conditioned. Bathrooms have all been refurbished and feature marble tiles with mahogany woodwork; many have bidets and all have a good array of toiletries. Hair dryers, trouser presses and satellite TV reflect the general care and attention to detail.

Harrington Hall ♪♪♪

5-15 HARRINGTON GDNS, SW7 4JW
020-7396 9696, FAX 020-7396 9090
WWW.HARRINGTONHALL.CO.UK
E-MAIL: HARRINGTONSALES@COMPUSERVE.COM
4 stes £220, 196 rms S/D £162-£180 inc service & VAT. 2 non-smoking stes 134 non-smoking rms. 24-hr rm service. Air cond.
U: Earls Court.

A 'Ⴑ' ▭ ▯

In South Kensington, this privately-owned hotel lies behind an original period façade. It's now a thoroughly modern hotel, with a formal entrance. There's a lounge bar with a marble fireplace and a well-decorated restaurant. Bedrooms are standard but comfortable, and many have king-size beds, plus all the facilities such as satellite TV, trouser press, voice-mail, modem points, etc. With good conference and banqueting facilities and excellent rates, it's appealing to the business traveller as well as the tourist.

K+K Hotel George ♪♪

1-15 TEMPLETON PL, SW5 9NB
020-7598 8707, FAX 020-7370 2285
WWW.HOTELGEORGE.CO.UK
E-MAIL: HOTELGEORGE@KKHOTELS.CO.UK
154 rms S £111-£150, D £133-£180 inc breakfast & VAT. 56 non-smoking rms. Air cond.
U: Earls Court.

A P ▤ ☼

From the outside, the George appears to be a fairly typical mid-Victorian terrace, step inside, however, and the high-tech, post-modernist décor comes as a complete surprise, but the bright sunshine yellow of the lobby is really very welcoming. Owned by the Austrian K+K group, the predominantly Austrian staff is extremely helpful and hospitable. Situated close to Earl's Court Exhibition Centre, the George is just a short tube ride away from the museums of South Kensington and the fashionable shopping of Knightsbridge. Most unusually for a London hotel, there is also a large private garden, which is overlooked by the breakfast room. The bar area is relaxed and has a strong local clientele as well as hotel guests. Bedrooms are of good size and well-appointed with thick down duvets, hairdryers, cable TV, safes and minibars. Bathrooms are similarly well-equipped. With breakfast included, this hotel really is a very good deal.

Kingsway Hall   ✓✓✓

GREAT QUEEN ST, WC2B 5BZ
020-7309 0909, FAX 020-7309 9696
WWW.KINGSWAYHALL.CO.UK
E-MAIL: KINGSWAYHALL@COMPUSERVE.CO.UK
2 stes £220-£240, 168 rms S £166-£195, D £178-£208 inc VAT. 65% non-smoking rms. 9 rms for disabled. Air cond. 24-hour rm service.
U: Covent Garden.

With Covent Garden on one side and the City of London on the other, this brand new hotel is likely to have a good mix of hedonistic theatregoing tourists and more sober, business travellers. A classical sandstone façade leads into a dramatic glass foyer with sweeping staircase and marble floor. Good sized bedrooms are traditionally furnished, and designed to appeal to both the business and leisure traveller, with interactive TVs, four ISDN lines, modem points and personal telephone numbers with voice-mail. The oak-timbered Harlequin restaurant features a three-and-a-half metre textured glass wall sculpture, while the kitchen is under the direction of chef Ian Hunt who produces a modern European menu. The bar area is handy for all-day snacks and as a useful meeting place. Conference facilities are excellent and can accommodate up to 150 delegates.

Knightsbridge Green Hotel   ✓✓

159 KNIGHTSBRIDGE, SW1X 7PD
020-7584 6274, FAX 020-7225 1635
E-MAIL: THEKGHOTEL@AOL.COM
12 stes £165, 16 rms S £105, D £145 inc VAT. Air cond.
U: Knightsbridge.

This small family-owned hotel on the first floor and upwards, is practically opposite Harrods and is ideal for anyone who wants to be in one of the most expensive areas of London without digging too deeply into the pocket. Barely noticeable from the road with just a small entrance with awning, it opens out quite considerably once inside. On the first floor is a comfortable lounge area with facilities for tea and coffee-making, and bar service is available from 11am to 8pm. Staircases and corridors are decorated in bold stripes. There is no restaurant, but the hotel is happy to recommend or book any of the numerous restaurants within walking distance. Rooms are large and well equipped with two phone lines modem points and satellite TV. All rooms are air-conditioned, a rarity in hotels in this price-range. Guests can use the health club and swimming pool at the nearby Berkley Hotel for an additional fee.

London Bridge Hotel   ✓✓✓

8-18 LONDON BRIDGE ST, SE1 9SG
020-7855 2200, FAX 020-7855 2233
E-MAIL: RESERVATIONS@LONDON-BRIDGE-HOTEL.CO.UK
3 stes £200-£375, 116 rms S £160, D £170-£195 inc VAT & service. Air cond. 24-hr rm service. Non-smoking rms. Rms for disabled.
U: London Bridge.

Right beside London Bridge Station, this modern hotel is ideal for City business visitors, but at the same time right in the middle of one of London's most exciting developing areas along the South Bank and near Shakespeare's Globe, the New Tate Gallery and Butlers Wharf. The lobby area is welcoming and traditionally furnished with comfortable tartan covered sofas and good lighting. Bedrooms carry on the traditional theme, but are equipped with every possible piece of technology. The restaurant is part of the Simply Nico chain and offers fixed-price all-inclusive menus, an idea which is proving popular in this restaurant chain. Hitchcock's City Bar serves light meals and drinks and understandably gets packed with local commuters each evening.

London Elizabeth Hotel ♪♪

LANCASTER TERRACE, W2 3PF
020-7402 6641, FAX 020-7224 8900
U.S. TOLL-FREE 1-800-721-5566
WWW.LONDONELIZABETHHOTEL.CO.UK
E-MAIL: RESERVATIONS@LONDONELIZABETHHO-
TEL.CO.UK
5 stes £180-£250, 44 rms S £110, D £125-£160 inc breakfast & VAT. 5 non-smoking stes, 17 non-smooking rms. 24-hr rm service. Air cond. U: Lancaster Gate.

A P ▦

Recently renovated and made up of three Victorian houses, this favourite small hotel, just near Hyde Park, is decorated in traditional style with comfortable bedrooms complete with individually controlled central heating, and good bathrooms. There's one four-poster room. Service is excellent as it's family-run, and this shows in the friendly welcome. The Rose Garden restaurant offers imaginative cooking and provides a good meeting place in an area not particularly well served. There's a cocktail bar and garden terrace.

Millennium Gloucester ♪♪♪

4 HARRINGTON GDNS, SW7 4LH
020-7373 6030, FAX 020-7373 0409
WWW.MILL-COP.COM
E-MAIL: SALES.GLOUCESTER@MILL-COP.COM
*6 stes £550-£1100, 610 rms S/D £225-£275 inc VAT. 240 non-smoking rms. Air cond. 24-hr rm service.
U:Gloucester Rd.*

A ᵞ ⟳ ⌨

Well situated just off Gloucester Road with its numerous restaurants and close to South Kensington, this modern hotel was extensively renovated when Millennium Hotels took over. The lobby exudes spaciousness and is an impressive focal point awash with marble, wood panelling and a vast chandelier centrepiece. Rooms have been revamped to high standards with fine fabrics, classic furniture and marble bathrooms. There are also Club rooms for executives, with a private lift, checkout and lounge with complimentary drinks. Italian and Californian-style food is served in the jazzed-up South West 7 restaurant.

There's also the fun Bugis Street Café, which reflects Millennium's Singapore origins and a spacious bar in the lobby for tea, drinks and light snacks. The 24-hour business centre is first-rate, with free fax service, and the hotel has extensive conference facilities.

Montague on the Gardens ♪♪♪

15 MONTAGUE ST, WC1B 5BJ
020-7637 1001, FAX 020-7637 2516
WWW.REDCARNATIONHOTELS.COM
E-MAIL: RESERVATIONSM@REDCARNATIONHO-
TELS.COM
*11 stes £250-£400, 93 rms S £130-£160, D £150-£180 plus VAT. 20 non-smoking rms. 24-hr rm service.
U: Holborn.*

A ᵞ ☎ ⟳ ⌨

A favourite of business travellers, owing to its proximity to London's financial district, Montague on the Gardens is also very close to the British Museum and the theatre district. Public rooms have been decorated in Victorian style, with tartan wall coverings in the bar and deep leather armchairs. The effect is very chintzy, and may be rather claustrophobic to those who don't like fabrics everywhere, including in one room, on the tented ceiling. The drawing room, where afternoon tea can be taken, is furnished with antiques and an eclectic collection of upholstered button-back chairs, including a Victorian loveseat. The Blue Door Bistro serves good, light meals. Bedrooms vary in size, but all are tastefully furnished and have plush bathrobes, hair dryers and an impressive assortment of toiletries. 'Executive business travel' rooms feature desk space with enhanced lighting, office supplies and speakerphones. Some rooms are specially designed for the female executive.

Number Eleven ♪♪

11 CADOGAN GDNS, SW3 2RJ
020-7730 7000, FAX 020-7730 5217
WWW.NUMBER-ELEVEN.CO.UK
E-MAIL: RESERVATIONS@NUMBER-ELEVEN.CO.UK
*6 stes £288-£398, 54 rms S £158-£178, D £198-£258 inc VAT. 24-hr rm service. Air cond. Limousine service.
U: Sloane Sq.*

A ᵞ ⟳

Number Eleven was one of the first townhouse hotels and remains delightfully Old World with a clubby atmosphere. In a

Victorian red brick terrace, the oak-panelled entrance hall leads to a warren of corridors leading to traditionally decked-out rooms, recently upgraded and some having four-poster beds. The Garden Suite has a splendid large drawing room with a grand plaster ceiling and many rooms overlook the gardens. The public drawing room is well-furnished with antiques, with a pretty conservatory off the back, and is excellent for tea in front of the roaring fire in wintertime. They offer complimentary homemade cake at teatime and sherry and canapés in the evening. In keeping with the area, and the pied-à-terre feeling, there is a chauffeured limousine service available. Most unusually in a small London hotel, there's an excellent state-of-the-art gym for workouts from 6.30am to 10.30pm. They can also arrange for a masseur to visit.

Number Sixteen ↙↙

16 SUMNER PL, SW7 3EG
020-7589 5232, FAX 020-7584 8615
U.S. TOLL-FREE 1-800-592-5387
WWW.NUMBERSIXTEENHOTEL.CO.UK
E-MAIL: RESERVATIONS@NUMBERSIXTEENHO-TEL.CO.UK
4 stes £205, 32 rms S £90-£125, D £160-£185 inc VAT and CB (served in the rm).
U: South Kensington.

A

Number Sixteen is undoubtedly the most upscale Bed and Breakfast in Sumner Place, a very smart street in South Kensington and a good location due to the many museums, shops and restaurants nearby. Planters on either side of the pillared entrance hint at the grand interior within. The comfortable drawing room is all chintz and swags and has an elegant fireplace and beautiful fresh flower arrangements. A trusting honor system operates in the library bar. The ample-sized rooms feature attractive chintz-covered furniture and include many antiques. Small and intimate, it feels like a private home, and many guests use it as a London pied-à-terre. A conservatory opens onto the secluded, award-winning walled garden. Three-quarters of the clientele are regulars with a high percentage of business people.

Pembridge Court Hotel ↙↙

34 PEMBRIDGE GDNS, W2 4DX
020-7229 9977, FAX 020-7727 4982
U.S. TOLL-FREE 1-800-709-9882
WWW.PEMCT.CO.UK
E-MAIL: RESERVATIONS@PEMCT.CO.UK
20 rms S £120-£160, D £150-£190 inc VAT. Air cond. in some rms. 24-hr rm service for light snacks and drinks.
U: Notting Hill.

A

Anyone who fell in love with the movie Notting Hill will make a bee-line for Pembridge Court, for this nineteenth-century townhouse faces a quiet, tree-lined garden in the heart of Notting Hill Gate. On the ground floor there's a comfortable well-furnished lounge; snacks can be taken in Caps restaurant downstairs, and drinks in the Cellar Bar. Bedrooms vary in size—some singles can be small—but the rooms on the top floor are spacious. Bathrooms have Italian tiles and are well equipped. Many of the antiques and objets d'art, including a large number of fans and the Victoriana in the rooms, come from the nearby antique shops of Portobello Road. In addition to an excellent long-standing staff, for whom nothing is too much trouble, guests may well be greeted by the two resident marmalade cats, Spencer and Churchill, who have recently starred in three television shows; they are even featured on the hotel's postcard.

Pippa Pop-ins ↙↙

430 FULHAM RD, SW6 1DU
020-7385 2458, FAX 020-7385 5706
1 night 5pm-10am £50, 24 hours £75, w/e £145. Accommodates up to 10 children.
U: Fulham Broadway.

A

Parental bliss—a hotel for children, minus their parents! This bright, west London Georgian townhouse specialises in accommodation for children only (aged two to twelve) and presents a loving, fun-filled environment under Montessori-influenced professional supervision. That means toys galore (teddy bears, clowns, games), for both education and play, and when the weather is good, a large private garden area. Arrival late afternoon, pick-up next day late morning, the package includes home-cooked suppers and breakfasts, magic bubble baths in the duck-and-clown bathroom, eight o'clock 'midnight' feasts, and bedtime stories. There are night-lights and baby-alarm intercoms in each room, and security is tight. Open for proper nursery school during the week during term time and on the holidays, Pippa is happy to take visiting children for short or longer periods. The service is also available for hourly baby-sitting, half-days and full-days. It also takes children, holed up at top hotels while parents work or shop, on their own outings. Even the brochure is fun.

Royal Lancaster Hotel ♪♪♪
LANCASTER TERR, W2 2TY
020-7262 6737, FAX 020-7724 3191
WWW.ROYALLANCASTER.COM
E-MAIL: BOOK@ROYALLANCASTERHOTEL.COM
20 stes £535-£1700, 398 rms S/D £220-£295 plus VAT. Air cond. Non-smoking rms. 24-hr rm service.
U: Lancaster Gate.

A ⟳ ⌨

This modern, functional hotel rises eighteen stories above the north side of Hyde Park and it goes without saying that the upper floors have great views across the park. Receiving accolades in the past for its extensive conference facilities, the Lancaster can cope with up to one thousand delegates. It has recently been refurbished, so from the entrance hall onwards, the feel is luxurious and modern. Rooms, which are standard size, are traditionally, though not spectacularly, furnished but have everything necessary for the modern traveller, including voice-mail and modem points; bathrooms are marble and with all the expected amenities like towelling bathrobes. Downstairs the lounge is a favourite place for tea or a drink; the newly opened Pavement is a Mediterranean-style brasserie while The Park restaurant serves Modern British food. The Nipa restaurant offers good Thai food.

The Rubens at the Palace ♪♪♪
39 BUCKINGHAM PALACE RD, SW1W 0PS
020-7834 6600, FAX 020-7233 6037
WWW.REDCARNATIONHOTELS.COM
E-MAIL: RESERVATIONS@RUBENS.REDCARNATION-HOTELS.COM
13 stes £220-£450, 161 rms S £126-£170, D £160-£220 plus VAT. Non smoking floors. Air cond. 24-hr rm service.
U: Victoria.

A ☎ ⟳ ⌨

As its name suggests, this comfortable, traditional hotel is situated bang opposite

Buckingham Palace. From the initial, instant check in, service is very friendly and attentive. Nice little extras like fresh flowers on arrival and good robes and slippers and a nightly selection of canapés make guests feel thoroughly pampered. Rooms are well furnished in traditional style and have a host of facilities: fax/modem lines, CD players, movie rental etc. Dedicated 'Business Ready' rooms have everything the busy executive could wish for: well-equipped desks, excellent lighting and speaker phones. The ambience of the public rooms is delightfully relaxed. The Cavalry Bar, decorated with comfortable love seats and wing chairs in red upholstery has a military theme and serves light meals all day. For more formal dining, guests have a choice of The Carvery offering traditional roasts, or The Library with a more intimate atmosphere and an international menu.

St. George's Hotel ♪♪♪
LANGHAM PL, W1N 8QS
020-7580 0111, FAX 020-7436 7997
8 stes £160-£235, 86 rms S £120-£165, D £130-£205 inc VAT. 4 non-smoking stes, 36 non-smoking rms. Air cond. 24-hr rm service.
U: Oxford Circus.

A ⟳

Few London hotels can boast panoramic views of the skyline, but **The Heights Bar** and restaurant on the fifteenth floor has a stunning view over London (see *Bars*). Most bedrooms also offer the same great perspective. The lobby is on the ground floor and the hotel occupies the ninth to fourteenth floors; external businesses occupy the intervening levels. Its position adjacent to the BBC ensures a regular celebrity clientele, while its proximity to Regent and Oxford Streets makes it a great base for shopaholics. Refurbishment has led to updated bedrooms and good bathrooms, although room sizes still vary.

The Selfridge ♪♪♪
ORCHARD ST, W1H 0JS
020-7408 2080, FAX 020-7409 2295
WWW.THISTLE.CO.UK
E-MAIL: SELFRIDGE@THISTLE.CO.UK
4 stes £300-£400, 290 rms S £124-£182, D £139-£204 inc VAT. 2 non-smoking stes, 145 non-smoking rms. Air cond. 24-hr rm service.
U: Bond St/Marble Arch.

A P ⟳ ⌨

Situated just behind Selfridges department store, on the heart of Oxford Street, this modern hotel is a great spot for shopaholics. The approach and driveway are impressive and the busy public rooms are attractive with light wood panelling and leather armchairs. Bedrooms are adequate and well equipped, with three phone lines and modem points. Décor is functional rather than luxurious, though housekeeping standards are good. There's a club-like feel to the first floor where you find a chintz-filled central lounge for tea, light meals and drinks. Also here are the Stoves Bar and the Orchard Terrace, an informal brasserie open from breakfast through dinner. Shoppers can leave bags at the hotel while they roam Oxford Street.

Shaw Park Plaza

100-110 EUSTON RD, NW1 2AJ
020-7666 9000, FAX 020-7666 9100
WWW.PARKPLAZAHOTELS.CO.UK
E-MAIL: SPPSALES@PARKPLAZAHOTELS.CO.UK
44 stes £185-£195, 268 rms D£145-£170 inc VAT. 44 non-smoking stes, 65 non-smoking rms. Air cond. 24-hour rm service. Limousine service. U: Euston/King's Cross.

This is Park Plaza's first hotel in the UK and has been designed very much with the business traveller in mind, being well located close to King's Cross, St. Pancras and Euston stations. One of the key features of the development has been the renovation of the Shaw Theatre, which is available for conferences as well as theatre productions. The outside of the building features a glass lift, giving arriving visitors spectacular views across London. Rooms are comfortably furnished and well equipped with ISDN phone lines and Internet access—they even have European plug sockets. Mirrors restaurant is quite large and bustling and offers a modern European menu.

Sloane Square Moat House

SLOANE SQ, SW1W 8EG
020-7896 9988, FAX 020-7824 8381
WWW.QUEENSMOAT.CO.UK
E-MAIL: LONDONAREA.SALES@QUEENSMOAT.CO.UK
3 stes £140-£230, 102 rms S £90-£150, D £90-£170 inc VAT. No air cond. 24-hr rm service. U: Sloane Sq.

Sloane Square is an impressive address, and great for the fashion-conscious, being on the corner of the King's Road (known for trendy, youthful fashion) and Sloane Street (with its designer boutiques). Public rooms are comfortable and have a kind of timeless elegance. The restaurant has recently become part of the Simply Nico chain. Barflies will find that the Tavern Pub gets pretty lively in the evenings and on weekends. Bedrooms are well-appointed and have oak furniture and soft colour schemes. Singles, however, are fairly small. Housekeeping standards are excellent, and the staff helpful.

Swallow Regents Plaza Hotel & Suites

PLAZA PARADE, MAIDA VALE, NW6 5RP
020-7543 6000, FAX 020-7543 2100
E-MAIL: REGENTSPLAZA@BTINTERNET.COM
17 stes from £250-£750, 204 rms from £185-£205 inc service & VAT. 8 non-smoking stes, 110 non-smoking rms. Air cond. U: Maida Vale.

The opening of the Heathrow Express put this modern hotel in Maida Vale just twenty-five minutes from the airport and makes it a great choice for the busy executive. Business facilities are excellent, with club floors, a club lounge and business centre, 23 meeting rooms, health club with swimming pool and car park. It looks spectacular, with a first-floor internal landscaped garden to sit in, as well as state-of-the-art technical facilities. Also on offer are good family packages, taking advantage of the close proximity to Madame Tussauds and London Zoo. Fratelli's offers good dining and, like the downstairs bar, is popular with locals, adding to the friendly atmosphere. For lighter meals, try the Café Maurice.

Swiss Cottage Hotel

4 ADAMSON RD, NW3 3HP
020-7722 2281, FAX 020-7483 4588
WWW.SWISSCOTTAGEHOTEL.CO.UK
E-MAIL: RESERVATIONS@SWISSCOTTAGEHOTEL.CO.UK
58 rms S £92, D £105-£126 inc VAT. U: Swiss Cottage.

Just two minutes from Swiss Cottage underground station, this attractive hotel has been converted from four Victorian terraced houses, dating from 1860. The rooms tend to be small, but well furnished, and as is the way with such hotels carved out of residences, there are numerous corridors and passages. But there is a delightful and gracious old-fashioned drawing room furnished with antiques and the view over the surrounding residential streets is leafy and restful. There's a restaurant also and a delightful bar; altogether this hotel makes a pleasant alternative to central London.

Thistle Hyde Park

90 LANCASTER GATE, W2 3NR
020-7262 2711, FAX 020-7262 2147
WWW.THISTLE.CO.UK
E-MAIL: HYDE.PARK@THISTLE.CO.UK
*14 stes £425, 40 rms S £215, D £279 inc VAT.
Air cond. 24-hr rm service.
U: Lancaster Gate.*

Formerly known as Whites Hotel, this pretty, gracious building, dating from 1866, is an excellent base from which to explore London; a walk across Kensington Gardens will bring you to Kensington Palace. Behind its imposing façade is a relatively unknown, charming hotel, which carries on the grand feeling of the outside into the reception area, with its marble fireplace and panelled, writing room. Good-sized bedrooms have comfortable chairs, lots of silk furnishings and well-equipped marble bathrooms. The Grill restaurant serves good English food and the bar area is a restful place for a drink.

Topham's Belgravia

24-32 EBURY ST, SW1W 0LU
020-7730 8147, FAX 020-7823 5966
E-MAIL: TOPHAMS-
BELGRAVIA@COMPUSERVE.COM
*1 ste £170-£260, 38 rms S£85-£150, D £100-£170 inc EB&VAT. 1 non-smoking ste, 20 non-smoking rms.
U: Victoria.*

There's something about Topham's that seems to conjure up Agatha Christie's ladies (nothing sinister though). Owned and run by the same family for more than 60 years, the hotel has been completely refurbished and all rooms now have bathrooms (two singles have exclusive use of non-en-suite). There is a pretty lounge area with comfortable armchairs in chintzy fabrics and pastel-coloured walls. The small conference room has a rather odd collec-

tion of large bright prints of jungle animals, which seem slightly distracting, but also rather charming. Bedrooms are newly decorated in pastel colours and are reasonably sized and well-equipped with voice-mail, TV and hair dryers. The new bathrooms are well-fitted and have excellent lighting. Topham's restaurant is a mix of English and French cooking, with large well-spaced tables. There is a small intimate bar on the lower ground floor, which used to be Topham's Club. They have many repeat clients, lots of them British, who swear by its efficiency and genuine convivial atmosphere.

ECONOMY

Abbey House

11 VICARAGE GATE, W8 4AG
020-7727 2594
*16 rms S/D £43-£68, triple/family £85-£95 inc breakfast & VAT.
U: High St Kensington.*

A great value and very well run bed-and-breakfast in an absolutely prime location just off Kensington Church Street. Don't expect luxury; bedrooms are simply, sometimes sparsely, furnished and the breakfast room is functional. But this is a pretty house, and the public areas, stairways and entrance are gracious and large. Built in 1860 in this classy residential area, the hotel is welcoming and particularly ideal for families since it's so close to the South Kensington museums.

Alison House Hotel

82 EBURY ST, SW1W 9QD
020-7730 9529, FAX 020-7730 5494
E-MAIL: ALIHOUSE82@AOL.COM
*2 stes £70-£95, 10 rms S £30-£38, D £50-£55, inc VAT.
U: Victoria.*

Though in Belgravia—one of the most expensive districts of London—Ebury Street is filled with small hotels, some good and some mediocre. The decoration at Alison House, big on pastels such as apricot, may not be inspiring, but the hotel is consistently commendable, clean and tidy. The hotel is privately owned and popular with an American clientele, many of them business people. All rooms have TVs, direct dial telephones, hair dryers and basins, though only two rooms have en-suite facilities. There's no restaurant, but plenty in the area.

Amber Hotel

101 LEXHAM GDNS, W8 6JN
020-7373 8666, FAX 020-7835 1194
38 rms S £65-£95, D £85-£110 inc breakfast &
VAT.
U: Earls Court.

In a very smart residential quarter of London, this hotel allows the visitor to be within easy reach of the major sights and yet soak up the feel of living in the city at a modest price. A generous buffet breakfast is served in the pleasant dining room, and service is warm and friendly. Bedrooms are nicely decorated with extremely good bathrooms and all have direct dial telephones, minibars and cable TV.

Amsterdam Hotel

7 TREBOVIR RD, SW5 9LS
020-7370 5084, FAX 020-7244 7608
WWW.AMSTERDAY-HOTEL.COM
E-MAIL: RESERVATIONS@AMSTERDAM-HOTEL.COM
8 stes £99-£146, 20 rms S £71, D £82-£105 inc
breakfast & VAT. 4 non-smoking stes, 10 non-
smoking rms.
U: Earls Court.

Very popular with families (several family rooms), this small friendly hotel is close to the Earl's Court Exhibition Centre and within easy reach of Knightsbridge and South Kensington. The whole hotel has recently been refurbished and decorated in attractive pastel colours and fabrics. The breakfast room has a pleasant summery feel and continental breakfast is included. There is a lift and all rooms have TV, telephone and individual heating controls.

Aster House

3 SUMNER PL, SW7 3EE
020-7581 5888, FAX 020-7584 4925
E-MAIL: ASTERHOUSE@BTINTERNET.COM
12 rms S £65-£90, D £135-£165 inc breakfast
& VAT. All non-smoking. Air cond.
U: South Kensington.

Sumner Place has a number of discreet B&B's, and this one has been routinely

endorsed by the British Tourist Authority as one of the best. It is family run, though beware the occasionally off-hand service. Set in the smart residential area of South Kensington, it features pretty bedrooms, many with four-poster beds, all with refrigerators, direct-dial telephones and cable TV. There is also a well-kept garden and a glassed-in conservatory to relax in after a hard day trawling the shops or museums. Good buffet breakfast.

The Claverley

13 BEAUFORT GDNS, SW3 1PS
020-7589 8541, FAX 020-7584 3410
U.S. TOLL FREE 1-800-747-0398
E-MAIL: CLAVERLEYHOTEL@NETSCAPEONLINE.CO.UK
7 stes £150-£200 22 rms S £85-£115, D £120-
£150 inc VAT. Air cond. some rms.
U: Knightsbridge.

A short walk from Harrods, this hotel, situated in a quiet garden square, is an elegant base from which to tour the shops of Knightsbridge and the museums in South Kensington. The Claverley is highly recommended by the British Tourist Authority and has won numerous awards. Rooms are decorated to a high standard, with a country-house feel and a strong emphasis on floral patterns. Bathrooms feature lots of marble. The hotel is justly proud of their fine English breakfasts, always cooked to order, and the attractive lounge area offers complimentary tea, coffee and newspapers.

Elizabeth Hotel

37 ECCLESTON SQ, SW1V 1PB
020-7828 6812, FAX 020-7828 6814
E-MAIL: ELIZABETH@ARGYLLHOTELS.COM
70 rms S £45-£70, D £68-£92, family £80-£120
inc VAT. Tennis nearby.
U: Pimlico/Victoria.

A good location in the heart of Pimlico on a historic square (the private gardens and tennis court are available to guests), and close to Victoria and Sloane Square make this simple family-run hotel a good choice. Great care has been taken to achieve an authentic mid-nineteenth-century décor, with carefully chosen prints and portraits in public rooms, reflecting the attention that the owners pay to detail. Bedrooms are modestly furnished and functional; only four are without bathrooms, but some rooms are very small and family rooms should be checked out for size when booking.

They also have longer-stay self-contained fully equipped apartments.

Five Sumner Place

5 SUMNER PL, SW7 3EE
020-7584 7586, FAX 020-7823 9962
E-MAIL: RESERVATIONS@SUMNERPLACE.COM
13 rms S £88-99, D £140-£152 plus VAT.
U: South Kensington.

Receiving numerous accolades, including on the hotel's tenth anniversary, the English Tourism Council's Bed & Breakfast of the Year 1999 award. Also its location in a smart, residential street in South Kensington, provide two very good reasons for choosing this upscale B&B. Recent refurbishments have improved it considerably with each bedroom being individually furnished and decorated to a high standard. There's a lift and all rooms have en-suite bathroom, TV, telephone, trouser presses, hair dryers and refrigerators. It's welcoming and friendly, and there's a Victorian-style conservatory in which to have breakfast—or just relax in.

Generator

COMPTON PLACE, OFF 37 TAVISTOCK PL, WC1H 9SD
020-7388 7666, FAX 020-7388 7644
WWW.THE-GENERATOR.CO.UK
E-MAIL: INFO@THE-GENERATOR.CO.UK
217 rms S £35-£39, D £40-£52.
U: Russell Sq.

Definitely budget and definitely for the young and (probably backpackers), nevertheless this is a great find. Everything is decorated like a generator, so expect functional décor and bunk beds in double rooms. It's more youth hostel that hotel in feel, but there's a bar and restaurant, Internet and games room. Staff is friendly and fun, and the place seems very safe, so you probably can send your teenagers here without too much worry.

Hotel 167

167 OLD BROMPTON RD, SW5 0AN
020-7373 0672, FAX 020-7373 3360
WWW.HOTEL167.COM
E-MAIL: ENQUIRIES@HOTEL167.COM
19 rms S £66-£72, D £90-£99 inc VAT.
U: South Kensington.

A great location, close to museums like the Victoria & Albert and the Natural History and to the shops in the Brompton Cross/Fulham Road area, makes this discreet Victoria hotel a good choice. The visitor is greeted by a muted, Scandinavian-influenced décor of soft grey and cream coordinated with many good antiques. Rooms are all different, with modern, stylish interiors, free from clutter. Double rooms have private baths, although singles only have nearby facilities. Staff is friendly and gracious.

Lincoln House Hotel

33 GLOUCESTER PL, W1H 3PD
020-7486 7630, FAX 020-7486 0166
WWW.LINCOLN-HOUSE-HOTEL.CO.UK
E-MAIL: RESERVATIONS@LINCOLN-HOUSE-HOTEL.CO.UK
22 rms S £55-£79, D/T £69-£95 inc EB, service & VAT.
U: Marble Arch.

Very handy for the shops of Oxford Street, this small hotel behind a Georgian façade is friendly and welcoming. Bedrooms, though modestly furnished, have facilities like hair dryers and trouser presses, tea and coffee-making, and all have en-suite bathrooms and direct-dial telephones. There's a small restaurant for breakfast.

Royal Park Hotel

5 WESTBOURNE TERR, W2 3UL
020-7402 6187, FAX 020-7224 9426
E-MAIL: RICHARDF@ARGYLLHOTELS.COM
58 rms S £62, D £84, triple £110- £125 inc breakfast & VAT.
U: Lancaster Gate.

In Bayswater, just north of Hyde Park, this hotel is taken from three mid-nineteenth-century townhouses, which have been modernised without losing their original character. The hotel has a free car park for guests, something which is almost unheard of in London, free or otherwise. Public areas consist of two lounges, an attractive bar and a Thai restaurant. Bedrooms are simply furnished and all have en-suite bathroom, TV and telephone.

Rushmore Hotel

11 TREBOVIR RD, SW5 9LS
020-7370 3839, FAX 020-7370 0274
22 rms S £59-£69, D £79-£85 inc breakfast & VAT.
U: Earls Court.

Situated on a street of hotels, the Rushmore stands out as being above average both in standards of décor and service. Being close to the Earl's Court Exhibition Centre, it is popular with a business clientele, but handy for tourists, too—just a couple of tube stops from the South Kensington museums and Knightsbridge. Rooms are individually decorated with use of trompe l'œil to great effect. The breakfast room has a very Mediterranean feel with lots of wrought iron and glass-topped tables. Temporary membership of a local health club can be arranged.

The Sanctuary House

33 TOTHILL ST, SW1H 9LA
020-799 4044, FAX 020-7799 3657
E-MAIL: SANCTUARY@FULLERS.CO.UK
1 ste £79-£99, 35 rms D £72-£89 inc VAT. 15 non-smoking rms. Air cond.
U: Victoria.

The aptly named Sanctuary House is built on the site of the almonry of Westminster Abbey from where monks dispensed food and shelter to the needy. Modern visitors will find a bit more comfort with well-equipped, air-conditioned rooms at a very reasonable price and in a great location for the main tourist sights of London. The Sanctuary Pub on the ground floor serves real ales and traditional English dishes.

Searcy's Roof Garden Bedrooms

30 PAVILION ST, SW1X 0HJ
020-7584 4921, FAX 020-7823 8694
E-MAIL: SEARCYGR@AOL.COM
1 ste £160, 10 rms S £90, D £130 inc VAT.
U: Knightsbridge.

One of the best deals around, Searcy's will appeal to anyone wanting a very comfortable room in a great location at an affordable price. Situated on a quiet street just behind Harrods, it doesn't offer the public rooms or amenities of a usual hotel, though a delicious continental breakfast is served in the room. What it does offer is an excellent base from which to explore London's many sights and restaurants. Rooms are extremely well-equipped and furnished, decorated tastefully with elegant fabrics and well-chosen pictures. Bathrooms are all marble and mahogany with proper cast-iron baths and nice little touches such as bottled water. There is a roof garden and a function centre, which caters for 20-250 guests. Apartments are also available.

University Women's Club

2 AUDLEY SQ, W1Y 6DB
020-7499 2268, FAX 020-7499 7046
E-MAIL: UWC@GLOBALNET.CO.UK
20 rms £43-£128 inc VAT.
U: Hyde Park Corner.

Just around the corner from the Dorchester, this private club is invaluable. Members and their guests will be accommodated if it is humanly possible, even if it means a sofa in the library as the club policy is committed to the concept of safety for women. London membership is £329, for country members it is £280, and for overseas members, it is only £197 per year. The restaurant for members operates seven days a week.

Willett Hotel

32 SLOANE GDNS, SW1W 8DJ
020-7824 8415, FAX 020-7730 4830
WWW.EEH.CO.UK; E-MAIL: WILLETT@EEH.CO.UK
19 rms S £79-£103, D £106-£176 inc breakfast plus VAT. Air cond in some rms.
U: Sloane Sq.

An excellent location, just around the corner from Sloane Square in fashionable Chelsea, makes this small townhouse hotel a very good budget choice. The whole hotel has been renovated to a high standard. Bedrooms are all individually decorated and feature hair dryers, trouser presses, refrigerators and satellite TV.

Looking for an address?
Refer to the index.

Windermere Hotel

142 WARWICK WAY, SW1V 4JE
020-7834 5163, FAX 020-7630 8831
E-MAIL: WINDERMERE@COMPUSERVE.COM
22 rms S £64-£88, D £75-£136, family rms £125-£142 inc VAT & EB.
U: Pimlico/Victoria.

Close to the Victoria Terminal, this welcoming and charming family-run hotel enjoys a high level of routine patronage. Soft drinks are available throughout the day in the pleasant lounge and in the basement is the Pimlico restaurant, serving a modern European menu. Bedrooms are simply furnished, but comfortable and immaculately kept by housekeeping. The needs of business clients are well served of with modem points, ISDN lines and video conference facilities.

THE CHAINS

Days Inn

New to Britain, this American giant plans to open 40 hotels during 2000 across the country. Already open is Days Inn Waterloo, 020-7922 1331, toll-free 0800 0280400, www.daysinn.com. Rates: £59.50.

Holiday Inn

Toll-free central booking 0800 897121, www.holidayinn.com. This worldwide chain needs no introduction and, as well as the Mayfair site (see above) has hotels in Kensington, Kings Cross, Docklands, Oxford Circus and Victoria. Rates: £75-£195.

Ibis

Part of the French Accor Group, of which Novotel is a part, these are moderately priced hotels with basic amenities and smaller rooms than Novotels. There are five branches in London: in Euston, 020-7388 7777, at Greenwich, 020-8305 1177, Docklands 020-8283 4550, East Barking 020-8477 4100 and Heathrow 020-8759 4917. Rates £45-£58. www.ibishotel.com.

Novotel

Central Bookings 020-8283 4530, www.novotel.com. Rapidly expanding French chain, with good, reasonably-sized rooms and

facilities now has hotels in Hammersmith, Heathrow and Waterloo (ideal for Eurostar). Rates £112-£165.

Radisson Edwardian Hotels

In addition to the three hotels mentioned above—The Hampshire (Leicester Square), The Mountbatten (Covent Garden) and the Radisson Edwardian (Heathrow)—this upscale chain operates seven other country-house-style hotels in central London: The Berkshire (Oxford Street), The Marlborough (Bloomsbury), The Pastoria (Leicester Square), The Kenilworth (Bloomsbury), The Grafton (Tottenham Court Road), The Vanderbilt (Kensington), and The Savoy Court (Marble Arch). All are decorated in the charmingly eclectic style of an Edwardian-era English home, and have excellent amenities for business travellers. Radisson Edwardian offers special programs at all their hotels, featuring guaranteed rates in U.S. dollars, full English breakfast, all taxes and service charges—and very reasonable prices (from £109, inc breakfast). Central reservations: U.S. toll-free 1-800-333-3333, 0800-37 44 11 in U.K., www.radisson.com.

Travel Inn

Rooms cost £62.95 a night. Locations are Belvedere Rd, Waterloo, SE1, 020-7902 1600; 141 Euston Rd, Euston, NW1, 020-7554 3400; 3 Putney Bridge Approach, Putney, SW6, 020-7471 8300. www.travelinn.co.uk

Travellodge

Rooms are £59.95 a night. Two locations at 200 York Rd, Battersea, SE11, 020-7228 5508; and Coriander Ave, East India Dock Rd, Docklands, E14, 020-7531 9705. www.travellodge.com.

AIRPORTS

Room rates vary enormously at the airport hotels, depending on whether you are staying mid-week (expensive) or weekend. Corporate rates, as with all hotels, vary considerably. Most airport hotels are used for conferences and business meetings, so many have day rates to accommodate international meetings. If you're travelling as a family, enquire about a family room and the possibility of your children staying free in your room. There's often an age limit, usually-16-years-old.

GATWICK

Copthorne London Gatwick ♪♪♪
COPTHORNE, NR CRAWLEY, WEST SUSSEX, RH10 3PG
01342-348800, FAX 01342-348833
WWW.MILL-COP.COM
E-MAIL: RESERVATIONS.GATWICK@MILL-COP.COM
5 stes £255, 222 rms S £130-£155, D £140-£165 inc service & VAT. 60% non-smoking rms. 24-hr rm service.

🅰 🏋 ♃ 🐎 ⩰ P ⌂ 🖥

Quite unlike the run-of-the-mill airport hotel, the Copthorne is built around an old sixteenth-century farmhouse and set in 100 acres of gardens and woods, yet is just six minutes from the airport. In keeping with its origins, log fires and oak beams grace the public rooms and many bedrooms are in traditional style, again beamed and with four-poster beds. Special rooms for the disabled are available. There are four banquet suites for business use. The Connoisseur Wing provides extra luxury, and each bathroom has a corner spa bath. There's a formal restaurant, The Lion d'Or, the informal Brasserie, the Library Bar and Lounge, and the White Swan Pub. For relaxation, there's a croquet lawn and jogging track and nearby golf and horse riding. The health club, located outside the hotel, includes a pool and squash courts.

Gravetye Manor ♪♪♪♪
VOWELS LANE, EAST GRINSTEAD, WEST SUSSEX, RH19 4LJ, 01342-810567, FAX 01342-810080
WWW.RELAISCHATEAUX.FR
E-MAIL: GRAVETYE@RELAISCHATEAUX.FR
18 rms S £90-£145, D from £120-£290 inc service plus VAT.

VISA MasterCard ♃ 🐎 P ⌂

This is as far from being an airport hotel as could be imagined, but arriving or leaving from Gatwick provides the perfect excuse for a deluxe stay and a delightful dining experience at celebrated Gravetye Manor, a member of the Relais et Châteaux group. One of the first country-house hotels in England, this Elizabethan stone mansion was built in 1598 and still retains its baronial feeling. Public downstairs rooms have magnificent panelled walls and moulded ceilings. Bedrooms are large, comfortable and beautifully furnished with antique furniture and glorious fabrics, while books and magazines are scattered around as if in a private home. The welcome given by owner Peter Herbert and his staff is proverbial. The gardens are the creation of William Robinson who bought Gravetye in 1884 and 1,000 acres of flowerbeds and lawns invite guests to stroll outside. People come from miles around to eat in the restaurant, from a menu that mixes the traditional with the modern. The wine cellar is formidable and contains 500 bins. If you feel expansive, or want a special treat on arrival or departure, Gravetye Manor is not to be missed.

Le Méridien Gatwick Airport ♪♪♪
NORTH TERMINAL, GATWICK AIRPORT
WEST SUSSEX, RH6 0PH
01293-567070, FAX 01293-567739
WWW.LEMERIDIEN-HOTELS.COM
8 stes from £255, 442rms S/D £180-£190 inc service & VAT. 8 non-smoking stes, 333 non-smoking rms. Air cond. 24-hr rm service.

🅰 🏋 ⩰ P ⌂ 🖥

A short covered walkway links Le Méridien to the North Terminal of the airport, so it couldn't be more convenient. The lobby area is dominated by an eight-storey atrium with a cocktail bar and café below and a grand piano as centrepiece. Décor is modern and minimal. The hotel has been refurbished; bedrooms are well equipped, and the TV system displays flight information. The new Royal Club occupies the eighth floor and offers luxury rooms, private check-in, business services and complimentary breakfast in Le Club Royal Lounge. Restaurants include the Brasserie with its extensive buffet, Café Montparnasse, and The Gatwick Oriental featuring Asian dishes. There's a spa and swimming pool.

London Gatwick Hilton ♪♪♪
GATWICK, WEST SUSSEX, RH11 0PD
01293-518080, FAX 01293-528980
WWW.HILTON.COM
E-MAIL: GATHITWGM@HILTON.COM
18 stes £260, 552 rms S £150-£219 inc VAT. Non-smoking floors. Air cond. 24-hr rm service.

🅰 🏋 ⚷ ♃ ⩰ P 🚆 ⌂ 🖥

One of the most impressive of Gatwick's hotels, it features a pedestrian walkway connecting to the South Terminal, and a four-storey central atrium where a life-size replica of Amy Johnson's biplane hangs from the ceiling. Bedrooms are good size and well-equipped and the TVs display the latest flight information. There's a fully equipped health club and pool, Amy's American Style Diner and the more formal Garden restaurant and two bars. Golf, tennis and squash are nearby.

HEATHROW

Heathrow Hilton ♪♪♪
TERMINAL 4, HOUNSLOW, MIDDLX, TW5 3AF
020-8759 7755, FAX 020-8759 7579
WWW.HILTON.COM
E-MAIL: GMHEATHROW@HILTON.COM
6 stes £430-£655, 395 rms S/D £110-£260 inc VAT. Non-smoking rms. Air cond.

A 'Y' ≈ P 📞 ❍ 🖥

Right beside Terminal 4, this is the most spectacular of Heathrow's hotels, all steel and glass and a landmark from the outside; you enter via a huge, high atrium which has a lounge and restaurant beneath it. Bedrooms are equipped with all the modern technology international travellers expect. Executive floor includes special check-in, lounge and complimentary breakfast and canapés; the business facilities are first rate. There are three restaurants, The Brasserie for informal dining, Zen with an oriental menu, and Oscar's, which specialises in grills. Direct access to Terminal 4 is via a covered walkway.

Le Méridien Excelsior ♪♪♪
BATH RD, WEST DRAYTON, MIDDLX, UB7 0DU
020-8759 6611, FAX 020-8759 3421
WWW.LEMERIDIEN-HOTELS.COM
10 stes from £250-£350, 527 rms S/D £64-£120, plus VAT. 6 non-smoking stes, 253 non-smoking rms. Air cond. 24-hr rm service.

A 'Y' ≈ P ❍ 🖥

This modern giant of a hotel was recently taken over by Le Méridien group and its refurbishment has ensured that it offers all the modern comforts. Some bedrooms are equipped for wheelchair-bound guests. There is a pool and the usual health and beauty facilities. Children under 14-years-old stay free in their parents' room. A grand entrance lobby

greets you and there are extensive conference facilities. Wheeler's of St. James's, the fish restaurant chain, runs one of the restaurants and there is a buffet in The Original Carvery and Grill. There are also two bars.

Radisson Edwardian Heathrow ♪♪♪
140 BATH RD, HAYES, MIDDLX, UB3 5AW
020-8759 6311, FAX 020-8759 4559
WWW.RADISSON.COM
17 stes £383-£723, 443 rms S £165, D£180-£210 plus VAT. Non-smoking rms. Air cond. 24-hr rm service.

A 'Y' ≈ P 📞 ❍ 🖥

The Radisson Edwardian Heathrow is a stylish hotel just five minutes from the airport and offering every comfort. Bedrooms are good size and well-decorated, some with four-poster beds; suites have spa baths. This is an important residential conference hotel; facilities are excellent for business travellers and include seventeen conference suites. Business Class, with its hallmark rooms, is aimed at the frequent traveller, with bigger rooms, full English breakfast and more. There is a pool, spa and beauty salon; The Brasserie for casual dining and Henley's for fine dining.

Sheraton Skyline ♪♪♪♪
BATH RD, HAYES, MIDDLX, UB3 5BP
020-8759 2535, FAX 020-8759 9150
WWW.SHERATON.COM
E-MAIL: RES268-SKYLINE@SHERATON.COM
5 stes £250-£750, 351 rms S £190-£231, D £200-£241 inc service & VAT. 177 non-smoking rms. Air cond. 24-hr rm service.

A 'Y' ≈ P 📞 ❍ 🖥

The Sheraton Skyline is known for the Patio Caribe—a large indoor tropical garden with swimming pool and bar. Bedrooms are excellently equipped; children up to 16-years-old stay free in their parents' room. Banqueting and conference facilities are what you would expect, and can accommodate up to 500. There is a choice of two restaurants, Le Jardin and the Colony restaurant, plus the more informal Sports Bar & Café.

NIGHTLIFE

CONTENTS

BARS & WINE BARS 204
    BELGRAVIA 204
    CHARING CROSS 204
    THE CITY 204
    COVENT GARDEN 205
    FITZROVIA 206
    FULHAM 206
    HOLBORN 206
    HOLLAND PARK 206
    ISLINGTON 207
    KNIGHTSBRIDGE 207
    LEICESTER SQUARE 207
    MAYFAIR 207
    NOTTING HILL GATE 208
    ST. JAMES'S 208
    SHOREDITCH 208
    SOHO 209
    VICTORIA 209
    WATERLOO 209
HOTEL BARS 210
PUBS 211
COMEDY CLUBS 222
MUSIC CLUBS 222
NIGHTCLUBS 224

BARS & WINE BARS

BELGRAVIA

Motcombs

26 MOTCOMB ST, SW1, 020-7235 6382
Open Mon.-Sat. 10am-midnight, Sun.11am-4pm.
U: Knightsbridge.

This pretty restaurant and bar is famous for its collection of oil paintings in all styles. The place has a club-like feeling, as there is a core of loyal, local patrons, but outsiders are made to feel welcome, too. Only a minute's walk from upmarket Sloane Street, it's an excellent stop for a lunch or a drink while shopping. There is an extensive wine list, and the food is Modern British with an emphasis on fresh fish. Diners are invited to go on celebrating in Motcomb's nightclub opposite until 3am.

CHARING CROSS

Gordon's

47 VILLIERS ST, WC2, 020-7930 1408
Open Mon.-Fri. 11am-11pm.
U: Embankment/Charing Cross.

Down past Charing Cross station towards the Embankment, in the last house on the left, and through an almost unmarked door, is an atmospheric cellar known as Gordon's wine bar. It is a place with old brick walls covered with newspaper clippings and tables lit with candles in nooks and corners. In the evenings, the clientele is a collection of regulars on their way home from the office and first-time passers-by on their way to town. There is a good selection of wines by the glass, which is useful as it's much easier to hold a glass rather than a bottle when you're standing in the crowd. They do simple, but good snacks, like cheese and quiches throughout the day. In warm weather, Gordon's opens its doors into the little backyard where a few tables look towards a small park.

Looking for an address?
Refer to the index.

THE CITY

Balls Brothers

158 BISHOPSGATE, EC2, 020-7626 7919
Open Mon.-Fri. 11am-9pm.
U: Liverpool St.

Balls Brothers started in the wine business more than twenty years ago, before the British had learnt to appreciate wines. Those were the days when some customers only knew Blue Nun and plonk de plonk. The eighties boom brought wine bars to Britain as a symbol of the yuppie culture; since then the tide has turned and today wine bars are an essential part of everyday British drinking life. The pioneering work of companies like Balls Brothers has borne fruit, and today patrons know exactly what they want and expect quality service from wine merchants. Balls Brothers ships its own wines and runs several excellent wine bars throughout London.

Corney & Barrow Champagne Bar

10 BROADGATE CIRCLE, EC2, 020-7628 1251
Open Mon.-Fri. 11am-10pm.
U: Liverpool St.

You find this branch of the Corney & Barrow chain high above Broadgate Circle, part of the modern development around Liverpool Street Station. The bar overlooks the Circle, which has constantly varied events and entertainment including ice skating in winter months. It's a good place to meet after work or to start a cultural evening in the nearby Barbican Centre. All Corney & Barrow bars offer a good selection of wines and snacks (see *Quick Bites*).

Pavilion

FINSBURY CIRCUS GNDS, EC2, 020-7628 8224
Open Mon.-Fri. noon-10pm.
U: Moorgate/Liverpool St.

Looking more like a glorified garden shed or a cricket pavilion, this bar is situated in peaceful Finsbury Circus Gardens just a few steps away from the buzzing City. The proximity of the money markets can be seen in the wine list: buying a bottle of champagne gives you membership of the Grande Marque Club, which entitles you to a free bottle for every ten bottles purchased. And yes, they do magnums and jeroboams of champagne to celebrate a good deal. The Pavilion is part of the Jamies chain of bars and restaurants.

COVENT GARDEN

Bar des Amis du Vin
11-14 HANOVER PL (OFF LONG ACRE), WC2
020-7379 3444
Open Mon.-Sat. 11.30am-11pm.
U: Covent Garden.

Famous for its excellent selection of French wines and award-winning cheese board, the Bar des Amis du Vin has become a landmark for quality in Covent Garden. Refurbished a couple of years ago, the bar now has more room for wine drinkers enjoying the mainly European list (with a decent sampling of the New World thrown in). The menu offers classic French food like, moules or steak frites throughout the day (see *Quick Bites*). It's a good place to start an evening of theatre or opera.

Crusting Pipe
27 THE MARKET, WC2, 020-7836 1415
Open Mon.-Sat. 11am-11.30pm, Sun. 11am-6pm.
U: Covent Garden.

This rambling wine bar fills a series of small, intimate nooks and vaults under Covent Garden's craft market. So it's easy to find a peaceful corner for a chat, or one can sit outside on the patio listening to classical music played by the ever-present pavement artists. There's sawdust on the floor, a good wine list and a substantial menu. The Crusting Pipe, situated on the lower level of the market building, is part of the ever-expanding Davy's chain of quality wine bars.

Denim
4 ST. MARTIN'S LANE, WC2, 020-7497 0376
Open Mon.-Sat. noon-1am, Sun. noon-10.30pm.
U: Leicester Sq.

Nice surprises are always...well, nice. When Denim opened it was talked about as the trendiest, and one of the snootiest, fashion bars in London. So it was, as we say, a nice surprise to walk in one quiet afternoon, have a friendly chat with the barmen and get a lesson on how to mix a perfect mojito with enough mint to make it really refreshing. It takes time, but is definitely worth it. Extra cool looks can be deceiving.

Navajo Joe
34 KINGLY ST, WC2, 020-7240 4008
Open Mon.-Sat. noon-11pm, Sun. noon-10.30pm.
U: Covent Garden.

According to the barman, they serve 231 different tequilas, but that was on the last count. One of life's basic rules is never to argue with a barman, and anyway the shelves here are full to overflowing with different shapes and sizes of tequila bottles. Stick to cocktails and tequilas either neat or mixed. You'll have a good time if you start from the left of the bottom shelf and take it from there to the right, then...

Oysters & Champagne

The fashion for the most fashionable pastime of sipping Champagne and downing oysters is well established in London. Oysters vary in price according to where you are, but reckon to pay around £12-£24 for a dozen. **Bibendum Oyster Bar**, 81 Fulham Rd, SW3, 020-7589 1480, is fashionable and good for people watching (see *Restaurants*). **Green's Restaurant & Oyster Bar**, 36 Duke St, SW1, 020-7930 4566, will see you seated among a business-suited crowd (see *Restaurants*), or you can eat at the splendid central bar. **The Rib Room & Oyster Bar** at the Hyatt Carlton Tower, Cadogan Pl, SW1, 020-7235 1234, is newly refurbished and delicious and comfortable with excellent oysters and interesting accompaniments (see *Restaurants*). Scott's, 20 Mount St, W1, 020-7629 5284, is a favourite place. If you're in The City, try **Sweeting's**, 39 Victoria St, EC4, 020-7248 3062 which has been serving oysters since 1889. Also try **Wiltons**, 55 Jermyn St, SW1, 020-7629 9955, which remains one of the establishment's favourite venues, so expect more captains of industry here (see *Restaurants*).

Light Bar

45 ST. MARTINS LANE, WC2, 020-7300 5599
Open Mon.-Sat. 5.30pm-3am, Sun. 5.30pm-10.30pm.
U: Leicester Sq.

The coolest of the cool London hotels, St. Martin's Lane has a light, airy bar on the ground floor. The minimalist lounge gives you the reflection of a goldfish bowl at the back and huge chess pieces as furniture. So, go to the right of the fishes and find a seat around the square bar at the centre of this clean-lined room. They serve all the classic cocktails and more. On our visit, the staff was not necessarily living up to the hype, but they are ironing out the early creases.

FITZROVIA

Matchbar

37-38 MARGARET ST, W1, 020-7499 3443
Open Mon.-Sat. 11am-midnight.
U: Oxford Circus.

Fitzrovia, or 'Noho', north of Oxford Street and Soho, is a buzzing and upwardly mobile area where bars are taking over from the rag trade. The first Match started in Clerkenwell, and this more central, second bar has proved to be at least as big a success as the original. The trick is to mix and match: try Match original cocktails from the list of the Magnificent Seven (named after film stars). You can stick to classics, sip a modern martini or go the whole hog for the Match Marathon (ten cocktails for £25 Monday to Wednesday only and served at the tables for obvious reasons). Pure indulgence. Match EC1 is at 45-47 Clerkenwell Rd, EC1, 020-7250 4002.

Jerusalem

33-34 RATHBONE ST, W1, 020-7255 1120
Open Mon.-Thurs. noon-2am, Fri. noon-3am, Sat. 7pm-3am.
U: Tottenham Court Rd.

During the day, Jerusalem serves food and drink to local office workers, but come the evening it turns into a pulsating music bar. A DJ gets this large cellar really going, ties are loosened and drinks flow. Another metamorphosis takes place at the weekend, when Jerusalem gets packed with young people just wanting to have fun. The long line outside is not just a bouncers' trick to advertise this fashionable bar. And no, we don't know why it's called Jerusalem.

FULHAM

Jim Thompson's

617 KING'S RD, SW6, 020-7731 0999
Open Mon.-Sat. noon-11pm, Sun. noon-10.30pm.
U: Fulham Broadway.

Take a cheaper route down the Silk Route and pop into this Fulham bar decorated with colourful silks and artefacts from the Far East. Before you ask, it's named after the American who introduced Thai silk to the West after World War II and then went mysteriously missing in Malaysia. A fun place to drink and meet friends.

HOLBORN

Bleeding Heart Wine Bar

BLEEDING HEART YARD, GREVILLE ST, EC2
020-7242 8238
Open Mon.-Fri. noon-11pm.
U: Farringdon.

Well hidden in a small courtyard just off Greville Street's Farringdon end, this charming bar and restaurant offers a mainly French menu and a sensibly priced wine list. The menu changes constantly and is one of the reasons why this place is always busy, (see *Quick Bites*). The poetic address was mentioned in Charles Dickens' novel *Little Dorritt*.

HOLLAND PARK

Julie's

137 PORTLAND RD, W11, 020-7727 7985
Open Mon.-Sat. 11.30am-11pm, Sun. 11.30am-10.30pm.
U: Holland Park.

A delightful place to relax or meet someone, Julie's has been for many years an essential feature of this rather posh part of London. Julie's wines can be a little pricey, but you pay happily for the atmosphere and highly convivial surroundings. The food gives another good reason for visiting.

ISLINGTON

Bierodrome

173 UPPER ST, N1, 020-7226 5835
Open Mon.-Sat. noon-midnight, Sun. noon-10.30pm.
U: Highbury & Islington.

This steel and concrete temple to Belgian beer is part of the fast expanding Belgo chain. About 200 different beers with flavours and names foreign to most people outside an inner circle of aficionados, and more than 100 genièvres (flavoured Belgian gins) keep the drinkers happy. The beers are strong and tasty (try 8 percent strong Kwak in its own round-bottomed glass on a wooden holder). To keep the nutritional balance just right, sample the filling wild boar sausages, mussels and lots of frites and mayo.

Also in **Clapham** at 44-48 Clapham High St, SW4, 020-7720 1118 and other branches opening.

Filthy McNasty's Whiskey Café

68 AMWELL ST, EC1, 020-7837 6067
Open Mon.-Sat. noon-11pm, Sun. noon-10.30pm.
U: Angel.

The meeting place of Islington's bohemia has actually cleaned up its act without losing any of its character. Writers, musicians and artists have been patronising this excellent, post-modern, Irish theme pub for years, and it has hosted various literary and film events for enthusiasts. Now there is also a varied menu offering dishes like lamb and tarragon burger, spinach crêpe, chicken Maryland and char-grilled eggplant stuffed with goat cheese. One of the places to remind us all that Guinness is good for you!

KNIGHTSBRIDGE

Le Shaker/Nam Long

159 OLD BROMPTON RD, SW3, 020-7373 1926
Open Mon.-Fri. noon-11pm, Sat. 6pm-midnight.
U: South Kensington.

'A superior cocktail bar also serving Vietnamese food' is the simplest way to describe Le Shaker. A creation by award-winning mixer master Marc Boccard-Schuster, Le Shaker is one of the best places for cocktails in London. It will not win prizes for a dashing interior or trendy designs, but it sure does exactly what it says at the door. Try a Formula One for an exploding start, then accelerate your evening with a Flaming Ferrari. It will burn your throat and wallet, but is definitely worth it.

LEICESTER SQUARE

Cork & Bottle

44-46 CRANBOURN ST, WC2, 020-7734 7807
Open Mon.-Sat. 11am-midnight, Sun. 11am-10pm.
U: Leicester Sq.

This charming, small wine bar stands right beside a porn shop, reminding us all about the charms and contradictions of Soho. But we reckon that the Cork and Bottle is a much more enjoyable alternative to its neighbour, with a wine list made very tempting by its Australian and Californian accent. The cellar stocks about 150 wines from all over the world, and the food is good, too.

MAYFAIR

Havana

17 HANOVER SQ, W1, 020-7629 2552
Open Mon.-Wed. 5pm-2am, Thurs.-Sat. noon-3am, Sun. 5pm-1am.
U: Oxford Circus.

It was a dark and stormy Sunday night when we stepped into this wonderful oasis of Latin rhythms and sexy dancing. The walls are decorated with modern metal sculptures, the colours are strong and warm, and the whole place just heaves to the music inviting you to dance. Serious dancers are respected on the floor, and there is a chance to dine if you feel peckish after the odd hot salsa. Sister bar is Havana, 490 Fulham Rd, SW6, 020-7381 5005, which was the starting point for the Cuban revolution in London.

Zeta

35 HERTFORD ST, W1, 20-7208 4067
Open Mon.-Sat. 11am-3am, Sun. 5pm-10pm.
U: Hyde Park Corner.

Zeta came, saw and conquered the London bar scene in a few months. And it added an extra ingredient—concern for health—into getting sloshed. Zeta offers a huge selection of alcoholic drinks with exotic mixers, but it also has a nutritional list with fruit and vegetable juices which double as a (healthy) liquid lunch. They have drinks to help—among other ailments—your virility, beauty, body cleansing, fatigue and insomnia. But, above all, stylish Zeta is one of the best cocktail bars in London. Choose from the Old Testament for classic drinks, or go for the original concoctions listed in the New Testament. Try Free Radical (vodka with apple, mango and pineapple juices muddled (sic) with blueberries and strawberries) to combat toxins in your body, or get energy directly from Buzz Lightyear (Bacardi with mango, guava, passion fruit and banana spiced with a teaspoon of guarana).

NOTTING HILL GATE

The Market Bar

240 PORTOBELLO RD, W11, 020-7229 6471
Open Mon.-Sat. 11am-1pm, Sun. noon-10.30pm.
U: Ladbroke Grove.

Not many bars can go from being trendy and fashionable to being friendly and local without problems, but let's face it, The Market Bar was never intended to be an average place. It has changed little of its Gothic interior of heavy curtains and wax-dripping huge chandeliers, but maybe it has shed the fashion-surfing part of its clientele. It is a good place to stop while browsing Portobello Market or in the evenings for meeting friends. And, of course, it is on the trail of that winner, the biggest-ever selling British comedy film that took its name from the surrounding area. The upstairs Thai restaurant is a real treat. It remains in the style of the downstairs bar, and the suitably strange interior is both exciting and relaxing. The service is warm and the food is worth a long walk down Portobello Road.

Pharmacy

150 NOTTING HILL GATE, W11, 020-7221 2442
Open Mon.-Thurs. noon-3pm & 5.30pm-1am, Fri.-Sat. noon-2am, Sun. noon-10.30pm.
U: Notting Hill.

When Pharmacy opened, it was instantly the trendiest of trendy London bars. With an interior designed by the bad boy of Modern Brit-art, Damien Hirst, famous for his pickled cow in formaldehyde, it became a haunt for the art crowd. The light comes in through large windows done up as a proper pharmacy, with huge amounts of medical boxes and parcels promising help for known and unknown diseases. In fact, the place looked so real that the Association of British Pharmacists complained about the name. So for a while, Pharmacy's sign became an anagram and read: The Army Chap—not that it fooled anyone. Today, Pharmacy has become a regular feature in Notting Hill, and it has widened its customer base. On the latest visit, drinkers were aged between 20 and 40 and represented a good cross-section of the local population, the Notting Hillbillies. But upmarket prices have driven the avant-garde bohemia to less expensive drinking dens (see *Restaurants*).

ST. JAMES'S

Che

23 ST. JAMES'S ST, SW1, 020-7747 9380
Open Mon.-Fri. 11am-11pm, Sat. 5pm-11pm.
U: Green Park.

Che was voted Cigar Bar of the Year in 1999—and boy, do they live up to their fame. There's a huge glass-fronted humidor, filled with boxes of new and vintage cigars covering all possible marques. Next door is the booze room, where the bar is stocked with an impressive selection of tequilas, bourbons and almost every other intoxicating liquor. The restaurant offers a varied menu from caviar to curry (see *Restaurants*).

SHOREDITCH

Cantaloupe

35-42 CHARLOTTE ST, EC2, 020-7613 4411
Open Mon.-Sat. noon-midnight, Sun. noon-11.30pm.
U: Old St.

Shock, horror—a trendy bar that turns out to be friendly and cosy! There is a small separate restaurant area in the back, but this is mainly a drinking place for a youngish audience. No nonsense, fully packed, welcoming—Cantaloupe has established its place in fashionable Shoreditch.

Great Eastern Dining Room

54-56 GREAT EASTERN ST, EC2, 020-7613 4545
Open Mon.-Fri. noon-midnight, Sat. 6pm-midnight.
U: Old St.

Stylish, rather minimalist bar just across the street from Cantaloupe. The well thought-out interior, no-fuss, good bar staff and interesting mix of customers make this an ideal place to start an evening. The restaurant side is part of the party-nisation of the area, there seem to be only creative firms, bars and restaurants in Shoreditch at the moment, (see *Restaurants*).

Shoreditch Electricity Showrooms
39 HOXTON SQUARE, N1, 020-7739 6934
Open Mon.-Sat. 11am-11pm, Sun. noon-10.30pm.
U: Old St.

Hoxton Square is an area where young creatives drink and have fun. There is a selection of bars close to each other in the area, but SES has been the most successful of the lot. Battered furniture, kitsch Alpine landscapes on the wall and huge windows onto the street give this bar a new lease on life as a showroom.

SOHO

Alphabet Bar
61-62 BEAK ST, W1, 020-7439 2190
Open Mon.-Sat. 11am-11pm.
U: Tottenham Court Rd.

In a few years, Alphabet has developed from an extremely cool bar to an extremely good, and still cool, establishment. There is usually standing room only, but if you get there early, it is possible to sit on leather sofas or armchairs. Drinking is the main attraction here, but they also do food. Downstairs there's a map of London painted on the floor to help customers plan a route after closing time.

Atlantic Bar & Grill
20 GLASSHOUSE ST, W1, 020-7734 4888
Open Mon.-Sat. noon-3am, Sun. 6pm-10.30pm.
U: Piccadilly Circus.

The Atlantic used to be notorious for its door policy, but it has luckily shown signs of relaxing. This spacious bar attracts a varied clientele, from suits on their way home from work to people on their way home from clubbing. Good cocktails; smart/casual atmosphere; late night drinking, (see *Restaurants*).

Shampers
4 KINGLY ST, W1, 020-7437 1692
Open Mon.-Sat. 11am-11pm.
U: Oxford Circus.

Resting serenely in a narrow street between Regent Street and that once again up-and-coming area, Carnaby Street, Shampers has built a reputation for good food and excellent wines. There are about 200 wines on the list, light food on the ground floor and more substantial dining downstairs. It is advisable to book for meals; or just pop in and pop a bottle of bubbly.

Titanic
81 BREWER ST, W1, 020-7437 1912
Open Mon.-Sat. 5.30pm-3am.
U: Piccadilly Circus.

There's quite a history between the Atlantic Bar (which came first), and the Titanic, which was opened directly above the former by Marco Pierre White clearly as a direct rival. Several brushes with the lawyers later, they both seem to have settled in happily, attracting the same kind of crowd. There's a huge bar at the front which heaves with singles all through the evening and an area for eating at the back (see *Restaurants*). All the usual cocktails, wines, beers are here. Try the Titanic and the Atlantic, then make your choice.

VICTORIA

Boisdale
15 ECCLESTON ST, SW1, 020-7730 6922
Open Mon.-Sat. noon-1am.
U: Victoria.

This Scottish whisky and cigar bar has been making waves with friends of these sinfully tempting vices for some years. Boisdale boasts of having the largest selection of whiskies in London, and there are more than 50 brands of Cuban cigars as well. There is also an excellent wine list, and a serious restaurant serving Modern British food (see *Restaurants*). Sure gets your tartans going.

WATERLOO

Archduke Wine Bar
CONCERT HALL APPROACH, SE1, 020-7928 9370
Open Mon.-Sat. 11am-11pm.
U: Waterloo.

A good starting/finishing/resting point on a cultural trek on the ever increasingly interesting south bank of the Thames. Wooden floors and brick walls echo gently to the sounds of the trains going past or to the regular live jazz sessions in the evenings. Situated half way between Waterloo Station and the cultural lure of the South Bank Centre, the Archduke gathers both commuters and concert-goers alike. Bar food is available.

HOTEL BARS

The American Bar

THE SAVOY, STRAND, WC2, 020-7836 4343
Open Mon.-Sat. 11am-11pm, Sun. noon-3pm.
U: Charing Cross.

This is a classic piano bar with a history of inventing cocktails, which have become classics. The Champagne cocktails seem to taste better here than anywhere else and the staff is seriously professional and attentive. We trusted a barman and asked for a drink based on how we felt (late night needing a kick-start), and went out happily refreshed.

Claridge's Bar

CLARIDGE'S, BROOK ST, W1, 020-7629 8860
Open Mon.-Sat.11am-11pm., Sun. noon-10.30pm.
U: Bond St.

Claridges' small, dark-panelled bar with its leather sofas, immediately gives you the urge to get luxuriously lubricated. The list of drinks is varied and includes all the classics as well as newer concoctions. The snacks are also on the deluxe side of bar food—try beluga caviar for your first helping, and take it from there. The bar is at its best on a quiet night, but is always worth a visit.

Dorchester Hotel Bar

THE DORCHESTER, 53 PARK LANE, W1
020-7629 8888
Open Mon.-Sat. 11am-11pm, Sun. noon-10.30pm.
U: Hyde Park Corner.

We always prefer to have a glass of champagne in the wonderful Promenade rather than going into the actual bar and certainly the lobby is an excellent place to watch people. However, the bar itself is a good one, all glitzy and glossy, and at the same time a throwback to the golden times of cocktail bars. There is a famously delicious Italian menu and jazz to entertain customers.

The Heights Bar

ST. GEORGE'S HOTEL, LANGHAM PL, W1
020-7580 0111
Open Mon.-Sat. 3pm-11pm, Sun. 3pm-10.30pm.
U: Oxford Circus.

Take a lift up to the 15th floor and enjoy the view, which is at its best after dark when London's lights illuminate the skyline. The bar is slightly soulless, but it serves an interesting variety of customers, and the staff is friendly. Drinks and food are also sensibly priced—which one cannot say about every plush hotel bar in London.

Library Bar

THE LANESBOROUGH, 1 LANESBOROUGH PL
HYDE PARK CORNER, SW1, 020-7259 5599
Open Mon.-Sat. noon-11pm, Sun. noon-10pm.
U: Hyde Park Corner.

Quiet as a library, with an undisturbing, but nonetheless entertaining pianist, and genteel chat in the background. The walls are covered with books, and one feels suitably relaxed in this pearl of a bar. Food is good and the fish and chips to die for. This is one of London's seriously charming meeting places; a place to have a glass of bubbly and forget your troubles.

Met Bar

METROPOLITAN, OLD PARK LANE, W1
020-7447 1000
Open daily 10am-6pm for public (after 5.30pm members only).
U: Hyde Park Corner.

When The Met Bar opened it took some harsh criticism about its door policy and snootiness. It is still members-only in the evenings, but mere mortals can sneak in during the afternoon. It is actually worth popping into, as bar staffers know their stuff and probably have degrees in modern mixology. If you stick around long enough, you may end up rubbing shoulders with Madonna, George Clooney and their ilk.

One Aldwych

ONE ALDWYCH, 1 ALDWYCH, WC2
020-7300 1000
Open daily 10am-11pm.
U: Covent Garden.

Almost austere in its spacious interior with its cool colours, the lobby bar of this top-class hotel is not the most inviting of places to pop into. On the other hand, it is internationally stylish, the service is professional and there is always room, so it is easy to arrange to meet someone here. The modern art in the lobby is more challenging and invigorating for the brain than the chintz one can still see in so many hotels.

The Ritz

THE RITZ, 150 PICCADILLY, W1, 020-7493 8181
Open Mon.-Sat. 11am-11pm, Sun. noon-10.30pm.
U: Green Park.

The place to try one of The Ritz's notoriously drinkable champagne cocktails and get into a 'putting-on-the-Ritz' mood. Try Marie-Antoinette (Champagne, strawberry liqueur, Cointreau, Calvados and lemon juice) and you'll know how it felt to lose one's head. Classic, traditional, but not snooty, is a good description for this famous bar.

The Stafford

THE STAFFORD, 16 ST. JAMES' PL, SW1
020-7493 0111
Open Mon.-Sat. 5.30pm-11pm, Sun. 6.30pm-10.30pm.
U: Green Park.

Just off Piccadilly, this compact bar is covered with sports memorabilia. There are American football helmets, ties of all possible clubs, baseball caps and whatever takes your fancy. It is a controlled and planned chaos; when the bar was renovated a few years back, they photographed everything carefully so it could be back together looking as spontaneous as before. A place to start a really successful evening out.

The Tenth

ROYAL GARDEN HOTEL
24 KENSINGTON HIGH ST, W8, 020-7937 8000
Open Mon.-Sat. noon-2.30pm, 5.30pm-11pm.
U: Kensington.

This is a bar best enjoyed after dark. The windows overlooking Kensington Palace Gardens toward the City offer a stunning view of London. The metropolis is really extraordinary from above. It is also the place to have a romantic drink or appetiser before settling down in the adjacent restaurant (see *Restaurants*).

Trader Vic's

LONDON HILTON ON PARK LANE
22 PARK LANE, W1, 020-7208 4113
Open Mon.-Sat. 5pm-midnight, Sun. 6pm-10pm.
U: Hyde Park Corner.

Decorated in kitschy desert island style, Trader Vic's could be the set for a romantic musical. Remarkably, it's a sunny place situated underground, with waitresses in South Sea outfits carrying large drinks loaded with fruit, parasols and straws. The menu is Asian, with grilled, fried or wood-oven prepared dishes. Dress for a colonial party.

Windows

LONDON HILTON ON PARK LANE
22 PARK LANE, W1, 020-7493 4957
Open Mon.-Sat. 11am-2am, Sun. 11am-3pm.
U: Hyde Park Corner.

The best place for an aerial view of London, this 28th-floor bar is worth a special visit. The view embraces most of central London, overlooking Hyde Park, the City and toward Chelsea. Have a small snack at the bar or dinner at the restaurant next door (see *Restaurants*). Dress code is smart-casual, with the emphasis on smart.

The Winter Garden

THE LANDMARK, 222 MARYLEBONE RD, NW1
020-7631 8000
Open Mon.-Thurs. 7am-1am, Fri.-Sat. 8am-2am, Sun. 9am-1am.
U: Marylebone.

This handsome atrium stands about six floors high, forming the central point for the Landmark Hotel. Guests can overlook the bar from balconies and visitors can sit in awe under the high ceiling. There is a good selection of bar food, or you can take tea or just a glass of wine while—for once in London—there is literally room for thoughts to wander.

PUBS

Many pubs serve snacks, and many now serve substantial meals. As a rule, the food stops at around 9pm, and is not always available on Sundays. And as they are not primarily restaurants, food can just run out. So if you plan to eat as well as drink in our selection, double check first.

BELGRAVIA

Antelope

22 EATON TERRACE, SW1, 020-7730 7781
Open Mon.-Sat. 11.30am-11pm, Sun. 1pm-10.30pm. Food served at lunch Mon.-Sat.
U: Sloane Sq.

Call me old-fashioned, but a pub without panelling just doesn't feel right. But here, the upstairs room in the Antelope is just as it should be, with dark panels adding to the pleasures of the food (only at lunchtime). The menu is written on a black board, and offers varied, hearty dishes. The wine list is another good reason to pop into this 200-year-old pub in the smart borderland between Belgravia and Chelsea.

Grenadier

18 WILTON ROW, SW1, 020-7235 3074
Open Mon.-Sat. noon-11pm, Sun. noon-10.30pm. Restaurant: lunch & dinner to 9pm.
U: Hyde Park Corner.

This establishment used to be an officers' mess during the Napoleonic wars. Today it boasts a good restaurant in the back, and a small, jolly bar in the front. The Grenadier is located in a quiet mews just off Belgrave Square—as a matter of fact, it is so far away from the main street that one has to look carefully for it. But it's worth the trouble, and you certainly feel well rewarded when sipping a refreshing pint at this well-decorated pub.

Star Tavern

6 BELGRAVE MEWS, SW1, 020-7235 3019
Open Mon.-Sat. 11.30am-11pm, Sun. noon-3pm, 7pm-10.30pm. Food served at lunch & dinner daily.
U: Hyde Park Corner.

In spite of being located in a mews behind the German Embassy, deep in the heart of Belgravia's Embassyland, the Star Tavern has kept its no-nonsense feel. It is a friendly local corner pub (but much better than your average local corner pub), with hanging flower baskets and tables outside in the cobbled mews. It's also a nice pub for intellectual conversation or good gossip, as, happily, there is no piped music to disturb the customers.

Looking for an address?
Refer to the index.

BERMONDSEY

Angel

101 BERMONDSEY WALL EAST, SE16
020-7237 3608
Open Mon.-Sat. noon-11pm. Restaurant: lunch daily, dinner Mon.-Sat.
U: Rotherhithe.

The riverside walk from Southbank along towards Rotherhithe is an excellent way to spend an afternoon. The development of old warehouses and wharves has brought this area up, and that can only be good for a classy pub like the Angel. The bar downstairs has a mixed clientele, a good cross-selection of East Enders—from greyhound racers to citywide boys. Upstairs the upmarket restaurant—with white tablecloths and a Thames view—serves typically British dishes like Scottish salmon and English cheeses.

BLOOMSBURY

Lamb

94 LAMB'S CONDUIT ST, WC1, 020-7405 0713
Open Mon.-Sat. 11am-11pm, Sun. noon-3.30pm, 7pm-10.30pm. Food served at lunch & dinner Mon.-Fri.
U: Russell Sq.

It's always a pleasure to pop into a city pub with a proper family feel such as you get here. The Lamb gives locals and regular customers a warm welcome that is extended to the steady stream of tourists from the nearby hotels. The bar is beautifully old-fashioned with original cut-glass snob screens—small screens that could be twisted to give privacy if you didn't want to be seen by your fellow drinkers. There is a good selection of pub games, a non-smoking room in the back and a couple of tables on the pavement.

CHALK FARM

The Enterprise

1 HAVERSTOCK HILL, NW3, 020-7485 2659
Open Mon.-Sat. 11am-11pm, Sun. noon-10.30pm. No food.
U: Chalk Farm.

The Enterprise is a landmark at this end of Camden market. Jolly, stripy colours invite you into this literature-themed pub with its bare wooden floors and rather rustic furniture.

Bookshelves and posters of famous authors strengthen the bookish atmosphere, and the function room is often the scene for readings and literary events. The Enterprise is also a good place for drinks before or after shows at the Roundhouse down the road.

CHARING CROSS

Sherlock Holmes

10 NORTHUMBERLAND ST, W1, 020-7930 2644
Open Mon.-Sat. 11am-11pm, Sun. noon-10.30pm. Restaurant: lunch & dinner Mon.-Wed., Thurs.-Sun. noon-10pm.
U: Charing Cross.

To be honest, usually themed pubs just don't work. But Sherlock Holmes is, of course, always an exception to the rule. It is an elementary pub for friends of the great detective, and author Arthur Conan Doyle used to visit the place. Then it was called The Northumberland Arms, and is mentioned in *The Hound of the Baskervilles*. The upstairs restaurant has dishes named after Sherlock Holmes' cases and the downstairs bar has lots of Holmes memorabilia around. On the first floor, they have even re-created the great detective's study.

CITY

Blackfriar

174 QUEEN VICTORIA ST, EC4, 020-7236 5650
Open Mon.-Fri. 11.30am-11pm. Food served at lunch only.
U: Blackfriars.

By the busy railway station and within reach of the hum of traffic crossing Blackfriars Bridge, stands this elegant and eccentric pub. The stylish outside indicates a well-kept watering hole, but it's the interior that has made the place famous. The Blackfriar is decorated all over with bronze reliefs and marble mosaics in splendid Art Nouveau style. The pictures depict the monks' lives, while the engraved proverbs instruct with sayings like: 'Wisdom is

rare' and 'Finery is foolery'. This exhilarating dottiness makes it quite easy to start talking to strangers—another unusual feature in a London pub.

The Cock Tavern

POULTRY MARKET, CENTRAL MARKETS, EC1
020-7248 2918
Open Mon.-Fri. 6am-3pm. Food served all day.
U: Farringdon/Barbican.

This pub has a license to cheer up its customers with breakfast and a pint in the early hours of the morning. These early birds often come direct from Smithfield Meat Market, which is literally above this cellar establishment. There is also a steady flow of clubbers and city businessmen either finishing a night out or starting their day with a fry-up and hearty meat from the market.

Counting House

50 CORNHILL, EC3, 020-7283 7123
Open Mon.-Fri. 11am-11pm. Food served daily noon-8pm.
U: Bank.

What was an old bank has been turned into a luxurious pub with an impressive glass dome as the centrepiece for the interior. A huge bar at the centre of the ground floor nicely splits the large room and a small balcony with tables is a good place to have an overview of this busy pub usually full of people in suits.

The Fox & Anchor

115 CHARTERHOUSE T, EC1, 020-7253 4838
Open Mon-Fri 7am-11pm. Food served all day (Fri. until 3pm).
U: Farringdon/Barbican.

It's no use taking your vegetarian friends to this pub situated right next door to Smithfield Market. The Fox and Anchor opens early to serve meaty breakfasts to a selection of people from the market and the City. You might find it advisable to book a table (at 7am!) to get a proper, huge English breakfast with all the classic trimmings.

Jamaica Wine House

ST. MICHAEL'S ALLEY, EC3, 020-7626 9496
Open Mon.-Fri. 11am-11pm. Food served at lunch only.
U: Bank.

An ancient coffee house has been turned into a wine house and a traditional pub to serve the busy people of the City. The old interior has been kept almost unchanged and the wooden panes feel seeped in history and tradition. The history of the 'Jam Pot' (as it is affectionately known in local parlance) is on display at the window.

CHELSEA

The Cross Keys

1 LAWRENCE ST, SW3, 020-7349 9111
Open Mon.-Sat. noon-11pm, Sun. noon-10.30pm. Food served at lunch & dinner daily.
U: Sloane Sq.

An open two-floor gallery gives height to this pub conversion on a quiet Chelsea side street. A few minutes' walk from the King's Road down towards the River Thames takes you to this modern bar/pub with its interesting selection of modern art and fashionable clientele. The airy conservatory is reserved for diners.

King's Head & Eight Bells

50 CHEYNE WALK, SW3, 020-7352 1820
Open Mon.-Sat. 11am-11pm, Sun. 11am-10.30pm. Food served all day.
U: Sloane Sq.

This is a good place to spend an evening or an afternoon playing pub games, like Shut the Box, Crib or Shoveha'penny. You can also dedicate a few hours to Monopoly or Scrabble. To keep the games going, there's a good selection of beers, wines and malts. Food is available all day during the week and most of the time on Sunday. Wondering about the intriguing name? Eight bells were rung to warn the locals to behave as the monarch sailed past on the river.

CLERKENWELL

Jerusalem Tavern

55 BRITTON RD, EC1, 020-7490 4281
Open Mon.-Fri. 9.30am-11pm. Food served at lunch only.
U: Farringdon.

This wonderfully rambling old pub was originally a merchant's house, then it was turned into workshops for watch and clock craftsmen like escapement-makers and fusee-cutters. The name comes from the Priory of St. John of Jerusalem, which stood since about 1140.

Today, only an ancient priory gate and this excellent old establishment—the building is from 1700s—recall the long history. Stick to the biblical theme and try some of the St. Peter's Brewery beers here in the Jerusalem.

O'Hanlon's

8 TYSOE ST, EC1, 020-7837 4112
Open Mon.-Sat. 11am-11pm. Food served at lunch only.
U: Farringdon.

London has so many mock-Irish pubs that it is a real pleasure to find one that honestly represents the good values of an Irish family-owned, corner pub. A good selection of beers from O'Hanlon's own micro-brewery is on sale; try Myrica Ale or Malster's Weiss to cure your thirst. The brewery also supplies other independent pubs and bars in London with its products. The food is hearty and filling, and the atmosphere is welcoming—what else can one ask for?

COVENT GARDEN

The Cross Keys

31 ENDELL ST, WC2, 020-7836 5185
Open Mon.-Sat. 11am-11pm, Sun. noon-10pm. Food served at lunch only.
U: Covent Garden/Holborn.

This small and little known local at the heart of the tourist land that is Covent Garden has kept its friendly character. The exterior is covered with hanging flower baskets; the interior is full of Beatles memorabilia and copper pans. There is an extra room upstairs if the bar gets too crowded and a few tables outside.

Lamb & Flag

33 ROSE ST, WC2, 020-7497 9504
Open Mon.-Sat. 11am-11pm, Sun. noon-10.30pm. Food served at lunch only.
U: Leicester Sq/Covent Garden.

One of the most attractive pubs in central London has come a long way since it was known as the 'Bucket of Blood' from the bare-fist boxing bouts arranged on its premises. Today, it is better known for good beer and food, and is very popular both with locals and tourists. Almost hidden in a quiet alley just off Garrick Street, the Lamb & Flag is busy and buzzing for all the right reasons.

The Maple Leaf
41 MAIDEN LANE, WC2, 020-7240 2843
Open Mon.-Sat. 11am-11pm, Sun. noon-10.30pm. Food served all day.
U: Covent Garden.

This large Canadian pub in London is, appropriately enough, decorated with ice hockey jerseys and flags. It always gets crowded when there is a good NHL match on satellite TV, and replays of the previous games are often shown again and again. The crowd is suitably well informed about the game, no matter from which winter sports country they come.

Salisbury
90 ST MARTIN'S LANE, WC2, 020-7836 5863
Open Mon.-Sat. 11am-11pm, Sun. noon-10.30pm. Food served all day.
U: Covent Garden/Leicester Sq.

One of the prettiest pubs in the West End, the Salisbury has an abundance of glittering cut-glass mirrors and brass fittings to dazzle its customers. This one-bar pub is an excellent meeting place after shopping or pre-theatre. It is often crowded, but the staff is friendly and the roaring gas fire at the back warms nicely after experiencing a brisk London breeze. One corner is dedicated to diners, as the Salisbury serves above-average pub grub.

FARRINGDON

Ye Old Mitre
1 ELY COURT (OFF HATTON GARDENS), ELY PL, EC1
020-7405 4751
Open Mon.-Fri. 11am-11pm. Food served all day.
U: Chancery Lane.

After a shopping spree at one of Hatton Gardens' jewelers, or a stroll around the City, one needs a place for a reflective drink. Ye Old Mitre is not hard to find as soon as you know what to look for. There are two ways into the extremely narrow lane that leads to its door, either via a sign-posted route from the southern end of Hatton Garden, or via Ely Place where St. Etheralda's church recalls the area's religious past—Ely Place used to be the property of the Bishops of Ely in Cambridgeshire. Ye Old Mitre boasts two bars, an upstairs room, plus a small back lane with conveniently

placed barrels to rest your pint on. This dark-panelled, historic pub has a welcoming staff serving beer, wine and sandwiches only to their numerous regulars and to those lucky enough to visit this establishment for the first time.

FLEET STREET

The Old Bank of England
194 FLEET ST, EC4, 020-7430 2255
Open Mon.-Fri. 11am-11pm. Food served all day.
U: Temple.

A handsome old bank has been turned into a handsome new pub, with all its murals and chandeliers left intact. The Old Bank is handy for lawyers in the nearby law courts, and for the suits from the City, but also welcomes whoever is walking down the former newspaper street of London. The Old Bank of England is part of Fullers Brewery's chain of ale and pie houses, which have regularly taken over old premises in London like banks. Good bar food is available and this flagship pub offers a wide selection of wines by the glass. Here is proof that one can feel rich while drinking in a pub.

Ye Olde Cheshire Cheese
145 FLEET ST, EC4, 020-7353 6170
Open Mon.-Fri. 11.30am-11pm, Sat. noon-3pm & 5-11pm, Sun. noon-3pm. Food served all day.
U: Temple.

When the last newspaper and its thirsty journalists left Fleet Street in the 1980s, we asked a member of the staff at Ye Olde Cheshire Cheese about the future. He was optimistic: after all, there had been a pub here long before something called a newspaper was invented and there will definitely be one long after we have forgotten that *The Times* ever existed. With such respect for tradition, this rambling, huge pub keeps going. There are small corners (rooms that serve hearty dishes) and bars with coal fires burning. There is a genuine feeling of history and one can easily imagine Charles Dickens or Dr. Johnston dropping in for an ale during a break from writing. A real gem.

GREENWICH

The Trafalgar Tavern
PARK ROW, SE10, 020-8858 2437
*Open Mon.-Sat. 11am-11pm, Sun. noon-
10.30pm. Food served at lunch & dinner daily.
Rail: Greenwich.*

A large, historic pub that offers an excellent view along the Thames, both towards the Millennium Dome and upriver towards Tower Bridge. In the 1800s, the Trafalgar was famous for its whitebait dinners attended by the then Prime Minister and his cabinet colleagues. The food is still good—and whitebait has returned to the menu. The Nelson room upstairs is a popular place for dinners and private functions. Built in Regency style in the 1830s, this magnificent tavern is always bustling with both tourists and locals.

The Plume of Feathers
19 PARK VISTA, SE10, 020-8293 3093
*Open Mon.-Sat. 11am-11pm, Sun. noon-
10.30pm. Food served all day.
Rail: Greenwich.*

'A country pub in town' is how they advertise this charming local near the eastern gate to Greenwich Park. Finding The Plume of Feathers was a lucky stroke, and happened by picking a side street away from the River Thames and stumbling by chance into this beautifully kept old building. The pub was built in 1691—although how much of the original establishment is left is a matter of opinion—and it claims to stand on the Meridian Line. The pub is adjacent to the National Maritime Museum and definitely worth a walk from further away in Greenwich. The Plume of Feathers takes its cooking seriously and offers both traditional pub food and international dishes.

HAMMERSMITH

Blue Anchor
13 LOWER MALL, W6, 020-8748 5774
*Open Mon.-Sat. 11am-11pm, Sun. noon-
10.30pm. Food served at lunch & dinner daily.
U: Hammersmith/Ravenscourt Park.*

On a summer evening the light turns the river view into an Impressionist painting, and this is one of the nicest places to share it with someone. There has been a licensed pub with the same name here since the 1700s, and still this small pub by the river attracts customers from near and far.

Dove
19 UPPER MALL, W6, 020-8748 5405
*Open Mon.-Sat. 11am-11pm, Sun. noon-
10.30pm. Food served at lunch & dinner daily.
U: Hammersmith/Ravenscourt Park.*

Over the 300 years of its existence, the Dove has seen monarchs, royal mistresses and the birth of the British national anthem on its premises. King Charles II entertained his mistress Nell Gwynne here, and James Thompson composed 'Rule Britannia' while drinking in the bar. Today, the patrons are still an interesting cross-section of humankind, enjoying a drink or a meal, either at the bar or on the terrace overlooking the river.

Rutland
15 LOWER MALL, W6, 020-8748 5586
*Open Mon.-Sat. 11am-11pm, Sun. noon-
10.30pm. Food served all day.
U: Hammersmith/Ravenscourt Park.*

A good place to forget all the problems of the world, have a pint and lean on the wall overlooking the Thames. It gets busy in warm weather when people want to enjoy a drink outside on the terrace while watching the oarsmen and women practising on the water below. The Blue Anchor is next door and the Dove just about 200 yards up the road.

HAMPSTEAD

Freemason's Arms
32 DOWNSHIRE HILL, NW3, 020-7433 6811
*Open Mon.-Sat. 11am-11pm, Sun. noon-
10.30pm. Food served all day.
U: Hampstead.*

A large garden is put to good use when the weather permits drinking and eating outside. Traditional English fare is served in this handsome, almost country-like pub right next to Hampstead Heath. It is a good stop before, during, or after a brisk walk around the Heath Ponds.

Holly Bush

22 HOLLY MOUNT, NW3, 020-7435 2892
*Open Mon.-Sat. 11am-11pm, Sun. noon-
10.30pm. Food served all day.*
U: Hampstead.

A walk along the narrow lanes up around
Hampstead's hilly streets to the Holly Bush is
one of life's great pleasures. This small, village-
style pub has almost a club-like feeling with
regular customers popping in and out all the
time. But it also warmly welcomes the occasional visitor to have a quiet drink or snack in
the small alcoves and nooks and crannies.
Regular literary events feed both the mind and
the soul as well.

Spaniard's Inn

SPANIARD'S LANE, NW3, 020-8731 6571
*Open Mon.-Sat. 11am-11pm, Sun. noon-
10.30pm. Food served all day.*
U: Hampstead.

The Spaniard's is named after the Spanish
Ambassador to the court of James I who lived
here; another historical anecdote concerns the
infamous highwayman Dick Turpin who,
allegedly, preyed on his victims from the
upstairs windows. The pub has an aviary and
roses in its pretty garden, and is just ten minutes' walk from Hampstead village's main
shopping street. Enjoy a pint or bar food by
an open fire in the busier downstairs bar or in
the more peaceful upstairs room.

HIGHGATE

Flask

77 HIGHGATE WEST HILL, N6, 020-8340 7260
*Open Mon.-Sat. 11am-11pm, Sun. noon-
10.30pm. Food served all day.*
U: Archway, then 10 minutes' walk.

This is one of the nicest places in London
for outdoor drinking on a summer's day. The
large front garden is full of tables and people
gather from near and far to meet friends or
have a drink in this old pub. In colder weather, the rambling interior has nice nooks and
corners for chatting or getting warm by the
fire. The Flask takes its name from the bottles
that people used to buy here to fill with water
from the Hampstead wells. The Flask also
boasts a colourful roster of customers: the
highwayman Dick Turpin once hid in the cellars; the artist William Hogarth used to sketch
here; and Karl Marx collected his thoughts

over a pint. Marx is buried in nearby Highgate
Cemetary, and there is a steady flow of well-
dressed Russians visiting his grave.

HOLBORN

Cittie of Yorke

22 HIGH HOLBORN, WC1, 020-7242 7670
*Open Mon.-Sat. 11am-11pm. Food served at
lunch & dinner daily.*
U: Holborn/Chancery Lane.

A huge copper sign and an enormous clock
outside announce this large, dark panelled pub
to the world. Popular with lawyers and office
workers from the nearby law courts, the Cittie
of Yorke offers its customers quiet alcoves in
which to discuss sensitive cases. Huge barrels,
a high ceiling and an extremely long bar all
add to the atmosphere of this lively meeting
place. Usually the front bar is populated by a
younger audience, with more mature customers in the main pub area.

ISLINGTON

Albion

10 THORNHILL RD, N1, 020-7607 7450
*Open Mon.-Sat. 11am-11pm, Sun. noon-
10.30pm. Food served at lunch & dinner daily.*
U: Angel/Highbury & Islington.

After bicycling by this almost country-like
pub, we were told that the Albion is well
established as a well-known 'secret'. In a quiet
side street, it serves the local community while
attracting knowledgeable customers from further away. It has a few tables in the front and a
huge garden in the back and the rooms inside
are spacious and unpretentious. A good and
popular place for Sunday lunch or for a
refreshing drink after exploring the pretty corners of Barnsbury and Islington and the
Estorick collection (see *Arts & Leisure*).

The Crown

116 CLOUDESLEY RD, N1, 020-7837 7107
*Open Mon.-Sat. noon-11pm, Sun. noon-
10.30pm. Food served at lunch & dinner daily.*
U: Angel.

A lucky mistake took us to The Crown a
couple of years back, and we've been going
back ever since. There are wooden floors, a
menu chalked on a blackboard, a leather sofa,
partitions and cut-glass windows. Tables out-

side overlook a quiet residential street, and it is actually possible to eat outside without inhaling the fumes from passing traffic. The food is seriously good, and a short and inexpensive wine list covers the world from France to South America.

KENSINGTON

Churchill Arms
119 KENSINGTON CHURCH ST, W8
020-7727 4242
Open Mon.-Sat. 11am-11pm, Sun. noon-10.30pm. Restaurant: lunch & dinner daily.
U: Notting Hill Gate.

The Churchill Arms has about the biggest collection of brass pots, kettles and other brass objects ever seen hanging from a pub ceiling. It is also a friendly place, where the staff quickly learns your name and locals enjoy an afternoon or early evening drink before giving way to (or being joined by) younger visitors from the area. Many come here for the excellent Thai restaurant at the back, but the Churchill Arms is also an excellent boozer in its own right. It is close enough to bohemian Notting Hill, but safely inside respectable Kensington so it attracts an interesting mix of visitors.

KENTISH TOWN

The Bull & Last
68 HIGHGATE RD, NW5, 020-7267 3641
Open Mon.-Sat. 11.20am-11pm, Sun. noon-10.30pm. Food served at lunch & dinner daily.
U: Kentish Town.

This is one of the few pubs where you often see more female customers than men, at lunchtime anyway. Good food is served in a cosy environment, which comes with changing art exhibitions and newspapers to read. It is situated right next to Parliament Hill, which offers long walks on the Hampstead Heath, playgrounds, paddling-pools, tennis courts and a bowling green. In the summer, the Parliament Hill Lido is only five minutes' walk away, giving the chance to swim and sunbathe. That is, if you feel you need an excuse to visit the charming Bull & Last.

MAIDA VALE

Warrington Hotel
93 WARRINGTON CRESCENT, W9, 020-7286 2929
Open Mon.-Sat. 11am-11pm, Sun. noon-10.30pm.
U: Maida Vale.

One of those huge, handsome gin-palaces built to drive people to drink during Victorian times. As the name indicates, this was originally a hotel and the main bar used to be the lobby. It is still very welcoming with its ornate interior and faded glory. There is a good quality Thai restaurant upstairs.

MARYLEBONE

O'Connor Don
88 MARYLEBONE LANE, W1, 020-7935 9311
Open Mon.-Fri. 11am-11pm, Sat. noon-10.30pm. Restaurant (Ard Ri): lunch & dinner Mon.-Fri.
U: Bond St.

Here you get a cosy, honestly Irish pub without any gimmicks. The O'Connor Don was the title of an ancient Irish prince and this pub carries its royal tradition with honours. A small bar is for drinkers enjoying quality snacks, and there is a good restaurant and vaulted cellar for those wanting a proper dinner (see *Quick Bites*).

MAYFAIR

Coach & Horses
5 BRUTON ST, W1, 020-7629 4123
Open Mon.-Fri. 11am-11pm, Sat. 11am-8pm. Food served all day.
U: Green Park.

The Coach & Horses is a place that makes you want to pop in every time you walk past it. It may be just around the corner from the exclusive shops of Bond Street, but it has managed to keep its unpretentious character. The building itself looks like a small country house and is rather incongruous beside the office blocks and commercial buildings of the area. This friendly pub is very popular with tourists, but during meal times there is also a steady influx of customers from neighbouring businesses.

Red Lion

1 WAVERTON ST, W1 020-7499 1307
*Open Mon.-Fri. 11am-11pm, Sat. noon -3pm,
6-11pm, Sun. noon -3pm & 6pm-10.30pm.
Food served all day.
U: Green Park.*

During lunchtime it's pretty easy to find the Red Lion—all you have to do is follow the flow of people down the small side street. This friendly, buzzing pub has a restaurant serving good food, and the locals know it well. It is full of people in business suits relaxing for a moment over a meal or grabbing a snack and a pint at the bar before returning to their offices. But as with all good pubs, it also welcomes anyone who visits.

Red Lion

23 CROWN PASSAGE, OFF PALL MALL, SW1
020-7930 4141
*Open Mon.-Sat. 11am-11pm, Sun. noon-10.30pm.
U: Green Park.*

The Red Lion hides down a narrow and cobbled alley just off Pall Mall. It has all the friendliness and feel of a village pub, which extends to official pub dogs wandering around. There is no hurry, no piped music nor jukebox no artificial buzz of the West End. But time doesn't stand still here; the service is efficient and there are sandwiches on offer all day.

PIMLICO

Orange Brewery

37 PIMLICO RD, SW1, 020-7730 5984
*Open Mon.-Sat. 11am-11pm, Sun. noon-10.30pm. Food served all day.
U: Sloane Sq.*

The Orange Brewery serves home-brewed beers, and home-cooked food is available from the Pie and Ale Shop next door. The house beers are varied: SW1 is suitable for beginners, while the stronger SW2 is more suited for the already initiated. The brewers here clearly respect the old German purity laws: Victoria lager is produced with no added chemicals. There are some tables outside, overlooking a small green, which are, there are tables available, which hardly surprisingly, are very popular on warm sunny days.

PRIMROSE HILL

The Queens

49 REGENT'S PARK RD, NW1, 020-7586 0408
*Open Mon.-Sat. 11am-11pm, Sun. noon-10.30pm. Food served at lunch & dinner daily.
U: Chalk Farm.*

The Queens stands majestically on Primrose Hill, its upstairs windows overlooking the hillside. Recently poshly renovated and firmly gastronomically orientated, this beautiful pub caters to the needs of both locals and tourists. A good place for a meal or a well-earned drink after walking around nearby Camden Market or Regent's Park. The wine list is suitably long for a place that takes such pride in its cooking (see *Quick Bites*).

The Engineer

65 GLOUCESTER AV, NW1, 020-7722 0950
*Open Mon.-Sat. 9am-11pm, Sun. 9am-10.30pm. Food served at breakfast, lunch & dinner daily.
U: Chalk Farm.*

The Engineer has found the perfect balance between being a breakfast joint, a serious restaurant and a comfy local pub. It can get so busy that booking is essential for a meal, but at the same time you can just enjoy a drink at the bar. Children are welcome, there is a little pretty garden in the back and the food is seriously delicious. In every way, this Primrose Hill establishment has taken its place at the forefront of London's gastro-pubs (see *Quick Bites*).

Lansdowne

90 GLOUCESTER AV, NW1, 020-7483 0409
*Open Mon.-Sat. noon-11pm, Sun. noon-4pm & 7pm-10.30pm. Food served at lunch Tues.-Sat., at dinner daily.
U: Chalk Farm.*

The Lansdowne is the third of Primrose Hill's gastro-pubs. It is also the most basic in its interior, but the simple and open rooms fill with families and other happy eaters daily. There are some tables outside on the pavement to enjoy your meal or drink. The beer selection is good (see *Quick Bites*).

RICHMOND

White Cross

RIVERSIDE, RICHMOND, SURREY, 020-8940 6844
*Open Mon.-Sat. 11am-11pm, Sun. noon-
10.30pm. Food served at lunch only.*
U: Richmond.

One of the few pubs to have a tide warning by its front door, this traditional hostelry offers a good view of the river. A central bar is the main attraction, but there are also pleasant tables on the patio. The interior has not made too many concessions to modern times—it still has thick carpets and colourful wallpaper. But, as we said before, the White Cross is a traditional pub in the best sense of the word with a friendly and peaceful atmosphere.

ROTHERHITHE

Mayflower

117 ROTHERHITHE ST, SE16, 020-7237 4088
*Open Mon.-Sat. 11am-11pm, Sun. noon-
10.30pm. Food served at lunch & dinner daily.*
U: Rotherhithe.

A historic pub, on the site from where the Pilgrim Fathers sailed for America. The best time to enjoy a pint in the Mayflower is on a warm and sunny day when you can sit on the jetty overlooking the Thames taking in the view of Tower Bridge and across the river to Wapping. The Mayflower has a nautical theme, with miniature ships and prints. It used to be the only place in Britain with a license to sell American stamps—not that anybody knew what use they might have had on this side of the pond.

Spice Island

163 ROTHERHITHE ST, SE16, 020-7394 7108
*Open Mon.-Sat.11am-11pm, Sun. noon-
10.30pm. Food served all day.*
U: Rotherhithe/Canada Water.

A modern warehouse-type building by the river offers handsome views over the Thames. The ground-floor bar divides the large room into small spaces, while the upstairs is dedicated to diners. The menu covers the world from Caribbean jerk chicken to Tex-Mex nachos. The warm wooden interior is welcoming and a variety of artefacts reminds you of the local history of docks and seafaring. During the weekend, the lively audience spills onto the patio by the riverside, watching the boats go by and considering their options for the evening.

ST. JOHN'S WOOD

The Clifton

96 CLIFTON HILL, NW8, 020-7624 5233
*Open Mon.-Sat. 11am-11pm, Sun. noon-
10.30pm. Food served at lunch & dinner Mon.-
Fri., all day Sat.-Sun.*
U: St. John's Wood/Maida Vale.

Even a very long walk gets its reward when you step into this upmarket pub on a leafy side street of residential St. John's Wood. The Abbey Road Studios, made famous by the Beatles, is nearby and the Saatchi Gallery offers another excuse (if one is really needed!) to look into this gem of a pub. There is a lively fire, pine panels and good food served in the back conservatory, while the tables at the front are protected by leafy climbing plants. The Clifton also has its own royal legend: Edward VII is said to have entertained his mistress Lily Langtry here when he was still the Prince of Wales.

Crocker's Folly

24 ABERDEEN PL, NW8, 020-7286 6608
*Open Mon.-Sat. 1am-11pm, Sun. noon-
10.30pm. Food served at lunch & dinner daily.*
U: Warwick Ave/Edgware Rd.

Inside information can have sad results if it turns out to be wrong! The hapless Frank Crocker had heard from 'a reliable source' that the new Marylebone Station would be built just next door, so he decided to catch thirsty travellers with this magnificent pub. Well, the station was built two miles away, and in 1899 Mr. Crocker jumped from the top of this handsome building. Today, Crocker's Folly stands in the middle of a residential area as a huge monument to days gone by. It is worth a visit, even if just for poor Mr. Crocker's sake.

The **prices** in this guide reflect what establishments were charging at press time.

SOHO

De Hems
11 MACCLESFIELD ST, W1, 020-7437 2494
Open Mon.-Sat. noon-midnight, Sun. noon-10.30pm. Food served all day.
U: Leicester Sq.

A sign of this most international of London areas, the Dutch pub De Hems has been a continental feature in Soho's cosmopolitan landscape for many years. A good selection of Dutch and Belgian beers are on offer to the international clientele, and there is vaguely Asian-spiced food available. There's frequently a comedy club performance upstairs and always a queue to get in on weekends.

French House
49 DEAN ST, W1, 020-7437 2799
Open Mon.-Sat. noon-11pm, Sun. noon-10.30pm.
U: Leicester Sq.

Probably the only pub in London not to serve pints, the French influence dictates the smaller measures for beer drinkers. Not that it affects the consumption—this excellently bohemian and cultured pub has been a home-away-from-home for Soho intellectuals and artists for many years. It is rumoured that the French House actually sells more wine than beer—whatever the case—it is definitely the place to visit. The upstairs dining room is also good (see *Restaurants*).

We're always interested to hear about your discoveries and to receive your comments on ours. Please let us know what you liked or disliked; **e-mail us** at gayots@aol.com.

Waxy O'Connors
14-16 RUPERT ST, W1, 020-7287 0255
Open Mon.-Sat. 11am-11pm, Sun. noon-10.30pm. Food served all day.
U: Piccadilly Circus/Leicester Sq.

This is a huge mock-Irish pub, with three bars on different levels. Waxy O'Connors is so over the top that it works. The audience is mainly reasonably young, but in the afternoon you can see everybody from businessmen to grandmothers having a well-earned drink under the huge tree which decorates the staircase at Waxy's or just under the pulpit. The menu has a strong Irish feel with oysters and other specialities.

SOUTHWARK

Anchor
34 PARK ST, BANKSIDE, SE1, 020-7407 1577
Open Mon.-Sat. 11.30am-11pm, Sun. noon-10.30pm. Food served at lunch & dinner daily.
U: London Bridge.

The south bank of the Thames is coming up fast, with Shakespeare's Globe Theatre and the new Tate Modern Gallery attracting even more visitors to the area. In all this frenzied activity, the Anchor remains an old, wonderfully rambling pub, serving food and drinks in various intimate bars and a restaurant overlooking the river. The original pub on this site was destroyed in the Great Fire of London in 1666; it is believed that the diarist Samuel Pepys stood here watching the old wooden city burn.

George Inn
77 BOROUGH HIGH ST., SE1, 020-7407 2056
Open Mon.-Sat. 11am-11pm, Sun. noon-10.30pm. Food served at lunch & dinner daily.
U: London Bridge.

Mentioned first in print in 1590, the George Inn was rebuilt after the Great Fire of 1666. The inn has not changed much since those days, and its sheltered courtyard is an oasis of calm in the middle of busy Southwark. The old galleried coaching inn has a restaurant upstairs, and at ground level there is a wine bar and a set of old-fashioned rooms for drinks and snacks. The courtyard was used in the past for performing plays written by a colourful local character named William Shakespeare.

WAPPING

Prospect of Whitby
57 WAPPING WALL, E1, 020-7481 1095
Open Mon.-Sat. 11am-11pm, Sun. noon-10.30pm. Food served at lunch & dinner daily.
U: Wapping.

Slate stone floors, dark wooden panels and beams make this east London pub a favourite with tourists. They come by the bus-load to drink, eat pub food and enjoy stories about the pub's history. Charles Dickens and Samuel Pepys used to drink here; criminals were hanged just near by and the painter JMW Turner searched for a liquid muse in this ancient establishment. This old tavern was built in the early 1500s and has never shown any signs of losing its position as one of the better beer houses in London.

WIMBLEDON

Fox & Grapes

CAMP RD, SW19, 020-8946 5599
Open Mon.-Sat. 11am-11pm, Sun. noon-10.30pm. Food served at lunch & dinner daily.
U, Rail: Wimbledon.

A nice Sunday walk to Cannizaro House and Southside House by Wimbledon Common is not complete without a refreshing pint in the Fox & Grapes. It's very popular with families for Sunday lunch and attracts golfers, shoppers, tennis fans and regular common walkers. The stable bar of the pub has high ceilings and wooden beams and is aimed mainly at diners.

COMEDY CLUBS

The British are famous for their sense of humour, but when it comes to describing this humour, opinions vary. It might be gentle as in P G Wodehouse; it could be the 1960s with Monty Python's Flying Circus, or today's stand-up comic type in pubs and clubs. For a visitor, live comedy is a two-edged affair: some of the verbal fireworks are comprehensible even to a foreigner, but many jokes and gags are based on current affairs in Britain. An essential part of club behaviour is heckling the comedian, but beware the wrath of the artist. You'd better be witty if you open your mouth; nothing is more embarrassing or received with such contempt as a boring heckler. The audience is a legitimate target for the artists and the verbal whipping can sometimes be extremely rude. Telephone to get information on artists and times. The weekly *Time Out* magazine has a good list of venues and acts and also consult the Thursday Hot Tickets section of the *Evening Standard*.

Comedy Store

HAYMARKET HOUSE, OXENDON ST, SW12
020-7344 4444
U: Piccadilly Circus.

The Comedy Store offers a staple diet of improvised comedy. The performers are supposed to make up a show from a given theme or style or from famous names.

Jongleurs

THE CORNET, 49 LAVENDER GARDENS, SW11
020-7228 3744
Rail: Clapham Junction.
DINGWALLS BUILDING, MIDDLE YARD, CAMDEN LOCK, CHALK FARM RD, NW1, 0171-267 1999
U: Camden Town.

Jongleurs has built up a steady following in both its venues. Well-known names from the club circuit perform here.

MUSIC CLUBS

London is full of live music every night. You can choose from acoustic folk in a quiet pub to hard-hitting heavy rock in a noisy club, to stylish jazz in a cosy dive. Telephone the venue first for artists and opening times. The weekly Time Out magazine and the Thursday Hot Tickets section of the Evening Standard has a good list of venues and acts.

Borderline

ORANGE YARD, OFF MANETTE ST, W1
020-7734 2095
U: Tottenham Court Rd.

A small and intimate place to hear music.

Bottom Line

SHEPHERD'S BUSH GREEN, W12, 020-8740 1304
U: Shepherd's Bush.

This is a mid-size rock venue in west London.

The Forum

9-17 HIGHGATE RD, NW5, 020-7344 0044
U: Kentish Town.

The Forum books established names in rock music to fill this 1,000-seater in north London.

The Jazz Café

5 PARKWAY, NW1, 020-7916 6060
U: Camden Town.

This serves the Camden Town trendies and serious music lovers with a daily dose of varied rhythm-orientated music.

The Mean Fiddler

28A HIGH ST, NW10, 020-8963 0940
Rail: Willesden Junction.

The Mean Fiddler in Harlesden is a bit out of central London but definitely worth a visit. It is at its best when well-known Irish artists play for London's Irish community.

The 100 Club

100 OXFORD ST, W1, 020-7636 0993
U: Tottenham Court Rd.

This is and has been a long-established venue for blues and its more rhythmic relations.

Ronnie Scotts

47 FRITH ST, W1, 020-7439 0747
U: Leicester Sq/Tottenham Court Rd.

Ronnie Scotts is a British institution. Though owner-saxophonist Scotts died some years ago, it is still as popular as ever. The club invariably books internationally known artists, and people go there to listen to the music rather than talk to friends.

The 606 Club

90 LOTS RD, SW10, 020-7352 5953
U: Fulham Broadway.

A real musicians' club, a cool cellar dive for the jazz-minded.

Eating & Entertainment

For a pretty mixed bag, try the following: **Elvis Gracelands Palace**, 81-83 Old Kent Rd, SW15, 020-7639 3961, the place where Chinese restaurant owner Paul Chan puts on the glitz and entertains you to his (Chinese) version of the great Elvis. Loved by hen parties. **The Brick Lane Music Hall**, 134-146 Curtain Rd, EC2, 020-7739 9997, recreates, in a limited way, the old-time music hall acts and atmosphere of the past. **Spaghetti Opera at Terraza-Est**, 109 Fleet St, EC4, 020-7353 2680, gives you some pretty powerful opera and some pretty standard Italian cooking in a lush, mock operatic setting. **Sarastro**, 126 Drury Lane, WC2, 020-7836 0101, is an opera-themed restaurant with all the gilt and red plush; diners can eat in an 'opera box'. Opera is sung on Monday nights.

The 12 Bar Club

DENMARK PL, WC2, 020-7916 6989
U: Tottenham Court Rd.

This is a small club for acoustic music, just off the musicians' place of pilgrimage—Denmark Street.

Other venues to look out for include:

Astoria, Charing Cross Rd, WC2, 020-7434 0403;

The Borderline, Orange Yard, Manette St, W1, 020-7734 Å2095;

The Garage, Highbury Corner, N5, 020-7607 1818;

Hammersmith Palais, Shepherd's Bush Rd, W12, 020-7734 8932;

Shepherd's Bush Empire, Shepherd's Bush Green, W12, 020-7771 2000.

NIGHTCLUBS

There are three important rules to remember before getting into the groove at London's most popular nightspots: One: Find out what the dress code is and abide by it. A suit and tie won't get you into the trendier haunts, while turning up in jeans and trainers at the more formal venues will see you standing on the pavement all evening. Two: Don't get too clever with the doormen—it never works. Three: Try turning up with an equal number of ladies in your party—groups of guys on their own stand less of a chance of getting in, particularly if they don't adhere to rules one and two. The weekly *Time Out* magazine and the Thursday Hot Tickets section of the *Evening Standard* has a good list of venues.

London's club scene is jumping, with a huge number of venues operating different nights of the week offering just about everything.

China White

6 AIR ST, PICCADILLY, W1, 020-7343 0040
Open Mon.-Sat. 8pm-3.30am.
U: Piccadilly Circus.

With a wide-ranging clientele, China White is a very popular club. On busy nights (Wednesdays, Fridays and Saturdays), you'll find top models strutting their stuff alongside pop stars, investment bankers, record producers, stylists and pretty much every profession in between. The dress code is fashionable rather than formal; men should avoid suits, although members can get away with work attire. Wednesday nights hosted by club supremos Jeanette Calliva and Sarah Woodhead are the busiest, but be warned: only the coolest faces will be admitted.

The Mayfair Club

15 BERKELEY ST, W1, 020-7629 0010
Open Mon.-Sat. 8pm-3am.
U: Green Park.

Glitzy in a 70s and 80s kind of way, this West End hot spot offers funky music, a cocktail and VIP bar and a good restaurant. Smart dress. If you don't want to spend a fortune, steer clear of ordering drinks at the tables—a

bottle of champagne with waitress service will set you back around £200.

Other venues to look out for include:

Camden Palace, 1A Camden High St, NW1, 020-7387 0428l

Electric Ballroom, 184 Camden High St, NW1, 020-7485 9006

The Empire Lounge, Leicester Sq, WC2, 020-7437 1446

The End, 16A West Central St, WC1, 020-7419 9199

Fabric, 77A Charterhouse St, EC1, 020-7490 0044

The Grand, St.John's Hill, SW11, 0800 783 7485

Heaven, Charing Cross Arches, WC2, 020-7930 2020

Home, Leicester Sq, WC2, 020-7909 0001/1116

Legends, 209 Old Burlington St, W1, 020-7437 9933

Leopard Lounge, 474 Fulham Rd, SW6, 0800 783 7485

The Ministry of Sound, 103 Gaunt St, SE1, 020-7378 6528

New Connaught Rooms, Gt. Queen St, WC2, 020-7263 6452

Oxygen, 18 Irving St, WC2, 020-7930 0905

Point 101, 101 New Oxford St, WC1, 020-7379 3112

Po Na Na, W8, 20 Kensington Church St, W8, 020-7795 6656

Sound Republic, 10 Wardour St, W1, 020-7287 1010

10 Tokyo Joes, 85 Piccadilly, W1, 020-7495 2595

Turnmills, 63B Clerkenwell Rd, EC1, 020-7250 3409

The Velvet Room, 143 Charing Cross Rd, WC2, 020-7439 4655.

SHOPPING

CONTENTS

ANTIQUES 226

AT YOUR SERVICE 244

BEAUTY 248

BOOKS 258

CHILDREN 264

DEPARTMENT STORES 269

FASHION FOR HIM & HER 271

FLOWERS & PLANTS 282

FOOD 284

GIFTS 300

HOME 305

JEWELRY 314

LEATHER & LUGGAGE 319

MENSWEAR 321

PHOTOGRAPHY & MUSIC 327

SPORTING GOODS 332

STATIONERY & PENS 336

TOBACCONISTS 337

WOMEN'S WEAR 338

ANTIQUES

ANTIQUES CENTRES

Alfie's
13-25 CHURCH ST, NW8, 020-7723 6066
Open Tues.-Sat. 10am-6pm.
U: Marylebone.

Established in 1974, Alfie's is one of London's most celebrated antique mazes where it is a delight to get lost amongst treasures from the past. About 200 expert dealers occupy a huge sprawling building (a one-time Victorian department store), specialising in everything from select pieces of furniture to advertising memorabilia, Victorian to Deco and toys to jewelry. Alfie's is a magpie's heaven indeed.

Antiquarius
131-141 KING'S RD, SW3, 020-7351 5353
Open Mon.-Sat. 10am-6pm.
U: Sloane Sq/South Kensington.

Smaller but select collection of about 100 or so dealers selling a choice range of specialist glass, porcelain, antique books and silver objets de vertu. The XS Baggage Co. deals in old champagne-coloured leather trunks and bags by such grandes marques as Hermès, Vuitton and Asprey. Geoffrey Waters sells superb ancient Oriental ceramics and works of art—and if you're looking for chic timepieces, you're in luck.

Bond Street Antiques Centre
124 NEW BOND ST, W1, 020-7493 1854
Open Mon.-Fri. 10am-5.45pm.
U: Bond St.

More than 30 dealers selling fine examples of antique jewels, glass, Oriental pieces, silver and vintage wristwatches. N. Boom & Son specialises in Victoriana, Edwardiana, Art Nouveau and Deco jewels, and there are dealers in fine cameos, and pretty antique rings, and paintings.

Bourbon-Handy Antiques Centre
151 SYDNEY ST, SW3, 020-7352 2106
Open Mon.-Sat. 10am-6pm, Sun. 11am-5pm.
U: Sloane Sq/South Kensington.

Eighteen shops within a pretty courtyard and a further twenty in an adjoining building set the scene for this Chelsea-based centre offering a trove of antique possibilities.

Covent Garden Centre
THE JUBILEE HALL, SOUTHAMPTON ST, WC2
020-7240 7405
Open Mon. 5.30am on.
U: Covent Garden.

Not only a huge selection of stalls but one of the better priced antique centres in town. There is always a buzz and sense of activity here, and many dealers, both old hands and newcomers, guarantee inspiration. Jewelry, buttons, vintage clothes, pictures and vintage watches change hands for very reasonable amounts. Look out also for the 'bargain tables' with prices starting from a few pounds for a world of chic antique detritus.

Georgian Village
Islington Green, N1, 020-7226 1571
Open Wed. 8am-4pm, Sat. 9am-4pm.
U: Angel.

A clutch of independent shops in this historic part of Islington dealing in mainly Art Nouveau and Deco artefacts that include ceramics and furniture. Look out for Titus Omega for vintage Liberty marque treasures.

Gray's Antique Market
58 DAVIES ST, W1, 020-7629 7032
Open Mon.-Fri. 10am-6pm.
U: Bond St.

More than 200 dealers with a variety of stock in this historic and exciting market. A tributary of the ancient River Tyburn flows through the basement—which is an attraction in itself—and you can muse on the Monet-style Japanese bridge built over it. Boasting the world's biggest collection of antique jewelry and acessories, there are also some superb books, paintings, objects, and miscellaneous bric-à-brac for the obsessed collector. There's everything from the gargantuan to the easily missed.

Gray's-in-the-Mews

1-7 DAVIES MEWS, W1, 020-7629 7034
Open Mon.-Fri. 10am-6pm.
U: Bond St.

This is a neighbouring market to Gray's. Elegant glassware in the form of scent bottles and Bohemian coloured glass in the displays set the sparkling scene, along with unusual and attractive ceramics. Teresa Clayton is a must for all such enthusiasts.

The Mall Antique Arcade

359 UPPER ST, CAMDEN PASSAGE, N1, 020-7354 2839
Open Wed. 7.30am-5pm, Sat. 9am-6pm, some shops Tues.-Fri. 10am-5pm.
U: Angel.

A long, thin strip of a space flanked on either side by tiny stalls selling everything from jewelry and china to Georgian glass and bakelite radios. Check out Count Alexander's Tsarist and Austro-Hungarian-style tiaras and parures just waiting for appropriate heads and necks.

ANTIQUE MARKETS

Bermondsey (New Caledonian) Market

LONG LANE & BERMONDSEY ST, SE1
Open Fri. 5am-2pm.
U: London Bridge.

This is one for die-hard enthusiasts only. Cheat time by staying up the night before and going straight to this historic market from a session of non-stop dancing in town. You are rarely disappointed as there is always something for everyone. Specialist stalls sit cheek-by-jowl with the more humble ones and the spirit is very much one of rummaging discovery. Tons of jewelry, exquisite and indifferent china, vintage watches and domestic detritus from the past are the usual stock-in-trade. But even if you don't buy anything, the atmosphere is great—particularly on crisp winter mornings when the sueded darkness adds a touch of mystery.

Brick Lane Market

BRICK LANE, E1
Open Sun. 6am on.
U: Aldgate East/Liverpool St.

Another charged atmosphere and again a historic market, which shares street space with fabric merchants, food stalls, electric acces-sories and dubious fashion outlets. Antique dealers get here very early, some goods hardly leaving the vans they arrive in before being snapped up. There is real motley selection of stuff—unprincipled but nonetheless rewarding. After this, take time out to fill your arms with fresh-cut flowers from nearby Columbia Road Market and consider couture rugs and jewelry by Annie Sherburne at 126 Columbia Rd, E2.

Camden Passage Market

OFF UPPER ST, N1, 020-7359 9969
Open Tues.-Sat. 10am-5pm, market days Wed. & Sat. 8am-4pm.
U: Angel.

Great for browsing and buying in a higgledy-piggledy ramshackle style reminiscent of *Les Puces* flea markets in Paris. A trove of trash and treasure, but all of it compelling and fun. Choose from piles of vintage buttons, elegant period prints, kitchenware, humidors, extravagances and eccentricities of every kind. Good prices; and a little polite haggling is never met unkindly A second book and antiquarian book

Useful Addresses

Antiquarian Booksellers Association, (ABA), Sackville House, 40 Piccadilly, W1, 020-7439 3118; **British Antique Dealers' Association, (BADA)**, 20 Rutland Gate, SW7, 020-7589 4128, www.bada.org; **Conservation Register**, Museums & Galleries Commission, 16 Queen Anne's Gate, SW1, 020-7233 4200; **Export Licensing Unit**, Dept of National Heritage, 2-4 Cockspur St, SW1, 020-7215 8564; **Furniture History Society**, c/o Dept. of Furniture and Woodwork Design, Victoria & Albert Museum, SW7, 020-7938 8282; **London & Provincial Antique Dealers' Association, (LAPADA)**, 535 King's Rd, SW10, 020-7823 3511; **National Association of Decorative & Fine Arts Societies (NADFAS)**, 8 Guildford St, WC1, 020-7430 0730; **Provincial Booksellers Fairs' Association (PBFA)**, 16 Melbourn St, Royston, Herts, 01763 248400; **Society of London Art Dealers**, 91A Jermyn St, SW1, 020-7930 6137.

market operates on Thursdays 9.30am-3.30pm.

Greenwich Market
COLLEGE APPROACH, SE10
Open Sat.-Sun. 9am-6pm.
U: Maze Hill.

Now that The Dome is close by, many more probably will visit this historic area of London to kill two birds (or even three) with one carefully aimed shot. Home to the Cutty Sark and the Observatory and now the Dome, too, Greenwich has boasted a great little market for years. Several 'uptown' dealers descend on the stalls here only to take their finds back up west and hike up the prices. The dealers at Greenwich are more than reasonable, and there is a great selection of secondhand clothing, books, china and jewelry. A nearby crafts market, conveniently covered, sells kids' clothes, wooden toys and handmade jewelry.

Hampstead Antiques Emporium
12 HEATH ST, NW3, 020-7794 3297
Open Tues.-Fri. 10.30am-5pm, Sat. 10am-6pm.
U: Hampstead.

Incorporating a crafts market, this Emporium runs the gamut from chic furniture to fun junk, silver and plenty of jewelry (real and faux). The small, independent venue has a decidedly bazaar feel about it. Very Hampstead.

Portobello Market
PORTOBELLO RD, W11, 020-7371 6960
Open Fri. 9am-4pm (under cover), Sat. 6am-4pm.
U: Notting Hill Gate/Ladbroke Grove/
Westbourne Park.

Immortalized in the fantasy film, *Bedknobs & Broomsticks*, Portobello Road has been one of London's best known markets for more than 150 years. On Friday mornings a tarpaulin-covered market operates, selling vintage clothes from the 1920s-1980s. They are well-priced and constantly changing. One stall sells army gear, another vintage clothes from the Deco period. Another deals in 1960s cashmere sweaters, and yet another in sharply tailored suits and outerwear. The earlier you get here the better. Just across the road from this section is an uncovered stalled-out area with wonderful hippy-chic dealers selling psychedelia and mod clothing along with others

offering all kinds of wardrobe horrors. Nearby shops on Portobello Road feature 1850s gems and theatrical memorabilia. All the way down Portobello Road and on to Golborne Road (towards the Harrow Road end) are stall after stall of untold junk and jewels.

On Saturdays, stretching back the other way toward Notting Hill Gate tube station, Portobello Road takes on a serious antique dealers' feel, with roadside stalls and shops within rabbit warren buildings, and arcades where everything from trophies to teacups, brassware to bags and furniture to fashion is sold, with goods changing hands from a few pounds to several thousands. There's a superb atmosphere and the several cafés and makeshift food stalls provide refreshing stops for refuelling.

Piccadilly Antiques Market
ST. JAMES'S CHURCHYARD, PICCADILLY, W1
Open Tues. 9am on.
U: Green Park/Piccadilly Circus.

Bijou market under the shadow of a beautiful and historic Wren church, an olive stone's throw from Fortnum & Mason. The gaily covered stalls sell a selection of clothes, jewelry and incidental objects, and although one of the smallest markets, you usually can turn up one or two exciting finds. The church itself offers pre- or post-wandering potential.

The Stables Antique Market
CHALK FARM RD, NW1, 020-7485 5511/5255
Open Sat.-Sun. 9am on.
U: Camden Town/Chalk Farm.

This is a must for the dedicated market rambler. This is a magnet for tourists and regulars alike, and the variety is astounding. Whether set outside or within the cavernous storehouse buildings, the stalls are brim full of everything from exceedingly cheap to very expensive goods: clothes, bric-a-brac, lamps and decorative items. The buzz is certainly alive and well and even when it rains, you somehow don't mind too much as there is always something to divert the attention.

ART DECO & ART NOUVEAU

Artemis Decorative Arts

36 KENSINGTON CHURCH ST, W8, 020-7376 0377
Open Mon.-Fri. 10.30am-6pm, Sat. noon-5.30pm.
U: High St Kensington.

This tempting shop specialises in superb examples of Galle, Daum and Lalique glass and intriguing furniture from the twentieth century—but only up to about the 1940s. Bronze incidental decorative pieces and clocks are also on sale, along with surprisingly sympathetic accessories from the eighteenth century.

Editions Graphiques Gallery

3 CLIFFORD ST, W1, 020-7734 3944
Open Mon.-Fri. 10am-6pm, Sat. 10am-2pm.
U: Bond St.

A corner haven founded in 1966 for lovers of Nouveau and Deco objects and sculptures. But where this specialist is a little different from many others is that it houses some truly unusual period stock—not just the standard 'new leafy' or 'architecturally angular' pieces sold by many others. Unusual and almost decadent ceramics, Erté posters and stunning Lalique vases are the collectable artefacts.

Gordon Watson

50 FULHAM RD, SW3, 020-7589 3108
Open Mon.-Sat. 11am-6pm.
U: South Kensington.

Stylish, sharp and very relevant to our own sleek, aerodynamic age, the stock here reflects especially the Deco period's obsession with edge and line. Specialities include metal furniture and objects, Daum glass, Puiforcat silver and signed jewels by such greats as Cartier and Van Cleef.

Haslam & Whiteway

105 KENSINGTON CHURCH ST, W8
020-7229 1239
Open Mon.-Fri. 10am-6pm, Sat. 10am-2pm.
U: High St Kensington.

Founded in 1972, this two-storey discovery box houses superb stock from Gothic Revival to the Arts and Crafts era. Look out for the great selection of William Morris tiles.

Mike Weedon

7 CAMDEN PASSAGE, N1, 020-7226 5319
Open Wed. & Sat. 10am-4pm, also by appointment.
U: Angel.

Among the classic Gallé, Daum and Lalique glass treasures are some stunning handmade lamps and lighting accessories—the Nouveau and Deco periods were typified by artistic luminations. Check out a few of the beautiful survivors.

Millinery Works Ltd
(The Antique Trader)

85-87 SOUTHGATE RD, N1, 020-7359 2019
Open Tues.-Sat. 11am-6pm, Sun. noon-5pm, also by appointment.

A wonderfully rambling set of rooms filled with carefully considered treasures from the Arts and Crafts Movement. Super signature shows are regular features, which highlight the directors' love and scholarship. You can certainly buy here—not only with pleasure but with confidence, too. Occasional modern and contemporary art is shown.

Pruskin Gallery

73 KENSINGTON CHURCH ST, W8, 020-7376 1285
Open Mon.-Fri. 10am-6pm, Sat. 11am-5pm.
U: High St Kensington.

Specialising in Decorative Arts (1880-1950), along with some important furniture by Ruhlmann, Royere, Arbus, Adnet and Brandt. This very well established haven is popular with serious collectors and those in the interiors' business. Classic bronzes and ivories—some by Chiparus—and a selection of Modern British paintings give the place a certain character.

Style

SHOP 1, ISLINGTON GREEN, N1, 020-7359 7867
Open Wed. 8am-3pm, Sat. 9am-4pm, also by appointment.
U: Angel.

Specialising in Liberty and WMF Pewter, bronzes, glass and jewelry, this shop is definitely one to visit when tracking down a variety of goods from this period. Liberty goods in particular show an elegance and grace with more than a little adventurous spirit.

Conservators/Restorers

BADA (020-7589 4128, www.bada.org), can advise. Also consult: **Association of British Picture Restorers**, Station Avenue, Kew TW9 3QA, 020-8948 5644; **British Antique Furniture Restorers' Association**, The Old Rectory, Warmwell, Dorchester, Dorset DT2 8HQ, 01305 854822; **British Horological Institute and Federation**, Upton Hall, Upton, Newark, Notts. NG23 5TE, 01636 813795; **Textile Conservation Centre**, Apt 22, Hampton Court Palace, East Molesey, Surrey KT8 9AU, 020-8977 4943; **United Kingdom Institute for Conservation**, 109 The Chandlery, 50 Westminster Bridge Rd, SE1 7QY, 020-7721 8721.

Tadema Gallery

10 CHARLTON PL, CAMDEN PASSAGE, N1
020-7359 1055
Open Wed. & Sat. 10am-5pm, also by appointment.
U: Angel.

Why not wear your antiques with a certain éclat and much élan? This shop specialises in beautiful Modernist jewelry in such materials as metal and shagreen. So much Modernist jewelry was so far ahead of its time, and the selection here certainly inspires today's designers. Abstract art is also on display.

Titus Omega

SHOP 18, ISLINGTON GREEN, N1, 020-7704 8003
Open Wed. 8am-4pm, Sat. 9am-4pm.
U: Angel.

Head straight to this space which boasts the largest selection of Art Nouveau pewter in the country—especially Liberty and WMF. A sprinkling of metalware and glass adds more style. Just try and leave without buying something.

Van Den Bosch

SHOP 14, ISLINGTON GREEN, N1, 020-7226 4550
Open Wed. & Sat. 8am-4pm, also by appointment.
U: Angel.

Art Nouveau and Arts and Crafts silver and jewelry set the period along with some very fetching ceramic and glass. The fact that the directors deal in stock right up to the 1950s extends the viewing and buying potential.

AUCTION HOUSES

Some of the daily newspapers give details of auctions; otherwise telephone to enquire which sales are coming up. Apart from the serious business of buying, previews of sales offer wonderful opportunities to look at antiques before they disappear back into private hands. Call for opening and viewing times; each auction house varies according to their sales programme.

Academy Auctioneers & Valuers

NORTHCOTE AVE, EALING, 020-8579 7466
U: Ealing Broadway.

Monthly, two-day auctions on Wednesdays and Thursdays of antiques and fine arts, as well as some specialist auctions.

Bonhams

MONTPELIER ST, SW7, 020-7393 3900
WWW.BONHAMS.COM
U: Knightsbridge.

Bonhams Chelsea

65-69 LOTS RD, SW10, 020-7393 3900
WWW.BONHANS.COM
U: Fulham Broadway.

Modern and antique guns, arms, armour and militaria, sporting memorabilia, vintage fountain pens, old masterpieces, nineteenth century paintings as well as modern British and continental pictures, furniture, clocks and watches, ceramics, books and many other antiquities all go under the gavel at the Knightsbridge auctioneers. Less formal than the main branch—and less expensive—the Lot's Road galleries hold regular sales of paintings, furniture, prints, silver, jewelry, ceramics and collectables.

Brooks Specialist (Cars & Motorcycles) Auctioneers

81 CLAPHAM COMMON, WEST SIDE, SW4
020-7228 8000, WWW.BROOKSAUCTIONS.COM
U: Clapham South.

Specialists in vintage, veteran and classic cars and motorcycles, they hold irregular auctions in different venues. Telephone for information.

Christie's

8 KING ST, SW1, 020-7839 9060
WWW.CHRISTIES.COM
U: Green Park.

Christie's South Kensington

85 OLD BROMPTON RD, SW7
020-7581 7611, WWW.CHRISTIES.COM
U: South Kensington.

A household name associated with the sale of fine paintings, this firm was established in 1766. It quickly became known for its sales of artists' studio works, starting with Gainsborough and continuing with Reynolds, Landseer, Rossetti, Burne-Jones, Leighton, Sargent and others. The smart galleries on King Street hold sales of important works of art and Old Master paintings. The range includes anything which collectors covet, from fine wines (for which they have made a name for themselves), to English furniture and decorative art objects. Christie's publishes many catalogues annually. The Brompton Road branch has a smaller display area and is less pricey but has an equally wide range of sale themes, often connected with seasonal subjects such as Valentine cards. Miniature aircraft, fans, dolls and teddy bears, posters, large Oriental carpets and much more are sold here.

Criterion Auction Rooms

53-55 ESSEX RD, ISLINGTON, N1, 020-7359 5707
WWW.CRITERION-AUCTIONEERS.CO.UK
U: Angel.

A good, less expensive auction house where you can really pick up the odd bargain. They concentrate on furniture, but have a good range of unusual accessories and small furnishings. On the first Monday of every month, there's an auction of higher quality items.

Lots Road Galleries

71 LOTS RD, SW10, 020-7351 7771
WWW.LOTSROAD.COM
U: Fulham Broadway.

A great place for some good deals at this slightly off-the-beaten-track auction house that covers a vast range of items.

Phillips

101 NEW BOND ST, W1, 020-7629 6602
WWW.PHILLIPS-AUCTION.COM
U: Bond St.
10 SALEM RD, W2, 020-7229 9090
U: Bayswater.

Established in 1796, Phillips has salesrooms throughout Britain, all staffed by specialists and experienced valuers who can advise on all aspects of buying and selling at auction. The Bond Street saleroom specialises in fine furniture, paintings, ceramics, jewelry, silver clocks, watches, Oriental artwork, textiles, books, musical instruments, stamps, medals and decorative arts. There's a new good café at the Salem Road location (see Quick Bites).

Sotheby's

34 NEW BOND ST, W1
020-7293 5000, WWW.SOTHEBYS.COM
Open Mon.-Fri. 9am-4.30pm, Sun. noon-4pm.
U: Bond St.

Founded in 1744, Sotheby's huge galleries are a traditional setting for the modern bustle of viewing days and the excitement of the crowds on sales days, when the atmosphere can heighten as lots are sold at the rate of two a minute for thousands of pounds—and a whole lot more. Like Christie's, Sotheby's offers an excellent advice and valuation service. The busy shop up-front sells its own range of catalogues and also beautifully illustrated books on art and the decorative arts, including specialist subjects. They also have an excellent café (see Quick Bites).

BOOKS & MANUSCRIPTS

The Charing Cross Road and Cecil Court areas are full of superb secondhand and specialist antique book dealers. Many are very affordable—and some simply outrageous—but you can leisurely spend a day merely browsing. Cecil Court in particular (off the Charing Cross Road and St. Martin's Lane), boasts shops specialising in the theatre, crime, cooking, first editions and travel. The shops featured below are to be found in other parts of the capital.

Adrian Harrington Rare Books

64A KENSINGTON CHURCH ST, W8
020-7937 1465
Open Mon.-Sat. 10am-6pm, also by appointment.
U: Notting Hill Gate.

Specialising in literature, first editions and bound library sets, this shop is a must. Whether you are looking for period reading material or collect books with engravings and illustrations there is sure to be something. Children's books and travel volumes, are regularly available.

Bernard Quaritch

5-8 LOWER JOHN ST, W1, 020-7734 2983
Open Mon.-Fri. 9.30am-5.30pm.
U: Piccadilly Circus.

Dating back to the 1840s, this is one of the oldest and largest antique book shops in London with departments specialising in art, architecture, travel, literature, philosophy and a sprinkling of fashion. Each department has its own knowledgeable director and the serious specialist collector certainly can buy with confidence. Medieval illustrated manuscripts provide a diversion. They are usually found in a display case at the entrance.

Bernard Shapero

32 ST. GEORGE ST, W1, 020-7493 0876
Open Mon.-Fri. 9.30am-6pm, Sat. 1am-5pm.
U: Green Park/Oxford Circus.

A handsome and inviting space with a somewhat studious atmosphere, it specialises in books on travel, art and a bit fashion with some colourplate books. There is a comprehensive range of Baedekers and early guidebooks provide interesting travel nostalgia.

Bertram Rota

FIRST FLOOR, 31 LONG ACRE, WC2
020-7836 0723
Open Mon.-Fri. 9.30am-5.30pm.
U: Covent Garden.

With a strong literary background, Rota pursues themes such as books published by particular firms and special short-run editions on distinctive paper. A bookworm's book shop, to be sure.

Biblion

GRAYS ANTIQUE MARKET
SOUTH MOLTON LANE, W1, 020-7629 1374
Open Mon.-Fri. 10am-6pm.
U: Bond St.

Biblion carries stock from about 100 top dealers in fine and rare books, creating one of the widest selections in the capital. Books are displayed in one hundred cabinets around the walls—each belonging to a separate dealer. Expert staff is on hand to offer advice.

Bloomsbury Workshop

2 GALEN PLACE, OFF BURY PLACE, WC1
020-7405 0632
Open Mon.-Fri. 10am-5.30pm.
U: Holborn/Tottenham Court Rd.

The Bloomsbury Group—featuring Virginia Woolf, Duncan Grant, Lytton Strachey, Clive Bell and Vanessa Bell—are the attractions here. There are many first editions. Changing shows of art by children of members of the group are charming.

Chelsea Gallery & Il Libro

G5 THE PLAZA, 535 KING'S RD, SW10
020-7823 3248
Open Mon.-Sat. 10am-7pm.
U: Sloane Sq.

A selection of antique books, maps and decorative prints make this one of Chelsea's few specialists to make a point of visiting.

G Heywood Hill

10 CURZON ST, W1, 020-7629 0647
Open Mon.-Fri. 9am-5.30pm, Sat. 9am-12.30pm.
U: Oxford Circus.

Specialists in antiquarian natural history illustrated books and volumes on architecture, the shop also deals in new and humbler, but no less interesting, secondhand tomes. There is a specialist children's book section downstairs.

Henry Sotheran

2/5 SACKVILLE ST, W1, 020-7734 1150
Open Mon.-Fri. 9.30am-6pm, Sat. 10am-4pm.
U: Piccadilly Circus.

One of the finest antiquarian book shops in the country. The vast selection includes books on art, architecture, travel and occasional oddities. Each department is presided over by an enthusiastic expert, and the friendly, though very serious atmosphere does encourage browsing as well, of course, as buying. Downstairs occasional print exhibitions are held.

Jarndyce Antiquarian Booksellers

46 GREAT RUSSELL ST, WC1, 020-7631 4220
Open Mon.-Fri. 10am-5pm.
U: Tottenham Court Rd.

Specialising in Charles Dickens, including first editions and celebrated eighteenth and nineteenth century literary books, this charming eighteenth century house is opposite the British Museum. One floor sells less expensive, but nonetheless interesting books. The upper floor is intended for the serious collector, who should make an appointment with the knowledgeable owners.

Maggs Brothers

50 BERKELEY SQ, W1, 020-7493 7160
Open Mon.-Fri. 9.15am-5pm.
U: Green Park.

One of the oldest and most respected antiquarian book shops in London. Early travel books and modern first editions include famous autographs from stage to royalty.

Pickering & Chatto

36 ST. GEORGE ST, W1, 020-7491 2656
Open Mon.-Fri. 9.30am-5.30pm.
U: Oxford Circus/Bond St.

They are specialists in medicine, science and humanities with a sprinkling of English literature from the late eighteenth century.

Robert Frew

106 GREAT RUSSELL ST, WC1, 020-7580 2311
Open Mon.-Fri. 10am-6pm, Sat. 10am-2pm.
U: Tottenham Court Rd.

Prints by Thomas Rowlandson, Arthur Rackham and David Roberts catch the eye in this handsome shop where books on travel and illustrated books on English literature are stocked. It also carries a good range of maps and atlases.

Sam Fogg

35 ST. GEORGE ST, W1, 020-7495 2333
Open Mon.-Fri. 9.30am-6pm.
U: Green Park

Established in 1971, this shop sells only manuscripts. In fact, it is reputedly the major manuscript dealer in the country. Medieval- and Renaissance-era manuscripts from Armenia, Indonesia, Ethiopia and Europe are featured.

Simon Finch Rare Books

53 MADDOX ST, W1, 020-7499 0974
Open Mon.-Fri. 10am-6pm.
U: Bond St.

Simon Finch carries a variety of literature and other subjects from the eighteenth century. Beautiful leather-bound and gilt tomes fill the elegant shop.

Also at 61A Ledbury Rd, W11, 020-7792 3303.

Sims Reed

43A DUKE ST, SW1, 020-7493 5660
Open Mon.-Fri. 9am-6pm.
U Green Park.

A specialist in rare, out-of-print and new reference books on fine and applied art from architecture to contemporary design. Sims Reed is probably the biggest dealer in decorative books with original prints.

Thomas Heneage

42 DUKE STREET, SW1, 020-7930 9223
Open Mon.-Fri. 9.30am-6pm.
U: Green Park.

Based in St. James's, this leading supplier of fine art books sells both newly published works and secondhand books for art collectors and dealers.

Ulysses

40 MUSEUM ST, WC1, 020-7831 1600
Open Mon.-Sat. 10.30am-6pm, Sun. noon-6pm.
U: Tottenham Court Rd.

One for dedicated browsers, where collector's items of modern first editions are readily available.

UK antiques trade website for information for domestic and international collectors: **www.antiques-web.co.uk.**

CLASSICAL ANTIQUITIES

Charles Ede Ltd
20 BROOK ST, W1, 020-7493 4944
*Open Tues.-Fri. 12.30pm-4.30pm, also by
appointment.*
U: Bond St.

A renowned expert in the classical and pre-
classical world of antiquities pre 600 A.D., the
contents of Charles Ede's gallery amazes, with
items such as Greek amphora decorated in the
black-figure style and Greek body armour usually found in museums.

CONTINENTAL & ENGLISH FURNITURE

Antoine Chenevière
27 BRUTON ST, W1, 020-7491 1007
Open Mon.-Fri. 10am-5pm.
U: Oxford Circus/Green Park.

These impressive showrooms are devoted to
ornately designed eighteenth- and nineteenth-
century Russian, Austrian, German and Italian
furniture along with many objets d'art.

Carlton Hobbs
8 LITTLE COLLEGE ST, SW1, 020-7340 1000
Open Mon.-Fri. 9am-6pm, Sat. by appointment.
U: Victoria.

This firm, established more than 22 years
ago, is a leading dealer in seventeenth, eighteenth and early nineteenth century English
and continental furniture, objets d'art, paintings and tapestries. Displayed in a dramatically
lit showroom, each piece has been researched
before going on sale.

Jeremy Ltd.
29 LOWNDES ST, SW1, 020-7823 2923
Open Mon.-Fri. 8.30am-6pm, Sat. 9am-1pm.
U: Sloane Sq.

Brothers Michael and John Hill carry on the
family tradition of selling high-quality English
and continental furniture from the eighteenth
and early nineteenth centuries in their smart
shop on a quiet Knightsbridge street. They
have outstanding examples of French, Russian
and English decorative art. Telephone first if
you would like to make sure that the Hills are
there.

O F Wilson
3-6 QUEENS ELM PARADE
OLD CHURCH ST, SW3, 020-7352 9554
*Open Mon.-Fri. 9.30am-5.30pm, Sat. 10.30am-
1pm.*
U: Sloane Sq.

The shop has a wide choice of eighteenth-
and early nineteenth-century English and continental furniture. Here you might see a pair
of Venetian armchairs and Roman gilt wood
console tables from the mid-eighteenth century and Italian statuary marble lions from the
nineteenth century. Marble mantelpieces and
architectural items are a speciality.

Partridge Fine Arts
144-146 NEW BOND ST, W1, 020-7629 0834
Open Mon.-Fri. 9am-5.30pm.
U: Green Park.

This large antiques firm is housed in an
impressive building with a grand staircase and
marble pillars, built in 1913 as showrooms for
Colnaghi, the art dealers. It is the only cus-
tom-built gallery of that era still used for the
original purpose of showing off masterpieces,
now in the form of continental furniture, silver, paintings of the English and Italian school
and terracottas.

Pelham Galleries
24-25 MOUNT ST, W1, 020-7629 0905
Open Mon.-Fri. 9am-5pm.
U: Bond St.

The emphasis here is on decorative arts and
furniture displayed in well laid-out, stylish galleries. Unusual forms of painted and lacquered
decoration are well represented. Exceptional
craftsmanship and interesting historical associations are appealing features of many pieces.

EIGHTEENTH- & NINETEENTH-CENTURY ENGLISH FURNITURE

Apter-Fredericks
265-267 FULHAM RD, SW3, 020-7352 2188
*Open Mon.-Fri. 9.30am-5.30pm, Sat. by
appointment.*
U: South Kensington.

The large windows of Apter-Fredericks, a
firm which goes back five generations, display
some fine eighteenth-century English furniture. Researching with meticulous care, they
know the provenance of most of this grand

furniture that illustrates the tastes of a past, more gracious age.

Brian Rolleston Antiques
104A KENSINGTON CHURCH ST, W8
020-7229 5892
Open Mon.-Fri. 10am-1pm & 2.30pm-5.30pm.
U: High St Kensington.

Eighteenth-century English furniture fills the three large showrooms here, where the pieces are of museum quality.

H Blairman & Sons
119 MOUNT ST, W1, 020-7493 0444
Open Mon.-Fri. 9am-5.30pm.
U: Bond St.

These discreet premises of a firm founded in 1884 are full of eighteenth- and early nineteenth-century English furniture and later English architect-designed furniture. To complement the furniture, you'll find related objects in the three showrooms.

Hotspur
14 LOWNDES ST, SW1, 020-7235 1918
Open Mon.-Fri. 8am-6pm, Sat. 9am-1pm.
U: Sloane Sq/Hyde Park Corner.

This family firm, run now by Robin Kern, specialises in fine eighteenth-century English furniture and works of art, trading from a delightful Regency townhouse which retains its original character. Established in 1924, Hotspur presents carefully selected rare and fine furniture from makers like Thomas Chippendale.

John Bly
27 BURY ST, SW1, 020-7930 1292
Open Mon.-Fri. 9.30am-5pm.
U: Green Park.

Comfortably laid out with eighteenth-century tables, desks and chairs, this firm was founded in 1891 by the grandfather of the present proprietor, John Bly. The present expert owner is something of a celebrity among the antique fraternity because of his television appearances and his *Daily Telegraph* column. This small, well-stocked shop has many stylish objets d'art to coordinate with the furniture. Knowledgeable and enthusiastic, he is one of the more forward-looking dealers. The firm has its own restoration workshop in Tring, Hertfordshire.

Mallett & Son
141 NEW BOND ST, W1, 020-7499 7411
Open Mon.-Fri. 9am-6pm, Sat. 10am-4pm.
U: Green Park.

Mallett at Bourdon House
2 DAVIES ST, W1, 020-7629 2444
Open Mon.-Fri. 9.30am-5.30pm.
U: Bond St.

Established in 1865, Mallet in Bond Street has five floors arranged into rooms, with richly coloured walls to show English furniture, paintings and decorative objects delightfully laid out as they would be in a fine home. One room is devoted to the later nineteenth and early twentieth centuries including interesting examples of Victorian Gothic Revival and the Arts and Crafts movement. The large antique glass department in the basement displays museum-standard pieces. At Mallett's charming Bourdon House premises (until 1953, the townhouse of the second Duke of Westminster), a more eclectic display of paintings, sculpture, objets d'art and garden statuary is on display.

Norman Adams
8-10 HANS RD, SW3, 020-7589 5266
Open Mon.-Fri. 9am-5.30pm.
U: Knightsbridge.

Opposite the west side of Harrods, this firm, established in 1923, has eighteenth-century English furniture and a wide variety of chandeliers, mirrors and barometers as well as objets d'art from England and France. Many are by well-known makers and have interesting histories.

Richard Courtney
112-114 FULHAM RD, SW3, 020-7370 4020
Open Mon.-Fri. 9.30am-5.30pm.
U: South Kensington.

One of the leading dealers in eighteenth-century furniture, the shop also specialises in fine Queen Anne walnut furniture. There are some beautiful choices in George III pieces, such as carved walnut library chairs and satinwood and marquetry inlaid tea tables.

Stair & Company

14 MOUNT ST, W1, 020-7499 1784
Open Mon.-Fri. 9.30am-5.30pm, Sat. by appointment.
U: Bond St.

Established in 1911, this firm has a huge stock of eighteenth-century English furniture and art. It is a place where you might find a fine set of dining chairs, a mahogany bookcase or Georgian mirrors.

GLASS

Jeanette Hayhurst

32A KENSINGTON CHURCH ST, W8
020-7938 1539
Open Mon.-Fri. 10am-5pm, Sat. noon-5pm.
U: High St Kensington.

A friendly and enthusiastic proprietor, Jeanette Hayhurst features eighteenth- to twentieth-century British glassware for collecting or using. There is a wide choice of Georgian decanters and Victorian sundae dishes and wine goblets. Modern glasswork is represented in a range of light fixtures, chandeliers and table ornaments.

ICONS

Maria Andipa Icon Gallery

162 WALTON ST, SW3, 020-7589 2371
Open Tues.-Sat. 11am-6pm.
U: South Kensington.

The golden glow of a medieval altar panel depicting saintly figures with halos sets the atmosphere of the window display and the exotic interior of this gallery. It is the home of one of Europe's largest collections of fourteenth- to nineteenth-century icons from Russia, Greece, the Balkans, Eastern Europe and Ethiopia. Maria Andipa was one of the first dealers to open a gallery specialising in Byzantine objects.

The Temple Gallery

6 CLARENDON CROSS, W11, 020-7727 3809
Open Mon.-Fri. 9am-6pm by appointment.
U: Holland Park.

From small, gold-leafed altar pieces of saints to large painted church doors, the collection of Greek and Russian icons and objects dates from the twelfth to sixteenth centuries. Established in 1960, Richard Temple's delightful little gallery is well known to collectors who head for this quiet corner, to appreciate Byzantine art at its finest. A noted expert, he has written several books about icons. The gallery is normally open during exhibitions; at other times, telephone in advance. Alternatively, get yourself on his mailing list. He publishes two to three catalogues a year, complete with illustrations and prices.

MAPS & PRINTS

Henry Sotheran

80 PIMLICO RD, SW1, 020-7730 8756
Open Mon.-Fri. 10am-6pm, Sat. 10am-4pm.
U: Sloane Sq.

Established in 1815 by Thomas Sotheran, whose family firm of booksellers had been founded in York in 1761 and is still a centre for booksellers today. This branch carries a huge range of topographical and architectural prints by artists such as Piranese, Roberts and Daniells and it welcomes browsers. The print department at 2-5 Sackville Street, W1 (020-7439 6151) concentrates mainly on original ornithological prints, especially by John Gould, although it is principally a book shop.

Japanese Gallery

66D KENSINGTON CHURCH ST, W8
020-7229 2934
Open Mon.-Sat. 10am-6pm.
U: High St Kensington.

Every inch of the walls in this small gallery is covered with colourful wood-block prints, mainly from the nineteenth century, though there are earlier works too. Birds and flowers jostle with portraits of beautiful women from masters like Utamaro. In the many cases dotted around, Satsuma medicine 'inros', incense burners, tea ceremony pots and Noh masks compete for your attention.

Jonathan Potter

125 NEW BOND ST, W1, 020-7491 3520
Open Mon.-Fri. 10am-6pm.
U: Bond St.

Ring the bell to gain entry to an upstairs gallery of early maps covering all parts of the known world—including the North American Great Lakes with the original Indian names. Jonathan Potter is one of the most important map dealers and offers a huge selection and range of prices.

The Map House

54 BEAUCHAMP PL, SW3, 020-7589 4325
Open Mon.-Fri. 9.45am-5.45pm, Sat. 10.30am-5pm.
U: Knightsbridge.

Besides antique maps, atlases and globes, the galleries offer reference books on maps and mapmaking, reproductions and prints, and decorative engravings, all beautiful and most published 1600-1900. Despite its size, it has a congenial atmosphere.

The O'Shea Gallery

120A MOUNT ST, SW1, 020-7629 1122
Open Mon.-Fri. 9.30am-6pm, Sat. 9.30am-1pm.

A must for any map enthusiast, there are thousands of examples contained in the plan chests. The shop is a specialist dealer in fifteenth- to nineteenth-century prints and maps. The stock can be viewed by county, country or by continent. Prints cover topographical, decorative, natural history, sporting and marine subjects.

The Parker Gallery

28 PIMLICO RD, SW1, 0171-730 6768
Open Mon.-Fri. 9.30am-5.30pm.
U: Victoria.

There is always a wide range of antique prints and engravings with the emphasis on marine, nautical and military sciences and personalities. They also stock prints on the more lighthearted side of life: games, pastimes and sports.

METALWARE

Jack Casimir

23 PEMBRIDGE RD, W11, 020-7727 8643
Open Mon.-Sat. 9.30am-5.30pm, also by appointment.
U: Notting Hill Gate.

From fireplaces to candle snuffers, the Casimirs carry on a third-generation family business in this well-stocked shop, specialising in the sixteenth to nineteenth centuries. The shelves are filled with British and European pewter tankards, copper pots, brass doorknobs and occasional rare items, such as fifteenth-century German braziers in either brass or bronze.

ORIENTAL ART

Barry Davies Oriental Art

1 DAVIES ST, W1, 020-7408 0207
Open Mon.-Fri. 10am-6pm.
U: Bond St.

Japanese works of art are the speciality of this smart gallery, which has some furniture and rare samurai armour. Behind small screens, shelves display fine netsuke, cloisonné, ivory and lacquer ware, such as a three-compartment inro after a print by Utamaro. The firm meticulously classifies individual artists and schools. To encourage modern craftsmen in the old traditions, the shop features contemporary lacquer work.

Eskenazi

10 CLIFFORD ST, W1, 020-7493 5464
Open Mon.-Fri. 9.30am-5.30pm, Sat. 10am-1pm.
U: Bond St.

More like a museum than a shop, this establishment's dramatically lit showcases display Ming porcelain, Tang figures, jade objets d'art and bronze pieces, many with BC dates. Museums and learned institutions refer to Eskenazi's expertise in Chinese antiquities. The netsuke collection is considered to be the best in Europe, with prices ranging from £1,000 to the sky.

John Eskenazi

15 OLD BOND ST, W1, 020-7409 3001
Open Mon.-Fri. 9am-6pm by appointment.
U: Green Park.

Previously with a Milan base, this gallery on the second floor of the building has a wide-ranging collection of artefacts from southeast Asia and the Himalayas including Buddhist and Tibetan sculptures, rugs, carpets, textiles and, on occasion, Chinese hangings.

Michael Goedhuis

116 MOUNT ST, W1, 020-7629 2228
Open Mon.-Fri. 9.30am-6pm.
U: Bond St.

Amid the Oriental works of art are such fine pieces as a gilt copper rakan, signed Kado from the eighteenth-century Edo period and a pair of bronze candelabra from the sixteenth-century Ming dynasty. Michael Goedhuis has a wide choice of sculptures, bronzes and ceramics from Japan and China and exhibits top Chinese contemporary artists.

Robert Hall

15C CLIFFORD ST, W1, 020-7734 4008
Open Mon.-Fri. 10am-5.30pm.
U: Bond St.

Established in 1976, and now probably the world's leading dealer in antique Chinese snuff bottles, Robert Hall opened this shop to show off hundreds of pieces. They are made of glass, agate, jade, enamel or porcelain and range in price from £200 to £400,000. They were originally made for the emperors of the Qing dynasty, becoming extremely popular in the mid-nineteenth century. The equivalent of the European snuffbox, the bottle would have a stopper and a little spoon for scooping out the snuff. Hall has written books, on sale at the shop, on collecting snuff bottles.

Rossi & Rossi

91C JERMYN ST, SW1, 020-7321 0208
Open Mon.-Fri. 10.30am-5.30pm, Sat. by appointment.
U: Green Park.

The friendly proprietors at this second-floor gallery specialise in top south Asian and Himalayan art, from the second century B.C. to the seventeenth century. Sculptures include

---

Crafts Flair

British crafts and crafts people are among the best in the world. You can see their work in exhibitions at the **Crafts Council Gallery Shop**, 44a Pentonville Rd, N1, 020-7278 7700, where there is also a 'library' of people you can commission. The Crafts Council also has an outlet in the **Victoria & Albert Museum**, South Kensington, SW7, 020-7938 8500 Another good source for top design is **Contemporary Applied Arts**, 2 Percy St, W1, 020-7436 344, which has changing exhibitions of textiles, ceramics, jewelry and printmaking. Worth a look, too, is the **Oxo Tower**, Bargehouse St, SE1, a converted warehouse building with a restaurant on top (see *Restaurants*), and many small units with all kinds of different crafts people. Many of them came originally from **Gabriel's Wharf**, 56 Upper Ground, SE1, an area with brightly painted, small craft shops.

---

bronze, stone and terra cotta pieces; they also stock textiles and paintings.

S Marchant & Son

120 KENSINGTON CHURCH ST, W8
020-7229 5319
Open Mon.-Fri. 9.30am-6pm.
U: High St Kensington

Sydney Marchant founded the firm in 1925 and it's still mainly family-owned and run. There are three floors of Chinese pottery and porcelain including a 'blue-and-white room', jade pieces, works of art and Chinese furniture and Japanese art, porcelain and ivory ware. And what a priceless collection it is. There are annual exhibitions on such themes as Qing mark and period wares, monochrome and two-coloured, and marked imperial pieces.

Sydney L Moss

51 BROOK ST, W1, 020-7629 4670
Open Mon.-Fri. 10am-6pm.
U: Bond St.

Chinese paintings, calligraphy and literati works, as well as bronzes, jades and furniture fill the large, sedate showrooms of this respected dealer. There are also Japanese paintings, calligraphy, netsuke, sculpture and lacquerware.

POTTERY & PORCELAIN

Alistair Sampson Antiques

120 MOUNT ST, W1, 020-7409 1799
Open Mon.-Fri. 9.30am-5.30pm, Sat. by appointment.
U: Bond St.

English pottery from the seventeenth and eighteenth centuries is the speciality of this shop, which has other decorative and interesting items from that period too, such as English naive painting, needlework and brassware. It also specialises in eighteenth-century English furniture.

Brian Haughton Antiques

31 OLD BURLINGTON ST, W1, 020-7437 0232
Open Mon.-Fri. 10am-5pm.
U: Bond St.

Brian Haughton specialises in English and continental ceramics and offers a wide range of objects from all factories like Chelsea 'Hans Sloane' plates with the red anchor mark

(1755-6). Other dramatic displays might include Sèvres parcel-biscuit gilt baskets and stands. Haughton is a ceramics specialist who organises the International Ceramics Fair and Seminar each June.

Constance Stobo

31 HOLLAND ST, W8, 020-7937 6282
Open Mon.-Fri. 11am-5pm, Sat. 10.30am-2pm.
U: High St Kensington.

Sunderland lustre figures depicting autumn and winter and Staffordshire pottery spaniel jugs from around 1850 might be found among the large choice of mantel dogs, and Staffordshire cow creamers and other pieces of eighteenth- and nineteenth-century pottery at this corner shop in a quiet enclave near Kensington High Street.

Jonathan Horne

66B & 66C KENSINGTON CHURCH ST, W8
020-7221 5658
Open Mon.-Fri. 9.30am-5.15pm.
U: High St Kensington.

From medieval pots and early English pottery up to the Arts and Crafts era, this firm has many delicious rarities. The two showrooms display Staffordshire cow creamers, Delftware and many tin-glazed tiles. Exhibitions about aspects of the collection are held every March.

London Curiosity Shop

66E KENSINGTON CHURCH ST, W8
020-7229 2934
Open Mon.-Sat. 10am-6pm.
U: High St Kensington.

Designed to look like a traditional 'Cabinet of Curiosities', this shop displays British china and Meissen cups and saucers as well as figures. It also specialises in French bisque dolls.

RUGS & TAPESTRIES

C John (Rare Rugs)

70 SOUTH AUDLEY ST, W1, 020-7493 5288
Open Mon.-Fri. 9.30am-5pm.
U: Bond St/Hyde Park Corner.

Established in 1947, this firm excels in its choice of French Aubusson and Savonnerie carpets from the eighteenth and nineteenth centuries. A mid eighteenth-century French Beauvais tapestry, finely woven in silk and wool, and a mid-Victorian English floral

needlework carpet are typical of the finds among the collection which includes handmade carpets, rugs, textiles and tapestries from Persia, Turkey, India, China, Spain, Italy, France, Portugal, Russia, the Caucuses and England.

David Black Oriental Carpets

96 PORTLAND RD, W11, 020-7727 2566
Open Mon.-Fri. 10am-6pm, Sat. 11am-5.30pm.
U: Holland Park.

Decorative carpets from Delhi to Donegal are displayed—or stand in rolled-up abundance—at this cheerful, informal shop. Here you see vintage carpets from Turkey, India and Persia as well as modern carpets brightly coloured with vegetable dyes, thanks to the Dobag project, which the shop started. Local craftsmen in Turkey are encouraged to use traditional handcraft methods in making carpets. Prices are excellent; restoration work is undertaken.

Linda Wrigglesworth

34 BROOK ST, W1, 020-7408 0177
Open Mon.-Fri. 10am-5.30pm, Sat. by appointment.
U: Bond St.

Specialising in Chinese costumes and textiles, this gallery and shop is arrayed with vibrantly coloured robes from the eighteenth and early nineteenth centuries, including a multihued wedding skirt, decorative panels and fans, as well as other accessories, such as hats and footwear, worn by attendants to the court. Linda Wrigglesworth established her business in 1978, intrigued by the symbolism, workmanship and colours of early Chinese costume. She has a special interest in the Qing period, 1644-1912.

Victor Franses Gallery

57 JERMYN ST, SW1, 020-7493 6284
Open Mon.-Fri. 10am-5pm.
U: Green Park.

Striking nineteenth-century bronze animal sculptures set this gallery apart. You'll find some of the best names here, like Pierre Jules Mene, one of the leading nineteenth-century Animalier sculptors. The animals and wildlife are very fine—capturing a dog pointing, or a horse pawing in all their glorious detail.

SCIENTIFIC INSTRUMENTS, CLOCKS & WATCHES

Arthur Middleton
12 NEW ROW, WC2, 020-7836 7042
Open Mon.-Fri. 10am-6pm, Sat. by appointment.
U: Leicester Sq.

Step back in time in this fascinating, old-fashioned shop where antique globes, including beautifully illustrated celestial varieties that depict constellations, are stocked alongside compasses, telescopes, sextants and other scientific and navigational instruments of the past. Globes range from several hundred pounds for early twentieth-century models, to many thousands for eighteenth-century examples. Only serious enquiries are welcome; ring the bell for entry.

Asprey & Garrard
165-169 NEW BOND ST, W1, 020-7493 6767
WWW.ASPREY-GARRARD.COM
Open Mon.-Fri. 9.30am-5.30pm, Sat. 10am-5pm.
U: Bond St.

Amid its comprehensive antique furniture selection, this famous store has a workshop for clock and watchmakers who undertake the restoration of timepieces and marine chronometers.

John Carlton-Smith
17 RYDER ST, SW1, 020-7930 6622
See below.

Camerer Cuss & Co
17 RYDER ST, SW1, 020-7939 1940
Open Mon.-Fri. 9.45am-5pm, also by appointment.
U: Green Park.

Sharing the same neat premises in the heart of St. James's are two experts. John Carlton-Smith specialises in longcase clocks, particularly up to 1830, and carriage clocks up to 1900, in addition to vintage barometers. Terence Cameron Cuss concentrates on watches, mostly up to 1910, as well as clocks.

Pendulum of Mayfair
51 MADDOX ST, W1, 020-7629 6606
Open Mon.-Fri. 10am-6pm, Sat. 10am-5pm.
U: Bond St.

This is a good place to come for a vast selection of longcase and bracket clocks as well as a wealth of advice and information from the knowledgeable and helpful staff. All the clocks are authenticated and none have been restored to more than 5 percent of the original works.

Raffety
34 KENSINGTON CHURCH ST, W8, 020-7938 1100
Open Mon.-Fri. 10am-6pm, Sat. by appointment.
U: High St Kensington.

George III mahogany longcases are some of the fine showpieces you might find in this shop. Even the doorway has a large clock face over it. The firm deals in English clocks, mostly from 1670 to 1860, and scientific instruments and barometers, in addition to exquisite examples of eighteenth-century English furniture.

Trevor Philip & Sons
75A JERMYN ST, SW1, 020-7930 2954
Open Mon.-Fri. 10am-6pm, Sat. 10.30-3.30pm, also by appointment.
U: Green Park.

Fine old clocks and some unusual objets d'art are displayed here along with scientific instruments, especially navigational varieties, which date back to 1450. Vintage globes are a speciality, particularly from the eighteenth century.

SILVER

Asprey & Garrard
165-169 NEW BOND ST, W1, 029-7493 6767
WWW.ASPREY-GARRARD.COM
Open Mon.-Fri. 9.30am-5.30pm, Sat. 10am-5pm.
U: Green Park.

With a large silver 'factory' on the premises, Asprey and Garrard offer their own designs of modern silverware and exquisite antique silver, especially from the Georgian era, such as sugar baskets and candlesticks. With its antique glass and furniture and its own workshops, the firm can comfortably be listed under every shopping category, from leather goods to fine jewelry.

J H Bourdon-Smith
24 MASON'S YARD, SW1, 020-7839 4714
Open Mon.-Fri. 9.30am-6pm.
U: Green Park.

In business for more than 50 years, John Bourdon-Smith believes antique silver should be bought 'for the love of the article and its useful purpose—and that it also makes a good long-term investment. In a secluded corner of St. James', this family-run shop gleams with coffeepots, platters, tankards, candlesticks, caskets, coasters, tureens, tea sets, snuffboxes and cutlery, mostly from the Georgian era.

London Silver Vaults

CHANCERY HOUSE
53-65 CHANCERY LANE, WC2, 020-7242 3844
Open Mon.-Fri. 9am-5.30pm (last entry 5.20pm), Sat. 9am-1pm (last entry 12.50pm).
U: Chancery Lane.

Going through the thick and heavy door, visitors may feel they are stepping into a giant underground safe. In fact, it turns out to house a series of little rooms where some 40 dealers show fine silver in a no-nonsense fashion. The vaults have the reputation for offering well-priced Sheffield plate and sterling silver.

Silver Galleries

111-112 NEW BOND ST, W1, 020-7493 6180
Open Mon.-Fri. 9am-5pm.
U: Green Park.

It may be a bit intimidating to climb the steps up to the clutch of serious-looking silver dealers but the exercise is worthwhile. For that special wedding present, search out silver and silver plate candelabras, tureens, teapots and platters, silver wine accessories and unusual silver objects.

SILVER & JEWELRY

Bentley & Skinner

8 NEW BOND ST, W1, 0120-7629 0651
Open Mon.-Sat. 10am-5.30pm.
U: Green Park.

This family-run business, established in 1934, has two floors to show off its antique silverware from the eighteenth century onward, including complete canteens of English cutlery and a broad choice of English period jewelry, plus pieces from Cartier and Fabergé.

D S Lavender

26 CONDUIT ST, W1, 020-7409 2305
Open Mon.-Fri. 9.30am-5.30pm.
U: Bond St/Oxford Circus.

The walls are bedecked with framed miniatures, a speciality of this firm since its founding in 1945. It has good antique jewelry and objets d'art—perhaps a Queen Anne snuffbox (1710) or a pair of eighteenth-century lorgnettes.

Hancocks & Co. Ltd.

52, 53 BURLINGTON ARCADE, W1, 020-7493 8904
Open Mon.-Fri. 9.30am-5.30pm, Sat. 10am-4pm.
U: Piccadilly Circus.

Like many of the specialist silver dealers, this firm, established in 1849, also has a wide array of jewelry from the Victorian, Edwardian and Art Deco eras. It also specialises in signed twentieth-century craftsmen items.

Harvey & Gore

41 DUKE ST, ST. JAMES'S, SW1, 020-7839 4033
Open Mon.-Fri. 10am-5pm.
U: Green Park.

A small, bright shop where the stock of silver and old Sheffield plate is the backbone of a firm founded in 1723. Its jewelry displays have included such choice items as a bracelet from the Imperial Russian collection, reported to have been worn by Catherine the Great. There's also a good collection of fine modern pieces.

Moira

10 NEW BOND ST, W1, 020-7629 0160
Open Mon.-Fri. 9.30am-5.30pm, Sat. 9.30am-5pm.
U: Green Park.

Established in 1985, this small, sleek shop always has eye-catching, high-quality antique jewelry, Art Deco earrings, signet rings and stylised floral Art Nouveau pieces. Well-represented are the repuatable Van Cleef & Arpels, Tiffany and Cartier.

N Bloom & Son

BOND STREET ANTIQUES CENTRE
124 NEW BOND ST, W1, 020-7629 5060
Open Mon.-Fri. 10am-5.30pm, Sat. 11am-5.30pm.
U: Green Park.

Proprietor Ian Harris, a celebrity expert, prides himself on unusual pieces. The jewelry is mostly from 1860 to 1960, ranging from approximately £200 to £30,000. There is some Georgian and Victorian silver, too. The firm, which also has pre-1920 Rolexes and other watches, has been welcoming connoisseurs since 1912, when it was founded by Ian Harris's maternal grandfather, Nathan Bloom.

S J Phillips

139 NEW BOND ST, W1, 020-7629 6261/2
WWW.SJPHILLIPS.COM
Open Mon.-Fri. 10am-5pm.
U: Bond St.

Nothing seems to change at this shop, founded in 1869, with its wide choice of fine silver on display in traditional glass-fronted showcases. Run by the Norton family, it has antique necklaces, brooches, rings, snuffboxes and a host of other exquisite pieces.

Sandra Cronan

18 BURLINGTON ARCADE, W1, 020-7491 4851
Open Mon.-Fri. 10am-5pm.
U: Green Park.

A polo player herself, Sandra Cronan usually has silver-plated polo trophies and related artefacts in her tiny arcade boutique, but her speciality is high-quality, rare antique jewelry. She stages interesting exhibitions on such topics as cufflinks through the ages and faux gems.

Tessier's

26 NEW BOND ST, W1, 020-7629 0458
Open Mon.-Fri. 10am-5pm, Sat. 10.30am-5pm.
U: Bond St.

There are coronets and tiaras in the window of this charming old shop where the silver tankards, tureens and candlesticks are of superb quality. There is a wide-ranging jewelry collection and many objets d'art, including Fabergé pieces.

Wartski

14 GRAFTON ST, W1, 020-7493 1141
Open Mon.-Fri. 9.30am-5pm.
U: Green Park.

Flower studies, snuffboxes and trinkets, including the famous eggs made with charm and humour by the legendary jeweller, Fabergé, make this shop somewhat of a retrospective museum of his work. Emmanuel Snowman, the father of the current chairman, A. Kenneth Snowman, made the first forays into post-Revolutionary Russia to save imperial works of art, so Wartski has a historic interest in maintaining its worldwide reputation as keepers of the Fabergé archives and remaining a centre for the study of Russian art. At the front, amid shelves of antique silver, the work of talented modern craftsmen is displayed.

SPORTING ANTIQUES

Sean Arnold SportingAntiques

21-22 CHEPSTOW CORNER
WESTBOURNE GROVE, W2, 020-7221 2267
Open Mon.-Sat. 10am-6pm.
U: Notting Hill Gate.

There are two floors now for this dealer in sporting items who moved from Gray's Market. Everything you could possibly imagine people needing for tennis, polo, golf, boating, yachting, shooting, hunting—in fact, all the traditional English country pursuits—is here. It's a fascinating shop and they also have a big library stocking books.

TEXTILES & CLOTHING

Blackout II

51 ENDELL ST, WC2, 020-7240 5006
Open Mon.-Fri. 11am-7pm, Sat. 11.30am-6.30pm.
U: Covent Garden.

Blackout II carries a trove of 1960s-70s collectables and wearables for men and women with a practically unrivaled selection of sunglasses, kitsch cufflinks and associated ephemera. Prices are keen but the turnover is considerable, so don't ponder too long. Wonderful 1960s evening gowns and unusual shoes are often in stock.

Cenci

31 MONMOUTH ST, WC2, 020-7836 1400
Open Mon.-Sat. 11am-6.30pm.
U: Covent Garden.

There are two floors of stupendous (mainly 1950s-70s) American clothes for men and women. They are well-priced and knowledgeably gathered by a duo who comb the U.S. for secondhand pieces. Look out for the stunning Lucite handbags and always wonderful selection of designer ties in pure silk or fashionable knits. Ski jumpers (snapped up by Japanese dealers and certain menswear designers), are always in stock as are golfing jumpers, hats and occasionally some period overcoats which put contemporary creators to shame. Super prices, and the basement is ultra-cheap, being the stock of past seasons.

David Ireland

283 WESTBOURNE GROVE, W11, 020-8968 8887
Open Sat. only 7am-3pm.
U: Notting Hill Gate.

A true connoisseur of costume and textiles, Ireland's knowledge allows you to buy with confidence, whether considering fragments of ancient fabric for preservation, or to make up into original garb, or picking over his breath-taking selection of eighteenth-century, hand-embroidered waistcoats. Ireland shares trading space with two other specialist clothes and fabric dealers, Briony and Eva. The former has worked as a costume supplier for several important films—selling rustic, agricultural and peasant wear, and the latter deals in exotic Asian and fine European textiles and clothes. David Ireland is a clothesaholics heaven. Many of these pieces are bought as investments rather than to wear, but there are certainly for your closet, too.

Gallery of Antique Costumes & Textiles

2 CHURCH ST, NW8, 020-7723 9981
Open Mon.-Sat. 10am-5.30pm.
U: Edgware Rd.

Lovers of lavish fabrics and costumes delight at this treasure-trove of a shop stocking exquisite quilts, antique velvets, brocades, silks and textiles dating back to the nineteenth century. Although the stock is international, there is a strong emphasis on English and French items, plus examples of Chinese, Indian, Russian and Turkish textiles. Cushions are covered in a riot of colours and flowers of the fields and chintzes hang beside antique tassles and swags. This is a wonderful place to pick up a shawl or a piece of antique material.

Lunn Antiques

86 NEW KING'S RD, SW6, 020-7736 4638
Open Mon.-Sat. 10am-6.30pm.
U: Sloane Sq.

Antique lace, textiles, clothing and costumes from the nineteenth century to the early 1960s are decked out in this little shop. Especially interesting are the beaded dresses from the 1920s. Linen, unusual bed covers and quilts, reproduction Victorian nightdresses (from £18) and children's smocks (from £15) are also available.

Steinberg & Tolkien

193 KING'S RD, SW3, 020-7376 3660
Open Mon.-Sat. 10.30am-7pm, Sun.noon-6.30pm.
U: Sloane Sq.

If you're after the best vintage fashion labels, look no further than Steinberg & Tolkien. Everything from Chanel and Schiaparelli jewelry to immaculate ensembles from Chanel and Pucci are always to be found here (that is if the fashion press don't pick them up first). A good place for inspiration as well as a great place to shop.

Yesterday's Bread

29 FOUBERT'S PL, W1, 020-7287 1929
Open Mon.-Fri. 11.30am-6.30pm, Sat. 11am-6pm.
U: Oxford Circus.

This psychedelic temple to the ever so hip 1960s is designed with brightly painted swirls that echo the stock within—hippy chic a go-go. And a special feature of this shop is that most of the stock is vintage but never worn before, from HM prison jackets and Afghans to all the rage drip-dry Swedish tops and flared jeans. The owners continually play a selection of vintage hits to get you in the mood. Pop in, drop out.

WALKING STICKS

Michael German

38B KENSINGTON CHURCH ST, W8
0171-937 2771
Open Mon.-Fri. 10am-5pm, Sat. 10am-1pm.
U: High St Kensington.

A walking stick was once a prestige decorative item shown off at court by royalty, then it became a necessary fashion accessory for gentlemen in the Victorian era. Today it is a collector's item. Here you'll find hundreds of walking sticks, 1650-1920, mostly with curiously carved handles. Prices are £60 to £200 and up to thousands of pounds for rare varieties. Collectors are very particular in their tastes; one customer collects only dogs'-head-handled sticks. Also stocks vintage guns.

WINE & WINE ANTIQUES

Emerson
SHOP 2, 151 SYDNEY ST, SW3, 020-7351 1807
Open Mon.-Sat. 10am-6pm, Sun. 11am-5pm.
U: Sloane Sq.

Corkscrews are a popular quarry for wine buffs and other collectors and the many varieties, some very comic and mischievous, can be found here in a variety of materials and ages. There are other wine-related products on view and for sale.

Hugh Johnson Collection
68 ST. JAMES'S ST, SW1, 020-7491 4912
Open Mon.-Fri. 9am-5pm.
U: Green Park.

Some antique glasses, decanters and antique corkscrews from Hugh Johnson, a wine critic.

WRISTWATCHES

Sugar Antiques
8/9 PIERREPOINT ARCADE, CAMDEN PASSAGE, N1
020-7354 9896
Open Wed. 8am-3.30pm, Sat. 9am-4pm, also by appointment.
U: Angel.

Specializing in beautiful and collectable wristwatches including much sought after models by such greats as Rolex and Longines.

AT YOUR SERVICE

CLOTHING REPAIRS

British Invisible Mending Service
32 THAYER ST, W1, 020-7487 4292
Open Mon.-Fri. 8.30am-5.45pm, Sat. 10am-1pm.
U: Bond St.

If you have something special you need mended, this is the place for invisible work that involves taking threads individually from a hem and reweaving them in elsewhere, changing buttonhole sizes and anything else required to make your clothes look as good as new. Items take approximately one week. Prices from £30 + VAT.

The Cashmere Clinic
11 BEAUCHAMP PL, SW3, 020-7584 9806
Open Mon.-Fri. 10am-5.45pm.
U: Knightsbridge.

Tired cashmere garments are given a new lease of life after a brief spell in Scotland where they are revitalised with careful washing and cleaned with specialist equipment. Any holes are expertly mended, those irksome bobbles are de-piled, and reshaping, if needed, is lovingly attended to. Prices don't come cheap, but neither would replacing your favourite cashmere piece: cleaning costs from £20 for a sweater, with hole repairs coming in at £10 per hole.

First Tailored Alterations
85 LOWER SLOANE ST, SW1, 020-7730 1400
Open Mon.-Sat. 9am-6pm.
U: Sloane Sq.

Specialising in leather and suede, although all fabrics are more than adequately fixed, this useful place can alter waistbands or reshape coats. Items take about one week.

DRY CLEANERS

Buckingham Dry-Cleaners
83 DUKE ST, W1, 020-7499 1253
Open Mon.-Fri. 8am-6pm, Sat. 9.30am-12.30pm.
U: Bond St.

Particularly noted for cleaning the gowns of the smart Mayfair set, they also clean waxed jackets and run a men's shirt service.

De-Luxe Cleaners
30 BREWER ST, W1, 020-7437 1187
Open Mon.-Fri. 8.30am-6pm.
U: Piccadilly Circus.

De-Luxe is used by local fashion houses, partly because they can clean so fast (one-two hours). They also undertake alterations, repairs and invisible mending.

Jeeves of Belgravia
8-10 PONT ST, SW1, 020-7235 1101
Open Mon.-Fri. 8.30am-6.30pm, Sat. 8.30am-5pm.
U: Sloane Sq.

For items that you truly treasure, take them to Jeeves, which has built an enviable reputation for great care and impeccable cleaning, with the added bonus of being packaged in tissue paper for collection. They also reproof raincoats and skiwear, clean and vacuum-pack wedding dresses, launder household linens (including duvets), and repair shoes, briefcase-boot zips and other leather repairs. Free collection/delivery. Prices: men's two-piece suit £17.85; blazers £9.95; and trousers £8.45. **Branches throughout London.**

DYEING

Chalfont Dyers & Cleaners
222 BAKER ST, NW1, 020-7935 7316
E-MAIL: WEWILLDYE@AOL.COM
Open Mon.-Fri. 8.30am-6pm, Sat. 9am-1pm.
U: Baker St.

Any natural fabric can be dyed with one of the fifteen standard colours from which Chalfont's has to choose. Synthetics also can take on a new personality, but the depth of colour cannot be guaranteed. The service takes between three to six weeks. Prices: from £40 for a sweater.

HIRE
....An Evening Dress

Bodie & Gibbs
8 HALKIN ARCADE, HALKIN ST SW1, 020-7259 6620
Open Mon.-Fri. 10am-6pm, Sat. 11am-5pm.
U: Knightsbridge.

Bodie & Gibbs hire the kind of dresses every woman would love to have in her wardrobe -if she could possibly afford them. Understated lines from classic designers like Vera Wang, Neil Cunningham, Amanda Wakeley, Tomasz Starzewski and Pearce Fionda are staples, with optional extras such as baby-soft pashminas, cashmere twinsets and velvet cloaks wrapping up the outfits. Jimmy Choo high heels and backless, strapless bras to try on with your outfit are thoughtful touches, as are the fake breasts on offer to give you the instant cleavage you've always wanted. Jewelry and handbags from Samantha Heskia, diamanté hairslides and real hairpieces assure you'll be the belle of any ball.

One Night Stand
44 PIMLICO RD, SW1, 020-7730 8708
Open Mon.-Fri. 10am-6.30pm, Sat. 10am-5pm
by appointment only.
U: Victoria.

For a really special occasion, this shop has cocktail dresses, ball gowns and all the accessories from evening wraps to handbags, everything, in fact, except shoes. Hire is £70-£90 for a short dress; £90-£140 for a long one.

....A Formal Gentleman's Outfit

Austin Reed
103-113 REGENT ST, W1, 020-7437 2140
Open Mon.-Tues. & Fri. 9.30am-6pm, Wed. 10am-6pm, Thurs. 9.30am-7pm, Sat. 9.30am-6.30pm.
U: Piccadilly Circus.

Formal wear for hire ranges from dinner jackets to morning suits for all special occasions. Evening suits £22.95-£46.95, morning suits £39.95 for weekend hire (Thurs.-Mon.).

Moss Bros
27 KING ST, WC2, 020-7497 9354
Open Mon.-Wed. & Fri. 9am-5.30pm, Thurs. 9am-6.30pm
U: Covent Garden.

The name in formal hire for men, Moss Bros has been kitting out gents for decades. A single-breasted or double-breasted dinner jacket with all the trimmings will cost £42.90 for a day's hire. Last fitting is 30 minutes before the shop closes and the length of time you can keep the suit is flexible; you can hire on a Thursday for a Saturday afternoon.

Tom Gilbey
2 NEW BURLINGTON PL, SAVILE ROW, W1
020-7734 4877
Open Mon.-Wed. & Fri. 10am-6pm, Thurs. 10am-7pm, Sat. 10am-5.30pm.
U: Piccadilly Circus.

Forget traditional morning dress; this designer, renowned for his opulent-looking waistcoats and flamboyant couture suits, has a hire service of suits and accessories for men who temporarily want to look like dandies. Choose your velvet suits, some with embroidered collars and pockets, and accessories; a complete outfit is £295 for four-day hire. It is a great way to look sumptuous without buying elaborate clothes you may not want to wear again.

....A Theatrical Costume

Angels & Bermans

119 SHAFTESBURY AVE, WC2, 020-7836 5678
Open Mon.-Fri. 9am-4.30pm for costume hire, 9am-5.30pm for returns.
U: Leicester Sq.

When you want to make an impression at a fancy dress party, call into Angels and Bermans for your costume. Maybe you fancy yourself as an authentic flapper or perhaps you want to step back in time to the medieval era, whatever the occasion or your particular preference, you're likely to find it here. Many outfits have been used in films and it's possible to hire one of the costume's Madonna wore in Evita or Kate Winslett wore in Titanic. Prices from £60 + VAT for seven-day hire.

The Costume Studio Montgomery House

159-161 BALLS POND RD, N1, 020-7388 4481
Open Mon.-Fri. 9.30am-6pm, Sat. 10am-5pm.
U: Highbury & Islington.

With a client list, which includes major television, promotional, public relations and production companies, the Costume Studio offers a comprehensive range of costumes, infinite in variety from historical, period and military to contemporary, fantasy and sci-fi. They also have an experienced team of professionals who can help with styling, hairdressing and make-up.

HIRED HANDS

Childminders

6 NOTTINGHAM ST, W1, 020-7935 3000
WWW.BABYSITTER.CO.UK
Open Mon.-Thurs. 8.45am-5.30pm, Fri. 8.45am-5pm.
U: Baker St.

With over 1,000 babysitters on their register, Childminders aim to provide the ideal childcare. All references are checked and most of the staff is off-duty nurses, nannies and primary school teachers with specific childcare experience.

Koala Nannies

22 CRAVEN TERR, SW10, 020-7402 4224
WWW.INFO@KOALANNANIES.COM
Open Mon.-Fri. 9.30am-5.30pm.
U: Lancaster Gate.

Originally started to provide Australian and New Zealand nannies and mother's helps, this agency finds carers, cooks, companions and housekeepers.

Nannies Incorporated

317 THE LINEN HALL, 162-168 REGENT ST, W1
020-7437 8989, WWW.NANNIESINC.COM
Open Mon.-Fri. 9am-6pm.
U: Piccadilly Circus.

This firm provides qualified maternity nurses, baby nurses and British nannies with experience and verified references. Worldwide placements.

Pippa Pop-ins

430 FULHAM RD, SW6, 020-7385 2457
U: Fulham Broadway.

London's only children's hotel also acts as creche and nursery school for children aged 2 to 12. The list of services on offer is staggering, covering things like creche workshops where participating children can learn to make exciting ice sculptures and pottery, or try out trampolining, either for a few hours (£33 from 8.15am-2.15pm; £25 from 2pm-6pm) or a whole day (£44-£50 from 9am-6pm). During school holidays the creche workshop provides extra activities such as pony riding, trips to Euro Disney, the theatre or Thorpe Park at the regular workshop prices, plus the price of admission. The hotel offers meals, activities and accommodation during the week for £40 per night (from 6pm-9am), and at weekends for £50 per night (from 5pm-10am), or a full weekend (from Friday 6pm-Sunday 6pm) at £145. The friendly company also extends to school runs and nanny service.

Top Notch Nannies & Brilliant Babysitters

22A CAMPDEN GROVE, W8, 020-7938 2006
WWW.TOPNOTCHNANNIES.COM
Open Mon.-Fri. 9am-5.30pm by appointment only.
U: Holland Park.

Jean Birtles will help you find a fully-vetted nanny, mother's helper or child minders with equal parts humour and sympathy.

Universal Aunts

P O BOX 304, SW4, 020-7738 8937

Established in 1921, Universal Aunts is famous for providing almost everything you need, from daily attendance at an embassy if you're after a visa, to escorting you wherever you want to go. They also act as an employment agency for staff, providing butlers for parties and the harrassed with a mother's helper. They are well-known for escorting unaccompanied children.

HOME DELIVERY

Deliverance

DELIVERANCE CENTRAL: 0800 019 2222;
DELIVERANCE SOUTH WEST: 0800 019 1111
WWW.DELIVERANCE.CO.UK.

Bringing all your favourite foods to your door without sacrificing quality or service. There are over 150 dishes to choose from including Chinese noodles, Thai curries, Indian bhajis and Italian pizzas. For the gourmet, there's Deliverance special lobster, tiger prawns with red peppers in a sweet tomato sauce, and Goan curry with freshly ground coconut, coriander and red chillies. The service operates throughout most of central London and Southwest London.

Food Ferry

020-7498 0827, WWW.FOODFERRY.COM

With its claim to be the fastest home delivery service in London, Food Ferry aims to deliver orders for fresh, frozen and packaged foods, plus household goods and pet foods placed by 10.30am the same day. £3 day delivery, £4 evening. Catalogue of over 2,500 lines.

Nappy Express

020-8368 0132 (24-HOUR PHONE/FAX ORDER-LINE)

Providing a nappy laundry service, baby products and household delivery service. Specify whether you require boy or girl nappies.

Room Service

020-7431 5555, WWW.ROOMSERVICE.CO.UK

Customers have a booklet listing a good selection of restaurants like Chutney Mary (see *Restaurants*), which offer special take-out

E-mail Home

EasyEverything, 020-7482 9502, www.easyeverything.com, is a neat idea—shops in busy High Streets with banks of computers for up to 400 people, open 24 hours a day. Costs are from £1 for one hour, no formal training offered. Also at Kensington High St, W8, 020-7938 1841; 9-16 Tottenham Court Rd, W1, 020-7436 1207; Wilton Rd, SW1, (opposite Victoria Station), 020-7233 8456 and other branches throughout London.

meals. You select your meal, phone your order and await your delivery (within the hour, unless it is very large). With some advance notice, you can have a whole restaurant meal for a dinner party.

PROPERTY MAINTENANCE

N D Management

41 BROXASH RD, SW11
TEL & FAX 020-7738 0151

Like all the companies recommended here, the two young directors Nicky Gill and Di Robertson have an efficient and enthusiastic team of helpers. This first-rate company undertakes everything to do with property. They will maintain your apartment or house while you're at home or away; clean, shop, garden, decorate and repair, as well as make travel bookings and theatre reservations. They will even start your Bentley once a week while it is sitting in the garage!

SHIPPERS

Trans Euro World Wide Movers

DRURY WAY, BRENT PARK, NW10 0JN
020-8784 0100

This company efficiently moves furniture all over the world and also has a helpful antiques and fine art division.

SHOE REPAIRS

Krantz & Son
180 DRURY LANE, WC2, 020-7405 0609
Open Mon.-Fri. 9am-4.30pm.
U: Covent Garden.

This company, established in 1905, is one of the few London shoe repairers still using traditional stitching machines. Prices for heels: men £8.50, ladies £4.50; leather half-sole and heels: £25 men, £15 ladies.

K G Shoes
253 EVERSHOLT ST, NW1, 020-7387 2234
Open Mon.-Fri. 8am-5.30pm, Sat. 9am-2pm.
U: Euston/Mornington Crescent.

With a client list including Gucci, Selfridges, Harrods and customers from all over the country, this family firm has built up a great reputation for quality repairs. Heels start at £6.50 for men, £4 for women; leather half-soles £15 for men; full remake from £40. K G is also popular for adjusting the 'bag factor' in women's boots.

The Complete Cobbler
26 TOTTENHAM ST, W1, 020-7636 9040
Open Mon.-Fri. 8am-6.30pm, Sat. 9.30am-1pm.
U: Goodge St.

At this family business, which includes an extensive dry cleaning service, George Zorlakkis specialises in trade repairs for big names like Gucci and Charles Jourdan and mends leather handbags and luggage. He can do repairs on the spot and also makes riding boots (he is on the premise Thursdays & Fridays from 5pm onwards). They will also restitch, replace trims and recover scuffed heels. Prices: £4.50 ladies heels, £6.50 men's; half rubber sole: £13.50 ladies, £17.50 men's.

We're always interested to hear about your discoveries and to receive your comments on ours. Please let us know what you liked or disliked; **e-mail us at gayots@aol.com.**

BEAUTY

ALTERNATIVE THERAPIES

Alternative Medicine Centre
56 HARLEY HOUSE, MARYLEBONE RD, NW1
020-7486 8087
Open Mon.-Thurs. 11am-7pm, Fri. 11am-8pm, Sat. 11am-1pm.
U: Baker St/Regents Park.

A variety of alternative therapies are offered in this 30-year-old practice. Everything from aromatherapy to zoning massage, Bach flower remedies to stress reduction, the female therapists combat a variety of problems using hypnotherapy and reflexology. They specialise in treating scarring, particularly with African and Asian skin.

Balance
250 KING'S RD, SW3, 020-7565 0333
Open Mon.-Fri. 9am-8pm, Sat. 10am-5pm, Sun. 10am-4pm.
U: Sloane Sq.

Walking into this clean, tranquil setting is a form of therapy in itself, with its whitewashed walls, suede camel-coloured banquettes, scented candles and serene therapists. Aromatherapy, herbalism, reflexogy, vacuflex, colonic hydrotherapy, kinesiology and manual lymphatic drainage, psychic surgery, reiki and weight management are some of the therapies offered. The perfect setting for the new-age devotee who still hankers after a little luxury.

Farmacia
169 DRURY LANE, WC2, 020-7831 0830
WWW.FARMACIA.CO.UK
E-MAIL HEALING@FARMACIA.CO.UK
Open Mon.-Fri. 8.30am-7pm, Sat. 9am-6pm.
U: Covent Garden/Holborn.

Devotees of natural remedies are well served in this modern, streamlined natural pharmacy. The ranges of supplements are particularly good and, if by chance you can't find what you're looking for, the well-trained staff will do their best to track it down for you. There are some excellent lines in aromatherapy-based skin and body care products as well as an herbal dispensary, on-site practitioners offering holistic aromatherapy, reflexology, dietary advice and some of the best freshly squeezed juices in town.

Also at 42 Short's Gardens, WC2, 020-7836 3179.

The Hale Clinic
7 PARK CRESCENT, W1, 020-7631 0156
NEW PATIENT ENQUIRY LINE: 01923-775 666
Open Mon.-Fri. 8.30am-9pm, Sat. 8.45am-4.30pm.
U: Regent's Park.

Thankfully, the clinic operates a new patient enquiry line to guide clients through the plethora of treatments and 100 or so private practitioners available at this popular clinic. They cover the familiar like aromatherapy, physiotherapy, chiropody and allergy testing, to more unusual therapies such as polarity, buteyko and kinesiology. If that list doesn't appeal, try out shyness counselling, colonic irrigation, Marma massage and a whole lot more. Prices vary in accordance with the practitioners. Call for details.

Natureworks
16 BALDERTON ST, W1, 020-7355 4036
Open Mon.-Fri. 10am-6pm.
U: Bond St.

If you want the more alternative treatments, spend an hour or two at Natureworks. Try out rebirthing, rejuvenessence, McTimoney chiropractice, kriyas or zero balancing; otherwise succumb to an Indian head massage, shiastu massage or Thai massage.

BEAUTY SALONS & SPAS

The Berkeley Health Club & Spa
THE BERKELEY, WILTON PL, SW1, 020-7235 6000
Open Mon.-Fri. 9am-9pm, Sat.-Sun. 9am-7pm.
U: Knightsbridge.

Wide range of facial treatments from specially trained Christian Dior specialists. From Prescription facial to a package called Perfect Retreat consisting of two hours of personalised skin care treatment, stress relief back massage and hydro-active mineral salt scrub (£105). Also great jet lag recovery package (£80). In addition, this is one of the few spas to get LaStone Therapy in London, where hot stones are used to achieve remarkable results in massage. They have a gym and swimming pool with retractable roof for summer days. Also on offer is the ultimate pampering treat,

the Silver Spirit Day, (£325) which offers treatments and use of the facilities—before being chauffeured home by the hotel's limousine.

Champneys Piccadilly
LE MERIDIEN, 21 PICCADILLY, W1
020-7255 8000
Open daily 6.45am-11pm.
U: Piccadilly Circus.

From the people who brought you Champneys in Tring, Hertfordshire, the first nature cure resort in England, the London-based club is every bit as luxurious. Set out in 40,000-square-feet and recently having been treated to a £1.5 million refurbishment programme, this Grade II listed building combines the stately pleasures of magnificient architecture with the latest exercise equipment, beauty treatments and light, modern cuisine. There's a Members' Services Team on hand to attend to all those irksome tasks like booking theatre tickets, flights, ordering flowers or even popping out to buy you a pair of trainers if you've forgotten to pack your own. Essentially a members-only club, you can make the most of the facilities and the excellent classes by signing up for the 'Top-to-Toe Day', consisting of morning coffee, heat treatment, half-hour body massage, Decleor Aromaplasty Facial, buffet lunch, manicure, pedicure, make-up, sunbed or body scrub (£175).

The Dorchester Spa
THE DORCHESTER, PARK LANE, W1, 020-7495 7335
Open daily 7am-9.30pm.
U: Hyde Park Corner.

As you'd expect from a beauty salon located in one of London's top hotels, The Dorchester Spa is the epitome of luxury. From the moment you walk into the lavish cream and gold spa area on the lower ground floor, all stresses and strains are left behind, freeing your mind to enjoy the hedonistic treats. Choose from half a dozen or so types of facials, manicures, pedicures and body treatments. Some of our favorites are Detoxifying Algae Wrap (£60), Holistic Aromatherapy Total Body care (£90), reflexogy, waxing and special packages like the Dorchester Spa Day which costs £230 for six-hour top-to-toe pampering. Men are more than adequately catered for with specially tailored programmes and individual treatments including the Gentlemen's Spa Day, five hours of grooming for £180, including light lunch.

Elizabeth Arden Red Door Hair & Beauty Spa

29 DAVIES ST, W1, 020-7629 4488
WWW.RED.DOOR@VIRGIN.NET
Open Mon.-Tues. & Fri.-Sat. 9am-6pm, Wed.-
Thurs. 9am-8pm.
U: Bond St.

Back in 1921 when the original salon opened, this was the place where all the beautiful people came to make themselves even more beautiful. The famous lacquer red door closed its London premises in 1981 but reopened again in May, 1997, in its new premises, a former bank spread over two floors on the corner of Grosvenor and Davies Streets. Treatments include Salt Glow to smooth away dry skin (£30), Body Wraps to detoxify and tone, Hot Mud foot treatment (£15), and a complete range of hair and make-up services to meet individual needs. The Arden Spa Packages such as Spa Body Retreat (£10) and Visible Difference Day (£130) are justifiably popular.

The Sanctuary

12 FLORAL ST, WC2, 020-7420 5151
Open Mon.-Tues. & Sat.-Sun. 10am-6pm,
Wed.-Fri. 10am-10pm.
U: Covent Garden.

As the name implies, this women-only pampering-zone is a haven in the centre of London. Entry is by membership which is £49.50 day or £29.50 evening (from 5pm-10pm on Wed.-Fri. only), and includes use of sauna, steam room, jacuzzi, meditation suite with massage chairs and the tropical swimming pool, complete with tinkling waterfall. The vast range of treatments available at extra cost include reflexology, body treatments, facials, manicures, pedicures, heat treatments, tanning sessions, waxing and make-up lessons.

Sher System Studio

30 NEW BOND ST, W1, 020-7499 4022
Open Mon.-Fri. 10am-6pm.
U: Bond St.

Helen Sher and daughter Glenda have developed their own unique beauty treatment, based on an easy warm-water therapy: just splash the face regularly in tap water specially treated with Sher crystals. A kit with four empty bottles for decanting comes in travel-pack form with lightweight plastic bottles and costs from £8; when filled, the kit should last

about six months. Despite the cost, enthusiastic clients with rejuventated faces keep rushing back for more.

The Urban Retreat & Aveda Concept Salon

4TH FLOOR, HARVEY NICHOLS
67 BROMPTON RD, SW3, 020-7201 8610
Open Mon.-Fri. 9am-8pm, Sat. 9am-7pm, Sun.
noon-6pm.
U: Knightsbridge.

An air of harmony prevails in this tailor-made, Feng Shui-designed beauty salon, devised to take the stress out of urban living. All treatments are based on the principles of Ayurveda, an ancient Indian healing philosophy.

COSMETICS

Cosmetics à la Carte

19B MOTCOMBE ST, SW1, 020-7235 0596
WWW.A-LA-CARTE.CO.UK
E-MAIL: COSMETICS@A-LA-CARTE.CO.UK
Open Mon.-Sat. 10am-6pm.
U: Knightsbridge.

Christina Stewart and Lynne Sanders produce hypoallergenic products for use in the make-up diagnosis and lessons which take place at the shop from their own factory. Price for 30 minutes: Express Make-up (£30 rising to £100 for a full make-up lesson). For information about other branches or to order the mail order catalogue, telephone 020-7622 2318.

Dickins & Jones

REGENT ST, W1, 020-7734 7070
Open Mon.-Tues. & Fri.-Sat. 10am-6.30pm,
Wed. 10am-7pm, Thurs. 10am-8pm, Sun.
11am-5pm.
U: Oxford Circus.

Since undergoing a £3.5 million facelift, Dickins & Jones has expanded and updated its cosmetic hall, making it one of the most spacious and unrivalled in town. Alongside the cosmetic giants such as Clarins, Estée Lauder, Christian Dior and Chanel, you'll find newer and fresher faces such as Bobbi Brown, Jurlique and Aveda. Exclusive lines include T. LeClerc and Make Up For Ever. Also home to John Gustafsson and his team of experts in the Personal Beauty Studios (women on second floor, men on the ground floor) where they offer unbiased, impartial advice on the best cosmetics to suit your skin type, lifestyle and budget. The service is complimentary and operates on an appointment basis. Telephone 020-7287 4947.

Joan Price's Face Place

4 CHELSEA MANOR STUDIOS
FLOOD ST, SW3, 020-7352 8113
Open Mon.-Tues. 10am-6pm, Wed.-Fri. 10am-10.30pm, Sat. 10am-5pm.
U: Sloane Sq.

From model to beauty editor, Joan Price opened the first salon in 1967 to offer make-up sessions as one-on-one lessons rather that just applications of cosmetics. A one-hour lesson is £40. The salon stocks twenty brands in all price ranges. Clients can buy at the salon and as the staff is not on commission, recommendations are genuine. An informal, welcoming approach attracts everyone from teenagers to seniors. Judge for yourself: Joan Price did the make-up for Mrs. Thatcher's TV appearances.

Liberty Perfumery

210-220 REGENT ST, W1, 020-7734 1234
WWW.LIBERTY-OF-LONDON.COM
Open Mon.-Wed. & Fri.-Sat. 10am-6.30pm, Thurs. 10am-7.30pm, Sun. noon-6pm.
U: Oxford Circus.

No bouffant-haired, overly made-up consultants here, just a team of friendly and helpful staff members who are passionate about their products. The cosmetics area is small, but still manages to create an illusion of light and space thanks to careful design and the natural light streaming in from Great Marlborough Street. Representation veers towards the new and natural rather than old-fashioned and established with skincare companies such as E'Spa, Kiehls, Aveda, Aesop and Philosophy and colour cosmetics from Shu Uemura and Face Stockholm.

MAC

109 KING'S RD, SW3, 020-7534 9222
Open Mon.-Sat. 10.30am-6.30pm, Sun. noon-5pm.
U: Sloane Sq.

Devised and formulated by a professional make-up artist and used by a host of supermodels, the two London MAC outlets and their area in Harvey Nichols are very much in vogue with Kate Moss wannabes and make-up artists. The company, which is under the giant Estée Lauder umbrella, operates a recycling

service whereby tokens are issued for each returned container, and when you have collected six tokens, you receive a free product.

Also at 28 Foubert's Pl, W1, 020-7439 0501.

Mary Quant

3 IVES ST, SW3, 020-7581 1811
WWW.MARYQUANT.COM
Open Mon.-Sat. 10am-6pm.
U: Sloane Sq/South Kensington.

A great place to shop for funky make-up colours which include 101 lipsticks in shades ranging from white to deepest violet, 80 nail colours and 120 eye shadows which can be handpicked then housed in daisy print compacts. Reasonable prices make this a popular spot for teen-agers; the wild and wacky colours appeal to fashionable types.

Also at 7 Montpelier St, SW7, 020-7581 5181.

Molton Brown Studio

58 SOUTH MOLTON ST, W1, 020-7499 6474
WWW.MOLTONBROWN.COM
Open Mon.-Wed. & Fri.-Sat. 10am-6.30pm, Thurs. 10am-7pm.
U: Bond St.

For the past 25 years, Molton Brown has been offering the best in natural-based, British products. For the millennium, the original outlet has been redesigned and streamlined to represent a new concept in cosmetic selection. Customers are free to try the products at the user-friendly 'play stations', then wash their hands at the stylish Philippe Starck sinks.

Origins

51 KING'S RD, SW3, 020-7823 6715
Open Mon.-Tues. & Thurs.-Sat. 10am-6.30pm, Wed. 10am-7pm, Sun. noon-6pm.
U: Sloane Sq.

Indulge yourself and all of your senses in this wonderful store filled with gorgeous goodies for body and soul. There are aromatic products for the home, face, hair, body, baby, even your dog, together with colour cosmetics, massage tools, books and a giant gum-ball machine dispensing 'Peace of Mind' bubble gums for instant stress relief.

Screenface

24 POWIS TERRACE, W11, 020-7221 8289
Open Mon.-Sat. 9am-6pm.
U: Westbourne Park.

Those in the beauty business stock up here on the tools of their trade. Make-up artists and famous faces like Cher, supermodels Helena Christensen and Linda Evangelista are among those in the know seeking out professional plastic eyelash curlers, illuminiser foundation and make-up palettes and containers.

Also at 48 Monmouth St, WC2, 020-7836 3955 which has less focus on professional compacts and products.

Shu Uemura

UNIT 16, THOMAS NEAL CENTRE
29-41 EARLHAM ST, WC2, 020-7379 6627
Open Mon.-Sat. 10.30am-6.30pm, Sun. noon-5pm.
U: Covent Garden.

For professionals and novices alike, these Japanese colour and skincare products are among the best around. The colour cosmetics are excellent—there are shades to suit every conceivable skin tone. To cleanse, try the excellent cleansing beauty oil, which washes away every trace of make-up.

Space NK

45-47 BROOK ST, W1, 020-7355 1727
Open Mon.-Sat. 10am-6pm.
U: Bond St.

Founder Nicola Kinnaird makes frequent trips abroad to source new and exciting cosmetic brands to add to the Space NK counters. Labels include François Nars, Stila, E'Spa, Antonias Flowers, Laura Mercier and Eve Lom. The colour cosmetics are arranged in customer-friendly 'play stations' where shoppers can test out the ranges without obligation or intimidation. The helpful staff, who do not work on a commission basis, are trained make-up artists who are knowledgeable on all of the products. Mail-order service available for customers outside London, while those within central London can take advantage of the to-your-desk courier service.

Also at 7 Bishopsgate Arcade, 135 Bishopsgate, EC2, 020-7256 2303; 307 Kings Rd, SW3, 020-7351 7209; 307 Brompton Rd, 020-7589 8250; 73 St. John's Wood High St, NW8, 020-7586 0607. Their first spa outlet is at 127-131 Westbourne Grove, W2, 020-7727 8002.

HAIR SALONS

Charles Worthington

7 PERCY ST, W1, 020-7631 1370
Open Mon.-Sat. 8am-7pm.
U: Goodge St.

Charles Worthington's salons are every bit as glitzy as his ever-increasing celebrity client roster. Worthington, an award-winning stylist, is at the salon one day a week, but the waiting list for an appointment is several weeks.

Also at The Dorchester, Park Lane, W1, 020-7629 8888; 34 Great Queen St, WC2, 020-7831 5303; 1 Exchange Pl, The Broadgate Club, EC2, 020-7838 0802.

Jo Hansford

19 MOUNT ST, W1, 020-7495 7774
Open Tues.-Sat. 9am-6pm.
U: Bond St.

One of London's top colourists, Jo Hansford is held in high esteem by the fashion press and her glitzy clients such as Lauren Hutton, Patsy Kensit and Melanie Griffith. Colour with Jo from £125 for half-head, £175 full-head; highlights from £95.

John Frieda

75 NEW CAVENDISH ST, W1, 020-7636 1401
Open Mon.-Sat. 9am-5pm.
U: Oxford Circus.

One of the top names in hairdressing and erstwhile spouse of pop singer Lulu, John Frieda no longer cuts hair himself but has an expert team of stylists. A cut and blow-dry for ladies is from £45.

Also at Claridge's Hotel, Brook St, W1, 020 7499 3617; 4 Aldford St, W1, 020 7491 0840.

Mahogany

17 ST. GEORGE ST
OFF HANOVER SQ, W1, 020-7629 3121
Open Mon.-Tues. & Fri. 10am-6.15pm, Wed-Thurs. 10am-7.45pm, Sat. 10am-4.45pm.
U: Bond St.

Already well-established in Bath and Oxford, this hairdressing firm has branched out into the London scene and is fast establishing a reputation for stylish haircuts and a welcoming approach. A ladies' cut is £36-£65. The name is derived from the handsome mahogany timber floors and fittings.

Michael Van Clarke

1 BEAUMONT ST, W1, 020-7224 3123
Open Tues. & Fri.-Sat. 8.30am-5pm, Wed.
8.30am-8pm, Thurs. 8.30am-6.30pm.
U: Baker St/Regent's Park.

Have you ever been disappointed by the difference in the colour you receive in the salon and the one that greets you in your bathroom mirror? Well, you're not alone. For this reason, Michael Van Clarke has built a daylight colour studio in his smart London salon, which also offers a selection of super-shiny hair conditioning treatments. Book your appointment around breakfast, lunch or supper time, and the two in-house chefs will prepare you something from the menu.

Richard Ward

162B SLOANE ST, SW1, 020-7245 6151
Open Mon.-Sat. 9am-6pm.
U: Sloane Sq.

This luxurious, air-conditioned salon purporting to be one of the largest in London, draws a galaxy of stars like Pierce Brosnan and Joanna Lumley. Be assured that you will be given a haircut that suits rather than what is currently in fashion. As well as full hairdressing facilities, there is also a Thalgo spa institute, offering a full range of beauty treatments. Cut and finish starts from £45 with a junior stylist for women, and from £25 for men.

Nicky Clarke

130 MOUNT ST, W1, 020-7491 4700
Open Mon.-Wed. & Fri.-Sat. 9am-6pm, Thurs.
9am-8pm.
U: Bond St.

A celebrity in his own right, Nicky Clarke, he of the shoulder-length mane and figure-hugging leather trousers, has cut Fergie's hair as well as tending to the tresses of, amongst others, Cindy Crawford, Greta Scaatchi, Paloma Picasso and Queen Noor of Jordan. A ladies' cut and blow-dry for a first-time visit with Clarke is a staggering £300, with subsequent visits at £200. For men, the initial visit is £220, then £175. Despite the hefty prices, there is always a waiting list. If you can't bear the wait (or the damage to your wallet), try an appointment with one of the junior stylists starting at £45. Arezoo, the beauty therapist in the first-floor salon, offers excellent Cathiodermie facials, manicures and pedicures, with lots of TLC.

Vidal Sassoon

130 SLOANE ST, SW1, 020-7730 7288
Open Mon.-Tues. & Sat. 9am-6pm, Wed. 9am-
7pm, Thurs. 9am-6.45pm.
U: Sloane Sq.

The reputation of this internationally known hairdresser is based on the Sassoon philosophy of cutting hair to suit the bone structure of the face and the commercial success of the sixties 'bob'. Prices are £45-£70 for a cut and finish. Manicures and pedicures are available. **Salons throughout London.**

MEN'S GROOMING

Adams

12 ST. GEORGE ST, W1, 020-7499 9779
Open Mon.-Fri. 9am-8pm, Sat. 10am-6pm.
U: Bond St.

For cool males who want their surroundings to match, this ultra-slick barbershop is hard to beat. Co-owned by one of the hottest names on London's club circuit, Piers Adams, where else can you have your shoes shined, your clothes dry cleaned, surf the net, send an E-mail, watch television or play a computer game specially inserted in the arm of your chair whilst succumbing to a hair cut, head massage and wet shave? A range of treatments is available including the save-it-for-a-rainy-day 'Hangover Package'.

Austin Reed

103-113 REGENT ST, W1, 020-7734 6789
E-MAIL: BARBERSHOP@AUSTINREED.CO.UK
Open Mon.-Wed & Fri. 10am-6.pm, Thurs.
10am-6.30pm, Sat. 10am-12.30pm.
U: Piccadilly Circus.

Step back in time and luxuriate in the glorious Art Deco setting of this wonderful barbershop. Victor Cook and his team are experts in the art of shaving, so just sit back, relax and soak up the atmosphere.

Chelsea Barbers

THE COURTYARD, 250 KING'S RD, SW3
020-7352 6888
Open Mon.-Fri. 10am-7pm, Sat. 9am-7pm,
Sun. 11am-5pm.
U: Sloane Sq.

A celebrity in his own right, owner Daniel Rouah was championing men's grooming techniques way before it was cool for men to admit they wore moisturiser, let alone treated themselves to the odd facial. His latest venture has room for just two men at a time so you can expect unrivalled service and attention to detail. Choose from an expert haircut, a variety of facials, waxing, electrolysis or a lesson in the much ill-practised art of shaving, or why not go for the full works and succumb to one of the 'Total Male Make Over' packages. All clients are treated to a complimentary shoeshine.

Geo F Trumper

9 CURZON ST, W1, 020-7499 1850
Open Mon.-Fri. 9am-6pm, Sat. 9am-5pm.
U: Green Park/Hyde Park Corner.

The granddaddy of them all, Trumper has tended to more locks and fingertips than most male salons put together. The Curzon Street shop opened in 1875 and is lovingly maintained with dark wood panelling and display cases of their male fragrances and shaving requisites, reflecting the fact that founder, George Trumper, ran one of the first exclusive barbershops in London and was court hairdresser. Both shops still provide a barber's service in a soothing and pampered ambience with face massage and moustache curling. Additionally, men who require advice on shaving reserve a lesson with one of the experts (£35 for an hour). They have wonderful colognes and aftershaves. Besides razors, soaps, shampoos, loofahs and sponges, a superior range of leather gifts includes flasks and cup sets, plus clothes and bathroom brushes. Hair cuts from £24.

Also at 20 Jermyn St, SW1, 020 7734 1370.

Ian Matthews

28 MADDOX ST, W1, 020-7499 4904
Open Mon., Wed. & Fri. 9am-6pm, Tues. 9am-7pm, Thurs. 9am-8pm, Sat. 10am-5pm by appointment only.
U: Bond St.

A winning combination of old-fashioned service and new-age treatments makes this the barber of choice for a growing number of men, including many politicians. The shaves are about as close as you'll get without shedding skin; and the haircuts, face and head massages are reputed to be first-rate.

Men's Grooming Studio at Dickins & Jones

LOWER GROUND FLOOR, 224 REGENT ST, W1
020-7734 7070, 020-7734 9719
Open Mon., Tues. & Fri. 10am-6.30pm, Wed. 10am-7pm, Thurs. 10am-8pm, Sat. 9.30am-6.30pm.
U: Oxford Circus.

It's all very well knowing that you have to tend to your skin, but choosing the correct products is where the nightmare starts. With this is mind, the brilliant team at Dickins & Jones have set up the Men's Grooming Studio where customers can receive expert, unbiased, and best of all, complimentary advice and tips on all aspects of skincare and grooming. The specially designed studio is conveniently located close to the Men's Personal Shopping Suite on the ground floor and features a consultation room and treatment room, complete with shower. Treatments available include facials, massage, manicures, pedicures, waxing and electrolysis.

Men's Salon at Selfridges

1ST FLOOR, 400 OXFORD ST, W1
020-7629 1234, 020-7318 3709
Open Mon.-Wed. 10am-7pm, Thurs.-Fri. 10am-8pm, Sat. 9.30am-7pm, Sun. noon-6pm.
U: Marble Arch.

Selfridges opened its men-only salon in November 1988, and along with all the establishments mentioned here, business is booming. The salon offers a mix of traditional and modern grooming techniques, ranging from a simple cut and blow dry, to the increasingly popular non-surgical facelift. Tailored grooming packages are also available. Why not try 'The Relaxer', a deep-cleansing steam facial, back and shoulder massage, manicure, scalp massage, shampoo and blow-dry starting at a reasonable £85.

The Refinery

60 BROOK ST, W1, 020-7409 2001
Open Mon.-Tues. 8am-7pm, Wed.-Fri. 8am-9pm, Sat. 8am-6pm.
U: Bond St.

The men's grooming sector is the fastest growing beauty market in the world, therefore it should come as no surprise to find that the first male-only spa has opened bang in the heart of London. Befitting its Mayfair location, The Refinery offers grooming services including face and body treatments, haircare and a comprehensive range of retail products. The club lounge offers an exclusive relaxing environment in which to unwind with Internet, E-mail and financial market access, as well as a quality snack menu and a selection of alcoholic and non-alcholic drinks. For those who are short of time, try the 15-minute Pit Stop treatments, but make sure you go back to try out one of the excellent spa days. Clothes pressing and shoe shine service available. There are nine hair-cutting stations fitted with computer consoles.

NAIL BARS

Nail bars are big business in the U.S., with one perched on almost every street corner. We Brits have been a little slower catching on to the trend, but now, with a handful of businesses which opened up last year, this looks set to change.

Nails Inc.

1ST FLOOR, DKNY, 27 OLD BOND ST, W1
020-7592 0145
Open Mon.-Sat. 10am-6pm.
U: Bond St/Green Park.
A ten-step manicure programme which aims to become a weekly necessity. £7 for 15-minute manicure; £15 for 25-minute pedicure; nail art £5 per nail.

The Nail Bar

37 MADDOX ST, W1, 020-7499 5898
Open Mon.-Wed. & Fri. 10am-7pm, Thurs. 10am-8pm.
U: Oxford Circus.
This bright pink-and-white salon has already earned a name for itself for its excellent manicures and pedicures. Organic juices are available and the customers just keep coming back for more. £15 for a 30-minute manicure; £22.50 for 40-minute pedicure; £9.50 for 15-minute reshape and revarnish.

The Nail Spa at F2

42 SHORTS GDNS, WC2, 020-7836 3192
Open Mon.-Sat. 10am-7pm.
U: Covent Garden.
Appointments are required for a manicure in this environmentally friendly salon. All the colours used are toluene- and formaldehyde-free so it's the perfect option for those who

want to lead as natural a life as possible. £15 for a 20-minute 'Rapido' manicure; £18 for a 45-minute holistic manicure; £25 for a 30-minute pedicure.

New York Nail Company

17 SOUTH MOLTON ST, W1, 020-7409 3332
Open Mon.-Sat. 10am-8pm.
U: Bond St.
Look out for this new nail company which aims to have a chain of salons sprouting over the next year. A training consultant from New York is on board to offer advice on fast and efficient service. If your manicure chips within five days, you're entitled to a revarnish. From £12.50 for a 30-minute manicure.
Also at 5 Upper James St, W1, 020-7659 4450; 21 Kensington High St, W8, 020-7938 3456.

SCENTS, SOAPS & TOILETRIES

Aveda Institute

28-29 MARYLEBONE HIGH ST, W1, 020-7224 3157
U: Baker St.
Settling nicely into the cool, laid-back Marylebone High Street vibe, the Aveda Institute offers two floors of eco-chic products. The ground floor is a showcase for the 1,000 or so Aveda products, which are thoughtfully divided into Self Select and Inter-Active shopping areas. Then there's Love, a lip-smacking organic restaurant, inspired bouquets from Parterre, and a range of first-class organic dietary supplements from Intelligent Nutrients. The lower floor is devoted to hair, skincare and make-up education, primarily aimed at professionals, but there are also consumer workshops on a regular basis—just ask for details.

L'Artisan Parfumeur

17 CALE ST, SW3, 020-7352 4196
Open Mon.-Fri. 10am-1pm, 2pm-6pm, Sat. 10am-5.30pm.
U: South Kensington.
There are several branches of this delightful perfumery in France but only one in Britain. L'Artisan sniffs out the scent to suit you. It's a little boutique where the art of fragrance is taken seriously and in addition to romantic potions, pot pourri and scented Gris Gris, you will be tempted by modern versions such as the French Dressing bath set including Bath Salts, Vinegar Tonic and Bath Oil.

Surprisingly, the precious bottles cost no more than a brand name, a 50 ml. bottle is £33.50.

The Body Shop

268 OXFORD ST, W1, 020-7629 9365
WWW.THE-BODY-SHOP.COM
Open Mon.-Wed. & Fri. 9.30am-7.30pm,
Thurs. 9.30am-8.30pm, Sun. 11am-6pm.
U: Oxford Circus.

Responsible for bringing affordable, environmentally friendly beauty products to the masses, this international chain, devised and set up by Anita Roddick, now has a prime position on most High Streets. The shops are filled with everyone from teen-agers seeking out the latest shade of lipstick, to grandmothers stocking up on jojoba shampoo, and young men buying skincare and shaving products from the hugely successful Mostly Men range. Besides a wide range of scents, cosmetics and grooming products, the Endangered Species range includes brightly coloured animal-shaped soaps and bath beads and is aimed at children. Basket assortments are popular presents.

Branches throughout London.

Crabtree & Evelyn

30 JAMES ST, WC2, 020-7379 0964
Open Mon.-Sat. 10am-8pm, Sun. noon-6pm.
U: Covent Garden.

Crabtree & Evelyn appeals to two distinct customers. The first is the loyalist who seeks out the prettily packaged hand and body lotions, soaps and bath products, homely preserves, vinegars and teas. The second is the more recent convert who has been seduced by the excellent aromatherapy products including oils, room fragrances, incense sticks and convenient bottles of pick-me-up oils to stroke on to pulse points. For both camps, Crabtree & Evelyn offers a wonderful and innovative selection of gift ideas, including the Cook's and Gardener's ranges.

The Crown Perfumery

51 BURLINGTON ARCADE, W1, 020-7408 0088
Open Mon.-Sat. 9.30am-5.30pm.
U: Green Park/Piccadilly Circus.

After extensive research, Barry Gibson has recreated the perfumes which British and European society enjoyed at the turn of the century, and has also revived the name of the firm which made the scents which include Sandringham and Tanglewood Bouquet.

Prices start from £30, although the Marechale brand, bottled in a limited edition Baccarat crystal bottle, will set you back £480. Soaps are modestly priced at £7.50-£13.50.

Culpeper

21 BRUTON ST, W1, 020-7629 4559
Open Mon.-Fri. 9.30am-6pm, Sat. 10am-5pm.
U: Bond St.

Aromatic food products add extra interest to these herbalist shops which have followed a 'green policy' since the company was founded in 1927. Sachets of curry powder, jars of ginger and spicy Major Grey's mango chutney tempt the palate and aromatherapy oils boxed in an attractive starter set lift the soul. There are also books, herb-filled pillows, prettily covered hot water bottles, 'make your own' potpourri, scented candles and aroma oil burners to enhance the home. Nutmeg graters, honey and ginger juice cordial and mulled wine spices are also available to liven up the larder.

Also at 8 The Market, Covent Garden, WC2, 020-7379 6698;

Czech & Speake

39C JERMYN ST, W1, 020-7439 0216
Open Mon. & Wed.-Fri. 9.30am-6pm, Tues.
10am-6pm, Sat. 10am-5pm.
U: Green Park/Piccadilly Circus.

Besides exotic bath oils of frankincense and myrrh, bathroom fittings designed to make even lavatory roll and brush holders look elegant are the showpieces of these smart little shops. A wall-mounted ivory-coloured porcelain lavatory-brush and holder with chrome finish costs about £195+VAT.

Also at 125 Fulham Rd, SW3, 020-7225 3667.

Floris

89 JERMYN ST, SW1, 020-7930 2885
Open Mon.-Fri. 9.30am-6pm, Sat. 10am-5pm.
U: Green Park/Piccadilly Circus.

Commissions to blend fragrances for the Queen and the Prince of Wales are all in a day's work for the Bodenham family, perfumiers for eight generations and direct descendants of a Spaniard, Juan Famenias Floris, who first set out his sign here in 1730. Now known for their English flower scents, such as rose, and lily of the valley, the shop sells old-fashioned perfume bottles with silk bulbs and tassels as well as crystal and cut-glass pot-pourri bowls, alabaster soap dishes and tortoiseshell combs.

D R Harris & Co

29 ST. JAMES'S ST, SW1, 020-7930 3915
Open Mon.-Fri. 8.30am-6pm, Sat. 9.30am-5pm.
U: Green Park.

The original 'Pick-Me-Up' specially devised by Victorian proprietor Daniel Rotely Harris is still sold (from £5.95). No doubt it always did well here since it is located near the gentlemen's clubs. This small shop offers lots of choices, such as cucumber and rose cream for facial care, the Arlington line of men's cologne, and shaving creams and soaps, plus Bewitch silky bath essence. It is a chemist shop where prescriptions can be filled, and thus adheres to the original purpose of the shop, which was co-founded in 1790 by a surgeon and one of the first pharmaceutical chemists.

Immaculate House

4-5 BURLINGTON ARCADE, W1, 020-7499 5788
Open Mon.-Sat. 10am-6pm.
U: Green Park/Oxford Circus.

A newcomer to Burlington Arcade, taking over two shops and adding a real zing to this venerable shopping area. Cakes of pure handmade soap adorn the windows, exciting looking jars are on the shelves inside. You can buy the soap by weight, or cut and packaged with other deliciously sensuous items. They use essential oils in scenting and natural food grade ingredients for colouring and texture. They also make their own toiletries and stock a range of French porcelain bathroom accessories, robes and pillows.

Jo Malone

150 SLOANE ST, SW3, 020-7581 1101
WWW.JOMALONE.CO.UK
Open Mon.-Tues. & Sat. 10am-6pm, Thurs.-Fri. 10am-7pm.
U: Sloane Sq.

London's queen of scent and skincare gets a new, super-chic address amidst some of the most covetable names in fashion. The classic elements originally in the Walton Street store are all here, together with a new technological edge to take the business into the new millennium. Sample the Jo Malone scents in one of the Fragrance Booths, where one touch of a button allows you to experience the scents in a pure-air environment. At the Skin Care Bar, you receive product information, demonstrations, or you can just drop by for a cleanse and tone or a fragrant arm massage. All the wonderful products, including delicious scented candles, linen sprays and skincare, are here. If you can't make it to the shop, the Send-A-Scent service on 020-7720 0202 will wrap your gift in signature cream and black, arriving at the recipient's door cushioned in lime-scented straw.

Also at 24 Royal Exchange, EC4, 020 7720 0202.

Lush

11 THE MARKET, THE PIAZZA
COVENT GARDEN, WC2, 020-7240 4570
Open Mon.-Sat. 10am-7pm, Sun. noon-6pm.
U: Covent Garden.

At first glance, Lush looks like a thriving delicatessen. Look a little closer at the packages in the chill cabinets and you'll find that they are in fact natural beauty products with edible-sounding names like Aroma Bread face mask, made from brown bread and garlic. Soaps can be bought by the chunk, similar to cheese, so you can buy as much or as little as you want. Customers serve themselves, scooping up the lotions and potions stored in the refrigerator into little tubs. Just like a deli, most products are labeled with a sell-by date as the company uses virtually no preservatives. New for 2000 are the ultra-fresh products neatly packaged in fruit and vegetable skins like orange, tomatoes and cucumbers.

Also at 123 King's Rd, SW3, 020-7376 8348; 40 Carnaby St, W1, 020-7287 5874.

Neal's Yard Remedies

2 NEAL'S YARD, WC2, 020-7379 7222
Open Mon. 10am-6pm, Tues.-Fri. 10am-7pm, Sat. 10am-5.30pm, Sun. 11am-5pm.
U: Covent Garden.

The striking deep-blue glass bottles, filled with shampoos, bath oils and ready-made lotions gleam on the shelves in the subdued lighting of this popular shop. The staff is kept busy measuring herbs, seeds, powders and leaves from giant glass jars for aficionados of natural remedies. To help decide what preparations can be used to cure which ailments, there is a shelf of relevant books to consult. Information on courses about herbalism, essential oils and homeopathy are on display.

Penhaligon's

18 BEAUCHAMP PL, SW3 020-7584 4008
WWW.PENHALIGONS.CO.UK
Open Mon.-Sat. 10am-6pm.
U: Knightsbridge.

The new, light and airy flagship is unlike any other Penhaligon's outfit. Unlike the prettily outfitted shops we all know and love, such as the Victorian-style interior of the Covent Garden premises or the tiny glass-roofed Mayfair shop, this streamlined version leads the company straight into the twenty-first century. The fragrances are still hand-blended to rediscovered recipes of William Penhaligon, court barber and perfumier extraordinaire in Queen Victoria's reign. The oldest, Hamman Bouquet, was created in 1872. Its exotic name and scent, including jasmine, lavender, rose and sandalwood was inspired by the Turkish baths situated next to his original shop. Antique perfume bottles and silver table accessories add to Penhaligon's charm. However, there are newer additions, such as the sleek, extremely well-priced leather wallets, make-up bags, jewelry rolls and vanity cases in delicious colours such as lipstick red, violet and yellow. You'll also find one of Britain's leading skincare experts, Janet Filderman, offering wonderful facials and her own skincare line in the Beauchamp Place store.

Also at 41 Wellington St, WC2, 020 7836 2150; 20a Brook St, W1, 020 7493 0002; 16 Burlington Arcade, Piccadilly, W1, 020 7629 1416; Royal Exchange, Cornhill, EC3, 020 7283 0711.

Les Senteurs Specialist Perfumery

227 EBURY ST, SW1, 020-7730 2322
Open Mon.-Sat. 10am-6pm.
U: Victoria.

VIP treatment is the norm at this sensually bedecked shop which stocks imported, independent, French and Italian brands. The proprietor, Karin Hawksley, takes time matching fragrances to a client's skin, which entails trying fragrances—whether flowery or pungent—on sample cards first. There are also lovely room fragrances and bath and beauty solutions. Prices for Eau de Toilette start at £15.95.

Zarvis

281 PORTOBELLO
4 PORTOBELLO GREEN, W10, 020-8968 5435
Open Wed. & Sat. 11am-5pm.
U: Ladbroke Grove/Westbourne Park.

This is a beautiful place to seek out more than 120 medicinal cosmetic herbs sold by the ounce, and a popular line of bath herbs and oils.

BOOKS

ARTS

A Zwemmer Arts Bookshop

24 LICHFIELD ST, WC2, 020-7240 4158
Open Mon.-Fri. 10am-6.30pm, Sat. 10am-6pm.
U: Leicester Sq.

Three floors are filled with books on artists and every facet of the visual arts with in-depth coverage of medieval, Oriental, twentieth-century art and art history. In the basement, shelves are packed with books on architecture and the decorative arts such as ceramics, fashion, textiles and other crafts. The sister shop at 80 Charing Cross Road, WC2, 020-7240 4157, specialises in media arts, stocking books on film, photography and graphic design.

Atrium

5 CORK ST, W1, 020-7495 0073
Open Mon.-Fri. 10am-6pm, Sat. 10am-4pm.
U: Piccadilly Circus.

This welcoming art book shop has a press book of current reviews to browse through on the new publications table. The shelves hold a comprehensive selection of books on photography, architecture, textiles and costume, sculpture, gardens, old masters, stained glass, Islamic and Indian art, Latin American arts, travel, interior design, icons and many other subjects. There are foreign language editions and many exhibition catalogues, and the staff takes a genuine interest in tracking down books. Events, festivals, readings and other events on the subject of literature and books take place regularly.

BBC Shop
Broadcasting House
PORTLAND PL, W1, 020-7765 0025
Open daily 9.30am-6pm.
U: Oxford Circus.

An outlet for all the BBC publications, tapes, videos and books, cards and posters, this is smaller than the spacious BBC World Service Shop, but jam-packed with the corporation's products which include coffee-table books on some of the most popular series and historical programmes.

BBC World Service Shop
BUSH HOUSE, STRAND, WC2, 020-7257 2576
Open Mon.-Sat. 9.30am-6pm.
U: Aldwych.

Shows broadcasted on the 'Beeb', as it is sometimes affectionately called, whether radio or TV, often produce a publication about the programme, the cast and compilations of favourite scripts. The shop started as an information centre for its million of listeners worldwide. There are videos, cassettes and CDs of some nostalgically remembered shows and current popular programmes, as well as short-wave radios.

Cinema Bookshop
13-14 GREAT RUSSELL ST, WC2, 020-7637 0206
Open Mon.-Sat. 10.30am-5.30pm.
U: Tottenham Court Rd.

The largest cinema book shop in Britain covers all aspects, catering for everyone from established cinematographers to students. It has biographies and technical books plus a good stock of ephemera, posters, photos and out-of-print books.

Dance Books
15 CECIL CT, WC2, 020-7836 2314
Open Mon.-Sat. 11am-7pm.
U: Leicester Sq.

Founded by a former Ballet Rambert dancer, this shop has books on all types of dance and human movement, plus videos, posters and prints, some of which decorate the walls.

French's Theatre Bookshop
52 FITZROY ST, W1, 020-7387 9373
Open Mon.-Fri. 9.30am-5.30pm, Sat. 11am-5pm.
U: Goodge St.

This firm, which has published plays since 1830, stocks more than 4,000 titles in well-assembled order. There are reading and acting versions of plays. It has a reference collection of sound effects and dialect recordings to help producers, playwrights and actors. There are also a few thousand books on the theatre.

National Portrait Gallery Shop
ST. MARTIN'S PL, WC2, 020-7306 0055
Open Mon.-Sat. 10am-6pm, Sun. noon-6pm.
U: Charing Cross/Leicester Sq.

Attached to the National Portrait Gallery, the store also boasts an extensive book shop, which is strong not only on books about art and related subjects, but also on biographies and critical appraisals of the people depicted in the gallery. Books by authors and painters are also included.

Royal Institute of British Architects
66 PORTLAND PL, W1, 020-7580 5533
Open Mon.-Fri. 9.30am-5.30pm, Sat. 10am-5pm.
U: Oxford Circus.

The RIBA, as it is known, has an excellent specialist book shop which includes foreign publications (020-7251 0791) for anyone interested in architecture, and (serious) landscape gardening in the context of the surrounding architecture. If you're in the building, take in the exhibitions which are often on show. There is also an excellent Pâtisserie Valerie café located here.

Victoria & Albert Museum Shop
CROMWELL RD, SW7, 020-7938 8500
Open daily 10am-5.30pm.
U: South Kensington.

Appealing range of art books in the V&A shop. Subjects include architecture, fashion design, pottery and general crafts.

Waterstone's Arts Bookshop
8 LONG ACRE, WC2, 020-7836 1359
Open Mon.-Sat. 9.30am-10pm, Sun. noon-7pm.
U: Covent Garden.

Housing a wonderful collection of art books and a huge range of fashion and art magazines, this bustling shop is a brilliant source for art books old and new.

CHILDREN

Children's Book Centre

237 KENSINGTON HIGH ST, W8, 020-7937 7497
WWW.CHILDRENSBOOKCENTRE.CO.UK
Open Mon.-Sat. 9.30am-6.30pm, Sun. noon-6pm.
U: High St Kensington.

This bright, well-organised shop with over 12,000 books thoughtfully arranged by age and subject, is usually full of children, sometimes sprawled on the floor, perusing a book or watching the latest video. It stocks a wide choice of fiction and educational books for young children as well as cuddly bears and toys by Galt, Fisher Price and Lego. Suitable for babies to teen-agers.

Daisy & Tom

181 KING'S RD, SW3, 020-7352 5000
Open Mon.-Tues. & Thurs.-Sat. 10am-6pm,
Wed. 10am-7pm, Sun. noon-6pm.
U: Sloane Sq.

The spacious, galleried book shop is the ideal environment to shop for children's books with or without the kids. The atmosphere is calming, the selection of books is extensive, and there's also a good selection of reference and audio material.

COMICS

Forbidden Planet

71 NEW OXFORD ST, WC1, 020-7836 4179
Open Mon.-Tues. & Sat. 10am-6pm, Thurs.-Fri. 10am-7pm.
U: Tottenham Court Rd.

This is one of London's largest stockers of comics and cartoons. Nobody has counted the selection, but the description is 'two full floors'. Forbidden Planet also sells novels and spin-offs from popular comics: models, T-shirts and memorabilia and there is a wide selection of videos.

COOKING & FOOD

Books for Cooks

4 BLEINHEIM CRESCENT, W11, 020-7221 1992
Open Mon.-Sat. 9.30am-6pm.
U: Ladbroke Grove.

There is a little café at the back of the shop. Cooking demonstrations by cooks/authors take place upstairs in the evening (£20 including a meal). Booking is essential. The shop is notable for its exhaustive selection of food and wine books and is one of the best in the country. From simple cookbooks to exotic cuisine, this shop is a must for anyone interested in the art of food.

CRIME

Murder One

71-73 CHARING CROSS RD, WC2, 020-7734 3483
Open Mon.-Wed. 10am-7pm, Thurs.-Sat. 10am-8pm.
U: Leicester Sq.

A huge stock of books covers crime and mystery, romantic fiction and science fiction. Many books are British, but there's a large selection from the U.S., too.

ECONOMICS & POLITICS

The Economist Shop

5 REGENT ST, SW1, 020-7839 1937
Open Mon.-Fri. 10am-6pm, Sat. 10am-5pm.
U: Piccadilly Circus.

Behind the handsome façade, this efficiently run shop stocks books on important issues in world affairs, especially in the economic, political and social fields. Countries and continents are divided into their own sections. The shop has their own range of publications that include titles such as the Economist Dictionary of International Finance.

Politico's

8 ARTILLERY ROW, SW1, 020-7828 0010
Open Mon.-Fri. 9am-5.30pm, Sat. 10am-5pm.
U: St. James's Park/Victoria.

Ian Dale used to be a political lobbyist, now while running the hugely popular Politico's, he's also writing books. Every book on every political party/movement is here, plus the history of politics, with a good secondhand section. There's also an excellent selection of funny postcards and a selection of unique gifts. A small café on the first floor gives refreshment to customers, many of whom are politicians or civil servants from the nearby government offices.

ESOTERICA

Mysteries New Age Centre

9-11 MONMOUTH ST, WC2, 020-7240 3688
Open Mon.-Sat. 10am-6pm.
U: Covent Garden.

A mystical purple façade sets the offbeat mood of this pyschic and new-age book shop which sells tarot cards, crystal balls, incense, pendulums and other devices for exploring the secrets of the universe. Tarot readings are available (from £20).

Skoob Two

17 SICILIAN AVE, WC1, 020-7405 0030
Open Mon.-Sat. 10.30am-6.30pm.
U: Tottenham Court Rd.

Part of Skoob, this shop specialises in new-age books, books on the occult, and subjects like Greek and Latin, archeology and ancient religions.

Watkins Books

19 CECIL CT, WC2, 020-7836 2182
Open Mon.-Wed. & Fri. 10am-6pm, Thurs. 10.30am-8pm, Sat. 10.30am-6pm.
U: Leicester Sq.

In this large modern shop, you'll find the widest range of books on esoteric themes to do with new-age philosophies: holistic health, Eastern religions and subjects connected with natural health therapies.

FASHION

R D Franks

KENT HOUSE, MARKET PL, W1, 020-7636 1244
E-MAIL: R.D.FRANKS@BTINTERNET.COM
Open Mon.-Fri. 9am-5pm.
U: Oxford Circus.

This well-stocked book shop is ideally located for designers in the rag trade and students at the nearby London College of Fashion and Central St. Martin's School of Art. The shelves are packed with books on everything to do with the fashion industry, including designers' biographies, encyclopedias and fashion illustration. All the major international fashion magazines such as Harper's Bazaar, Allure, Donna and every issue of Vogue are represented here along with the bumper seasonal fabric and trend reports from all the fashion capitals.

FEMINIST

Silver Moon Women's Bookshop

68 CHARING CROSS RD, WC2, 020-7836 7906
Open Mon.-Sat. 10am-6.30pm, Sun. 2pm-6pm.
U: Leicester Sq.

All Virago's titles are stocked here, along with books relating to women's issues from women's rights to giving birth. They hold regular readings; consult the listings magazines or telephone for details.

GARDENING

Garden Books

11 BLENHEIM CRESCENT, W11, 020-7792 0777
Open Mon.-Sat. 9am-6pm.
U: Notting Hill Gate.

Delightful book shop with wonderfully well informed owners who will guide you through the stock with pleasure. Books on gardening, and related subjects covering interior design and architecture. Mail-order available.

GAY

Gay's the Word

66 MARCHMONT ST, WC1, 020-7278 7654
Open Mon.-Sat. 10am-6.30pm, Sun. 2pm-6pm.
U: Russell Sq.

A well-stocked shop covering all aspects of gay life, including sexuality, living with AIDS, and general information and advice. Occasional author readings are held; telephone for details.

GENERAL INTEREST

Blackwell's

100 CHARING CROSS RD, WC2, 020-7292 5100
Open Mon.-Sat. 9.30am-8.30pm, Sun. noon-6pm.
U: Leicester Sq.

Originally set up in Oxford, this renowned company has moved to London's famous book shop street. The large store premises stocks 50,000 titles and although Blackwell's is strong on academic subjects such as economics, history, computing, social science, psychology, architecture, archeology and busi-

ness, it has a good general-interest section for fiction, biographies and travel.
Branches throughout London.

Books Etc.
421 OXFORD ST, W1, 020-7495 5850
Open Mon.-Tues. & Sat. 9.30am-8pm, Thurs.-Fri. 9.30am-8.30pm, Sun. noon-6pm.
U: Tottenham Court Rd.

Well-stocked and organised, this popular chain, particularly good for discounted and discontinued lines, was founded in 1981 and is now found throughout London.

Borders Books & Music
203-207 OXFORD ST, W1, 020-7292 1600
Open Mon.-Sat. 8am-11pm, Sun. noon-6pm.
U: Oxford Circus.

Working on the premise that shopping for books should be a positive pleasure, the Borders chain has arrived in Britain and encouraged a new breed of bookworm. It has to be said that many of them are shopping for partners as well as the latest novel, thanks to the laid-back atmosphere, comfy seats and late operating hours. For the serious shopper, there are 150,000 books, 50,000 CDs and music tapes and 5,000 videos, plus a huge selection of newspapers and magazines and Paperchase, an in-house stationers. Regular readings and events, a café where you can sample the pages of your book whilst sipping a leisurely cappuccino, make this one of the busiest book shops in town.

Also at 20 Charing Cross Rd, WC2, 020-7379 8877.

W & G Foyle
113-119 CHARING CROSS RD, WC2, 020-7437 5660
Open Mon.-Wed. & Fri.-Sat. 9am-6pm, Thurs. 9am-7pm.
U: Leicester Sq.

This giant, old-fashioned shop with its countless corridors and heavily laden shelves and tabletops is probably London's most famous bookseller, an old-fashioned place, constantly bustling with browsers overwhelmed with choice. Fiction is confusingly displayed by the publisher. It has become a running joke that the store definitely has the book you want somewhere, but can't necessarily find it.

Hatchards
187 PICCADILLY, W1, 020-7439 9921
Open Mon., Wed.-Fri. 9 am-6pm, Tues. & Sat. 9.30am-6pm, Sun. noon-6pm.
U: Piccadilly Circus.

Now part of the Dillons chain, Hatchards is still the book shop with cachet. This is the place where discerning readers while away their time browsing in the genteel, carpeted rooms. It has three Royal Warrants on display and traditionally sends a selection of books for royal summer holiday reading. There are five floors of books on general subjects with the latest hardbacks by the entrance.

John Sandoe
10 BLACKLANDS TERR, SW3, 020-7589 9473
Open Mon.-Tues. & Thurs.-Sat. 9.30am-5.30pm, Wed. 9.30am-7.30pm.
U: Sloane Sq.

Locals speak with real affection about this shop, just off the King's Road near Sloane Square. Sandoe's is particularly strong on literature and the arts, but, along with the latest hard covers also stocks lots of paperbacks of fiction, poetry and classics.

W H Smith & Son
36 SLOANE SQ, SW1, 020-7730 0351
Open Mon.-Sat. 8.30am-7pm, Sun. 11am-5pm.
U: Sloane Sq.

One of the longest established newsagents and booksellers in Britain, W H Smith & Son continues to act as a good general book shop, with an emphasis on fiction and travel. Many of their shops concentrate on stationery or computer supplies, but they remain one of the most reliable sources for newspapers and magazines as well as books.

Branches throughout London and well-represented at mainline train stations and airports.

Talking Bookshop
11 WIGMORE ST, W1, 020-7491 4117
Open Mon.-Fri. 9.30am-5.30pm, Sat. 10am-5pm.
U: Bond St.

This smart, modern shop covering everything from Shakespeare to Dame Edna Everage's *Memoirs*, stocks Britain's largest selection of spoken-word CDs and cassettes, including unabridged versions of fiction, biography and drama. There is also a small French selection.

Waterstone's

82 GOWER ST, WC1, 020-7636 1577
Open Mon.-Wed. & Fri. 9.30am-8pm, Tues.
10am-8pm, Sat. 9.30am-7pm, Sun. 11am-5pm.
U: Euston Sq.

This store is huge and since it is in the midst of London University, it has a strong academic section. It is housed in a Victorian building with a fantastically decorated façade. Some of the branches specialise, like Waterstone's Arts Bookshop.

Waterstone's

203-206 PICCADILLY, W1, 020-7851 2400
Open Mon.-Sat. 8.30am-11pm, Sun. noon-6pm.
U: Piccadilly Circus.

The new Waterstone's flagship store in the former Simpsons of Piccadilly site is the largest bookstore in Europe. This colossal branch of Waterstone's stocks over 265,000 titles and a million and a half books, which laid end-to-end would stretch from Piccadilly Circus to the Hook of Holland. There are four restaurants ranging from the smart Red Room on the lower ground floor (see *Restaurants*), through to the buzzing News Café also on the lower ground floor. The Creative Juice Bar in the children's department on the second floor offers something for the health-conscious and the Studio Lounge bar is a smart place to drop by for an after-work drink (see *Quick Bites*). The store also offers twelve Internet stations, a small gift shop, magazine and newspaper department, personal shopping, regular events, exhibitions and art spaces, and private meeting and dining rooms.
Branches throughout London.

Waterstone's at Harrods

HARRODS, KNIGHTSBRIDGE, SW1, 020-7730 1234
Open Mon.-Tues. & Sat. 10am-6pm, Wed.-Fri.
10am-7pm.
U: Knightsbridge.

As expected in a department store of such calibre, Harrods has a well-stocked book shop, managed by Waterstones with the same keen enthusiasm which characterises this chain's many branches nationwide. There is a strong emphasis on literary book launches and a good selection of finely bound and printed books. The department occupies about an eighth of the second floor, with a well-stocked magazine and periodicals area next to it.

LANGUAGES

European Bookshop

5 WARWICK ST, W1, 020-7734 5259
Open Mon.-Sat. 9.30am-6pm.
U: Oxford Circus/Piccadilly Circus.

As the name implies, this shop specialises in European books. The emphasis is on French, German, Spanish, Italian, Portuguese and Scandinavian books, plus books on English as a foreign language. There are also many language course books and learning materials.

Grant & Cutler

55-57 GREAT MARLBOROUGH ST, W1
020-7734 2012
Open Mon.-Wed. & Fri.-Sat. 9am-5.30pm,
Thurs. 9am-7pm.
U: Oxford Circus.

This impressively stocked language book shop has publications in languages you may never even have heard of, ranging from Afrikaans and Albanian to Yoruba and Zulu. For mainstream languages, there are learn-at-your-leisure language cassettes and videos as well as handy tourist travel packs of essential phrases. You can also find literature, drama and poetry in the original languages and sometimes in English translation. There are also some videos of popular cinema releases in foreign languages.

SECOND-HAND

Skoob Books

11A-17 SICILIAN AVE
SOUTHAMPTON ROW, WC1, 020-7404 3063
Open Mon.-Sat. 10.30am-6.30pm.
U: Tottenham Court Rd.

The largest secondhand book shop in London, with around 50,000 titles always in stock. Although essentially Skoob is a second-hand book shop, it also specialises in up-to-date academic books and is the only specialist in scientific and technical titles. There is also a small antiquarian department and a host of other titles. Although slightly shabby, this is a great shop for browsing in a truly serendipitous manner.

SPORTS

Sportspages

CAXTON WALK, 94-96 CHARING CROSS RD, WC2
020-7240 9604
Open Mon.-Sat. 9.30am-7pm.
U: Leicester Sq.

'The book shop that takes sport seriously' runs the slogan for this specialist shop with a selection of 8,000 international titles. If it's not here, it isn't a recognised sport, as this shop has books, magazines and videos for all sports' enthusiasts (with the exception of chess, board and card games). Titles cover all aspects from training to tactics, from biographies to medical studies.

TRAVEL

Daunt Books for Travellers

83 MARYLEBONE HIGH ST, W1, 020-7224 2295
Open Mon.-Sat. 9am-7.30pm, Sun. 11am-6pm.
U: Baker St/Bond St.

This delightful, airy shop laid out on three floors carries a vast and varied stock of 25,000 travel books. Upstairs is devoted to the British Isles, while the ground floor concentrates on Europe; and for books on the rest of the world, look no further than downstairs. According to James Daunt, the owner, they file books the way people read them, so sitting alongside the Cuban shelves, you'll find the latest book on Caribbean communism and Graham Greene's *Our Man in Havana*. They also have large stockrooms, so if you're after a particular title not displayed on the shelves, the chances are it might be stacked away.

Also at 196 Haverstock Hill, NW3, 020-7794 4006.

Stanford

12-14 LONG ACRE, WC2, 020-7836 1321
Open Mon.-Sat. 9am-7.30pm, Sun. 10am-7pm.
U: Covent Garden/Leicester Sq.

A travel specialist, this shop has a large ground floor devoted to books and guides to international destinations. Books on Britain and a well-organised department of maps, including the Ordnance Survey series, for which this shop is justly famous are downstairs.

Also at 52 Grosvenor Gdns, SW1, 020-7730 1314, and in the British Airways Shop, 156 Regent St, W1, 020-7434 4744.

The Travel Book Shop

13 BLENHEIM CRESCENT, W11, 020-7229 5260
Open Mon.-Sat. 10am-6pm.
U: Ladbroke Grove.

The shelves of this small, interesting shop are jam-packed with travel books to take your mind off the British weather. They stock the usual quota of guides, plus some rare books kept locked up. For a small fee, the staff will try to trace any title. This is a real enthusiast's shop.

CHILDREN

Some womens wear chains like Next, Monsoon, Jigsaw, Laura Ashley and French Connection also stock very good children's lines.

CLOTHING & SHOES

Anthea Moore Eade

16 VICTORIA GROVE, SW3, 020-7584 8826
Open Mon.-Sat. 10am-6pm.
U: Gloucester Rd.

If you yearn for your child to resemble a Kate Greenaway drawing, this is the place to go. Featuring hand-smocked dresses, white taffeta and velvet party wear, crisp cotton nightgowns, tweed coats and traditional boy's shirts, the Anthea Moore Eade label represents the best in classic childrenswear.

Buckle-My-Shoe

19 ST. CHRISTOPHER'S PL, W1, 020-7935 5589
Open Mon.-Wed. & Fri.-Sat. 10am-6pm,
Thurs. 10am-7pm.
U: Bond St.

Bright and fashionable shoes, boots, sandals and trendy trainers rather than the sports variety are sold in this busy shop which caters for children up to ten years old. Even the most particular child (and parent) should find something from the 85 different styles of shoes, boots and slippers in 300 colourways, both from well-known designers and their own range.

Looking for an address?
Refer to the index.

Children's Pavilion

7 PAVILION RD, SW1, 020-7235 6513
Open Mon.-Sat. 10am-6pm.
U: Knightsbridge.

This smart children's shop sells French and Italian clothes for boys and girls up to twelve, but no shoes or outerwear. Styles range from very dressy to casual play clothes.

Createx

27 HARRINGTON RD, SW7, 020-7589 8306
Open Mon.-Sat. 10am-6pm.
U: South Kensington.

A very well-stocked shop, including footwear, with high-fashion French and Italian clothes for infants to 14 year-olds. Brand names include Catimini, David Charles, Simonetta and Baby Bottle.

The Disney Store

140-141 REGENT ST, W1, 020-7287 6558
Open Mon.-Sat. 10am-8pm, Sun. noon-6pm.
U: Oxford Circus/Piccadilly Circus.

Expect to see all the Disney characters—Winnie-the-Pooh, Pocohontas and 101 Dalmations—depicted on casual clothes including T-shirts, baseball caps, sweaters, jackets, trousers and underwear. The costumes are fun too, as are the hair accessories and jewelry. The Disney Store is always a favourite with children.

Jakss

319 UPPER ST, N1, 020-7359 4942
Open Tues.-Fri. 10am-5.30pm, Sat. 10.30am-6pm.
U: Angel.

If money is no option and you'd rather your child grew up as well versed in his/her DKNY's and Versace's as his/her ABC's, then this is the place for you. The labels are impressive, even by adult standards, ranging from Calvin Klein and Donna Karan to Paul Smith and Dries Van Noten. The shop is very popular and mothers will cross town to dress their tots up in the new season's collections. **Also at** 463 Roman Rd, E3, 020-8981 9451; 469 Roman Rd, E3, 020-8981 2233.

Joanna's Tent

289B KING'S RD, SW3, 020-7352 1151
Open Mon.-Tues. & Thurs.-Sat. 9.45am-6pm, Wed. 9.45am-7pm.
U: Sloane Sq.

The childrenswear department in the basement is very well-stocked and includes a wide range of accessories such as gloves, belts, bags and hats. Designer names include NoNo, Hakka Kids, Paul Smith, DKNY, Junior Armani, Blu Kids, Les Enfants and Joanna's Tent own collection.

Kent & Carey

10 WEST HALKIN ST, SW1, 020-7838 9431
Open Mon.-Sat. 9.30am-5.30pm.
U: Knightsbridge.

Ten years ago, after the birth of her daughter Jessica, Julie Kent produced her first Sleepcozy. A cross between a quilted cotton sleeping bag and a nightdress, the product proved to be so innovative and practical that soon she was designing a small range of nightwear from the kitchen table of her Wiltshire farmhouse. Now Kent's vision has bloomed into a thriving business with three shops of her own and a string of department stores stocking her designs. Kent & Carey offers English-style childrenswear from birth to teens and also includes a couture line of special-occasion wear. There is also a full interior design service. **Also at** 154 Wandsworth Bridge Rd, SW6, 020-7736 5554; 6 Northcote Rd, SW11, 020-7350 1879.

Oilily

9 SLOANE ST, SW1, 020-7823 2505
Open Mon.-Tues. & Thurs.-Sat. 10am-6pm, Wed. 10am-7pm.
U: Knightsbridge.

Colourful stripes, bold florals and bright patterns are the trademarks of this Dutch company specialising in fun and funky yet traditional clothes for children up to 12. The vast range includes pretty dresses, smocks, dungarees, casual beach wear, jackets, coats and accessories. Also stocks a range of ladies clothing following the same casual and colourful styling.

Patrizia Wigan

19 WALTON ST, SW3, 020-7823 7080
Open Mon.-Fri. 10am-6pm, Sat. 10am-5.30pm.
U: Knightsbridge/South Kensington.

Special clothes in pretty styles and fabrics. Patrizia Wigan's designer clothes, which include casual wear and intricate dressy garments, are known on the international circuit for their quintessential English look.

Paul Smith for Children

40-44 FLORAL ST, WC2, 020-7379 7133
Open Mon.-Wed. & Fri. 10.30am-6.30pm,
Thurs. 10am-7pm, Sat. 10am-6.30pm.
U: Covent Garden.

Paul Smith's style lends itself well to miniature fans. Even traditional parents will find little to offend with the chunky fisherman's sweaters, Fair Isle knits and trendy but classical shirts and tops.

Also at Westbourne House, 122 Kensington Park Rd, W11, 020-7727 3553.

Polo Ralph Lauren

143 NEW BOND ST, W1, 020-7535 4600.
Open Mon.-Wed. & Fri. 10am-6pm, Thurs.
10am-7pm.
U: Bond St/Green Park.

Label queens watch out, the King of American Cool has designs on your tots. Ralph Lauren's first freestanding children's store is the swankiest place for chic all-in-ones and hand-knits for newborns through to hip and colourful fashion items for the fussiest 16-year-olds. The interior is conventional, with a twist. Rich mahogany wood-paneling and nautical pictures create a restful mood for parents, while the salt-water fish tank is a welcome diversion for the kids. Not that they'll need it. With clothes as cool as this, a fish, however colourful, will be the last thing on their minds.

Tartine et Chocolat

66 SOUTH MOLTON ST, W1, 020-7629 7233
Open Mon.-Sat. 10am-6pm.
U: Bond St.

French flair is evident in the clothes and accessories sold at this shop which features clothes by Catherine Painvin, a Parisian designer. The range is for babies to 12-year-olds and includes coats, dressy outfits and play clothes.

Trotters

34 KING'S RD, SW3, 020-7259 9620
Open Mon.-Tues. & Thurs.-Sat. 9am-6.30pm,
Wed. 9am-7pm, Sun. 10am-6pm.
U: Sloane Sq.

Trotters is an ideal one-stop shop for parents and children alike. Parents can take their time choosing from the clothes, shoes, toys, videos, books and games whilst children are distracted as they have their hair cut by the goldfish swimming in the tanks.

Also at 127 Kensington High St, W8, 020-7937 9373.

Warner Brothers Studio Store

178-182 REGENT ST, W1, 020-7434 3334
Open Mon.-Wed. & Fri.-Sat. 10am-7pm,
Thurs. 10am-8pm, Sun. noon-6pm.
U: Oxford Circus/Piccadilly Circus.

Head for the first floor to find children's clothes (the larger ground floor is reserved for grown-ups with a penchant for baseball caps, jackets and quirky T-shirts). Kid's clothes include pinafore dresses, T-shirts, dressing gowns, underwear, baseball caps and fringed leather jackets. Sylvester the Cat and Tweetie Pie are popular motifs along with Bugs Bunny, Daffy Duck and Taz, the cartoon Tazmanian Devil.

Young England

47 ELIZABETH ST, SW1, 020-7259 9003
Open Mon.-Fri. 10am-5.30pm, Sat. 10am-3pm.
U: Sloane Sq/Victoria.

Hand-smocked and formal dresses, tailored coats, swimwear, nightdresses and dressing gowns, all with a traditional appeal, are sold in this well-stocked shop catering to children up to the age of 7. Natural fabrics such as taffeta, wool and cotton are favoured. Everything is well made with conscientious touches like generous hem allowances, linings on wool products, net petticoats with party dresses and matching accessories. Wool coatdresses and sailor-look outfits are popular.

SPECIALIST SHOPS

Green Baby

345 UPPER ST, N1, 020-7226 4345
WWW.GREENBABYCO.COM
Open Tues.-Sat. 10am-6pm, Sun. 10am-2pm.
U: Angel.

If you seek out organic produce for yourself, it stands to reason that you should want the purest possible products for your baby. Devised by Canadian Jill Barker, a former City worker, this environmentally friendly shop sells washable nappies, baby toiletries, jogging strollers and slings, and the wonderful Boo Boo Bears, aromatherapy teddy packs filled with wheat and natural herbs for soothing restless babies.

TOYS, GAMES & BOOKS

Beatties

202 HIGH HOLBORN, WC1, 020-7405 6285
Open Mon.-Fri. 9am-6pm, Sat. 9.30am-5.30pm.
U: Holborn.

This is a huge shop with everything for the model maker, with all kinds of kits, plus electronic games and more.
Branches throughout London.

Benjamin Pollock's Toy Shop

44 THE MARKET, COVENT GARDEN, WC2
020-7379 7866
Open Mon.-Sat. 10.30am-6pm, Sun. noon-5pm.
U: Covent Garden.

Model theatres and intricate cardboard cutouts of old-fashioned theatres with all the accouterments are the delightful wares at this shop, which has puppets, traditional toys and teddy bears.

Big Kids Store

394 KING'S RD, SW10, 020-7795 0801
Open Mon.-Sat. 10am-6pm.
U: Sloane Sq.

Kids from 1-100 will find something to bring a smile to their face in this store. All-time favourites such as Babar, Tintin, Asterix and Noddy sit together with newcomers such as the popular Beanie Babies.

Daisy & Tom

181 KING'S RD, SW3, 020-7352 5000
Open Mon.-Tues. & Thurs.-Sat. 10am-6pm,
Wed. 10am-7pm, Sun. noon-6pm.
U: Sloane Sq.

Offering everything for children under one roof. The fairground carousel is one of the attractions, along with the bright and cheerful soda bar. There is also a children's hairdressing salon, galleried book department and the best in toys, games, clothes and shoes. Regular events, activities, competitions and author visits are held within this busy and popular store.

The Disney Store

140-141 REGENT ST, W1, 020-7287 6558
Open Mon.-Sat. 10am-8pm, Sun. noon-6pm.
U: Oxford Circus/Piccadilly Circus.

Mickey Mouse and all the other Walt Disney characters are represented on mugs, toys, games and other products. Adults and children can be seen singing along with the characters on the multiscreen video. There are two floors, with the lower level filled with stuffed toys and its own travel centre which arranges trips to the various Disneyland destinations.
Also at 360-366 Oxford St, W1, 020-7491 9136.

Early Learning Centre

36 KING'S RD, SW3, 020-7581 5764
Open Mon.-Tues. & Thurs.-Sat. 9am-6pm,
Wed. 9am-7pm, Sun. 11am-5pm.
U: Sloane Sq.

Always very busy, this welcoming shop, geared to children, has a wide selection of games, books, puzzles and other cheerful products aimed at making learning fun. There is a special area where kids are usually erecting giant building blocks or trying their hand at the latest game.
Branches throughout London.

Hamleys

188 REGENT ST, W1, 020-7734 3161
WWW.HAMLEYS.COM
Open Mon.-Tues. & Sat. 10am-7pm, Thurs.-Fri. 10am-8pm, Sun. noon-6pm.
U: Oxford Circus/Piccadilly Circus.

This is a large, five-storey department store entirely devoted to toys and games for children. It is always heaving with children looking at toys ranging from the cheap and cheerful varieties to top-of-the-range computer games. Adults are just as likely as children to find entertaining toys—but beware—prices are higher than in many other toyshops.

Also at Unit 3, The Piazza, Covent Garrden, WC2, 020-7240 4646.

The Kite Store

48 NEAL ST, WC2, 020-7836 1666
Open Mon.-Wed. & Fri. 10am-6pm, Thurs. 10am-7pm, Sat. 10.30am-6pm.
U: Covent Garden.

The cheerful window display of brightly coloured kites says it all. Inside there are high-powered designer kites in every shape imaginable.

Playin' Games

33 MUSEUM ST, WC1, 020-7323 3080
Open Mon.-Sat. 10am-6pm, Sun. 11am-4pm.
U: Tottenham Court Rd.

Small, but busy shop on two floors with lots of classic and new board games, card games and more on the ground floor. Models, paints and games of the Dungeons and Dragons genre are downstairs.

Pollock's Toy Theatres

1 SCALA ST, W1, 020-7636 3452
Open Mon.-Sat. 10am-5pm.
U: Goodge St.

Two small houses, with a shop on the ground floor selling theatres to make up, plus all the characters and more. This theatre was originally published by Benjamin Pollock, one of the last publishers of toy theatre sheets sold in Victorian times for 'a penny plain and two pence coloured'. Upstairs, there's a delightful museum (admission adults £3, child £1.50), full of old toys as well as theatres.

The Singing Tree

69 NEW KING'S RD, SW6, 020-7736 4527
Open Mon.-Sat. 10am-5.30pm.
U: Sloane Sq.

Everything you could possibly want for a dolls' house is available here in either kit form or made up, including a selection of perfectly scaled-down furniture spanning the eras and styles. Much of the furniture is made by quality craftsmen and pieces are perfect replicas, so be warned, prices are justifiably high. This fascinating shop is as much, if not more, for adult collectors and enthusiasts as it is for children.

Warner Brothers Studio Store

178-182 REGENT ST, W1, 020-7434 3334
Open Mon.-Wed. & Fri. 10am-7pm, Thurs. & Sat. 10am-8pm, Sun. noon-6pm.
U: Oxford Circus/Piccadilly Circus.

Kid's toys, stuffed animals and videos take up the first floor. There are hands-on activities to try, including Paint Shack, a computer colouring-by-numbers and a video screen showing cartoons or action scenes from shows like the *Adventures of New Superman*. Naturally the company's animated characters are emblazoned on mugs, watches and lots of accessories. There is a large animation art gallery for adults, selling original hand-painted drawings on celluloid, some signed by the company's famous cartoonists, ranging in price from about £150 to £1,000.

WHERE TO ENTERTAIN CHILDREN

The Little Angel Marionette Theatre

14 DAGMAR PASSAGE, CROSS ST, N1, 020-7226 1787
U: Angel.

The Ugly Duckling, Sleeping Beauty, Christmas opera and much more, all expressed with delightful marionettes have been captivating children for years at this tucked-away theatre in Islington.

Polka Theatre for Children

240 THE BROADWAY, WIMBLEDON, SW19
020-8543 4888
U: Wimbledon.

Well worth making the trek to Wimbledon for the wonderful performances at the Polka Theatre. Arrive early and enjoy a meal in the railway restaurant. Children enjoy sitting in the brightly-coloured carriages after making their choice from the menu which features favourites such as baked potatoes, toasted sandwiches, fish fingers and freshly baked cakes. If it's sunny, children enjoy running about in the garden, complete with climbing frames and a large wooden play house.

DEPARTMENT STORES

Debenhams

334-348 OXFORD ST, W1, 020-7408 4444
Open Mon.-Tues. 9.30am-7pm, Wed. 10am-8pm,
Thurs. 10am-9pm, Fri. 10am-8pm, Sat. 9am-
7pm, Sun. noon-6pm.
U: Oxford Circus.

The great thing that Debenhams boasts is the brilliant 'Designers' selection, incorporating everything from jewelry, fashion and homewares. On the fashion front, they have commissioned prolific British designers such as Pearce Fionda, Ben de Lisi, Maria Grachvogel and Jasper Conran to produce a fantastic range of affordable day and eveningwear for women, with Ozwald Boeteng and John Richmond providing stylish dressing options for the men. Chic homewares come from Jasper Conran and Kelly Hoppen; accessories from Dinny Hall, Lulu Guiness, Van Peterson, Philip Treacy and Neisha Crosland. Debenhams is definitely worth a look.

Dickins & Jones

222-224 REGENT ST, W1, 020-7734 7070
Open Mon.-Tues. & Fri. 10am-6.30pm, Wed.
10am-7pm, Thurs. 10am-8pm, Sun. 11am-5pm.
U: Oxford Circus.

This department store is mainly devoted to fashion and beauty, from the perfume and cosmetics on the ground floor to the extensive designer ranges on the upper floors. All the top, classic designer names are here—Karl Lagerfeld, Max Mara, Escada, Calvin Klein, George Rech—plus House of Fraser, their own label. In addition, it has contemporary fashions from Whistles, Hobbs, Monix and Betty Jackson. The stylish 'At Home' department on the fourth floor is the place for exclusive gifts, from soaps from Marseilles to contemporary or reproduction silverware, and individual, elegant pieces for the home. There are beauty and hair salons, personal shopping services for men and women, and the Albert Roux café.

Fenwick

63 NEW BOND ST, W1, 020-7629 9161
Open Mon.-Wed. & Fri.-Sat. 9am-6pm, Thurs.
9am-8pm.
U: Bond St.

Founded in 1891 in its present corner location on prestigious Bond Street, this is one of the less hectic department stores. High-fashion accessories such as quality bags by Hervé Chapelier, scarves, gloves and a good range of jewelry occupy the ground floor. Concessions include Maison de la Fourrure dedicated to fake fur clothing, accessories and home furnishings. On the upper floors you find designers you can rely on to pull together a good working wardrobe like Paul Costelloe, Joseph and Jasper Conran. Menswear, located on the lower ground floor with gifts, is also well stocked. The lingerie department is worth seeking out for seductive little numbers. Round off your shopping trip with refreshment from the excellent Joe's Restaurant Bar on the second floor.

Fortnum & Mason

181 PICCADILLY, W1, 020-7734 8040
WWW.FORTNUMANDMASON.COM
Open Mon.-Sat. 9am-6pm.
U: Green Park/Piccadilly Circus.

Fortnum & Mason stays in an agreeable time warp with its glittering chandeliers, opulent packaging and the world-famous array of luxury food and wine. And though prices have changed from the early eighteenth-century days when a baronet in Berkeley Square paid a mere £5 for six dozen bottles of the finest claret, this very traditional department store is a monument to the elegance of a bygone era. The exterior is famous for its clock—the figures of Mr. Fortnum and Mr. Mason greet each other as the hour is struck. The original duo founded this remarkable store in 1707 to cater for the aristocracy of St. James's. Mr. Fortnum was a footman in the Royal Household who knew the exact grocery requirements of the royal family and Mr. Mason supplied the delivery wagons. However, there is life beyond the food hall; upstairs, a further four floors provide women's fashions, millinery, lingerie, jewelry, accessories, menswear, stationery and gifts, plus a china and glass department on the lower ground floor. Also, top-quality restaurants and a Salmon & Champagne bar (see *Quick Bites*).

Harrods

KNIGHTSBRIDGE, SW1, 020-7730 1234
WWW.HARRODS.COM
Open Mon.-Tues. & Sat. 10am-6pm, Wed.-Fri.
10am-7pm.
U: Knightsbridge.

Harrods is so vast (it occupies a 4.5 acre block) and so famous that it has become a tourist attraction in its own right. And justifiably so, with its magnificent exterior and equally impressive departments inside, which include, on the ground floor alone, the Egyptian Hall for gifts, a glittering perfumery hall and the renowned food hall—well known for its Edwardian picture-tiles and daily changing displays of fish. Harrods began as a small Victorian grocery store, but from its humble beginnings was always in the forefront of fashion. It was the first London shop to install an escalator—because the manager hated lifts. This 1898 novelty proved such an excitement for the first clients that an attendant had to be stationed at the top to hand out brandy or salvolatile for the gentlemen and ladies overcome by the experience. These days, the list of its departments and services goes on and on, and includes a bank, theatre ticket services and safe-deposit boxes, justifying its claim to sell

anything and everything. There are sixteen restaurants and bars. The January sale, opened by a celebrity, always starts on the first Wednesday of the year and brings Knightsbridge to a halt.

Harvey Nichols

109-125 KNIGHTSBRIDGE, SW1, 020-7235 5000
Open Mon.-Tues. & Thurs.-Sat. 10am-7pm,
Wed. 10am-8pm, Sun. noon-6pm.
U: Knightsbridge.

If Harrods is the grande dame of Knightsbridge shopping, then Harvey Nichols is the funkier sister. Harvey Nicks, as it is known in fashion circles, is a shiny, streamlined temple for label addicts wishing to get their fix from the latest international designer looks. It has everything from the most coveted cosmetic brands to the hottest fashion labels, scrumptious food to enjoy on the premises or the most desirable ingredients to rustle something gorgeous up at home—at a price of course. The ground floor is hallowed ground for make-up and fragrance, with many companies signing deals to launch their products exclusively in the store. The first floor is given over to Contemporary Collections and big name International Designers. Further up on two you'll find the successful Personal Shopping suites and more Designer Collections from the likes of Nicole Farhi and Joan & David. Three is the place for casual wear and lingerie, whilst four houses the luxurious Aveda Concept salon. Five is dedicated to the finest food: eat in the ultra-fashionable Fifth Floor restaurant, the Fifth Floor Café (see *Quick Bites*) or buy from the equally fashionable food supermarket.

Liberty

214-220 REGENT ST, W1, 020-7734 1234
WWW. LIBERTY-OF-LONDON.COM/EXCLUSIVE-PREVIEWS
Open Mon.-Wed. & Fri.-Sat. 10am-6pm,
Thurs. 10am-7.30pm, Sun. noon-6pm.
U: Oxford Circus.

There are two faces to Liberty. One is romantic, from the mock-Tudor, half-timbered façade and quaint, rambling departments—many of which are filled with the famous Liberty print fabrics, Oriental departments and gifts; the other is cutting-edge. Founded in 1875 at the height of the aesthetic movement, Liberty has become one of the best London stockers of contemporary designers with global representation from Alexander

Local Shopping

Many areas of London are becoming mini shopping areas, and these can be as small as one street or passageway. The following are worth seeking out for a very pleasant wander. **St. Christopher's Place,** just off Oxford Street, W1, on the north side opposite Bond Street Underground Station has a selection of good small shops like *The Changing Room* and *Mulberry*. **James Street,** running off it, has good small restaurants and cafés.

Walton Street, SW3, running between Brompton Road and Hans Place, is a pretty street, with many small boutiques including *Contessa Ghisi* for stunning unique mink-fringed cashmere stoles as well as the excellent *Baker & Spice* for top breads and pastries.

The area now known as '**Belgravia Village**', centred around Motcomb Street and Halkin Street, is the place for small, upmarket boutiques including *Henry Beguelin* for shoes, small leather goods and items for the home and *Elspeth Gibson* in Pont Street.

Seek out the unusual in '**Clarendon Cross**', around Clarendon and Portland Roads, W11, for shops like *Summerill & Bishop* for their wonderful kitchen items on Portland Road.

McQueen flying the flag for Britain, to Yohji Yamamoto representing Japan. The light, airy cosmetics hall, although small in comparison to some of London's other department stores, is gaining a reputation as being one of the best places to shop, thanks to new and exciting ranges like E'Spa, Philosophy, François Nars and Face Stockholm and the beauty bonus of being lit by natural daylight. Elsewhere, you'll find a good selection of Oriental rugs, furnishings and accessories, exotic jewelry, a good range of furnishing and dress fabrics, plus the excellent ground-floor Bath Shop.

Marks & Spencer
458 OXFORD ST, W1, 020-7935 7954
Open Mon.-Fri. 9am-8pm, Sat. 9am-7pm, Sun. noon-6pm.
U: Marble Arch.

Although it has suffered losses of late, Marks & Spencer is still one of the busiest stores on the high street. Whether it's a packet of briefs from the underwear department or a three-seater sofa from furnishings, there's something for everyone at Marks & Spencer. The M&S logo has become synonymous with quality and value worldwide. The company, which began life in 1884 as a penny stall business, seeks out the design skills of the leaders in their field and employs them in everything from the clothing (Tania Sarne at Ghost), to leading make-up artist Charlie Green for the colour cosmetics, while a team of chefs develops new flavours for its phenomenally successful ready-meals. Grab a coffee and freshly baked pastry in the recently opened coffee shop in the basement of the Marble Arch store.
Branches throughout London.

Peter Jones
SLOANE SQ, SW1, 020-7730 3434
Open Mon.-Tues. & Thurs.-Sat. 9.30am-6pm, Wed. 9.30am-7pm.
U: Sloane Sq.

Chelsea's only department store, and part of the John Lewis chain, holds the wedding lists for the well-born, well-heeled and well-connected town-and-country set. It's the ideal place for distinctive fabrics, linens, china, glass, antiques and fashionable gifts as well as clothes and accessories. A bonus here is that both its coffee shop and licensed restaurant have views over London's rooftops.

Selfridges
400 OXFORD ST, W1, 020-7629 1234
Open Mon.-Tues. 10am-7pm, Wed.-Fri. 10am-8pm, Sat. 9.30am-7pm, Sun. noon-6pm.

Having recently undergone major cosmetic surgery, Selfridges is back in the running with the other big-league department stores. Although undeniably one of the biggest and busiest stores on Oxford Street, it was beginning to look a little ragged around the edges, but now under the direction of Vittoro Radice (who previously spruced up Habitat and doubled its turnover in three years), Selfridges' future is looking bright. The fashions for men and women have reaped the benefits of the change, as has the cosmetics hall and beautiful home furnishings department. A central atrium houses new glass-encased escalators and a sculpture of Josephine Baker by Sir Eduardo Paolozzi is an added touch.

FASHION FOR HIM & HER

DESIGNER LABELS
For more designer-fashion shops, see separate Menswear and Women's wear sections.

Adolfo Dominguez
129 REGENT ST, W1, 020-7494 3395
Open Mon.-Sat. 10am-6.30pm, Sun. noon-6pm.
U: Piccadilly Circus.

Prices are surprisingly reasonable for the elegant suits, separates, casual and eveningwear and accessories from this much overlooked Spanish design firm. Designs are classic with modern touches giving them a distinctive look. The shop also sells luggage, bags and a very desirable range of footwear.
Also at 15 Endell St, WC2, 020-7836 5013.

Agnès b
35-36 FLORAL ST, WC2, 020-7379 1992
Open Mon.-Wed. & Fri.-Sat. 10.30am-6.30pm, Thurs. 10am-7pm, Sun. noon-5pm.
U: Covent Garden.

The Agnès b label is synonymous with understated elegance—think Jean Seberg and Audrey Hepburn and you've got the idea. The range of mix-and-match separates and suitings, all impeccably designed and finished, work just as well in the boardroom as they do for a casual weekend stroll. Agnès b, the label's designer and creator, has never been influenced by passing fashion trends, hence the clothes are bought to be worn (and re-worn), not found gathering dust in the closet. Signature styles include quality T-shirts, simple knitwear, slim-fitting suits and leather coats and jackets, in men's and women's wear, plus a line for children and teen-agers. While you're there, stock up on the cosmetics and fragrance lines.

Also at 111 Fulham Rd, SW3, 020-7225 3477; 235 Westbourne Grove, W11, 020-7792 1947; 58-62 Heath St, NW3, 020-7431 1995.

Alexander McQueen

47 CONDUIT ST, W1, 020-7734 2340
Open Mon.-Wed. & Fri.-Sat. 10.30am-6.30pm, Thurs. 10.30am-7pm.
U: Oxford Circus.

Now that McQueen has upped and gone to New York to show his spectacular collections, he has branched out with his first stand-alone outlet here. Fashion fans who can't afford the ticket to the Big Apple can come and admire his handiwork at close range, including his ballerina crinoline skirts in filigree metal, lace embroidered with crystals and his razor-sharp tailoring for men.

Amanda Wakeley

80 FULHAM RD, SW3, 020-7584 4009
Open Mon.-Tues. & Thurs.-Sat. 10am-6pm, Wed. 10am-7pm.
U: South Kensington.

This young, successful British designer has won the coveted Glamour Designer of the Year twice in a row. She sells ready-to-wear clothes for women but also continues her cou-ture business, by appointment only, at the same premises. Understated and elegant, the dresses, suits, knitwear and separates make a striking impact matched up with shoes and accessories, but eveningwear is her forte.

Browns

23-27 SOUTH MOLTON ST, W1, 020-7491 7833
Open Mon.-Tues. & Fri.-Sat. 10am-6pm, Thurs. 10am-7pm.
U: Bond St.

You don't need to have confidence to walk through the number of doors leading into this stalwart among the favourite places to find top designer looks, but it certainly helps. At first glance, the sales assistants may seem like they will be haughty, but once you've managed to overcome their sleek, almost superior appear-ance, they are friendly and extremely helpful. Walk through the interconnecting rooms for the world's most desirable labels such as Jil Sander, Shirin Guild, Anna Sui, Dries van Noten, Alexander McQueen, Prada, Missoni and Helmut Lang, in fact, all of the designers with that 'must-have' appeal. They also stock a capsule collection Dosa clothing and home accessories.

Also at 6c Sloane Street, SW1, 020-7493 4232.

CK Calvin Klein

53-55 NEW BOND ST, W1, 020-7491 9696
Open Mon.-Wed. & Fri.-Sat. 10am-7pm, Thurs. 10am-8pm, Sun. noon-6pm.
U: Bond St.

Clean, simple lines are the trademarks of Calvin Klein. Although there is a diffusion line, aimed at a younger audience, his famous uncluttered lines are prevalent. Expect lots of earthy tones such as stone, graphite and putty, put together to create a sleek, sporty style.

The Changing Room

THOMAS NEAL'S CENTRE, EARLHAM ST, WC2
020-7379 4158
Open Mon.-Fri. 11am-7pm, Sat. 10.30am-7pm, Sun. 12.30pm-5.30pm.
U: Covent Garden.

A butcher's block and a large wood framed mirror provide a simple backdrop for designs from Lezley George, Betty Jackson, Sara Sturgeon, John Rocha, Pleats Please by Issey Miyake, Tehen and half-a-dozen or so more.

Also at 10 Gees Court, W1, 020-7408 1596.

Comme des Garçons

59 BROOK ST, W1, 020-7493 1258
Open Mon.-Wed. & Fri. 10am-6pm, Thurs. 10am-7pm, Sat. 10am-5pm.
U: Bond St.

Minimalist to the point that you feel your presence upsets the balance, this small shop tucked away in Mayfair, appeals to confident fashion types. The mere fact that you have to ring the bell for entry is enough to send the uninitiated running in the opposite direc-tion—and that's before they catch sight of the price tags.

DKNY

27 OLD BOND ST, W1, 020-7499 8089
Open Mon.-Wed & Fri. 10am-6pm, Thurs.
10am-7pm, Sat. 10am-6.30pm.
U: Green Park.

If you want to buy into the Donna Karan lifestyle without paying for the hugely expensive 'black label' clothes from the designer's mainline collection further along the street, this is the place to come. The audience is younger, the atmosphere noisier, and the prices marginally cheaper for the sportswear-influenced and diffusion line designer clothes. There's a juice bar and video banks to add to the busy floor space, plus a heavy security guard presence.

Dolce & Gabbana

6-8 OLD BOND ST, W1, 020-7659 9000.
Open Mon.-Fri. 10am-6pm, Sat. 10am-7pm.
U: Bond St.

Always producing collections that send fashion editors into a flutter, Domenico Dolce and Stephano Gabbana make the most of manipulating the female form, having fun and producing dynamic clothes at the same time. Leopard print and mafiosa-style trouser suits usually make an appearance. Sunglasses, beautiful bags, T-shirts and, more recently, a line of cushions adds more affordable access to the D&G club.

Also at 175 Sloane St, SW1, 020-7235 0335.

Donna Karan

19 NEW BOND ST, W1, 020-7495 3100
Open Mon.-Wed. & Fri.-Sat. 10am-6pm,
Thurs. 10am-7pm.
U: Green Park.

In sharp contrast to the DKNY store, Donna Karan is sleek, serene, and for the seriously monied. The clothes are beautiful—well-cut suits and separates in the menswear department in the basement and Oscar-winning evening dresses and power dressing for women spread over two floors.

Emporio Armani

57-59 LONG ACRE, WC2, 020-7917 6882
Open Mon.-Wed & Fri. 10am-6.30pm, Thurs.
10am-7.30pm, Sun. 11.30am-5.30pm.
U: Covent Garden.

Understated, classic and elegant, the Armani label oozes the smooth taste of Italy like melting mozzarella. Men's and women's styles work just as well on the young as they do on the old and the colour choice is suited to all but the wildly eccentric. Includes jeans, underwear, childrenswear and desirable accessories.

Etro

14 OLD BOND ST, W1, 020-7495 5767
Open Mon.-Sat. 10am-6pm.
U: Green Park.

This family-run business is steeped in tradition and Milanese style. Nice touches like the inclusion of paintings and furniture from the Etro family's antique collection make customers feel they are entering the home of an affluent friend. This store is famous for their gloriously mismatched and paisley velvets for men and women and exotic fragrances and candles.

Gianni Versace

34-36 OLD BOND ST, W1, 020-7499 1862
Open Mon.-Sat. 10am-6pm.
U: Green Park.

Three things spring to mind when Versace's name is mentioned. Firstly, there is the designer himself, then there is his friend, Diana, Princess of Wales, both of whom died tragically in the same year. Lastly, there is Elizabeth Hurley who made the headlines of every tabloid when she wore 'that dress' at the première of Four Weddings and a Funeral. The label is mostly known for excess and brash colours (largely due to the Liz Hurley exposure), less for the classic and tasteful designs favoured by Diana.

Gucci

17-18 SLOANE ST, SW1, 020-7235 6707
Open Mon.-Tues. & Thurs.-Fri. 9.30am-6pm,
Wed. 10am-7pm, Sat. 10am- 6pm.
U: Knightsbridge.

After a metamorphosis by Texan designer, Tom Ford, the Gucci label is the epitome of clothes and stylish accessories with attitude. The globally recognised snaffle loafers are still present, along with gravity-defying stilettoes and a variety of other shoe styles. The men's collection borders on the sleek, modern-day playboy, while the women's clothes encompass everything from chic executive to disco diva.

Also at 32-33 Old Bond St, W1, 020-7629 2716.

Hermès

179 SLOANE ST, SW1, 020-7823 1014
Open Mon.-Sat. 10am-6pm.
U: Knightsbridge.

A covetable label since 1837, the Hermès insignia, brandished on clothes, fragrances, scarves and accessories, is the stamp of international style. Grace Kelly popularised the 'Kelly' bag during her pregnancy, since then Elle 'The Body' MacPherson has had her name immortalised in the 'Elle' bag, with handy, supermodel compartments for make-up and accessories.
Also at 155 New Bond St, W1, 020-7499 8856; 3 Royal Exchange, EC3, 020-7626 7794.

Issey Miyake

270 BROMPTON RD, SW3, 020-7581 3760
Open Mon.-Sat. 10am-6pm.
U: Knightsbridge.

Origami as clothing, the original concept and a hugely profitable one this successful Japanese designer created. Clients include architects, artists, actresses, and members of the fashion fraternity. The perma-pleats are perfect for travelling which, apart from the stylish look, may be the reason for the huge success.

Jean Paul Gaultier

GALERIE GAULTIER
171-175 DRAYCOTT AVE, SW3, 020-7584 4648
Open Mon.-Tues. & Thurs.-Sat. 10am-6pm,
Wed. 10am-7pm.
U: South Kensington.

Before Paris took on John Galliano, it had its own enfant terrible, Jean Paul Gaultier, a designer who always cited London as being the source of his inspiration. His shop,

---

Arcade Shopping

The **Burlington Arcade**, W1, running between Piccadilly and Burlington Gardens has a whole variety of small shops, including *N Peal* for cashmere, *The Irish Linen Company* for home linens, *Immaculate House* for beautiful soaps and toiletries and *Georgina von Etzdorf* for highly individual, beautiful clothes in stunning fabrics.

---

designed to resemble a Parisian courtyard, holds his bold, bright and exotic creations for men and women, including the JPG and jeans ranges as well as his successful lines of fragranced products encased in an hourglass female form.

Jitrois

6F SLOANE ST, SW1, 020-7245 6300
Open Mon.-Sat. 10am-7pm.
U: Knightsbridge.

Jean Claude Jitrois is already established in France; now he brings his sexy, innovative leather designs to London with the assistance of Arsenal footballer, Emmanuel Petit, who co-owns the swanky shop. The collection features modern, immaculately tailored leather and suede pieces for men and women, together with a selection of more unusual styles using leather appliquéd onto fabrics such as silk organza and mohair. The store also stocks the Jitrois jeans label, purely for the skinnies out there. The unique lambskin and cotton fabric stretches to the skin and clings to every curve. Items can be made up to your specifications in a wide range of colours.

Joseph

77 FULHAM RD, SW3, 020-7823 9500
Open Mon.-Tues. & Thurs.-Fri. 10am-6.30pm,
Wed. 10am-7pm, Sat. 10am-6pm, Sun. noon-
5pm.
U: South Kensington.

When it comes to striking the right fashion note, Moroccan-born Joseph Ettedgui hits it perfectly every time. For the past ten years, he has carved out a niche for delivering cool, classic and contemporary clothes in a fashionable but friendly environment. Both men and women can slip into the designer's own label products or eye up the ranges from Martin Margiela, Prada and Helmut Lang. The first exclusively menswear store in the Joseph stable includes Gucci and Jil Sander in a minimal, arty setting. **Men's store** at 74 Sloane Ave, SW3, 020- 590 6200.
Branches throughout London.

Krizia

24-25 CONDUIT ST, W1, 020-7491 4987
Open Mon.-Wed. & Fri.-Sat. 10am-6pm,
Thurs. 10am-7pm.
U: Bond St.

Super-sleek and stylish, Krizia's first British outlet sits comfortably in Conduit Street, a relatively new designer enclave. Men's, women's wear and the Casa Krizia homewares collection are on offer, together with the not much cheaper Krizia diffusion lines.

Nicole Farhi

158 NEW BOND ST, W1, 020-7499 8368
Open Mon.-Wed. & Fri.-Sat. 10am-6pm, Thurs. 10am-7pm.
U: Bond St/Green Park.

Thanks to designers like Nicole Farhi, the British fashion industry is booming. She might not produce headline-grabbing collections or send her models down the catwalks with outrageous accessories, but she consistently manages to create clothes that men and women buy and will wear forever. This ultra-sleek flagship store is in keeping with the luxurious but minimalist interiors of the international names who have found their way to Bond Street. Take time to admire the clothes then book yourself a table in her restaurant Nicole's (see *Restaurants*).

Paul Smith

WESTBOURNE HOUSE, 122 KENSINGTON PARK RD, W11, 020-7727 3553
Open Mon.-Thurs. 10.30am-6.30pm, Fri.-Sat. 10am-6pm.
U: Ladbroke Grove.

Having already claimed Covent Garden's Floral Street as his own, Paul Smith is aiming to do the same in trendy Notting Hill Gate. Not wishing to settle for anything as mundane as a run-of-the-mill shop, he has taken over a former private house and kept the feel of his store as homely as possible. Antiques and paintings have been chosen to add a relaxed, informal air and, just like the men's, women's and children's collections, accessories and novelty gifts, each piece is for sale.

Also at 49 Floral St, WC2, 020-7379 7133; 84 Sloane Ave, SW3, 020-7589 9139; 52 Thrale St, SE1, 020-7378 9933; and sale shop at 23 Avery Row, W1, 020-7493 1287.

Polo Ralph Lauren

1 NEW BOND ST, W1, 020-7535 4600
Open Mon.-Wed. & Fri.-Sat. 10am-6pm, Thurs. 10am-7pm.
U: Bond St/Green Park.

A new palatial location for the man who serves up an Americanised version of British style to his loyal customer base. Feeling like it takes up the whole of Bond Street, the five-storey building is home to the mainline Ralph Lauren collection, the Ralph Lauren Cruise collection, Polo Sport featuring shirts and sporty items, the Ralph collection which is aimed at a younger audience, the Polo and Golf collections, and the funky RXL sportsline range.

Prada

44-45 SLOANE ST, SW1, 020-7235 0008
Open Mon.-Tues. & Thurs.-Sat. 10am-6pm, Wed. 10am-7pm.
U: Knightsbridge.

Head here for the so-trendy-it-hurts nylon rucksacks, gorgeous leather shoes and some of the most influential designs of the past decade. The calming green interior allows even the most anti-fashion person to appreciate the precision detailing of Miuccia Prada's collections of cool utility chic clothing.

Also at 15-16 Old Bond St, W1, 020-7647 5000.

Vivienne Westwood

6 DAVIES ST, W1, 020-7629 3757
Open Mon.-Wed. & Fri.-Sat. 10am-6pm, Thurs. 10am-7pm.
U: Bond St.

In the days when London's fashion designers were regarded as experimentalists of little substance, only one was making headlines for clothes, which combined wit, wisdom and wearability. People may have mocked Vivienne Westwood for her seemingly outrageous creations, but they could never deny the fact that she was, and still is, one of Britain's hottest fashion exports. Her collections always have some historical references and feature smartly tailored tweeds, clingy dresses and endless suits with neat little nipped-in waists and leg-o'-mutton sleeves. You'll find the demi-couture 'Gold Label' at Davies Street, and the funkier 'Red Label' at Conduit Street and a selection of Westwood classics in the shop where it all started in World's End.

Also at 43 Conduit St, W1, 020-7439 1109; World's End, 430 King's Rd, SW10, 020-7352 6551.

Voyage

115 & 177 FULHAM RD, SW3, 020-7823 9581
Open Mon.-Tues. & Thurs.-Fri. 10.30am-6.30pm, Wed. 10.30am-7pm, Sat. 10.30am-6pm.
U: South Kensington.

Hippy-chic label for the ultra-hip. Fans of the bohemian, ancient velvet trim and creased silk creations of Tiziano and Louise Mazzilli, former designers at Valentino, include Jemima Khan, Nicole Kidman, Emma Thompson, Melanie Griffith, and any self-respecting fashion editor. Entry is selective and operates on a ring-the-doorbell policy. If your face fits, the staff will let you in to admire the colourful garments hanging from the bamboo rails and wooden shelves, otherwise they won't. Don't take it too personally, though, refuses extend to fashion editors and major celebrities. Prices are high: cardigans start from £395. The recently opened men's store down the road at 177 Fulham Rd offers the same flamboyant styles for men.

Yohji Yamamoto
14-15 CONDUIT ST, W1, 020-7491 4129
Open Mon.-Wed. & Fri.-Sat. 10am-6pm,
Thurs. 10am-7pm.
U: Bond St/Oxford Circus.

Purity and elegance are the two words that spring to mind when describing the mainly monochromatic collections Yohji Yamamoto produces for men and women. The styling is ingenious yet comes across as being deceptively simple. It is wonderful that the designer now has his first outlet in London.

Yves Saint Laurent Rive Gauche
137 NEW BOND ST, W1, 020-7493 1800
Open Mon.-Wed. & Fri. 9.30am-6pm, Thurs.
9.30am-7pm, Sat. 10am-6pm.
U: Bond St/Green Park.

That old adage, (if it ain't broke, why fix it?) springs to mind when describing Yves Saint Laurent's collections as he sees no harm in giving his customers variations of the same theme year after year. The YSL staple is the classic, black Le Smoking, the perfect trouser suit, which he first introduced to an appreciative public in 1966. His skirt suits, coats, jackets, dresses and shirts are finished to perfection and allow any woman to look and feel like a star.

GENERAL FASHION

All the major department stores carry very good ranges of all kinds of clothes for both sexes, from major international designers to general labels. Here we recommend some top British clothing companies.

Aquascutum
100 REGENT ST, W1, 020-7734 6090
WWW.AQUASCUTUM.CO.UK
Open Mon.-Wed. & Fri.-Sat. 9.30am-6pm,
Thurs. 9.30am-7pm, Sun. noon-6pm.
U: Piccadilly Circus.

The first Aquascutum shower-proof coat went on sale in 1851, the year of the Victorian Great Exhibition held to show off the best British inventions. Some things have not changed. Today, the Aquascutum name is still highly regarded and the distinctive 'club check' in khaki and red appears in numerous guises. They have even extended the range to include slim tailoring and nylon coats aimed at a younger audience with an eye for quality.

Also at 9-13 Brompton Rd, SW1, 020-7581 4444.

Austin Reed
103-113 REGENT ST, W1, 020-7734 6789
WWW.AUSTINREED.CO.UK
Open Mon.-Wed. & Fri.-Sat. 10am-6.30pm,
Thurs. 10am-7.30pm, Sun. noon-5pm.
U: Piccadilly Circus.

This shop is a four-storey delight of moderately conservative, but well-designed and well-made clothes. Males are spoiled for choice from the smart ranges of casual, work and special occasion wear and a well-priced made-to-measure suit service. Women, meanwhile, have a good selection of all of the above, minus made-to-measure suits. The store is also a good source for smart and reasonably priced accessories.

Burberry
18-22 HAYMARKET, W1, 020-7930 3343
Open Mon.-Wed. & Fri.-Sat.10am-6pm, Thurs.
10am-7pm, Sun. noon-6pm.
U: Piccadilly Circus.

That distinctive check is seen all over the world, most famously in outerwear. Burberry stocks a good selection of women's wear, particularly now that the company has taken stock of its design directive and sharpened up its image to appeal to a young and fashion-conscious audience. The funky, reasonably priced Thomas Burberry range is aimed at the smarter end of the street-wear market. Find bargain priced seconds in the factory shop tucked away in the East End at 29-53 Chatham Pl, E9, 020-8985 3344.

Also at 165 Regent St, W1, 020-7734 4060.

Jaeger

200-206 REGENT ST, W1, 020-7200 4000
Open Mon.-Wed. & Fri.-Sat. 10am-6.30pm,
Thurs. 10am-7.30pm, Sun. noon-5pm.
U: Oxford Circus.
Jaeger is a byword in conservative dressing.
The clothes are well designed and cut, trans-
lating to garments you'll wear for years to
come. There's also a good selection of clothes from
the classical and classic Jean Muir collection.

OUTERWEAR

For specific sporting outerwear, see the
Sporting Goods section.

Aquascutum

100 REGENT ST, W1, 020-7734 6090
WWW.AQUASCUTUM.CO.UK
Open Mon.-Wed. & Fri.-Sat. 10am-6.30pm,
Thurs. 10am-7pm, Sun. noon-5pm.
U: Piccadilly Circus.
Coincidentally, the first Aquascutum shower-
proof coat went on sale in 1851, the year of
the Victorian Great Exhibition held to show
off the best British inventions. Some things
have not changed. Today, the Aquascutum
name is still highly regarded and the understated 'club check' in khaki and red appears in
numerous guises. They have even extended
the range to include slim-fitting tailoring and
nylon coats aimed at a younger—though no
less discerning—customer.
Also at 9-13 Brompton Rd, SW1, 020-7581
4444.

Burberry

18-22 HAYMARKET, SW1, 020-7930 3343
Open Mon.-Wed. & Fri.-Sat. 10am-6pm,
Thurs. 10am-7pm, Sun. noon-6pm.
U: Piccadilly Circus.
That distinctive Burberry check appears as a
lining on solid trench coats, which have
earned a worldwide reputation for being quintessential rainwear. It was created by Thomas
Burberry in the 1870s and fast gained the reputation of being untearable and rainproof, yet
cool and comfortable. Meryl Streep wore one
in *Kramer vs. Kramer*, Michael Douglas in
Wall Street and Warren Beatty in *Dick Tracy*.
More recently, though, Burberry has reinvented itself as the label of choice with the fashion
cognoscenti. Leather coats, sexy knitwear in
jewel shades, funky ball skirts fashioned in the
red, black, cream and red check—all very
British and very, very desirable.

Also at 165 Regent St, W1, 020-7734
4060.

Cordings

19 PICCADILLY, W1, 020-7734 0830
WWW.CORDINGS.CO.UK
Open Mon.-Fri. 9.30am-6pm, Sat. 10am-6pm.
U: Piccadilly Circus.
John Charles Cordings went into business in
1839 to provide classic country clothes for the
hunting, shooting and fishing fraternity. The
refurbished shop has been at this site since
1890. Occasional adventurers included Sir
Henry Morton Stanley, who in 1871 was outfitted in Cordings apparel for his expedition to
find Dr. Livingstone in Africa. Cordings is
renowned for using materials such as moleskin, corduroy and traditional tweeds in
colours inspired by the Scottish moors. The
store has the appeal of one-stop shopping for
all-weather coats, jackets and boots as well as
shirts, knitwear, ties, shoes, socks, luggage and
accessories. A made-to-order service is also
available.

Farlow's

5 PALL MALL, SW1, 020-7839 2424
Open Mon.-Fri. 9am-6pm, Sat. 9am-1pm.
U: Green Park.
Besides stocking a comprehensive range of
fishing tackle, this shop has separate premises
devoted to country clothes, including an
adjoining shop for women. Farlow's probably
has the largest selection of waxed Barbour
clothing in London as well as other well-
known clothing and footwear brands.

The General Leather Company

56 CHILTERN ST, W1, 020-7935 1041
Open Mon.-Fri. 9am-6pm, Sat. 9am-4pm.
U: Baker St.
Made-to-measure leather, suede and sheep-
skin designs are The General Leather
Company's forté. In business since 1970, they
also alter old models and offer repairs.

R M Williams

223 REGENT ST, W1, 020-7629 6222
Open Mon.-Wed. & Fri.-Sat. 10am-6.30pm,
Thurs. 10am-7.30pm, Sun. 11am-pm.
U: Hyde Park Corner.
The classic Akubra bushwhacker hats that
Prince Charles wears during his Australian vis-

its are one of the best-selling items here, along with Australian-made moleskin trousers, oil skin jackets and handcrafted boots. The racks are full of cotton, denim and linen shirts and jeans, trousers and shirts for men and women. Established more than 60 years ago, this Aussie firm pays attention to detail, using only the best-quality buttons, zips and rivets. The overall great outdoors look is devastatingly romantic à la Indiana Jones.

SHOES

Audley
96 MOUNT ST, W1, 020-7491 3441
Open Mon.-Fri. 10am-6pm, Sat. 10am-5pm.
U: Bond St.

A glorious shoe shop with a difference, combining bespoke and ready-to-wear in a clever way. Each season the company produces a collection in a standard range of leather, from £65 for women and £95 for men. Leather in different colours is also offered and for a mere £50 more, you can get a pair made-to-order. Going the whole bespoke route costs from £500 for women to £600 for men. There's a one-time charge of £200, which is much less than most such services.

Bertie
36 SOUTH MOLTON ST, W1, 020-7493 5033
Open Mon.-Wed. & Fri.-Sat. 10am-7pm,
Thurs. 10am-8pm, Sun. noon-5.30pm.
U: Bond St.

Fashion dictates it and this shop caters to it—a wide choice of reasonably comfortable shoes, mostly in varying shades of brown and black. However, more delicate dressy shoes in lighter colours have been making an appearance in theline, no doubt to 'lift' the uniform of black, grey and brown outfits which continue to dominate the nation's wardrobes.
Branches throughout London.

Church's
58-59 BURLINGTON ARCADE, W1, 020-7493 8307
Open Mon.-Sat. 9.30am-6pm.
U: Piccadilly Circus

This shop is one of the branches of a famous Northampton-based manufacturer. A pair of Oxford brogues or penny loafers is £195. All styles, many in the timeless English classic mode, are well made, in narrow and wide fit-

tings, and tend to last forever. Some of the women's shoes look like clones of men's styles, sensible and comfortable with old-fashioned styling, but there are many surprises in store and they have started a line of high-fashion designs.
Branches throughout London and in major department stores.

D L Lord
70 BURLINGTON ARCADE, W1, 020-7493 5808
Open Mon.-Sat. 9.30am-5.45pm.
U: Piccadilly Circus.

The classic shoe styles have made this shop a must for men who appreciate quality. It has a bespoke service for men's shoes, run by the Grenson firm, shoemakers since 1866. A Grenson consultant is available by appointment and it takes several fittings and eight to ten weeks to make the shoes. The shop stocks traditional, ready-to-wear shoes for men starting at £145.

Deliss
15 ST. ALBAN'S GROVE, W8, 0207-938 2255
Open Mon.-Fri. 9.30am-5.30pm, Sat. 10am-2pm.
U: High St Kensington.

With animal skins making a resurgence in the fashion world, Deliss will undoubtedly become one of the most treasured addresses for any fashionista worth her weight in designer logos. Lizard, crocodile, elephant and ostrich skin are among the shoe and boot coverings available in this working cobbler's shop, where you can spy customers being measured for handmade shoes through the front window. For a real treat, splurge on a matching bag and belt. Men's shoes start from £512 + VAT; women's are from £425 + VAT. Items take three to four weeks.

Edward Green
12-13 BURLINGTON ARCADE, W1, 020-7499 6377
Open Mon.-Sat. 9am-5.30pm.
U: Piccadilly Circus.

Smart men's shoes are available from stock or made-to-order, from £395; boots from £400. However, they do not have a made-to-measure service.

Emma Hope

33 AMWELL ST, EC1, 020-7833 2367
E-MAIL: MAIL@EMMAHOPE.CO.UK
Open Mon.-Wed. & Fri.-Sat. 10am-6pm,
Thurs. 10am-7pm.
U: Angel.

Emma Hope makes beautiful shoes with a hint of the baroque. Her designs are elegant and timeless, coming in a choice of leathers such as nappa, suede, morroco and snakeskin and fabrics such as silk velvet and satin, often with delightful bows and distinctive decoration. She also produces a collection of bridal shoes, which can be made with the fabric of the chosen dress.
Also at 53 Sloane Sq, SW1, 020-7259 9566.

Gina Shoes

9 OLD BOND ST, W1, 020-7409 7090
Open Mon.-Wed. & Fri.-Sat. 10am-6pm,
Thurs. 10am-7pm.
U: Bond St.

A second outlet for the wonderful shoes by Gina. An English, in fact London-based firm, their shoes are highly individual and stylish. They stock a particularly good and popular line in high-heeled glamour shoes attracting a host of celebrity customers.
Also at 189 Sloane St, SW1, 020-7235 2932.

Hobbs

UNIT 17, THE PIAZZA, COVENT GDN, WC2
020-7836 9168
Open Mon.-Wed. & Fri.-Sat. 10.30am-7pm,
Thurs. 10.30am-7.30pm, Sun. noon-5pm.
U: Covent Garden.

Well-known for its fashionable but functional shoes in conservative colours, Hobbs also makes women's clothes and accessories, thus creating a totally coordinated look.
Branches throughout London.

Jimmy Choo

20 MOTCOMB ST, SW1, 020-7235 6608
Open Mon.-Sat. 10am-6pm.
U: Knightsbridge.

Previously, the Malaysian designer produced his custom-made, delicate satin shoes in a workshop in Hackney. His well-heeled client list must be thanking their lucky stars that Jimmy is now located so much nearer to their homes. The shop has been designed according to Feng Shui principles to improve mental, physical and financial wellbeing. It must be doing the trick because his classic ready-to-wear shoes seem to just walk out of the door.

Joan & David

150 NEW BOND ST, W1, 020-7499 7506
Open Mon.-Wed. & Fri.-Sat. 10am-6pm,
Thurs. 10am-7pm.
U: Bond St.

This sophisticated store fits well into Bond Street, offering expensive American-designed footwear to both men and women in a minimalist setting.

John Lobb

88 JERMYN ST, SW1, 020-7930 8089
Open Mon.-Wed. & Fri.-Sat. 10am-6pm,
Thurs. 10am-7pm.
U: Green Park.

Not to be confused with the John Lobb bootmakers (see below), this shop is owned by Hermès, Paris. The firm makes beautiful classically styled pret-à-porter shoes for men, average price £395. They offer a service for clients in hotels, and can arrange for a representative to call with different styles. They also make classic women's shoes.

John Lobb Bootmaker

9 ST. JAMES'S ST, SW1, 020-7930 3664
Open Mon.-Fri. 9am-5.30pm, Sat 9am-4.30pm.
U: Green Park.

Possibly one of the most famous shoemakers in the world, set in a delightfully old-fashioned shop. Here you'll be fitted with dream shoes to last a lifetime; the lasts, dating back to figures like the Duke of Wellington, are all kept downstairs in carefully labeled boxes. Handmade to the highest specification and of the finest leathers, the shoes here may be expensive (from £1500) but what price luxury, expert craftsmanship and comfort?

Joseph Azagury

73 KNIGHTSBRIDGE, SW1, 020-7259 6887
Open Mon.-Wed. & Fri.-Sat. 10am-6pm,
Thurs. 10am-7pm.
U: Knightsbridge.

Designer Azagury comes up with all the right styles to keep fashion addicts at bay, whether the vogue is for high-steppin' strappy sandals or low-heeled town shoes. The shop also offers a good range of all-year-round bridal shoes and matching evening bags. And the best bit is, the majority of styles are available up to size 10 (43), so even if your feet are on the large side, you don't need to forfeit fashion for fit.

Kurt Geiger

49 NEW BOND ST, W1, 020-7491 8562
Open Mon.-Wed. & Fri.-Sat. 9.30am-6pm, Thurs. 9.30am-7pm.
U: Bond St.

Part of the Ferragamo and Bruno Magli group of companies, Kurt Geiger sells women's and men's shoes from £80-£250. The shop features mostly Continental designers, but some styles come from their American suppliers in U.S. sizes.

L K Bennett

130 LONG ACRE, WC2, 020-7379 1710
Open Mon.-Wed. & Fri.-Sat. 10.30am-7.30pm, Thurs. 10.30am-8pm.
U: Covent Garden.

Linda Bennett's shops bridge that hard-to-fill gap between high street and designer, both in the styles and quality of the shoes, boots and clothing ranges and the all-too-important price tag. The evening shoes are always inspirational.
Branches throughout London.

Manolo Blahnik

49-51 OLD CHURCH ST, SW3, 0207-352 3863
Open Mon.-Fri. 10am-6pm, Sat 10.30am-5pm.
U: Sloane Sq.

Dramatic, seductive, totally 'wantable' are the words that sum up Manolo Blahnik's shoes for women. Many women will sacrifice the discomfort of the impossibly high heels for the instant sex appeal they experience when slipping into a pair of Mr. B's finest. Shoes are made in limited edition batches of fifteen, which just increase the glamour. They are on display in this minimalist shop in a charmingly quiet residential corner of Chelsea.

The **prices** in this guide reflect what establishments were charging at press time.

New & Lingwood

53 JERMYN ST, SW1, 020-7493 9621
Open Mon.-Fri. 9am-5.30pm, Sat. 10am-5.30pm.
U: Piccadilly Circus/Green Park.

Best known for their excellent range of shirts, this shop has wonderfully woody brown shades in its classic men's shoes. You can buy them made-to-measure or ready-to-wear. Velvet slippers are around £120, but are more expensive with a hand-embroidered monogram or crest and take three months to make. Old Etonians continue to shop here, having been introduced as boys to the firm's branch near the famous school.

Patrick Cox

129 SLOANE ST, SW3, 020-7730 8886
Open Mon.-Tues. & Thurs.-Sat. 10am-6pm, Wed. 10am-7pm, Sun. 11am-5pm.
U: Sloane Sq.

It all started with a loafer that everyone just had to have and Patrick Cox's status was confirmed. His store is a mixture of coveted shoes and equally desirable furniture, both of which do a brisk trade for the Canadian designer.

Small & Tall Shoe Shop

71 YORK ST, W1, 020-7723 5321
Open Mon.-Wed. & Fri.-Sat. 10am-5pm, Thurs. 10am-7pm.
U: Marylebone.

As the name suggests, this shop caters to those who have difficulty finding the right size, either because their feet are bigger or smaller than average. Shoes range from $13\text{-}2^{1/2}$ in small sizes (American $1\text{-}4^{1/2}$, European 31 to 34), and large English sizes $8^{1/2}\text{-}11$ (American $10^{1/2}\text{-}13$, European 42 to 46). The shoes are stylish and foreign made. They also specialise in special-occasion and party shoes for all sizes. A useful find.

Tricker's

67 JERMYN ST, SW1, 020-7930 6395
Open Mon.-Fri. 9.30am-5.30pm, Sat. 9.30am-5pm.
U: Piccadilly Circus/Green Park.

The all-leather shoes for men are made in Northampton, the historic centre of the English footwear industry. This old-fashioned shop offers a made-to-measure service where classic brogues and tasseled penny loafers are popular styles. The walls are lined with wooden lockers, adding to the olde-worlde charm.

SWEATERS & WOOLLENS

Belinda Robertson
4 WEST HALKIN ST, SW1, 020-7235 0519
WWW.SHORTANDROBERTSON.CO.UK.
Open Mon.-Tues. & Thurs.-Sat. 10am-6pm,
Wed. 10am-7pm.
U: Knightsbridge.
　If you like your cashmere on the bright and fashionable side, this is the place to find it. Take your pick from the excellent styles hanging in this clean and stylish boutique, or—better still—ask for something from the made-to-order service, which has more than 100 delicious colours to choose from.

Berk
46 BURLINGTON ARCADE, W1, 020-7493 0028
Open Mon.-Sat. 9am-5.30pm.
U: Piccadilly Circus.
　A small shop stocked with neatly folded piles of cashmere sweaters, Berk has its own label and also stocks 'the world's largest selection of Ballantyne products'. Two additional Berk branches are within Burlington Arcade: at No. 6 (020-7493 1430), there is more women's knitwear, including throws; at No.20 (020-7493 6558), there are assorted designer labels, including Mulberry and Burberry accessories for men and women.

Lucien Pellat-Finet
9 POND PLACE, SW3, 020-7584 9458
Open Mon.-Wed. & Fri.-Sat. 10am-6pm,
Thurs. 10am-7pm.
U: South Kensington.
　Lucien Pellat-Finet, the chic cashmere label finally gets its own London outlet. Check out the luxurious men's, women's and children's cashmere clothing and accessories which you can try on in the cashmere-draped dressing rooms.

N Peal
37 BURLINGTON ARCADE, W1, 020-7493 9220
Open Mon.-Fri. 10am-6.30pm, Sat. 10am-6pm.
U: Piccadilly Circus.
　This roomy branch in Piccadilly stocks a wide selection of famous cashmere goods from N Peal, the company that was one of the first to redesign the ordinary cardigan or twin set and turn it into a high-fashion item. They offer elegant cashmere separates in fashionable colours for men and women. At the other (Piccadilly) end of the arcade at No. 71 (020-7493 0912), the cashmere sweaters are for men only.

Scotia
IVORY HOUSE, ST. KATHARINE'S DOCK, E1
020-7481 2556
Open daily 10am-6pm.
U: Tower Hill.
　Near the Tower of London, this is both a tartan and knitwear shop for men and women, stocking tartan kilts, capes, blankets and clothes for children as well as knitwear in cotton and wool. There is also a wide selection of Burberry and Pringle products.

Shirin Cashmere
11 BEAUCHAMP PL, SW3, 020-7581 1936
Open Mon.-Tues. & Thurs.-Fri. 10am-6pm,
Wed. 10am-7pm, Sat. 10.30am-6pm.
U: Knightsbridge.
　Founded in 1982, this family business designs and makes in its own factory, glamorous but wearable dresses, coats, jackets, separates and leg wear for women either in cashmere or silk knits. Each season brings its own new clever motif in the patterns. The styles are timeless. Upstairs, there is a useful cashmere clinic, which will wash and redress any cashmere garments to make them look like new. There are also classic cashmere sweaters for men.

The Scotch House
2 BROMPTON RD, SW1, 020-7581 2151
Open Mon.-Tues. & Thurs.-Sat. 9am-6pm,
Wed. 10am-7pm.
U: Kightsbridge.
　Located in Scotch Corner, the Scotch House has a wonderful collection of cashmere, lambswool and Shetland knits for men and women. Most are traditional in style and colouring, but a younger audience is catching on to the classic shapes and well-made knits (particularly the Barrie knitwear Tartan Rose twin sets with bold rose prints against a tartan backdrop), which look contemporary when worn with jeans. There is also an extensive selection of pure new wool tartans as well as a tartan room, where you can seek out your clan's tartan.
　Also at 84-86 Regent St, W1, 020-7734 0203; 165 Regent St, W1, 020-7734 4816.

Westaway & Westaway

65 GREAT RUSSELL ST, WC1, 020-7405 4479
Open Mon.-Sat. 9am-5.30pm, Sun. 11am-5.30pm.
U: Tottenham Court Rd.

There is something reassuring about shops like this one, where shelves are lined with sweaters and the tables are laden with tartan scarves, which match the sensible skirts hanging on the rack. A wonderful place for traditional woollens for men and women at reasonable prices and particularly favoured by chic young Italian and Spanish visitors.

UMBRELLAS

T Fox

118 LONDON WALL, EC2, 020-7606 4720
Open Mon.-Fri. 9am-5.15pm.
U: Moorgate.

Deep in the city, and good for all those rolled umbrellas types, Fox offers good made-to-order tailoring as well as services like engraving. They repair their own umbrellas. Mail-order on 020-8642 9561.

James Smith & Sons

3 NEW OXFORD ST, WC1, 020-7836 4731
Open Mon.-Fri. 9.30am-5.30pm, Sat. 10am-5.30pm.
U: Tottenham Court Rd.

Although very traditional, with umbrellas still made on the premises, this large shop is fun and pleasant to visit, thanks to its vast array of styles including frilly parasols in wonderful colours. There are also walking sticks in various lengths. The handsome façade, with its Victorian touches, is worth a photograph. It has been here since 1857; the shop was established in 1830.

Swaine Adeney

54 ST. JAMES'S ST, SW1, 020-7409 7277
Open Mon.-Sat. 10am-6pm.
U: Green Park.

Longtime fans of this fine riding and country clothes shop remember when 'Briggs' was part of the store name. The firm still holds the Royal Warrant as the umbrella maker to the Queen Mother and the quality Briggs umbrellas are still an important accessory sold in a variety of styles. There are golf umbrellas (from £50-£64) and the famous, collapsible 'stubby' (from £45-£55). This store now only focuses on menswear; women's wear is only

available from the factory shop at Nursery Rd, Saffron Waldon, Great Chesterford, Essex, 01799 530521.

FLOWERS & PLANTS

FLOWER SHOPS

Cameron Shaw

279 NEW KING'S RD, SW6, 020-7371 8175
Open Mon.-Fri. 9am-6pm, Sat. 10am-5pm.
U: Sloane Sq.

Dried flower sculptures are created with wit and humour by Kerry Longmuir. The final effect might be a moss-covered bicycle or the corner of a wheat field. A small rose pot is £18. The shop also supplies top furnishing stores.

Edward Goodyear

45 BROOK ST, W1, 020-7629 1508
Open Mon.-Fri. 8.30am-5.30pm.
U: Bond St.

Located inside Claridge's, this long-established florist has been arranging country flowers for high society since 1880 and holds four Royal Warrants—the most you can get.

Fast Flowers

339 FULHAM RD, SW10, 020-7352 8618
Open Mon.-Fri. 10am-6pm, Sat. 10.30am-4pm.
U: South Kensington.

The turquoise-fronted shop has eye-catching displays and the pretty jugs of flowers look picturesque against the red-tiled floor. A small bunch costs £20 plus delivery charge.

Also at 609 Fulham Rd, SW6, 020-7381 6422.

Felton & Sons

220 BROMPTON RD, SW3, 020-7589 4433
Open Mon.-Fri. 9am-5.30pm, Sat. 9am-11am.
U: South Kensington.

From its large corner shop in the heart of fashionable Kensington, Felton's—lit by a chandelier—offers good service to a regular clientele who appreciate traditional arrangements.

Flowercity

40 CITY RD, EC1, 020-7336 6337
WWW.FLOWERCITY.CO.UK.
Open Mon. 7am-6.30pm, Tues. 8am-6pm,
Wed.-Fri. 8am-7pm.
U: Old St.

The curved glass frontage reveals an array of dazzling flowers, exotic plants and a cool coffee shop decked out in stainless steel and glass. Of the many ingenious services offered by this new firm, the Espresso Delivery Service is tops. You call when you are five minutes away from the store and your flowers and coffee will be brought directly to your car (Thursday and Friday evenings only). 'Petal Points' is an incentive for anyone who regularly orders flowers to redeem their points for a free bouquet or a lunchtime Flower Masterclass. A small line of gifts and cards is also available.

The Flower Store

282 SEVEN SISTERS RD, N4, 020-7561 9287
Open Mon.-Sat. 9am-7.30pm.
U: Finsbury Park.

If, by chance, you happen to find yourself near Finsbury Park, reawaken your senses at this eye-catching store. Maybe the reason it stands out so much is because everything else in the vicinity is so drab, but the colourful, exotic flowers sing out from the minimalist shop. Speaking of singing, rumour has it that even Madonna has made note of the address. If this Material Girl were to pull up outside in her limo, the locals probably wouldn't believe it.

Kenneth Turner

125 MOUNT ST, W1, 020-7355 3880
Open Mon.-Fri. 9.30am-5.30pm, Sat. 10am-4pm.
U: Bond St.

Quite simply, the best designer of dried flower arrangements in Britain, possibly in the world. Kenneth Turner creates the most fabulous decorations for private homes, weddings, clubs and hotels and flies around the world for clients. In the sweetly scented shop you can be inspired by wonderful aromatic candles, dried arrangements and a good selection of candlesticks and holders.
Also at 18 Russell St, WC2, 020-7240 6026.

McQueens

126 ST JOHN ST, EC1, 020-7251 5505
Open Mon.-Fri. 8.30am-6pm, Sat. 9am-3pm.
U: Barbican.

Maybe it's a coincidence but McQueens, like British fashion's hottest export of the same name, produces some of the best floral designs around. The window display is minimal and modernist with the kind of artistic displays that stop you dead in your tracks.
Also at 130 Lauriston Rd, E9, 020-8510 0123.

Moyses Steven

157-158 SLOANE ST, SW1, 020-7259 9303
Open Mon.-Fri. 8.30am-5.30pm, Sat. 8.30am-4.30pm.
U: Knightsbridge.

Masses of seasonal flowers and a selection of garden ornaments greet discerning customers at this top florist shop that's filled with imaginative designs.

Parterre

8 MARYLEBONE PASSAGE, W1, 020-7323 1623
Open Mon.-Fri. 9am-5.30pm.
U: Oxford Circus.

The stunning impact of this shop is due to the well-laden baskets of fabulous flowers, including exotic varieties. There is a dried-flower room and a floristry school, all run by the talented owners, Jane Durbridge and Nigel Wooller.
Also at Aveda, 28-29 Marylebone High St, NW1, 020-7935 9507.

Pont

104 KENSINGTON CHURCH ST, W8
020-7727 6060, WWW.PONT.CO.UK
Open Mon.-Fri. 7.30am-9pm, Sat. 8am-8pm,
Sun. 9.30am-3.30pm.
U: High St Kensington.

The wonderful scent of fresh flowers greets you the minute you step into this nautically themed shop. All the flowers are transported in water, right from the time they are picked in Holland ensuring that they are in optimum condition. Beautiful bouquets wrapped in navy paper and raffia cost from £10; swags from £5.50 per foot and table arrangements to your design start from £20.

Pulbrook & Gould

127 SLOANE ST, SW1, 020-7730 0030
Open Mon.-Fri. 9am-5.30pm, Sat. 10am-2pm.
U: Knightsbridge.

A large, glamorous showplace, established more than 30 years ago by Lady Susan Pulbrook and Rosamund Gould, the eponymous shop became known for its innovative, natural approach to flower arranging and for its use of masses of white flowers. They also sell their own line of reviving lotions such as herbal hand cream and hand scrub gel as well as scented candles. The Lady Pulbrook Flower School passes on its techniques in one-day sessions, which include flowers and lunch.

FLOWER MARKET

Columbia Road Market

COLUMBIA RD, E2
Open Sun. 7am-3pm.
U: Old St.

There's a wonderful atmosphere at this busy Sunday market. Pick up bargain bedding plants by the tray, house plants and bunches of fresh and dried flowers. The shops on this picturesque Victorian street cater to the gardening fan and are full of delightful ceramics, urns, garden furniture, vases and accessories. Even if you don't want to buy plants, you can still enjoy the bustling environment and take in a bagel, bun or tea in a number of good small cafés.

GARDENING

Avant Garden

77 LEDBURY RD, W11, 020-7229 4408
Open Mon.-Sat. 10am-5pm.
U: Westbourne Park.

Joan Clifton runs this delightful shop which is an inspiration to the aspiring indoor and outdoor gardener. You'll find original candelabra, amphorae and pot stands, as well as gardening tools like her 'Monet' watering cans, buckets and jugs. Wire work is a specialty and comes in various shapes to use as topiary frames. Also, a good range of English-made terracotta plant pots.

The Chelsea Gardener

125 SYDNEY ST, SW3, 020-7352 5656
Open Mon.-Sat. 10am-6pm, Sun. noon-6pm.
U: Sloane Sq.

Being located in trendy Chelsea means this garden centre is always up-to-date with the latest fashions in gardening plants. The various plots are well labeled, helpfully pointing out which plants are suitable for shady or sunny spots. Inside, there is a wide choice of unusual houseplants, cacti and dried and silk flowers.

Clifton Nurseries

5a Clifton Villas, W9, 020-7289 6851
Open Mon.-Sat. 8.30am-6pm, Sun. 10.30am-4.30pm.
U: Warwick Ave.

Popular, well tended centre, which caters to everyone from patio gardeners to those fortunate to have a larger plot or even an estate. Staff is extremely friendly and very helpful; the selection is one of the best in London and gives you great inspiration.

FOOD

Anyone even moderately interested in food should visit the food halls of the big department stores. The 'Big Four' are Harrods, Fortnum & Mason, Selfridges and Harvey Nichols. We also have included here several smaller shops that also cover the gastronomic spectrum.

BAKERIES

& Clarkes

122 KENSINGTON CHURCH ST, W8
020-7229 2190
Open Mon.-Fri. 8am-8pm, Sat. 9am-4pm.
U: High St Kensington.

Bread doesn't come much tastier than the delicious loaves baked by Sally Clarke and her team. If plain old whole wheat is too run-of-the-mill, treat your taste buds to one of the 35 freshly baked varieties. There's Parmesan, apricot, black olive, fig and fennel or rye with poppy-seed varieties, plus ciabatta, sourdough and yummy baguettes. The cakes are special, too, as are the wines, Neal's Yard cheeses, homemade ginger nut and gingerbread men cookies, Whittard's teas and Monmouth's coffees.

Bagatelle Boutique

44 HARRINGTON RD, SW7, 020-7581 1551
WWW.BAGETELLE.CO.UK
Open Mon.-Sat. 8am-8pm, Sun. 8am-6pm.
U: South Kensington.

You don't have to cross the channel to sink your teeth into a chunk of real French bread, Bagatelle Boutique brings the flavour of France right to the centre of London. Using flour produced by owner Lessellier's family mill in France, the company produces crusty baguettes, rustic loaves and a selection of melt-in-the-mouth pastries. The ready-made dishes and hams, terrines, patés, quiches and fresh foie gras when in season, make delightful additions to dinner parties or a sumptuous feast on your own.

Baker & Spice

46 WALTON ST, SW3, 020-7589 4734
Open Mon.-Sat. 7am-7pm, Sun. 8.30am-2pm.
U: South Kensington.

Big advice if you're on a diet: don't walk anywhere near Baker & Spice. Even if you manage not to spy the brioche, croissants, pastries and tartes Tartin whispering 'eat-me-now' from the window, your nostrils will be teased by their intoxicating aromas spilling out to the street. Give in graciously, all of the delicacies here are well worth the horrific calorie count. Cakes made to order. Outside catering service also available.

Beverly Hills Bakery

3 EGERTON TERR, SW3, 020-7584 4401
E-MAIL: SALES@BEVERLEYHILLSBAKERY.COM
Open Mon.-Sat. 7.30am-6pm, Sun. 8am-5.30pm.
U: South Kensington.

Mmm is for the delicious all-American muffins at this small café/bakery. If your eyes are bigger than your stomach, no doubt you'll succumb to the hefty muffins in tempting fruity flavours or moreish chocolate. Those with smaller appetites can savour the same tastes in the dinky bite-sized varieties. The bakery also does a fine job with cookies, pastries, cakes and jams. The gift baskets make popular and tasty presents.

Bread Shop

65 ST. JOHN'S WOOD HIGH ST, NW8
020-7586 5311
Open Mon.-Sat. 7am-6.30pm, Sun. 8am-4.30pm.
U: St. John's Wood.

Super new bakery with unusually modern décor, offering a wonderfully large choice of organic, freshly baked breads, including a spelt loaf that's wheat flour and gluten free. Also here you'll find traditional cheesecake, danish filled with curd cheese, and the Parisian cream cake with custard cream.

Café Mezzo

100 WARDOUR ST, W1, 020-7314 4000
WWW.CONRAN.COM.
Open Mon.-Sat. 8.30am-11pm, Sun. noon-10pm.
U: Leicester Sq.

Trust Terence Conran to serve up his gourmet range of specialty breads and pastries in one of the most foody areas of London. Standards are high and the taste is exquisite (well, what do you expect, the bakery supplies the adjoining Mezzo restaurant). If your budget doesn't allow for a sit-down meal next door, pick up designer sandwiches and hot takeaway dishes from the refurbished café.

Carmelli Bakeries

126-128 GOLDERS GREEN RD, NW11, 020-8455 2074
Open Mon.-Wed. 7am-1pm, Fri. 7am-until one hour before sunset, Sat. 7am-one hour after sunset.
U: Golders Green.

You don't have to be Jewish to appreciate the fine specimens of breads on sale at this popular north London bakery. Go for challah, bulka, Russian black rye and plain, sesame and rye bagels, as well as an assortment of cakes, including Jewish delicacies, cheesecakes and strudels.

De Baere

101 NOTTING HILL GATE, W11, 020-7792 8080
Open Mon.-Sat. 8.30am-6.30pm, Sun. 9am-1pm.
U: Notting Hill Gate.

This is a Belgian chocolate firm, need we say more? The chocolate cakes here are to die for, but they also make all kinds of excellent pastries and breads. There's a tea-room for those who can't wait to sample them at home.
Also at 5-6 William St, SW1, 020-7235 4040; 24 Bute St, SW7, 020-7591 0606; 3 Shepherd St, W1, 020-7408 1991.

De Gustibus

6 SOUTHWARK ST, SE1, 020-7407 0020
WWW.DEGUSTIBUS.CO.UK
Open Mon.-Fri. 7am-7pm, Sat. 7am-3pm.
U: London Bridge.

When it comes to bread, there's more than good old-fashioned white sliced and whole wheat. If you need proof, take a look at the bakers at work at the recently opened De Gustibus on Southwark Street to find out. Dan and Annette Schickentanz's new second London outlet puts the focus on the craftsmanship of breadmaking. Their bakers take centre stage in the front of the shop where customers can watch them creating the most original and tastiest loaves in town. If honey-lavender, pumpkin, Alpine museli or coriander-ginger foccacia don't tickle your fancy, then maybe the raisin walnut & stout, date-honey-mixed fruit, or savoury potato breads might. There are plainer varieties from which to choose such as farmhouse, plain ciabatta, white bloomers, challah, crusty whole wheat and a host of ryes. It almost seems a shame to deny your taste buds the privilege of the more unusual flavours, which run to so many mouthwatering options. The company also runs day courses on bread making for both beginners and experienced bakers.
Also at 53 Blandford St, W1, 020-7486 6608.

Bagels

There are some great places for bagels in London, either to take home, or to eat, filled with smoked salmon, cream cheese and more in the early hours of the morning after (or during) clubbing.
Check out: **Angel Bagel**, 53 Goodge St, W1, 020-7636 0561; **Brick Lane Beigel Bake**, 159 Brick Lane, E1, 020-7729 0616, open 24 hours for well-filled bagels at any time, plus challah, rye and cheesecake. **Carmelli Bakeries**, 128 Golders Green Rd, NW11, 020-8455 3063 for a huge range of breads and traditional bagels. **Great American Bagel Factory**, 18 Endell St, WC2, 020-7497 1115, 20 Charlotte St, W1, 020-7631 0790; **Harry Morgan**, 31 St. John's Wood High St, NW8, 020-7722 1869, a restaurant and deli for bagels and classic fare like gefilte fish, latkes and more.

Euphorium Bakery

203 UPPER ST, N1, NO TELEPHONE NUMBER
Open Mon.-Sat. 8am-5pm, Sun. 9.30am-3.30pm.
U: Angel.

Every morning you'll find lengthy queues for the delicious freshly made croissants, French sticks, baguettes and feathery crisp Danish pastries. In the afternoon, the emphasis shifts to the pizza slices, focaccia and ciabatta sandwiches, sweet tartlets and tempting cakes.

Jane Asher Party Cakes

22-24 CALE ST, SW3, 020-7584 6177
WWW.JANE-ASHER.CO.UK
Open Mon.-Sat. 9.30am-5.30pm.
U: Sloane Sq/South Kensington.

Let your imagination run wild at this specialist cake shop run by actress Jane Asher. Spaceships, guitars, buildings, animals—there's no limit to what this team can do with a fruitcake or sponge base and colourful fondant icing. Start off by looking through the catalogue of over 2,000 designs, but if you have a special theme or design in mind, the team of experts will rise to the occasion. Cakes are (from £120 to £600 for a large, intricate design). The small tearoom serves morning coffee, set afternoon tea and light lunches.

Maison Blanc

102 HOLLAND PARK AVE, W11, 020-7221 2494
Open Mon.-Thurs. 8am-7pm; Fri. 8am-7.30pm, Sat. 8am-7pm, Sun. 8.30am-6pm.
U: Holland Park.

Cake and pastry lovers travel miles for the exquisite concoctions available at the pâtisserie counter of this popular small chain. The 30 or so varieties of bread are baked according to French regulations, so you can be sure of that certain ooh la la in every bite.
Also in **Chelsea** at 11 Elystan St, SW3, 020-7584 6913; Fulham at 303 Fulham Rd, SW10, 020-7795 2663; **Hampstead** at 62a Hampstead High St, NW3, 020-7431 8338; **Holland Park** at 102 Holland Park Ave, W11, 020-7221 2494; **St. John's Wood** at 37 St. John's Wood High St, NW8, 020-7586 1982; **Richmond** at 27B The Quadrant, Richmond, Surrey, 020-8332 7041; **Turnham Green** at 26-28 Turnham Green Terrace, W4, 020-8995 7220.

Pâtisserie Valerie

44 OLD COMPTON ST, W1, 020-7437 3466
Open Mon.-Sat. 7.30am-10pm, Sun. 9.30am-7pm.
U: Leicester Sq.

Pâtisserie Valerie has expanded, but this, the original, is our favourite. It's small and cosy with wood-panelled walls and always crowded with locals and tourists alike. The gâteaux are a treat to the eye, and the profiteroles to die for.

Also at 215 Old Brompton Rd, SW3, 020-7823 9971; 105 Marylebone High St, W1, 020-7935 6240; 8 Russell St, WC2, 020-7240 0064; RIBA, 66 Portland St, W1, 020-7631 0467.

CHEESES

Barstow & Barr Fine Cheeses

204 Upper St, N1, 020-7359 4222
Open Mon.-Wed. 10am-7pm, Thurs.-Fri. 10am-8pm, Sat. 9am-6pm, Sun. 10am-3pm.
U: Angel.

In its new location, right next door to Euphorium Bakery, At Barstow & Barr Fine Cheeses, Islingtonians are in a state of perpetual bliss. The shop is also sought out by those from slightly further afield for its delicious ranges of British unpasteurised cheeses such as Colston Bassett Stilton, Tyning and cheeses from the Isle of Mull and Gubbeen. This shop also carries the French farmhouse cheeses, which include Coulommiers and a prize-winning Brie de Meaux. Make a meal by adding pickles, mustards, olives and, of course, a good loaf of Euphorium bread, also in stock.

Also at 32-34 Earl's Court Rd, W8, 020-7937 8004.

Cheeses

13 FORTIS GREEN RD, N10, 020-8444 9141
Open Tues.-Thurs. 10am-6.30pm, Fri. 10am-6pm, Sat. 9.30am-6pm.
U: None nearby.

You could easily miss this tiny shop in Muswell Hill, but cheese lovers should make a special attempt to find it. Although the shop is small, around 150 cheeses are stocked with an emphasis on farm-made varieties. Mainly from France and Britain, the cheeses include the unusual, such as goat's milk from the Canary Islands as well as cheeses made from ewe's milk, but you'll also find a small and good range of Italian and Spanish names. If you

don't know where to start, ask owners Trevor Crane and Vanesa Wilby for their expert advice and a sample.

International Cheese Centre

21 GOODGE ST, WC2, 020-7631 4191
Open Mon.-Fri. 9am-6.30pm, Sat. 9.30am-6.30pm.
U: Goodge St.

With anything from 350-400 cheeses from ten countries available at any given time, the International Cheese Centre offers an impressive range. English cheeses, mostly farmhouse varieties, are best represented, with France not far behind. A good proportion is made with unpasteurised milk and many use vegetarian rennet. Also a good selection of biscuits, jams, sauces and mustards made by small suppliers. Mail-order also available.

Also at The Parade, Victoria Station, SW1, 020-7828 2886.

Jeroboam's

51 ELIZABETH ST, SW1, 020-7823 5623
WWW.JEROBOAMS.CO.UK
Open Mon.-Fri. 9am-7pm, Sat. 9am-4pm.
U: Sloane Sq.

French and British farmhouse cheeses are the mainstay of this, one of London's best known and most popular cheese shops. The cheeses are beautifully presented and the staff is justifiably proud and knowledgeable about their excellent products, which encompass wines, pastas, oils, vinegars, and about 160 or so first-rate cheeses. You can join the monthly cheese club; you'll get a good return for your money.

Also at 96 Holland Park Ave, W11, 020-7727 9359.

La Fromagerie

30 HIGHBURY PARK, N5, 020-7359 7440
Open Mon.-Sat. 9.30am-7.30pm, Sun. 10am-5pm.
U: Arsenal.

If every neighbourhood had a cheese shop as delightful as this, supermarkets would have a much harder time shifting their blocks of bland Cheddars. As it is, devoted customers are prepared to travel miles for the array of mainly French and Italian cheeses stocked in Patricia Michelson's picturesque shop. Real devotees know that this is the place where they can find rarities such as Rogallais, creamy Butte or Pecorino Foglie di Noce matured in walnut leaves and shells. A small selection of unpasteurised British cheeses such as

Montgomery Cheddar are also stocked and you'll be encouraged to try before you buy, so expect to come away with a new taste sensation. You might also want to pick up a home-made tart (or two) or a loaf of Poilâne bread delivered weekly from Paris. Mail-order also available.

Neal's Yard Dairy

17 SHORTS GARDENS, WC2, 020-7379 7646
Open Mon.-Sat. 9am-7pm, Sun. 10am-5pm.
U: Covent Garden.

It is probably true to say that Randolph Hodgson has single-handedly saved true British and Irish cheeses from extinction. The shop opened in 1979 with Hodgson making and selling his own cheese. Now the business has expanded to include farm-produced cheeses from throughout Britain and Ireland. Every cheese in this shop has been handmade by a real person using real milk from real animals, properly 'brought up' on the premises. The cheeses are turned by hand and aged to perfection. Hodgson puts the maker's name on the cheese he or she produces. The vast majority is made from unpasteurised cow's, sheep's and goat's milk. Also yoghurt, olives and chutneys, and breads from Sally Clarke. Mail-order also available.

Paxton & Whitfield

93 JERMYN ST, SW1, 020-7930 0259
WWW.CHEESEMONGERS.CO.UK
Open Mon.-Fri. 9.30am-6pm, Sat. 9am-5.30pm.
U: Green Park.

Sir Winston Churchill once said, 'A gentleman only buys his cheese from Paxton & Whitfield' and those who have shopped there are inclined to agree. Like a good, ripe Brie, it oozes taste and quality, and its location, in the heart of the prestigious gentleman's district, St. James's, makes it the cheesemonger of choice with London's elite. The business has reigned supreme since 1797 and, despite changing hands and undergoing a delightful refurbishment, it still retains its original charm. There are around 200 British and European cheeses in stock, as well as a good selection of hams, meats, hand-raised pies and relishes. Sign up to become a member of the cheese society and receive special offers and tutored tastings. Mail-order service also available.

CHOCOLATE & CONFECTIONERY

Charbonnel et Walker

ONE THE ROYAL ARCADE, 28 OLD BOND ST, W1
020-7491 0939
Open Mon.-Fri. 9am-6pm, Sat. 10am-6pm.
U: Piccadilly Circus.

Don't be fooled by the name, Charbonnel et Walker is steeped in British history. Founded in 1875 when the Prince of Wales persuaded Madame Charbonnel to set up a confectionery establishment in London with a Mrs. Walker, Charbonnel et Walker continues to sell fabulous chocolates, made in oh-so-British Tunbridge Wells. Still using many of the original recipes from Mme. Charbonnel's book, you can discover the taste of real drinking chocolate or treat someone special to the Célébration Boîte Blanche, where your personal message can be spelled out in foil-covered chocolates. The company will courier chocolates the same day to addresses within London, and they also operate a mail-order service.

Also at 20 Royal Exchange, EC3, 020-7283 5843.

The Chocolate Society

36 ELIZABETH ST, SW1, 020-7259 9222
WWW.CHOCOLATE.CO.UK
Open Mon.-Fri. 10am-5pm, Sat. 10am-3pm.
U: Sloane Sq.

This is where foodies shop for chocolate in its purest form. Using high cocoa content, unrefined cocoa butter, natural vanilla and minimal sugar, chocolate becomes less of a cloying confection and more of a delicious luxury. From a caddy of first-class chocolate biscuits for after dinner nibbles to fresh, hand-made truffles with Champagne or raspberry filling for pure decadence, the Chocolate Society offers everything for the epicurean.

Godiva

247 REGENT ST, W1, 020-7495 2845
WWW.GODIVA.COM
Open Mon.-Sat. 9.30am-7pm, Sun. noon-6pm.
U: Oxford Circus.

Just Before Christmas, Easter and Valentine's Day, these chic little Belgian confectioners are in their element. Although the fabulous displays of luxury Belgian chocolates imported from Belgium on a weekly basis are always a feast to the eye, it is on the aforementioned chocolate-giving occasions that you find the real treats. Children will adore the huge chocolate Easter bunnies and Santas, while any woman probably will fall for the red Valentine's boxes.

Also at 150 Fenchurch St, EC3, 020-7623 2287; Harrods, 87-135 Brompton Rd, SW1, 020-7730 1234 & 4199; Selfridges, 400 Oxford St, W1, 020-7629 1234 ext. 3798.

Prestat
14 PRINCES ARCADE, W1, 020-7629 4838
Open Mon.-Fri. 9.30am-6pm, Sat. 10am-5.30pm.
U: Green Park.

A world of pure indulgence, strictly for real chocolate-lovers. The new décor gives this small shop a real chocolate-box appearance, thanks to the ornate mirrored walls and rich pink and royal blue shelves. Prestat supplies its sumptuous chocolates to Her Majesty The Queen. All the chocolates and truffles are handmade in England. A favourite is the velvety, cocoa-dusted, fresh cream Napoleon III truffles made to a nineteenth-century recipe and the recently launched Royal Tokaji Napoleon III truffle, infused with Louis XIV's favourite wine.

Rococo
321 KING'S RD, SW3, 020-7352 5857
WWW. VENUS@ROCOCHOCOLATES.DEMON.CO.UK
Open Mon.-Sat. 10am-6.30pm, Sun. noon-5pm.
U: Sloane Sq.

If you have a genuine passion for real chocolate, a visit to this shop is a must. Set up by Chantal Coady, who, whilst looking for part-time employment to finance her art degree, worked at Harrods' chocolate counter. She took her job very seriously and after exhaustive research, opened up shop, wrote the authorative books *Chocolate: Food of Gods* and *The Chocolate Companion* and founded The Chocolate Society. In her exquisite shop, which has become a mecca for those seeking chocolate in its purest form, you find bars of 'cru' chocolate—each type originating from specific beans from specific plantations. There are three Grand Cru bars made by the French Valrhona firm of which the top is made from the Criollo cocoa bean produced on an island in the Indian Ocean. Coady also stocks handmade English truffles. Try to get there as early in the day as possible: chocolates arrive daily and sell quickly. The shop has a great sense of fun: some of the gourmet chocolates are wrapped in painted silver to resemble brightly coloured fishes; there are scary-looking chocolate dinosaurs, and seasonal delights like snowballs and holly berries at Christmas.

COFFEE & TEA

Algerian Coffee Stores
52 OLD COMPTON ST, W1, 020-7437 2480
WWW.ALGCOFFEE.CO.UK
Open Mon.-Sat. 9am-7pm.
U: Leicester Sq.

The big-bucks coffee chains may come and go, but this shop is destined to outlive them all. Serving aromatic coffee and teas since 1887, the shop is something of an institution amongst aficionados, particularly as all the varieties are produced solely for the shop. Try the Lebanese with cardamom and Maragogype, the largest coffee bean in the world. If you're a tea drinker, have a field day selecting from more than 200 varieties. The company also sells an array of coffee-making equipment and operates a mail-order service.

Angelucci Coffee Merchants
23B FRITH ST, W1, 020-7437 5889
Open Mon.-Wed. & Fri.-Sat. 9am-5pm, Thurs. 9am-1pm.
U: Tottenham Court Rd.

This tiny corner shop, still run by the Angelucci family, has stood on the same site for its entire 70-year history. Its appearance suggests that very little has changed in that time. If it's razzamatazz you're after, you're in the wrong place—this is purely a no-frills, no-fuss operation. Choose from 35 international coffees from such places as Puerto Rico, Angola, Kenya and Haiti. Make up your own blend or go for their best-selling Mokital coffee. Mail-order also available.

Drury Tea & Coffee Co
3 NEW ROW, WC2, 020-7836 1960
WWW.DRURY.UK.COM
Open Mon.-Fri. 8.30am-6pm, Sat. 11am-5pm.
U: Leicester Sq.

This well-known company has been in London for more than 50 years. Much of its business is in the catering trade which goes some way in explaining its popularity. The shop is bright, friendly and traditional. Teas are from Sri Lanka, India, China, Formosa and Africa together and there are a range of flavoured infusions. Try China Rose Tippy

Golden Darjeeling or one of Drury's traditional blends, like English Breakfast and pick up all the paraphernalia like infusers, teapots and accessories whilst you're here.

Also at 37 Drury Lane, WC2, 020-7836 2607; 1 York Rd, SE1, 020-7928 0144.

H R Higgins

79 DUKE ST, W1, 020-7491 8819
Open Mon.-Wed. 8.45am-5.30pm, Thurs.-Fri. 8.45am-6pm, Sat. 10am-5pm.
U: Bond St.

More than fifty years in business and still in family hands, H R Higgins' coffees are sold by appointment to The Queen. Given its impressive status, you can be assured that the quality is first-rate. There are coffees from Colombia, India, Sumatra, Costa Rica, Mexico, Tanzania, Jamaica, Guatemala, Ethiopa, Brazil and Java.The many teas are equally sought after and you can sip one in the small tearoom downstairs.

L Fern & Co

27 RATHBONE PL, W1, 020-7636 2237
Open Mon.-Fri. 8.30am-5.30pm, Sat. 10am-4pm.
U: Tottenham Court Rd.

The company was originally a Covent Garden coffeehouse when it set up business in 1863. Despite a change of address, Fern's has still managed to retain an olde-worlde image. It's all aged wooden dressers, brass-plated labels and antique caddies, providing the ideal showcase for its 14 coffee blends, dozen or so teas and coffee-making equipment.

Monmouth Coffee Company

27 MONMOUTH ST, WC2, 020-7836 5272
WWW.COFFEE@MONMOUTH.CO.UK
Open Mon.-Sat. 9am-6.30pm.
U: Leicester Sq.

Many claim that this is one of the best places to buy coffee in London. With good reason. In addition to being retailers, the Monmouth Coffee Company imports its own Arabica beans from Colombia, Kenya, Nicaragua, Costa Rica and Papua New Guinea. The beans are roasted on the premises six days a week and each is available in medium and dark roasts. You can even buy green (unroasted) coffee beans and roast them yourself (instructions provided). Sit and sip the varieties at the back of the shop.

The Tea House

15 NEAL ST, WC2, 020-7240 7539
Open Mon.-Sat.10am-7pm, Sun. noon-6pm.
U: Covent Garden.

Depending on your personality, looking through the windows of this shop will either entice you or make you turn on your heels and run a mile. There are novelty teapots shaped like elephants—Sherlock Holmes and dragons are not everybody's cup of tea. However, even those who prefer their cuppa from plain, white china will find the perfect infusion to brew in this wonderful shop stocking loose leaves from China, India, Japan, Sri Lanka, Taiwan, Kenya, Russia, Turkey and South Africa. For a lighter, fresher taste, try one of the fruit, flower and flavoured teas such as mango, caramel, coconut, honey, passion fruit and vanilla.

Twinings

216 STRAND, WC2, 020-7353 3511
Open Mon.-Fri. 9.30am-4.45pm.
U: Aldwych.

The Twinings name is highly regarded in the tea business, which is not surprising as the family firm's long history dates back to 1706. In this wonderful, rather eccentric shop, you'll find a wide selection of all Twinings' varieties, together with tea towels, teapots, infusers and a small museum at the back to trace how it all began. Mail-order also available.

FISH & GAME

B & M Seafoods

258 KENTISH TOWN RD, NW5, 020-7485 0346
Open Mon.-Sat. 9am-5.45pm.
U: Kentish Town.

A bonus for those living in Kentish Town and further north, B & M has carved out a real market, with a good range of flappingly fresh fish, including smoked swordfish and cooked crabs. The Pure Meat Company supplies the other half of the business—top organic meat. Their sausage list is also great, covering Toulose and wild boar. Other specialities include crown of lamb and rôti de veau.

The Caviar House

161 PICCADILLY, W1, 020-7409 0445
Open Mon.-Sat. 9am-9pm.
U: Green Park.

If you have a passion for caviar, this Danish-owned firm in a prominent site on Piccadilly is among the best places to indulge it. Operating internationally since 1950, the company offers Iranian sevruga, oscietre, beluga, imperial, royal black and classic grey caviars, all packed and imported daily from the Caspian. The staff are happy to answer any questions you might have. They will also advise on complementary products such as wine, smoked wild Norwegian salmon, vodka and chocolates, all of which are also available in the shop. For a treat, enjoy a caviar-based meal in La Cave, an on-site restaurant

John Blagden
65 PADDINGTON ST, W1, 020-7935 8321
Open Mon.-Fri. 7.30am-5pm.
U: Baker St.
This pretty, blue-glazed brick shop is sought out for its fish and game. It's a family-run business, so you can expect lots of friendly banter amid the knowledgeable advice on the displays of seabass, red mullet, wild Scotch lobsters and native oysters. The game—Aylesbury and Barbary ducks, teal and grey-legged partridge—are all hung and plucked on the premises.

R H Jarvis & Sons
56 COOMBE RD, KINGSTON-UPON-THAMES, SURREY, 020-8546 0989
Open Mon.-Fri. 8.30am-5.30pm, Sat. 7.30am-4.30pm.
Rail: Norbiton.
Those in the know think nothing of venturing out to Kingston to get their hands on the first-rate sushi and sashimi and other delights such as sea urchins. Even those with less adventurous palates are more than delighted with the flappingly fresh fish and British delicacies such as Devon-smoked sprats and jellied eels. Make a point of going in the winter months for the wild duck, pheasant, quail, grouse, hare and venison.

Steve Hatt
88-90 ESSEX RD, N1, 020-7226 3963
Open Tues.-Sat. 7am-5pm.
U: Angel.
This fourth-generation fishmonger sells only prime quality fresh fish like brill, turbot, John Dory and halibut. He also smokes his own haddock, trout and mackerel on the premises. From Dover sole to Devon squid, everything is amazingly fresh and there is an enormous range. Fish specially flown in include tuna,

swordfish, snapper and doranda as well as fresh, raw king prawns. Of course, there is also a wide array of cod, plaice, herrings, mackerel, trout, salmon (wild and farmed), sea bream, monkfish, skate and red mullet. Most importantly, they are happy to advise and provide on-the-spot processing of cuts required for recipes.

GOURMET SHOPS & EMPORIUMS

Bluebird
350 KING'S RD, SW3, 020-7559 1141
WWW.CONRAN.COM
Open Mon.-Wed. 9am-8pm; Thurs.-Sat. 9am-9pm; Sun. noon-6pm.
U: Sloane Sq.
Conran's stylish emporium, housed in the former Bluebird garage, is as much a place to be seen as it is to purchase delectable produce. Where the petrol pumps once were, there's now a long stand of fruit and vegetables lit by magnificent flares at each end at night and protected somewhat by a glass canopy. The whole of the ground floor, with the exception of a café, is taken up by a food, wine and cook shop. The selection is admirable: excellent Bresse chickens, exceptional cheeses, all the speciality foreign labels and Conran's own label, too, in sauces and preserves, biscuits and pastas. Prices are high, but so is quality.

Butlers Wharf Gastrodome
36 SHAD THAMES, SE1, 020-7403 4030
WWW.CONRAN.COM
Open Mon.-Fri. 8.30am-7.30pm, Sat.-Sun. 10am-6pm.
U: Tower Hill.
The way to a man's heart is through his stomach, so they say, in which case, Sir Terence Conran must be one of the world's happiest and most contented men. Good food is his passion and bringing together the best ingredients in British surroundings has been his mission for a number of years. Like his other gourmet haven, Bluebird, the emphasis is on food shopping par excellence. Therefore, you'll find an oil and spice shop offering around 90 spices (all ground on the premises), fragrant vinegars and olive oils all open for tasting. There's a food store (see above) stocking cooked meats, Neal's Yard cheeses, jams and splendid breads baked in-store and a smoked fish crustacea shop displaying an impressive selection of seafood.

Fortnum & Mason

188 PICCADILLY, W1, 020-7734 8040
WWW.FORTNUMANDMASON.COM.
Open Mon.-Sat. 9.30am-6pm.
U: Piccadilly Circus.

Fortnum & Mason is definitely one of the must-see experiences for food lovers in London. Established in 1707 and with three Royal Warrants under its belt, the Fortnum's experience is enough to make anyone feel like royalty. The food hall is very grand and traditional. Most of the myriad goods here are Fortnum & Mason's own label. Then, of course, there are wines, a range of fresh fruits and vegetables and an excellent selection of cigars. Around 200 cheeses are available at any one time, as well as sausages, smoked fish, pâtés, hams, fresh pasta, traditional English pies and freshly ground coffee. For those with a sweet tooth, there are delicious pastries and a large chocolate counter. The tea section is always busy, with visitors buying phenomenal amounts. In summer and at Christmas, their food hampers are the most sought after in the world.

Green's Picnics & Hampers

36 DUKE ST, ST. JAMES'S, SW1, 020-7493 4097;
ORDERS 020-7930 3146. WWW.GREENS.ORG.UK
Open Mon.-Fri. 9am-6pm.
U: Green Park.

Although Green's doesn't operate as a retail outlet, this smart restaurant in St. James's will prepare some of the best gift boxes and hampers in town. Choose from Mixed Hampers consisting of an enviable collection of food and drink; the Cognac and Champagne Hamper made up of four quality French brandies and two Riedel brandy balloons; the Cigar Hamper, dubbed as the complete kit for the cigar connoisseur, including ten Montecristo No. 4 cigars and a smoking cap. The company can also tailor-make hampers and gift boxes. Call for details.

Harrods Food Hall

KNIGHTSBRIDGE, SW1, 020-730 1234
WWW.HARRODS.COM
Open Mon.-Tues. & Sat. 10am-6pm, Wed.-Fri. 10am-7pm.
U: Knightsbridge.

Harrods started life as a top quality grocer in 1849, and, befitting its roots, it is now one of the largest food stores in London. Within its huge space, there are seven rooms and eighteen departments—each with lavish marble tiles. Follow your nose to the charcuterie and dairy hall where you'll find 250 cheeses and dishes from around the world. The pâtisserie hall is like Billy Bunter's dreams, filled with richly decorated cakes, pastries, flans and tarts and 300 types of top-quality chocolate. Traditional British fare sits beside Continental and Aisan delicacies. There are also Harrods wines, as well as native oysters—in fact almost anything you can think of—in stunning surroundings.

Harvey Nichols Food Hall

109-125 KNIGHTSBRIDGE, SW1, 020-7235 5000
Open Mon.-Tues. & Sat. 10am-7pm, Wed.-Fri. 10am-8pm, Sun. noon-6pm.
U: Knightsbridge.

The airy, chrome-filled food department is like a temple to avid Sloane Street shoppers who like their food as stylish as their designer clothing labels. The entire fifth floor is devoted to food and drink in one form or another and there's a bar, café (see *Quick Bites*) and famous restaurant (see *Restaurants*). It's all very high-tech and very, very stylish. There are great cheeses, fruit and vegetables on display, meats and fish and a good traiteur selection. For fashion-conscious foodies image is all, so they absolutely adore the glam packaging, which looks great on the kitchen shelves. Designer olive oils are very much in evidence and the wine shop is first-rate.

Partridges

132 SLOANE ST, SW1, 020-730 0651
WWW.PARTRIDGES.CO.UK
Open daily 8am-10pm.
U: Sloane Sq.

As you might expect of an establishment situated just a stone's throw away from Sloane Square and boasting a Royal Warrant to Her Majesty the Queen, Partridges caters to the rich. The space may be small, but they pack in a lot of quality: exotic fruits and vegetables, wine, freshly baked breads, ground-to-order coffees, cold meats, caviar, biscuits and an assortment of ready-made dishes. Partridges also roasts their own free-range chickens, Barbary ducks and gammon knuckles daily, which makes it an ideal place to buy an impromptu meal. For a luxurious picnic, why not order a tailor-made hamper—it'll turn the day into a real event. Mail-order also available.

The Real Food Store
14 CLIFTON RD, LITTLE VENICE, W9
020-7266 1162
Open Mon.-Sat. 8am-8pm, Sun. 10am-5pm.
U: Warwick Ave.

When whole food addicts need an instant fix, they head straight to The Real Food Store. A cross between a health food and gourmet store, it successfully combines the best of both worlds without using refined sugar, MSG or E numbers. There are vitamins, smoked tofu and organically grown vegetables and carefully chosen products from around the world. There's lavender honey from Provence, organically grown almonds from Spain, Iranian dried apricots, Neal's Yard cheeses, olive oils and the shop's own label produce. A demonstration kitchen makes dishes for the shop and also for their catering service.

Selfridges Food Hall
400 OXFORD ST, W1, 020-7629 1234
WWW.SELFRIDGES.CO.UK
Open Mon.-Wed. 10am-7pm, Thurs.-Fri. 10am-8pm, Sat. 9.30am-7pm, Sun. noon-6pm.
U: Marble Arch.

Unlike the quintessentially English Harrods and Fortnum & Mason, Selfridges has a truly international flavour. Taste your way around the world, picking up British meats, cheeses, biscuits and mustards; Lebanese sweets, pistachios, pastries and honey; Indian, Chinese and Thai takeaway dishes; and all manner of Mediterannean treats. If the delightfully pungent aromas catch you on an empty stomach, take a seat at Yo! Sushi, oyster bar or Prêt-à-Manger before leaving (see *Quick Bites*).

GOURMET SPECIALIST, ETHNIC FOODS & TAKE-AWAY

Bonsai Catering
41 LOWNDES ST, SW1, 020-7460 0200/07768 897733. WWW.BONSAI-CATERING.COM

To give your dinner party or business function that 'wow' factor, just call Bonsai Catering. The new company, originated and run by friends Amanda Hale and Divia Lalvani, specialises in delicious, bite-sized Asian cuisine made with organic products where possible. The delicacies include mini yakitori, lemon soya chicken, aromatic crispy duck and assorted dim sum.

Carluccio's
30 NEAL ST, WC2, 020-7240 1487
Open Mon.-Sat. 11am-7pm, Sun. noon-6pm.
U: Covent Garden.

Owners Antonio and Priscilla Carluccio take your taste buds on a gastronomic tour of Italy. Delicacies might include the latest food finds for their annual 'hunting trips' such as fresh cuttlefish pasta, white Alba truffles in brine, and top-notch olive oils. A wide choice of Italian cheeses and salamis, cooked pasta dishes and antipasti are available, as are some of the best Tuscan wild boar and pork sausages (slasiccia di cingale). The lazy cook can choose from set-price, ready-prepared meals which the company can deliver. Antonio Carluccio is a self-confessed fungophile, so you'll find a wonderful assortment of hand-picked mushrooms gathered from secret sources around the suburbs (there is a wider choice in September and October), as well as truffles flown in fresh from Italy. Try Carluccio's latest venture at 8 Market Pl, W1, 020-7636 2228, which incorporates a café and food shop.

Drones The Grocer
3 PONT ST, SW1, 020-7259 6166
Open Mon.-Fri. 8.30am-10pm, Sat.-Sun 9.30am-10pm.
U: Knightsbridge.

Rhyming with the name given to those living in the vicinity (Sloanes), this shop is filled with gourmet treats like olive oils, relishes, sauces, antipasti and cheeses. They also sell take-out dishes served in the next-door café and offer complete meals for the harrassed host or hostess.

Finns
4 ELYSTAN ST, SW3, 020-7225 0733
Open Mon.-Fri. 8am-7pm, Sat. 8am-2pm.
U: South Kensington.

For those days when you can barely move, let alone cook, Finns always comes to the rescue. Each day they offer two or three seasonally driven soups, and prepared meat, vegetable and fish dishes. They also offer those little extras like quality preserves, flavoured olive oils and fragrant mustards made on the premises. If you're planning a dinner party but can't work your way around a recipe book, leave it all to Finn's.

Fratelli Camisa

53 CHARLOTTE ST, W1, 020-7255 1240
Open Mon.-Sat. 8.30am-6pm.
U: Oxford Circus/Tottenham Court Rd.

This is what delis in Italy must have looked like in the good old days—hams hanging from the ceiling, fresh and dried pastas piled high on the counter and a knowledgeable staff who takes pride in their produce and their work. The shop is filled with Italy's finest, like balsamic vinegars, olive oil, prosciutto, good cheeses, grappas and lip-smacking apéritifs.

The Hive

53 WEBB'S RD, SW11, 020-7924 6233
Open Mon.-Fri. 10am-5pm, Sat. 10am-6pm.
U: None nearby.

Honey-lovers should make a beeline for this delightful shop where owner James Hamill and his team make more than 100 honey-based products. These range from fresh-cut honeycomb and tangy honey mustards, to the most delicious honey and rum raisin fudge sauce. Take time to admire the five-foot glass beehive wall containing live bees at the back of the shop.

I Camisa & Son

61 OLD COMPTON ST, W1, 020-7437 7610
Open Mon.-Sat. 9am-6pm.
U: Leicester Sq.

Fancy, high-tech gastrodomes are all well and good, but pile-'em-high-and-sell-'em-with-care delis like this have a charm all their own. Most of the customers are regulars, picking up fresh (different varieties are made daily) and dried pastas, salamis, own-brand olive oils from Tuscany and Liguria, breads and fresh white truffles in season. However, passersby seem to gravitate to the shop thanks to the great smells and lengthy queues, which serve as a welcome mat.

La Grande Bouchée

31 BUTE ST, SW7, 020-7589 8346
Open Mon.-Fri. 8am-7pm, Sat. 8am-6pm.
U: South Kensington.

A well-stocked French deli, selling specialities like foie gras, truffles and great French cheeses. They also stock delicious filled sandwiches and baguettes.

Limoncello

402 ST. JOHN ST, EC1, 020-7713 1678
Open Mon.-Fri. 9am-7pm, Sat. 9.30am-2.30pm.
U: Angel.

A cool, bright and breezy traiteur deli, which successfully combines old-fashioned standards with modern flavours and style. The wide range of takeout foods, which include couscous and pot-roasted boned lamb, are all made in Limoncello's own kitchens and can be ordered in bulk for parties. There is a range of goods such as organic flour, dry-cured bacon, farmhouse cheeses, dried fruits, free-range eggs, speciality breads, wine, fresh fruit and vegetables and excellent olive oils.

Lina Stores

18 BREWER ST, W1, 020-7437 6482
Open Mon.-Fri. 7am-5.45pm, Sat. 7am-5pm.
U: Piccadilly Circus.

Brewer Street is famous for two things: one is slightly dubious, the other is this deli, which has stood on this site for 60 years. Lina's is filled with all of those scrumptious Italian basics like fresh and dried pasta, a variety of hams, Parmesan, risotto rice, pesto and polenta. The lip-smacking, award-winning ravioli is made daily on the premises and is stuffed with delicious flavours like pumpkin, sun-dried tomato and ricotta, and artichoke and truffle oil. Coffee can be ground to order.

Lisboa

54 GOLBORNE RD, W10, 020-8969 1052
Open Mon.-Sat. 9.30am-7.30pm, Sun. 10am-1pm.
U: Ladbroke Grove/Westbourne Park.

A well-known name in London both for its delicatessen (Notting Hillbillies love it on a sunny day, see *Quick Bites*), and a wide range of Portuguese delicacies, running from hams to spices, traditional bread to beers.

Mauro's

229 MUSWELL HILL BROADWAY, N10
020-8883 2848
Open Tues.-Sat. 10am-6pm, Sun.11am-4pm.
U: None nearby.

The front window is bright with Mauro's multicoloured fresh pastas in various shape, lengths and sizes made with spinach, saffron, beetroot and squid ink. Mauro also makes dried pasta with unusual flavours like wild mushroom, carrot, anchovy and bitter chocolate. To complement them there are ten to fifteen homemade sauces available daily, home-made sausages, marinated grilled aubergines and more.

Monte's
23 CANONBURY LANE, N1, 020-7354 4335
Open Mon.-Sat. 10am-7pm.
U: Highbury & Islington.

Monte's provides edible proof that food can be as good as sex. Their densely coloured pastas alone are enough to produce moans of delight, and their sauces, well, let's just say they're made to make your mouth water. The funky pasta bows come in a variety of flavours and colours—your dinner party guests will love the electric-blue pasta; the red-and-yellow striped bows (cumin and tomato); red-and-black striped (chilli and squid ink) or yellow-and-black striped (cumin and squid ink). For a tasty introduction, try a bag of several coloured pastas, with beetroot, tomato, carrot, spinach, chilli, pepper, cumin and squid ink providing the flavours. There are a number of sauces including five pestos (aubergine, basil, sun-dried tomato, roquette and mixed pepper), harissa, and meatballs in tomato sauce, all of which make the ideal accompaniment. Julia Monte makes all the takeout dishes and is happy to cater for dinner paties large or small. Favourites include chicken escalopes, baked risotto slices and stuffed peppers with goat cheese; for dessert, try pear and polenta cake, baked pears or her speciality, tiramisù. Yum!

Mr Christian's
11 ELGIN CRES, W11, 020-7221 0501
Open Mon.-Fri. 6am-7pm, Sat. 5.30am-6pm,
Sun.7am-4pm.
U: Ladbroke Grove.

Make a date with Mr. Christian's if you're looking for food with flair. This bustling deli has its own chef and kitchen to prepare their wide range of takeout food including roast chickens, risotto, salads and daily specials. There is a good selection of wines, Champagne and chocolates (made on the premises), plus pastries, 60 varieties of bread and up to 35 different salamis. If you want to catch this store at its peak, drop by on a Saturday afternoon when the crowds from Portobello Road market pile in to stock up on

foodie treats for their designer kitchens. On the other hand, if you want to shop in peace, go at another time.

Mortimer & Bennett
33 TURNHAM GRN TERR, W4, 020-8995 4145
Open Mon.-Fri. 8.30am-6.30pm, Sat. 8.30am-5.30pm.
U: Turnham Green.

Many products stocked by Mortimer & Bennett are exclusive to the shop and even those that aren't seem exclusive. There's a wide range of gourmet foods, including pasta sauces from Mauro's (see above), cheeses from France, Italy, Spain and Britain, smoked salmon, fresh pasta and agnolotti, coffee, tea, twelve varieties of olives and a good stock of Sally Clarke's breads.

Outpatients
154 NOTTING HILL GATE, W11, 020-7221 9777
E-MAIL: OUTPATIENTS@AOL.COM
Open Mon.-Fri. 10am-8pm, Sat. 9am-7pm,
Sun. 11am-5pm.
U: Notting Hill Gate.

They are a clever lot, those people who own Pharmacy restaurant (see *Restaurants*). What other name would you give your takeaway division than Outpatients? The prescriptions range from funky hampers, packed with their own-label collection of gourmet foods, plus little extras from big brands like Carluccio's. The shop is small, but manages to cram in lots of goodies like freshly baked organic breads, pastries and tarts, handmade chocolates, old-fashioned candies, fruit smoothies, own-estate olive oils, jams, pickles and organic Scottish smoked salmon. Takeout lunch foods include filled bagels, freshly made sandwiches, pizzolas and pots of salads. The 'Home Meal Replacement' offers a special menu-planning service, which allows customers to experience the Pharmacy menu in their own homes. Destined to be a big hit.

R Garcia & Sons
248-256 PORTOBELLO RD, W11, 020-7221 6119
Open Tues.-Sat. 8.30am-6pm.
U: Notting Hill Gate.

Catering to North Kensington's large Spanish and Portuguese community, this lively, well-stocked deli sells salted pigs' feet, tinned tripe, hams, salamis, olives, threads of saffron, piquillo peppers and Spanish cheeses.

The Rosslyn Delicatessen

56 ROSSLYN HILL, NW3, 020-794 9210
Open Mon.-Sat. 8am-8.30pm, Sun. 8am-8pm.
U: Hampstead.

You'll find marinated baby figs, cranberry and raspberry relishes, flavoured mustards, oils, vinegars, teas and coffees. Service is friendly and knowledgeable, and you can taste any of the 100 or so cheeses in stock before buying. This shop is famous for its freshly baked croissants and pastries, and the wide range of cheese and charcuterie. The lazy gourmet can enjoy prepared salads and several cooked dishes daily, such as chicken roulade and beef Wellington. Christmas hampers are a speciality. Catalogue available.

The Spice Shop

1 BLENHEIM CRESCENT, W11, 020-7221 4448
Open Mon.-Sat. 9.30am-6pm, Sun. 11am-5pm.
U: Ladbroke Grove.

It's hard not to come away from this aromatic shop without some spice. Owner Brigit Erath offers about 1,700 herbs and spices including twenty different chillies and about a dozen paprikas. The displays are small, which keeps them fresh. The mixes are tantalising; the possibilities of new tastes endless.

Talad Thai

320 UPPER RICHMOND RD, SW15, 020-8789 8084
Open Mon.-Sat. 9am-10pm, Sun. 10am-8pm.
Rail: Putney.

Well-stocked store with everything you've tried in Thai restaurants and more: chili sauces, herbs, coconuts among the fresh fruit and vegetables and Thai beers. There is also tableware.

Tom's

226 WESTBOURNE GROVE, W11, 020-7221 8818
Open Mon.-Fri. 8am-10pm, Sat. 8am-6pm,
Sun. 10am-4pm.
U: Bayswater.

It's not surprising that Tom's does so well, its owner certainly has a good pedigree. 'Tom' is Tom Conran, son of restaurateur Sir Terence and nephew by marriage of Antonio Carluccio. As you might expect, the surroundings are stylish with food to match. The influence is largely Italian, with a selection of single-estate olive oils, but France is not left out with a French cheese selection that includes Reblochon and Epoisses. There is a selection of ready-prepared dishes to take out and the best gourmet sandwiches, which you can have with a coffee at the coffee counter. Trendy Notting Hillbillies wouldn't shop anywhere else.

Villandry

170 GREAT PORTLAND ST, W1, 020-7631 3131
Open Mon.-Sat. 8.30am-8pm, Sun. noon-4pm.
U: Great Portland St.

Jean-Charles Carratini supplies top gourmet foods (at prices to match), all beautifully packaged and arranged in this impressive store. They sell rare cheeses from France as well as top British varieties, fresh vegetables, freshly baked bread, hams, pâtés and a delicious range of charcuterie. Sample the delights of the restaurant at the back (see *Restaurants*).

HEALTH FOOD

Bennett & Luck

212 UPPER ST, N1, 020-7226 3422
Open Mon.-Fri. 9am-7pm, Sat. 9am-6pm, Sun.
noon-5pm.
U: Angel.

Surprsingly, for an area brimming with hippy throwbacks and young bohos, there is only one major independent health food shop in central Islington. Luckily, this one stocks a large range of vitamins, skin and body care products, pulses, grains and whole-grain breads. A small selection of organic fruit and vegetables is available. The shop also has two alternative treatment rooms.

Freshlands

49 PARKWAY, NW1, 020-7428 7575
Open daily 8am-9.30pm.
U: Camden Town.

North London's finest health food store. The emphasis is on organic and unrefined food including grains, pulses, biscuits, cereals, pasta and coffee. There are plenty of wines, an array of vitamins and a good selection of take-out dishes and power juices.
Also at 196 Old St, EC1, 020-7250 1708.

Planet Organic

42 WESTBOURNE GROVE, W2, 020-7221 7171
Open Mon.-Sat. 9am-8pm, Sun. 11am-5pm.
U: Ladbroke Grove.

Now it is possible to lead a totally unblemished, environomentally friendly lifestyle, despite inhaling London's fumes. The large, bright, modern premises houses a bakery, delicatessen, wine department, butcher and fishmonger and a huge selection of fresh and packaged organic foods. All the meats have certificates from the appropriate authorised organisations attesting to the conditions under which they are reared. Organic sausages (free Saturday tastings) include the Arbroath fish sausage with smokey-flavoured fish blended with lemongrass and herbs. Aside from food, there's an extensive selection of vitamins, household cleaners, body care products and pet foods. 'Health-conscious customers can shop without having to read every label because each product conforms to our high standards', say the innovative owners Jonathan Dwek and Rene Elliott. There is also a coffee bar (organic, of course) and an on-site nutritionist. Delivery service available.

Sesame Health Foods

128 REGENT'S PARK RD, NW1, 020-7586 3779
Open Mon.-Fri. 9am-6pm, Sat. 10am-6pm, Sun. noon-5pm.
U: Chalk Farm.

Be careful not to swing around too quickly or you might find yourself crashing into one of the displays in this small, friendly whole food store. An excellent stock of organic produce and health remedies available, together with tasty takeout dishes that will make you feel virtuous for being so health-conscience.

Wholefood Ltd.

24 PADDINGTON ST, W1, 020-7935 3924
Open Mon.-Thurs. 8.45am-6pm, Fri. 8.45am-6.30pm, Sat. 9am-1pm.
U: Baker St.

Wholefood's offers products without artificial colourings, flavours or chemical additives. Seasonal, organically grown vegetables are available, as are breads, preserves, free-range eggs, fruit juices, pasta, cheese and organic wine. They have incorporated the old Wholefood butchers and packaged organic meat is available; and they take orders for fresh cuts. The shop also stocks a good range of books and health care products.

Covent Garden

The former fruit and vegetable market, immortalised in Shaw's *Pygmalion* and later the *My Fair Lady* movie, is now a covered shopping enclave called The Piazza. Its success with shops of every kind—food, fashion, gifts—has inspired the streets around to become a lively shopping and restaurant quarter. Don't miss pedestrianised **Neal Street** which also has the enclosed shopping mall, Thomas Neal's.

Wild Oats

210 WESTBOURNE GROVE, W11, 020-7229 1063
Open Mon.-Fri. 9am-8pm, Sat. 9am-7pm, Sun. 10am-5pm.
U: Ladbroke Grove.

A three-storey whole food emporium selling everything the health food buff might need. There are organic baby foods, an array of breads, cereals, grains and pulses, all sold by friendly, helpful staff.

MEAT & GAME

A Dove & Son

71 NORTHCOTE RD, SW11, 020-7223 5191
Open Mon.-Sat. 8am-1pm.
U: None nearby.

You only need to see the queues to know that Dove's is more than just a run-of-the-mill butcher. It was established 111 years ago and is still going strong under the direction of the third generation of the family business. The meat is mostly free-range and features Welsh lamb, Aberdeen beef and a wide range of game when in season. Their home-cooked hams and a good selection of British and French cheeses, specially sourced from small suppliers, add to the attraction. While you're here, stock up on a few of Lynda Dove's homemade pies such as the Highland with Highland beef flamed in whisky, beef Bourguignon, Moroccan chicken and fish pies.

Allen & Co

117 MOUNT ST, W1, 020-7499 5831
Open Mon.-Fri. 4am-4pm, Sat. 5am-12.30pm.
U: Bond St.

With its plush Mayfair address, you can't help but expect great things and, thankfully, Allen's doesn't disappoint. With more than two hundred years in the business, 141 of them spent in these premises, the company has carved out a great career. The meat is first-class and is sought out by many of the best kitchens in London.

Biggles

66 MARYLEBONE LANE, W1, 020-7224 5937
Open Mon.-Sat. 9.30am-6pm.
U: Bond St.

You can't beat a great British banger and the bangers here are among the best. Biggles is London's main dedicated sausage maker, and produces 60 handmade varieties. Try classics such as Toulouse and Cumberland, or go for something a little more unusual like Swedish potato or Beaujolais Nouveau. All sausages contain a minimum of 85 percent meat and are made on the premises each day.

Frank Godfrey

7 HIGHBURY PARK, N5, 020-7226 2425
Open Mon.-Fri. 8am-6pm, Sat. 9am-5pm.
U: Arsenal.

You'd never guess from the length of the queues that there are at least another three butchers in the immediate vicinity. Customers prefer to wait for the choice cuts of meat. Godfrey's buys them from small producers who rear their meat and game to excellent standards. For those who want the hard work done for them, Godfrey's offers ready-seasoned meats, including chicken and lamb kebabs, which kids seem to love.

The Highgate Butchers

76 HIGHGATE HIGH ST, N6, 020-8340 9817
Open Mon.-Fri. 7.30am-5.30pm, Sat. 7am-5pm.
U: Highgate.

This is everything a butcher's shop should be, and locals consider themselves blessed to have it right on their doorstep. It's a small shop, tucked into a row of small shops in Highgate's picturesque High Street. The meat is of an excellent quality and the butchers can handle special requests for customers, such as crown roast of lamb, boned saddle of lamb,

and Dutch veal. A list of sixteen sausages are made on the premises, including the traditional British favourite of Cumberland, alongside the more adventurous lamb and mint, and beef and Guinness, to name a few.

The House of Albert Roux

539 WANDSWORTH RD, SW8, 020-7720 4915
Open Mon.-Fri. 9.30am-7pm.
U: Clapham Common.

For a real boudin blanc or a few boudin noir sausages, this traiteur, inspired by top chef Albert Roux gets our vote every time. The meats can be prepared and tied and there is a good selection of hams and charcuterie. There is a vast selection of quality produce, including cheeses from Paris, a yummy pâtisserie section with breads and pastries baked in the Roux kitchens, exotic fruit and vegetables, confectionery and a fine choice of wines. Try any of the seasonally inspired, prepared dishes to takeout, like roulade of salmon or stuffed quails.

Lidgate's of Holland Park

110 HOLLAND PARK AVE, W11, 020-7727 8243
Open Mon.-Fri. 7am-6pm, Sat. 7am-5pm.
U: Holland Park.

Without doubt, one of the finest butchers/charcutiers in the country. Founded in 1850, the family business has earned numerous awards, which line the panelled walls. The beef, lamb, pork, chicken and eggs are all organic or free-range, and proprietor David Lidgate keeps in touch with the farmers who rear the animals that end up in the shop. Prince Charles' Highgrove Farm is one of the more wellknown suppliers. Exotic products include marinated wild boar cutlets (in season), bison, kangaroo and ostrich. Not to be missed are Lidgate's famous pies (lamb and leek, steak and kidney, cottage, game and coq au vin). They also stock a wide selection of English and French cheeses and preserves.

Richardson's of Ealing

88 NORTHFIELD AVE, W13, 020-8567 1064
Open Mon.-Thurs. 8am-5.30pm, Fri. 8am-6pm, Sat. 8am-4.30pm.
U: Northfields.

Admittedly the organically fed beef, free-range lamb and home-cured bacon are extremely popular, but Richardson's is renowned for its own-made, award-winning sausages. They also stock a selection of cheeses and cold meats.

Also at 110 South Ealing Rd, W5, 020-8567 4405.

Simply Sausages

341 CENTRAL MARKETS, EC1, 020-7329 3227
Open Mon.-Fri. 8am-6pm, Sat. 9.30am-1.30pm.
U: Farringdon.

Like its name says, this is a good place to shop for sausages. The range of handmade, preservative-free bangers is good, with about 35 varieties on offer, including seven types for vegetarians. Popular choices include, beef and Guinness and duck and orange.

South Kensington Butchers

19 BUTE ST, SW3, 020-7581 0210
Open Mon.-Fri. 7.30am-5.30pm, Sat. 7.30am-5pm.
U: South Kensington.

The French are renowned for their fastidiousness, so when they give something their seal of approval, you know that it is not exactly run-of-the-mill. The popular shop, in the heart of a large French community, stocks fine cuts of Scotch beef, Dutch veal, English lamb, game and free-range poultry. French cuts of meat are always possible, and perfectly complement the French tinned goods available.

WINES & SPIRITS

A visit to any of the main wine shop chains (liquor stores in Britain are known as 'off-licences'), will reveal an excellent selection of wines from around the world—from California, New Zealand, South Africa, France, Italy, Romania and Chile. The best wine shop chains are Oddbins with a very wide choice and its own selections and Nicolas, which offers some top French wines (look in the telephone directory for your local branch). For the avid wine buff, the following independent shops are recommended:

Berry Bros & Rudd

3 ST. JAMES'S ST, SW1, 020-7396 9600
WWW.BERRY-BROS.CO.UK.
Open Mon.-Fri. 9am-5.30pm, Sat. 10am-4pm.
U: Green Park.

Berry Bros. possesses the olde-worlde charm of a Dickens' novel with its creaky floorboards,

low ceilings and polished wood-panelled interior. It's little wonder really, since its stood on the same spot since the mid-eighteenth century and very little in the shop has changed. The stock is still amongst the best in London with fine traditional red Bordeaux and vintage ports along with newer varieties from California, Australia and New Zealand. The company stocks an array of single-malt Scotch whiskies, and has more recently branched out into coffees and some exclusive liqueurs. The advice given here is invaluable, the efficient staff can help with everything from building up your own wine cellar to the perfect wine to lay down as a Christening present.

Also at Terminal 3, Heathrow airport. Mail-order also available.

Bibendum

113 REGENT'S PARK RD, NW1, 020-7722 5577
WWW.BIBENDUM-WINE.CO.UK
Open Mon.-Sat. 10am-5.30pm.
U: Chalk Farm.

For wine expertise without the pomp and circumstance, this large warehouse is hard to beat, offering a mail-order only service. Used by many of London's top restaurants for its expertise in sourcing unusual names, its credentials are highly regarded. In addition to the more usual European wines, Bibendum offers some of the great full-bodied Australian, New Zealand, North and South American wines. Make a date for their regular tastings.

Corney & Barrow

194 KENSINGTON PARK RD, W11, 020-7221 5122
Open Mon.-Sat. 10.30am-9pm.
U: Ladbroke Grove.

With its main office in the ultra-conservative City, London's financial district, and a shop in the eternally arty Portobello area, Corney & Barrow attracts wine lovers from a wide spectrum. The Bordeaux first growths and top-name Burgundies keep the pin-striped City gents fulfilled, while the well-chosen list of house wines from the New World is just the thing for the boho crowd. A great source for good quality.

Justerini & Brooks

61 ST. JAMES'S ST, SW1, 020-7493 8721
Open Mon.-Fri. 9am-5.30pm.
U: Green Park.

Despite its plush address and sophistication, it's possible to find wines that are friendly on the wallet in this 250-year old wine merchants. The Bordeaux is very popular, as are the Burgundy and Rhône wines. The company also ventures further afield to the rest of Europe and the new world. Excellent, friendly service. Mail-order also available.

La Vigneronne

105 OLD BROMPTON RD, SW7, 020-7589 6113
WWW.LAVIG@AOL.COM
Open Mon.-Fri. 10am-8pm, Sat. 10am-6pm.
U: South Kensington.

Master of wine Liz Berry, the 'vigneronne' herself, is the genius behind this well-stocked little shop. Berry makes frequent travels to the Continent, particularly France, and knows all the producers' wines—and most of the producers themselves on a first-name basis. This being the only La Vigneronne, Berry is not confined by size, so if there's something good, but not much of it, she is happy to stock it. There are wines here that you won't find elsewhere. Speciality areas are Alsace and the Languedoc-Rousillon region in southern France, on which Liz is an expert.

GIFTS

Upmarket gifts are available at many of the shops listed under sections such as china, leather, jewelry and department stores, but this list features some small and specialist shops worth a visit. In keeping with the times, museum shops have greatly improved beyond the well-stocked postcard counter and we have noted our favourites here. If you have a specialist interest, check in the museum section for more.

Animation Art Gallery

13-14 GREAT CASTLE ST, W1, 020-7255 1456
Open Mon.-Thurs. & Sat. 10am-6pm, Fri. 10am-7pm.
U: Oxford Circus.

Disney characters are the stars at this unusual gallery which specialises in drawings made on celluloid (called 'cels') of cartoon characters such as Bugs Bunny, Peanuts or characters in movies such as *Snow White* and *101 Dalmatians*. The price range is from £20 to about £20,000. A video shows you exactly which frame of the final film you have purchased. Some original drawings are also on sale, plus a few limited editions.

Annabel Jones

52 BEAUCHAMP PL, SW3, 020-7589 3215
Open Mon.-Fri. 10am-5.30pm, Sat. 10.30am-5.30pm.
U: Knightsbridge.

The ground floor has delightful jewelry (look for the star and flower lines) and giftware, which includes glass globes in blue, green and yellow used as matching strikers. Heart-shaped clocks, dice-shaped paperweight clocks, egg-timers, cigar tubes, champagne coolers, novelty pepper mills, picture frames, pens and enamel cufflinks are among the silver items.

Asprey & Garrard

165-169 NEW BOND ST, W1, 020-7493 6767
Open Mon.-Fri. 10am-6pm, Sat. 10am-5pm.
U: Green Park.

'It can be done' is the motto of the resident artists, so expect to see an extravagant showpiece on display by the entrance. From the filigreed white wrought-iron trim and arches around the outside to the fifth floor, this is the ultimate gift shop with both tradition and a sense of frivolity. Look for the leather-bound photograph albums and agendas, playing cards, roulette wheels and dice on the ground floor.

Barclay & Bodie

7-9 BLEINHEIM TERR, NW8, 020-7372 5705
Open Mon.-Sat. 9.30am-5.30pm.
U: St. John's Wood.

This elegant shop is a wonderful source of gifts and some delightful boxes in which to put them. Practical as well as pretty, their French Provençal oven-to-tableware consists of hand-painted dishes designed to come straight from the oven or microwave to sit neatly into pretty woven baskets. They stock all sorts of goodies like bags, pewter boxes, initialled ladies handkerchiefs and wonderful miniature teapots in the shape of garlic heads, cabbages and cauliflowers. Just the thing for a collector.

British Museum

GREAT RUSSELL ST. WC1, 020-7636 1555
Open Mon.-Sat. 9:30am-6pm, Sun. noon-6pm.
U: Tottenham Court Rd.

There is a book shop, a children's shop and a gift shop which sells good reproductions of items from the museum's impressive collections, from Roman ear-rings to Egyptian cats. Recently opened on the corner of Gt. Russsell St and Bloomsbury at 22 Bloomsbury St, WC1, 020-7637 9449, is a stand-alone shop, impressively stocked with more British Museum items and a larger general stock than in the museum itself.

China House
160 PICCADILLY, W1, 020-7499 6996
WWW.CHINAHOUSE.CO.UK.
Open Mon.-Sat. 10am-10pm, Sun. noon-10pm.
U: Green Park.
All the merchandise such as the scented Feng Shui candles, lacquered boxes and bowls from Vietnam and Laos, Chinese wind chimes, Japanese kimono fabrics and aromatic bath and bodylines have been specifically chosen for their interpretation of the China House theme. You'll also find China House pandas, Chinese teas, handmade enamelled cufflinks and ladies watches.

Cologne & Cotton
791 FULHAM RD, SW6, 020-7736 9261
Open Mon.-Sat. 9.30am-7pm.
U: Fulham Broadway.
The cotton part of the title comes from the ranges of crisp cotton products ranging from bed linen and embroidered nightdresses to baby clothes and accessories. The cologne part comes into play with the ranges of eau de toilette and pure vegetable soaps, which are made especially for the company.
Also at 9 Kensington Church St, W8, 020-7376 0324; 88 Marylebone High St, W1, 020-7486 0595.

The Conran Shop
MICHELIN HOUSE, 81 FULHAM RD, SW3
020-7589 7401, WWW.CONRAN.COM
Open Mon.-Tues. & Fri. 10am-6pm,
Wed.-Thurs. 10am-7pm, Sat. 10am-6.30pm,
Sun. noon-6pm.
U: South Kensington.
The shopping list is endless and the products are irrestistible at Terence Conran's stylish emporium. There is china, stationery, toys, kitchenware, glassware, candles and holders, posh gardening tools, Indian textiles, and a small range of wonderful baby clothes. It would be virtually impossible not to find something for everyone in this wonderful store.

Also at 55 Marylebone High St, NW1, 020-7723 2223; 12-13 Conduit St, W1, 020-7399 0710.

Contemporary Applied Arts
2 PERCY ST, W1, 020-7436 2344
WWW.CCA.ORG.UK
Open Mon.-Sat. 10.30am-5.30pm.
U: Goodge St.
A light, bright and airy art gallery, filled with original, high-quality artefacts. Beautifully crafted and designed vases, pitchers and bowls are always on show along with changing displays of baskets, ceramics, textiles, glassware, metal, woodwork and more. Although you can buy the exhibits from the upstairs gallery, you can't take them away until the end of the exhibitions, which run for approximately six weeks. If you do want something you can walk away with, stick to the jewelry and crafts in the gallery shop downstairs.

Contessa Ghisi
25 WALTON ST, SW3, 020-7581 1373
Open Mon.-Sat. 10am-6pm.
U: South Kensington.
Sanna-Maria Chebanne and Marie Storm's cosy little shop is a wonderful place for seeking out gifts for very dear friends, or even better, for personal treats. The gorgeous mink-trimmed stoles, scarves, earmuffs and 'scrunches' are the creations of Sanna-Maria; the hand-blown Venetian glass jewelry and masks are designed and sought out by Marie Storm. Both women are equally passionate about the other's products as their own, so much so that you'll probably depart with something from each collection. A gem of a neighbourhood shop where the owners regularly invite their clients for lunch or tea in the charming room at the back of the shop.

Crafts Council
44A PENTONVILLE RD, N1, 020-7278 7700
Open Tues.-Sat. 11am-6pm, Sun. 2pm-6pm.
U: Angel.
Well away from the city centre, this shop has a constantly changing range of contemporary crafts created by artists who make sculpture, design scarves, carve wood and produce ceramics, pottery and glass. The handmade jewelry is wonderful, but it is possible to buy handmade automata too. It is part of the National Centre for the Crafts and houses a reference centre, exhibition space and café.

The Crafts Council also produces booklets and information on working in the crafts, and runs regular workshops and offers advice on funding, awards and bursaries. Some items sold at the Victoria and Albert Museum Shop.

The Cross

141 PORTLAND RD, W11, 020-7727 6760
Open Mon.-Sat. 10.30am-6pm.
U: Holland Park.

The area around Notting Hill Gate and Portobello Road seems to have cornered the market for stylish independent boutiques selling a variety of covetable products. The Cross is one such place, frequented by people seeking out beautiful home accessories and clothes, including delightful Irish candles, hand-painted glass, woven baskets, picture frames and mirrors. Well worth visiting.

Eximious

4 PONT ST, SW1, 020-7235 7828
WWW.EXIMIOUS.COM
Open Mon.-Fri. 9.30am-5.30pm, Sat. 10am-4pm
U: Knightsbridge.

This beautiful shop looking like an elegant private drawing room contains a first-class collection of gifts and accessories for the home. By appointment to the Prince of Wales, they sell a wide range from lacquered wooden planters to architectural bookends. They can monogram items for you, and produce personalised enamel boxes with photographs of your house, favourite animal or just a message. Their mail-order catalogue is a delight.

Gosh!

39 GREAT RUSSELL ST, WC1, 020-6373 1011
Open Mon.-Sat. 10am-6pm.
U: Tottenham Court Rd.

Gosh now stocks a great range of all types of comics, both new and collectors' editions. Having taken over the London Cartoon Gallery, now in the basement, there's the added fun of browsing through the work of eminent cartoonists for *Private Eye*, *The Guardian*, *Oldie* and many more. Also interesting playing cards.

Graham & Green

4, 7 & 10 ELGIN CRESCENT, W11, 020-7727 4594
Open Mon.-Sat. 10am-6pm.
U: Holland Park.

Eye-catching windows in the middle of the Portobello district attract passersby into this shop. Crammed full of original items such as planters, exotic candle sticks, ornate mirrors, glassware, rustic earthenware plates, linens and many intricate wrought-iron decorative items, you'll find kitchen and garden utensils in the basement and the remainder of the desirable stock on the ground floor. Cross the road for more of the same at Number 4, and Number 10 for clothing.

Also at 164 Regents Park Rd, NW1, 020-7586 2960.

Halcyon Days

14 BROOK ST, W1, 020-7629 8811
WWW.HALCYONDAYS.CO.UK
Open Mon.-Sat. 9.30am-6pm.
U: Bond St.

Charming enamel boxes are decorated with themes like Victorian flowers from the Victoria and Albert Museum archives or specific designs made for anniversaries or celebrations. Some have messages like 'Thank You'; others display sporting pursuits. There is always a Christmas, New Year and Valentine's Day box on offer for those who are stuck for gift ideas. The enamel is fired onto copper in Bilston, West Midlands, and each box has a certificate of authenticity. Antique enamel boxes and other wares such as pot-pourri baskets, mirrors, spill vases and photo frames fill the shelves and cabinets.

Also at 4 Royal Exchange, EC3, 020-7626 1120.

Irish Shop

14 KING ST, WC2, 020-7379 3625
Open Mon.-Thurs. 10.30am-7pm, Sun. noon-6pm.
U: Covent Garden.

Quality products from Ireland include fine Waterford, Galway and Tyrone crystal, Belleek and Royal Tara china, hand-knit Aran sweaters and a wide range of capes, jackets and outerwear.

Lady Daphne

145 SLOANE ST, SW1, 020-7235 2905
Open Mon.-Tues. & Thurs.-Sat. 9.30am-6.30pm, Wed. 9.30am-7pm.
U: Sloane Sq.

Hand-painted artefacts and decorative bits and pieces for the home have been designed by Lady Daphne Bailey using motifs such as the fleur de lys, flowers and butterflies. Items include waste paper baskets, table lamps, cache pots, umbrella stands and silk cushions.

Links of London

160 SLOANE ST, SW1, 020-7730 3133
WWW.LINKSOFLONDON.COM
Open Mon.-Tues. & Thurs.-Sat. 9.30am-6pm,
Wed. 9.30am-7pm.
U: Sloane Sq.

The cool cream walls are the perfect back-drop for the sleek, mainly silver, jewelry and accessories. Stylish novelty gifts are big business, particularly for men. You'll find cufflinks bearing cricket bats and balls, binoculars, footballs and boots and golfbags and balls. There are keyrings with Formula-One cars and sailing boats and numerous accessories for the male executive's desk, including a multifaced clock for keeping up with international time zones, perpetual calendars and paperweights. Women will love the sinuous lipstick cases, with an enclosed mirror, the neat compacts, bullet-like atomisers, handbag mirrors and the silver and recently launched gold jewelry collection. A thoughtful addition is the chill-out zone at the back of the shop where weary partners can recharge their batteries whilst surfing the Internet or catching up on the latest magazines.

London Transport Museum

33 EARLHAM ST, WC2, 020-7379 6344
WWW.LTMUSEUM.CO.UK
Open Sat.-Thurs. 10am-6pm, Fri. 11am-6pm.
U: Covent Garden.

The London Underground map is the most popular selling item, but reproductions of the best transport posters of previous decades make great souvenirs. The posters were works of art commissioned regularly to promote the destinations along the route and run from the opulent Art Deco styles of the 1920s through to today's modern graphics. Also worth looking out for are the recently introduced T-shirts and boxer shorts aimed at a younger audience. They include logos such as Hold Tight, Push Once and All Zones on the skinny-fit T-shirts, and Open Flap for Ventilation, Emergency Exit and Fire Extinguisher on the boxer shorts.

National Gallery Shop

TRAFALGAR SQ, WC2, 020-7747 2885
Open Mon.-Tues. & Thurs.-Sun.
10am-5.45pm,Wed. 10 am-8.45pm.
U: Charing Cross.

A splendid shop, full of posters, great range of art books and gifts centred mostly around

the gallery's splendid collections. They operate special shopping evenings just before Christmas.

National Portrait Gallery Shop

ST. MARTIN'S PL, WC2, 020-7306 0055
Open Mon.-Sat. 10am-6pm, Sun. noon-6pm.
U: Leicester Sq.

A wonderful shop with a large range of art books, many published by National Gallery Publications, prints, gifts and, of course, postcards and posters of many of the exhibitions.

National Trust

BLEWCOAT SCHOOL, 23 CAXTON ST, SW1
020-7222 2877
Open Mon.-Fri. 10am-5.30pm.
U: Victoria.

Inside this early 1800s building, a historic attraction in its own right, are products designed and produced for the National Trust, the organisation which maintains stately homes, country houses and much of the English countryside. The building was once a school for poor children: look for the little figure of a boy and girl on the back outside wall. The fabric designs of the aprons, tea towels, tea cosies and the printed designs of diaries and paper products are based on authentic patterns from National Trust properties like palatial Ickworth in Suffolk or are specially commissioned.

Neal Street East

5 NEAL ST, WC2, 020-7240 0135
Open Mon.-Wed. 11am-7pm, Tues.-Sat. 10am-7pm, Sun. noon-6pm.
U: Covent Garden.

More like a bazaar than a shop, covering all things Asian, from cards and notebooks to kimonos, folk craft, brightly coloured bed

For the Left-Handed

This is a wonderful shop and a delight to visit. Their best-selling line is scissors, but they also sell a left-handed sickle and additional useful items. **Anything Left-Handed**, 57 Brewer St, W1, 020-7437 3910, open Mon.-Fri. 9.30am-5pm, Sat. 10am-5pm. Mail-order catalogue available.

coverings, cloth bags, scarves, I Ching books and sculptures of Buddha.

Nina Campbell

9 WALTON ST, SW3, 020-7225 1011
WWW.NINACAMPBELL.COM
Open Mon.-Fri. 9.30am-5.30pm, Sat. 10am-4pm.
U: South Kensington.

A delightful shop well worth a visit for its mixture of goods, many of which you will be tempted to buy for your own home as well as for gifts. Items include beeswax bamboo-shaped candles, a variety of lamps and shades, lustrous flower pots, traditional and unusual photograph frames, cut cystal and silver dressing table bottles, hand-painted coffee cup and saucer sets, and glamorous Fortuny silk vases. You'll find beautiful fabrics at the fabric shop at 7 Milner St, SW3, 020-7589 8589.

Oggetti

135 FULHAM RD, SW3, 020-7581 8088
Open Mon.-Sat. 9.30am-6pm, Sun. noon-5pm.
U: South Kensington.

A temple for high-tech and the unusual. Expect the unexpected: domino sets composed of a variety of woods, a letter opener inlaid with pear, cherry, apple and other fruit woods and beautiful coloured glass tumblers. A branch a few doors away at 143 Fulham Rd, SW3, 020-7584 9808, stocks ultra-smart Alessi kitchenware, including their distinctively shaped kettles.

Past Times

146 BROMPTON RD, SW3, 020-7581 7616
Open Mon.-Sat. 9am-6pm, Sun. 11am-5pm.
U: South Kensington.

All eras of history are represented in this shop's gifts, whether it be a medieval manuscript jigsaw puzzle or a compact disc of Georgian chants. Laid out in chronological order, the varied giftware includes tapestry kits, jewelry, card games, calendars, satchels, candles and cards. Good mail-order catalogue.

Also at 179 Kensington High St, W8, 020-7795 6344; 155 Regent St, W1, 020-7734 3728.

Royal Academy of Arts

BURLINGTON HOUSE, PICCADILLY, W1
020-7300 8000
Open Mon.-Thurs. 10am-6pm, Fri. 10am-5.30pm.
U: Piccadilly Circus.

You'll find finely designed gifts here, most of them unique to the Royal Academy. They commission work in connection with their exhibitions and also stock a very good range of designs commissioned from the Royal Academicians. Their ceramic plates and bowls are exquisite.

Tate Gallery Shop

MILLBANK, SW1, 020-7887 8000
WWW.TATE.ORG.UK
Open Mon.-Sat. 10.30am-5.40pm, Sun. 10am-5.40pm.
U: Pimlico.

From a 20p bookmark to gorgeous coffee table books, this spacious shop has wonderful art publications and fun art T-shirts. It also carries a good range of exhibition catalogues.

Tiffany & Co

25 OLD BOND ST, W1, 020-7409 2790
WWW.TIFFANY.COM
Open Mon.-Fri. 10am-5.30pm, Sat. 10am-6pm.
U: Green Park.

What could be nicer than a gift presented in that distinctive duck-egg blue box secured with a simple white ribbon? Surprisingly, it is possible to buy a present from this smartly turned-out store without breaking the bank. Teen-agers will either love or appreciate the 'Teengage Book of Manners' at £10, while it would be hard to offend anyone with a gift of a smart key-ring from approximately £25. Christening gifts are also a forte here with Christening sets starting from £55 for a three-piece china set. Of course it is the jewelry which has earned Tiffany its impeccable reputation, and you will find Tiffany cross pendants in 18-carat gold at £1,450, in platinum with eleven diamonds on a gold chain for £1,650. Spend time browsing around the three-storey shop, as you'll find leather and silver gifts, scarves, picture frames, clocks, cutlery, china and crystal, plus the wonderful collections by Elsa Perretti and Paloma Picasso.

The Tintin Shop

34 FLORAL ST, WC2, 020-7836 1131
Open Mon.-Sat. 10am-6pm.
U: Covent Garden.

The Belgian cartoon character has inspired a range of gifts including stationery, jigsaws, T-shirts, watches, badges, books, videos and audiocassettes.

Victoria & Albert Museum Shop

CROMWELL RD, SW7, 020-7938 8500
WWW.VAM.AC.UK
Open daily 10am-5.45pm.
U: South Kensington.

With its spacious room and its constantly evolving stock, this is good gift-hunting ground, especially for exclusive items made to coincide with exhibitions. There are also limited-edition products matching up with the newer galleries, such as the Glass and the Silver galleries. There are excellent books on the decorative arts, plus a Crafts Council shop with a range of beautifully designed, one-of-a-kind products like ceramics, glassware, textiles and handmade jewelry.

HOME

CHILDREN'S FURNITURE

Dragons

23 WALTON ST, SW3, 020-7589 3795
Open Mon.-Fri. 10.30am-5.30pm, Sat. 10am-6pm.
U: Knightsbridge/South Kensington.

A white four-poster bed has pride-of-place in the back of this long shop which has miniature armchairs, tables, desks and hand-painted furniture by several artists, including one who specialises in Beatrix Potter animals. All decorative techniques feature on the designs like sponging, gilding and lacquering. The shop stocks everything from rag dolls to handsome, handcrafted rocking horses to take pride-of-place in any nursery.

The Nursery Window

83 WALTON ST, SW3, 020-7581 3358
Open Mon.-Sat. 10am-5.30pm.
U: Knightsbridge/South Kensington.

Fabrics and wallcoverings for the smartest nurseries are in abundance at this shop which also stocks a wide choice of changing mats and bags, cot and pram quilts, hooded towels, lampshades and blankets.

CHINA & GLASS

Bridgewater

739 FULHAM RD, SW6, 020-7371 9033
Open Mon.-Fri. 10am-5.30pm, Sat. 10am-5pm.
U: Fulham Broadway.

Emma Bridgewater has revived the old-fashioned spongewear technique of decorating pottery, and the process lends itself well to her quintessentially English china. Everything is included in her collections, from delightful children's mugs to large pasta and salad dishes in a variety of colours. You can have items personalised with your choice of name or commission pieces specially. She also sells a few designs at Harrods and the General Trading Company; Harvey Nichols houses a Bridgewater shop with the complete range. Check out the shop in January and the summer when there are good sales of seconds.

Contemporary Ceramics

7 MARSHALL ST, W1, 020-7437 7605
Open Mon.-Wed. & Fri.-Sat. 10am-5.30pm,
Thurs. 10am-7pm.
U: Oxford Circus.

Since 1960, the members of the Craft Potters Association have had a large, bright gallery in which to sell their distinctive, highly original pieces. The pottery on sale ranges from simple yet stunning everyday domestic ware to collectable statuary, pots and vases, and a small collection of jewelry. There are changing exhibitions and a large stock of books and magazines on ceramics, plus a selection of tools for the trade. The wide-ranging display makes for excellent browsing.

Famous Names

6 & 7 COLONNADE WALK, 123 BUCKINGHAM
PALACE RD, SW1, 020-7233 9313
E-MAIL: KARIM@CBT-FN.FREESERVE.CO.UK
Open Mon.-Sat. 9am-6pm.

This is primarily a china shop with many
lines of English-made tableware but it also carries the Swarovski jewelry and charm lines.

Hugh Johnson Collection

68 ST. JAMES'S ST, SW1, 020-7491 4912
Open Mon.-Fri. 9am-5pm.
U: Green Park.

Wine critic Hugh Johnson has gathered an
elegant array of wine accessories, including
fine decanters and glasses, some antique, plus
magnificent corkscrews—in fact everything for
the wine connoisseur (except the wine).

Lalique

162 NEW BOND ST, W1, 020-7499 8228
Open Mon.-Fri. 10am-6pm, Sat. 10am-5pm.
U: Bond St.

The trademark crystal created in 1913 sits in
fine company with scarves, handbags, fragrance, jewelry and a limited-edition line of
children's crockery. Following the tradition set
by the Art Deco craftsman René Lalique, the
finely turned crystal sculptures still manage to
captivate. The shop displays glow in the illu-
minated interior where the crystalware is beautifully offset by Limoges porcelain pieces and
Christofle silverware.

Also at 201 Sloane St, SW1, 020-7245
9090.

Portobello China & Woollens

89 PORTOBELLO RD, W11, 020-7727 3857
Open Mon.-Sat. 10am-5pm.
U: Notting Hill Gate.

Choc-a-bloc with tableware from all over
Britain and Ireland including many discontinued lines, this shop also sells knitwear including scarves, shawls, Aran sweaters and lambswool ranges at very good prices.

Looking for an address?
Refer to the index.

Chinacraft

134 REGENT ST, W1, 020-7434 2502
WWW.CHINACRAFT.CO.UK
*Open Mon.-Wed. & Fri.-Sat. 9am-6pm, Thurs.
9am-8pm, Sun. 11am-5pm.*
U: Piccadilly Circus.

When this company opened more than 35
years ago, an abundance of 'seconds' were
being released by the china manufacturers, so
the original shop in Beauchamp Place seemed
like a good idea for bargain hunters. Today,
although the company trades under the same
name their shops stock mostly high-quality
china, though still retaining a seconds area,
clearly distinguished by labels and a more cluttered display. There are lots of amusing items
such as teapots on legs.

Also at 183 Brompton Rd (corner of
Beauchamp Pl), 020-7581 0739.

Royal Doulton

167 PICCADILLY, W1, 020-7493 9121
Open Mon.-Sat. 9.30am-6pm.
U: Piccadilly Circus.

This is the main shop for the famous china
company with a huge display of their tableware including famous brands such as Royal
Albert, all displayed with the company's glassware.

The Tea House

15 NEAL ST, WC2, 020-7240 7539
Open Mon.-Sat. 10am-7pm, Sun. noon-6pm.
U: Covent Garden.

Astonishingly shaped teapots attract visitors
as much as the wide variety of teas. Sherlock
Holmes looking for a clue, a couple dancing, a
snowman, a cottage—any subject can inspire a
teapot maker. Brightly coloured, plain-shaped
teapots make an appearance, as do teacups for
fortune telling, plus a range of books.

Thomas Goode

19 SOUTH AUDLEY ST, W1, 020-7499 2823
WWW.THOMASGOODE.CO.UK
Open Mon.-Sat. 10am-6pm.
U: Hyde Park Corner.

Not only does the exterior look like a grand
townhouse, the interior feels like one as well.
The elegant appearance reflects Thomas
Goode's status as an institution for sophisticated shopping since 1845. There is a flamboy-
ance along with tradition and unexpected
nooks in the various rooms, several with tables
lavishly decked out with a wide array of

coloured glassware. For those seeking a contemporary touch, look for Peter Ting's collection of china and glass or consider the bespoke service where you can order a dinner service made to your exact specifications. This is an exclusive shop; the Wall of China in the basement depicts various designs over the decades, and there's a little museum on the ground floor.

Villeroy & Boch
267 MERTON RD, SW18, 020-8875 6006
Open daily 10am-5pm.
U: Southfields.
This is a factory shop for the famous brand name of fine, distinctive tableware. Rich colours used within distinctive designs have been the trademark of this firm's tableware since its formation in 1748. It stocks ends of lines and special offers, with sales taking place twice a year.

Waterford Wedgwood
158 REGENT ST, W1, 020-7734 7262
WWW.WEDGWOOD
Open Mon.-Wed. & Fri.-Sat. 9.30am-6.30pm,
Thurs. 9.30am-7pm, Sun. noon-6pm.
U: Piccadilly Circus.
Stretching an impressive length while remaining on one level, the shop stocks all the ranges produced by these two famous manufacturers. At Christmas, it decorates its trees beautifully. You'll find inspiration in the elegant tables laid out for different occasions, including a formal dinner party and a summer picnic.
Also at 173 Piccadilly, SW1, 020-7629 2614.

FABRICS, FURNISHINGS & INTERIOR DESIGN

The English Style
Before World War II, Paris and New York were the most important centres for interior decoration. But for the last few years, it has been London that people look to for inspiration. In 1972, Mrs. Munro (see below) helped organise an exhibition in Paris called Le Style Anglaise, which consolidated the English approach to interior design. Unlike much European design which is often very formal, it is based both on practical consideration and on the eternally beautiful English style as epit-

omised by the chintzes and antiques found in English country houses. From its start as an exclusive look, it can now be seen everywhere, a move helped by the early popularity of the late Laura Ashley. But English design is not all chintz and grand country houses. We have also included shops that practice a very different style. Many of the shops we recommend here undertake commissions and offer an interior decorating service; others may just sell wallpapers and fabrics.

Andrew Martin
200 WALTON ST, SW3, 020-7584 4290
Open Mon.-Fri. 9am-5.30pm, Sat. 10.am-5pm.
U: Knightsbridge.
Much of his inspiration is Chinese and becomes bold, swirling designs in strong colours. Good source for unusual fabrics.

Barclay & Bodie
7-9 BLEINHEIM TERR, NW8, 020-7372 5705
Open Mon.-Sat. 9.30am-5.30pm.
U: St. John's Wood.
You could actually be stepping into somebody's drawing room in this shop. They stock a fair amount of Victorian antiques, but this is mainly a shop for well-designed accessories for the home with items ranging from a Parisian navy gingham cotton frame for photographs to candle sconces, padded hangers and rugs. Look out for unusual things like sepia-coloured ironing board covers with the image of a male nude.

Cath Kidson
8 CLARENDON CROSS, W11, 020-7221 4000
Open Mon.-Fri. 10.30am-6pm, Sat. 11am-6pm.
U: Holland Park.
Cath Kidson's interior style achieves an unfussy, bright look, based on her own taste for unusual fabrics, wallpaper designs, and a love for 1950s simplicity. She opened this fun shop in a village-like corner of posh Holland Park to sell renovated tables, chairs and dressers from her favourite era, as well as interesting fabrics and artefacts from her visits to antique and bric-a-brac markets. Some of these finds are still sold but Kidson has now branched out to design her own stationery and a range of fabrics using 1950s items as her inspiration.
Also at 8 Elystan St, SW3, 020-7584 3232.

Colefax & Fowler

39 BROOK ST, W1, 020-7493 2231
Open Mon.-Fri. 9.30am-5.30pm.
U: Bond St.

When the firm started in the 1930s, John Fowler took the romantic spirit of late eighteenth-century decoration as his inspiration. Now the famous Colefax and Fowler firm is located in an authentic Georgian house in Mayfair which shows off the great swags of fabrics, floral wallpapers and antique furniture to perfection. The firm is famous for creating that certain English style so characteristic of grand English country houses.

Designers Guild

267-271 & 277 KING'S RD, SW3
020-7243 7300, WWW.DESIGNERSGUILD.COM
Open Mon.-Tues. 10am-5.30pm, Wed.-Sat. 10am-6pm, Sun. noon-5pm.
U: Sloane Sq.

Tricia Guild's innovative firm has sold fabrics, wall coverings, upholstery and accessories since the 1970s. Every decorative device combined with stunning, often dramatic wallpapers and curtain fabrics make these showrooms inspiring to visit. Number 277 King's Road offers the exclusive Designers Guild fabric and wallpaper ranges, including printed floral, geometric patterns, woven plain, checks and stripes, silks, velvets, jacquards and children's designs. The two-storey sister shop sells furniture, kelims, one-of-a-kind crafts, jewelry, unusual garden accessories and brightly coloured stationery. Woven and embroidered cotton bed linen, wool blankets, rugs, cushions, tableware and even gourmet food — Italian and French olive oils, English jams and chutney—are also sold. They also offer a complete design service. Mail-order catalogue available.

Jane Churchill

151 SLOANE ST, SW3, 020-7730 9847
Open Mon.-Sat. 10am-6pm.
U: Sloane Sq.

A good source for innovative and stylish wallpapers and fabrics, which are matched up with a coordinated range of lampshades, towels, bedlinens and accessories.

Joanna Wood

48A PIMLICO RD, SW3, 020-7730 5064
Open Mon.-Fri. 10am-6pm, Sat. 10am-4pm.
U: Sloane Sq/Victoria.

Another shop offering the quintessential English look. Go for the large, distinctive furniture and fabrics or add an instant stately feel to your home with the prettily finished objects, such as hat boxes, stationery and desk accessories and lampshades. There are also miniature china boxes, visitors' books, freeze-dried rose heads with pungent aromas and cushion covers.

Laura Ashley

256 REGENT ST, W1, 020-7437 9760
WWW.LAURA-ASHLEY.COM
Open Mon.-Tues. 10am-6.30pm, Wed. 10am-7pm, Thurs. 10am-8pm, Sat. 9.30am-7pm, Sun. noon-6pm.
U: Oxford Circus.

The company prides itself on holding onto their customers from childhood to old-age, designing patterns for home furnishings which mix and match in the long-admired Laura Ashley style. These days the company has extended their collections to include funkier cushions and accessories with a broader appeal. Only the larger women's wear shops have a home furnishings department, a curtain and blind making service and a styling interior service (the direct line to the stylist at this shop is 020-7434 1343; also try 9 Harriet St, SW1, 020-7823 2287).

Branches throughout London include three Homebase shops which stock home furnishings only, such as 193 Warwick Rd, W14, 020-7603 2285.

Mary Fox Linton

4 HEWLETT HOUSE, HAVELOCK TERR, SW8
020-7622 0920
By appointment.
Rail: Battersea Park.

There are two sides to this firm. Under the Mary Fox Linton banner, they sell decorative objects and fabrics in ranges exclusive to them, such as Dedar and Gland, Jim Thompson, Thai Silks and Fabergé, all of which can be seen at her two showrooms at Chelsea Harbour (020-7351 9908), along with contemporary furniture for the home and office. Fox Linton Associates, established in 1962, is the design practice side of the business and is called on to decorate house and corporate buildings all over the world, whether it's a Georgian-style house in Tokyo or modern-looking flats with the emphasis on interesting uses of space for which the designer, Mary Fox Linton, has become well-known.

Mrs Munro Ltd

JUBILEE HOUSE, 70 CADOGAN PL, SW1
020-7235 0326
Open Mon.-Thurs. 9.30am-5.30pm, Fri. 9.30am-5pm.
U: Knightsbridge.

Set up in 1926 by Geraldine Munro, the company is now run by her daughter Jean, whose particular passion is eighteenth-century style. Her most public work was decorating and furnishing Number 1 Royal Crescent, Bath (see Bath in Out-of-London). But mostly Jean Munro and director John Lusk work privately, creating delightful replicas of the English country style all over the world. Although primarily an interior design firm, they also stock a range of chintzes, the designs for which have been researched and discovered in old books and houses. They then have them made up either for private clients or for their showroom.

Osborne & Little

304-308 KING'S RD, SW3, 020-7352 1456
WWW.OSBORNE&LITTLE.COM
Open Mon.-Fri. 9.30am-6pm, Sat. 10am-5.30pm.
U: Sloane Sq.

Although mainly regarded for its take on the English look, which includes a strongly traditional range of floral and striped wallpapers, it is worth noting that Osborne & Little include a good range of modern looks from designers such as Nina Campbell (see above). A great place to shop for a good range of fabrics.

The Shaker Shop

322 KING'S RD, SW3, 020-7352 3918
WWW.SHAKER.CO.UK
Open Mon.-Sat. 10am-6pm.
U: Sloane Sq.

Admiration of the simple and practical style of the furniture of the Shakers in America—a religious group who broke away from the Quakers in the late 1700s—led Liz Shirley and Tim Lamb to open their first shop. They sell chairs, tables and other products made at the Shaker Workshops in Massachussetts. The unusual and definitely un-English sight of chairs hung from peg rails on the wall first brought customers into the shop out of curiosity, and the superior craftsmanship of the products enticed them to buy. The pure lines and first-rate woods employed in the trestle and candle tables, wall cupboards, pegrails and Shaker boxes are breathtaking.

Also at 25 Harcourt St, W1, 020-7724 7672.

Simon Horn Furniture

117-121 WANDSWORTH BRIDGE RD, SW6
020-7731 1279
Open Mon.-Sat. 9.30am-5.30pm.
U: Parsons Green.

Europe's leading specialist in French and classical wooden beds, Simon Horn offers 60 traditional designs from the Lit Bateau to splendid four posters. His antique replicas are made from solid woods such as rose and cherry, and clients can also specify their preferred stain or patina. For children's rooms, the Simon Horn Cot is a real treat since the design, based on the classic French Lit Bateau, serves first as cot, then a child's bed and finally a sofa. Prices for a Lit Bateau start from £1,595.

Timney Fowler

388 KING'S RD, SW3, 020-7351 6562
Open Mon.-Fri. 9.30am-6pm, Sat. 10am-6pm.
U: Sloane Sq.

Definitely not for shrinking violets, the bold, mainly monochrome prints inspired by dramatic images such as medieval stained glass, rococo panache or even the crown jewels, make a dramatic statement. Colour has been introduced to the range of fabrics, cushions, wraps, scarves and boxes to equally breathtaking effect. Devotees of their signature range of Roman emperors' head and mythological scenes will be pleased to know these are still available. The shop now offers an extensive range of home accessories such as picture frames, mugs and mirrors which coordinate with Timney Fowler fabrics.

Viaduct

1-10 SUMMER'S ST, EC1, 020-7278 8456
WWW.VIADUCT.CO.UK
Open Mon.-Fri. 9.30am-6pm, Sat. 10.30am-4pm.
U: Farringdon.

Former architect James Mair stocks cutting-edge furniture in his showroom on the ground floor of an old print warehouse in Clerkenwell. In the huge well-lit space, he sells Martin

Ryan's Romany chair with birch ply seat and back, Philippe Starck's teardrop door handles and lights and accessories by top European and British designers.

GENERAL

Aero

96 WESTBOURNE GROVE, W2
020-7221 1950, WWW.AERO-FURNITURE.COM
Open Mon.-Sat. 10am-6.30pm, Sun. noon-5pm.
U: Bayswater.

A treat for those seeking a company that manufactures, retail and promotes modern furniture, lighting and accessories. Stocking everything from animal-shaped CD holders to stainless-steel wall panels to hang kitchen equipment, this shop sells designer products, which stylishly solve practical problems in the home. Lamps, ultra-modern tables and chairs for home and office all have a minimalist flair.

Aria

133 & 295-297 UPPER ST, N1
020-7704 1999, WWW.ARIA-SHOP.CO.UK.
Open Mon.-Fri. 10am-7pm, Sat. 10am-6.30pm,
Sun. noon-5pm.
U: Angel.

Starting out as a small shop selling contemporary home accessories, Aria has spread its vision of home modernity to three shops along Upper Street. The first outlet at No. 135 is where you'll find great gift ideas, while over the road the through shop at Nos. 295-297 is the place for a range of stylish bathroom accessories. The latest addition to the Aria emporium houses the full range of Alessi products in well-lit cabinets and a good collection of Philippe Starck homewares.

Ciel Décor

187 NEW KING'S RD, SW6, 020-7731 0444
Open Mon.-Sat. 10am-5.30pm.
U: Sloane Sq.

Besides its own range of fabrics, this shop stocks the sunny Provençal fabrics produced by the Les Olivades company. There are accessories such as table mats, lampshades, wash bags and towels.

The Conran Shop

MICHELIN HOUSE, 81 FULHAM RD, SW3
020-7589 7401, WWW.CONRAN.COM
Open Mon. & Thurs.-Fri. 9.30am-6pm, Tues.
10am-6pm, Wed, 9.30am-7.30pm, Sat. 10am-
6.30pm, Sun. noon-5.30pm.
U: South Kensington.

Some consider this the most exciting shop in London, both for its wide range of specially commissioned merchandise and for its location. You'll find it inside the fantastic Art Nouveau building which was once the headquarters of the Michelin tyre company. It's impossible to miss, with its motoring motif tiled murals and stained-glass windows. The shop's buyers travel extensively to find new and unusual products, so there are antiques and artefacts from all over the world. Conran works with contemporary designers and manufacturers and much of the furniture collection is exclusive to the store. They also stock more than 200 fabric designs, exclusive bed linens, garden furniture, a small but wonderful range of children's toys and clothes, lovely accessories and gifts.

Also at 55 Marylebone High St, NW1, 020-723 2223; 12-13 Conduit St, W1, 020-7399 0710.

Crucial Trading

79 WESTBOURNE PARK RD, W2, 020-7221 9000
WWW.CRUCIAL-TRADING.COM
Open Tues.-Sat. 10am-6pm.
U: Westbourne Park.

As specialists in supplying natural floor coverings, this shop has a choice of 120 designs in materials such as sisal, seagrass, jute and wool. Prices start from £8 per square metre.

Also at 535 The Plaza, Lots Rd, SW10, 020-7376 7100.

The Dining Room Shop

62-64 WHITE HART LANE, BARNES, SW13
020-8878 1020
Open Mon.-Fri. 10am-5.30pm, Sat. 10.15am-
5.30pm.
Rail: Barnes Bridge.

The name lives up to its promise of supplying everything for the dining room. You'll find all the furniture including antique tables and chairs, plus the necessary accoutrements for a well-dressed table such as china, linen, glass, lace and cutlery.

Elephant

230 TOTTENHAM COURT RD, W1, 020-7439 3353
*Open Mon.-Fri. 10am-6.30pm, Sat. 10am-6pm,
Sun. 11am-5.30pm.*
U: Warren St.

This shop carries desirable furniture and accessories to transform your house into a home. Very strong on ethnic furniture and sofas that make you want to hibernate all winter. Also, there's a good range of casual accessories from lamps to vases.

Also at 94 Tottenham Court Rd, W1, 020-7813 2092; 18 Westbourne Gr, W2, 020-7243 0203; 167 Queensway, W2, 020-7467 0630.

The General Trading Company

144 SLOANE ST, SW1, 020-7730 0411
WWW.GENERAL-TRADING.CO.UK
*Open Mon.-Tues. & Thurs.-Sat. 9.30am-6pm,
Wed. 9.30am-7pm.*
U: Sloane Sq.

A place where you can find every kind of household object from a candlestick to a library pole holder with antiqued hide covering. This is an institution among the local 'Sloane Ranger' set and still one of the top places for a traditional wedding list for young brides. All the departments—antiques, upholstery and furniture, Asian, garden, stationery, kitchen, linen, cutlery, china, glass—cater to shoppers with an appreciation of good design. The shop holds all four Royal Warrants (a Royal Warrant is granted by the Queen, the Queen Mother, the Duke of Edinburgh and the Prince of Wales) and is only one of six other companies in the country to share this honour.

Habitat

196 TOTTENHAM COURT RD, W1, 020-7631 3880
WWW.HABITAT.NET
*Open Mon.-Wed. & Fri. 10am-6pm, Thurs.
10am-8pm, Sat. 9.30am-6.30pm, Sun. noon-6pm.*
U: Goodge St.

After losing direction slightly, Habitat is back delivering well-designed furniture and accessories for the style-conscious with more dash than cash. A good all-round place for ready-made or custom-made curtains, bold cushion covers, basic furniture including lines for children's bedrooms, plain or bright bed linen, glass, china, lamps and cutlery. Branches include 206 King's Rd, SW3, 020-7351 1211.

Heal's

196 TOTTENHAM COURT RD, W1, 020-7636 1666
*Open Mon.-Wed. 10am-6pm, Thurs. 10am-
8pm, Fri. 10am-6.30pm, Sat. 9.30am-6.30pm.*
U: Goodge St.

Heal's is a must for those who appreciate good craftsmanship and design. With three floors of stylish, modern furniture, and a wide range of imaginative and exciting accessories to choose from, it's almost impossible to leave empty-handed (unless your budget gets the better of you). The company began as bed-makers and its handmade beds are still sought after. Heal's reputation for being a forerunner in the 1920s is maintained today: it is a good place for exclusive designs.

Also at 234 King's Rd, SW3, 020-7349 8411.

The Holding Company

241-2 KING'S RD, SW3, 020-7352 1600
Open Mon.-Sat. 10am-7pm, Sun. noon-6pm.
U: Sloane Sq.

Sometimes the best business ideas are the most obvious ones, and this was certainly the case for American Donna Walter who set up her thriving business when she moved to London and wanted storage solutions in her London flat. The company offers every kind of object to organise your home and office: wicker baskets, hessian and plastic containers, card drawer dividers (to keep socks and knickers

Accessorize Yourself

Accessories are the items which brighten up your home (and in this case, also your wardrobe). **V.V. Rouleaux,** 54 Sloane Sq, SW1, 020-7730 3125, open Mon.-Sat. 9.30am-6pm (Wed. 10.30am-6.30pm), stocks just about every conceivable design and kind of ribbons, braids, trimmings and more, a treasure house for designers, milliners, stylists and ordinary people.

The Stencil Store, 89 Lower Sloane St, SW1, 020-7730 0728, open Mon-Sat. 10am-5.30pm, Wed. 10am-6.30pm, inspires you to transform your room, your furniture, your walls, anything that stands still. There are stencilling workshops for beginners and helpful staff to start you on the right track.

tidy). Many lines are in bright colours and unusual patterns or natural fabrics to blend in beautifully with minimalist surroundings.

India Jane

140 SLOANE ST, SW1, 020-7730 1070
Open Mon.-Sat. 10am-6pm.
U: Sloane Sq.

Everything here (with the very odd exception) is imported from India, hence the name. It has a good collection of colourful and fashionable furniture and small objects, linens, rugs, planters and china.

Jerry's Home Store

163-167 FULHAM RD, SW3, 020-7581 0909
Open Mon.-Sat. 10am-6pm, Sun. 11.30am-5.30pm.
U: South Kensington.

The stylish simplicity of American homes appealed to Jeremy Sacher so much he decided to introduce the look to London. The airy store is filled with novelty items such as popcorn makers and functional products such as cookie jars, brightly coloured crockery and extensive kitchenwares and equipment. The large room downstairs has a New England feel, from the expensive sofas, handsome wooden tables, gleaming lamps and accessories. Much of the merchandise is made in America.
Also in Harvey Nichols; 57 Heath St, NW3, 020-794 8622; The Bentall Centre, Kingston-upon-Thames, Surrey, 020-8549 5393.

Maryse Boxer
at Joseph Penthouse

26 SLOANE ST, SW1, 020-7245 9493
WWW.MARYSEBOXER.COM
Open Mon.-Fri. 10am-6.30pm, Sat. 10am-6pm.
U: Knightsbridge.

From her gallery-shop space on the top floor of Joseph's emporium, Maryse Boxer sells beautifully designed china, glassware, gorgeous linens and cotton throws. Her taste is impeccable and her stock is of the must-have variety.

Mint

70 WIGMORE ST, W1, 020-7224 4406
Open Mon.-Wed. & Fri.-Sat. 11am-6.30pm, Thurs. 11am-7pm.
U: Bond St.

Whether you're a fan of African and Moroccan homewares and accessories or not,

you'll appreciate the finely crafted goods, hand picked by the owner Lina Kanafani, a former stylist. Her taste is impeccable—everything from the notebooks to the large furniture makes you wish you had at least four homes to fill with the whole lot.

Mulberry Home

219 KING'S RD, SW3, 020-7352 1937
WWW.MULBERRY-ENGLAND.CO.UK
Open Mon.-Tues. & Thurs.-Sat. 10am-6pm, Wed. 10am-7pm.
U: Sloane Sq.

Walking into the Mulberry Home store is like walking into a lavish film set. The look, inspired by romantic and medieval themes, is rich and warming with harmonious blues, reds and golds creating an inviting homey environment. The furniture consists of Chesterfield sofas covered in beautiful brocades, handsome wooden chests and ottomans, while accessories include imposing wooden candlesticks, throws, suede and brocade cushions and refined crockery. Mulberry also offers an interior design service.

Nicole Farhi Home

17 GRAFTON ST, W1, 020-7494 9051
Open Mon.-Wed. & Fri.-Sat. 10am-6pm, Thurs. 10am-7pm.
U: Green Park.

Proving that clothing design is not the only thing at which Nicole Farhi excels, her first outlet dedicated to homewares is a must for all style gurus. Antique furniture, sourced by Nicole herself, ceramics, bedding, and beautiful tableware fill the shop.

Purves & Purves

80-81, 83 TOTTENHAM COURT RD, W1
020-7580 8223
Open Mon.-Wed. & Fri.-Sat. 9.30am-6pm, Thurs. 9.30am-7.30pm.
U: Goodge St.

Whatever your taste, it's virtually impossible to walk past the Purves & Purves stores without glancing at their eye-catching furniture and accessories. Like a beacon, the jewel-bright colours, flamboyant shapes and unique designs capture the imagination, enticing you into the light-hearted and unfussy store to take a closer look at the plethora of wonderful creations. The furniture may be a bit on the pricey side, but you can always brighten up your washing line with funky flying fish clothes pegs or add a bit of character to your kitchen with the quirky, but well-designed Garbo wastebasket.

KITCHENWARE

David Mellor
4 SLOANE SQ, SW1, 020-7730 4259
Open Mon.-Sat. 9.30am-6pm.
U: Sloane Sq.

Devoted to the well-appointed kichen featured in interior magazines, the ground floor stocks glassware from Poland, Finland and Spain as well as English Dartington. Downstairs there are clay cooking pots, bright blue earthenware, corkscrews, aluminium moulds and many other products designed to make cooking easy, enjoyable and stylish. The shop also stocks bottles of special olive oils, jars of sauces, aromatic olives, olive pesto and sun-dried tomatoes.

Divertimenti
45-47 WIGMORE ST, W1, 020-7935 0689
Open Mon.-Fri. 9.30am-6pm, Sat. 10am-6pm.
U: Bond St.

This is what the kitchen in foodie heaven must look like—all gleaming surfaces and shiny utensils. The shop is always busy with people looking for the perfect kitchen accessory—whether it be the best pot to cook in, pretty ochre-toned earthenware, the right coffeepot, or the white net coverings for storing food. It is perfect for browsing, with two floors devoted to pots, plates and cookbooks.

Also at 39-141 Fulham Rd, SW3, 020-7581 8065.

Richard Dare
93 REGENT'S PARK RD, NW1, 020-7722 9428
Open Mon.-Fri. 9.30am-6pm, Sat. 10am-6pm.
U: Chalk Farm.

This kitchenware shop may seem small-fry but it carries an excellent range of professional kitchenware—suspended from the ceiling, piled high on shelves and stacked on the floor. Good earthenware pottery includes Quimper faience crockery alongside fish kettles, pots and pans in a delightful residential neighbourhood shop.

Summerill & Bishop
100 PORTLAND RD, W11, 020-7221 4566
Open Mon.-Sat. 10am-6pm.
U: Holland Park.

A truly delightful and inspiring kitchen shop that mixes the old with the new and French and British in such a way that you imagine yourself in a Provençal farm or on a patio in the South of France. Plenty of items here make this worth a good look.

LIGHTING

Besselink & Jones
99 WALTON ST, SW3, 020-7584 0343
Open Mon.-Fri. 10am-5.30pm, Sat. 10am-4.30pm.
U: South Kensington.

The sign says 'wonderful lamps' and the clutter of lamps in the window is an indication of how jam-packed the shop is with antique lamps, handmade lampshades and many new lamps designed in traditional style. The firm also sells in Harvey Nichols although vintage lamps are found mostly at this shop.

Christopher Wray Lighting
600 KING'S RD, SW6, 020-7736 8434
Open Mon.-Sat. 9.30am-6pm.
U: Sloane Sq.

Christopher Wray stocks a dazzling array of one-of-a-kind and Tiffany-style lamps. Prices vary, depending on whether you go for a reproduction or original item to light up your life.

Also at 199 Shaftesbury Ave, WC2, 020-7437 6199.

London Lighting Company
135 FULHAM RD, SW3, 020-7589 3612
Open Mon.-Sat. 9.30am-6pm, Sun noon-5pm.
U: South Kensington..

Almost 80 manufacturers from all over Europe are represented in this huge gallery devoted to contemporary lighting. One of their suppliers has the rights to the Bauhaus designs and makes lamps based on the original styles. There is also a wide choice of lights that illuminates pictures.

LINEN

Cologne & Cotton

791 FULHAM RD, SW6, 020-7736 9261
Open Mon.-Sat. 9.30am-7pm.
U Fulham Broadway.

Delightful shop selling beautiful crisp matching bed linen in pretty designs that you can buy in sets or singly. Also a good range of toiletries.

Also at 39 Kensington Church St, W8, 020-7376 0324; 88 Marylebone High St, W1, 020-7486 0595.

Descamps

197 SLOANE ST, SW1, 020-7235 6957
Open Mon.-Tues. & Thurs.-Sat. 10am-6.30pm, Wed. 10am-7.30pm.
U: Knightsbridge.

Pyjamas in classic styles plus a selection of fun designs, this bright shop has a large selection of French lines, which include bed linen, towels, bathrobes, and baby accessories.

Frette

98 NEW BOND ST, W1, 020-7629 5517
Open Mon.-Wed. & Fri. 10am-6pm, Thurs. 10am-7pm, Sat. 10am-5.30pm.
U: Bond St.

The colour choice of Frette's cool, crisp linens, sink-into towels and Hollywood-style bathrobes span the spectrum and the quality is unrivalled. All of the items on sale in the long galleried room can be matched or fully coordinated.

The Irish Linen Company

35 BURLINGTON ARCADE, W1, 020-7493 8949
Open Mon.-Thurs. 11am-7pm, Fri.-Sat. 10.30am-7pm, Sun. noon-6pm.
U: Piccadilly Circus.

A wonder in white is how this little corner shop looks with all its stock draped around, but there are colour ranges should you wish to add a little variety. The linen is Irish and of the finest quality, and the shop monograms to your own wishes. They can supply table linen for palaces, as well as the more modest home.

The Linen Merchant

11 MONTPELIER ST, SW7, 020-7584 3654
Open Mon.-Sat. 9.30am-6pm.
U: Knightsbridge.

A charming shop full of reasonably priced and beautiful linens. Their lines of Belgian linen cushions and tablecloths in both bold and pastel colours are particularly eye-catching. They also have a good range of embroidered Maderian cotton. All items can be gift-wrapped.

The Monogrammed Linen Shop

168 WALTON ST, SW1, 020-7589 4033
Open Mon.-Fri. 10am-6pm, Sat. 10am-5.30pm.
U: South Kensington.

With lots of bed linen, towels and children's clothing, this pretty white-fronted shop can personalise almost any item in a week.

Ruffle & Hook

123-124 ST. JOHN ST, EC1, 020-7490 4321
Open Mon.-Fri. 10am-5.30pm, Sat. 10am-2pm.
U: Farringdon.

Clean, crisp linens and muted sari fabrics for the best dressed-windows in town. Also a small range of candles, soaps, cushions and room fragrances.

JEWELRY

CONTEMPORARY DESIGNERS

Crazy Pig Designs

38 SHORTS GDNS, WC2, 020-7240 4305
Open Mon.-Sat. 10.30am-6.30pm.
U: Covent Garden.

The chunky silver jewelry made on the premises of Crazy Pig Designs appeals to rock and rollers like Ozzie Osbourne and The Rolling Stones. Little wonder really, as the styles include skull motifs, heavy identity bracelets and Batman logos, all of which go down equally well in photographic sessions as they do on stage. Semi-precious stones feature in some of the work. Customers' own designs can be made up in either silver or gold.

Dinny Hall

200 WESTBOURNE GROVE, W11, 020-7792 3913
Open Mon.-Fri. 11am-7pm, Sat. 10am-6pm.
U: Bayswater.

A former British Accessory Designer of the Year, Dinny Hall is known for her fine, delicate jewelry, mostly in silver, from which hand-cut, semi-precious stones are suspended. She also creates pieces in 18-carat gold and precious stones and will undertake commissions. Her range includes a small collection of bath oils, with floral or spicy notes, housed in 'gold' or 'silver' aluminium cans created by the designer. Exhibitions of other designers' work are held at her **other shop** at 44 Fulham Rd, SW3, 020-7589 9192.

Electrum Gallery

21 SOUTH MOLTON ST, W1, 020-7629 6325
Open Mon.-Fri. 10am-6pm, Sat. 10am-7pm.
U: Bond St.

Barbara Cartlidge's small but comprehensive showcase for contemporary jewelry by more than 80 international designers still looks fresh despite being founded more than 20 years ago. There is usually an exhibition following a theme or promoting a new artist; Vicki Ambery-Smith, for instance, produces architecturally inspired jewelry, like Shakespeare's Globe. Wendy Ramshaw, who creates the distinctive ring sets you can find here, received an OBE honour for her contribution to the art.

The Great Frog

51 CARNABY ST, W1, 020-7734 1900
Open Mon.-Sat. 10.30am-6.30pm.
U: Oxford Circus.

You need a big personality and it helps if you have a penchant for black leathers and Harley Davidsons to fully appreciate the wide range of jewelry available at this shop. Carol and Pat Reilly's creations have attracted rock star attention for over twenty years, and there are photographs displayed of groups wearing wild-faced belt buckles and articulated rings to prove it. Skull motifs are popular themes as is the spooky enamelled 'eyeballs'.
Also at 10 Ganton St, W1, 020-7439 9357.

Janet Fitch

25 OLD COMPTON ST, W1, 020-7287 3789
Open Mon.-Sat. 11am-7pm, Sun. 1pm-6pm.
U: Leicester Sq.

This is an exciting showcase for British craftsmen. The work of some of the country's most talented jewelry designers is displayed in a stylish contemporary setting where prices run from approximately £14 to £400. For aspiring jewellers, Janet Fitch has compiled the ultimate book called The Art and Craft of Jewelry.
Also at 37 Neal St, WC2 020-7240 6332; 188a King's Rd, SW3, 020-7352 4401.

Jess James

3 NEWBURGH ST, W1, 020-7437 0199
Open Mon., Wed. & Fri. 11am-6.30pm, Tues. noon-6.30pm, Thurs. 11am-7pm, Sat. 11am-6pm.
U: Oxford Circus.

Among the innovative designs of jewelry on display, Jess James has a range of diamond navel jewels and nipple rings made in platinum with diamonds from £825. This shop is a showcase for top international designers such as Jacqueline Rabun, Wright & Teague, Dinny Hall, plus Jess James' own line.
Also at 13 Lowndes St, SW1, 020-7235 7171.

Kiki McDonough

77 WALTON ST, SW3, 020-7581 1777
Open Mon.-Fri. 9.30am-5.30pm, Sat. 10am-4.30pm.
U: South Kensington.

A favourite with the Chelsea set, Kiki McDonough designs and produces delightful jewelry, drawing on inspirations from all ages and all over the world. Using precious metals and stones, a gold, pearl and diamond choker at £5,200, or an 18-carat gold, diamond and sapphire eternity ring at £1,900, is a well-worth investment. She creates a range of understated earrings for day wear in both 9- and 18-ct. gold, for approximately £425, plus a range of cufflinks for females. Catalogue available.

Lesley Craze Gallery

34 CLERKENWELL GN, EC1, 020-7608 0393
Open Mon.-Sat. 10am-5.30pm.
U: Farringdon.

A showcase for some of the best contemporary designers set in a thriving area of creativity. It is made up of two gallery spaces—one area displays work in precious metals, while Craze 2 sells jewelry made from a variety of non-precious metals including brightly coloured acrylic, papier-maché and tin. There are always works on display and regular exhibitions. Lesley Craze is keen to promote commissions for her stable of jewellers and some of the exhibitions include technical drawings which add to the interest.

Merola

195 FULHAM RD, SW3, 020-7351 9338
Open Mon.-Sat. 10am-6pm.
U: South Kensington.

Imaginative designs by Maria Merola include novelties such as cherub earrings and a wide range of decorative crosses. This new enlarged shop glitters with vintage costume pieces from the 1920s to the 1950s sourced by Merola all over the country, particularly from the designer Miriam Haskell. A good spot for pieces in crystal, jet beads, dazzling wedding tiaras and the cutest vintage handbags.

Obelle

92 MARYLEBONE HIGH ST, W1, 020-7487 4151
E-MAIL: INFO@OBELLE.CO.UK, WWW.OBELLE.COM
Open Mon.-Sat. 10am-6pm.
U: Bond St.

From the moment you step over the threshold, you know you're in for a thrilling surprise. For a start, the interior—all sinuous and aquatic in feel—is unlike any other jewelry shop and provides the perfect foil for the beautiful contemporary designs that lie in wait. The shop is divided into two sections: one is home to the funky, chunky stainless-steel and silver designs (check out the rubber jewelry studded with diamonds); the other is where you find the exquisite platinum and 18- and 22-carat gold pieces. Prepare to spend an hour or more as you ooh and aah at the myriad trinkets just begging to be taken home. Prices are reasonable, considering the originality, ranging from £100 to £1,200. The work of more than twenty designers work is on display. Their jewelry works so beautifully together, it's easy to mix-and-match collections throughout the shop. Look for the highly stylised and original Reflexx rings and bangles—new from Germany.

Solange Azagury-Partridge

171 WESTBOURNE GROVE, W2, 020-7792 0197
Open Mon.-Sat. 11am-6pm.
U: Bayswater.

Big, bold jewelry is made by Azagury-Partridge for people who like unconventional designs. She chooses striking gemstones like rose quartz, aquamarine, citrine and peridot. Her informal and friendly shop is as striking as the jewelry she creates, with a purple velvet

sofa, orange walls and jewelry designed by Tom Dixon. It also stocks her other interests, such as 1960s vases by Vallauris, modern chandeliers by Droog, sculptures by Roger Partridge and leather goods by William Wallace.

Theo Fennell

169 FULHAM RD, SW3, 020-7591 5000
Open Mon.-Thurs. 10am-6pm, Fri.-Sat. 10am-5pm.
U: South Kensington.

Theo Fennell designs, makes and sells his witty but stylish pieces in this smart three-storey shop. In addition to the beautiful traditional jewelry, Fennell offers a range of hugely popular quirky items such as a silver and gold tubs for placing your Hagen Daaz ice-cream, silverscrew lid tops for jars of Marmite and sleeves for vinegar bottles. His 'London charms with miniature London icons such as traditional telephone booths and post boxes are also on sale at Harrods.

Wright & Teague

1A GRAFTON ST, W1, 020-7629 2777
WWW.WRIGHTANDTEAGUE.COM
Open Mon.-Wed. & Fri.-Sat. 10am-6pm, Thurs. 10am-7pm.
U: Bond St.

For those who shun the showy diamond clusters and shiny gold school of jewelry, this husband-and-wife design team offer a stylish and simple alternative. Wright & Teague are famous for their organic shapes—be they fashioned in chunky pendants suspended from silver chains, or fabulous hand-hewn pieces adorning the wrists or fingers. Many of the gold and silver pieces bear intricately engraved messages, like 'I love you' or 'Amore' making ideal presents for loved ones. Check out the engagement and eternity rings for men and women, which are made to order in sterling silver or gold. Items take four to six weeks to be made.

COSTUME JEWELRY

The Amber Centre

24 ST. CHRISTOPHER'S PL, W1, 020-7224 2953
Open Mon.-Wed. & Fri.-Sat. 10am-6pm, Thurs. 10am-7pm.
U: Bond St.

If you like amber, you'll love this shop devoted entirely to Baltic amber jewelry. The items, which run into the hundreds, include chunky and delicate earrings, pendants, bracelets, necklaces and objets d'art. Prices range from £10 to £1,000.

Butler & Wilson

20 SOUTH MOLTON ST, W1, 020-7409 2955
Open Mon.-Wed. & Fri.-Sat. 10am-6pm, Thurs. 10am-7pm.
U: Bond St.
Owners Nicky Butler and Simon Wilson were originally antique jewellers and still display some Victorian and Art Deco pieces in their stores. They are more popular for their lines of costume jewelry, which include jet, diamanté and silver baubles.
Also at 189 Fulham Rd, SW3, 020-7352 3045.

Cobra & Bellamy

149 SLOANE ST, SW1, 020-7730 2823
Open Mon.-Fri. 10.30am-5.30pm, Sat. 10.30am-5pm.
U: Sloane Sq.
Tania Hunter and Veronica Manussis create their own distinctive designs, including amber and jet, at their little black-and-white boutique. Look for silver pieces and objets d'art. They also sell exclusive jewelry made by Italian designer Barbara Bertagnolli in applied 24-carat gold with gemstones.

Fior

31 NEW BOND ST, W1, 020-7493 0101
Open Mon.-Fri. 9.30am-6pm, Sat. 9.30am-5.30pm.
U: Bond St.
A shimmering array of bejewelled evening bags, silk, satin or handmade gold and silver-plated, are specialities here. Styles come in scrunchy as well as square, round, oval and novelty shapes. Their costume jewelry is celebrated for its styling which rivals the designs in the fine jewelry world. Discreetly displayed inside the shop is a Royal Warrant, 'By appointment to HRH the Prince of Netherlands'.
Also at 27 Brompton Rd, SW3, 020-7589 0053.

Van Peterson Designs

194-195 WALTON ST, SW3, 020-7584 1101
Open Mon.-Tues. & Thurs.-Sat. 10am-6pm, Wed. 10am-7pm.
U: South Kensington.
Run by a husband-and-wife team who design fashionable statement jewelry, mostly in silver and gold. The shop also sells elegant designs by other vogue-ish designer including Ericsson Beamon and Linda Levinson. Also in Liberty.

FINE JEWELRY

Adler

13 NEW BOND ST, W1, 020-7409 2237
Open Mon.-Fri. 9.30am-5.30pm, Sat. 10am-5pm.
U: Bond St.
The third generation of the Adler family keeps the opulent influence of the Ottoman civilisation in striking pieces influenced by the designs of their grandfather, Jacques Adler, who had a workshop in Constantinople in 1910. Look for the Seraglio multiple ring with gold hoops linked by a bar, studded with diamonds and set off by round sapphires, rubies and emeralds. In-house designer, Dominque Bott, will undertake commissions or redesign old jewelry.

Asprey & Garrard

165-169 NEW BOND ST, W1, 020-7493 6767
WWW.ASPREY-GARRARD.COM
Open Mon.-Fri. 9.30am-5.30pm, Sat. 10am-5pm.
U: Green Park.
When Asprey and Garrard joined forces, one instinctively knew that it would be the most agreeable partnership. An institution, full of beautiful pieces, including their own designs. This is also a place to come to for antique jewelry, plus a range of Art Deco pieces.

Boodle & Dunthorne

128-130 REGENT ST, W1, 020-7437 5050
Open Mon.-Sat. 9am-6pm.
U: Piccadilly Circus.
Established in 1798, this family business started in Liverpool and its three London showrooms pride themselves on offering something for everyone. It has its own in-house designers, undertakes commissions and also offers good-value jewelry and watches by top international designers. Its specialist shop

in Harrods features pieces by goldsmith Leo de Vroomen.
Also at 1 Sloane Sq, SW1, 020-7235 0111.

Cartier
175 NEW BOND ST, W1, 020-7493 6962
Open Mon.-Fri. 10am-6pm, Sat. 10am-5pm.
U: Green Park.

The name speaks for itself, but if you need verification of the appeal just remember that Richard Burton gave Elizabeth Taylor a Cartier 69-carat diamond for one of her birthdays. Synonymous with classic French design since it opened in 1909, the London branch sells its own range of watches. Gift items include a monogrammed inkwell. The shop has a showcase of vintage Cartier pieces on sale and sometimes advertises its search for Cartier objects, jewels and watches made before 1970.

Collingwood
171 NEW BOND ST, W1, 020-7734 2656
Open Mon.-Fri. 10am-5.30pm, Sat. 10am-5pm.
U: Green Park.

Collingwood, in existence for two hundred years and holding Royal Warrants from the Queen and the Queen Mother, stocks watches and classic jewelry including some vintage pieces. They also undertake commissions.

David Morris
18 NEW BOND ST, W1, 020-7499 2200
Open Mon.-Fri. 10am-5.30pm, Sat. 10.30am-4.30pm.
U: Bond St.

This small shop carries a range of David Morris's distinctive designs, making him one of Europe's foremost jewellers. There is a 'boutique range' of signature pieces. He will undertake commissions and is especially popular for jewelry set with pink and yellow diamonds.

Hennell
12 NEW BOND ST, W1, 020-7629 6888
Open Mon.-Fri. 9.30am-5.30pm, Sat. 10am-4.30pm.
U: Green Park.

The gold and platinum jewelry on sale here is dazzling. Established in 1736, the firm has design books dating back to the 1850s, and therfore employs many traditional, classic features in its necklaces, rings, bracelets and brooches. The gift selection—which includes silver pencils, glassware, inkwells and blotters—is equally stylish and popular.

Ilias Lalaounis
5 SLOANE ST, SW1, 020-7235 9253
Open Mon.-Sat. 10am-6pm.
U: Knightsbridge.

At their Athens workshops, the four daughters of the family are the sixth generation to carry on the tradition of producing high-quality, opulent-looking gold jewelry, inspired by Greek tradition and Byzantine influences.

Longmire
12 BURY ST, SW1, 020-7930 8720
Open Mon.-Fri. 9.30am-5.30pm.
U: Green Park.

This small, handsome shop has three Royal Warrants and the world's largest selection of cufflinks. Designs include traditional, modern, estate or custom-made to include a monogram, crest or the image of your choice (prices from approximately £240).

Philip Antrobus
11 NEW BOND ST, W1, 020-7493 4557
Open Mon.-Sat. 9.30am-5pm.
U: Bond St.

This venerable firm founded in 1815 made the engagement ring given to the Queen by HRH Prince Philip. It carries a good range of antique and Victorian pieces plus a selection of modern jewelry. It is known for its workshop, which makes up specially commissioned pieces.

Richard Ogden
28 BURLINGTON ARCADE, W1, 020-7493 9136
Open Mon.-Fri. 9.30am-5.15pm, Sat. 9.30am-5pm.
U: Piccadilly Circus.

Well-known for fine antique and traditional jewelry, all British hand-crafted, this family-run firm, established in 1948, has a wide selection of engagement and wedding rings (from £200 to £15,000).

Tiffany & Co
25 OLD BOND ST, W1, 020-7409 2790
Open Mon.-Sat. 10am-5.30pm.
U: Green Park.

Understated surroundings for some of the world's most famous jewelry, which includes designer rings, brooches and necklaces in organic shapes from Paloma Picasso and Elsa Perretti on the ground floor. There is also the Tiffany signature collection.

The Watch Gallery

129 FULHAM RD, SW3, 020-7930 9488
Open Mon.-Sat. 10.30am-6pm.
U: South Kensington.

From their traditional and popular Swiss watch brands like Breitling, Jaeger-Le Coultre and Audermars Piguet, through to the more unusual such as Ulysee Nardin, Girard-Perragaux and IWC, customers take their time while considering a purchase from the myriad timepieces at this excellent shop. They specialise in selling and reparing vintage watches and are often supplied with the first of a limited-edition piece making this shop the ideal hunting ground for serious watch collectors.

Watches of Switzerland

16 NEW BOND ST, W1, 020-7493 2716
Open Mon. & Wed.-Fri. 9.30am-5.30pm, Tues. & Sat. 10am-5.30pm.
U: Piccadilly Circus.

There are many branches of this company, selling a wide range of watches, but in this corner of New Bond Street are such specialist showrooms as the Rolex centre and a Patek Phillipe salon.
Branches throughout London.

LEATHER & LUGGAGE

Anya Hindmarch

15-17 PONT ST, SW3,
Open Mon.-Sat. 10am-6pm.
U: Knightsbridge/Sloane Sq.

The chicest bags in a variety of shapes and sizes from one of Britain's foremost handbag designers. The new shop on Pont Street is the ideal location for those who have enjoyed a shopping trip on Sloane Street and need the perfect beaded or shiny leather bag to complete their outfit. Also offers a good range of stylish agendas and accessories.
Also at 91 Walton St, (first floor), SW3, 020-7584 7644.

Asprey & Garrard

165-169 NEW BOND ST, W1, 020-7493 6767
WWW.ASPREY-GARRARD.COM
Open Mon.-Fri. 9.30am-5.30pm, Sat. 10am-5pm.
U: Bond St.

Asprey & Garrard dates back to the 1780s when an ancestor of Huguenot descent worked as a silk printer and craftsman of fitted dressing cases. His son, Charles, went on to make more portable cases in leather and moved in 1848 to the present premises where luggage is still hand-stitched and gold-tooled.

Bill Amberg

10 CHEPSTOW RD, W2, 020-7727 3560
Open Mon.-Tues. & Fri.-Sat. 10am-6pm, Wed.-Thurs. 10am-7pm, Sun. noon-5pm.
U: Bayswater.

The modern British name to tote on your fashionable handbag. At this, his first independent outlet, you will love his beautiful bags, briefcases and luggage. Commissions are undertaken for luggage, furniture and leather flooring.

The Bridge

25 BEAUCHAMP PL, SW3, 020-7589 8055
Open Mon.-Tues. & Thurs.-Sat. 10am-6pm, Wed. 10am-7pm.
U: Knightsbridge.

The Bridge offers the best of Florentine flair. The range includes suitcases and carriers, travel bags, briefcases, holdalls, Filofaxes and accessories, all designed by Fernando Biagioni and produced in Italy (prices from around £20 for a key ring).

Coach

8 SLOANE ST, SW1, 020-7235 1507
Open Mon.-Tues. & Thurs.-Fri. 10am-6pm, Wed. 10am-7pm.
U: Knightsbridge.

The American company Coach has been making high-quality, durable, classic handbags and small leather goods since 1941. Their handsome designs, hand-crafted in the finest leather, might be on the expensive side (from £75 to £390) but the bags last forever and improve with age.

Connolly

41 CONDUIT ST, W1, 020-7439 2510
Open Mon.-Sat. 10am-6pm.
U: Oxford Circus

You can trust the people who make the sleek leather interiors for Rolls Royce, Aston Martin and Jaguar to deliver something a little bit special when it comes to leather bags and accessories. The luggage has a smooth walnut frame, the credit card holders, agendas and road maps are encased in melt-in-your-mouth, buttersoft leather. This, their new marvellous shop, is opening as we go to press.
Also at 32 Grosvenor Crescent Mews, SW1, 020-7235 3883.

Gucci

18 SLOANE ST, SW1, 020-7235 6707
Open Mon.-Tues. & Thurs.-Sat. 10am-6pm,
Wed. 10am-7pm.
U: Knightsbridge.

Gucci bags inspire as many ripoffs as they do sales from their beautiful store. Their bamboo-handled shoulder bags spawned a bamboo-fest on the high street with nearly every major retailer following the inspiration of designer Tom Ford. However, despite the price tag, only a real Gucci carries the necessary panache.
Also at 17 Sloane St, SW1, 020-7235 6707.

Henry Beguelin

17 MOTCOMB ST, SW1, 020-7245 6161
Open Mon.-Sat. 10am-6pm.
U: Knightsbridge.

You can't help but stop dead in your tracks when you first stumble across this gorgeous shop in increasingly popular Belgravia Village. Unusual leather goods many of which are handmade of every description including shoes, luggage, homewares with an ethnic bias and pretty bags.

Hermès

155 NEW BOND ST, W1, 020-7499 8856
Open Mon.-Sat. 10am-6pm.
U: Bond St.

Grace Kelly sparked off the worldwide love affair with Hermès bags. And, believe it or not, the waiting list for a 'Kelly' bag is still at least a couple of years. Those who neither have the patience (or the money) can console themselves with the recently introduced lines of shoes, belts and horse motif scarves.

Also at 179 Sloane St, SW1, 020-7823 1014.

J & M Davidson

42 LEDBURY RD, W11, 020-7313 9532
Open Mon.-Sat. 10am-6pm.
U: Ladbroke Grove.

Before the clothing ranges and the home-wares collections, this husband-and-wife team focused their energy on producing some of the finest leather goods in the country. Consequently, their bags, belts and luggage are still among the many highlights of their tasteful shops, although it seems that everything they turn their hands to looks like a design classic.

Loewe

130 NEW BOND ST, W1, 020-7493 3914
Open Mon-Sat. 9.30am-6pm.
U: Bond St.

From luxurious suede suits to leather and suede luggage are the elegant products from Narcisco Rodriguez, formerly of Cerruti, that include purses and briefcases embellished with a logo that is one of the most prestigious among leatherware shops.

Louis Vuitton

17-18 NEW BOND ST, W1, 020-7399 4050
Open Mon.-Sat. 9.30am-6pm.
U: Bond St.

Marc Jacobs takes over the helm at Louis Vuitton. The new global flagship store, which is the second largest in the world opened earlier this year amid a blaze of publicity. The Jacob's touch on the clothes, shoes and accessories is awaited with bated breath.
Also at 198 Sloane St, SW1, 020-7235 3356.

Mulberry

41-42 NEW BOND ST, W1, 020-7491 3900
Open Mon.-Wed. & Fri.-Sat. 10am-6pm,
Thurs. 10am-7pm.
U: Bond St.

For that perfect English country look, this large shop is the place to find everything from satchels to chic little handbags, from laptop cases to belts, sturdy Filofaxes to nifty little manicure cases and key rings. The range on display on the first floor includes suitcases and overnight bags.

Also at 11-12 Gees Ct, St. Christopher's Pl, W1, 020-7493 2546; 185 Brompton Rd, SW1, 020-7225 0313.

Osprey

11 ST. CHRISTOPHER'S PL, W1, 020-7935 2824
Open Mon.-Wed. & Fri.-Sat. 10am-6pm,
Thurs. 10am-7pm.
U: Bond St.

Osprey produces fashionable, smart, hand-made leather handbags and accessories, including genuine looking Kelly bags you might not be able to find at Hermès. They have expanded their range to include luggage, gloves, hand-sewn suede and leather-bound folios, diaries and photo frames.

Pickett Fine Leather

41 BURLINGTON ARCADE, W1, 020-7493 8939
Open Mon.-Sat. 9am-6pm.
U: Piccadilly Circus.

One person makes a crowd in this cupboard of a shop, but what a marvellous cupboard, packed with hundreds of wallets, handbags and briefcases in a variety of colours. Catalogue from 020-7493 1053.
Also at 6 Royal Exchange, EC3, 020-7283 7636.

Revelation

170 PICCADILLY, W1, 020-7493 4138
Open Mon.-Sat. 9.30am-6pm, Sun. 11am-5pm.
U: Piccadilly Circus.

A good choice of prices and labels from this leather and luggage specialist. For the young and street-conscious, there's Hervé Chapelier, Le Sac and Sequoia, while the more classically-minded can choose from Mulberry and The Bridge amongst others.
Also at 5 St. John's Wood High St, NW8, 020-7483 0166.

Tanner Krolle

38 OLD BOND ST, W1, 020-7493 6302
Open Mon.-Sat. 10am-6pm.
U: Green Park.

Once upon a time, Tanner Krolle was a good old reliable British firm making sturdy, mainly city-type briefcases. Nowadays the company is on level pegging with the big international players that make chic leather handbags, laptop carriers, beaded purses and their ever-popular circles and square collection.

W & H Gidden

15 CLIFFORD ST, W1, 020-7734 2788.
Open Mon.-Sat. 9am-6pm.
U: Bond St.

The smart wallets, purses, handbags, document holders and briefcases have the respected Gidden logo. Gidden's is famous for its equestrian products, which are also available within the store.

MENSWEAR

The area in and around Jermyn Street is a good starting point for any man wanting to cut a dash in the best of British style.

DESIGNER LABELS

Ermenegildo Zegna

37-38 JERMYN ST, SW1, 020-7493 4471
Open Mon.-Wed. & Fri.-Sat. 10am-6pm,
Thurs. 10am-7pm.
U: Green Park.

If classic Italian design is your passion, Zegna should be your label of choice. All the clothes are well cut, the fabrics used luxurious, and the staff is relaxed and helpful enough to make male shopping a pleasurable experience. Made-to-measure suits are available along with luxurious leather accessories, casual wear and gorgeous movie star-like pajamas. Be warned: don't touch the Casa Zegna cashmere blankets unless you intend to buy them, they're so beautiful, you won't want to be parted.

Jones

13 & 15 FLORAL ST, WC2, 020-7240 8312
E-MAIL: INFO@JONES-CLOTHING.CO.UK
Open Mon.-Sat. 10am-6.30pm, Sun. 1pm-5pm.
U: Covent Garden.

For men looking for a good cross-section of the hottest international designer names, this is the perfect place. The Active-wear shop at Number 13 houses the latest, hip sporty fashions; the designer shop at Number 15 is given over to labels like Dries van Noten, Helmut Lang, Alexander McQueen and Dirk Bikkembergs.

Jermyn Street Cachet

This delightful street, running parallel to Piccadilly, W1, has always been known as the place for bespoke gentlemen's clothing, a reputation it still retains today. Go here for handmade shirts, shoes, dressing gowns and more.

Joseph

74 SLOANE AVE, SW3, 020-7590 6200
Open Mon.-Tues. & Thurs.-Sat. 10am-6.30pm, Wed. 10am-7.30pm, Sun. noon-6pm.
U: South Kensington.

For the fashionable man around town, this, the first of Joseph Ettedgui's exclusively menswear stores, provides myriad dressing options. Label addicts will be drawn to the collections from Jil Sander, Prada and Gucci as well as the sleek lines from Joseph himself. Accessories include J. P. Tod, Granello and Duchamp.

The Library

268 BROMPTON RD, SW3, 020-7589 6569
Open Mon.-Tues. & Thurs.-Sat. 10am-6.30pm, Wed. 10am-7pm, Sun. 12.30pm-5pm.
U: Kightsbridge/South Kensington.

Fashion-conscious males are well served at this shop which gets its name from the backdrop of books on show. Seek out the latest collections from menswear designers such as Alexander McQueen, Dirk Bikkembergs, Martin Kidman, Dries van Noten and YMC.

HATS

Bates

21A JERMYN ST, SW1, 020-7734 2722
Open Mon.-Fri. 9am-5.15pm, Sat. 9.30am-4pm.
U: Green Park.

Established in 1902, Bates know a thing or two when it comes to the art of making splendid hats. The company offers a wide range of styles including top hats, felt trilbys and the largest selection of tweed flat caps, selling from £35. Good mail-order catalogue available.

Herbert Johnson

54 ST. JAMES'S ST, SW1, 020-7408 1174
Open Mon.-Sat. 10am-5pm.
U: Green Park.

Jack Nicholson in Batman, Harrison Ford in Raiders of the Lost Ark, Rex Harrison in My Fair Lady and Peter Sellars in Inspector Clouseau, what do they all have in common? They all wear hats made by this traditional hatters which has catered to high society and the military since 1899. This family business has an in-house design team for such interesting cinematic projects as well as your ordinary trilby. Accessories like fancy waistcoats, scarves and silk dressing gowns are always on display, too.

James Lock & Co

6 ST. JAMES'S ST, SW1, 020-7930 5849
WWW.LOCKHATTERS.CO.UK
E-MAIL: SALES@LOCKHATTERS.CO.UK
Open Mon.-Fri. 9am-5.30pm, Sat. 9.30am-5.30pm.
U: Green Park.

A legendary hat-maker established in 1676 to kit out the nearby court of St. James, this shop became famous for the 'coke', or the 'bowler' hat as it is more commonly known. It was made for William Coke in 1850 and was transported to America to become the 'Derby'. Hats have made a comeback and this is the place to find anything from a cap for country pursuits to a straw boater for watching cricket. Although a venerable institution, the store has a friendly and helpful staff.

LARGE SIZES

High & Mighty

83 KNIGHTSBRIDGE, SW1, 020-7589 7454
Open Mon. 10am-6pm, Tues.-Sat. 9am-6pm.
U: Knightsbridge.

The ready-to-wear suits and separates here are designed for men who are over six-foot-three inches, or whose chest sizes are from 40 to 60 inches.

Also at The Plaza, 120 Oxford St, W1, 020-7436 4861; 145-147 Edgware Rd, W2, 020-7723 8754.

Rochester Big & Tall

90 BROMPTON RD, SW3, 020-7838 0018
Open Mon.-Tues. & Thurs.-Sat. 9.30am-6pm,
Wed. 9.30am-7pm.

This firm, well known in America, has a popular shop here, which caters to men who are more than six-feet-tall and shorter men with chest sizes from 44 to 64 inches. Among their famous brands are Burberry, Gieves and Hawkes, Ermenegildo Zegna, Aquascutum, DKNY and Jhane Barnes. The store carries shoes by Allen-Edmonds, Cole Haan and New Balance.

SHIRTS & TIES

Emma Willis

66 JERMYN ST, SW1, 020-7930 9980
Open Mon.-Sat. 10am-6pm.
U: Green Park.

A female shirt-maker on Jermyn Street has caused quite a stir. Emma Willis designs and makes wonderful shirts for both gentlemen and ladies in top cottons and silks, as well as her own designs of wool and cashmere tops. Bespoke shirts take four to six weeks to make (from £125 for cotton to £220 for silk).

Harvie & Hudson

77 & 97 JERMYN ST, SW1, 020-7839 3578
WWW.INFO@HARVEYHUDSON.COM
Open Mon.-Fri. 9am-5.30pm, Sat. 9am-5.15pm.
U: Green Park.

Rolls of striped, checked and plain blue, navy or pink cotton poplin line the back of Number 97, ready for measurement here to be made up at the workshop at Number 77. Thomas Harvey and George Hudson set up business three generations ago and their shirt-making expertise is maintained by their direct descendants to this day. Keeping to a very traditional look, the company's own designers come up with the large range of classic stripes and solid colours in the finest two-fold poplins, Oxfords, batistes and voiles. A range of ties complement your chosen shade to perfection. Shirts can be made to measure or bought from stock in sizes 14 1/2 to 18 1/2 collar in link or button cuff styles. A range of blazers is also available.

Also at 55 Knightsbridge, SW1, 020-7235 2651.

Hilditch & Key

73 JERMYN ST, SW1, 020-7734 4707
WWW.HILDITCH.CO.UK
Open Mon.-Fri. 9.30am-6pm, Sat. 9.30am-5pm.

The classic white shirt is still the favourite at this company, in business since 1899. The ready-to-wear range is excellently made, with hand cutting and using two-fold poplin in a variety of stripes and plain colours. Famous for a distinctively shaped collar, the shirts have fine single-needle stitching, extra body length and are finished with real mother-of-pearl buttons. The handmade-to-order shirts are cut and made at Number 73. This shop also sells hand-slipped ties, plus fine quality pajamas and dressing gowns. Both shops sell ladies' cotton shirts.

Also at 88 Jermyn St, SW1, 020-7930 2329.

Thomas Pink

85 JERMYN ST, SW1, 020-7930 6364
WWW.THOMASPINK.CO.UK
Open Mon.-Wed. & Fri. 9.30am-6pm, Thurs.
9.30am-7pm, Sun. noon-5pm.
U: Green Park.

Quality, a certain cachet and reasonable prices make this shop a must for young city types. Appropriately enough, there are two outlets in the City of London, both of which sell the best-selling pure cotton poplin shirts, priced from a modest £49.50. Little silk knot cufflinks, which punctuate the cuffs with clever twists of colour are £5. Boxer shorts retail at £15.

Branches throughout London.

T M Lewin

106 JERMYN ST, SW1, 020-7930 4291
WWW.TMLEWIN.CO.UK
Open Mon.-Wed. & Fri.-Sat. 9.30am-6pm,
Thurs. 9.30am-7pm.
U: Green Park.

Established more than 100 years ago, this firm makes classic shirts from the finest two-fold poplin or pinpoint Oxford cotton, and the colours match up perfectly with the ties and quality cufflinks on offer. There are also striped and checked shirts and dress shirts. Accessories can be fun, with teddy bear images on braces and novelty cufflinks in the shape of sink taps, scissors, knife and fork, pewter pigs or with dollar and pound symbols for those on the trading floor. There is a large women's wear shop next door.

Turnbull & Asser

71-72 JERMYN ST, SW1, 020-7808 3000
Open Mon.-Fri. 9am-6pm, Sat. 9.30am-6pm.
U: Green Park.

James Bond was always partial to a Turnbull & Asser shirt or two, so too were the likes of Katharine Hepburn, Naomi Campbell and Winston Churchill. It's the impeccable quality and fine details such as hand-stitching, bone collar stays and shell buttons which brings customers through the door, as well as the attentive after-sales service which includes replacement collars and cuffs. The minimum order is six shirts, which will last for years. There is a large ready-to-wear selection and the firm holds a Royal Warrant as shirt maker to the Prince or Wales.
Also at 23 Bury St, SW1, 020-7930 0502.

Savile Row Style

Savile Row is associated with the best of British quality, with tailoring establishments that have been here for generations, as well as a few newcomers on the scene.

SUITS, SPORTSWEAR & GENERAL

Alfred Dunhill

48 JERMYN ST, SW1, 020-7290 8600
Open Mon.-Fri. 9.30am-6pm, Sat. 10am-6pm.
U: Green Park.

You could easily spend the whole day in this wonderfully light and airy store. It was founded in 1893, but having undergone a total transformation. First, the clothes are excellent, appealing to everyone from the most conservative dresser to those looking for casual but elegant sportswear. If you don't trust your own taste, simply enlist the help of one of the personal dressing stylists who will happily advise on cut and colour to suit your style and budget. The jewelry line is first-rate, as are the briefcases and luggage. Other treats within the store include a tie-loan service, complimentary jewelry polishing, tailoring service (available on items bought in the store only) and a fine humidor with complimentary whisky tastings. The company has also installed a fax so you can catch up on the latest share prices. In the basement, you can marvel at the archive products in the Alfred Dunhill museum. This is one of the best men's shops around.

Eden Park

16 CONDUIT ST, W1, 020-7408 0037
Open Mon.-Sat. 10am-6pm.
U: Piccadilly Circus.

Created by members of the French rugby team, Eden Park is a highly sought-out label in its native France. Since arriving in London two years ago, the company has carved out a niche for its luxury menswear, sportswear and Town Line collection, as well as a small women's wear and children's collection.

Hackett

85 JERMYN ST, SW1, 020-7930 1300
WWW.HACKETT.CO.UK
Open Mon.-Wed. & Fri.-Sat. 9.30am-6pm,
Thurs. 9.30am-7pm.
U: Green Park.

For a while the description 'young fogey' was bandied about to describe that conservative look reminiscent of previous decades. This firm started to make its own garments in 1984, borrowing details from the vintage clothing the founders came across in market stalls. The firm now sells brushed cotton shirts, tweed sports jackets, hand-knit sweaters, plus-fours and all manner of clothing which cover everything from attending events like polo and race meetings to looking well-turned out at the office.
Also at 137-138 Sloane St, SW1, 020-7730 3331.

Kent & Curwen

30 ST. JAMES'S ST, SW1, 020-7409 1955
Open Mon.-Sat. 9.30am-6pm.
U: Green Park/Piccadilly Circus.

A jaunty air prevails in this shop with the premier location, thanks to the brightly striped blazers and caps, usually worn at sporting events like Henley Regatta. Many of these are official colours to be worn strictly by the members of a particular club, regiment or school, but there are many adaptations of the striped look. The jackets are sometimes bought by overseas' visitors for occasions when an English look is de rigueur. Chunky cricket sweaters with their bold stripe trims are popular for men and women.

Moss Bros

27 KING ST, WC2, 020- 7632 9700
*Open Mon.-Wed. & Fri. 9am-5.30pm, Thurs.
9am-6.30pm.*
U: Covent Garden.

Moses Moses started selling second-hand suits in 1860; his sons, under a new company name, Moss Bros, found themselves lending a formal suit to an unsuccessful stockbroker just once too often, and started charging him for the loans in 1897. Thus, suit hire was born. Still outfitting men for formal occasions, this Covent Garden shop has dark panelled walls stretching back to rooms, which include a traditional barbershop. Among the many racks of men's clothes are Hugo Boss, Pierre Cardin and Chester Barrie lines of suits and cashmere coats.

Also at 88 Regent St, W1, 020-7494 0666; 33 Eastcheap, EC3, 020-7626 4247.

Natural Blue

52 ARTILLERY LANE, E1, 020-7377 8755
*Open Mon.-Wed. & Fri. 10am-6.30pm, Thurs.
10am-7.30pm, Sun. 11am-5pm, closed Sat.*
U: Liverpool St.

The calm stainless steel, glass and natural wood interior is the perfect backdrop for the casual clothing collections from Natural Blue. Originally sought out for their knitwear, the label now extends from streamlined leather jackets (£290), to the down vest with mobile phone and minidisc pocket (£55).

TAILORS

Anderson & Sheppard

30 SAVILE ROW, W1, 020-7734 1420
Open Mon.-Fri. 8.30am-5pm.
U: Bond St.

In this brash world of aggressive advertising, it makes a refreshing change to come across an industry where quality and expertise are allowed to speak for themselves. Anderson & Sheppard, established in 1906, is held in high esteem and is considered to be the tops in the tailoring network. British maverick designer, Alexander McQueen, sharpened his cutting skills here and the results of his training can be witnessed in his impeccable tailoring. If you are recommended by someone, the team at A&S will match the cutter your friend had to achieve a similar look or feel. Prince Charles has his double-breasted suits made here.

Dege

10 SAVILE ROW, W1, 020-7287 2941
WWW.DEGESAVILEROW.CO.UK
*Open Mon.-Fri. 9.15am-5.15pm, Sat. 9.30am-
12.30pm.*
U: Piccadilly Circus.

Founded in 1856, the firm holds three Royal Warrants including one from the Sultan of Oman, and makes bespoke suits, shirts and military uniforms. The firm's styles are influenced by its equestrian, military and sporting background. Representatives regularly visit Europe, the Gulf, U.S. and Japan.

Gieves & Hawkes

1-2 SAVILE ROW, W1, 020-7434 2001
E-MAIL: GIEVES@GIEVESANDHAWKES.COM
Open Mon.-Sat. 9am-6pm.
U: Piccadilly Circus.

A large shop with a genteel ambience featuring wood paneling and Schooner prints, the firm sells mostly ready-to-wear suits and shirts using the latest computer technology. Past clients included Admiral Nelson and the Duke of Wellington. It is well stocked with scarves, belts, shirts and accessories and has a casual range of clothing in the shop next door. Younger clients particularly like the recently launched Gieves collection. The lines are a modification of Gieves & Hawkes traditional look, brought bang up-to-date with contemporary fabrics and styling.

Also at 18 Lime St, EC3, 020-7283 4914.

Henry Poole

15 SAVILE ROW, W1, 020-7734 5985
Open Mon.-Fri. 9am-5.15pm.
U: Piccadilly Circus.

In typically discreet Savile Row style where it was the first tailor to open a showroom on Savile Row, this firm has been going since 1806 and has occupied the present building since 1887. It received its first Royal Warrant from Queen Victoria, an honour still bestowed today by Queen Elizabeth.

Hogg Sons & J B Johnstone

19 CLIFFORD ST, W1, 020-7734 5915
Open Mon.-Fri. 8.45am-4.45pm.
U: Piccadilly Circus.

Two tailoring establishments share these traditional-looking premises. The cutting room is on the ground floor where customers can catch a glimpse of the meticulous attention to detail. The front shop stocks ready-to-wear trousers, shirts, waistcoats and ties. Sara Haydon is the only female proprietor in Savile Row, and the shop makes suits for women.

H Huntsman & Sons

11 SAVILE ROW, W1, 020-7734 7441
Open Mon.-Fri. 9am-1pm & 2pm-5.30pm.
U: Piccadilly Circus.

One of the venerable vendors of Savile Row, this firm has been making top-of-the-line menswear since the 1920s. It has a distinctive line of well-fitted jackets and blazers and offers a bespoke service where customers are fitted four times before walking off with their suit. Like many other Savile Row tailors, Huntsman sends staff to the U.S. twice a year to fit customers.

Kilgour, French & Stanbury

8 SAVILE ROW, W1, 020-7734 6905
WWW.8SAVILEROW.COM
Open Mon.-Fri. 9am-5.30pm, Sat. 10am-4pm.
U: Piccadilly Circus.

There are some 5,000 fabrics to choose from at this traditional tailor where everything is made by hand. The company shares the premises with another famous tailor, the equestrian specialist Bernard Weatherill, which is why a saddle prop is on hand to ensure measurements are accurate. You can be sure its good, too—it's sent to Buckingham Palace when the Queen orders new riding wear.

Maurice Sedwell

19 SAVILE ROW, W1, 020-7734 0824
WWW.SAVILEROWTAILOR.COM
Open Mon.-Fri. 9am-5.30pm, Sat. 9am-1pm.
U: Piccadilly Circus.

Maurice Sedwell died in 1991, but his tradition lives on. About 90 percent of the company's bespoke suits are made from British worsted cloth, involve a three-stage fitting process and some 60 hours of highly skilled hand stitching until the final fitting. There is an in-house shirt maker and a bespoke shoemaker who visits the shop by appointment. Accessories include silk ties, antique cufflinks, cummerbunds, braces and handkerchiefs.

Ozwald Boeteng

9 VIGO ST, W1, 020-7734 6868
Open Mon.-Sat. 10am-6pm.
U: Piccadilly Circus.

Ozwald Boeteng is a dream advertisement for his sharp tailoring. His lean, six-foot-plus frame and smooth, dark complexion show off his bright suits and clashing shirts to perfection. It's not every man who can carry off a fuschia shirt or a lime green tie, however, but clients such as Wesley Snipes and Mick Jagger are willing to give it a try.

Richard James

31 SAVILE ROW, W1, 020-7434 0605
Open Mon.-Fri. 10am-6pm, Sat. 11am-5pm.
U: Piccadilly Circus.

One of the newest tailors on the block, Richard James brings with him a modern approach to tailoring. The genial and good-humoured James has both ready-to-wear and following the tradition of Savile Row, bespoke suits and boasts a glitzy client list that includes Liam and Patsy Gallagher, Elton John, Jarvis Cocker, Viscount Linley and Christian Lacroix. A two-piece suit (men's only) starts at £625; a bespoke suit is £1,350 + VAT and takes six to eight weeks to make. There are also sharp-looking off-the-peg jackets, shirts and knitwear.

Tom Gilbey

2 NEW BURLINGTON PL, SAVILE ROW, W1
020-7734 4877
Open Mon.-Wed. & Fri. 10am-6pm, Thurs. 10am-7pm, Sat. 10am-5.30pm.
U: Oxford Circus.

From wildly flamboyant to traditional Savile Row, this designer's made-to-measure suits always have a distinctive flair. The fabrics used include silks, velvets, brocades and wools.

WAISTCOATS

Favourbrook

9-21 PICCADILLY ARCADE, JERMYN ST, SW1
020-7491 2337
Open Mon.-Tues. 9am-6pm, Wed.-Thurs. 9am-7pm, Sat. 10am-6pm.
U: Green Park.

The fabulous waistcoats, smoking jackets, frock coats and tasseled, fez-style hats bearing the Favourbrook label are made with the highest quality of fabrics. It makes for a unique, dandified look, as famously portrayed in the film Four Weddings and a Funeral, where one of the characters wore a hand-painted waistcoat from this store festooned with angels. The women's wear includes the same English-meets-Asian style with a full range of waistcoats, beautifully tailored Nehru jackets and coats.

Tom Gilbey Waistcoat Gallery

2 NEW BURLINGTON PL, SAVILE ROW, W1
020-7734 4877
Open Mon.-Wed. & Fri. 10am-6pm, Thurs. 10am-7pm, Sat. 10am-5.30pm.
U: Oxford Circus.

Waistcoats are the main selling point of Tom Gilbey's business. His designs are often likened to works of art due to the decorative processes and fine materials employed in his clothing. His distinctive waistcoats are popular with the pop and film set. Prices start at £150. Although this shop is devoted to accessories, you can order a gorgeous made-to-measure suit or rent an outfit for a wedding.

PHOTOGRAPHY & MUSIC

PHOTOGRAPHY

Camera Clinic

SUITE 240-241, THE LINEN HALL
162 REGENT ST, W1, 020-7734 6629
Open Mon.-Fri. 9am-6pm.
U: Oxford Circus/Piccadilly Circus.

As the name indicates, this company repairs all major makes of cameras and camcorders, all done on site. Camera Clinic is one of the few shops in London advertising their language skills—when needed, they serve customers in French and Spanish.

Also at 26 North End Crescent, W14, 020-7602 7976.

Jessop Photo Centre

67 NEW OXFORD ST, WC1
020-7240 6077, WWW.JESSOPS.COM
Open Mon.-Wed. & Sat. 9am-6pm, Thurs. 9am-8pm, Fri. 9am-7pm, Sun. 11am-5pm.
U: Tottenham Court Rd.

A good stop for eager amateur photographers, since the staff is friendly and helpful.

There's a large selection of cameras and equipment from cheap and cheerful to the reassuringly expensive.

Joe's Basement

113 WARDOUR ST, W1, 020-7439 3210
WWW.JOESBASEMENT.CO.UK
Open daily 24 hours.
U: Tottenham Court Rd.

For amateurs and professionals needing to process film at any time of the day or night. There's a 4-hour service for films, also a small counter for films, batteries and accessories.

Also at 82 Clerkenwell Rd, EC1, 020-7253 3210; 247 Euston Rd, NW1, 020-7388 3210; 111 Hammersmith Rd, W6, 020-7371 3210.

Keith Johnson & Pelling

93 DRUMMOND ST, NW1
020-7380 1144, WWW.KJP.CO.UK
Open Mon.-Fri. 8.30am-6.30pm.
U: Euston.

A real professional's place with a superb range of equipment and film, plus hire and repair service and knowlegeable staff. It is said to be the largest photographic company in Europe.

Also at 175 Wardour St, W1, 020-7434 1848; 10 Heathmans Rd, SW6, 020-7384 3270.

London Camera Exchange

98 STRAND, WC2
020-7379 0200, WWW.LCEGROUP.CO
Open Mon.-Fri. 9am-5.30pm, Sat. 11am-5.30pm.
U: Charing Cross.

This chain of 24 shops specialises in good secondhand cameras and photographic equipment. There is a selection of new cameras, too—but the emphasis is on pre-loved items. A good place to re-equip.

Metro Imaging

76 CLERKENWELL RD, EC1, 020-7865 0000
WWW.METROIMAGING.CO.UK
Open daily 24 hours.
U: Barbican/Farringdon.

Terrific service from this 24-hour place, who caters mainly to professionals. All types of services are offered here.

Also at 3 Jubilee Pl, SW3, 020-7376 8999; 3 Great Marlborough St, EC1, 020-7543 4000.

Museum Cameras

4-11 PIED BULL COURT, WC1, 020-7831 9200
Open Mon.-Fri. 10am-6pm, Sat. 10am-1pm.
U: Holborn.

Huge collection of historical still and moving picture cameras dating from 1840 are carried here. Expert staff will discuss technicalities with you.

Silverprint

12 VALENTINE PL, SE1, 020-7620 0844
WWW.SILVERPRINT.CO.UK
Open Mon.-Fri. 9.30am-5.30pm.
U: Southwark.

Everything one needs (and a bit more), for processing, developing and printing photographs. Special papers and chemicals for photographers.

Snappy Snaps

170 KING'S RD, SW3, 020-7351 4472
WWW.SNAPPYSNAPS.COM
Open Mon.-Sat. 8.30am-6.30pm, Sun. 10am-5.30pm.
U: Sloane Sq.

One-or three-hour developing of most films, cropping to your liking and small wonders performed on those 'almost there'-type of holiday snaps. Used also by professionals, although the results may vary from branch to branch.

Also at 127 Camden High St, NW1, 020-7284 2264; 359 Strand, WC2, 020-7836 6644; and branches throughout London.

Techno

154 TOTTENHAM CT RD, W1, 020-7387 7001
Open Mon.-Wed. & Fri. 9am-6pm, Thurs. 9am-7pm, Sat. 9am-5.30pm.
U: Tottenham Court Rd.

These specialists in secondhand cameras used to be called Fox Talbot, but now they go under the banner of their parent company. They stock serious Leicas, Nikons, and virtually any other make of camera that you could fancy. One often sees professionals sneaking in to check for possible bargains.

Also at 443 Strand, WC2, 020-7379 6522.

Looking for an address?
Refer to the index.

MUSICAL INSTRUMENTS

General

Blanks

273 KILBURN HIGH RD, NW6, 020-7624 7777
Open Mon.-Sat. 10am-5pm.
U: Kilburn.

A shop serving up musical products and instruments from traditional Irish folk to guitars, brass and sheet music.

Foote's

10 GOLDEN SQ, W1
020-7734 1822 FOR PERCUSSION
020-7437 1811 FOR ORCHESTRAL INSTRUMENTS
WWW.FOOTESMUSIC.COM
Open: Mon.-Fri. 9am-6pm, Sat. 9am-5pm.
U: Piccadilly Circus

The two floors of this long-established Soho shop are split between percussion and orchestral instruments. Foote's also has a hire service for children, believing it important to practise on a good instrument from an early age. So if your daughter suddenly decides to become a world-class percussionist, you don't have to buy a full kit straight away.

Rose Morris

11 DENMARK ST, WC2
020-7836 0991 FOR EQUIPMENT
020-7836 4766 FOR PRINTED MUSIC
WWW.ROSE-MORRIS.CO.UK
Open Mon.-Tues. & Fri.-Sat. 10am-6.30pm, Thurs. 10am-7pm.
U: Tottenham Court Rd.

This superstore includes six floors of instruments, amplification, recording equipment and sheet music. All the floors have their own sector covered, and if Rose Morris doesn't have what you are looking for, then you are in for a long search.

Specialists

Accordions of London

365 KILBURN HIGH RD (CORNER OF LOVERIDGE RD), NW6, 020-7935 3339
Open Mon.-Sat. 10am-5pm.
U: Kilburn.

The accordion may not be the trendiest of instruments, but it enjoys strong support among those who are hooked on its sound.

This specialist shop sells everything from beginners' instruments to concert-level accordions. Accessories, repairs and spare parts are also available.

All Flutes Plus

5 DORSET ST, W1 020-7935 3339
WWW.ASP@ALLFLUTESPLUS.CO.UK
Open Mon.-Fri. 10am-6pm, Sat. 10am-4.30pm.
U: Baker St.

Why bother with a complicated name? Sales, repairs and rentals of quality flutes plus recorders and saxophones. They also sell second-hand instruments and accessories.

Andy's

27 DENMARK ST, WC2, 020-7916 5080
WWW.ANDYSGUITAR.NET.COM
Open Mon.-Sat. 10am-7pm, Sun. 12.30pm-6.30pm.
U: Tottenham Court Rd.

A long-time favourite among guitar enthusiasts all over the world. A small shop, crammed full of electric guitars downstairs and acoustics upstairs. The list of customers includes many top musicians from Bob Dylan downwards. Andy's is also famous for their finder service; if you are looking for that favourite guitar you sold to pay the mortgage and desperately want it back, they're the people to talk to. Andy's repairs are good enough for world famous professionals.

The Bass & Acoustic Centre

131 WAPPING HIGH ST, E1, 020-7265 1567
WWW.BASSCENTRE.COM
Open Mon.-Sat. 10am-5.30pm.
U: Wapping.

When you need more bottom end for your band, or just want to enjoy the kick of a bass guitar, head for Wapping. The Bass Centre claims to be the biggest of its kind in the world, and it certainly serves up a huge selection of wonderful and practical instruments. The selection of acoustic guitars is also excellent.

J & A Beare

7 BROADWICK ST, W1
020-7437 1449, WWW.BEARES.COM
Open Mon.-Fri. 9am-12.15pm & 1.30pm-5pm.
U: Piccadilly Circus.

One hundred years of experience and tradition in dealing with violins and cellos gives J & A Beare a pretty decent pedigree. They are the specialists in building, repairing, restoring and retailing stringed instruments. Their selection of antique instruments is by appointment only.

Hobgoblin Music

24 RATHBOURNE PL, W1
020-7323 9040, WWW.HOBGOBLIN.COM
Open Mon.-Sat. 10am-6pm.
U: Tottenham Court Rd.

Musical instruments for folk enthusiasts, guitars and mandolins galore, Hobgoblin is a fascinating shop on two floors just north of Oxford Street specialising in English folk music, plus everything that is needed when playing it. There are also boddhrans and other percussion instruments from around the globe, and even kits to build your own early lute. There's also a small selection of folk and world music recordings from all corners of the earth.

Macari's

92-92 CHARING CROSS RD, WC2
020-7836 2856, WWW.MACARIS.CO.UK
Open Mon.-Sat. 10.30am-5.30pm.
U: Tottenham Court Rd.

A shop to go to for vintage guitars and amplifiers. If you know your Gretch from your Gibson, and your Rickenbacker from your Danelectro, you'll find a lot to admire in this excellent shop around the corner from Denmark Street. The selection on two floors includes both acoustics and electrics and everything from bargains for beginners to classic instruments for top professionals.

Professional Percussion

205 KENTISH TOWN RD, NW5, 020-7485 0822
Open Mon.-Sat. 10am-6pm.
U: Kentish Town.

A toy and tool shop for all those interested in everything you can bang —and tops for professional percussionists, too. This first-floor shop has percussion instruments for classical orchestras, schools and all those young pop bands dreaming about being the Next Big Thing. There are talking drums, kettle drums, practise kits for quiet rehearsals, vibrafones and bongos. Staff is professional, knowledgeable and friendly. The customers include 10-year olds having their first drumming lesson at the shop and top-level musicians spending serious time thoroughly testing the new equipment.

Ray Man

54 CHALK FARM RD, NW1, 020-7692 6261
Open daily 10.30am-6pm.
U: Chalk Farm/Camden Town.

Ray Man used to be a small, cramped shop in Covent Garden with exotic instruments piled high. A move to bigger premises in Chalk Farm has given the shop a chance to display its goods properly and these beautiful—as well as playable—instruments from Asia are a pleasant sight. Ray Man has everything from Chinese temple gongs to one-stringed violins.

Spanish Guitar Centre

36 CRANBOURNE ST, WC2, 020-7240 0754
Open daily 10.30am-6pm.
U: Leicester Sq.

This emporium of acoustic guitars was started by Len Williams, whose son John is one of the world's leading classical guitarists. Be amazed at the beauty of instruments, and astonished at the scale of prices, ranging from under £100 to more than £10,000. The shop also offers guitar tuition and accessories. A place worth a pilgrimage.

T W Howarth

311-35 CHILTERN ST, W1
020-7935 2407, WWW.HOWARTH.CO.UK
Open Mon.-Fri. 10am-5.30pm, Sat. 10am-3pm.
U: Baker St.

All woodwind instruments in one stop, and also three shops in one, T W Howarth has secured its place as the leading London specialist for bassoons, oboes, saxophones and clarinets. The shop also does repairs, has a hire service and appraises instruments.

MUSICAL RECORDINGS

Classical, Jazz, Pop, Easy Listening

Dress Circle

57-59 MONMOUTH ST, WC2
020-7240 2227, WWW.DRESSCIRCLE.CO.UK
Open Mon.-Sat. 10am-7pm.
U: Leicester Sq.

Music and memorabilia: from soundtracks and videos of musicals to nostalgic items of the golden stage. For those who want to be entertained in an old-fashioned way.

HMV

150 OXFORD ST, W1
020-7631 3423, WWW.HMV.CO.UK
Open Mon.-Sat. 9am-8pm, Sun. noon-6pm.
U: Oxford Circus/Tottenham Court Rd.

HMV covers all musical styles from avant-garde to mainstream pop, from rap to rhapsodies. It is especially good on jazz, folk and international music. This huge store is a one-stop place for musical souvenirs.

Intoxica

231 PORTOBELLO RD, W11
020-7229 8010, WWW.INTOXICA.CO.UK
Open Mon.-Sat. 10.30am-6.30pm, Sun. 11am-4pm.
U: Ladbroke Grove.

This mini-megastore in trendy Notting Hill Gate is a gold mine for those interested in music outside the latest pop charts. A good selection of dance music from the latest beats to chill-out records and classic soul (they named the downstairs the 'bass-ment') and loads of indie, trash, noise and psychedelia. There are collectors' items and a good second-hand department.

Tower Records

1 PICCADILLY CIRCUS, W1
020-7439 2500, WWW.TOWERRECORDS.CO.UK
Open Mon.-Sat. 9am-midnight, Sun. noon-6pm.
U: Piccadilly Circus.

A huge megastore with late hours for those who decide after dinner that they need some music for the night. The ground floor is full of pop, rock and imports; the first floor covers classical, jazz, country and world music. The monthly magazine *Top* tells you about the latest releases and concerts in London.

Also at 162 Camden High St, NW1, 020-7424 2810.

Virgin

225-229 PICCADILLY, W1
020-7930 4208, WWW.VIRGIN.COM
Open Mon.-Sat. 9.30am-9pm, Sun. noon-6pm.
U: Tottenham Court Rd.

Virgin started the whole business of music megastores in Britain back in the 1970s. Today they sell everything from records to travel tickets, books, computer games and mobile telephones. Music is extremely well represented and well organised in different categories.

Also at 14-30 Oxford St, W1, 020-7631 1234; Kings Walk Mall, 122 King's Rd, SW3, 020-7591 0957; Unit V30, Brent Cross Shopping Centre, NW4, 020-8202 3815; Wimbledon Centre Court Shopping Centre, Queens Rd, SW19, 020-8944 7691.

Specialists

Beano's

7 MIDDLE ST, CROYDON, SURREY
020-8680 1202, WW.BEANOSRECORDSHOP.CO.UK
Open Mon.-Fri. 10am-6pm, Sat. 9am-6pm.
Rail: East Croydon/West Croydon
This is the largest second-hand record store in Europe and is reasonably priced for ordinary records and hugely expensive for collectors' items. It has to be seen to be believed. Beano's mail-order service covers most of the world.

Cheapo Cheapo

53 RUPERT ST, W1, 020-7437 8272
Open Mon.-Sat. noon-10pm.
U: Leicester Sq.
Pile them high and sell them cheapo cheapo! A huge selection of records from children's songs to psychedelia, from folk to classical. A place to spend time browsing through thousands of records, but luckily there are lots of bars and cafés nearby to park your partner while shopping.

D.O.C. Records

5 CARDWELL TERRACE (CARDWELL ST), N7
020-7700 0081
Open Mon.-Sat. 10am-7pm, Sun. 11am-5pm.
U: Holloway Rd.
A place for collectors and all friends of good music, this small, two-room shop is packed full of CDs, vinyl singles and albums, videos and memorabilia. This is a place to talk about music, listen before you buy and spend a small fortune!

Daddy Kool

12 BERWICK ST, W1, 020-7437 3535
Open Mon.-Sat. 10.30am-6.30pm.
U: Leicester Sq.
Caribbean beats, Jamaican reggae and ska, loads of good old vinyl and rarities for those enjoying sunny rhythms and roots music.

Honest Jon's

276-278 PORTOBELLO RD, W10, 020-8969 9822
Open Mon.-Sat. 10am-6pm, Sun. 11am-5pm.
U: Ladbroke Grove.
A respected specialist in R&B music, lovingly covering everything from jazz to dance. Situated at the end of the famous Portobello Road market, this shop always draws a varied clientele of jazzers and hipsters.

Mole Jazz

311 GRAY'S INN RD, WC1
020-7278 8623, WWW.MOLEJAZZ.CO.UK
Open Mon.-Thurs. & Sat.10am-6pm, Fri. 10am-8pm.
U: King's Cross.
One of the brighter spots in the scruffy King's Cross area, Mole Jazz brings the message of music to these corners. Records, cassettes, books and posters, a chance to listen properly to the music before buying—no wonder the place draws music lovers from near and far. And as with all good jazz shops, it also has a corner for rarities, a selection for those who already have all the records we mere mortals are still thinking of buying.

Ray's Jazz

180 SHAFTESBURY AVE, WC2, 020-7240 3969
Open Mon.-Sat. 10am-6.30pm, Sun. 2pm-5.30pm.
U: Leicester Sq/Covent Garden.
The two floors of this compact shop are full of jazz from sunny Dixieland to serious European avantgarde, plus a collection of world music from Lappish joiku to country yodel. Good listening facilities, friendly and knowledgeable staff, central location—there is a lot going for Ray's. It is always refreshing to find a store where the staff gives honest comments about the music they are selling. Valuations for secondhand records.

Rough Trade

130 TALBOT RD, W11
020-7229 8541, WWW.ROUGHTRADE.COM
Open Mon.-Sat. 10am-6.30pm, Sun. 1pm-5pm.
U: Ladbroke Grove
Rough Trade remains one of the shops at the forefront of independent music. All the obscure record labels you have heard-of or can only imagine—are here. The shop also has a good selection of fanzines, those small publications written by music fans for music fans.

Also, rather eccentrically, a decent amount of surf and skateboard gear and T-shirts.
Also at 16 Neal's Yard, WC2, 020-7240 0105.

Sound of China
6 GERRARD ST, W1, 020-7734 1970
Open daily 11am-7pm.
U: Leicester Sq.

In the heart of China Town, this small shop sells both classical and popular Chinese music on cassettes and CDs. They also carry books and magazines.

Stern's African Record Centre
116 WHITFIELD ST, W1
020-7387 5550, WWW.STERNMUSIC.COM
Open Mon.-Sat.10.30am-6.30pm.
U: Warren St.

An institution among world music shops, Stern's has been the place to go to for African, Caribbean and Latin music for years. It's not just a record shop, it also acts as a good information point for concerts and other world music happenings in London.

SHEET MUSIC

Argent's Music
20 DENMARK ST, W1, 020-7240 4159
Open Mon.-Fri. 9am-6pm, Sat. 10am-6pm.
U: Tottenham Court Rd.

A wide selection of sheet music from quiet classical to evergreens and heavy rock are available.

Boosey & Hawkes
295 REGENT ST, W1, 020-7580 2060
WWW.BOOSEY.COM/MUSICSHOP
Open Mon.-Fri. 9.30am-6pm, Sat. 10am-5pm.
U: Oxford Circus.

Walking into B&H is like walking into an office, as there is a reception desk in the lounge guarding the firms upstairs from music lovers. On the ground floor is a wide selection of classical sheet music and a good selecion of jazz and popular music from different decades. Boosey & Hawkes also has a collection of music-related gifts, like notated socks, 'Chopin lists' and 'Bach in a minuet'-type cards.

Foyle's
119 CHARING CROSS RD, WC1, 020-7437 5660
Open Mon.-Wed. & Fri.-Sat. 9am-6pm, Thurs. 9am-7pm.
U: Tottenham Court Rd.

The third floor of this old, massive, and rambling book shop is partly dedicated to sheet music and related books. That is, if you can find them in this eccentrically arranged store.

Schott
48 GREAT MARLBOROUGH ST, W1
020-7437 1246, WWW.SCHOTTMUSIC.COM
Open Mon.-Fri. 9am-5.30pm.
U: Oxford Circus.

Printed classical music from different ages—from early times to contemporary works, miniature scores for orchestras, solo pieces for recorders and educational music and books are available.

SPORTING GOODS

CLOTHING & EQUIPMENT

Lillywhites
PICCADILLY CIRCUS, SW1, 020-7930 3181
Open Mon.-Fri. 9.30am-7pm, Sat. 9.30am-6pm, Sun. 11am-5pm.
U: Piccadilly Circus.

This six-storey department store has the widest choice of sportswear and equipment in town. There are departments devoted to baseball, hockey, squash, golf, tennis, badminton, darts, football—in fact, this is the place to find everything you need for any sport, ranging from ski clothing and equipment to Wimbledon products. There is also an entire floor dedicated to footwear for over 30 sports, and a comprehensive book and video section. It may be a little daunting finding your way around this rambling series of rooms and departments, but don't worry, the staff is particularly helpful and knowledgeable.

NikeTown

236 OXFORD ST, W1, 020-7612 0800
WWW.NIKE.COM/WWW.EASTBAY.COM
Open Mon.-Thurs. 10am-7pm, Fri.-Sat. to 8pm,
Sun. noon-6pm.
U: Oxford Circus.

The largest NikeTown in the world set up shop in London less than a year ago. Set over 70,000 sqare feet and spread over three floors are separate buildings each housing areas devoted to specific sports. There's an area devoted to youngsters that includes footwear, clothing and interactive displays; a men's football pavilion with a turnstile hatch, astro-turf and stadium roof, an area for golf fans, basketball heroes and women's sports. NikeTown also encourages workers in the area to become fitter by joining the NikeTown Runners, a free weekly running club taking 3, 5 and 8 mile routes.

Sam de Téran

151 FULHAM RD, SW7, 020-7460 3216
Open Mon.-Fri. 10am-6.30pm, Sat. 10am-7pm,
Sun. noon-6pm.
U: South Kensington.

When you take your annual snow in Cloisters and soak up the sun in Mustique, the only place to buy your sportswear is from Sam de Téran. Since she created her first swimwear collection in 1992, this designer has gone on to produce the most coveted tennis, gym, swim and skiwear that appeals to the jet set. The clothes are displayed on a table and glass shelving spanning the length of the shop and the spacious dressing rooms are made ultra-luxurious with the inclusion of sofas.

Soccer Scene

56 CARNABY ST, W1, 020-7439 0778
Open Mon.-Sat. 9.30am-7pm, Sun. 11am-5pm.
U: Oxford Circus.

The best place to outfit yourself in the home—and away is full of all of the British teams, plus some foreign teams and other sporting gear. Sizes from infants to adults.

YHA Adventure Shop

14 SOUTHAMPTON ST, WC2, 020-7836 8541
Open Mon.-Wed. 10am-7pm, Thurs.-Fri.
10am-7pm, Sat. 9am-6.30pm, Sun. 11am-5pm.
U: Covent Garden.

Sir Ranulph Fiennes (the arctic explorer) and Sir Chris Bonnington (the mountaineer), use YHA cooking and camping equipment on their adventures. The staggering selection of parkas, knapsacks, sleeping bags and all the necessary equipment for camping and mountain-climbing is verification that this shop is serious about its business. Even in winter, when the ski equipment takes up valuable floor space, there is a geodesic dome tent set up and the staff talks to customers through the intricacies of its maintenance. Once part of the Youth Hostel Association, the company is now privately owned but there is a membership department at the shop for people who wish to join and want to make bookings at a hostel (020-7836 1036). The company also runs the Campus Travel Agency (020-7836 3343).

Also at 174 Kensington High St, W8 020-7938 2948; 120 Victoria St, SW1, 020-7233 6500.

FISHING

Farlow's

5 PALL MALL, SW1, 020-7839 2423
Open Mon.-Fri. 9am-6pm, Sat. 9am-4pm.
U: Piccadilly Circus.

Established in 1840 and sheltered under a banner at the corner of the Royal Opera Arcade, this neat row of three delightful shops is home to everything connected with angling. Farlow's, London's oldest fishing tackle shop, specialises in trout and salmon fishing but has departments for coarse, sea, big-game and saltwater enthusiasts. Among its stock of leading manufacturers' products, it carries the entire House of Hardy line of rods, reels and accessories. You'll also find multi-pocketed fishing bags, fishing glasses, books and lots of fishing paraphrenalia, plus tweed breeks, windstopper sweaters, furlined hats and boots. The firm offers an invaluable fishing rod repair service and sells game guns and shooting accessories.

House of Hardy

61 PALL MALL, SW1, 020-7839 5515
Open Mon.-Fri. 9am-6pm, Sat. 9am-5pm.
U: Green Park.

A distinguished name in angling circles and a rival to Farlow's (see above), Hardy's stocks all the best-quality fishing requisites in a neatly arrnaged modern shop. These include cane rods, special salmon flies, its own brand of safety vest, Barbour garments, unusual carved walking sticks, videos on angling, hand warmers and sporting prints. It has a computerised service for booking services like salmon fishing on the Tweed.

HUNTING & SHOOTING

Asprey & Garrard
165-169 NEW BOND ST, W1, 020-7493 6767
WWW.ASPREY-GARRARD.COM
Open Mon.-Fri. 10am-6pm, Sat. 10am-5pm.
U: Bond St.

In 1990, this luxury store started producing handmade English shotguns, bolt and double rifles, all bearing the distinguished Asprey hallmark. It also has a wide selection of quality secondhand guns from other famous gunmakers such as Holland & Holland, Purdey and Boss. Its handsome Gun Room has everything from cartridge holders to cufflinks with sporting motifs in addition to weatherproof clothing and well-tailored tweed and whipcord garments.

Boss & Co
13 DOVER ST, W1, 020-7493 0711
Open Mon.-Fri. 10am-5pm.
U: Green Park.

There is nothing grand about this Dickensian-looking shop but this is the specialist maker of Boss single trigger guns, including the famous Boss Over and Under in 410 inch, 12, 20 and 28 gauge. The firm, now under the expert eye of managing director Tim Robertson, the great-grandson of the founder, still hand makes 'Best Guns Only' to the original specifications which includes side-

I-Spy

For those seriously worried about security, those wanting toys and James Bond wannabes, check out the spy shops. These include **Queensway Spy Shop**, 56a Queensway, W2, 020-7221 9029; **Spymaster**, 3 Portman Sq, W1, 020-7486 3885, E-mail: spymaster@compuserve.com; and the **Counter Spy Shop**, 62 South Audley St, W1, 020-7408 0287, www.spyzone.co.uk. Everything from concealed TV cameras and microphones to bugging and de-bugging devices.

by-side Express Double rifles. All firearms are made-to-order, taking from eighteen months to three-and-a half years.

Holland & Holland
31-33 BRUTON ST, W1, 020-7499 4411
Open Mon.-Sat. 9.30am-6pm.
U: Bond St.

Established in 1835, this famous gun-maker holds the Royal Warrant of the Duke of Edinburgh for rifles and the Prince of Wales for shotguns, country clothing and accessories. In its Gun Room, customers have preliminary fittings for bespoke weapons or choose from antique, secondhand or imported makes. Their top range of 'Best London' guns includes 'royal models' with the highest standard of hand craftsmanship and technical excellence. The shop has an extensive range of practical country shoes and accessories for men and women as well as books and gifts. Its art gallery has sporting and wildlife pictures and sculptures and its Sporting Agency can tailor-make sporting tours in almost any country.

Also at 171-172 Sloane St, SW1, 020-7235 3475.

James Purdey & Sons
57 SOUTH AUDLEY ST, W1, 020-7499 1801
Open Mon.-Fri. 9.30am-5.30pm, Sat. 10am-5pm.
U: Hyde Park Corner.

Old Royal Warrants remain painted on the window frontage of this top people's gunmaker, obscuring the view inside except for the mounted big-game heads. Inside there is an established-for-decades feel, where guns and rifles, all handmade, are works of art and collector's items. They are displayed and sold in the corner shop, which has an adjoining, more modern shop on Mount Street for accessories and a line of first-class outdoor clothing and footwear from woollen shawls for women to tweed hats for men.

William Evans
67A ST. JAMES'S ST, SW1, 020-7493 0415
Open Mon.-Fri. 9.30am-5.30pm, Sat. 10am-4pm (shop only on Sat., not gun room).
U: Green Park.

Smart apparel for the country, including leather-lined Wellington boots and Barbour waxed coats, plus cartridge bags, belts and framed shooting caricatures. An order for a pair of guns, which can cost over £54,000, takes about two years to complete. Besides new Sidelock and Boxlock game guns and rifles, there is a wide range of secondhand guns, both William Evans' own brand and other well-known makes.

RIDING

Swaine Adeney

54 ST. JAMES'S ST, SW1, 020-7409 7277
Open Mon.-Sat. 10am-6pm.
U: Green Park.

A new address for this firm (whose illustrious history dates back to 1750 when Captian John Ross got the initial carriage whip business off the ground). It was sold to James Swaine and his son and son-in-law 48 years later and has become one of the brand leaders in the whips, canes and leather goods world. Its fashions for men have classic style and the store is well-stocked with outdoor clothing such as Klondike waxed jackets with leather trim. Swaine Adeney holds three Royal Warrants including umbrella makers to the Queen Mother. Women's clothes available from the factory shop at Nursery Rd, Saffron Waldon, Great Chesterford, Essex, 01799 530521.

SAILING

Arthur Beale

194 SHAFTESBURY AVE, WC2, 020-7836 9034
Open Mon.-Fri. 9am-6pm, Sat. 9.30am-1pm.
U: Tottenham Court Rd.

This shop's history dates back some 400 years to a rope chandler's business. It stocks marine hardware, fixtures and fittings and has some bright weatherproof clothing and boots. Because of its location in fashionable Covent Garden, its wares are often bought for adding a twist to shop window displays, fashion photographic shoots and artistic sculptures as well as providing necessary support for barrier ropes at restaurants and nightclubs.

Captain O M Watts

5-7 DOVER ST, W1, 020-7493 4633
Open Mon.-Fri. 9am-6pm, Sat. 9am-5pm.
U: Green Park.

Walk into this specialist sailing suppliers and you can almost smell the sea. They stock everything for the dinghy and keelboat sailor including charts and yachting clothing labels like Henri Lloyd and Musto. The knowledgable staff offers expert advice when needed.

SKIING & MOUNTAINEERING

Black's

176 KENSINGTON HIGH ST, W8, 020-7361 0060
Open Mon., Wed., Fri. 9.30am-6pm, Tues. 10am-6pm, Thurs. 9.30am-7pm, Sat. 9.30am-5.30pm, Sun. 11am-5pm.
U: High St Kensington.

In winter, colourful skiwear and a wide range of equipment are in abundance; in summer, camping and climbing gear takes its place. However, there is always a choice of country clothes and walking boots.

Also at 10 Holborn, EC1, 020-7404 5681; 53 Rathbone Pl, W1, 020-7636 6645.

Ellis Brigham Mountain Sports

30-32 SOUTHAMPTON ST, WC2, 020-7240 9577
Open Mon.-Wed. & Fri. 10am-7pm, Thurs. 10am-7.30pm, Sat. 9.30am-6.30pm, Sun. 11.30am-5.30pm.
U: Covent Garden.

You know things are serious when the even the door handles are ski-shaped! This specialist shop sells snowboards along with Raichle and Solomon ski boots, and also has a good choice of back-up products for winter and summer sports.

Snow & Rock

188 KENSINGTON HIGH ST, W8, 020-7937 0872
Open Mon.-Fri. 10am-7pm, Sat. 9am-6pm, Sun. 11am-5pm.
U: High St Kensington.

The name says it all succinctly since this large shop stocks skiwear and trekking gear in a good range of styles at reasonable prices. It has a climbing wall for customers to try out boots. In summer, there is a good selection of tents and camping equipment. The range of essentials is wide from thermal silk underwear to hand-and-finger exercise gadgets.

STATIONERY & PENS

Alastair Lockhart
97 WALTON ST, SW3, 020-7581 8289
Open Mon.-Fri. 10am-6pm, Sat. 10am-5pm.
U: South Kensington.

As you'd expect from any establishment on this delightful street, Alastair Lockhart specialises in some of the most beautiful writing papers almost too good on which to write. The tiny shops stocks Crane's cotton paper in a host of colours, and takes orders for engraving and printing.

Blade Rubber Stamps
2 NEAL'S YARD, WC2, 020-7379 7391
Open Mon.-Sat. 10.30am-6pm, Sun. 11.30am-5pm.
U: Covent Garden.

Design your own stationery or get into stamp design art at this little shop which stocks hundreds of rubber stamps and pads in a variety of designs. Children's kits are also available.

Bureau
10 GREAT NEWPORT ST, WC2, 020-7379 7898
Open Mon.-Fri. 10am-7.45pm, Sat. 10am-7pm.
U: Oxford Circus.

A rainbow of colours greets you as you walk into this modern stationery shop which stocks pens, papers, notebooks and accessories to brighten up the dullest office. No decorative process is left unexplored, with notepaper taking cover in fake leopard skin and dalmation hide, acid-bright prints and glitter.

Faccessory
43 BROADWICK ST, W1, 020-7734 5034
Open Mon.-Fri. 9am-6pm, Sat. 10am-5.30pm.
U: Oxford Circus.

All the big names in loose-leaf diary and organisers are neatly arranged in this small shop which also sells pens and pencils from prestige companies.

Filofax
69 NEAL ST, WC2, 020-7836 1977
Open Mon.-Fri. 9.30am-6pm, Sat. 10.30am-6.30pm.
U: Covent Garden.

The whole range of Filofax and Lefax products are on display as well as many top pens.
Also at 21 Conduit St, W1, 020-7499 0457.

Paperchase
213 TOTTENHAM COURT RD, W1
020-7580 8496, WRITE@PAPERCHASE.CO.UK.
Open Mon.-Wed. & Fri.-Sat. 9.30am-6.30pm, Thurs. 9.30am-7.30pm, Sun. 11am-5pm.
U: Tottenham Court Rd.

With its recent facelift, the main Paperchase store already a popular destination—has become even better. Not that it would take much to improve one of the most popular stationery stores in town. It's always packed with bright, exciting stationery-based products for the office and home. The store is filled with cards, diaries, wrapping paper, pens and pencils, photograph albums and frames, gift ideas and a wide selection of storage boxes. This branch has a good selection of art materials and, in season (September to January) a great range of Christmas decorations.
Branches throughout London.

Papyrus
48 FULHAM RD, SW3, 020-7584 8022
Open Mon.-Sat. 9.30am-6pm.
U: South Kensington.

This shop has two sides to its services. In true cottage-industry style, a team of craftsmen carry out their own designs, book-binding and marbling to produce photo albums and all manner of desk accessories, including leather book jackets. The second arm is a design and print business, specialising in letterheads, invitations and personalised stationery.

Penfriend
BUSH HOUSE, STRAND, WC2, 020-7836 9809
Open Mon.-Fri. 9.30am-5.30pm.
U: Aldwych.

You could describe this shop as a little museum devoted to the craft of writing utensils and curios like Georgian skirt-lifters, lorgnettes and early pencil sharpeners. The shop has a genial proprietor, Peter Woolf, who is invariably available when visitors come to browse in the shop located in an offbeat arcade that includes the BBC World Service Shop. Woolfe sells fully restored vintage pens such as Mentmore, Conway Stewart, Parker and Swan, which he often supplies for films and photographic shoots. The shop also includes a huge range of modern pens and the workshop repairs pens.

Also at 34 Burlington Arcade, W1, 020-7499 6337.

Smythson

44 NEW BOND ST, W1, 020-7629 8558
Open Mon.-Fri. 9.15am-5.30pm, Sat. 10am-5.30pm.
U: Bond St.

As stationers to the Queen, Smythson wears the paper products crown. The store offers some of the most beautiful diaries, notebooks, pocketbooks, organisers and quality papers to be found anywhere in London. There is hand-bordered, water-marked stationery (at £17 for 25 sheets and matching envelopes), wine connoisseurs' notebooks, handsome atlases and the smartest leather-bound photograph albums. Among the elegant pens for sale are novelties such as American edition diaries. Some of the more extravagant items include a deluxe leather picnic case for two with china plates and cups at approximately £995. If you want to create a good impression, Smythson offers a hand- engraving and printing service.

Also at 35 Sloane St, SW1, 020-7730 5520.

The Stationery Department

181 NEW KING'S RD, SW6, 020-7384 1871
Open Mon.-Sat. 10am-6pm.
U: Sloane Sq.

For an excellent choice of high-quality writing paper and envelopes in a colour palette that spans the spectrum and invitation printing.

TOBACCONISTS

Alfred Dunhill

27 JERMYN ST, SW1, 020-7499 9566
Open Mon.-Fri. 9.30am-6pm, Sat. 10am-6pm.
U: Green Park.

On the first floor of this men's fashion store is a large, specially set aside area, which is a walkin humidor room with an extensive choice of cigars from Cuba and the Dominican islands. Sitting pride-of-place is a magnificient humidor specially commissioned from David Linley. Regular customers store their cigars in 306 lockers, all original cedar cabinets dating to the store's origins as a tobacconist shop founded by Alfred Dunhill in 1907. Aromatic loose tobacco is sold, including Alfred's own and Blenders' Own. Customers also can enjoy a complementary whisky.

Benson & Hedges

13 OLD BOND ST, W1, 020-7493 1825
Open Mon.-Fri. 9am-5.30pm, Sat. 10am-5pm.
U: Green Park.

The cool, clean-cut, efficient look of the shop belies its historic tradition of selling tobacco products, pipes and cigarettes since 1870. There is also a range of small leather gifts.

Davidoff

35 ST. JAMES'S ST, SW1, 020-7930 3079
Open Mon.-Fri. 9am-5.45pm, Sat. 9.30am-5.45pm.
U: Green Park.

A showy, spacious store with one of the best selections of Havana cigars in town, Davidoff has its own humidor and sells all of the smoking requisites like Cognac, lighters and top-quality accessories.

Desmond Sauter

106 MOUNT ST, W1, 020-7499 4866
Open Mon.-Fri. 9am-6pm, Sat. 9am-4pm.
U: Bond St.

The antique smoking memorabilia is one of the attractions in this old square-shaped shop with its glass walk-in humidor standing pride-of-place among the wooden fixtures. They specialise in Cuban cigars and sell hallmarked silver boxes and decorative pipes.

James J Fox & Robert Lewis

19 ST. JAMES'S ST, SW1, 020-7493 9009
Open Mon.-Sat. 9am-5.30pm.
U: Green Park.

The sign says James J Fox, but this little shop is home to two well-known cigar merchants. It is devoted to cigars made with care and attention to detail from all over the world. James Fox also runs a tobacco department at Harrods and Selfridges.

Shervington

337-338 HIGH HOLBORN, WC1, 020-7405 2929
Open Mon.-Fri. 9am-6pm.
U: Holborn.
Established in 1864, this shop is set in a half-timbered building which dates back to 1845. Not surprisingly, there is a specialist atmosphere to enjoy while perusing the full range of pipes, tobaccos and smoking products.

G Smith & Sons

74 CHARING CROSS RD, WC2, 020-7836 7422
Open Mon.-Fri. 9am-6pm, Sat. 9.30am-5.30pm.
U: Leicester Sq.
A specialist in hand-blended snuff, which is available in some 50 aromatic varieties, this small shop stocks its own brand of tobacco as well as antique snuffboxes and little spoons for taking snuff.

WOMEN'S WEAR

AFFORDABLE CHIC

Episode

172 REGENT ST, W1, 020-7439 3561
Open Mon.-Tues. 10am-6.30pm, Wed. & Fri.-Sat. 10am-7pm, Thurs. 10am-8pm, Sun. noon-6pm.
U: Piccadilly Circus.
It's easy to pull together a coordinated look from the smart collections in easy-on-the-eye colours like cream, red, navy and black. Since it concentrates on strong and elegant knits, simple dresses and neatly tailored trouser suits in fabrics such as wool, silk and cashmere, Episode is good for the classic working wardrobe.
Also at 53 Brompton Rd, SW3, 020-7589 5274; Bishopsgate Arcade, Liverpool St, Station, EC2, 020-7628 8691.

French Connection

249 REGENT ST, W1, 020-7493 3124
Open Mon.-Wed. & Fri.-Sat.10am-7pm, Thurs. 10am-8pm, Sun. noon-6pm.
U: Piccadilly Circus.
This firm, winner of fashion awards such as More Dash Than Cash and High Street Retailer of the Year, offers well-made directional clothes at very attractive prices.
Branches throughout London.

Hobbs

84 KING'S RD, SW3, 020-7581 2914
Open Mon.-Tues. & Thurs.-Sat. 10am-6.30pm, Wed. 10am-8pm, Sun. noon-6pm.
U: Sloane Sq.
Linen-mix suits, cashmere-blend coats and a good range of lean knitwear make this shop a popular choice with career women with more dash than cash. The own-label shoes, boots and bags complete the look.
Branches throughout London.

Jane & Dada

20 ST. CHRISTOPHER'S PL., W1, 020-7486 0977
Open Mon.-Wed. & Fri.-Sat. 9.30am-6pm, Thurs. 9.30am-7pm.
U: Bond St.
For more than 20 years, this shop has been offering women's wear at affordable prices. Ranges include Fenn, Wright & Manson, In Wear, Marina Rinaldi and Jackpot.
Also at 59 Hampstead High St, NW3, 020-7431 0708.

Jigsaw

126-127 NEW BOND ST, W1, 020-7491 4484
Open Mon.-Wed. & Fri. 10.30am-7pm, Thurs. 10.30am-7.30pm, Sat. 10am-6.30pm.
U: Green Park.
Created by the minimalist interior designer, John Pawson, this flagship Jigsaw store hosts regular exhibitions amidst the well-designed contemporary clothing collections. Don't let the modernist surroundings put you off because the prices are surprisingly realistic (particularly for a store on this street). Four branches are dedicated exclusively to menswear; some stores feature clothes for both men and women.
Branches throughout London.

Karen Millen

46 SOUTH MOLTON ST, W1, 020-7495 5297
Open Mon.-Wed. & Fri.-Sat. 10am-6.30pm, Thurs. 10am-.30pm.
U: Bond St.
Since opening her first store at the age of 21, this designer has become known for her combination of fine tailoring and cutting skills. There is a good line of understated separates in neutral colours, with jackets from £150, skirts from £59.95 and dresses from £89.95. Millen also uses strong colours in her more offbeat styles, which appeal to younger audience.
Branches throughout London.

Mango

8-12 NEAL ST, WC2, 020-7240 9312
WWW.MANGO.ES
Open Mon.-Sat. 10am-7pm, Sun. noon-6pm.
U: Covent Garden.

London's first Mango store opened in late November, 1999, just in time for the Christmas and millennium rush. Since then the crowds have not abated, having sampled the high style and low- price ethos which has made this Spanish design firm one of the top two chains in its homeland. The clothes are strongly influenced by the latest catwalk trends, the only drawback is that they are only cut to fit small-boned women.

Monsoon

264 OXFORD ST, W1, 020-7499 2578
MONSOON@MONSOON.CO.UK
Open Mon.-Sat. 9.30am-6.30pm, Sun. noon-6pm.
U: Oxford Circus.

Sought out for Nehru-collared jackets, structured coats and long dresses, often edged with embroidery or beads, this smart chain offers some of the best eveningwear on the high street.
Branches throughout London.

Oasis

13 JAMES ST, WC2, 020-7240 7445
Open Mon.-Wed. & Fri.-Sat. 10am-7pm,
Thurs. 10am-8pm, Sun. noon-6pm.
U: Covent Garden.

Even label snobs can pick up some good little finds in this dependable high street chain which always has the pick of the hottest trends before they have made it off the catwalk. The accessories are particularly impressive.
Branches throughout London.

Phase Eight

28A KENSINGTON CHURCH ST, W8
020-7937 5438
Open Mon.-Wed. & Fri.-Sat. 9.30am-6pm,
Thurs. 9.30am-7pm.
U: High St Kensington.

A well coordinated shop, selling clothes for casual/smart occasions. Lines include Fenn, Wright & Manson, Sasperilla and the Patsy Seddon Collection. It's a good place for everything from a dress or linen separates for a summery event, to tailored clothes and stylish wedding outfits. They also offer a wide range of casual silks, knitwear and accessories.
Branches throughout London.

Pied-à-Terre

31 OLD BOND ST, W1, 020-7629 0686
Open Mon.-Wed. & Fri.-Sat. 10am-6.30pm,
Thurs. 10am-7pm.
U: Bond St.

To many, the name Pied a Terre means shoes, but there are many branches, including the one on South Molton Street, which incorporate 'Basics for Women' clothes, that are designed to complement the shoes. The garments are designed in-house using the latest catwalk trends as inspiration. Separates and dresses (from approximately £80).
Branches throughout London.

Whistles

12 ST. CHRISTOPHER'S PL, W1, 020-7487 4484
Open Mon.-Wed. & Fri.-Sat. 10am-6pm,
Thurs. 10am-7pm.
U: Bond St.

With up to 50 new lines a season, the shop's philosophy is to spot up-and-coming designers before they hit the big time. Owner Lucille Lewin's success has been built on her foresight to bridge the gap between High Street and high design—something she does exceedingly well.
Branches throughout London.

Zara

118 REGENT ST, W1, 020-7534 9500
Open Mon.-Wed. & Fri.-Sat. 10am-7pm,
Thurs. 10am-8pm, Sun. noon-6pm.
U: Piccadilly Circus.

Anyone who prides themself on finding stylish bargains will already have Zara's address firmly fixed in their mind. The great thing about this Spanish firm, laid out over three floors, is that the flattering grey wool trousers you bought for £35 are unlikely to still be on the shop floor in three weeks time, so you can wear your cut-price chic proudly without bumping into carbon copies of your outfit everywhere you look. A smart place to pick up well-made basics, plus directional fashion finds, accessories and shoes.

BESPOKE WEAR

More tailors in Savile Row are making suits for women and bespoke shirts can be ordered on Jermyn Street.

Emma Willis

66 JERMYN ST, SW1, 020-7930 9980
Open Mon.-Sat. 10am-6pm.
U: Green Park.

A female shirt-maker in Jermyn Street has caused quite a stir. Emma Willis designs and makes wonderful shirts for both gentlemen and ladies in top cottons and silks, as well as stocking wool and cashmere tops to her own design. Bespoke shirts take four to six weeks to make (from £125 for cotton to £220 for silk).

DESIGNER LABELS

A la Mode

36 HANS CRESCENT, SW1, 020-7584 2133
E-MAIL: ALAMODE@DIRCON.CO.UK
Open Mon.-Sat. 10am-6pm.
U: Knightsbridge.

Owners Peter and Josephine Turner, are blessed with the eyes and instincts for what is going to be 'the next big thing.' They were the first to stock Julien MacDonald's cob-webbed knits and the acid-bright creations from Matthew Williamson, Britain's latest fashion genius. Amanda Wakeley, Chloe, Jemima Khan and breathtaking evening wear from John Galliano are also carried. Free alterations and overseas delivery.

Alberta Ferretti

205 SLOANE ST, SW1, 020-7235 2349
Open Mon.-Tues. & Thurs.-Sat. 10am-6pm,
Wed. 10am-7pm.
U: Knightsbridge.

London showcase for the first lady of Italian fashion. And what a showcase it is. Unless you're very confident, you'll probably be too intimidated to make it past the front door. It's worth plucking up the courage, though. With her state-of-the-art manufacturing company, Aeffe, producing collections for the likes of Jean Paul Gaultier, Moschino and Narciso Rodriguez, high-quality workmanship is assured. Ferretti designs beautiful clothes for real women. Her trademarks include lace, chiffon and appliqué detail. The first-floor restaurant is popular with ladies who make an art of lunching without food ever touching their lips.

Amanda Wakeley

80 FULHAM RD, SW3, 020-7590 9105
Open Mon.-Tues. & Thurs.-Sat. 10am-6pm,
Wed. 10am-7pm.
U: South Kensington.

This young, beautiful and very successful British designer has won the coveted *Glamour Designer of the Year* award twice in a row. She sells ready-to-wear clothes for women but also continues her couture business, by appointment only, at the same premises. Understated and elegant, the dresses, suits, knitwear and separates make a striking impact, especially when matched with shoes and accessories. Nevertheless, eveningwear is Wakeley's forte.

Anna Molinari Blumarine

11A OLD BOND ST, W1, 020-7493 4872
Open Mon.-Sat. 10am-6pm.
U: Green Park.

Not for shy, retiring types, Anna Molinari designs for women who like showing off their assets. Colours are bright, fabrics mostly clinging and the effect is pure drama.

Betty Jackson

311 BROMPTON RD, SW3, 020-7589 7884
Open Mon.-Fri. 10.30am-6.30pm, Sat. 10.30-6pm, Sun. noon-5pm.
U: South Kensington.

Always managing to keep a finger firmly on the pulse of fashion, Betty Jackson, MBE, has built up a loyal customer base who love her simple designs. Her knitwear is always worth seeking out, as are her flattering separates and coats.

Catherine Walker

65 SYDNEY ST, SW3, 020-7352 4626
Open Mon.-Sat. 10am-6pm.
U: Sloane Sq/South Kensington.

French-born designer Catherine Walker produces classic clothes for the rich and famous. Her clients include the Duchess of Kent, Shakira Caine and the ballerina Darcey Bussell. The late Diana, Princess of Wales, was also a fan. Walker also has a bridal shop at 46 Fulham Rd, SW3, 020-7581 8811.

Caroline Charles

56-57 BEAUCHAMP PL, SW3, 020-7589 5850
Open Mon.-Tues. & Thurs.-Sat. 10am-6pm,
Wed. 10am-6.30pm.
U: Knightsbridge.

Well-established with the town-and-country set, Caroline Charles is one of Britain's most successful designers. Her clothes are aimed at business women who want to put together a look that is classic, practical and stylish. It's reserved and, therefore, not for those who want to make bold fashion statements.

Chanel

26 OLD BOND ST, W1, 020-7493 5040
Open Mon.-Sat. 10am-6pm.
U: Bond St.

The Chanel label needs no introduction. Those interlocking 'Cs' embossed on everything from the cap of the best-selling No. 5 perfume and shiny black powder compacts to quilted leather bags and the lining of chic tweed suits are coveted the world over. Amidst the black lacquer fittings, beige carpeting and sumptuous suede banquettes, you'll find the latest mix of traditional and sometimes quirky offerings from Chanel maestro Karl Lagerfeld. Cosmetics, watches and accessories are also part of the empire.

Also at 31 Sloane St, SW1, 020-7235 6631.

Christian Dior

31 SLOANE ST, SW1, 020-7235 1357
Open Mon.-Fri. 10am-6pm, Sat. 10.30am-6pm.
U: Knightsbridge.

Since John Galliano took the helm at Dior, the sensible suits and wonderfully crafted but 'safe' dresses associated with 'the House' are a distant memory. Galliano cuts to create drama—even simple sweaters are given a sexy twist. The accessories are just as coveted as the clothing, particularly the jewelry, shoes and city bags.

The Cross

141 PORTLAND RD, W11, 020-7727 6760
Open Mon.-Sat. 10.30am-6pm.
U: Holland Park.

Virtually every fashionista in town makes it their business to own at least one ultra-hip garment from this shop. Sam Robinson and Sarah Kean have the knack of tapping into trends just before they happen, stocking ranges from cult names like Tracy Boyd,

Bond Street

Bond Street, along with Sloane Street, is London's premier shopping street, containing many flagship stores of top designer names, plus Sotheby's auction house, many top art dealers, and top jewelers towards the Piccadilly end.

Old Bond Street, dating from 1686, starts at Piccadilly and runs to Clifford Street where the name changes to New Bond Street, which was laid out in the early eighteenth century.

Anna Molinari Blumarine, 11a Old Bond St, 020-7493 4872; **Calvin Klein,** 53-55 New Bond St, 020-7491 9696; **Cerruti 1881,** 106 New Bond St, 020-7495 5880; **Chanel,** 26 Old Bond St, 020-7493 5040; **Donna Karan,** 19 New Bond St, 020-7495 3100; **DKNY,** 27 Old Bond St, 020-7499 8089; **Emporio Armani,** 112a New Bond St, 020-7491 8080; **Gianni Versace,** 34-36 Old Bond St, 020-7499 1862; **Gucci,** 32-33 Old Bond St, 020-7629 2716; **Guess?,** 95 New Bond St, 020-7629 2716; **Hermès,** 155 New Bond St, 020-7499 8856; **Joan & David,** 150 New Bond St, 020-7499 7506; **Karl Lagerfeld,** 173 New Bond St, 020-7493 6277; **Loewe,** 130 New Bond St, 020-7493 3914; **Louis Vuitton,** 17-18 New Bond St, 020-7499 4050; **Max Mara,** 153 New Bond St, 020-7491 4748; **Miu Miu,** 123 New Bond St, 020-7409 0900; **Nicole Farhi,** 158 New Bond St, 020-7499 8368; **Polo Ralph Lauren,** 1 New Bond St, 020-7491 4967; **Yves Saint Laurent,** 137 New Bond St, 020-7493 1800.

Gharani Strok, Antoni & Allison and Mark Whitaker. As well as clothes for women and children, The Cross also offers its interpretation of what the best-dressed homes should be wearing.

Egg

36 KINNERTON ST, SW1, 020-7235 9315
Open Tues.-Sat. 10am-6pm.
U: Knightsbridge.

This glorious shop with its regular exhibits of ceramics and paintings has a wonderful range of zen-like clothing, including reasonably priced Khadi cotton basic designs made in India (from £60 for trousers to £130 for jackets). More intricate designs can cost up to £2,000 and feature the djellabah style popularised by Jemima Khan.

Elspeth Gibson

7 PONT ST, SW3, 020-7235 0601
WWW.LATERAL.NET/ELSPETH.GIBSON
Open Mon.-Sat. 10am-6pm
U: Knightsbridge.

Like a breath of cool, clean air, Elspeth Gibson's vision of femininity is decidedly refreshing. Romantic, pretty and totally alluring, the clothing has inspired older women to yearn to be young again. The fabrics are

Sloane Street

Sloane Street, running from Knightsbridge to Sloane Square, shares the crown with Bond Street as London's premier shopping street for designer names. Many of the big designers have shops in both locations.
Alberta Ferretti, 205 Sloane St, 020-7235 2349; **Chanel,** 167-170 Sloane St, 020-7235 6631; **Christian Dior,** 31 Sloane St, 020-7235 1357; **Christian Lacroix,** 8a Sloane St, 020-7235 2400; **Dolce & Gabbana,** 175 Sloane St, 020-7235 0335; **Emmanuel Ungaro,** 36 Sloane St, 020-7259 6111; **Giorgio Armani,** 37 Sloane St, 020-7235 6232; **Gucci,** 17 Sloane St, 020-7235 6707; **Hermès,** 179 Sloane St, 020-7823 1014; **Kenzo,** 15 Sloane St, 020-7235 4021; **Louis Vuitton,** 198 Sloane St, 020-7235 3356; **Max Mara,** 32 Sloane St, 020-7235 7941; **Prada,** 43-45 Sloane St, 020-7235 0008; **Valentino,** 174 Sloane St, 020-7235 5855; **Yves Saint Laurent,** 33 Sloane St, 020-7235 6706.
The Sloane Square end has a more neighbourly feel, thanks to some small shops and the church. There are some excellent interior designer shops like **The General Trading Company,** 144 Sloane St, 020-7730 0411; **Lady Daphne,** 145 Sloane St, 020-7730 1131; **India Jane,** 140 Sloane St, 020-7730 1070; and **Jane Churchill,** 151 Sloane St, 020-7730 9847.

luxurious, attention to detail meticulous and the overall effect is distinctively Elspeth.

Ghost

13 HINDE ST, W1, 020-7486 0239
WWW.GHOST.LTD.UK
Open Mon.-Wed. & Fri.-Sat. 10am-6pm,
Thurs. 10am-7pm.
U: Bond St.

Hugely popular for their modern Victoriana dresses, peasant skirts and little puffed sleeved blouses, Tarna Sarne's collections now include a number of directional pieces including pedal pushers with velcro fastenings and simple dresses with dramatic slashes of colour.
Also at 36 Ledbury Rd, W11, 020-7229 1057.

Koh Samui

65 MONMOUTH ST, WC2, 020-7240 4280
Open Mon.-Sat. 10am-7pm.
U: Covent Garden.

Laura Dern, Amber Valetta and Kylie Minogue are just a few of the many celebrity clients who seek out the hottest and newest British fashion labels stocked at Koh Samui. Collections include designs by Elspeth Gibson above), Gharni Strok, Clements Ribeiro, Lainey Keogh and Tristan Webber.
Also at 28 Lowndes St, SW1, 020-7828 9292.

Liza Bruce

9 PONT ST, SW1, 020-7235 8423
Open Mon.-Sat. 11am-6pm.
U: Knightsbridge.

When it comes to bravado, designer Liza Bruce has it in spades. Not just in the cut of her second-skin skirts, tops, swimwear and PVC coats, but in her determination to rebuild her business after an unsuccessful and costly legal case against retail giants Marks & Spencer a few years ago. Her latest venture will appeal to body-conscious, clubby types with credit limits to match their attitudes.

Margaret Howell

29 BEAUCHAMP PL, SW3, 020-7584 2462
Open Mon.-Sat. 10am-6pm.
U: Knightsbridge.

Mannish, beautifully tailored clothes are Margaret Howell's hallmark. The shop is pristine yet homey and, similarly, the clothes—often featuring linens and crisp cottons—are smart whilst still possessing a relaxed air. Look for the beautiful homeware collection with pajamas, bathrobes, wash bags and toiletries.

Nitya

118 NEW BOND ST, W1, 020-7495 6396
Open Mon.-Wed. & Fri. 10am-6pm, Thurs. & Sat. 10am-7pm.
U: Bond St.

The easy elegance of Nitya's simple, fluid and layered designs lends itself to women who do not let fashion trends dictate their look. It's also a godsend for those with fuller figures.

Paul Costelloe

156 BROMPTON RD, SW3, 020-7589 9480
Open Mon.-Tues. & Thurs.-Sat. 10am-6pm, Wed. 10am-7pm.
U: Knightsbridge.

One of the best known of the new breed of Irish designers, Costelloe loves producing clothes in natural fabrics, particularly Irish linen. His collection includes everything from jeans to eveningwear. The Dressage collection includes separates for day wear and stylish dress suits.

Valentino

174 SLOANE ST, SW1, 020-7235 4526
Open Mon.-Fri. 10am-6pm, Sat. 10.30am-6pm.
U: Sloane Sq.

A glamorous shop filled with glamorous clothes. The spiral staircase leads up to the women's collections, which include sumptuous eveningwear such as long column dresses and sophisticated daywear. Downstairs is devoted to men with suits, shirts and sweaters for the elegant man-around-town.

Wardrobe

42 CONDUIT ST, W1, 020-7494 1131
Open Mon.-Wed. & Fri.-Sat. 10am-7pm, Thurs. 10am-8pm.
U: Bond St.

Since 1973, Susie Faux has been a fairy godmother to busy, high-powered women who come to her shop for advice on a complete look—everything from hosiery to make-up. Waving her magic wand, Faux and her team prescribe clothes from her stock of mainly Italian, French and German designers including Erruno, Mani, Strenesse, Jil Sander and Antonio Fusco. The staff is attentive, advising on cut, colour and styles to suit individuals,

and records are kept for regular customers so new purchases will be in keeping with their coordinated wardrobes. This also helps dutiful partners buy the appropriate gift without making a costly mistake. There is also a beauty treatment salon in the store.

Yasmin Cho

LEVEL ONE, 22 POLAND ST, W1, 020-7287 6922
Open Mon.-Sat. 10am-7pm.
U: Oxford Circus.

For the ultimate fashion fix, Yasmin Cho (gorgeous wife of gorgeous actor Rufus Sewell) offers her pick of the best new designs in clothes, shoes, jewelry and cosmetics. The cool, loft setting makes the store even more desirable and cult-like, and the occasional vintage finds add further excitement to the mix. Labels include Madame à Paris, Jurgi Persoons, Alicia Lawhorn and Handmaid from LA.

EVENING & SPECIAL OCCASION

Anouska Hempel

2 POND PL, SW3, 020-7589 4191
Open Mon.-Fri. 9am-6pm by appointment.
U: South Kensington.

When she isn't tending to the design details at her hotels, The Hempel and Blakes, Lady Weinberg—or Anouska Hempel as she is more commonly known—is designing gorgeous frocks for her equally blessed clientele. Exquisite details and precision cutting put her couture garments in the £2,000+ bracket. Clothes to die for.

Basia Zarzycka

52 SLOANE SQ, SW3, 020-7351 7276
100622.1656@COMPUSERVE.COM
Open Mon.-Sat. 11am-7.30pm. Also by appointment.
U: Sloane Sq.

Stunning eveningwear and bridal gowns and all the appropriate accessories, beautiful hats and beaded shoes, handbags and jewelry are the mainstay of this pretty shop. Zarzycka's custom-made, special-occasion, intricately decorated clothes in velvets, laces and silks are one-of-a-kinds. Handbags are also special—often a combination of antique frames and lavish fabrics. There are approximately 500 tiara-style headdresses for brides (there is a choice of about one hundred, including antique models dating from 1790, for hire). Zarzycka also has designed waistcoats and posh slippers for celebrities. This is a friendly shop and customers are welcome even if they just want to buy a silk flower or merely browse. Overseas shipping available.

Bellville Sassoon

18 CULFORD GDNS, SW3, 020-7581 3500
Open Mon.-Fri. 9.30am-5.30pm.
U: Sloane Sq.

This large, highly stylised showroom has racks of breathtaking evening gowns, cocktail dresses and special-occasion wear, all in jewel colours and designed and made in Britain under the Belville Sassoon/Lorcan Mullany label.

Ben de Lisi

40 ELIZABETH ST, SW1, 020-7730 2994
Open Mon.-Fri. 10am-6pm, Sat. noon-5pm.
Also by appointment.
U: Victoria.

For evening dresses with attitude, you won't find better than Ben de Lisi. Simple, elegant and oozing with sexuality, this cool American even cuts everyday items to make women feel like sirens. For a cheaper alternative, seek out the BDL collection at Debenhams.

Droopy & Browns

99 ST. MARTIN'S LANE, WC2, 020-7379 4514
Open Mon.-Wed. 10.30am-6.30pm, Thurs. 10.30am-7.30pm, Fri. 10.30am-7pm, Sat. 9.30am-5.30pm.
U: Leicester Sq.

Founded in York in 1972, Angela Holmes's company is strong on wedding dresses (best to make an appointment), eveningwear and smart day suits and dresses. All fabrics are coloured, dyed and woven to Angela's specifications to complement her designs. The dress racks are always brimming with romantic clothes and matching hats. It is an informal, fun place to browse for ready-to-wear special occasion-clothes.
Also at 16-17 St. Christopher's Pl, W1, 020-7486 6458.

Tatters

74 FULHAM RD, SW3, 020-7584 1532
Open Mon.-Fri. 10am-6pm, Sat. 10am-5pm.
U: South Kensington.

For everyone from 13-year-old girls to 70 year-old grandmother, this shop is the place to

go for off-the-rack evening wear including frothy little dresses, regal ballgowns and a mélange of velvet and satin garments.

Tomasz Starzewski

20 SLOANE ST, SW1, 020-7235 4526
Open Mon.-Sat. 10am-6pm.
U: Knightsbridge.

London-born but of Polish heritage, Tomasz Starzewski combines fun and elegance in his daywear, short, sexy cocktail dresses and dramatic evening gowns. His designs are big hits with the high society set and past clients include the late Diana, Princess of Wales. His shop encompasses three floors of ready-to-wear, including the Gold Label line, which is exclusive to the shop, couture garments and a bridal collection.

HATS

The British Hatter

36B KENSINGTON CHURCH ST, W8
020-7361 0000
Open Tues.-Sat. 10.30am-6pm.
U: High St. Kensington.

A good source for the mother-of-the-bride and the kind of frothy confections favoured by traditional Ascot-goers. In addition to the swathes of silk, owner Pamela Bromley stocks a selection of big, bold and brash hats guaranteed to stop the traffic.

Fred Bare

118 COLUMBIA RD, E2, 020-7247 9004
Open Sun. 10am-2pm only.
U: Old St.

The eclectic hat collections in the shop are ideal for the myriad visitors to Columbia Road market. Men can choose from trilbys, straw pork pie hats and puffa hats while younger women will veer towards the colourful, floral, woolly or fluffy hats. For granny, there are even nylon sou'westers. A wonderful shop for tantalising tifters. A warehouse sale is held twice a year in the studio at 134-136 Curtain Rd, EC2, 020-7739 4612.

Herald & Heart

131 ST. PHILIP ST, SW8, 020-7627 2414
Open Mon.-Fri. 10am-6pm, Sat. 9.30am-5pm.
Rail: Queen's Rd (Battersea).

With screen credits such as *Four Weddings and a Funeral* and *101 Dalmations* under their belts, Herald & Heart are reaping the rewards they deserve. The team produces two dramatic collections annually. Felt and straw are usually the basis, with individual touches such as embroidery, and beaded feathers adding the necessary flair.

Herbert Johnson

54 ST. JAMES'S ST, SW1, 020-7408 1174
Open Mon.-Sat. 10am-6pm.
U: Green Park.

Founded in 1899, this family business boasts a millinery department for women and an in-house design team. Dozens of styles are on display, including some famous headgear from films such as Batman, My Fair Lady and Raiders of the Lost Ark.

James Lock & Co

6 ST. JAMES'S ST, SW1, 020-7930 5849
E-MAIL: LOCKHATTERS@LOCKHATTERS.CO.UK.
Open Mon.-Fri. 9am-5.30pm, Sat. 10am-5.30pm.
U: Green Park.

This shop sees more women entering its hallowed portals since it opened a millinery department (with four milliners, two on the premises), to offer pretty hats for occasions like Ascot and garden parties.

Philip Treacy

69 ELIZABETH ST, SW1, 020-7259 9605
Open Mon.-Fri. 10am-6pm.
U: Sloane Sq.

Philip Treacy's hats are works of art. That's why designers like Karl Lagerfeld seek him out to create the dream toppings for their creations. His own catwalk shows are one of the hottest tickets in London Fashion Week and each time you think he has surely run out of ways to twist, bend and shape a hat, the unassuming, softly spoken Irish designer comes back with an even stronger collection. His salon in Belgravia is the epitome of elegance. The striking designs are displayed on milky-coloured mannequins, the perfect foil to show off the often gravity-defying shapes and imaginative use of colour. He also designs a small handbag collection, which includes satin paisley shapes with tassles and simple suede clutch bags.

Stephen Jones

36 GREAT QUEEN ST, WC2, 020-7242 0770
Open Tues.-Wed. & Fri. 11am-6pm., Thurs. 11am-5pm.
U: Covent Garden.

Another of the great British modern milliners, Stephen Jones has created hats for designers such as John Galliano, Claude Montana, Antonio Berardi and Vivienne Westwood. His shapes are sharp and often witty featuring nifty little flowerpots, mini bowlers and flirty feathery concoctions. In his lilac boutique, customers can buy ready-to-wear hats (£100), and custom-made (£100 to £1,000). The latter may involve discussions on fabric and colour and two or three fittings. Miss Jones, a diffusion line is available from major stores including Harvey Nichols.

LARGE SIZES

Also try Selfridges for their large size collections and Hennes for the Big & Beautiful line.

Base

55 MONMOUTH ST, WC2, 020-7240 8914
Open Mon.-Sat. 10am-6pm.
U: Covent Garden.

Rushka Murganovic designs a range of separates in sizes 16-28. There are also clothes from Scandinavia, Germany, America and Israel.

Long Tall Sally

21 CHILTERN ST, W1, 020-7487 3370
Open Mon.-Wed. & Fri.-Sat. 9.30am-5.30pm, Thurs. 10am-7pm.
U: Baker St.

One of twenty outlets nationwide, this popular shop commissions manufacturers who supply the High Street fashion stores to re-proportion the current styles to fit women from five-foot-nine inches and taller. From teen-age to any age, the range of clothes includes casual wear, business suits and special-occasion dresses.

We're always interested to hear about your discoveries and to receive your comments on ours. Please let us know what you liked or disliked; **e-mail us** at gayots@aol.com.

1647

69 GLOUCESTER AVE, NW1, 020-7483 0733
Open Tues.-Sat. 10am-6pm.
U: Chalk Farm.

Set up by comedienne Dawn French and ex-architect Helen Teague, this company produces a range of casual and stylish clothes for big women. The name has a double meaning; it refers to the fact that that 47 percent of British women are size 16 or over, it also states the store's sizing which goes from a modest 16 to a more generous 47. They produce two main collections a year in fabrics like linen, jersey and silk. Prices are reasonable, starting at around £40. Styles are deliberately loose and made in 1647's workshops. The higher-priced designer label, French & Teague, is available at Liberty.

LINGERIE

Agent Provocateur

6 BROADWICK ST, W1, 020-7439 0229
Open Mon.-Sat. 11am-7pm.
U: Tottenham Court Rd.

Joe Corre, Vivienne Westwood's son, runs this salon-like, specialist lingerie shop with his partner' Serena. They believe in the appeal of seductive, beautiful underwear and spread their gospel to the masses. Decked out like a boudoir with ornate chairs, ostrich-feather fans and swans-down powder puffs setting the mood, the lingerie includes hour-glass corsets, delicate slips, negligees and matching bras and knickers, and extends to belly chains and decorative nipple clamps. Not for the fainthearted.
Also at 16 Pont St, SW1, 020-7235 0229.

Bradleys

57 KNIGHTSBRIDGE, SW1, 020-7235 2902
Open Mon.-Fri. 9.30am-6pm, Sat. 10am-6pm.
U: Knightsbridge.

The lingerie ranges from hot and spicy French briefs, baby doll nightdresses and saucy bras to cocoa and slipper snug cotton nightgowns, sensible pajamas and slippers. Top designers from all over the world are represented here, including Christian Dior, Nina Ricci, Aubade and Cotton Club.

Femme Fatale

64 HIGH ST, WIMBLEDON VILLAGE, SW19
020-8947 8588
Open Mon.-Sat. 10am-6pm, Sun. 11am-5pm.
U: Wimbledon.

When you have a penchant for the finest lingerie and you can't find it where you live, it makes sense to open your own shop. That's what model Tamzin Greenhill did three years ago, and judging by the number of locals who are big on her smalls, it seems she hit the proverbial nail right on the head. There's nothing overtly sexual here, the draped ceilings and chaise lounges create a romantic feel and provide the perfect backdrop for delicious lingerie, swimwear, nightwear and hosiery from Cotton Club, Gottex, Hanro, Huit and Marie Jo.

Fogal

36 NEW BOND ST, W1, 020-7493 0900
Open Mon.-Sat. 9.30am-6pm.
U: Bond St.

Luxury hosiery up to £165 is the main product in this shop. It is the quality of the fibres and the finishing techniques, which make some of the products so pricey. One style has 1000 crystals sewn up the side.
Also at 3a Sloane St, SW1, 020-7235 3115.

Janet Reger

10 BEAUCHAMP PL, SW3, 020-7584 9360
Open Mon.-Sat. 10am-6pm.
U: South Kensington.

Janet Reger was responsible for putting the 'oomph' back into lingerie when she draped Joan Collins in glamorous satin in the film The Bitch. In her elegant whitewashed walled shop, skimpy knickers hang importantly and incongruously, each pair on its own little hanger. Mail-order available.

Rigby & Peller

2 HANS RD, SW3, 020-7589 9293
Open Mon.-Tues. & Thurs.-Sat. 9.30am-6pm, Wed. 9.30am-7pm.
U: Knightsbridge.

As corset-makers to the Queen and Queen Mother, this firm displays two Royal Warrants and offers a discreet, unrivalled made-to-measure service for underwear, which has been operating for more then fifty-years. As well as their own label, designed by June Kenton, the shop sells ranges from Lejaby, Primadonna and Marie Jo, and offers a wide choice of swimwear. The demand for its expert fittings has led to the opening of an additional shop at 22a Conduit St, W1, 020-7491 2200.

MATERNITY

Formes

33 BROOK ST, W1, 020-7493 2783
Open Mon.-Wed. & Fri.-Sat. 10am-6pm, Thurs. 10am-6.30pm.
U: Bond St.
Pregnant women have no need to feel frumpy in the clever designs dreamed up by Daniel Boudon. Styles include adjustable cropped jackets with nipped-in waists, day dresses, trousers and flamboyant eveningwear, all in flattering shapes and fabrics.
Also at 313 Brompton Rd, SW3, 020-7584 3337; 28 Henrietta St, WC2, 020-7240 4777.

Maman Deux

79 WALTON ST, SW3, 020-7589 8414
Open Mon.-Sat. 9.30am-6pm.
U: South Kensington.
A curious little shop which sells unusual gifts such as pillows with slogans like 'Never complain, never explain', also has clothes for pregnant women who don't want to look dull. The stock includes jeans, smart suits, dresses and bathing suits.

Night Owls & Great Expectations

78 FULHAM RD, SW3, 020-7584 2451
Open Mon.-Tues. & Thurs.-Sat. 10am-6pm, Wed. 10am-7pm.
U: South Kensington.
Everything from stretchy jeans to formal evening wear can be found in this shop, which carries labels that include Pertesi, Pringle and Neuf Lune.

Telephone numbers in England have eleven digits, beginning with a zero. The initial zero must be omitted if you are calling England from abroad. Within the country, dial the entire eleven digits.

PETITE SIZES

Next

160 REGENT ST, W1, 020-7434 2515
Open Mon.-Wed. 10.30am-7pm, Thurs. 10.30am-8pm, Fri.-Sat. 10am-7pm, Sun. noon-6pm.
U: Oxford Circus.
In the 1980s, this chain of unisex fashion shops delivered coordinated high street fashions at affordable prices. Next has since introduced a welcome line of well-proportioned petite sizes for women, five-foot-three and under, in sizes 6 to 14. Clothes tend to be polyester-mix and can be found at the chain's larger branches.

Principles

419 OXFORD ST, W1, 020-7493 5371
Open Mon.-Wed. & Fri.-Sat. 10am-7pm, Thurs. 10am-8pm, Sun. noon-6pm.
U: Bond St.
Another popular chain of reasonably priced fashionable clothes for men and women. The collection includes a line for women under five-foot-three inches tall in sizes 6 to 16. The fit is very good and has received favourable reviews in the fashion press.
Branches throughout London.

SCARVES

Georgina von Etzdorf

50 BURLINGTON ARCADE, W1, 020-7409 7789
Open Mon.-Sat. 10am-6pm.
U: Green Park.
For an instant, opulent lift to any outfit, Georgina von Etzdorf's beautiful scarves, shawls and stoles are unbeatable. The colour blends are superb; the fabrics (which include plain and elaborate devore velvet, organza devoré linens, lace and silks) are truly magical

YOUNG STREET FASHION

Amazon

7A KENSINGTON CHURCH ST, W8
NO TELEPHONE NUMBER
Open Mon.-Sat. 10am-5pm.
U: High St Kensington.
Amazon started as one small shop and has proceeded to take over its neighbours, now

stretching over five premises in fashionable Kensington Church Street at 1, 3, 7a, 7b, 19 to 22. The company buys up seconds and discontinued lines from a variety of sources and offers labels such as Ralph Lauren, Nicole Farhi, Katharine Hamnett Jeans and Jasper Conran at up to 60 percent off. Expect even greater reductions on mid-range items from French Connection and In Wear. The stock changes rapidly, so if you see something you like, buy it.

American Classics

398 & 400 KING'S RD, SW10
020-7352 2853/7352 3248
Open Mon.-Sat. 11am-7pm.
U: Sloane Sq.

These shops sell new and secondhand clothing, styled on the classic American 1950s look. Think James Dean in Rebel Without a Cause or Marlon Brando in On the Waterfront and you've got the idea. Popular items include monogrammed, satin baseball jackets, flying jackets, checked cotton shirts and original, red label Levi 501s.

Also at 20 Endell St, WC2, 020-7831 1210.

American Retro

35 OLD COMPTON ST, W1, 020-7734 3477
Open Mon.-Sat. 10.15am-7pm.
U: Leicester Sq.

Highly stylish American clothes and accessories made in the fashions of the past. The stock is varied and fast-moving and includes men's fashions from W&LT, Ben Sherman and John Smedley, plus lingerie, underwear, sunglasses, cigarette lighters and books. Their own-label motorcycle bags are extremely popular.

Bond

10 NEWBURGH ST, W1, 020-7437 0079
WWW.BONDINTERNATIONAL.COM
Open Mon.-Sat. 10.30am-6pm.
U: Oxford Circus.

This cheerful sportswear shop is aimed at skateboarders. Labels carried include Stussy, Zoo York and Addict plus all of the latest trainers. Bond also stocks a range of sports magazines and hip-hop tapes. Catalogue available.

Boxfresh

UNIT 6, THOMAS NEAL'S, EARLHAM ST, WC2
020-7240 4742, WWW.BOXFRESH.CO.UK.
Open Mon.-Sat. 11am-6.30pm.
U: Covent Garden.

Stocker of British and American urban sportswear labels, such as Carhartt, Spiewack, Blue Marlin and Yak Pak Boys. Also stocks its own exclusive collection which is designed and produced in Los Angeles four times a year.

Browns Focus

38-39 SOUTH MOLTON ST, W1
020-7629 0666, E-MAIL: BROWNSSMS@AOL.COM
Open Mon.-Wed. & Fri.-Sat. 10am-6pm,
Thurs. 10am-7pm.
U: Bond St.

Younger, funkier sister to the exclusive Browns store down the street. Prices are still, well, pricey but the collections are geared more towards the street-smart who want to keep one step ahead of the fashion-pack. Many designs, such as the oversized Phat pants are imported, and devotees think nothing of parting with their cash to get their hands on the latest styles. Along with Hysteric Glamour T-shirts, Orla Kiely bags, there are diffusion lines from designers such as Helmut Lang, Dolce & Gabbana, Lilly Pulitzer and Vivienne Westwood. Another treat is the modern-art installations and window displays created by young artists. A great place to immerse yourself in emerging trends before they hit the high street.

Diesel

43 EARLHAM ST, WC2, 020-7497 5543
WWW.UKSTOREDIESEL.COM.
Open Mon.-Wed. & Fri.-Sat. 10.30am-7pm,
Thurs. 10.30am-8pm, Sun. noon-6pm.
U: Covent Garden.

A perfect hang-out for the young and impressionable. The interior is fun and funky with an in-your-face glass stairway, fish-headed mannequins and almost cheesy 1970s attention-grabbing décor. The clothes veer towards 1950s trailer park trash, with about 140 styles of jeans including skinny and 'Wanker' pants. There are also retro shirts and childrenswear.

Dr Martens Dept Store

1-4 KING ST, WC2, 020-7497 1460
Open Mon.-Wed. & Fri.-Sat. 10am-7pm,
Thurs. 10am-8pm, Sun. noon-6pm.
U: Covent Garden.

The minimalist factory look of this shop is an apt background for the sturdy range of clothes for men, women and children, all of which complement the Dr. Marten range of chunky footwear. There is also a hairdresser and a café.

Duffer of St. George

29 SHORTS GDNS, WC2, 020-7379 4660
Open Mon.-Fri. 10.30am-7pm, Sat. 10.30am-
6.30pm, Sun. 1pm-5pm.
U: Covent Garden.

Women can now buy into the successful street-smart Duffer style with neat suedette jackets and hipsters to match their boyfriend's ultra-smooth Duffer button-down shirts, flat-front hipsters, Evisu jeans and Gloverall duffle coats. The company's own label products include everything from knitwear to denim, and many items prove to be so popular, they end up being on a waiting list.

High Jinks Clothing

UNIT 25, THOMAS NEAL'S, EARLHAM ST, WC2
020-7240 5580
Open Mon.-Sat. 10am-7pm, Sun. noon-6pm.
U: Covent Garden.

Specialising in club, street and skate wear for young, hip men and women. Labels include Technics, Arc, One World, Komodo and Custard Shop

Mambo

UNITS 2 & 3 THOMAS NEAL'S, EARLHAM ST, WC2
020-7379 6066, WWW.MAMBO.COM.AU
Open Mon.-Sat. 10am-7pm, Sun. noon-6pm.
U: Covent Garden.

We may not have the climate or facilities for it, but surf-wear is proving popular in London. Mambo, originating in surfing country, Australia, provides some of the best up-to-the minute styles for active surfers as well as those who only make waves.

Also at 26-27 Carnaby Street, W1, 020-7434 2404.

Mash

73 OXFORD ST, W1, 020-7434 9609
Open Mon.-Wed. & Fri.-Sat. 10am-7pm,
Thurs. 10am-8pm, Sun. 11am-6pm.
U: Oxford Circus.

Favourite Saturday afternoon haunt for clubbers searching for the perfect outfit for the weekend. The dance music is loud and appeals to the crowd looking out for the latest hip-hop sportswear labels like Spiewack, North Star, Carhartt and Evisu to wear on the dance floor later in the evening.

O'Neill

9-15 NEAL ST, WC2, 020-7836 7686
E-MAIL: ONEILLUK@MSN.COM.
Open Mon.-Sat. 10am-7pm, Sun. noon-6pm.
U: Covent Garden.

When Californian surfer Jack O'Neill invented the first wetsuit in 1952, little did he know he was starting a style, which would adapt and become as fashionable on the street as in the water. The first London outlet is spread over three floors and each has its own characteristics. The ground floor and basement is modern and urban, featuring simplistic steel interiors. The mezzanine has traditional wooden fixtures with authentic memorabilia. The store holds all of O'Neill's four clothing lines, Boardcore, O'52, Main line and Boardbabes, as well as a year-round supply of swimwear and wetsuits.

Red or Dead

41-43 NEAL ST, WC2, 020-7379 7571
Open Mon.-Sat. 10am-6.30pm.
U: Covent Garden.

Red or Dead's designs are an injection of humour to the often too serious world of fashion. The designs are bold, often brash, sometimes tasteful but never boring. Owner Wayne Hemingway and his wife Geraldine have a tongue-in-cheek approach to their collections; however, their efforts have earned them the British Street Designer of the Year award on a fairly regular basis.

Looking for an address?
Refer to the index.

Shop

4 BREWER ST, W1, 020-7437 1259
Open Mon.-Sat. 10am-6pm.
U: Piccadilly Circus.

A babe's delight—all girly pink, upbeat and doll-like with a range of well-sourced clothes to put the fun back into shopping. Expect lots of T-shirts and dresses with attitude from labels like Anna Sui, Hysteric Glamour, Stussy Sister and Fiorucci. At the higher end of the price range, you'll find gorgeous Tocca dresses and a few pieces from Sofia Ford Coppola's Milk Fed line.

Top Shop

214 OXFORD ST, W1, 020-7636 7700
Open Mon.-Wed. & Fri.-Sat. 9am-8pm, Thurs. 9am-8.30pm, Sun. noon-6pm.
U: Oxford Circus.

With its recent revamp, Top Shop (or ToSho as it has been dubbed by fashion luvvies) is a heady mix of good-value clothing, accessories, shoes and cosmetics much adored by clubbers and fashion editors alike. You'll find all the latest catwalk trends here, set against a pumping in-house radio station delivering music, messages and store information. There are regular public appearances by the latest pop/dance acts and competitions. The clothes are designed to last a couple of seasons only, so don't go looking for expert finishing.

YOUNG STREET SHOE FASHION

Buffalo

47-49 NEAL ST, WC2, 020-7379 1051
WWW.BUFFALO-BOOTS.COM
Open Mon.-Sat. 10.30am-7pm, Sun. 2pm-6pm.
U: Covent Garden.

From the outset of their career, Buffalo shoes have had the Spice Girls stamp of approval, which probably explains the mass appeal of these over-sized, built-up trainers and shoes. No matter that Baby Spice made the front pages of the tabloids when she took a tumble from her colossal wedges, Buffalo have become the fashionable way to walk tall.

Dr Martens Dept Store

1-4 KING ST, WC2, 020-7497 1460
Open Mon.-Wed. & Fri.-Sat. 10am-7pm, Thurs. 10am-8pm, Sun. noon-6pm.
U: Covent Garden.

As the name suggests, shoppers find more than shoes here (clothes, jeans, accessories, gifts, a café and a hairdresser for men and women). But, there certainly are lots of styles of this famous brand name which are both practical and fashionable. Some of the chunky boots and shoes come in zany patterns and colours; others come with laminated sequins. There are also myriad dressing options for the kids, including floral patterns to soften the look of these tough leather boots. The fourth floor has an exhibition on the company's history.

Office

57 NEAL ST, WC2, 020-7379 1896
Open Mon.-Sat. 10am-7pm, Sun. noon -6pm.
U: Covent Garden.

Their own line features good-value, high-fashion shoes that look straight to the catwalk for inspiration—from a distance you'd never know the difference. Elsewhere in the shop, there are collections from footwear designers like Robert Clergerie, Maud Frizon and Nicholas Deakins, which appeal to a much broader audience.

Branches throughout London.

Red or Dead Shoes

33 NEAL ST, WC2, 020-7379 7571
Open Mon.-Fri. 10.30am-7pm, Sat. 10am-6.30pm, Sun. noon-5pm.
U: Covent Garden.

Red or Dead makes shoes, which are a far cry from slim and elegant Italian classics. These shoes for men and women evoke memories of the extremes of the 1970s platform days and some are clearly inspired by Frankenstein's monster. More fun than most shoe shops!

Shellys

266-270 REGENT ST, W1, 020-7287 0939
Open Mon.-Wed. & Fri.-Sat. 9.30am-6.30pm, Thurs. 9.30am-7.30pm.
U: Oxford Circus.

The three-storey shop is always busy with men, women and children on the look out for fashionable shoes without exorbitant price tags. There's Shellys' own line, which features everything from chunky platforms to toe-crunching stilettos, plus trainers styles and boots. They also sell a good line of Dr. Marten products and shoes from Kickers, No Box and LA Gear.

ARTS & LEISURE

CONTENTS

ART GALLERIES 352
   COMMERCIAL ART GALLERIES 352
   EIGHTEENTH-, NINETEENTH-
   & TWENTIETH-CENTURY ART 358
   OLD MASTER SPECIALISTS 361
ART MUSEUMS 362
ATTRACTIONS 367
CHURCHES 376
HOBBIES & SPORTS 377
   ART COURSES 377
   BICYCLING... 379
   BRASS RUBBING 379
   COOKING 379
   DANCE.. 380
   FITNESS & SPORTS CLUBS........................... 380
   GARDENING 383
   GOLF 383
   HOT AIR BALLOONING.............................. 383
   ICE SKATING 383
   NEEDLEWORK COURSES 384
   RIDING... 384
   SHOOTING 385
   SWIMMING....................................... 385
   TENNIS & SQUASH 385
   WATER SPORTS 386
   WINE COURSES 386
HOUSES TO VISIT.................................... 386
INNS OF COURT 392
MUSEUMS 393
PARKS & GARDENS 401
THEATRE & MUSIC 405
   THEATRE 405
   MUSIC 410

ART GALLERIES

COMMERCIAL ART GALLERIES

London boasts some 400 commercial galleries. Rich cultural pickings for the determined art lover indeed—with everything from the calm and classical to the purposefully maverick. Today, art dealing is no longer simply in and around celebrated Cork Street, but goes right across the capital. There's certainly a buzz about the London art scene, which sees regular hoards of visitors and international dealers speculating on the regularly changing shows.

Check on all opening times before making a visit as some galleries are only open when an exhibition is on show. *Galleries* a free, updated and handy pocket-sized guide is available from most major galleries.

Air Gallery
32 DOVER ST, W1, 020-7409 1255
Open Mon.-Fri. 11am-7pm.
U: Green Park.
This is one of London's largest commercial spaces operating as a hire gallery, and it's justifiably popular with both artists and dealers. Its 2,000 square feet show-space is divided into two distinct galleries, staging almost weekly exhibitions guaranteeing something for everyone. Paintings, drawings and sculpture from a selection of UK and foreign contemporary creators are always on view.

Adonis Art
1A COLEHERNE RD, SW10, 020-7460 3888
Open Mon.-Fri. 10.30am-5pm, Sat. 10.30am-6.30pm.
U: Earl's Court.
One of London's very few established spaces specialising in the male nude. From stock, there are some fine, classically conceived drawings and paintings, but the regularly changing shows of new and often young masters of the genre are the ones to watch. Drawings and photographs—some alarmingly frank, are the sensual fare for all who appreciate a lean muscle or two.

Alan Cristea
31 CORK ST, W1, 020-7439 1866
Open Mon.-Fri. 10am-5.30pm, Sat. 10am-1pm.
U: Piccadilly Circus.
When Alan Cristea took over the premises of Waddington Graphics in 1995, he continued the role of the gallery as the major print venue on Cork Street. Here are prime examples of contemporary and master prints from artists like Picasso and Matisse, alongside changing exhibitions of recent printed editions by artists such as Jim Dine, Antoni Tapies, Mick Moon and new names.

Albemarle Gallery
49 ALBEMARLE ST, W1, 020-7499 1616
Open Mon.-Fri. 10am-6pm, Sat. 10am-4pm.
U: Green Park.
A strikingly spartan space, cool with very clean lines, is the setting for some decidedly classically inspired paintings and sculptures in the British and European tradition. Portraits, landscapes and some very clever trompe l'œil creations make regular appearances in group or one-person shows which are invariably accompanied by full-size, handsome catalogues.

Annely Juda Fine Art
23 DERING ST, W1, 020-7629 7578
Open Mon.-Fri. 10am-6pm, Sat. 10am-1pm.
U: Oxford Circus.
Founded in 1960 by Annely Juda, this gallery is known worldwide for its exhibitions of Constructivism, Dada, Russian Avant-Garde, Bauhaus and de Stijl. Some of the best international contemporary artists like Ackling, Edwina Leapman, Nash, Anthony Caro and Christo now join such classics as Kandinsky, Mondrian, Rodchenko, Schwitters and Chillida.

Anthony d'Offay Gallery
20 DERING ST, W1, 020-7499 4100
Open Mon.-Fri. 10am-5.30pm, Sat.10am-1pm.
U: Bond St.
Without peer, the most stylish, and certainly among the most influential, commercial galleries in Europe, d'Offay's spaces in Dering Street are a mecca for all serious contemporary buyers and art students with their eye on the future. D'Offay regularly shows international art stars such as Joseph Beuys, Gilbert & George, Carl Andre, Andy Warhol and James

Turrell (whose 'Heaven's Waiting Room' installation can be seen at the faith zone of The Dome). The gallery often intersperses its big-name artists with the work of younger ones who just might be the superstars of tomorrow. A regular magnet for celebrity art shoppers.

Art Space Gallery

84 ST. PETER'S ST, N1, 020-7359 7002
Open Tues.-Sat. 11am-7pm.
U: Angel.

Michael Richardson's gallery in Islington is a delight, showing new names like Andrea McLean and Nigel Massey and top contemporary artists like Anthony Whishaw and George Rowlett, with prices from £500 to £40,000.

Association of Photographers

9-10 DOMINGO ST, EC1, 020-7739 3631
Open Mon.-Fri. 9.30am-6pm, Sat. noon-4pm.
U: Barbican/Old St.

The gallery of the Association of Photographers shows work from professional photographers in a series of themed exhibitions, which might cover 'The Dog' or geographical areas such as East or South Asia.

BCA Boukamel Gallery

9 CORK ST, W1, 020-7734 6444
Open Mon.-Fri. 10am-6pm, Sat. 10am-2pm.
U: Piccadilly Circus.

Originally a German gallery, this space continues to show some German talents such as the inspiring Rainer Fetting, but there is a distinct international feel in the choice of other artists. Who, although all very distinct, somehow are recognizably part of the BCA Boukamel stable. Bold painting and often uncomfortable, uncompromising subjects typify the kind of work regularly on show from such young greats as Cuttie, Sherman and Serrano.

Beardsmore Gallery

22 PRINCE OF WALES RD, NW5, 020-7485 0923
Open Tues.-Fri. 10am-6pm, Sat. noon-6pm.
Also by appointment.
U: Kentish Town.

Small, excellent gallery of architect Brian Beardsmore and his wife in part of their architectural offices. Seek this gallery out; the Beardsmores' selection is highly regarded.

They have about 20 regular artists in stock with changing one-man and group exhibitions of paintings, works on paper, ceramics and sculpture from artists like Royal Academician Lisa Wright, Stathis Logoudakis, Michael Druks, sculptor Oliver Barratt and Henry Moore Fellow.

Beaux Arts

22 CORK ST, W1, 020-7437 5799
Open Mon.-Fri. 10am-6pm, Sat. 10am-2pm.
U: Piccadilly Circus.

With a huge reputation and regular sell-out shows, this is one of the busiest and most successful commercial galleries. The directors are passionate about new painting with a definite edge, whether that happens to be the seeming aggressiveness of Ray Richardson's subjects or the tantalizing discomfiture and sinister quality of Jonathan Leapman—both much awaited by regulars. A host of new, young talent is occasionally premiered.

Bernard Jacobson Gallery

14A CLIFFORD ST, W1, 020-7495 8575
Open Mon.-Fri. 10am-6pm, Sat. 10am-1pm.
U: Oxford Circus.

The results of Bernard Jacobson's decades of dealing in this area are on the walls, from Bomberg, Abrahams, Rauschenberg, Nicholson and Weight, to the new additions of Glynn Williams and Maggi Hambling. Comprehensive gallery publications sometimes include conversations with the artists providing personal insight into their works.

Blains

23 BRUTON ST, W1, 020-7495 5050
Open Mon.-Fri. 10am-6pm, Sat. 10am-5pm.
U: Bond St.

With its 5,000 square feet of showing space, Blains is the largest privately owned commercial gallery in the West End. Now in its third year, the directors have certainly established it as a hip venue, throwing some of the best parties where a lot of rubber-necking goes on and adopting a very hands-on approach to the showing and selling of art. The gallery's client base is young, wealthy and distinctly non-establishment. This it seems is the perfect crowd for works by Degas, Giacometti, Moore, Matisse and Warhol. Sexy but serious.

Chinese Contemporary

21 DERING ST, W1, 020-7734 9808
Open Mon.-Fri. 10am-6pm, Sat. 11am-4pm.
U: Bond St.

What a find. As Europe's only space so far showcasing the works of contemporary mainland Chinese artists, it certainly rules the roost. Expect the unexpected and even the decidedly weird, as Eastern and Western influences get mixed together and served up to savour—from monumental paintings in oil to painstakingly worked pencil drawings.

Cross Street Gallery

40 CROSS ST, N1, 020-7226 8600
Open Tues.-Sat. 10.30am-6pm.
U: Angel.

Bijou space that packs a punch. The gallery specialises in showing works from about the 1960s on with a nod to some contemporary creators. Showcase exhibitions for British stars such as John Hoyland and Peter Blake have been held and there is also an emphasis on the St. Ives' artists and the Modern Movement. Big, bold and competitively priced prints are always in stock.

The Eagle Gallery

159 FARRINGDON RD, EC1, 020-7833 2674
Open Wed.-Fri. 11am-6pm, Sat. 11am-4pm.
U: Farringdon.

Situated above the famous Eagle public house, haunt of media types and arty souls, the Eagle Gallery is a feisty little powerhouse of a space showing the best in new, young and recently graduated artists. There is an emphasis on esoteric, atmospheric and often abstract work. Proximity to the pub affords the chance of considering a purchase over a pint or a meal (see *Quick Bites*).

England & Co

216 WESTBOURNE GROVE, W11, 020-7221 0417
Open Mon.-Sat. 11am-6pm.
U: Notting Hill Gate.

After twelve years of trading in a very small space, this new venue is more like an ocean-going liner. Beautifully and sympathetically designed, the gallery boasts a huge floor-to-ceiling plate-glass frontage and a supreme lighting system to show off to its best advantage, unusual and elegant early modern and contemporary works. Look out for the annual *Art in Boxes* show, and several others dedicated to characters such as Adrian Bannon, Elspeth Juda and Chris Kenny.

Flowers East

199-205 & 282 RICHMOND RD, E8
020-8985 3333
Open Tues.-Sun. 10am-6pm.
Rail: Hackney Central.

One of the East End's finest. Angela Flowers has built up her reputation over the years and can be relied upon for some truly riveting shows. Regulars include Peter Howson, Patrick Hughes, Trevor Sutton and Kevin Sinott—all well established, but Flowers and son Matthew have not lost their appetite for discovery and revel in showing new works often on a grand scale. There is also a separate graphics and prints area, which affords more browsing potential. A one-time warehouse, it is being put to far better use than simply storage.

Frith Street Gallery

60 FRITH ST, W1, 020-7494 1550
Open Wed.-Fri. 10am-6pm, Sat. 11am-4pm,
Tues. by appointment.
U: Leicester Sq.

Jane Hamlyn has united two houses to create a haven of calm in the middle of bustling Soho. The spaces are interconnected on several levels and the spare style of the architecture is reflected in the careful selection of contemporary art from the most innovative artists of the international scene.

London's Crafts Markets

There are plenty of open-air craft markets in London—try the stalls in the middle of **Covent Garden** for interesting handmade items by young designers, the daily market at the church of **St. Martin-in-the-Fields** and on Fridays and Saturdays the collection of stalls at **St. James's Church**, Piccadilly. On Sunday the **Brixton Market** offers bric-a-brac; and **Greenwich** is also a very good hunting ground at weekends.

Gallery K

101-103 HEATH ST, NW3, 020-7794 4949
Open Tues.-Fri. 10am-6pm, Sat. 11am-6pm,
Sun. 2.30pm-6.30pm.
U: Hampstead.

One of Hampstead's many quality galleries and a very real specialist at that. Contemporary Greek paintings and sculpture are invariably on view, along with the occasional showcase of Alexander the Great-inspired jewelry, gargantuan glass and stone worry beads, ceramics and writing table-sized sculpture by Edward Bell. Some contemporary British and European work does get a viewing, too—and every year *The Kiss Show* is staged—an exhibition based on the fine art of osculation.

Gimpel Fils

30 DAVIES ST, W1, 020-7493 2488
Open Mon.-Fri. 10am-5.30pm, Sat. 10am-1pm.
U: Bond St.

In business for over 50 years, the Gimpel family has built its reputation on showing established artists. But they are certainly not content to play it safe, exhibiting challenging and frankly difficult art which often has a socio-political edge. The handsome sweep of the gallery enables some enormous canvases and vast sculptures to be shown.

Hamiltons

13 CARLOS PL, W1, 020-7499 9493
Open Tues.-Sat. 10am-6pm.
U: Bond St/Green Park.

Certainly one of the most chic photographic venues in the capital, showing the work of celebrity snappers and superstars along with that of newcomers. Vintage works are also often on display. The gallery, more like a grand vestibule on two levels, is no stranger to the click of heels belonging to the seriously glamorous. When there's a party, you invariably read about it the next day.

Hanina Gallery

180 WESTBOURNE GROVE, W11, 020-7243 8877
Open Mon.-Sat. 10am-6pm.
U: Notting Hill Gate.

An elegant and handsome space is the setting for the gallery's changing stock of Post-Impressionist and early Modern paintings and sculpture, and there are many focus exhibitions held throughout the year. A private viewing room is available for buyers who want to muse far from the maddening crowd. Others,

less coy, can take in the magnificent design of the space and its use of natural and artificial light.

Helly Nahmad

2 CORK ST, W1, 020-7494 3200
Open Mon.-Fri. 10am-6pm, Sat. 10am-1pm.
U: Green Park.

No visit to London's art world is complete without a visit to this space, one of the newest and most important. Helly Nahmad is not yet 30, but has already racked up museum-quality shows by such masters as Picasso and Miro. The group shows are always brilliant and whatever and whoever is on view, there is more than a strong chance that you will be suitably impressed.

Jason & Rhodes Gallery

4 NEW BURLINGTON PL, W1, 020-7434 1768
Open Mon.-Fri. 10am-6pm, Sat. 10.30am-1pm.
U: Bond St/Green Park.

This is an understated gallery with a very English feel. It is committed to searching out new art but within a traditional arena. It has a wide scope with an adventurous feel and show photographs, videos and paintings from artists like Robert Davies and Paul Storey.

Jay Jopling/White Cube

44 DUKE ST, 2ND FLOOR ST. JAMES'S, SW1
020-7930 5373
Open Fri.-Sat. 10am-6pm. Also by appointment.
U: Green Park.

Ironically named as the gallery is practically no bigger than the expanse of a double sheet, White Cube has spawned one controversy after another. Shock and irony are tenets here and no more shocking and ironic than when in the hands of Damien Hirst, Tracey Ermin, Gary Hume and Mona Hatoum, who have all shown here and gone on to enjoy the buzz of fame. Decide for yourself how deeply their tongues are in their cheeks. Jay Jopling has also opened a new, large space in fashionable Hoxton at 48 Hoxton S, N1.

Jill George Gallery

38 LEXINGTON ST, W1, 020-7439 7343
Open Mon.-Fri. 10am-6pm, Thurs. 10am-8pm,
Sat. 11am-5pm.
U: Oxford Circus.

Slap bang in the middle of bustling Soho is this corner site showing large-scale and unusual portraits, narrative paintings and abstracts.

Limited edition and monoprints are for sale in the gallery downstairs, whereas the ground-floor space showcases new, contemporary, one-person shows. Established more than 12 years, George's stable of about twenty artists includes such talent as Rod Judkins, Alison Lambert and David Hosie.

Lisson Gallery

52/54 BELL ST & 67 LISSON ST, NW1
020-7724 2739
Open Mon.-Fri. 10am-6pm, Sat. 10am- 5pm.
U: Baker St/Marylebone.

Nicholas Logsdail has been based in this London backwater for more than 30 years, but geography in his case is not a problem. Everyone travels to see what he shows. Both spaces around the corner from one another are stunning, and the perfect partners to match the work on view, ranging from Dan Graham and Tony Craig, to Anish Kapoor and Juan Munoz. One of the more unusual art spaces in the capital.

Marlborough Fine Art

6 ALBEMARLE ST, W1, 020-7629 5161
Open Mon.-Fri. 10am-5.30pm, Sat. 10am-12.30pm.
U: Green Park.

One of London's most significant arty heavyweights dealing with the estates of, amongst others, Francis Bacon, Barbara Hepworth, Kurt Schwitters and Graham Sutherland. Mature and young contemporary stars such as Paula Rego, RB Kitaj and Steven Campbell show regularly in one-person presentations. The emphasis is squarely on the efficacy of painting—in all its guises—with a nod to the scholarly or a flirtation with the experimental.

Mayor Gallery

22 CORK ST, W1, 020-7734 3558
Open Mon.-Fri. 10am-5.30pm, Sat. 10am-1pm.
U: Green Park.

Commanding a huge respect amongst dealers and collectors, the Mayor has been a focus of attention for more than 50 years, originally as the famed Unit One. Amongst the big name stars are some fun but serious finds, particularly from the U.S. British Surrealism is of special interest. Anthropologist Desmond Morris is also a surrealist painter and shows here occasionally, as does Conroy Maddox, the world's oldest surviving (and practicing) surrealist.

Mercury Gallery

26 CORK ST, W1, 020-7734 7800
Open Mon.-Fri. 10am-5.30pm, Sat. 10am-12.30pm.
U: Green Park.

Another important stalwart in the gallery stakes showing superb painting and occasional sculpture. Director Gillian Raffles has a passion for early twentieth-century art and, in particular, the work of the fated Henri Gaudier-Brzeska, killed during the last days of World War I. Several excellent shows have been staged on various aspects of his sinuous and beautiful work. Objets d'art, maquettes and the like are on permanent display.

O'Shea Gallery

120A MOUNT ST, W1, 020-7629 1122
Open Mon.-Fri. 9.30am-6pm, Sat. 9.30am-1pm.
U: Marble Arch.

A sumptuous and very English setting for superb prints, engravings, hand-coloured etchings and maps from the eighteenth century to the present. Specialties include interior design studies and architectural drawings and the lively and amusing cartoons of Annie Tempest, who regularly contributes to, amongst others, *Country Life*. Related stationery, books and ceramics bearing Tempest's vignette cartoons are on sale. Look out also for the intricate and compelling work of Peter Coke, who makes stately objects constructed from thousands of tropical shells.

Paton Gallery

LONDON FIELDS, 282 RICHMOND RD, E8
020-8986 3409
Open Tues.-Sat. 11am-6pm, Sun. noon-6pm.
Rail: Hackney Central.

Since his earliest days in the art world, Graham Paton has championed the work of new, emerging and, indeed, totally unheard-of artists. He is famous for combing through the graduation shows of the London art colleges and presenting a showcase of talent. His choice is bold, brave and often surprising, but always compelling. His large warehouse-style space is perfect for the usually large-scale paintings on display.

The Photographer's Gallery

5 & 8 GREAT NEWPORT ST, WC2, 020-7831 1772
Open Mon.-Sat. 11am-6pm.
U: Leicester Sq.

This was the first independent gallery in Britain devoted to photography, and since its foundation in 1971 by Sue Davies OBE, it has maintained its reputation as *the* venue for contemporary photographic work. It has always shown innovative work alongside classic images, playing a major role in establishing such key names as Irving Penn, André Kertesz and Lartigue. Housed in two buildings, it holds exhibitions in several gallery spaces, the largest of which is in No. 8 Newport Street, along with the excellent bookshop. The print sales room and library are in No. 5 over another extensive showing area.

Portal Gallery

43 DOVER ST, W1, 020-7493 2667
Open Mon.-Fri. 10am-5.30pm, Sat. 10am-4pm. U: Green Park.

A specialist, indeed, the Portal has, for a number of years shown a peculiarly British phenomenon—the naïve artist. Scorned by many more academic purists, but adored by countless enthusiasts, naïve art is often frank, funny and a riot of colour, evoking very real moods and atmospheres. Think 'calendar or greeting card' by Beryl Cook (perhaps the most famous exponent of the style) and you have an inkling. But, of course, it doesn't just end with guffawing girls looking into the posing pouch of a male stripper...

Purdy Hicks

65 HOPTON ST, SE1, 020-7401 9229
Open Mon.-Fri. 10am-5.30pm, Wed. 10am-7pm, Sat. 10am-3pm. U: Tower Hill.

Thames-side gallery close to the new Tate, specialises in all kinds of contemporary painting from the esoteric to the classically considered. The light, airy space shows regularly such talent as Estelle Thompson (buzzing chunks of pure colour), Hughie O'Donoghue (bold, large-scale works), and Arturo Di Stefano (brooding, atmospheric and intriguing paintings). The stable of artists is well established, all different but each relentlessly pursuing the power of paint.

Rebecca Hossack Gallery

35 WINDMILL ST, W1, 020-7436 4899
Open Mon.-Sat. 10am-6pm. U: Goodge St.

This important gallery has two areas of specialisation: a selection of contemporary British art; plus art from a non-European tradition from names like Alaisdair Wallace, Jan

Williams and Abigail McLellan. Several specialised shows each year feature work by Australian Aboriginal artists and contemporary African artists.

Redfern Gallery

20 CORK ST, W1, 020-7734 0578
Open Mon.-Fri. 10am-5.30pm, Sat. 10am-1pm. U: Piccadilly Circus.

From its beginning in 1936, Redfern's gave one-man exhibitions to young painters, printmakers and sculptors, and the inclusion of young artists in mixed shows and in published print editions has never changed. Famous for its stock of works by well-known artists, including paintings by Gauguin, Van Gogh, Matisse, Monet, Hockney, Bacon and Tapies, and for artists established in the 1950s-1960s, it remains true to the tradition of Proctor, Tindle and Neiland.

Special Photographers Company

21 KENSINGTON PARK RD, W11, 020-7221 3489
Open Mon.-Thurs. 10am-6pm, Fri. 10am-5.30pm, Sat. 11am-5pm. U: Ladbroke Grove.

This is a fine art photography gallery and agency which introduces unknown and internationally recognised photographers, such as Herman Leonard, Edward Sheriff Curtis, Joyce Tennison, Holly Warburton and Laura Wilson in both group and one-person shows. There is always plenty to see on the two floors of this small gallery and it is all very well presented.

Thompson's Gallery

18 DOVER ST, W1, 020-7629 6878
Open Mon.-Fri. 10am-6pm, weekends by appointment. U: Green Park.

The rate of show turnover here is quite phenomenal. Stop by every two weeks or so and you'll see something entirely new on the walls—and occasionally on plinths in the form usually of balletic studies and polite nudes. Paintings tend to be big and bold and feature flower imagery, still-life works and seascapes by a selection of gallery artists. Set on two levels in a charming and traditional space, Thomspon's is certainly one to watch for endless variety.

Timothy Taylor Gallery

1 BRUTON PL, W1, 020-7409 3344
Open Mon.-Fri. 10am-6pm, Sat. 11am-2pm.
U: Bond St.

An exciting gallery which has rapidly established itself as one of the most important venues in London, in a small but dramatic space just off Bruton Street. Timothy Taylor represents major artists like Julian Schnabel, Miguel Barcel and Jonathan Lasker.

Victoria Miro Gallery

21 CORK ST, W1, 020-7734 5082
Open Mon.-Fri. 10am-5.30pm, Sat. 11am-1pm.
U: Piccadilly Circus.

Victoria Miro picks her artists with care and presents precise exhibitions in her equally precise space, redesigned by Claudio Silberstrin in 1990. The mood of the gallery suits works by Alan Charlton, Ian Hamilton Finlay and Richard Tuttle, although some may find the austerity a little severe.

Waddington Galleries

11/12 & 34 CORK ST, W1, 020-7437 8611
Open Mon.-Fri. 10am-5.30pm, Sat. 10am-1pm.
U: Piccadilly Circus.

Hailing from the heady 1960s, this art scene stalwart is the home of Leslie Waddington, who like Anthony d'Offay and Nicholas Logsdail of the Lisson, has been instrumental internationally due to his fine selective eye and bravado. Waddington has certainly been—and continues to be—a very important part of the London art scene. Stop by to see the best of Modern British, Continental and some challenging contemporary work.

Zelda Cheatle Gallery

99 MOUNT ST, WI, 020-7408 4448
Open Mon. by appointment, Tues.-Fri. 10am-6pm, Sat. 11am-4pm.
U: Bond St.

An impressive variety of photographic work in a gem of a gallery. It was started in Cecil Court in 1989 (the year photography was 150 years old) by Zelda Cheatle, whose previous experience running the Print Room at the Photographer's Gallery shows in the sure choice of stock. The range from Magnum professionals like Sebastiao Salgado, to contemporary art photographers such as Hannah Collins, is not only comprehensive but purposeful in its selection.

EIGHTEENTH-, NINETEENTH- & TWENTIETH-CENTURY ART

As London's dealers in eighteenth- and nineteenth-century art are amongst the best in the world, many of them exhibit at the international fairs and may be closed during these times. Therefore, be sure to check in advance.

Agnew's

43 OLD BOND ST, W1, 020-7629 6176
Open Mon.-Wed. & Fri. 9.30am-5pm, Thurs. 9.30am-6.30pm.
U: Green Park.

Established in 1867 and situated in a very atmospheric building, this family firm is no stranger to elegant and important historic works of art. Paintings are shown throughout the many smaller rooms and larger vestibule display areas—not under the scrutiny of overbright lights, but in an environment that just shrieks 'baronnial hall'. Among the many English eighteenth and nineteenth century paintings and prints, take a look at the French masters—Vuillard, Redon, Bonnard, Lautrec and Picasso. Some contemporary work is often on show simultaneously.

Burlington Paintings

10 & 12 BURLINGTON GDNS, SW1
020-7734 9984
Open Mon.-Fri. 9.30am-5.30pm. Also by appointment.
U: Piccadilly Circus.

Despite the fact that this gallery deals in fine nineteenth- and twentieth- century British and European paintings, it is resolutely not tied to the past. Having had an 'on-line' exhibition transmitted to hundreds via the Internet, it also continues to show more usual and very elegant stock.

Chris Beetles

8 & 10 RYDER ST, SW1, 020-7839 7551
Open Mon.-Sat. 10am-5.30pm.
U: Green Park.

Surely the home of British illustrations, cartoons and caricatures. With several viewing areas and very regular changing exhibitions, a vast variety of work is able to be aired. Chris Beetles seems particularly good at focusing attention on often forgotten or neglected artists and subjects, and the scholarship of his catalogues is always reassuring. A must for anyone who collects or is interested in the print medium. The stock includes more than 100 artists from 1780 to the present.

The Fine Art Society

148 NEW BOND ST, W1, 020-7629 5116
Open Mon.-Fri. 9.30am-5.30pm, Sat. 10am-1pm.
U: Piccadilly Circus.
Arguably one of the most distinguished galleries in London. This space specialises in showing work from the late nineteenth century—including Art Nouveau masters through the excitingly turbulent 1920s-1930s Deco period and right up to today with artists such as Emma Sargeant. There are, along with the fine selection of paintings, always wonderful ceramics, glassware, and incidental but compelling (and curiously affordable) objects.

Frost & Reed

2 KING ST, ST. JAMES'S, SW1, 020-7839 4645
Open Mon.-Fri. 9am-5.30pm.
U: Green Park.
Very close to celebrating 200 years of fine art dealing, Frost & Reed houses its stock and changing shows in a bright, large space. Around six major shows are organised a year, often of a sporting and equestrian nature with a sprinkling of establishment moderns or respected, older contemporaries.

The Lefevre Gallery

30 BRUTON ST, W1, 020-7493 2107
Open Mon.-Fri. 10am-5pm.
U: Bond St.
Well-established family business selling the choicest examples of French Impressionism and occasionally some twentieth-century giants such as Picasso and Georgia O'Keefe.

The Maas Gallery

15A CLIFFORD ST, W1, 020-7734 2302
Open Mon.-Fri. 10am-5.30pm.
U: Piccadilly Circus.
Despite being the size of a rather small sitting room, this gallery is one to treasure. The gallery director is certainly in love with his period—Victorian—with a particular relish for Pre-Raphaelite drawings, paintings and watercolours. The roaring fire, lit on cold days, compounds the cosy atmosphere, and the elegant moulded windows advertise the gallery's wares. Often the works of Burne-Jones and

Alma-Tadema are on view. Contemporary shows are slotted in between the period ones.

The Mallet Gallery

141 NEW BOND ST, W1, 020-7499 7411
Open Mon.-Fri. 9.30am-5.30pm, Sat. 10am-4pm.
U: Piccadilly Circus.
One of the foremost specialists in fine Victorian, Edwardian and Pre-Raphaelite pictures and works of art, showing nineteenth- and twentieth-century English and European paintings, as well as sculpture, ceramics, nineteenth-century Gothic furniture and works of art. One gallery is devoted to eighteenth- and nineteenth-century watercolours and drawings.

Mathaf Gallery

24 MOTCOMB ST, SW1, 020-7235 0010
Open Mon.-Fri. 9.30am-5.30pm.
U: Knightsbridge.
The Mathaf sits squarely in a small but influential art enclave and, as a specialist, is on the map of collector and browser alike. This gallery features 'Orientalist' art—grand and invariably atmospheric glamorous images of old Araby, complete with glistening tenting, bedecked camels, treasures, silken palaces and marble halls. Some European and British artists were so captivated by the Near East in the nineteenth century that they dedicated their lives to depicting it. Most images are framed within heavy gold leaf structures (works of art in their own right), emphasising the imposing grandeur. Coloured lithographs by David Roberts complement dramatic oils by Deutsch and Gerome.

Drinking Fountains

In 1859 the **Metropolitan Free Drinking Fountain Association** was established to supply drinking water to combat the dreadful water shortages, cholera and intemperance rife in London's poorer areas. By 1886 they had established 594 though few remain today.

Peter Nahum
at the Leicester Galleries

3-5 RYDER ST, ST. JAMES'S, SW1, 020-7930 6059
Open Mon.-Fri. 9.30am-6pm.
U: Green Park.

Leaving auction house Sotheby's in 1984, Peter Nahum set up this gallery specialising in high-quality paintings, drawings and sculpture from the nineteenth and twentieth centuries. A television personality, lecturer and author to boot, Nahum is also advisor to several official departments of art. Expect to see works by Burne-Jones, Millais, Tissot and Alma-Tadema.

Pyms Gallery

9 MOUNT ST, W1, 020-7629 2020
Open Mon.-Fri. 9.30am-5.30pm, Sat. only for special exhibitions.
U: Bond St.

Located on a street of chic antique shops and restaurants, Pyms deals in a wide range of work concentrating on the Irish eighteenth, nineteenth and twentieth centuries, including work by Lavery and Orpen. French Naturalism is represented by the Barbizon School and there are some British late nineteenth- and early twentieth-century paintings.

Richard Green

44 DOVER ST, W1, 020-7493 3939
Open Mon.-Fri. 10am-6pm, Sat. 10am-noon.
Also by appointment.
U: Green Park.

Mainly sporting and marine paintings which find favour with several international collectors. The handsome and relatively new setting provides an impressive backdrop for some of the most celebrated sporting paintings in history, many with more than significant provenances. Impressionist, Post-Impressionist, Modern British and Scottish Colourists are also on view and over at the gallery's other space at 39 Dover St., W1, Victorian paintings and nineteenth-century European works are on view.

Richard Philp

59 LEDBURY RD, W11, 020-7727 7915
Open Mon.-Sat. 10am-6pm (but check opening times before visiting).
U: Ladbroke Grove/Notting Hill Gate.

On two floors of an elegant building just off Portobello Road, Richard Philp has a stock, which spans centuries. Roman and Greek sculpture occupy the same space as Old Master drawings alongside early Elizabethan or Jacobean portraits. However, this is no casual selection—there is a genuine delight in the works of art here.

Shapero Gallery

24 BRUTON ST, W1, 020-7491 0330
Open Mon.-Fri. 9.30am-6.30pm, Sat. 11am-5pm.
U: Bond St.

Antique prints, watercolours, photographs and maps are the stock-in-trade here. Already famed for his superb bookshop around the corner on St. George St. Bernard Shapero wanted his new space to cater especially to younger people familiar with the lure of Bond Street and its environs. Decorative prints, vintage travel and ethnographic photographs and maps can be set in handmade picture frames. Regular themed exhibitions are held through the year.

Spink & Son

5-7 KING ST, SW1, 020-7930 7888
Open Mon.-Fri. 9am-5.30pm.
U: Green Park.

Established in 1666, Spink comprises several showrooms and galleries with various specialities. Famed for their Eastern art, jewelry, carpets and sculpture, Spink also has a keen interest in medals and coins and occasionally shows nineteenth- and twentieth-century art. A superb backdrop for some rare and unusual pieces gathered from across the globe.

Spink-Leger

13 OLD BOND ST, W1, 020-7629 3538
Open Mon.-Fri. 9am-5.30pm.
U: Green Park.

Continual selection of prime, classic work often dating from the sixteenth century, but usually the last two hundred years ago or so. Themed exhibitions are held at regular intervals at this relatively new salon-style space.

Waterhouse & Dodd

110 NEW BOND ST, W1, 020-7491 9293
Open Mon.-Fri. 9.30am-6pm.
U: Bond St.

The no-nonsense approach to buying quality period paintings and sculptures is evident here. A helpful newsletter published frequently not only keeps potential buyers up-to-date, but also advises on how to buy, what to look for, and includes prices so that one knows instantly the cost of something without having to ask. There is always something marvelous to look at here—slices of grand nineteenth-century life, rural studies, cool marble busts and occasional portraits. French, Belgian and British artists make up the bulk of the stock.

OLD MASTER SPECIALISTS

Derek Johns

12 DUKE ST, ST JAMES, SW1, 020-7839 7671
Open Mon.-Fri. 9.30am-5.30pm.
U: Green Park.

As a specialist in Old Masters, Derek Johns has achieved international acclaim for discovering lost masterpieces and showing rare works never previously exhibited. In addition, annual shows present displays of European painting and sculpture.

John Mitchell & Son

160 NEW BOND ST, W1, 020-7493 7567
Open Mon.-Fri. 9.30am-5.30pm, Sat. by appointment.
U: Bond St.

This independent family firm was established in 1930 and is a well-known specialist in flower paintings. It offers a small, rigorously selected stock of paintings, watercolours and drawings from the seventeenth to nineteenth centuries.

P & D Colnaghi & Co

14 OLD BOND ST, W1, 020-7491 7408
Open Mon.-Fri. 10am-6pm.
U: Green Park.

A reverential hush pervades the interior, hinting at the impeccable provenance of Colnaghi's. The company goes all the way back to 1760, and whilst concentrating on Italian and French schools up to the early 1800s, also has carefully selected Old Master paintings on view, including English paintings. The plush surroundings complement the works, which are allowed ample viewing space—as befits the quality of paintings destined for major collections in the world.

Looking for an address?
Refer to the index.

Raphael Valls

11 DUKE ST, ST. JAMES'S, SW1, 020-7930 1144
Open Mon.-Fri. 10am-5.30pm & by appointment.
U: Green Park.

In a bustling, rather faded, atmosphere, are paintings, drawings and watercolours from the Dutch and Flemish tradition. European Old Masters such as Ruisdael, Arellano and Van Goyen are often on display. Relax and browse through the hubbub—it's well worth it.

Simon Dickinson Ltd

58 JERMYN ST, SW1, 020-7493 0340
Open Mon.-Fri. 10am-5pm.
U: Green Park.

Whilst it is possible for the casual visitor to see the selection of Old Master and British paintings on show, the strength of this organisation is in finding important pictures from private collections.

Van Haeften Gallery

13 DUKE ST, SW1, 020-7930 3062
Open Mon.-Fri. 10am-6pm.
U: Green Park.

Here, on green beize-lined walls, are gems of seventeenth-century Dutch and Flemish Old Masters. Johnny Van Haeften has extended family in Holland, but is not Dutch; however, it is hard to imagine anyone more in tune with Dutch painting. These are works to be enjoyed and marvelled over in a small gallery before they are whisked off to some lucky museum.

Whitfield Fine Art

180 NEW BOND ST, W1, 020-7499 3592
Open by appointment.
U: Bond St.

Clovis Whitfield is one of the most important and charismatic dealers in Old Master Italian paintings from the sixteenth to late eighteenth centuries. Drawings are also shown, along with Florentine and Venetian frames from the same period.

Wildenstein & Co

147 NEW BOND ST, W1, 020-7629 0602
Open by appointment.
U: Bond St.

A venerable institution which deals in Impressionist and Old Master paintings. Shimmering silver-gray crushed velvet walls and period furniture set the scene for the occasional van Gogh or Leonardo da Vinci sketch. Handy for the auction rooms and perfect for those dreaming of owning a masterpiece.

ART MUSEUMS

Please note that admission charges were correct at press time, but that museums and galleries may alter their admission charges. If you are in London over a public holiday, please check opening times. The main museum sites are **www.24hourmuseum.org.uk** and **www.exhibitionsnet.com**.

The **London GoSee** card gives you unlimited admission to seventeen major museums and galleries. Three-day (£16) and seven-day passes (£26) are available from participating museums, the Tourist Information Centre at Victoria Station, and many hotel concierges (**www.london-gosee.com**).

The **London Pass** gives admission to 40 attractions in and around London. You can either buy just this card or buy a pass that also gives free travel in zones 1-6, guide book, map, £5 of telephone calls and also discounts on services like open-top bus tours and canal boat trips. Without travel: 1, 3, 6 days: adults £13.50, £29, £43; children £9, £15, £26. With travel: 1, 3, 6, days; adults £18, £42, £74; children £11, £22, £38. Passes can be booked over the telephone (0870-2429 988), or over the web (www.londonpass.com). The pass is sent to you by mail, or you can get it from the Britain Visitor Centre at 1 Lower Regent St, SW1. Once at the attraction, you swipe the pass through a machine and you're on your way.

For information on **events in 2000 in London**: 09068-66 33 44. For London Tourist Board recorded information on **current exhibitions**: 09068-505 440. For **what's on this week**: 09068-505 440. For **what's on in next three months**: 09068-505 490. For **museums and galleries**: 09068-505 462. For **palaces**: 09068-505 466. For **famous houses and gardens**: 09068-505 468. For **other visitor attractions**: 09068-505 465. For **attractions in Greenwich**: 09068-505 467. For **day trips from London**: 09068-505 479.

Please note that all 09068 calls are currently charged at 60p per minute.

The official **London Tourist Board web site** is www.londontown.com.

Barbican Gallery

BARBICAN CENTRE, SILK ST, EC2
020-7638 4141, WWW.BARBICAN.ORG.UK
Open Mon.-Sat. 9am-11pm, Sun. & public holidays noon-11pm. Admission free, but charge for some exhibitions.
U: Barbican.

Top art exhibitions are held in the art gallery, found on the third level of this product of 1960s' city planning. The residential, commercial and arts complex was built on a site destroyed during World War II and opened to the public in the 1980s. It contains two theatres, a concert hall, cinema, library and a conservatory on the roof. The exhibitions are of major importance and it's always a lively place to visit with frequent free performances.

College Art Collections

STRANG PRINT ROOM, UNIVERSITY COLLEGE LONDON, GOWER ST, WC1, 020-7387 7050
Open Wed.-Fri. 1pm-5pm (term time), or by appointment. Admission free.
U: Euston Sq.

Old Master prints and drawings plus collections of the famous Slade School of Art drawn from more than 7,000 prints, 600 paintings and drawings and 150 sculptures.

Courtauld Institute

SOMERSET HOUSE, STRAND, WC2
020-7872 0220, WWW.COURTAULD.AC.UK
Open Mon.-Sat. 10am-6pm, Sun. noon-6pm. Adults £4, under 18 free. Joint ticket with the Gilbert Collection: adults £7, concessions £5.
U: Covent Garden/Temple (not Sun.)

Housed in the glorious former palace of Somerset House (1776-86), the Courtauld Institute galleries hold one of the best collections of Impressionist and Post-Impressionist paintings outside France. Apart from masterpieces from the Impressionists like Manet's *Bar at the Folies-Bergères* and van Gogh's *Self-Portrait*—part of the original gift of textile magnate, Samuel Courtauld (1865-1947)—you can feast your eyes on paintings by Rubens, Tiepolo and Van Dyck, as well as British paintings, Roger Fry's pictures, artworks by the early twentieth-century London Bloomsbury Group and the Omega Workshops, drawings and more. The Witt Library boasts one of the largest photographic collections of Western paintings in the world. It's an important collection housed in impressive surroundings and there's a good book-shop attached.

Crafts Council Gallery

44A PENTONVILLE RD, N1, 020-7278 7700
WWW.CRAFTSCOUNCIL.ORG.UK
Open Tues.-Sat. 11am-6pm, Sun. 2pm-6pm.
Admission free.
U: King's Cross/Angel.

The national centre for crafts shows work by Britain's foremost talents. Britain has always had a reputation for producing first-rate craft items and this gallery demonstrates this pre-eminence. Frequently changing exhibitions of silver, jewellery, woodcarvings, pottery and more are always interesting. The shop is an excellent source of high-quality unique items. The *Crafts Index* holds details and pictures of hundreds of craftsmen for those who want to commission works.

Dulwich Picture Gallery

COLLEGE RD, SE21, 020-8693 5254
WWW.DULWICHPICTUREGALLERY.ORG.UK
Open Tues.-Fri. 10am-5pm, Sat. 11am-5pm,
Sun. 2pm-5pm. Adults £3, children free.
Rail: West Dulwich.

Although England's oldest public art gallery was designed by Sir John Soane (see the John Soane Museum) and opened in 1814, it has been magnificently refurbished. Soane's use of skylights, which gave the rooms natural light, made it the model for subsequent art galleries. The twelve galleries and mausoleum contain a splendid collection of Old Master paintings belonging to Dulwich College and some excellent exhibitions are mounted throughout the year.

Estorick Collection of Modern Italian Art

NORTHAMPTON LODGE, 39A CANONBURY SQ, N1
020-7704 9522, WW.ESTORICKCOLLECTION.COM
Open Tues.-Sat. 11am-6pm. Adults £3.50,
children £2.50.
U: Highbury & Islington.

This hugely important collection of early twentieth-century artists of the avant-garde Futurist movement opened as a gallery early in 1998. Boccioni, Severini and Russolo are just a few of the many artists exhibited from the

original private collection Eric Estorick (1913-1993), an American sociologist, dealer, collector and writer who gave his collection to Britain. Also featured: an excellent café and good shop.

European Academy & Accademia Italiana

8 GROSVENOR PL, SW1, 020-7235 0303
Open Tues. & Thurs.-Sat. 10.30am-6pm,
Wed. 10.30am-8pm. Adults £5, under 16 £2,
concessions £3.40.
U: Hyde Park Corner.

Open for specific exhibitions only on contemporary European artists, so please check in advance.

Gilbert Collection

SOMERSET HOUSE, STRAND, WC2, 020-7240 4080
WWW.GILBERT-COLLECTIONS.ORG.UK
Open Mon.-Sat. 10am-6pm, Sun. & bank holidays noon-6pm. Last admission 5.15pm. Adults £4, under 18 free, concessions £3. Joint ticket with Courtauld Gallery: adults £7, concessions £5.
U: Covent Garden/Temple (not Sun.)

This is one of the most exciting and important private collections to be opened to the public in recent times. It was bequeathed to Britain in its entirety by Sir Arthur Gilbert, who was born in London in 1913, but moved to California in 1949. There are 800 works of

𝒥riends

If you're in London for any length of time, consider becoming a Friend of one of your favourite museums. Although the main purpose of these organisations is to raise much-needed funds, becoming a Friend is rather like joining a club. You pay a yearly membership and receive news about the museum, free admission to exhibitions as well as the possibility of enjoying specially arranged holidays. Many of them also organise evening viewings which are only open to Friends. The Friends of the Royal Academy can take guests to private views for free, and use the special club room which is one of the best in London.

art displayed, a collection of wonderful European silver, gold snuff boxes and Italian mosaics, now housed in the South Building of Somerset House (which also houses the Courtauld Collection). One of the few private collections to be given in its entirety and displayed similarly, this is a gift to the nation, which should be treasured for its unique appeal. Whereas museums will hold only a few specific examples of works of art or styles, a private collector can indulge his or her particular passion and collect multiple examples of one style. From exquisite gold snuffboxes made in all the major manufacturing centres, to rare silver drinking cups and beakers, this is a rich experience.

Hayward Gallery

SOUTH BANK CENTRE, SE1
020-7928 3144, WWW.HAYWARD-GALLERY.ORG.UK
Open for exhibitions only Tues.-Wed. 10am-8pm, Thurs.-Mon. 10am-6pm. Adults £6, under 12 free, concessions £4.
U: Waterloo.
Part of the South Bank complex, this is one of London's main venues for major exhibitions of international importance. Check in the national newspapers for current shows.

Hulton Getty Picture Gallery

3 JUBILEE PL, SW3
020-7376 4525, WWW.GETTY-IMAGES.COM
Open Mon.-Fri.10am-6pm, Sat. noon-6pm. Admission free.
U: South Kensington.
The Hulton Getty collection is one of the best in the world. Changing exhibitions are on display, which are sometimes thematic, sometimes based on a particular photographer. All the images are for sale.

Courses & Lectures

Most of the big museums offer all kinds of lectures, tours and courses, frequently on the subject of their current exhibitions. Ring each museum separately for details.

Institute of Contemporary Arts

CARLTON HOUSE TERRACE, SW1
020-7930 6393 (RECORDED INFORMATION)
WWW.ICA.ORG.UK
Open (galleries) daily noon-7.30pm, Fri. noon-9.30pm. Adults £1.50, concessions £1.
U: Charing Cross/Piccadilly Circus.
The ICA was established in 1947 by art critics Herbert Read and Roland Penrose to help British artists in the way American artists were assisted by the Museum of Modern Art in New York. Many leading figures had their first British exhibitions here, from Picasso and Max Ernst, to contemporary names like Helen Chadwick and Damien Hirst. The Institute, which has always promoted the more avant-garde aspects of modern culture, holds a lively and continual series of exhibitions, films, theatre, performances and talks. The ICA Café is excellent (see *Quick Bites*).

London International Gallery of Children's Art

02 CENTRE, 255 FINCHLEY RD, NW3
020-7435 0903
Open Tues.-Thurs. 4pm-6pm, Fri.-Sun. noon-6pm. Admission free.
U: Finchley Rd.
The only gallery in London for art produced by children; there are many exhibitions and good workshops throughout the year.

National Gallery

TRAFALGAR SQ, WC2
020-7839 3321, WWW.NATIONALGALLERY.ORG.UK
Open daily 10am-6pm, Wed. 10 am-9pm. Admission free, but charge for major exhibitions.
U: Charing Cross.
The National Gallery opened in 1824, much later than other national galleries in Europe, after King George IV persuaded a philistine government to buy 38 major paintings, including works by Raphael and Rembrandt. Today, this large and comprehensive collection, housed in the neo-classical William Wilkins nineteenth-century building, and in the new Sainsbury Wing, provides a first-class panorama of European painting from Giotto to the French Impressionists. (Modern and British paintings are housed in the new Tate Britain and Tate Modern.) The masterpieces here are well known: the Leonardo da Vinci cartoon, Velazquez's *Rokeby Venus*, *The*

Baptism of Christ by Pierro della Francesca, Van Eyck's *Arnolfini Marriage,* and *The Haywain* by John Constable. Divided into sections covering Early Renaissance (1260-1510) in the Sainsbury Wing, High Renaissance (1520-1600), English, French and German Painting (1800-1900) and more, the galleries are compact and well laid out.

National Portrait Gallery

ST. MARTIN'S PL, WC2
020-7306 0055, WWW.NPG.ORG.UK
Open Mon.-Sat. 10am-6pm, Sun. noon-6pm.
Admission free, but charge for certain exhibitions.
U: Leicester Sq.

With a new wing and a major redevelopment, this wonderful gallery has been revitalised. If you want to know what a favourite, famous or infamous British writer, King, Queen, Prince or Princess, poet, artist or villain looked like, go to the National Portrait Gallery which shows British history through its people. Covering five centuries of portraiture, the earliest portraits include a Hans Holbein cartoon of King Henry VIII, while the newest galleries display photographs, sculptures and pictures of contemporary figures. The latter is a more controversial section: who will be considered important enough to be preserved in years to come? As the collection concentrates on the sitter rather than the artist, it is a mixture, with works by some of the world's great artists hanging alongside more mundane efforts. The collection, arranged chronologically, gives an insight into different ideals of beauty, from the sloping shoulders and long noses of the eighteenth century, to the gamin waif-like looks of the 1990s. Good rooftop café run by Searcy's and a good shop.

Percival David Foundation of Chinese Art

53 GORDON SQUARE, WC1
020-7387 3909, WWW.SOAS.AC.UK
Open Mon.-Fri. 10.30am-5pm. Admission free.
U: Euston Sq.

This important and relatively unknown collection of beautiful Chinese ceramics made between the tenth and eighteenth centuries is a must for anyone with an interest in the subject. Percival David (1892-1964) was a Governor of the School of Oriental and African Studies and gave his collection to London University. It is exquisite; many of the pieces once belonged to the Chinese Imperial dynasty.

Queen's Gallery

BUCKINGHAM PALACE RD, SW1
020-7799 2331, WWW.ROYAL.GOV.UK
U: Victoria.

The Queen's Gallery is currently closed for refurbishment and reopens in 2002.

RIBA Architecture Gallery

66 PORTLAND PL, W1
020-7307 3699, WWW.RIBA.NET.
Open Mon., Tues. & Thurs.-Sat. 10am-6pm,
Wed. 10am-9pm. Admission free.
U: Oxford Circus/Regent's Park.

The gallery of the Royal Institute of British Architects holds regular exhibitions and special events, which include distinguished architects airing their views and speaking on their work.

Royal Academy of Arts

BURLINGTON HOUSE, PICCADILLY, W1
020-7300 8000, WWW.ROYALACADEMY.ORG.UK
Open Mon.-Thurs. & Sat.-Sun. 10am-6pm, Fri.
10 am-8.30pm. Admission charges vary with
different exhibitions.
U: Green Park.

A splendid institution housed in the equally splendid Burlington House in Piccadilly—and approached through a newly refurbished courtyard—the Royal Academy of Arts was founded in 1768 by Sir Joshua Reynolds with King George III as patron. Although probably best known for its Annual Summer Exhibition (held for over 200 years), the Royal Academy hosts some of the most important general exhibitions and shows of major individual artists, though none of them living figures. Each elected Academician has to give a piece of work before receiving a Diploma signed by the Sovereign. Along with bequests, gifts and purchases, this makes for an impressive collection of British Art over the past 217 years. There's a roster of names which includes every major British artist including Alan Jones, David Hockney and Elisabeth Frink, and architects Richard Rogers and Norman Foster. Good shop and restaurant (see *Quick Bites*).

Royal College of Art

KENSINGTON GORE, SW7
020-7590 4444, WWW.RCA.AC.UK
*Open Sat.-Tues.10am-6pm, Fri. 10am-9pm
(during exhibitions only). Admission charges
vary by exhibition.*
U: High St Kensington.

The Royal College of Art is primarily a post-graduate college, among the best in the world. They also hold exhibitions on a wide range of subjects throughout the year, from vehicle design to fine art, as well as hosting some of the big annual art fairs.

Saatchi Collection

98A BOUNDARY RD, NW8, 020-7624 8299
*Open Thurs.-Sun. noon-6pm. Closed Aug. &
Dec. Adults £4, under 12 free, concessions £2.*
U: St. John's Wood.

This spectacular space—converted by architect Max Gordon from an old paint factory for Charles Saatchi, the advertising mogul in 1985—is one of the few venues for viewing large-scale contemporary work in an appropriate setting. The private Saatchi Collection of International Contemporary Art is displayed in changing exhibitions, including the annual one, *Young British Artists,* which always causes a stir.

Serpentine Gallery

GALLERY LAWN, KENSINGTON GARDENS, W2
020-7289 1515, WW.SERPENTINEGALLERY.ORG.UK
Open daily 10am-6pm. Admission free.
U: Lancaster Gate/South Kensington.

Devoted to modern art, this refurbished gallery continues its reputation for showing some of the most controversial artists of the day, like Damian Hirst, in a series of highly publicised exhibitions.

Tate Britain

MILLBANK, SW1
020-7887 8000, WWW.TATE.ORG.UK
*Open daily 10am-5.50pm. Admission free, but
charge for major exhibitions.*
U: Pimlico.

The original Tate Gallery has been relaunched as Tate Britain, holding and exhibiting the greatest collection of British art in the world from the sixteenth century to today, in a wonderful series of new displays and exhibitions in theme-based galleries. The expansion allows a far greater proportion of the Tate's huge holdings to be displayed. The rest of the original collection is displayed in the new Tate Modern (see below). The two galleries are linked by a shuttle bus and boat service. The Millbank gallery was originally built through the generosity of sugar millionaire Sir Henry Tate, who also gave his own collection. The Clore Gallery, designed by Sir James Stirling and an architectural sight in its own right, houses the extensive collection of JMW Turner's works.

Tate Modern

25 SUMNER ST, BANKSIDE, SE1
020-7887 8000, WWW.TATE.ORG.UK
*Open Sun.-Thurs. 10am-6pm, Fri.-Sat. 10am-
10pm. Admission free, but charge for major
exhibitions.*
U: Southwark.

This new gallery is housed in the vast former Bankside Power Station by the Thames (now totally remodelled and refurbished) and has had an enormous impact on the regeneration of the South Bank. Designed by Swiss architects, Herzog and de Meurona, and costing £134 million, it's Britain's first museum of modern art with a magnificent series of displays and special exhibitions. It now contains the second part of the Tate's holdings—international twentieth-century art. It's among the three or four most important such collections in the world featuring major works by all the influential artists of the last century, from Picasso, Matisse and Duchamps to Bacon, Rothko and Warhol. Its policy is also to exhibit new art as it is being created. Under Nicholas Serota, the Tate has established a reputation as a major institution often at the centre of controversy. It's linked to St. Paul's Cathedral by the first new bridge built in central London since 1894. There is a shuttle bus and boat service linking the new gallery to the Tate in Millbank.

Two 10 Gallery

WELLCOME TRUST, 210 EUSTON RD, NW1
020-7611 7211, WWW.WELLCOME.AC.UK
Open Mon.-Fri. 9am-6pm. Admission free.
U: Euston Sq/Warren St.

A range of good temporary exhibitions, including photography exhibitions concentrating on the interaction between contemporary medical science and art.

Wallace Collection

HERTFORD HOUSE, MANCHESTER SQUARE, W1
020-7935 0687
WWW.THE-WALLACE-COLLECTION.ORG.UK
Open Mon.-Sat. 10am-5pm, Sun. 2pm-5pm.
Admission free.
U: Bond St.

Originally built for the Duke of Manchester, Hertford House was bought by the Marquess of Hertford in 1797. The family was a great patron of the arts and what you see is one of the finest private collections of French art, including porcelain and sculpture. There's also an eclectic mix of arms and armour and furniture in a delightful setting that imparts a feeling of an aristocratic family's tastes and lifestyle. Four new galleries and a lecture theatre provide additional spaces for exhibitions.

Whitechapel Art Gallery

80 WHITECHAPEL HIGH ST, E1
020-7522 7878 (RECORDED INFORMATION)
WWW.WHITECHAPEL.ORG
Open Tues. & Thurs.-Sun. 11am-5pm, Wed 11am-8pm. Admission free, but charge for certain exhibitions.
U: Aldgate East.

Founded at the end of the nineteenth century to bring the West End to the East End, this has been the mecca for innovative art under a series of high-profile directors since the 1960s. Housed in a splendid Art Nouveau building, there are two elegant main galleries, the upper one totally top-lit, that are used for one-person contemporary shows and retrospectives. The *Whitechapel Open*, devoted to east London's growing and significant artists, is held every two years, the next one being in 2000.

ATTRACTIONS

Please note that admission charges were correct at press time, but that museums and galleries may alter their admission charges. If you are in London over a public holiday, please check opening times. The main museum sites are **www.24hourmuseum.org.uk** and **www.exhibitionsnet.com.**

The **London GoSee** card gives you unlimited admission to seventeen major museums and galleries. Three-day (£16) and seven-day passes (£26) are available from participating museums, the Tourist Information Centre at Victoria Station, and many hotel concierges (**www.london-gosee.com**).

The **London Pass** gives admission to 40 attractions in and around London. You can either buy just this card or buy a pass that also gives free travel in zones 1-6, guide book, map, £5 of telephone calls and also discounts on services like open-top bus tours and canal boat trips. Without travel: 1, 3, 6 days: adults £13.50, £29, £43; children £9, £15, £26. With travel: 1, 3, 6, days; adults £18, £42, £74; children £11, £22, £38. Passes can be booked over the telephone (0870-2429 988), or over the web (www.londonpass.com). The pass is sent to you by mail, or you can get it from the Britain Visitor Centre at 1 Lower Regent St, SW1. Once at the attraction, you swipe the pass through a machine and you're on your way.

For information on **events in 2000 in London**: 09068-66 33 44. For London Tourist Board recorded information on **current exhibitions**: 09068-505 440. For **what's on this week**: 09068-505 440. For **what's on in next three months**: 09068-505 490. For **museums and galleries**: 09068-505 462. For **palaces**: 09068-505 466. For **famous houses and gardens**: 09068-505 468. For **other visitor attractions**: 09068-505 465. For **attractions in Greenwich**: 09068-505 467. For **day trips from London**: 09068-505 479.

Please note that all 09068 calls are currently charged at 60p per minute.

The official **London Tourist Board** web site is www.londontown.com.

Walks Around London

Many excellent companies offer top walks, concentrating on different areas or themes. Many also do historic pub walks which is a good way to meet people. Check out the following: **Architectural Dialogue,** 020-8341 1371; **Historical Walks,** 020-8668 4019; **The Londoner Pub Walks,** 020-8883 2656; **The London Walking Forum,** 01992-717 711; **Mystery Walks,** 020-8558 9446; **The Original London Walks,** 020-7264 3978; **Pied Piper Walks,** 020-7435 4782; **Stepping Out Walking Tours,** 020-8881 2933; **Walk the Millennium Mile,** 020-7261 9211.

Albert Memorial

KENSINGTON GDNS, SW7, 020-7495 0916
Open for guided group tours Sun. 2pm, 3pm.
Telephone for times and information.
U: High St Kensington.

This magnificent memorial built by Queen Victoria to commemorate her husband, has been restored to its former, gilded glory and now gleams impressively in Kensington Gardens. Guided tours take you inside the memorial. Otherwise just stand and admire from outside.

Banqueting House

WHITEHALL, WC2
020-7930 4179, WWW.HRP.ORG.UK
Open Mon.-Sat. 10am-5pm (last admission 4.30pm). Closes at short notice for government functions, so please check in advance. Adults £3.60, ages 5-15 £2.30, concessions £2.80.
U: Westminster.

All that is left of the old Westminster Palace is the magnificent Banqueting House with its double cube room built by Inigo Jones in the then new Italianate-style from 1619 to 1622. The Rubens ceiling is magnificent, painted in 1634 for Charles I to honour his father, James I of England. Charles I was beheaded on a scaffold erected outside; also here is his son Charles II who celebrated his restoration to the throne. It's a good place to watch the mounted Changing the Guard ceremony opposite.

BBC Experience

BROADCASTING HOUSE, PORTLAND PL, W1
0870 6030304, WWW.BBC.CO.UK/EXPERIENCE
Open daily first tour 10am, last tour 4.30pm (Mon. first tour 11am). Adults £6.95, children £5.95, families £19.95.
U: Oxford Circus.

The BBC's own show, with a behind-the-scenes look at how the BBC works, what its future might be and a lot of archive material from great events. It also gives you the chance to help make a radio drama and test your editing abilities. Good café and shop.

> **Telephone numbers** in England have eleven digits, beginning with a zero. The initial zero must be omitted if you are calling England from abroad. Within the country, dial the entire eleven digits.

BFI London IMAX Cinema

1 CHARLIE CHAPLIN WALK, SOUTH BANK, SE1
020-7902 1234
Daily show times noon, 1.15pm, 2.30pm, 3.30pm, 5pm, 6.50pm, 8.30pm. Adults £8.50, ages 5-15 £5.50, concessions £6.50.
U: Waterloo.

Part of the British Film Institute, the new circular, glass-walled, £20 million IMAX cinema sits impressively at the bottom end of Waterloo Bridge, with a huge seven-storey artwork by Howard Hodgkin stretched around the circumference. The 482-seat, 14-tiered, state-of-the-art, large-format cinema has a huge screen for showing 2D and 3D films. The choice is still fairly limited, but films like *Destiny in Space* and *Into the Deep* are worth the trip.

British Airways London Eye

JUBILEE GARDENS, SOUTH BANK, SE1
0870-5000 600, WWW.BA-LONDONEYE.COM
Open Nov.-Mar. daily 10am-6pm, Apr.-Oct. daily 9am-late evening. Adults £7.45, children £4.95, under 5 free.
U: Waterloo.

There was some trouble erecting this huge, magnificent piece of engineering. At 135 metres high, it's the world's highest observation wheel—more than 120 feet taller than Big Ben and a third taller than the Statue of Liberty. Its magnificent glittering appearance dominates the skyline, fitting in beautifully by the river. It gives visitors, travelling in huge pods, a 30-minute, slow-moving 'flight' observing the heart of London and seeing 25 miles in each direction.

British Library

EUSTON RD, NW1
020-7412 7332, WWW.BL.UK
Open Mon. & Wed.-Fri. 9.30am-6pm, Tues. 9.30am-8pm, Sat. 9.30am-5pm, Sun. & bank holiday Mon. 11am-5pm. Admission free.
U: Euston/King's Cross/St. Pancras.

Finally working as the nation's main research library after a 30-year-long building programme, the public areas include four permanent exhibitions showing the works and the work of the library. Also houses temporary exhibitions. Tickets to use the reading room are only obtainable with an academic's or publisher's recommendations.

Cabinet War Rooms

CLIVE STEPS, KING CHARLES ST, SW1
020-7930 6961
Open Oct.-Mar. daily 10am-6pm (last admission 5.15pm), Apr.-Sept. daily 10am-6pm.
Adults £4.80, children £2.30, under 5 free, concessions £3.50.
U: St. James's Park/Westminster.

These are underground war rooms from where Sir Winston Churchill, his chiefs of staff and his cabinet directed the war. It's a fascinating place, full of old equipment, furniture and all the paraphernalia of war like charts, models and radios. Small, good gift shop.

Changing the Guard

BUCKINGHAM PALACE/HORSE GUARDS, WHITEHALL, SW1, 0839-123411 (60P PER MINUTE, RECORDED INFORMATION)
Open Apr.-July/Aug. daily 11.30am, rest of the year even or odd dates depending on the month. Call for details. Free.
U: St. James's Park/Westminster.

The Foot Guards of the Household Division of the Cavalry, the Queen's personal guards, leave Wellington Barracks at 11.27am precisely and march along Bird Cage Walk to Buckingham Palace. There's usually a band playing, but the ceremony is scaled down when the Queen is not in residence (look for the Royal Standard flying at Buckingham Palace when she is there) and can be cancelled if the weather is very bad. In crowded summer months, get to the palace by at least 10.30am. The mounted guard changing ceremony by the Household Cavalry in Whitehall takes place daily at 11am, Sun. at 10am. Stand in Whitehall or in Horse Guards Parade, or for a bird's-eye view, see it from the Banqueting House (see above for details).

Clockmakers' Company Collection

GUILDHALL LIBRARY, ALDERMANBURY, EC2
020-7332 1868
Open Mon.-Fri. 9.30am-4.45pm. Admission free.
U: Moorgate/St. Paul's.

Try to go to the museum in the morning when this large collection (about 600 watches and 30 clocks dating from the sixteenth to the nineteenth centuries) chimes, bongs and tinkles the hours. But at any time, the collection holds surprises. The oldest surviving clocks are from the 1300s. By 1675, English watches,

using hairsprings, could run to within an accurate two minutes a day. In 1752, the world's first watch to compensate against the effects of heat and cold was made. By 1785, there were self-winding watches. Good small, general, Guildhall shop.

College of Arms

QUEEN VICTORIA ST, EC4, 020-7248 2762
WWW.HWTELECOM\HERALD\COLLARMS
Open Mon.-Fri. 10am-4pm. Admission free.
U: Blackfriars.

Housed in a delightful seventeenth-century mansion, the College of Arms grants coats-of-arms and checks family pedigrees. Casual visitors may see the entrance room only. Groups may book a tour to see the Record Room and artists at work on certificates. To trace your roots, contact the Officer in Waiting (fee charged).

Cutty Sark

KING WILLIAM WALK, SE10
020-8858 3445, WWW.CUTTYSARK.ORG.UK
Open daily 10am-5pm. Adults £3.50, under 5 free, families £8.50, concessions £2.50.
Rail: Greenwich.

This absurdly small vessel now permanently marooned in Greenwich, was built at Dumbarton, Scotland in 1869 as one of the fast clippers that raced across the Atlantic and Pacific Oceans in the nineteenth century carrying first tea, then wool. In 1871, she won the annual China to London clipper race taking a mere 107 days. The brave clipper's last sea voyage was in 1938; she became a museum in 1957. On board you see the complex rigging and masts characteristic of the great days of sail; below deck the cramped quarters of the seamen are full of prints, instruments, odd personal artefacts and a collection of wooden figureheads.

Dennis Severs' House

18 FOLGATE ST, E1, 0220-7247 4013
Open first Sun. of each month 2pm-5pm & first Mon. 6pm-9pm for candle-lit viewing. Also, three times per week for theatrical performances (telephone for details). Performances £30, house admission: Sun. £7, Mon. £10.
U: Liverpool St.

American Dennis Severs was one of the first enthusiasts to buy a house in the historic area of Spitalfields and save it from destruction. In line with many of the people in the street, he authentically restored the house to its state 200 years ago. A tour of the house takes you through two centuries of east London life. Telephone first to book.

The Dome
GREENWICH, SE19
0870 606 2000, WWW.DOME2000.CO.UK
Open daily 9am (gates open), entrance to the dome 10am-6pm. Adults £20, ages 5-15 £16.50, under 5 free, family of five £57, concessions £16.50-£18.
U: North Greenwich. City cruises run from Waterloo & Blackfriars, White Horse Fast Ferries run from Greenwich to Millennium Pier.

The Dome, subject of huge and fierce public debate and costing £758 million which many say should have been spent on health, education, transport and other major aspects of life, is a massive venture in a run-down part of Greenwich. The structure is space age—a huge tent suspended from poles. That is the most impressive part of the attraction. Inside, fourteen zones encircle a central performance area where 200 live performers and stunning visual effects created by Mark Fisher and Peter Gabriel entertain the audience several times a day. The fourteen themed zones celebrate British ideas and technology and are designed to make you ponder the twenty-first century. They cover themes like how we work, rest and play, how our bodies and minds work and our beliefs and faiths. Skyscape, which is beside the Dome, is a futuristic entertainment venue with two huge cinemas/live performance venues. There are many cafés and restaurants and shops on the site. The exhibition in the Dome is projected to last only through 2000; what happens after that is currently under debate.

Eltham Palace
COURT RD, ELTHAM, SE9
020-8294 2548, WWW.ENGLISH-HERITAGE.ORG.UK
Open Apr.-Sept. Wed.-Fri. & Sun. 10am-6pm; winter months 10am-4pm. Adults £5.50, children £2.75, concessions £4.10. Ground only: adults £3.30, children £1.65, concessions £2.50.
Rail: Eltham Station.

The interiors of this wonderful example of 1930s style and glamour were recreated from photographs and archive material by English Heritage and reopened in mid-1999. The Art Deco house, adjoining the medieval Great

Hall of the original Eltham Palace (the boyhood home of Henry VIII), is dramatic and evokes the sophisticated and glamorous lifestyle of millionaire Stephen Courtauld and his wife Virginia, one of the great society couples of the 1930s.

Fawcett Library
LONDON GUILDHALL UNIVERSITY
OLD CASTLE ST, E1, 020-7320 1189
Open (term time) Mon. 10.15am-8.30pm, Wed. 9am-8.30pm, Thurs.-Fri. 9am-5pm. Holidays closed at 5pm. Annual membership £30, one-time visits £3.
U: Aldgate East.

Britain's main reference collection on women is the direct descendant of the London Society for Women's Suffrage, founded in 1867. It holds over 50,000 books, pamphlets and leaflets, periodicals, boxes of papers on relevant organisations, newspaper cuttings and photographs, autographed letters and posters. The library is part of the university, but non-members can use it on a daily basis for a small fee. Dedicated feminists, as well as those with a general interest in the women's movement, will find it invaluable. From autumn, 2000, the library—renamed the National Library of Women—will be housed in a huge new building which will also hold exhibitions.

Fulham Palace
BISHOP'S AVE
OFF FULHAM PALACE RD, SW6, 020-7736 3233
Open (museum) Mar.-Oct.: Wed.-Sun. 2-5pm; Nov.-Feb.: Thurs.-Sun. 1pm-4pm. Adults 50p, tours £2, under 16 free.
U: Putney Bridge.

The official residence of the Bishops of London until 1973, the present brick house dates from the beginning of the sixteenth century. Much rebuilt in various styles and at various dates, visitors may see the interior, the Victorian chapel and the museum. Tours are good, held twice a month in summer and once a month in winter; telephone for details.

Fuller's Brewery
GRIFFIN BREWERY, CHISWICK LANE SOUTH, W4
020-8996 2063, WWW.FULLERS.DEMON.CO.UK
Tours Mon. & Wed.-Fri., 11am, noon, 1pm, 2pm. Adults £5, under 14 £3.50.
U: Stamford Brook.

London's oldest brewery shows off its history in 90-minute tours. Watch the art of brewing, then sample some of the results. You must book in advance.

Golden Hinde

ST MARY OVERIE DOCK, CATHEDRAL ST, SE1
020-7403 0123
Open daily 10am-6pm (but telephone to check on weekends when it can be closed for private parties). Adults £2.50, children £1.75, concessions £2.10.
U: London Bridge/Monument.

This is a perfectly reconstructed vessel, done with painstaking detail to illustrate exactly what Sir Francis Drake's sixteenth-century flagship was like. There are actors in Elizabethan costume to tell you stories of the bad old days. Great for children.

Guildhall

GUILDHALL YARD, GRESHAM ST, EC2
020-7606 3030, WWW.CITYOFLONDON.GOV.UK
Open daily 10am-5pm. Admission free.
U: Bank/St. Paul's.

The seat of the City of London's municipal government since 1192, the Guildhall is a beautiful old building, though very little of the original remains. The Great Hall, largely destroyed in 1666 and during the Blitz has been wonderfully restored and is the scene of the Lord Mayor's annual banquet and other important occasions. There is also the new Guildhall Art Gallery, with about 250 works on display drawn from the City's collection (1660-present) of about 4,000 paintings, drawings and sculptures.

HMS Belfast

MORGAN'S LANE, TOOLEY ST, SE1
020-7940 6300, WWW.HMSBELFAST.ORG.UK
Open Mar.-Oct. daily 10am-6pm; Nov.-Feb. daily 10am-5pm. Adults £4.70, under 15 free.
U: London Bridge.

The cruiser HMS Belfast, the Royal Navy's last big-gun ship, became a museum in 1971. During World War II, this floating city with 800 men on board had the unenviable task of guarding Russian convoys and in 1943 helped sink the greatest single danger to the Russian lifeline, the German battle cruiser *Scharnhorst*. Part of the ship has been left as it was; the rest relates to the history of the Royal Navy. In these days of nuclear weapons, the whole ship has a strange, outdated feel; was war really like this?

Houses of Parliament

PARLIAMENT SQ, SW1
020-7219 4272, WWW.PARLIAMENT.UK
See text for free admission times.
U: Westminster.

More correctly the Palace of Westminster, this splendid, flamboyant and rather pompous-looking building was designed by Sir Charles Barry and built from 1837-1858 when the Clock Tower housing Big Ben was finished. The site is ancient, bound up with British history from the start, as the first Palace was built for Edward the Confessor before 1066. There is a very good exterior view from the river and from Westminster or Lambeth Bridges. To go inside, you either have to make arrangements through your MP, or, as a visitor, turn up when the House is sitting after 2.30pm (Mon. to Thurs.). Once inside, queue to get into the Stranger's Gallery, which looks over the Chamber of the Commons and seats 100 to 150 people. Friday is Private Members' Bill day. Get there early, but check first: no bills mean the House doesn't sit.

Jewel Tower

ABINGDON ST, SW1
020-7222 2219, WWW.ENGLISH-HERITAGE.ORG.UK
Open Apr.-Sept. daily 10am-6pm; Oct.-Mar. daily 10am-4pm. Adults £1.50, children 80p. concessions £1.10
U: Westminster.

Built in 1365 from Kentish ragstone on three storeys and surrounded by a moat, it was used to keep the King's valuables such as his jewels, clothes, furs and gold vessels. In 1621-1864 it housed Parliamentary records, and now has an exhibition and video on Parliament past and present.

Lauderdale House

HIGHGATE HILL, WATERLOW PARK, N6
020-8348 8716/8341 2032
Open Tues.-Fri. 11am-4pm, Sun. noon-5pm. Admission free.
U: Archway.

An excellent local community arts centre with concerts, antique fairs, workshops, exhibitions and more, Lauderdale House was built in 1580 in pretty Waterlow Park. Good small café.

Looking for an address?
Refer to the index.

London Aquarium

COUNTY HALL, RIVERSIDE BUILDING
WESTMINSTER BRIDGE RD, SE1, 020-7967 8000
*Open daily 10am-6pm, last admission 5pm.
Adults £8, children £5, familes £22, under 3
free. concessions £6.50.
U: Waterloo.*

This is a huge aquarium beside the Thames
in the former County Hall Building, showing
an international variety of fish and sea life.
Sharks are a great attraction, as is the pool
where visitors can touch some of the fish.
There is a good shop.

London Balloon

SPRING GARDENS, 4 AUCKLAND ST, SE11
0345-023 842
*Open daily 10am-5pm or dusk. Evening flights
for pre-booked groups. Adults £12, under 12
£7.50, under 2 free, families £35.
U: Vauxhall.*

Look at London below you from a tethered
balloon up 400 feet. Spectacular views give
you an idea of how vast the metropolis is. The
balloon carries up to 30 people and the ride
takes 15 minutes. If it's winter, or very bad
weather, check first.

London Dungeon

28-34 TOOLEY ST, SE1, 020-7403 7221
*Open daily 10.30am-5pm, last admission one
hour before closing. Adults £9.50, children £6.50.
U: London Bridge.*

The sort of ghoulish place children love and
parents shudder at, full of the more blood-
thirsty parts of British history and naturally
accompanied by shrieks and groans. Even the
entrance is fun: you enter a dark and different
world, lit by candles. Their most popular
exhibit? The *Jack the Ripper Experience*, they
cheerfully tell you.

London Planetarium

MARYLEBONE RD, NW1
020-7935 6861, WWW.MADAME-TUSSAUDS.CO.UK
*Open June-Aug. daily 10am-5pm; Sept.-May
Mon.-Fri. noon-5pm, Sat.-Sun. 10am-5pm.
Adults £6.30, under 16 £4.20, concessions
£4.85. Combined ticket with Madame
Tussaud's: adults £12.95, under 16 £8.50,
concessions £9.80.
U: Baker St.*

Part of Madame Tussaud's, here the galaxies
are explored in the space show, Planetary

Quest, which projects the story of the heavens
onto a huge dome every 40 minutes.

London Zoo

REGENT'S PARK, NW1
020-7722 3333, WWW.WEBOFLIFE.CO.UK
*Open Mar.-Oct. daily 10am-5.30pm; Nov.-Feb.
daily 10am-4pm. Adults £9, children £7, under
3 free.
U: Baker St/Camden Town.*

Though relatively small, the zoo in Regent's
Park is a delightful family destination, with a
good children's zoo, an emphasis on conservation, a penguin pool, large animals and more.
The new *Web of Life* exhibition is a fascinating
look at the Earth's biological interactions. The
architectural delights include *Lubetkin and
Tecton's Penguin Pool* (1936), *Lord Snowdon's
big Aviary* (1963) and *Sir Hugh Casson's
Elephant House* (1965).

Lord's Cricket Ground Tours & Museum

ST. JOHN'S WOOD, NW8, 020-7289 1611
TOURS: 020-7432 1033/7266 3825
WWW.LORDS.ORG
*Open daily in winter for tours (which include a
visit to the museum) noon and 2pm, except for
match days during the season (late Apr.-Sept.).
In summer 10am, noon and 2pm. Book in
advance. Adults £5.80, children £4.20.
U: St. John's Wood.*

A visit to the Cricket Museum will not give
you a huge insight into the rules and conven-
tions of a game that many find distressingly
obscure, but it will provide you with a bit of
amusement (if such a thing can be allowed
with such a revered pastime). It was not, it
turns out, such a gentleman's game: the first
rules state the width of the bat as early cads
were making bats wider than the wicket
behind them. There are paintings and objects,
a talking head of WG Grace and eccentric
objects like the stuffed sparrow killed by a
cricket ball in play. And you do see the famous
and very beautiful rooms and grounds.
Telephone ahead for details and booking.

Telephone numbers in England have
eleven digits, beginning with a zero. The
initial zero must be omitted if you are
calling England from abroad. Within the
country, dial the entire eleven digits.

Madame Tussaud's Waxworks

MARYLEBONE RD, NW1
020-7935 6861, WWW.MADAME-TUSSAUDS.CO.UK
Open Mon.-Fri. 10am-5.30pm, Sat.-Sun.
9.30am-5.30pm. Adults £10.50, children £7,
under 5 free, concessions £8. Combined ticket
with London Planetarium: adults £12.95,
under 16 £8.50, concessions £9.80.
U: Baker St.

One of London's greatest tourist attractions, Madame Tussaud's began as a museum in 1835 when the redoubtable lady stopped touring England with her waxworks—originally death masks of many of the best-known victims of the French Revolution—and made a permanent exhibition. The scope is endless and international: from King Henry VIII to Nelson Mandela and is continually being expanded. In the *Garden Party* section, you mingle with lifelike models of celebrities. Man's gruesome side is displayed with a grim catalogue of torture and punishment in the ever-popular *Chamber of Horrors;* a high-tech replica London taxi cab journey takes you through London's history in *The Spirit of London.* Try to avoid Madame Tussaud's at peak times like school holidays.

Monument

MONUMENT ST, EC2, 020-7626 2717
Open Mon.-Fri. 10am-5.40pm, Sat.-Sun. 2pm-
5.40pm. Adults £1, children 50p.
U: Monument.

Built by Sir Christopher Wren to commemorate the Great Fire of London in 1666, it stands 202 feet, the distance from the start of the conflagration in a baker's shop in Pudding Lane.

Old Bailey

NEWGATE ST & OLD BAILEY, EC4, 020-7248 3277
Open Mon.-Fri. 10.30am-1pm & 2pm-4.30pm.
Admission free (ages 14-16 accompanied only,
no under 14 allowed).
U: St. Paul's.

The Central Criminal Court (or Old Bailey as it is more familiarly known) is Britain's major court dealing with notorious cases over the centuries from Oscar Wilde in 1895 to the more recent Peter Sutcliffe, the 'Yorkshire Ripper,' in 1981. It was built on the site of Newgate Prison and opened in 1907 by King Edward VII.

Royal Courts of Justice

STRAND, WC2, 020-7936 6000
Open Mon.-Fri. 9.30am-4.30pm. Closed Aug.
& Sept. Admission free.
U: Temple.

The nineteenth-century Law Courts were built to try all civil cases. This huge building has more than 1,000 rooms and more than three miles of corridors. You can tell when a controversial case is being heard; the media camp outside the building in the Strand. The public is admitted to any of the 88 working courts.

Royal Horticultural Society Halls

GREYCOAT ST VINCENT SQ, SW1
020-7834 4333, WWW.RHS.ORG.UK
U: Pimlico.

The Royal Horticultural Society has its main gardens at Wisley, Surrey (01483 224234), but here at their magnificent central London halls, they hold monthly flower weekend specialist and seasonal flower shows.

Royal Mews

BUCKINGHAM PALACE RD, SW1
020-7799 2331 (RECORDED INFO)
Open Aug.-Sept. Mon.-Thurs. 10.30am-4.30pm,
last admission 3.30pm; Oct.-July Tues.-Thurs.
noon-4pm. Adults £4.30, children £2.10.
U: St. James's Park/Victoria.

This collection of royal vehicles is housed in the old stables and coach houses of Buckingham Palace. It was built by John Nash in 1825. Of major interest is the 1761 gold state coach of George III, which weighs a massive four tons and is pulled at walking pace by eight horses. Don't miss the glass coach used for royal weddings or the splendid royal cars. The harnesses are among the finest in the world and some of the magnificent heavy horses are stabled here. Closed during Royal Ascot Week in June.

St. Paul's Cathedral

ST. PAUL'S CHURCHYARD, EC4, 020-7236 4128
WWW.STPAULS.LONDON.ANGLICAN.ORG
Open Mon.-Sat. 9am-5pm, Sun. 11am-5pm.
Cathedral, crypt & galleries: adults £7.50, chil-
dren £3.50. Cathedral & crypt only: adults £4,
children £2.
U: St. Paul's.

Apparently on the site of a Roman temple dedicated to the goddess Diana, the present cathedral was designed by Sir Christopher Wren after the Great Fire of London in 1666. Taking 35 years to build, Wren went every week to superintend the work. Toward the end, he was hoisted up to the lantern in a basket and appropriately was one of the first of many distinguished people to be buried in the crypt. You can climb the 627 steps into the dome for a fabulous, if windy, view of London, via the Whispering, Stone and Golden Galleries.

Shakespeare's Globe Exhibition

NEW GLOBE WALK, BANKSIDE, SE1
020-7401 9919, WWW.SHAKESPEARES-GLOBE.ORG
Open daily May-Sept. 9am-noon, Oct.-Apr. 10am-5pm. Adults £7.50, under 16 £5.
U: London Bridge.

Shakespeare's Globe Theatre on the old Bankside site is a reconstruction of Shakespeare's original wooden 'O'. Elizabethan-style, the thatched roof only partially covers the audience; the main auditorium is open to the elements, though the stage is also covered. It's a glorious experience to sit in this remarkably small space and the audience tends to react as an Elizabethan one, hissing or cheering according to whether villain or hero is on stage. Beneath the theatre itself, there's a separate huge and very effective exhibition on Shakespeare's influence—from Elizabethan times to today. It is well worth visiting for its insights into the playwright and Tudor London. It shows how the costumes were made and how the plays were printed; has the recorded voices of great Shakespearean actors from Herbert Beerbohm Tree, to Richard Burton, to Dame Judi Dench. Good restaurant, café (see *Quick Bites*), and shop.

Skyline Millennium Balloon

TOOLEY ST, CORNER OF TOWER BRIDGE RD, SE1
020-7378 8252, WWW.SKYLINEBALLOONS.COM
Open daily 9am-10pm, last flight 9.45pm. Adults £10, children £7.50, under 3 free, families £31.50.
U: London Bridge/Tower Hill.

A tethered balloon giving wonderful views of the city and Millennium Dome from 400 feet. They are 15-minute flights and are subject to weather.

Southwark Cathedral

MONTAGUE CLOSE, SE1
020-7407 3708, WWW.DSWARK.ORG.UK
Open daily 9am-6pm. Closing times depend on religious holidays. Admission free.
U: London Bridge.

This delightful church (which became a cathedral in 1905) was originally the monastic church of St. Mary Overie. It was heavily restored during Victorian times, though much of the old buildings remain intact. John Harvard, benefactor of Harvard University, was born in Southwark in 1607 and baptised here. In this rapidly changing area of Southwark, there are new facilities including a visitor centre and refectory.

Thames Barrier Visitors Centre

UNITY WAY, SE19, 020-8854 1373
WWW.ENVIRONMENTAGENCY.GOV.UK
Open Mon.-Fri. 10am-5pm, last admission 4pm, Sat.-Sun. 10.30am-5.30pm, last admission 4.30pm. Adults £3.40, children £2, families £7.50, concessions £2.
Rail: Charlton, Riverboat from Westminster to Thames Barrier Pier (not Nov.-Mar.), & from Greenwich (not Dec.-Jan.).

This is a great piece of engineering running across the Thames to be used if ever the river threatens to rise and flood the rest of London. The Visitor Centre shows you how it all works, and occasionally you can see the Barrier being put into position.

Tower Bridge Experience

TOWER BRIDGE, SE1, 020-7378 1928
Open Apr.-Oct. daily 10am-6.30pm, last admission 5.15pm; Nov.-Mar. daily 9.30am-6pm, last admission 4.45pm. Adults £6.15, children £4.15, under 5 free, concessions £4.15.
U: Tower Hill.

Tower Bridge (1886-94) was one of London's wonders with its ability to open 135-feet-high for ships to steam through. The museum has been rebuilt and has all sorts of animatronic characters and special effects, which recreate the past. It's also a good place to go for the spectacular views and, cleverly, there are pictures of the same views through the ages, showing just how much London has changed. The Bridge is not only for show; it is still opened to allow tall ships to pass.

Tower of London
TOWER HILL, EC3
020-7709 0765, WWW.HRP.ORG.UK
Open Mon.-Sat. 9am-5pm, Sun. 10am-5pm.
Adults £11, children £7.30, families £33.
U: Tower Hill.

The finest medieval fortress in Britain, the Tower was begun by William 1 after 1066 to keep his subjects subdued, and added to through the ages. It's been a palace, prison and place of execution; it housed the Royal Armouries, the Mint, the Royal Observatory, the Royal Zoo, the Public Records and still houses the Crown Jewels—one of the major attractions of the Tower. Yeomen Warders, the 'Beefeaters' who live in the casements, will regale you with stories of blood-thirsty happenings in the small towers that dot the walls. They are ripping good yarns and great fun.

Vinopolis—City of Wine
1 BANK END, SE1
0870-4444 777, WWW.EVINOPOLIS.COM
Open daily 10am-5.30pm. Tickets £11.50.
U: London Bridge.

A theme park for adults. It's a tour through the world's great wine-making countries on The Wine Odyssey, the opportunity to look up any and every aspect of the subject on a vast computerised encyclopedia and the chance to taste five wines. Vinopolis is, in fact, a strange place, housed in splendid former railway arches and with the aim of assuring us that London is the centre of the wine-buying world. There are restaurants, including Cantina Vinopolis (see Restaurants), a wine bar, a top wine accessories shop which also has cheese, bread and coffee and a wine shop run by Majestic, which delivers your purchases anywhere in Britain for free.

Wembley Stadium Tours
WEMBLEY STADIUM, MIDDLESEX
020-8902 8833, WWW.WEMBLEYSTADIUM.COM
Open daily: 10am-4pm, except event days;
telephone first to check. Adults £7.45, children
£5.25, families £22.50.
U: Wembley Park.

Take a behind-the-scenes tour to see the pitch, the players' changing rooms, and the most impressive control room. Also the Royal Box where the FA cup is presented. Tours last around 45 minutes and take place continuously. The Stadium closes in September, 2000 for a massive rebuilding programme.

Westminster Abbey
BROAD SANCTUARY, SW1, 020-7222 5152
WWW.WESTMINSTER-ABBEY.ORG
Open Mon.-Fri. 9.20am-3.45pm, Sat. 9am-1.45pm & 3.45pm-5pm, Sun. services only.
Main body of the nave free, Royal chapels, nave, cloisters: adults £5, children £2, Abbey Museum, Pyx Chamber and Chapter House extra £1.
U: Westminster.

Probably best known for its spectacular Royal marriages, coronations and funerals, Westminster Abbey has served for hundreds of years as the focal point of Westminster. It is full of treasures. The Royal chapels are magnificent, the Henry VII chapel awe-inspiring with its fabulous roof and colourful banners. The scope runs from tombs and memorials of the famous and highborn to the infamous and plain odd (like Jonas Hanway, founder of the Marine Society, known for being the first man in London to carry an umbrella). The architectural details like the tiled floor of the Chapter House and the quiet oasis of the cloisters are impressive as well.

Westminster Cathedral
FRANCIS ST, SW1, 020-7798 9055
WWW.WESTMINSTERCATHEDRAL.ORG.UK
Open Sun.-Fri. 7am-7pm, Sat. 8am-7pm.
Admission free.
U: Victoria.

This Roman Catholic cathedral is a magnificent piece of Victorian Byzantine architecture, full of mosaics and ornamented with more than 100 different kinds of marble from all over the world. The tombs and memorials are no less interesting; don't miss Eric Gill's sculptures of the Stations of the Cross created during World War I. The view from the tower (when open—-March-Nov. daily 9am-5pm; Dec.-Feb. Thurs.-Sun. 9am-5pm) is wonderful. If you have the chance, attend a concert here.

Winston Churchill's Britain at War Experience
64-65 TOOLEY ST, SE1
020-7403 3171, WWW.BRITAIN-AT-WAR.CO.UK
Open Apr.-Sept. daily 10am-5.30pm, 5.30 last admission; Oct.-Mar. daily 10am-4.30pm, 4.30 last admission. Adults £5.95, children £2.95, families £14, concessions £3.95.
U: London Bridge.

Make your way through civilian London life in World War II from air raids to rationing.

There are plenty of items to look at and it's an atmospheric place. Good shop.

Young's Brewery Visitor Centre

THE RAM BREWERY, WANDSWORTH HIGH ST, SW19
020-8875 7000, WWW.YOUNGS.CO.UK.
Open for tours Tues.-Thurs. 10am, noon, 2pm,
Sat. noon, 2pm. Shop & bar Mon.-Fri. 11am-
5pm, Sat. noon-5pm. Adults £5.50, children £3.50.
Rail: Wandsworth Town.

Young's was one of the last breweries to deliver its beer by horse-drawn drays, and its splendid teams of Suffolk Punches, black and white Shires, dappled grey Percherons and Clydesdales still appear at horse shows around the country.

CHURCHES

One of the great pleasures of wandering around London lies in visiting the different churches, particularly in the City of London. The Great Fire of 1666 destroyed 87 churches within the old City walls. The great architect, Sir Christopher Wren, was responsible for rebuilding some 51 of them. World War II destroyed 11 of them; an IRA bomb in 1993 did huge damage to St Ethelburgh's in Bishopsgate, which is being restored. Many of them hold lunchtime concerts that are well worth attending.

All Hallows

BY THE TOWER, BYWARD ST, EC3, 020-7481 2928
Open Mon.-Fri. 9am-5.45pm, Sat.-Sun. 10am-
5pm.
U: Tower Hill.

Largely bombed during World War II, but rebuilt, it contains some old remains and a delightful collection of model ships. Samuel Pepys watched the Great Fire from the tower; William Penn was baptised here and John Quincy Adams married here.

St. Bartholomew-the-Great

WEST SMITHFIELD, EC1, 020-7606 5171
Open Mon.-Fri. 8.30am-4pm, Sat. 10.30am-
1.30pm, Sun. 2pm-5pm.
U: Farringdon.

London's oldest church, you get to it through a Tudor gateway, which along with the church managed to survive the Great Fire.

It's a delightful place, founded in 1123 by Rahere, Henry I's court jester, after a vision. He then became the first prior. The painter William Hogarth was baptised here; Benjamin Franklin worked as a printer in the chapel.

St. Bride's

FLEET ST, EC4, 020-7353 1301
Open Mon.-Tues. & Thurs.-Fri. 8am-4.45pm,
Wed. 8am-6pm, Sat. 9am-4.30pm, Sun. 11am-
6.30pm.
U: Blackfriars.

Known affectionately as the wedding cake church because of its ornate steeple, it was finished by Wren in 1703 in Italian style. Once the printers' and journalists' church, before the industry deserted Fleet Street, St. Bride's was the site where Wynken de Worde set up London's first printing press in. There are interesting Roman and Saxon remains on display in the crypt.

St. Helen Bishopsgate

GREAT ST. HELEN'S, EC3, 020-7283 2231
Open Mon.-Fri. 9am-5pm, Sun. for church services.
U: Bank/Liverpool St.

Originally founded in the thirteenth century, but badly bombed by the IRA in 1992, it was a double-naved church. It contains wonderful medieval and Tudor monuments to City dignitaries.

St. Mary Abchurch

ABCHURCH YARD, ABCHURCH LANE, EC4
020-7626 0306
Open Mon.-Thurs. 10.30am-2.30pm, Fri.
10.30am-noon.
U: Bank/Cannon St.

Rebuilt by Wren, 1681-6, it has a beautiful interior, complete with a splendid dome and seventeenth-century woodwork. The reredos was carved by the incomparable Grinling Gibbons.

St. Mary-le-Bow

CHEAPSIDE, EC2, 020-7248 5139
Open Mon.-Thurs. 7am-6pm, Fri. 7am-4pm.
U: Bank/St. Paul's.

One of Wren's masterpieces, built in the early 1670s, the interior was rebuilt after bombing during World War II. There is a tradition that only those born within the sound of the ringing of 'Bow bells' can claim to be true cockneys. In the crypt there is a good vegetarian restaurant, The Place Below (see *Quick Bites*).

St. Mary Woolnoth
LOMBARD ST, EC2, 020-7626 9701
Open Mon.-Fri. 8.30am-4.30pm.
U: Bank.

Originally a Saxon church, what you mainly see today is a beautiful interior by Nicholas Hawksmoor (1716-17), based on the Egyptian Hall of Vitruvius. It is also the only church with a tube station in its crypt.

St. Stephen Walbrook
39 WALBROOK, EC4, 020-7283 4444
Open Mon.-Thurs. 10am-4pm, Fri. 10am-3pm.
U: Bank/Mansion House/Monument.

If you only get to see one Wren church, try to make it this one, which is generally held to be his masterpiece. Many of the architectural features were later incorporated into his grand design for St. Paul's Cathedral. The Henry Moore central altar is startling. Dr. Chad Varah founded the Samaritans here in 1953, an organisation which is hugely effective in counseling the suicidal and despairing.

HOBBIES & SPORTS

ART COURSES

London's local authorities run large numbers of courses on every subject under the sun. *Floodlight*, from any bookstore, is a useful booklet published annually and lists all courses with full details from butterfly spotting to macramé. For private courses, try Sotheby's and Christie's. They both run a variety of courses, some lasting a year and leading to an academic qualification, others lasting anywhere from a day to a month and aimed at the person with a general interest in the subject. *Time to Learn*, published by the National Institute of Adult Continuing Education, 21 De Montfort St, Leicester LE1 7GE, 0116 2044200, gives details of learning holidays throughout Britain. Send a cheque or a postal order for £4.95 for details.

Christie's Education
63 OLD BROMPTON RD, SW7
020-7581 3933, FAX 020-7589 0383
U: South Kensington.

Evening courses cover fine and decorative arts and music (there's a very good opera course, for instance), plus a professional course.

The New Study Centre
21 PALACE GARDENS TERRACE, W8
020-7229 3393, FAX 020-7229 4220

Previously the Study Centre for the History of the Fine and Decorative Arts, this well-established school offers a variety of courses and lectures covering all interests and expertise. Ranging from arts and crafts traditions from the sixteenth century to the Post-Modern era, most lectures are at the Royal Entomological Society, 41 Queen's Gate, SW7, U: South Kensington.

Sotheby's Institute
30 OXFORD ST, W1
020-7323 5775, FAX 020-7580 8160
U: Tottenham Court Rd.

Apart from offering master degrees in fine and decorative arts, the Institute runs a large number of excellent specialised courses throughout the year. There are also evening study courses, day and weekend courses in fine arts, ceramics, furniture and wine (see below).

Art Supplies

Brodie & Middleton
68 DRURY LANE, WC2
020-7836 3289, FAX 020-7497 8425
Open Mon.-Fri. 8.30am-5pm.
U: Covent Garden.

In the heart of London's theatre world, a major shop for stage design and theatrical make-up since 1840. Brodie and Middleton sell everything for thespians from stage dyes and blood capsules to special brushes and paints for theatre sets.

Falkiner Fine Papers
76 SOUTHAMPTON ROW, WC1
020-7831 1151, FAX 020-7430 1248
Open Mon.-Sat. 9.30am-5.30pm.
U: Holborn.

Falkiner stocks a wide range of good and rare international handmade papers for watercolours, drawings and printmaking such as kozo (Oriental mulberry paper), vellum, parchment and beautiful hand-marbled papers in both large and small quantities.

Green & Stone

259 KING'S RD, SW3
020-7352 0837, FAX 020-7351 1098
Open Mon.-Sat. 9am-6pm, Wed. 9.30am-7pm, Sun. noon-5pm.
U: Sloane Sq.

Near the Chelsea College of Art, Green & Stone sell almost everything for the artist. This is also the place to go if you want gilding materials such as real or fake gold, glazes for special effects and varnishes that will give a surface the aged or cracked look of an instant antique. And at the back there are a number of antiques, particularly glasses, for sale as well.

L Cornelissen & Son

105 GT. RUSSELL ST, WC1
020-7636 1045, FAX 020-7636 3655
Open Mon.-Fri. 9.30am-5.30pm, Sat. 9.30am-5pm.
U: Tottenham Court Rd.

We love the old-fashioned wooden chests of drawers and displays in this 'Artists' Colourmen' specialists, established in 1855. You'll find unusual items like lapis lazuli paints, and an extensive range of the best brushes, painting knives, glues and pastels, gilding materials and papers.

London Graphics Centre

16-18 SHELTON ST, WC2
020-7240 0095, WWW.LONDONGRAPHICS.CO.UK
Open Mon.-Fri. 9.30am-6pm, Sat. 10.30am-6pm.
U: Covent Garden.

This is a large store with helpful staff stocking specialist materials for both fine art and graphics. Branches throughout London.

Rowney

12 PERCY ST, W1
020-7636 8241, FAX 020-7580 7534
Open Mon.-Fri. 9am-5.30pm, Sat. 10am-5pm.
U: Tottenham Court Rd.

Established in 1789 as a perfumery selling paints and pigments for cosmetics, Rowney's is now the largest UK manufacturer of artists' paints. Their shop contains the widest possible range of colours.

Russell & Chapple

68 DRURY LANE
(UNDER BRODIE & MIDDLETON), WC2
020-7836 7521
Open Mon.-Fri. 8.30am-5pm, Sat. 10am-5pm.
U: Covent Garden.

Everyone goes here for canvases, both prime and unprimed, and wooden stretcher pieces. They also stock a wide range of materials used by theatres and loft-dwellers eager to keep up with the latest fashions in velour, jutes, muslins and hessian. This shop is much smaller than their former one, so much of what you see here is samples only, and they then order what you need from the warehouse.

T N Lawrence & Son

117-119 CLERKENWELL RD, EC1
020-7242 3534, FAX 020-7430 2234
Open Mon.-Fri. 9am-5pm, Sat. 10am-4pm.
U: Farringdon.

Founded in 1859 in Bleeding Heart Yard, this shop has moved and expanded. Apart from being the major place for wood-engraving materials, they also specialise in tools for all kinds of engraving, You'll find 'Golden' acrylics from the U.S., materials for etching and ranges of paints and paper for bookbinders. In fact if it's paper you're after, Lawrence is world-famous for their wide range of rare supplies.

Tiranti

27 WARREN ST, W1, TEL & FAX: 020-7636 8565
Open Mon.-Fri. 9am-5.30pm, Sat. 9.30am-1pm.
U: Warren St.

Tiranti's has been supplying materials for sculptors for more than100 years. But added to the mallets and chisels for stone sculpting and clays for modelling in the past, they now also supply dental plaster (apparently good for modelling), silicon rubber resins and more for the contemporary artists.

Winsor & Newton

51 & 52 RATHBONE PL, W1, 020-7636 4231.
Open Mon.-Fri. 9.30am-5.30pm, Sat. 9.30am-5pm.
U: Tottenham Court Rd.

In business for 150 years, they produce a very wide range of paper and paint and are particularly useful for supplying oil paints in unusually small sizes.

BICYCLING

Bicycling in London, as in any city, can be hazardous and should be undertaken with caution. The following shops carry a wide range of accessories including protective helmets, which you should wear. You will have to leave a deposit, which is returned when the bike is safely back.

Bikefix

48 LAMB'S CONDUIT ST, WC1
020-7405 1218, WWW.BIKEFIX@DIRCON.CO.UK
Open Mon.-Fri. 8.30am-7pm, Sat. 10am-5pm.
U: Holborn.
Bikefix rents several different kinds of bicycles, plus all accessories.

Country Lanes

01425 655022, WWW.COUNTRYLANES.CO.UK
Top bicycle touring specialist runs day trips by rail from London to the New Forest and Cotswolds. Hire, tea and good routes. From £25.

London Bicycle Tour Company

1A GABRIEL'S WHARF, 56 UPPER GROUND, SE1
020-7928 6838. WWW.LONDONBICYCLE.COM
Open Easter-Oct daily 10am-6pm, Nov-Easter by appointment.
U: Waterloo.
Bicycle hire and routes. Plus rent of rollerblades and bicycle rickshaws.

On Your Bike

52-54 TOOLEY ST, SE1, 020-7357 6958
Open Mon.-Fri. 9am-6pm, Sat. 9.30am-5.30pm, Sun. 11am-4pm.
U: London Bridge.
Major stockers of mountain, touring and racing bikes, they rent by the day, week, month or longer.

BRASS RUBBING

This peculiarly English hobby has many devotees. You'll find a lot of them carefully rubbing the impressions of knights and ladies, dogs and coats-of-arms at the two main brass rubbing centres.

London Brass Rubbing Centre

ST. MARTIN-IN-THE-FIELDS CHURCH
TRAFALGAR SQ, WC2, 020-7930 9306
Open Mon.-Sat. 10am-6pm, Sun. noon-6pm.
U: Charing Cross/Leicester Sq.

Westminster Abbey Brass Rubbing Centre

NORTH CLOISTER, WESTMINSTER ABBEY, SW1
020-7222 4589
Open Mon.-Sat. 9.30am-5pm.
U: Westminster.

COOKING

Books for Cooks

4 BLENHEIM CRESCENT, W11, 020-7221 1992
Open Mon.-Sat. 9.30am-6pm.
U: Ladbroke Grove.
Wide range of cookery classes.

Butlers Wharf Chef School

CARDAMOM BUILDING, 31 SHAD THAMES, SE1
020-7357 8842, FAX 020-7403 2638
WWW.CONRAN.COM
U: London Bridge/Tower Hill.
Part of the Conran empire, there are both beginners and advanced courses, though the school concentrates on the professional. Many of the trainees go on to work in Conran's restaurants.

Le Cordon Bleu

14 MARYLEBONE LANE, W1
020-7935 3503, FAX 020-7935 7621
U: Baker St/Bond St.
Attracting professionals and amateurs, Le Cordon Bleu offers a wide range of specialised short courses, demonstrations and daytime courses in classic cuisine, guest-chef lecturers, tastings and advanced patisserie training. It issues certificates and diplomas on the professional courses. Facilities are excellent and the school offers restaurant-like conditions for the aspiring chef.

Looking for an address?
Refer to the index.

Leith's School of Food & Wine

21 ST. ALBAN'S GROVE, W8 5BP, 020-7229 0177
FAX 020-7937 5257, WWW.LEITHS.COM
U: Gloucester Rd.

If you want to learn about restaurant management, wine or just how to plan a sophisticated dinner party menu in one easy Saturday morning lesson, this is the place to come. Leith's is top also for people who want to go into catering as a career. Course lengths vary; many offer professional qualifications recognised worldwide.

The Mosimann Academy

STUDIO 5, THE WILLIAM BLAKE HOUSE
THE LANTERNS, BRIDGE LANE, SW11 3AD
020-7326 8366, FAX 020-7326 8360
No underground or rail station nearby.

Seminars and demonstrations from chefs and teachers for both professional companies and corporations like British Airways and for the amateur wanting to know everything about creating the proper dinner party. This school is inspired and under the direction of top chef Anton Mosimann, who recently received a Royal Warrant from Prince Charles for his catering.

DANCE

Danceworks

16 BALDERTON ST, W1
020-7629 6183, FAX 020-7499 -9087
Open Mon.-Fri. 8am-10pm, Sat.Sun. 9am-6pm.
U: Bond St.

Danceworks offers more than 100 classes, including Russian classical ballet, contemporary, salsa and tap, all taught by experts. They also teach martial arts, hold aerobics classes, have various fitness studios and a rehearsal space. There's a Natureworks complementary therapy centre with a range of treatments including homeopathy.

Pineapple Covent Garden

7 LANGLEY ST, WC2
020-7836 4004, FAX 020-7836 0806
Open Mon.-Fri. 9am-9pm, Sat. 9am-6.30pm.
U: Covent Garden.

Seven studios offer 180 classes a week in every kind of dance from contemporary to jazz. They also have a hydra gym.

FITNESS & SPORTS CLUBS

There are a number of excellent health and fitness clubs in London. Although the most economical way to enjoy them is to take out a year's membership, many offer shorter memberships of one month, one week or just one day. In addition, many offer special days, which include use of the facilities and special offers on beauty treatments. All clubs try to be flexible. Make an appointment or speak to the membership secretary to see what you can arrange. Most also offer beauty treatments and it is not necessary to take out membership for those.

Academy Fitness Centre

16 HOXTON SQ, N1, 020-7729 5789
Open Mon.-Fri. 10am-10pm, Sat. 10am-4pm.
U: Old St.

Gyms and full range of aerobics, but their main specialty is martial arts.

Berkeley Health Club & Spa

BERKELEY HOTEL, WILTON PL, SW1
020-7235 6000, WWW.SAVOY-GROUP.CO.UK
Open Mon.-Fri. 9am-9pm, Sat.-Sun. 9am-7pm.
U: Knightsbridge.

This is one of London's great venues, a club on the seventh floor that has a swimming pool complete with retractable roof. On a sunny day, the terrace with its deck chairs, and the view over the greenery of Hyde Park is quite a sensation. The small gym shares the view, and more to the point is equipped with state-of-the-art fitness equipment. Treatment rooms below offer all kinds of therapies, including La Stone (using heated flat stones on oiled skins for deep massage). The Christian Dior Beauty rooms offer all the usual facials, cathiodermie, and aromatherapy in luxurious surroundings, and the staff are extremely relaxed and friendly.

Broadgate Club

1 EXCHANGE PL, EC2
020-7422 6400, WWW.BROADGATE-CLUB.CO.UK
Open Mon.-Thurs. 6.30am-10.20pm, Fri.
6.30am-10pm, Sat.-Sun. 10am-6pm.
U: Liverpool St.

Great City hangout where tense traders work it all off. Good six-lane swimming pool, fully equipped gym, squash courts, spa, sauna and steam rooms. There are many classes from karate to yoga. Top restaurant run by the Roux brothers.

Cannons Health Club & Spa

COUSIN LANE, EC4
020-7283 0101, WWW.CANNONSCLUBS.CO.UK
*Open Mon.-Fri. 6.30am-10.30pm, Sat.-Sun.
10am-7pm.*
U: Cannon St.

Great for those city folks in need of keeping fit, this large club was one of the first of the health clubs. Apart from the aerobics studio, cardio theatre and more, there's a women's running club, hairdressing salon and café.

Central YMCA

112 GREAT RUSSELL ST, WC1, 020-7343 1700
*Open Mon.-Fri. 7am-10.30pm, Sat.-Sun.
10am-9pm.*
U: Tottenham Court Rd.

Accessible to the general public and with top facilities, they offer a swimming pool, fitness classes, weight training, badminton, squash, basketball and gymnastics. Large range of classes in their two dance studios. You can join as a member or just turn up and take temporary membership for the day. Rates are low for central London.

Champneys
The London Club

LE MERIDIEN, 21 PICCADILLY, W1
020-7255 8000, FAX 020-7494 0876
Open Mon.-Fri. 7am-11pm, Sat.-Sun. 8am-9pm.
U: Piccadilly Circus.

A fabulous marble swimming pool, fully equipped gym, cardiovascular room, two dance studios and squash courts are some of the many facilities this luxurious club offers. They have a Health and Fitness Day and a Top-to-Toe day. The club's facilities are free to hotel guests.

The Club at County Hall

COUNTY HALL, SE1, 020-7928 4900
WWW.THECLUBATCOUNTYHALL.COM
Open daily 24 hours.
U: Waterloo.

The only 24-hour club in London, you're likely to find jet-setting stars along with night workers like chef Gordon Ramsay and concierges at the top hotels here. On two top floors, there are wonderful views of the Houses of Parliament. Facilities include a gym, swimming pool, steam rooms and more. Wide range of beauty and health treatments from Indian head massage to body wraps. Many weekly classes in the aerobics studio.

Crystal Palace National Sports Centre

NORWOOD, SE19, 020-8778 0131
*Open Mon.-Fri. 8am-10pm, Sat. 8am- 8pm,
Sun. 8am-6pm.*
Rail: Crystal Palace.

This huge and impressive complex is the premier sports centre in Britain. While it holds leading competitions on both the international and national circuit (frequently televised), it is also open to the public. Facilities are superb and include an Olympic-size pool, a diving pool, football pitches as well as six floodlit all-weather courts and ten squash courts.

The Dorchester Spa

THE DORCHESTER, PARK LANE, W1
020-7495 7335, WWW.DORCHESTERHOTEL.COM
Open daily 7am-9.30pm.
U: Hyde Park Corner.

The place to come to for pampering, the Art Deco Spa offers everything from eyelash tinting to assorted body wraps, massage, waxing and much more. There is also a fully equipped gym and work-out studio, solarium and whirlpool bath. The celebrity list is endless, from George Bush to Goldie Hawn. Hotel guests have free use of the club.

Earls Court Gym

254 EARLS COURT RD, SW5, 020-7370 1402
*Open Mon.-Fri. 6.30am-10pm, Sat. 10am-
10pm, Sun. 10am-6pm.*
U: Earls Court.

Great selection of programmes in the gym and studio from t'ai chi to yoga, circuits to aerobics. Not luxurious, but very welcoming.

Ellements Womens Health & Fitness

40 VAUXHALL BRIDGE RD, SW1, 020-7834 2289
Open Mon.-Fri. 7am-9pm, Sat.-Sun 9am-6pm.
U: Pimlico.

A big women-only health club with personalised sessions, classes from step to body conditioning and a beauty salon.

The Harbour Club

WATER MEADOW LANE, SW6, 020-7371 7700
FAX 020-7371 7770, WWW.HARBOURCLUB.COM
Open daily 6.30am-11.30pm.
U: Fulham Broadway.

This spectacular, exclusive club is impressive. Spread over four levels, the club, which opened in 1993, never feels crowded. There's a 25-metre ozone pool, crèche, ten indoor and four outdoor tennis courts, gym, saunas, steam rooms and health and beauty clinics. Membership is expensive, and you are likely to run into international celebrities like former English rugby captain Will Carling, Greg Rusedski and jockey Richard Dunwoody at this ultra-fashionable place.

Jubilee Hall Clubs
30 THE PIAZZA, WC2
020-7379 0008, FAX 020-7379 8503
Open Mon.-Fri. 7am-10pm, Sat., Sun. 10am-5pm.
U: Covent Garden.

In Covent Garden's former Flower Market, this popular club offers membership and is also open to nonmembers. Huge number of classes include contemporary jazz, cardio fitness and more. The gym is large and light and includes martial arts classes and a treatment centre. Prices are good and vary according to whether you want to include use of the gym or just go for the classes.

Jubilee Sports Centre
CAIRO ST, W10
020-8960 9629, FAX 020-8960 9661
Open Mon.-Fri. 7am-10pm, Sat.-Sun. 8am-8pm.
U: Goldhawk Rd./Westbourne Park.

A 30-metre pool, sports hall, squash courts, tanning beds and multipurpose gym are just a few of the facilities at this excellent centre. To use the gym, you have to take out membership; other facilities like squash courts you pay for when you use.

Life Centre
15 EDGE ST, W8, 020-7221 4602
Open Mon.-Sat. 8am-9.30pm, Sun. 9.30am-7pm.
U: Notting Hill Gate.

One-stop health centre with many alternative therapies and exercise classes including yoga and t'ai chi classes.

The Peak
THE HYATT CARLTON TOWER, CADOGAN PL, SW1
020-7858 7008, FAX 020-7245 6570
WWW.LONDON.HYATT.COM
Open Mon.-Fri. 6.30am-10pm, Sat.-Sun. 7.30am-9pm.
U: Knightsbridge.

On the ninth floor of the hotel, The Peak offers a great day of pampering which includes a personal health counsellor, a recommended exercise regime on top equipment, a buffet lunch, Clarins body treatment and more from 9am-5pm daily.

The Sanctuary
11 FLORAL ST, WC2
020-7420 5151, FAX 020-7497 0410
Open (Health Spa) Wed-Fri. 10am-10pm, all other days 10am-6pm.
U: Covent Garden.

A great place in the middle of Covent Garden for women only. Housed in an old banana warehouse, it's one of our favourite locations for swimming, tanning beds and aromatherapy. Membership is annual and varies according to times. If you book treatments, you don't need membership.

Soho Gym
10 MACKLIN ST, WC2, 020-7242 1290
Open Mon.-Fri. 6.30am-10pm, Sat. 10am-10pm, Sun. noon-6pm.
U: Covent Garden.

Former banana warehouse has sleek décor and full programme in new aerobics studio, therapy rooms and more.

There are many chains with branches throughout London. We list here the main health club in each chain. Check in the telephone book for a branch near you.

Cannons
COUSIN LANE, EC4, 020-7283 0101

Fitness Exchange
179A TOTTENHAM COURT RD, W1
020-7436 9266

Fitness First
105-109 SALUSBURY RD, NW6, 020-7328 8333

Holmes Place Health Club
188A FULHAM RD, SW10, 020-7352 9452

LA Fitness
20 LITTLE BRITAIN, EC1, 020-7600 0900

LivingWell Health Club
32 WOBURN PL, WC1, 020-7291 6500

Mecklenburgh Health Club
MECKLENBURGH PL, WC1, 020-7813 0555

GARDENING

The English Gardening School
66 ROYAL HOSPITAL RD, SW3
020-7352 4347, FAX 020-7376 3936
WWW.THEENGLISHGARDENINGSCHOOL.COM
U: Sloane Sq.
Established in 1983, the school, which is for both professionals and amateurs, offers various options. There are one-day workshops on general subjects such as the English cottage garden tradition, roses and plant groupings, and one-year courses in subjects like 'garden design' and 'botanical illustration' which lead to a professional qualification.

The Royal Horticultural Society
80 VINCENT SQUARE, SW1
020-7834 4333, WWW.RHS.ORG.UK
U: St. James's Park/Victoria.
The RHS as it's popularly known, runs the famous Chelsea Flower Show. But they also hold monthly flower shows in their splendid halls in Vincent Square. Like a mini-Chelsea but entirely indoors, each show concentrates on a theme or species from dahlias and rhododendrons to their Great Autumn Show. Telephone for further information and also for details of admission to their comprehensive Lindsay library.

GOLF

Regent's Park Golf & Tennis School
OUTER CIRCLE, REGENT'S PARK, NW1
020-7724 0643
Open daily 8am-9pm.
U: Baker St.
Telephone for details.

Richmond Park
ROEHAMPTON GATE, RICHMOND PARK, SW15
020-8876 3205
No underground or rail nearby.
Two beautiful 18-hole golf courses to play on from only £14 a day Monday to Friday, or £17.50 Saturday or Sunday (the rate lowers each hour and starts at 11.30am. To get in a full round, you need to start by 1pm). They rent golf clubs, but you must have your own golf shoes.

HOT AIR BALLOONING

Balloon Safaris
15-17 CHURCH ST, STAINES, MIDDLESEX
01784-451007, FAX 01784-440200
For a truly different view of England, try going up in the skies in a hot-air balloon for £120. If two or more book, it's £115 per person. The company flies from different venues in the southeast from March to October or November, depending on the weather. Balloons can take up to sixteen people, and, yes, you do have a pilot on board, and Champagne at the end of the flight.

ICE SKATING

Broadgate Ice Rink
BROADGATE CIRCLE, EC2, 020-7505 4068
Open Oct.-Apr. Mon.-Fri. noon-2.30pm &
3.30pm-6pm, Fri. also 7pm-10pm, Sat.-Sun.
11am-1pm & 2pm-4pm, also Sat. 5pm-8.30pm,
Sun. 5pm-7pm.
U: Liverpool St.
Britain's only open-air ice rink and consequently operating only in wintertime, it's a pretty place in the middle of the impressive new Broadgate development in the City. You can rent skates, buy equipment and book skating lessons.

Queen's Ice Bowl
17 QUEENSWAY, W2, 020-7229 0172
Open daily 10am-10pm in 2- or 3-hour sessions,
charged variously.
U: Bayswater.
You can rent skates at this renovated ice ring.

We're always interested to hear about your discoveries and to receive your comments on ours. Please let us know what you liked or disliked; **e-mail us at gayots@aol.com.**

NEEDLEWORK COURSES

The Embroiderers' Guild
APT 41, HAMPTON COURT PALACE, EAST
MOLESEY, ST, KT8 9AU
020-8943 1229, FAX 020-8977 9882,
WWW.ADMINISTRATOR@EMBROIDERERSGUILD.ORG.UK
Open Mon.-Fri. 10.30am-4pm.
Rail: Hampton Court.
   Exhibitions, classes, a library, shop and study
schemes are all run by this crafts-based organi-
sation. They have thousands of members in
the UK and overseas who receive a newsletter
relaying information about the Guild's activities.

Royal School of Needlework
APT 12A, HAMPTON COURT PALACE, EAST
MOLESEY, SURREY, KT8 9AU
020-8943 1432, FAX 020-8943 4910
Rail: Hampton Court.
   The School was founded in 1872 by a
daughter of Queen Victoria and friends, with
the purpose of showing the beauty of hand-
crafted needlework and of finding suitable
employment for ladies of gentle birth in strait-
ened circumstances. Today the school designs
and makes banners for the military, undertakes
all kinds of commissions, does smocking and
stretches customers' own work—everything,
in fact, to do with the gentle art of needlework. They also hold open days, exhibitions,
classes and private lessons throughout the year.

Suppliers

Colourway
112A WESTBOURNE GROVE, W2, 020-7229 1432
WWW.YARNS@COLOURWAY.DEMON.CO.UK
Open Mon.-Sat. 10am-6pm.
U: Notting Hill Gate.
   Tapestry kits and Kaffe Fassett patchwork
kits here, plus wools and patterns.

Ehrman
28A LANCER SQUARE, KENSINGTON CHURCH ST
W8, 020-7937 8123, WWW.EHRMANTAPESTRY.COM
*Open Mon.-Fri. 9.30am-5.30pm, Sat. 11am-
4.30pm.*
U: High St Kensington.
   A treasure trove for needlework enthusiasts,
Ehrman's stocks Kaffe Fassett, Annabel
Nellist, Candace Bahouth and other designers.
You can see everything made up before you

buy the kit or appropriate material. They also
sell loose canvases, tapestry wools and stationery.

Liberty
210-220 REGENT ST, W1, 020-7734 1234
WWW.LIBERTY-OF-LONDON.COM
*Open Mon.-Sat. 10am-6.30pm, Thurs. to
7.30pm.*
U: Oxford Circus.
   This department store has an excellent
needlework department staffed by people who
are experts.

Tapisserie
54 WALTON ST, SW3, 020-7581 2715
WWW.TAPISSERIE.CO.UK
Open Mon.-Fri. 10am-5.30pm, Sat. to 4pm.
U: South Kensington.
   If you're after one-of-a-kind traditional
English and Continental designs, make your
way to this small but well-stocked shop.
Antique themes are designed by their own
team and you can get a photograph of your
own adapted to a canvas. All their canvases
come with wools.

WHI Tapestry Shop
85 PIMLICO RD, SW1, 020-7730 5366
Open Mon.-Fri. 9.30am-5pm.
U: Victoria.
   Good specialist supplier with all the best
yarns and canvases. They will also make up a
set to your own design.

RIDING

   Book in advance at any of the following stables for every day except Mondays. Prices are
about £25 per hour and they can rent you hats
if necessary. If you want to go further afield,
Richmond Park is delightful. **Trent Park
Equestrian Centre** is cheaper and very good
for children as well as expert adults interested
in dressage.

Hyde Park Stables
63 BATHURST MEWS, W2, 020-7723 2813

Ross Nye
8 BATHURST MEWS, W2, 020-7262 3791

Roehampton Gate Stables
PRIORY LANE, SW15, 020-8876 7089

Trent Park Equestrian Centre
BRAMLEY RD, SOUTHGATE, N14, 020-8363 8630

Wimbledon Village Stables
24 A/B HIGH ST, WIMBLEDON VILLAGE, SW19
020-8946 8579

SHOOTING

Holland & Holland
DUCKS HILL RD, NORTHWOOD, MIDDLSEX, HA6 2SS
01923-825 349, FAX 01923-836 266
WWW.HOLLANDANDHOLLAND.COM

The famous gunmakers Holland and Holland have a shooting school 50 minutes by underground from central London where for £63 (cartridges and clay extra), you can clay-pigeon shoot for an hour under supervision.

SWIMMING

Apart from pools attached to health clubs (see above), there are a number of good central London pools. Local authorities have swimming pools; lists are available at local libraries. Also for indoor swimming try:

Chelsea Sports Centre
CHELSEA MANOR ST, SW3, 020-7352 6985

Crystal Palace National Sports Centre
LEDRINGTON RD, NORWOOD, SE19
020-8778 0131

Porchester Centre
QUEENSWAY, W2, 020-7792 2919

TENNIS & SQUASH

Squash is difficult to play on a casual basis in London. You either have to be a member of a club or book a local authority court. **The Jubilee Sports Centre** (020-7335 4900), **Porchester Centre** (020-7792 2919) and **Crystal Palace National Sports Centre** (020-8778 0131) are good bets. **The Squash Rackets Association** (0161-231 4499) will fax you a list of clubs in your area, outside London.

The top tennis tournament is, of course, the **All England Lawn Tennis Championships** (Wimbledon) first held in 1877, (All England Lawn Tennis & Croquet Club, Church Rd, Wimbledon SW19, 020-8946 2244). It's difficult to get tickets for this world-class event, but if you want to pay a premium, ticket agencies can often supply tickets—look in the classified section of major national newspapers. The enthusiastic can try queuing for return tickets after lunch on the day; it's fun, cheap and you often get to see a good four hours or so of tennis.

An equally enjoyable event (though less prestigious), played on grass courts in a club small enough to see the players properly, is the **Stella Artois Tournament at Queen's Club** (the run-up to Wimbledon).

For information on tennis and where to play in London, contact the **Lawn Tennis Association**, 020-7381 7000, Fax 020-7381 6050, at Queen's Club, Barons Court, W14, 020-7385 3421. For private clubs, try the following:

The Carlton Tennis & Health Club
ALFRED RD, WESTBOURNE GREEN, W2
020-7286 1985, FAX 020-7940 7141
Open daily 7am-11pm, Sun. 8am-11pm.
U: Westbourne Park.

Three indoor courts with well-laid Escotennis carpet surfaces and good lighting. There is also a fitness studio and more facilities. No temporary membership; though off-peak and full membership available. Gym membership is separate.

David Lloyd Club Finchley
LEISURE WAY, HIGH RD, N12, 020-8446 8704
Open Mon.-Fri. 7am-11.30pm, Sat., Sun. 8am-11.30pm.
U: East Finchley, then 263 bus.

Twelve indoor and six outdoor courts at this very well-equipped centre, which also offers aerobics, pool, sauna, shop and more. Monthly membership available. Branches throughout London.

The Vanderbilt Racquet Club

31 STERNE ST, W12
020-8743 9816/9822, FAX 020-8740 0440
Open daily 7am-11pm.
U: Shepherd's Bush.

This club offers eight indoor tennis courts and one show court with good spectator facilities, stretch and fitness classes, a beautician, bar and restaurant and special treatment centre for sports injuries and general conditions such as stress, spinal pain and migraine. Yearly membership and temporary membership for overseas residents.

WATER SPORTS

Within London, water sports centres are concentrated in **Docklands**. Getting out on one of the old docks is an exhilarating experience. Hours vary according to the time of year and amount of daylight.

Docklands Water Sports Club

KING GEORGE V DOCK, GATE 14, WOOLWICH
MANOR WAY, E14
020-7511 7000, FAX 020-7511 9000
Open summer daily, winter Thurs.-Sun.
DLR: West India Quay.

This is the club to go to for wet-biking and jet-skiing. You can either bring your own craft or rent from the centre.

Docklands Sailing & Watersports Centre

WEST FERRY RD, MILLWALL DOCKS, E14
020-7537 2626, FAX 020-7537 7774
Open summer daily, winter times vary.
DLR: West India Quay.

A session fee means you can windsurf by the day, or sail, canoe and go dragon-boating where you sit in a canoe with 22 people accompanied by a dragon and a gong.

WINE COURSES

Christie's Education

63 OLD BROMPTON RD, SW7 3JS, 020-7581 3933
FAX 020-7589 0383, WWW.CHRISTIES.COM
U: South Kensington.

Christie's auctions some of the world's greatest wine. It also runs quality wine cours-

es, an introductory evening course and a special master class course which takes a closer look at classic wines and vintages.

International Wine & Food Society

9 FITZMAURICE PL, BERKELEY SQ, W1X 6JD
020-7495 4191, WWW.BRODIE.CO.UK/IWFS
U: Green Park.

Annual membership gives you tastings, dinners and lectures.

Sotheby's Educational Studies

30 OXFORD ST, W1R 1RE, 020-7323 5775
FAX 020-7580 8160, WWW.SOTHEBYS.COM
U: Tottenham Court Rd.

Both varietal and regional courses are offered throughout the year, covering tastings of old and new wines, varietals and more.

Wine & Spirit Education Trust

FIVE KINGS HOUSE, 1 QUEEN ST PL, EC4R 1QS
020-7236 3551, WWW.WSET.CO.UK
U: Mansion House.

Top courses; beginner's course; and single events.

Wine Wise

107 CULFORD RD, N1 4HL, 020-7254 9734
U: Angel.

Wine expert and author Michael Schuster holds tastings on wines ranging from everyday drinking wines to the world's great vintages.

HOUSES TO VISIT

Please note that admission charges were correct at press time, but that museums and galleries may alter their admission charges. If you are in London over a public holiday, please check opening times. The main museum sites are **www.24hourmuseum.org.uk** and **www.exhibitionsnet.com**.

The **London GoSee** card gives you unlimited admission to seventeen major museums and galleries. Three-day (£16) and seven-day passes (£26) are available from participating museums, the Tourist Information Centre at Victoria Station, and many hotel concierges (**www.london-gosee.com**).

The **London Pass** gives admission to 40 attractions in and around London. You can either buy just this card or buy a pass that also gives free travel in zones 1-6, guide book, map, £5 of telephone calls and also discounts on services like open-top bus tours and canal boat trips. Without travel: 1, 3, 6 days: adults £13.50, £29, £43; children £9, £15, £26. With travel: 1, 3, 6, days; adults £18, £42, £74; children £11, £22, £38. Passes can be booked over the telephone (0870-2429 988), or over the web (www.londonpass.com). The pass is sent to you by mail, or you can get it from the Britain Visitor Centre at 1 Lower Regent St, SW1. Once at the attraction, you swipe the pass through a machine and you're on your way.

For information on **events in 2000 in London:** 09068-66 33 44. For London Tourist Board recorded information on **current exhibitions:** 09068-505 440. For **what's on this week:** 09068-505 440. For **what's on in next three months:** 09068-505 490. For **museums and galleries:** 09068-505 462. For **palaces:** 09068-505 466. For **famous houses and gardens:** 09068-505 468. For **other visitor attractions:** 09068-505 465. For **attractions in Greenwich:** 09068-505 467. For **day trips from London:** 09068-505 479.

Please note that all 09068 calls are currently charged at 60p per minute.

The official **London Tourist Board web site** is www.londontown.com.

Buckingham Palace

SW1, INFORMATION LINE 020-7799 2331
BOOKING LINE 020-7839 1377
WWW.ROYALINSIGHT.GOV.UK
Open State rooms Aug.-Sept. daily 9.15am-4.15pm. Admission £10.50, over 60 £8.
U: *St. James's Park/Victoria.*

Buckingham Palace opened to the general public for the first time in August, 1993, to help fund the restoration of parts of Windsor Castle after a hugely damaging fire. Imposing? Yes. Comfortable, beautiful, homely? No. But what everyone agrees on is the quality of the art, much of which was purchased by the (thankfully) spendthrift George IV. It's a huge palace, functioning as both office and home and used for ceremonial state occasions like banquets for visiting heads of state. What the visitor sees are the Throne Room, Picture Gallery, Drawing Rooms, Grand Staircase and other impressive State rooms. The general opinion is that this is a place for the art lover,

Who Lived Where

Walking around London's streets you'll notice **blue plaques** on the sides of houses telling you which famous personage lived there and when. You'll be surprised—an Indian poet in the Vale of Health on Hampstead Heath, **Mozart** in Ebury Street, **Handel** in Brook Street. There are some surprising finds as well as some obscure ones. To qualify a candidate must have been dead for at least twenty years and born more than one hundred years ago and to have made some positive and important contribution to human welfare or happiness.

rather than royal watchers. Although you do see the door through which the Royal family makes a sudden and dramatic entrance before formal dinners and pass through the Music Room where the late Princess Diana used to tap dance. You can purchase souvenirs on your way out; each based on a different room in the palace.

Carlyle's House

24 CHEYNE ROW, SW3, 020-7352 7087
INFORMATION LINE: 01494 755559
Open Easter-Oct Wed-Sun., bank holiday Mon. 11am-5pm. National Trust. Adults £3.50, children £1.75.
U: *Sloane Sq.*

'A most massive, roomy, sufficient old house...Rent £35'. So wrote Thomas Carlyle in 1834 of his new lodging in fashionable Chelsea. Left as he and his wife Jane had it, it's a modest house where he wrote some of his greatest books like *The French Revolution* and *Frederick the Great*. Personal touches—his hat hanging by the garden door, a screen his wife decorated—bring this little house to life. Events include evening performances of works by Chelsea writers; telephone for details.

Dickens House Museum

48 DOUGHTY ST, WC1, 020-7405 2127
WWW.RMPLC.CO.UK
Open Mon.- Sat. 10am-5pm. Adults £4, children £2, concessions £3.
U: *Russell Sq.*

Many of the rooms are laid out exactly as they were when Dickens sat at his desk and wrote *Oliver Twist* and *Nicholas Nickelby* and finished *Pickwick Papers*. The only one of Dickens' London homes to survive (he lived here from 1837 to 1839) was bought by the Dickens Fellowship in the 1920s. It has enough mementos to satisfy the most enthusiastic fan: first editions, portraits, his desk, chair and such personal items as marked-up copies for his lucrative public readings.

Dr Johnson's House

17 GOUGH SQ, EC4
020-7353 3745, WWW.DRJH.DIRCON.CO.UK
Open May-Sep. Mon.-Sat. 11am-5.30pm; Oct.-Apr. Mon.-Sat. 11am-5pm. Adults £3, children £1, under 10 free, concession £2.
U: Aldwych/Chancery Lane.

Dive into Hind Court off Fleet Street and then into Gough Square for a glimpse of eighteenth-century life. Dr. Samuel Johnson (1709-84) lived here from 1749 to 1759, compiling his great dictionary in the attic, surrounded by six assistants and scribes who stood at high desks, industriously scratching away with their quill pens. But go for the atmosphere and the sense of peace in this hectic part of the City of London. As the day comes to an end, it's easy to imagine the good Doctor putting down his pen, snuffing out his candle, and walking out for ale and good company at one of the nearby taverns. As you go out, look for the statue of the doctor's cat, Hodge, in Gough Square.

Fenton House

20 HAMPSTEAD GROVE, NW3, 020-7435 3471
INFORMATION LINE 01494 755563
Open Apr.-Oct. Wed.-Fri. 2pm-5pm, Sat.-Sun. & bank holiday Mon. 11am-5pm. National Trust. Adults £4.20, children £2.10, families £10.50.
U: Hampstead.

This pretty, gracious William and Mary house, built in 1693, is full of early keyboard instruments (kept in full working order and used for concerts here), fine eighteenth-century furniture and a magnificent collection of porcelain. The formal walled garden is a delight on a sunny day, and as the house is surrounded by other old Hampstead houses, the sense of the past is very real.

Freud Museum

20 MARESFIELD GDNS, NW3
020-7435 2002, WWW.FREUD.ORG.UK
Open Wed.-Sun. noon-5pm. Adults £4, children £2, concessions £2.
U: Finchley Rd.

In 1938, Sigmund Freud (1856-1939), the founder of psychoanalysis, escaped wartime Vienna and arrived in leafy Hampstead. Until his death here a year later, he worked surrounded by his possessions in what was a replica of his Vienna consulting rooms. His collection of antiquities, working library, papers and the famous desk and couch are all on display. Upon his death in 1939, his daughter Anna kept the house as it was; it opened as a museum in 1986.

Ham House

HAM ST, RICHMOND, TW10, 020-8940 1950
WWW.NATIONALTRUST.ORG.UK/SOUTHERN
Open house Apr.-Oct. Mon.-Wed., Sat.-Sun. 1pm-5pm; gardens all year Mon.-Wed, Sat.-Sun. 10.30am-6pm. National Trust. House & garden: adults £5, children £2.50, families £12.50, garden only: adults £1.50, children 75p, families £3.75.
U: Richmond, then 371 bus.

Standing by the Thames, Ham House was built in 1610, but came into its own with the redoubtable Countess of Dysart (c1626-98) and her second husband, the Duke of Lauderdale. In an age that valued comfort and elegance, the Duchess spared no expense. The house passed to the Duchess' son by her first marriage, a man as miserly as his mother was prodigal, and declined. But as a result the house remained in its original form and now appears locked in the past. The grand rooms contain wonderful furniture and fabrics, while the kitchens are full of roasting spits, scrubbed wooden tables and even a seventeenth-century mousetrap. They hold events, special tours and concerts; telephone for details. The restored gardens are historically important and delightful to walk through.

Hogarth's House

HOGARTH LANE, GT. WEST RD, W4
020-8994 6757
Open Apr.-Oct. Tues.-Fri. 1pm-5pm, Sat.-Sun. 1pm-6pm; Nov.-Mar. Tues.-Fri. 1pm-4pm, Sat.-Sun. 1pm-5pm. Admission free.
U: Turnham Green.

This eighteenth-century brick house, now just off a busy roundabout on the road to

Heathrow and the west, was originally the painter William Hogarth's country retreat from 1749 until the night before he died in 1764 in his town house in Leicester Fields (now Leicester Square). It was first opened as a museum in 1909 and now houses over 200 of his works (though the original *of The Rake's Progress* is on display in the Sir John Soane Museum, see below).

John Wesley's House, Chapel & Museum

49 CITY RD, EC1, 020-7253 2262
Open Mon.-Sat. 10am-4pm, Sun. noon-2pm (after the service). Adults £4.
U: Old St.

John Wesley, the founder of the Methodist church, laid the chapel's foundation stone in 1777 and lived in the house next door in the last years of his life. Five storeys high but only two rooms deep, it's plain with bare wood floors and little furniture. The chapel where Baroness Thatcher was married is austere, with columns made from ships' masts.

Keats House

KEATS GROVE, NW3, 020-7435 2062
Open Apr.-Oct. Mon.-Sat. 10am-1pm & 2pm-5pm, Sun. 2pm-5pm; Nov.-Mar. Mon.-Fri. 1pm-5pm, Sat. 10am-1pm & 2pm-5pm, Sun. 2pm-5pm. Admission free.
U: Belsize Park/Hampstead.
Rail: Hampstead Heath.

Delightful, countrified house lived in by the poet John Keats in 1819 where he wrote his famous poem, *Ode to a Nightingale*. Fanny Browne, his fiancée, lived next door and the two houses later became Keats House. Many personal items and memorabilia are on display.

Kensington Palace

KENSINGTON GARDENS, W8
020-7937 9561, WWW.HRP.ORG.UK
Open daily 10am-5pm, tours 10.30am-4pm. Adults £9.50, children £7.10.
U: High St Kensington.

Built in 1605 and beautifully sited in Kensington Gardens in some delightful grounds of its own, the palace is an architectural delight as well as providing private homes to various members of the Royal Family, including the late Princess Diana. The King's Gallery is spectacular—all the public rooms have been restored. The Royal Ceremonial Dress

Collection, which is by guided tour only, is arranged in different settings, all around the theme of presentation at court. You go through a tailor's workshop, a gentlemen's outfitters and more, complete with sound effects and special fibre optics displays.

Kenwood House

HAMPSTEAD LANE, NW3
020-8348 1286, WWW.ENGLISH-HERITAGE.ORG.UK
Open Apr.-Sept. daily 10am-6pm or dusk; Oct. daily 10am-5pm; Nov.-Mar. daily 10am-4pm. Admission free.
U: Archway/Golders Green/Hampstead.

A magnificent mansion remodelled by Robert Adam in 1764, this neo-classical house set high on Hampstead Heath in landscaped gardens was rescued by Edward Cecil Guinness, 1st Earl of Iveagh, in 1925, and later given to London. The library is the architectural highlight, but the real glory of the house is its collection of treasures: paintings many national galleries covet and the very finest English eighteenth-century furniture. It's beloved by locals—children and dogs play in the grounds, families picnic beside the lake. Now administered by English Heritage, it holds a series of highly popular open-air summertime concerts by the lake. (Look in national newspapers for details.)

Leighton House

12 HOLLAND PARK RD, W14, 020-7602 3316
Open Mon.-Sat. 11am-5.30pm. Admission free.
U: High St Kensington.

The flamboyant, purpose-built studio and house of Pre-Raphaelite artist Lord Leighton, is a rare sight in fashionable Kensington. Built in 1866 at the height of the Victorian Aesthetic movement for the wildly fashionable portrait painter, the high point is the Arab Hall added in 1879 to accommodate the Islamic tiles he acquired on his travels, and Walter Crane's gilt mosaic frieze. Paintings by Leighton and his contemporaries hang in the richly decorated rooms.

Linley Sambourne House

18 STAFFORD TERR, W8, 020-8994 1019
Open Mar.-Oct. Wed. 10am-4pm, guided tours only 2.15pm, 3.15pm, 4.15pm, Sun. 2.15pm. Adults £3.50, children £2, concessions £3.
U: High St Kensington.

Built in the 1870s, No. 18 was the home from 1874 to 1910 of Linley Sambourne, book illustrator and political cartoonist for the satirical magazine *Punch*. As you enter the cluttered, olive-green hall with its small fireplace, dinner gong and heavy curtains to keep dangerous draughts at bay and wander through the rooms, the years slip away. The house is a perfect, almost totally intact example of a late Victorian, early Edwardian home.

Marble Hill House

RICHMOND RD, TWICKENHAM, MIDDX
020-8892 5115, WWW.ENGLISH-HERITAGE.ORG.UK
Open Apr.-mid-Oct. daily 10am-6pm; mid-Oct.-Mar. Wed.-Sun. 10am-4pm. Adults £3.30, children £1.70, concessions £2.50. English Heritage.
U: Richmond.

Overlooking the Thames in rolling parkland at Twickenham, Marble Hill House is a perfect Palladian villa. This small, white house was built by Henrietta Howard, the mistress of Frederick, Prince of Wales (later George II). Restored with original Georgian furniture, it is a delightful, quiet house. Summer open-air concerts add to the pleasure. (Look in local and national newspapers for details.)

Osterley Park

JERSEY RD, ISLEWORTH, MIDDX
020-8560 3918
INFORMATION LINE: 01494 755566
Open park daily dawn-dusk; house Apr.-Oct. Wed.-Sun. 1pm-4.30pm. Park adults £4.10, children £2.05, families £10.25, concessions £2.05. National Trust. House: adults £4.20, families £10.50.
U: Osterley.

Originally built by the founder of the Royal Exchange, the financier, Thomas Gresham in the sixteenth century, the present house is the work of Robert Adam who completely transformed it in 1761. The house is lovely; the neo-classical interior was conceived by Adam as 'all is delicacy, gaiety, grace and beauty'. The State Rooms are magnificent, and much of the original furniture designed by Adam is still in the house. Horace Walpole described the house in 1783 as 'the palace of palaces'. The house and glorious grounds remained in the Jersey family until 1949 when the ninth Earl gave the property to the nation.

Queen's House

ROMNEY RD, SE10, 020-8858 4422
Open daily 10am-5pm. Adults £7.50, children £3.75, concessions £6.
Rail: Greenwich.

Designed by Inigo Jones and finished in 1637, this charming small palace became home to many of England's queens. Now restored and furnished to be as perfect a replica of a seventeenth-century house as possible, it is bright—almost garish—in its decorations. The 'tulip staircase' is a famous architectural feature.

Ranger's House

CHESTERFIELD WALK, SE10
020-8853 0035, WWW.ENGLISH-HERITAGE.ORG.UK
Open Apr.-Oct. daily 10am-6pm; Nov.-Mar. Wed.-Sun. 10am-5pm. Adults £2.50, children £1.30, concessions £1.90. English Heritage.
Rail: Blackheath/Maze Hill.

An early eighteenth-century house perched high up overlooking Greenwich, its most famous inhabitant was Philip, Fourth Earl of Chesterfield, author of the famous letters. It contains the Suffolk collection of Jacobean and Stuart portraits and holds contemporary art exhibitions.

Sir John Soane Museum

14 LINCOLN'S INN FIELDS, WC2
020-7430 0175/7405 2107, WWW.SOANE.ORG.UK
Open Tues.-Sat. 10am-5pm, first Tues. of each month 6pm-9pm. Guided tours 2.30pm (£3). Admission free.
U: Holborn.

The son of a bricklayer, John Soane (1753-1837) rose to become one of Britain's leading architects. He designed the Bank of England, Dulwich Picture Gallery and more, and as an art patron, accumulated and commissioned a wide variety of works. The astonishing result is an eclectic collection remaining much as he left it, and both the house and the collection are full of surprises. The already crowded walls of the picture gallery unfold to reveal yet more paintings (such as William Hogarth's *Rake's Progress* series which cost £570 in 1802); the Monk's Parlour is full of grotesque Gothic casts; a vast sarcophagus stands in the crypt. Seek out the design of wife's tombstone: it inspired Britain's old-style red telephone boxes.

Southside House

WIMBLEDON COMMON, SW19, 020-8946 7643
*Open Jan.-mid-summer guided tours only
Wed. & Sat.-Sun. 2pm, 3pm, 4pm. Telephone to
book and check times and prices.
U: Wimbledon.*

This is a house where the phrase 'entering a time warp' has real meaning. Lived in continuously by the same family since it was built in 1687, this small red-brick mansion has been left mercifully unrestored. It is full of odd family treasures—the pearls worn by Marie Antoinette at her execution and the cufflinks given by King Edward VII to Axel Munthe, the doctor who became famous for his work with the poor in southern Italy and who wrote the 1920s best-seller *The Villa of San Michele*. To the surprise of the fashionable world, Munthe wooed and married the society beauty Hilda Pennington, whose family owned the house...but that's another story. Visit this atmospheric home, so full of ghosts. Each time you enter a room you feel that the occupants of the past have just closed the far door quietly behind them, leaving you to enjoy their house for a few minutes before they return.

Spencer House

27 ST. JAMES'S PL., SW1, 020-7499 8620
*Open every Sun. except in Jan. & Aug. Guided
tours only 11.15am-4.45pm. Timed tickets
available from 10.30am on the day of the tour.
Adults £6, under 16 £5 (no children under 10
allowed), concessions £5.
U: Green Park.*

Spencer House was built in the mid-eighteenth century for John, first Earl of Spencer. It's in fashionable St. James's, conveniently close to the monarch at St. James's Palace. The former London home of the late Princess of Wales' family, it has been sumptuously and correctly restored by Lord Rothschild, who currently leases the house, and is one of the very few surviving examples of an eighteenth-century townhouse. The Spencer family was noted for its art collection and legendary and lavish entertaining, and for a few thousand pounds, you too can hire the house and dine in the gilded surroundings.

Sutton House

2 & 4 HOMERTON HIGH ST, E9, 020-8986 2264
INFORMATION LINE: 01494 755569
*Open Feb.-Nov. Wed., Sun. & bank holidays
11.30am-5.30pm, Sat. 2pm-5.30pm. Adults
£2.10, under 16 60p, families £4.80. National
Trust.
Rail: Homerton.*

Built for a Tudor politician in 1535 when Hackney was a country village, this red-brick Tudor house is the oldest surviving domestic building in East London. It has been beautifully restored. Good small café and shop open all year round.

Syon House

SYON PARK, BRENTFORD, MIDDX, 020-8560 0883
*Open house mid-Mar.-Oct. Wed.-Thurs., Sun &
public holidays 11am-5pm; gardens daily 10am-
dusk. House & garden: adults £6, children £4,
concessions £4; gardens only: adults £3, children
£2, concessions £2.
U: Gunnersbury, then bus 237, 267. Rail: Kew
Bridge, then bus 237, 267.*

Robert Adam's masterpiece, since 1594, the house has been the home of the Percys, Dukes of Northumberland. The interiors are gorgeous, with all the architectural glories of the day: Doric columns, Roman-style decorations, columns and domes. The house stands in magnificent grounds, with botanical gardens, a lake and parkland, much of it remodelled by 'Capability' Brown. Visitors can see the nineteenth-century conservatory, steam train, garden centre and the London Butterfly House.

2 Willow Road

2 WILLOW RD, NW3, 020-7435 6166,
INFORMATION LINE 01494 755570
*Open Apr.-Oct. Thurs.-Sat. noon-5pm, entry by
timed ticket only. Admission £4.20. National
Trust.
U: Hampstead. .*

The great twentieth-century architect Erno Goldfinger designed and built 2 Willow Road for himself in 1939. The house is one of Britain's best examples of modernist architecture. The rooms contain furniture Goldfinger designed, personal items like his passport and family photographs, and works by contemporaries like Henry Moore, Man Ray and Max Ernst.

INNS OF COURT

Today there are four Inns of Court, originally called inns because barristers trained, lodged and ate here. Today all barristers have to work from, and eat a certain number of dinners at one of them. All are independent, self-governing bodies with some powers delegated to the Senate of the Inns of Court. They are delightful places to wander around and give the casual visitor a very real feeling of old London. All are free and the grounds are open to visitors.

Gray's Inn

GRAY INN RD, WC1, 020-7458 7810
Open Mon.-Fri. 10am-4pm, hall for guided tours by appointment.
U: Chancery Lane/Holborn.

Founded in 1569 on the site of the manor house of Sir Reginald le Grey, Chief Justice of Chester who died in 1308, the hall is impressive. It contains a screen said to be constructed from the wood of a captured Spanish Armada galleon. Shakespeare's *Comedy of Errors* was first staged here in 1594 as the Earl of Southampton, the playwright's patron, was a member of the Inn. The hall is open for guided tours only by appointment; write to the Under Treasurer, Treasury Office, No 8 South Sq, WC1R 5EQ.

Lincoln's Inn

LINCOLN'S INN FIELDS, WC2
020-7405 1393, WWW.LINCOLNSINN.CO.UK
Open grounds Mon.-Fri. 9am-6pm, chapel noon-2.30pm.
U: Chancery Lane/Holborn

Founded on this site in 1422, Lincoln's Inn is a wonderful oasis in the city with its quiet alleyways, chapel (open to the public), and halls (open for guided tours only, telephone for details). Many of the buildings date from the fifteenth and sixteenth centuries. The playwright Ben Jonson worked as a bricklayer on the chapel, a trowel in his hand, a book in his pocket. New Square dates from 1682-93; Stone Buildings from 1774-80, and the New Hall and Library from 1843-5. Sir Thomas More, Lord Hailsham and Lord Denning. Walpole, Oliver Cromwell, William Penn, Disraeli and Gladstone, John Donne, David Garrick and John Galsworthy were among the many students enrolled here. Charles Dickens' famous and savage case, Jarndyce v Jarndyce in *Bleak House*, is set here. To visit the buildings

with a guide, write to the Treasury Office, Lincoln's Inn, WC2A 3TL

The Temple

EC4
Open grounds Mon.-Fri. 8.30am-9pm.
U: Temple

The Temple is made up of the Inner and the Middle Temple, all housed in the same area between Fleet Street and the River Thames.

Inner Temple

INNER TEMPLE TREASURY OFFICE, EC4
020-7797 8250, WWW.INNTEMPL.ORG.UK

Temple Church

INNER TEMPLE, KING'S BENCH WALK, EC4
020-7353 3470
Open Wed.-Fri. 11am-4pm (telephone first to check any special opening times).

Middle Temple

MIDDLE TEMPLE LANE, EC4, 020-7427 4800
MIDDLE TEMPLE HALL
Open Mon.-Fri. 10am-noon.
U: Temple.

The Knights Templars, founded originally to protect pilgrims, established themselves in the twelfth century, making their base here in 1162 around the New Temple's Round church. Suppressed in 1312 because of their wealth and power, their properties passed to the Knights Hospitallers who leased the land to students and professors of the Common Law. It wasn't until 1609 that James I gave the ownership of the Temple to the two Inns. Middle Temple Hall, dating from around 1320 and open to the public, has a striking oak double hammerbeam roof and screen. Used formally and for lavish entertainments, Shakespeare's *Twelfth Night* was first performed here on February 2, 1601. Names associated with the Middle Temple include Sir Francis Drake and Sir Walter Ralegh, William Wycherley, the Duke of Monmouth, John Evelyn, Henry Fielding, Charles Dickens and Thomas de Quincey. Temple Church, based, it is believed, on the Church of the Holy Sepulchre in Jerusalem, contains the tombs of thirteenth-century knights from the Holy Land. For special tours of the Inner Temple Hall, write to the Inner Temple Treasury Office, EC4Y 7HL, or fax 020-7797 8178.

MUSEUMS

Please note that admission charges were correct at press time, but that museums and galleries may alter their admission charges. If you are in London over a public holiday, please check opening times. The main museum sites are **www.24hourmuseum.org.uk** and **www.exhibitionsnet.com**.

The **London GoSee** card gives you unlimited admission to seventeen major museums and galleries. Three-day (£16) and seven-day passes (£26) are available from participating museums, the Tourist Information Centre at Victoria Station, and many hotel concierges (**www.london-gosee.com**).

The **London Pass** gives admission to 40 attractions in and around London. You can either just buy this card or buy a pass that also gives free travel in zones 1-6, guide book, map, £5 of telephone calls and also discounts on services like open-top bus tours and canal boat trips. Without travel: 1, 3, 6 days: adults £13.50, £29, £43; children £9, £15, £26. With travel: 1, 3, 6, days; adults £18, £42, £74; children £11, £22, £38. Passes can be booked over the telephone (0870-2429 988), or over the web (www.londonpass.com). The pass is sent to you by mail, or you can get it from the Britain Visitor Centre at 1 Lower Regent St, SW1. Once at the attraction, you swipe the pass through a machine and you're on your way.

For information on **events in 2000 in London**: 09068-66 33 44. For London Tourist Board recorded information on **current exhibitions**: 09068-505 440. For **what's on this week**: 09068-505 440. For **what's on in next three months**: 09068-505 490. For **museums and galleries**: 09068-505 462. For **palaces**: 09068-505 466. For **famous houses and gardens**: 09068-505 468. For **other visitor attractions**: 09068-505 465. For **attractions in Greenwich**: 09068-505 467. For **day trips from London**: 09068-505 479.

Please note that all 09068 calls are currently charged at 60p per minute.

The official **London Tourist Board web site** is www.londontown.com.

Telephone numbers in England have eleven digits, beginning with a zero. The initial zero must be omitted if you are calling England from abroad. Within the country, dial the entire eleven digits.

Artillery Museum
THE ROTUNDA, REPOSITORY RD, SE18
020-8781 3127
Open Mon.-Fri. 1pm-4pm. Admission free.
Rail: Woolwich Dockyard.

Interesting for its eighteenth-century architecture by John Nash, it also has artillery of all kinds, from Tudor times to the Gulf War.

Apsley House
149 PICCADILLY, HYDE PARK CORNER, W1
020-7499 5676, W.VAM.AC.UK\COLLECTIONS\APSLEY
Open Tues.-Sun. 11am-5pm. Adults £4.50, under 18 free, concessions £3.
U: Hyde Park Corner.

Originally built by Robert Adam between 1771 and 1778 as just one part of a spectacular neo-classical terrace, Apsley House was lived in by the Duke of Wellington, or the 'Iron Duke' as he was familiarly known after he won the Battle of Waterloo in 1817. Known as 'Number One, London' because it was the first major building you saw on entering London from the west, it is now full of a priceless collection of furniture, fabrics, china and mementos of his battles and political career.

Bank of England Museum
BANK OF ENGLAND, BARTHOLOMEW LANE, EC2
020-7601 5545, WWW.BANKOFENGLAND.CO.UK
Open Mon.-Fri. 10am-5pm, except bank holidays. Admission free.
U: Bank.

'The Old Lady of Threadneedle Street' (as the Bank was named by the playwright and politician Sheridan), was set up in 1694 to raise money for foreign wars, came under government control in 1766 and was nationalised in 1946. The museum tells the story of the 'Banker's Bank' (and a surprisingly exciting one it is) and the story of the development of the financial system, with displays from glittering gold bars to dealing desks and interactive exhibits.

Bethnal Green Museum of Childhood
CAMBRIDGE HEATH RD, E2, 020-8983 5200
WWW.VAM.AC.UK\COLLECTIONS\BRANCHMUSEUMS
Open Mon.-Thurs. & Sat. 10am-5.50pm, Sun. 2.30pm-5.30pm. Admission free.
U: Bethnal Green.

This delightful treasure house in the East End of London is housed in one of the temporary train-shed buildings put up for the original Victoria and Albert Museum (of which it is still part) in South Kensington. Re-erected piece-by-piece in 1872, the cast-iron building now contains the nation's toy box. Walk inside and you're magically transported back in time through your own childhood to the seventeenth century. What delights and reassures is the fact that children's pleasures have changed so little. Dolls' houses from three centuries still attract crowds of small children pointing out miniature pianos, plates and furniture; others put money into the machine that makes the model trains go around an eternal circle. It's a wonderful mix of toys and games, dolls and magic lantern shows, model railways and board games from all over Europe. They hold special children's workshops every Saturday.

Bramah Tea & Coffee Museum

BUTLERS WHARF, SE1, 020-7378 0222
WWW.BRAMAHMUSEUM.CO.UK
Open daily 10am-6pm. Adults £4, children £3.
U: London Bridge.

This museum, devoted to the history of the much-loved beverages is housed down by the warehouses where cargoes were brought ashore. It's the brainchild of Edward Bramah, former tea merchant and taster, whose huge and comprehensive collection of teapots, coffeepots and general tea- and coffee-making machinery forms the main bulk of the museum. And do have a cup of tea or coffee in the café—the taste (particularly of the tea)—will remind you of the past glories of the drink before the almost universal use of the dreaded tea bag. Good small shop.

British Museum

GREAT RUSSELL ST, WC1
020-7636 1555, WWW.BRITISH-MUSEUM.AC.UK
Open Mon.-Sat. 10am-5pm, Sun. 2.30pm-6pm.
Admission free. Special evening opening first
Tues. of the month 6pm-9pm. Admission £5, free
for members of the Friends of the British
Museum.
U: Tottenham Court Rd/Holborn/Russell Sq.

The British Museum, one of the world's greatest museums, was started by physician Sir Hans Sloane (1660-1753), who suggested in his will that the government buy his private collection. This they did and in 1753 passed the British Museum Act for London's (and the

world's) first public museum. Benefactors gave generously and the collection rapidly outgrew the original location in Montagu House, Bloomsbury. George II bequeathed the Royal Library of 10,500 volumes (1757); Sir William Hamilton gave his antique vase collection (1772); the famous Greek Marbles from the Parthenon and Erechtheum from Greece were bought from Lord Elgin in 1816, and George III donated his library of 120,800 books in 1823. The present neo-classical building (1823-38), designed by Robert Smirke, now houses some four million objects, divided between different departments (Greek and Roman, Egyptian, Ethnography, Prehistory and Roman Britain, Oriental, Coins and Medals, Medieval and Later Antiquities, Prints and Drawings, Western Asiatic and Japanese Antiquities). There are so many treasures—Egyptian mummies, the Portland Vase, the glorious Lindisfarne gospels, the Sutton Hoo ship burial, magnificent Chinese art—it is impossible to see them all in one visit. Having received a massive amount of money in the late 1990s, both public and private, the museum has reconstructed the whole of the central court, incorporating the old round Reading Room which ceased to function as such when the British Library moved to St. Pancras (see British Library). The result is a vast new exhibition space in the Great Court, plus refurbishment of some of the major spaces, taking this important museum into the twenty-first century. The best way to explore the museum is to pick up a map in the front hall and choose one or two particular topics or galleries. And then go back for more.

Canal Museum

12-13 NEW WHARF RD, N1, 020-7713 0836
WWW.CHARITYNET.ORG\~LCANALMUS
Open Tues.-Sun., 10am-4.30pm. Adults £2.50,
children £1.25, concessions £1.25.
U: King's Cross.

This is a former mid-nineteenth century warehouse that held imported ice from Norway. It was built in the 1850s Carlo Gatti, an Italian immigrant who ran his lucrative business from here. It tells the story of Gatti and how London's canals were built and developed. Many models are on display.

Cuming Museum

155-157 WALWORTH RD, SE17, 020-7701 1342
Open Tues.-Sat. 10am-5pm. Admission free.
U: Elephant & Castle.

The museum houses the Cuming family's wonderful collection of worldwide objects of archaeology, ethnography and decorative arts, gathered between 1780 and 1900. The museum also tells Southwark's history and is full of artefacts relating to the life of Londoners.

Design Museum

BUTLERS WHARF, SHAD THAMES, SE1
020-7378 6055 (RECORDED INFO)
020-7403 6937, WWW.DESIGNMUSEUM.ORG.UK
Open Mon.-Fri. 11.30am-6pm, Sat.-Sun. 10.30am-6pm. Adults £5.50, families £15, concessions £4.
U: London Bridge.

This museum, the brainchild of Sir Terence Conran, is devoted to the design of mass-produced everyday objects from chairs to cars, lemon squeezers to radios. International design is displayed in temporary exhibitions with different themes, and there's an exciting interactive section where you can research details on the history and design of every object imaginable. You want to know about chairs? Legs of chairs? History? Famous designers? Just follow the instructions on the screen. There is a shop and café.

Fan Museum

12 CROOMS HILL, GREENWICH, SE10
020-8305 1441, WWW.FAN-MUSEUM.ORG.UK
Open Tues.-Sat. 11am-5pm, Sun. noon-5pm.
Adults £3.50, under 7 free, concessions £2.50.
Rail: Greenwich.

Fans may seem at first an unlikely subject for a museum, but this one is full of surprises. The museum shows fans in themed exhibitions like those decorated with children or flowers. There is a permanent display on the history and materials used in fan making and a craft workshop, which holds fan-making classes and undertakes conservation and restoration.

Faraday Museum

ROYAL INSTITUTION, 21 ALBEMARLE ST, W1
020-7409 2992
Open Mon.-Fri. 9.30am-5.30pm. Admission £1.
U: Green Park.

A small museum telling the story of Michael Faraday, who began as assistant to Humphry Davy in 1812 at 12 shillings a week then became Professor of Chemistry at the Royal Institution (1833-67). Better known as the 'father of electricity', there's a recreation of the lab where he discovered the laws of electromagnetics.

Florence Nightingale Museum

ST THOMAS'S HOSPITAL, LAMBETH PALACE RD, SE1
020-7620 0374,
WWW.FLORENCE-NIGHTINGALE.CO.UK
Open Mon.-Fri. 10am-5pm, Sat.-Sun. & bank holiday Mon. 11.30am-4.30pm. Adults £4.80, children £3.60, families £10, concessions £3.60.
U: Waterloo.

Florence Nightingale, born into a well-to-do Victorian family, became a nurse (at that time, not considered a profession for a lady) and was sent to the Crimean War. Her reorganisation of Scutari Hospital and fame as 'the lady with the lamp' (she sat at the deathbeds of 2,000 men, believing no one should die alone), turned out to be only a small part of her achievements. On her return home, she became a tireless campaigner for hospital reform and set the standards of nursing care and training we know today. The museum tells the story of this formidable lady's remarkable life with room sets, pictures, and personal memorabilia.

Freemasons' Hall

60 GT. QUEEN ST, WC2, 020-7395 9254
Open Mon.-Fri. 10am-5pm, Sat. 10.15am (pre-booked tour only). Admission free.
U: Covent Garden/Holborn.

It may seem odd that an organisation shrouded in secrecy should have its own museum, but the library and museum of the United Grand Lodge of England sheds light on the history of Freemasonry in Britain from the sixteenth century.

Geffrye Museum

KINGSLAND RD, E2
020-7739 9893, WWW.GEFFRYE-MUSEUM.ORG.UK
Open Tues.-Sat. 10am-5pm, Sun.-Mon. & public holidays noon-5pm. Admission free.
U: Old St, then 243 bus.

This charming and unusual museum is housed in a collection of alms-houses, which were built for the poor in 1715. In the centre of the former furniture-making area in the

East End, it became a museum in 1911. The interior is arranged as a series of room settings (taking you through the story) of English furnishings and decorative tastes. From a 1600-style paneled Elizabethan room through the elegance of the Georgians to the present with a series of wonderful new twentieth-century galleries, which also house special exhibitions. Outside there's a walled herb garden. It's a charming place and, because of their displays, especially good to visit around Christmas. Good café and shop.

Guards Museum

WELLINGTON BARRACKS, BIRDCAGE WALK, SW1
020-7930 4466 EXT. 3271
Open Mon.-Thurs. & Sat.-Sun. 10am-4pm.
Adults £2, children £1, families £4.
U: St. James's Park.

If you're a military enthusiast, this is a must, full of tableaux, weapons, uniforms, models and dioramas to illustrate the battles in which the five famous Guards regiments have taken part.

Horniman Museum

100 LONDON RD, FOREST HILL, SE23
020-8699 1872, WWW.HORNIMAN.DEMON.UK
Open Mon.-Sat. 10.30am-5.30pm, Sun. 2pm-5.30pm. Admission free.
Rail: Forest Hill.

Frederick Horniman, the tea merchant, clearly a man with a tremendous curiosity about his fellow human beings, had this Art Nouveau museum built in 1901 to house all the odd objects he had collected on his travels. This includes everything from Navajo paintings to objects you'd be hard put to name if there wasn't a handy description nearby. Most famous is the collection of 1,500 musical instruments from all over the world. Displayed in the music room, you can hear through headphones hundreds of different instruments. The museum is set in sixteen acres of gardens with extensive views of London.

Imperial War Museum

LAMBETH RD, SE1
020-7416 5320, WWW.IWM.ORG.UK
Open daily 10am-6pm. Adults £5.20, children free. Free admission after 4.30pm.
U: Lambeth North.

Perhaps it is appropriate that the Imperial War Museum, dedicated to the paraphernalia and story of twentieth-century war, should be housed in the former Bethlehem Hospital for the Insane ('Bedlam'), built in 1811. The museum, with its huge guns outside and the machinery of war inside, is impressive. So, too, is the story of the social effects of war: the deprivation, food rationing, air raid precautions and censorship. This is a particularly effective museum: extracts from wartime films, radio programmes and literature, paintings and photographs are on display, as are strange artefacts like Montgomery's caravan office and the German straw over-boots for protection against Russia's cold. The museum is kept up-to-date with the inclusion of information about recent wars like the Gulf War of 1991.

Jewish Museum

RAYMOND BURTON HOUSE, 129-131 ALBERT ST
CAMDEN TOWN, NW1
020-7284 1997, WWW.ORT.ORG/JEWMUSM
Open Sun.-Thurs. 10am-4pm. Adults £3, children £1.50, concessions £2.
U: Camden Town.
ALSO AT 80 EAST END RD, FINCHLEY, N3
020-8349 1143. WWW.ORT.ORG/JEWMUSM
Open Mon.-Thurs. 10.30am-5pm, Sun. 10.30am-4.30pm. Closed on Jewish Festivals. Adults £3, children £1.50.
U: Finchley Central.

With one of the world's finest collections of Jewish ceremonial art, including highly decorated documents, wedding rings, curtains and more, it also shows the lives of British Jews. There is a fascinating interactive map showing Jewish settlement in Britain. Finchley houses the social history collections including an Oral History Archive, a Photographic Archive and many documents. There are frequently changing exhibitions.

Kew Bridge Steam Museum

GREEN DRAGON LANE, BRENTFORD, MIDDLESEX
020-8568 4757
Open daily 11am-5pm. Adults £2.80, ages 5-15 £1, families £7.
U: Gunnersbury/Kew Gardens.

In an unmistakable, extraordinary nineteenth-century pumping station next to Kew Bridge, this fascinating and idiosyncratic museum illustrates how steam engines pumped west London's water supply. The award-winning Water for Life gallery is interactive. Telephone in advance for information on days when the engines are in steam; normally it's every weekend.

London Transport Museum

THE PIAZZA, COVENT GARDEN, WC2
020-7379 6344, WWW.LTMUSEUM.CO.UK
Open Sat.-Thurs. 10am-6pm, Fri.11am-6pm.
Adults £5.50, children £2.95, under 5 free,
families £13.95.
U: Covent Garden.

Don't pass this one by thinking it's just full of old vehicles. It's a lively place, with lots of hands-on exhibits for children and, yes, lots of old but interesting vehicles from the original horse-bus of 1829 to trams and tube trains. The art collection fascinates, too: London Transport has always commissioned first-rate artists for their posters, including Graham Sutherland and Paul Nash. Special events keep people coming back. There's a good shop.

London Transport Museum Depot

118-120 GUNNERSBURY LANE, W3
020-7565 7299 (RECORDED INFORMATION)
WWW.LTMUSEUM.CO.UK
Open days only for guided tours, telephone
020-7379 6344.
U: Acton Town.

A new depot holding the museum's behind-the-scenes collection, also a wonderful place full of surprises like a locomotive from the world's first electric underground railway, tiles, clocks, posters and more. Good shop.

Museum of Garden History

LAMBETH PALACE RD, SE1, 020-7401 8864
WWW.MUSEUMGARDENHISTORY.ORG.UK
Open first Sun. Mar.-mid-Dec.: Mon.-Fri.
10.30am-4pm, Sun. 10.30am-5pm. Admission
free, but donation requested.
U: Lambeth North.

This was started as a labour of love by Rosemary Nicholson in what was the shut and decaying church of St. Mary-at-Lambeth, beside the Archbishop of Canterbury's London home, Lambeth Palace. With the help of dedicated gardeners, who included Lady Salisbury of Hatfield House and the Queen Mother, the church opened as a museum in 1979, dedicated to the history of gardening in Britain. It's officially the Tradescant Trust, called after the Tradescants, father and son, who were gardeners to seventeenth-century monarchs and dedicated plant hunters in Russia, Europe and particularly the Americas. They were also the Salisbury family's gardeners. The museum has good changing exhibi-

tions and the churchyard, which has a knot garden planted with seventeenth-century plants, is a delightful place on a summer afternoon. The Tradescants are buried in the churchyard, alongside Captain Bligh of Bounty fame. A very good shop for individual items and small café.

Museum of London

150 LONDON WALL, EC2, 020-7600 0807
WWW.MUSEUMOFLONDON.ORG.UK
Open Mon.-Sat. 10am-5.50pm, public holidays
& Sun. noon-5.50pm. Adults £5, under 16 free,
concessions £3.
U: Barbican/Moorgate.

Arranged chronologically, the museum tells the story of London in an intriguing way with each section providing a vivid idea of what living in London was like through the ages up to the present. You pass through the Roman section complete with Roman kitchens, see the Cheapside Hoard of jewelry cascading down a chimney just as it was found. Walk past eighteenth-century prisons, grocers' shops, through elegant Regency London to the city of the suffragettes, the Blitz and the swinging sixties. One of the high points is the cinematic experience of watching the Great Fire of London. Samuel Pepys' contemporary account is read with suitable solemnity while London (in model form) burns and crashes to the ground in front of your eyes. The museum offers a delightful visual experience, holds frequent exhibitions and in the cinema, shows a changing programme of classic British movies from the days when Britain had a viable movie industry.

Museum of Rugby

TWICKENHAM RUGBY STADIUM, RUGBY RD,
TWICKENHAM, 020-8892 2000, WWW.RFU.COM
Open Tues.-Sat. 10.30am-5pm, Sun. 2pm-5pm.
Museum or tour only: adults £3, children £2;
combined ticket: adults £5, children £3.
Rail: Twickenham.

One of the great sports finally has gotten a museum worthy of it, though it's a museum for the aficionado rather than the casual visitor. Beneath Twickenham's famous stand, you can either see the Museum alone or combine it with a tour of the stadium and see behind the scenes. The museum has caps and kits from past heroes, paintings, prints, trophies as well as ceramics, silver and bronze. There also are touch-screen information points on players and their clubs.

Museum of the Order of St. John

ST. JOHN'S GATE, EC1, 020-7253 6644
Open Mon.-Fri. 9am-5pm, Sat. 10am-4pm.
Tours Tues. & Fri.-Sat. 11am, 2.30pm.
Donation requested.
U: Barbican/Farringdon.

The stone 1504 gateway was once the entrance to the twelfth-century Priory of St John of Jerusalem, now the HQ of the British Order of St. John. Originally the Knights Hospitallers, the museum has various artefacts of the order, up to today's St John Ambulance Brigade.

Musical Museum

368 HIGH ST, BRENTFORD, MIDDX
020-8560 8108
Open Apr.-June & Sept.-Oct.: Sat.-Sun. 2pm-5pm; July-Aug: Wed. 2pm-4pm, Sat.-Sun 2pm-5pm. Adults £3.20, children £2.50, concessions £2.50.
U: Gunnersbury.

In a converted church, this idiosyncratic collection covers mechanical musical instruments of all types, all self-playing and restored. Guided 90-minute tours give you a real insight.

National Army Museum

ROYAL HOSPITAL RD, SW3, 020-7730 0717
Open daily 10am-5.30pm. Admission free.
U: Sloane Sq.

The museum records five centuries of the British Army from 1485 to the present day with weapons, paintings, tableaux, dioramas and film clips. Students of military history can write or telephone for a reader's ticket to the comprehensive, rare collection of manuscripts, books, maps, drawings and more.

National Maritime Museum

ROMNEY RD, GREENWICH, SE10
020-8312 6565, WWW.NMM.AC.UK
Open daily 10am-5pm. Adults £7.50, ages 5-16 free, concessions £8.40; combined with Royal Observatory: adults £9.50, ages 5-16 free, concessions £7.60.
Rail: Greenwich.

This large museum, founded in 1934, is devoted to Britain's great maritime history. The superb collections include models of ships from all ages and of all types, the finest collection of globes in the world, early charts and instruments. An interactive gallery occupies an entire wing. The 'All Hands' centre concentrates on the lives of people connected with the sea. Each year, there are major long-running exhibitions. The museum gives a wonderful insight into the importance of maritime developments, and goes a long way to helping understand British pride in past exploits and successes around the world. The museum is part of the complex, which includes the Royal Observatory and The Queen's House. A £20-million refurbishment has given the museum 20 new gallery spaces, housed under a 2,500 square metre free-span glass roof—the largest of its kind in Europe. The spacious, airy interior features an open space with access to every new gallery. High drama comes with artefacts like a giant cube covering environmental issue. Many of the treasures on view have never been shown before because of lack of space.

Natural History & Geological Museum

CROMWELL RD, SW7
020-7942 5000, WWW.NHM.AC.UK
Open daily 10am-5.50pm. Adults £6.50, under 17 free, concessions £3.60. Also, free Mon.-Fri. after 4.30pm, Sat.-Sun. after 5pm.
U: South Kensington.

More than 65 million species make up one of the world's largest collections of animals, plants, fossils and minerals. It was founded originally on the private collection of the celebrated physician Sir Hans Sloane, whose collection also helped found the main British Museum. Traditional displays alongside interactive techniques prompt questions about ecology and evolution, the origin of the species and how human beings have developed. There are now two major sections: the Life Galleries and the Earth Galleries (which are in effect the old Geological Museum and which make the subject come to life starting with an escalator ride through a revolving globe.) It has some spectacular new exhibits including the popular permanent Dinosaur Exhibition and one on insects (Creepy-Crawlies), both of which display lifelike models. The building is worth a visit in itself: a huge cathedral-like space designed by Alfred Waterhouse using revolutionary Victorian building techniques and covered outside with a stone façade of a veritable zoo of animals as well as plants.

Old Operating Theatre Museum & Herb Garret

9A ST. THOMAS'S ST, SE1, 020-7955 4791
Open daily 10.30am-5pm. Adults £3.25,
children £1.60, under 8 free, concessions £2.25.
U: London Bridge.

The oldest surviving operating theatre in the country was built in 1822 from part of the herb garret. With its banked seats for students to watch as surgeons performed their grisly tasks before the days of anaesthetics and antiseptic surgery, it is just like a theatre. The herb garret, used by the Apothecary of nearby St. Thomas's, has objects like instruments for the ancient art of cupping and trepanning. With such reminders of the crude medicine of the past, you emerge doubly grateful for being born in the twentieth century. They hold lectures at 2.30pm on the first Sunday of every month on the history of Old St. Thomas's Hospital and Guy's and the history of health care, as well as frequent events, so check in advance.

Petrie Museum of Egyptian Archaeology

UNIVERSITY COLLEGE LONDON
MALET ST, WC1, 020-7504 2884
Open Mon.-Fri. 1pm-5pm, Sat. 10am-1pm.
Admission free.
U: Euston Sq.

Part of London University, this relatively unknown museum houses one of the greatest collections of Egyptian archaeology in the world, showing life in the Nile Valley from prehistory to Islamic times. The world's earliest surviving dress (circa 2,800 B.C.), epitomises a collection that is rich in personal items that bring the ancient world to life.

Pitshanger Manor & Gallery

WALPOLE PARK, MATTOCK LANE, EALING, W5
020-8567 1227
Open Tues.-Sat. 10am-5pm. Admission free.
Rail: Ealing Broadway.

The delightful Pitshanger Manor was once owned by the architect Sir John Soane (1753-1837), who designed the Bank of England and Dulwich Picture Gallery. Set in beautiful parkland, John Soane largely rebuilt the house in his highly individual style. The gallery houses contemporary art exhibitions and a

Victorian wing houses a large collection of Martinware pottery. There is always an excellent series of lectures and events.

Ragged School Museum

46-48 COPPERFIELD RD, E3, 020-8980 6405
Open Wed.-Thurs. 10am-5pm, first Sun. of each
month 2pm-5pm. Admission free.
U: Mile End.

The philanthropist Dr. Barnardo converted these Victorian warehouses beside the canal a century ago for orphans. East End local history is on display here in a reconstructed Victorian schoolroom. Enough to convince today's school children that theirs is a happier lot than they might think. They regularly hold excellent activities for children, so check in advance.

Royal Air Force Museum

GRAHAM PARK WAY, NW9, 020-8205 2266
Open daily 10am-6pm. Adults £6.50, children
£3.25, families £16.60, concessions £4.90.
U: Colindale. Rail: Mill Hill Broadway.

A must for anyone interested in the history of aviation and the story of the Royal Air Force. The museum has three separate sections: the RAF Museum, the Battle of Britain Museum, and the Bomber Command Museum. There are also effective exhibits of room settings, air-raid shelters and command posts which convey a very real atmosphere, as well as an excellent 'fun 'n flight' interactive gallery particularly loved by children and budding bomber pilots. Aircraft is displayed in the vast hall.

Royal College of Music Museum of Instruments

PRINCE CONSORT RD, SW7, 020-7589 3643
Open Wed. (term time) 2pm-4pm.
U: South Kensington.

Housed in the prestigious Royal College of Music (which Benjamin Britten, Ralph Vaughan Williams and other leading British musicians were schooled) this valuable collection of around 500 instruments must be on your list if you have an interest in music and the ways of making it.

Royal College of Surgeons of England

35-43 LINCOLN'S INN FIELDS, WC2
020-7973 2190
Open Mon.-Fri. 10am-5pm.
U: Holborn.

Vast treasures on display. There are more than 3000 specimens of human and animal anatomy and pathology, gathered by John Hunter Fellow of the Royal Society (1728-1793). There are also paintings this famous surgeon commissioned. A display on the work of Joseph Lister (1827-1912) completes the museum.

Royal Observatory

GREENWICH PARK, SE10
020-8858 4422, WWW.NMM.AC.UK
Open daily 10am-5pm. Adults £6, ages 5-16 free, concessions £4.80; combined with National Maritime Museum (see above): adults £10.50, ages 5-16 free, concessions £8.90.
Rail: Greenwich.

Flamsteed House, originally built for John Flamsteed, the first Astronomer Royal appointed by King Charles II, was the official government observatory from 1675 to 1948. That is when London's lights became too bright to see the heavens and it moved to Sussex. Today it is full of astronomical instruments, clocks and chronometers, but is perhaps best known as the home of the Prime Meridian (0 longitude), dividing the eastern and western hemispheres. The Observatory is part of the National Maritime Museum.

Science Museum

EXHIBITION RD, SW7, 020-7938 8000
020-7938 8123 (RECORDED INFORMATION)
WWW.NMSI.AC.UK
Open daily 10am-6pm. Adults £6.50, under 16 free, concessions £3.50. Free after 4.30pm.
U: South Kensington.

The Science Museum will thrill even the most unscientific-minded. Leaving aside the Space Exploration Galleries and Launch Pad (a first-class hands-on exhibition for children), the museum, with its five floors of exhibits, brings such varied subjects as medical history, the art of navigation, the weather, computers and transport to life. Exhibits range from a magnificent collection of scientific instruments and apparatus originally belonging to King George III in the eighteenth century and

Puffing Billy, the earliest surviving locomotive (1813), to Apollo 10. How scientific discoveries and progress have transformed our lives plays an equally important part, and there are enough interactive displays to satisfy the most avid seeker of scientific discovery, from age three upwards. The new Wellcome Wing, between the Natural History Museum, Imperial College and the Science Museum will be devoted to contemporary science, medicine and technology and includes a 450-seat IMAX cinema. Good cafés and shop.

Sherlock Holmes Museum

221B BAKER ST, NW1, 020-7935 8866
Open daily 9.30am-6pm. Adults £5, children £3.
U: Baker St.

A faithful reconstruction of Holmes' rooms at 221b Baker Street, this small museum with its memorabilia of the world's most famous sleuth is a must for Holmes' fans. Good small shop.

Sovereign Gallery

THE ROYAL MINT
7 GROSVENOR GARDENS, SW1, 020-7931 7977
Open Mon.-Fri. 10am-4pm. Admission free.
U: Victoria.

Run by The Royal Mint, it tells the story of the sovereign, the gold coin King Henry VII introduced. Also all the new issues are on show (and many are on sale) here.

Theatre Museum

7 RUSSELL ST, WC2, 020-7836 2330
WWW.THEATREMUSEUM.VAM.AC.UK
Open Tues.-Sun. 10am-6pm. Adults £4.50, under 16 free, concessions £2.50.
U: Covent Garden.

There's a fascinating collection of theatrical memorabilia, from death masks to playbills, costumes to make-up boxes, a model of Shakespeare's Globe to a jumpsuit of Mick Jagger's. They hold different exhibitions and workshops throughout the year, and have on display the important Somerset Maugham collection of theatrical paintings. If you love the theatre it's worth a visit.

Looking for an address?
Refer to the index.

Victoria & Albert Museum

CROMWELL RD, SW7, 020-7938 8500
020-7938 8441 (RECORDED INFORMATION)
WWW.VAM.AC.UK
Open daily 10am-5.45pm, late viewing Wed.
6.30pm-9.30pm. Adults £5, under 18 & special
concessions free. Also free after 4.30pm.
U: South Kensington.

The V and A as it is popularly known, officially the National Museum of Art and Design, is the largest decorative arts museum in the world, covering a mind-boggling seven miles of galleries. Opened in 1857 with the accent on design and craft in commerce, it was the brainchild of Prince Albert and civil servant Sir Henry Cole (who, incidentally, sent the first Christmas card in 1843). The massive, comprehensive museum is arranged in a unique way. It is divided into galleries devoted to art and design to express the style of an age (such as Europe from 1600 to 1800) and into study collections, which concentrate on materials and techniques. The Dress Collection, the Historic Musical Instruments Collection, the Indian Gallery (which contains the greatest collection of Indian Art outside India, a legacy of the British Empire), the Chinese Gallery, the Japanese Gallery, the Samsung Gallery of Korean Art, the Glass Galleries, the Silver Galleries, the Raphael Cartoons and the Jewellery Gallery all merit visits. Unless you have a specific purpose in mind, the best way to enjoy the museum is to wander through at random. That way you discover sections like the vast metalwork department, full of snuff-boxes, arms and armour, watches, clocks, locks and salt cellars. You also don't want to miss the extraordinary Cast Courts, which turn out to be two galleries containing Victorian plaster casts of Europe's great sculptures and masonry originally made as teaching aids. As so much of Europe's art is eroding with pollution, this was not such a bad idea.

William Morris Gallery

LLOYD PARK, FOREST RD, E17, 020-8527 3782
Open Tues.-Sat. & first Sun. every month
10am-1pm & 2pm-5pm. Admission free.
U: Walthamstow Central.

The childhood home of the famous late-Victorian designer, craftsman and socialist, this eighteenth-century house exhibits all aspects of the world of William Morris and Co., as well as telling his biography including his political writings. For the devotee, this place—which also has works by Frank Brangwyn and other examples of Victorian style—is a must-see.

Wimbledon Lawn Tennis Museum

CHURCH RD, WIMBLEDON, SW19, 020-8946 6131
Open daily 10.30am-5pm. (Open during
Wimbledon fortnight for ticket holders only.)
Adults £5, children £4, concessions £4.
U: Southfields.

Lawn tennis grew out of real tennis in the 1870s, when in 1875, one croquet lawn at the All England Croquet Club was transformed into a tennis court and the new game became all the rage. The museum is both great fun (lots of good exhibits often displayed in appropriate room settings), and informative. Did you know that Bunny Austin was the first man to wear shorts on the Centre Court (1933), that each racket uses 33 feet of animal gut and that 33,000 bath buns and 18 tons of strawberries are consumed every Wimbledon fortnight?

PARKS & GARDENS

Alexandra Park

ALEXANDRA PALACE, MUSWELL HILL, N22
020-8365 2121, WWW.ALEXANDRAPALACE.COM
Open daily 24 hours.
U: Wood Green. Rail: Alexandra Palace.

Go to this 22-acre park for superb views all over London. Ally Pally, as Alexandra Palace is locally known, opened in 1873 as North London's answer to Crystal Palace, but burnt down after only 16 days. It was rebuilt and used extensively: as a barracks during World War I, then for Belgian refugees and German prisoners of war who landscaped the grounds. In 1936, it became the BBC's first TV studio. Today it's an entertainment and exhibition centre and has an indoor ice-rink and sports facilities. It holds regular antiques fairs and events plus a great Bonfire Night fireworks display (the Saturday nearest 5 Nov).

Battersea Park

ALBERT BRIDGE RD, SW11, 020-8871 7530
Open daily dawn-dusk.
Rail: Battersea Park.

London's second largest park created for Londoners (the first being Victoria Park in the

East End). It was opened on marshy fields beside the river by Queen Victoria in 1853. Its delightful ornamental lake, Old English Garden and carriage drives made it an instant success with the Victorians, who used it almost exclusively for the great new craze of bicycling which was forbidden in Royal Hyde Park. In 1985 the Peace Pagoda, one of more than 70 built around the world, was opened. Today the park contains a botanical garden, deer park, the Festival Pleasure Gardens (part of the 1951 Festival of Britain), tennis courts, boating lake and a children's zoo with monkeys, snakes, deer, otters and a reptile house.

Chelsea Physic Garden

SWAN WALK, SW3, 020-7352 5646
Open Apr.-Oct. Wed. noon-5pm, Sun. 2pm-6pm, Feb. for special days (telephone in advance to check). Adults £4, children £2, concessions £2. U: Sloane Sq.

Tucked away in a peaceful corner of Chelsea, this delightful garden was founded by the Worshipful Society of Apothecaries in 1673 to grow plants for medical study, following Pisa (1543) and Oxford (1621). Internationally important, the garden conducted two-way traffic: plants were sent from all over the known world to be cultivated and studied here, while the first cotton seeds were packed up here and sent down the Thames and on to the new colony of Georgia. Today it is a small, pretty four-acre garden of herbs, flowers, trees, and medicinal plants grown in a newly established area. Pharmaceutical companies around the world are once again researching the uses of natural drugs from plants grown in Chelsea—the garden has come full circle, it seems. It's a wonderful place for a summer afternoon. To the sound of bird song and the distant hum of traffic on the Chelsea Embankment, you can stroll around the ancient trees, historical walks and the first rock garden created in this country (1772).

We're always interested to hear about your discoveries and to receive your comments on ours. Please let us know what you liked or disliked; **e-mail us at gayots@aol.com.**

Chiswick House & Gardens

BURLINGTON LANE, W4, 020-8995 0508
WWW.ENGLISH-HERITAGE.ORG.UK
Open Apr.-Sept. daily 10am-6pm, Nov.-Mar. Wed.-Sun. 10am-4pm. Adults £3.30, ages 5-16 £1.60, concessions £2.50.
Rail: Chiswick.

Though called Chiswick House, the gardens are what people really come to see. The house, modelled on a Palladian villa, was never intended to be lived in, but was built in 1725-1729 by the 3rd Earl of Burlington, specifically to show off his works of art and as a place to entertain his friends. The gardens, full of delightful eighteenth-century temples and grottoes, were the first to move away from the formal Dutch-style so popular at that time and epitomised by those at Hampton Court Palace. Only one or two of the little buildings remain, but the garden makes a delightful informal park and people come from miles around to see the camellias housed in the early nineteenth-century conservatory.

Crystal Palace Park

SYDENHAM, SE19
Open daily dawn-dusk.
Rail: Crystal Palace.

This park where Joseph Paxton's great glass house was re-erected after the Great Exhibition in 1851, was formally opened in 1854 by Queen Victoria and became one of the showplaces of Victorian London. Fires in the vulnerable glass 'Crystal Palace' however took their toll and the park's importance and attraction gradually declined. The last and most disastrous fire was in 1936 when the flames were visible from Brighton, 60 miles away. Today it is best known for the Victorian prehistoric stone monsters; there's also a boating lake, a children's zoo and the Crystal Palace National Sports Centre (see above).

Green Park

PICCADILLY, SW1
Open daily 5am-dusk.
U: Green Park/Hyde Park Corner.

Full of daffodils in springtime, this small 53-acre park was once part of Henry VIII's hunting ground. Charles II made it into a royal park, and being a monarch who liked his pleasures, built a snow-house in the middle of it to keep his wines cool in summertime (you can still see the mound). During the eighteenth century, it was a known haunt for duelling, highwaymen, ballooning and grand fireworks displays, which reached their height in 1748 at the celebration of the end of the War of the Austrian Succession. Today it's a good place to rent a deck chair on a summer afternoon, or just to stroll around away from the hustle and bustle of capital life.

Greenwich Park

GREENWICH, SE10
Open daily 6am-dusk.
Rail: Greenwich.

The park was first enclosed in 1433, but what we see today was created later by Louis XIV's gardener, Le Nôtre, who designed the gardens at Versailles and was invited by Charles II to do a similar job for him. Greenwich enjoyed its best days under the Tudors. Henry VIII was born here and retained a particular fondness for the park where he hunted deer and jousted. The park is magnificent, rising from river level gently to the Queen's House and up to the top of the hill and the Royal Observatory. It's worth the climb to the top, though the wonderful symmetry of the original design is marred today by towering Canary Wharf.

Hampstead Heath

HAMPSTEAD, NW3
Open daily 24 hours.
U: Hampstead. Rail: Gospel Oak/Hampstead Heath.

Some 790 acres of rolling hills, meadows, woods, ponds and lakes, this is one of London's wonders, an area of open spaces and great vistas which through legislation is kept in perpetuity for the people's enjoyment. Lying between the hilltop villages of Hampstead and Highgate, it's a collection of properties added to the original Heath over the years. Parliament Hill became part of the Heath in 1889, Golders Hill Park in 1898 and Kenwood in the 1920s. Further small areas were added subsequently (such as the delightful, secret Hill Garden signposted off the road beyond Jack Straw's Castle) and today it constitutes a 'green lung' for Londoners. At weekends it's full of people flying kites, jogging, having picnics and exercising their dogs. On the three main holiday weekends of Easter, May and late summer, there's a popular fun fair at South End Green.

Highgate Cemetery

SWAIN'S LANE, N6, 020-8340 1834
Open East Cemetery Apr.-Oct.: Mon.-Fri. 10am-5pm, Sat.-Sun. 11am-5pm, Nov.-Mar.: Mon.-Fri. 10am-4pm, Sat.-Sun., 11am-4pm; West Cemetery tours Apr.-Oct.: Mon.-Fri. noon, 2pm, 4pm, Sat.-Sun. hourly 11am-4pm, Nov.-Mar.: Sat.-Sun. 11am-3pm. East Cemetery £1, West Cemetery tour £3.
U: Archway.

The most fascinating of all London's Victorian cemeteries, Highgate opened its western part in 1839. A perfect example of exotic High Victorian taste with an Egyptian Avenue, a street of family vaults and the Circle of Lebanon, famous names which lie peacefully here include Tom Sayers (last of the barefisted fighters, scientist Michael Faraday, the poetess Christina Rossetti and writer Mary Ann Evans (George Eliot). Many have elaborate tombstones, with dogs, angels and other figures watching beside them. Rescued by the Friends of Highgate Cemetery, it is being sensitively restored and remains one of London's great nature reserves. In the newer East Cemetery, the most famous tomb is that of Karl Marx.

Holland Park

ABBOTSBURY RD, W14
Open Apr.-late Oct. daily 7.30am-10pm (can vary); late Oct.-Mar. 7.30am-4.30pm (can vary).
U: Holland Park.

A relatively late addition to London's parks, this small, intimate place full of wooded areas, rhododendrons and azaleas as well as the odd unexpected peacock was made into a public park in 1950. It stands on the former grounds of Holland House, a splendid mansion bombed during World War II. Holland House, now a student hostel, forms the backdrop for the annual outdoor Holland Park Theatre which performs mainly opera (for details call the Central Library, 020-7937 2542). The former Garden Ballroom is now The Belvedere Restaurant.

Keeping Out of Step

If you're crossing **Albert Bridge** in Chelsea, look for the sign that demands that troops break step while marching over it. The vibrations, it was felt, might cause it to collapse.

Hyde Park

HYDE PARK, W2
Open daily 5am-midnight.
U: Hyde Park Corner/Marble Arch/Lancaster
Gate/Knightsbridge/High St Kensington.

This huge 619-acre park, made up of Hyde Park and Kensington Gardens, has been a royal park since 1536 when King Henry VIII seized the lands of Westminster Abbey at the Dissolution of the Monasteries. The monk's loss is the public's gain: it was turned from a hunting and hawking park for the indefatigable Henry VIII into a public park by Charles I. Protector Cromwell sold it off; Charles II took it back again and created the road which became the place for polite society to see and be seen. When William and Mary came to live in Kensington Palace they had 300 lamps hung from the trees along the route du roi (or Rotten Row as it became anglicised as). However even this eminently sensible precaution did nothing to deter the gangs of notorious highwaymen who, along with the duellists, continued to haunt the park. The Serpentine was created by damming the Westbourne River in 1730, and during the 1814 celebrations for the defeat of Napoleon, the complete Battle of Trafalgar was reenacted on the lake. The park continues to be a place for entertainment with huge open-air concerts. Speaker's Corner (by Marble Arch) provides a platform for anyone with a cause and a loud voice.

Regent's Park

REGENT'S PARK, NW1
Open daily 5am-dusk.
U: Baker St/Camden Town/Regent's Park.

Another acquisition by Henry VIII, it became part of the town plans of the Prince Regent who commissioned John Nash in the early nineteenth century to design an extremely grand 'garden city' for his aristocratic friends within the park. Fifty-six villas in a variety of classical styles were planned though only eight were finally built. It's a beautiful and gracious park with Nash's Terraces around the edge and Queen Mary's Rose Garden in the centre. In the summer, the Open Air Theatre puts on a season of plays. The boating lake is famous for its wide variety of water birds. London Zoo has been updated, and now contains an important extra section on the biodiversity of life on the planet.

Richmond Park

KINGSTON VALE, SW15
Open daily 7.30am-dusk.
U: Richmond.

King Charles I first enclosed this huge park of 2,470 acres in 1637 with an eight-mile wall to form a hunting park. Today herds of deer still wander through these relatively wild areas of woods and bracken-covered heath. Big enough to absorb five cricket pitches, two golf courses and twenty-four football grounds without the public being aware of them, the park has two eighteenth-century lakes, beloved by anglers, and the Isabella Plantation, full of rhododendrons.

Royal Botanic Gardens

KEW, RICHMOND, SURREY
020-8940 1171 (RECORDED INFORMATION)
Gardens open daily in daylight hours. Telephone first for seasonal house and museum opening hours. Adults £5, children £2.50, families £13, concessions £3.50.
U: Kew Gardens.

First planted in 1759 by George III's mother, this 288-acre garden is the most complete public garden in the world. Sir Joseph Banks (1743-1820) who went round the world with Captain Cook, established the garden as an international plant centre, sending gardeners and plant-hunters off to every known continent to collect specimens for the magnificent collection. The gardens contain glorious Victorian heated palm houses (wonderful to dash into on a cold winter's day), trees, flowers, formal and informal gardens as well as royal buildings like tiny Kew Palace, the Orangery and much more.

Victoria Park

OLD FORD RD, E3
Open daily 6am-dusk.
U: Mile End.

The idea for a public park in London's East End was mooted in the 1840s; the park was opened in 1845 and the lakes excavated in 1846. Today, it's a welcome 'lung' for built-up Hackney, and has a small children's zoo and tearooms.

Waterlow Park

HIGHGATE HILL, N6
Open daily 7.30am-dusk.
U: Archway.

This beautifully landscaped park next to Highgate Cemetery, with its meandering paths, formal flowerbeds and mature trees, was bequeathed to the people by Sydney Waterlow. Today with tennis courts and a garden café (wonderful in the summer) in Lauderdale House, it's an active place for locals.

THEATRE & MUSIC

No city in the world has a richer or more varied theatrical life than London. Always the capital of English-speaking theatre, as well as a melting-pot of international talents, in the last decades of the twentieth century, Andrew Lloyd Webber and a small group of British directors and designers made London a serious competitor to New York for the musical crown as well. Today Disney and Broadway have begun to reassert American dominance here and the British blockbuster musicals are looking a bit long in the tooth. Opera and dance are benefiting from exciting new or refurbished venues made possible by generous grants from the National lotteries to celebrate the Millennium.

For information on **West End shows**, 09068 505 473; for **non-West End shows** 09068 505 476. All 09068 numbers are currently charged at 60p per minute. The **Society of London Theatre**'s website gives a lot of information; visit it at **www.officiallondontheatre.co.uk**

THEATRE
Musicals

On any given night in the West End, more people are watching musicals than all the other forms of theatre combined. The names of many of the fifteen or more shows will be familiar since the musical is international. Many of the current crop of musicals have come from Andrew Lloyd Webber and have been occupying the same theatres for years. But, there are good reasons for seeing such familiar works in London—this is where many originated and the eagle-eye of the original

director ensures standards are maintained. Competition to take over leading roles is intense, and many of the theatres the directors occupy are among the West End's most beautiful. London's high standards make it an excellent place to catch shows, which may have originated elsewhere. While the crop of Broadway musicals changes fairly regularly, some, such as Disney's *Lion King*, look to become scenic permanent features of the West End.

Drury Lane Theatre Royal

CATHERINE ST, WC2, 020-7930 8800
U: Covent Garden.

This is one of the most magnificent of London theatres and the oldest site in continuous use (since 1663). It deserves its royal title; it was here that Nell Gwynne delighted King Charles II and both King George I and George III survived assassination attempts. On a more artistic plane, David Garrick played in the eighteenth century; the mighty Edmund Kean in the nineteenth. The present vast edifice (it seats 2,237), with its classical exterior, cupola-topped entrance and twin staircases leading to the Grand Salon Bar, was designed by Benjamin Wyatt in 1812.

The West End

The West End is London's equivalent of Broadway—a relatively small area bounded by Shaftesbury Avenue and the Strand, which for 300 years or so has been the heart of theatreland. Most theatres in this area were built between 80 and 110 years ago. Beautiful gilded interiors, a sense of history, and occasional discomfort can help or hinder your enjoyment, so choose carefully. The West End has too many theatres producing too many different plays to mention more than a few and to give some guidelines as to what to expect. But, if you are uncertain what to see, check *Time Out* (weekly), *Where London* (monthly and free in four- and five-star hotels) or *Hot Tickets*, a Thursday supplement to the *Evening Standard*. The weekend quality national newspapers publish helpful summaries of all the main plays and performances.

Backstage Tours

One of the best ways to discover more about the theatre is to go on a backstage tour. The three mentioned here also take you beyond the stage, into the auditorium and the changing rooms and give you a good history of the place. There's nothing more exciting—and daunting—than standing on the stage staring out into the footlights and beyond. The experience should sort out the serious from the dilettante aspiring thespians. **Drury Lane Theatre Royal,** Catherine St, WC2, 020-7494 5060; **London Palladium Theatre,** Argyll St, W1, 020-7494 5454; **National Theatre,** South Bank, SE1, 020-7452 3400; **Royal Shakespeare Company,** Barbican Centre, Silk St, EC1, 020-7628 3351, **Royal Opera House,** Covent Garden, Bow St, WC2, 020-7304 4000.

Her Majesty's

HAYMARKET, SW1, 020-7494 5400
U: Piccadilly Circus.

Phantom of the Opera is one of Andrew Lloyd Webber's most popular shows and opened ten years ago at this attractive 1896 theatre, which changes its gender to Her or His Majesty's according to who is on the British throne at the time.

London Palladium

ARGYLL ST, W1, 020-7494 5020
U: Oxford Circus.

Another huge theatre (capacity 2,298), the Palladium was for many years the home of variety shows and 'to play the Palladium' was the ambition of every singer and comedian on both sides of the Atlantic. For the past few years, these lavish acts have been replaced by musicals.

Lyceum

WELLINGTON ST, WC2, 0870 243 9000
U: Aldwych.

The home of Henry Irving and the most famous theatre of Victorian London, the Lyceum had an unhappy twentieth-century, declining from music hall to dance hall, and

was only refurbished as a theatre at the very end of the last century. Today it is home to Disney's universally acclaimed *The Lion King*, likely to be a permanent fixture for many years.

New London

167 DRURY LANE, WC2, 020-7405 0072
U: Covent Garden.

Designed in 1973 by theatre designer Sean Kenny, the New London has been home to *Cats* since Trevor Nunn's first production opened here in 1981. Be warned 'latecomers are not admitted while the auditorium is in motion!'

Palace

CAMBRIDGE CIRCUS, W1, 020-7434 0909
U: Leicester Sq.

Owned by Andrew Lloyd Webber, this magnificent former large opera house, dating from 1891, is one of the few West End theatres not hosting one of his works. Beautifully refurbished inside and out, it became home to director Trevor Nunn's production of *Les Misérables* in 1985.

Subsidised Theatre

One of the reasons London retains its pre-eminence in the English-speaking theatre is because of state subsidy. The subsidised theatres not only offer some of the best productions of a range of plays from the classic to the contemporary, they are also a training ground for Britain's best actors, directors and designers, as well as first stops for productions heading for the commercial West End. The two main companies are the **Royal National Theatre** and the **Royal Shakespeare Company**, both of which occupy permanent, purpose-built London homes.

Royal National Theatre

SOUTH BANK, SE1
020-7452 3000, WWW.NT-ONLINE.ORG
U: Waterloo.

Opened in 1976, Sir Denys Lasdun's Royal National Theatre is a modernist concrete and glass building beside the Thames. It offers three contrasting theatre spaces and includes areas to relax with a drink and a snack, admire the sunset over the river or enjoy a free informal concert or exhibition. t teems with life before or after the show and is always a pleasure to visit. The public foyers were enlarged, a road separating the theatre from the river removed and backstage facilities enhanced with Lottery funding during 1997. Remarkably not one performance was missed during these works!

In 1997, Sir Trevor Nunn took over the artistic directorship from Sir Richard Eyre, whose 10-year reign had been the finest and most varied in the National's history. Nunn is maintaining this excellence and vitality and is a worthy heir to Lord Lawrence Olivier, Sir Peter Hall, and Eyre. He continues to pursue a deliberately eclectic policy using directors from other companies around the country and top British stage and screen actors in conjunction with a dedicated ensemble permanently attached to the company. This marriage of the established with the new offers constant surprises and revelations and is reflected also in the breadth of works presented—native and foreign, originals and translations. Nunn is himself one of the finest theatrical directors of the century. It was Nunn whose long reign at the rival Royal Shakespeare Company (RSC) made it the best company in the English-speaking world in the 1970s-80s. It is ironic that at a time when the National was strengthening an already supreme position in London, its only rival, the Royal Shakespeare Company chose to abandon its main London venue, the Barbican for the six months of summer (see below).

The three auditoria offer distinct theatrical experiences. The largest, the Olivier, seats 1,100 in an amphitheatre facing a large, open stage equipped with magical mechanical devices for spectacles in large-scale works. The most conventional is the proscenium-arched Lyttleton, which seats 900. The experimental Cottesloe seats up to 400, has flexible seating and offers everything from theatre-in-the-round to more conventional layouts. Despite the greater comfort and luxury of the two larger theatres, the Cottesloe can often be the most thrilling because it offers wonderful intimacy with the actors. Many of the National's finest productions sell out completely. But don't despair—a limited number of seats for each production is sold on the day of performance at 9.30am. Queue from 8.30am or before to be sure of a chance.

Royal Shakespeare Company

BARBICAN CENTRE, SILK ST, EC2
020-7638 8891, WWW.RSC.ORG.UK
U: Barbican.

As its name suggests, one of the main purposes of the RSC is to produce the works of the Bard, but it also embraces new plays and classics from the entire world repertoire. Originally based in Stratford, Shakespeare's birthplace, where it was founded 120 years ago, the company now divides itself between its three theatres there and its two in the Barbican in London. The RSC is more of a repertory company than the National in that one team of actors plays first the Stratford theatres and six months later comes to London. The Artistic Director, Adrian Noble, has almost as wide a range of directors as the National, and productions are exciting and innovative.

The building itself is something of an architectural folly: it opened in 1982, but dates in conception from a futuristic vision of the 1960s. Inside the building it's easy to get lost—get there early. But the two auditoria are magnificent. The main theatre is almost spherical giving even those in the remotest seats—the 'gods'—a good view of the large stage. The Pit is also impressive: it is small with a capacity of only 180-240, with the action three-quarters in the round so the audience feels a real involvement. Unfortunately, the RSC has decided to spend six months every summer away from London touring provincial cities. The management of the Barbican has responded imaginatively to this blow and every summer mounts a festival of international theatre, together with some dance and small-scale opera. British theatre is sometimes accused of being parochial, so the annual presence in London of the world's leading companies is a stimulus hugely to be welcomed.

Royal Court

SLOANE SQ, SW1, 020-7565 5000
U: Sloane Sq.

London's principal theatrical beneficiary of the National Lottery is the Royal Court, which reopened early in 2000 after a £26 million refurbishment. This left its two historic auditoria more or less as they have always been, but added much improved backstage facilities, easier access for all, and a sparkling new bar/restaurant excavated under Sloane Square. Originally built in1889, the Royal

Court has always been an important venue for new writers. Once it was George Bernard Shaw, Sir Arthur Pinero and Granville Barker, then, in the 1950s, John Osborne and the revival of realistic English drama, and since 1998, it has had a new, exciting, young Artistic Director, Ian Rickson. The minute studio Theatre Upstairs continues to be an important venue for radical new writing.

West End/ Mainstream Theatres

Plays—with the notable exception of *The Mousetrap* at St. Martin's Theatre—do not have long runs, but a few pointers as to what to look for can be given. Such is the excellence of the National and the RSC that transfers of their most popular productions can be amongst the best bets for quality serious theatre in the West End.

Albery Theatre

ST. MARTIN'S LANE, WC2, 020-7369 1730
U: Leicester Sq/Charing Cross.

This delightful theatre is now often the West End venue for major productions originating at the Almeida or Donmar (see below) looking for larger audiences.

Donmar Warehouse

EARLHAM ST, WC2, 020-7369 1732
U: Covent Garden.

This small theatre has been carved out of the upper floors of a magnificent Victorian warehouse in Covent Garden. Under the dynamic direction of the young Sam Mendes, it offers an exciting programme of classic revivals and small-scale, experimental musicals. Mendes, now a major film director (the Oscar-winning film "American Beauty"), is often successful in attracting very major stars from both sides of the Atlantic to appear in this intimate space.

Haymarket (Theatre Royal)

HAYMARKET, SW1, 020-7930 8800
U: Piccadilly Circus.

Second only to the Drury Lane Theatre Royal for a sense of history, the Haymarket was originally built in 1720 and rebuilt in 1821 by John Nash. A beautiful theatre is not in itself a reason to choose a production, but it is a wonderful bonus and the Theatre Royal's track record in choosing productions is good.

Old Vic

THE CUT, SE1, 020-7369 1722
U: Waterloo.

Opened in 1818, the Old Vic has had a central place in the development of London theatre, particularly through the twentieth century. The first permanent home for Shakespeare in London, the theatre was the inspiration for the development of both the National Theatre and Sadler's Wells. Beautifully refurbished in the 1980s, today it is home to a variety of excellent visiting companies and original productions.

Shakespeare's Globe

NEW GLOBE WALK, SE1, 020-7401 9919
Adult £7.5, child £4, family £15
U: London Bridge.

Shakespeare's 'wooden O' is a perfect reconstruction of a theatre designed in 1599, open to the elements for the audience but with a partially covered stage. Inspired originally by the late Sam Wannamaker, it took many years in the building, but now gives the viewer a superb experience. Part of the regeneration of the South bank of the Thames, the small theatre with its white-washed walls with half-timbering and thatched roof evokes a London of long ago. The season runs May to September and plays are performed almost whatever the weather. The audience sits on banked wooden benches, or stands in the pit below. You're very close to the action, and this combined with the intimacy of the space, often means audience participation, which reflects the theatre of Shakespeare's day perfectly. Each season under artistic director, Mark Rylance, presents a series of Shakespeare's plays, plus plays by his contemporaries. Get there early to walk around the complex, and if possible give yourself time to visit the exhibition (see above).

Young Vic

66 THE CUT, SE1, 020-7928 6363
U: Waterloo.

The Young Vic has no direct connection with the Old Vic, but has a similar policy of hosting visiting major companies—for example, it shares the Royal Shakespeare Company's London run with the Barbican. It also stages its own original productions in a modern two-thirds in the round purpose built auditorium.

Fringe Theatre

West End theatre is fed by the creative ferment of the fringe, London's equivalent of New York's 'Off Broadway'. It ranges from the well-established—indeed subsidised—theatre to small rooms in pubs.

Almeida

ALMEIDA ST, N1, 020-7359 4404
U: Angel/Highbury & Islington.

Since the artistic direction was taken over by actors Iain McDiarmid and Jonathan Kent, this tiny 1837 building has become acknowledged as the most exciting theatre outside the West End. It stages a mixture of premieres (by authors as notable as Harold Pinter) and the classics, adorned by stars who give their services for the Actors Equity minimum wage and directed by the two principals and celebrated guests. With a capacity of only 300 in an arena layout, intimacy as well as excitement is guaranteed. Located in Islington (near Camden Passage Antique market), the theatre is an easy ten-minute walk from the Angel or Highbury & Islington underground station.

Hackney Empire

291 MARE ST, E8, 020-8985 2424
Rail: Cambridge Heath.

Frank Matcham was England's most prolific and successful theatre architect—he designed 150 theatres between 1879 and 1912 as well as lots of pubs and early cinemas before his death in 1920. The Empire, which opened as a provincial variety house in 1901, is perhaps his most imaginative and now most beautifully preserved. Today, it offers a very varied mix of variety/music hall, plays, opera and music. Pantomime is especially notable at Christmas. Above all, it caters to the richly multicultural local community. At its best, it is an incomparable theatrical experience.

Hampstead

SWISS COTTAGE CENTRE, AVE RD, NW3
020-7722 9301
U: Swiss Cottage.

Housed in a shed-like building, the Hampstead Theatre in its almost 30 years of existence has sent many successes to the West End. Most productions are of new plays so prediction of what you might see is impossible, but this is the sort of venue always worth giving the benefit of the doubt. With perma-

nent tiered seating, this is an unusually comfortable way of visiting the fringe. The theatre is adjacent to Swiss Cottage underground station. Currently Lottery-backed plans for a new enlarged permanent theatre are beset with planning problems! If the outcome is successful, this will probably be a building site for the next two years.

King's Head Islington

115 UPPER ST, N1, 020-7226 1916
U: Angel.

This is deservedly the most famous of all London's pub theatres. It puts on a broad repertoire of new plays in a cramped room where you can eat beforehand (honest, good-value-for-money, ordinary food). The atmosphere is special and on the right night can offer great excitement. It is located in Upper Street 100 yards before Almeida Street.

Soho Theatre & Writers' Centre

21 DEAN ST, W1, 020-7478 0100
U: Tottenham Court Rd.

Opened in early 2000, this is a purpose-built centre for the Soho Theatre Company, which has been nurturing new talent for 30 years. Inside a striking modern building, there's an air-conditioned theatre, a studio and rehearsal room and a space for writers to work in, plus rooms for seminars and workshops. On the ground floor and in the basement, Café Lazeez operates a café and a more serious restaurant. The Centre has a great buzz to it, and there are some exciting plays on offer. With tickets at £5, it is fulfilling what it aims to do—bringing new work to a wide audience.

Theatre Royal Stratford East

GEORGE RAFFLES SQ, E15, 020-8534 0310
U: Stratford.

A tiny Victorian theatre located deep in the East End of London but conveniently close to Stratford tube station and subsidised mostly by local government, this theatre caters primarily for the local community. It also has a long history of developing popular works, which transfer to the West End from its days as the Theatre Workshop under Joan Littlewood in the 1960s. Often the work will be of only parochial interest, but look for their enjoyable and traditional Christmas pantomimes (a strange mixture of fairy tales, comedy and modern bawdy that is uniquely English). This theatre is another beneficiary of Lottery funds and enjoyed a well-merited refurbishment in 1998.

Tricycle Theatre

269 KILBURN HIGH RD, NW6, 020-7328 1000
U: Kilburn.

Another intimate theatre with an excellent track record of producing exciting new plays often with an Irish or Caribbean background.

Buying Tickets

The most convenient way is by phone direct to the theatre box office; only rarely is a booking charge made and tickets can be paid for by credit card or reserved up to 30 minutes before curtain-up. Most theatres are centrally located so you can often stop by in person to buy your tickets and check seat locations. For sell-out musicals try reputable theatre ticket agencies who make a booking charge (enquire the percentage). The cheapest way to buy tickets for many shows is at the Leicester Square Half Price Ticket Booth. Theatres with a surplus of unsold tickets deliver them for sale at half price plus a £2 service fee or £1 for tickets with a face value of £5 or less. Tickets go on sale for the day of performance only at 12noon for matinees and from 1pm to 6.30pm for evening performances, with a limit of 4 tickets per person. You have no choice of seats (you get the best available), but for the cost of a half hour in the queue this is a great way of economising on the cost. As seats for the English National Opera, The National and the RSC are often included the choice is wide. So successful is the official half price booth that unscrupulous competitors have set up on the streets leading into the square advertising similar offers, but delivering much less. Remember the genuine booth is inside the gardens of the Square itself on the south side opposite the Radisson Edwardian Hampshire Hotel.

MUSIC

London offers daily more than a dozen chances to listen to classical or contemporary music with artists varying from international stars to ambitious students. It has four symphony orchestras and a host of excellent chamber music groups.

Major Venues

Barbican

BARBICAN CENTRE, SILK ST, EC2
INFORMATION & BOOKINGS 020-7638 8991
U: Barbican.

There's anything from full-scale symphonies in the main concert hall to performances of chamber and folk music in the various foyers.

Royal Albert Hall

KENSINGTON GORE, SW7
020-7589 8212, WWW.ROYALALBERTHALL.COM
U: High St Kensington.

A beautiful round building with everything from Eric Clapton to the best symphony concerts. It's probably best known, in Britain at least, as the home of the annual BBC Promenade concerts ('the Proms'). Tickets for the Proms can be bought on the day of performance, but long queues build up early, so take a cushion or camping stool with you. The 'Promenaders' then sit in the middle of the hall or high up in the balconies.

St. John's Smith Square

SMITH SQUARE, SW1, 020-7222 1061
U: St. James's Park/Westminster.

Chamber and symphony orchestras play in this converted church. Concerts are frequently recorded by the BBC and the atmosphere is very special. The Footstool is a good wine bar/restaurant in the crypt.

South Bank Centre

SOUTH BANK, SE1
020-7960 4242, WWW.SBC.ORG.UK
U: Waterloo.

Three halls with music from pop to Prokofiev. The Royal Festival Hall is the biggest venue with good acoustics for symphonies or great choral works. The Queen Elizabeth Hall is smaller, suitable for chamber music and visiting opera productions. The Purcell Room seats under 400 people and is used for recitals, readings and debut concerts by new artists. Book shops, bars, cafés, exhibitions and foyer concerts make the South Bank Centre a pleasant place for a concert-goer.

Wigmore Hall
36 WIGMORE ST, W1, 020-7935 2141
U: Bond St.
The refurbished Wigmore Hall is an intimate and pleasant place for small-scale concerts. Good acoustics and a friendly atmosphere have made it probably the most loved of London's classical venues. There is music every night.

Music Festivals

London offers a number of music festivals but two offer special excellence not only of performance, but also of unique locations, some of which are usually closed to the public. **The City of London Festival** at the end of June and the beginning of July stages concerts in St. Paul's Cathedral, many of Sir Christopher Wren's beautiful City churches and historic City livery halls. **The Covent Garden Music Festival** in the late spring also gives the chance to enjoy a Handel opera in a Wren church. It also features Gilbert & Sullivan at Bow Street Magistrate's court or the mysteries of the Masonic Temple in Gt. Queen Street for a musical revival or an oratorio.

Other Regular Music Venues

London's cathedrals all offer wonderful church music with magnificent choirs and organists, and many churches hold frequent secular concerts. The principal music colleges' concerts give you the chance to enjoy young talent for a modest cost.

British Music Information Centre
10 STRATFORD PL, W1, 020-7499 8567
U: Bond St.
The BMIC, which promotes contemporary British music and has a music library, also

hosts small concerts and recitals of twentieth-century music on Tuesdays and Thursdays at 7.30pm. Telephone for programmes.

Cecil Sharp House
2 REGENT'S PARK RD, NW1
020-7485 2206, WWW.EFDSS.ORG
U: Camden Town.
The home of the English Folk Dance and Song Society and the Vaughan Williams Memorial Library (England's leading multimedia folk archive), Cecil Sharp House boasts two concert halls, training and meeting rooms, bar, café and more. Frequent concerts and recitals.

Christ Church, Spitalfields
COMMERCIAL ST, EC1, 020-7344 0287
U: Aldgate East.
Nicholas Hawksmoor's magnificent church is the scene of a very fine musical festival every June and a series of concerts leading up to Christmas.

Guildhall School of Music
BARBICAN CENTRE, SILK ST, EC2
020-7628 2571
U: Barbican.
This prestigious music school holds regular concerts and events by students, mostly free. Telephone for programmes.

Royal Academy of Music
MARYLEBONE RD, NW1, 020-7873 7373
U: Baker St.
One of London's trio of outstanding schools of music that gives regular concerts.

Royal College of Music
PRINCE CONSORT RD, SW7, 020-7589 3643
U: South Kensington.
The place for students' showcases top concerts. Telephone for programmes.

St. James Piccadilly
197 PICCADILLY, W1, 020-7381 0441
U: Piccadilly Circus.
A lovely church in a convenient location, which holds regular lunchtime concerts.

St. Mary-le-Bow
CHEAPSIDE, EC2, 020-7248 5139
U: St. Paul's.
They hold series of concerts on Thursdays at
1.05pm.

St. Martin-in-the Fields
TRAFALGAR SQUARE, WC2, 020-7839 8367
U: Charing Cross/Leicester Sq.
St. Martin's is world-famous for its concerts,
which range from lunchtime recitals to Mozart
by candlelight in the evening. On the east side
of Trafalgar Square, the church is one of
London's landmarks. There's a good café in
the crypt.

Opera & Dance

Britain's National Lottery built up a fund to
celebrate the millennium. Opera and dance
were major beneficiaries with the Royal Opera
House virtually rebuilt around its original
auditorium and Sadler's Wells built completely
new.

Coliseum
ST. MARTIN'S LANE, WC2, 020-7632 8300
U: Leicester Square.
London's largest theatre, with 2,356 seats,
has been home to the English National Opera
(ENO) since 1968. Built in 1904 by prolific
theatre architect, Frank Matcham, the
Coliseum was originally a variety theatre, then
home to lavish spectaculars and briefly a
down-at-heel cinema before its rebirth as an
opera house. ENO's present singular character
stems from its origins as a touring company
with the mission to bring opera to new audiences in the provinces. To do this it needed a
permanent company, mostly British—soloists
as well as chorus—and it's directors decided
everything would be sung in English for
greater accessibility. Today, it has turned these
traditions to good effect: its soloists are drawn
from a small but increasingly excellent pool of
largely British talent. Because they work closely together, more of an ensemble feel has
developed, and with it a more committed acting style than is usual in opera. Under Paul
Daniel, its dynamic, young music director,
musical and artistic standards are very high.

Royal Opera House
BOW ST, WC2, 020-7304 4000
WWW.ROYALOPERAHOUSE.ORG.UK
U: Covent Garden.
After a refurbishment costing more than
£220 million, only the magnificent auditorium
and façade remain of the original 1858 building. 'Covent Garden' as the Royal Opera is
invariably known, boasts a completely rebuilt
backstage with ample rehearsal rooms and
scenery storage facilities. The rebuilt Floral
Hall (part of the original flower market), and
Linbury Studio, a totally new experimental
theatre are wonderful. In return for a large
government subsidy, Covent Garden promised
to reduce its prices to encourage greater
access. Eccentrically it has drastically cut the
price of the best seats for the most prestigious
operas, but increased the cost of the mass of
seats. Unfortunately, seats only for sale on the
day of performance have been dropped, so
book ahead!

Sadler's Wells
ROSEBERY AVE, EC1, 020-7863 8000
WWW.SADLERS-WELLS.COM
U: Angel.
Totally rebuilt with Lottery funding, the
new Sadler's Wells stages a variety of touring
opera and dance companies, giving London
the opportunity to enjoy visits from the Welsh
National Opera and Glyndebourne, as well as
international visitors. The new auditorium is
somewhat stark, but is a welcome and important addition to London's cultural riches.

Experimental Venues for Music & Dance

The Drill Hall
CHENIES ST, WC1, 020-7637 8270
U: Warren St.
For small-scale opera, dance and offbeat
drama, often with a gay orientation, this venue
offers an exciting and innovative programme.

The Place
17 DUKES RD, WC1, 020-7387 0031
U: Euston.
This is the principal experimental venue for
dance.

OUT OF LONDON

CONTENTS

INTRODUCTION 414

BATH 414

OXFORD 419

WINDSOR 424

YORK 425

GREAT BRITAIN

⑤ YORK

❷BATH

❸ OXFORD

WINDSOR❹

LONDON ❶

©2000 GP

413

INTRODUCTION

Though London may seem to be the centre of the world, there's plenty to see and enjoy within a very short distance. With **Bath** a mere 90 minutes away by train, **Oxford** and **Windsor** about an hour, and **York** only two hours away, it's worth taking a trip into the green and pleasant countryside. On the practical side: we have indicated published hotel prices, and where breakfast is included. However, there are often weekend/weekday/special breaks, and prices may also vary according to the season and availability.

BATH

The onset of Spring transforms the English landscape as hedgerows blossom, crocuses, daffodils and tulips fill rural gardens, apple blossoms appear and the countryside takes on that glorious colour of fresh limes. But the weather, particularly in March, can be cruel, so go prepared. Whether you choose the **Cheltenham Gold Cup** meeting in early Spring, or book for the **Bath International Music Festival**, this great Roman city, a World Heritage Site, is enjoyable at any time.

If you take the train, you can stay for a weekend without a car. Otherwise, it's about a two-hour drive by the M4 motorway. If you're prepared to take a slower route and see a little of the countryside, go via Andover then on towards Salisbury. The tiny village of **Pitton** is a good place for a country lunch stop. The Silver Plough was a farmhouse until it became a pub. Traditionally decorated, it serves good homemade food, from winter soups to fresh pastas, smoked trout to smoked pork sausages and British puds like treacle tart. There are two afternoon possibilities. **Wilton House** is a wonderful seventeenth-century mansion still owned by the Earls of Pembroke. The neoclassical interiors of architect Inigo Jones are echoed in the pretty Palladian bridge standing on the grounds. **Stonehenge** is Europe's most famous and complex prehistoric monument—still presenting a mystery as to its original purpose. Then it's on to Bath and a spectacular stay in the heart of the city.

Bath has been a visitor destination since Roman times when the discovery of **hot springs** led to a complex of baths plus a temple to the goddess Minerva in the city the Romans called Aqua Sulis. By AD 410, the Romans had abandoned their most northerly province of Britain, and the baths fell into disuse; the Roman buildings were plundered for their valuable stone. It wasn't until the early eighteenth century that Bath was once again on the map, put there by Queen Anne who was advised by her doctors that the waters would cure her gout. Three men were largely responsible for the city we see today: Ralph Allen, a stone quarry owner, and the architects John Wood the Elder and John Wood the Younger. Together they set about building the most splendid new Georgian city, with terraces and crescents and circles of houses in mellow, golden Bath stone. Throughout the eighteenth century, fashionable society came here to take the waters and enjoy the balls and assemblies. In the early nineteenth century, the young and fashionable followed the Prince Regent to the newly discovered seaside resort of Brighton for their summers and Bath once again was left to the staid and the elderly. But in 1879, when digging out new sewers, the borough engineer discovered the remains of the Roman Baths. Extensive excavations were made and ever since, tourists have flocked here. Currently a state-of-the-art spa is being constructed. Facilities will include a rooftop pool and terrace, more pools on other levels, treatments rooms, whirlpools, solarium, steam room, gym, shop and café. (*For more information: www.bathspa.co.uk*).

The city's attractions are many and varied. Starting at the beginning, go to the **Roman Baths** themselves, sulphurous, smoky and subterranean. A light lunch in the nearby Pump Room keeps you rooted in the past, so an afternoon visit to the **Museum of Costume** and the perfect Georgian interior of **No 1 Royal Crescent** fits the mood perfectly.

Bath is famous for many things, not least the **Bath Bun** which you can buy at any bakery. For something equivalent, try Sally Lunn's buns at—where else?—*Sally Lunn's Refreshment House*, which claims to be the oldest house in Bath and certainly has one of the most interesting cellars and original bakeries.

Bath **has become more of a serious restaurant city lately**, led initially by the hotels, but now with an excellent choice of exciting venues in the city centre. Top of the list, however, is *Lettonie*, which moved from Bristol to Bath a few years ago and has remained consistently top of the range.

A good city to walk, Bath has beautifully proportioned streets and crescents full of **plaques to the famous and infamous** who came here for the waters and for the entertainment—aristocratic gamblers, architects, statesmen, Sir William Herschel, the potter Josiah Wedgwood, the soldier General Wolfe. A walk over **Pulteney Bridge** takes you to the **Holburne of Menstrie Museum** with its collection of great English paintings, furniture and silver. The no.18 bus drops you at **The Avenue** and a ten-minute walk to the unusual **American Museum in Britain**, showing domestic life in America from colonial times to the end of the nineteenth century. It's a delightful manor house, with good grounds and a café for light lunches. You can just spend a day in Bath, which will give you a tantalising glimpse of the place and the desire to return, but to get the full flavour of this historic city, take a few days.

HOTELS

Apsley House Hotel ♪♪
NEWBRIDGE HILL, BATH BA1 3PT
01225-336 966, FAX 01225-425 462
WWW.APSLEY-HOUSE.CO.UK
E-MAIL: INFO@APSLEY-HOUSE.CO.UK
9 rms £65-£130 inc English breakfast.

A P 🛏 *(English breakfast)*
Delightful house built in 1830 as the country residence for the Duke of Wellington, Apsley House has pretty gardens and a warm welcome. Antiques and oil paintings furnish the good-sized, period rooms and the drawing room and breakfast room open up into the garden. The welcome is genuine, the breakfast very good, and the centre of Bath is just a 20 minutes' walk.

Bath Priory ♪♪♪
WESTON RD, BATH BA1 2XT
01225-331 922, FAX 01225-448 276
E-MAIL: BATHPRIORYHOTEL@COMPUSERVE.COM
28 rms £140-£300 inc English breakfast.

A 🛏 *(English breakfast)* 🍴 ≋ P
This delightful hotel occupies a Bath stone house and is set in its own grounds a little away from the centre. There's a gracious drawing room, and throughout the public rooms, traditional furnishings and good antiques along with the smell of wood smoke give a homey feel. Bedrooms are individually decorated with good antiques, paintings and English country-style fabrics. A recent refurbishment has added more rooms and a new spa, putting it in the first league of Bath's hotels.

Holly Lodge ♪♪
8 UPPER OLDFIELD PARK, BATH BA2 3JZ
01225-424 042, FAX 01225-481 138
WWW.HOLLYLODGE.CO.UK
E-MAIL: STAY@HOLLYLODGE.CO.UK
7 rms inc English breakfast S £48-£33, D £79-£97.

A P 🛏 *(English breakfast) No Smoking throughout.*
With views over the city and a truly charming welcome, Holly Lodge is a popular place. Beautifully decorated and maintained with a comfortable sitting room and luxurious furnishings, bedrooms are a large and bathrooms have everything you need, including a heated mirror. Breakfast, taken in the light and airy Mediterranean-style room, offers more than the usual standard fare like smoked salmon; croissants are home baked.

Lettonie ♪♪
35 KEDLESTON RD, BATH BA1 3QH
01225-446 676, FAX 01225-447 541
WWW.BATH.CO.UK/LETTONIE
2 double rms £95, 2 four-poster rms £150.

A P
For years, we have been championing Martin and Siân Blunos for their top restaurant; now their refurbished, elegant Georgian house, on the outskirts of the city, offers good accommodations also, with comfortable rooms and breakfast served in the bedroom.

Queensbury Hotel ♪♪♪♪
RUSSEL ST, BATH, BA1 2QF
01225-447 928, FAX 01225-446 065
E-MAIL: QUEENSBERRY@DIAL.PIPEX.COM
29 rms £90-£185, 1 four-poster rm £210.

A P
This stylish townhouse hotel, owned by Stephen and Penny Ross, is delightful and in a residential street near the centre. It's welcoming and gracious with eighteenth-century features retained from the original house. There is no chintz in sight, but instead a sophisticated, elegant feel to the furnishings. Bathrooms are of a top standard coming with all the expected toiletries and plush bathrobes. Its flower-filled restaurant, The Olive Tree, offers good Modern British cooking. The many awards and accolades The Queensbury has

received has kept it in position as one of the best country house hotels in Britain.

Royal Crescent Hotel 🍴🍴🍴🍴

16 ROYAL CRESCENT, BATH, BA1 2LS
01225-823 333, FAX 01225-339 401
30 rms £190-£290, 15 stes £380-£695.
Set lunch £18; set dinner £36, à la carte dinner for two is around £90.

A ≈ **P** ⬡ *Holistic spa.*

In the centre of Bath's most famous crescent, the Royal Crescent Hotel is set up high enough to give wonderful views over the city and out to the rolling countryside beyond. There are four-poster beds in the bedrooms, and antique furniture throughout in this period hotel which still has many of its historic features intact. The Spa is magnificent, housed in the splendid Bath House and offering special package retreats for three nights. Treatments include all the main massages, detoxifying wraps and facials you would expect in a relaxing and elegant setting. Dinner in the refurbished Pimpernel's, now in the Dower House looking across a garden, offers good Modern British cooking, combining classic dishes with Eastern influences.

RESTAURANTS

Bath Priory

CONTEMPORARY EUROPEAN 14/20 👨‍🍳
WESTON RD, BATH BA1 2XT
01225-331 922, FAX 01225-448 276
E-MAIL: BATHPRIORYHOTEL@COMPUSERVE.COM
Lunch & Dinner daily. £££

A ☎

The refurbishment of the Bath Priory has brought a new spa and huge improvements in the dining room, which welcomes with comfortable banquettes and pretty colours. Chef Robert Clayton's modern style offers well-sourced ingredients cooked well in a straightforward style. A three-course dinner at £39 offered seven starters and main dishes and eight desserts. The cooking is confident: scallops pan-fried to a delightful caramel consistency with fresh salad leaves, and a rich braised duck leg in Madeira with creamed potatoes with flecks of truffle. A main dish of sea bass came lightly sautéed with tagliolini and a delicate basil velouté; guinea fowl came as a tender steamed breast with lime and a herb-roasted leg with red wine sauce. Desserts tread a

rewarding path: pear poached in vanilla with a properly bitter dark chocolate sorbet, and fresh raspberry and crisp coconut tuiles with hazelnut creams. For those who cannot make up their mind, an extra £5 brings the whole selection. The wine list goes around the world; service is charming. Set 2-course lunch £17.50, 3 courses £23.50, Sun. lunch £35; set 3-course dinner £39.

Browns

FRENCH 11/20
THE OLD POLICE STATION, ORANGE GROVE, BATH
01225-461 199
Open Mon.-Sat. 11am-11.30pm, Sun. noon-10.30pm. £

A

Part of the Browns' chain—and as always in an interesting old building—this one retaining a detention cell which is now a private dining room. The menu is good standard fare such as Caesar salad, duck liver parfait to start, pastas, salads and main courses from confit of duck to salmon fishcakes. Good for families and open all day, you can spend as much or as little as you like.

Clos du Roy

FRENCH/BRITISH 11/20
1 SEVEN DIALS, SAW CLOSE, BATH
01225-444 450, FAX 01225-404 044
Lunch & Dinner daily. £

A ☎

Now something of an institution, the musical theme dominates in this rather idiosyncratic restaurant with images of instruments everywhere, even framing the windows. Good bistro-style menu of favourites like steak béarnaise, plus good fish imaginatively treated as in crab cheesecake with dill sauce, and spicy seafood hotpot with cumin risotto. Desserts equally attract with interesting combinations: try coconut and mango crème brûlée. Set lunch Mon.-Sat. 2 courses £9.95, 3 courses £13.95; set Sun. lunch £11.95; set 2-course dinner £16.50, 3 courses £19.50.

Looking for an address?
Refer to the index.

Lettonie

FRENCH   17/20   🍴🍴🍴

35 KELSTON RD, BATH
01225-446 676, FAX 01225-447 541
WWW.BATH.CO.UK/LETTONIE
Lunch & Dinner Tues.-Sat. £££

A ☎

Since moving from their first small place in Bristol to Bath, Siân and Martin Blunos' enterprise has gone from strength to strength, becoming a known destination in its own right. As before, Martin Blunos' culinary genius is at once apparent in a menu which excites the eyes as well as the palate. His self-confident cooking is full of visual surprises, as in the now famous starter of flaming duck egg, topped with sevruga caviar that comes with ice-cold vodka (though this particular treat does attract a £5 supplement). Another surprise is the pheasant tortellinis which come with a grain mustard sauce and the crab mousse with a cream sauce laced with Cognac. French classics are given a new Eastern—but this time Eastern European orientation (Martin Blunos is from Latvia)—in subtle counterpoints of sweet and savoury, as in honey-glazed belly of pork with truffle cream sauce, or loin of venison with haggis and liquorice-infused sauce. He is not afraid to experiment and the results can be spectacular, very rarely missing their target. Desserts get similar treatment: try the hot rhubarb soufflé with cardamom ice cream; or for a savoury, the cannelloni of goat cheese on an onion marmalade with a lemon-butter sauce. The Blunos family has worked hard for their success, and the proof is on your plate. Set 2-course lunch £20; set 4-course dinner £47.50.

The Moody Goose

MODERN BRITISH   13/20   🍴

7A KINGSMEAD SQ, BATH
TEL/FAX 01225-466 688
Lunch & Dinner Mon.-Sat. £

A ☎

This basement restaurant in Bath's centre is light and airy with cream colours and quality pictures on the walls. The eponymous goose sits in the middle of the three interconnecting spaces, keeping an eye on things. Innovative cooking brings a mixture of influences as in crab with pancetta and tarragon mayonnaise; sea bass with a sharp horseradish; and roast breast of guinea fowl with a smoked-chicken

ravioli. Game is to the fore in winter. Desserts bring out the glutton: as in caramelised rich pudding with glazed pears, excellent chocolate concoctions and a classic tarte Tatin. Good wine list; friendly service. Set 2-course lunch & 6pm-7.15pm £10; set dinner £20.

No 5 Bistro

FRENCH   12/20

5 ARGYLE ST, BATH
01225-444 499, FAX 01225-318 668
E-MAIL: CHOME@GLOBALNET.CO.UK
Lunch Tues.-Sat., Dinner Mon.-Sat. ££

A ☎

Centrally located by gracious Pulteney Bridge, No. 5 Bistro has brought good casual-style dining to Bath. The setting is informal: wooden floors, poster-covered walls and candles on tables. Food is attractive, with dishes like Provençale fish soup, and warm chicken with tarragon mousse as starters; well-sourced main dishes of meat and game given an Asian touch with lemon grass and lime, and good desserts like cinnamon tart with light fromage frais. The wine list, too, sticks to well-tried wines at reasonable prices.

Olive Tree

MODERN BRITISH   14/20   🍴

QUEENSBURY HOTEL, RUSSEL ST, BATH, BA1 2QF
01225-447 928, FAX 01225-446 065
E-MAIL: QUEENSBERRY@DIAL.PIPEX.COM
Lunch Mon.-Sat., Dinner nightly. £££

A 💳 **P**

In a bright, airy, colourful basement dining room, Matthew Prowse and proprietor/chef Stephen Ross continue to attract a local regular crowd as well as visitors to the hotel with their excellent cooking, using well-sourced ingredients in classic style. The menu is seasonally driven, and fish is particularly favoured. Expect seared Cornish scallops with pumpkin and cardamom risotto; pot-roasted halibut with roasted tomatoes and fennel; Gressingham duck with cucumber couscous, grilled spring onion and sweet chilli sauce; and delightful desserts like lemon curd tart with lemon confit; chocolate and pistachio tart; and imaginative ice creams. Set lunch £15.50; set 3-course dinner Sun.-Fri. £24.

Woods

MODERN BRITISH 11/20
9-13 ALFRED ST, BATH
01225-314 812, FAX 01225-443 146
Lunch & Dinner Mon.-Sat. ££

A 🏠 🍴

Pleasant brasserie just opposite the Assembly Rooms, Woods has continued to hoe a modern British path very successfully. Wooden floors, high ceilings and an informal bar at one end of three interconnecting dining rooms give a good first impression, carried through a meal which might start with roasted pigeon breast salad or soup and move on to casseroles and dishes like lambs' kidneys with mustard sauce. The formula is for a simple lunch—excellent if you're on a serious sightseeing day—and a more elaborate dinner. Set 2-course lunch £7; set 2-course dinner £12.25, 3 courses £22.50.

PUBS & CAFÉS

Old Green Tree

12 GREEN ST, BATH, 01225-448 259
Mon.-Sat. 11am-11pm, Sun. 7pm-10.30pm

Small, delightful local pub with home-cooked lunchtime bar food (soups, open sandwiches) and daily specials. Good beer selection.

Sally Lunn's Refreshment House & Museum

4 NORTH PARADE PASSAGE, BATH, 01225-461 634
Daily 10am-11pm.

Silver Plough

PITTON, WILTSHIRE, 01722-712 266
Lunch & Dinner daily.

Telephone numbers in England have eleven digits, beginning with a zero. The initial zero must be omitted if you are calling England from abroad. Within the country, dial the entire eleven digits.

Near Newbury

The Vineyard at Stockcross 💰💰💰

NEWBURY, BERKS RG20 8JU
01635-528 770, FAX 01635-528 398
WWW.THE-VINEYARD.CO.UK
E-MAIL: GENERAL@THE-VINEYARD.CO.UK
33 rms £139, D £165-£445 plus VAT. Air cond.

A 🍴 **P** ≈ 🔾

Conveniently close to Newbury, The Vineyard at Stockcross, which opened in 1998, is a very well-refurbished hotel, set in delightful countryside. The first view is of an ornamental small lake in front of the low building, lit by flaming torches; once inside there is all the charm of a gracious house with very touches. Bedrooms are decorated prettily with plenty of luxurious touches in both the furnishings and the bathrooms. Public rooms are a mix of old and new, with lovely views onto the surrounding grounds. The spa and fully equipped gym are good, with treatments ranging from thalgo to all the necessary aromatherapy today's spa guests expect.

The Vineyard at Stockcross Restaurant

CONTEMPORARY EUROPEAN 14/20 👨‍🍳
SEE ADDRESS ABOVE
Lunch Sun.-Fri., Dinner daily. ££££

A 🏠 **P**📷

The arrival of Billy Reid, formerly at L'Escargot, has brought a new edge to the kitchen. His classic French style with a modern light twist that was so successful at the London restaurant has resulted in a self-confident, contemporary menu—starters like roasted escalope of foie gras with pear chutney, potato crisps and a salad dressed with a light sherry vinaigrette; and beignet of black pudding with a pomme purée given a grain mustard twist and tart apple jus. Mains might include a robust Goosnargh duckling with choucroute, dauphinoise potatoes and red wine jus; and a sublime roast Dover sole unusually coming with peas, beans, tomato, basil and potato purée and rösti, all with a delicate vermouth cream. This is a fine mixing of tastes, and Billy Reid pulls it off supremely well. Desserts, too, are given a new look, as in a stem ginger brûlée with poached rhubarb and rhubarb sorbet, or chocolate ice cream with vanilla cheesecake crumble. It's set in a split-level restaurant with a stone floor and a steel balustrade depicting a vineyard, the large windows giving light and views to the outside. The wine list is comprehensive, with stars like bottles from the California vineyard of the owner, Sir Peter Michael. Set 2-course lunch £16, 3 courses £22; set 3-course dinner Sun.-Thurs. £42, set 6-course 'Fusion' menu £75 inc 4 glasses of wine.

OXFORD

Oxford is a bustling, lively place at any time of the year with a life independent of the university for which the city is famous. You can get there easily by train; alternatively it's about a one-hour, 15 minute drive from London. If time is short, take the M40 motorway; otherwise go by the prettier road to **Henley**, then through some charming countryside and **Nettlebed** and **Dorchester**. Oxford offers three good small hotels. Or, as many do, and everyone who can afford it should do, book in at one of Britain's very best country-house hotels, Le Manoir aux Quat'Saisons, with an internationally renowned restaurant.

Oxford is well known for **Frank Cooper's Oxford Marmalade** (no longer made here), **Oxford University Press**, the **covered market**—which nobody should miss—and lately for the fictional but oh-so-believable **Inspector Morse**, and, of course, its **ancient university** which is the main visitor attraction. If you want a guide, the Oxford Information Centre organises walking tours of the colleges and the city conducted by Blue Badge Guides which last two hours. Or you can wander at will through the halls, quads and gardens of the medieval and later buildings. Oxford's beauty is not so immediate as that of its rival university town, Cambridge; you have to seek it out down small passages, through gateways into College quads (at Cambridge they're called 'courts') and along semi-hidden alleyways.

Now with **35 colleges**, the University began when a group of English students were expelled from Paris in 1167. But it was not until 1249 that the first college, **University College**, was founded. For a good walk, start at the centre of the old city, **Carfax** ('the crossing of the four ways'). South along St. Aldate's you come to **Christ Church**, the grandest college and the home of *Alice in Wonderland*; Lewis Carroll, a mathematics don here, wrote it for Alice Liddell, the dean's daughter. Along Blue Boar Street, you come to **Corpus Christi College**, founded in 1517 and the first college at which Greek was taught. Nearby **Merton College** possesses some of the oldest buildings in Oxford; its gateway tower was built in 1418, the chapel was built in the last decade of the thirteenth century. The library is one of the oldest medieval libraries in England (1371-78), and was the first to store books upright in shelves instead of laying them flat in presses.

Along **High Street** (east of Carfax), you come across the university church of **St. Mary's**. It's well worth climbing up the spire high above the rooftops. From here you look out over the mellow buildings and understand the nineteenth-century poet Matthew Arnold who described Oxford as '*That sweet city with her dreaming spires*'.

Behind the church there's a cluster of buildings: **Brasenose College** (so called after its brazen or brass door knocker) and **All Souls College**, founded in 1438 by King Henry VI and dedicated to the souls of all those who fell in the Hundred Years War against the French. The **Sheldonian Theatre** was the first work of Sir Christopher Wren and was built 1663-1669. Impossible to miss is the splendid **Radcliffe Camera**, built to house Dr. Radcliffe's science library, and now part of the world famous **Bodleian Library**, one of the six copyright libraries in Britain.

Oxford is a city where you wander at will, either discovering new sights, or if you are a frequent visitor, rediscovering your favourites. Try to see **New College** in New College Lane, founded in 1379, with a particularly fine chapel adorned with Epstein's statue of Lazarus and gardens bounded by the old city wall. **Magdalen College** (1458) is worth seeking out for its famous fifteenth-century Bell Tower, lawns, river walk and deer park, as well as its three quads; **Worcester College** (1713) for its delightful gardens and lake.

If colleges pall, Oxford has other attractions. The **Botanical Garden** on High Street—the oldest in Britain—was founded as a 'Physic Garden' in 1621. The **Ashmolean Museum** on Beaumont Street contains the university's art and archaeological collections. The **Pitt Rivers Museum** is one of the world's great anthropological collections in an extraordinary Victorian setting. **Blackwell's bookshop** in Broad Street is a large and comprehensive bookshop, a delight to browse through. And **The Oxford Story** gives you the chance to take a ride through scenes from the University's past.

Oxford can easily occupy you for a whole weekend, but if you want to see a little of the English countryside, go out to **Woodstock**, a typical old market town, slightly sleepy but kept permanently on the visitor map by the splendid palace of **Blenheim**, a huge baroque edifice built by Sir John Vanbrugh for the first Duke of Marlborough. Lunch at The Feathers Hotel is a delight, the welcoming hotel offering both bar snacks and more substantial meals and, should you decide to stay here peace and quiet in the centre of the small town. *Further information from the Oxford Information Centre, St. Aldate's, 01865-726 871.*

HOTELS

Bath Place Hotel
4 & 5 BATH PL., HOLYWELL ST, OXFORD OX1 3SU
01865-791 812, FAX 01865-791 834
WWW.BATHPLACE.CO.UK
10 rms £90-£130 inc continental breakfast.

Small hotel in the centre of Oxford, in a seventeenth-century house located in its own small courtyard. The restaurant Il Cortile serves classic Italian food, offering dishes from light pastas to wild duck with citrus fruits. Set lunch is £19.50, set dinner £25, à la carte for 2 is around £70.

Old Bank Hotel
92-94 HIGH ST, OXFORD OX1 4BN
01865-799 599, FAX 01865-799 598,
WWW.OXFORD-HOTELS-RESTAURANTS.CO.UK
E-MAIL: INFO@OLDBANK-HOTEL.CO.UK
44 rms £135-£225, 3 stes £255-£300, inc breakfast. Air cond.

The latest venture from Jeremy Mogford, founder and former owner of Browns restaurants and owner of the Old Parsonage Hotel. The Old Bank in a building dating back to Tudor times is just that, a former Barclays in the centre of Oxford. Rooms in this old listed building are prettily decorated with Stanley Spencer pencil sketches on the walls. There are all the state-of-the-art facilities in the rooms and all have excellent marble bathrooms. Most

rooms look out over the dreamy spires of this university city, plus there's a private rooftop viewing platform for one of the best photo opportunities around. Large twentieth-century paintings hang throughout the hotel. The public rooms are just as delightful, while the Quod Bar and Grill has a contemporary look with cream-coloured and bare brick walls, wood and leather chairs and a stone floor. Cooking is Italian based.

Old Parsonage Hotel
BANBURY RD, OX2 6NN
01865-310 210, FAX 01865-311 262
WWW.OXFORD-HOTELS-RSTAURANTS.CO.UK
E-MAIL: OLDPARSONAGE@DIAL.PIPEX.COM
30 rms £125-£170. 1 ste £195, inc breakfast. A meal for two in the bar is around £50.

In a delightful old building, this hotel has history, dating back, the owners claim, to 1308. Inhabitants have been many and varied, including Oscar Wilde, who was a student here when it was owned by University College. A warm Cotswold stone 1660s building, the hotel was refurbished and re-opened in 1991 by Jeremy Mogford, the founder of the successful Browns chain. Today it is one of Oxford's few hotels, with 30 pretty, comfortably and elegantly decorated rooms, all with en-suite marble bathrooms with good showers. There's a pretty secluded walled garden which many rooms look on to, and in the summer you can eat outside on the front terrace. The all-day Parsonage bar is equally welcoming with its huge stone fireplace, lit in winter and serves a good modern menu with plenty of well prepared modish ingredients like guinea flow, red mullet and couscous. There is 24-hour service, which is unusual in a small hotel.

RESTAURANTS

Al-Shami
LEBANESE   12/20
25 WALTON CRES, OXFORD
01865-310 066, FAX 01865-311 241
Open daily noon-midnight. ££

This good Lebanese restaurant is popular with locals who come for classic, fresh Lebanese cooking in a pretty, greenery-filled setting. Raw vegetables appear when you sit down, then go for the mezze which covers all the bases, or grilled mains of perhaps lamb or chicken kebabs. Desserts are good; service is friendly; Château Musar is on the wine list.

Browns

INTERNATIONAL   11/20
5-11 WOODSTOCK RD, OXFORD, 01865-319 600
Mon.-Sat. 11am-11.30pm, Sun. noon-10.30pm. £

A

Opened in 1976 in an old garage, this is one of Oxford's great eating places for students, as well as providing sustenance to all and sundry throughout the day. The succcessful Browns' menu formula is pursued here (see Bath), and as with all Browns, it's a very good choice for children.

Cherwell Boathouse

MODERN BRITISH   12/20
BARDWELL RD, OXFORD, TEL/FAX 01865-52746
Lunch Tues.-Sun., Dinner Tues.-Sat. ££

A 🕿 ♟ 📷 *(No smoking)*

Charming restaurant, set—as you've probably guessed—in an old boathouse, this is a simple place with similarily styled cooking. Expect dishes like fishcakes with a sweet sesame sauce or black pudding with bacon salad and balsamic vinaigrette as starters; pork with braised Puy lentils in a tomato and basil sauce or sautéed chicken with herb mash and tarragon jus for mains. Desserts go the tasty route of sticky toffee puddings with toffee nut sauce and homemade ice creams. The wine list is excellent, and very good value. Set lunch Tues.-Fri. £18.50, Sat.-Sun. £19.50; set dinner £20.50.

Lemon Tree

CONTEMPORARY EUROPEAN   12/20
268 WOODSTOCK RD, OXFORD
TEL/FAX 01865-311 936
Daily 11am-11pm. ££

A 🕿 ♟

Something of a revelation in Oxford, the Lemon Tree is modern and bright, with a large bar at the front, a glassed-over dining room and a delightful garden for summer dining. Colours are natural—sands and ochre, and the design is bold with large paintings, much greenery and big mirrors. Food is equally bold, mixing and matching as in chicken

liver in a salad dressed with mango-based sauce; Thai prawns; duck confit with baby figs, and confit of lamb with borlotti beans enlivened with chorizo. Desserts might include Normandy apple tart; cheeses are English. Service is young and friendly; and there is a short, good wine list.

Le Petit Blanc

FRENCH   13/20   ♟
71-72 WALTON ST, OXFORD
01865-510 999, FAX 01865-510 700
Open daily 11am-11pm (9.45pm Sun.) ££

A 🕿 ♟

This Raymond Blanc-inspired and run chain (there are Le Petit Blanc brasseries in Cheltenham and Birmingham), aims to serve good, value-for-money meals in a brasserie setting. Chef Martin White treads the set wide path very well, offering regional French dishes from chargrilled tuna Niçoise (£3.75) and parfait of foie gras and chicken liver with a girolles salad (£6.50), to Toulouse sausage with mousseline potatoes and rich devil sauce, and braised pig cheek with glazed onion and girolles as mains (£8.50, £11.50). The menu also includes more straightforward pastas, risottos, rump of lamb, and ribeye steak. Excellent choice of wines, and friendly atmosphere in this popular, often noisy, restaurant which welcomes children with open arms. There's also the Blanc Vite of 'Fast, Fresh food' like soup du jour and baguette (£3.75) and moules marinière with frites (£.6.75.) Set 2-course menu £12.50, 3 courses £15; child's menu (up to 12 years old), £5.95, £7.95.

The White House

MODERN BRITISH   12/20
2 BOTLEY RD, OXFORD
01865-242823, FAX 01865-793 331
Lunch & Dinner daily. £

A 🕿 ♟

This 'gastro-pub' has been achieving great things with its menu of well-cooked modish dishes, served in a former pub with a garden at the back. Dishes might include tuna fish cake with a coriander and coconut dressing, tender grilled calf's liver or roast salmon. Portions are generous. The wine list is good; service is friendly. The place gets very busy at weekends.

PUBS

The Bear
ALFRED ST, OXFORD, 01865-721 783
Mon.-Sat. noon-11pm, Sun. noon-10.30pm.
Lunch daily.
Dating from 1242, this friendly pub has a collection of ties that has to be seen to be believed.

Eagle & Child
49 ST. GILES, OXFORD, 01865-310 154
Open Mon.-Sat. 11am-11pm, Sun. noon-10.30pm..
Locally known as the Bird and Baby, J. R. Tolkein and C.S. Lewis drank here; today it's patronised by all.

Kings Arms
40 HOLYWELL ST, OXFORD, 01865-242 369
Open Mon.-Sat. 11am-11pm, Sun. noon-10.30pm. Bar food all day.
Busy pub with small comfortable small rooms, with a dictionary for crossword fiends in the Dons Bar. Decent bar food like baked potatoes and homemade soups.

Turf Tavern
TAVERN BATH PL, HOLYWELL ST, OXFORD
01865-243 235
Open Mon.-Sat 11am-11pm, Sun. noon-10.30pm.
Picturesque low-ceilinged beamed pub described in Thomas Hardy's *Jude the Obscure*. Simple food, good beer, courtyards for summer eating. In winter, they put up braziers so you can still sit the outdoors.

At Great Milton

Le Manoir
aux Quat' Saisons ♪♪♪♪
CHURCH RD, GREAT MILTON, OXFORD OX44 7PD
01844-278 881, FAX 01844-278 847
WWW.MANOIR.COM
E-MAIL: LEMANOIR@BLANC.CO.UK
TOLL FREE (FROM USA ONLY) 1-800-845-4274
32 rms £230-£550. Air cond.

🅰 ⋔ ♈ 🐎 *nearby* P ⌬ ☱
Le Manoir's setting, in beautifully restored gardens in the small village of Great Milton

eight miles outside Oxford, is idyllic, and so is the experience of staying here. Le Manoir is now as Raymond Blanc envisaged it. From the wood-panelled Tudor entrance a bar and drawing rooms lead off to the right for coffee, pre-dining drinks or afternoon tea in winter. Luxurious furnishings, mixing a range of beautifully textured fabrics in natural colours, and original art on the walls, much of it twentieth century and open fires and glorious flower arrangements decorate the well proportioned rooms. To the left, you walk through a bright traditional dining room into the light, spacious conservatory restaurant looking out onto landscaped gardens, lit at night. Bedrooms and suites are designed to evoke very different moods. The Provençale room with its high beamed ceiling is furnished with polished old French furniture; Anais is a tribute to sensuality—of a pre-war kind—where a long cigarette holder and flapper-style clothes would not be out of place and a fur rug invites 'Eleanor Glynn to sin'. In the main building, a Tudor room is furnished with a four-poster bed and exquisite seventeenth-century antiques. Bathrooms are large and luxurious, each in keeping with the style of the room. It is the attention to detail which marks out Le Manoir and includes touches such as the hi-fi system which extends to the bathroom, a good range of toiletries, as well as fresh flowers, drinks and fruit in your room on arrival. Staff ratios are suitably high, and the young, enthusiastic and professional team are always discreetly on hand. The gardens fit seamlessly into the picture. Kitchen gardens are planted with neat rows of vegetables, all freshly used daily in the restaurant. Green lawns are surrounded by herbaceous borders; shrubs and climbing plants cascade in glorious profusion over the walls; and there's even a pond and a little stream behind a half-ruined wall. Le Petit Blanc cooking school operates here, its kitchen attached to part of the main kitchen. The hotel holds a wedding licence, and there are rooms for private parties. But despite all this extra activity, it is all so well organised and run that nothing intrudes on the individual. No expense has been spared at Le Manoir, and it shows. Relais & Châteaux.

Le Manoir
aux Quat'Saisons Restaurant
FRENCH 19/20 ♛♛♛♛
SEE ADDRESS ABOVE
Lunch & Dinner daily. ££££

🅰 ☎ 🚗 🎄📷☕

The final completion of the new kitchens and the settling in of chef Gary Jones from Cliveden has confirmed Raymond Blanc's restaurant as one of the very best. A truly memorable experience starts with drinks and canapés, taken either in the glorious, comfortable drawing rooms, or if the weather is fine, outside looking out at the green sweeping lawns punctuated by flower beds and stone walls. Tables in the airy conservatory are well spaced; service from the young staff is superb—thoroughly professional and unobtrusive. The atmosphere buzzes both at lunch and dinner and there is none of that hushed reverence which such top cooking might induce in a less self-confident restaurant. The menu, which is seasonally led and uses to the full Le Manoir's fresh organic garden produce picked daily, shows off Raymond Blanc's superb skill in mixing ingredients, tastes and textures, a true balancing act which never seems to fail. An 'assiette apéritive' of superb scallops and seafood kicked off a memorable meal which began with starters of foie gras with quince, unified with a gelée of aged balsamic vinegar, and foie gras with delicate leeks and truffle sauce. Luxury ingredients are treated with proper respect here, but so is the more humble oxtail, filled with a mixture of shallots and wild mushrooms, with a beautifully reduced red wine sauce and offset by a creamy parsnip purée. Roasted Anjou pigeon was served as its leg and breast, with foie gras, rolled and deep fried, and a truffle jus providing an extra rich element that elevated the intensely flavoured dish to food of the gods while the fresh green taste of broad and French beans kept it rooted on Earth. Others have remarked on a spectacular meltingly tender squab baked in a salt crust with foie gras on the side. Roasted monkfish was contrasted with cockles and mussels; pan-fried sea bass and roasted langoustine came with a punchy basil oil and raw tomato coulis. A mango soup with passion fruit sorbet, and a sharp citrus jelly with orange butter sauce provides a little light relief before spectacular desserts—hot chocolate fondant with its rich chocolate interior accompanied by a bitter almond cream and pistachio ice cream. This is just one of the homemade ice creams and sorbets, which in one dish comes as a visual joke as mounds of ice cream placed on a 'palette' of biscuit base looking like the real thing. This element of innovation typifies Raymond Blanc's approach, which combines an inspired individual's knowledge and imagination with a kitchen that is known for its real craftsmanship and superb technical skill. Exquisite petits fours and coffee in one of the drawing rooms round off the perfect dinner. The wine list is long and serious, French dominated but with the New World and other European countries getting a good showing. Serious clarets and Burgundies lead, but there are some excellent, good-value wines and a selection of half bottles like a Pernand-Vergelesses 1997 and a top Savigny-lès-Beaune 1995. The whole package comes at a price of course, but this is one to save for, and the set lunch is a remarkable value. Set lunch Mon.-Fri. £35; Menu Gourmand £84.

At Woodstock

The Feathers Hotel ♪♪♪
MARKET ST, WOODSTOCK, OXFORDSHIRE, OX20 1SX
01993-812 291, FAX 01993-813 158
WWW.FEATHERS.CO.UK
E-MAIL: ENQUIRIES@FEATHERS.CO.UK
18 rms £95-£220, 3 stes £220-£275, inc breakfast.

🅰P🍽♻🛁

Eight miles from Oxford in the country town of Woodstock, just outside the gates to Blenheim Palace, the privately owned seventeenth-century Feathers is a pretty warren of rooms. Originally four houses, there are unexpected staircases and odd corners which add to the charm. Bedrooms are in English country house style; there are good antiques, red and green colours, luxurious fabrics and comfortable chairs and sofas. The Windchat bar is a favourite local place; the restaurant attracts people from far and wide.

We're always interested to hear about your discoveries and to receive your comments on ours. Please let us know what you liked or disliked; e-mail us at gayots@aol.com.

The Feathers Hotel Restaurant

CONTEMPORARY EUROPEAN **14/20** ♟
Lunch & Dinner daily. £££
SEE ADDRESS ABOVE

🅰 ☎

The restaurant is charming, with panelled walls and filled bookshelves, a fireplace, crisp linen, candles and fresh flowers. The cooking may be rooted in France with recognition of British tradition, but it's done with plenty of invention as well as expertise. On the menu, it sounds as if tastes will clash; in reality, they work beautifully together, each flavour adding to a satisfying whole. Starters might include roasted scallops with split-pea casserole, smoked pancetta bacon and deep-fried onion rings, or deep-fried battered langoustines beignets with herbed purée potato and tartare sauce. A main dish of herbed cannon of lamb wrapped in puff pastry rosemary and garlic velouté came with buttered carrots and spinach; a baked sea bass with ratatouille, black olives, balsamic vinegar, roasted tomato, rouille and pesto. Desserts are simpler, as in warm plum tart with amaretto and almonds or the hot chocolate sponge with dark chocolate sauce and vanilla ice cream. Set 2-course lunch £17.50, 3 courses £21.

WINDSOR

Windsor Castle, where the kings and queens of England have lived for 900 years, dominates the small town and the surrounding countryside. First a wooden fortress built by William the Conqueror in 1066—a day's march, or twenty-two miles from his other castle, the Tower of London—the present collection of buildings is a mixture of architectural styles. Three sections—**Upper**, **Middle** and **Lower Wards**—give dramatic views over the river and countryside. Within the castle, you see the small houses of the **Military Knights of Windsor**, an order founded by King Edward III as the 'Poor Knights of Windsor', and **St. George's Chapel**, begun in 1478. Reminiscent of King's College Chapel, Cambridge, it is full of tombs (ten monarchs are buried here) and monuments to various royal figures. But most visitors come to see the **State Apartments**, the formal rooms used by the reigning monarch for ceremonial, state and official occasions. Open to the public when the Royal Family is not in residence, they are now beautifully restored after a huge and very destructive fire. Some of the Queen's impressive art collection is on display on the walls. Also within the castle is the delightful **Queen Mary's Dolls' House**, created by the architect Sir Edwin Lutyens for the young Queen Mary and given to her by the nation in 1923. It's a wonderful world in miniature. You can combine a trip to Windsor with a trip to the Waterside Inn at Bray, one of Britain's best restaurants (with rooms attached) or eat at the excellent Fat Duck.

Windsor is about 27 miles west of London and a short car journey. Trains from Waterloo Station run regularly and take about 45 minutes.

Bray-on-Thames

Fat Duck

FRENCH **17/20** ♟♟♟
1 HIGH ST, BRAY-ON-THAMES, BERKS
01628-580 333, FAX 01628-776 188
Lunch Tues.-Sun., Dinner Tues.-Sat. £££

🅰 ☎

This was once a pub, although that is hard to believe, particularly since the recent renovations which have added a little more comfort for diners and vastly improved the kitchen space. Prepare yourself for a most unusual voyage, chef Heston Blumenthal is entirely self-taught, completely obsessive and almost universally praised for his involved, complex cooking. He approaches his subject with scientific zeal, analysing and dissecting dishes only to rebuild them with extraordinary wit, skill and not a little complexity. Some maintain his cooking is overworked, dishes containing one ingredient too many, but others marvel at his confidence. He plays superbly well both with taste and texture—cuttlefish cannelloni for example, the body stuffed with duck confit, foie gras and maple syrup and served on a purée of parsley which send taste buds on an odyssey. Main courses are no less involved, game and offal being particular favourites, although fish is deftly handled, too. Veal sweetbreads, for example, roasted in a salt crust and hay and served with confit parsnips, lettuce and truffle cream and grilled clams. Desserts may appear simple, as in spiced ice cream with pineapple and chilli jelly, but wait until you taste the jelly. Wine is another Blumenthal passion and the list is enormous.

It's well-stocked and largely, although by no means exclusively, French, and fair in its pricing with plenty to offer the cautious.

Waterside Inn

FRENCH   18/20   ♔♔♔
FERRY RD, BRAY-ON-THAMES
01628-620 691, FAX 01628-620 691
Lunch Wed.-Sun., Dinner Tues.-Sun. ££££

A ☎ ❚ ⚲⌨

The setting is totally pastoral: right beside the river Thames, where willow trees move gently in the light breeze, and the whole place imparts the feeling that all is well with the world. The sense of wellbeing extends to the food and the service at the Waterside, which continues to be run by Michel Roux with consumate care, maintaining the kind of precise cooking and attention to technical detail that can make a meal here a once-in-a-lifetime experience. Start with an apéritif under the weeping willow or in a little gazebo, then move into the light, airy dining room. The menu is to linger over, particularly if you choose the à la carte where prices rise to £34.50 for a lobster starter. But once served, any reservations disappear: this was perfectly timed pan-fried lobster with a delectable white port sauce and a vegetable julienne subtly flavoured with ginger to give it extra punch. The combinations of taste and the perfection of the saucing is impressive, as in a mains of turbot grilled on the bone that comes with either a tomato béarnaise sauce or a chive-infused olive oil. The Spring menu offers seven dishes under 'Les Potages, Hors d'Œuvres et Œufs' including a foie gras terrine flavoured with Sauternes and gooseberry, the fruit again providing an unexpected but totally compatible flavour. 'Les Crustacés et Coquillages' offers five dishes—such as lobster appearing in a salad with avocado pear and grapefruit, dressed with a citrus vinaigrette. As we have remarked before, it is the intensity of flavour that so impresses: as in a masterly veal dish that comes stuffed with a duxelle of cèpes, grilled kidney on braised lettuce and the sweetbreads en croûte with a white wine and parsley jus. The cheese board is exceptional, bringing French and English unpasteurised farm cheeses to the fore. But leave room for desserts, the Waterside is well known for them: perhaps a raspberry gratin with orange and Grand Marnier sauce, or for those who cannot make up their minds, a selection of chocolate treats, or the selection of six desserts. The wine list is magisterial, firmly French-based and with some real treats (at a price), though there are a few affordable bottles, and the house wine is £19. Service is excellent, efficient but self-effacing, reflecting the total professionalism of the place. Set lunch Tues.-Fri. £30.50, Sat. £69, Sun. £44.50; set 5-course dinner £69.50; Menu Exceptionnel (must be taken by everyone in the group) 7 courses £71.50.

YORK

Of all Britain's great historic cities, York inspires huge admiration and devotion in Brits and visitors alike. **One of Britain's best preserved medieval cities**, it's only two hours from London by train. But that apart, it's also an extremely friendly city and an easy one for visitors to get to know quickly. Taken as a whole, you have a magical experience.

York is a city for walking, another of those places where you discover its corners only on foot. Founded by the Romans in AD 71 as a fortress to quell the rebellious northerners, York was first known as 'Eboracum'. With the departure of the Romans successive invasions followed, but it was the Vikings who left the greatest mark on the city, not least by the fact that the gates are still called bars and the streets are called gates (the Danish word for street is gaten). The eleventh-century Norman conquerors found a thriving little city which they promptly sacked but they did build the magnificent city walls which you can still walk on today. In the Middle Ages, York became the most important city in the north as its massive **Minster**—the largest north of the Alps—testifies. By the eighteenth century, York was also the most fashionable, welcoming the 'Beau Monde' from far and wide for the balls and assemblies, who found graceful Georgian houses to stay in. By great good fortune, the Victorian Industrial Revolution largely passed York by, and instead the city became a refuge for the mill owners of the neighbouring towns, leaving it wonderfully preserved and unspoilt by Victorian 'improvements'.

The best way to start a visit to this intriguing city is to **walk around the walls** which enclose the 263 acres of medieval York. From here you look down on the web of narrow streets whose names read like a history lesson: **Spurriergate** named after the spur makers, the **Shambles** from 'fleshammels' (once a row of butchers' shops) and the curiously named

Whip-Ma-Whop-Ma Gate, derived from a whipping post where criminals were thrashed. Dominating the skyline is the great **York Minster** which took more than 200 hundred years to build. It has some of the finest medieval stained glass in Britain and is a must for any visitor to York. One of the most exciting developments in recent years was the excavation of the Viking settlement in **Coppergate** and the opening of the **Yorvik Centre**. The visitor boards a 'time car' and is whisked back through history to a reconstruction of the Viking community of over 1,000 years ago. The car passes through the actual excavation site and finally the visitor walks through an exhibition of everyday items from the dig: woolen socks, shoes and, rather surprisingly, hornless Viking helmets.

No visit to York is complete without seeing the **Castle Museum**. Partly housed in the old prison, visitors see the highwayman Dick Turpin's cell (the residents of York are particularly proud of this famous inhabitant) and walks through reconstructed Victorian streets. It is essentially a museum of everyday life and some of the twentieth-century exhibits—vacuum cleaners, television sets and so on from the recent past—bring a pang of nostalgia. Medieval buildings such as the **Merchant Adventurer's Hall**, scores of churches, narrow streets, the **National Railway Museum**, the eighteenth-century **Fairfax House**, the city walls and gates, the Minster, the Yorvik Centre and excellent shops make York a city with something for everyone.

Further information from York Tourist Office, De Grey Rooms, Exhibition Sq, York, 01904-621 756.

HOTELS

The Grange ✔✔

1 Clifton, York YO30 6AA
01904-644 744, Fax 01904-612 453
WWW.GRANGEHOTEL.CO.UK
E-MAIL: INFO@GRANGEHOTEL.CO.UK
30 rms £99-£180, 3 stes £210. Set lunch £11.50; set 4-course dinner £25.

🅰 ⟳P

This Regency townhouse is usefully located near the centre of town. It's a comfortable hotel, furnished in traditional style and with open fires. The public rooms are welcoming, particularly the sunny morning room. The Ivy Restaurant serves a good British/French menu with plenty of contemporary dishes like rack of lamb with polenta and ratatouille; there's also a sea bar and brasserie for more casual dining. Bedrooms have facilities like ISDN line and voice mail.

Middlethorpe Hall ✔✔✔

BISHOPSTHORPE RD, YORK, YO2 1QB
01904-641 241, FAX 01904-620 176
E-MAIL: INFO@MIDDLETHORPE.U-NET.COM
23 rms £99-£165, 7 stes £185-£250.

🅰 ⛽ ≈ ⟳P

Set in its own grounds of 26 odd acres, Middlethorpe is a beautiful William & Mary seventeenth-century house in warm red brick. It's owned by the small but excellent Historic House Hotels and has recently added a spa with swimming pool to its attractions. Public rooms are gracious; bedrooms are elegant, all are decorated with good antiques and have original moulded ceilings and plenty of wood panelling. Once belonging to the writer Lady Mary Wortley Montagu whose portrait hangs in the stairwell, it makes an excellent base for exploring York (a mile and a half south of the city), as well as some glorious surrounding countryside.

Mount Royale Hotel ✔✔

THE MOUNT YO2 2DA
01904-628 856, FAX 01904-611 171
WWW.MOUNTROYALE.CO.UK
E-MAIL: STUART@MOUNTROYALE.CO.UK
17 rms £78-£95, 6 stes £135.

🅰 ≈ ⟳P

A family-run hotel which is both professional and friendly. The house and more expensive garden rooms are decorated with antiques; there's a cosy bar and public rooms such as a conservatory and two lounges where you can take an apéritif and study the menu, all accompanied by a pianist. The cooking is good, seasonally led and using fresh local ingredients, and is simply but well cooked.

RESTAURANTS

Melton's

CONTEMPORARY EUROPEAN 13/20
7 SCARCROFT RD, YORK
01904-634 341, FAX 01904 635 115
Lunch Tues.-Sun., Dinner Mon.-Sat. ££

This pretty restaurant with its coral-coloured walls continues to please the regulars in York, who appreciate the fact that mineral water, bread, service and coffee is included in the prices. The monthly changing menu offers six starters which might include fresh mackerel escabèche with ginger and coriander or terrine of gravad lax with Jerusalem artichoke and langoustine, and mains which run from a vegetarian grilled polenta with wild mushrooms and herb dressing, to an excellent home-cured poached fillet of pork with a nicely sharp horseradish and apple compote, pommes Anna and green cabbage. British and Irish cheeses fill a good cheeseboard; otherwise try the superb tuile basket of vanilla ice cream with Ximenez sherry and cherry and nut brittle. There is much explanation on the menu, which typifies the friendly and helpful approach of the staff. The wine list is good and the mark-ups modest. Set lunch & 6pm-7.45pm departure £15; set dinner £20.

Middlethorpe Hall

MODERN BRITISH 13/20
BISHOPSTHORPE RD, YORK, YO2 1QB
01904-641 241, FAX 01904-620 176
Lunch & Dinner daily. ££

Suitably grand dining room in this lovely seventeenth-century house. In such surroundings, you expect luxurious food and this is what chef Martin Barker provides. A robust boudin blanc came with artichokes, veal sweetbreads and a delicious truffle hollandaise; the light soup of seafood with cucumber and sevruga caviar carried a £2.90 supplement, but merited the extra. Self confidence shines through in the mains—where a tender wood pigeon came wrapped in Parma ham and cabbage with thyme fondants and roast garlic, while an herbed loin of lamb was accompanied by stuffed courgettes and black olives, the whole evoking just the right amount of Provençale sunshine. Desserts might be a citrus fruit trio of lemon tart, passion fruit sorbet and a masterful orange and Grand Marnier soufflé, or a rich tarte Tatin of figs with amaretto ice cream and raspberry sauce. As both these take an extra 20 minutes, it's wise to ask for the dessert menu at the beginning. There's also a good vegetarian menu. The wine list covers both new and old worlds. Set 2-course lunch £14.50, 3 courses £17.50; set dinner £32.

PUBS & CAFÉS

Bettys Café

6-8 ST. HELEN'S SQ, YORK, 01904-659 142
Open daily 9am-9pm.

Wonderful institution, which has spawned a whole lot more 'Bettys' across north England. Great cakes, tea, and light meals.

The Black Swan Pub

PEASEHOLME GREEN, YORK, 01904-686 911
Open Mon.-Sat. 11am-11pm, Sun. noon-10.30pm.

Lovely half-timbered building with proper old lead-latticed windows and a black-beamed bar, complete with wooden settles and fireplace for chilly Yorkshire days. Good bar with food-like soups, baked potatoes and the like, plus daily specials on the lines of sausages and pastas. Range of good beers.

The Old Starre Pub

STONEGATE, YORK, 01904-623 063
Open Mon.-Sat. 11am-11pm, Sun. noon-10.30pm.

York's oldest licensed pub (1644), though some of the building is even older. The interior is delightful with original panelling on the walls, and many small cosy rooms, plus a flowery garden and courtyard with views of the famous minster. Good bar food like steak and kidney pie, Cumberland sausages and fish. Range of good beers. It's on Stonegate, a pedestrian-only street.

Telephone numbers in England have eleven digits, beginning with a zero. The initial zero must be omitted if you are calling England from abroad. Within the country, dial the entire eleven digits.

BASICS

CONTENTS

ARRIVING IN LONDON 430

GETTING AROUND 431

TOURS 433

USEFUL ADDRESSES & PHONE NUMBERS 435

CALENDAR OF EVENTS 438

ARRIVING IN LONDON

Getting into London from any of the major airports is relatively easy.

The London Tourist Board's official Internet site for London is www.LondonTown.com

FROM HEATHROW
(15 MILES WEST OF LONDON)

The **Heathrow Express**, a dedicated high-speed rail link, runs between the airport and Paddington Station every 15 minutes between 5.20am and 11.40pm. The trip takes 15 minutes from Terminals 1, 2, & 3 and around 20 minutes from Terminal 4. Paddington Station has full airline passenger and luggage check-in facilities for all major airlines. The fare is £12 single, £22 return (valid for one month), under-15s free. For information on airlines at Paddington Station call 0845-600 1515, or visit www.heathrowexpress.co.uk.

The **Piccadilly Line** underground departs for London every few minutes; the trip takes about 50-60 minutes. The first departure from Terminal 4 then all three other Terminals is at 4.58pm, the last at 11.34pm. The first arrivals at Terminal 4 are at 6.28am and the last at 11.55pm. The fare is £3.40 single. But note: There are only escalators to get you down to the trains at Heathrow and few stations in central London have lifts, so if you have a lot of luggage, this may present problems. For information call 020-7222 1234.

Information desks operate in each terminal.

Airport Travel Line	0990-747 777
Airport Police	020-8897 1212
Flight Arrivals	020-8759 4321
General Enquiries	020-8759 4321
Lost Property	020-8745 7727
Left luggage	
Terminal 1	020-8745 5301
Terminal 2	020-8759 3344
Terminal 3	020-8745 4599
Terminal 4	020-8745 7460
Medical Helpline	01276-685 040
Skycaps (porters)	020-874 5727

The **Berkeleys Hotel Connections** operates from desks in Terminals 3 and 4 and meets clients in Terminals 1 and 2 to take them in a new 14-seat bus to their central London hotel. £12 per person each way. Booking should be made in advance on 01442-298 507, fax on 01442-255 656, on www.berkeleys.co.uk, or via E-mail on sales@berkeleys.co.uk.

Airbus Heathrow Shuttle takes about one hour to King's Cross, running every 15 minutes and taking about 60 minutes. The cost is £7 single, £12 return (within 3 months), under 16s free.

National Express operates roughly the same hours. The cost is £6 single, £8 return. Signs at the airport indicate the route and the stops.

The **N97** night bus links Heathrow with central London every 30 minutes between 11.35pm and 5.35pm. The fare is £1.50. For information call 020-7722 1234.

A **black taxi** costs from £50. Be sure to only take a licensed black cab. Beware mini cabs or private drivers touting for custom in the airport as they can be expensive and they may not be adequately insured.

FROM GATWICK
(30 MILES SOUTH OF LONDON)

Fast and frequent train services run by different train companies depart about every 15 minutes and take 30 minutes into Victoria Station. They run every hour between midnight and 5am, then every twenty minutes. Single fare is £10.20, return is £20.40. **Rail enquiries**: 0345-484 950. **Gatwick Express**: 0990-301 530.

Jetline Buses 777 to Victoria Coach Station depart at 5am and 6.30am, then about every hour until 5.40pm. The last bus is at 8.10pm. The bus trip takes about 75 minutes depending on the time of day and costs £9 single, £13 return.

The Berkeleys Hotel Connections operates with the Gatwick Express, meeting clients in the airport arrivals area and transferring onto the Gatwick Express. At Victoria station, clients are met and taken, via coach to their hotel. £18 per person each way. Booking should be made in advance on 01442-298 507, fax on 01442-255 656, on www.berkeleys.co.uk or via E-mail on sales@berkeleys.co.uk.

National Express coaches to Victoria Coach Station runs at 7.15am, then from 9.45am every hour to 9.35pm, and 11.35pm, taking between one hour and one hour and twenty minutes. The cost is £8 single, £12 open

Information desks operate in both terminals.

General Enquiries	
& Flight Arrivals	01293-535 353
Airport Police	01293-531 122
Lost Property	01293-503 162
Left Luggage	
North Terminal	01293-502 013
South Terminal	01293-502 014
Medical assistance	01293-507 400

return for 3 months. Tel: 0990-808 080; or www.nationalexpress.co.uk.
A **taxi** will cost from £60 and take from an hour-and-a-half to two hours.
There are **Internet Exchange cafés** in Gatwick South and North Terminals, landside, open daily 6am-9pm. www.internet-exchange.co.uk.

FROM STANSTED
(35 MILES NORTH EAST OF LONDON)
Skytrain Express trains depart at 5am, 6am, then every 30 minutes on the half hour 6.30am-11pm. Services are less frequent at weekends. They take 45 minutes to Liverpool Street Station. The fare is £11 single, £22 return, but there are special deals available. Tel: 0345-484 950.
Jetlink runs coaches to Victoria Coach Station about every hour, taking 1 hour 40 minutes. The fare is £9 single, £13 return. Tel 0990-747 777.
National Express coaches run hourly 6am-7pm, taking 1 hour and 40 minutes. The fare is £9 single, £13 return. Tel 0990-808 080; www.nationalexpress.co.uk.
A **taxi** will cost from £50 and takes about 90 minutes.
There are **Internet Exchange cafés** at Stansted, landside, open daily 6am-9pm. www.internet-exchange.co.uk.

Information desks operate in the terminal building.

General Enquiries	
& Flight Arrivals	01279-680 500
Left luggage	01279-663 213
Lost property	01279-680 500
Medical assistance	01279-680 500

FROM LONDON CITY AIRPORT
(9 MILES EAST OF CENTRAL LONDON)
London City Airport only handles European flights. Assistance line—020-7646 0088. General Enquiries, Flight arrivals & Lost property—020-7646 0000.
Shuttle buses run every 10 minutes from the airport to Liverpool Street Station (about 30 minutes) and to Canary Wharf (10 minutes).
Docklands Light Railway links Bank station and Tower Gateway to Canary Wharf and connects with the Airport Shuttle Bus. Tel 020-7222 1234.
The easiest way into central London is by **taxi**.

FROM LUTON
(30 MILES NORTH OF LONDON)
Trains run from Luton Central to King's Cross, via a shuttle bus service from the airport to the station. Trains run frequently through the day from 3am-1am. The fare is £10.60 single, open return £19.20. Tel 0345-484950.
National Express coaches run 1.30am, 5am, 6.30am, 8am, 9am, every half hour to 5.30pm, then at 6.15pm. Fare is £7 return. Tel 0990-808080; www.nationalexpress.co.uk.

BY TRAIN
Eurostar comes from Paris or Brussels via the Channel Tunnel: The trip takes around 3 hours, with trains arriving at and departing from London Waterloo International Station. Tel 0990-186 186.

GETTING AROUND

PUBLIC TRANSPORT SYSTEM
London's public transport system is **one of the biggest, oldest and most complex in Europe,** so expect overcrowding at peak times—between 8am and 9.30am and 4.30pm to 6.30pm. It is also expensive compared to other cities. The most economical tickets are *Travelcards*—daily, weekly or monthly passes giving you unlimited travel on all forms of transport in set zones. Make sure you get the right ticket for the right zone as there are six zones which stretch from city centre into outer suburbia. Most major sights are

contained within Zones One and Two. You can buy these tickets at underground stations and at newsagents showing a special Red Pass agent sign. Weekly and monthly passes require a passport-sized photograph. One-day Travelcards (no photo needed) cannot be used before 9.30am Monday to Friday. Central London bus and underground guides are available from underground stations and at Heathrow.

For multiple trips, ask about *The Carnet*, a book of ten single tube tickets for travel in Zone One costing £11 and saving £4; a *Family Travelcard*, giving various savings on buses, the underground, Docklands Light Railway and some trains within the greater London area; and a Weekend Travelcard offering a 25 percent discount. Information: 020-7222 1234.

AIR CHARTER

Falcon Jet Centre—020-8897 6021
Heathrow Jet Charter—020-8759 5560
International Sky Charter—
020-7242 9501
Southern Air—01273-461 661

BUSES

The best way to travel around London for a visitor is by bus. Bus stops are either compulsory stops (London Transport signs on a white background) or request stops (Request Stop signs on a red background). At the latter, hold out your hand to indicate to the driver to stop.

> **London Buses**
> **& Underground**—020-7222 1234
>
> **Lost Property**
> 200 Baker St, NW1—020-7486 2496

Most new buses are one-man operated and you pay your fare to the driver as you get on. Do not try to pay with large notes—you risk the wrath of the queue. Night Buses exist on several popular routes from 11pm to 6am. The routes are prefixed with the letter 'N'. One day Travelcards do not operate on night buses. Bus guides are available from Travel Information Centres at Underground stations and airports.

If you want to take a bus to almost anywhere outside central London, from Aberdeen to

Athens, you'll probably go from the main Victoria coach station on Buckingham Palace Road (about three minutes walk from Victoria railway station). The main company for national travel is National Express, 0990-808080; www.nationalexpress.co.uk.

CARS

Driving in London can be a nightmare if you don't know your way around. And there is the added hazard of possible clamping for illegal parking or overrunning time on a meter. **National Car Parks** (NCP) run 24-hour car parks in central London, 020-7404 3777. If you plan to go outside London into the countryside, hiring a car is a good idea, particularly from an airport.

Avis—020-8848 8733
Budget—800-181 181
Dimple—020-7243 4400, 020-8205 1200
Europcar—020-7834 8484
Hertz—020-7730 8323
Hertz Worldwide Reservations—
0990-996 699
National Car Rental—0990-365 365
Thrifty—020-7262 2223

TAXIS

There are taxi ranks at railway stations and throughout London. **You can hail a cab** on the street whenever you see the yellow 'Taxi' or 'For Hire' sign lit up. A tip of between ten and fifteen percent of the cost of the journey is usual. You can call a taxi on *Radio Taxicars*, 020-7272 0272, or *Computer Cabs*, 020-7286 0286.

Although we only recommend minicabs from your hotel concierge who will know reliable companies, **lone women travellers** can contact *Lady Cabs*, 020-7272 3019 or 020-7254 3314.

Motorbike cabs are fast but only for the intrepid. But drivers are superb (they have to be!) and prices are good—around £15 to go across London. Contact: *Addison Lee*, 020-7387 8888; *Floyd's Flyers Chauffeurs*, 020-7801 6233; *Virgin LimoBikes*, 020-7499 6233.

For **lost property in taxis**, telephone 020-7833 0996, open Mon.-Fri. 9am-4pm.

TRAINS

To get to outer London and beyond, trains run every day except Christmas Day and

Boxing Day (December 25 and 26). For all national enquiries: 0345-48 49 50. Please note that all mainline stations share the same national enquiry number.

Charing Cross Station—Strand, WC2. For connections to south London and the southeast of England.

Docklands Light Railway (DLR)—Connects Docklands with the City, Stratford and Greenwich. The driverless trains run Mon.-Fri. 5.30am-12.30am, Sat. 6am-12.30am, Sun. 7.30am-11.30pm. Many special ticket deals are available; ask for details at 020-7363 9700.

Euston Station—Euston Rd, NW1. For connections to northwest London and northwest England, the Midlands, North Wales, Scotland and Ireland via Holyhead.

King's Cross Station—Euston Rd, NW1. For connections to northeast London, the east and northeast of England, and the east coast of Scotland.

NO SMOKING on London Transport—you can be fined up to £1,000 for the offense.

Liverpool Street Station—Bishopsgate, EC2. For connections to east and northeast London, Essex and East Anglia.

Paddington Station—Praed St, W2. For connections to west London, Oxford, Bristol, Plymouth, the west of England, South Wales and Ireland via Fishguard.

Thameslink Service—Connects Luton Airport with south London, Gatwick Airport and Brighton via West Hampstead and Blackfriars.

Victoria Station—Buckingham Palace Rd, SW1. For connections to south London, Gatwick airport, southwest England and the Channel ports for Europe.

Waterloo Station—Waterloo Rd, SE1. For south London and the south of England.

Waterloo International—Waterloo Rd, SE1. For connections to Paris, Brussels and other European destinations via the Channel tunnel.

UNDERGROUND

Known as the 'tube', the London underground has twelve lines and more than 275 stations and is the oldest in the world, having opened on January 10, 1863. Tube trains run every day except Christmas Day from around 5.30am to just after midnight, but this is not always the case on lines running to outlying stations. Get tickets either from a ticket office or an automatic machine which indicates whether it will give change or not. Keep your ticket as you will need it at the end of the journey. Information at 020-7222 1234.

TOURS

BY BUS/COACH

A good way to see London is from the top of a double-decker open-topped bus. **The Original London Sightseeing Tour** (020-8877 1722, www.TheOriginalTour.co) runs hop-on, hop-off service, 8.30am-5pm, from 90 different stops including four points close to underground stations: Baker Street, Marble Arch, Piccadilly Circus and Victoria Station. Buy tickets (adult £12.50, children under 16 £7) on the bus, from London Transport stations, London Tourist Board Information Centres and at many central London hotels.

The Big Bus Company (020-7233 9533, www.bigbus.co.uk) offers much the same hop-on, hop-off service, all with live commentary, departing from central points like Marble Arch, Green Park Underground (by The Ritz Hotel), Victoria (Royal Westminster Hotel) and Victoria Coach Station. Prices are £15 for adults, £6 for children (5-15 years old).

City Garden Tours (020-8693 6620, E-mail: info@citygardentours.com, www.citygardentours.co.uk) is a specialist company offering minibus tours to London's prize-winning private gardens where you meet the owners.

If you want to go outside London, try **Visitor Sightseeing** (020-7636 7175, www.visitorsightseeing.co.uk) which includes trips around Britain, as well as London half-day tours. For small minibus tours, try Berties at 020-8402 2480, or mobile 0973 839377.

Other companies offering bus tours lasting from two hours to a full day in or outside London include: **Evan Evans Tours**, 020-7950 1777, E-mail: webmaster@evanevans.co.uk, www.evanevans.co.uk); **Frames Rickards**, 020-7837 3111, E-mail: reservations@framesrickards.co.uk); **Golden Tours**, 020-7233 6668, E-mail: goldtour@aol.com, www.goldentours.co.uk); **Harrods**, 020-7581 3603; **London Millennium Tours**. 020-7706 2220, www.londonsight.com); **London Pride Sightseeing** , 01708-631122).

BY CHAUFFEURED CAR OR LIMOUSINE

Avis—0990-900 500
Berkeley Square Chauffeur Services—
020-7629 3939
Browns Chauffeur Hire—020-7493 4851
Carey Camelot Chauffeur Drive—
020-7235 0234
Chauffeurdrive—0541-536 537
Europcar Chauffeur Drive—020-7834 6701
Guy Salmon—0345-886 688
Kensington & Chelsea Cars—
020-7603 6660

By Private Car & Driver-Guide

Take-a-Guide Ltd.
34 Finstock Rd, W10, 020-8960 0459,
Fax 020-8964 0990. One of the oldest
and best driver-guide companies.

Good Company
48 Prince of Wales Rd, NW5, 020-
7267 5340, Fax 020-7284 0765
E-mail: good-company@psilink.co.uk.

James & Company
PO Box 549, SW18, Tel/Fax 020-8875
0755; E-mail:james@jamestours.com;
www.jamestours.com.

London Chauffeur Drive—020-7633 9410
Miles & Miles—020-7591 0888
PrimeAce Chauffeur Service—
0118 979 3324

BY HELICOPTER

Cabair Helicopters—020-8953 4411

BY RIVER & CANAL

Travelling through London by river is **a
wonderful experience** as you see the riverside
buildings from a different angle and travel
effortlessly. Sightseeing trips go from
Westminster Pier and Charing Cross Pier regularly, winter and summer, from around 10am
to 5pm. They take 25-30 minutes to the
Tower of London and 60 minutes to
Greenwich. You can just go to the piers and
take the next boat; they depart every 30 to 45
minutes, depending on the time of year, and
cost around £5 single to the Tower of
London, £6 return, and around £7 single to
Greenwich, £7.50 return. For general information, call the LTB Info line at 0839-123
432. For information on sightseeing tours, call
Bateaux London Thames Circular Cruises,
020-7925 2215; *City Cruises*, 020-7237
5134; **Thames Cruises**, 020-7930 3373;
Westminster Passenger Service Association,
020-7930 4097/1661. **White Horse Fast
Ferry**, 01793-618 566, www.whitehorse.co.uk/
fastferries, operates from Canary Wharf to
Embankment with six stops in between, and
costs £1.90 per journey.

New Millennium River Link, 020-7740
0400, operates four new boats for up to 515
passengers from piers at Waterloo and
Blackfriars to the Dome, leaving at regular
intervals. Return tickets: adults £8.40, child
£5.20. Combined return river travel and
admission to the Dome: adults £27, child
£20.

London Frog Tours, 020-7721 8228,
www.frogtours.com, is a new company operating road and river adventurers using 30-seat
amphibious vehicles, including sightseeing
through the heart of London, followed by a
30-minute cruise along the Thames, all in the
same vehicle.

The **Regent's Park Canal** is worth seeing.
Narrow boat cruises on Jason's Trip start
opposite 60 Blomfield Rd, Little Venice, W9,
daily at regular intervals, 020-7286 3428.
From Camden Town, try the Jenny Wren at
Camden Lock, 020-7485 4433. The same
company runs *My Fair Lady*. You get a good
lunch (Sundays only) or dinner and a trip past
London Zoo to Little Venice and back. My
Fair Lady, 250 Camden High St, NW1, 020-
7485 4433 or 020-7485 6210. The costs vary
from around £17.95 (lunch) to £31.95 (dinner).

Lunch & Evening Dinner/Dance Cruises

They offer different dates, winter and sum-
mer, so telephone for details:
Bateaux London Catamaran Cruisers—
Charing Cross Pier, Victoria Embankment,
WC2, 020-7987 1185/925 2215. A restau-
rant cruiser offering lunch (£20) and dinner
(£69) cruises. Board at Temple Pier on
Victoria Embankment.
London Showboat—Westminster Pier, WC1,
020-7237 5134, Fax 020-7237 3498, has

evening cruises to the Thames Barrier with cabaret, 5-course dinner and dancing. £42 per person.

Silver Sturgeon—Savoy Pier (by the Savoy Hotel), Embankment, SW1, 020-7480 7770. Luxury restaurant river boat with bars, dance floor and two restaurants. £54 per person.

BY TAXI

Black Taxi Tours—Tours last 2 hours and cost £65 per taxi cab (maximum of 5 people). They can pick you up and return you to your hotel and give you a real insider's knowledge and point of view. Information at 020-7289 4371, or 0956-384 124

GUIDE BOOKING AGENCIES

The official body of the professions is the Guild of Registered Tourist Guides:

The Guild House—52d Borough High St, SE1, 020-7403 1115, Fax 020-7378 1705
Professional Guides—020-8874 2745
Professional Guide Services—020-8874 2745, www.highway57.co.uk/pgs, for badged tourist guides and translators nationwide.
Tour Guides Ltd.—020-7495 5504, E-mail: tours@tourguides.co.uk, www.tourguides.co.uk. For nationwide registered tour guides, coach, car, walking, specialists and linguists.
Clerkenwell & Islington Guides Associations—020-7622 3278, www.hawkins.ndirect.co.uk. To book guides for Islington and environs.

TOURIST INFORMATION CENTRES

Britain Visitor Centre
1 Regent St, SW1. Personal callers only: *Open Mon.-Fri. 9am-6.30pm, Sat.-Sun. 10am-4pm (June-Oct. Sat. 9am-5pm).*
City of London Tourist Information
St. Paul's Churchyard, EC4, 020-7332 1456. *Open daily Easter-Oct 1 9am-5pm, then Mon.-Fri. 9am-5pm, Sat. 9.30am-12.30pm.*
Greenwich Tourist Information Centre
Pepys Building, Cutty Sark Gardens, SE10, 0870-608 2000. *Open daily 10am-5pm.*
Heathrow Terminals 1, 2, 3
Underground Station Concourse, Heathrow Airport, Middlesex. *Open daily 8.30am-6pm.*
Islington Tourist Information Centre
44 Duncan St, N1, 020-7278 8787, Fax 020-7833 2193, www.discoverislington.co.uk. *Open Apr.-end Oct.: Mon. 2pm-5pm, Tues.-*

Sat. 10am-5pm (closed Sat. 1.30pm-2.30pm).
Liverpool Street Underground Station EC2. *Open Mon.-Fri. 8am-6pm, Sat.-Sun. 9am-5.30pm.*
London Tourist Board & Convention Bureau
26 Grosvenor Gdns, SW1, 020-932 2000. No personal callers. Instead the LTB runs information lines which you can reach by telephone only. Calls cost 60p per minute. Check in the London telephone book for details of services like: *Accommodation Information*, 0891-505 487; *Events*, 0839-123 4000; *Changing the Guard*, 0891-505 452.
Southwark Tourist Information Centre
Corner of London Bridge & Duke St, SE1, 020-7403 8299. *Open Mon.-Fri. 10am-6pm, Sat.-Sun. 10am-5.30pm.*
Victoria Station Forecourt
Victoria Station, SW1, (no phone). *Open daily 8am-7pm.*
Waterloo
Waterloo International Station, SE1. *Open daily 8am-10.30pm.*

USEFUL ADDRESSES & PHONE NUMBERS

BUREAUX DE CHANGE

Almost every bank in central London operates a bureau de change and there are also numerous private enterprises which change money also. Exchange rates vary widely, sometimes with differences at branches of the same bank. Otherwise try:
American Express—
Haymarket, SW1, 020-7930 4411 or
24-hour Travellers Cheque Refund—
0800-521 313.

BUSINESS FACILITIES

Kinko's
326-328 HIGH HOLBORN, WC1
020-7539 2900, WWW.KINKOS.COM.
U: Holborn.
29-35 MORTIMER ST, W1, 020-7643 1900.
U: Oxford Circus.
24-hour computer services, printing, shipping, video conferencing available.

Looking for an address?
Refer to the index.

Office 24
38 NEW OXFORD ST, WC1
020-7616 7300, WWW.OFFICE24.COM.
U: Tottenham Court Rd.

Digital printing, colour and B/W, full range of finishing services, walk-in self-service PC's and printers, internet and E-mail, rental of laptops/PCs/projectors/mobile phones etc; videoconferencing/boardroom hire.

Service Point
32 GRESSE ST, W1
020-7631 0222, WWW.PICKINGPACK.NET.
Open Mon.-Fri. 24 hours, Sat. 9am-1am.
U: Oxford Circus.
UNIT 3, WILLIAM RD, NW1, 020-7387 6071
Open Mon.-Thurs. 24 hours, Fri. 9am-10pm,
Sat. 9am-12noon. U: Gt. Portland St.
U: Euston Sq/Warren St.
Everything to do with printing and graphics.

Time Zone Express
19 AIR ST, W1
020 7287 6563, WWW.MALL.CO.UK.
Open Mon.-Sat. 9am-7.30pm.
U: Piccadilly Circus.

Mailing address and voice mail, website facilities, couriers, stationery, mobile phones, bureau de change and more.

COMPUTER HIRE
Elbow Room—020-7629 2200
Micro-Rent—020-7700 4848
Short Term Rental Systems—
020-8330 4106
Vernon Computer Rentals—020-7720 7000

COMPUTER REPAIRS
Companies charge from £50-£100 per hour plus VAT for brought-in machines. On-site services vary from £60-£125 per hour plus VAT.
Albion Computers—020-7323 0220.
General repairs, accessories and upgrades for Apple Macs and PCs.
Computeq—020-7231 3144. Repairs PCs, also arranges repairs on Apple Macs.
DNA Computer Services—020-8742 3524.
Repair and upgrade of Apple Macs.
Honeylight Computers—020-8871 4187.
Repairs PCs and Apple Macs. Also data recovery service.
PC Computer Problems—020-7371 0201.
Specialises in home users of PCs, can upgrade and repair.
20/20—020-7771 2020. Full repair service

for Apple Macs.
Hardware Support—01159 711 000. Repair service on PCs.

Helplines

20/20 Business Support—0897 501 352 (calls cost £1 per minute)
IBM—0990 727 272
Apple—0990 127 753

EMBASSIES
Australian High Commission
Australia House, Strand, WC2, 020-7379 4334. *U: Temple.*

Canadian High Commission
Macdonald House, 1 Grosvenor Square, W1, 020-7258 6600. *U: Bond St.*

Chinese Embassy
49 Portland Pl, SW1, 020-7631 1430. *U: Oxford Circus.*

Finnish Embassy
32 Chesham Pl, SW1, 020-7838 6200. *U: Hyde Park Corner.*

French Consulate Général
21/23 Cromwell Rd, SW7, 020-7201 1000. *U: South Kensington.*

German Embassy
23 Belgrave Sq, SW1, 020-7824 1300. *U: Hyde Park Corner.*

India High Commission
India House, Aldwych, WC2, 020-7836 8484. *U: Temple/Covent Garden.*

Japanese Embassy
101 Piccadilly, SW1, 020-7465 6500. *U: Hyde Park Corner.*

New Zealand High Commission
New Zealand House, 80 Haymarket, SW1, 020-7930 8422. *U: Piccadilly Circus.*

Russian Embassy & Consulate
5-6 Kensington Palace Gardens, W8, 020-7229 8027. *U: Notting Hilll Gate.*

South Africa High Commission
South Africa House, Trafalgar Sq, WC2, 020-7930 4488. *U: Charing Cross.*

Swedish Embassy
11 Montagu Pl, W1, 020-7724 2101. *U: Baker St.*

United States Embassy
24 Grosvenor Square, W1, 020-7499 9000. *U: Bond St.*

EMERGENCY PHONE NUMBERS

Accident & Emergency Wards in London hospitals:

Charing Cross Hospital—Fulham Palace Rd, W6, 020-8846 1234

Royal Free Hospital—Pond St, NW3, 020-7794 0500

University College Hospital—Gower St, WC1, 020-7387 9300

Whittington Hospital—Highgate Hill, N19, 020-7272 3070

Emergency Dentist—Guy's Hospital Dental School, 020 7955 5000

Emergency Doctor—Doctorcall, 020 7225 1111; Medcall, 0800 136 106; SOS Doctors, 020 7603 3332

Emergency Optician—Opticall, 020 7495 4915

Lost Credit Cards—*American Express*, 01273 696 933, 01273-689 955; *Diners Club*, 0800 460 800; *Mastercard*, 0800 964 767; *Visa*, 0800 895 082

Police, Fire & Ambulance Services—999 or 112.

LATE OPENING PHARMACISTS

Bliss Chemists—5 Marble Arch, W1, 020-7723 6116. *Open daily 9am-midnight. U: Marble Arch.*

Boots—Piccadilly Circus, W1, 020-7734 6126. *Open daily 9am-8pm. U: Piccadilly Circus.* Also 74 Queensway, W2, 020-7229 9266. *Open Mon.-Sat. 9am-10pm, Sun. 2pm-10pm. U: Bayswater.*

I Warman Freed—45 Golders Green Rd, NW11, 020-8455 4351. *Open daily 8.30am-midnight. U: Golders Green.*

Zafash Pharmacy—233-235 Old Brompton Rd, SW5, 020-7373 2798. *Open 24 hours. U: West Brompton.*

MOBILE PHONE HIRE

Cellhire—0990 610 610. Next day delivery.
Charles Street Communications—020-7451 1313. Deliveries until 8pm daily.

MONEY TRANSFER

Western Union—0800-833 833

PHOTOGRAPHIC DEVELOPMENT

Compton Photos—Old Compton St/Wardour St, W1, 020-7437 7329

Joe's Basement—113-117 Wardour St, W1, 020-7439 3210, *open 24 hours*; 247 Euston Rd, NW1, 020-7388 3210, *open Mon.-Fri. 8am-8pm*; 111 Hammersmith Rd, W14, 020-7371 3210 *open Mon.-Fri. 8am-8pm*; 82 Clerkenwell Rd, EC1, 020-7253 3210

Metro Imaging—76 Clerkenwell Rd, EC1, 020-7865 0000 (24 hours); 3 Gt Marlborough St, W1, 020-7543 4000, *open 24 hours*; 3 Jubilee Pl, SW3, 020-376 8999, *open Mon.-Fri. 24 hours, Sat.-Sun. 7am-midnight.*

REFERENCE LIBRARIES

Chamber of Commerce & Industry Reference Library—33 Queen St, EC4, 020-7248 4444. *U: Blackfriars.* Export and international trade.

City Business Library—1 Brewers Hall Garden (off London Wall), EC2, 020-7638 8215. *U: Barbican/Moorgate/St. Paul's.* Newspaper cuttings, world directories and other reference material.

EC Information Unit—8 Storeys Gate, SW1, 020-7973 1992. *U: St. James's Park/Westminster.* Information about the European Commission's decisions and initiatives.

London Business School Library—Sussex Pl, NW1, 020-7262 5050. *U: Baker St/Marylebone.* Library and research service.

RELIGIOUS SERVICES

Baptist—London Baptist Association, 1 Merchant St, E3, 020-8980 6818

Buddhist—The Buddhist Society, 58 Eccleston Sq, SW1, 020-7834 5858

Jewish—Liberal Jewish Synagogue, 28 St. John's Wood Rd, NW8, 020-7286 5181; United Synagogue (Orthodox), 735 High Road, N2, 020-8343 8989

Moslem—Islamic Cultural Centre, 146 Park Rd, NW8, 020-7724 3363

Protestant—Church of England, St. Paul's Cathedral, EC4, 020-7248 2705, Information line 020-7236 0752

Quakers—Religious Society of Friends, 173-177 Euston Rd, NW1, 020-7387 3601

Roman Catholic—Westminster Cathedral, Victoria St, SW1, 020-7798 9055, Service information 020-7798 9099

TAX-FREE SHOPPING

Value added tax (VAT) of 17.5% is charged on almost all goods in Britain except, most notably, on books, food and all children's clothes, and is almost always included in the advertised price. Non-European Community visitors to Britain staying for less than three months **can claim back VAT**. Take your passport with you when shopping. You must fill in a form in the store when you buy the goods and then give a copy to Customs when you leave the country. You may also have to show the goods to Customs, so make sure they are accessible. The tax refund will either be returned by cheque or attributed to your credit card, although in that case you may pay a service charge. Most stores have a minimum purchase threshold, often £50 or £75. If your goods are shipped directly home from the shop, VAT should be deducted before you pay.

TRANSLATION SERVICES

All Languages Ltd.—020-7739 6641
Berlitz International—020-7629 7360
Multilingual Services—020-7930 5110
Universal Translations—020-7248 8707

CALENDAR OF EVENTS

There is so much going on in London it is difficult to decide what to see and do, but here we give a brief summary.

English National Holidays: January 1, Good Friday, Easter Monday, the first and last Mondays in May, last Monday in August, December 25, 26. When December 25, 26 fall on a weekend, extra holidays are given on the preceding Friday or following Monday/Tuesday. If New Year's Day falls on a weekend, the first Monday in January is usually a public holiday.

JANUARY

London International Boat Show—Earl's Court Exhibition Centre, SW5. Huge exhibition of large and small craft.

Contemporary Art Show—Business Design Centre, Upper St, Islington, N1. Annual, very prestigious exhibition of work by living artists from around the world, with prices ranging from £50 to £20,000.

Decorative Antiques & Textiles Fair—The Marquee, Riverside Terraces, Battersea Park, SW11. Wonderful home decorative fair.

West London Antiques & Fine Art Fair—Kensington Town Hall, Hornton St, W8. Vetted fair with plenty of stands and a good range of items and styles.

London International Mime Festival—Venues throughout London. Two-week festival of mime with artists from around the world.

World of Drawings & Watercolours Fair—The Dorchester Hotel, Park Lane, W1. A wonderful fair with drawings from Victorian country gardens to Old Masters (sometimes runs in February).

FEBRUARY

Chinese New Year—Celebrations throughout Chinatown, around Gerrard St, W1.

Art on Paper Fair—Royal College of Art, Kensington Gore, SW7. Relatively new but already distinguished fair devoted to all works on paper.

Fine Arts & Antiques Fair—Olympia, Hammersmith Rd, W14. Another of London's prestigious antiques fairs.

MARCH

British Antique Dealers' Fair—Duke of York's Headquarters, SW3. Run by one of the two official antique dealers' organisations, the BADA show is a popular, excellent antiques fair with an international clientele.

Daily Mail Ideal Home Show—Earl's Court Exhibition Centre, SW5. Annual show offering everything for the house and garden, a major event in many people's calendar.

Chelsea Antiques Fair—Chelsea Old Town Hall, King's Rd, SW3. Vetted and fun, with a good range.

London Original Print Fair—Royal Academy of Arts, Piccadilly, W1. The longest-running event of its kind, attracting print dealers from around the world.

Country Living Spring Fair—Business Design Centre, Upper St, N1. Big crafts and home fair sponsored and run by the magazine *Country Living*. Great for ideas.

London International Book Fair—Olympia, Hammersmith Rd, W14. Big international trade show for the book industry.

Oxford & Cambridge Boat Race—From Putney to Mortlake, a 4-mile course (sometimes held in April).

APRIL

The Decorative Antiques & Textiles Fair—The Marquee, Riverside Terraces, Battersea Park, SW11. Another of the big decorative fairs (see *January*).

London Marathon—From Greenwich Park to central London.

MAY

Royal Windsor Horse Show—Home Park, Windsor. A long-running popular event with show-jumping, dressage and Country Fair.

Chelsea Flower Show—Royal Hospital, Chelsea, SW3. Probably the most famous flower show in the world and one of the most difficult to get tickets to. Contact the Royal Horticultural Society for details, 020-7834 4333, www.rhs.org.uk.

Covent Garden Festival—Various venues throughout Covent Garden and surrounds. Great theatre and music festival often in unusual venues.

Royal Academy Summer Exhibition—Royal Academy of Arts, Piccadilly, W1. One of the largest public art exhibitions in the world and the event that, in the days when such things mattered, announced the beginning of the London social season. Runs until August.

JUNE

Beating Retreat by the Massed Bands of the Household Division—Horse Guards Parade, SW1. A wonderful piece of pageantry with various regiments taking part.

Trooping the Colour—Horse Guards Parade, SW1. Celebration of the Queen's official birthday on June 11.

Antiquarian Book Fair—Olympia 2, Kensington Olympia, W14. A huge antiquarian book fair with dealers offering a great range of subjects and prices.

Fine Art & Antiques Fair—Olympia, Kensington, W14. One of the great fine arts fairs held this month.

Stella Artois Championship—Queen's Club, W14. The 'run-up' to Wimbledon—small and delightful.

Grosvenor House Art & Antiques Fair—Grosvenor House Hotel, Park Lane. The most prestigious antiques and fine art fair in the world, with top dealers mainly from Europe and the United States. Not to be missed.

International Ceramics Fair & Seminar—The Park Lane Hotel, Piccadilly, W1. This ceramic fair of the most commonly collected of all antiques combines the best dealers and an interesting lecture programme.

City of London Antiques Fair—Honourable Artillery Company, Armoury House, City Rd, EC1. Large fair in the City offering plenty of choice.

Covent Garden Flower Festival—Covent Garden Piazza, WC2.

Royal Ascot Race Meeting—Ascot, Berks. One of the best flat race meetings in the world.

Daily Telegraph House & Garden Fair—Olympia, Hammersmith Rd, W14. Another celebration of the house and garden, with plenty of ideas for your own patch.

Wimbledon Lawn Tennis Championships—All England Lawn Tennis Club, SW19, 0181-946 2244. One of the world's major sporting events, always the last week of June and the first of July.

Henley Royal Regatta—Henely-on-Thames, Oxfordshire. Glorious regatta usually running the last week of June and first week of July.

Greenwich & Docklands International Festival—Various venues in Greenwich, SE10. Excellent music, theatre and arts festival running into July.

JULY

Hampton Court Palace International Flower Show—Hampton Court Palace, East Molesey, Surrey. This new event has become one of the major UK horticultural events of the year. The largest of its kind in the world, it features landscaped garden displays, marquees, water gardens, crafts and more.

BBC Henry Wood Promenade Concerts—Royal Albert Hall, Kensington Gore, SW7. One of London's best loved annual events, with concerts nightly in the Royal Albert Hall and many premieres. Runs until September. Don't miss it.

AUGUST

Kensington Antiques Fair & Contemporary Art Fair—Kensington Town Hall, Hornton St, W8.

Notting Hill Gate Carnival—Notting Hill Gate, W8. A celebration of Caribbean culture and music in London.

SEPTEMBER

Chelsea Antiques Fair—Chelsea Old Town Hall, SW3. A popular antiques event stretching over ten days and held twice a year (also March).

20th Century British Art Fair—Royal College of Art, Kensington Gore, SW7. Important view of the contemporary art scene, much sought-after by serious collectors and those interested in today's artists.

Horse of the Year Show—Wembley Arena, Wembley. Show-jumping from the world's top competitors (sometimes held in October).

OCTOBER

International Festival of Fine Wine & Food-Olympia—Hammersmith Rd, W14. Extravaganze for foodies and lovers of fine wine.

Chelsea Crafts Fair—Chelsea Old Town Hall, King's Rd, SW3. One of the most important crafts fairs in Europe, stretching over two sessions with different craftsmen in each, offering a huge range of high quality items from jewellery to textiles.

LAPADA (London & Provincial Antique Dealers' Association) Arts & Antiques Fair—Royal College of Art, Kensington Gore, SW7. The biggest London fair from this antique dealers' association.

NOVEMBER

Chelsea Book Fair—Chelsea Old Town Hall, SW3. Vetted, high quality antiquarian and second hand book fair, vetted, no dateline.

The Fine Art & Antiques Fair—Olympia, W14. One of London's prestigious arts events.

RAC London to Brighton-Veteran Car Run—Hyde Park, London to Brighton. When the 'old crocks' gather to drive in stately manner to Brighton from Hyde Park.

Lord Mayor's Show—The new Lord Mayor parades through the streets of the City of London. It always takes place on the second Sunday in November, with fireworks along the river at the end of the day.

Remembrance Sunday Ceremony—Cenotaph, Whitehall, W1. Ceremony attended by the Queen and the Royal Family commemorating the dead of both world wars.

World Travel Market—Earl's Ct, SW5. One of the biggest travel trade shows in the world.

Little Chelsea Antiques Fair—Chelsea Old Town Hall, King's Rd, SW3. Autumn equivalent of the Spring fair.

DECEMBER

Olympia International Show Jumping Championships—Olympia, W14. A great show-jumping international event.

Menu Savvy

A Guide to International Food Terms

French

Agneau: lamb
Aïoli: garlicky mayonnaise
Américaine or **armoricaine**: sauce of white wine, Cognac, tomatoes and butter
Ananas: pineapple
Andouille: smoked tripe sausage, usually served cold
Anglaise (à l'): boiled meats or vegetables
Anguille: eel
Asperges: asparagus
Ballottine: boned, stuffed and rolled poultry
Bar: bass
Bâtarde: sauce of white roux (a mixture of flour and butter or other fat, usually in equal proportions, cooked together slowly and used to thicken sauces and soups)
Béarnaise: sauce made of shallots, tarragon, vinegar and egg yolks, bound with butter
Béchamel: sauce made of flour, butter and milk
Beurre blanc: sauce of wine and vinegar boiled down with minced shallots, then thickened with butter
Beurre noisette: lightly browned butter
Bière: beer
Bigarade: bitter orange used in sauces and marmalade
Bisque (crayfish, lobster, etc.): rich, velvety soup, usually made with crustaceans, flavored with white wine and Cognac
Blinis: small, thick crêpes made with eggs, milk and yeast
Bœuf: beef
Bœuf bourguignon: beef stew with red wine, onions and lardons (lardons: small chunks of slab bacon)
Bombe glacée: molded ice cream dessert
Bordelaise: fairly thin brown sauce of shallots, red wine and tarragon
Boudin noir: blood sausage
Bouillabaisse: various fish (including scorpion fish) cooked in a soup tomatoes, garlic, saffron and olive oil
Bourride: sort of bouillabaisse, usually made with large white fish; the creamy broth is thickened with aïoli and poured over slices of bread
Brie: cow's milk cheese with a soft, creamy inside and a thick crust, made in the shape of a disk and sliced like a pie
Brioche: a soft loaf, often sweet yeast or roll enriched with eggs and butter
Brochette: on a skewer
Brochet: pike
Buiscuits: cookies
Caille: quail
Calvados: distilled apple cider
Canapé: small piece of bread topped with savory food
Canard: duck
Carbonnade: pieces of lean beef, first sautéed then stewed with onions and beer
Carrotte: carrot
Carré d'agneau: rack of lamb
Cèpes: prized wild mushroom, same family as the Italian porcini
Cerises: cherries
Champignons: mushrooms
Chanterelles: prized wild mushroom, trumpet-shaped
Charcutière: sauce of onions, white wine, beef stock and gherkins
Charlotte: dessert of flavored creams and/or fruit molded in a cylindrical dish lined with ladyfingers (if served cold) or strips of buttered bread (if served hot)
Chasseur: brown sauce made with shallots, white wine and mushrooms
Chèvre: goat cheese
Chevreuil: venison
Chou: cabbage
Choucroute: sauerkraut; often served with sausages, smoked bacon, pork loin and potatoes
Citron: lemon
Citron vert: lime
Chou-fleur: cauliflower
Clafoutis: a dessert of fruit (usually cherries) baked in an eggy batter
Confit: pork, goose, duck, turkey or other meat and sealed in its own fat
Coquilles St-Jacques: sea scallops
Côtes d'agneau: lamb ribs
Coulis: thick sauce or purée, often of vegetables or fruit
Court-bouillon: stock in which fish, meat and poultry are cooked
Crème chantilly: sweetened whipped cream
Crêpe Suzette: crêpe stuffed with a sweetened mixture of butter, ground almonds, Grand Marnier, orange juice and peel
Crevette: shrimp
Croque-monsieur: grilled ham and cheese sandwich
Croûte (en): in pastry crust
Crudités: raw vegetables
Crustacés: shellfish
Daube: beef braised in red wine
Daurade or **dorade**: sea bream
Ecrevisses: crayfish
Entrecôte: 'between the ribs'; steak cut from between the ribs

Epinards: spinach
Escalope: slice of meat or fish, flattened slightly and sautéed
Escargots (à la bourguignonne): snails (with herbed garlic butter)
Faisan: pheasant
Financière: Madeira sauce enhanced with truffle juice
Fish: poisson
Florentine: with spinach
Foie gras: liver of a specially fattened goose or duck
Fondue: a bubbling pot of liquid into which pieces of food are dipped, most commonly cheese and bread; can also be chocolate and fruit or various savory sauces and cubes of beef; also, vegetables cooked at length in butter and thus reduced to pulp
Forestière: garnish of sautéed mushrooms and lardons (lardons: small chunks of slab bacon)
Fraise: strawberry
Framboise: raspberry
Frangipane: almond pastry cream
Galantine: boned poultry or meat, stuffed and pressed into a symmetrical form, cooked in broth and coated with aspic
Galettes and **crêpes** (Brittany): galettes are thin pancakes made of buckwheat flour and are usually savory; crêpes are made of wheat flour and are usually sweet
Gâteau: cake
Gelée (en): in aspic (gelatin usually flavored with meat, poultry or fish stock)
Génoise: sponge cake
Gibier: game
Glace: ice cream
Granité: lightly sweetened fruit ice
Gratin dauphinois: sliced potatoes baked in milk, cream and grated Gruyère
Grenouille: frog (frogs' legs: cuisses de grenouilles)
Hollandaise: egg-based sauce thickened with butter and flavored with lemon
Homard: lobster
Huître: oyster
Jambon: ham
Julienne: shredded vegetables;

also a consommé garnished with shredded vegetables
Jus: juice; also a reduction or essence used as a sauce
Lait: milk
Langouste: rock or spiny lobster
Langoustine: saltwater crayfish
Lapereau: young rabbit
Lapin: rabbit
Lièvre: hare
Lotte: monkfish or anglerfish; sometimes called 'poor man's lobster'
Madrilène (la): jellied tomato consommé
Magret (Maigret): breast of fattened duck, cooked with the skin on; usually grilled
Médaillon: food, usually meat, fish or foie gras, cut into small, round pieces
Morue: salt cod
Moules (marinières): mussels (cooked in the shell with white wine, shallots and parsley)
Nantua: sauce of crayfish, white wine, butter and cream with a touch of tomato
Navets: turnips
Noisettes: hazelnuts; also, small, round pieces of meat (especially lamb or veal)
Nougat: sweet made with roasted almonds, egg whites, honey and sugar
Oeufs: eggs
Pain: bread
Parfait: sweet or savory mousse; also a layered ice cream dessert
Parisienne: garnish of fried potato balls
Pâtisserie: pastry
Paupiettes: thin slices of meat stuffed with forcemeat and shaped into rolls
Pêche: peach
Pigeonneau: squab
Pintade: guinea hen
Pissaladière: tart with onions, black olives and anchovy filets
Poireau: leek
Poire: pear
Pomme: apple
Pomme de terre: potato
Potée: various vegetables and meats boiled together
Poulet: chicken
Profiteroles: small puffs of

choux paste often filled with whipped cream of crème pâtissière and piled high in a dish with chocolate sauce poured over
Provençale (à la): with garlic or tomato and garlic
Quiche: savory tart of eggs filled with a mixture of cream, and various fillings (such as ham, spinach or bacon)
Raisin: grape
Ratatouille: stew of eggplant, tomatoes, bell peppers, zucchini, onion and garlic, all sautéed in oil
Rémoulade: tangy cold sauce often flavored with capers, onions, parsley, gherkins or herbs
Ris de veau: sweetbreads
Rissoles: type of small pie filled with forcemeat
Rognon: kidney
Rouget: red mullet
Rouille: a Provençal sauce, so called because of the red chilies and sometimes saffron which give it a 'rust' color; chilies are pounded with garlic and breadcrumbs and blended with olive oil; the sauce being served with bouillabaisse, boiled fish or octopus
Sabayon: fluffy, whipped egg yolks, sweetened and flavored with wine or liqueur; served warm
Saint-Pierre: John Dory, a white-fleshed fish
Salade niçoise: salad of tomatoes, hard-boiled egg, anchovy filets, tuna, sweet peppers, celery and olives (also can include green beans, potatoes, basil, onions and/or broad beans)
Saumon: salmon
Sole meunière: sole dipped in flour and sautéed in butter with parsley and lemon
Soissons: garnished with green beans
Sorbet: sherbet
Spätzle: round noodles, often made from eggs
Steak au poivre: pepper steak; steak covered in crushed peppercorns, browned in a frying pan, flambéed with

Cognac, often served in a cream sauce

Tapenade: a paste of black olives, often capers and anchovies, crushed in a mortar with lemon juice and pepper

Tartare: cold sauce for meat or fish: mayonnaise with hard-boiled egg yolks, onions and chopped olives

Tarte: tart, round cake or flan; can be sweet or savory

Tarte Tatin: upside-down apple tart, invented by the Tatin sisters

Tortue: turtle; also, a sauce made with various herbs, tomato, Madeira

Tournedos Rossini: beef sautéed in butter, served with pan juices, foie gras

Truffe: truffle; highly esteemed subterranean fungus, especially from Périgord

Truite: trout

Vacherin: ice cream served in a meringue shell; also, creamy, pungent cheese from Switzerland or Eastern France

Viande: meat

Volaille: poultry

ITALIAN

Acciughe: anchovies
Aceto: vinegar
Aglio: garlic
Agnello: lamb
Agnolotti: crescent-shaped, meat-filled pasta
Agrodolce: sweet-and-sour
Amaretti: crunchy almond macaroons
Anatra: duck
Anguilla: eel
Aragosta: spiny lobster
Arrosto: roasted meat
Baccalá: dried salt cod
Bagna cauda: hot, savory dip for raw vegetables
Bierra: beer
Biscotti: cookies
Bistecca (alla fiorentina): charcoal-grilled T-bone steak (seasoned with pepper and olive oil)
Bolognese: pasta sauce with tomatoes and meat

Bresaola: air-dried spiced beef; usually thinly sliced, served with olive oil and lemon juice
Bruschetta: toasted garlic bread topped with tomatoes
Bucatini: hollow spaghetti
Calamari (calamaretti): (baby) squid
Calzone: stuffed pizza-dough turnover
Cannellini: white beans
Cappelletti: meat- or cheese-stuffed pasta ('little hats')
Carbonara: pasta sauce with ham, eggs, cream and grated cheese
Carciofi (alla giudia): (flattened and deep-fried baby) artichokes
Carpaccio: paper thin, raw beef (or other meats)
Cassata: ice cream bombe
Cavolfiore: cauliflower
Ceci: chickpeas
Cipolla: onion
Conchiglie: shell-shaped pasta
Coniglio: rabbit
Coppa: cured pork fillet encased in sausage skin
Costata: rib steak
Costoletta (alla milanese): (breaded) veal chop
Cozze: mussels
Crespelle: crêpes
Crostata: tart
Fagioli: beans
Fagiolini: string beans
Farfalle: bow-tie pasta
Fegato: liver
Fegato alla veneziana: calf's liver sautéed with onions
Fichi: figs
Finocchio: fennel
Focaccia: crusty flat bread
Formaggio: cheese
Frittata: Italian omelet
Fritto misto: mixed fry of meats or fish
Frutti di mare: seafood (especially shellfish)
Funghi (trifolati): mushrooms (sautéed with garlic and parsley)
Fusilli: spiral-shaped pasta
Gamberi: shrimp
Gamberoni: prawns
Gelato: ice cream
Gnocchi: dumplings made of cheese (di ricotta), potatoes (di patate), cheese and spinach (verdi), or semolina (alla romana)

Grana: hard grating cheese
Granita: sweetened, flavored grated ice
Griglia: grilled
Insalata: salad
Involtini: stuffed meat or fish rolls
Lenticchie: lentils
Maccheroni: macaroni pasta
Manzo: beef
Mela: apple
Melanzana: eggplant
Minestra: soup; pasta course
Minestrone: vegetable soup
Mortadella: large, mild Bolognese pork sausage
Mozzarella di bufala: fresh cheese made from water-buffalo milk
Noce: walnut
Orecchiette: ear-shaped pasta
Osso buco: braised veal shanks
Ostriche: oysters
Pane: bread
Panettone: brioche-like sweet bread
Panna: heavy cream
Pancetta: Italian bacon
Pappardelle: wide, flat pasta noodles
Pasta asciutta: pasta served plain or with sauce
Pasticceria: pastry; pastry shop
Pasticcio: pie or mold of pasta, sauce and meat or fish
Patate: potatoes
Pecorino: hard sheep's-milk cheese
Penne: hollow, ribbed pasta
Peperoncini: tiny, hot peppers
Pepperoni: green, red or yellow sweet peppers
Pesca: peach
Pesce: fish
Pesce spada: swordfish
Pesto: cold pasta sauce of crushed basil, garlic, pine nuts, parmesan cheese and olive oil
Piccata: thinly sliced meat with a lemon or Marsala sauce
Pignoli: pine nuts
Polenta: cornmeal porridge
Pollo: chicken
Polipo: octopus
Pomodoro: tomato
Porcini: prized wild mushrooms, known also as boletus
Prosciutto: air-dried ham
Ragú: meat sauce
Ricotta: fresh sheep's-milk cheese

Rigatoni: large, hollow ribbed pasta

Riso: rice

Risotto: braised rice with various savory items

Rucola: arugula

Salsa (verde): sauce (of parsley, capers, anchovies and lemon juice or vinegar)

Salsicce: fresh sausage

Saltimbocca: veal scallop with prosciutto and sage

Sarde: sardines

Semifreddo: frozen dessert, usually ice cream, with or without cake

Sgombro: mackerel

Sogliola: sole

Spiedino: brochette; grilled on a skewer

Spumone: light, foamy ice cream

Tartufi: truffles

Tiramisú: creamy dessert of rum-spiked cake and triple-crème Mascarpone cheese

Tonno: tuna

Torta: cake

Tortelli: pasta dumplings stuffed with greens and ricotta

Tortellini: ring-shaped dumplings stuffed with meat or cheese and served in broth or in a cream sauce

Trenette: thin noodles served with potatoes and pesto sauce

Trota: trout

Uovo (sodo): egg (hard-boiled)

Uva: grapes

Uva passa: raisins

Verdura: greens, vegetables

Vitello (Tonnato): veal (in a tuna and anchovy sauce)

Vongole: clams

Zabaglione: warm whipped egg yolks flavored with Marsala

Zafferano: saffron

Zucchero: sugar

Zucchine: zucchini

Zuppa: soup

Zuppa inglese: cake steeped in a rum-flavored custard sauce

SPANISH & LATIN AMERICAN

Because there are so many regional dialects in Spain and Latin America, the term for one food product might easily have four or five variations.

Aceite: oil

Ajo: garlic

Al ajillo: with olive oil and garlic

A la marinera: fish or seafood cooked with garlic, onions and white wine

All-i-oli: aïoli; garlicky mayonnaise

Almendras: almonds

Almejas: clams

Anchoas: anchovies

Arroz: rice

Asado: roast

Atœn or **bonito**: tuna

Bacalao: dried, salted codfish

Besugo: sea bream

Boquerones: marinated anchovies

Bullabesa: Catalàn fish stew similar to bouillabaisse

Burrito: soft, wheat-flour tortilla rolled and stuffed with various meats, refried beans, cheese and vegetables

Calamares: squid

Caldo: broth

Callos: tripe

Camarones: shrimp

Carne: meat

Cerveza: beer

Ceviche: raw fish marinated in citrus juice

Chalupa: a small, thick corn tortilla folded into a boat shape, fried and filled with a mixture of shredded meat, cheese and/or vegetables

Chiliquile: flat tortilla layered with beans, meat, cheese and tomato sauce

Chili relleno: large, mild chili pepper, stuffed with cheese and fried in an egg batter

Chorizo: spicy pork sausage flavored with garlic and spices

Cigallas: crayfish or langoustines

Conejo: rabbit

Cordero: lamb

Crema catalana: custard with burnt sugar on top like a crème brûlée, but less creamy than the French dish

Empanada: pie or tart filled variously with meat, seafood or vegetables

Empanadita: a small empanada

Enchilada: a tortilla, fried and stuffed variously with meat, cheese and/or chilies

Entremeses: appetizers

Escalivada or **Escalibada**: chargrilled or roasted peppers, onions, aubergines or other Mediterranean vegetables

Flan: a baked custard with a caramel coating (also crema caramela)

Frito (frita): fried

Gambas: shrimp

Garbanzos: chickpeas

Gazpacho: Andalusian; a cold soup of fresh tomatoes, peppers, onions, cucumbers, olive oil, vinegar and garlic (also celery, breadcrumbs)

Guacamole: an avocado dip or filling, with mashed tomatoes, onions, chilies and citrus juice

Habas: broad beans

Higado: liver

Huachinango: red snapper

Huevos: eggs

Huevos rancheros: tortillas topped with eggs and a hot, spicy salsa

Huevos revueltos: scrambled eggs

Jalapeño: very common hot chili pepper, medium size

Jamón: ham

Jamón Ibérico: delicacy from the native Iberian breed of pig

Jamón Serrano: dry-cured ham, like Parma ham

Lenguado: sole

Licuado: fruit milkshake
Lima: lime
Limón: lemon
Linguiça: garlicky pork sausage
Mantequilla: butter
Mariscos: shellfish
Masa: cornmeal dough; essential for making tortillas
Menudo: a stew featuring tripe
Mole: sauce; most often a thick, dark sauce made with mild chilies and chocolate
Morcilla: black, blood sausage
Nachos: a snack dish of tortilla chips topped with melted cheese and chilies
Nopales: leaves of the prickly pear cactus; simmered and used in various dishes
Ostras: oysters
Paella: a dish of saffron-flavored rice studded with meat (chicken, ham, sausages, pork), shellfish and vegetables
Papas: potatoes (also, patatas)
Papas fritas: literally 'fried potatoes'; french fries
Parrillada: grilled
Pechuga de pollo: chicken breast
Pescado: fish
Pez espada: swordfish
Pimiento: red chili-pepper; can be sweet or hot
Plátano: plantain; a starchy, mild-tasting variety of banana popular in Latin America; usually cooked and served as a side dish
Pollo: chicken
Poblano: large, mild, dark green chili pepper; used for chili rellenos
Puerco: pig
Pulpo: octopus
Quesadilla: a soft, folded tortilla filled with cheese (and/or other savory stuffings) and toasted or fried
Queso: cheese
Rape: monkfish
Riñón: kidneys
Salchicha: sausage
Salsa: sauce; also, an uncooked condiment of fresh tomatoes, onions and chilies
Salsa borracha: 'drunken

sauce'; salsa made with tequila
Sangría: Spanish drink made with red wine, soda water, chopped fresh fruits and sugar, often with a touch of brandy; served on ice
Setas: wild mushrooms
Seviche: raw fish marinated in citrus juice (also, cebiche)
Sopa: soup
Sope: a small cornmeal bun cooked and filled with savory stuffing
Taco: a folded, fried tortilla filled with ground beef (or other meats or fish), refried beans, shredded lettuce, tomatoes, onion, cheese and salsa
Tamale: corn dough made with lard, filled with a savory stuffing, wrapped up in a piece of corn husk, and steamed
Tapa: appetizer, Spanish in origin; usually enjoyed with an apéritif such as dry sherry
Tortilla: a flat, unleavened, crêpe-like bread made with cornmeal flour (masa) or wheat flour
Tostada: a fried tortilla topped with a salad-like mix of ground beef or chicken, beans, lettuce, tomato and guacamole
Zorza: pork marinated in wine and herbs

ASIAN

Chinese

Bao bun: dim sum item; small, steamed buns, white in color, stuffed with a variety of minced fillings (often chicken, shrimp, pork or lotus beans)
Bird's-nest soup: soup that has been thickened and flavored with the gelatinous product derived from soaking and cooking the nests of cliff-dwelling birds

Bok choy: Chinese white cabbage
Chop suey: strictly a Chinese American dish; meat or shrimp and vegetables (mushrooms, water chestnuts, bamboo shoots, bean sprouts) stir-fried together and served over rice
Chow mein: strictly a Chinese American dish; meat or shrimp and vegetables (mushrooms, water chestnuts, bamboo shoots, bean sprouts) stir-fried and served over crispy egg noodles
Dim sum: figuratively, 'heart's delight'; a traditional meal featuring a variety of small dumplings, buns, rolls, balls, pastries and finger food, served with tea in the late morning or afternoon
Egg roll: filo-like wrapper stuffed with pork, cabbage or other vegetables, rolled up, and deep-fried or steamed
Fried rice: cooked, dried rice quickly fried in a wok with hot oil, various meats or vegetables and often an egg
Hoisin: a sweet, rich, dark brown sauce made from fermented soy beans; used as a base for other sauces
Lo mein: steamed wheat-flour noodles stir-fried with bean sprouts and scallions and either shrimp, pork, beef or vegetables
Lychee: small, round, fleshy fruit; used fresh, canned, preserved and dried
Mu shu: a delicate dish of stir-fried shredded pork and eggs rolled up in thin pancakes oyster sauce: a thick, dark sauce of oysters, soy and brine
Oyster sauce: a thick, dark sauce of oysters, soy and brine
Peking duck: an elaborate dish featuring duck that has been specially prepared, coated with honey and cooked until the skin is crisp and golden; served in pieces with thin pancakes or steamed

buns and hoisin

Pot sticker: dim sum item; dumpling stuffed with meat, seafood or vegetables, fried and then steamed

Shark's fin soup: soup thickened and flavored with the cartilage of shark's fins, which provides a protein-rich gelatin

Shu mai: dim sum item; delicate dumpling usually filled minced pork and vegetables

Spring roll: a lighter version of the egg roll, with fillings such as shrimp or black mushrooms

Szechuan: cuisine in the style of the Szechuan province, often using the peppercorn-like black Chinese pepper to make hot, spicy dishes

Thousand-year-old eggs: chicken, duck or goose eggs preserved for 100 days in ashes, lime and salt (also, 100-year-old eggs)

Wonton: paper-thin, glutinous dough wrapper; also refers to the dumpling made with this wrapper, stuffed with minced meat, seafood or vegetables

Wonton soup: a clear broth in which wontons are cooked and served

Indian

Aloo: potato

Aloo papri chat: crisp poori stuffed with chickpeas and potatoes and served with a sour sauce with spicy yoghurt

Bhajia (or Bhaji): deep-fried snacks of vegetables in a spicy batter; usually onions and potatoes served with spicy flavored chutney

Bharta: a dish cooked and puréed

Bhatura: round, lightly leavened and deep fried bread

Bhel poori: crisp poori piled with puffed rice, potatoes, onions, sev (vermicelli), and with fresh coriander; usually served with tamarind sauce and chutneys; not to be con-

fused with poori (bread)

Bhindi: okra, ladyfingers

Bhuna gosht: dry, spicy lamb dish

Biryani: Moghul dish of seafood, meat or chicken marinated in lemon juice, yoghurt, onions, garlic and ginger and stewed with saffron rice

Channa: chickpeas

Chapati: unleavened, thin, round bread made from whole-meal flour and in central India often used instead of rice

Dal (Dahl): lentils

Garam masala: best known of the ground, aromatic Indian spice mixtures, containing no turmeric

Ghee: clarified butter, regarded in India as the purest food because it comes from the sacred cow, giving a rich, buttery taste

Gosht: lamb

Kachori: pastry stuffed with spiced mung beans, served with tamarind chutney

Kofta: balls or dumplings of ground or mashed meat or vegetables, grilled or fried and often stuffed with spices or diced nuts

Korma: powder or aromatic spice, with white pepper instead of chili powder and used in mild curries cooked with yoghurt

Kulfi: milk ice cream flavored with mango, pistachios or almonds

Masala (masaladar): with spices

Masala dosai: ground rice or semolina and lentil pancake filled with potatoes and onion, served with spicy coconut chutney

Mughlai: method of cooking using cream, yoghurt, almonds and pistachios

Murgh: chicken

Naan: soft textured bead made from white flour leavened with natural yeast and baked by moistening one side and attaching it to the inside of a

tandoor oven; may have poppy or sesame seeds or onion added

Paper dosai: very thin pancakes with potato and onion, served with coconut chutney

Parathas: crisp, layered, buttery breads served plain or stuffed

Pilau (pillau, pulao): rice stir-fried in ghee then cooked in stock and served with fish, vegetables or meat

Poori: whole-wheat bread, like a chapati, fried, usually in ghee, and puffed into a ball; served with vegetarian foods, particularly dal (lentil), potato and bean dishes (cooked pooris can be stuffed with hot curried fillings as a quick snack)

Poppadum: flat, dried wafers of lentil, rice or potato flour, deep fried and served as a snack; can be highly spiced

Potato poori: crisp poori piled with potatoes and onions, sweet and sour sauce, yoghurt and sev (vermicelli)

Raita: yoghurt relish

Saag: spinach

Samosas: crisp, deep-fried triangular pastry stuffed with spiced vegetables like onions, or meat, served with chutney or yoghurt

Seekh kebab: skewered and grilled meat

Sev poori: crisp poori piled with potato and onions and sweet and sour sauce and with sev (vermicelli)

Tamarind: tree producing flat, bean-like pods which have become essential in Indian cooking; often made into a chutney as a dip for deep-fried snacks and the juice is used extensively in South Indian cooking

Tandoor: barrel-shaped mud or clay oven used for roasting meats and baking bread (moistened and placed against the sides of the oven)

Thali: complete meal on a tray with each curry, relish and dessert in separate bowls or katori, plus bread or rice

Tikka: small pieces of chicken or lamb served as an appetizer

Vindaloo: very hot dish seasoned with ground-roasted spices and chilies with vinegar and/or tamarind; a specialty of central and western coastal India with a strong flavor

Japanese

Amaebi: sweet shrimp

Anago: sea eel

Awabi: abalone

Azuki: dried bean; azuki flour is often used for confections

Bento: meal served in a box with different compartments

Daikon (Mooli): long, white radish, usually grated or cut into strips

Donburi: bowl of boiled rice with different toppings like chicken, egg or beef

Ebi: shrimp

Edamame: fresh soy beans boiled in their pods and sprinkled with salt

Enoki (Enokitake): delicate mushrooms with long stems and small caps

Gohan: rice

Hamachi: yellowtail, often used for sushi or grilled

Hashi: chopsticks

Hibachi: small, open charcoal grill

Hirame: flounder

Ikura: salmon roe

Kaiseki: multicourse menu of luxury dishes reflecting the seasons with the use of seasonal foods and artistic dinnerware and presentation

Kani: crab

Kappa: cucumber

Kobe beef: cattle raised in exclusive conditions (frequent massages and a diet featuring large quantities of beer), which results in an extraordinarily tender, very expensive beef

Konbu: dried kelp; used in soup stock, for sushi and as a condiment

Maguro: tuna

Maki: rolled

Mako: shark

Mirugai: giant clam

Miso (soup): soybean paste from which a savory broth is made, usually served with cubes of tofu or strips of seaweed

Ono: wahoo fish; a relative of the mackerel often compared in taste to albacore

Ramen: Chinese soup noodles

Saba: mackerel

Sake: salmon

Saké: traditional rice wine served hot or cold

Sashimi: thinly sliced raw fish on rice, usually served with soy sauce and wasabi

Shabu shabu: similar to sukiyaki; beef and vegetables cooked tableside in a broth

Shiitake: prized cultivated mushroom, dark brown with a large cap

Shoya: soy sauce

Soba: buckwheat noodles

Sukiyaki: braised beef and vegetable dish with broth added after cooking

Sushi: rounds of vinegared rice wrapped in dried seaweed with a center of raw fish or vegetables, served with wasabi and soy

Tai: snapper

Tako: octopus

Tamago: egg

Tamari: dark sauce similar in composition and taste to soy; often used for dipping

Tempura: deep-fried, batter-dipped fish or vegetables

Teriyaki: a marinade of soy and sweet saké used on meats, fish and poultry

Tofu: bean curd, processed into a liquid and then molded into large cubes

Toro: fatty belly cut of tuna

Udon: wheat noodles

Unagi: freshwater eel

Uni: sea-urchin roe

Wasabi: a hot, spicy condiment made from the roots of Japanese horseradish, chartreuse in color

Yakitori: a dish of pieces of chicken and vegetables, marinated in a spicy sauce, skewered and grilled

Thai

Kaeng (or Gaeng): large and diverse category of dishes; loosely translates as "curry"

Kaeng massaman: a variety of coconut-milk curry

Kaeng phed: a red, coconut-cream curry

Kaeng som: a hot-sour curry

Kapi: fermented shrimp paste; vital ingredient in nam phrik, or dishes flavored with hot chili sauce

Kai (or Gai): chicken

Khai: egg

Khao: rice

Khao suai: white rice

Khao phad: fried rice

King: ginger

Kung: prawns

Lab (or Larb): dish of minced meat with chilies and lime juice

Mu: pork

Nam: sauce

Nam pla: fish sauce

Nam phrik: a hot chili sauce

Nuea: beef

Ped: duck

Phad: fried

Phad king: fried with ginger

Phad phed: fried hot and spicy

Phad Thai: pan-fried rice noodles with chicken, shrimp, eggs, peanuts and bean sprouts

Phrik: chili pepper

Pla: fish

Si racha (or Sri racha): spicy chili condiment

Tom: boiled; often refers to soup

Tom kha kai: chicken coconut-cream soup flavored with lemongrass and chilies

Tom yam kung: hot-sour shrimp soup flavored with lemongrass, lime and chilies

Yam: flavored primarily with lime juice and chilies, resulting in a hot-sour taste; usually 'salads' but can also be noodle dishes or soup

Yam pla: raw fish spiked with lime juice, chili, lemongrass, mint and fish sauce

GENERAL INDEX

A

A Dove & Son, 297
A la Mode, 340
A Zwemmer Arts Bookshop, 258
Abbey House, 196
Academy Auctioneers & Valuers, 230
Academy Fitness Centre, 380
Academy Town House, 185
Accordions of London, 328
Adam's Café, 137
Adams, 253
Addison Lee, 432
Adler, 317
Admiral Codrington, 110
Admiralty, The, 109
Adolfo Dominguez, 271
Adonis Art, 352
Adrian Harrington Rare Books, 232
Aero, 310
Agent Provocateur, 346
Agnès b, 271
Agnew's, 358
AIR CHARTER, 432
Air Gallery, 352
Airbus Heathrow Shuttle, 430
AIRPORTS, 430, 431
- HOTELS, 200
Al's Café & Bar, 114
Al Duca, 80
Al Hamra, 62
Al-Shami, 420
Alain Ducasse, 97
Alan Cristea, 352
Alastair Little, 86
- Lancaster Gate, 72
Alastair Lockhart, 336
Albemarle Gallery, 352
Albert Bridge, 403
Albert Memorial, 368
Albert Roux, 67
- Café, 146
Alberta's Café, 146
Alberta Ferretti, 340, 342
- QUICK BITE, 146
Albery Theatre, 408
Albion, 217
Albion Computers, 436
Alexander McQueen, 272
Alexandra Park, 401
Alfie's, 226
Alfred, 27
Alfred Dunhill, 337
Algerian Coffee Stores, 289
Alison House Hotel, 196
Alistair Sampson Antiques, 238
All England Lawn Tennis
    Championships, 385

All Flutes Plus, 329
All Hallows, 376
All Languages Ltd., 438
Allen & Co, 298
Almeida, 409
Alounak, 123
Alphabet Bar, 209
Alternative Medicine Centre, 248
ALTERNATIVE THERAPIES, 248
Amanda Wakeley, 272, 340
Amandier, 23
Amber Centre, The, 316
Amber Hotel, 197
Ambulance, 437
American Bar, The, 210
American Classics, 348
American Express, 435
American Museum in Britain, 415
American Retro, 348
Amsterdam Hotel, 197
Anchor, 221
& Clarkes, 284
Anderson & Sheppard, 325
Andrew Edmunds, 138
Andrew Martin, 307
Andy's, 329
Andy's Taverna, 107
Angel, 212
Angel Bagel, 286
Angels & Bermans, 246
Angelucci Coffee Merchants, 289
Anglesea Arms, 137
Animation Art Gallery, 300
Anna Molinari Blumarine, 340, 341
Annabel Jones, 300
Annely Juda Fine Art, 352
Anouska Hempel, 343
Antelope, 212
Anthea Moore Eade, 264
Anthony d'Offay Gallery, 352
Antiquarian Book Fair, 439
Antiquarian Booksellers
    Association, 227
Antiquarius, 226
ANTIQUES, 226
- CENTRES, 226
- MARKETS, 227
Antoine Chenevière, 234
Anya Hindmarch, 319
Anything Left-Handed, 303
APARTMENT RENTAL
    SERVICES, 153
Apartment Service, The, 153
Apple, 436
Apsley House, 393
Apsley House Hotel, 415
Apter-Fredericks, 234

Aquascutum, 276, 277
Archduke Wine Bar, 209
Architectural Dialogue, 367
Ard Ri Dining Room, 125
Argent's Music, 332
Aria, 310
Arkansas Café, 112
Arlington House Restaurant, 81
Aroma, 31
ARRIVING IN LONDON, 430
ART COURSES, 377
ART DECO, 229
ART GALLERIES, 352
ART MUSEUMS, 362
ART NOUVEAU, 229
Art Space Gallery, 353
ART SUPPLIES, 377
Artemis Decorative Arts, 229
Arthur Beale, 335
Arthur Middleton, 240
Artillery Museum, 393
Asakusa, 107
Ascott Mayfair, The, 153
Ashmolean Museum, 419
Asia de Cuba, 40
Asprey & Garrard, 240, 300, 317,
    319, 334
Assaggi at The Chepstow, 73
Association of British Picture
    Restorers, 230
Association of Photographers, 353
Aster House, 197
Aston's apartments, 154
Astoria, 223
Athenaeum, The, 161
Atlantic Bar & Grill, 74, 209
Atlas, The, 119
Atrium, 258
ATTRACTIONS, 367
Aubergine, 27
AUCTION HOUSES, 230
Audley, 278
Aurora, 34, 139
Austin Reed, 245, 253, 276
Australian High Commission, 436
Avant Garden, 284
Aveda Institute, 255
Avenue, 80
Avis, 432, 434
Axis, 40

B

B & M Seafoods, 290
Babe Ruth's, 121
Back to Basics, 126
BACKSTAGE TOURS, 406
BADA, 230
Bagatelle Boutique, 285

Bagels, 286
Baker & Spice, 135, 270, 285
BAKERIES, 284
Balance, 248
Bali Sugar, 73
Balloon Safaris, 383
Balls Brothers, 204
Bank, 41, 135
Bank of England Museum, 393
Banqueting House, 368
Bar des Amis du Vin, 205
Bar Italia, 139
Barbican Centre, 410
- RESTAURANT, 37
Barbican Gallery, 362
Barclay & Bodie, 300, 307
Barclay International Group, 153
Barry Davies Oriental Art, 237
BARS, 204
Barstow & Barr Fine Cheeses, 287
Base, 48, 345
Basia Zarzycka, 343
Basil Street Hotel, The, 185
- TEA ROOM, 147
Bass & Acoustic Centre, The, 329
Bateaux London Catamaran
        Cruisers, 434
Bateaux London Thames Circular
        Cruises, 434
BATH, 414
- Bun, 414
- Hot Springs, 414
Bath International Music Festival, 414
Bath Place Hotel, 420
Bath Priory, 415, 416
Battersea Park, 401
BBC Experience, 368
BBC Henry Wood Promenade
        Concerts, 439
BBC Shop Broadcasting House, 258
BBC World Service Shop, 259
BCA Boukamel Gallery, 353
Beak Street, 86
Beano's, 331
Bear, The, 422
Beardsmore Gallery, 353
Beating Retreat by the Massed
        Bands of the Household
        Division, 439
Beatties, 267
Beaufort, The, 177
Beaufort House, 154
BEAUTY, 248
- SALONS, 249
Beaux Arts, 353
BED & BREAKFAST, 155
Belair House, 45
Belgo Noord, 27
Belgravia Village, 270
Belinda Robertson, 281
Bellville Sassoon, 344
Belvedere, The, 52

Ben de Lisi, 344
Bengal Trader, 112
Benjamin Pollock's Toy Shop, 267
Bennett & Luck, 296
Benson & Hedges, 337
Bentley & Skinner, 241
Berk, 281
Berkeley, The, 156
- Health Club & Spa, 380
- RESTAURANT, 57, 59
Berkeley Square Chauffeur
        Services, 434
Berkeleys Hotel Connections, 430
Berlitz International, 438
Bermondsey (New Caledonian)
        Market, 227
Bernard Jacobson Gallery, 353
Bernard Quaritch, 232
Bernard Shapero, 232
Berners Hotel, 186
Berry Bros & Rudd, 299
Bertie, 278
Bertorelli's Café Italian, 96
Bertram Rota, 232
Besselink & Jones, 313
Bethnal Green Museum
        of Childhood, 393
Betty Jackson, 340
Bettys Café, 427
Beverly Hills Bakery, 285
Beyoglu, 104
BFI London IMAX Cinema, 368
Bibendum, 92, 299
- Oyster Bar, 92, 205
Biblion, 232
BICYCLING, 379
Bierodrome, 207
Big Bus Company, The, 433
Big Easy, 110
Big Kids Store, 267
Biggles, 298
Bikefix, 379
Bill Amberg, 319
Birdcage, The, 96
Bistro Daniel, 105
Black's, 335
Black Swan Pub, The, 427
Black Taxi Tours, 435
Black Truffle, The, 134
Blackfriar, 213
Blackout II, 242
Blackwell's, 261
Blackwell's Bookshop, 419
Blade Rubber Stamps, 336
Blains, 353
Blakes Hotel, 161
Blanc, Raymond, 422
Blanks, 328
Bleeding Heart, 115
- Wine Bar, 206
Blenheim, 420
Bliss Chemists, 437

Blooms Hotel, 186
Bloomsbury Workshop, 232
Blue Anchor, 216
Blue Elephant, 46
Blue Print Café, 98
Bluebird, 291
- Café, 110
- Restaurant, 28
Blunos, Martin, 417
Blunos, Siân, 417
Bodie & Gibbs, 245
Bodleian Library, 419
Body Shop, The, 256
Boisdale, 99, 209
Bombay Brasserie, 92
Bond, 348
Bond Street, 341
- Antiques Centre, 226
Bonhams, 230
- Chelsea, 230
Bonsai Catering, 293
Boodle & Dunthorne, 317
BOOKS, 231, 258, 267
Books for Cooks, 129, 260, 379
Books Etc., 262
Boosey & Hawkes, 332
Boots, 437
Borderline, The, 222, 223
Borders Books & Music, 262
Boss & Co, 334
Botanical Garden, 419
Bottom Line, 222
Bourbon-Handy Antiques Centre, 226
Bourdin, Michel, 64
Boxfresh, 348
Brackenbury, The, 85
Bradleys, 346
Brady's, 145
Bramah Tea & Coffee
        Museum, 147, 394
Brasenose College, 419
BRASS RUBBING, 379
Brasserie, The, 135
Brasserie St. Quentin, 55
BRAY-ON-THAMES, 424
Bread Shop, 285
BREAKFAST, 135
Brian Haughton Antiques, 238
Brian Rolleston Antiques, 235
Brick Lane Beigel Bake, 286
Brick Lane Market, 227
Brick Lane Music Hall, The, 223
Bridge, The, 319
Bridgewater, 305
Brilliant, 142
Britain Visitor Centre, 435
British Airways London Eye, 368
British Antique Dealers'
        Association, 227
British Antique Dealers' Fair, 438
British Antique Furniture
        Restorers' Association, 230

British Hatter, The, 344
British Horological Institute & Federation, 230
British Invisible Mending Service, 244
British Library, 368
British Museum, 300, 394
British Music Information Centre, 411
Brixton Market, 354
Broadgate Club, 380
Broadgate Ice Rink, 383
Brodie & Middleton, 377
Brooks Specialist (Cars & Motorcycles) Auctioneers, 230
Brown's Hotel, 162
- RESTAURANT, 64
- TEA ROOM, 147
Browns Restaurant & Bar, 115
Browns, 272, 416, 421
Browns Chauffeur Hire, 434
Browns Focus, 348
Bruce Poole, 55
Buckingham Dry-Cleaners, 244
Buckingham Palace, 387
Buckle-My-Shoe, 264
Buddhist Society, The, 437
Budget, 432
Buffalo, 350
Builder's Arms, 110
Bull & Last, The, 218
Bulldog Club, 155
Burberry, 276, 277
Bureau, 336
BUREAUX DE CHANGE, 435
Burlington Arcade, 274
Burlington Paintings, 358
busaba eathai, 139
Busabong Tree, 28
BUSES, 432
BUSINESS FACILITIES, 435
Butler & Wilson, 317
Butlers Wharf Chef School, 379
Butlers Wharf Chop House, 98
Butlers Wharf Gastrodome, 291
Buying Tickets, 410

C

C John (Rare Rugs), 239
Cabair Helicopters, 434
Cabinet War Rooms, 369
Cadogan, The, 162
Café in the Crypt, 144
Café Delancey, 107
Café des Amis du Vin, 116
Café du Jardin, 41
Café Flo, 132
Café Japan, 48
Café Med, 129
Café Mezzo, 139, 285
Café at Phillips, The, 105
Café Spice Namaste, 34
CAFÉS, 104
Caffè Nero, 128
CALENDAR OF EVENTS, 438

Calvin Klein, 341
Calzone, 130
Cambio de Tercio, 92
Camden Brasserie, 107
Camden Palace, 224
Camden Passage Market, 227
Camera Clinic, 327
Camerer Cuss & Co, 240
Cameron Shaw, 282
Canadian High Commission, 436
Canadian Muffin Company, 128
CANAL CRUISES, 434
Canal Museum, 394
Cannizaro House, 147, 186
Cannons, 382
- Health Club & Spa, 381
Cantaloupe, 208
Cantina Vinopolis, 104
Capital, The, 162
- RESTAURANT, 56
- TEA ROOM, 148
Captain O M Watts, 335
Carey Camelot Chauffeur Drive, 434
CARFAX, 419
Carlton Hobbs, 234
Carlton Tennis & Health Club, 385
Carluccio's, 293
Carluccio's Caff, 132
Carlyle's House, 387
Carmelli Bakeries, 285, 286
Caroline Charles, 341
Cartier, 318
Cashmere Clinic, The, 244
Cassia Oriental, 62
Castle Museum, 426
Cath Kidson, 307
Catherine Walker, 340
Cavallini, Stephano, 26
Cavendish, The, 187
Caviar House, The, 290
Cecil Sharp House, 411
Cellhire, 437
Cenci, 242
Central YMCA, 381
Centuria, 121
Cerruti, 1881, 341
CHAINS HOTELS, 200
Chalfont Dyers & Cleaners, 245
Chamber of Commerce & Industry Reference Library, 437
Champneys The London Club, 381
Champneys Piccadilly, 249
Chanel, 341, 342
Changing the Guard, 369
Changing Room, The, 270, 272
Charbonnel et Walker, 288
Charing Cross Hospital, 437
Charing Cross Station, 433
Charles Ede Ltd, 234
Charles Street Communications, 437
Charles Worthington, 252
Charlotte Street Hotel, 177

Chauffeurdrive, 434
CHAUFFEURED CAR, 434
Chavot, Eric, 56
Che, 80, 208
Cheapo Cheapo, 331
CHEESES, 287
Chelsea Antiques Fair, 438, 440
Chelsea Barbers, 253
Chelsea Book Fair, 440
Chelsea Crafts Fair, 440
Chelsea Flower Show, 439
Chelsea Gallery & Il Libro, 232
Chelsea Gardener, The, 284
Chelsea Physic Garden, 402
Chelsea Ram, 110
Chelsea Sports Centre, 385
Chelsea Village Hotel, 187
Cheltenham Gold Cup, 414
Cherwell Boathouse, 421
Chesterfield, The, 187
Chez Bruce, 100
Chez Gérard at the Opera Terrace, 116
Chez Marcelle, 138
Chez Max, 46
Chez Moi, 50
Chez Nico, 63
Childminders, 246
CHILDREN, 264
- ENTERTAINMENT, 268
- FURNITURE, 305
Children's Book Centre, 260
Children's Pavilion, 265
CHINA, 305
China House, 132, 301
China White, 224
Chinacraft, 306
Chinese Contemporary, 354
Chinese Embassy, 436
Chinese New Year, 438
Chinon, 85
Chiswick, The, 112
Chiswick House & Gardens, 402
CHOCOLATE, 288
Chocolate Society, The, 288
Chor Bizarre, 63
Chris Beetles, 358
Christ Church, 419
- Spitalfields, 411
Christian Dior, 341, 342
Christian Lacroix, 342
Christie's, 231
- Education, 377, 386
- South Kensington, 231
Christopher's American Grill, 41
Christopher Wray Lighting, 313
Church's, 278
Church of England, 437
CHURCHES, 376
Churchill Arms, 218
Churchill Inter-Continental, The, 163
Chutney Mary, 47
Cibo, 52

Ciel Décor, 310
Cinema Bookshop, 259
Cinnamon Bar, The, 135
Circus, 87
Citadines Barbican, 154
Cittie of Yorke, 217
City Business Library, 437
City Garden Tours, 433
City of London Antiques Fair, 439
City of London Festival, The, 411
City of London Tourist
    Information, 435
City Rhodes, 34
CK Calvin Klein, 272
Clarendon Cross, 270
Claridge's, 156
- BAR, 210
- HAIR SALON, 252
- RESTAURANT, 63
- TEA ROOM, 148
Clark & Sons, 114
Clarke's, 53
Claverley, The, 197
Clerkenwell & Islington Guides
    Associations, 435
Clifton, The, 220
Clifton Ford Hotel, 188
Clifton Nurseries, 284
Cliveden Town House, The, 178
Clockmakers' Company
    Collection, 369
CLOCKS, 240
Clos du Roy, 416
CLOTHING, 271, 321, 338
- ANTIQUES, 242
- CHILDREN, 264
- REPAIRS, 244
Club at County Hall, The, 381
Club Gascon, 35
Coach, 319
Coach & Horses, 218
Coast, 64
Cobra & Bellamy, 317
Cock Tavern, The 135, 213
COFFEE, 128, 289
Coffee Gallery, 106, 135
Colefax & Fowler, 308
Coliseum, 412
College of Arms, 369
College Art Collections, 362
College Farm, 148
Collingwood, 318
Cologne & Cotton, 301, 314
Colonnade Town House, The, 188
Colourway, 384
Columbia Road Market, 284
COMEDY CLUBS, 222
Comedy Store, 222
COMICS, 260
Comme des Garçons, 272
Complete Cobbler, The, 248
Compton Photos, 437

Computeq, 436
Computer Cabs, 432
COMPUTERS, 436
Concert Hall Approach (WINE
    BAR), 209
Condotti, 128
Connaught, The, 156
- Grill Room & Restaurant, The, 64
- TEA ROOM, 148
Connolly, 320
Conrad, The, 163
Conran Shop, The, 301, 310
Conservation Register, 227
CONSERVATORS, 230
Conservatory, The, 148
Constance Stobo, 239
Contemporary Applied Arts, 238, 301
Contemporary Art Show, 438
Contemporary Ceramics, 305
Contessa Ghisi, 270, 301
CONFECTIONERY, 288
COOKING, 379
Coppergate, 426
Copthorne London Gatwick, 201
Cordings, 277
Cork & Bottle, 207
Corney & Barrow, 117, 204, 299
Corpus Christi College, 419
Corrigan, Richard, 88
COSMETICS, 250
Cosmetics à la Carte, 250
Costas Fish Restaurant, 130
Costume Studio Montgomery
    House, The, 246
Counter Spy Shop, 334
Counting House, 213
Country Lanes, 379
Country Living Spring Fair, 438
County Hall Restaurant, 91, 148
Courses & Lectures, 364
Courtauld Institute, 362
Covent Garden, 297, 354
Covent Garden
- Centre, 226
- Festival, 439
- Flower Festival, 439
- Hotel, 178
- Music Festival, The, 411
Cow Dining Room, The, 130
Crabtree & Evelyn, 256
Crafts Council, 301
- Gallery, 363
- Gallery Shop, 238
Crafts Markets, 354
Cranks, 139
Cranley, The, 188
Cranley Gardens Hotel, 188
Crazy Pig Designs, 314
Createx, 265
Creative Juice Bar, 116
Crescent, The, 60
Criterion Auction Rooms, 231

Criterion Marco Pierre White, 74
Crocker's Folly, 220
Cross, The, 302, 341
Cross Keys, The, 214
Cross Street Gallery, 354
Crown, The, 217
Crown & Goose, The, 108
Crown Perfumery, The, 256
Crowne Plaza St. James's, 163
- RESTAURANT, 99
Crucial Trading, 310
CRUISES, 434
Crussh, 116
Crusting Pipe, 205
Crystal Palace National Sports
    Centre, 381, 385, 402
Culpeper, 256
Cumberland Hotel, 188
Cuming Museum, 395
Cutty Sark, 369
Cyberia Café, 142
Czech & Speake, 256

D

D L Lord, 278
D R Harris & Co, 257
D S Lavender, 241
Daddy Kool, 331
Daily Mail Ideal Home Show, 438
Daily Telegraph House
    & Garden Fair, 439
Daisy & Tom, 260, 267
DANCE, 380, 412
Dance Books, 259
Danceworks, 380
Daphne, 108
Daphne's, 93
Daquise, 142
Daunt Books for Travellers, 264
David Black, 239
David Ireland, 243
David Lloyd Club Finchley, 385
David Mellor, 313
David Morris, 318
Davidoff, 337
Days Inn, 200
De Baere, 130, 285
De Gustibus, 286
De Hems, 221
De-Luxe Cleaners, 244
Debenhams, 269
Decorative Antiques & Textiles
    Fair, 438, 439
Dege, 325
Del Buongustaio, 79
Delfina Studio Café, 26
Deliss, 278
Deliverance, 247
Denim, 205
Dennis Severs' House, 369
DEPARTMENT STORES, 269
Derek Johns, 361
Descamps, 314

Design Museum, 395
- RESTAURANT, 98
Designers Guild, 308
Desmond Sauter, 337
Dickens House Museum, 387
Dickins & Jones, 146, 250, 269
Diesel, 348
Dimple, 432
Dining Room Shop, The, 310
Dinny Hall, 315
Disney Store, The, 265, 267
Divertimenti, 313
Diwana Bhel Poori House, 119
DKNY, 273, 341
- NAIL BARS, 255
- QUICK BITE, 146
DNA Computer Services, 436
D.O.C. Records, 331
Docklands, 386
Docklands Light Railway, 431, 433
DOCKLANDS (QUICK BITES), 118
Docklands Sailing & Watersports
    Centre, 386
Docklands Water Sports Club, 386
Dr Johnson's House, 388
Dr Martens Dept Store, 349, 350
Dolce & Gabbana, 273, 342
Dome, The, 370
Don Pepe, 125
Donmar Warehouse, 408
Donna Karan, 273, 341
Dorchester, The, 157
DORCHESTER, 419
Dorchester, The, 157
- BAR, 210
- HAIR SALON, 252
- The RESTAURANTS, 66, 69
- SPA, 249, 381
- TEA ROOM, 148
Dorset Square, 179
Dove, 216
Drabble, William, 27
Dragons, 305
Draycott House, 154
Dress Circle, 330
Drill Hall, The, 412
Drinking Fountains, 359
Drones The Grocer, 293
Droopy & Browns, 344
Drury Lane Theatre Royal, 405, 406
Drury Tea & Coffee Co, 289
DRY CLEANERS, 244
Ducasse, Alain, 97
Duffer of St. George, 349
Duke of Cambridge, 105, 122
Dukes, 164
Dulwich Picture Gallery, 363
Durley House, 154
Durrants, 189
DYEING, 245

Eagle, 115

Eagle & Child, 422
Eagle Gallery, The, 354
Earls Court Gym, 381
Early Learning Centre, 267
EasyEverything, 247
EAT, 133
Eating & Entertainment, 223
Ebury Wine Bar International, 144
EC Information Unit, 437
Eco Pizzeria, 114
Economist Shop, The, 260
Eden Park, 324
Editions Graphiques Gallery, 229
Edward Goodyear, 282
Edward Green, 278
Edwards, Mark, 69
Egerton House, 179
Egg, 341
Ehrman, 384
1837, 64
Elbow Room, 436
Electric Ballroom, 224
Electrum Gallery, 315
Elephant, 311
Elizabeth Arden Red Door Hair
    & Beauty Spa, 250
Elizabeth Hotel, 197
Ellements Womens Health
    & Fitness, 381
Ellis Brigham Mountain Sports, 335
Elspeth Gibson, 270, 342
Eltham Palace, 370
Elvis Gracelands Palace, 223
E-MAIL, 247
EMBASSIES, 436
Embroiderers' Guild, The, 384
Emergency Dentist, 437
Emergency Doctor, 437
Emergency Optician, 437
EMERGENCY PHONE
    NUMBERS, 437
Emerson, 244
Emma Hope, 279
Emma Willis, 323
Emmanuel Ungaro, 342
Empire Lounge, The, 224
Emporio Armani, 273, 341
- QUICK BITE, 146
End, The, 224
Engineer, The, 135, 219
England & Co., 354
English Garden, The, 28
English Gardening School, The, 383
In the English Manner, 153
English National Holidays, 438
English Style, The, 307
Enterprise, The, 212
Episode, 338
Eric Chavot, 56
Ermenegildo Zegna, 321
Eskenazi, 237
Estorick Collection of Modern
    Italian Art, 363

ETHNIC
- FOODS, 293
- RESTAURANTS, 104
Etro, 273
Euphorium, 50
- Bakery, 286
Europcar, 432
- Chauffeur Drive, 434
European Academy & Accademia
    Italiana, 363
European Bookshop, 263
Eurostar, 431
Euston Station, 433
Evan Evans Tours, 433
Evening Dress, 245
EVENTS INFORMATION, 362, 438
Executive Hotel, 189
EXHIBITIONS
    INFORMATION, 362
Eximious, 302
Export Licensing Unit, 227
Eyre Bros, 133

F Cooke, 120, 138
Fabric, 224
FABRICS, 307
Faccessory, 336
Fairfax House, 426
Falcon Jet Centre, 432
Falkiner Fine Papers, 377
Famous Names, 306
Fan Museum, 395
Faraday Museum, 395
Farlow's, 277, 333
Farmacia, 116, 248
Farmacia II, 116
Farmers Market
    (QUICK BITE), 111
FASHION, 271
Fast Flowers, 282
Fat Duck, 424
Faulkener's, 120
Favourbrook, 326
Fawcett Library, 370
Feathers Hotel, The, 423, 424
Felton & Sons, 282
Femme Fatale, 346
Fenton House, 388
Fenwick, 269
- QUICK BITE, 146
Fifth Floor, The, 56
- Café, 124, 146
Filofax, 336
Filthy McNasty's Whiskey Café, 207
Fine Art & Antiques Fair, 438-440
Fine Art Society, The, 359
Finnish Embassy, 436
Finns, 293
Fior, 317
Fire, 437
Firebird, 65
First Floor, 73

First Tailored Alterations, 244
FISH, 290
FISHING, 333
FITNESS CLUBS, 380
Fitness Exchange, 382
Fitness First, 382
Five Sumner Place, 198
Flask, 217
Flemings Mayfair, 154, 189
Florence Nightingale Museum, 395
Floriana, 57
Floris, 256
Flower Store, The, 283
Flowercity, 283
FLOWERS, 282
- MARKETS, 284
Flowers East, 354
Floyd's Flyers Chauffeurs, 432
Fluid, 116
Fogal, 346
Foliage, 56
FOOD, 284
- TAKE-AWAY, 293
Food Ferry, 247
Food for Thought, 117
Foote's, 328
Forbidden Planet, 260
Formal Gentleman's Outfit, 245
Formes, 347
Fortnum & Mason, 269, 292
- QUICK BITE, 133, 146
- TEA ROOM, 148
Forum, The, 189, 223
Foundation, The, 146
Fountain Restaurant, 133
Fountains, 154
Four Seasons Hotel, The, 158
- TEA ROOM, 149
Four Seasons Hotel Canary
    Wharf, The, 158
- RESTAURANT, 37
47 Park Street, 157
Fox & Anchor, The, 135, 213
Fox Club, The, 179
Fox & Grapes, 222
Foyle's, 332
Frames Rickards, 433
Frank Cooper's Oxford
    Marmalade, 419
Frank Godfrey, 298
Franklin, The, 179
Fratelli Camisa, 294
Fred Bare, 344
Freemason's Arms, 216
Freemasons' Hall, 395
French Connection, 338
French Consulate Général, 436
French House, 221
- Dining Room, 87
French's Theatre Bookshop, 259
Freshlands, 296
Frette, 314

Freud Museum, 388
Friends of the Royal Academy, 363
Fringe Theatre, 409
Frith Street Gallery, 354
Frost & Reed, 359
Fulham Palace, 370
Fuller's Brewery, 370
Fung Shing, 31
FURNISHINGS, 307
FURNITURE, 234
Furniture History Society, 227

G

G Heywood Hill, 232
G Smith & Sons, 338
Gabriel's Wharf, 238
Gainsborough, 190
GALLERIES INFORMATION, 362
Gallery of Antique Costumes
    & Textiles, 243
Gallery Hotel, 190
Gallery K, 355
Galvin, Chris, 61
GAME, 290, 297
GAMES, 267
Garage, The, 223
Garden Books, 261
Garden Restaurant General Trading
    Company, The, 111, 146
GARDENING, 284, 383
GARDENS, 401
Gastro, 114
GATWICK, 430
- HOTELS, 201
Gatwick Express, 430
Gaudi, 38
Gay's the Word, 261
Geffrye Museum, 395
General Leather Company, The, 277
General Trading Company,
    The, 311, 342
- QUICK BITE, 111, 146
Generator, 198
Geo F Trumper, 254
George Inn, 221
Georgian Restaurant, 146
Georgian Village, 226
Georgina von Etzdorf, 274
German Embassy, 436
GETTING AROUND, 431
Ghost, 342
Gianni Versace, 273, 341
Gieves & Hawkes, 325
GIFTS, 300
Gilbert Collection, 363
Gimpel Fils, 355
Gina Shoes, 279
Giorgio Armani, 342
GLASS, 236, 305
Glasshouse, The, 55
Globe Café, 142
Godiva, 288
Golden Hind, 126

Golden Hinde, 371
Golden Tours, 433
GOLF, 383
Good Company, 434
Gordon's, 204
Gordon Ramsay, 29
Gordon Watson, 229
Gore, The, 180
Goring, The, 164
- TEA ROOM, 149
Gosh!, 302
Gourmet Pizza, 142
GOURMET SHOPS, 291
GOURMET SPECIALISTS, 293
Graham & Green, 302
Grand, The, 224
Grange, The, 426
Granita, 51
Grano, 33
Grant & Cutler, 263
Gravetye Manor, 201
Gray's Antique Market, 226
Gray's Inn, 392
Gray's-in-the-Mews, 227
Great American Bagel Factory, 286
Great Eastern Dining Room, 85, 208
Great Eastern Hotel, 164
- BREAKFAST, 135
- QUICK BITE, 113
Great Frog, The, 315
GREAT MILTON, 422
Great Nepalese, 119
Green Baby, 267
Green Olive, The, 125
Green Park, 402
Green's Picnics & Hampers, 292
Green's Restaurant
    & Oyster Bar, 81, 205
Green & Stone, 378
Greenhouse, The, 65
Greenwich, 354
- Tourist Information Centre, 435
Greenwich & Docklands
    International Festival, 439
Greenwich Market, 228
Greenwich Park, 403
Grenadier, 212
Gresslin's, 49
Grill Room, The, 66
Grosvenor House, 154
- RESTAURANT, 63
Grosvenor House Art
    & Antiques Fair, 439
Guards Museum, 396
Gucci, 273, 320, 341, 342
Guess?, 341
GUIDE BOOKING AGENCIES, 435
Guild House, The, 435
Guildhall, 371
- School of Music, 411
Guy Salmon, 434

H

H Blairman & Sons, 235, 326
H R Higgins, 290
Habitat, 311
- QUICK BITE, 146
Hackney Empire, 409
HAIR SALONS, 252
Halcyon, The, 165
- RESTAURANT, 50
Halcyon Days, 302
Hale Clinic, The, 249
Halepi, 121
Halkin, The, 159
- RESTAURANT 26
Ham House, 388
Hamiltons, 355
Hamleys, 267
Hammersmith Palais, 223
Hampstead, 409
Hampstead Antiques Emporium, 228
Hampstead Heath, 403
Hampton Court Palace
    International Flower Show, 439
Hancocks & Co. Ltd., 241
Handel, 387
Hanina Gallery, 355
Harbour Club, The, 381
Hard Rock Café, 133
Hardware Support, 436
Harrington Hall, 190
Harrods, 269
- Food Hall, 292
- QUICK BITE, 146
Harry Morgan, 286
Harvey & Gore, 241
Harvey Nichols, 270
- Food Hall, 292
- QUICK BITES, 124, 146
- RESTAURANT, 56
Harvie & Hudson, 323
Haslam & Whiteway, 229
Hatchards, 262
HATS, 322, 344
Havana Sq, 207
Haymarket (Theatre Royal), 408
Hayward Gallery, 364
Hazlitt's, 180
Heal's, 311
HEALTH FOOD, 296
HEATHROW, 430
- HOTELS, 202
Heathrow Express, 430
Heathrow Hilton, 202
Heathrow Jet Charter, 432
Heaven, 224
Heights Bar, The, 210
HELICOPTER, 434
Helly Nahmad, 355
Hempel, The, 159
HENLEY, 419
Henley Royal Regatta, 439
Hennell, 318

Henry Beguelin, 270, 320
Henry Poole, 325
Henry Sotheran, 232, 236
Her Majesty's, 406
Herald & Heart, 344
Herbert Johnson, 322, 345
Hermès, 274, 320, 341, 342
Hertz, 432
Heston Blumenthal, 424
High Jinks Clothing, 349
High & Mighty, 322
Highgate Butchers, The, 298
Highgate Cemetery, 403
Hilaire, 93
Hilditch & Key, 323
Hilton Hotels, 168, 201, 202
HIRE, 245
- HANDS, 246
Historical Walks, 367
Hive, The, 294
HMS Belfast, 371
HMV, 330
HOBBIES, 377
Hobbs, 279, 338
Hobgoblin Music, 329
Hogarth's House, 388
Hogg Sons & J B Johnstone, 325
Holburne of Menstrie Museum, 415
Holding Company, The, 311
Holiday Inn, 200
- Mayfair, 165
Holland & Holland, 334, 385
Holland Park, 403
Holly Bush, 217
Holly Lodge, 415
Holmes Place Health Club, 382
Home, 224
HOME, 305
- DELIVERY, 247
Home from Home, 153
At Home in London, 155
Honest Jon's, 331
Honeylight Computers, 436
Horniman Museum, 396
Horse of the Year Show, 440
HOSPITALS, 437
HOT AIR BALLOONING, 383
Hot stuff, 144
Hotel, 167, 198
HOTELS, 151
- BARS, 210
- RATING SYSTEM, 152
- SYMBOLS, 155
Hotspur, 235
House, The, 29
House of Albert Roux, The, 298
House of Hardy, 333
Houses of Parliament, 371
HOUSES TO VISIT, 386
Howard Hotel, The, 165
Hugh Johnson Collection, 244, 306
Hulton Getty Picture Gallery, 364

HUNTING, 334
Hyatt Carlton Tower, The, 159
- RESTAURANT, 25
Hyatt Hotel, 169
Hyde Park, 169, 404
- Residence, 155
- Stables, 384

I

I Camisa & Son, 294
I Warman Freed, 437
Ian Matthews, 254
Ibis, 200
Ibla, 60
IBM, 436
ICA Café, 144
ICE SKATING, 383
Ichi-Riki Sushi House, 145
ICONS, 236
Idaho, 49
Ikkyu, 143
Il Forno, 87
Ilias Lalaounis, 318
Immaculate House, 257, 274
Imperial War Museum, 396
Incognito, 63
India High Commission, 436
India Jane, 312, 342
Indigo, 42
Inner Temple, 392
INNS OF COURT, 392
Inspector Morse, 419
Institute of Contemporary Arts, 364
Inter-Continental Hotels, 163,
    166, 170
- RESTAURANT, 67
Intercafé, 142
INTERIOR DESIGN, 307
International Ceramics Fair
    & Seminar, 439
International Cheese Centre, 287
International Festival of Fine
    Wine & Food-Olympia, 440
International Sky Charter, 432
International Wine & Food
    Society, 386
INTERNET CAFÉS, 142, 431
Intoxica, 330
Irish Linen Company, The, 274, 314
Irish Shop, 302
Islamic Cultural Centre, 437
ISLINGTON
- Tourist Information Centre, 435
Isola, 58
Issey Miyake, 274
Istanbul Iskembecisi, 143
Itsu, 93
Ivy, The, 42

J

J & A Beare, 329
J H Bourdon-Smith, 240
J & M Davidson, 320
J Sheekey, 42

Jack Casimir, 237
Jacques Rolancy, 71
Jaeger, 277
Jakss, 265
Jamaica Wine House, 213
James's Church, 354
James & Company, 434
James J Fox & Robert Lewis, 337
James Lock & Co, 322, 345
James Purdey & Sons, 334
James Smith & Sons, 282
James Street, 270
Jane Asher Party Cakes, 286
Jane Churchill, 308, 342
Jane & Dada, 338
Janet Fitch, 315
Janet Reger, 346
Japanese Canteen, 122
Japanese Embassy, 436
Japanese Gallery, 236
Jarndyce Antiquarian Booksellers, 233
Jason & Rhodes Gallery, 355
Jay Jopling/White Cube, 355
Jazz Café, The, 223
Jean-Georges Vongerichten, 59
Jean Paul Gaultier, 274
Jeanette Hayhurst, 236
Jeeves of Belgravia, 244
Jenny Lo's Tea House, 145
Jeremy Ltd, 234
JERMYN STREET, 322
Jeroboam's, 287
Jerry's Home Store, 312
Jerusalem, 206
- Tavern, 214
Jess James, 315
Jessop Photo Centre, 327
Jetline Buses, 430
Jetlink, 431
Jewel Tower, 371
JEWELRY, 241, 314
Jewish Museum, 396
Jigsaw, 338
Jill George Gallery, 355
Jim Thompson's, 206
Jimmy Choo, 279
Jitrois, 274
Jo Hansford, 252
Jo's at Joseph (QUICK BITES), 146
Jo Malone, 257
Joan & David, 279, 341
Joan Price's Face Place, 251
Joanna's Tent, 265
Joanna Wood, 308
Joe's, 146
Joe Allen, 43
Joe's Basement, 327, 437
John Blagden, 291
John Bly, 235
John Carlton-Smith, 240
John Eskenazi, 237
John Frieda, 252

John Lobb, 279
John Mitchell & Son, 361
John Sandoe, 262
John Wesley's House, Chapel & Museum, 389
Jonathan Horne, 239
Jonathan Potter, 236
Jones, 321
Jones, Gary, 423
Jongleurs, 222
Joseph, 274, 322
Joseph Azagury, 279
Jubilee Hall Clubs, 382
Jubilee Sports Centre, 382, 385
Juicemoose, 116
JUICES, 116
Julie's, 206
Jury's International Regent Park Hotel (RESTAURANT), 84
Jus Café, 133

K

K G Shoes, 248
K+K Hotel George, 190
Karen Millen, 338
Karl Lagerfeld, 341
Kashinoki, 84
Kastoori, 143
Keats House, 389
Keeping Out of Step, 403
Keith Johnson & Pelling, 327
Kenneth Turner, 283
Kensington Antiques Fair & Contemporary Art Fair, 439
Kensington & Chelsea Cars, 434
Kensington Palace, 389
- QUICK BITE, 123
Kensington Place, 53
Kent & Carey, 265
Kenwood House, 389
Kenzo, 342
Kettners, 140
Kew Bridge Steam Museum, 396
Kiki McDonough, 315
Kilgour, French & Stanbury, 326
King's Cross Station, 433
King's Head & Eight Bells, 214
King's Head Islington, 409
Kings Arms, 422
Kingsway Hall, 191
Kinko's, 435
KITCHENWARE, 313
Kite Store, The, 268
Knightsbridge Green Hotel, 191
Koala Nannies, 246
Koffmann, Pierre, 57
Koh Samui, 342
Krantz & Son, 248
Krizia, 274
Kulu Kulu Sushi, 140
Kurt Geiger, 280

L

L'Artisan Parfumeur, 255

L Cornelissen & Son, 378
L Fern & Co, 290
L K Bennett, 280
La Delizia, 111
LA Fitness, 382
La Fromagerie, 287
La Grande Bouchée, 294
La Porte des Indes, 60
La Spighetta, 128
La Tante Claire, 57
Ladenis, Nico, 63
Lady Cabs, 432
Lady Daphne, 302, 342
Lalique, 306
Lamb, 212
Lamb & Flag, 214
Landmark, The, 166
- BAR, 211
- TEA ROOM, 149
Lanesborough, The, 160
- BAR, 210
- TEA ROOM, 148
Langan's Brasserie, 67
Langham Hilton, The, 166
- TEA ROOM, 149
Lansdowne, The, 135, 219
Lauderdale House, 371
Launceston Place, 53
Laura Ashley, 308
Lawn Tennis Association, 385
Le Caprice, 81
Le Colombier, 29
Le Coq d'Argent, 35
Le Cordon Bleu, 379
Le Gavroche, 67
Le Manoir aux Quat' Saisons, 422, 423
Le Méridien, 167
- Excelsior Hotel, 202
- Gatwick Airport, 201
- Grosvenor House, 167
- Grosvenor House RESTAURANT, 63
- RESTAURANT, 75
- Waldorf, 168
- Waldorf TEA ROOM, 149
Le Métro, 124
Le Petit Blanc, 421
Le Pont de la Tour, 98
Le Shaker/Nam Long, 207
Le Soufflé, 67
LEATHER, 319
Lefevre Gallery, The, 359
LEFT-HANDED, 303
Legends, 224
Leicester Square Half Price Ticket Booth, 410
Leighton House, 389
Leith's at Dartmouth House, 129
Leith's School of Food & Wine, 380
Lemon Tree, 421
Lemonia, 136
Leonard, The, 180

Leopard Lounge, 224
Les Senteurs Specialist Perfumery, 258
L'Escargot, 88
Lesley Craze Gallery, 315
Lettonie, 415, 417
L'Hôtel, 181
Liberal Jewish Synagogue, 437
Liberty, 270, 384
- Perfumery, 251
- QUICK BITE, 146
LIBRARIES, 437
Library, The, 322
Library Bar, 149, 210
Lidgate's of Holland Park, 298
Life Centre, 382
Light Bar, 206
LIGHTING, 313
Lillywhites, 332
Limani, 136
Limoncello, 294
LIMOUSINE, 434
Lina Stores, 294
Lincoln House Hotel, 198
Lincoln's Inn, 392
Linda Wrigglesworth, 239
Lindsay House, The
    (RESTAURANT), 88
LINEN, 314
Linen Merchant, The, 314
Lingerie, 346
Links of London, 303
Linley Sambourne House, 389
Lisboa, 294
- Pâtisserie, 131
Lisson Gallery, 356
Little Angel Marionette
    Theatre, The, 268
Little Chelsea Antiques Fair, 440
Livebait, 43
Liverpool Street Station, 433, 435
LivingWell Health Club, 382
Liza Bruce, 342
L'Odéon, 76
Loewe, 320, 341
Lola's, 51
Lomo, 30
London Aquarium, 372
London
- Balloon, 372
- Baptist Association, 437
- Bicycle Tour Company, 379
- Brass Rubbing Centre, 379
- Bridge Hotel, 191
- Business School Library, 437
- Camera Exchange, 327
- Chauffeur Drive, 434
- City Airport, 431
- Curiosity Shop, 239
- Dungeon, 372
- Elizabeth Hotel, 192
- Frog Tours, 434
- Gatwick Hilton, 201

- GoSee, 362
- Graphics Centre, 378
- Hilton on Park Lane, 168
- -RESTAURANT, 71
- -BARS, 211
- Hong Kong, 111
- International Boat Show, 438
- International Book Fair, 438
- International Gallery
    of Children's Art, 364
- International Mime Festival, 438
- Jade Garden, 31
- Lighting Company, 313
- Marathon, 439
- Marriott County Hall, 169
- Marriott County Hall
    RESTAURANT, 91
- Marriott, 169
- Millennium Tours, 433
- Original Print Fair, 438
- Outpost, 181
- Palladium, 406
- Palladium Theatre, 406
- Pass, 362
- Planetarium, 372
- Pride Sightseeing, 433
- & Provincial Antique Dealers'
    Association, 227
- Showboat, 434
- Silver Vaults Chancery House, 241
- Tourist Board, 362
- Tourist Board & Convention
    Bureau, 430, 435
- Transport Museum, 303, 397
- Transport Museum Depot, 397
- Walking Forum, The, 367
- Zoo, 372
Londoner Pub Walks, The, 367
Long Tall Sally, 345
Longmire, 318
L'Oranger, 81
Lord's Cricket Ground Tours
    & Museum, 372
Lord Mayor's Show, 440
Lost Credit Cards, 437
Lost Property, 432
- In Taxis, 432
Lots Road Galleries, 231
Louis Pâtisserie, 121
Louis Vuitton, 320, 341, 342
Lowndes Hyatt, 169
Lucien Pellat-Finet, 281
LUGGAGE, 319
Lundum's, 94
Lunn Antiques, 243
Lush, 257
LUTON, 431
LUXURY, 161
Lyceum, 406

m

Ma Goa, 79
Maas Gallery, The, 359

MAC, 251
Macari's, 329
McQueens, 283
Madame Tussaud's Waxworks, 373
Magdalen College, 419
Maggs Brothers, 233
Mahogany, 252
Maison Bertaux, 140
Maison Blanc, 136, 286
Maison Bouquillon, 105
Major Venues, 410
Mallet Gallery, The, 359
Mallett at Bourdon House, 235
Mallett & Son, 235
Maman Deux, 347
Mambo, 349
Mandalay, 126
Mandarin Kitchen, 24
Mandarin Oriental Hyde Park, 169
- RESTAURANT, 56
Mango, 339
Mango Room, 108
Manolo Blahnik, 280
Mantanah, 95
MANUSCRIPTS, 231
Map House, The, 237
Maple Leaf, The, 215
MAPS & PRINTS, 236
Marble Hill House, 390
Marco Pierre White, 74
Marcus Wareing, 82
Margaret Howell, 342
Maria Andipa Icon Gallery, 236
Marine Ices, 108
Market Bar, The, 208
Market Thai, The, 131
Marks & Spencer, 271
Marlborough Fine Art, 356
Marmaris, 145
Marriott Hotels, 169
Martin Blunos, 417
Martinez, Nacho, 38
Mary Fox Linton, 308
Mary Quant, 251
Maryse Boxer at Joseph
    Penthouse, 312
Mash, 349
Masons Arms, 105
Matchbar, 206
MATERNITY, 347
Mathaf Gallery, 359
Matsuhisa, Nobuyuki, 69
Matsuri, 82
Maurice Sedwell, 326
Mauro's, 294
Max Mara, 341, 342
Mayfair Club, The, 224
Mayfair Inter-Continental, 170
Mayflower, 220
Mayor Gallery, 356
Mean Fiddler, The, 223
MEAT, 297

Mecklenburgh Health Club, 383
Medina's, 115
Mela, 44
Melton's, 427
MEN'S GROOMING, 253
Men's Grooming Studio
    at Dickins & Jones, 254
Men's Salon at Selfridges, 254
MENSWEAR, 321
Merchant Adventurer's Hall, 426
Mercury Gallery, 356
Merola, 316
Merton College, 419
Met Bar, 210
METALWARE, 237
Metro Imaging, 327, 437
Metropolitan, 170
- BAR, 210
- RESTAURANT, 69
Metropolitan Free Drinking
    Fountain Association, 359
Mezzo, 88
Michael German, 243
Michael Goedhuis, 237
Michael Van Clarke, 253
Michel Roux, 67, 425
Micro-Rent, 436
Middle Temple, 392
Middlethorpe Hall, 426, 427
Mike Weedon, 229
Miles & Miles, 434
Milestone, The, 181
Military Knights of Windsor, 424
Millennium Britannia, 171
Millennium Gloucester, 192
Millennium Knightsbridge, The, 171
Millinery Works Ltd (The Antique
    Trader), 229
Ming, 32
Ministry of Sound, The, 224
Minster church, 425
Mint, 312
Mirabelle, 67
Mrs Munro Ltd, 309
Mr Christian's, 295
Mr Kong, 32
Miu Miu, 341
Miyama, 68
Mó, 134
MOBILE PHONE HIRE, 437
Moira, 241
Mole Jazz, 331
Molton Brown Studio, 251
Momo, 75
Mon Plaisir, 44
MONEY TRANSFER, 437
Monmouth Coffee Company, 290
Monmouth Coffee House, 117
Monogrammed Linen Shop, The, 314
Monsoon, 339
Montague on the Gardens, 192
Montcalm, The, 171

- RESTAURANT, 60
- TEA ROOM, 149
Monte's, 295
Monument, 373
Moody Goose, The, 417
Moro, 38
Mortimer & Bennett, 295
Moshi Moshi Sushi, 112
Mosimann Academy, The, 380
Moss Bros, 245, 325
Motcombs, 204
Motorbike cabs, 432
Mount Royale Hotel, 426
MOUNTAINEERING, 335
Moyses Steven, 283
Mozart, 387
Mulberry, 270, 320
Mulberry Home, 312
Multilingual Services, 438
Murder One, 260
Museum Cameras, 328
Museum of Costume, 414
Museum of Garden History, 397
- QUICK BITE, 109
Museum of London, 397
Museum of the Order of St. John, 398
Museum of Rugby, 397
MUSEUMS, 393
- INFORMATION, 362
MUSIC, 327, 405, 410
- CLUBS, 222
- FESTIVALS, 411
MUSICAL INSTRUMENTS, 328
Musical Museum, 398
MUSICAL RECORDINGS, 330
MUSICALS, 405
Mysteries New Age Centre, 261
Mystery Walks, 367

n

N Bloom & Son, 241
N D Management, 247
N97, 430
N Peal, 274, 281
Nacho Martinez, 38
Nail Bar, The, 255
NAIL BARS, 255
Nail Spa at F2, The, 255
Nails Inc, 255
Nannies Incorporated, 246
Nappy Express, 247
National Army Museum, 398
National Association of
    Decorative & Fine Arts
    Societies, 227
National Car Parks, 432
National Car Rental, 432
National Express, 430, 431
National Gallery, 364
- QUICK BITE, 109
- Shop, 303
National Maritime Museum, 398
National Portrait Gallery, 365

- QUICK BITE, 109
- Shop, 259, 303
National Railway Museum, 426
National Theatre, 406
National Trust, 303
Natural Blue, 325
Natural History & Geological
    Museum, 398
Natureworks, 249
Navajo Joe, 205
Nayab, 120
Neal Street, 297
Neal Street East, 303
Neal's Yard Bakery & Tearoom, 117
Neal's Yard Dairy, 288
Neal's Yard Remedies, 257
NEEDLEWORK, 384
Nell Gwynn House, 155
NETTLEBED, 419
New College, 419
New Connaught Rooms, 224
New Diamond, 32
New End, 49
New & Lingwood, 280
New London, 406
New Millennium River Link, 434
New Study Centre, The, 377
New Tayyab, 113
New York Nail Company, 255
New Zealand High Commission, 436
NEWBURY, 418
News Café, 146
Next, 347
Nicky Clarke, 253
Nico Ladenis, 63
Nicole's, 68, 146
Nicole Farhi, 275, 312, 341
- QUICK BITES, 146
Night Owls & Great Expectations, 347
NIGHTCLUBS, 224
NikeTown, 333
Nina Campbell, 304
Nitya, 343
Noble Rot, 68
Nobu, 69
Nobuyuki Matsuhisa, 69
Noho, 143
Norman Adams, 235
Novelli Restaurant, 39
Novotel, 200
Number, 41, 182
Number Eleven, 192
No 5, 181
No 5 Bistro, 417
No 1 Royal Crescent, 414
Number Sixteen, 193
Nursery Window, The, 305

o

O F Wilson, 234
Oak Room, The, 75
Oasis, 339
Obelle, 316

O'Connor Don, 125, 218
Odette's, 78
Office, 350, 436
Oggetti, 304
O'Hanlon's, 214
Oilily, 265
Old Bailey, 373
Old Bank of England, The, 215
Old Bank Hotel, 420
Old Delhi, 24
Old Green Tree, 418
Old Operating Theatre Museum
   & Herb Garret, 399
Old Parsonage Hotel, 420
Old Starre Pub, The, 427
Old Vic, 408
Olive Tree, 417
Olivo, 24
Olympia International Show
   Jumping Championships, 440
On Your Bike, 379
One Aldwych, 172
- BAR, 210
- BREAKFAST, 135
100 Club, The, 223
1 Lombard Street, 35
One Night Stand, 245
192, 73
One Thirty, 155
O'Neill, 349
OPERA, 412
Orange Brewery, 219
Orangery, The, 123
Organic Café, 124
Oriental, The, 69
ORIENTAL ART, 237
Original London Sightseeing
   Tour, The, 433
Original London Walks, The, 367
Original Maids of Honour, 149
Origins, 251
Orrery, 61
Orso, 44
Osborne & Little, 309
O'Shea Gallery, The, 237, 356
Osprey, 321
Osteria Antica Bologna, 22
Osteria Isola, 58
Osterley Park, 390
OUTERWEAR, 277
Outpatients, 295
OXFORD, 419
- & Cambridge Boat Race, 438
- Information Centre, 420
- Story, The, 419
- University Press, 419
Oxo Tower, 238
- Restaurant Bar & Brasserie, 91
Oxygen, 224
OYSTERS, 205
Ozer, 76
Ozwald Boeteng, 326

P

P & D Colnaghi & Co, 361
Pacific Oriental, 36
Paddington Station, 433
Palace, 406
Palaces, 367
Palm Court, 149
Paperchase, 336
Papyrus, 336
Parade, 46
Paris-London Café, 104
Park Lane Hotel, The, 172
- Apartments, 153
Parker Gallery, The, 237
PARKS, 401
Parterre, 283
Partridge Fine Arts, 234
Partridges, 292
Pascal Proyart, 58
Pasha, 122
Passione, 143
Past Times, 304
Pâtisserie Valerie, 140, 287
Paton Gallery, 356
Patrick Cox, 280
Patrizia Wigan, 266
Paul Costelloe, 343
Paul Smith, 275
- for Children, 266
Pavilion, 204
Paxton & Whitfield, 288
PC Computer Problems, 436
Peak, The, 382
Pelham, The, 182
Pelham Galleries, 234
Pembridge Court Hotel, 193
Pendulum of Mayfair, 240
Penfriend, 336
Penhaligon's, 258
PENS, 336
Percival David Foundation
   of Chinese Art, 365
Peter Jones, 271
Peter Nahum at the Leicester
   Galleries, 360
PETITE SIZES, 347
Petrie Museum of Egyptian
   Archaeology, 399
Pétrus, 82
PHARMACISTS, 437
Pharmacy, 74, 208
Phase Eight, 339
Philip Antrobus, 318
Philip Treacy, 345
Phillips, 231
Phoenicia, 54
PHONE NUMBERS, 435
Photographer's Gallery, The, 356
PHOTOGRAPHY, 327
- DEVELOPMENT, 437
Piazza, The, 297
Piccadilly Antiques Market, 228

Piccadilly Line, 430
Pickering & Chatto, 233
Pickett Fine Leather, 321
Pied-à-Terre, 97, 339
Pied Piper Walks, 367
Pierre Koffmann, 57
Pineapple Covent Garden, 380
Pippa Pop-ins, 193, 246
Pitshanger Manor & Gallery, 399
Pitt Rivers Museum, 419
Pizza Express, 140
Pizza on the Park, 125
Place, The, 412
Place Below, The, 113
Planet Hollywood, 134
Planet Organic, 296
PLANTS, 282
Playin' Games, 268
Plume of Feathers, The, 216
Po Na Na, 224
Poetry Café, The, 117
Point, 224
Police, 437
Politico's, 145, 260
Polka Theatre for Children, 268
Pollock's Toy Theatres, 268
Polo Ralph Lauren, 266, 275, 341
Pomegranates, 78
Pont, 283
Poole, Bruce, 55
Poons in the City, 36
Poons & Co, 33
PORCELAIN, 238
Porchester Centre, 385
Portal Gallery, 357
Portobello China & Woollens, 306
Portobello Gold's, 142
Portobello Hotel, The, 182
Portobello Market, 228
Portrait Restaurant & Bar, The, 109
POTTERY, 238
Prada, 275, 342
Premier, 146
Prestat, 289
Prêt-à-Manger, 133
PrimeAce Chauffeur Service, 434
Primrose Pâtisserie, 136
Prince Bonaparte, 131
Principles, 347
Prism, 36
Professional Guide Services, 435
Professional Guides, 435
Professional Percussion, 329
PROPERTY MAINTENANCE, 247
Prospect Grill, 118
Prospect of Whitby, 221
Provincial Booksellers Fairs'
   Association, 227
Proyart, Pascal, 58
Pruskin Gallery, 229
PUBLIC TRANSPORT
   SYSTEM, 431

PUBS, 211
Pulbrook & Gould, 284
Pulteney Bridge, 415
Punjab, 118
Purdy Hicks, 357
Purple Sage, 127
Purves & Purves, 312
Putney Bridge, 79
Pyms Gallery, 360

Q

Quadrato, 37
Quaglino's, 83
Quality Chop House, 39
Queen's Gallery, 365
Queen's House, 390
Queen's Ice Bowl, 383
Queen Mary's Dolls' House, 424
Queens, The, 136, 219
Queensbury Hotel, 415
Queensway Spy Shop, 334
QUICK BITES, 103
Quilon, 99
Quo Vadis, 89

R

R D Franks, 261
R Garcia & Sons, 295
R H Jarvis & Sons, 291
R M Williams, 277
RAC London to Brighton-
    Veteran Car Run, 440
Radcliffe Camera, 419
Radio Taxicars, 432
Radisson Edwardian Hotels, 200
- Heathrow, 202
- Mountbatten, 172
Radisson Hampshire, The, 173
Radisson SAS Portman, 173
Raffety, 240
Ragged School Museum, 399
Rail enquiries, 430
Randall & Aubin, 141
Ranger's House, 390
Ransome's Dock, 22
Raphael Valls, 361
Rasa Samudra, 97
Rasa W1, 69
Ray's Jazz, 331
Ray Man, 330
Raymond Blanc, 422
Real Food Store, The, 293
Real Greek, The, 86
Rebecca Hossack Gallery, 357
Red or Dead, 349
- Shoes, 350
Red Fort, 89
Red Lion, 219
Red Pepper, The, 125
Red Room, The, 76
Redfern Gallery, 357
Redmond's, 79
Refinery, The, 254
Regent's Park, 404

- Golf & Tennis School, 383
Reid, Robert, 75
RELIGIOUS SERVICES, 437
Religious Society of Friends, 437
Remembrance Sunday Ceremony, 440
RESERVATION SERVICE, 152
Restaurant One-O-One, 58
RESTAURANTS, 11
- BY CUISINE, 17
- DRESS CODE, 13
- LATE NIGHT, 19
- BY NOTABLE FEATURES, 19
- OPEN SUNDAY, 20
- PRICING SYSTEM, 14
- RATING SYSTEM, 13
- RESERVATIONS, 13
- SAVVY, 13
- SERVICE, 13
- SYMBOLS, 14
- TALLY, 15
- VEGETARIAN, 20
RESTORERS, 230
Revelation, 321
Rhodes in the Square, 78
Rib Room & Oyster Bar, The, 25, 205
RIBA Architecture Gallery, 365
Richard Corrigan at Lindsay
    House, 88
Richard Courtney, 235
Richard Dare, 313
Richard Green, 360
Richard James, 326
Richard Ogden, 318
Richard Philp, 360
Richard Ward, 253
Richardson's of Ealing, 298
Richmond Park, 383, 384, 404
RIDING, 335, 384
Rigby & Peller, 346
Riso, 33
Ritz, The, 160
- BAR, 211
- Palm Court, The, 150
- RESTAURANT, 83
- TEA ROOM, 150
Riva, 22
River Café, The, 48
RIVER CRUISES, 434
River Room, The, 95
RK Stanley's, 127
Robert Frew, 233
Robert Hall, 238
Robert Reid, 75
Rococo, 289
Roehampton Gate Stables, 385
Roman Baths, 414
Ronnie Scotts, 223
Rookery, The, 183
Room at The Halcyon, The, 50
Room Service, 247
Rose Morris, 328
Ross Nye, 384

Rossi & Rossi, 238
Rosslyn Delicatessen, The, 296
Rôtisserie, 138
Rôtisserie Jules, 131
Rough Trade, 331
Roussillon, 25
Roux, Albert, 67
Roux, Michel, 67, 425
Rowney, 378
Royal Academy of Arts, 304, 365
- QUICK BITE, 109
- RESTAURANT, 134
Royal
- Academy of Music, 411
- Academy Summer Exhibition, 439
- Air Force Museum, 399
- Albert Hall, 410
- Ascot Race Meeting, 439
- Botanic Gardens, 404
- College of Art, 366
- College of Music, 411
- College of Music Museum
    of Instruments, 399
- College of Surgeons of England, 400
- Court, 407
- Courts of Justice, 373
- Crescent Hotel, 416
- Doulton, 306
- Free Hospital, 437
- Garden Hotel, 173
- Garden Hotel BAR, 211
- Garden Hotel RESTAURANT, 55
- Horseguards Thistle, 174
- Horticultural Society, The, 383
- Horticultural Society Halls, 373
- Institute of British Architects, 259
- Lancaster Hotel, 194
- Mews, 373
- National Theatre, 406
- Observatory, 400
- Opera House, 406, 412
- Park Hotel, 198
- School of Needlework, 384
- Shakespeare Company, 406, 407
- Windsor Horse Show, 439
Rubens at the Palace, The, 194
Ruffle & Hook, 314
RUGS, 239
Rules, 45
Rushmore Hotel, 199
Russell & Chapple, 378
Russian Embassy & Consulate, 436
Rutland, 216

S

S J Phillips, 242
S Marchant & Son, 238
S & R Kelly, 106
Saatchi Collection, 366
Sabras, 100
Sadler's Wells, 412
Saga, 70
Saigon Thuy, 146

Saigon Times, 113, 135
SAILING, 335
Sainsbury Wing Brasserie, The, 109
St. Bartholomew-the-Great, 376
St. Bride's, 376
St. Christopher's Place, 270
St. George's Chapel, 424
St. George's Hotel, 194
- George's Hotel BAR, 210
St. Helen Bishopsgate, 376
St. James Piccadilly, 411
St. James Restaurant, 146
St. John, 39
St. John's Smith Square, 410
St. Johns, 104
Saint M, 45
St. Martin-in-the Fields, 354, 412
- QUICK BITE, 144
St. Martins Lane Hotel, 174
- RESTAURANT, 40
St. Mary's, 419
St. Mary Abchurch, 376
St. Mary-le-Bow, 376, 412
- QUICK BITE, 113
St. Mary Woolnoth, 377
St. Paul's Cathedral, 373
St. Stephen Walbrook, 377
Salisbury, 215
Salloos, 25
Sally Lunn's Refreshment House
    & Museum, 418
Salmon & Champagne Bar, 146
Salt House, The, 137
Sam de Téran, 333
Sam Fogg, 233
Sanctuary, The, 250, 382
Sanctuary House, The, 199
Sanderson, 175
- RESTAURANT, 97
Sandra Cronan, 242
Sandringham Hotel, 183
SANDWICHES, 133
Sarastro, 223
Sarkhel's, 101
Sartoria, 77
Sauce Bar Organic Diner, 108
Savile Row, 324
Savoy, The, 160
- BAR, 210
- RESTAURANT, 95
- TEA ROOM, 150
SCARVES, 347
SCENTS, 255
Schott, 332
Science Museum, 400
SCIENTIFIC INSTRUMENTS, 240
Scotch House, The, 281
Scotia, 281
Scott's, 205
Screenface, 252
Sean Arnold Sporting Antiques, 242
Searcy's at the Barbican, 37

Searcy's Roof Garden Bedrooms, 199
Seashell, 137
Selfridge, The, 194
Selfridges, 271
- Food Hall, 293
- MEN'S SALON, 254
- QUICK BITE, 146
Sequel, The, 114
Serpentine Gallery, 366
Service Point, 436
Sesame Health Foods, 297
Seven Deadly Sins Breakfast, 135
Shaker Shop, The, 309
Shakespeare's Globe, 408
- Exhibition, 374
- QUICK BITE, 109, 142
Shambles, 425
Shampers, 209
Shanghai, 120
Shapero Gallery, 360
Shaw Park Plaza, 195
SHEET MUSIC, 332
Sheldonian Theatre, 419
Shellys, 350
Shepherd's Bush Empire, 223
Sher System Studio, 250
Sheraton Belgravia, 175
Sheraton Park Tower, 175
Sheraton Skyline, 202
Sherlock Holmes, 213
- Museum, 400
Shervington, 338
SHIPPERS, 247
Shirin Cashmere, 281
SHIRTS, 323
SHOES, 278
- CHILDREN, 264
- REPAIRS, 248
SHOOTING, 334, 385
Shop, 350
Shoreditch Electricity
    Showrooms, 209
Short Term Rental Systems, 436
Shu Uemura, 252
Siàn Blunos, 417
SILVER, 240, 241
Silver Galleries, 241
Silver Moon Women's
    Bookshop, 261
Silver Plough, 418
Silver Sturgeon, 435
Silverprint, 328
Simon Dickinson Ltd, 361
Simon Finch Rare Books, 233
Simon Horn Furniture, 309
Simply Sausages, 299
Simpson's-in-the-Strand
    Grand Divan, 135
Sims Reed, 233
Singing Tree, The, 268
Sir John Soane Museum, 390
Sir Terence Conran, 61

606 Club, The, 223
1647, 346
SKIING, 335
Skoob Books, 263
Skoob Two, 261
Skyline Millennium Balloon, 374
Skytrain Express, 431
Sloane Hotel, The, 183
Sloane Square Moat House, 195
Sloane Street, 342
Small & Tall Shoe Shop, 280
Smythson, 337
Snappy Snaps, 328
Snow & Rock, 335
SOAPS, 255
Soccer Scene, 333
Society of London Art Dealers, 227
Society of London Theatre, 405
Sofra, 118
Soho Gym, 382
Soho Soho, 90
Soho Spice, 141
Soho Theatre & Writers' Centre, 409
Solange Azagury-Partridge, 316
Somerset House
    (QUICK BITE), 109
Sonny's, 22
Sotheby's, 231
- Café, 129
- Educational Studies, 386
- Institute, 377
Souls College, 419
Sound of China, 332
Sound Republic, 224
Soup, 127
Soup Opera, 127
Soup Works, 127
Soupdouper, 127
South Africa High Commission, 436
South Bank Centre, 410
South Kensington Butchers, 299
Southern Air, 432
Southside House, 391
Southwark Cathedral, 374
Southwark Tourist Info. Centre, 435
Sovereign Gallery, 400
Soviet Canteen, 30
Space NK, 252
Spaghetti Opera at Terraza-Est, 223
Spaniard's Inn, 217
Spanish Guitar Centre, 330
SPAS, 249
Special Photographers Company, 357
Spencer House, 391
Spice Island, 220
Spice Shop, The, 296
Spiga, 141
Spink-Leger, 360
Spink & Son, 360
SPIRITS, 299
Spoon+ at Sanderson, 97
SPORTING ANTIQUES, 242

SPORTING GOODS, 332
SPORTS, 377
Sportspages, 264
Sportswear, 324
Springbok Café, 112
Spurriergate, 425
Spymaster, 334
Square, The, 70
SQUASH, 385
Squeeze, 116
Stables Antique Market, The, 228
Stafford, The, 176
- BAR, 211
- RESTAURANT, 83
Stair & Company, 236
Stanford, 264
STANSTED, 431
Star of India, 94
Star Tavern, 212
State Apartments, 424
Station Grill, 51
STATIONERY, 336
Stationery Department, The, 337
Stefano Cavallini at The Halkin, 26
Steinberg & Tolkien, 243
Stella Artois Championship, 439
Stella Artois Tournament at
    Queen's Club, 385
Stencil Store, The, 311
Stephen Bull, 61
Stephen Bull Smithfield, 40
Stepping Out Walking Tours, 367
Stepping Stone, 23
Stern's African Record Centre, 332
Steve Hatt, 291
Sticky Fingers, 123
Stonehenge, 414
Style, 229
Subsidised Theatre, 406
Sugar Antiques, 244
Sugar Club, 90
Suits, 324
Summerill & Bishop, 270, 313
Suntory, 84
Suppliers, 384
Sutton House, 391
Swaine Adeney, 282, 335
Swallow Regents Plaza Hotel
    & Suites, 195
SWEATERS, 281
Swedish Embassy, 436
Sweeting's, 205
SWIMMING, 385
Swiss Cottage Hotel, 195
Sydney House Hotel, 184
Sydney L Moss, 238
Syon House, 391

T

T Fox, 282
T M Lewin, 323
T N Lawrence & Son, 378
T W Howarth, 330

Table Café, 146
Tadema Gallery, 230
Tailors, 325
Tajine, 61
Take-a-Guide Ltd, 434
Talad Thai, 296
Talking Bookshop, 262
Tamarind, 31
Tanner Krolle, 321
Tao, 113
TAPESTRIES, 239
Tapisserie, 384
Tartine et Chocolat, 266
Tate Britain, 366
- QUICK BITE, 109
Tate Gallery Shop, 304
Tate Modern, 366
- QUICK BITE, 109
Tatsuso, 37
Tatters, 344
TAX-FREE SHOPPING, 438
TAXIS, 432, 435
TEA, 289
Tea House, The, 290, 306
- TEA ROOM, 148
Teca, 71
Techno, 328
Temple, The, 392
Temple Church, 392
Temple Gallery, The, 236
Ten Manchester Street, 184
10 Tokyo Joes, 224
TENNIS, 385
Tentazioni, 99
Tenth, The, 55, 211
Terminus, 113, 135
Terrace, 54
Tessier's, 242
Textile Conservation Centre, 230
TEXTILES, 242
Thai Pavilion, 90
Thames Barrier Visitors Centre, 374
Thames Cruises, 434
Thames Wharf Studios
    (RESTAURANT), 48
Thanh Binh, 109
THEATRE, 405
Theatre Museum, 400
Theatre Royal Stratford East, 409
Theatrical Costume, 246
Theo Fennell, 316
Thistle Charing Cross, 176
Thistle Hyde Park, 196
Thistle Tower Hotel, 176
Thomas Goode, 306
Thomas Heneage, 233
Thomas Pink, 323
Thompson's Gallery, 357
Thrifty, 432
Ties, 323
Tiffany & Co, 304, 318
Tiger Lil's, 111

Time Zone Express, 436
Timney Fowler, 309
Timothy Taylor Gallery, 358
Tinseltown, 115
Tintin Shop, The, 305
Tiranti, 378
Titanic, 77, 209
Titus Omega, 230
TOBACCONISTS, 337
TOILETRIES, 255
Tokyo Diner, 111
Tom's, 296
Tom Gilbey, 245, 326
- Waistcoat Gallery, 327
Tomasz Starzewski, 344
Top Notch Nannies & Brilliant
    Babysitters, 246
Top Shop, 350
Topham's Belgravia, 196
Tour Guides Ltd, 435
TOURIST INFORMATION
    CENTRES, 435
TOURS, 433
- BACKSTAGE, 406
Tower Bridge Experience, 374
Tower of London, 375
Tower Records, 330
Townhouse Brasserie, 106
TOWNHOUSE HOTELS, 152, 177
TOYS, 267
Trader Vic's, 211
Trafalgar Tavern, The, 216
TRAINS, 432
Trans Euro World Wide Movers, 247
TRANSLATION SERVICES, 438
Travel Book Shop, The, 264
Travel Inn, 200
Travelcards, 431
Travellers Cheque Refund, 435
Travellodge, 200
Trent Park Equestrian
    Centre, 384, 385
Trevor Philip & Sons, 240
Tricker's, 280
Tricycle Theatre, 410
Trooping the Colour, 439
Trotters, 266
Turf Tavern, 422
Turnbull & Asser, 324
Turner's, 94
Turnmills, 224
12 Bar Club, The, 223
20th Century British Art Fair, 440
Twenty Nevern Square, 185
23 Greengarden House, 155
20/20, 436
22 Jermyn Street, 184
Twentyfour, 38
Twinings, 290
Two Brothers Fish Restaurant, 119
Two, 10 Gallery, 366
2 Willow Road, 391

U

Ulysses, 233
UMBRELLAS, 282
UNDERGROUND, 7, 433
Union Café, 128
United Kingdom Institute
 for Conservation, 230
United States Embassy, 436
Universal Aunts, 247
Universal Translations, 438
University College, 419
University College Hospital, 437
University Women's Club, 199
Upper Street Fish Shop, 122
Uptown Reservations, 155
Urban Retreat & Aveda Concept
 Salon, The, 250

V

Vale, The, 126
Valentino, 342, 343
Vama, 30
Van Den Bosch, 230
Van Haeften Gallery, 361
Van Peterson Designs, 317
Vanderbilt Racquet Club, The, 386
Vasco & Piero's Pavilion, 91
VAT, 438
Veeraswamy, 77
VEGETARIAN RESTAURANTS, 20
Velvet Room, The, 224
Vernon Computer Rentals, 436
Viaduct, 309
Victor Franses Gallery, 239
Victoria & Albert Museum, 401
- QUICK BITE, 109
- Shop, 238, 259, 305
Victoria Miro Gallery, 358
Victoria Park, 404
Victoria Station, 433
- Forecourt, 435
Vidal Sassoon, 253
Villandry, 62, 296
Villeroy & Boch, 307
Vineyard at Stockcross, The, 418
Vingt-Quatre, 120
Vinopolis-City of Wine, 375
Virgin, 330
Virgin LimoBikes, 432
Visitor Sightseeing, 433
Vivienne Westwood, 275
Vong, 59
Voyage, 275
Vuitton, Louis, 320, 341, 342
V.V. Rouleaux, 311

W

W & G Foyle, 262
W & H Gidden, 321
W H Smith & Son, 262
Waddington Galleries, 358
Wagamama, 106
Waistcoats, 326

Walk the Millennium Mile, 367
WALKING STICKS, 243
Walks Around London, 367
Wallace Collection, 367
Walton Street, 270
Wardrobe, 343
Wareing, Marcus, 82
Warner Brothers Studio
 Store, 266, 268
Warrington Hotel (BAR), 218
Wartski, 242
Watch Gallery, The, 319
WATCHES, 240
Watches of Switzerland, 319
WATER SPORTS, 386
Waterford Wedgwood, 307
Waterhouse & Dodd, 360
Waterloo, 435
Waterloo International, 433
Waterloo Station, 433
Waterlow Park, 405
Waterside Inn, 425
Waterstone's, 263
- QUICK BITE, 146
Waterstone's Arts Bookshop, 259
Waterstone's at Harrods, 263
Watkins Books, 261
Waxy O'Connors, 221
Wembley Stadium Tours, 375
West End, The, 405
West London Antiques & Fine
 Art Fair, 438
Westbourne, The, 131
Westbury, The, 177
Western Union, 437
Westminster Abbey, 375
- Brass Rubbing Centre, 379
Westminster Apartment Services, 153
Westminster Cathedral, 375, 437
Westminster Passenger Service
 Association, 434
WHI Tapestry Shop, 384
Whip-Ma-Whop-Ma Gate, 426
Whistles, 339
White Cross, 220
White Horse, The, 132
White Horse Fast Ferry, 434
White House, The, 421
White Onion, 123
Whitechapel Art Gallery, 367
Whitfield Fine Art, 361
Whittington Hospital, 437
Who Lived Where, 387
Wholefood Ltd., 297
Wigmore Hall, 411
Wild Oats, 297
Wildenstein & Co, 361
Willett Hotel, 199
William Evans, 334
William IV, 123
William Morris Gallery, 401
Wilsons, 138

Wilton, 205
Wilton House, 414
Wiltons, 84
Wimbledon Lawn Tennis
 Championships, 439
Wimbledon Lawn Tennis
 Museum, 401
Wimbledon Village Stables, 385
Windermere Hotel, 200
Windows, 71, 211
WINDSOR, 424
WINE, 244, 299
- BARS, 204
- COURSES, 386
Wine & Spirit Education Trust, 386
Wine Wise, 386
Winsor & Newton, 378
Winston Churchill's Britain at War
 Experience, 375
Winter Garden, The, 211
Wolsey Lodges Ltd., 155
WOMEN'S WEAR, 338
Woods, 418
WOODSTOCK, 420, 423
WOOLLENS, 281
Worcester College, 419
World of Drawings
 & Watercolours Fair, 438
World Travel Market, 440
Wright & Teague, 316
WRISTWATCHES, 244

Y

Yas, 124
Yasmin Cho, 343
Ye Old Mitre, 215
Ye Olde Cheshire Cheese, 215
Yellow River Café, 118
Yesterday's Bread, 243
YHA Adventure Shop, 333
Yima, 109
Yo! Sushi/Yo! Belo, 141
Yohji Yamamoto, 276
YORK, 425
- Minster, 426
- Tourist Office, 426
Yorvik Centre, 426
Young's Brewery Visitor Centre, 376
Young England, 266
Young Vic, 408
Yves Saint Laurent, 341, 342
- Rive Gauche, 276

Z

Zafash Pharmacy, 437
Zafferano, 26
Zaika, 47
Zara, 339
Zarvis, 258
Zelda Cheatle Gallery, 358
Zen Central, 72
Zen Chelsea, 30
Zen Garden, 72
Zeta, 207

GAYOT